8 Pract Tests for the ACT®

8 Practice Tests for the ACT®

KAPLAN PUBLISHING

New York

Published by Kaplan Publishing, a division of Kaplan, Inc.
750 Third Avenue
New York, NY 10017

10 9 8 7 6 5 4

ISBN-13: 978-1-5062-3512-7

Kaplan Publishing print books are available at special quantity discounts to use for sales promotions, employee premiums, or educational purposes. For more information or to purchase books, please call the Simon & Schuster special sales department at 866-506-1949.

Table of Contents

Practice Makes Perfect

Don't be scared of the ACT. Why? Because we know what's on the exam, and we know exactly how you should prepare for it. Kaplan has been teaching kids how to succeed on standardized tests for more than 75 years—longer than anyone else, period.

This book contains 8 practice exams that mirror the ACT you will face on Test Day—more ACT practice than can be found between the covers of any other book. Practice is one of the keys to mastery, and these 8 exams give you plenty of practice to assess your strengths and weaknesses before you take the real thing.

Just as important as taking practice tests is understanding why you got a question right or wrong when you're done. The detailed answers and explanations that follow each practice test provide you with a thorough explanation of the correct answer as well as strategic advice, so you will start to learn some ways you can approach similar questions on Test Day. In addition, every answer explanation lets you know the difficulty level of each question. If you're missing a lot of "Low" difficulty questions, you might need to do some extra review. If you are acing many of the "High" difficulty questions, you're on the right track.

Every practice question and answer explanation in this book is geared toward one thing—getting you more points on the actual ACT. So don't stress out—Kaplan's got you covered.

HOW TO USE THIS BOOK

This book is filled with over 1,700 practice questions to help you master the ACT. Follow these steps to get the most out of these 8 practice tests:

1. Read about the ACT structure in the next section. This way, you'll know what to expect—not only as you work through the book but, more importantly, on Test Day.

2. Begin your practice! Buying this book has given you an advantage—after you've worked your way through the exams, the format and timing of the ACT will be second nature to you. All you will have to concentrate on is improving your skills in the areas that need work.

3. Keep track. Turn to the Score Tracker on page xi, where you can track your score as you take each exam. Keep a record of your scores and watch how much you improve from test to test.

4. Assess your strengths and weaknesses. After you finish each test, carefully read the detailed explanations—pay attention to the questions you got wrong, but don't forget to read about the ones you got right. It's important to note your areas of strength as well as weakness. Take your own personal inventory of the skills you've mastered and the skills you need to work on.

5. Watch your scores improve! After you've made your way halfway through the book, compare your scores on Test 1 and Test 4. You've made progress, haven't you? See if your strengths and weaknesses have changed. Then work your way through the remaining tests, building skills and ACT competency along the way.

After making your way through these steps, we guarantee that you will have the test expertise and improved skills to tackle the ACT with confidence.

ACT TEST DATES

As a general rule, students take the ACT at least once in their junior year, often taking it for the first time in the early spring. The ACT is administered on select Saturdays during the school year. Sunday testing is also available for students who cannot take the Saturday test because of religious observances. Check the official ACT website at actstudent.org/regist/dates.html for the most up-to-date test dates.

ACT REGISTRATION

To register for the ACT by mail, you'll need to get an ACT Paper Registration Guide from your high school guidance counselor.

You can register online at actstudent.org/regist/. Note: Not all students are eligible to register online, so read the instructions and requirements carefully.

Register early to secure the time you want at the test center of your choice and to avoid late registration fees.

Students with disabilities can go to actstudent.org/regist/disab/ to learn how to apply for accommodations.

In the United States, the fee for the ACT is $62.50 with the writing test, and $46.00 without the writing test. This price includes reports for you, your high school, and up to four colleges and scholarship programs. To get the most up-to-date information on test fees, please check actstudent.org/regist/actfees.html.

You will receive an admission ticket at least a week before the test. The ticket confirms your registration on a specified date, at a specified test center. Make sure to bring this, along with proper identification, to the test center. Some acceptable forms of identification include photo IDs such as a driver's license, a school identification card, or a valid passport. (Unacceptable forms of identification include a Social Security card, credit card, or birth certificate.)

Your ACT scores will be available online approximately three weeks after the test.

Remember to check act.org for all the latest information on the ACT. Every effort has been made to keep the information in this book as up-to-date as possible, but changes may occur after the book is published.

Finally, bookmark the ACT's website: act.org.

HOW THE ACT IS STRUCTURED

The ACT is about three hours long (three and a half with the Writing Test). The test consists of four subject tests, with a total of 215 scored multiple-choice questions, and one optional essay.

Below is the breakdown of the test:

Test	Questions	Timing	Content
English	75 questions	45 minutes	Measures standard written English and rhetorical skills.
Mathematics	60 questions	60 minutes	Measures mathematical skills students have typically acquired in courses taken up to the beginning of grade 12.
Reading	40 questions	35 minutes	Measures reading comprehension.
Science	40 questions	35 minutes	Measures the interpretation, analysis, evaluation, reasoning, and problem-solving skills required in the natural sciences.
Optional Writing Test	1 prompt	40 minutes	Measures writing skills emphasized in high school English classes and in entry-level college composition courses.

* There will be a short break between the Math and Reading subject tests.

HOW THE ACT IS SCORED

The ACT is scored differently from most tests that you take at school. Your ACT score on a test section is not reported as the total number of questions you answered correctly, nor does it directly represent the percentage of questions you answered correctly. Instead, the test makers add up all of your correct answers in a section to get what's called your raw score. They then use a conversion chart, or scale, that matches up a particular raw score with what's called a scaled score. The scaled score is the number that gets reported as your score for that ACT subject test.

You gain one point for every question you answer correctly. You lose no points for answering a question wrong OR for leaving a question blank. This means you should ALWAYS answer EVERY question on the ACT—even if you have to guess.

SCORE TRACKER

1. **Figure out your raw score for each subject test.** Refer to the answer keys to determine how many questions you answered correctly. Enter the results in the chart:

RAW SCORES

	TEST 1	TEST 2	TEST 3	TEST 4	TEST 5	TEST 6	TEST 7	TEST 8
English:								
Math:								
Reading:								
Science:								

2. **Convert your raw scores to scaled scores for each subject test.** Locate your raw score for each subject test in the following table. The score in the far left column indicates your estimated scaled score if this were an actual ACT. Enter your scaled scores in the chart that follows the table.

SCALED SCORE	RAW SCORES			
	English	**Mathematics**	**Reading**	**Science**
36	75	60	40	40
35	74	–	–	–
34	73	59	39	39
33	72	58	–	–
32	71	57	38	38
31	70	55–56	37	37
30	69	53–54	36	36
29	68	50–52	35	35
28	67	48–49	34	34
27	65–66	45–47	33	33
26	63–64	43–44	32	32
25	61–62	40–42	31	30–31
24	58–60	38–39	30	28–29
23	56–57	35–37	29	26–27
22	53–55	33–34	28	24–25
21	49–52	31–32	27	21–23
20	46–48	28–30	25–26	19–20
19	44–45	26–27	23–24	17–18
18	41–43	23–25	21–22	16
17	39–40	20–22	19–20	15
16	36–38	17–19	17–18	14
15	34–35	15–16	15–16	13
14	30–33	13–14	14	12
13	28–29	11–12	12–13	11
12	25–27	9–10	10–11	10
11	23–24	8	9	9
10	20–22	7	8	8
9	17–19	6	7	7
8	14–16	5	6	6
7	12–13	4	5	5
6	9–11	3	4	4
5	7–8	2	3	3
4	4–6	–	2	2
3	3	1	1	1
2	2	–	–	–
1	0–1	0	0	0

SCALED SCORES

	TEST 1	TEST 2	TEST 3	TEST 4	TEST 5	TEST 6	TEST 7	TEST 8
English:								
Math:								
Reading:								
Science:								

3. **Calculate your estimated Composite score.** Simply add together your scaled scores for each subject test and divide by four. Keep track of your composite score for each test in the chart below.

COMPOSITE SCORES

TEST 1	TEST 2	TEST 3	TEST 4	TEST 5	TEST 6	TEST 7	TEST 8

ACT ESSAY SCORING RUBRIC

There are four separate scoring domains for the ACT Essay: Ideas and Analysis, Development and Support, Organization, and Language Use. Two trained readers score your essay on a scale of 1–6 for each of the four Writing test domains; those scores are added to arrive at your four Writing domain scores (each from 2 to 12). You will also receive an overall Writing test score ranging from 2 to 12, which is determined by a rounded average of the four domain scores. The graders will use a rubric similar to the following to determine each domain score.

6	5	4
Ideas and Analysis		
• Skillfully explores multiple perspectives on the given issue • Includes a comprehensive, detailed, and insightful thesis • Establishes thorough context for analysis of the issue and its perspectives • Evaluates implications, intricacies, and/or assumptions	• Effectively explores multiple perspectives on the given issue • Includes a detailed, insightful thesis • Establishes effective context for analysis of the issue and its perspectives • Discusses implications, intricacies, and/or assumptions	• Adequately explores multiple perspectives on the given issue • Includes a detailed thesis • Establishes adequate context for analysis of the issue and its perspectives • Identifies implications, intricacies, and/or assumptions
Development and Support		
• Provides additional insight and context • Skillfully provides relevant reasoning • Explores the significance of the argument	• Provides additional understanding • Effectively provides relevant reasoning • Discusses the significance of the argument	• Provides additional clarity • Adequately provides relevant reasoning • Identifies the significance of the argument
Organization		
• Demonstrates a skillful structure • Focuses on a well-defined main idea • Includes transitions that skillfully connect ideas	• Demonstrates an effective structure • Focuses on a main idea • Includes transitions that effectively connect ideas	• Demonstrates an adequate structure • Reflects a main idea • Includes transitions that adequately connect ideas
Language Use		
• Features skillful, precise, appropriate word choice • Consistently includes varied sentence structure • May include a few minor errors in grammar that do not distract from clarity or readability	• Features precise, appropriate word choice • Often includes varied sentence structure • May include minor errors in grammar that do not distract from clarity or readability	• Features appropriate word choice • Sometimes includes varied sentence structure • Includes minor errors in grammar that rarely distract from clarity or readability

3	2	1
Ideas and Analysis		
• Somewhat explores multiple perspectives on the given issue • Includes a thesis • Establishes some context for analysis of the issue and its perspectives • May mention implications, intricacies, and/or assumptions	• Somewhat responds to multiple perspectives on the given issue • Does not include a clear thesis • Does not provide context for analysis of the issue and its perspectives • Does not discuss implications, intricacies, and/or assumptions	• Fails to explore multiple perspectives on the given issue • Does not include a thesis • Does not provide context for analysis of the issue and its perspectives • Does not identify implications, intricacies, and/or assumptions
Development and Support		
• Provides general information • Provides relevant reasoning in a redundant or inexact way	• Weakly provides information • Inadequately provides relevant reasoning	• Lacks development • Does not provide relevant reasoning
Organization		
• Demonstrates a basic structure • Contains a main idea • Includes transitions that sometimes connect ideas	• Demonstrates a simplistic structure • May not reflect a main idea • Does not use transitions that adequately connect ideas	• Demonstrates a confusing structure • Does not reflect a main idea • Does not use transitions that adequately connect ideas
Language Use		
• Features basic word choice • Rarely includes varied sentence structure • Includes errors in grammar that somewhat distract from clarity and readability	• Features unclear word choice • Often includes unclear sentence structure • Includes numerous errors in grammar that distract from clarity and readability	• Features confusing word choice • Often includes unclear, confusing sentence structure • Includes numerous errors in grammar that distract from clarity and readability

ACT Practice Test 1
ANSWER SHEET

ENGLISH TEST

1. (A) (B) (C) (D) 11. (A) (B) (C) (D) 21. (A) (B) (C) (D) 31. (A) (B) (C) (D) 41. (A) (B) (C) (D) 51. (A) (B) (C) (D) 61. (A) (B) (C) (D) 71. (A) (B) (C) (D)
2. (F) (G) (H) (J) 12. (F) (G) (H) (J) 22. (F) (G) (H) (J) 32. (F) (G) (H) (J) 42. (F) (G) (H) (J) 52. (F) (G) (H) (J) 62. (F) (G) (H) (J) 72. (F) (G) (H) (J)
3. (A) (B) (C) (D) 13. (A) (B) (C) (D) 23. (A) (B) (C) (D) 33. (A) (B) (C) (D) 43. (A) (B) (C) (D) 53. (A) (B) (C) (D) 63. (A) (B) (C) (D) 73. (A) (B) (C) (D)
4. (F) (G) (H) (J) 14. (F) (G) (H) (J) 24. (F) (G) (H) (J) 34. (F) (G) (H) (J) 44. (F) (G) (H) (J) 54. (F) (G) (H) (J) 64. (F) (G) (H) (J) 74. (F) (G) (H) (J)
5. (A) (B) (C) (D) 15. (A) (B) (C) (D) 25. (A) (B) (C) (D) 35. (A) (B) (C) (D) 45. (A) (B) (C) (D) 55. (A) (B) (C) (D) 65. (A) (B) (C) (D) 75. (A) (B) (C) (D)
6. (F) (G) (H) (J) 16. (F) (G) (H) (J) 26. (F) (G) (H) (J) 36. (F) (G) (H) (J) 46. (F) (G) (H) (J) 56. (F) (G) (H) (J) 66. (F) (G) (H) (J)
7. (A) (B) (C) (D) 17. (A) (B) (C) (D) 27. (A) (B) (C) (D) 37. (A) (B) (C) (D) 47. (A) (B) (C) (D) 57. (A) (B) (C) (D) 67. (A) (B) (C) (D)
8. (F) (G) (H) (J) 18. (F) (G) (H) (J) 28. (F) (G) (H) (J) 38. (F) (G) (H) (J) 48. (F) (G) (H) (J) 58. (F) (G) (H) (J) 68. (F) (G) (H) (J)
9. (A) (B) (C) (D) 19. (A) (B) (C) (D) 29. (A) (B) (C) (D) 39. (A) (B) (C) (D) 49. (A) (B) (C) (D) 59. (A) (B) (C) (D) 69. (A) (B) (C) (D)
10. (F) (G) (H) (J) 20. (F) (G) (H) (J) 30. (F) (G) (H) (J) 40. (F) (G) (H) (J) 50. (F) (G) (H) (J) 60. (F) (G) (H) (J) 70. (F) (G) (H) (J)

MATHEMATICS TEST

1. (A) (B) (C) (D) (E) 11. (A) (B) (C) (D) (E) 21. (A) (B) (C) (D) (E) 31. (A) (B) (C) (D) (E) 41. (A) (B) (C) (D) (E) 51. (A) (B) (C) (D) (E)
2. (F) (G) (H) (J) (K) 12. (F) (G) (H) (J) (K) 22. (F) (G) (H) (J) (K) 32. (F) (G) (H) (J) (K) 42. (F) (G) (H) (J) (K) 52. (F) (G) (H) (J) (K)
3. (A) (B) (C) (D) (E) 13. (A) (B) (C) (D) (E) 23. (A) (B) (C) (D) (E) 33. (A) (B) (C) (D) (E) 43. (A) (B) (C) (D) (E) 53. (A) (B) (C) (D) (E)
4. (F) (G) (H) (J) (K) 14. (F) (G) (H) (J) (K) 24. (F) (G) (H) (J) (K) 34. (F) (G) (H) (J) (K) 44. (F) (G) (H) (J) (K) 54. (F) (G) (H) (J) (K)
5. (A) (B) (C) (D) (E) 15. (A) (B) (C) (D) (E) 25. (A) (B) (C) (D) (E) 35. (A) (B) (C) (D) (E) 45. (A) (B) (C) (D) (E) 55. (A) (B) (C) (D) (E)
6. (F) (G) (H) (J) (K) 16. (F) (G) (H) (J) (K) 26. (F) (G) (H) (J) (K) 36. (F) (G) (H) (J) (K) 46. (F) (G) (H) (J) (K) 56. (F) (G) (H) (J) (K)
7. (A) (B) (C) (D) (E) 17. (A) (B) (C) (D) (E) 27. (A) (B) (C) (D) (E) 37. (A) (B) (C) (D) (E) 47. (A) (B) (C) (D) (E) 57. (A) (B) (C) (D) (E)
8. (F) (G) (H) (J) (K) 18. (F) (G) (H) (J) (K) 28. (F) (G) (H) (J) (K) 38. (F) (G) (H) (J) (K) 48. (F) (G) (H) (J) (K) 58. (F) (G) (H) (J) (K)
9. (A) (B) (C) (D) (E) 19. (A) (B) (C) (D) (E) 29. (A) (B) (C) (D) (E) 39. (A) (B) (C) (D) (E) 49. (A) (B) (C) (D) (E) 59. (A) (B) (C) (D) (E)
10. (F) (G) (H) (J) (K) 20. (F) (G) (H) (J) (K) 30. (F) (G) (H) (J) (K) 40. (F) (G) (H) (J) (K) 50. (F) (G) (H) (J) (K) 60. (F) (G) (H) (J) (K)

READING TEST

1. (A) (B) (C) (D) 6. (F) (G) (H) (J) 11. (A) (B) (C) (D) 16. (F) (G) (H) (J) 21. (A) (B) (C) (D) 26. (F) (G) (H) (J) 31. (A) (B) (C) (D) 36. (F) (G) (H) (J)
2. (F) (G) (H) (J) 7. (A) (B) (C) (D) 12. (F) (G) (H) (J) 17. (A) (B) (C) (D) 22. (F) (G) (H) (J) 27. (A) (B) (C) (D) 32. (F) (G) (H) (J) 37. (A) (B) (C) (D)
3. (A) (B) (C) (D) 8. (F) (G) (H) (J) 13. (A) (B) (C) (D) 18. (F) (G) (H) (J) 23. (A) (B) (C) (D) 28. (F) (G) (H) (J) 33. (A) (B) (C) (D) 38. (F) (G) (H) (J)
4. (F) (G) (H) (J) 9. (A) (B) (C) (D) 14. (F) (G) (H) (J) 19. (A) (B) (C) (D) 24. (F) (G) (H) (J) 29. (A) (B) (C) (D) 34. (F) (G) (H) (J) 39. (A) (B) (C) (D)
5. (A) (B) (C) (D) 10. (F) (G) (H) (J) 15. (A) (B) (C) (D) 20. (F) (G) (H) (J) 25. (A) (B) (C) (D) 30. (F) (G) (H) (J) 35. (A) (B) (C) (D) 40. (F) (G) (H) (J)

SCIENCE TEST

1. (A) (B) (C) (D) 6. (F) (G) (H) (J) 11. (A) (B) (C) (D) 16. (F) (G) (H) (J) 21. (A) (B) (C) (D) 26. (F) (G) (H) (J) 31. (A) (B) (C) (D) 36. (F) (G) (H) (J)
2. (F) (G) (H) (J) 7. (A) (B) (C) (D) 12. (F) (G) (H) (J) 17. (A) (B) (C) (D) 22. (F) (G) (H) (J) 27. (A) (B) (C) (D) 32. (F) (G) (H) (J) 37. (A) (B) (C) (D)
3. (A) (B) (C) (D) 8. (F) (G) (H) (J) 13. (A) (B) (C) (D) 18. (F) (G) (H) (J) 23. (A) (B) (C) (D) 28. (F) (G) (H) (J) 33. (A) (B) (C) (D) 38. (F) (G) (H) (J)
4. (F) (G) (H) (J) 9. (A) (B) (C) (D) 14. (F) (G) (H) (J) 19. (A) (B) (C) (D) 24. (F) (G) (H) (J) 29. (A) (B) (C) (D) 34. (F) (G) (H) (J) 39. (A) (B) (C) (D)
5. (A) (B) (C) (D) 10. (F) (G) (H) (J) 15. (A) (B) (C) (D) 20. (F) (G) (H) (J) 25. (A) (B) (C) (D) 30. (F) (G) (H) (J) 35. (A) (B) (C) (D) 40. (F) (G) (H) (J)

ENGLISH TEST

45 Minutes—75 Questions

Directions: Each passage has certain words and phrases that are underlined and numbered. The questions in the right column will provide alternatives for the underlined segments. Most questions require you to choose the answer that makes the sentence grammatically correct, concise, and relevant. If the word or phrase in the passage is already the correct, concise, and relevant choice, select Choice A, NO CHANGE. Some questions will ask a question about the underlined segment. When a question is presented, choose the best answer.

Some questions will ask about part or all of the passage. These questions do not refer to a specific underlined segment. Instead, these questions will accompany a number in a box.

For each question, choose your answer and fill in the corresponding bubble on your answer sheet. Read the passage once before you answer the questions. You will often need to read several sentences beyond the underlined portion to be able to choose the correct answer. Be sure to read enough to answer each question.

Passage I

Origins of Urban Legends

[1]

Since primitive times, societies have <u>created, and told</u> legends. Even before the development of written language, cultures would orally pass down these popular stories. The legends were told and retold, passing from generation to generation.

1. **A.** NO CHANGE
   B. created then subsequently told
   C. created and told
   D. created, and told original

GO ON TO THE NEXT PAGE

[2]

2 The stories served the dual purpose of enter-

taining audiences and of transmitting values

2. The writer wants to add a sentence that describes the different kinds of oral stories told by these societies. Which of the following true statements would most clearly and effectively accomplish the writer's goal?

    F. These myths and tales varied in substance, from the humorous to the heroic.

    G. These myths and tales were often recited by paid storytellers.

    H. Unfortunately, no audio recording of the original myths and tales exists.

    J. Sometimes it took several evenings for the full story to be recited.

and beliefs. <u>Indeed</u> today we have many more perma-
          3

nent ways of handing down our beliefs to future genera-

tions, we continue to create and tell legends.

3. **A.** NO CHANGE

    B. However,

    C. Because

    D. Although

In our technological society, a new form of folktale has

emerged: <u>the</u> urban legend.
     4

[3]

4. **F.** NO CHANGE

    G. it is called the

    H. it being the

    J. known as the

    Urban legends are stories we all have heard; they

are supposed to have really happened, but are never

verifiable. It seems that the people involved can never be

found. Researchers of the urban legend call the elusive

participant in such supposed "real-life" events a

<u>FOAF; a Friend of a Friend.</u> [A]
      5

[4]

5. **A.** NO CHANGE

    B. FOAF . . . a Friend of a Friend.

    C. FOAF a Friend of a Friend.

    D. FOAF: a Friend of a Friend.

    Urban legends have some characteristic features.

They are often humorous in nature with a surprise

GO ON TO THE NEXT PAGE ⟶

ending and a conclusion. [B] One such legend is the tale
       6
of the hunter who was returning home from an unsuc-

cessful hunting trip. On his way home, he accidentally

hit and killed a deer on a deserted highway. Even though

he knew it was illegal, he decided to keep the deer, and

he loads it in the back of his station wagon.
    7

As the hunter continued driving, the deer, he was only
                   8
temporarily knocked unconscious by the car, woke up

and began thrashing around. The hunter panicked,

stopped the car, ran to hide in the roadside ditch, and

watched the enraged deer destroy his car.

[5]

[C] One legend involves alligators in the sewer

systems of major metropolitan areas. According to the

story, before alligators were a protected species, people
                                   9
vacationing in tropical locations purchased baby alliga-

tors to take home as souvenirs.

6. F. NO CHANGE
   G. ending.
   H. ending, which is a conclusion.
   J. ending or conclusion.

7. A. NO CHANGE
   B. loaded it in
   C. is loading it in
   D. had loaded it in

8. F. NO CHANGE
   G. which being
   H. that is
   J. which was

9. A. NO CHANGE
   B. species; people
   C. species. People
   D. species people

GO ON TO THE NEXT PAGE

After the pet alligators proved to be nuisances, many
10
people heartlessly discarded their alligators.
10
Legend has it that the baby alligators found a perfect

growing and breeding environment in city sewer sys-

tems, where they thrive to this day on the ample supply

of rats.

[6]

In addition to urban legends that are told from

friend to friend, a growing number of urban legends are

passed along through the Internet and email. One of the

most popular stories are about a woman who was unwit-
11
tingly charged $100 for a cookie recipe she requested at

an upscale restaurant. To get her money's worth,

this woman supposed copied the recipe for the deli-
12
cious cookies and forwarded it via email to everyone she

knew. [D]

[7]

Although today's technology enhances our ability to

tell and retell urban legends, the Internet can also serve

as a monitor of urban legends. Dedicated to commonly
13
told urban legends, research is done by many websites.
13
According to those websites, most legends, including

the ones told here, have no basis in reality.

10. Which choice maintains the essay's humorous tone and most clearly conveys the legend being described at this point in the essay?

F. NO CHANGE

G. When pet alligators turned out to be less fun than many people assume, their owners got rid of them.

H. Once people deduced that alligators were unsafe companions, they resorted to using industrial plumbing to dispose of the reptiles, disseminating the creatures among miles of municipal distribution pipes.

J. After the novelty of having a pet alligator wore off, many people flushed their baby souvenirs down city toilets.

11. A. NO CHANGE

B. would be about

C. is about

D. is dealing with

12. F. NO CHANGE

G. woman supposedly

H. women supposedly

J. women supposed to

13. A. NO CHANGE

B. Many websites are dedicated to researching the validity of commonly told urban legends.

C. Researching the validity of commonly told urban legends, many websites are dedicated.

D. Dedicated to commonly told urban legends, the validity of them is researched by many websites.

GO ON TO THE NEXT PAGE →

> Questions 14 and 15 ask about the preceding passage as a whole.

14. The writer wants to add the following sentence to the essay:

> Other urban legends seem to be designed to instill fear.

The sentence would most logically be placed at Point:

F. A.

G. B.

H. C.

J. D.

15. Suppose the writer's primary purpose had been to compare the purposes and topics of myths and legends in primitive societies and in our modern society. Would this essay accomplish that purpose?

A. Yes, because the essay describes myths and legends from primitive societies and modern society.

B. Yes, because the essay provides explanations of possible purposes and topics of myths and legends from primitive societies and modern society.

C. No, because the essay does not provide enough information about the topics of the myths and legends of primitive societies to make a valid comparison.

D. No, because the essay does not provide any information on the myths and legends of primitive societies.

GO ON TO THE NEXT PAGE

Passage II

Henry David Thoreau: A Successful Life

What does it mean to be successful? <u>Do one</u> meas-
16
ure success by how much money someone earns?

<u>When</u> I told you about a man who worked as a teacher,
17
a land surveyor, and a factory worker (never holding

any of these jobs for more than a few years), would that

man sound like a success to you? If I told you that

<u>he spent two solitary years living alone</u> in a small cabin
18
that he built for himself and that he spent those years

looking at plants and writing in a diary, would you think

of him as a celebrity or an important figure? What if I

told you that he rarely ventured far from the town where

he was <u>born—that he was thrown in jail for refusing to</u>
19
<u>pay his taxes, and</u> that he died at the age of 45? Do any
19
of these facts seem to point to a man whose life should

be studied and emulated?

You may already know about this man. You

may even have read some of his writings. His name

<u>was, Henry David Thoreau and he</u> was, in addition to
20
the jobs listed above, a poet, an essayist, a naturalist, and

a social critic. Although the facts listed about

16. **F.** NO CHANGE
    G. Does we
    H. Do you
    J. Did one

17. **A.** NO CHANGE
    B. If
    C. Despite the fact that
    D. Before

18. **F.** NO CHANGE
    G. two solitary years all by himself
    H. he spent two years living alone
    J. he spent a couple of years alone living in solitude

19. **A.** NO CHANGE
    B. born that he was thrown in jail for refusing to pay his taxes and
    C. born—that he was thrown in jail for refusing to pay his taxes and
    D. born, that he was thrown in jail for refusing to pay his taxes, and

20. **F.** NO CHANGE
    G. was Henry David Thoreau he
    H. was, Henry David Thoreau; and he
    J. was Henry David Thoreau, and he

GO ON TO THE NEXT PAGE

him may not seem to add up to much, he <u>was, in fact a</u>
₂₁
tremendously influential person. Along with writers
such as Ralph Waldo Emerson, Mark Twain, and Walt
Whitman, Thoreau helped to create the first literature
and philosophy that most people identify as <u>uniformly</u>
₂₂
American.

In 1845 <u>Thoreau, built a cabin</u> near Walden Pond
₂₃
and remained there for more than two years. He lived
alone, fending for himself, and observing the nature
around him. He kept scrupulous notes in his diary,
which he wrote in <u>daily; he later</u> distilled those notes
₂₄
into his most famous work titled *Walden*.

[1] To protest slavery, Thoreau refused to pay his
taxes in 1846. [2] Thoreau was a firm believer in the
abolition of slavery, and he objected to slavery's extension into the new territories of the West. [3] For this act
of rebellion, he was thrown in the Concord jail. [25]

Thoreau used his writing to spread his message of
resistance and <u>activism; he published</u> an essay entitled
₂₆
Civil Disobedience (also known as *Resistance to Civil
Government*). In it, he emphasized the importance of
prioritizing one's consciousness over legal traditions.
Thoreau was wholeheartedly unapologetic in arguing for
the right to refuse to obey unjust laws.

21. **A.** NO CHANGE
    B. was, in fact, a
    C. was in fact a
    D. was in fact, a

22. **F.** NO CHANGE
    G. uniquely
    H. obliquely
    J. deplorably

23. **A.** NO CHANGE
    B. In 1845, Thoreau built a cabin,
    C. Thoreau in 1845 built a cabin
    D. In 1845, Thoreau built a cabin

24. Which of the following alternatives to the un-
    derlined portion would NOT be acceptable?
    F. daily—he
    G. daily, and he
    H. daily. He
    J. daily, he

25. What is the most logical order of sentences in
    this paragraph?
    A. NO CHANGE
    B. 3, 2, 1
    C. 2, 1, 3
    D. 3, 1, 2

26. **F.** NO CHANGE
    G. activism, he published:
    H. activism, he published
    J. activism, he published,

GO ON TO THE NEXT PAGE ⟶

<u>Given that</u> Thoreau's life was very brief, his works
                27
and his ideas continue to touch and influence people.

Students all over the country—all over the world—

continue to read his essays and hear his unique voice,

urging them to lead lives of principle, individuality, and

freedom. To be able to live out ideas that have so

much meaning—surely <u>you</u> would agree that is the
                                  28

meaning of success. 29

27. **A.** NO CHANGE
    B. Even though
    C. Because
    D. Despite the true fact that

28. **F.** NO CHANGE
    G. they
    H. they all
    J. everyone

29. This paragraph primarily serves to:
    A. explain why Thoreau was put in jail.
    B. prove a point about people's conception of success.
    C. suggest that Thoreau may be misunderstood.
    D. discuss Thoreau's importance in today's world.

> Question 30 asks about the preceding passage as a whole.

30. By including questions throughout the entire first paragraph, the writer encourages the reader to:
    F. answer each question as the passage proceeds.
    G. think about the meaning of success.
    H. assess the quality of Thoreau's work.
    J. form an opinion about greed in modern society.

GO ON TO THE NEXT PAGE

Passage III

The Sloth: Slow but Not Slothful

[1]

More than half of the world's currently living plant
                                                    31
and animal species live in tropical rain forests. Four

square miles of a Central American rain forest can be

home to up to 1,500 different species of flowering plants,

700 species of trees, 400 species of birds, and 125 species

of mammals. Of these mammals, the sloth is one of the

most unusual. [A]

[2]

Unlike most mammals, the sloth is usually upside

down. A sloth does just about everything upside down,

including sleeping, eating, mating, and giving birth.

Its' unique anatomy allows the sloth to spend most of
   32
the time hanging from one tree branch or another, high

in the canopy of a rain forest tree. [B] About the size of

a large domestic cat, the sloth hangs from its unusually
               33
long limbs and long, hooklike claws.

Specially designed for limbs, the sloth has muscles that
                                   34
seem to cling to things.
        34

31. A. NO CHANGE
　　B. currently existing plant
　　C. living plant
　　D. plant

32. F. NO CHANGE
　　G. It's unique
　　H. Its unique
　　J. Its uniquely

33. A. NO CHANGE
　　B. cat; the
　　C. cat. The
　　D. cat, but the

34. F. NO CHANGE
　　G. The sloth's muscles seem to cling to things for specially designed limbs.
　　H. The muscles in a sloth's limbs seem to be specially designed for clinging to things.
　　J. Specially designed for limbs, clinging to things is how the sloth uses its muscles.

GO ON TO THE NEXT PAGE

[3]

In fact, a sloth's limbs are so <u>defiantly</u> adapted to
          35
upside-down life that a sloth is essentially incapable of

walking on the ground.

35. **A.** NO CHANGE
    B. enthusiastically
    C. painstakingly
    D. specifically

<u>Instead, it must crawl, or drag itself</u> with its massive
            36
claws. This makes it easy to see why the sloth rarely

leaves its home in the trees.

36. **F.** NO CHANGE
    G. Instead, it must crawl or drag itself
    H. Instead, it must crawl, or drag itself,
    J. Instead it must crawl or drag itself,

<u>Because</u> it cannot move swiftly on the ground, the sloth
    37
is an excellent swimmer.

37. **A.** NO CHANGE
    B. Despite
    C. Similarly,
    D. Though

[4]

[38] A sloth can hang upside down and, without

38. Which of the following true statements would provide the best transition from the preceding paragraph to this paragraph?
    F. Of course, many other animals are also excellent swimmers.
    G. Another unique characteristic of the sloth is its flexibility.
    H. In addition to swimming, the sloth is an incredible climber.
    J. Flexibility is a trait that helps the sloth survive.

moving the rest of its <u>body, has the ability to be able to</u>
                                39
<u>turn</u> its face 180 degrees so that it
 39

39. **A.** NO CHANGE
    B. body, turns
    C. body, has the ability to turn
    D. body, turn

GO ON TO THE NEXT PAGE ⟶

was looking at the ground. A sloth can rotate its fore-
 40
limbs in all directions, so it can easily reach the leaves

that make up its diet.

40. F. NO CHANGE
    G. had been looking
    H. will have the ability to be looking
    J. can look

Also roll itself up into a ball in order to protect itself
 41
from predators.

41. A. NO CHANGE
    B. The sloth is known also
    C. The sloth is to also
    D. The sloth can also

The howler monkey, another inhabitant of the rain
                        42
forest, is not as flexible as the sloth.
             42
                    [5]

    The best defense a sloth has from predators such as

jaguars and large snakes, though, is its camouflage. Dur-

ing the rainy season, a sloth's thick brown or gray fur is

usually covered with a coat of blue-green

42. If the writer were to delete the underlined
    sentence, the paragraph would primarily lose:
    F. an important detail that highlights the
        distinctiveness of the sloth.
    G. a statement that provides a logical transi-
        tion from the ideas in one paragraph to
        the next.
    H. affirmation that the sloth lives in a
        habitat with different species, such as the
        howler monkey.
    J. an unnecessary detail that does not provide
        additional information about the writer's
        main idea.

algae. Which helps it blend in with its forest surround-
 43
ings. [C] Another type of camouflage is the sloth's

incredibly slow movement: it often moves less than 100

feet during a 24-hour period.

                    [6]

    It is this slow movement that earned the sloth its

name. *Sloth* is also a word for laziness or an aversion to

work. But even though it sleeps an average of

43. A. NO CHANGE
    B. algae, which
    C. algae, being that it
    D. algae

GO ON TO THE NEXT PAGE

15 hours a day, the sloth is not necessarily lazy. [D] It just moves, upside down, at its own slow pace through its world of rain forest trees. [44]

44. The writer is considering deleting the last sentence of Paragraph 6. This change would:

    F. diminish the amount of information provided about the habits of the sloth.

    G. make the ending of the passage more abrupt.

    H. emphasize the slothful nature of the sloth.

    J. make the tone of the essay more consistent.

Question 45 asks about the preceding passage as a whole.

---

45. The writer wants to add the following sentence to the essay:

> An observer could easily be tricked into thinking that a sloth was just a pile of decaying leaves.

The sentence would most logically be placed at Point:

    A. A.

    B. B.

    C. C.

    D. D.

GO ON TO THE NEXT PAGE

Passage IV

Fires in Yellowstone

During the summer of 1988, I watched Yellowstone National Park go up in flames. In June, <u>fires ignited by lightning</u> had been allowed to burn unsuppressed

46
because park officials expected that the usual summer rains would douse the flames. However,

the rains never <u>will have come.</u> A plentiful fuel supply

47
of fallen logs and pine needles was available, and winds of up to 100 miles per hour whipped the spreading fires along and carried red-hot embers to other areas, creating new fires. By the time park officials succumbed to the pressure of public opinion and <u>decide</u> to try to

48

extinguish the <u>flames. It's</u> too late. The situation

49
remained out of control in spite of the efforts of 9,000 firefighters who were using state-of-the-art equipment. By September, more than 720,000 acres of Yellowstone had been affected by fire. <u>Nature was only able to curb the destruction</u>; the smoke did not begin to clear until

50
the first snow arrived on September 11.

<u>Being that I was</u> an ecologist who has studied

51
forests for 20 years, I know that this was not nearly the tragedy it seemed to be.

46. **F.** NO CHANGE
    G. fires having been ignited by lightning
    H. fires, the kind ignited by lightning,
    J. fires ignited and started by lightning

47. **A.** NO CHANGE
    B. came.
    C. were coming.
    D. have come.

48. **F.** NO CHANGE
    G. are deciding
    H. decided
    J. DELETE the underlined portion.

49. **A.** NO CHANGE
    B. flames, it's
    C. flames, it was
    D. flames; it was

50. **F.** NO CHANGE
    G. Only curbing the destruction by able nature
    H. Only nature was able to curb the destruction
    J. Nature was able to curb only the destruction

51. **A.** NO CHANGE
    B. Being that I am
    C. I'm
    D. As

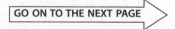
GO ON TO THE NEXT PAGE

Large fires are, after all, necessary <u>despite</u> the continued
                                        52
health of the forest ecosystem. Fires thin out

overcrowded areas and <u>allow it</u> to reach species of plants
                          53
stunted by shade. Ash fertilizes the soil, and fire smoke

kills forest bacteria. In the case of the lodgepole pine,

fire is essential to reproduction:

the <u>pines' cone</u> open only when exposed to tempera-
        54
tures greater than 112 degrees.

    The fires in Yellowstone did result in some loss of

wildlife, but overall, the region's animals proved to be

fire-tolerant and fire-adaptive. <u>However,</u> large animals
                                    55
such as bison were often seen grazing and bedding

down in meadows <u>close to and near</u> burning forests.
                        56
Also, the fire posed little threat to the members of any

endangered animal species in the park.

    My confidence in the natural resilience of the forest

has been borne out in the years since the fires ravaged

Yellowstone. [57]

52. **F.** NO CHANGE
    G. without
    H. beside
    J. for

53. **A.** NO CHANGE
    B. allows it
    C. allow the sun
    D. allows the sun

54. **F.** NO CHANGE
    G. pines cones'
    H. pine's cones
    J. pine's cone

55. **A.** NO CHANGE
    B. Clearly,
    C. In fact,
    D. Instead,

56. **F.** NO CHANGE
    G. close to, and near
    H. near,
    J. near

57. In the preceding sentence, the clause "has been borne out" primarily serves to indicate that:

    A. the forest's animal population thrived in years directly following the fire.

    B. the fire created new species of vegetation, which were better suited to survive harsh conditions.

    C. other forests may not have survived a wildfire as well as Yellowstone National Park did.

    D. the writer's assessment that the fire was not a catastrophe was accurate.

GO ON TO THE NEXT PAGE

<u>Judged from recent pictures of the park,</u> the forest was
58
not destroyed; it was rejuvenated.

58. **F.** NO CHANGE

    G. Recent pictures of the park show that

    H. Judging by the recent pictures of the park,

    J. As judged according to pictures taken of the park recently,

---

Questions 59 and 60 ask about the preceding passage as a whole.

---

59. The author is considering inserting the following true statement after the first sentence of the second paragraph:

> Many more acres of forest burned in Alaska in 1988 than in Yellowstone Park.

Would this addition be appropriate for the essay?

    A. Yes, the statement would add important information about the effects of large-scale forest fires.

    B. Yes, the statement would provide an informative contrast to the Yellowstone fire.

    C. No, the statement would not provide any additional information about the effect of the 1988 fire in Yellowstone.

    D. No, the statement would undermine the writer's position as an authority on the subject of forest fires.

60. Suppose that the writer wishes to provide additional support for the claim that the fire posed little threat to the members of any endangered animal species in the park. Which of the following additions would be most effective?

    F. A list of the endangered animals known to inhabit the park

    G. A discussion of the particular vulnerability of endangered species of birds to forest fires

    H. An explanation of the relative infrequency of such an extensive series of forest fires

    J. A summary of reports of biologists who monitored the activity of endangered species in the park during the fire

GO ON TO THE NEXT PAGE

Passage V

My First White-Water Rafting Trip

[1]

White-water rafting has been a favorite pastime of mine for several years. I have drifted down many challenging North American rivers, including the Snake, the Green, and the <u>Salmon, and there are many other rivers</u> $\overline{}$ 61
<u>in America as well that I have not rafted.</u> I have spent
 61
some of my best moments in dangerous rapids, yet nothing has matched the thrill I experienced facing

my <u>first, rapids, on the Deschutes River.</u> [A]
 62

[2]

<u>My father and me</u> spent the morning floating down
 63
a calm stretch of the Deschutes in his wooden McKenzie river boat.

This trip <u>being</u> the wooden boat's first time down rapids,
 64
as well as mine. While I enjoyed the peacefulness, I was eager for the thrill yet to come. [B]

[3]

<u>Roaring, I was in the boat approaching Whitehorse</u>
 65
<u>Rapids.</u> I felt much like a novice skier peering down my
65
first steep slope: I was scared, but even more exhilarated.

61. A. NO CHANGE
    B. Salmon, just three of many rivers existing in North America.
    C. Salmon; many other rivers exist in North America.
    D. Salmon.

62. F. NO CHANGE
    G. first: rapids on the Deschutes River.
    H. first rapids; on the Deschutes River.
    J. first rapids on the Deschutes River.

63. A. NO CHANGE
    B. Me and my father
    C. My father and I
    D. I and my father

64. F. NO CHANGE
    G. happened that it was
    H. been
    J. was

65. A. NO CHANGE
    B. It roared, and the boat and I approached the Whitehorse Rapids.
    C. While the roaring boat was approaching the Whitehorse Rapids, I could hear the water.
    D. I could hear the water roar as we approached the Whitehorse Rapids.

GO ON TO THE NEXT PAGE

The water churned and swirled, covering me with a
66
refreshing spray. My father, toward the stern, controlled

the oars. The carefree expression he usually wore

on the river had been replaced, and instead adopted a
67
look of intense concentration as he maneuvered around

boulders dotting our path. To release tension, we began

to holler like kids on a roller coaster, our voices echoing

across the water as we lurched violently about.

[4]

Eventually we came to a jarring
68

halt; and the left side of the bow was wedged on a large
69
rock. [C] A whirlpool swirled around us; if we capsized,

we would be sucked into the undertow. Instinctively,

I threw all of my weight toward the right side of the

tilting boat. Luckily, it was just enough force to dislodge
70
us, and we continued on downstream to enjoy about 10

more minutes of spectacular rapids. [D]

[5]

Later that day, we went through Buckskin Mary

Rapids and Boxcar Rapids. When we pulled up on the

bank that evening, we saw that the boat had received

their first scar: a small hole on the upper bow from the
71
boulder we had wrestled with. In the years to come,

66. F. NO CHANGE
    G. churning and swirling, covering me
    H. churning, covering me
    J. churned, covering me

67. A. NO CHANGE
    B. replaced with
    C. replaced by another countenance alto-
       gether:
    D. replaced; instead

68. F. NO CHANGE
    G. Not surprisingly
    H. Without a doubt
    J. Suddenly

69. A. NO CHANGE
    B. halt. And
    C. halt
    D. halt;

70. F. NO CHANGE
    G. it's
    H. it is
    J. its

71. A. NO CHANGE
    B. their extremely visible
    C. its very ghastly
    D. its

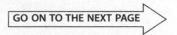
GO ON TO THE NEXT PAGE

Practice Test 1

we went down many rapids and the boat received many

bruises, Whitehorse remains the most memorable
     72

rapids of all. 73

72. F. NO CHANGE
    G. bruises, but Whitehorse
    H. bruises even though Whitehorse
    J. bruises Whitehorse

73. Which choice most effectively concludes the essay?
    A. The brutal calamities that it presented the unwary rafter were more than offset by its beguiling excitement.
    B. Perhaps it is true that your first close encounter with white water is your most intense.
    C. Or, if not the most memorable, then at least a very memorable one!
    D. Call me crazy or weird if you want, but white-water rafting is the sport for me.

Questions 74 and 75 ask about the preceding passage as a whole.

74. Suppose the writer's primary purpose had been to focus on the techniques of white-water rafting. Would this essay accomplish that purpose?
    F. No, because the essay's main focus is on a particular experience, not on techniques.
    G. No, because the essay mostly deals with the relationship between family members.
    H. Yes, because specific rafting techniques are the essay's main focus.
    J. Yes, because it presents a dramatic story of a day of white-water rafting.

75. The writer wants to add the following sentence to the essay:

    It was such a mild summer day that it was hard to believe dangerous rapids awaited us downstream.

    The sentence would most logically be placed at Point:
    A. A in Paragraph 1.
    B. B in Paragraph 2.
    C. C in Paragraph 4.
    D. D in Paragraph 4.

IF YOU FINISH BEFORE TIME IS CALLED, YOU MAY CHECK YOUR WORK ON THIS SECTION ONLY. DO NOT TURN TO ANY OTHER SECTION IN THE TEST. STOP

Practice Test 1

MATHEMATICS TEST

60 Minutes—60 Questions

Directions: Choose the correct solution to each question and fill in the corresponding bubble on your answer sheet.

Do not continue to spend time on questions if you get stuck. Solve as many questions as you can before returning to any if time permits.

You may use a calculator on this test for any question you choose. However, some questions may be better solved without a calculator.

Note: Unless otherwise stated, you can assume:

1. Figures are NOT necessarily drawn to scale.

2. Geometric figures are two dimensional.

3. The word *line* indicates a straight line.

4. The word *average* indicates arithmetic mean.

1. In a recent survey, 14 people found their mayor to be "very competent." This number is exactly 20% of the people surveyed. How many people were surveyed?

   A. 28

   B. 35

   C. 56

   D. 70

   E. 84

2. A train traveled at a rate of 90 miles per hour for x hours, and then at a rate of 60 miles per hour for y hours. Which expression represents the train's average rate, in miles per hour, for the entire distance traveled?

   F. $\dfrac{540}{xy}$

   G. $\dfrac{90}{x} \times \dfrac{60}{y}$

   H. $\dfrac{90}{x} + \dfrac{60}{y}$

   J. $\dfrac{90x + 60y}{x + y}$

   K. $\dfrac{150}{x + y}$

GO ON TO THE NEXT PAGE

3. In a certain string ensemble, the ratio of men to women is 5:3. If there are a total of 24 people in the ensemble, how many women are there?

    A. 8

    B. 9

    C. 10

    D. 11

    E. 12

4. What is the value of $-|-6| - (-6)$?

    F. −36

    G. −12

    H. 0

    J. 12

    K. 36

5. Martin's average score after four tests is 89. What score on the fifth test would bring Martin's average up to exactly 90 ?

    A. 90

    B. 91

    C. 92

    D. 93

    E. 94

6. What is the sum of $\frac{3}{16}$ and 0.175 ?

    F. 0.3165

    G. 0.3500

    H. 0.3625

    J. 0.3750

    K. 0.3875

7. Which of the following is less than $\frac{3}{5}$?

    A. $\frac{4}{6}$

    B. $\frac{8}{13}$

    C. $\frac{6}{10}$

    D. $\frac{7}{11}$

    E. $\frac{4}{7}$

8. An ice cream parlor offers five flavors of ice cream and four different toppings (sprinkles, hot fudge, whipped cream, and butterscotch). There is a special offer that includes one flavor of ice cream and one topping, served in a cup, sugar cone, or waffle cone. How many ways are there to order ice cream with the special offer?

    F. 4

    G. 5

    H. 12

    J. 23

    K. 60

9. At a recent audition for a school play, 1 out of 3 students who auditioned were asked to come to a second audition. After the second audition, 75% of those asked to the second audition were offered parts. If 18 students were offered parts, how many students went to the first audition?

    A. 18

    B. 24

    C. 48

    D. 56

    E. 72

GO ON TO THE NEXT PAGE

Use the following information to answer questions 10–12.

The following table shows the results of a study about the benefits of eating breakfast as it relates to maintaining a healthy weight.

Breakfast Study Results

	Breakfast ≤ 1 time per week	Breakfast 2–4 times per week	Breakfast 5–7 times per week	Total
Within healthy weight range	6	15	36	57
Outside healthy weight range	38	27	9	74
Total	44	42	45	131

10. What percent of the participants who were outside a healthy weight range ate breakfast one or fewer times per week?

F. 29.00%

G. 37.15%

H. 51.35%

J. 56.49%

K. 86.36%

11. If two of the participants from this study are selected at random to complete a follow-up survey, which expression represents the probability that neither of the participants ate breakfast more than 1 time per week?

A. $\dfrac{44}{131} + \dfrac{43}{130}$

B. $\dfrac{44}{131} \times \dfrac{43}{130}$

C. $\dfrac{44}{131} \times \dfrac{44}{131}$

D. $\dfrac{87}{131} \times \dfrac{86}{130}$

E. $\dfrac{87}{131} \times \dfrac{87}{131}$

12. A large company that provides breakfast for all its employees 5 days a week wants to use the results of the original study to determine how many of its employees are likely to be within a healthy weight range, given that all the employees take advantage of the free breakfast all 5 weekdays. If the company has 3,000 employees, and assuming the participants in the study were a good representative sample, about how many of the employees are likely to be within a healthy weight range?

F. 825

G. 1,030

H. 1,300

J. 1,900

K. 2,400

13. How many positive integers less than 50 are multiples of 4 but NOT multiples of 6 ?

A. 4

B. 6

C. 8

D. 10

E. 12

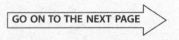
GO ON TO THE NEXT PAGE

14. Given that $f(x) = (8 - 3x)(x^2 - 2x - 15)$, what is the value of $f(3)$?

    F. -30

    G. -18

    H.   6

    J.   12

    K.   24

15. At most colleges, students receive letter grades, which correspond to a GPA score, rather than a numerical grade, such as 92. The following figure shows the distribution of grades and corresponding GPA scores among students in a biology class. What is the approximate mean biology GPA for this class of students?

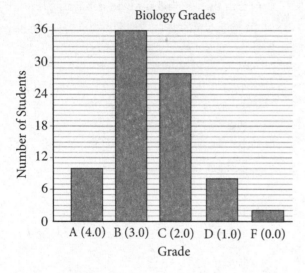

    A.   2.0

    B.   2.5

    C.   2.8

    D.   3.0

    E.   3.2

16. In triangle XYZ shown, $\overline{XS}$ and $\overline{SZ}$ are 3 and 12 units long, respectively. If the area of triangle XYZ is 45 square units, how many units long is altitude $\overline{YS}$?

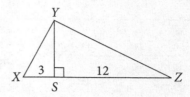

    F.   3

    G.   6

    H.   9

    J.   12

    K.   15

17. At which y-coordinate does the line described by the equation $6y - 3x = 18$ intersect the y-axis?

    A.   2

    B.   3

    C.   6

    D.   9

    E.   18

18. If $x^2 - y^2 = 12$ and $x - y = 4$, what is the value of $x^2 + 2xy + y^2$?

    F.   3

    G.   8

    H.   9

    J.   12

    K.   16

GO ON TO THE NEXT PAGE

19. What is the area in square units of the following figure, given that the angle in the lower right corner has a measure of 45° ?

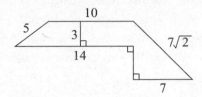

A. $39 + 7\sqrt{2}$

B. 60.5

C. 91

D. 108.5

E. 147

20. A carpenter is cutting wood to make a new bookcase with a board that is 12 feet long. If the carpenter cuts off three pieces, each of which is 1 foot, 5 inches long, how many inches long is the remaining part of the board? (A foot contains 12 inches.)

F. 36

G. 51

H. 93

J. 108

K. 144

21. What two numbers should be placed in the blanks below so that the difference between successive entries is the same?

26, ___, ___, 53

A. 36, 43

B. 35, 44

C. 34, 45

D. 33, 46

E. 30, 49

22. If −3 is a solution for the equation $x^2 + kx - 15 = 0$, what is the value of k ?

F. −5

G. −2

H. 2

J. 5

K. Cannot be determined from the given information

23. In the standard (x,y) coordinate plane, three corners of a rectangle are $(2,-2)$, $(-5,-2)$, and $(2,-5)$. Where is the rectangle's fourth corner?

A. (2,5)

B. (−2,5)

C. (−2,2)

D. (−2,−5)

E. (−5,−5)

24. For the two functions $f(x)$ and $g(x)$, tables of values follow. What is the value of $f(g(1))$?

x	$f(x)$
−2	8
−1	6
0	4
1	2

x	$g(x)$
−1	−4
1	0
2	2
4	6

F. 0

G. 1

H. 2

J. 4

K. 6

GO ON TO THE NEXT PAGE

Practice Test 1   25

25. The following sketch shows the dimensions of a flower garden. What is the area of this garden in square meters?

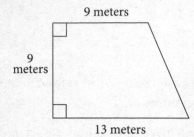

9 meters

9 meters

13 meters

A. 31

B. 85

C. 99

D. 101

E. 117

26. In a certain cookie jar containing only macaroons and gingersnaps, the ratio of macaroons to gingersnaps is 2 to 5. Which of the following could be the total number of cookies in the cookie jar?

F. 20

G. 35

H. 39

J. 48

K. 52

27. A store is running a sale, discounting merchandise by a specific percentage. Margo purchases a coffee maker with an original price of $62.00. After the sale discount, she gets an additional 10% off for using her store credit card. She ends up paying $41.85, not including tax. What was the amount of the original sale discount?

A. 15%

B. 20%

C. 25%

D. 30%

E. 40%

28. What is the maximum possible area, in square inches, of a rectangle that has a perimeter of 20 inches?

F. 15

G. 18

H. 20

J. 25

K. 32

29. $\dfrac{\dfrac{3}{2} + \dfrac{7}{4}}{\left(\dfrac{15}{8} - \dfrac{3}{4}\right) - \left(\dfrac{4+3}{-4+3}\right)} = ?$

A. $\dfrac{3}{8}$

B. $\dfrac{2}{5}$

C. $\dfrac{9}{13}$

D. $\dfrac{5}{2}$

E. $\dfrac{8}{3}$

GO ON TO THE NEXT PAGE

Practice Test 1

30. If $x - 15 = 7 - 5(x - 4)$, then $x = $?

    F.   0

    G.   2

    H.   4

    J.   5

    K.   7

31. Julie can type 3 pages in x minutes. How many minutes will it take her to type 11 pages?

    A. $33x$

    B. $\dfrac{3}{11x}$

    C. $\dfrac{11}{3x}$

    D. $\dfrac{3x}{11}$

    E. $\dfrac{11x}{3}$

32. What is the slope of the line described by the equation $6y - 3x = 18$?

    F. -2

    G. $-\dfrac{1}{2}$

    H. $\dfrac{1}{2}$

    J.   2

    K.   3

33. Which of the following logarithmic equations is equivalent to the exponential equation $10^2 = 100$?

    A. $\log_{10} 100 = 2$

    B. $\log_{10} 2 = 100$

    C. $\log_{100} 10 = 2$

    D. $\log_{100} 2 = 10$

    E. $\log_{2} 100 = 10$

34. Line t in the standard (x,y) coordinate plane has a y-intercept of -3 and is parallel to the line having the equation $3x - 5y = 4$. Which of the following is an equation for line t ?

    F. $y = -\dfrac{3}{5}x + 3$

    G. $y = -\dfrac{5}{3}x - 3$

    H. $y = \dfrac{3}{5}x + 3$

    J. $y = \dfrac{5}{3}x + 3$

    K. $y = \dfrac{3}{5}x - 3$

35. If the vector $\mathbf{w}$ is given by $\mathbf{w} = \langle -8, 12 \rangle$, which of the following represents $-\dfrac{3}{4}\mathbf{w}$?

    A. $\langle 6, -9 \rangle$

    B. $\langle -6, -9 \rangle$

    C. $\langle -6, 9 \rangle$

    D. $\langle 6, 12 \rangle$

    E. $\langle -8, -9 \rangle$

GO ON TO THE NEXT PAGE

Practice Test 1

36. A scientist has 100 grams of a radioactive substance that has a half-life of 28 days. The table below shows the number of grams of the substance remaining after a certain number of days.

Number of days	0	28	56	84	112
Number of grams remaining	100	50	25	12.5	6.25

Which equation best represents the number of grams of the substance remaining as a function of the number of days, t, that have passed?

F. $f(t) = 28 \cdot \left(\dfrac{1}{2}\right)^t$

G. $f(t) = 28 \cdot 2^{\frac{t}{100}}$

H. $f(t) = 100 \cdot 2^{\frac{t}{28}}$

J. $f(t) = 100 \cdot \left(\dfrac{1}{2}\right)^{\frac{t}{28}}$

K. $f(t) = 100 \left(\dfrac{1}{2}\right)^t$

37. Which of the following is an equation for the circle in the standard (x,y) coordinate plane that has its center at $(-1,-1)$ and passes through the point $(7,5)$?

A. $(x - 1)^2 + (y - 1)^2 = 10$

B. $(x + 1)^2 + (y + 1)^2 = 10$

C. $(x - 1)^2 + (y - 1)^2 = 12$

D. $(x - 1)^2 + (y - 1)^2 = 100$

E. $(x + 1)^2 + (y + 1)^2 = 100$

38. For all $x \neq 8$, $\dfrac{x^2 - 11x + 24}{8 - x} = ?$

F. $8 - x$

G. $3 - x$

H. $x - 3$

J. $x - 8$

K. $x - 11$

39. Points A and B lie in the standard (x,y) coordinate plane. The (x,y) coordinates of A are $(2,1)$, and the (x,y) coordinates of B are $(-2,-2)$. What is the distance from A to B ?

A. $3\sqrt{2}$

B. $3\sqrt{3}$

C. 5

D. 6

E. 7

40. In the following figure, $\overline{AB}$ and $\overline{CD}$ are both tangent to the circle as shown, and $ABCD$ is a rectangle with side lengths $2x$ and $5x$. What is the area of the shaded region?

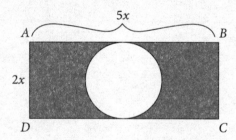

F. $10\pi x^2$

G. $10x^2 - \pi x^2$

H. $10x^2 - 2\pi x$

J. $9\pi x^2$

K. $6\pi x^2$

GO ON TO THE NEXT PAGE

Practice Test 1

41. A tree is growing at the edge of a cliff, as shown in the figure that follows. From the tree, the angle between the edge of the cliff and the base of the house is 62°. If the distance between the base of the cliff and the base of the house is 500 feet, which expression represents the height of the cliff in feet?

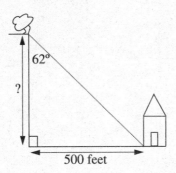

A. 500 cos 62°

B. 500 tan 62°

C. $\dfrac{500}{\sin 62°}$

D. $\dfrac{500}{\cos 62°}$

E. $\dfrac{500}{\tan 62°}$

42. Consider fractions of the form $\dfrac{7}{n}$, where n is an integer. How many integer values of n make this fraction greater than 0.5 and less than 0.8 ?

F. 3

G. 4

H. 5

J. 6

K. 7

43. The figure that follows shows two tangent circles. The circumference of circle X is 12π, and the circumference of circle Y is 8π. What is the greatest possible distance between two points, one of which lies on the circumference of circle X and one of which lies on the circumference of circle Y ?

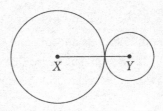

A. 6

B. 10

C. 20

D. 10π

E. 20π

44. $\sqrt{\left(x^2 + 4\right)^2} - (x + 2)(x - 2) = ?$

F. $2x^2$

G. $x^2 - 8$

H. $2(x - 2)$

J. 0

K. 8

45. If $t = -3$, then $5(t + 1) - 1 = ?$

A. -15

B. -11

C. -9

D. 9

E. 11

GO ON TO THE NEXT PAGE

46. How many unique solutions does the equation $2x + 6 = (x + 5)(x + 3)$ have?

    F. 0

    G. 1

    H. 2

    J. 3

    K. Infinitely many

47. Calleigh puts 5 nickels into an empty hat. She wants to add enough pennies so that the probability of drawing a nickel at random from the hat is $\frac{1}{6}$. How many pennies should she put in?

    A. 1

    B. 5

    C. 10

    D. 25

    E. 30

48. In the function $g(r) = (2)^{\frac{1}{r}}$, r represents a positive integer. As r increases without bound, the value of the function:

    F. gets closer and closer to 0.

    G. gets closer and closer to 1.

    H. gets closer and closer to 2.

    J. remains constant.

    K. increases without bound.

49. In the following figure, O is the center of the circle, and C, D, and E are points on the circumference of the circle. If $\angle OCD$ measures 70° and $\angle OED$ measures 45°, what is the measure of $\angle CDE$?

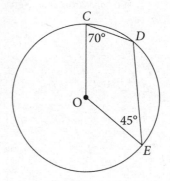

    A. 25°

    B. 45°

    C. 70°

    D. 90°

    E. 115°

50. Which of the following systems of equations has no solution?

    F. $\begin{cases} x + 3y = 19 \\ 3x + y = 6 \end{cases}$

    G. $\begin{cases} x + 3y = 19 \\ x - 3y = 13 \end{cases}$

    H. $\begin{cases} x - 3y = 19 \\ 3x - y = 7 \end{cases}$

    J. $\begin{cases} x + 3y = 6 \\ 3x + 9y = 7 \end{cases}$

    K. $\begin{cases} x + 3y = 19 \\ 9x + 3y = 6 \end{cases}$

GO ON TO THE NEXT PAGE

51. What is the 46th digit to the right of the decimal point in the decimal equivalent of $\frac{1}{7}$?

    A. 1

    B. 2

    C. 4

    D. 7

    E. 8

52. If a and b are real numbers, and $\sqrt{3\left(\frac{a^2}{b}\right)} = 2$, then what must be true of b ?

    F. b must be positive

    G. b must be negative

    H. b must equal $\frac{2}{3}$

    J. b must equal 3

    K. b may have any value

53. Which of the following best describes the graph on the number line that follows?

    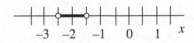

    A. $-|x| = 0.5$

    B. $-|x| > 0.5$

    C. $-3 < x < -1$

    D. $-1.5 < x < -2.5$

    E. $-2.5 < x < -1.5$

54. In the following diagram, $\overline{CD}$, $\overline{BE}$, and $\overline{AF}$ are all parallel and are intersected by two transversals as shown. What is the length of $\overline{EF}$?

    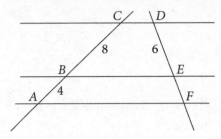

    F. 2

    G. 3

    H. 4

    J. 6

    K. 9

55. Given that the complex number i is defined as $i^2 = -1$, which of the following is equivalent to $(i + 1)^2(i - 1)$?

    A. $i - 1$

    B. $i - 2$

    C. $-i + 2$

    D. $-2i + 2$

    E. $-2i - 2$

56. Compared to the graph of the function $f(\theta) = \cos \theta$, the graph of $g(\theta) = 2 \cos \theta$ has:

    F. twice the period and the same amplitude.

    G. half the period and the same amplitude.

    H. twice the period and half the amplitude.

    J. half the amplitude and the same period.

    K. twice the amplitude and the same period.

GO ON TO THE NEXT PAGE

57. Which of the following is equivalent to the product $\sqrt{2} \times \sqrt[4]{2}$?

   A. $\sqrt[4]{8}$

   B. $\sqrt[6]{2}$

   C. $\sqrt[8]{2}$

   D. $\sqrt[8]{4}$

   E. It is not possible to multiply the two numbers.

58. One empty cylinder has three times the height and twice the diameter of another empty cylinder. How many fillings of the smaller cylinder would be equivalent to one filling of the larger cylinder? (Note: The volume of a cylinder of radius r and height h is $\pi r^2 h$.)

   F. 6

   G. $6\sqrt{2}$

   H. 12

   J. 18

   K. 24

59. What is the perimeter of a 30°-60°-90° triangle that has a long leg of length 12 inches?

   A. $5\sqrt{3} + 12$

   B. $4\sqrt{3} + 18$

   C. $8\sqrt{3} + 18$

   D. $12\sqrt{3} + 12$

   E. $12\sqrt{3} + 18$

60. A baseball team scores an average of x runs in its first n games, and then scores y runs in its next and final game of the season. Which of the following expressions represents the team's average score for the entire season?

   F. $x + \dfrac{y}{n}$

   G. $x + \dfrac{y}{n + 1}$

   H. $\dfrac{x + ny}{n + 1}$

   J. $\dfrac{nx + y}{n + 1}$

   K. $\dfrac{n(x + y)}{n + 1}$

IF YOU FINISH BEFORE TIME IS CALLED, YOU MAY CHECK YOUR WORK ON THIS SECTION ONLY. DO NOT TURN TO ANY OTHER SECTION IN THE TEST. **STOP**

READING TEST

35 Minutes—40 Questions

Directions: The Reading Test includes multiple passages. Each passage includes multiple questions. After reading each passage, choose the best answer and fill in the corresponding bubble on your answer sheet. You may review the passages as often as necessary.

Passage I

PROSE FICTION: This passage is adapted from the novel *Emma* by Jane Austen. It was originally published in 1815.

Emma Woodhouse, handsome, clever, and rich, with a comfortable home and happy disposition, seemed to unite some of the best blessings of existence. She had lived nearly twenty-one years
5 in the world with very little to distress or vex her. She was the youngest of the two daughters of a most affectionate, indulgent father, and had, in consequence of her sister's marriage, been mistress of his house from a very early period. Her mother
10 had died too long ago for her to have more than an indistinct remembrance of her caresses, and her place had been taken by an excellent governess who had fallen little short of a mother in affection.

Sixteen years had Miss Taylor been in Mr.
15 Woodhouse's family, less as a governess than a friend, very fond of both daughters, but particularly of Emma. Between them it was more the intimacy of sisters. Even before Miss Taylor had ceased to hold the nominal office of governess, the mildness
20 of her temper had hardly allowed her to impose any restraint. The shadow of authority being now long passed away, they had been living together as friend and friend very mutually attached, and Emma doing just what she liked, highly esteeming
25 Miss Taylor's judgment, but directed chiefly by her own. The real evils, indeed, of Emma's situation were the power of having rather too much her own way, and a disposition to think a little too well of herself; these were the disadvantages

30 which threatened alloy to her many enjoyments. The danger, however, was at present so unperceived, that they did not by any means rank as misfortunes with her.

Sorrow came—a gentle sorrow—but not at all in the shape of any disagreeable consciousness. Miss
35 Taylor married. It was Miss Taylor's loss which first brought grief. It was on the wedding-day of this beloved friend that Emma first sat in mournful thought of any continuance. The wedding over, and the bride-people gone, she and her father were
40 left to dine together, with no prospect of a third to cheer a long evening. Her father composed himself to sleep after dinner, as usual, and she had then only to sit and think of what she had lost.

The marriage had every promise of happiness
45 for her friend. Mr. Weston was a man of unexceptionable character, easy fortune, suitable age, and pleasant manners. There was some satisfaction in considering with what self-denying, generous friendship she had always wished and promoted the
50 match, but it was a black morning's work for her. The want of Miss Taylor would be felt every hour of every day. She recalled her past kindness—the kindness, the affection of sixteen years—how she had taught her and how she had played with her
55 from five years old—how she had devoted all her powers to attach and amuse her in health—and how she had nursed her through the various illnesses of childhood. A large debt of gratitude was owing

GO ON TO THE NEXT PAGE

60 equal footing and perfect unreserve which had soon
followed Isabella's marriage, on their being left to
each other, was yet a dearer, tenderer recollection.
She had been a friend and companion such as few
possessed: intelligent, well-informed, useful, gentle,
65 knowing all the ways of the family, interested in
all its concerns, and peculiarly interested in her, in
every pleasure, every scheme of hers—one to whom
she could speak every thought as it arose, and who
had such an affection for her as could never find
70 fault.

How was she to bear the change? It was true that
her friend was going only half a mile from them, but
Emma was aware that great must be the difference
between a Mrs. Weston, only half a mile from them,
75 and a Miss Taylor in the house. With all her advantages, natural and domestic, she was now in great
danger of suffering from intellectual solitude.

1. According to the passage, what are the greatest disadvantages facing Emma?

   A. Her father is not a stimulating conver-
      sationalist, and she is bored.

   B. She is lonely and afraid that Mrs.
      Weston will not have a happy
      marriage.

   C. She is used to having her way too
      much, and she thinks too highly of
      herself.

   D. She misses the companionship of her
      mother, her sister, and Miss Taylor.

2. In lines 38—43, the author describes Emma's
   solitary thoughts after dinner in order to:

   F. illustrate her anger regarding Miss
      Taylor's marriage.

   G. emphasize her feelings of sadness and
      loneliness.

   H. suggest her disappointment in her father.

   J. indicate her dislike of Mr. Weston.

3. As described in the passage, Emma's relationship
   with Miss Taylor can be characterized as:

   A. more loving than a parent-child relation-
      ship.

   B. similar to the relationship of sisters or
      best friends.

   C. weaker than Emma's relationship with her
      sister.

   D. stronger than Miss Taylor's relationship
      with her new husband.

4. As used in line 28, *disposition* can most closely
   be defined as:

   F. a tendency.

   G. control.

   H. placement.

   J. transfer.

GO ON TO THE NEXT PAGE

5. Which of the following are included in Emma's memories of her relationship with Miss Taylor?

    I. Miss Taylor taking care of Emma during childhood illnesses

    II. Miss Taylor entertaining Emma

    III. Miss Taylor teaching her mathematics

    IV. Miss Taylor scolding her for being selfish

  A. I, III, and IV only

  B. I and III only

  C. II, III, and IV only

  D. I and II only

6. According to the passage, since the death of her mother, Emma has led a:

  F. desolate life.

  G. restricted life.

  H. happy life.

  J. confused life.

7. Based on the passage, Emma could best be described as:

  A. obedient.

  B. unappreciative.

  C. headstrong.

  D. bitter.

8. The passage suggests that the quality Emma values most in a friend is:

  F. intelligence.

  G. devotion.

  H. honesty.

  J. charisma.

9. How does Emma view Mr. Weston?

  A. She thinks that he is an excellent match, and it required considerable self-sacrifice not to pursue him herself.

  B. She considers him to be a respectable if somewhat average match for her friend.

  C. She sees him as an intruder who has carried away her best friend in "a black morning's work" (line 50).

  D. She believes he is an indulgent, easily-swayed man, reminiscent of her father.

10. The author feels that Emma is accustomed to:

  F. behaving according to the wishes of her affectionate father.

  G. taking the advice of Miss Taylor when faced with deciding upon a course of action.

  H. doing as she pleases without permission from her father or governess.

  J. abiding by strict rules governing her behavior.

GO ON TO THE NEXT PAGE ⇨

Practice Test 1

Passage II

SOCIAL SCIENCE: The period of active experimentation to develop the airplane began in the 1890s. Many scientists and engineers attempted to solve the problem in the decade following, but with limited progress until Orville and Wilbur Wright made the first successful powered, heavier-than-air flight in 1903. Both of the passages below discuss aspects of the Wright brothers' invention.

Passage A

What about the method used by the Wright brothers allowed them to succeed where so many scientists, engineers, and crackpots had failed to make progress for a dozen years? In the decade
5 leading up to their success, there had been so many unsuccessful attempts that newspaper reporters became jaded, tired of investigating each yokel who claimed to have made an airplane. In fact, the reporter present at that historical first flight did
10 not even bother to take his camera out of its bag, deciding that two unassuming brothers from Ohio without college educations would be two more in a long line. Instead, the Wrights, quite systematically and without much fuss or outside assistance,
15 changed the world dramatically in 1903. What made Orville and Wilbur so different from the rest of the pack?

Most inventors of the time were working on their planes with a fairly simple and logical
20 approach: They would design an airplane, build it, test it in the field, and then use the results of that test to tinker with their designs in an attempt to improve the next model. There was no way of knowing whether the wings were good
25 but the engine was bad, or the shape was right but the materials were too heavy. With no way of discerning which parts worked and which parts did not, inventors' second attempts often flew worse than their initial ones, because their creators had
30 inadvertently removed design features that were

effective and exaggerated features that were not.

The Wright brothers proved to be adept scientists. With their keen analytical insight and love of engineering and all things mechanical,
35 they were able to escape that endless loop of misguided "improvements." They worked on their machine one aspect at a time. After familiarizing themselves with all the published literature on flight, they began working on a method of control.
40 They theorized that twisting the wings one way or another would steer a craft. Instead of building an entire airplane to test their theory, they built a five-foot biplane kite. Sure enough, twisting the wings controlled the craft laterally. Having settled that as-
45 pect of the craft's design, they turned to wing shape.

After building two failed gliders based on their original design, they invented the first wind tunnel with instruments capable of quantifying the lift and drag of wing segments. In this wind tunnel, they
50 could test wings alone for their efficiency and aero-dynamics. In the process of testing 80 to 200 wing shapes in this way, they disproved a commonly accepted component of the theory of lift (called "Smeaton's coefficient") and settled on a new and
55 highly efficient wing shape for their craft.

The Wrights returned to the wind tunnel to perfect designs for their propeller and then designed an effective four-cylinder engine to power the craft. When the time came to marry all of these carefully
60 designed components into a complete craft, there was no guesswork involved. That first historic flight was merely proof of their scientific genius.

GO ON TO THE NEXT PAGE ⟶

Passage B

Few people recognize that the Wright brothers are tragic figures in American history. Today, they
65 are hailed as great inventors, but during their lives they were scorned and discredited publicly, even though the entire world copied their successful designs. The prevailing opinion among those who made airplanes was that two rustic, uneducated
70 fellows from Ohio could never have accomplished such a historic feat, let alone deliberately marry the disparate components of air travel that are required for successful flight. The secrecy of Orville and Wilbur during the years in which they prepared their
75 patents only fueled doubts about their skill.

While the Wright brothers finally received a U.S. patent for their system of lateral control in May of 1906, manufacturers were unwilling to pay the modest fee the brothers asked for use of their
80 system. The companies launched a sadly successful smear campaign against the brothers, impugning the importance of their contribution to flight. Some European airplane manufacturers were even allowed to legally copy the Wrights' technology.

85 In the midst of the legal battle over rights and license fees against several airplane manufacturers, Wilbur sadly succumbed to typhoid fever. He was thus deprived of seeing his claims vindicated in court, and, though Orville was accorded a tidy sum,
90 this small victory was hardly commensurate with the enormous contribution the two brothers had made. The court case also did nothing to compensate the brothers for the taxing and unfair period of ridicule and doubt and the obstinate refusal by
95 much of the world to acknowledge their achievements. Perhaps most tellingly, the Smithsonian Museum did not display the brothers' historic craft until 1948, when it finally bestowed on them the title of the first men to fly in a heavier-than-air craft.
100 Sadly, this was too little, too late, as the brothers had both passed away.

Questions 11–13 ask about Passage A.

11. The main purpose of Passage A is to:

    A. describe how the Wright brothers were regarded.

    B. emphasize the process of designing the airplane.

    C. criticize the attitude of other inventors.

    D. explore the practical application of science.

12. As it is used in line 7, the word *jaded* most nearly means:

    F. excited.

    G. valuable.

    H. bored.

    J. critical.

13. Passage A suggests that the wind tunnel played what role in the Wright brothers' research?

    A. It provided more reliable data than their experiments with kites.

    B. It allowed them to isolate single aspects of design from other considerations.

    C. It helped them develop a method of twisting the wings to control the plane laterally.

    D. It confirmed the accuracy of Smeaton's coefficient.

Questions 14–16 ask about Passage B.

14. In Passage B, the author mentions a "legal battle" (line 85) in order to:

    F. emphasize the harsh way in which the Wright brothers were treated.

    G. illustrate the dangers of publicizing new knowledge.

    H. help explain why the Wright brothers' discovery was of little importance.

    J. suggest a reason for Wilbur's fatal illness.

GO ON TO THE NEXT PAGE

15. What does Passage B suggest about the Smith-sonian Museum's choice to display the brothers' historic craft in 1948 ?

   A. It was a small victory for Orville, who lost his brother Wilbur to typhoid fever.

   B. It was a direct result of the obstinate refusal by much of the world to acknowledge their achievements.

   C. While it was a great honor, it did not fully atone for the poor treatment of the brothers.

   D. The historic craft would have been displayed sooner if European countries had issued the brothers a patent.

16. Based on the passage, it can be concluded that the author feels others characterized the Wright brothers as:

   F. meticulous in their research.

   G. prepared to design an airplane.

   H. well-compensated for their work.

   J. unlikely pioneers of flight.

Questions 17–20 ask about both passages.

---

17. The author of Passage B would likely agree that the "inventors of the time" (line 18) mentioned in Passage A:

   A. thought that the Wright brothers did not actually make the first airplane.

   B. did not believe that the Wright brothers deserved credit for the magnitude of their achievement.

   C. were grateful for the breakthrough that the Wrights had engineered.

   D. felt the Wright brothers had likely copied the design from a more accomplished inventor.

18. In lines 59 and 71, *marry* most nearly means:

   F. prove.

   G. test rigorously.

   H. bring together.

   J. satisfy.

19. According to Passage A, while the brothers "were scorned and discredited publicly" (line 66), as mentioned in Passage B, they were indeed skilled inventors because:

   A. they designed an airplane, built it, tested it in the field, and then used the results of that test to adjust their designs.

   B. they used analytical insight to work on machines one aspect at a time to perfect their design.

   C. they invented the first wind tunnel, which was a greater accomplishment than inventing the first successful aircraft.

   D. their claims were eventually vindicated in court, and Orville received monetary reimbursement.

20. Both passages provide support for the idea that the Wright brothers:

   F. used a method of scientific inquiry that was different from everyone else's.

   G. were poorly treated following their discovery.

   H. were exceptional inventors.

   J. should have protected the rights to their discovery more carefully.

GO ON TO THE NEXT PAGE

Passage III

HUMANITIES: This passage is excerpted from *A History of Women Artists*, © 1975 by Hugo Munsterberg; Clarkson N. Potter (a division of Random House, Inc.), publisher. Reprinted by permission of the author's family.

There can be little doubt that women artists have been most prominent in photography and that they have made their greatest contribution in this field. One reason for this is not difficult to ascertain. As
5 several historians of photography have pointed out, photography, being a new medium outside the traditional academic framework, was wide open to women and offered them opportunities that the older fields did not.

10 All these observations apply to the first woman to have achieved eminence in photography, and that is Julia Margaret Cameron. Born in 1815 in Calcutta into an upper-middle-class family and married to Charles Hay Cameron, a distinguished
15 jurist and member of the Supreme Court of India, Julia Cameron was well-known as a brilliant conversationalist and a woman of personality and intellect who was unconventional to the point of eccentricity. Although the mother of six children,
20 she adopted several more and still found time to be active in social causes and literary activities. After the Camerons settled in England in 1848 at Freshwater Bay on the Isle of Wight, she became the center of an artistic and literary circle that included
25 such notable figures as the poet Alfred Lord Tennyson and the painter George Frederick Watts. Pursuing numerous activities and taking care of her large family, Mrs. Cameron might have been remembered as still another rather remarkable and
30 colorful Victorian lady had it not been for the fact that, in 1863, her daughter presented her with photographic equipment, thinking her mother might enjoy taking pictures of her family and friends. Although forty-eight years old, Mrs. Cameron took
35 up this new hobby with enormous enthusiasm and dedication. She was a complete beginner, but

within a very few years she developed into one of the greatest photographers of her period and a giant in the history of photography. She worked cease-
40 lessly as long as daylight lasted and mastered the technical processes of photography, at that time far more cumbersome than today, turning her coal house into a darkroom and her chicken house into a studio. To her, photography was a "divine art," and
45 in it she found her vocation. In 1864, she wrote triumphantly under one of her photographs, "My First Success," and from then until her death in Ceylon in 1874, she devoted herself wholly to this art.

Working in a large format (her portrait studies
50 are usually about 11 inches by 14 inches) and requiring a long exposure (on the average five minutes), she produced a large body of work that stands up as one of the notable artistic achievements of the Victorian period. The English art critic Roger
55 Fry believed that her portraits were likely to outlive the works of artists who were her contemporaries. Her friend Watts, then a very celebrated portrait painter, inscribed on one of her photographs, "I wish I could paint such a picture as this." Her
60 work was widely exhibited, and she received gold, silver, and bronze medals in England, America, Germany, and Austria. No other female artist of the nineteenth century achieved such acclaim, and no other woman photographer has ever enjoyed such
65 success.

Her work falls into two main categories on which her contemporaries and people today differ sharply. Victorian critics were particularly impressed by her allegorical pictures, many of them
70 based on the poems of her friend and neighbor Tennyson. Contemporary taste much prefers her portraits and finds her narrative scenes sentimental and sometimes in bad taste. Yet, not only Julia Cameron, but also the painters of that time loved to
75 depict subjects such as *The Five Foolish Virgins* or *Pray God, Bring Father Safely Home*. Still, today her fame rests upon her portraits for, as she herself said, she was intent upon representing not only the outer

GO ON TO THE NEXT PAGE ⟩

likeness but also the inner greatness of the people
80 she portrayed. Working with the utmost dedication,
she produced photographs of such eminent Victorians as Tennyson, Browning, Carlyle, Trollope,
Longfellow, Watts, Darwin, Ellen Terry, Sir John
Herschel, who was a close friend of hers, and Mrs.
85 Duckworth, the mother of Virginia Woolf.

21. Which of the following conclusions can
    be reasonably drawn from the passage's
    discussion of Julia Margaret Cameron?

    A. She was a traditional homemaker
       until she discovered photography.

    B. Her work holds a significant place in
       the history of photography.

    C. She was unable to achieve in her
       lifetime the artistic recognition she
       deserved.

    D. Her eccentricity has kept her from
       being taken seriously by modern
       critics of photography.

22. According to the passage, Cameron is most
    respected by modern critics for her:

    F. portraits.

    G. allegorical pictures.

    H. use of a large format.

    J. service in recording the faces of so
       many twentieth-century figures.

23. The author uses which of the following methods
    to develop the second paragraph (lines 10—48)?

    A. A series of anecdotes depicting Cameron's
       energy and unconventionality

    B. A presentation of factual data demon-
       strating Cameron's importance in the
       history of photography

    C. A description of the author's personal
       acquaintance with Cameron

    D. A chronological account of Cameron's
       background and artistic growth

24. As it is used in the passage, *cumbersome* (line
    42) most closely means:

    F. difficult to manage.

    G. expensive.

    H. intense.

    J. enjoyable.

25. When the author says that Cameron had found
    "her vocation" (line 45), his main point is that
    photography:

    A. offered Cameron an escape from the
       confines of conventional social life.

    B. became the main interest of her life.

    C. became her primary source of income.

    D. provided her with a way to express her
       religious beliefs.

26. The main point of the third paragraph is that
    Cameron:

    F. achieved great artistic success during her
       lifetime.

    G. is the greatest photographer who ever
       lived.

    H. was considered a more important artist
       during her lifetime than she is now.

    J. revolutionized photographic methods in the
       Victorian era.

GO ON TO THE NEXT PAGE

27. In line 6, the author refers to photography as a "new medium" in order to:

  A. describe why it was so popular at the time.

  B. explain why the equipment was so cumbersome.

  C. express Cameron's desire to be a trend-setter.

  D. account for the importance of women photographers.

28. *The Five Foolish Virgins* and *Pray God, Bring Father Safely Home* (lines 75–76) are examples of:

  F. portraits of celebrated Victorians.

  G. allegorical subjects of the sort that were popular during the Victorian era.

  H. photographs in which Cameron sought to show a subject's outer likeness and inner greatness.

  J. photographs by Cameron that were scoffed at by her contemporaries.

29. According to the passage, which of the following opinions of Cameron's work was held by Victorian critics but is NOT held by modern critics?

  A. Photographs should be based on poems.

  B. Her portraits are too sentimental.

  C. Narrative scenes are often in bad taste.

  D. Her allegorical pictures are her best work.

30. The author's treatment of Cameron's development as a photographer can best be described as:

  F. admiring.

  G. condescending.

  H. neutral.

  J. defensive.

GO ON TO THE NEXT PAGE

Passage IV

NATURAL SCIENCE: This passage discusses aspects of the harbor seal's sensory systems.

The harbor seal, *Phoca vitulina*, lives amphibiously along the northern Atlantic and Pacific coasts. This extraordinary mammal, which does most of its fishing at night when visibility is
5 low and in places where noise levels are high, has developed several unique adaptations that have sharpened its acoustic and visual acuity. The need for such adaptations has been compounded by the varying behavior of sound and light in each of the
10 two habitats of the harbor seal—land and water.

While the seal is on land, its ear operates much like the human ear, with sound waves traveling through air and entering the inner ear through the auditory canal. The directions from which sounds
15 originate are distinguishable because the sound waves arrive at each inner ear at different times. In water, however, where sound waves travel faster than they do in air, the ability of the brain to differentiate arrival times between each ear is severely
20 reduced. Yet it is crucial for the seal to be able to pinpoint the exact origins of sound in order to locate both its offspring and its prey. Therefore, the seal has developed an extremely sensitive quadraphonic hearing system, composed of a specialized
25 band of tissue that extends down from the ear to the inner ear. In water, sound is conducted to the seal's inner ear by this special band of tissue, making it possible for the seal to identify the exact origins of sounds.

30 The eye of the seal is also uniquely adapted to operate in both air and water. The human eye, adapted to function primarily in air, is equipped with a cornea, which aids in the refraction and focusing of light onto the retina. As a result, when
35 a human eye is submerged in water, light rays are further refracted and the image is blurry. The seal's cornea, however, refracts light as water does. Therefore, in water, light rays are transmitted by the cornea without distortion and are clearly
40 focused on the retina. In air, however, the cornea

is astigmatic, resulting in a distortion of incoming light rays. The seal compensates for this by having a stenopaic pupil, which constricts into a vertical slit. Since the astigmatism is most pronounced in the
45 horizontal plane of the eye, the vertical pupil serves to minimize its effect on the seal's vision.

Since the harbor seal hunts for food under conditions of low visibility, some scientists believe it has echolocation systems akin to those of bats, por-
50 poises, and dolphins. This kind of natural radar involves the emission of high-frequency sound pulses that reflect off obstacles such as predators, prey, or natural barriers. The reflections are received as sensory signals by the brain, which processes them
55 into an image. The animal, blinded by unfavorable lighting conditions, is thus able to perceive its surroundings. Such echolocation by harbor seals is suggested by the fact that they emit "clicks," high-frequency sounds produced in short, fast bursts
60 that occur mostly at night, when visibility is low.

Finally, there is speculation that the seal's whiskers, or vibrissae, which are unusually well developed and highly sensitive to vibrations, act as additional sensory receptors. Scientists speculate
65 that the vibrissae may sense wave disturbances produced by nearby moving fish, allowing the seal to home in on and capture prey.

GO ON TO THE NEXT PAGE

Practice Test 1

31. The harbor seal's eye compensates for the distortion of light rays on land by means of its:

    A. vibrissae.

    B. cornea.

    C. stenopaic pupil.

    D. echolocation.

32. The passage implies that a harbor seal's vision is:

    F. inferior to a human's vision in the water, but superior to it on land.

    G. superior to a human's vision in the water, but inferior to it on land.

    H. inferior to a human's vision both in the water and on land.

    J. equivalent to a human's vision both in the water and on land.

33. According to the passage, scientists think vibrissae help harbor seals to catch prey by:

    A. improving underwater vision.

    B. sensing vibrations in the air.

    C. camouflaging predator seals.

    D. detecting underwater movement.

34. According to the passage, the speed of sound in water is:

    F. faster than the speed of sound in air.

    G. slower than the speed of sound in air.

    H. the same as the speed of sound in air.

    J. unable to be determined exactly.

35. According to the passage, which of the following have contributed to the harbor seal's need to adapt its visual and acoustic senses?

    I. Night hunting

    II. The need to operate in two habitats

    III. A noisy environment

    A. I and II only

    B. II and III only

    C. I and III only

    D. I, II, and III

36. Which of the following statements expresses an opinion, not a fact?

    F. Seals' eyes are adapted to function primarily in air.

    G. When the seal is on land, its ear operates like a human ear.

    H. The "clicks" emitted by the harbor seal mean it uses echolocation.

    J. The need for adaptation is decreased if an animal lives in two habitats.

37. The writer would most likely agree that the harbor seal's vibrissae are:

    A. proof of their use as sensory receptors.

    B. similar to those of bats.

    C. possible means by which the seals locate food.

    D. required to offset blurry conditions in water.

GO ON TO THE NEXT PAGE

38. According to the passage, a special band of tissue extending from the ear to the inner ear enables the harbor seal to:

    F. make its distinctive "clicking" sounds.

    G. find prey by echolocation.

    H. breathe underwater.

    J. determine where a sound originated.

39. The author compares harbor seal sensory organs to human sensory organs primarily in order to:

    A. point out similarities among mammals.

    B. explain how the seal's sensory organs function.

    C. prove that seals are more adaptively successful than humans.

    D. prove that humans are better adapted to their environment than seals.

40. According to the passage, one way in which seals differ from humans is:

    F. that sound waves enter a seal's inner ear through the auditory canal.

    G. the degree to which their corneas refract light.

    H. that the seal has learned to camouflage itself to avoid predators.

    J. that seals have adapted to live in a certain environment.

IF YOU FINISH BEFORE TIME IS CALLED, YOU MAY CHECK YOUR WORK ON THIS SECTION ONLY. DO NOT TURN TO ANY OTHER SECTION IN THE TEST. STOP

SCIENCE TEST

35 Minutes—40 Questions

Directions: The Science Test includes multiple passages. Each passage includes multiple questions. After reading each passage, choose the best answer and fill in the corresponding bubble on your answer sheet. You may review the passages as often as necessary.

You may NOT use a calculator on this test.

Passage I

Table 1 contains some physical properties of common optical materials. The refractive index of a material is a measure of the amount by which light is bent upon entering the material. The transmittance range is the range of wavelengths over which the material is transparent.

Table 1				
Physical Properties of Optical Materials				
Material	Refractive index for light of 0.589 μm	Transmittance range (μm)	Useful range for prisms (μm)	Chemical resistance
Lithium fluoride	1.39	0.12−6	2.7−5.5	Poor
Calcium fluoride	1.43	0.12−12	5−9.4	Good
Sodium chloride	1.54	0.3−17	8−16	Poor
Quartz	1.54	0.2−3.3	0.2−2.7	Excellent
Potassium bromide	1.56	0.3−29	15−28	Poor
Flint glass*	1.66	0.35−2.2	0.35−2	Excellent
Cesium iodide	1.79	0.3−70	15−55	Poor

*Flint glass is lead oxide-doped quartz.

1. According to Table 1, which material(s) will transmit light at 25 μm ?

   A. Potassium bromide only

   B. Potassium bromide and cesium iodide

   C. Lithium fluoride and cesium iodide

   D. Lithium fluoride and flint glass

2. A scientist hypothesizes that any material with poor chemical resistance would have a transmittance range wider than 10 μm. The properties of which of the following materials contradicts this hypothesis?

   F. Lithium fluoride

   G. Flint glass

   H. Cesium iodide

   J. Quartz

3. When light travels from one medium to another, total internal reflection can occur if the first medium has a higher refractive index than the second. Total internal reflection could occur if light were traveling from:

   A. lithium fluoride to flint glass.

   B. potassium bromide to cesium iodide.

   C. quartz to potassium bromide.

   D. flint glass to calcium fluoride.

4. Based on the information in the table, how is the transmittance range related to the useful prism range?

   F. The transmittance range is always narrower than the useful prism range.

   G. The transmittance range is narrower than or equal to the useful prism range.

   H. The transmittance range increases as the useful prism range decreases.

   J. The transmittance range is wider than and includes within it the useful prism range.

5. The addition of lead oxide to pure quartz has the effect of:

   A. decreasing the transmittance range and the refractive index.

   B. decreasing the transmittance range and increasing the refractive index.

   C. increasing the transmittance range and the useful prism range.

   D. increasing the transmittance range and decreasing the useful prism range.

6. Which of the following materials would provide the greatest range of transmittance as well as the greatest useful range for prisms?

   F. Lithium fluoride

   G. Sodium chloride

   H. Quartz

   J. Flint glass

GO ON TO THE NEXT PAGE

Passage II

Osmosis is the diffusion of a solvent (often water) across a semipermeable membrane from the side of the membrane with a lower concentration of dissolved material to the side with a higher concentration of dissolved material. The result of osmosis is an equilibrium—an even distribution—on both sides of the membrane. In order to prevent osmosis, external pressure must be applied to the side with the higher concentration of dissolved material. *Osmotic pressure* is equivalent to the minimum external pressure required to prevent osmosis. The apparatus shown in Diagram 1 was used to measure osmotic pressure in the following experiments.

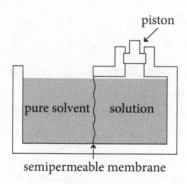

Diagram 1

Experiment 1

Aqueous (water-based) solutions containing different concentrations of sucrose were placed in the closed side of the apparatus. The open side was filled with water. The sucrose solutions also contained a blue dye that binds to sucrose. The osmotic pressure created by the piston was measured for each solution at various temperatures. The results are given in Table 1.

Table 1		
Concentration of sucrose solution (mol/L)	Temperature (K)	Osmotic pressure (atm)
1.00	298.0	24.47
0.50	298.0	12.23
0.10	298.0	2.45
0.05	298.0	1.22
1.00	348.0	28.57
0.50	348.0	14.29
0.10	348.0	2.86
0.05	348.0	1.43

GO ON TO THE NEXT PAGE

Experiment 2

Sucrose solutions of four different organic solvents were investigated in the same manner as in Experiment 1 with all trials at 298 K. The results are shown in Table 2.

Table 2		
Solvent	Concentration of sucrose solution (mol/L)	Osmotic pressure (atm)
Ethanol	0.50	12.23
Ethanol	0.10	2.45
Acetone	0.50	12.23
Acetone	0.10	2.45
Diethyl ether	0.50	12.23
Diethyl ether	0.10	2.45
Methanol	0.50	12.23
Methanol	0.10	2.45

7. Osmotic pressure can be calculated using the formula $\Pi = MRT$, where Π represents the calculated osmotic pressure, M is the concentration in mol/L, R is a constant equal to 0.0821, and T is temperature in Kelvins. Which of the following can be inferred from this equation and the data in Table 1 ?

    I. As temperatures increases, osmotic pressure decreases.

    II. To maintain a constant osmotic pressure, temperature must be decreased if concentration increases.

    III. Osmotic pressure increases as concentration increases.

  A. I only

  B. II only

  C. III only

  D. II and III only

8. According to the experimental results, osmotic pressure is dependent upon the:

  F. solvent and temperature only.

  G. solvent and concentration only.

  H. temperature and concentration only.

  J. solvent, temperature, and concentration.

9. According to Experiment 2, when methanol is used as a solvent, what is the minimum pressure that must be applied to a 0.5 mol/L solution of sucrose at 298 K to prevent osmosis?

  A. 1.23 atm

  B. 2.45 atm

  C. 12.23 atm

  D. 24.46 atm

10. A 0.10 mol/L aqueous sucrose solution is separated from an equal volume of pure water by a semipermeable membrane. If the solution is at an external pressure of 1 atm and a temperature of 298 K:

  F. water will diffuse across the semipermeable membrane from the sucrose solution side to the pure water side.

  G. water will diffuse across the semipermeable membrane from the pure water side to the sucrose solution side.

  H. water will not diffuse across the semipermeable membrane.

  J. water will diffuse across the semipermeable membrane, but the direction of diffusion cannot be determined.

GO ON TO THE NEXT PAGE

11. In Experiment 1, the scientists investigated the effect of:

    A. solvent and concentration on osmotic pressure.

    B. volume and temperature on osmotic pressure.

    C. concentration and temperature on osmotic pressure.

    D. temperature on atmospheric pressure.

12. Which of the following conclusions can be drawn from the experimental results?

    I. Osmotic pressure is independent of the solvent used.

    II. Osmotic pressure is only dependent upon the temperature of the system.

    III. Osmosis occurs only when the osmotic pressure is exceeded by the external pressure.

    F. I only

    G. III only

    H. I and II only

    J. I and III only

13. What was the most likely purpose of the dye placed in the sucrose solutions in Experiments 1 and 2 ?

    A. The dye showed when osmosis was completed.

    B. The dye showed the presence of ions in the solutions.

    C. The dye was used to make the experiment more colorful.

    D. The dye was used to make the onset of osmosis visible.

Passage III

A series of experiments was performed to study the environmental factors affecting the size and number of leaves on the *Cycas* plant.

Experiment 1

Five groups of 25 *Cycas* seedlings, all 2–3 cm tall, were allowed to grow for three months, each group at a different humidity level. All of the groups were kept at 75°F and received 9 hours of sunlight a day. The average leaf lengths, widths, and densities are given in Table 1.

Table 1			
% Humidity	Average length (cm)	Average width (cm)	Average density* (leaves/cm)
15	5.6	1.6	0.13
35	7.1	1.8	0.25
55	9.8	2.0	0.56
75	14.6	2.6	0.61
95	7.5	1.7	0.52

*Number of leaves per 1 cm of plant stalk

Experiment 2

Five new groups of 25 seedlings, all 2–3 cm tall, were allowed to grow for 3 months, each group receiving different amounts of sunlight at a constant humidity of 55%. All other conditions were the same as in Experiment 1. The results are listed in Table 2.

Table 2			
Sunlight (hrs/day)	Average length (cm)	Average width (cm)	Average density* (leaves/cm)
0	5.3	1.5	0.32
3	12.4	2.4	0.59
6	11.2	2.0	0.56
9	8.4	1.8	0.26
12	7.7	1.7	0.19

*Number of leaves per 1 cm of plant stalk

GO ON TO THE NEXT PAGE

Practice Test 1

Experiment 3

Five new groups of 25 seedlings, all 2–3 cm tall, were allowed to grow at a constant humidity of 55% for three months at different daytime and nighttime temperatures. All other conditions were the same as in Experiment 1. The results are shown in Table 3.

Table 3			
Day/night temperature (°F)	Average length (cm)	Average width (cm)	Average density* (leaves/cm)
85/85	6.8	1.5	0.28
85/65	12.3	2.1	0.53
65/85	8.1	1.7	0.33
75/75	7.1	1.9	0.45
65/65	8.3	1.7	0.39

*Number of leaves per 1 cm of plant stalk

14. Based on the data in Experiment 3, which day/night temperatures (in degrees Fahrenheit) produced the smallest leaves?

   F. 85/85

   G. 85/65

   H. 75/75

   J. 65/85

15. Which of the following conclusions can be made based on the results of Experiment 2 alone?

   A. The seedlings do not require long daily periods of sunlight to grow.

   B. The average leaf density is independent of the humidity the seedlings receive.

   C. The seedlings need more water at night than during the day.

   D. The average length of the leaves increases as the amount of sunlight increases.

16. Seedlings grown at a 40% humidity level under the same conditions as in Experiment 1 would most likely have average leaf widths closest to:

   F. 1.6 cm.

   G. 1.9 cm.

   H. 2.2 cm.

   J. 2.5 cm.

17. According to the experimental results, under which set of conditions would a *Cycas* seedling be most likely to produce the largest leaves?

   A. 95% humidity and 3 hours of sunlight

   B. 75% humidity and 3 hours of sunlight

   C. 95% humidity and 6 hours of sunlight

   D. 75% humidity and 6 hours of sunlight

18. Which variable remained constant throughout all of the experiments?

   F. The number of seedling groups

   G. The humidity level

   H. The daytime temperature

   J. The nighttime temperature

19. It was assumed in the design of the three experiments that all of the *Cycas* seedlings were:

   A. more than 5 cm tall.

   B. equally capable of germinating.

   C. equally capable of producing flowers.

   D. equally capable of further growth.

20. As a continuation of the three experiments listed, it would be most appropriate to investigate next:

   F. how many leaves over 6.0 cm long there are on each plant.

   G. which animals consume *Cycas* seedlings.

   H. how mineral content of the soil affects leaf size and density.

   J. what time of year the seedlings have the darkest coloring.

GO ON TO THE NEXT PAGE

Passage IV

The resistance (R) of a conductor is the extent to which it opposes the flow of electricity. Resistance depends not only on the conductor's resistivity (ρ) but also on the conductor's length (L) and cross-sectional area (A). The resistivity of a conductor is a physical property of the material that varies with temperature.

A research team designing a new appliance was researching the best type of wire to use in a particular circuit. The most important consideration was the wire's resistance. The team studied the resistance of wires made from four metals—gold (Au), aluminum (Al), tungsten (W), and iron (Fe). Two lengths and two gauges (see Diagram 1) of each type of wire were tested at 20°C. The results are recorded in Table 1.

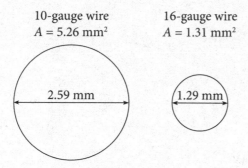

10-gauge wire
$A = 5.26$ mm²

16-gauge wire
$A = 1.31$ mm²

2.59 mm

1.29 mm

Note: area of circle $= \pi r^2$

Diagram 1

Table 1				
Material	Resistivity (mV-cm)	Length (cm)	Cross-sectional area (mm²)	Resistance (mV)
Au	2.44	1.0	5.26	46.4
Au	2.44	1.0	1.31	186.3
Au	2.44	2.0	5.26	92.8
Au	2.44	2.0	1.31	372.5
Al	2.83	1.0	5.26	53.8
Al	2.83	1.0	1.31	216.0
Al	2.83	2.0	5.26	107.6
Al	2.83	2.0	1.31	432.1
W	5.51	1.0	5.26	104.8
W	5.51	1.0	1.31	420.6
W	5.51	2.0	5.26	209.5
W	5.51	2.0	1.31	841.2
Fe	10.00	1.0	5.26	190.1
Fe	10.00	1.0	1.31	763.4
Fe	10.00	2.0	5.26	380.2
Fe	10.00	2.0	1.31	1,526.7

21. Of the wires tested, resistance increases for any given material as which parameter is decreased?

A. Length

B. Cross-sectional area

C. Resistivity

D. Gauge

22. Given the data in the table, which of the following best expresses resistance in terms of resistivity (ρ), cross-sectional area (A), and length (L) ?

F. $\dfrac{\rho A}{L}$

G. $\dfrac{\rho L}{A}$

H. ρAL

J. $\dfrac{AL}{\rho}$

GO ON TO THE NEXT PAGE

23. Which of the following wires would have the highest resistance?

    A. A 1-cm aluminum wire with a cross-sectional area of 0.33 mm²

    B. A 2-cm aluminum wire with a cross-sectional area of 0.33 mm²

    C. A 1-cm tungsten wire with a cross-sectional area of 0.33 mm²

    D. A 2-cm tungsten wire with a cross-sectional area of 0.33 mm²

24. According to the information given, which of the following statements is (are) correct?

    I. 10-gauge wire has a larger diameter than 16-gauge wire.

    II. Gold has a higher resistivity than tungsten.

    III. Aluminum conducts electricity better than iron.

    F. I only

    G. II only

    H. III only

    J. I and III only

25. Which of the following graphs best represents the relationship between the resistivity of a tungsten wire and its length?

    A.
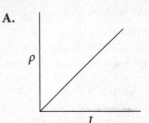

    B.
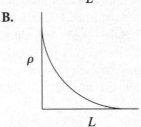

    C.
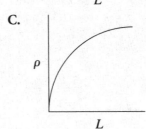

    D.
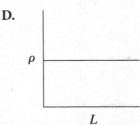

26. If the length of the wires were increased to 4 cm, what effect would this most likely have on the wires' resistance values?

    F. Resistance would increase, but only with a 10-gauge wire.

    G. Resistance would decrease, but only with a 16-gauge wire.

    H. Resistance would not change because 2 cm is the maximum length that affects resistance.

    J. Resistance would increase on both the 10- and 16-gauge wires.

GO ON TO THE NEXT PAGE

Passage V

How does evolution occur? Two scientists offered their own answers to the question.

Scientist 1

Evolution occurs by natural selection. Random mutations are continually occurring in a species as it propagates. A number of these mutations result in traits that help the species adapt to environmental changes. Because these mutant traits are advantageous, the members of the species who possess them tend to survive and pass on their genes more often than those who do not have these traits. Therefore, the percentage of the population with an advantageous trait increases over time. For example, long necks evolved in giraffes by natural selection. The ancestors of giraffes had necks of various sizes; however, their average neck length was much shorter than the average neck length of modern-day giraffes. Since the food supply was limited, the individuals with necks on the long range of the spectrum had access to more food (the leaves of trees), and therefore were more likely to survive and pass on their traits than individuals with shorter necks. Thus, the proportion of the individuals with long necks was slightly greater in each subsequent generation.

Scientist 2

Evolution occurs by the inheritance of acquired characteristics. Characteristics that are acquired by an individual member of a species during its lifetime are passed on to its offspring. Therefore, each generation's traits are partially accounted for by all the changes that occurred in the individuals of the previous generation. This includes changes that occurred as a result of accidents, changes in the environment, overuse of muscles, and so on. The evolution of the long necks of giraffes is an example. Ancestors of giraffes had short necks and consequently had to stretch their necks to reach the leaves of trees that were their main source of food. This repeated stretching of their necks caused them to elongate slightly. This trait was passed on so that the individuals of the next generation had slightly longer necks. Each

subsequent generation also stretched their necks to feed; therefore, each generation had slightly longer necks than the previous generation.

27. Both scientists agree that:

   A. the environment affects evolution.

   B. the individuals of a generation have identical traits.

   C. acquired characteristics are inherited.

   D. random mutations occur.

28. How would the two hypotheses be affected if it were found that all of the offspring of an individual with a missing leg due to an accident were born with a missing leg?

   F. It would support Scientist 1's hypothesis, because it is an example of a random mutation occurring within a species.

   G. It would refute Scientist 1's hypothesis, because it is an example of a random mutation occurring within a species.

   H. It would support Scientist 2's hypothesis, because it is an example of an acquired characteristic being passed on to the next generation.

   J. It would refute Scientist 2's hypothesis, because it is an example of an acquired characteristic being passed on to the next generation.

GO ON TO THE NEXT PAGE

29. Which of the following characteristics can be inherited, according to Scientist 2 ?

    I. Fur color

    II. Bodily scars resulting from a fight with another animal

    III. Poor vision

A. I only

B. II only

C. I and III only

D. I, II, and III

30. Scientist 1 believes that the evolution of the long neck of the giraffe:

F. is an advantageous trait that resulted from overuse of neck muscles over many generations.

G. is an advantageous trait that resulted from random mutations.

H. is an advantageous trait that resulted from mutations that occurred in response to changes in the environment.

J. is a disadvantageous trait that resulted from random mutations.

31. The fundamental point of disagreement between the two scientists is whether:

A. giraffes' ancestors had short necks.

B. traits evolve from random mutations or from acquired characteristics.

C. the environment affects the evolution of a species.

D. the extinction of a species could be the result of random mutations.

32. Suppose evidence suggested that before the discovery of fire, human skin lacked the nerve endings necessary to detect extreme heat. Which of the following pieces of additional information, if true, would most seriously weaken the hypothesis of Scientist 2 ?

F. Human skin is capable of generating nerve endings with new functions during life.

G. The total number of nerve endings in the skin of a human is determined at birth and remains constant until death.

H. An excess of nerve endings that are sensitive to extreme heat is a relatively common human mutation.

J. There is no evidence that an excess of nerve endings that are sensitive to heat could be acquired through mutations.

33. The average height of a fully grown human today is significantly greater than was the average height of a fully grown human 1,000 years ago. If it were true that the increase in average height was due only to evolutionary changes, how would Scientist 1 most likely explain this increase?

A. Humans genetically prone to growing taller have been more likely to produce offspring over the last 1,000 years.

B. Over the last 1,000 years, improvements in nutrition and medicine have led to greater average growth over a lifetime, and this growth has been passed on with each new generation.

C. Over the last 1,000 years of civilization, humans have had to stretch to reach items placed on high shelves, resulting in small height increases that are inherited each generation.

D. Measurements of average height were less accurate 1,000 years ago than they are today.

GO ON TO THE NEXT PAGE

Practice Test 1

Passage VI

Bovine spongiform encephalopathy (BSE) is caused by the spread of a misfolded protein that eventually kills infected cattle. BSE is diagnosed postmortem from the diseased cavities that appear in brain tissue and is associated with the use in cattle feed of ground-up meat from scrapie-infected sheep. A series of experiments was performed to determine the mode of transmission of BSE. The results of both experiments are provided in Table 1.

Experiment 1

Sixty healthy cows were divided into two equal groups. Group A's feed included meat from scrapie-free sheep; and Group B's feed included meat from scrapie-infected sheep. Eighteen months later, the two groups were slaughtered and their brains examined for BSE cavities. The results can be found in Table 1.

Experiment 2

Researchers injected ground-up sheep brains directly into the brains of two groups of 30 healthy cows each. The cows in Group C received brains from scrapie-free sheep. The cows in Group D received brains from scrapie-infected sheep. Eighteen months later, both groups were slaughtered and their brains examined for diseased cavities. The results can be found in Table 1.

Table 1			
Group	Mode of transmission	Scrapie present	Number of cows infected with BSE*
A	feed	no	1
B	feed	yes	12
C	injection	no	0
D	injection	yes	3

*As determined visually by presence/absence of spongiform encephalopathy

34. Based on the information provided in Table 1, a cow is at greatest risk for contracting BSE if the cow:

    F. consumes meat from scrapie-free sheep.

    G. consumes meat from scrapie-infected sheep.

    H. is injected with ground-up sheep brains from scrapie-free sheep.

    J. is injected with ground-up sheep brains from scrapie-infected sheep.

35. Which of the following hypotheses was investigated in Experiment 1 ?

    A. The injection of scrapie-infected sheep brains into cows' brains causes BSE.

    B. The ingestion of wild grasses causes BSE.

    C. The ingestion of scrapie-infected sheep meat causes scrapie.

    D. The ingestion of scrapie-infected sheep meat causes BSE.

36. What is the purpose of Experiment 2 ?

    F. To determine whether BSE can be transmitted by injection

    G. To determine whether BSE can be transmitted by ingestion

    H. To determine whether ingestion or injection is the primary mode of BSE transmission

    J. To determine the healthiest diet for cows

37. Which of the following assumptions is made by the researchers in Experiments 1 and 2 ?

    A. Cows do not suffer from scrapie.

    B. A year and a half is a sufficient amount of time for BSE to develop.

    C. Cows and sheep suffer from the same diseases.

    D. Cows that eat scrapie-free sheep meat will not develop BSE.

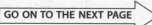
GO ON TO THE NEXT PAGE

38. A researcher wishes to determine whether BSE can be transmitted through scrapie-infected goats. Which of the following experiments would best test this?

F. Repeating Experiment 1, but using a mixture of sheep and goat meat in Group B's feed

G. Repeating Experiments 1 and 2, but replacing all the sheep with scrapie-infected goats

H. Repeating Experiments 1 and 2, but replacing healthy sheep with healthy goats and scrapie-infected sheep with scrapie-infected goats

J. Repeating Experiment 2, but replacing healthy cows with healthy goats

39. What is the control group in Experiment 1?

A. Group A

B. Group B

C. Group C

D. Group D

40. Which of the following conclusions can be drawn based on the results of the experiments?

    I. Cows raised in proximity to scrapie-infected sheep are more likely to develop BSE than cows that are not.

    II. BSE is only transmitted by eating scrapie-infected sheep meat.

    III. A cow that eats scrapie-infected sheep meat is more likely to develop BSE than a cow that is injected with scrapie-infected sheep brains.

F. II only

G. III only

H. I and III only

J. II and III only

IF YOU FINISH BEFORE TIME IS CALLED, YOU MAY CHECK YOUR WORK ON THIS SECTION ONLY. DO NOT TURN TO ANY OTHER SECTION IN THE TEST. **STOP**

56 Practice Test 1

WRITING TEST

40 Minutes—1 Question

Directions: The essay is used to evaluate your writing skills. You will have **40 minutes** to review the prompt and plan and write an essay in English. Before you begin, read everything in this test booklet carefully to make sure you understand the task.

Your essay will be judged based on the evidence it provides of your ability to do the following:

- Assert your own perspective on a complex issue and evaluate the relationship between your perspective and at least one other perspective

- Use reasoning and evidence to refine and justify your ideas

- Present your ideas in an organized way

- Convey your ideas effectively using standard written English

Write your essay on the lined essay pages in the answer booklet. All writing on those lined pages will be scored. Use the unlined pages in this test booklet to plan your essay. Your work on these unlined pages will not be scored.

Put your pencil down as soon as time is called.

DO NOT OPEN THIS BOOKLET UNTIL TOLD TO DO SO.

GO ON TO THE NEXT PAGE

Career Readiness Programs

High school curricula are designed to ready students for future career paths, many of which include higher education. Whether or not students choose to attend college, a comprehensive high school education provides an essential foundation. Some educators argue that high schools have an obligation to provide career readiness training for students who do not intend to pursue a college degree. Should high schools invest time and money to develop programs for students who do not wish to continue their education beyond 12th grade? Given the many factors that students weigh when considering if, where, and when to attend college, it is prudent for educators to explore programs that contribute to a better-skilled workforce.

Read and carefully consider these perspectives. Each offers suggestions regarding high school-based career readiness programs.

Perspective One	Perspective Two	Perspective Three
Rather than concentrating solely on students who may not pursue higher education, high schools should help all students develop valuable skills for the workforce. Requiring students to complete classes that focus on key cognitive strategies, content knowledge, and relevant skills and techniques will help them enter the workforce, either immediately after high school or later in their lives.	Career-readiness training should be provided for students who do not wish to pursue college, and it should be particularly targeted at students who are at risk for dropping out. When their high school experience is reframed as training for successful careers rather than government-mandated learning, students can succeed where they may previously have failed.	Students who do not want to pursue higher education should not be given additional accommodations in high school, because they should not be provided any incentives to not attend college. College is the best way to learn how to be productive in the workforce, and students should be encouraged to attend since it is in their best interest.

Essay Task

Write a clear, well-reasoned essay evaluating multiple perspectives on high school-based career readiness programs. In your essay, be sure to:

- Assert your own perspective on the issue and evaluate the relationship between your perspective and at least one other perspective

- Use reasoning and evidence to refine and justify your ideas

- Present your ideas in an organized way

- Convey your ideas effectively using standard written English

Your perspective may be fully, somewhat, or not at all in agreement with one or more of the three perspectives in the prompt.

GO ON TO THE NEXT PAGE

Planning Your Essay

These pages are not scored.

Use the space below to brainstorm and plan your essay. Consider the following as you think about the prompt:

- Strengths and weaknesses of the three perspectives in the prompt

  ◦ What observations do they offer, and what do they overlook?

  ◦ Why are they persuasive or why are they not persuasive?

- Your own background and identity

  ◦ What is your perspective on this issue, and what are its strengths and weaknesses?

  ◦ What evidence will you use in your essay?

GO ON TO THE NEXT PAGE

GO ON TO THE NEXT PAGE ⟶

Practice Test 1

GO ON TO THE NEXT PAGE

_____
_____
_____
_____
_____
_____
_____
_____
_____
_____
_____
_____
_____
_____
_____
_____
_____
_____
_____
_____
_____
_____

IF YOU FINISH BEFORE TIME IS CALLED, YOU MAY CHECK YOUR WORK ON THIS SECTION ONLY. DO NOT TURN TO ANY OTHER SECTION IN THE TEST. STOP

PRACTICE TEST 1 ANSWER KEY

ENGLISH TEST

1. **C**	16. **H**	31. **D**	46. **F**	61. **D**
2. **F**	17. **B**	32. **H**	47. **B**	62. **J**
3. **D**	18. **H**	33. **A**	48. **H**	63. **C**
4. **F**	19. **D**	34. **H**	49. **C**	64. **J**
5. **D**	20. **J**	35. **D**	50. **H**	65. **D**
6. **G**	21. **B**	36. **G**	51. **D**	66. **J**
7. **B**	22. **G**	37. **D**	52. **J**	67. **B**
8. **J**	23. **D**	38. **G**	53. **C**	68. **J**
9. **A**	24. **J**	39. **D**	54. **H**	69. **D**
10. **J**	25. **C**	40. **J**	55. **C**	70. **F**
11. **C**	26. **F**	41. **D**	56. **J**	71. **D**
12. **G**	27. **B**	42. **J**	57. **D**	72. **G**
13. **B**	28. **F**	43. **B**	58. **G**	73. **B**
14. **H**	29. **D**	44. **G**	59. **C**	74. **F**
15. **C**	30. **G**	45. **C**	60. **J**	75. **B**

MATHEMATICS TEST

1. **D**	13. **C**	25. **C**	37. **E**	49. **E**
2. **J**	14. **J**	26. **G**	38. **G**	50. **J**
3. **B**	15. **B**	27. **C**	39. **C**	51. **E**
4. **H**	16. **G**	28. **J**	40. **G**	52. **F**
5. **E**	17. **B**	29. **B**	41. **E**	53. **E**
6. **H**	18. **H**	30. **K**	42. **H**	54. **G**
7. **E**	19. **B**	31. **E**	43. **C**	55. **E**
8. **K**	20. **H**	32. **H**	44. **K**	56. **K**
9. **E**	21. **B**	33. **A**	45. **B**	57. **A**
10. **H**	22. **G**	34. **K**	46. **G**	58. **H**
11. **B**	23. **E**	35. **A**	47. **D**	59. **D**
12. **K**	24. **J**	36. **J**	48. **G**	60. **J**

READING TEST

1. **C**	9. **B**	17. **B**	25. **B**	33. **D**
2. **G**	10. **H**	18. **H**	26. **F**	34. **F**
3. **B**	11. **B**	19. **B**	27. **D**	35. **D**
4. **F**	12. **H**	20. **H**	28. **G**	36. **H**
5. **D**	13. **B**	21. **B**	29. **D**	37. **C**
6. **H**	14. **F**	22. **F**	30. **F**	38. **J**
7. **C**	15. **C**	23. **D**	31. **C**	39. **B**
8. **G**	16. **J**	24. **F**	32. **G**	40. **G**

SCIENCE TEST

1. **B**	9. **C**	17. **B**	25. **D**	33. **A**
2. **F**	10. **G**	18. **F**	26. **J**	34. **G**
3. **D**	11. **C**	19. **D**	27. **A**	35. **D**
4. **J**	12. **F**	20. **H**	28. **H**	36. **F**
5. **B**	13. **D**	21. **B**	29. **D**	37. **B**
6. **G**	14. **F**	22. **G**	30. **G**	38. **H**
7. **D**	15. **A**	23. **D**	31. **B**	39. **A**
8. **H**	16. **G**	24. **J**	32. **G**	40. **G**

ANSWERS AND EXPLANATIONS

ENGLISH TEST

Passage I

1. C   Difficulty: Medium

Category: Punctuation

Getting to the Answer: Choice (C) is the correct and most concise choice. Choice A uses an unnecessary comma. Choice B is unnecessarily wordy. Choice D is redundant—if the societies created the legends, there is no need to describe the legends as *original*.

2. F   Difficulty: High

Category: Topic Development / Supporting Material

Getting to the Answer: The question stem gives an important clue to the best answer: The purpose of the inserted sentence is "to describe the different kinds" of stories. Choice (F) is the only choice that does this. Choice G explains how the stories were told. Choice H explains why more is not known about the stories. Choice J describes the length of some stories.

3. D   Difficulty: Medium

Category: Organization, Unity, and Cohesion / Transitions

Getting to the Answer: Choices A and B create run-on sentences. Choice C fixes the run-on, but the cause-and-effect transition does not make sense in context. Choice (D) correctly describes a relationship that makes sense between our "many more permanent ways of handing down our beliefs" and the fact that "we continue to create and tell legends," and it creates a complete sentence.

4. F   Difficulty: Low

Category: Usage

Getting to the Answer: A colon is used to introduce a short phrase, quotation, explanation, example, or list. The sentence is correct as written because "the urban legend" is the writer's example of "a new form of folktale." Choices G, H, and J add unnecessary words after the colon.

5. D   Difficulty: Medium

Category: Punctuation

Getting to the Answer: If an underlined segment contains punctuation, check to make sure it is correct. The semicolon needs to be changed to a colon; colons are used to introduce a short phrase, quotation, explanation, example, or list. The phrase "a Friend of a Friend" explains what the acronym FOAF stands for, so a colon is necessary. Choices A, B, and C do not include the necessary colon.

6. G   Difficulty: Low

Category: Knowledge of Language / Concision

Getting to the Answer: Choices F, H, and J are all redundant. The word *conclusion* is unnecessary because the word *ending* has already been used, so (G) is correct.

7. B   Difficulty: Medium

Category: Usage

Getting to the Answer: Choice (B) is the only choice that is consistent with the past tense established by *knew* and *decided*. Choices A, C, and D use incorrect verb tenses.

8. J   Difficulty: Medium

Category: Usage

Getting to the Answer: Choice F creates a run-on sentence and also makes it seem that the hunter, not the deer, "was only temporarily knocked unconscious by the car." Choices G and H use incorrect verb tenses. Choice (J) fixes the run-on and the modifying phrase confusion.

9. A   Difficulty: High

Category: Sentence Structure and Formation

Getting to the Answer: The sentence is correct as written. Choice B is incorrect because the words preceding the semicolon are not a complete sentence on their own. Choice C creates a sentence fragment. Choice D creates a run-on sentence.

10. J Difficulty: High

Category: Knowledge of Language / Style and Tone

Getting to the Answer: Eliminate choices F and G because they do not clearly convey the legend; they do not specifically state how the baby alligators found their way to city sewers. Choices H and (J) describe how the alligators came to live in sewers, but H is too formal and wordy. Choice (J) is correct.

11. C Difficulty: Medium

Category: Usage

Getting to the Answer: The subject of the sentence is *One*, so the verb must be singular, which matches (C). Choice A incorrectly uses a plural verb. Choices B and D use incorrect verb tenses.

12. G Difficulty: Low

Category: Usage

Getting to the Answer: Choice F creates a sentence that does not make sense, as it incorrectly uses the adjective *supposed* to describe the verb *copied*. Choices H and J incorrectly use the plural *women* instead of the singular *woman*. Choice (G) uses the correct noun and adverb.

13. B Difficulty: Medium

Category: Sentence Structure and Formation

Getting to the Answer: Choices A and D misplace the modifying phrase "Dedicated to commonly told urban legends," which should describe the *websites*, and C is not clear. Choice (B) provides the most clear and correct option.

14. H Difficulty: High

Category: Organization, Unity, and Cohesion / Passage Organization

Getting to the Answer: Paragraph 4 describes an urban legend that is "humorous in nature." Paragraph 5 describes a rather frightening legend: alligators living underneath the city in the sewer system. The sentence "Other urban legends seem to be designed to instill fear" is an appropriate topic sentence for Paragraph 5, and it also serves as a needed transition between Paragraph 4 and Paragraph 5. Therefore, (H) is correct.

15. C Difficulty: Medium

Category: Topic Development / Writer's Purpose

Getting to the Answer: Although Paragraph 1 provides a bit of general information about the purpose and topics of the myths and legends of primitive societies, no specifics are given. This makes (C) the best answer.

Passage II

16. H Difficulty: Medium

Category: Usage

Getting to the Answer: Choice (H) correctly pairs a singular verb with a singular subject, and the pronoun *you* matches how the author addresses the reader throughout the first paragraph. Choices F and G are grammatically incorrect. Choice J uses both a verb tense and pronoun that do not match the surrounding text.

17. B Difficulty: Medium

Category: Organization, Unity, and Cohesion / Transitions

Getting to the Answer: If a transition is underlined, check to make sure it is logical in context. As written, the sentence does not make sense. Only (B) conveys the writer's intended meaning: a hypothetical. Choice C indicates a contrast the writer is not making, and D is not logical.

18. H Difficulty: Medium

Category: Knowledge of Language / Concision

Getting to the Answer: As written, the sentence is redundant because *solitary* and *living alone* have the same meaning. Eliminate J because it is even wordier than the original. Choice G is more concise, but it creates a run-on sentence. Choice (H) provides the most concise, clear answer.

19. D Difficulty: Low

Category: Punctuation

Getting to the Answer: Items in a list must be punctuated properly. In this sentence, a comma is required after the words *born* and *taxes*, so (D) is correct. Choices A, B, and C do not offer correct punctuation.

20. J   Difficulty: Medium

Category: Sentence Structure and Formation

Getting to the Answer: As written, the sentence is a run-on. Choice (J) offers a common fix for run-ons: a FANBOYS conjunction (in this case, the word *and*) as well as a comma. Choice G deletes the word *and*, which does not fix the run-on. Choice H inserts a semicolon, which can fix a run-on, but the semicolon should not be paired with a FANBOYS conjunction.

21. B   Difficulty: Medium

Category: Punctuation

Getting to the Answer: The phrase *in fact* is nonessential, so it should be set off by commas, as shown in (B). Choices A, C, and D do not punctuate the phrase correctly.

22. G   Difficulty: Medium

Category: Knowledge of Language / Precision

Getting to the Answer: This question provides four adverbs to chose from, only one of which is correct based on the context. The writer is saying that Thoreau is distinctly American, which matches (G). Choices F, H, and J do not reflect the writer's intended meaning; *uniformly* implies that Thoreau was following other people's ideas, *obliquely* means indirectly, and *deplorably* means shamefully.

23. D   Difficulty: Low

Category: Punctuation

Getting to the Answer: The phrase "In 1845 Thoreau, built a cabin" places the comma in the wrong spot—the comma should appear after the introductory phrase "In 1845." Choice (D) corrects the error and does not introduce new issues. Choice B puts a comma after the introductory phrase, but introduces a new error by placing an unnecessary comma after *cabin*. Choice C is incorrect because moving *in 1845* after *Thoreau* creates an unclear sentence that is not grammatically correct.

24. J   Difficulty: Medium

Category: Sentence Structure and Formation

Getting to the Answer: As written, the sentence correctly joins two independent clauses with a semicolon.

The clauses can also be punctuated using a dash, joined with a comma and FANBOYS conjunction, or separated by a period. The clauses cannot be separated by just a comma because it creates a run-on sentence, so (J) is correct.

25. C   Difficulty: High

Category: Organization, Unity, and Cohesion / Passage Organization

Getting to the Answer: Sentence 3 logically follows sentence 1. Choice (C) is the only choice that lists this correct order.

26. F   Difficulty: Medium

Category: Sentence Structure and Formation

Getting to the Answer: There is one independent clause on each side of the semicolon, so the sentence is punctuated correctly. Choices G, H, and J create run-on sentences.

27. B   Difficulty: Medium

Category: Organization / Transitions

Getting to the Answer: When a transition is underlined, read the sentence for context to determine what type of transition is needed. The sentence requires a contrast transition, so you can eliminate A and C. Choices (B) and D offer contrast transitions, but D is too wordy. Choice (B) is correct.

28. F   Difficulty: Medium

Category: Sentence Structure and Formation

Getting to the Answer: When a pronoun is underlined, check to see if it makes sense in context. The sentence is correct as written because the writer addresses the reader as *you*, as seen in the introductory paragraph. Choices G, H, and J unnecessarily shift the pronoun.

29. D   Difficulty: Medium

Category: Topic Development / Writer's Purpose

Getting to the Answer: This paragraph discusses Thoreau's impact on modern society; only (D) expresses the correct topic.

30. G **Difficulty:** High

Category: Topic Development / Writer's Purpose

Getting to the Answer: The use of questions prompts a reader to think about the answers to those questions, so (G) is correct. Choice F is too literal, and J is out of scope for the topic of the essay. Choice H is incorrect because the writer establishes the quality of Thoreau's work.

Passage III

31. D **Difficulty:** Medium

Category: Knowledge of Language / Concision

Getting to the Answer: Because the word *live* is used later in the sentence, A, B, and C contain redundant information. Choice (D) is correct.

32. H **Difficulty:** Low

Category: Punctuation

Getting to the Answer: In this sentence, the *its* must be possessive because the *unique anatomy* belongs to the sloth. The word describing the noun *anatomy* must be an adjective, not an adverb. Choice (H) is the only choice that meets both requirements.

33. A **Difficulty:** Medium

Category: Punctuation

Getting to the Answer: The comma is correctly used in (A) to separate the nonessential descriptive phrase "about the size of a large domestic cat" from the rest of the sentence. Choices B, C, and D do not offer correct punctuation.

34. H **Difficulty:** Medium

Category: Sentence Structure and Formation

Getting to the Answer: Choices F, G, and J all misplace the modifying phrase "specially designed for limbs." Choice (H) clearly and directly expresses how the sloth's muscles are designed to allow this animal to cling to things.

35. D **Difficulty:** Low

Category: Knowledge of Language / Precision

Getting to the Answer: The question provides four words, and you must choose the word that best fits the context of the sentence. The sentence indicates that the sloth's

limbs have a distinct design that makes it easy for them to live in the trees. Choice (D), *specifically*, reflects this idea. Choices A, B, and C do not make sense in context; *defiantly* means resistantly or disobediently, *enthusiastically* means eagerly, and *painstakingly* means very carefully.

36. G **Difficulty:** Medium

Category: Punctuation

Getting to the Answer: As written, the underlined portion includes an unnecessary comma after *crawl* in the compound verb *crawl or drag*, so F is incorrect. Eliminate H because it does not remove the unnecessary comma, and it adds an additional unnecessary comma. Choice J removes the comma after *crawl*, but it adds an unnecessary comma after *itself* and omits the necessary comma after *Instead*. Choice (G) correctly retains the comma after the introductory transition *Instead* and deletes the comma after *crawl*.

37. D **Difficulty:** Medium

Category: Organization, Unity, and Cohesion / Transitions

Getting to the Answer: Choice (D) is the only choice that correctly establishes the relationship between the sloth's inability to "move swiftly on the ground" and its ability to swim.

38. G **Difficulty:** High

Category: Topic Development / Supporting Material

Getting to the Answer: Choice (G) is the only choice that connects the sloth's unique characteristics discussed in Paragraph 3 with the description of its flexibility in Paragraph 4.

39. D **Difficulty:** Medium

Category: Knowledge of Language / Concision

Getting to the Answer: Choice A can be eliminated because it is unnecessarily wordy. Choice C is a bit more concise, but (D) is even more concise than C. Choice B is a short option, but it includes an incorrect shift in verb tense.

40. J **Difficulty:** Medium

Category: Usage

Getting to the Answer: Choice (J) is the only choice that reflects the present tense, which is consistent with the sentence.

41. D   Difficulty: Low

Category: Sentence Structure and Formation

Getting to the Answer: As written, the sentence is a fragment. Choices B and C each lack a complete verb phrase. Only choice (D) corrects the run-on.

42. J   Difficulty: Medium

Category: Topic Development / Supporting Material

Getting to the Answer: This information about the howler monkey is irrelevant to the topic of the passage.

43. B   Difficulty: Medium

Category: Sentence Structure and Formation

Getting to the Answer: Choice A creates a sentence fragment. Choice C is unnecessarily wordy and awkward. Choice D creates a run-on sentence. Choice (B) changes the period to a comma to correctly combine the clauses.

44. G   Difficulty: Medium

Category: Topic Development / Supporting Material

Getting to the Answer: The last sentence aptly concludes the entire passage, and removing it would end the essay before the author provides a concluding expression.

45. C   Difficulty: High

Category: Organization, Unity, and Cohesion / Passage Organization

Getting to the Answer: The description of the sloth's camouflage is in Paragraph 5, so (C) is correct. Choices A, B, and D each place the sentence in an illogical spot.

Passage IV

46. F   Difficulty: Medium

Category: Sentence Structure and Formation

Getting to the Answer: The underlined portion is best left as is, so (F) is correct. The other answer choices make the sentence unnecessarily wordy.

47. B   Difficulty: Low

Category: Usage

Getting to the Answer: The verb tense must agree with the tense that has been established up to this point. The passage is in the past tense, so (B) is correct. Choices A, C, and D do not reflect the correct tense.

48. H   Difficulty: Medium

Category: Usage

Getting to the Answer: As with the answer to the previous question, the simple past tense is needed, so (H) is correct. Choices F and G use the incorrect tense, and J creates a fragment.

49. C   Difficulty: Medium

Category: Sentence Structure and Formation

Getting to the Answer: Choice A contains a sentence fragment and uses an incorrect present verb tense. Choice (C) fixes both issues. Choice B fixes the fragment but uses the incorrect verb tense. Choice D fixes the verb tense but incorrectly uses a semicolon, as the words preceding the semicolon do not constitute an independent clause.

50. H   Difficulty: High

Category: Sentence Structure and Formation

Getting to the Answer: In the context of the rest of the passage, only (H) makes sense by correctly placing the modifying word *only*. The firefighters' attempts to extinguish the flames failed; only nature could stop the fire with the first snowfall.

51. D   Difficulty: Medium

Category: Knowledge of Language / Concision

Getting to the Answer: Choices A and B are unnecessarily wordy and awkward. Choice C creates a run-on sentence. Choice (D) is concise and correct.

52. J   Difficulty: Medium

Category: Organization, Unity, and Cohesion / Transitions

Getting to the Answer: The sentence requires a continuation transition, so you can eliminate F and G because they are contrast transitions. Choice H does not make sense in context. Choice (J) is both logical and grammatically correct.

53. C   Difficulty: High

Category: Knowledge of Language / Ambiguity

Getting to the Answer: The pronoun *it* does not have a clear antecedent, so A is incorrect. Choices B and D each change the verb form, which introduces a new error; the word *Fires* is plural, so the plural verb form *allow* is required. Only (C) specifies what *it* means and retains the correct verb tense.

54. H   Difficulty: Medium

Category: Punctuation

Getting to the Answer: From the plural verb *open*, you can determine that the best answer will contain *cones*, so eliminate F and J. This makes (H) the only possible answer, as the apostrophe is incorrectly used in G.

55. C   Difficulty: Medium

Category: Organization, Unity, and Cohesion / Transitions

Getting to the Answer: Choice (C) is the only option that makes sense in the context of the passage. The sighting of the large animals near burning forests is used as evidence that the animals of the region were "fire-tolerant and fire-adaptive."

56. J   Difficulty: Medium

Category: Knowledge of Language / Concision

Getting to the Answer: Eliminate F and G because *close to* and *near* have the same meaning. Choices H and (J) are more concise, but H introduces an error by adding an unnecessary comma. Choice (J) is correct.

57. D   Difficulty: High

Category: Topic Development / Writer's Purpose

Getting to the Answer: The phrase *borne out* means proven, so look for an answer choice that is true based on the information the writer provides. Choice (D) reflects the writer's conclusion that the fire was not a tragedy. Choices A, B, and C may be true, but there is no evidence in the essay to support those statements.

58. G   Difficulty: High

Category: Sentence Structure and Formation

Getting to the Answer: The problem with "judging from recent pictures of the park" is that the phrase is modifying *forest*, and a forest cannot judge anything. The phrase would have been correct if the sentence had read "judging from the recent pictures of the park, I think that the forest was not destroyed." In this case, the phrase would modify *I*, the writer, who is capable of judging. Choice (G) fixes the issue by rewriting the sentence to eliminate the modifying phrase.

59. C   Difficulty: Medium

Category: Topic Development / Supporting Material

Getting to the Answer: The introduction of information about fires in Alaska is unwarranted, so A and B can be eliminated. Choice D is incorrect because the additional information would actually uphold the writer's position as an authority. Choice (C) is correct.

60. J   Difficulty: High

Category: Topic Development / Supporting Material

Getting to the Answer: The reports mentioned in (J) directly substantiate the writer's claims regarding the threat to endangered animal species. Choice F would not provide information regarding the effect on the animals. Choice G is too narrow to provide enough information about multiple animal species, and H isn't related to animals at all.

Passage V

61. D   Difficulty: Medium

Category: Knowledge of Language / Concision

Getting to the Answer: The final part of the sentence, "and there are many other rivers in America as well," is completely irrelevant to the rest of the paragraph and to the essay, which discusses white-water rafting and the rivers the writer has rafted.

62. J   Difficulty: Medium

Category: Punctuation

Getting to the Answer: Choice F is incorrect because *rapids* is essential information and should not be set off by commas. Choice G is incorrect because what follows the colon is not an explanation. Choice H is incorrect because what follows the semicolon cannot stand alone as a sentence. Choice (J) is correctly punctuated.

63. C   Difficulty: Medium

Category: Usage

Getting to the Answer: When a pronoun is underlined, make sure it is used properly. Choices A and B use the objective pronoun *me*, which is incorrect. While D uses the subjective pronoun *I*, it is not placed correctly. Only (C) reflects correct pronoun usage and placement.

64. J   Difficulty: Medium

Category: Usage

Getting to the Answer: Choices F and H create sentence fragments, and G is both wordy and awkward. Choice (J) is correct.

65. D   Difficulty: Medium

Category: Sentence Structure and Formation

Getting to the Answer: This sentence makes it sound as though the writer were *roaring*, not the rapids; roaring is a misplaced modifier. Choice B does not fix the problem because the reader has no idea what *it* refers to. Choice C has the *boat* roaring. Choice (D) is the clearest choice.

66. J   Difficulty: Medium

Category: Knowledge of Language / Concision

Getting to the Answer: The sentence is redundant because *churned* and *swirled* both mean that the water was turbulent. Choices G and H introduce new errors by changing the verb tense. Choice (J) retains the correct verb tense and eliminates the redundancy.

67. B   Difficulty: Medium

Category: Sentence Structure and Formation

Getting to the Answer: Choices A and D create run-on sentences. While C is grammatically correct, (B) is the

clearest, most concise way of expressing the writer's intended meaning.

68. J   Difficulty: Low

Category: Organization, Unity, and Cohesion / Transitions

Getting to the Answer: Choices F, G, and H make it sound as though the writer was expecting the boat to hit the rock. Choice (J) is the most accurate wording: a jarring halt.

69. D   Difficulty: Medium

Category: Sentence Structure and Formation

Getting to the Answer: "Suddenly we came to a jarring halt" and "the left side of the bow was wedged on a large rock" are independent clauses that must be properly combined. Choice (D) correctly uses a semicolon to join the clauses. Choices A and B incorrectly place the word *and* in front of the second independent clause, and C creates a run-on sentence.

70. F   Difficulty: Low

Category: Punctuation

Getting to the Answer: *It was* is correct here because the writer is telling the story in the past tense. Choices G and H are in the present tense, and J incorrectly introduces the possessive form.

71. D   Difficulty: Medium

Category: Usage

Getting to the Answer: When a pronoun is underlined, make sure it agrees with its antecedent. Choices A and B use the plural pronoun *their*, which does not match the singular subject *the boat*. Choice C uses the word *its*, but (D) is the correct wording to match the *small hole* and thus the correct answer.

72. G   Difficulty: Medium

Category: Sentence Structure and Formation

Getting to the Answer: The sentence is a run-on because a comma cannot separate two independent clauses without including a coordinating conjunction directly after the comma. Choice (G) adds in the missing coordinating conjunction. Choice H fixes the run-on by making the second clause dependent, but it does not make sense in context. Choice J deletes the comma, which does not fix the run-on.

73. B   Difficulty: Medium

Category: Topic Development / Supporting Material

Getting to the Answer: Choice A would not work as a concluding sentence because its style and tone are off; nowhere in the passage does the writer use language such as *brutal calamities* and *beguiling excitement*. Also, the writer and the writer's father were not *unwary rafters*. Choice C contradicts the writer's main theme that nothing was as memorable as the writer's first ride through the rapids. This is also a sentence fragment. The tone in D—"call me crazy or weird"—is much different from the writer's. Choice (B) closely matches the writer's style and tone while restating the main theme of the passage.

74. F   Difficulty: Medium

Category: Topic Development / Writer's Purpose

Getting to the Answer: This essay relates a personal experience of the writer and includes very little mention of the techniques of white-water rafting, so the essay would not meet the requirements of the assignment. Choice G is incorrect because the essay does not focus on the relationship between family members, but on their first rafting experience together. Choice (F) is correct.

75. B   Difficulty: High

Category: Organization, Unity, and Cohesion / Passage Organization

Getting to the Answer: The sentence foreshadows things to come, so it must appear toward the beginning of the essay. That eliminates C and D. The second paragraph is about the peaceful setting, so (B) is correct.

MATHEMATICS TEST

1. D   Difficulty: Low

Category: Essential Skills / Rates, Percents, Proportions, and Unit Conversion

Getting to the Answer: You know that 14 people make up 20% of the total, and you need to find 100% of the total. You could set up an equation, or you could multiply

14 by 5, because 100% is 5 times 20%. The number of people surveyed is 14×5, or 70. Choice (D) is correct.

2. J   Difficulty: Medium

Category: Essential Skills / Expressions and Equations

Getting to the Answer: One strategic way to answer this question is by Picking Numbers. For instance, if you let $x = 2$ and $y = 3$, the train would have traveled $(90 \times 2) + (60 \times 3) = 360$ miles in $2 + 3 = 5$ hours, or $\frac{360}{5} = 72$ miles per hour. If you then plug $x = 2$ and $y = 3$ into the answer choices, you find that (J) is correct. No other answer choice equals 72 when $x = 2$ and $y = 3$.

You can also answer the question using algebra. First, the train traveled 90 miles per hour for x hours, so it traveled a distance of $90x$ miles. Next, the train traveled 60 miles per hour for y hours, which is a distance of $60y$ miles. Now put the two legs of the trip together. The train traveled a total distance of $90x + 60y$ miles in a total time of $x + y$ hours, for an average rate of $\frac{90x + 60y}{x + y}$ miles per hour, which matches (J).

3. B   Difficulty: Medium

Category: Essential Skills / Rates, Percents, Proportions, and Unit Conversion

Getting to the Answer: If the ratio of men to women is 5:3, then the ratio of women to the total is $3:(3 + 5) = 3:8$. Because you know the total number of string players is 24, you can set up the proportion $\frac{3}{8} = \frac{x}{24}$, and then solve using cross-multiplication to find that $x = 9$, which is (B).

4. H   Difficulty: Low

Category: Essential Skills / Numbers and Operations

Getting to the Answer: Use the order of operations. In PEMDAS, absolute value counts as parentheses, so you must evaluate it first.

$$-|-6| - (-6) = -(6) - (-6) = -6 + 6 = 0$$

Choice (H) is correct.

5. E   Difficulty: Medium

Category: Essential Skills / Statistics and Probability

Getting to the Answer: The best way to deal with changing averages is to make use of the sums. Use the old average to figure out the total of the first four scores:

$$\text{Sum of first 4 scores} = 4 \times 89 = 356$$

Then use the new average to figure out the total he needs after the fifth score:

$$\text{Sum of five scores} = 5 \times 90 = 450$$

To raise the sum from 356 to 450, Martin needs to score $450 - 356 = 94$. Choice (E) is correct.

6. H   Difficulty: Low

Category: Essential Skills / Numbers and Operations

Getting to the Answer: This question is a great opportunity to use your calculator. Notice that all the answer choices are decimals. In order to solve, convert $\frac{3}{16}$ into a decimal and add that to 0.175; $\frac{3}{16} = 0.1875$, so the sum equals $0.1875 + 0.175 = 0.3625$. Thus, (H) is correct.

7. E   Difficulty: Low

Category: Essential Skills / Numbers and Operations

Getting to the Answer: On the ACT Mathematics test, you have an average of one minute per question. If a question can be solved quickly using your calculator, take advantage of it. For example, you can use your calculator to compare fractions by finding the decimal equivalents.

$$\frac{3}{5} = 0.6$$

A: $\frac{4}{6} = 0.\overline{6} = 0.666\ldots$

B: $\frac{8}{13} = 0.61538\ldots$

C: $\frac{6}{10} = 0.6$

D: $\frac{7}{11} = 0.\overline{63}$

(E): $\frac{4}{7} = 0.57142\ldots$

Only (E) is smaller than 0.6.

8. K   Difficulty: Low

Category: Higher Math / Statistics and Probability

Getting to the Answer: To determine the total number of possible arrangements, simply determine the number of possibilities for each option and then multiply them together. There are three ways of serving the ice cream (cup, sugar cone, or waffle cone), five flavors, and four toppings. Therefore, there are $3 \times 5 \times 4 = 60$ ways to order ice cream with the special offer, and (K) is correct.

9. E   Difficulty: Medium

Category: Essential Skills / Rates, Percents, Proportions, and Unit Conversion

Getting to the Answer: Backsolving is a great technique to use for this question. Start with C: The director asked 1 out of 3 students to come to the second audition and $\frac{1}{3}$ of 48 is 16, so 16 students were invited to a second audition. Then 75% of 16, which is $\frac{3}{4}(16) = 12$, students were offered parts. The question states that 18 students were offered parts, so you already know that C is too small. (You can also, thus, eliminate A and B.) Because the director invited $\frac{1}{3}$ of the students to a second audition, the number of students at the first audition must be divisible by 3. (You can't have a fraction of a student.) That eliminates D, leaving only (E).

10. H   Difficulty: Medium

Category: Higher Math / Statistics and Probability

Getting to the Answer: The question only asks about participants who were outside a healthy weight range, so focus on the middle row of numbers: 38 out of the 74 participants who were outside a healthy weight range ate breakfast one or fewer times per week. This represents $\frac{38}{74} \approx 0.5135$, or 51.35%, which matches (H).

11. B   Difficulty: High

Category: Higher Math / Statistics and Probability

Getting to the Answer: This question requires some rewording in order to use the table. "Neither participant ate breakfast more than 1 time per week" can be restated as "both participants ate breakfast less than or equal to 1 time per week," so the column you're interested in is the "Breakfast ≤ 1 time per week" column. Of the 131 participants, 44 ate breakfast less than or equal to 1 time per week, so the probability that the first person chosen for the follow-up survey fits the criteria is $\frac{44}{131}$. Now there are 43 out of 130 remaining participants who fit the criteria, so the probability that the second person chosen for the follow-up survey fits the criteria is $\frac{43}{130}$.

The probability that both people chosen for the follow-up survey fit the criteria (neither of the participants ate breakfast more than 1 time per week) is the product of the two probabilities, or $\frac{44}{131} \times \frac{43}{130}$, which is (B).

12. K   Difficulty: High

Category: Higher Math / Statistics and Probability

Getting to the Answer: The question asks about employees who eat breakfast every weekday, so focus on the "5-7 times per week" column in the table. The question states that the participants in the study were a good representative sample, so you can use the results of the study to approximate the number of employees that are likely to be within a healthy weight range: 36 out of 45, or 80%, of the company's 3,000 employees are likely to be within a healthy weight range. Multiply 0.8 × 3,000 to arrive at 2,400, which is (K).

13. C   Difficulty: Low

Category: Essential Skills / Numbers and Operations

Getting to the Answer: The safest strategy is to list out the possibilities. It's also helpful to realize that multiples of both 4 and 6 are multiples of 12 (the least common multiple between the two), so skip over all multiples of 12:

4, 8, ~~12~~, 16, 20, ~~24~~, 28, 32, ~~36~~, 40, 44, ~~48~~

There are 8 in all, making (C) correct.

14. J   Difficulty: Medium

Category: Higher Math / Functions

Getting to the Answer: Don't be intimidated by the function notation—you do not need to multiply the two expressions together. Here, you can just substitute the number that appears in the parentheses, 3, for each x in

the expression given:

$$f(3) = [8 - 3(3)][(3)^2 - 2(3) - 15]$$

Once you get to this point, use PEMDAS:

$$[8 - 3(3)][(3)^2 - 2(3) - 15]$$
$$= (8 - 9)(9 - 6 - 15) = (-1)(-12) = 12$$

Choice (J) is correct.

15. B   Difficulty: Medium

Category: Higher Math / Statistics and Probability

Getting to the Answer: The mean of a set of numbers is the same as the average, which is the sum of the terms divided by the number of terms. Use the graph to find the sum of the GPA values, and then calculate the mean. Read the graph carefully—each grid line represents one student. To save time, multiply the frequency in each category by the GPA value and then divide by the total number of students: $(10 \times 4) + (36 \times 3) + (28 \times 2) + (8 \times 1) + (2 \times 0) = 212 \div 84 = 2.524$, or about 2.5, which is (B).

16. G   Difficulty: Medium

Category: Essential Skills / Geometry

Getting to the Answer: The formula for finding the area of a triangle is $A = \frac{1}{2}$ (base)(height). You're given the area and the length of the base (after a simple calculation), so plug these values in and solve for the height (altitude). The area of the triangle is 45 square units and the length of the base is $3 + 12 = 15$ units. Let h be the length of altitude $\overline{YS}$. Plug these into the area formula to get $45 = \frac{15h}{2} \rightarrow 90 = 15h \rightarrow h = \frac{90}{15} = 6$. Choice (G) is correct.

17. B   Difficulty: Low

Category: Higher Math / Algebra

Getting to the Answer: Every point along the y-axis has an x-coordinate of 0 (because the points are neither left nor right of the y-axis). This means you can substitute 0 for x into the equation and solve for y:

$$6y - 3(0) = 18$$
$$6y = 18$$
$$y = 3$$

Choice (B) is correct. Note that you could also rewrite the given equation in slope-intercept form ($y = mx + b$), in which case the value of b gives you the y-intercept.

18. H   Difficulty: High

Category: Higher Math / Algebra

Getting to the Answer: This question involves special quadratics (a difference of squares and the square of a binomial), so the key is to write these quadratic expressions in their other forms. For instance, $x^2 - y^2 = 12$ can be written as $(x + y)(x - y) = 12$. Because $x - y = 4$, you now have $(x + y)(4) = 12$, which means $x + y = 3$. Finally, $x^2 + 2xy + y^2 = (x + y)^2 = (3)^2 = 9$, making (H) the correct answer.

19. B   Difficulty: High

Category: Higher Math / Geometry

Getting to the Answer: This composite shape can be divided into three simple shapes. By drawing two perpendicular line segments down from the endpoints of the side that is 10 units long, you are left with a 3×10 rectangle, a triangle with a base of 4 and a height of 3, and a triangle with a base of 7 and a hypotenuse of $7\sqrt{2}$. The rectangle has an area of $3 \times 10 = 30$ square units. The smaller triangle has an area of $\frac{1}{2}(4 \times 3) = 6$ square units. The larger triangle is a 45°-45°-90° triangle, so the height must be 7. Therefore, it has an area of $\frac{1}{2}(7 \times 7) = 24.5$ square units. The entire shape has an area of $30 + 6 + 24.5 = 60.5$ square units, (B).

20. H   Difficulty: Low

Category: Essential Skills / Rates, Percents, Proportions, and Unit Conversion

Getting to the Answer: Although Backsolving is certainly possible with this question, it's probably quicker to solve using arithmetic. To keep the calculations organized, convert all the measures to inches. The board is 12 feet long, which means it is $12 \times 12 = 144$ inches. Each of the three pieces the carpenter cuts off is 1 foot, 5 inches, or $12 + 5 = 17$ inches. Thus, the carpenter cuts off $3 \times 17 = 51$ inches. That leaves $144 - 51 = 93$ inches for the remaining part of the board. Choice (H) is correct.

21. B   Difficulty: Low

Category: Higher Math / Functions

Getting to the Answer: In this arithmetic sequence, you can think of the terms as 26, $26 + s$, $26 + s + s$, and $26 + s + s + s$. In this example, s represents the difference between successive terms. The final term is 53, so set up an algebraic equation: $26 + s + s + s = 53$. Solve this equation for s by first combining like terms: $26 + 3s = 53$. Subtract 26 from both sides to get $26 - 26 + 3s = 53 - 26$, or $3s = 27$. Divide both sides by 3 to find that s, the difference between terms, is 9. Therefore, the terms are 26, $26 + 9$, $26 + 9 + 9$, and 53, or 26, 35, 44, and 53, making (B) the correct answer.

22. G   Difficulty: Medium

Category: Higher Math / Algebra

Getting to the Answer: Here's another question that tests your factoring ability, but you have to be careful. The question states that -3 is a solution for the equation $x^2 + kx - 15 = 0$, so in its factored form, one set of parentheses with a factor inside must be $(x + 3)$. Because the last term in the given equation is -15, and $3 \times (-5)$ is -15, the entire factored equation must look like $(x + 3)(x - 5) = 0$, which in its expanded form is equivalent to $x^2 - 2x - 15 = 0$. Thus, $k = -2$ and (G) is correct.

Note that, because you're told that -3 is a solution to the equation, you could also plug in -3 for each x and solve for k.

$$x^2 + kx - 15 = 0$$
$$(-3)^2 + k(-3) - 15 = 0$$
$$9 - 3k - 15 = 0$$
$$-3k - 6 = 0$$
$$-3k = 6$$
$$k = -2$$

23. E   Difficulty: Low

Category: Essential Skills / Geometry

Getting to the Answer: Draw a quick sketch. Notice that the answers are fairly different, so you just need a general idea in order to get the correct answer.

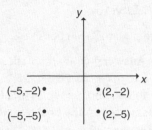

As you can see in the diagram above, the fourth coordinate must be (E), $(-5,-5)$.

24. J   Difficulty: Medium

Category: Higher Math / Functions

Getting to the Answer: Don't let the nested function (composition) scare you. Work from the inside out. To find $g(1)$, find $x = 1$ in the x column of the $g(x)$ table and read the corresponding $g(x)$ value, 0. Now repeat the process with the $f(x)$ table, using the x-value 0 to find that $f(g(1))$ is $f(0) = 4$, which is (J).

25. C   Difficulty: Medium

Category: Essential Skills / Geometry

Getting to the Answer: Break strange figures like this one up into shapes that are more familiar and easier to handle. In this case, the quadrilateral can be split into a square and a right triangle. The square is 9×9, so the area of that part of the figure is 81 square meters. The right triangle has a height of 9 and a base of 4, so the area of the triangle, in square meters, is:

$$\frac{1}{2}bh = \frac{1}{2}(4 \times 9) = \frac{1}{2}(36) = 18$$

Therefore, the total area of the figure is $(81 + 18)$ square meters = 99 square meters, (C).

26. G   Difficulty: Low

Category: Essential Skills / Rates, Percents, Proportions, and Unit Conversion

Getting to the Answer: If the ratio of the parts (macaroons to gingersnaps) is 2:5, then the total number of parts is $2 + 5 = 7$. Thus, the actual total number of cookies must be a multiple of 7. The only choice that's a multiple of 7 is (G), 35.

27. C   Difficulty: High

Category: Essential Skills / Rates, Percents, Proportions, and Unit Conversion

Getting to the Answer: This is a question where you will need to work backward. Normally, when there is a sale, you take the original price and multiply it by the discount to find the amount the shopper saved. But here, you know how much she paid and one discount amount, but not the other, so to work backward, you'll need to divide.

Divide the amount Margo paid, $41.85, by 0.9 (because the discount for using her store credit card was 10%, or 0.1). This will tell you how much she would have paid if she hadn't used her store credit card: $41.85 ÷ 0.9 = $46.50. To find the amount of the sale discount, divide this by the original price: $46.50 ÷ $62.00 = 0.75, which means she paid 75% of the price. In other words, the discount was 25%, making (C) the correct choice.

You could also try each answer choice, one at a time, but this will use up valuable time on Test Day.

28. J   Difficulty: Medium

Category: Essential Skills / Geometry

Getting to the Answer: When you are given a perimeter for a rectangle, the rectangle with the greatest possible area for that perimeter will always be a square. So you are looking for the area of a square with a perimeter of 20. The perimeter of a square equals $4s$, where s is the length of one side of the square. If $4s = 20$, then $s = 5$. The area of the square equals $s^2 = 5^2 = 25$, (J).

29. B   Difficulty: Medium

Category: Essential Skills / Numbers and Operations

Getting to the Answer: Be careful on this one. You can't start plugging numbers into your calculator without paying careful attention to the order of operations. This one is best solved by hand. A common denominator for the entire expression is not required. Instead, simplify the numerator and the denominator independent of each other:

$$\frac{\frac{3}{2}+\frac{7}{4}}{\left(\frac{15}{8}-\frac{3}{4}\right)-\left(\frac{4+3}{-4+3}\right)}=\frac{\frac{6}{4}+\frac{7}{4}}{\left(\frac{9}{8}\right)-\left(\frac{7}{-1}\right)}$$

$$=\frac{\frac{13}{4}}{\frac{65}{8}}=\frac{13}{4}\times\frac{8}{65}=\frac{2}{5}$$

This matches (B).

30. K   Difficulty: Low

Category: Essential Skills / Expressions and Equations

Getting to the Answer: You could solve this algebraically for x as follows:

$$x-15=7-5(x-4)$$
$$x-15=7-5x+20$$
$$x-15=-5x+27$$
$$6x=42$$
$$x=7$$

Choice (K) is correct. Remember also that if you are ever stuck, you can Backsolve using the answer choices. Here, if you try each one, only 7 works:

$$7-15=7-5(7-4)$$
$$-8=7-5(3)$$
$$-8=7-15$$
$$-8=-8$$

31. E   Difficulty: Medium

Category: Essential Skills / Rates, Percents, Proportions, and Unit Conversion

Getting to the Answer: When the answer choices include variables, Picking Numbers may make the question look less complicated. Choose a small, easily workable number to replace the variable. Suppose $x=3$. If it takes Julie 3 minutes to type 3 pages, her rate is 1 page per minute. So it will take her 11 minutes to type 11 pages. Now plug 3 into each of the answer choices, and you will find that (E) gives you the same answer, 11 minutes.

Want to solve the question using algebra? Let m equal the number of minutes it takes for Julie to type 11 pages.

If she types 3 pages in x minutes, you can use the proportion:

$$\frac{m}{11}=\frac{x}{3}$$
$$m=\frac{11x}{3}$$

32. H   Difficulty: Low

Category: Higher Math / Algebra

Getting to the Answer: To answer this question, write the equation in slope-intercept form, $y=mx+b$, where m equals the slope. In other words, you need to isolate y:

$$6y-3x=18$$
$$6y=3x+18$$
$$y=\frac{3x+18}{6}$$
$$y=\frac{1}{2}x+3$$

So the slope equals $\frac{1}{2}$, which is (H).

33. A   Difficulty: Medium

Category: Higher Math / Functions

Getting to the Answer: Don't let logarithmic functions scare you. They are simply another way of arranging exponential equations. The general terminology and rule to follow is that "base^{exponent} = amount" translates to "log $_{\text{base}}$ amount = exponent." Start with the base: The base in the given exponential equation is 10, so the logarithm must also be base 10. This means either (A) or B is correct. Now the exponent: The exponent in the given expression is 2, so the number to the right of the equal sign in the logarithm must be 2, making (A) the correct answer.

34. K   Difficulty: Medium

Category: Higher Math / Algebra

Getting to the Answer: When a linear equation is written in $y=mx+b$ form, b tells you the y-intercept. Because the question gives the y-intercept (-3), it is easy to look at the answer choices and rule out F, H, and J. To decide between the two remaining choices, put the equation from the question in slope-intercept form to find its slope (m):

Answers & Explanations

$$3x - 5y = 4$$
$$-5y = -3x + 4$$
$$y = \frac{-3x + 4}{-5}$$
$$y = \frac{3}{5}x - \frac{4}{5}$$

Because line t is parallel, it has the same slope, $\frac{3}{5}$, so (K) must be correct.

35. A   Difficulty: Medium

Category: Higher Math / Number and Quantity

Getting to the Answer: Even if you know absolutely nothing about vectors, answering this question works exactly like you would think. The $-\frac{3}{4}$ is called a scalar, and it behaves the same way any number being multiplied by a quantity does: Multiply the scalar by each of the numbers that represent the two components of the vector to get:

$$-\frac{3}{4}\mathbf{w} = \left\langle -\frac{3}{4} \cdot -8, \ -\frac{3}{4} \cdot 12 \right\rangle = \langle 6, -9 \rangle$$

This matches (A).

36. J   Difficulty: High

Category: Higher Math / Functions

Getting to the Answer: The term *half-life* means the length of time needed for the amount of a radioactive substance to be reduced by half. The amount of the substance will decrease by half every 28 days, so the base of the power will be $\frac{1}{2}$. The exponent should be t days divided by the half-life, in days. Because the scientist started with 100 grams of the substance, the correct function is $f(t) = 100 \cdot \left(\frac{1}{2}\right)^{\frac{t}{28}}$, which is (J).

Note that this is a fairly advanced topic, so you may want to skip it and come back. If you have time, you could choose one (or more) pairs of values from the table and substitute them into each function until you find the correct one. For example, if $t = 0$ days, the correct function must return a value of 100. This works for H, (J), and K. So, choose another pair of values. If $t = 28$, H returns a value of 200, (J) returns a value of 50, and K returns a value of a teeny-weeny decimal. Thus, (J) must be correct (because the table indicates that the number of grams remaining should be 50).

37. E   Difficulty: High

Category: Higher Math / Functions

Getting to the Answer: If you find the distance from the center to the given point on the circle, you'll have the radius. Using the distance formula, you'll find that the radius is:

$$\sqrt{(7 - (-1))^2 + (5 - (-1))^2} = \sqrt{8^2 + 6^2}$$
$$= \sqrt{64 + 36}$$
$$= \sqrt{100} = 10$$

Now you can plug the radius and the coordinates of the center point into the general form of the equation of a circle:

$$(x - h)^2 + (y - k)^2 = r^2$$
$$(x - (-1))^2 + (y - (-1))^2 = 10^2$$
$$(x + 1)^2 + (y + 1)^2 = 100$$

Choice (E) is correct.

38. G   Difficulty: High

Category: Higher Math / Algebra

Getting to the Answer: While you could try factoring the numerator, you'll find that you can't easily cancel out the denominator by doing so. Instead, use the Picking Numbers strategy. Choose a simple number, such as $x = 2$, and substitute it into the given expression. The result is:

$$\frac{x^2 - 11x + 24}{8 - x} = \frac{(2)^2 - 11(2) + 24}{8 - 2}$$
$$= \frac{4 - 22 + 24}{6}$$
$$= \frac{6}{6} = 1$$

So 1 is your target number. When you plug $x = 2$ into the answer choices, the only choice that gives you 1 is (G).

39. C   Difficulty: Medium

Category: Higher Math / Geometry

Getting to the Answer: The textbook method for this question would be to use the distance formula, but that's time-consuming. Instead, it may help to draw a picture. Draw a right triangle on the coordinate plane as shown below:

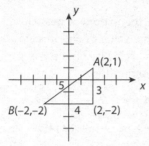

Note that the distance between the two points represents the hypotenuse of the triangle. The legs of the triangle have lengths of 3 and 4, so the distance between the two points must be 5, (C).

40. G   Difficulty: Medium

Category: Higher Math / Geometry

Getting to the Answer: To find the area of the shaded region, you must subtract the area of the circle from the area of the rectangle. Because the sides of the rectangle are $2x$ and $5x$, it has an area of $2x \cdot 5x = 10x^2$. By examining the diagram, you can see that the circle has a diameter of $2x$, so it has a radius of x. Its area is, therefore, πx^2. Thus, the shaded region has an area of $10x^2 - \pi x^2$, which matches (G).

41. E   Difficulty: High

Category: Higher Math / Geometry

Getting to the Answer: Use SOHCAHTOA. Your first step should be to identify the sides you're given and the side you're trying to find. Then figure out which trig function gives you a relationship between the side you know and the side you want to know. The distance between the cliff and the house is opposite the given angle. The height of the cliff is adjacent to that angle. The trig function that gives a relationship between the opposite and the adjacent sides is tangent.

$$\tan 62° = \frac{500}{\text{height}}$$
$$\text{height} \times \tan 62° = 500$$
$$\text{height} = \frac{500}{\tan 62°}$$

Choice (E) is correct.

42. H   Difficulty: Medium

Category: Essential Skills / Numbers and Operations

Getting to the Answer: To answer this question using algebra, set up and solve two inequalities. The calculations will be easier if you write the decimal numbers as fractions and use cross-multiplication. First, $\frac{7}{n} > \frac{1}{2} \rightarrow 14 > n$, or n is less than 14. Next, $\frac{7}{n} < \frac{8}{10} \rightarrow 70 < 8n \rightarrow 8.75 < n$, or n is greater than 8.75. The integer values that work for both inequalities are $n = 9, 10, 11, 12,$ and 13. Five integer values work, making (H) correct.

Note that you could also use brute force and your calculator: Divide 7 by integer values for n, and look for values between 0.5 and 0.8. Begin by looking for the integer values of n where $\frac{7}{n}$ is greater than 0.5. If $n = 14$, then $\frac{7}{n} = 0.5$ exactly, so n must be less than 14. Work through values of n until you get to the point where $\frac{7}{n}$ is less than 0.8. When $n = 9$, $\frac{7}{n} = 0.778$, but when $n = 8$, $\frac{7}{n} = 0.875$. So the integer values that work are $n = 9, 10, 11, 12,$ and 13.

43. C   Difficulty: Medium

Category: Higher Math / Geometry

Getting to the Answer: The points are as far apart as possible when separated by a diameter of X and a diameter of Y as shown here:

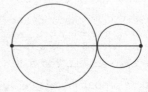

The circumference of a circle is π × (diameter), so the diameter of circle *X* is 12, and the diameter of circle *Y* is 8. The greatest possible distance between points then is $12 + 8 = 20$, which is (C).

44. K   Difficulty: Medium

Category: Higher Math / Algebra

Getting to the Answer: Begin by getting rid of the square root sign. For all $a \geq 0$, $\sqrt{a^2} = a$, so $\sqrt{(x^2 + 4)^2} = x^2 + 4$ (because a quantity squared is always greater than or equal to 0). Then $(x + 2)(x - 2) = x^2 - 4$, so you now have $(x^2 + 4) - (x^2 - 4) = ?$ Get rid of the parentheses by distributing the minus in the middle to arrive at $x^2 + 4 - x^2 + 4 = 8$, which is (K).

45. B   Difficulty: Low

Category: Essential Skills / Expressions and Equations

Getting to the Answer: Here, you need to substitute −3 for *t* in the expression and simplify using the correct order of operations (PEMDAS). That gives you the expression $5(-3 + 1) - 1$, which equals $5(-2) - 1 = -10 - 1 = -11$. Choice (B) is correct.

46. G   Difficulty: High

Category: Higher Math / Algebra

Getting to the Answer: Be careful on this one. Begin by simplifying the equation by FOILing the right-hand side:

$$2x + 6 = (x + 5)(x + 3) \rightarrow 2x + 6 = x^2 + 8x + 15$$

Then make the left side of the equation equal zero by subtracting 2x and 6 from both sides: $0 = x^2 + 6x + 9$.

The right-hand side of the new equation is the perfect square $(x + 3)^2$, so $(x + 3)^2 = 0$, which has only one unique solution, $x = -3$. Choice (G) is correct.

47. D   Difficulty: Medium

Category: Essential Skills / Statistics and Probability

Getting to the Answer: This is a great candidate for Backsolving. For each answer, add that number to 5 to find the total. Is the probability of getting a nickel $\frac{1}{6}$? If the total is 30 coins, 5 will be $\frac{1}{6}$ the number of coins, so Calleigh needs to add $30 - 5 = 25$ pennies, (D).

48. G   Difficulty: High

Category: Higher Math / Functions

Getting to the Answer: You can make abstract questions more concrete by Picking Numbers. When the denominator of a fraction gets larger while the numerator stays constant, the value of the fraction gets closer to 0. Thus, the exponent $\frac{1}{r}$ gets closer to 0 as *r* gets larger and larger. Because the exponent gets closer and closer to 0, and $2^0 = 1$, the value of $g(r)$ gets closer and closer to 1 as *r* increases, so (G) is correct. You can plug in a few values of *r* to confirm this.

If $r = 1$, then $g(1) = (2)^{\frac{1}{1}} = 2^1 = 2$.

If $r = 2$, then $g(2) = 2^{\frac{1}{2}} \approx 1.414$.

If $r = 10$, then $g(10) = 2^{\frac{1}{10}} \approx 1.072$.

If $r = 100$, then $g(100) = 2^{\frac{1}{100}} \approx 1.007$.

The values are indeed getting closer to 1.

49. E   Difficulty: Medium

Category: Higher Math / Geometry

Getting to the Answer: Triangles are the secret to answering this question. Drawing $\overline{OD}$ divides quadrilateral *OCDE* into two triangles, *OCD* and *ODE*. Both triangles are isosceles because $\overline{OC}$, $\overline{OD}$, and $\overline{OE}$ are all radii of circle *O*. Angles *ODC* and *OCD* have equal measures, because they're opposite equal sides, so $\angle ODC$ measures 70°. Similarly, $\angle ODE$ measures 45°. Together, angles *ODC* and *ODE* make up $\angle CDE$, so its measure is $70° + 45° = 115°$. This matches (E).

50. J   Difficulty: High

Category: Higher Math / Algebra

Getting to the Answer: The solution to a system of equations is the point or points at which the graphs of the two equations intersect. A system that has no solution indicates two graphs that never intersect—for linear equations, this means the lines have the same slope and are parallel. To answer this question, find the pair of equations representing lines that have the same slope. Writing the equations in (J) in slope-intercept form gives:

$$y = -\frac{1}{3}x + 2, \; y = -\frac{1}{3}x + \frac{7}{9}$$

The slope is $-\dfrac{1}{3}$ for both lines, and the y-intercepts are different, so the lines are parallel and do not intersect.

51. E   **Difficulty:** Medium

Category: Essential Skills / Numbers and Operations

Getting to the Answer: To solve a repeating decimal question, begin by determining the pattern of the decimal using your calculator:

$\dfrac{1}{7} = 1 \div 7 = 0.\overline{142857}\ \overline{142857}$ ... so you know that this fraction repeats every six decimal places. Because you are looking for the 46th decimal place, you need to determine where in the six-term pattern you would be at the 46th place. Divide 46 by 6 and look for the remainder. The remainder in this case is 4, so you are looking for the 4th term in the sequence, which is 8, (E).

52. F   **Difficulty:** High

Category: Higher Math / Number and Quantity

Getting to the Answer: Think of a few possible values for a and b and use these values to evaluate the answer choices. First, simplify the expression by getting rid of the radical:

$$\sqrt{3\left(\dfrac{a^2}{b}\right)} = 2$$

$$\left(\sqrt{3\left(\dfrac{a^2}{b}\right)}\right)^2 = 2^2$$

$$3\left(\dfrac{a^2}{b}\right) = 4$$

$$\dfrac{a^2}{b} = \dfrac{4}{3}$$

If $\dfrac{a^2}{b} = \dfrac{4}{3}$, then one set of possible values is $a = 2$ and $b = 3$. This eliminates G and H. Another set of possible values is $a = 4$ and $b = 12$. This eliminates J. Now, since $\dfrac{a^2}{b}$ results in $\dfrac{4}{3}$, which is positive, and because a^2 will always be positive, you know that b CANNOT be a negative number, because a positive number divided by a negative number would result in a negative number. Therefore, you can eliminate K. The correct answer is (F).

53. E   **Difficulty:** Medium

Category: Higher Math / Number and Quantity

Getting to the Answer: If you're not sure which answer is correct, try plugging in points from the number line. Plugging in $x = -2$ eliminates A, B, and D (the inequality in D includes values to the left of -2.5 and at the same time to the right of -1.5, which is not possible). Choice C includes numbers that aren't in the shaded region, such as -2.9, so (E) is correct. Using a more general approach also works: The shaded region includes all the values between -1.5 and -2.5. Because -1.5 is larger than -2.5, the inequality should be $-2.5 < x < -1.5$.

54. G   **Difficulty:** Medium

Category: Higher Math / Geometry

Getting to the Answer: When transversals intersect parallel lines, corresponding line segments on the transversals are proportional. In this figure, $\dfrac{DE}{CB} = \dfrac{EF}{BA}$. Thus, $\dfrac{6}{8} = \dfrac{EF}{4}$, and using cross-multiplication, $8EF = 24$ or $EF = 3$. Choice (G) is correct.

55. E   **Difficulty:** Medium

Category: Higher Math / Number and Quantity

Getting to the Answer: A complex number can seem scary on the ACT, but this question defines it for you, so treat it like you would any other variable that you plug numbers into. In this question, the key is swapping every i^2 with a -1. Begin by simplifying the first factor in the expression:

$$(i + 1)^2 = (i + 1)(i + 1)$$
$$= i^2 + 2i + 1$$
$$= -1 + 2i + 1 = 2i$$

Multiplying this by the second factor yields:

$$2i(i - 1) = 2i^2 - 2i = 2(-1) - 2i = -2 - 2i$$

That's the same as (E).

56. K   **Difficulty:** Medium

Category: Higher Math / Functions

Getting to the Answer: First, recall a couple of definitions: The *amplitude* of a trigonometric function refers to how high or low the curve moves from the horizontal axis (indicated by *y*-values of points on the curve). The *period* refers to the distance required to complete a single wave along the horizontal axis (indicated by *x*-values of points along the curve). Now compare the equation for each function: The only transformation to the standard cosine function here is the 2 in front. The 2 is not grouped with the argument (θ), so you are doubling the *y*-coordinates of all the points on the graph. Thus, you are doubling the original amplitude, making (K) the correct answer.

57. A   Difficulty: High

Category: Higher Math / Number and Quantity

Getting to the Answer: When written in radical form, it is not possible to add, subtract, multiply, or divide roots that have different indexes (such as a square root and a cube root). However, if you rewrite the radicals using fraction exponents, then you can use rules of exponents to combine them.

Write each radical using a fraction exponent, and then use the rule $a^x \times a^y = a^{x+y}$ to combine them:

$$\sqrt{2} \times \sqrt[4]{2} = 2^{\frac{1}{2}} \times 2^{\frac{1}{4}}$$
$$= 2^{\frac{1}{2}+\frac{1}{4}}$$
$$= 2^{\frac{2}{4}+\frac{1}{4}}$$
$$= 2^{\frac{3}{4}}$$

The answers are written as radicals, so convert back to radicals using the saying "power over root." The result is $\sqrt[4]{2^3} = \sqrt[4]{8}$, which is (A).

58. H   Difficulty: High

Category: Higher Math / Geometry

Getting to the Answer: You're given the formula for the volume of a cylinder in the question, so you can find the volume of both cylinders described. Then this becomes a ratio question in which you're comparing the volumes of both cylinders. Pick Numbers and plug them into the volume formula to make this question more concrete. Let's say the smaller cylinder has a height of 1 and a radius of 1 (diameter of 2), resulting in a volume of $\pi(1)^2 \times 1 = \pi$. The larger cylinder would then have a height of 3 and a radius of 2 (diameter of 4), resulting in a volume of $\pi(2)^2 \times 3 = 12\pi$. Thus, it would take 12

fillings of the smaller cylinder to fill the larger cylinder. Choice (H) is correct.

59. D   Difficulty: High

Category: Higher Math / Geometry

Getting to the Answer: Draw a picture of the triangle and carefully apply your knowledge of the ratio of the lengths of the sides of a 30°-60°-90° triangle $(x:x\sqrt{3}:2x)$. If the longer leg has a length of 12, the shorter leg has a length of:

$$\frac{12}{\sqrt{3}} = \frac{12\sqrt{3}}{\sqrt{3} \times \sqrt{3}} = \frac{12\sqrt{3}}{3} = 4\sqrt{3}$$

Then, the hypotenuse is twice this, or $8\sqrt{3}$. Finally, the perimeter is the sum of the three sides, or:

$$4\sqrt{3} + 12 + 8\sqrt{3} = 12\sqrt{3} + 12$$

Choice (D) is correct.

60. J   Difficulty: Medium

Category: Essential Skills / Expressions and Equations

Getting to the Answer: Use the definition of average to answer this question: $\text{Average} = \dfrac{\text{sum of the terms}}{\text{number of terms}}$. To find the *total* average, find the total sum and divide it by the total number of terms. If a team averages *x* points in *n* games, then it scored *nx* points in *n* games. In the final game of the season, it scored *y* points. So the total sum of points for the season is $nx + y$, and the total number of games is $n + 1$. Thus the team's average score for the entire season is $\dfrac{nx + y}{n + 1}$, which matches (J).

READING TEST

Passage I

Suggested Passage Map notes:

¶1: Emma (E) 20 yrs old, indulgent father, no mother

¶2: Miss Taylor (T) governess 16 yrs like sister; E used to getting own way

¶3: T now married

¶4: T's husband not exceptional but nice

¶5: E very lonely w/o T

1. C   Difficulty: Medium

Category: Key Ideas and Details / Detail

Getting to the Answer: The answer can be found in lines 26−30: "The real evils, indeed, of Emma's situation were the power of having rather too much her own way, and a disposition to think a little too well of herself; these were the disadvantages which threatened alloy to her many enjoyments." This matches (C). Choices A, B, and D are distortions—they do not directly reflect the author's intended meaning.

2. G   Difficulty: Medium

Category: Key Ideas and Details / Detail

Getting to the Answer: The dinner takes place on the evening of Miss Taylor's wedding day, as "she [Emma] and her father were left to dine together, with no prospect of a third to cheer a long evening" (lines 39−41). The mood is sad, and Emma longs for the past when Miss Taylor was an integral and enjoyable member of the family. This matches (G). Choice F is out of scope; Emma was certainly sad, but the author never says she was angry. Choices H and J are also out of scope; Emma is not disappointed in her father, and she seems to like Mr. Weston, whom she recognizes as a good man and suitable husband (line 45−47).

3. B   Difficulty: Medium

Category: Key Ideas and Details / Detail

Getting to the Answer: The answer can be found in lines 17−18: "Between them it was more the intimacy of sisters." Choice (B) is correct. Choice A is a misused detail; while Miss Taylor "had fallen little short of a mother in affection" (line 13), the author does not imply that Miss Taylor loved Emma more than a parent loves a child. Choices C and D are distortions—the author does not make those comparisons in the text.

4. F   Difficulty: Low

Category: Craft and Structure / Vocab-in-Context

Getting to the Answer: As it is used in the sentence, "disposition" means a tendency or inclination. Choices G, H, and J are incorrect because it would not make sense for Emma to have a *control, placement,* or *transfer* "to think a little too well of herself" (lines 28−29).

5. D   Difficulty: High

Category: Key Ideas and Details / Detail

Getting to the Answer: The answer can be found in lines 52−58: "She recalled her past kindness—the kindness, the affection of sixteen years—how she had taught her and … how she had devoted all her powers to attach and amuse her in health—and how she had nursed her through the various illnesses of childhood." Only (D) matches perfectly.

6. H   Difficulty: Medium

Category: Key Ideas and Details / Detail

Getting to the Answer: The author writes that Emma had "very little to distress or vex her" (line 5), had "a most affectionate, indulgent father" (lines 6−7), and "an excellent governess who had fallen little short of a mother in affection" (lines 12−13). All this adds up to a happy life, which matches answer choice (H). Choice F is opposite. Choice G is opposite because the author writes that Emma does what she pleases without needing permission, and J is out of scope: there is no evidence that Emma is confused.

7. C   Difficulty: Medium

Category: Key Ideas and Details / Inference

Getting to the Answer: Emma is described as "having rather too much her own way" (lines 27−28), which matches (C). Choice A is opposite because *obedient* and *headstrong* are antonyms. Emma's love for Miss Taylor shows her appreciation of her, making B incorrect. Lines 1−4 speak of Emma's happy life, so she would not be bitter, eliminating D.

8. G   Difficulty: Medium

Category: Key Ideas and Details / Global

Getting to the Answer: Emma's description of her friendship with Miss Taylor suggests that Emma most highly values devotion—(G)—in her friends, as evidenced in lines 64−70. Choice F is a misused detail: Emma mentions that Miss Taylor is intelligent, but Emma does not indicate that intelligence is most highly valued. While H and J are plausible, there is no direct evidence in the text to support those answers.

9. B   Difficulty: Medium

Category: Key Ideas and Details / Detail

Getting to the Answer: The description of Mr. Weston is in lines 44−47: "The marriage had every promise of happiness for her friend. Mr. Weston was a man of unexceptionable character, easy fortune, suitable age, and pleasant manners." Choice (B) matches. Choices A, C, and D do not reflect this description.

10. H   Difficulty: Medium

Category: Craft and Structure / Writer's View

Getting to the Answer: In lines 21−22, when describing the relationship between Emma and her governess, Miss Taylor, the author writes that the "shadow of authority" was "now long passed away," meaning that Emma is no longer under the control of Miss Taylor. As for Emma's father, he was "affectionate" and "indulgent," another person whose permission Emma would not need. The correct answer then is (H), which describes Emma as her own independent person. Choice F is out of scope; there's no reference to her father's wishes. Choice G is tempting, but the author writes that though Emma "highly esteemed" Miss Taylor's advice, she goes her own way. Choice J is opposite of the information in the passage.

Passage II

Suggested Passage Map notes:

Passage A

¶1: 1903 - W bros successful

¶2: other inventors tested models

¶3: W bros tested 1 aspect at a time

¶4: W bros invented wind tunnel

¶5: no guesswork

Passage B

¶1: peopled doubted W bros

¶2: companies fought W bros patent

¶3: finally, public support, but after death

11. B   Difficulty: Medium

Category: Key Ideas and Details / Global

Getting to the Answer: Passage A discusses the Wright brothers' process for designing a successful airplane; (B) is correct. Although the passage mentions how the Wright brothers were regarded, A, this information appears in the first paragraph only, and is not the main focus of the passage. The passage discusses the approaches used by other inventors, but the author does not criticize them, as represented in C. The practical application of science, D, is too broad to be correct.

12. H   Difficulty: High

Category: Craft and Structure / Vocab-in-Context

Getting to the Answer: When answering a Vocab-in-Context question, be sure to read the word in the context of the sentence in which is appears. The word *jaded* is followed by "tired of investigating each yokel who claimed to have made an airplane," and the next sentence describes a reporter who is so bored with attempts at flight that he does not even touch his camera. Based on this context, *jaded* means something like bored or uninterested, which matches (H). Choice F is opposite. Choice G is out of scope; something made of jade may be valuable but this is irrelevant to the passage. Choice J implies enough interest to have a negative opinion, and "jaded" means lack of interest, so J is incorrect.

13. B   Difficulty: High

Category: Key Ideas and Details / Inference

Getting to the Answer: The passage says that the Wright brothers invented the wind tunnel as an alternative to building and testing "whole machines." They tested only parts of their design in the tunnel, such as wing shape. You can infer that the wind tunnel made it possible for them to deal with their airplane design one piece at a time, which matches (B). The author never implies that the data from the kites, A, was inaccurate. To work on controlling the plane laterally, they used a five-foot biplane kite rather than the wind tunnel, which rules out C. Choice D is opposite; they proved that a commonly accepted component of the theory of lift (called Smeaton's coefficient) was wrong.

14. F   Difficulty: High

Category: Craft and Structure / Function

Getting to the Answer: Passage B deals mainly with how the Wright brothers were treated publicly following their discovery. The *legal battle* is mentioned as another example of how the brothers did not receive the money and respect they deserved for their important contribution, (F). The author does not imply that it is unwise to publicize knowledge, G. Choice H is opposite; the author feels that their discovery was quite important. Choice J is not directly related to the court case.

15. C   Difficulty: Medium

Category: Key Ideas and Details / Inference

Getting to the Answer: In the last paragraph, the author states that "this was too little, too late," which suggests that the honor did not properly compensate for the poor treatment of the brothers, (C). It was not a victory for Orville, A, because both brothers had passed away by 1948. The Smithsonian's choice was not a result of the refusal to recognize the brothers' achievements, B, because it was a great honor. There is no evidence to suggest that the craft would have been displayed sooner if European countries had issued the brothers a patent, D.

16. J   Difficulty: High

Category: Craft and Structure / Writer's View

Getting to the Answer: The passage talks about how "those who made airplanes" thought little of the Wright brothers' accomplishments. In lines 93–96, it says the brothers went through an "unfair period of ridicule and doubt and the obstinate refusal by much of the world to acknowledge their achievements." This suggests that others characterized the Wright brothers as "unlikely pioneers of flight," (J). It also cancels out F, G, and H, which suggest positive assessments of the Wright brothers.

17. B   Difficulty: Medium

Category: Integration of Knowledge and Ideas / Synthesis

Getting to the Answer: The passage says "the prevailing opinion among those who made airplanes was that two rustic, uneducated fellows from Ohio could never have accomplished such a historic feat." From this, you can infer that those who made airplanes did not think that the Wright brothers were exceptional; in their eyes, the brothers' discovery must have been sheer luck, not the result of scientific experimentation, which matches (B).

Eliminate A because the passage never says that they thought the Wrights had not made a working airplane, only that they thought little of the accomplishment. Choice C is opposite; they had a negative opinion of the Wrights' breakthrough. Choice D is a distortion; they felt the brothers were lucky, not dishonest.

18. H   Difficulty: Low

Category: Integration of Knowledge and Ideas / Synthesis

Getting to the Answer: The authors state that the Wrights were able to "marry all of these carefully designed components into a complete craft" (lines 59–60) and "deliberately marry the disparate components of air travel that are required for successful flight" (lines 71–73). So the Wright brothers brought together all the separate pieces into a whole airplane. Predict that *marry* means "bring together," (H). The airplane did prove, F, that the components worked when together, but it does not make sense to say that the brothers were able to deliberately prove the components. The Wright brothers had already rigorously tested each component separately, so G is incorrect. Airplane components cannot be satisfied, so J does not work.

19. B   Difficulty: Medium

Category: Integration of Knowledge and Ideas / Synthesis

Getting to the Answer: At the beginning of Paragraph 3, Passage A states, "The Wright brothers proved to be adept scientists. With their keen analytical insight and love of engineering and all things mechanical, they were able to escape that endless loop of misguided 'improvements.'" This matches perfectly with (B). Choice A describes the approach that other, unsuccessful inventors used. Passage A does not provide evidence that the invention of the wind tunnel was a greater accomplishment than the airplane, C. The court case cited in D is included in Passage B, not in Passage A.

20. H   Difficulty: Low

Category: Integration of Knowledge and Ideas / Synthesis

Getting to the Answer: Wrong answer choices for this type of question are commonly those that are true for one passage but not the other. Both passages agree that the Wright brothers did something great that no one else was capable of at the time, which is reflected in (H). The brothers' method of inquiry, F, is discussed in Passage A only. Choices G and J are included in Passage B, but not in Passage A.

Passage III

Suggested Passage Map notes:

¶1: photography not traditional, so allowed women

¶2: Cameron (C) 1st famous woman photographer

¶3: C's work notable in Victorian period

¶4: Victorian critics liked C's allegorical pics; today's critics prefer C's portraits

21. B   Difficulty: Medium

Category: Key Ideas and Details / Inference

Getting to the Answer: In lines 10–11, Julia Margaret Cameron is described as "the first woman to have achieved eminence in photography," which matches (B). Choices A, C, and D contradict information supplied in the passage.

22. F   Difficulty: Medium

Category: Key Ideas and Details / Detail

Getting to the Answer: The answer to this question can be found in lines 71–72, "Contemporary taste much prefers her portraits," and in lines 76–77, "today her fame rests upon her portraits." Choices G, H, and J do not match the information regarding modern critics' opinions.

23. D   Difficulty: High

Category: Key Ideas and Details / Detail

Getting to the Answer: The dates used in the passage tell you that this is a chronological account; the author begins with Cameron's birth in 1815, and then tells of her marriage and her move to England in 1848. The author points out that she received her first photographic equipment in 1863, describes one of her photographs from 1864, and then concludes the paragraph with her death in 1874. Only (D) matches the method the author uses.

24. F   Difficulty: Medium

Category: Craft and Structure / Vocab-in-Context

Getting to the Answer: The passage indicates that *cumbersome* means not easy to handle. Choice (F) most closely

fits this definition, and it is the only answer choice that makes sense within the context of the sentence.

25. B   Difficulty: Medium

Category: Key Ideas and Details / Inference

Getting to the Answer: Lines 47–48 describe how Cameron "devoted herself wholly to this art," which matches (B). Choice A contradicts information from the passage, which suggests that Cameron led anything but a conventional life. Neither the money that Cameron earned as a photographer nor her religious beliefs are discussed in the passage, making C and D incorrect.

26. F   Difficulty: Medium

Category: Key Ideas and Details / Global

Getting to the Answer: Lines 52–54 say, "she produced a large body of work that stands up as one of the notable artistic achievements of the Victorian period," which matches (F). Choice G is incorrect because to say that she "is the greatest photographer who ever lived" goes beyond anything stated or implied in the passage. The third paragraph does not compare her importance as an artist during her lifetime to her importance today, so H is incorrect. You can eliminate J because the passage also does not state that she "revolutionized" any photographic methods.

27. D   Difficulty: Medium

Category: Key Ideas and Details / Detail

Getting to the Answer: Think about how the author supports this choice of words: he writes that "women artists have been most prominent in photography and that they have made their greatest contribution in this field," (lines 1–3) and that photography was "outside the traditional academic framework," thus "wide open to women" (lines 6–8). So photography, the new medium, was a field not overpopulated or controlled by men, offering women an area in which they could not only participate but also shine, as (D) states. Choice A is a faulty use of detail; *new medium* refers to opportunities for women, not to general popularity. Choice B is true, but not why the author used the words he chose. Choice C is out of scope; Cameron took photographs in order to represent "not only the outer likeness but also the inner greatness of the people she portrayed" (lines 78–80), not to be a trendsetter.

28. G   Difficulty: Low

Category: Key Ideas and Details / Detail

Getting to the Answer: These titles refer to allegorical pictures, as described in lines 68–71: "Victorian critics were particularly impressed by her allegorical pictures, many of them based on the poems of her friend and neighbor Tennyson." This information matches (G). Choices F, H, and J are incorrect because they are not relevant to allegorical pictures.

29. D   Difficulty: Medium

Category: Key Ideas and Details / Detail

Getting to the Answer: The answer to this question can be found in lines 71–73: "Contemporary taste much prefers her portraits and finds her narrative scenes sentimental and sometimes in bad taste." Only (D) matches perfectly. Choice A is a distortion. While the photographs were based on poems, the author doesn't say that the Victorian critics thought that photographs *should* be based on poems. Choice B is opposite; modern critics like her portraits because they are not sentimental. Choice C is opposite; modern critics, not Victorian critics, thought her narrative scenes were in bad taste.

30. F   Difficulty: Low

Category: Craft and Structure / Writer's View

Getting to the Answer: The author says that Cameron "achieved eminence" (line 11) in her field, that she "devoted herself wholly to this art" (line 48), and that "no other woman photographer has ever enjoyed such success" (lines 63–65). Only (F) fits with these descriptions. Choices G and J are too negative, and H is not positive enough.

Passage IV

Suggested Passage Map notes:

¶1: harbor seal adapted

¶2: quadraphonic hearing = pinpoint location

¶3: eye refracts light in water = better vision

¶4: echolocation

¶5: whiskers sense vibration

31. C   Difficulty: Low

Category: Key Ideas and Details / Detail

Getting to the Answer: For details about the eye, look at Paragraph 3. Only the cornea and stenopaic pupil are relevant, eliminating A and D. The cornea, B, is helpful underwater, not on land. Choice (C) is correct.

32. G   Difficulty: Medium

Category: Key Ideas and Details / Inference

Getting to the Answer: The eye is covered in Paragraph 3. The seal's cornea improves vision in the water (note the comparison to human underwater vision), but it distorts light moving through the air. Another adaptation was then needed to *minimize* (line 46) distortion, but that does not mean distortion is completely eliminated, so the seal's vision in the air is distorted, (G). Choice F is opposite, and H and J do not reflect the correct comparison.

33. D   Difficulty: Low

Category: Key Ideas and Details / Detail

Getting to the Answer: The vibrissae are discussed only in Paragraph 5. Seals sense wave disturbances made by nearby moving fish, so (D) is correct. Choice A is a misused detail; underwater vision is mentioned in Paragraph 3, not Paragraph 5. Choice B, by using the phrase "in the air," distorts information in the passage. Choice C is incorrect because camouflage is not mentioned in the passage, so it is out of scope.

34. F   Difficulty: Low

Category: Key Ideas and Details / Detail

Getting to the Answer: The correct answer, (F), is stated in the second paragraph, where the seal's hearing is discussed. Choices G and H contradict the information in the passage, and J does not make sense because the speed of sound can be calculated.

35. D   Difficulty: Medium

Category: Key Ideas and Details / Detail

Getting to the Answer: This appears in the first paragraph, which introduces the influences on the seal's adaptations. They include that the seal "does most of its fishing at night," that "noise levels are high," and that these factors are compounded by the seal's "two habitats," so all three statements are correct. Choice (D) is the only option that includes all three.

36. H   Difficulty: Medium

Category: Craft and Structure / Writer's View

Getting to the Answer: Choice (H) is *suggested* as an opinion scientists hold (lines 48–50). Choice G is a fact from the passage. Choices F and J are distortions of information in the passage.

37. C   Difficulty: High

Category: Craft and Structure / Writer's View

Getting to the Answer: The author discusses vibrissae, or whiskers, in the last paragraph, in which he uses the words *speculate* and *speculation*. To *speculate* is to theorize without firm evidence, so it must be that the scientists who speculate, and the author who reports that speculation, can only guess at the real function of the whiskers. Thus, the author would not agree that the use is proven, as A states, but that vibrissae may help harbor seals locate food by sensing "wave disturbances produced by nearby moving fish" (lines 65–66). That agrees with (C) because the word *possible* leaves room for doubt. Choices B and D reflect misused details; bats are comparable to seals in terms of the use of echolocation, not whiskers, and blurry conditions in water refer to the human eye underwater.

38. J   Difficulty: Medium

Category: Key Ideas and Details / Detail

Getting to the Answer: This feature is mentioned at the end of Paragraph 2, and it matches (J). It should not be confused with distinctive "clicking" sounds or echolocation, as mentioned in F and G respectively, which is discussed in Paragraph 4, not Paragraph 2. Choice H is a distortion; the author does not say that harbor seals can breathe underwater.

39. B   Difficulty: Medium

Category: Craft and Structure / Function

Getting to the Answer: The entire passage is about how the seal's sensory organs have adapted to life on land and in the water, making (B) the best choice. Generally, you are told about differences, not similarities, between the sensory organs of humans and harbor seals, eliminating A. The relative success of human and seal adaptation to their environments is not discussed, thus eliminating C and D.

40. G   Difficulty: Medium

Category: Key Ideas and Details / Detail

Getting to the Answer: In Paragraph 3, we see that human corneas refract light badly in water, while the seal's corneas perform well. This information matches (G). Choice F is incorrect because it is a similarity among seals and humans. Choice H is out of scope; the author does not mention camouflage. Choice J is also not mentioned in the passage and humans *have* adapted to live in certain environments.

SCIENCE TEST

Passage I

1. B   Difficulty: Medium

Category: Interpretation of Data

Getting to the Answer: To answer this question, you have to examine the third column of Table 1, transmittance range. For a material to transmit light at a wavelength of 25 μm, its transmittance range—the range of wavelengths over which the material is transparent—must include 25 μm. Only potassium bromide (0.3–29 μm) and cesium iodide (0.3–70 μm) have transmittance ranges that include 25 μm, so (B) is correct.

2. F   Difficulty: Medium

Category: Interpretation of Data

Getting to the Answer: The material that contradicts the hypothesis will have poor chemical resistance but a transmittance range less than 10 μm. Lithium fluoride, (F), fits the bill: its chemical resistance is poor, and its transmittance range is less than 6 μm wide. Choices G and J are wrong because both flint glass and quartz have excellent chemical resistance. Choice H is out because cesium iodide has a transmittance range nearly 70 μm wide.

3. D   Difficulty: High

Category: Interpretation of Data

Getting to the Answer: The correct answer will be a pair of materials in which the refractive index of the first material is greater than that of the second. In A, B, and C, the refractive index of the first material is less than that of the second. In (D), however, flint glass has a refractive index of 1.66, while calcium fluoride's refractive index is only 1.43. That makes (D) the correct answer.

4. J   Difficulty: Medium

Category: Interpretation of Data

Getting to the Answer: The easiest way to answer this question is to examine the first few materials in the table and test each hypothesis on them. Choices F and G are incorrect because the transmittance range of lithium fluoride is wider than its useful prism range. Comparing the data on lithium fluoride and calcium fluoride rules out H because transmittance range does NOT increase as useful prism range decreases. In fact, based on other values in the table, transmittance range seems to *decrease* as useful prism range decreases. Choice (J) is the only one left, and the data on lithium fluoride and calcium fluoride (as well as all the other materials) confirm that the transmittance range is always wider than, and includes within it, the useful prism range.

5. B   Difficulty: High

Category: Interpretation of Data

Getting to the Answer: According to the footnote to Table 1, quartz infused with lead oxide is flint glass. Comparison of the properties of pure quartz and flint glass shows that the transmittance range of flint glass is narrower than that of quartz, but its refractive index is greater. This supports (B).

6. G   Difficulty: Medium

Category: Interpretation of Data

Getting to the Answer: Begin this question by looking at the answer choices and finding the transmittance range and useful range for prisms for lithium fluoride, sodium chloride, quartz, and flint glass. A quick glance at the chart shows that the ranges for lithium fluoride (for transmittance and prisms, respectively) are slightly below 6 and less than 3. Sodium chloride shows ranges of 16.7 and 8. Quartz has ranges of 3.1 and 2.5, while flint glass has ranges of less than 2 for both categories. Therefore, sodium chloride, (G), is the correct answer.

Passage II

7. D   Difficulty: High

Category: Interpretation of Data

Getting to the Answer: Because a higher temperature leads to a higher osmotic pressure at a given concentration, as seen in Table 1, statement I is false and choice A can be eliminated. (This can also be determined by noticing the direct relationship between Π and T in the equation.) Statement II suggests that temperature must be decreased to keep the osmotic pressure constant when concentration is increased. According to the given equation, osmotic pressure (Π) is simply equal to the concentration (M), a constant (R), and the temperature (T) multiplied together. That means that increasing the concentration will normally just increase the osmotic pressure. However, if the temperature is lowered by the appropriate amount, it could offset the increase in osmotic pressure that would be caused by a concentration increase. Because R is a constant, it can never change, so only decreasing the temperature would allow the osmotic pressure to stay constant with an increasing concentration. Consequently, statement II is true, which means choice C can be eliminated. For statement III, Tables 1 and 2 both show that higher concentrations result in higher osmotic pressures at constant temperature. (This can also be seen by noticing the direct relationship between Π and M in the equation.) Because statement III is also true, (D) is correct.

8. H   Difficulty: Medium

Category: Interpretation of Data

Getting to the Answer: Use the results of both experiments to answer this question. The answer choices all involve temperature, concentration, and solvent in different combinations. To determine whether osmotic pressure is dependent upon a variable, look for a pair of trials in which all conditions except for that variable are identical. In doing so, you can see that temperature and concentration affect osmotic pressure, but choice of solvent does not. Choice (H) is correct.

9. C   **Difficulty:** Low

Category: Interpretation of Data

Getting to the Answer: Find methanol at 0.5 mol/L, which is in Table 2. The text above the table states that all the trials were conducted at the same temperature (298 K). Therefore, simply look across the row that you identified. The osmotic pressure (the minimum external pressure required to prevent osmosis) is 12.23, (C).

10. G   **Difficulty:** High

Category: Scientific Investigation

Getting to the Answer: To figure out what will happen under the conditions described in the question, go back to the definition of osmotic pressure given in the introduction. Once the external pressure reaches the osmotic pressure, osmosis will not occur. In order for osmosis to occur, then, the external pressure must be less than the osmotic pressure of the solution. The solution in this question is a 0.10 mol/L aqueous sucrose solution at 298 K; according to Table 1, those conditions correspond to an osmotic pressure of 2.45 atm. Because the external pressure is 1 atm, which is less than the osmotic pressure, osmosis will occur. From the definition of osmosis in the passage, it is clear that the solution will diffuse from the side of the membrane with a lower concentration of dissolved material (in this case, pure water) to the side with a higher concentration (in this case, the sucrose solution). Choice (G) is correct.

11. C   **Difficulty:** Medium

Category: Evaluation of Models, Inferences, and Results

Getting to the Answer: To determine what the scientists investigated in Experiment 1, look at what they varied and what they measured. In Experiment 1, the scientists varied the concentration and the temperature of sucrose solutions, and they measured the osmotic pressure. Therefore, they were investigating the effect of concentration and temperature on osmotic pressure, (C). Watch out for A: it states what was investigated in Experiment 2, not Experiment 1.

12. F   **Difficulty:** High

Category: Evaluation of Models, Inferences, and Results

Getting to the Answer: The results in Table 2 demonstrate that osmotic pressure doesn't depend on the solvent, as indicated by the fact that the values remain constant for a particular concentration, irrespective of solvent used. So statement I is a valid conclusion, and G can be eliminated. Statement II is false: The results in Table 1 indicate that osmotic pressure is dependent on concentration as well as temperature. So H can be ruled out. Now consider statement III. It is not a valid conclusion because, according to the definition provided in the passage, osmotic pressure is the minimum pressure required to prevent osmosis, so osmosis will occur only if the external pressure is less than the osmotic pressure. Because only statement I is true, (F) is correct.

13. D   **Difficulty:** Medium

Category: Scientific Investigation

Getting to the Answer: The passage explains that osmotic pressure is equal to the minimum external pressure required to prevent osmosis. In order to measure the osmotic pressure of a solution, scientists need to be able to tell whether osmosis is occurring. If you have two clear solutions, it could be difficult to tell when osmosis has begun to occur, that is, when the solvent begins to move from the less concentrated solution to the more concentrated one. However, if the sucrose is dyed, the blue solution will start to become a lighter shade of blue when osmosis starts. Therefore, (D) is correct.

Passage III

14. F   **Difficulty:** Low

Category: Interpretation of Data

Getting to the Answer: The question refers to Experiment 3, so look at Table 3. According to that table, when the temperature is 85°F during the day and 85°F at night, the leaves have the smallest measurements. Choice (F) is correct.

15. A   Difficulty: Low

Category: Evaluation of Models, Inferences, and Results

Getting to the Answer: The question refers to Experiment 2 only, so the correct answer will involve sunlight. Neither humidity nor watering is relevant to Experiment 2, so B and C can be eliminated. Table 2 shows that the average length of the leaves increased from 5.3 cm to 12.4 cm as the amount of sunlight increased from 0 to 3 hours per day. But as the amount of sunlight increased further, leaf size decreased. Therefore, D is incorrect, leaving (A) as the correct answer. Choice (A) is supported by the data in Table 2 showing that only 3 hours of sunlight resulted in optimal leaf growth.

16. G   Difficulty: Low

Category: Interpretation of Data

Getting to the Answer: Table 1 gives leaf widths at 35% and 55% humidity at 1.8 cm and 2.0 cm, respectively. The leaf width at 40% humidity would most likely be between those two figures. Choice (G) is the only option within that range.

17. B   Difficulty: Medium

Category: Scientific Investigation

Getting to the Answer: All the answer choices involve humidity and sunlight, which were investigated in Experiments 1 and 2, respectively. In Table 1, leaf length and width were greatest at 75% humidity. In Table 2, they were greatest at 3 hours per day of sunlight. Combining those two conditions, as in (B), would most likely produce the largest leaves.

18. F   Difficulty: Medium

Category: Scientific Investigation

Getting to the Answer: This question concerns the methods of the studies. Each experiment begins with a statement that five groups of seedlings were used. Therefore, (F) is correct. The other choices list variables that were manipulated in one of the experiments.

19. D   Difficulty: High

Category: Evaluation of Models, Inferences, and Results

Getting to the Answer: Choice (D) is an assumption that underlies the design of all three experiments. If the

seedlings were not equally capable of further growth, then changes in leaf size and density could not be reliably attributed to researcher-controlled changes in humidity, sunlight, and temperature. Choice A is incorrect because all the seedlings were 2–3 cm tall. The seedlings' abilities to germinate, B, or to produce flowers, C, were not mentioned in the passage.

20. H   Difficulty: Medium

Category: Scientific Investigation

Getting to the Answer: According to the first paragraph of the passage, the purpose of the three experiments was "to study the environmental factors affecting the size and number of leaves on the *Cycas* plant." Consequently, to continue in this vein, it would be appropriate to choose another environmental factor to manipulate and to examine its impact on the plant's leaf growth, just as was done in the other experiments. Choice (H) presents exactly such an option, by proposing a study of the impact of soil mineral content on leaf size and density. None of the other choices relate directly to the stated purpose of the experiments.

Passage IV

21. B   Difficulty: Medium

Category: Interpretation of Data

Getting to the Answer: According to Table 1, decreasing the cross-sectional area of a given wire always increases resistance, so (B) is correct. The table also shows that if length decreases, resistance decreases, too, so A is incorrect. Choice C is incorrect because resistivity, displayed in the second column, is constant for each material and thus cannot be responsible for variations in resistance for a given material. Gauge varies inversely with cross-sectional area (as seen in Diagram 1), which means that resistance decreases as gauge decreases, so D is also incorrect.

22. G   Difficulty: High

Category: Interpretation of Data

Getting to the Answer: According to Table 1, resistance increases when resistivity increases and when length increases, but resistance decreases as cross-sectional area increases. The only answer choice that shows a direct relationship between resistance and both resistivity and length (placing both ρ and *L* in the numerator) and an inverse relationship between resistance and cross-sectional area (placing *A* in the denominator) is (G).

23. D   Difficulty: Medium

Category: Interpretation of Data

Getting to the Answer: Compare the choices two at a time. The wires in A and B are made of the same material and have the same cross-sectional area; only their length is different. Doubling the length doubles the resistance, as can be seen in Table 1, so B would have a higher resistance than A. By similar reasoning, (D) would have a higher resistance than C. That means both A and C can be eliminated. The only difference between B and (D) is the material. Even though the research team didn't test wires with a 0.33 mm² cross-sectional area, Table 1 shows that tungsten wire has higher levels of resistance than aluminum wire when length and area are held constant. Thus, (D) is correct.

24. J   Difficulty: Medium

Category: Interpretation of Data

Getting to the Answer: According to Diagram 1, the larger circle with a diameter of 2.59 mm represents 10-gauge wire, while the smaller circle with a diameter of only 1.29 mm represents 16-gauge wire. Consequently, statement I is true, allowing you to eliminate G and H. Statement II must be false since it doesn't appear in any of the remaining choices, and this can be confirmed by comparing the resistivity values for gold (Au) and tungsten (W) in Table 1. For statement III, the table shows that the resistance of an iron (Fe) wire is much higher than that of an aluminum (Al) wire with the same length and cross-sectional area. The first sentence of Paragraph 1 defined the resistance of a conductor as "the extent to which it opposes the flow of electricity." Because iron has a higher resistance than aluminum, iron must not conduct electricity as well. Therefore, statement III is also true, and (J) is correct.

25. D   Difficulty: Medium

Category: Interpretation of Data

Getting to the Answer: The data indicate that the resistivity of a material doesn't change when wire length changes. Therefore, the graph of resistivity versus length for tungsten (or any other) wire is a horizontal line, as in (D).

26. J   Difficulty: Medium

Category: Interpretation of Data

Getting to the Answer: Refer to Table 1 to see the effect that wire length has on resistance. Regardless of wire gauge, resistance increases for each material when length is increased. Choice (J) is thus correct.

Passage V

27. A   Difficulty: Medium

Category: Evaluation of Models, Inferences, and Results

Getting to the Answer: According to Scientist 1, some "mutations result in traits that help the species adapt to environmental changes." Similarly, Scientist 2 states that acquired characteristics inherited by subsequent generations include modifications that result from "changes in the environment." In addition, both scientists use the example of giraffes to show how scarcity of food and the need to reach higher and higher branches led to the evolution of long necks. Thus, both agree that the environment affects evolution, (A).

28. H   Difficulty: Medium

Category: Evaluation of Models, Inferences, and Results

Getting to the Answer: This question requires you to determine how new evidence affects the two hypotheses. Scientist 2 claims that characteristics acquired by an individual over a lifetime, including "changes that occurred as a result of accidents," are passed on to its offspring. The scenario presented in the question stem describes such an accidental change being passed on to offspring, so Scientist 2's hypothesis would be supported, making (H) correct.

29. D   Difficulty: Medium

Category: Evaluation of Models, Inferences, and Results

Getting to the Answer: Scientist 2 suggests that all of the changes that occur during an individual's life can be passed on to its offspring. The scientist states that such acquired characteristics include "changes that occurred as a result of accidents, changes in the environment, overuse of muscles, and so on." Because Scientist 2 puts no limits on the sort of traits that can be passed on to subsequent generations, it is reasonable to conclude that characteristics I, II, and III can all be inherited, so (D) is correct.

30. G   Difficulty: Medium

Category: Evaluation of Models, Inferences, and Results

Getting to the Answer: According to the passage, Scientist 1 claims that random mutations continually occur within a species as it propagates and that advantageous mutations, such as increasingly longer necks on giraffes, become more prevalent within a species over time because they help the species adapt to environmental changes. Thus, because Scientist 1 would say that a giraffe's long neck resulted from random mutations and that it is an advantageous trait, (G) is correct. Choice H is incorrect because the mutations did not occur "in response to" environmental changes; rather, the mutations were random, and they happened to be advantageous because of the type of environment that the ancestors of modern giraffes lived in, in which access to the leaves of trees was beneficial for their survival.

31. B   Difficulty: Low

Category: Evaluation of Models, Inferences, and Results

Getting to the Answer: The crux of the scientists' disagreement is over how evolution occurs—whether through random mutations that become more prevalent as a result of natural selection or through the inheritance of characteristics acquired during the lifetimes of previous generations. Choice (B) is thus correct.

32. G   Difficulty: High

Category: Evaluation of Models, Inferences, and Results

Getting to the Answer: Recall that Scientist 2 claims that evolution occurs through the inheritance of acquired characteristics. In order to account for humans possessing nerve endings now that were not present before the discovery of fire, Scientist 2 would have to believe that new nerve endings could be acquired during an individual's lifetime. Choice (G) directly contradicts this idea and would therefore undermine Scientist 2's hypothesis.

33. A   Difficulty: Medium

Category: Evaluation of Models, Inferences, and Results

Getting to the Answer: Recall that Scientist 1 explains that evolution occurs as a result of random mutations that become more prevalent through natural selection, while Scientist 2 claims that evolution occurs as a result of the inheritance of acquired characteristics. Choices B and C can then be eliminated, because they are explanations that Scientist 2 might offer. Choice D is irrelevant because it would not explain the height increase. Only (A) provides a valid explanation for the increase in average height that is based on the natural selection of adaptive mutations described by Scientist 1.

Passage VI

34. G   Difficulty: Low

Category: Interpretation of Data

Getting to the Answer: According to the passage, each group consisted of exactly 30 cows, so the greatest risk will correspond to the circumstances of the group with the greatest absolute number of BSE infections. Table 1 shows that Group B had the greatest number of cows infected with BSE. Group B was fed meat from scrapie-infected sheep, so (G) is correct.

35. D   Difficulty: Medium

Category: Scientific Investigation

Getting to the Answer: The first paragraph of the passage suggests that the purpose of the experiments was "to determine the mode of transmission of BSE." In Experiment 1, the researchers fed one group of cows meat from scrapie-free sheep and another group meat from scrapie-infected sheep, then later examined the cows for signs of BSE. Thus, the purpose and design of the experiment suggest that it was intended to investigate the hypothesis that ingesting scrapie-infected sheep will cause cows to develop BSE, as in (D).

36. F   Difficulty: Medium

Category: Scientific Investigation

Getting to the Answer: As noted in the explanation to the previous question, the general purpose of the two experiments was "to determine the mode of transmission of BSE." Experiment 2, in particular, tested whether injection of scrapie-infected sheep brains directly into cows' brains could cause BSE. Thus, the purpose of Experiment 2 is to investigate whether injection can cause the transmission of BSE, as in (F).

37. B   Difficulty: Medium

Category: Scientific Investigation

Getting to the Answer: In Experiments 1 and 2, the researchers examined the brains of cows 18 months (a year and a half) after the cows were fed sheep meat or were injected with sheep brains. In both experiments, the experimental groups received scrapie-infected sheep while the control groups received scrapie-free sheep. For the experiments to yield useful results, 18 months must be enough time for BSE to develop. Otherwise, there could not be a reasonable expectation of different results for the control and experimental groups—since all the cows were healthy at first, none of them would have had time to develop BSE if it took longer than 18 months. Thus, (B) is correct. Choices A and C are incorrect because the passage never discusses whether cows can suffer from scrapie nor whether cows and sheep are susceptible to the same diseases. Choice D is incorrect because it is not relevant to Experiment 2 and because it is subject to investigation in Experiment 1—the researchers don't just assume that cows fed scrapie-free sheep won't develop BSE, but rather they actually make the effort to examine the cows' brains postmortem to see whether they do.

38. H   Difficulty: Low

Category: Scientific Investigation

Getting to the Answer: The experiments discussed in the passage investigate whether scrapie-infected sheep can cause the transmission of BSE to cows. To test whether scrapie-infected goats can do the same, a researcher would merely need to replace the sheep with goats, but otherwise preserve the conditions of the experiments. This means that the control groups should receive scrapie-free goats rather than scrapie-free sheep and that the experimental groups should receive scrapie-infected goats rather than scrapie-infected sheep. This matches exactly with (H).

39. A   Difficulty: Medium

Category: Scientific Investigation

Getting to the Answer: Remember that control groups are used in experiments as standards of comparison. To investigate whether ingesting scrapie-infected sheep causes BSE, it would not be enough simply to look at the effects of eating such infected meat on a group of cows, because there could be some unknown factor at work, other than eating the infected meat, that is responsible for causing BSE. A good experiment will instead involve comparing this experimental group to another group, the control group, which is subject to almost the same conditions as the experimental group, with the only difference being that they are not fed the scrapie-infected sheep. For Experiment 1, this describes the group that is fed scrapie-free sheep, Group A, so (A) is correct.

40. G   Difficulty: High

Category: Evaluation of Models, Inferences, and Results

Getting to the Answer: Statement I concerns cows raised in proximity to scrapie-infected sheep, but this was not studied in either experiment, so statement I could not be a valid conclusion drawn from the experiments' results. This means that H can be eliminated. Statement II is also invalid, since the results of Experiment 2 suggest that cows can develop BSE through injection, too—some cases of BSE were discovered in Group D, as seen in Table 1. Choices F and J can thus also be eliminated. Since I and II are both invalid, only statement III can be a valid conclusion and (G) must be correct. This can be confirmed by comparing the results for Groups B and D in Table 1. The passage suggests that both groups consisted of 30 cows, but Group B had 12 BSE-infected cows while Group D only had 3.

WRITING TEST

MODEL ESSAY

Below is an example of what a high-scoring essay might look like. Notice that the author states her position clearly in the introductory paragraph and supports that position with evidence in the following paragraphs. This essay also uses transitions, some advanced vocabulary, and an effective "hook" to draw in the reader.

Children are often asked, "What do you want to be when you grow up?" Little do they know, whether or not they go to college has a huge impact on their career choices. The issue under discussion is whether or not schools should develop dual curricula to serve both those students who are college bound and those who intend to forego college, instead entering a career directly after high school graduation. The fundamental concern is how to best serve all students, which I believe should be through two curricula working together.

The first point of view supports having all students pursue the same curriculum, one primarily directed at college-bound students. It essentially states that an academic-only curriculum is valuable for all students, regardless of their future plans. It is true that the ability to think critically, have a wide range of content knowledge, and be adept at the skills and techniques required to live a full and productive life are important to all students. A well-rounded person is able to take advantage of many more opportunities than those with limited skills. Furthermore, should a career-bound student change his mind and decide to go to college, he will have the basic requirements for a successful college experience. However, if a student is determined to start his career directly after high school, the college curriculum could be a waste of his time, and he would be better served by taking courses that prepare him for his career. I am in partial agreement with option one, since a broad, basic education is important for all students. However, it is similarly important to prepare students for their future lives, which may begin immediately after high school.

The second option supports career-readiness education. As stated above, it is important to recognize that some students are set on a embarking on a career after high school rather than on going to college. High school is the place to prepare these students, since it can offer the courses that are most applicable to them. Furthermore, students in danger of dropping out of high school are generally those who are uninterested in or bored by the academic curriculum. Such students would be more engaged and successful if they were able to take classes that fit their goals and interests, and they would be more likely not only to stay in school but also to be well-prepared for their careers. This option purposes a dual curriculum, one for the college bound and one for career readiness, and thus provides the best education for both. On the assumption that non-college-bound students are also taking an adequate number of general education classes, and supplementing them with courses designed to provide them with the skills they need for their careers, these students will now have a solid academic foundation as well as career skills. College-bound students will still have the option to take more academic classes. Thus, I support this option because it provides the best solution for both groups.

Those who agree that students who are not planning on going to college should not be offered career-centered classes are denying the fact that not all students go to college, even if given incentives to do so. This option does not take into consideration the numerous facts that can affect whether or not a student goes to college. Some students cannot afford college fees, even with scholarships; some have a low GPA that would prohibit their acceptance at college; and some do poorly on pre-college tests such as the ACT. Encouraging students to go to college is not enough to ensure that they will. Though it may be true that college teaches how to be productive in the workforce, it is also true that being a fully qualified mechanic or electrician after high school is extremely productive for those who choose these careers. This option is an elitist one that would disregard those for whom college is not a goal, and it is one with which I completely disagree.

It is vital to all students that high schools prepare them for their future, whatever that may be. Those who choose college are well-served by an intensive academic curriculum that gives them a solid foundation for college. On the other hand, for those who choose, or are forced by circumstances, to forego college in favor of immediate entry into the workforce, it is important that, along with a sufficient academic foundation, they also receive training in their intended careers. Thus the second perspective, that of providing both an academic and a career-oriented curriculum, serves the needs of both and is the most effective one for all students.

You can evaluate your essay and the model essay based on the following criteria:

- Is the author's own perspective clearly stated?
- Does the body of the essay assess and analyze an additional perspective?
- Is the relevance of each paragraph clear?
- Does the author start a new paragraph for each new idea?
- Is each sentence in a paragraph relevant to the point made in that paragraph?
- Are transitions clear?
- Is the essay easy to read? Is it engaging?
- Are sentences varied?
- Is vocabulary used effectively? Is college-level vocabulary used?

ACT Practice Test 2
ANSWER SHEET

ENGLISH TEST

1. Ⓐ Ⓑ Ⓒ Ⓓ   11. Ⓐ Ⓑ Ⓒ Ⓓ   21. Ⓐ Ⓑ Ⓒ Ⓓ   31. Ⓐ Ⓑ Ⓒ Ⓓ   41. Ⓐ Ⓑ Ⓒ Ⓓ   51. Ⓐ Ⓑ Ⓒ Ⓓ   61. Ⓐ Ⓑ Ⓒ Ⓓ   71. Ⓐ Ⓑ Ⓒ Ⓓ
2. Ⓕ Ⓖ Ⓗ Ⓙ   12. Ⓕ Ⓖ Ⓗ Ⓙ   22. Ⓕ Ⓖ Ⓗ Ⓙ   32. Ⓕ Ⓖ Ⓗ Ⓙ   42. Ⓕ Ⓖ Ⓗ Ⓙ   52. Ⓕ Ⓖ Ⓗ Ⓙ   62. Ⓕ Ⓖ Ⓗ Ⓙ   72. Ⓕ Ⓖ Ⓗ Ⓙ
3. Ⓐ Ⓑ Ⓒ Ⓓ   13. Ⓐ Ⓑ Ⓒ Ⓓ   23. Ⓐ Ⓑ Ⓒ Ⓓ   33. Ⓐ Ⓑ Ⓒ Ⓓ   43. Ⓐ Ⓑ Ⓒ Ⓓ   53. Ⓐ Ⓑ Ⓒ Ⓓ   63. Ⓐ Ⓑ Ⓒ Ⓓ   73. Ⓐ Ⓑ Ⓒ Ⓓ
4. Ⓕ Ⓖ Ⓗ Ⓙ   14. Ⓕ Ⓖ Ⓗ Ⓙ   24. Ⓕ Ⓖ Ⓗ Ⓙ   34. Ⓕ Ⓖ Ⓗ Ⓙ   44. Ⓕ Ⓖ Ⓗ Ⓙ   54. Ⓕ Ⓖ Ⓗ Ⓙ   64. Ⓕ Ⓖ Ⓗ Ⓙ   74. Ⓕ Ⓖ Ⓗ Ⓙ
5. Ⓐ Ⓑ Ⓒ Ⓓ   15. Ⓐ Ⓑ Ⓒ Ⓓ   25. Ⓐ Ⓑ Ⓒ Ⓓ   35. Ⓐ Ⓑ Ⓒ Ⓓ   45. Ⓐ Ⓑ Ⓒ Ⓓ   55. Ⓐ Ⓑ Ⓒ Ⓓ   65. Ⓐ Ⓑ Ⓒ Ⓓ   75. Ⓐ Ⓑ Ⓒ Ⓓ
6. Ⓕ Ⓖ Ⓗ Ⓙ   16. Ⓕ Ⓖ Ⓗ Ⓙ   26. Ⓕ Ⓖ Ⓗ Ⓙ   36. Ⓕ Ⓖ Ⓗ Ⓙ   46. Ⓕ Ⓖ Ⓗ Ⓙ   56. Ⓕ Ⓖ Ⓗ Ⓙ   66. Ⓕ Ⓖ Ⓗ Ⓙ
7. Ⓐ Ⓑ Ⓒ Ⓓ   17. Ⓐ Ⓑ Ⓒ Ⓓ   27. Ⓐ Ⓑ Ⓒ Ⓓ   37. Ⓐ Ⓑ Ⓒ Ⓓ   47. Ⓐ Ⓑ Ⓒ Ⓓ   57. Ⓐ Ⓑ Ⓒ Ⓓ   67. Ⓐ Ⓑ Ⓒ Ⓓ
8. Ⓕ Ⓖ Ⓗ Ⓙ   18. Ⓕ Ⓖ Ⓗ Ⓙ   28. Ⓕ Ⓖ Ⓗ Ⓙ   38. Ⓕ Ⓖ Ⓗ Ⓙ   48. Ⓕ Ⓖ Ⓗ Ⓙ   58. Ⓕ Ⓖ Ⓗ Ⓙ   68. Ⓕ Ⓖ Ⓗ Ⓙ
9. Ⓐ Ⓑ Ⓒ Ⓓ   19. Ⓐ Ⓑ Ⓒ Ⓓ   29. Ⓐ Ⓑ Ⓒ Ⓓ   39. Ⓐ Ⓑ Ⓒ Ⓓ   49. Ⓐ Ⓑ Ⓒ Ⓓ   59. Ⓐ Ⓑ Ⓒ Ⓓ   69. Ⓐ Ⓑ Ⓒ Ⓓ
10. Ⓕ Ⓖ Ⓗ Ⓙ   20. Ⓕ Ⓖ Ⓗ Ⓙ   30. Ⓕ Ⓖ Ⓗ Ⓙ   40. Ⓕ Ⓖ Ⓗ Ⓙ   50. Ⓕ Ⓖ Ⓗ Ⓙ   60. Ⓕ Ⓖ Ⓗ Ⓙ   70. Ⓕ Ⓖ Ⓗ Ⓙ

MATHEMATICS TEST

1. Ⓐ Ⓑ Ⓒ Ⓓ Ⓔ   11. Ⓐ Ⓑ Ⓒ Ⓓ Ⓔ   21. Ⓐ Ⓑ Ⓒ Ⓓ Ⓔ   31. Ⓐ Ⓑ Ⓒ Ⓓ Ⓔ   41. Ⓐ Ⓑ Ⓒ Ⓓ Ⓔ   51. Ⓐ Ⓑ Ⓒ Ⓓ Ⓔ
2. Ⓕ Ⓖ Ⓗ Ⓙ Ⓚ   12. Ⓕ Ⓖ Ⓗ Ⓙ Ⓚ   22. Ⓕ Ⓖ Ⓗ Ⓙ Ⓚ   32. Ⓕ Ⓖ Ⓗ Ⓙ Ⓚ   42. Ⓕ Ⓖ Ⓗ Ⓙ Ⓚ   52. Ⓕ Ⓖ Ⓗ Ⓙ Ⓚ
3. Ⓐ Ⓑ Ⓒ Ⓓ Ⓔ   13. Ⓐ Ⓑ Ⓒ Ⓓ Ⓔ   23. Ⓐ Ⓑ Ⓒ Ⓓ Ⓔ   33. Ⓐ Ⓑ Ⓒ Ⓓ Ⓔ   43. Ⓐ Ⓑ Ⓒ Ⓓ Ⓔ   53. Ⓐ Ⓑ Ⓒ Ⓓ Ⓔ
4. Ⓕ Ⓖ Ⓗ Ⓙ Ⓚ   14. Ⓕ Ⓖ Ⓗ Ⓙ Ⓚ   24. Ⓕ Ⓖ Ⓗ Ⓙ Ⓚ   34. Ⓕ Ⓖ Ⓗ Ⓙ Ⓚ   44. Ⓕ Ⓖ Ⓗ Ⓙ Ⓚ   54. Ⓕ Ⓖ Ⓗ Ⓙ Ⓚ
5. Ⓐ Ⓑ Ⓒ Ⓓ Ⓔ   15. Ⓐ Ⓑ Ⓒ Ⓓ Ⓔ   25. Ⓐ Ⓑ Ⓒ Ⓓ Ⓔ   35. Ⓐ Ⓑ Ⓒ Ⓓ Ⓔ   45. Ⓐ Ⓑ Ⓒ Ⓓ Ⓔ   55. Ⓐ Ⓑ Ⓒ Ⓓ Ⓔ
6. Ⓕ Ⓖ Ⓗ Ⓙ Ⓚ   16. Ⓕ Ⓖ Ⓗ Ⓙ Ⓚ   26. Ⓕ Ⓖ Ⓗ Ⓙ Ⓚ   36. Ⓕ Ⓖ Ⓗ Ⓙ Ⓚ   46. Ⓕ Ⓖ Ⓗ Ⓙ Ⓚ   56. Ⓕ Ⓖ Ⓗ Ⓙ Ⓚ
7. Ⓐ Ⓑ Ⓒ Ⓓ Ⓔ   17. Ⓐ Ⓑ Ⓒ Ⓓ Ⓔ   27. Ⓐ Ⓑ Ⓒ Ⓓ Ⓔ   37. Ⓐ Ⓑ Ⓒ Ⓓ Ⓔ   47. Ⓐ Ⓑ Ⓒ Ⓓ Ⓔ   57. Ⓐ Ⓑ Ⓒ Ⓓ Ⓔ
8. Ⓕ Ⓖ Ⓗ Ⓙ Ⓚ   18. Ⓕ Ⓖ Ⓗ Ⓙ Ⓚ   28. Ⓕ Ⓖ Ⓗ Ⓙ Ⓚ   38. Ⓕ Ⓖ Ⓗ Ⓙ Ⓚ   48. Ⓕ Ⓖ Ⓗ Ⓙ Ⓚ   58. Ⓕ Ⓖ Ⓗ Ⓙ Ⓚ
9. Ⓐ Ⓑ Ⓒ Ⓓ Ⓔ   19. Ⓐ Ⓑ Ⓒ Ⓓ Ⓔ   29. Ⓐ Ⓑ Ⓒ Ⓓ Ⓔ   39. Ⓐ Ⓑ Ⓒ Ⓓ Ⓔ   49. Ⓐ Ⓑ Ⓒ Ⓓ Ⓔ   59. Ⓐ Ⓑ Ⓒ Ⓓ Ⓔ
10. Ⓕ Ⓖ Ⓗ Ⓙ Ⓚ   20. Ⓕ Ⓖ Ⓗ Ⓙ Ⓚ   30. Ⓕ Ⓖ Ⓗ Ⓙ Ⓚ   40. Ⓕ Ⓖ Ⓗ Ⓙ Ⓚ   50. Ⓕ Ⓖ Ⓗ Ⓙ Ⓚ   60. Ⓕ Ⓖ Ⓗ Ⓙ Ⓚ

READING TEST

1. Ⓐ Ⓑ Ⓒ Ⓓ   6. Ⓕ Ⓖ Ⓗ Ⓙ   11. Ⓐ Ⓑ Ⓒ Ⓓ   16. Ⓕ Ⓖ Ⓗ Ⓙ   21. Ⓐ Ⓑ Ⓒ Ⓓ   26. Ⓕ Ⓖ Ⓗ Ⓙ   31. Ⓐ Ⓑ Ⓒ Ⓓ   36. Ⓕ Ⓖ Ⓗ Ⓙ
2. Ⓕ Ⓖ Ⓗ Ⓙ   7. Ⓐ Ⓑ Ⓒ Ⓓ   12. Ⓕ Ⓖ Ⓗ Ⓙ   17. Ⓐ Ⓑ Ⓒ Ⓓ   22. Ⓕ Ⓖ Ⓗ Ⓙ   27. Ⓐ Ⓑ Ⓒ Ⓓ   32. Ⓕ Ⓖ Ⓗ Ⓙ   37. Ⓐ Ⓑ Ⓒ Ⓓ
3. Ⓐ Ⓑ Ⓒ Ⓓ   8. Ⓕ Ⓖ Ⓗ Ⓙ   13. Ⓐ Ⓑ Ⓒ Ⓓ   18. Ⓕ Ⓖ Ⓗ Ⓙ   23. Ⓐ Ⓑ Ⓒ Ⓓ   28. Ⓕ Ⓖ Ⓗ Ⓙ   33. Ⓐ Ⓑ Ⓒ Ⓓ   38. Ⓕ Ⓖ Ⓗ Ⓙ
4. Ⓕ Ⓖ Ⓗ Ⓙ   9. Ⓐ Ⓑ Ⓒ Ⓓ   14. Ⓕ Ⓖ Ⓗ Ⓙ   19. Ⓐ Ⓑ Ⓒ Ⓓ   24. Ⓕ Ⓖ Ⓗ Ⓙ   29. Ⓐ Ⓑ Ⓒ Ⓓ   34. Ⓕ Ⓖ Ⓗ Ⓙ   39. Ⓐ Ⓑ Ⓒ Ⓓ
5. Ⓐ Ⓑ Ⓒ Ⓓ   10. Ⓕ Ⓖ Ⓗ Ⓙ   15. Ⓐ Ⓑ Ⓒ Ⓓ   20. Ⓕ Ⓖ Ⓗ Ⓙ   25. Ⓐ Ⓑ Ⓒ Ⓓ   30. Ⓕ Ⓖ Ⓗ Ⓙ   35. Ⓐ Ⓑ Ⓒ Ⓓ   40. Ⓕ Ⓖ Ⓗ Ⓙ

SCIENCE TEST

1. Ⓐ Ⓑ Ⓒ Ⓓ   6. Ⓕ Ⓖ Ⓗ Ⓙ   11. Ⓐ Ⓑ Ⓒ Ⓓ   16. Ⓕ Ⓖ Ⓗ Ⓙ   21. Ⓐ Ⓑ Ⓒ Ⓓ   26. Ⓕ Ⓖ Ⓗ Ⓙ   31. Ⓐ Ⓑ Ⓒ Ⓓ   36. Ⓕ Ⓖ Ⓗ Ⓙ
2. Ⓕ Ⓖ Ⓗ Ⓙ   7. Ⓐ Ⓑ Ⓒ Ⓓ   12. Ⓕ Ⓖ Ⓗ Ⓙ   17. Ⓐ Ⓑ Ⓒ Ⓓ   22. Ⓕ Ⓖ Ⓗ Ⓙ   27. Ⓐ Ⓑ Ⓒ Ⓓ   32. Ⓕ Ⓖ Ⓗ Ⓙ   37. Ⓐ Ⓑ Ⓒ Ⓓ
3. Ⓐ Ⓑ Ⓒ Ⓓ   8. Ⓕ Ⓖ Ⓗ Ⓙ   13. Ⓐ Ⓑ Ⓒ Ⓓ   18. Ⓕ Ⓖ Ⓗ Ⓙ   23. Ⓐ Ⓑ Ⓒ Ⓓ   28. Ⓕ Ⓖ Ⓗ Ⓙ   33. Ⓐ Ⓑ Ⓒ Ⓓ   38. Ⓕ Ⓖ Ⓗ Ⓙ
4. Ⓕ Ⓖ Ⓗ Ⓙ   9. Ⓐ Ⓑ Ⓒ Ⓓ   14. Ⓕ Ⓖ Ⓗ Ⓙ   19. Ⓐ Ⓑ Ⓒ Ⓓ   24. Ⓕ Ⓖ Ⓗ Ⓙ   29. Ⓐ Ⓑ Ⓒ Ⓓ   34. Ⓕ Ⓖ Ⓗ Ⓙ   39. Ⓐ Ⓑ Ⓒ Ⓓ
5. Ⓐ Ⓑ Ⓒ Ⓓ   10. Ⓕ Ⓖ Ⓗ Ⓙ   15. Ⓐ Ⓑ Ⓒ Ⓓ   20. Ⓕ Ⓖ Ⓗ Ⓙ   25. Ⓐ Ⓑ Ⓒ Ⓓ   30. Ⓕ Ⓖ Ⓗ Ⓙ   35. Ⓐ Ⓑ Ⓒ Ⓓ   40. Ⓕ Ⓖ Ⓗ Ⓙ

ENGLISH TEST

45 Minutes—75 Questions

Directions: Each passage has certain words and phrases that are underlined and numbered. The questions in the right column will provide alternatives for the underlined segments. Most questions require you to choose the answer that makes the sentence grammatically correct, concise, and relevant. If the word or phrase in the passage is already the correct, concise, and relevant choice, select Choice A, NO CHANGE. Some questions will ask a question about the underlined segment. When a question is presented, choose the best answer.

Some questions will ask about part or all of the passage. These questions do not refer to a specific underlined segment. Instead, these questions will accompany a number in a box.

For each question, choose your answer and fill in the corresponding bubble on your answer sheet. Read the passage once before you answer the questions. You will often need to read several sentences beyond the underlined portion to be able to choose the correct answer. Be sure to read enough to answer each question.

Passage I

Duke Ellington, a Jazz Great

[1]

By the time Duke Ellington published his autobiography, *Music Is My Mistress,* in <u>1973 he had</u> traveled
¹
to dozens of countries and every continent. "I pay rent in New York City," he answered when asked of his residence. [A]

[2]

In the 1920s, though, Ellington <u>pays</u> more than rent
²
in New York; he paid his dues on the bandstand. Having moved to Harlem from Washington, D.C., in 1923,

Ellington <u>established: his own</u> band and achieved criti-
³
cal recognition with a polished sound and appearance.

As Ellington made a name for himself

1. A. NO CHANGE
    B. 1973. He had
    C. 1973, it had
    D. 1973, he had

2. F. NO CHANGE
    G. paid
    H. has to pay
    J. pay

3. A. NO CHANGE
    B. established the following: his own
    C. established his own
    D. took the time and effort to establish his own

GO ON TO THE NEXT PAGE

as a <u>leader arranger and pianist,</u> his Harlem Renaissance
₄
compositions and recordings highlighted two enduring

characteristics of the man. First, Ellington lived for jazz.

Second, Harlem sustained <u>it,</u> physically and spiritually.
₅

[3]

[B] Ellington himself admitted he was not a very

<u>good pianist. As a teenager</u> in Washington.
₆

He missed more piano <u>lessons then he took</u> with his
₇
teacher, Mrs. Clinkscales, and spent more time going to

dances than practicing the piano.

<u>Mrs. Clinkscales was really the name of his piano</u>
₈
<u>teacher!</u>
₈

In the clubs, <u>therefore,</u> Ellington and his friends eventu-
₉
ally caught word of New York and the opportunities

<u>that awaited and were there for</u> young musicians.
₁₀
Ellington wrote, "Harlem, to our minds, did indeed have

the world's most glamorous atmosphere. We had to go

there."

4. F. NO CHANGE
   G. leader arranger, and pianist,
   H. leader, arranger, and pianist
   J. leader, arranger, and pianist,

5. A. NO CHANGE
   B. him,
   C. them,
   D. itself,

6. F. NO CHANGE
   G. good pianist as a teenager
   H. good pianist, a teenager
   J. good pianist, as a teenager

7. A. NO CHANGE
   B. lessons then he had taken
   C. lessons; he took
   D. lessons than he took

8. F. NO CHANGE
   G. That was really the name of his piano
      teacher: Mrs. Clinkscales!
   H. Mrs. Clinkscales was really the name of
      his piano teacher.
   J. DELETE the underlined portion.

9. A. NO CHANGE
   B. however,
   C. despite,
   D. then,

10. F. NO CHANGE
    G. awaiting and being there for
    H. that awaited
    J. that were there for

GO ON TO THE NEXT PAGE

He promptly left Washington with drummer <u>Sonny Greer, before they</u> could even unpack in Harlem, they found themselves penniless. Not until Ellington was lucky enough to find fifteen dollars on the street could he return to Washington and re-collect himself.

[4]

Ellington eventually did return to Harlem, and he achieved great success as the bandleader at the Cotton Club from 1927 to 1932. [C] Located in the heart of Harlem at 142nd Street and Lenox Avenue, <u>he played at the Cotton Club, which was frequented</u> by top entertainers and rich patrons. Harlem's nightlife, "cut out of a very luxurious, royal-blue bolt of velvet," was an inspirational backdrop, and Ellington composed, arranged, and recorded prolifically to excited critical acclaim. "Black and Tan Fantasy," "Hot and Bothered," and "Rockin' in Rhythm" were Ellington's early hits during this period. [13] They exhibited his unique ability to compose music that animated both dancers in search of a good time and improvising musicians in search of good music. [D]

11. A. NO CHANGE
    B. Sonny Greer but before they
    C. Sonny Greer, but before they
    D. Sonny Greer, they

12. F. NO CHANGE
    G. he played at the Cotton Club, a club that was frequented
    H. the Cotton Club, which was frequented
    J. the Cotton Club was frequented

13. The purpose of including the names of Ellington's songs is to:
    A. provide some details about Ellington's early music.
    B. contradict an earlier point that Ellington did not create his own music.
    C. illustrate the complexity of Ellington's music.
    D. discuss the atmosphere at the Cotton Club.

Practice Test 2

GO ON TO THE NEXT PAGE

Before long, the once fumbling pianist from Washington, D.C., became the undisputed leader of hot jazz in decadent Harlem. 14

14. The purpose of Paragraph 4, as it relates to the previous paragraphs, is primarily to:

F. demonstrate how accomplished Ellington had become.

G. suggest that Ellington did not like living in New York.

H. remind us how difficult it is to be a musician.

J. make us skeptical of Ellington's abilities.

Question 15 asks about the preceding passage as a whole.

15. The writer is considering adding the following sentence to the essay:

The combination of fun and seriousness in his music led to critical acclaim and mass appeal.

If the writer were to add this sentence, it would most logically be placed at Point:

A. A in Paragraph 1.

B. B in Paragraph 3.

C. C in Paragraph 4.

D. D in Paragraph 4.

GO ON TO THE NEXT PAGE

Passage II

> The following paragraphs may or may not be in the most logical order. Each paragraph is numbered in brackets, and question 29 will ask you to choose the appropriate order.

Coloring as Self-Defense in Animals

[1]

Some animals change <u>its</u> coloring with the seasons.
16

The ptarmigan sheds its brown plumage <u>in winter, re-</u>
17
<u>placing</u> it with white feathers. The stoat, a member of
17

the <u>weasel family is known</u> as the *ermine* in winter
18
because its brown fur changes to white.

The chameleon is perhaps the most versatile of all

animals <u>having changed</u> their protective coloration. The
19
chameleon changes its color in just a few minutes to that

of whatever surface it happens to be sitting on.

[2]

While animals like the chameleon <u>use their coloring</u>
20
as a way of hiding from predators, the skunk uses its

distinctive white stripe as a way of standing out from its

surroundings.

16. **F.** NO CHANGE
    G. their
    H. it's
    J. there

17. **A.** NO CHANGE
    B. in winter and replacing
    C. in winter: replacing
    D. in winter replacing

18. **F.** NO CHANGE
    G. weasel family known
    H. weasel family, which is known
    J. weasel family, is known

19. **A.** NO CHANGE
    B. who changes
    C. that change
    D. that changed

20. **F.** NO CHANGE
    G. their use coloring
    H. use coloring their
    J. coloring their use

GO ON TO THE NEXT PAGE

Far from placing it in danger, <u>the skunk's visibilities</u>
                                              21
actually protects it. By distinguishing itself from

other <u>animals. The</u> skunk warns its predators to avoid its
         22
infamous stink. Think about it:

<u>the question is would your appetite be whetted by the</u>
                                    23
<u>skunk's odor?</u>
       23

[3]

Researchers <u>have been investigating</u> how animal
                              24
species have come to use coloring as a means of pro-

tecting themselves. One study has shown that certain

animals have glands that release special hormones,

resulting in the change of skin or fur color. <u>Therefore,</u>
                                                     25
not all the animals that camouflage themselves have

these glands.

The topic <u>remains and endures as</u> one of the many mys-
                        26
teries of the natural world.

21. **A.** NO CHANGE
    B. the skunk's visibility
    C. the skunks' visibility
    D. it is the skunk's visibilities

22. **F.** NO CHANGE
    G. animals, therefore, the
    H. animals because
    J. animals, the

23. **A.** NO CHANGE
    B. would your appetite be whetted by the skunk's odor?
    C. the question is as follows, would your appetite be whetted by the skunk's odor?
    D. the question is would your appetite be whetted by the odor of the skunk?

24. **F.** NO CHANGE
    G. investigated
    H. were investigating
    J. investigate

25. **A.** NO CHANGE
    B. Nevertheless,
    C. However,
    D. Finally,

26. **F.** NO CHANGE
    G. remaining and enduring as
    H. remains and endures
    J. remains

GO ON TO THE NEXT PAGE

[4]

Animals have a variety of ways of protecting themselves from enemies. Some animals adapt in shape and color to their environment. The tree frog, for example, blends perfectly into its surroundings. When it sits motionless, <u>a background of leaves completely hides the tree frog.</u>
27

27. **A.** NO CHANGE
   B. the tree frog is completely hidden in a background of leaves.
   C. completely hidden is the tree frog in a background of leaves.
   D. a background of leaves and the tree frog are completely hidden.

<u>This camouflage enables the tree frog to hide from other</u>
28
<u>animals that would be interested in eating the tree frog.</u>
28

28. **F.** NO CHANGE
   G. This camouflage enables the tree frog to hide from predators.
   H. This camouflage enables the tree frog to hide from other animals interested in eating the tree frog.
   J. DELETE the underlined portion.

Questions 29 and 30 ask about the preceding passage as a whole.

29. What would be the most logical order of paragraphs for this essay?
   A. 3, 1, 4, 2
   B. 1, 2, 4, 3
   C. 4, 1, 2, 3
   D. 2, 1, 3, 4

30. Suppose the writer's primary purpose had been to write an essay on how animals use their coloring to protect themselves in the wild. Would this essay accomplish that purpose?
   F. Yes, because the author covers several aspects of how animals use their coloring to protect themselves.
   G. Yes, because the author thoroughly investigates how one animal protects itself with its coloring.
   H. No, because the author does not consider animals that exist in the wild.
   J. No, because the author does not include information from research studies.

GO ON TO THE NEXT PAGE

Passage III

The History of Chocolate

The word *chocolate* is used to describe a variety of
<u>foods and made</u> from the beans of the cacao tree.
  31

The first people known to have made chocolate were the
Aztecs, who used cacao seeds to make a bitter but tasty
drink. <u>Therefore,</u> it was not until Hernán Cortés
      32

exploration of Mexico in <u>1519. That</u> Europeans first
                            33
learned of chocolate.

[34] When Cortés returned to Spain, his ship's cargo
included three chests of cacao beans. It was from these
beans that Europe experienced its first taste of what
seemed to be a very unusual but desirable beverage.

31. A. NO CHANGE
    B. foods, which are cultivated and made
    C. foods, which made
    D. foods made

32. F. NO CHANGE
    G. Additionally,
    H. As a result,
    J. However,

33. A. NO CHANGE
    B. 1519 that
    C. 1519, that
    D. 1519:

34. Which of the following true statements would
    provide the best transition from the preceding
    paragraph to this paragraph?

    F. The Aztecs successfully drove the Spanish
       from Tenochtitlan at first, but Cortés
       returned to defeat them and take hold of
       the city in 1521.

    G. Just four years after Cortés set off to
       explore Mexico, King Charles I appointed
       him governor of New Spain.

    H. Cortés came to the New World in search
       of gold, but his interest was also fired by
       the Aztecs' strange drink.

    J. Cortés befriended some of the people he
       met, but mostly he used deadly force in his
       quest to conquer Mexico.

GO ON TO THE NEXT PAGE

Even so, the drink soon became popular among those
35
people wealthy enough to afford it.

35. **A.** NO CHANGE

    B. Soon,

    C. Nonetheless,

    D. Not surprisingly,

Over the next century cafés specializing in chocolate
36

36. **F.** NO CHANGE

    G. Over the next century cafés specialize

    H. Over the next century, cafés specializing

    J. Over the next century, there were cafés specializing

drinks began to appear throughout Europe. [37]

37. The author is considering the addition of another sentence here that briefly describes one of the first European cafes to serve a chocolate drink. This addition would:

    A. weaken the author's argument.

    B. provide an interesting detail that is relevant to the essay.

    C. contradict the topic of the paragraph and the essay as a whole.

    D. highlight the author's opinion of chocolate.

      Of course, chocolate is very popular today. People all over the world enjoy chocolate bars chocolate sprin-
38
kles and even chocolate soda.
38

38. **F.** NO CHANGE

    G. chocolate, bars, chocolate, sprinkles, and even chocolate soda.

    H. chocolate bars chocolate sprinkles—even chocolate soda.

    J. chocolate bars, chocolate sprinkles, and even chocolate soda.

In fact, Asia has cultivated the delicacy of chocolate-
39
covered ants! People enjoy this food as a snack at the movies or sporting events.

39. **A.** NO CHANGE

    B. Unfortunately,

    C. In spite of this,

    D. The truth is,

GO ON TO THE NEXT PAGE

The chocolate ant phenomenon has yet to take over America, <u>but enjoy their chocolate Americans do</u> none-
40
theless.

    Many chocolate lovers around the world were ecstatic to hear that chocolate may actually be good for you. Researchers <u>say: chocolate contains</u> a chemical that
41
could prevent cancer and heart disease. New research measures the amount of catechins, the chemical thought to be behind the benefits, in different types of chocolate. <u>The substance is also found in tea.</u>
42

<u>They show</u> that chocolate is very high in catechins.
43

The research <u>has yet to be officially verified by the Food</u>
44
<u>and Drug Administration, though, so an appropriate</u>
44
<u>level of caution is warranted.</u>
44

40. **F.** NO CHANGE

    G. but Americans enjoy their chocolate

    H. but enjoy their chocolate is what Americans do

    J. but Americans do enjoy their chocolate

41. **A.** NO CHANGE

    B. have said the following: chocolate contains

    C. say that chocolate contains

    D. say: chocolate contained

42. **F.** NO CHANGE

    G. Another place where the substance is found is tea.

    H. Also, tea contains the substance.

    J. DELETE the underlined portion.

43. **A.** NO CHANGE

    B. It shows

    C. The studies show

    D. The scientist shows

44. Which choice most effectively concludes the sentence and the essay?

    F. NO CHANGE

    G. may prove to be less than helpful to people with multiple risk factors for cancer and heart disease; they should ask their doctors for additional prevention information.

    H. should be used to design similar experiments to test the efficacy of consuming other types of catechin-rich sustenance as a means of prevention.

    J. is likely to be welcomed by chocolate lovers everywhere, although dentists may be less pleased.

GO ON TO THE NEXT PAGE →

Question 45 asks about the preceding passage as a whole.

45. Suppose the writer's primary purpose had been to write about culinary trends in history. Would this essay accomplish that goal?

   A. Yes, because the essay discusses many culinary trends in history.

   B. Yes, because the essay shows how chocolate has been used over time.

   C. No, because the essay focuses too much on chocolate in present times.

   D. No, because the essay only covers chocolate.

Passage IV

The Military Uniform of the Future

[1]

Scientists, in programs administers by the United
                                      46
States Army, are experimenting to develop the military

uniform of the future.

As imagined, it would be light as silk, bulletproof, and
                                                      47
able to rapidly change at the molecular level to adapt to
 47
biological or chemical threats. In response to a detected

anthrax threat, for example, it would become an imper-

meable shield.

46. F. NO CHANGE

   G. administering by

   H. administered by

   J. administers with

47. A. NO CHANGE

   B. would: be light as silk, bulletproof, and able to

   C. would be light as silk bulletproof and able to

   D. light as silk, bulletproof, and was able to

GO ON TO THE NEXT PAGE

Practice Test 2

The pant leg of a <u>soldier who's</u> leg had been broken
48

<u>would have been</u> able to morph into a splint or
49

even form an artificial muscle. 50

[2]

[A] The especially promising Invisible Soldier

program aims to make the long-held dream of human

invisibility a reality by using <u>technology. To create</u> a
51

48. **F.** NO CHANGE
   G. soldier whose
   H. soldier, who's
   J. soldier that's

49. **A.** NO CHANGE
   B. would be
   C. will have been
   D. is

50. The writer wants to add a sentence that describes an additional feature that the uniform of the future would include. Given that all of the following statements are true, which one, if added here, would most clearly and effectively accomplish the writer's goal?

   F. If a broken leg is not attended to properly, a soldier could suffer from bone deformity, nerve damage, and muscle atrophy.

   G. Nanosensors would transmit vital signs back to a medical team or monitor breathing for increased nitric oxide, a sign of stress.

   H. One issue the military uniform of the future would not address is the need for fresh water and ample supplies in even the most remote locations.

   J. Deep pockets would provide room for soldiers to store a myriad of important supplies such as ammunition, first aid kits, and batteries.

51. **A.** NO CHANGE
   B. technology to create
   C. technology, which were creating
   D. technology; create

GO ON TO THE NEXT PAGE

covering capable of <u>confounding</u> a soldier from
52

most wavelengths of visible light. 53 54

[3]

A solution proposed in the early stages of the Invisible Soldier program's development was to construct <u>something that would sense the environment around</u> the soldier.
55

<u>the soldier.</u>
55

52. F. NO CHANGE
    G. obfuscating
    H. concealing
    J. eliminating

53. The writer's description of the US Army's Invisible Soldier program seems to indicate that the army's opinion of the program is:
    A. skeptical.
    B. curious.
    C. enthusiastic.
    D. detailed.

54. This paragraph primarily serves to:
    F. highlight one of the successes of the scientists' programs.
    G. predict the future of US military uniforms.
    H. outline what will follow in the essay.
    J. introduce a specific example of the uniform of the future.

55. Which choice maintains the essay's tone and most clearly explains the solution being described at this point in the essay?
    A. NO CHANGE
    B. a really special outfit with super helpful sensors that can figure out what the world around the soldier looks like.
    C. a suit or cape from fabric linked to sensors that could identify the coloring and pattern of the background.
    D. a garment made from sensor-infused textile that could detect the previously-imperceptible intricacies of a military personnel's surrounding environment.

Practice Test 2

GO ON TO THE NEXT PAGE

The sensors would then send varying intensities of electrical current to the appropriate areas of the fabric, <u>they</u> would be infused with chemicals sensitive to electricity. The coveralls would change colors continually as the soldier moved. [B]

[4]

[C] The problem with this solution from a military standpoint, <u>you know, is</u>

power: <u>the fact that the suit</u> would require a continuous flow of electricity means that a soldier would have to carry a large number of batteries, which would hardly contribute to ease of movement and camouflage. [D]

[5]

[1] To address this problem, Army researchers have developed a new kind of color-changing pixel, known as the interferometric modulator or IMOD. [2] The researchers hope that a flexible suit made of IMOD pixels could completely blend into any background. [3] In addition to matching a background, the pixels could also be set to show other colors, for example, a camouflage mode that would render a soldier effectively invisible in the forest and a flash mode that would enhance a soldier's visibility in a rescue situation. [4] Changing the distance between the mirrors changes the color of the light that they reflect.

56. F. NO CHANGE
    G. that
    H. it
    J. which

57. A. NO CHANGE
    B. is, like,
    C. however, is
    D. therefore, is

58. F. NO CHANGE
    G. power; the fact that the suit
    H. power the fact that the suit
    J. power the fact that, the suit

GO ON TO THE NEXT PAGE

[5] Each IMOD pixel is made up of a pair of tiny mirrors. [59]

59. Which of the following sequences of numbered sentences would make Paragraph 5 most logical?

    A. 2, 4, 5, 3, 1

    B. 2, 3, 1, 5, 4

    C. 1, 4, 5, 2, 3

    D. 1, 5, 4, 2, 3

Question 60 asks about the preceding passage as a whole.

---

60. The writer is considering adding the following sentences to the essay:

> When H. G. Wells wrote *The Invisible Man*, there was no interest in camouflaging soldiers; the British army was garbed in bright red uniforms. Since that time, governments have learned the value of making soldiers difficult to see, first by using camouflage fabrics and today by envisioning something even more effective that would change color to match the terrain.

If the writer were to add these sentences, they would most logically be placed at Point:

    F. A in Paragraph 2.

    G. B in Paragraph 3.

    H. C in Paragraph 4.

    J. D in Paragraph 4.

GO ON TO THE NEXT PAGE

Practice Test 2

Passage V

California: A State Built on Dreams

It lasted fewer than 10 years, but when it was over, the United States had been radically and forever changed. The population had exploded on the country's west coast, <u>fortunes had been made and those same for-</u>
<u>tunes were lost,</u> and a new state had entered the union—
61
a state that would become a state of mind

for all <u>Americans: California.</u>
62

The United States <u>acquiring</u> the territory that
63
would later become California during the Mexican War (1846–1848). One of the many settlers who traveled to

the new territory was <u>John Sutter who was a shopkeeper</u>
64
from Switzerland who had left behind his wife, his

children, and his debts, in search of a new life.

<u>Hired he did</u> a carpenter named James Marshall to build
65
a sawmill for him on the American River in the foothills

of the Sierra Nevada mountains.

61. A. NO CHANGE
  B. fortunes had been made and lost,
  C. fortunes, which had been made, were then lost,
  D. made and lost were fortunes,

62. F. NO CHANGE
  G. Americans, and that place was called California.
  H. Americans, California.
  J. Americans. California.

63. A. NO CHANGE
  B. has acquired
  C. is acquiring
  D. acquired

64. F. NO CHANGE
  G. John Sutter, a shopkeeper
  H. John Sutter; a shopkeeper
  J. John Sutter, who was a shopkeeper

65. A. NO CHANGE
  B. He hired
  C. Hiring
  D. He did hire

GO ON TO THE NEXT PAGE

On January 24, 1848, while <u>probing</u> the mill's run-
                              66
off into the river, Marshall saw two shiny objects below
the surface of the water. He took the nuggets to Sutter,
who was annoyed by the discovery; Sutter didn't want
<u>them</u> mill workers distracted by gold fever.
 67

<u>Keeping the discovery</u> quiet for a while, but then he
            68
couldn't resist bragging about it. Word got out, and
workers began quitting their jobs and heading into the
hills to look for the source of the gold that had washed
down the river.

[69] Thousands of people poured into California in
search of fortune and glory.

66. F. NO CHANGE
    G. computing
    H. reading into
    J. investigating

67. A. NO CHANGE
    B. this
    C. his
    D. there

68. F. NO CHANGE
    G. The discovery he was keeping
    H. Marshall kept the discovery
    J. Keeps he the discovery

69. Which of the following true statements would
    provide the best transition from the preceding
    paragraph to this paragraph?

    A. Sutter and Marshall did not make a
       profit.
    B. The gold rush had officially begun.
    C. Can you image how a small discovery led
       to such a large state?
    D. Most of the "gold" turned out to be a
       hoax.

GO ON TO THE NEXT PAGE

[70] During the two years after Marshall's discovery, more than 90,000 people made their way to California, looking for gold.

70. The author is considering inserting the following true statement at this point in the fourth paragraph:

> This is similar to recent stock market increases.

Would this addition be appropriate for the essay?

F. Yes, the statement would add important information about a similar unexpected increase.

G. Yes, the statement would provide an informative contrast to the gold rush.

H. No, the statement would undermine the writer's position as an authority on the gold rush.

J. No, the statement would not provide any additional information about the gold rush.

In fact, so many people moved west in just <u>singularly one</u> of those years, 1849, that all the prospectors,

71
regardless of when they arrived, became known as forty-niners. By 1850, so many people had moved to the California territory that the United States Congress was forced to declare it a new state. In 1854, the population had increased by another 300,000 people. <u>In fact</u>, one

72
out of every 90 people in the United States at that time was living in California.

71. A. NO CHANGE
B. one
C. one and only one
D. singular

72. F. NO CHANGE
G. In spite of this,
H. Believe it or not,
J. Therefore,

GO ON TO THE NEXT PAGE

Even after all of the gold had been taken from the ground, California remained a magical place in the American imagination. The 31st state had become a place <u>that</u> lives could change, fortunes could be made, and dreams could come true.

73. **A.** NO CHANGE
    B. where
    C. through which
    D. in

For many <u>people, and California</u> is still such a place.

74. **F.** NO CHANGE
    G. forty-niners, California
    H. people and California
    J. people, California

Question 75 asks about the preceding passage as a whole.

75. Suppose the writer's primary purpose had been to write a brief essay detailing the life of a forty-niner during the California gold rush. Would this essay accomplish that purpose?

    A. No, because the essay does not discuss forty-niners.

    B. No, because the essay covers a historical rather than biographical perspective of the gold rush.

    C. Yes, because one can imagine the life of a forty-niner from the details provided in the essay.

    D. Yes, because the essay tells about the lives of John Sutter and James Marshall.

IF YOU FINISH BEFORE TIME IS CALLED, YOU MAY CHECK YOUR WORK ON THIS SECTION ONLY. DO NOT TURN TO ANY OTHER SECTION IN THE TEST. **STOP**

MATHEMATICS TEST

60 Minutes—60 Questions

Directions: Choose the correct solution to each question and fill in the corresponding bubble on your answer sheet.

Do not continue to spend time on questions if you get stuck. Solve as many questions as you can before returning to any if time permits.

You may use a calculator on this test for any question you choose. However, some questions may be better solved without a calculator.

Note: Unless otherwise stated, you can assume:

1. Figures are NOT necessarily drawn to scale.

2. Geometric figures are two dimensional.

3. The word *line* indicates a straight line.

4. The word *average* indicates arithmetic mean.

1. The regular price for a certain bicycle is $125.00. If that price is reduced by 20%, what is the new price?

    A. $100.00

    B. $105.00

    C. $112.50

    D. $120.00

    E. $122.50

2. If $x = -5$, then $2x^2 - 6x + 5 = ?$

    F. −15

    G. 15

    H. 25

    J. 85

    K. 135

3. How many distinct prime factors does the number 36 have?

    A. 2

    B. 3

    C. 4

    D. 5

    E. 6

4. In the following figure, what is the value of x ?

    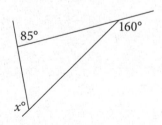

    F. 105

    G. 115

    H. 135

    J. 245

    K. 255

GO ON TO THE NEXT PAGE

5. What is the average of $\frac{1}{20}$ and $\frac{1}{30}$?

 A. $\frac{1}{25}$

 B. $\frac{1}{24}$

 C. $\frac{2}{25}$

 D. $\frac{1}{12}$

 E. $\frac{1}{6}$

6. In the figure of parallelogram $RSTU$, the length of $\overline{ST}$ is 8 feet. If the parallelogram's perimeter is 42 feet, how many feet long is $\overline{UT}$?

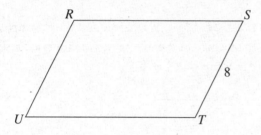

 F. 34

 G. 26

 H. 21

 J. 13

 K. 5.25

7. For all x, the product $3x^2 \cdot 5x^3 = $?

 A. $8x^5$

 B. $8x^6$

 C. $15x^5$

 D. $15x^6$

 E. $15x^8$

8. What is the positive difference between the mean and the median of the data set {12, 21, 29, 34} ?

 F. 0

 G. 1

 H. 2

 J. 5

 K. 23

9. In a group of 25 students, 16 are female. What percentage of the group is female?

 A. 16%

 B. 40%

 C. 60%

 D. 64%

 E. 75%

10. For how many integer values of x is the statement $\frac{1}{4} < \frac{7}{x} < \frac{1}{3}$ true?

 F. 6

 G. 7

 H. 12

 J. 28

 K. Infinitely many

11. What is the value of $\left(\frac{|3(2) - 14|}{|-4|} - (4 - 7)^2 \right)^{-1}$?

 A. -7

 B. $-\frac{1}{7}$

 C. $\frac{1}{7}$

 D. $1\frac{1}{7}$

 E. 7

GO ON TO THE NEXT PAGE

12. Which of the following is the solution statement for the inequality $-3 < 4x - 5$?

F. $x > -2$

G. $x > \dfrac{1}{2}$

H. $x < -2$

J. $x < \dfrac{1}{2}$

K. $x < 2$

13. In the following figure, $\overline{AD}$, $\overline{BE}$, and $\overline{CF}$ all intersect at point G. If the measure of $\angle AGB$ is $40°$ and the measure of $\angle CGE$ is $105°$, what is the measure of $\angle AGF$?

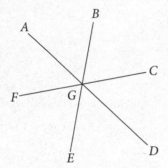

A. $35°$

B. $45°$

C. $55°$

D. $65°$

E. $75°$

14. Which of the following graphs represents the solutions for x in the inequality $5x - 2(1 - x) \geq 4(x + 1)$?

F.
```
<----+--+--⊕--+--+--+--+--+--+-->
    -4 -3 -2 -1  0  1  2  3  4
```

G.
```
<----+--+--●--+--+--+--+--+--+-->
    -4 -3 -2 -1  0  1  2  3  4
```

H.
```
<----+--+--●--+--+--+--+--+--+-->
    -4 -3 -2 -1  0  1  2  3  4
```

J.
```
<----+--+--+--+--+--+--⊕--+--+-->
    -4 -3 -2 -1  0  1  2  3  4
```

K.
```
<----+--+--+--+--+--+--●--+--+-->
    -4 -3 -2 -1  0  1  2  3  4
```

15. In the following figure, BD bisects $\angle ABC$. The measure of $\angle ABC$ is $100°$, and the measure of $\angle BAD$ is $60°$. What is the measure of $\angle BDC$?

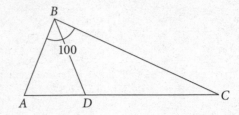

A. $80°$

B. $90°$

C. $100°$

D. $110°$

E. $120°$

16. If $x + 2y - 3 = xy$, where x and y are positive, then which of the following equations expresses y in terms of x?

F. $y = \dfrac{3 - x}{2 - x}$

G. $y = \dfrac{3 - x}{x - 2}$

H. $y = \dfrac{x - 3}{2 - x}$

J. $y = \dfrac{x - 2}{x - 3}$

K. $y = \dfrac{6 - x}{x - 2}$

17. In a group of 50 students, 28 speak English and 37 speak Spanish. If everyone in the group speaks at least one of the two languages, how many speak both English and Spanish?

A. 11

B. 12

C. 13

D. 14

E. 15

GO ON TO THE NEXT PAGE

18. A car travels 288 miles in 6 hours. At that rate, how many miles will it travel in 8 hours?

    F. 216

    G. 360

    H. 368

    J. 376

    K. 384

19. When $\dfrac{4}{11}$ is written as a decimal, what is the 100th digit after the decimal point?

    A. 3

    B. 4

    C. 5

    D. 6

    E. 7

20. What is the solution for x in the following system of equations?

    $$3x + 4y = 31$$
    $$3x - 4y = -1$$

    F. 4

    G. 5

    H. 6

    J. 9

    K. 10

Use the following information to answer questions 21–22.

Ariel, Lisa, and Jared participated in a snowboarding competition. The scores for each of their six qualifying runs are in the table shown here.

	Ariel	Lisa	Jared
Run 1	8.3	8.5	8.4
Run 2	7.7	8.0	8.0
Run 3	7.1	8.5	7.5
Run 4	6.6	7.8	9.0
Run 5	8.0	8.1	7.5
Run 6	6.6	7.5	7.2
Mean Score	7.38	8.07	7.93
Standard Deviation	0.73	0.39	0.67

21. According to the data in the table, which of the following is a valid conclusion?

    A. Ariel had the lowest mean score, so her performance was the least consistent.

    B. Lisa had the smallest standard deviation, so her performance was the most consistent.

    C. Ariel had the largest standard deviation, so her performance was the most consistent.

    D. Jared had the highest score on any one run, so his performance was the most consistent.

    E. It is not possible to determine whose performance was the most consisent without finding the mode of the data.

GO ON TO THE NEXT PAGE

Practice Test 2

22. Based on the qualifying-run mean scores, a friend predicts that if all three compete, they will finish in the order Ariel, then Jared, then Lisa. If the friend instead uses the mode score for each person to make the prediction, in which order should he predict that the three will finish?

    F. Ariel, Lisa, Jared

    G. Lisa, Jared, Ariel

    H. Lisa, Ariel, Jared

    J. Jared, Ariel, Lisa

    K. He should predict the same order.

23. In the following figure, the circle centered at P is tangent to the circle centered at Q. Point Q is on the circumference of circle P. If the circumference of circle P is 6 inches, what is the circumference, in inches, of circle Q?

    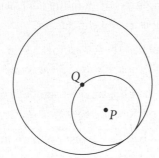

    A. 12

    B. 24

    C. 36

    D. 12π

    E. 36π

24. If $f(x) = 1 - x^2$, then $f(x + h) = ?$

    F. $1 - x^2 + h$

    G. $1 - x^2 - h$

    H. $-x^2 - 2xh - h^2$

    J. $1 - x^2 - 2xh - h^2$

    K. $1 - x^2 + 2xh + h^2$

25. What is the volume, in cubic inches, of the cylinder shown in the following figure?

    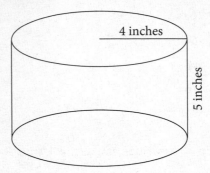

    A. 20π

    B. 40π

    C. 60π

    D. 80π

    E. 100π

26. What is the complete factorization of $2x + 3x^2 + x^3$?

    F. $x(x^2 + 2)$

    G. $x(x - 2)(x + 3)$

    H. $x(x - 1)(x + 2)$

    J. $x(x + 1)(x + 2)$

    K. $x(x + 2)(x + 3)$

27. If $xyz \neq 0$, which of the following is equivalent to $\dfrac{x^2 y^3 z^4}{\left(xyz^2\right)^2}$?

    A. $\dfrac{1}{y}$

    B. $\dfrac{1}{z}$

    C. y

    D. $\dfrac{x}{yz}$

    E. xyz

GO ON TO THE NEXT PAGE

28. As a decimal, what is the sum of $\frac{2}{3}$ and $\frac{1}{12}$?

    F. 0.2

    G. 0.5

    H. 0.75

    J. 0.833

    K. 0.875

29. In the following figure, all angles are right angles and all lengths are in feet. What is the perimeter, in feet, of the figure?

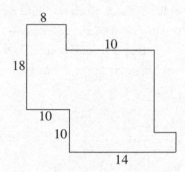

    A. 70

    B. 76

    C. 84

    D. 92

    E. 104

30. A jar contains 4 green marbles, 5 red marbles, and 11 white marbles. If 1 marble is chosen at random, what is the probability that it will be green?

    F. $\frac{1}{3}$

    G. $\frac{1}{4}$

    H. $\frac{1}{5}$

    J. $\frac{1}{16}$

    K. $\frac{5}{15}$

31. What is the average of the expressions $2x + 5$, $5x - 6$, and $-4x + 2$?

    A. $x + \frac{1}{3}$

    B. $x + 1$

    C. $3x + \frac{1}{3}$

    D. $3x + 3$

    E. $3x + 3\frac{1}{3}$

32. A system of two linear equations in two variables has NO solution. One of the equations is graphed in the (x,y) coordinate plane as shown below. Which of the following could be the equation of the other line?

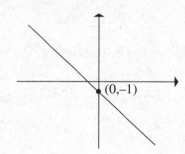

    F. $y = x + 1$

    G. $y = -x - 1$

    H. $y = x + 2$

    J. $y = -x + 2$

    K. $y = 1$

GO ON TO THE NEXT PAGE

33. In the following figure, $\overline{QS}$ and $\overline{PT}$ are parallel and the lengths of $\overline{QR}$ and $\overline{PQ}$ are as marked. If the perimeter of $\triangle QRS$ is 11 units long, how many units long is the perimeter of $\triangle PRT$?

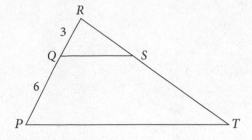

A. 22

B. 33

C. 66

D. 88

E. 99

34. The figure shown belongs in which of the following classifications?

    I. Polygon

    II. Quadrilateral

    III. Rectangle

    IV. Trapezoid

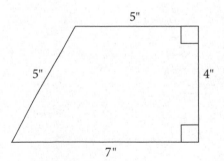

F. I only

G. II only

H. IV only

J. I, II, and III only

K. I, II, and IV only

35. A polynomial function is defined by the equation $p(x) = 2x^2 + ax - 4x - 2a$. If $p(-3) = 0$, what is the value of a?

A. 0

B. 2

C. 4

D. 6

E. 12

36. A menu offers 4 choices for the first course, 5 choices for the second course, and 3 choices for dessert. How many different meals—consisting of a first course, a second course, and a dessert—can one choose from this menu?

F. 12

G. 24

H. 30

J. 36

K. 60

37. If an integer is divisible by 6 and by 9, then the integer must be evenly divisible by which of the following?

    I. 12

    II. 18

    III. 36

A. I only

B. II only

C. I and II only

D. I, II, and III

E. None

GO ON TO THE NEXT PAGE

38. If $\begin{bmatrix} x & 5 \\ -1 & x \end{bmatrix} + \begin{bmatrix} 2 & 3y \\ -1 & y \end{bmatrix} = \begin{bmatrix} 7 & 17 \\ -2 & z \end{bmatrix}$, what is the value of z?

    F.   4

    G.   5

    H.   8

    J.   9

    K.   13

39. Joan has q quarters, d dimes, n nickels, and no other coins in her pocket. Which of the following expressions represents the total number of coins in Joan's pocket?

    A. $q + d + n$

    B. $5q + 2d + n$

    C. $0.25q + 0.10d + 0.05n$

    D. $(25 + 10 + 5)(q + d + n)$

    E. $25q + 10d + 5n$

40. What value or values of x satisfy the equation $|2x + 1| = \dfrac{7}{6}$?

    F. $-\dfrac{13}{12}$ only

    G. $-\dfrac{1}{12}$ only

    H. $\dfrac{1}{12}$ only

    J. $-\dfrac{1}{12}$ and $\dfrac{1}{12}$

    K. $-\dfrac{13}{12}$ and $\dfrac{1}{12}$

41. If w, x, y, and z are all positive real numbers and $w^{-1} > x^{-1} > y^{-1} > z^{-1}$, which of the numbers has the least value?

    A. w

    B. x

    C. y

    D. z

    E.   Cannot be determined from the given information

42. What is the amplitude of the graph of the trigonometric function $y + 3 = 4 \sin(5\theta)$?

    (Note: The amplitude is $\dfrac{1}{2}$ the difference between the maximum and minimum values of y.)

    F.   3

    G.   4

    H.   5

    J.   7

    K.   10

43. If $f(x) = 9^{2x-1}$ and $g(x) = 3^{3x+3}$, for what value of x does $f(x) - g(x) = 0$?

    A. -4

    B. $-\dfrac{7}{4}$

    C. $-\dfrac{10}{7}$

    D.   2

    E.   5

GO ON TO THE NEXT PAGE

44. From 1970 through 1980, the population of City Q increased by 20%. From 1980 through 1990, the population increased by 30%. What was the combined percent increase for the period 1970–1990 ?

F. 25%

G. 36%

H. 50%

J. 54%

K. 56%

45. Which of the following is an equation for the graph shown in the standard (x,y) coordinate plane?

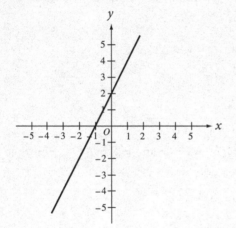

A. $y = -2x - 1$

B. $y = -x + 2$

C. $y = x - 1$

D. $y = 2x + 1$

E. $y = 2x + 2$

46. Which of the following is the graph, in the standard (x,y) coordinate plane, of the rational function $f(x) = \dfrac{3x^2 + 2x}{x}$?

F.

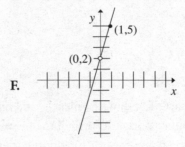

G.

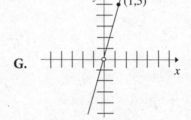

H.

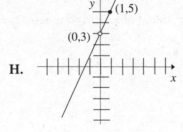

J.

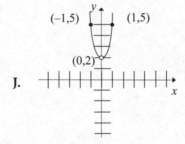

K.

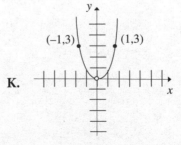

GO ON TO THE NEXT PAGE

47. In complex numbers, where $i^2 = -1$, what is the simplified form of the expression $\dfrac{(i+1)(i+1)}{(i-1)(i-1)}$?

   A. $\dfrac{i+1}{i-1}$

   B. $\dfrac{i}{2}$

   C. $\dfrac{2}{i}$

   D. $2i$

   E. -1

48. What is $\dfrac{1}{4}$% of 16 ?

   F. 0.004

   G. 0.04

   H. 0.4

   J. 4

   K. 64

49. For all s, $(s+4)(s-4) + (2s+2)(s-2) = ?$

   A. $s^2 - 2s - 20$

   B. $3s^2 - 12$

   C. $3s^2 - 2s - 20$

   D. $3s^2 + 2s - 20$

   E. $5s^2 - 2s - 20$

50. Which of the following is an equation of the quadratic function graphed in the following (x,y) coordinate plane?

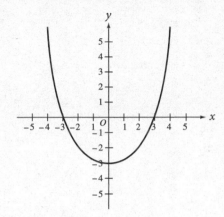

   F. $f(x) = \dfrac{x^2}{3} - 3$

   G. $f(x) = \dfrac{x^2 - 3}{3}$

   H. $f(x) = \dfrac{x^2}{3} + 3$

   J. $f(x) = \dfrac{x^2 + 3}{3}$

   K. $f(x) = 3x^2 - 3$

GO ON TO THE NEXT PAGE

51. In the following figure, $\sin a = \dfrac{4}{5}$. What is $\cos b$?

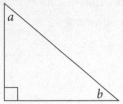

A. $\dfrac{3}{4}$

B. $\dfrac{3}{5}$

C. $\dfrac{4}{5}$

D. $\dfrac{5}{4}$

E. $\dfrac{4}{3}$

52. If the first term in a geometric sequence is x and the second term is nx, what is the 30th term in the sequence?

F. $n^{29}x$

G. $n^{30}x$

H. $n^{31}x$

J. $(nx)^{29}$

K. $(nx)^{30}$

53. The formula for the surface area S of a rectangular solid with square bases (shown in the figure) is $S = 4wh + 2w^2$, where w is the side length of the bases and h is the height of the solid. Doubling each of the dimensions (w and h) will increase the surface area to how many times its original size?

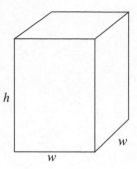

A. 2

B. 4

C. 6

D. 8

E. 24

54. A yogurt factory fills cylindrical containers 80% of the way to the top, putting 6 ounces of yogurt in each cup. The containers are 4 inches tall and 2.5 inches wide. Approximately how many cubic inches of space does one ounce of yogurt take up?

F. 2.1

G. 2.3

H. 2.6

J. 3.3

K. 4.2

GO ON TO THE NEXT PAGE

55. In $\triangle RST$, $\angle R$ is a right angle and $\angle S$ measures 60°. If $\overline{ST}$ is 8 inches long, what is the area of $\triangle RST$ in square inches?

 A. 8

 B. $8\sqrt{3}$

 C. 16

 D. 32

 E. $32\sqrt{3}$

56. Right triangle ABC has lengths as marked in the following figure. If $\overline{DE}$ is the perpendicular bisector of $\overline{AC}$, what is the ratio of the length of $\overline{AB}$ to the length of $\overline{DE}$?

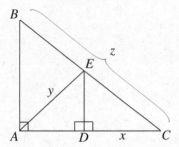

 F. $\dfrac{1}{2}$

 G. $\dfrac{x}{y}$

 H. $\dfrac{y}{x}$

 J. $\dfrac{y}{z}$

 K. $\dfrac{z}{y}$

57. In a certain club, the average age of the male members is 35 and the average age of the female members is 25. If 20% of the members are male, what is the average age of all the club members?

 A. 26

 B. 27

 C. 28

 D. 29

 E. 30

58. To determine the height h of a tree, Roger stands b feet from the base of the tree and measures the angle of elevation to be θ, as shown in the figure. Which of the following relates h and b ?

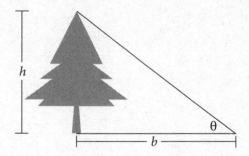

 F. $\sin\theta = \dfrac{h}{b}$

 G. $\sin\theta = \dfrac{b}{h}$

 H. $\sin\theta = \dfrac{b}{\sqrt{b^2 + h^2}}$

 J. $\sin\theta = \dfrac{h}{\sqrt{b^2 + h^2}}$

 K. $\sin\theta = \dfrac{\sqrt{b^2 + h^2}}{b}$

GO ON TO THE NEXT PAGE

59. The formula for the lateral surface area S of a right circular cone is $S = \pi r\sqrt{r^2 + h^2}$, where r is the radius of the base and h is the altitude. What is the lateral surface area, in square feet, of a right circular cone with base radius 3 feet and altitude 4 feet?

A. $3\pi\sqrt{5}$

B. $3\pi\sqrt{7}$

C. 15π

D. 21π

E. $\dfrac{75\pi}{2}$

60. A circle in the standard (x,y) coordinate plane has the equation $(x+2)^2 + (y-2)^2 = 5$. What is the radius of the circle?

F. $\sqrt{2}$

G. 2

H. $\sqrt{5}$

J. 5

K. 25

IF YOU FINISH BEFORE TIME IS CALLED, YOU MAY CHECK YOUR WORK ON THIS SECTION ONLY. DO NOT TURN TO ANY OTHER SECTION IN THE TEST. STOP

READING TEST

35 Minutes — 40 Questions

Directions: The Reading Test includes multiple passages. Each passage includes multiple questions. After reading each passage, choose the best answer and fill in the corresponding bubble on your answer sheet. You may review the passages as often as necessary.

Passage I

PROSE FICTION: This passage is adapted from *Bleak House* by Charles Dickens, which was first published in 1853. In this excerpt, Esther recounts some of her childhood experiences.

I can remember, when I was a very little girl indeed, I used to say to my doll when we were alone together, "Now, Dolly, I am not clever, you know very well, and you must be patient with me, like a dear!"

5 My dear old doll! I was such a shy little thing that I seldom dared to open my lips, and never dared to open my heart, to anybody else. It almost makes me cry to think what a relief it used to be to me when I came home from school of a day to run upstairs

10 to my room and say, "Oh, you dear faithful Dolly, I knew you would be expecting me!" and then to sit down on the floor, leaning on the elbow of her great chair, and tell her all I had noticed since we parted.

I was brought up, from my earliest remem-

15 brance—like some of the princesses in the fairy stories, only I was not charming—by my godmother. At least, I only knew her as such. She was a good, good woman! She went to church three times every Sunday, and to morning prayers on Wednesdays

20 and Fridays, and to lectures whenever there were lectures, and never missed. She was handsome; and if she had ever smiled, would have been (I used to think) like an angel—but she never smiled. She was always grave and strict. She was so very good

25 herself, I thought, that the badness of other people made her frown all her life. It made me very sorry to consider how good she was and how unworthy of her I was, and I used ardently to hope that I might have a better heart; and I talked it over very

30 often with the dear old doll, but I never loved my godmother as I ought to have loved her and as I felt I must have loved her if I had been a better girl.

I had never heard my mama spoken of. I had never been shown my mama's grave. I had never

35 been told where it was.

Although there were seven girls at the neighboring school where I was a day boarder, and although they called me little Esther Summerson, I knew none of them at home. All of them were older than

40 I, to be sure (I was the youngest there by a good deal), but there seemed to be some other separation between us besides that, and besides their being far more clever than I was and knowing much more than I did. One of them in the first week of my go-

45 ing to the school (I remember it very well) invited me home to a little party, to my great joy. But my godmother wrote a stiff letter declining for me, and I never went. I never went out at all.

It was my birthday. There were holidays at school

50 on other birthdays—none on mine. There were rejoicings at home on other birthdays, as I knew from what I heard the girls relate to one another—there were none on mine. My birthday was the most melancholy day at home in the whole year.

55 Dinner was over, and my godmother and I were sitting at the table before the fire. The clock ticked, the fire clicked; not another sound had been heard in the room or in the house for I don't know how long. I happened to look timidly up from my stitch-

60 ing, across the table at my godmother, and I saw in her face, looking gloomily at me, "It would have been far better, little Esther, that you had had no birthday, that you had never been born!"

GO ON TO THE NEXT PAGE ⟶

I broke out crying and sobbing, and I said, "Oh,
65 dear godmother, tell me, pray do tell me, did Mama
die on my birthday?"

"No," she returned. "Ask me no more, child!"

I put up my trembling little hand to clasp
hers or to beg her pardon with what earnestness
70 I might, but withdrew it as she looked at me, and
laid it on my fluttering heart. She said slowly in
a cold, low voice—I see her knitted brow and
pointed finger—"The time will come—and soon
enough—when you will understand this better and
75 will feel it too. I have forgiven her"—but her face
did not relent—"the wrong she did to me, and I say
no more of it, though it was greater than you will
ever know. Forget your mother and leave all other
people to forget her. Now, go!"

80 I went up to my room, and crept to bed, and laid
my doll's cheek against mine wet with tears, and
holding that solitary friend upon my bosom, cried
myself to sleep. Imperfect as my understanding of
my sorrow was, I knew that I had brought no joy
85 at any time to anybody's heart and that I was to no
one upon earth what Dolly was to me.

Dear, dear, to think how much time we passed
alone together afterwards, and how often I repeated
to the doll the story of my birthday and confided to
90 her that I would try as hard as ever I could to repair
the fault I had been born with. I hope it is not
self-indulgent to shed these tears as I think of it.

1. By writing "Dolly, I am not clever" (line 3), "how unworthy of her I was" (lines 34–35), and " I knew that I had brought no joy at any time to anybody's heart" (lines 84–85), the author intends to give the impression that the narrator:

A. is an especially mean and unintelligent girl.
B. has a low opinion herself because of her upbringing, not because of her character.
C. resents and rejects her godmother's statement that she should never have been born.
D. hates her godmother for not celebrating her (the narrator's) birthday.

2. The author refers to Esther's doll as a "solitary friend" (line 82) in order to emphasize that the doll is:

F. only an amusing plaything.
G. Esther's only kind companion and confidante.
H. a princess in a fairy tale.
J. a beautiful toy that was too fragile to touch.

3. As it is used in line 47, the word *stiff* most nearly means:

A. difficult to bend.
B. rigidly formal.
C. unchanging.
D. not moving easily or freely.

GO ON TO THE NEXT PAGE

4. Which of the following most likely contributed to Esther's belief that she had been born with a fault (lines 90–91)?

   F. She is not very clever.

   G. Her birthday was never celebrated.

   H. She did not have any friends at school.

   J. Her mother died in childbirth.

5. Esther's godmother's words, actions, and facial expression as described in the tenth paragraph (lines 68–79) suggest that she:

   A. had a change of heart about celebrating Esther's birthday.

   B. did not know what had happened to Esther's mother.

   C. continued to resent Esther's mother.

   D. had truly forgiven Esther's mother.

6. According to the passage, Esther's childhood could be most accurately characterized as:

   F. an adventure.

   G. a time of loneliness and confusion.

   H. a period of dedication to education and self-improvement.

   J. a period of attempting to become more like her godmother.

7. From Esther's statement, "I was to no one upon earth what Dolly was to me" (lines 85–86), it is reasonable to infer that Esther:

   A. believed that her godmother loved her.

   B. believed that she would be able to become friends with the girls at school.

   C. believed that no one loved her.

   D. believed that her mother was alive.

8. In the passage, it is implied that all of the following contributed to separating Esther from the other girls at her school EXCEPT:

   F. the other girls were older than Esther.

   G. Esther's godmother did not allow Esther to socialize with the other girls outside of school.

   H. Esther believed that the other girls were much smarter.

   J. Esther was self-indulgent.

9. According to the passage, one reason that Esther thinks of her godmother as a "good, good woman" (lines 17–18) is that:

   A. when she smiles, she looks like an angel.

   B. she forgave Esther's mother.

   C. she frequently attends church services.

   D. she gave Esther a doll.

10. In the passage, Esther describes herself as a child as:

    F. self-indulgent and not very clever.

    G. shy and not very clever.

    H. shy and faithful.

    J. self-indulgent and faithful.

GO ON TO THE NEXT PAGE

Passage II

SOCIAL SCIENCE: This passage is excerpted from "The Return of the Big Cats" by Mac Margolis, *Newsweek*, December 11, 2000, © 2000 by Newsweek, Inc. All rights reserved. Reprinted by permission.

Marcos Nunes is not likely to forget his first holiday in Brazil's Pantanal wilderness. One afternoon last October, he was coaxing his horse through a lonely tuft of woods when he suddenly found him-
5 self staring down a fully grown spotted jaguar. He held his breath while the painted cat and her cub paraded silkily through the grove, not 10 meters away. "Thank you," he wrote later in a hotel visitor's log, "for the wonderful fright!"

10 As Nunes and other ecotourists are discovering, these big, beautiful animals, once at the brink of extinction, are now staging a comeback. Exactly how dramatic a comeback is difficult to say because jaguars—*Panthera onca*, the largest feline
15 in the New World—are solitary, secretive, nocturnal predators. Each cat needs to prowl at least 35 square kilometers by itself. Brazil's Pantanal, vast wetlands that spill over a 140,000-square-kilometer swath of South America the size of Germany,
20 gives them plenty of room to roam. Nevertheless, scientists who have been tagging jaguars with radio transmitters for two decades have in recent years been reporting a big increase in sightings. Hotels, campgrounds, and bed-and-breakfasts have sprung
25 up to accommodate the half-million tourists a year (twice the number of five years ago) bent on sampling the Pantanal's wildlife, of which the great cats must be the most magnificent example.

Most sightings come from local cattle herd-
30 ers—but their jaguar stories have a very different ring. One day last September, ranch hand Abel Monteiro was tending cattle near the Rio Vermelho, in the southern Pantanal, when, he says, a snarling jaguar leaped from the scrub and killed his two
35 bloodhounds. Monteiro barely had time to grab his .38 revolver and kill the angry cat. Leonelson Ramos da Silva says last May he and a group of field hands had to throw flaming sticks all night to keep

a prowling jaguar from invading their forest camp.
40 The Brazilian interior, famous for its generous spirit and cowboy *bonhomie*, is now the scene of a political catfight between the scientists, environmentalists, and ecotourists who want to protect the jaguars and the embattled ranchers who want to protect
45 themselves and their livelihood.

The ranchers, to be sure, have enough headaches coping with the harsh, sodden landscape without jaguars attacking their herds and threatening their livelihoods. Hard data on cattle losses due to
50 jaguars in the Pantanal are nonexistent, but there are stories. In 1995, Joo Julio Dittmar bought a 6,200-hectare strip of ideal breeding ground, only to lose 152 of his 600 calves to jaguars, he claims. Ranchers chafe at laws that forbid them to kill the
55 jaguars. "This is a question of democracy," says Dittmar. "We ranchers ought to be allowed to control our own environment."

Man and jaguar have been sparring for territory ever since 18th-century settlers, traders, and herds-
60 men began to move into this sparsely populated *serto*, or back lands. By the 1960s, the Pantanal was a vast, soggy canvas, white with gleaming herds of Nelore cattle. Game hunters were bagging 15,000 jaguars a year in the nearby Amazon Basin (no fig-
65 ures exist on the Pantanal) as the worldwide trade in pelts reached $30 million a year. As the jaguars grew scarce, their chief food staple, the capybara— a meter-long rodent, the world's largest—overran farmers' fields and spread trichomoniasis, a live-
70 stock disease that renders cows sterile.

Then in 1967, Brazil outlawed jaguar hunting, and a world ban on selling pelts followed in 1973. Weather patterns also shifted radically—due most likely to global warming—and drove annual floods
75 to near-biblical proportions. The waters are only now retreating from some inundated pasturelands. As the Pantanal herds shrank from 6 million to about 3.5 million head, the jaguars advanced. Along the way they developed a taste for the bovine

GO ON TO THE NEXT PAGE →

80 intruders. The ranchers' fear of the big cats is partly cultural. The ancient Inca and Maya believed that jaguars possessed supernatural powers. In Brazil, the most treacherous enemy is said to be *o amigo da onca*, a friend to the jaguar.

85 Some people believe there may be a way for ranchers and jaguars to coexist. Sports hunters on "green safaris" might shoot jaguars with immobilizing drugs, allowing scientists to fit the cats with radio collars. Fees would help sustain jaguar research

90 and compensate ranchers for livestock losses. (Many environmentalists, though, fear fraudulent claims.) Scientists are setting up workshops to teach ranchers how to protect their herds with modern husbandry, pasture management, and such gadgets

95 as blinking lights and electric fences.

Like many rural folk, however, the wetland ranchers tend to bristle at bureaucrats and foreigners telling them what to do. When the scholars go home and the greens log off, the *pantaneiros* will

100 still be there—left on their own to deal with the jaguars as they see fit.

11. As it is used in line 62, the word *canvas* most nearly means:

   A. a survey of public opinion.
   B. a background.
   C. a coarse cotton fabric.
   D. a painting.

12. The author's purpose in retelling Nunes's experience is to:

   F. describe the dangers of encountering wild animals.
   G. suggest the excitement of unexpected jaguar sightings.
   H. support the ranchers' claim that jaguars threaten their herds.
   J. argue that ecotourism is unsafe.

13. According to the passage, it is difficult to determine the extent of the jaguar's comeback because:

   A. the area the jaguars inhabit is so large.
   B. the stories that the local ranchers tell about jaguars contradict the conclusions reached by scientists.
   C. jaguars are solitary, nocturnal animals that can have a territory of 35 square kilometers.
   D. scientists have only used radio transmitters to track the movements of the jaguar population.

14. The information about ecotourism in the first and second paragraphs of the passage (lines 1–28) suggests that:

   F. the jaguars are seen as a threat to the safety of tourists.
   G. the jaguars are important to the success of Brazil's growing ecotourism industry.
   H. the growth of the ecotourism industry is threatening the habitat of the jaguars.
   J. it is common for ecotourists to spot one or more jaguars.

15. According to the passage, which of the following is NOT a method scientists are teaching ranchers in order to protect cattle herds?

   A. "Green safaris"
   B. Pasture management
   C. The use of blinking lights and electric fences
   D. Modern husbandry

GO ON TO THE NEXT PAGE ▷

16. The author of the passage most likely included the jaguar stories of three ranchers in order to:

    F. express more sympathy toward the ranchers than toward the environmentalists and scientists.

    G. illustrate the dangers and economic losses that the jaguars currently pose to ranchers.

    H. show the violent nature of the ranchers.

    J. provide a complete picture of the Pantanal landscape.

17. From information in the passage, it is most reasonable to infer that the cattle herds "shrank from 6 million to about 3.5 million head" (lines 77–78) because:

    A. the jaguars had killed so many cattle.

    B. environmentalists and scientists worked to convert pastureland into refuges for the jaguars.

    C. many cows had become sterile from trichomoniasis, and annual floods submerged much of the pastureland used by ranchers.

    D. the cattle could not tolerate the increase in the average temperature caused by global warming.

18. The main conclusion the passage reaches about the future of the relationship between the people and the jaguars in the Pantanal is that:

    F. the increase in ecotourism will ensure the continued growth of the jaguar population.

    G. the ranchers themselves will ultimately determine how they will cope with the jaguars.

    H. the jaguar population will continue to fluctuate with the number of tourists coming into the Pantanal.

    J. the scientists' new ranching methods will make it easy for the ranchers and jaguars to coexist.

19. Given the adjectives the author uses to describe the jaguar, his attitude toward the animal is one of:

    A. admiration.

    B. fear.

    C. revulsion.

    D. concern.

20. Based on the passage, the author would most likely agree that:

    F. ranchers have a stronger argument than do environmentalists.

    G. jaguars are too shy to be seen by ecotourists.

    H. the resurgence of jaguars can be a positive development.

    J. the conflict between jaguars and ranchers is a recent problem.

GO ON TO THE NEXT PAGE

Passage III

HUMANITIES: This passage is excerpted from *Music Through the Ages: Revised Edition*, © 1987 by Marion Bauer and Ethel R. Peyser, edited by Elizabeth E. Rogers, copyright © 1932 by Marion Bauer and Ethel R. Peyser, renewed copyright © 1960 by Ethel R. Peyser. Reprinted by permission of G. P. Putnam's Sons, a division of Penguin Group (USA), Inc.

Greek instruments can be classified into two general categories—string and pipe, or lyre and aulos. Our knowledge of them comes from representations on monuments, vases, statues, and
5 friezes and from the testimony of Greek authors. The lyre was the national instrument and included a wide variety of types. In its most antique form, the chelys, it is traced back to the age of fable and allegedly owed its invention to Hermes. Easy to
10 carry, this small lyre became the favorite instrument of the home, amateurs, and women, a popular accompaniment for drinking songs and love songs as well as more noble kinds of poetry. Professional Homeric singers used a kithara, a larger, more pow-
15 erful instrument, which probably came from Egypt. The kithara had a flat wooden sound box and an upper horizontal bar supported by two curving arms. Within this frame were stretched strings of equal length, at first but three or four in number.
20 Fastened to the performer by means of a sling, the kithara was played with both hands. We are not sure in just what manner the instrument was used to accompany the epics. It may have been employed for a pitch-fixing prelude and for interludes, or it
25 may have paralleled or decorated the vocal melody in more or less free fashion.

Two types of tuning were used: the dynamic, or pitch method, naming the degrees "according to function," and the thetic, or tablature, naming them
30 "according to position" on the instrument.

As early as the eighth century BCE, lyres of five strings appeared. Terpander (fl. c. 675 BCE), one of the first innovators, is said to have increased the number of strings to seven. He is also supposed to
35 have completed the octave and created the Mix-

olydian scale. Aristoxenos claimed that the poetess Sappho, in the seventh century BCE, in addition to introducing a mode in which Dorian and Lydian characteristics were blended, initiated use of the
40 plectrum or pick. At the time of Sophocles (495–406 BCE), the lyre had eleven strings.

Another harplike instrument was the magadis, whose tone was described as trumpetlike. Of foreign importation, it had twenty strings, which,
45 by means of frets, played octaves. As some of the strings were tuned in quarter tones, it was an instrument associated with the enharmonic mode. Smaller versions, the pectis and the barbitos, were also tuned in quarter tones. Greek men and boys
50 had a style of singing in octaves that was called magadizing, after the octave-playing instruments.

The kithara was identified with Apollo and the Apollonian cult, representing the intellectual and idealistic side of Greek art. The aulos or reed pipe
55 was the instrument of Dionysians, who represented the unbridled, sensual, and passionate aspect of Greek culture.

Although translated as "flute," the aulos is more like our oboe. Usually found in double form, the
60 pipes set at an angle, the aulos was imputed to have a far more exciting effect than that produced by the subdued lyre. About 600 BCE, the aulos was chosen as the official instrument of the Delphian and Pythian festivals. It was also used in performances of
65 the Dionysian dithyramb as well as a supplement of the chorus in classic Greek tragedy and comedy.

There was a complete family of auloi covering the same range as human voices. One authority names three species of simple pipes and five
70 varieties of double pipes. (The double pipe was the professional instrument.) An early specimen was supposed to have been tuned to the chromatic tetrachord D, C sharp, B flat, A—a fact that points to Oriental origin. Elegiac songs called aulodia
75 were composed in this mode to be accompanied by an aulos. Although the first wooden pipes had

GO ON TO THE NEXT PAGE ⟶

only three or four finger holes, the number later
increased so that the Dorian, Phrygian, and Lydian modes might be performed on a single pair.
80 Pictures of auletes show them with a bandage or
phorbeia over their faces; this might have been
necessary to hold the two pipes in place, to modu-
late the tone or, perhaps, to aid in storing air in the
cheeks for the purpose of sustained performance.

21. The passage suggests that the aulos was
considered "the instrument of Dionysians"
(line 55) because:

  A. it expressed the excitement and
passion of that aspect of Greek
culture.

  B. it was chosen as the official instrument of the Delphian and Pythian
festivals.

  C. it represented the intellectual and
idealistic side of Greek art.

  D. it was invented around the time that
the Dionysian cult originated.

22. The statement that the chelys can be "traced
back to the age of fable" (line 8) implies that
the chelys:

  F. was invented by storytellers.

  G. was used to accompany the epics.

  H. probably existed in legend only.

  J. was a particularly ancient instrument.

23. As it is used in line 25, the word *decorated* most
nearly means:

  A. adorned.

  B. embellished.

  C. increased.

  D. made pretty.

24. According to the passage, the kithara was:

  F. most likely of Greek origin.

  G. played with one hand.

  H. used by professional musicians.

  J. less powerful than a chelys.

25. Which of the following is NOT cited as a change
that occurred to the lyre between the eighth and
fifth centuries BCE?

  A. Musicians began to use a plectrum.

  B. Lyres featured increasing numbers of
strings.

  C. Musicians began to use different scales
and modes.

  D. Lyres were used to accompany dramatic
productions.

GO ON TO THE NEXT PAGE

26. The author most likely views ancient Greek instruments as:

    F. interesting and integral to Greek culture.

    G. too ancient to be relevant to today's instrumental music.

    H. complicated in design and use.

    J. primitive when compared to modern instruments.

27. The author's approach to Greek music and instruments is that of:

    A. an historian.

    B. a professional musician.

    C. a music teacher.

    D. a Greek scholar.

28. According to the passage, one of Sappho's contributions to ancient Greek music was that she:

    F. completed the octave and created the Mixolydian scale.

    G. introduced a mode blending Dorian and Lydian characteristics.

    H. incorporated poetry into recitals of lyre music.

    J. helped increase the number of strings on the lyre.

29. According to the passage, which of the following is/are characteristic(s) of the aulos?

    I. It was used in performances of the Dionysian dithyramb.

    II. It sounded more exciting than the lyre.

    III. It resembled the modern-day flute more than it did the oboe.

    A. I only

    B. I and II only

    C. II and III only

    D. I, II, and III

30. Which of the following does the passage suggest is true about our knowledge of ancient Greek instruments?

    F. Our knowledge is dependent on secondary sources.

    G. Little is known about how instruments were tuned.

    H. Very few pictures of ancient Greek instruments have survived.

    J. More is known about stringed instruments than about pipe instruments.

GO ON TO THE NEXT PAGE

Passage IV

NATURAL SCIENCE: The immune system can be divided into two major divisions: nonspecific and specific. The nonspecific immune system is composed of defenses that are used to fight off infection in general and are not targeted at specific pathogens. The specific immune system is able to attack very specific disease-causing organisms by means of protein-to-protein interaction and is responsible for our ability to become immune to future infections from pathogens we have fought off already.

Passage A

Nonspecific defenses serve as the first line of defense for the body to fight off infection. The skin and mucous membranes form one part of these nonspecific defenses, which our body uses against
5 foreign cells or viruses. Intact skin cannot normally be penetrated by bacteria or viruses, and oil and sweat secretions give the skin a pH that ranges from 3 to 5, which is acidic enough to discourage most microbes from growing there. In addition, saliva,
10 tears, and mucous all contain the enzyme lysozyme, which can destroy bacterial cell walls (causing bacteria to rupture due to osmotic pressure) and some viral capsids. Mucous is able to trap foreign particles and microbes and transport them to the
15 stomach through swallowing or to the outside during coughing or blowing the nose. Also, movement in the stomach due to peristalsis and in the airways due to cilia helps remove harmful agents.

Certain white blood cells are another part of
20 the nonspecific defense systems. Macrophages are large white blood cells that circulate, looking for foreign material or cells to engulf, which they do through phagocytosis. Macrophages circulate through the blood and are able to transport them-
25 selves through capillary walls and into tissues that have been infected or wounded. Macrophages are called antigen-presenting cells (APCs) because of their ability to display on their own cell surface the proteins that were on the surface of the cell or viral
30 particle they have just digested.

Neutrophils are white blood cells that are actively phagocytic like macrophages but are not APCs. Our bodies normally produce approximately 1 million neutrophils per second, and they can be
35 found anywhere in the body. They usually destroy themselves as they fight off pathogens.

People who have decreased numbers of neutrophils circulating through their blood are extremely susceptible to bacterial and fungal infections. Other
40 white blood cells that secrete toxic substances without fine-tuned specificity include the eosinophils, basophils, and mast cells.

Passage B

The major specific defense of the immune system includes specialized white blood cells known as
45 lymphocytes, which come in two varieties: B cells and T cells. Both are produced by stem cells in the bone marrow, and although T cells mature in the thymus, B cells do not. The thymus is essential for "educating" T cells; those that recognize "self" anti-
50 gens (proteins found on one's own cell surfaces) are killed off to prevent the body from attacking itself. This negative selection results in the development of T cell tolerance, a necessity of the specific immune system. Yet a positive selection process also
55 exists whereby T cells that do not react to a specific set of glycoproteins, called MHC (major histocompatibility complex) proteins, are killed off because T cells need to be able to bond to both self-MHC and foreign antigens simultaneously.

60 There are three types of T cells: helper (TH), cytotoxic (TC), and suppressor (TS). While TH cells are mediators between macrophages and B cells, TC cells are essential in defending against viruses because they can kill virally infected cells
65 directly. Since virally infected cells display some viral proteins on their surfaces, TC cells can bind to those proteins and secrete enzymes that tear the cell membrane, thereby killing the cell. TS cells are in-

GO ON TO THE NEXT PAGE

volved in controlling the immune response so that
70 it does not run amok; they do this by suppressing
the production of antibodies by B cells.

T cells cannot detect free antigens; they can only
respond to displayed antigens and MHC on the surfaces of cells. When they do recognize a displayed
75 antigen, it is always in combination with a self-
MHC protein displayed along with the antigen on
the host cell surface.

Every B cell has surface receptors that can
recognize a specific set of foreign antigens (proteins
80 found on the surfaces of foreign cells and viruses).
B cells can be "activated" in one of two ways: either
they can come into contact with a foreign antigen
that can bind to the B cell surface receptors, or they
can engulf a pathogen, displaying its antigens on
85 the B cell surface much as a macrophage would.

B and T cells each have unique cell receptors.
That means that almost every one of the several billion B and T cells in the body is capable of responding to a slightly different foreign antigen. When
90 a particular B or T cell gets activated, it begins to
divide rapidly to produce identical clones.

In the case of B cells, these clones will all produce antibodies of the same structure, capable of
responding to the same invading antigens. B cell
95 clones are known as plasma B cells and can produce
thousands of antibody molecules per second as
long as they live.

Questions 31–33 ask about Passage A.

---

31. In line 17, the author mentions peristalsis in
order to:

  A. describe the functioning of the
      stomach.

  B. define cilia.

  C. give an example of a defense against
      infection.

  D. identify a specific pH range.

32. Which specific characteristic of macrophages
often results in a more intensive immune response?

  F. The specific immune system detects
      the pathogens that the macrophage is
      engulfing.

  G. Macrophages are antigen-presenting cells.

  H. Macrophages will pass "non-self" proteins
      to the specific immune system division.

  J. Foreign particles are digested within mac-
      rophage lysosomes.

33. According to the passage, neutrophils:

  A. may cause people to be more susceptible
      to disease.

  B. are similar to macrophages because they
      engulf foreign material.

  C. display non-self proteins on their cell
      walls as do macrophages.

  D. will always destroy themselves in battling
      pathogens.

Questions 34–36 ask about Passage B.

---

34. As it is used in line 62, the word *mediators* most
nearly means:

  F. regulators.

  G. peacemakers.

  H. instigators.

  J. intermediaries.

GO ON TO THE NEXT PAGE

35. According the passage, once a particular B cell gets activated, the cell:

    A. divides quickly to create plasma B cells.

    B. produces a foreign antigen.

    C. uses pseudopodia to destroy foreign particles.

    D. creates identical clones called neutrophils.

36. The passage describes a B cell as:

    F. a type of macrophage that can display antigens on its surface.

    G. using entirely different methods to capture foreign antigens than do macrophages.

    H. maturing in the thymus, where those that recognize "self" antigens are killed off.

    J. able to detect proteins found on the surfaces of foreign cells and viruses.

Questions 37–40 ask about both passages.

---

37. The specific immune system differs from the nonspecific immune system in that it:

    A. is more complicated.

    B. uses white blood cells.

    C. is responsible for the body's ability to become immune.

    D. does not target specific pathogens.

38. Which of the following statements provides the most accurate comparison of the passages?

    F. Passage A provides a generic overview, while Passage B provides specific details.

    G. Passage A includes nonspecific information about a concept, while Passage B provides specific information.

    H. Passage A provides information about one aspect of a system, while Passage B provides additional information about that system.

    J. Passage A provides an explanation of a process, while Passage B provides a different explanation of that same process.

39. It can be most reasonably inferred from both passages that:

    A. certain nonspecific defenses are required to occur before certain specific defenses can commence.

    B. nonspecific and specific defenses of the immune system operate independently.

    C. nonspecific defenses serve to communicate information to specific defenses.

    D. specific defenses are more important than nonspecific passages.

40. It can reasonably be assumed that both authors are writing for an audience comprised primarily of:

    F. physicians specializing in immunology.

    G. nonprofessional but interested readers.

    H. daily newspaper readers.

    J. science teachers.

IF YOU FINISH BEFORE TIME IS CALLED, YOU MAY CHECK YOUR WORK ON THIS SECTION ONLY. DO NOT TURN TO ANY OTHER SECTION IN THE TEST. | **STOP**

SCIENCE TEST

35 Minutes—40 Questions

Directions: The Science Test includes multiple passages. Each passage includes multiple questions. After reading each passage, choose the best answer and fill in the corresponding bubble on your answer sheet. You may review the passages as often as necessary.

You may NOT use a calculator on this test.

Passage I

Blood samples of equal volume were collected from five students on one day immediately after waking in the morning and one hour after a breakfast of pancakes and syrup with orange juice. The samples were then analyzed. Tables 1 and 2 show the color, mass, and sugar concentration of the blood samples taken before and after breakfast, respectively. *Sugar concentration* was calculated in milligrams per deciliter (mg/dL) as follows:

$$\text{sugar concentration (mg/dL)} = \frac{\text{mass of sugars(mg)}}{\text{volume of blood(dL)}}$$

The normal range for blood sugar concentration is 90 mg/dL–120 mg/dL.

Table 1			
Before-breakfast blood samples			
Student	Color*	Mass(g)	Sugar concentration (mg/dL)
A	9	1.067	116
B	4	1.049	93
C	3	1.051	94
D	6	1.058	108
E	7	1.064	112

*Note: Color values were assigned according to the following scale: 0 = pale red; 10 = dark red

Table 2			
After-breakfast blood samples			
Student	Color*	Mass(g)	Sugar concentration (mg/dL)
A	8	1.069	119
B	5	1.051	96
C	4	1.055	102
D	6	1.060	110
E	7	1.066	115

*Note: Color values were assigned according to the following scale: 0 = pale red; 10 = dark red

GO ON TO THE NEXT PAGE

1. Based on the information presented in the passage, which of the following blood samples most likely had the highest water content per milliliter?

   A. The before-breakfast blood sample from Student A

   B. The before-breakfast blood sample from Student B

   C. The after-breakfast blood sample from Student C

   D. The after-breakfast blood sample from Student D

2. Do the data in Tables 1 and 2 support the conclusion that as the mass of a given volume of blood decreases, blood color darkens?

   F. Yes, because blood samples with the lowest masses had lower color values.

   G. Yes, because blood samples with the lowest masses had higher color values.

   H. No, because blood samples with the lowest masses had lower color values.

   J. No, because blood samples with the lowest masses had higher color values.

3. Based on the results provided, as the sugar concentration of a given volume of blood increases, the mass of that volume of blood:

   A. increases, then decreases.

   B. decreases, then increases.

   C. increases only.

   D. decreases only.

4. One of the five students had a cold on the day the blood samples were collected. Given that the sugar concentration of blood tends to increase during periods of illness, the student with a cold was most likely:

   F. Student A.

   G. Student B.

   H. Student C.

   J. Student D.

5. A volume of 0.5 mL from which of the following blood samples would weigh the most?

   A. The before-breakfast blood sample from Student B

   B. The before-breakfast blood sample from Student D

   C. The after-breakfast blood sample from Student C

   D. The after-breakfast blood sample from Student E

6. What is the positive difference in mass, in milligrams, between the before and after samples from Student C ?

   F. 0.000004

   G. 0.004

   H. 0.04

   J. 4.0

GO ON TO THE NEXT PAGE

Passage II

The following experiments were performed to study the effects of adding various amounts of a *solute* (a substance that is dissolved in a solution) on the boiling points and freezing points of two different *solvents* (substances that dissolve other substances). The two solvents, isopropyl alcohol (IPA) and acetone, boil at 108°C and 56°C, respectively, and freeze at −88°C and −95°C, respectively, at standard atmospheric pressure.

Experiment 1

A student dissolved 0.05 moles of potassium chloride (KCl) in 200 g of IPA. Each mole of KCl produces 2 moles of solute particles: 1 mole of potassium ions (K^+) and 1 mole of chloride ions (Cl^-) in solution. After the KCl dissolved, the boiling point of the solution was determined. This procedure was repeated, dissolving different amounts of KCl in IPA and acetone (using 200 g of solvent for each solution). The results are shown in Table 1.

Table 1			
Solution	Solvent	Amount of KCl added (moles)	Boiling point (°C)
1	IPA	0.05	109.5
2	IPA	0.1	111.2
3	IPA	0.2	114.4
4	IPA	0.4	119.7
5	acetone	0.05	56.4
6	acetone	0.1	56.8
7	acetone	0.2	57.9
8	acetone	0.4	59.2

Note: Boiling points were measured at standard atmospheric pressure.

Experiment 2

A student dissolved 0.05 moles of KCl in 200 g of IPA. After the KCl dissolved, the freezing point of the solution was determined. The procedure was repeated using various amounts of KCl. The results are shown in Table 2.

Table 2		
Solution	Amount of KCl added (moles)	Freezing point (°C)
9	0.05	−88.5
10	0.1	−89.0
11	0.2	−90.0
12	0.4	−92.0

Note: Freezing points were measured at standard atmospheric pressure.

7. A solution containing 200 g of IPA and an unknown amount of KCl freezes at −93.0°C. Based on the results of Experiment 2, the number of moles of KCl dissolved in the solution is closest to:

   A. 0.4.
   B. 0.5.
   C. 0.6.
   D. 0.7.

8. Which of the following factors was NOT directly controlled by the student in Experiment 2 ?

   F. The substance added to the IPA
   G. The amount of IPA used
   H. The amount of solute added to the IPA
   J. The freezing points of the IPA solutions

GO ON TO THE NEXT PAGE

9. From the results of Experiment 2, which of the following statements most accurately reflects the effect of the number of solute particles dissolved in IPA on the freezing point of a solution?

   A. The number of solute particles produced does not affect the freezing point.

   B. The more solute particles present, the higher the freezing point will be.

   C. The more solute particles present, the lower the freezing point will be.

   D. No hypothesis can be made because only one solute was tested.

10. According to the results of Experiments 1 and 2, which of the following conclusions can be made about the changes in the boiling point and freezing point of IPA solutions when 0.4 moles of KCl are added to 200 g of IPA ? The boiling point is:

   F. raised more than the freezing point is lowered.

   G. raised less than the freezing point is raised.

   H. lowered more than the freezing point is lowered.

   J. lowered less than the freezing point is raised.

11. Based on the results of Experiment 1, as the number of potassium particles and chloride particles in 200 g of IPA increased, the boiling point of the solution:

   A. increased only.

   B. decreased only.

   C. increased, then decreased.

   D. remained the same.

12. $MgCl_2$ produces 3 moles of solute particles per mole when dissolved. Experiment 1 was repeated using a solution containing 200 g of IPA and 0.2 moles of $MgCl_2$. Assuming that $MgCl_2$ has the same effect on the boiling point of IPA as does KCl per particle produced when dissolved, the boiling point of the solution would most likely be:

   F. between 109.5°C and 111.2°C.

   G. between 111.2°C and 114.4°C.

   H. between 114.4°C and 119.7°C.

   J. above 119.7°C.

13. Based on the relationship between moles and boiling point in Table 1 and the trend with the freezing point of IPA in Table 2, which value is the best approximation of the freezing point, in °C, for acetone when 0.1 moles of KCl are added?

   A. −88.5

   B. −89.0

   C. −95.0

   D. −95.5

GO ON TO THE NEXT PAGE

Passage III

The study of carbon isotopes present in an archaeological sample can allow researchers to approximate the age of the sample. To do this, the ratio of the isotopes ^{14}C and ^{12}C in a sample of formerly living tissue, such as skeletal remains, is compared to the $^{14}C/^{12}C$ ratio in a sample of air from Earth's *biosphere*. The biosphere is the layer of the atmosphere closest to Earth's surface, in which living organisms constantly exchange carbon isotopes with the environment. The comparison of a sample's ratio to that of the biosphere is called the *C-14 index* ($\delta\,^{14}C$). The $\delta\,^{14}C$ is calculated using the following formula:

$$\delta\,^{14}C = \frac{\left(^{14}C/^{12}C\right)_{biosphere} - \left(^{14}C/^{12}C\right)_{sample}}{\left(^{14}C/^{12}C\right)_{biosphere}} \times 100$$

Scientists conducted 3 studies to examine the C-14 index of human remains excavated from sites in Mexico and Mali in order to learn more about the ancient civilizations that once existed in those locations.

Study 1

Human remains from 10 different tombs throughout Mexico were examined, and the average C-14 index was calculated for each tomb. Figure 1 shows a comparison between the calculated values of $\delta\,^{14}C$ and the ages of the remains as determined by other methods.

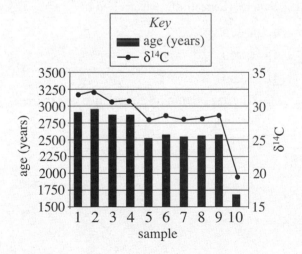

Figure 1

Study 2

The remains from a different archaeological site in Mexico were organized according to the depth beneath the surface from which they were excavated. Since layers of soil and rock were deposited at a known rate at this location, each depth corresponded to a different sample age. In total, 20 m of earth represented the last 11,000 years of soil and rock accumulation. The calculated values of $\delta\,^{14}C$ for samples taken from different depths are shown in Figure 2.

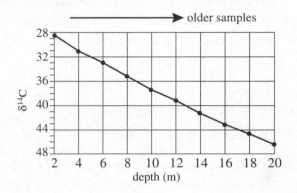

Figure 2

Study 3

The procedures of Study 2 were repeated for samples excavated from an archaeological site in Mali in western Africa. The past 11,000 years of soil and rock accumulation was represented by 40 m of depth. The calculated values of $\delta\,^{14}C$ for the samples are shown in Figure 3.

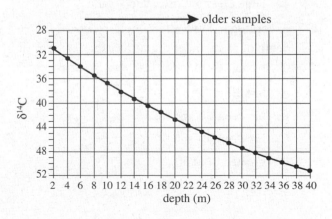

Figure 3

GO ON TO THE NEXT PAGE

14. According to Study 1, average δ ^{14}C values for the samples from Mexico were closest for which of the following pairs of tombs?

F. Tomb 2 and Tomb 3

G. Tomb 4 and Tomb 5

H. Tomb 5 and Tomb 10

J. Tomb 6 and Tomb 9

15. According to Study 1, which of the following best describes the relationship between the average C-14 index and the ages of the samples from Mexico? As the ages of the samples increased, the average δ ^{14}C of the samples:

A. increased only.

B. decreased only.

C. increased, then decreased.

D. decreased, then increased.

16. Which of the following statements best describes why Mexico and Mali were chosen as locations for these studies? The locations had to have:

F. sample ages greater than 2,000 years for all tomb sites.

G. sites over which a significant amount of soil and rock was deposited over the last 11,000 years.

H. several sites at which little soil and rock was deposited over the last 11,000 years.

J. large areas of undeveloped land.

17. According to Study 2, a sample excavated from a depth of 25 m under the surface in Mexico most likely had a C-14 index that was:

A. less than 30.

B. between 30 and 40.

C. between 40 and 50.

D. greater than 50.

18. According to Studies 2 and 3, 11,000 years of soil and rock accumulation was represented by 20 m of earth in Mexico and 40 m of earth in Mali. Which of the following statements best explains why the relationships between time and depth were different? The average rate of soil and rock accumulation over that time period in Mali:

F. was less than the rate in Mexico.

G. was the same as the rate in Mexico.

H. was greater than the rate in Mexico.

J. could not be determined in comparison with the rate in Mexico.

19. According to the information provided, a sample that has a calculated δ ^{14}C of zero must have a ^{14}C/^{12}C ratio that compares in which of the following ways to the ^{14}C/^{12}C ratio of the biosphere? The sample's ^{14}C/^{12}C ratio is:

A. 1/4 of the ^{14}C/^{12}C ratio of the biosphere.

B. 1/2 of the ^{14}C/^{12}C ratio of the biosphere.

C. the same as the ^{14}C/^{12}C ratio of the biosphere.

D. twice as large as the ^{14}C/^{12}C ratio of the biosphere.

20. What is the approximate age, in years, of a sample from the Mexican tomb that was unearthed 5 meters beneath the surface?

F. 2,600

G. 2,900

H. 3,200

J. The age can not be determined due to the decomposition of the soil.

GO ON TO THE NEXT PAGE

Passage IV

The last of the dinosaurs went extinct approximately 65 million years ago. Two scientists present their hypotheses about events that may have caused this extinction.

Scientist 1

The extinction of the dinosaurs was caused by a meteorite of about 10 km in diameter that struck Earth at a location along what is now the northwestern coast of the Yucatan Peninsula in Mexico. The initial impact incinerated everything on Earth's surface within a radius of approximately 500 km from the point of impact. The resulting shock wave set massive fires and generated tidal waves that caused destruction across much larger distances.

In addition, trillions of tons of debris were thrown into the air, blocking light from the sun and causing a significant decrease in global temperatures. The worldwide fires and the large amounts of CO_2 they released later resulted in an equally significant increase in temperatures and caused chemical reactions that led to downpours of acid rain.

Scientist 2

The extinction of the dinosaurs was caused by an extended period of widespread volcanic activity. Volcanic eruptions around the world introduced large amounts of soot into the atmosphere, causing dramatic climatic changes. Combined with the excess CO_2 released by fires ignited by lava flows, the soot in the atmosphere led to the production of acid rain. Before long, sources of food and water became too toxic for the dinosaurs.

The volcanoes also expelled huge amounts of sulfates (SO_4) into the atmosphere; the mixing of sulfates with water vapor caused more acid rain. Moreover, SO_4 in the atmosphere led to a breakdown of the ozone layer, allowing high levels of ultraviolet radiation to reach the surface.

21. Which of the following statements best explains why Scientist 1 mentions acid rain?

    A. Acid rain is beneficial to many living things.

    B. Acid rain is harmful to many living things.

    C. Acid rain helps create CO_2 in the atmosphere.

    D. Acid rain results in fires.

22. Suppose that sulfates in the atmosphere help to reflect solar radiation back into space, resulting in a reduction of Earth's surface temperature. Based on the passage, this new information would most likely weaken the viewpoint(s) of:

    F. Scientist 1.

    G. Scientist 2.

    H. both Scientist 1 and Scientist 2.

    J. neither Scientist 1 nor Scientist 2.

23. Scientist 2 would most likely agree that the ozone layer present in today's atmosphere is maintained, at least in part, by:

    A. frequent meteor showers.

    B. periodically active volcanoes.

    C. the high level of CO_2 in the atmosphere.

    D. the low level of SO_4 in the atmosphere.

24. Both scientists would most likely agree that worldwide climate changes occurred partially as a result of:

    F. the impact of a meteorite.

    G. tidal waves.

    H. the presence of high levels of CO_2 in the atmosphere.

    J. the presence of high levels of SO_4 in the atmosphere.

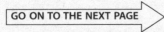

GO ON TO THE NEXT PAGE

Practice Test 2

25. According to the information provided, radio-active dating of fragments of the meteorite described by Scientist 1 should show the fragments to be about how many million years old?

    A. 2

    B. 10

    C. 50

    D. 65

26. Sulfates are produced in large amounts by a variety of industrial processes. Scientist 2 would most likely predict that in an area of many sulfate-producing industries, if the industries were to alter their processes so that sulfates were no longer produced, the climatic effect in that area would be an increase in the:

    F. average pH of rainfall.

    G. amount of rainfall.

    H. acidity of rainfall.

    J. amount of ultraviolet radiation reaching Earth's surface.

27. *Inorganic sulfates*, such as barium sulfate ($BaSO_4$), are substances that are formed when minerals combine with sulfates in a high-temperature environment. If scientists found that large amounts of inorganic sulfates had formed about 65 million years ago, this discovery would most likely support the viewpoint(s) of:

    A. Scientist 1.

    B. Scientist 2.

    C. both Scientist 1 and Scientist 2.

    D. neither Scientist 1 nor Scientist 2.

GO ON TO THE NEXT PAGE

Passage V

Under certain conditions, mixtures of hydrogen and chlorine will form hydrochloric acid (HCl). In their chemistry class, students performed the following experiments to study how HCl forms.

Experiment 1

A clear, thick-walled gas syringe was filled with 20 mL of hydrogen gas (H_2) and 20 mL of chlorine gas (Cl_2), as shown in Diagram 1.

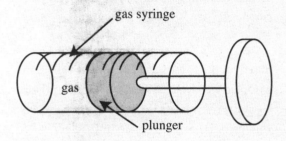

Diagram 1

The syringe's plunger was then locked into place, and the syringe was covered in a black cloth. After a few minutes, the cloth was removed and an ultraviolet lightbulb was flashed to illuminate the gas briefly from close range. A reaction occurred, forming droplets of HCl. The plunger was then released, and the final volume of gas was recorded after the system was allowed to adjust to room temperature. The composition of the remaining gas, if any, was analyzed. The procedure was repeated with different gas volumes, and the results were recorded in Table 1.

Table 1				
	Volume (mL)			
Trial	Initial H_2	Initial Cl_2	Final H_2	Final Cl_2
1	20	20	0	0
2	20	30	0	10
3	20	40	0	20
4	10	40	0	30
5	40	40	0	0
6	30	20	10	0

Since equal numbers of different gas molecules are known to occupy equal volumes at the same pressure and temperature, the students proposed the following equation:

$$H_2 + Cl_2 \rightarrow 2\ HCl$$

Experiment 2

As shown in Diagram 2, streams of silicon tetrachloride ($SiCl_4$) and hydrogen (H_2) gases were allowed to mix in a high-temperature furnace, producing HCl vapor and solid Si. The vapor was released into a cooler chamber, where it condensed to form liquid HCl.

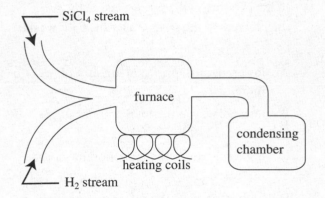

Diagram 2

The changes in mass of the contents of the furnace and condensing chamber were used to calculate the masses of $SiCl_4$ and H_2 reacted and the mass of HCl formed. It was determined that 4 molecules of HCl were produced for every 1 molecule of $SiCl_4$ and every 2 molecules of H_2 reacted:

$$SiCl_4 + 2\ H_2 \rightarrow Si + 4\ HCl$$

GO ON TO THE NEXT PAGE

28. When sodium hydroxide (NaOH) and HCl are combined, both compounds decompose, and sodium chloride (NaCl) and H_2O are formed. Which of the following correctly represents this reaction?

   F. $NaCl + H_2O \rightarrow NaOH + HCl$

   G. $NaCl + 2 H_2O \rightarrow NaOH + HCl$

   H. $NaOH + HCl \rightarrow NaCl + H_2O$

   J. $NaOH + HCl \rightarrow NaCl + 2 H_2O$

29. In Trial 5 of Experiment 1, immediately after the reaction began but before the syringe plunger was released, one would predict that, compared to the pressure in the syringe before the flash, the pressure in the syringe after the flash would be:

   A. lower, because the total amount of gas increased.

   B. lower, because the total amount of gas decreased.

   C. higher, because the total amount of gas increased.

   D. higher, because the total amount of gas decreased.

30. If 10 mL of H_2 and 20 mL of Cl_2 were reacted using the procedure from Experiment 1, the final volume of Cl_2 would most likely be:

   F. 0 mL.

   G. 5 mL.

   H. 10 mL.

   J. 20 mL.

31. In Experiment 1, which of the following assumptions about the chemical reactions were made before the final measurements were taken?

   A. Each reaction had run to completion.

   B. Excess Cl_2 must be present for HCl to form.

   C. HCl vapor is not absorbed by solid Si.

   D. $SiCl_4$ and H_2 will only react when heated.

32. When oxygen gas (O_2) is reacted with H_2 under certain conditions, the following reaction occurs:

$$2 H_2 + O_2 \rightarrow 2 H_2O$$

Based on the results of Experiment 1, if 10 mL of O_2 were completely reacted with 25 mL of H_2 at the same pressure and temperature, what volume of H_2 would remain unreacted?

   F. 0 mL

   G. 5 mL

   H. 10 mL

   J. 15 mL

33. Which of the following events would NOT cause an error in interpreting the results of Experiment 2 ?

   A. Other reactions occurring between $SiCl_4$ and H_2 that produced different products

   B. HCl condensing before it reached the condensing chamber

   C. Using $SiCl_4$ contaminated with nonreactive impurities

   D. Using H_2 contaminated with reactive impurities

34. In which trial is Cl_2 a limiting reagent?

   F. Trial 2

   G. Trial 3

   H. Trial 4

   J. Trial 6

GO ON TO THE NEXT PAGE

Passage VI

A wooden box was held in place on a plastic track a distance, d_0, from one end of the track, which was inclined at an angle, θ, above the floor, as shown in Diagram 1.

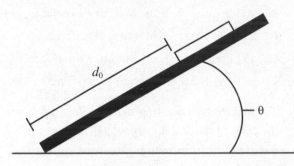

Diagram 1

When the box was released, it slid down the plane, as shown in Diagram 2.

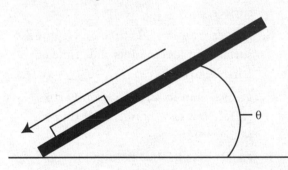

Diagram 2

The *slide time* was the time required for the leading face of the box to reach the end of the track. The slide time is graphed in Figure 1 for a fixed θ and various values of d_0 on the surfaces of Neptune, Earth, and Mercury. The slide time is graphed in Figure 2 for $d_0 = 60$ cm and various values of θ on the same three surfaces. The acceleration due to gravity on these planets' surfaces is shown in Table 1.

Table 1	
Planet	Acceleration due to gravity on surface of planet (m/sec^2)
Neptune	13.3
Earth	9.8
Mercury	3.6

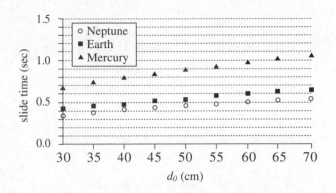

Figure 1

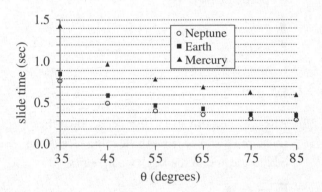

Figure 2

GO ON TO THE NEXT PAGE

35. Which pair of values for θ produce slide times that are approximately equal for Earth and Mercury, respectively?

    A. 45° and 85°

    B. 35° and 65°

    C. 45° and 55°

    D. 35° and 55°

36. Based on Figure 1, if d_0 were 25 cm, the slide time on Mercury would be closest to:

    F. 0.3 sec.

    G. 0.4 sec.

    H. 0.6 sec.

    J. 1.1 sec.

37. According to Figure 2, the box with $d_0 = 60$ cm will have a slide time on Mercury of 1.2 sec if θ is approximately:

    A. 27°.

    B. 30°.

    C. 38°.

    D. 51°.

38. After the box traveled a distance x down the track, the distance from the leading face of the box to the end of the track would equal:

    F. $d_0 - x$.

    G. $d_0 + x$.

    H. d_0.

    J. x.

39. Suppose the box represented in Figure 2 has a 0.8 second slide time on Mercury's surface. For the same box released from the same d_0 to have a 0.8 second slide time on Earth's surface, θ on Earth's surface would have to be approximately:

    A. 23° greater than on Mercury's surface.

    B. 23° less than on Mercury's surface.

    C. 17° greater than on Mercury's surface.

    D. 17° less than on Mercury's surface.

40. The acceleration due to gravity on the surface of the planet Jupiter is approximately 24.9 m/sec². Based on the information presented in the passage, a box's slide time on Jupiter's surface, for a given θ and a given d_0, would be:

    F. less than its slide time on Neptune's surface.

    G. greater than its slide time on Neptune's surface but less than its slide time on Earth's surface.

    H. greater than its slide time on Earth's surface but less than its slide time on Mercury's surface.

    J. greater than its slide time on Mercury's surface.

YOU FINISH BEFORE TIME IS CALLED, YOU MAY CHECK YOUR WORK ON THIS SECTION ONLY. DO NOT TURN TO ANY OTHER SECTION IN THE TEST. **STOP**

WRITING TEST

40 Minutes—1 Question

Directions: The essay is used to evaluate your writing skills. You will have **40 minutes** to review the prompt and plan and write an essay in English. Before you begin, read everything in this test booklet carefully to make sure you understand the task.

Your essay will be judged based on the evidence it provides of your ability to do the following:

- Assert your own perspective on a complex issue and evaluate the relationship between your perspective and at least one other perspective

- Use reasoning and evidence to refine and justify your ideas

- Present your ideas in an organized way

- Convey your ideas effectively using standard written English

Write your essay on the lined essay pages in the answer booklet. All writing on those lined pages will be scored. Use the unlined pages in this test booklet to plan your essay. Your work on these unlined pages will not be scored.

Put your pencil down as soon as time is called.

DO NOT OPEN THIS BOOKLET UNTIL TOLD TO DO SO.

GO ON TO THE NEXT PAGE

Student Engagement

Studies show that students not only retain more information but also enjoy learning more when they actively participate in the classroom. Teachers therefore strive to optimize engagement to foster a positive, effective instructional environment. In an effort to increase student interaction in the high school classroom, some educators argue that curriculum should take into account the interests and suggestions of students. Since teachers cannot allow students to choose every aspect of a lesson, is it worth the time and effort to actively seek relevant student feedback? As high schools aim to improve the quality of the education they offer to students, student opinion may prove to be valuable.

Read and carefully consider these perspectives. Each discusses the relevance of student feedback in lesson planning.

Perspective One	Perspective Two	Perspective Three
Many colleges require students to complete a course survey before they are eligible to receive their semester grades. Colleges use students' responses to evaluate course materials to ensure quality education. High schools would benefit from implementing a similar system of regular feedback on classroom lesson plans by students.	Students are not qualified to provide insight regarding lesson planning or curriculum design. Improving the quality of education is the responsibility of educators, and they are rightfully in charge of making effective changes.	Many school districts evaluate teachers using students' test scores and by conducting in-classroom observations. Information gathered from student surveys could not only inform lesson design, but also provide another source of evaluation by which to measure teacher effectiveness.

Essay Task

Write a clear, well-reasoned essay evaluating multiple perspectives on student feedback in lesson planning. In your essay, be sure to:

- Assert your own perspective on the issue and evaluate the relationship between your perspective and at least one other perspective

- Use reasoning and evidence to refine and justify your ideas

- Present your ideas in an organized way

- Convey your ideas effectively using standard written English

Your perspective may be fully, somewhat, or not at all in agreement with one or more of the three perspectives in the prompt.

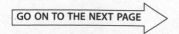
GO ON TO THE NEXT PAGE

Practice Test 2

Planning Your Essay

These pages are not scored.

Use the space below to brainstorm and plan your essay. Consider the following as you think about the prompt:

- Strengths and weaknesses of the three perspectives in the prompt
  - What observations do they offer, and what do they overlook?
  - Why are they persuasive or why are they not persuasive?
- Your own background and identity
  - What is your perspective on this issue, and what are its strengths and weaknesses?
  - What evidence will you use in your essay?

GO ON TO THE NEXT PAGE

GO ON TO THE NEXT PAGE

Practice Test 2

GO ON TO THE NEXT PAGE

PRACTICE TEST 2 ANSWER KEY
ENGLISH TEST

1. **D**	16. **G**	31. **D**	46. **H**	61. **B**
2. **G**	17. **A**	32. **J**	47. **A**	62. **F**
3. **C**	18. **J**	33. **B**	48. **G**	63. **D**
4. **J**	19. **C**	34. **H**	49. **B**	64. **G**
5. **B**	20. **F**	35. **D**	50. **G**	65. **B**
6. **G**	21. **B**	36. **H**	51. **B**	66. **J**
7. **D**	22. **J**	37. **B**	52. **H**	67. **C**
8. **J**	23. **B**	38. **J**	53. **C**	68. **H**
9. **B**	24. **F**	39. **A**	54. **J**	69. **B**
10. **H**	25. **C**	40. **G**	55. **C**	70. **J**
11. **C**	26. **J**	41. **C**	56. **J**	71. **B**
12. **J**	27. **B**	42. **J**	57. **C**	72. **F**
13. **A**	28. **G**	43. **C**	58. **F**	73. **B**
14. **F**	29. **C**	44. **J**	59. **D**	74. **J**
15. **D**	30. **F**	45. **D**	60. **F**	75. **B**

MATHEMATICS TEST

1. **A**	13. **D**	25. **D**	37. **B**	49. **C**
2. **J**	14. **K**	26. **J**	38. **J**	50. **F**
3. **A**	15. **D**	27. **C**	39. **A**	51. **C**
4. **G**	16. **F**	28. **H**	40. **K**	52. **F**
5. **B**	17. **E**	29. **E**	41. **A**	53. **B**
6. **J**	18. **K**	30. **H**	42. **G**	54. **H**
7. **C**	19. **D**	31. **A**	43. **E**	55. **B**
8. **G**	20. **G**	32. **J**	44. **K**	56. **K**
9. **D**	21. **B**	33. **B**	45. **E**	57. **B**
10. **F**	22. **K**	34. **K**	46. **F**	58. **J**
11. **B**	23. **A**	35. **D**	47. **E**	59. **C**
12. **G**	24. **J**	36. **K**	48. **G**	60. **H**

READING TEST

1. **B**	9. **C**	17. **C**	25. **D**	33. **B**
2. **G**	10. **G**	18. **G**	26. **F**	34. **J**
3. **B**	11. **B**	19. **A**	27. **A**	35. **A**
4. **G**	12. **G**	20. **H**	28. **G**	36. **J**
5. **C**	13. **C**	21. **A**	29. **B**	37. **C**
6. **G**	14. **G**	22. **J**	30. **F**	38. **H**
7. **C**	15. **A**	23. **B**	31. **C**	39. **A**
8. **J**	16. **G**	24. **H**	32. **G**	40. **G**

SCIENCE TEST

1. **B**	9. **C**	17. **D**	25. **D**	33. **C**
2. **H**	10. **F**	18. **H**	26. **F**	34. **J**
3. **C**	11. **A**	19. **C**	27. **B**	35. **A**
4. **F**	12. **H**	20. **G**	28. **H**	36. **H**
5. **D**	13. **D**	21. **B**	29. **B**	37. **C**
6. **J**	14. **J**	22. **G**	30. **H**	38. **F**
7. **B**	15. **A**	23. **D**	31. **A**	39. **D**
8. **J**	16. **G**	24. **H**	32. **G**	40. **F**

ANSWERS AND EXPLANATIONS

ENGLISH TEST

Passage I

1. D   Difficulty: Medium

Category: Punctuation

Getting to the Answer: A comma is needed to set off the introductory phrase, so choice A cannot be correct. Choice B creates a sentence fragment, and the pronoun *it* in C does not match the subject of the sentence, Duke Ellington.

2. G   Difficulty: Low

Category: Sentence Structure and Formation

Getting to the Answer: The whole passage is in past tense, and there is no reason why this verb should not be in past tense as well. Also, the part of the sentence on the other side of the semicolon gives you a big clue by using *paid*. Choice (G) is correct.

3. C   Difficulty: Medium

Category: Punctuation

Getting to the Answer: The colon is used incorrectly in the original sentence, and B does not solve the problem. Choice D is unnecessarily wordy. Therefore, choice (C) is correct.

4. J   Difficulty: High

Category: Punctuation

Getting to the Answer: Commas are needed between items in a series, so eliminate F and G. A comma is also needed to set off the introductory phrase, so eliminate H. Choice (J) is therefore correct.

5. B   Difficulty: Medium

Category: Usage

Getting to the Answer: In order to figure out the appropriate pronoun, identify the noun to which the pronoun

refers. The only possible corresponding noun is *Ellington*; therefore, (B) is the correct answer.

6. G   Difficulty: High

Category: Sentence Structure and Formation

Getting to the Answer: "As a teenager in Washington" is not a complete sentence, so F is incorrect. Choice H does not make sense, and J is incorrect because the comma is unnecessary. Therefore, (G) is correct.

7. D   Difficulty: Medium

Category: Usage

Getting to the Answer: The word *then* should be *than*—(D) makes this correction.

8. J   Difficulty: Low

Category: Knowledge of Language / Concision

Getting to the Answer: Even though the piano teacher's name is mentioned in the preceding sentence, more information about her name is unnecessary, and this sentence is not relevant to the passage. Therefore, choice (J) is correct.

9. B   Difficulty: Medium

Category: Organization, Unity, and Cohesion / Transitions

Getting to the Answer: There is a contrast between Ellington's not being a good pianist and his hearing about the opportunities for musicians in New York. The correct contrast is established by (B).

10. H   Difficulty: Medium

Category: Knowledge of Language / Concision

Getting to the Answer: *Awaited* and *were there for* mean the same thing, so one part of the underlined portion should be deleted—that eliminates F and G. Choice J is also unnecessarily wordy. Therefore, (H) is correct.

11. C   Difficulty: Medium

Category: Sentence Structure and Formation

Getting to the Answer: Eliminate A because, as written, the sentence is a run-on. Choice (C) correctly inserts a FANBOYS conjunction (in this case, the word *but*) after the comma to correct the run-on sentence. Choice B replaces the comma with the word *but*, which doesn't fix the run-on, and D creates a fragment.

12. J   Difficulty: Medium

Category: Usage

Getting to the Answer: The subject of the sentence is the Cotton Club, so choices with the pronoun *he*—F and G—should be eliminated. Choice H creates a sentence fragment. Choice (J) is correct.

13. A   Difficulty: Low

Category: Topic Development / Writer's Purpose

Getting to the Answer: This list of songs follows a description of Ellington's early musical career, so (A) is correct. The songs do not contradict anything, so eliminate B. The names of the songs themselves do not illustrate complexity; therefore, C is incorrect. This part of the paragraph is no longer about the Cotton Club, so eliminate D.

14. F   Difficulty: Medium

Category: Topic Development / Writer's Purpose

Getting to the Answer: The last paragraph of the essay lists Ellington's accomplishments. Choice (F) is the only answer choice that makes sense.

15. D   Difficulty: High

Category: Organization, Unity, and Cohesion / Passage Organization

Getting to the Answer: Paragraph 4 is the only paragraph that covers elements of Ellington's music. The logical place for the insertion of this sentence that mentions both *fun* and *seriousness* is after the sentence that claims his music appealed both to those seeking *a good time* and *good music*.

Passage II

16. G   Difficulty: Medium

Category: Usage

Getting to the Answer: The subject is *animals*, so a plural pronoun is needed. Choice F is a singular pronoun, H is a contraction, and J uses *there* instead of *their*. Choice (G) correctly uses the plural pronoun *their*.

17. A   Difficulty: Medium

Category: Punctuation

Getting to the Answer: The comma is needed to set off the second clause from the first, so eliminate B and D. Choice C incorrectly uses a colon. Choice (A) is correct.

18. J   Difficulty: High

Category: Punctuation

Getting to the Answer: The phrase "a member of the weasel family" is a nonessential clause and should be set off by commas, so (J) is correct. Choice F is incorrect because it is missing a necessary comma. Choices G and H are incorrect because they create sentence fragments.

19. C   Difficulty: Medium

Category: Usage

Getting to the Answer: *Having changed* is the incorrect verb tense. Ermines are nonhuman, so B is incorrect. Choice (C) uses *that* correctly. The whole passage is in present tense, so eliminate D because it is in past tense.

20. F   Difficulty: Medium

Category: Sentence Structure and Formation

Getting to the Answer: Choose the most logical order of the words. Choice (F) makes the most sense.

21. B   Difficulty: Medium

Category: Usage

Getting to the Answer: The sentence is describing just one skunk, so the singular *visibility* is correct; eliminate A and D. To show singular possession, place the apostrophe between the noun and the letter *s*, with the resulting word being *skunk's*. Choice (B) is correct. Choice C shows plural possession, which doesn't make sense in context.

22. J   Difficulty: Medium

Category: Sentence Structure and Formation

Getting to the Answer: "By distinguishing itself from other animals" is a sentence fragment. These words make sense as an introductory phrase and should therefore be set off by a comma. Choice (J) is the only choice that accomplishes this concisely.

23. B   Difficulty: Low

Category: Knowledge of Language / Concision

Getting to the Answer: The unnecessary phrase "the question is" should be eliminated. Choice (B) is the simplest and most correct way to phrase the question.

24. F   Difficulty: High

Category: Usage

Getting to the Answer: The investigating has occurred in the past, and it is still occurring. Therefore, the present perfect progressive tense, as used in (F), is correct. Choices G and H only refer to the past, and J refers only to the present.

25. C   Difficulty: Medium

Category: Organization, Unity, and Cohesion / Transitions

Getting to the Answer: The previous sentence speaks of special glands, but this sentence says that some animals do not have these glands. This is a contrast, and *however*, (C), sets it up correctly.

26. J   Difficulty: Low

Category: Knowledge of Language / Concision

Getting to the Answer: *Remains* and *endures as* mean the same thing, so the correct choice will eliminate one of them. Choice (J) does just that.

27. B   Difficulty: Low

Category: Sentence Structure and Formation

Getting to the Answer: The pronoun *it* refers to the tree frog, not a background of leaves. Choice (B) fixes this modifier error by placing "the tree frog" after the modifying phrase.

28. G   Difficulty: Medium

Category: Knowledge of Language / Concision

Getting to the Answer: The information pertains to the paragraph's topic, so eliminate J. Choice (G) is a simple and logical way of rephrasing all of the excess words.

29. C   Difficulty: High

Category: Organization, Unity, and Cohesion / Passage Organization

Getting to the Answer: Paragraph 4 begins with an introduction, and Paragraph 3 ends with a conclusion. Choice (C) is the only option that features this correct order.

30. F   Difficulty: Medium

Category: Topic Development / Writer's Purpose

Getting to the Answer: The author covers a range of topics in the area and uses several animals as examples, so (F) is correct. All of the other answer choices are incorrect because they contradict things that the author does in the essay.

Passage III

31. D   Difficulty: Medium

Category: Sentence Structure and Formation

Getting to the Answer: The word *and* interrupts the flow of the sentence and should be removed. Choice (D) corrects the original error and does not introduce new issues. Choices B and C delete the word *and*, but each choices creates a new error; B is unnecessarily wordy, and C creates a fragment.

32. J   Difficulty: Medium

Category: Organization, Unity, and Cohesion / Transitions

Getting to the Answer: Based on the context of the essay, a contrast transition word is needed, which matches (J). Choices F and H are cause-and-effect transitions, and G is a continuation transition.

33. B   Difficulty: High

Category: Sentence Structure and Formation

Getting to the Answer: The sentences on both sides of the period are fragments. The best way to fix this mistake is to simply combine the sentences as (B) does.

34. H   Difficulty: High

Category: Topic Development / Supporting Material

Getting to the Answer: The first paragraph states that Europeans first learned of chocolate because of Cortés's exploration of Mexico in 1519, and the second paragraph provides additional information about how the cacao beans traveled to Europe. Choice (H) provides information about why Cortés was in Mexico and how it is relevant to the history of chocolate. Choices F, G, and J provide information about Cortés's exploration of Mexico but do not mention chocolate at all.

35. D   Difficulty: Medium

Category: Organization, Unity, and Cohesion / Transitions

Getting to the Answer: Based on the context, a continuation transition is needed: because the drink was desirable, it became popular. Choice (D) correctly includes a continuation transition and makes sense in context. Eliminate A and C because they are contrast transitions. Choice B is incorrect because it is redundant to use the word *soon* twice in the same sentence.

36. H   Difficulty: Medium

Category: Sentence Structure and Formation

Getting to the Answer: "Over the next century" is an introductory phrase and should be set off by a comma. Choices (H) and J add the comma, but J also adds unnecessary words.

37. B   Difficulty: Medium

Category: Topic Development / Supporting Material

Getting to the Answer: This description would provide new information that is pertinent to the history of chocolate, so (B) is correct. Eliminate A and C because the description would not weaken or contradict anything. It would not say anything about the author's opinion of chocolate either, so eliminate D.

38. J   Difficulty: Low

Category: Punctuation

Getting to the Answer: Commas are needed between items in a series. Choice G is incorrect because there are too many commas.

39. A   Difficulty: Medium

Category: Organization, Unity, and Cohesion / Transitions

Getting to the Answer: The sentence provides an example of the uses of chocolate worldwide. Choices B and C set up an unwarranted contrast. Choice D is not a good transition between the two sentences.

40. G   Difficulty: Medium

Category: Sentence Structure and Formation

Getting to the Answer: The word *do* is unnecessary in the sentence, especially with the presence of *nonetheless*. Choice (G) is the most concise statement of the information.

41. C   Difficulty: Medium

Category: Punctuation

Getting to the Answer: The sentence is incorrect as written because the colon is not introducing a short phrase, quotation, explanation, example, or list. Eliminate B and D because they each include a colon. Choice (C) is correct.

42. J   Difficulty: Low

Category: Knowledge of Language / Concision

Getting to the Answer: Tea has nothing to do with the topic, so the sentence should be eliminated.

43. C   Difficulty: High

Category: Knowledge of Language / Ambiguity

Getting to the Answer: The sentence does not indicate what or who *It* refers to, so the sentence is unclear. Eliminate A and B because they have ambiguous pronouns. Because *Researchers say* appears earlier in the paragraph, it doesn't make sense to say that the research was conducted by just one scientist, so D is incorrect. Choice (C) corrects the ambiguity error and is logical in context.

44. J   Difficulty: Medium

Category: Topic Development / Supporting Material

Getting to the Answer: Choices F and H use language that is too formal to match the rest of the passage and do not provide appropriate conclusions for the topic. Choices G and (J) use appropriate language, but G is off-topic, focusing on cancer and heart disease prevention rather than chocolate. Choice (J) is correct.

45. D   Difficulty: Medium

Category: Topic Development / Writer's Purpose

Getting to the Answer: This essay is about only chocolate, and it does not cover any other culinary trends in history. Therefore, it would not meet the requirement. Choice (D) is correct.

Passage IV

46. H   Difficulty: Medium

Category: Usage

Getting to the Answer: Here, the verb is being used as part of a modifying phrase. Choice (H) is idiomatically correct.

47. A   Difficulty: Medium

Category: Punctuation

Getting to the Answer: Commas are needed in a series, so eliminate C. A colon is not appropriate; eliminate B. Choice D incorrectly switches to the past tense. The original punctuation, (A), is correct.

48. G   Difficulty: Medium

Category: Usage

Getting to the Answer: The form needed is the possessive of *who,* so (G) is correct.

49. B   Difficulty: Medium

Category: Usage

Getting to the Answer: This sentence is part of a list of proposed "uniform of the future" developments. The other sentences in that list use the verbs *would be* and *would become*; the correct form is (B).

50. G   Difficulty: High

Category: Topic Development / Supporting Material

Getting to the Answer: Choice (G) describes a great potential benefit of the uniform of the future. Choice J is tempting, but deep pockets are not considered a break-through technology. Choices F and H discuss information relevant to soldiers in general but do not present an additional feature of the uniform of the future.

51. B   Difficulty: Low

Category: Sentence Structure and Formation

Getting to the Answer: Be wary of sentences that begin with *to*; they are often fragments like the one here. Choice (B) is the best and most concise way to combine the two parts of the sentence.

52. H   Difficulty: Medium

Category: Knowledge of Language / Precision

Getting to the Answer: Predict that the Invisible Soldier program aims to use technology that is capable of *hiding* a soldier from most wavelengths of visible light. Choice (H) matches this prediction. Choices F, G, and J don't make sense in context; *confounding* and *obfuscating* mean confusing, and *eliminating* implies that the technology is capable of removing the soldier altogether.

53. C   Difficulty: Medium

Category: Topic Development / Writer's Purpose

Getting to the Answer: To determine the US Army's opinion of the Invisible Soldier program, look at the words used to introduce and describe it: the Army has dreamed of such a program and invested in it. So the Army's attitude is positive; eliminate the negative word *skeptical* in A and the neutral words *curious* and *detailed* in B and D, leaving *enthusiastic*, (C).

54. J   Difficulty: High

Category: Topic Development / Writer's Purpose

Getting to the Answer: In context, this paragraph offers a specific example of the more general issues raised in Paragraph 1, so (J) is correct.

55. C   Difficulty: Medium

Category: Knowledge of Language / Style and Tone

Getting to the Answer: Look for the option that maintains the essay's informative tone and clearly explains the solution being described. As written, the sentence does not clearly describe the solution; the word *something* is vague. Choice B is more specific, but the tone is too casual to match the rest of the essay. Choices (C) and D are both very specific, but D is overly formal and wordy. Choice (C) is correct.

56. J   Difficulty: Medium

Category: Sentence Structure and Formation

Getting to the Answer: As written, this is a run-on sentence, so eliminate F. To correct it, the new clause should be made subordinate by replacing the pronoun with a relative pronoun, so eliminate H. The correct form, because it follows a comma, is *which* rather than *that*, so eliminate G.

57. C   Difficulty: Medium

Category: Knowledge of Language / Precision

Getting to the Answer: The passage has a formal, technical tone. It would, therefore, be inappropriate for the author to use the highly informal expressions *you know*, or *is, like*. Eliminate A and B. Choice (C), *however, is*, is appropriate because this paragraph contrasts with the preceding one. Choice D would be appropriate if this paragraph drew a conclusion based on the prior paragraph, but it doesn't.

58. F   Difficulty: High

Category: Punctuation

Getting to the Answer: A colon is correct punctuation here because the material that follows it is an explanation of what precedes it, so (F) is correct.

59. D   Difficulty: Medium

Category: Organization, Unity, and Cohesion / Passage Organization

Getting to the Answer: Only Sentence 2 and Sentence 1 are choices for a first sentence. To put the sentences in logical order, first look for a good transition

from Paragraph 4, which discusses a problem. Sentence 1 explicitly refers to addressing the problem, so it's the better choice. Eliminate A and B. The second sentence should follow logically from Sentence 1's description of the new color-changing pixel, so your choices are Sentences 4 and 5. Sentence 4 in C refers to mirrors, which we haven't encountered before in the passage, rather than pixels, so eliminate C. That leaves us with Sentence 5 in (D), which refers to the pixels introduced in the first sentence. Choice (D) is therefore correct.

60. F   Difficulty: Medium

Category: Organization, Unity, and Cohesion / Passage Organization

Getting to the Answer: To answer this question, you need an idea of the purpose of each paragraph. Paragraph 1 introduces the "uniform of the future," Paragraph 2 the Invisible Soldier program, Paragraph 3 the program's early-stage solution, Paragraph 4 a problem with that solution, and Paragraph 5 a new advance that may solve that problem. The new sentences to be inserted do not discuss a problem with such a program. You can therefore eliminate G, H, and J. The material properly belongs in Paragraph 2, (F), because it introduces camouflage generally.

Passage V

61. B   Difficulty: Low

Category: Sentence Structure and Formation

Getting to the Answer: Choices A and C are too wordy, and D does not continue the verb tense established in the series. Choice (B) concisely and correctly phrases the sentence.

62. F   Difficulty: Medium

Category: Punctuation

Getting to the Answer: The colon in (F) is used here to dramatically introduce California. The commas in G and H do not do this well, and the separate sentence in J does not work either.

63. D **Difficulty:** Low

Category: Sentence Structure and Formation

Getting to the Answer: This paragraph is in the past tense, so the introductory sentence should be in the past tense as well. Choice (D) is correct.

64. G **Difficulty:** Medium

Category: Punctuation

Getting to the Answer: This is a long nonessential clause that should be set off by a comma—eliminate F and H. Choice J is incorrect because it unnecessarily adds more words. Choice (G) is correct.

65. B **Difficulty:** Medium

Category: Sentence Structure and Formation

Getting to the Answer: The word order is incorrect in A. Choice C creates a sentence fragment, and *did* in D is unnecessary. Therefore, (B) is correct.

66. J **Difficulty:** Medium

Category: Knowledge of Language / Precision

Getting to the Answer: You can predict that Marshall was *looking closely* at the mill's runoff when he "saw two shiny objects below the surface of the water." Choice (J) matches your prediction. The other options don't make sense in context; *probing* means physically exploring, *computing* means calculating, and *reading into* means finding an extra meaning in a word or phrase.

67. C **Difficulty:** Low

Category: Usage

Getting to the Answer: The only choice that works here is (C), which uses the correct possessive form.

68. H **Difficulty:** Medium

Category: Sentence Structure and Formation

Getting to the Answer: Choice F is a sentence fragment. Choices G and J are very awkward. Choice (H) is correct.

69. B **Difficulty:** Medium

Category: Organization, Unity, and Cohesion / Transitions

Getting to the Answer: The last sentence of the previous paragraph talks about how workers began to quit their jobs to join the gold rush. The first sentence of this paragraph magnifies this point. Choice (B) is the only logical transition.

70. J **Difficulty:** Medium

Category: Topic Development / Supporting Material

Getting to the Answer: This information is not pertinent to the gold rush back in 1849. Choice (J) is correct because it contains the correct answer, ("No"), and the correct reason.

71. B **Difficulty:** Low

Category: Knowledge of Language / Concision

Getting to the Answer: *Singularly* and *one* are redundant, so A is incorrect. Choice C is too wordy, and D is incorrect within the context of the sentence. Choice (B) is correct.

72. F **Difficulty:** Medium

Category: Organization, Unity, and Cohesion / Transitions

Getting to the Answer: This sentence is a more specific detail that illustrates the preceding sentence. Choice (F) is the best transition between the two sentences.

73. B **Difficulty:** Medium

Category: Usage

Getting to the Answer: Choice A makes it sound as though lives are changing the place rather than the other way around. Choice C does not make sense, and D is grammatically incorrect. Choice (B) contains the correct phrasing.

74. J **Difficulty:** Medium

Category: Sentence Structure and Formation

Getting to the Answer: Choices F and H do not make sense because of the word *and*. Choice G is incorrect because the sentence is talking about people today, not the forty-niners. Therefore, (J) is correct.

75. B   **Difficulty:** High

Category: Topic Development / Writer's Purpose

Getting to the Answer: Though the forty-niners are mentioned, the focus of the essay is on the history of the California gold rush. Therefore, the essay would not meet the requirements of the assignment, so (B) is correct.

MATHEMATICS TEST

1. A   **Difficulty:** Low

Category: Essential Skills / Rates, Percents, Proportions, and Unit Conversion

Getting to the Answer: To reduce a number by 20%, you could take 20% of the original number and subtract the result, or you could just take 80% (because you are only paying 100% − 20% = 80%) of the original number:

$$\text{New price} = 80\% \text{ of original price}$$
$$= (0.80)(\$125)$$
$$= \$100$$

Choice (A) is correct.

2. J   **Difficulty:** Low

Category: Essential Skills / Expressions and Equations

Getting to the Answer: Plug in $x = -5$ and simplify using the correct order of operations:

$$2x^2 - 6x + 5 = 2(-5)^2 - 6(-5) + 5$$
$$= 2 \times 25 - (-30) + 5$$
$$= 50 + 30 + 5$$
$$= 85$$

Choice (J) is correct.

3. A   **Difficulty:** Low

Category: Essential Skills / Numbers and Operations

Getting to the Answer: A prime factor is a factor that can be divided by only 1 and itself. The prime factorization of 36 is $2 \times 2 \times 3 \times 3$. That factorization includes two distinct prime factors, 2 and 3, so (A) is correct.

4. G   **Difficulty:** Low

Category: Essential Skills / Geometry

Getting to the Answer: The exterior angles of a triangle (or any polygon, for that matter) add up to 360°, so $x° + 85° + 160° = 360°$. Solving this equation for x yields $x = 115$, which is (G).

5. B   **Difficulty:** Medium

Category: Essential Skills / Numbers and Operations

Getting to the Answer: Don't jump to hasty conclusions—you can't just average the denominators. Instead, add the fractions and divide by 2. To do this, you'll need to find a common denominator for the fractions:

$$\frac{\frac{1}{20} + \frac{1}{30}}{2} = \frac{\frac{3}{60} + \frac{2}{60}}{2} = \frac{\frac{5}{60}}{2} = \frac{\frac{1}{12}}{2} = \frac{1}{12} \times \frac{1}{2} = \frac{1}{24}$$

Choice (B) is correct. Note that you could also use your calculator here. Just be careful to enter each fraction using parentheses: Enter (1/20) + (1/30), hit Enter, then divide by 2. The result is 0.041666 . . . , which is equivalent to choice (B).

6. J   **Difficulty:** Medium

Category: Essential Skills / Geometry

Getting to the Answer: In a parallelogram, opposite sides have the same length, so $RU = ST = 8$ and $RS = UT$. The perimeter is the sum of all the sides, so $RS + ST + UT + RU = 42$. Substitute the known side lengths ($RU = ST = 8$ and $RS = UT$) and solve for the length of UT:

$$UT + 8 + UT + 8 = 42$$
$$2UT + 16 = 42$$
$$2UT = 26$$
$$UT = 13$$

Choice (J) is correct.

7. C   **Difficulty:** Low

Category: Essential Skills / Expressions and Equations

Getting to the Answer: Multiply the coefficients and add the exponents: $3x^2 \cdot 5x^3 = (3 \times 5)(x^2 \cdot x^3) = 15x^{(2+3)} = 15x^5$. This matches (C).

8. G **Difficulty:** Low

Category: Essential Skills / Statistics and Probability

Getting to the Answer: This is a fairly straightforward question as long as you know your statistics definitions. The *mean* of a data set is the sum of the terms divided by the number of terms. For this data set, the mean is $\frac{12 + 21 + 29 + 34}{4} = \frac{96}{4} = 24$. The *median* is the value that is in the middle of the set when the values are arranged in order. When there are an even number of terms, as in this question, the median is the average of the two middle terms, which is $\frac{21 + 29}{2} = \frac{50}{2} = 25$. The positive difference between the mean and median is $25 - 24 = 1$, (G).

9. D **Difficulty:** Low

Category: Essential Skills / Rates, Percents, Proportions, and Unit Conversion

Getting to the Answer: Use the three-part percent formula, Percent times whole (25) equals part (16):

$$\text{Percent} \times 25 = 16$$
$$\text{Percent} = \frac{16}{25} = 0.64 = 64\%, \text{(D)}$$

10. F **Difficulty:** Medium

Category: Higher Math / Number and Quantity

Getting to the Answer: The easiest way to solve this compound inequality is to break it into two pieces and use cross-multiplication.

First, $\frac{1}{4} < \frac{7}{x} \rightarrow 1x < 4(7) \rightarrow x < 28$.

Next, $\frac{7}{x} < \frac{1}{3} \rightarrow 7(3) < x \rightarrow x > 21$.

Together the two pieces tell you that x can be any of the integers 22 through 27, of which there are 6. Choice (F) is correct.

11. B **Difficulty:** Medium

Category: Higher Math / Number and Quantity

Getting to the Answer: Use the order of operations (PEMDAS), the definition of absolute value, and the rule $a^{-1} = \frac{1}{a}$.

$$\left(\frac{|3(2) - 14|}{|-4|} - (4 - 7)^2 \right)^{-1} = \left(\frac{|-8|}{4} - (-3)^2 \right)^{-1}$$
$$= \left(\frac{8}{4} - 9 \right)^{-1}$$
$$= (2 - 9)^{-1}$$
$$= (-7)^{-1} = -\frac{1}{7}$$

Choice (B) is correct.

12. G **Difficulty:** Medium

Category: Essential Skills / Expressions and Equations

Getting to the Answer: You solve an inequality just like you solve an equation: Do the same things to both sides until you've isolated the variable. (Just remember to flip the symbol if you ever multiply or divide both sides by a negative number.) Here, you want to isolate x:

$$-3 < 4x - 5$$
$$2 < 4x$$
$$\frac{2}{4} < x$$
$$x > \frac{1}{2}$$

This matches (G).

13. D **Difficulty:** Medium

Category: Essential Skills / Geometry

Getting to the Answer: When you're given a geometric figure and angle measures, be sure to add those measures to the figure as you work. $\angle CGE$ and $\angle BGF$ are vertical angles, so $\angle BGF$ measures 105°. If you subtract $\angle AGB$ from $\angle BGF$, you're left with $\angle AGF$, the angle you're looking for.

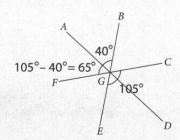

So $\angle AGF$ measures $105° - 40°$, or 65°, which is (D).

14. K   Difficulty: Medium

Category: Higher Math / Algebra

Getting to the Answer: Before jumping into the algebra, you can eliminate F and J right away because the inequality symbol is ≥, which is represented on a number line by a solid (closed) dot. Next, isolate the variable by using the Distributive Property on both sides and then a series of inverse operations. (Just remember to flip the symbol if you multiply or divide both sides by a negative number.)

$$5x - 2(1 - x) \geq 4(x + 1)$$
$$5x - 2 + 2x \geq 4x + 4$$
$$5x + 2x - 4x \geq 4 + 2$$
$$3x \geq 6$$
$$x \geq 2$$

The "greater than or equal to" symbol means you want numbers that are larger than (to the right of) 2 on the number line, so (K) is correct.

15. D   Difficulty: Medium

Category: Essential Skills / Geometry

Getting to the Answer: Because BD bisects $\angle ABC$, the measure of $\angle ABD$ is 50°. Now you know two of the three angles of $\triangle ABD$, so the third angle measures $180° - 60° - 50° = 70°$.

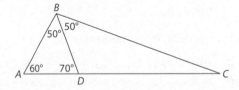

$\angle BDC$, the angle you're looking for, is supplementary to the 70° angle, so $\angle BDC$ measures $180° - 70° = 110°$, which is (D).

16. F   Difficulty: High

Category: Higher Math / Algebra

Getting to the Answer: To express y in terms of x, you need to isolate y. To do this, you need to first gather all the y-terms on one side of the equation and all the terms that don't contain y on the other. Then factor the y out and divide both sides by what's left:

$$x + 2y - 3 = xy$$
$$2y - xy = -x + 3$$
$$y(2 - x) = 3 - x$$
$$y = \frac{3 - x}{2 - x}$$

This matches (F).

17. E   Difficulty: Medium

Category: Higher Math / Statistics and Probability

Getting to the Answer: Think this question through logically: If you add the number of English speakers to the number of Spanish speakers, you get $28 + 37 = 65$. But there are only 50 students, so $65 - 50 = 15$ of them are being counted twice—because those 15 speak both languages. Choice (E) is correct.

18. K   Difficulty: Low

Category: Essential Skills / Rates, Percents, Proportions, and Unit Conversion

Getting to the Answer: Set up a proportion in the form "miles to hours" equals "miles to hours":

$$\frac{288 \text{ miles}}{6 \text{ hours}} = \frac{x \text{ miles}}{8 \text{ hours}}$$
$$6x = 288 \times 8$$
$$6x = 2,304$$
$$x = 384$$

The car will travel 384 miles in 8 hours. This means (K) is correct.

19. D   Difficulty: Low

Category: Essential Skills / Numbers and Operations

Getting to the Answer: To convert a fraction to a decimal, divide the numerator by the denominator. Use your calculator to save time. Clearly, the calculator won't produce 100 places after the decimal point, so there must be a pattern you can take advantage of. Your calculator should return $0.363636 \ldots$

Each first, third, fifth, etc. digit is a 3; and each second, fourth, sixth, etc. digit is a 6. In other words, each odd-numbered digit is a 3 and each even-numbered digit is a 6. The 100th digit is an even-numbered digit, so it's a 6. Choice (D) is correct.

20. G   Difficulty: Low

Category: Higher Math / Algebra

Getting to the Answer: Because it's *x* you're looking for, eliminate *y*. Fortunately, the equations are ready for you to solve using elimination—just add them and the $+ 4y$ cancels with the $- 4y$:

$$
\begin{aligned}
3x + 4y &= 31 \\
+\ 3x - 4y &= -1 \\
\hline
6x &= 30 \\
x &= 5
\end{aligned}
$$

Choice (G) is correct.

21. B   Difficulty: Medium

Category: Higher Math / Statistics and Probability

Getting to the Answer: Consider the difference between mean and standard deviation: Mean is a measure of center, while standard deviation is a measure of spread. The five answers all involve consistency, which means the explanation should involve standard deviation. Based on this, you can eliminate A, D, and E. Higher consistency means lower standard deviation (and vice versa); the only choice that reflects this—and correctly represents the data in the table—is (B).

22. K   Difficulty: Low

Category: Higher Math / Statistics and Probabilty

Getting to the Answer: The mode of a data set is the value that occurs most often. The modes are: Ariel = 6.6, Lisa = 8.5, and Jared = 7.5. Based on the modes, the friend should predict the same order, which is (K).

23. A   Difficulty: Medium

Category: Higher Math / Geometry

Getting to the Answer: The center of *Q* is on *P*'s circumference, and the radius of circle *Q* is twice the radius of circle *P*. You could use the circumference of circle *P* to find the radius of circle *P*, then double that radius to get the

radius of circle *Q*, and finally use that radius to calculate the circumference of circle *Q*. It's much easier and faster, however, if you realize that double the radius means double the circumference (because both the radius and the circumference are one-dimensional geometries). If the circumference of circle *P* is 6, then the circumference of circle *Q* is twice that, or 12. This makes (A) correct.

24. J   Difficulty: High

Category: Higher Math / Functions

Getting to the Answer: Don't let function notation scare you. All you need to do is a little substitution. To find $f(x + h)$ from $f(x)$, plug in $(x + h)$ wherever you see *x*. Don't forget to use parentheses, and be careful—you'll need to square a binomial and distribute a negative, so take your time.

$$
\begin{aligned}
f(x + h) &= 1 - (x + h)^2 \\
&= 1 - (x + h)(x + h) \\
&= 1 - \left(x^2 + xh + xh + h^2\right) \\
&= 1 - x^2 - 2xh - h^2
\end{aligned}
$$

This matches (J).

25. D   Difficulty: Medium

Category: Essential Skills / Geometry

Getting to the Answer: The formula for the volume of a cylinder is $V = \pi r^2 h$, where *r* is the radius of the circular base and *h* is the height. Here $r = 4$ and $h = 5$, so:

$$
\begin{aligned}
\text{Volume} &= \pi r^2 h \\
&= \pi (4)^2 (5) \\
&= \pi (16)(5) \\
&= 80\pi
\end{aligned}
$$

Choice (D) is correct.

26. J   Difficulty: Medium

Category: Higher Math / Algebra

Getting to the Answer: First factor out an *x* from each term, then write the remaining terms in descending order and factor what's left—it will be a nice quadratic, so look for the factors of the constant term that sum to the coefficient of the middle term:

$$2x + 3x^2 + x^3 = x(2 + 3x + x^2)$$
$$= x(x^2 + 3x + 2)$$
$$= x(x + 1)(x + 2)$$

This matches (J).

27. C   Difficulty: Medium

Category: Higher Math / Algebra

Getting to the Answer: Get rid of the parentheses in the denominator (by distributing the square to each variable) and then cancel factors the numerator and denominator have in common:

$$\frac{x^2 y^3 z^4}{\left(xyz^2\right)^2} = \frac{x^2 y^3 z^4}{x^2 y^2 z^4} = \frac{x^2}{x^2} \cdot \frac{y^3}{y^2} \cdot \frac{z^4}{z^4} = y$$

Choice (C) is correct.

28. H   Difficulty: Low

Category: Essential Skills / Numbers and Operations

Getting to the Answer: Normally, you would have a choice: Either convert the fractions to decimals first and then add, or add the fractions first and then convert the sum to a decimal. In this case, however, both fractions would convert to endlessly repeating decimals, which would be unwieldy when adding—so it makes sense to add first, then convert:

$$\frac{2}{3} + \frac{1}{12} = \frac{8}{12} + \frac{1}{12} = \frac{9}{12} = \frac{3}{4} = 0.75$$

Choice (H) is correct. Note that you could also use your calculator here—just be sure to enter each fraction using parentheses to be safe: (2/3) + (1/12) = 0.75.

29. E   Difficulty: Medium

Category: Essential Skills / Geometry

Getting to the Answer: You don't always need to add up all the sides—because all angles are right angles, just find the total vertical distance and the total horizontal distance. On the left side, the distance up is 10 + 18 = 28, so this must be the sum of the vertical sides on the right as well. The total vertical distance along both sides is 2(28) = 56. Similarly, from the bottom, the total distance from left to right is 10 + 14 = 24, so the total horizontal

distance along the top and bottom is 2(24) = 48. The total perimeter is 56 + 48 = 104, or (E).

30. H   Difficulty: Low

Category: Essential Skills / Statistics and Probability

Getting to the Answer: Probability equals the number of favorable outcomes divided by the total number of possible outcomes. In this question, a favorable outcome is choosing a green marble—that's 4. The total number of possible outcomes is the total number of marbles, or 20:

$$\text{Probability} = \frac{\text{number of favorable outcomes}}{\text{total number of possible outcomes}}$$
$$= \frac{4}{20}$$
$$= \frac{1}{5}$$

That makes (H) the correct answer.

31. A   Difficulty: Medium

Category: Essential Skills / Expressions and Equations

Getting to the Answer: To find the average of three numbers—even if they're algebraic expressions—add them and divide by 3:

$$\text{Average} = \frac{\text{sum of terms}}{\text{number of terms}}$$
$$= \frac{(2x + 5) + (5x - 6) + (-4x + 2)}{3}$$
$$= \frac{3x + 1}{3}$$
$$= \frac{3x}{3} + \frac{1}{3}$$
$$= x + \frac{1}{3}$$

This matches (A).

32. J   Difficulty: Medium

Category: Higher Math / Algebra

Getting to the Answer: When a system of linear equations has NO solution, you are dealing with parallel lines. How can you tell if any of the equations form a line parallel to the one in the graph? Parallel lines have the same slope but different y-intercepts. The given equations are all in the same form: $y = mx + b$, where m is the slope. You don't know the exact slope of the line in the graph, but you can see that it has a negative slope because it decreases from left to right. Therefore, you can eliminate F, H, and K because they do not have negative slopes. Next, you can eliminate G because it has the same y-intercept as the line in the figure. That leaves you with the correct answer, (J).

33. B   Difficulty: Medium

Category: Higher Math / Geometry

Getting to the Answer: When parallel lines are the bases of a little triangle inside a big triangle with a shared vertex, as they are here, the triangles are similar (because they have the same angle geometries). Side $\overline{PR}$ is three times the length of $\overline{QR}$, so each side of the big triangle is three times the length of the corresponding side of the smaller triangle, and therefore the ratio of the perimeters is also 3:1. This means the perimeter of $\triangle PRT$ is $3 \times 11 = 33$ units, which is (B).

34. K   Difficulty: Low

Category: Essential Skills / Geometry

Getting to the Answer: The figure is a polygon because it is closed and composed of straight line segments. It is a quadrilateral because it has four sides. It is not a rectangle because opposite sides are not equal. It is a trapezoid because it has one pair of parallel sides. Thus, (K) is correct.

35. D   Difficulty: High

Category: Higher Math / Functions

Getting to the Answer: Start by translating the function notation into a more understandable form: "If $p(-3) = 0$" translates to "If you plug -3 into the equation for each x, then the value of the expression is 0." This tells you how to answer the question: Substitute -3 for each x, set the whole expression equal to 0, and solve for a:

$$2x^2 + ax - 4x - 2a = 0$$
$$2(-3)^2 + a(-3) - 4(-3) - 2a = 0$$
$$18 - 3a + 12 - 2a = 0$$
$$30 - 5a = 0$$
$$-5a = -30$$
$$a = 6$$

Choice (D) is correct.

36. K   Difficulty: Low

Category: Higher Math / Statistics and Probability

Getting to the Answer: The total number of combinations of a first course, a second course, and dessert is equal to the product of the three numbers: total possibilities $= 4 \times 5 \times 3 = 60$, which is (K).

37. B   Difficulty: Medium

Category: Essential Skills / Numbers and Operations

Getting to the Answer: An integer that's divisible by 6 has at least one 2 and one 3 in its prime factorization. An integer that's divisible by 9 has at least two 3s in its prime factorization. Therefore, an integer that's divisible by both 6 and 9 has at least one 2 and two 3s in its prime factorization. That means it's divisible by 2, 3, $2 \times 3 = 6$, $3 \times 3 = 9$, and $2 \times 3 \times 3 = 18$. It's not necessarily divisible by 12 or 36, each of which includes two 2s in its prime factorization. Thus, (B) is correct.

Note that you could also answer this question by Picking Numbers. Think of a common multiple of 6 and 9 and use it to eliminate some options. For example, $6 \times 9 = 54$ is an obvious common multiple—and it's not divisible by 12 or 36, but it is divisible by 18. The *least* common multiple of 6 and 9 is 18, which is also divisible by 18. In fact, every common multiple of 6 and 9 is also a multiple of 18.

38. J   Difficulty: High

Category: Higher Math / Number and Quantity

Getting to the Answer: To add matrices of the same size, add corresponding entries (entries that sit in the same spot). Here, you can use the upper left entries to find x, the upper right entries to find y, and the lower right entries to find z as follows:

$$x + 2 = 7 \rightarrow x = 5$$
$$5 + 3y = 17 \rightarrow 3y = 12 \rightarrow y = 4$$
$$x + y = z \rightarrow z = 5 + 4 = 9$$

Choice (J) is correct.

39. A **Difficulty:** Medium

Category: Essential Skills / Expressions and Equations

Getting to the Answer: Read carefully. This question's a lot easier than you might think. It's asking for the total *number* of coins, not the total *value*, so all you need to do is add the variables that represent the numbers of different coins: q quarters, d dimes, and n nickels add up to a total of $q + d + n$ coins. Therefore, choice (A) is correct.

40. K **Difficulty:** High

Category: Higher Math / Algebra

Getting to the Answer: You could use Backsolving here, but doing the algebra is probably quicker due to all the fractions. Because the absolute value of a number represents its distance from zero on the number line, the solutions to $|x| = c$ are the coordinates of the two points that lie exactly c units from 0, which are $+c$ and $-c$. Thus, to solve the given equation, you can break it into two linear equations: one that is equal to $+\frac{7}{6}$ and another that is equal to $-\frac{7}{6}$:

$$2x + 1 = \frac{7}{6} \qquad\qquad 2x + 1 = -\frac{7}{6}$$
$$2x = \frac{7}{6} - \frac{6}{6} \qquad\qquad 2x = -\frac{7}{6} - \frac{6}{6}$$
$$2x = \frac{1}{6} \qquad\qquad 2x = -\frac{13}{6}$$
$$x = \frac{1}{6} \cdot \frac{1}{2} = \frac{1}{12} \qquad x = -\frac{13}{6} \cdot \frac{1}{2} = -\frac{13}{12}$$

Choice (K) is correct.

41. A **Difficulty:** Medium

Category: Higher Math / Number and Quantity

Getting to the Answer: You can use Picking Numbers when there are variables in the answer choices and the question stem. When you work with an exponent of -1, write the reciprocal of the number. First, rewrite the inequality using fractions, as $\frac{1}{w} > \frac{1}{x} > \frac{1}{y} > \frac{1}{z}$. In a

unit fraction, as the denominator becomes smaller, the value of the fraction becomes greater—for example, $\frac{1}{2}$ is greater than $\frac{1}{3}$. Based on the question stem, $\frac{1}{w}$ has the greatest value, so w must have the least value. If you Pick Numbers, let $w = 2$, $x = 3$, $y = 4$, and $z = 5$:

$$\frac{1}{2} > \frac{1}{3} > \frac{1}{4} > \frac{1}{5}$$

This supports the conclusion that w has the least value, meaning choice (A) is correct.

42. G **Difficulty:** High

Category: Higher Math / Functions

Getting to the Answer: A graphing calculator can be a good backup, but understanding the math will always be faster. You could plug this equation into your graphing calculator, find the highest and lowest values, find their difference, and divide by 2. Alternatively, you could use algebra. Rewrite the equation as $y = 4 \sin(5\theta) - 3$, then use rules for transformations. The -3 at the end moves the entire graph down by 3; it doesn't affect the difference between the largest and smallest values. The 5 inside the argument (the parentheses) affects how often the function repeats itself in the same space on the x-axis, which again doesn't impact the amplitude. It's the 4 in front that multiplies the y-values and makes the extreme values of the function higher and lower. Sine usually goes from -1 to 1, so if you multiply all the values by 4, it will go from -4 to 4. The difference is 8, and half of the difference is 4. So the amplitude is 4, meaning (G) is correct.

43. E **Difficulty:** High

Category: Higher Math / Functions

Getting to the Answer: The first step here is understanding what the question asks. If $f(x) - g(x) = 0$, then $f(x)$ and $g(x)$ must have the same value—or in mathematical terms, $f(x) = g(x)$. Thus, all you need to do is set the expressions for the functions equal to each other and solve for x. The equation becomes $9^{2x-1} = 3^{3x+3}$, which is an exponential equation (because the variable is in the exponent). To solve the equation using algebra, start by rewriting the left side with a base of 3 so that both sides have the same base:

$$9^{2x-1} = 3^{3x+3}$$

$$(3^2)^{2x-1} = 3^{3x+3}$$

$$3^{4x-2} = 3^{3x+3}$$

Now that the bases are the same, set the exponents equal to each other and solve for x:

$$4x - 2 = 3x + 3$$

$$4x - 3x = 3 + 2$$

$$x = 5$$

Choice (E) is correct.

44. K   Difficulty: Medium

Category: Essential Skills / Rates, Percents, Proportions, and Unit Conversion

Getting to the Answer: Be careful with combined percent increases. You cannot just add the two percents, because they're generally percents of different wholes. In this instance, the 20% increase is based on the 1970 population and the 30% increase is based on the larger 1980 population.

The best way to answer a question like this is to choose a number for the original whole and just see what happens. As usual with percents, the best number to choose is 100. (That may be a small number for the population of a city, but realism is not important here—all that matters is the math.)

If the 1970 population was 100, then a 20% increase would put the 1980 population at 120. Now, to figure the 30% increase, multiply 120 by 130% to get 1.3(120) = 156. The population went from 100 to 156, which is a 56% increase. This means (K) is correct.

45. E   Difficulty: Low

Category: Higher Math / Algebra

Getting to the Answer: When a linear equation is written in the form $y = mx + b$, as these answer choices are, m gives the slope of the line and b gives the y-intercept.

From the graph, you can see that the y-intercept is 2, so the correct answer is either B or (E). To choose between the two, look at the way the line moves from left to right—it rises, so the slope must be positive, making the (E) the correct answer. You could also use the intercepts, $(-1,0)$ and $(0,2)$, to find the slope if you're not sure:

$$\text{Slope} = \frac{y_2 - y_1}{x_2 - x_1} = \frac{2 - 0}{0 - (-1)} = 2$$

The correct equation is $y = 2x + 2$, which is (E).

46. F   Difficulty: High

Category: Higher Math / Functions

Getting to the Answer: When matching an equation to a graph, always look for ways to simplify the algebra before graphing the equation. Here, you can factor an x out of each term in the numerator and then cancel that x with the one in the denominator.

$$y = \frac{3x^2 + 2x}{x} = \frac{x(3x + 2)}{x} = 3x + 2$$

Even though the equation looks complicated at first, it's really just a line. The graph is a line with y-intercept 2 and slope 3. Only (F) fits this description. The missing point (the hole) at $x = 0$ is there because x cannot equal 0 in the original equation—that would be dividing by 0, which is undefined.

47. E   Difficulty: High

Category: Higher Math / Number and Quantity

Getting to the Answer: You don't have to know anything about complex numbers ahead of time. All the information you need is in the question stem. Treat i as a variable, FOIL as usual, and replace i^2 with -1 whenever it appears:

$$\frac{(i + 1)(i + 1)}{(i - 1)(i - 1)} = \frac{i^2 + 2i + 1}{i^2 - 2i + 1}$$

$$= \frac{-1 + 2i + 1}{-1 - 2i + 1}$$

$$= \frac{2i}{-2i} = -1$$

Choice (E) is correct.

48. G   Difficulty: Medium

Category: Essential Skills / Rates, Percents, Proportions, and Unit Conversion

Getting to the Answer: Be careful. The question is not asking, "What is $\frac{1}{4}$ of 16?" It's asking, "What is $\frac{1}{4}$ % of 16?" One-fourth of 1% is 0.25%, or 0.0025:

$$\frac{1}{4}\% \text{ of } 16 = 0.0025 \times 16 = 0.04$$

Choice (G) is correct.

49. C   Difficulty: Medium

Category: Higher Math / Algebra

Getting to the Answer: Use FOIL to get rid of each pair of parentheses, then combine like terms:

$$(s + 4)(s - 4) + (2s + 2)(s - 2)$$
$$= \left(s^2 - 16\right) + \left(2s^2 - 2s - 4\right)$$
$$= s^2 + 2s^2 - 2s - 16 - 4$$
$$= 3s^2 - 2s - 20$$

This matches (C).

50. F   Difficulty: Medium

Category: Higher Math / Functions

Getting to the Answer: The easiest way to find the equation of a given parabola is to take a point or two from the graph and plug the coordinates into the answer choices, eliminating the choices that don't work. Start with a point with coordinates that are easy to work with. Here, you could start with (3,0). Plug $x = 3$ and $y = 0$ into each answer choice and you'll find that only (F) works. Note that you could also strategically eliminate some of the answer choices using rules of transformations. The vertex of the parabola in the graph is 3 units below the origin, so the equation must include a -3 (not attached to the x), which means you don't even need to check G, H, and J.

51. C   Difficulty: Medium

Category: Higher Math / Geometry

Getting to the Answer: Use SOHCAHTOA: Because $\sin a = \frac{4}{5}$, you can think of this as a 3-4-5 triangle. Add

labels to the sketch provided in your test booklet—label the side opposite a with a 4 and the hypotenuse with a 5. The remaining side has length 3:

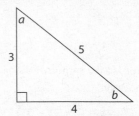

Cosine is "adjacent over hypotenuse." Here, the leg adjacent to b is 4 and the hypotenuse is 5, so $\cos b = \frac{4}{5}$. Choice (C) is correct. (Notice that the sine of one acute angle in a right triangle is equal to the cosine of the other acute angle; this is always the case.)

52. F   Difficulty: High

Category: Higher Math / Functions

Getting to the Answer: In a geometric sequence, you calculate each successive term by multiplying the previous term by the same value. If the first number in a geometric sequence is x and the second number is nx, then the third number will be $(n)(n)x$, or n^2x, and the fourth number will be $(n)(n)(n)x$, or n^3x, and so on. As you can see, the exponent of n will always be *one less* than the number of the term in the sequence. The 30th term in the sequence, then, will be $n^{30 - 1}x$, or $n^{29}x$. Choice (F) is therefore correct.

53. B   Difficulty: Medium

Category: Higher Math / Geometry

Getting to the Answer: Picking Numbers is a great way to deal with abstract questions like this one. Say the original dimensions were $w = 2$ and $h = 3$. The surface area would be $S = 4(2)(3) + 2(2)^2 = 24 + 8 = 32$. If you double each dimension, you'll have $w = 4$, $h = 6$, and $S = 4(4)(6) + 2(4)^2 = 96 + 32 = 128$. The surface area has gone up by a factor of 4, (B), because $32 \cdot 4 = 128$.

54. H   Difficulty: High

Category: Higher Math / Geometry

Getting to the Answer: Find the volume of the container using the formula for the volume of a cylinder, $V = \pi r^2 h$.

The question gives you the width, or the diameter of the container, so divide by 2 to get the radius.

$$\text{Volume} = \pi r^2 h$$

$$= \pi(1.25)^2(4)$$

$$= \pi(1.5625)(4)$$

$$= 6.25\pi$$

The factory only fills the cup 80% of the way up, so multiply the container volume by 0.8 to find that the actual volume of the yogurt is $6.25\pi \times 0.8 = 5\pi$, or about 15.708 cubic inches. Divide this by 6 ounces to determine that 1 ounce takes up approximately 2.6 cubic inches of space, which matches (H).

55. B   **Difficulty:** High

Category: Higher Math / Geometry

Getting to the Answer: Did you recognize that $\triangle RST$ is a 30°-60°-90° triangle? You should always be on the lookout for special triangles. Drawing a quick diagram of $\triangle RST$ may help you to organize the information in this question. Since $\angle R$ is a right angle, you know that the side opposite $\angle R$, $\overline{ST}$, will be the hypotenuse.

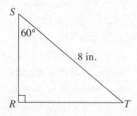

Remember that a 30°-60°-90° triangle has sides in the ratio $x:x\sqrt{3}:2x$. This allows you to calculate the other two sides of $\triangle RST$. Since $2x = 8$, $x = 4$. $\overline{SR}$ is 4 inches long and $\overline{RT}$ is $4\sqrt{3}$ inches long. These two sides are the base and height of $\triangle RST$, so you can plug their lengths into the formula for finding the area of a triangle:

$$A = \frac{1}{2}bh$$

$$= \frac{1}{2}(4)(4\sqrt{3})$$

$$= 8\sqrt{3}$$

Choice (B) is correct.

56. K   **Difficulty:** High

Category: Higher Math / Geometry

Getting to the Answer: Whenever there doesn't seem to be enough information to solve a geometry question, look for special or similar triangles. You know that $\triangle ABC$ is similar to $\triangle DEC$ because both are right triangles that share $\angle DCE$. $\triangle DEC$ is the same as $\triangle DEA$ because the two triangles that share height $\overline{DE}$ are both right triangles and have bases of the same length. (Since $\overline{DE}$ bisects $\overline{AC}$, $\overline{AD}$ and $\overline{DC}$ are the same length.) Therefore, $CE = y$. The ratio between corresponding sides of similar triangles is the same, so $\dfrac{AB}{DE} = \dfrac{BC}{CE} = \dfrac{z}{y}$, which is (K).

57. B   **Difficulty:** High

Category: Higher Math / Statistics and Probability

Getting to the Answer: The overall average is not simply the average of the two average ages. Because there are a lot more women than men and the average age of the women is 25, women carry more weight and the overall average will be closer to 25 than 35. Pick particular numbers for the females and males that meet the criteria that 80% are female and 20% are male. For example, say 8 members are female and 2 are male. The ages of the 8 females total 8 times 25, or 200, and the ages of the 2 males total 2 times 35, or 70. The average, then, is (200 + 70) divided by 10, or 27. Choice (B) is correct.

58. J   **Difficulty:** High

Category: Higher Math / Geometry

Getting to the Answer: The height h of the tree is the leg opposite θ. The distance b from the base of the tree is the leg adjacent to θ. "Opposite over adjacent" is tangent, but all the answer choices involve sine. Sine is "opposite over hypotenuse," so you're going to have to figure out the hypotenuse. Use the Pythagorean theorem:

$$(\text{hypotenuse})^2 = (\text{leg}_1)^2 + (\text{leg}_2)^2$$

$$(\text{hypotenuse})^2 = b^2 + h^2$$

$$\text{hypotenuse} = \sqrt{b^2 + h^2}$$

Now, to get the sine, write the opposite, h, over the hypotenuse, $\sqrt{b^2 + h^2}$, to get $\sin \theta = \dfrac{h}{\sqrt{b^2 + h^2}}$, which is (J).

59. C   Difficulty: Medium

Category: Higher Math / Geometry

Getting to the Answer: This question is simply testing your ability to use a geometric formula. All you need to do is plug in the given value for each variable and simplify using the correct order of operations:

$$S = \pi r \sqrt{r^2 + h^2}$$
$$= \pi(3)\sqrt{3^2 + 4^2}$$
$$= 3\pi\sqrt{9 + 16}$$
$$= 3\pi\sqrt{25}$$
$$= 3\pi \times 5$$
$$= 15\pi$$

Choice (C) is correct.

60. H   Difficulty: Medium

Category: Higher Math / Functions

Getting to the Answer: This question is much simpler than it first appears. You just need to know the formula for the equation of a circle. The formula for the equation of a circle is $(x - h)^2 + (y - k)^2 = r^2$, where the center of the circle is (h,k) and r is the radius of the circle. Therefore, in this question, (H) is correct because:

$$r^2 = 5$$
$$r = \sqrt{5}$$

READING TEST

Passage I

Suggested Passage Map notes:

¶1-2: Esther (E) remembers love for Dolly (D)

¶3: E's godmother (g) - stern, churchgoing

¶4: E doesn't know mother

¶5: E doesn't have friends

¶6: g doesn't celebrate E's bday

¶7-10: g says would have been better if E never born

¶11-12: E cries self to sleep, thankful for D

1. B   Difficulty: High

Category: Craft and Structure / Writer's View

Getting to the Answer: The narrator's opinion of herself is based purely on her godmother's words, deeds, and general negativity toward her (the narrator). The author is implying that there is no real truth to the narrator's perception of herself, which matches answer choice (B). Choice A is the opposite of the author's intention. Choices C and D are also opposites; the narrator believes her godmother's statement, and though she calls her birthday "the most melancholy day at home in the whole year" (lines 53–54), there is no hint that the narrator hates her godmother for not celebrating her birthday.

2. G   Difficulty: Medium

Category: Craft and Structure / Function

Getting to the Answer: From the description of Dolly in the first two paragraphs, it is clear that Esther views her doll as her only friend. "I was such a shy little thing that I seldom dared to open my lips, and never dared to open my heart, to anybody else" (lines 5–8). This idea is repeated in lines 80–83: "I went up to my room, and crept to bed, and laid my doll's cheek against mine wet with tears, and holding that solitary friend upon my bosom, cried myself to sleep." Choice (G) is correct. Choices F and J are opposites; Esther clearly cherishes her doll for far more than amusement, and she sleeps with her cheek touching the doll's. Choice H is a misused detail; the reference to a princess in a fairy tale describes Esther's being brought up by her godmother.

3. B   Difficulty: Medium

Category: Craft and Structure / Vocab-in-Context

Getting to the Answer: In this case, *stiff* is used to describe the tone of the letter that Esther's godmother wrote to decline the invitation to another student's birthday party. Choice (B), *rigidly formal*, is the most appropriate definition in this context. Choice A, C, and D are incorrect because they don't make sense in context.

4. G   Difficulty: High

Category: Key Ideas and Details / Inference

Getting to the Answer: This is a Global question. Esther mentions that her birthday was never celebrated, and the pivotal scene in the passage happens on her birthday. In lines 3–4, Esther tells her doll that she is not very clever, but that is not the focus of the passage. In lines 44–46, she mentions being invited to a friend's home for a party, so H is not correct. In lines 64–67, you find out that Esther's mother did not die on her birthday, so J is not correct. This leaves only (G), which is correct.

5. C   Difficulty: Medium

Category: Key Ideas and Details / Inference

Getting to the Answer: Although Esther's godmother says that she has forgiven Esther's mother, her facial expression directly contradicts this. As it says in lines 72–76, "I see her knitted brow and pointed finger . . . her face did not relent." This is reflected in (C). Choices A and B are not supported in the passage, and D can be inferred as opposite of the information given.

6. G   Difficulty: Low

Category: Key Ideas and Details / Detail

Getting to the Answer: Esther is clearly lonely, as evidenced by her description of Dolly as her only friend and her explanation that there is a divide between her and the other girls at school. The birthday scene with her godmother also shows that Esther is quite confused about her own family's past. All this evidence matches (G). None of the other choices is supported in the passage.

7. C   Difficulty: Medium

Category: Key Ideas and Details / Inference

Getting to the Answer: Her confrontation with her godmother gives Esther further reason to believe that no one loves her. The phrase before the cited line also points to (C) as the best answer: "I knew that I had brought no joy at any time to anybody's heart" (lines 84–85). The cited quote makes A and B opposites. Choice D is both irrelevant to the quote and not given any support in the passage.

8. J   Difficulty: Medium

Category: Key Ideas and Details / Detail

Getting to the Answer: Choices F, G, and H are all mentioned in the fifth paragraph (lines 36–48). At the end of

the passage, Esther says, "I hope it is not self-indulgent to shed these tears as I think of it" (lines 91–92), so (J) is correct.

9. C   Difficulty: Low

Category: Key Ideas and Details / Detail

Getting to the Answer: Esther's evidence that her godmother is a "good, good woman" is explained in lines 18–21: "She went to church three times every Sunday, and to morning prayers on Wednesdays and Fridays, and to lectures whenever there were lectures, and never missed." This is reflected in (C). Esther says her grandmother never smiles, which eliminates A. It is clear that the grandmother has not truly forgiven Esther's mother, so B is incorrect. Choice D is incorrect because we do not know that the doll was a gift from the grandmother.

10. G   Difficulty: High

Category: Key Ideas and Details / Detail

Getting to the Answer: In the first paragraph, Esther says, "Now, Dolly, I am not clever" (line 3). In the second paragraph, Esther describes herself as "such a shy little thing" (line 5). Both of these match (G). None of the other answers reflect how Esther thinks of herself.

Passage II

Suggested Passage Map notes:

¶1: jaguar (j) surprised tourist in Brazil

¶2: j comeback difficult to determine

¶3: ranchers afraid of j, kill in self-defense

¶4: ranchers want right to kill j

¶5: 1967 - Brazil outlawed j hunting, j population

¶6: may be way for ranchers and j to coexist

¶7: ranchers deal with j as they see fit

11. B   Difficulty: Medium

Category: Craft and Structure / Vocab-in-Context

Getting to the Answer: In the phrase "the Pantanal was a vast, soggy canvas, white with gleaming herds of Nelore cattle," (lines 61–63), *canvas* is used to mean "a background." Choices A, C, and D don't make sense in context.

12. G   Difficulty: Medium

Category: Craft and Structure / Function

Getting to the Answer: Nunes's encounter with a jaguar opens the passage and ends with his describing the experience as a *wonderful fright!* The word *wonderful* and the exclamation point suggest that this event was unexpected and thrilling, as choice (G) also reflects. Choice F may be true, but Nunes's story is not about dangers—it is about his enjoyment of the experience. Choice H is irrelevant to the story, and choice J is out of scope; the author never suggests that ecotourism is unsafe overall.

13. C   Difficulty: Medium

Category: Key Ideas and Details / Detail

Getting to the Answer: The answer to this question can be found in lines 12–17: "Exactly how dramatic a comeback is difficult to say because jaguars—*Panthera onca*, the largest feline in the New World—are solitary, secretive, nocturnal predators. Each cat needs to prowl at least 35 square kilometers by itself," as (C) says. This is the only answer supported in the passage.

14. G   Difficulty: Medium

Category: Key Ideas and Details / Inference

Getting to the Answer: The last sentence of the second paragraph provides the answer: "Hotels, campgrounds, and bed-and-breakfasts have sprung up to accommodate the half-million tourists a year . . . bent on sampling the Pantanal's wildlife, of which the great cats must be the most magnificent example" (lines 23–28). Tourists want to see the jaguars, and not having the jaguars might negatively affect the booming ecotourist business, which matches (G).

15. A   Difficulty: Low

Category: Key Ideas and Details / Detail

Getting to the Answer: The "green safari" example is mentioned as a way for "scientists to fit the cats with radio collars" (lines 88–89), not a way to protect cattle. This matches (A). The other three examples provided are listed in lines 92–95 as methods the scientists are teaching the ranchers.

16. G   Difficulty: Medium

Category: Craft and Structure / Function

Getting to the Answer: In lines 49–50, the author says, "Hard data on cattle losses due to jaguars in the Pantanal are nonexistent." One reason for providing anecdotal information, then, is to tell the story of the hardships that the jaguars cause for the ranchers. The author does not suggest that he empathizes with the ranchers more than the jaguars—in fact, he refers to the jaguars as "magnificent." The only examples that show rancher violence are Abel Monteiro's shooting an attacking jaguar that had killed his two dogs (lines 31–36) and Leonelson Ramos da Silva's throwing burning sticks at a jaguar that was trying to invade his camp (lines 36–39), both acts of self-defense. The landscape of the Pantanal is not the focus of these two paragraphs, so J can be eliminated.

17. C   Difficulty: Medium

Category: Key Ideas and Details / Inference

Getting to the Answer: The passage explains that because of the decrease in the jaguar population, the capybara population increased. These rodents "spread trichomoniasis, a livestock disease that renders cows sterile" (lines 69–70). Lines 73–76 describe the effect of weather patterns and floods on the ranchers' land: "Weather patterns also shifted radically—due most likely to global warming—and drove annual floods to near-biblical proportions. The waters are only now retreating from some inundated pasturelands." These statements make only (C) correct.

18. G   Difficulty: Medium

Category: Key Ideas and Details / Detail

Getting to the Answer: The last sentence of the passage reads, "When the scholars go home and the greens log off, the *pantaneiros* will still be there—left on their own to deal with the jaguars as they see fit" (lines 98–101), which matches (G). None of the other answers reflect the author's conclusion.

19. A   Difficulty: Medium

Category: Craft and Structure / Writer's View

Getting to the Answer: The author uses the most descriptive language when he introduces the jaguar in the second paragraph. He calls the animal *big* and *beautiful* (line 11), and *magnificent* (line 28). These words indicate the author's admiration for the jaguar, despite the fact that the bulk of the passage details the problems ranchers have with jaguars. Though the author notes that jaguars are "solitary, secretive, nocturnal predators" (lines 15–16), he is stating facts, not showing fear. That makes B incorrect. Choice C—revulsion, meaning extreme dislike—is the opposite of the author's attitude. And though the author is concerned for both jaguars and ranchers, his descriptive words are mostly reserved for showing his admiration of the big cat, making D incorrect.

20. H   Difficulty: Medium

Category: Craft and Structure / Writer's View

Getting to the Answer: In the second paragraph, the author links the jaguar's comeback to a large increase in ecotourism, and in lines 66–70, he writes that as the jaguar population declined, disease and rodents took over. It can be assumed that though the jaguar was still a problem for farmers, its resurgence helped to restore ecological balance and increase tourism. Thus it is likely that the author would agree with positive aspects of the jaguar's resurgence, which matches (H). Choice F is incorrect because the author doesn't take sides. As a matter of fact, the second-to-last paragraph argues for compromise. Choice G is a distortion; though the author writes that jaguars are solitary (line 15), he doesn't say they are too shy to be seen. Choice J is the opposite; the fifth paragraph contradicts this answer.

Passage III

Suggested Passage Map notes:

¶1: 2 types of Greek instruments: string/lyre & pipe/aulos

¶2: 2 types of tuning

¶3: lyre started with 5 strings → 11 strings

¶4: similar to lyre = magadis, pectis, barbitos

¶5: kithara = intellect & aulos = passion

¶6: aulos similar to oboe

¶7: family of auloi = same range as human voice

21. A   Difficulty: Medium

Category: Key Ideas and Details / Inference

Getting to the Answer: This question asks you why the aulos was considered "the instrument of Dionysians." In the fifth paragraph, you find out that the Dionysians "represented the unbridled, sensual, and passionate aspect of Greek culture" (lines 55–57). The passage also says that the aulos had a "far more exciting effect" (line 61) than that of the lyre. The suggestion here is clearly that the aulos must have been able to express the unbridled passion and excitement of the Dionysians, making (A) the best answer. Choice B is out because the fact that the aulos was chosen as the official instrument of the Delphian and Pythian festivals doesn't explain why it was the instrument of the Dionysians. Choice C contradicts the passage. The kithara, not the aulos, represented the intellectual, idealistic side of Greek art. Finally, the author never says when the Dionysian cult originated, so D is also out.

22. J   Difficulty: Medium

Category: Key Ideas and Details / Detail

Getting to the Answer: All the author means by saying that the chelys can be "traced back to the age of fable" is that it is an ancient instrument, which matches (J). The chelys was an actual, not an imaginary, instrument, so H is incorrect. Choice G is incorrect because the kithara, not the chelys, was used to accompany epics.

23. B   Difficulty: Medium

Category: Craft and Structure / Vocab-in-Context

Getting to the Answer: Since it's important to read the word in question in the context of the sentence in which is appears, go back to the passage and read the entire sentence. It's about the possible way in which the kithera was used, so the answer will have to do with how an instrument could be used in making music. Choice C doesn't make a lot of sense, since *increased* is not relevant to making music. Choice D is incorrect because while "to decorate" can mean "to make pretty," this definition is more relevant to something seen or used than to making music. Choice A also means "to make more beautiful" and is incorrect for the same reason as D. Choice (B) is correct because to embellish something is to make it more interesting by adding details, which is exactly what a kithara would do if it were to embellish a singer's voice by adding musical flourishes or other musical details.

24. H   Difficulty: Medium

Category: Key Ideas and Details / Detail

Getting to the Answer: The first thing the author says about the kithara is that it was used by "professional Homeric singers" (lines 13–14), which matches (H). The kithara, according to the author, probably came from Egypt, so F is incorrect. Choices G and J contradict information in the paragraph that the kithara was more powerful than the chelys and was played with both hands.

25. D   Difficulty: Medium

Category: Key Ideas and Details / Detail

Getting to the Answer: Skim through the third paragraph to find the changes that occurred to the lyre between the eighth and fifth centuries BCE. Musicians began to use a plectrum in the seventh century BCE, so A is incorrect; lyres featured an increasing number of strings during this period, so B is incorrect; and musicians also began to use different scales and modes, so C is incorrect. That leaves (D). Nothing in the paragraph indicates that lyres were used to accompany dramatic productions.

26. F   Difficulty: Medium

Category: Craft and Structure / Writer's View

Getting to the Answer: The author writes that ancient Greek instruments were used by many types of people, that the "lyre was the national instrument" (line 6), and that the different instruments which represented gods were played at official festivals. All this indicates the author's belief that instruments were important and essential parts of Greek culture, which matches (F). Choices G, H, and J are all out of scope; the author does not include information that supports them.

27. A   Difficulty: Medium

Category: Craft and Structure / Writer's View

Getting to the Answer: The author writes about Greek instruments and music, but always in terms of history—when, how, and why they were used, and what they

represented in Greek life. Match this with (A). Choice B is incorrect because a professional musician would be far less interested in history and culture than in music. Choice C would be correct only if the music teacher were also a talented historian; teaching music is not the same as knowing music's place in an ancient culture. Choice D is incorrect because the passage is specific to music, not Greece in general.

28. G   Difficulty: Medium

Category: Key Ideas and Details / Detail

Getting to the Answer: Sappho did two things that you know about from lines 37–40. She introduced a mode "in which Dorian and Lydian characteristics were blended," and she "initiated the use of the plectrum," which matches (G). None of the other answers is attributed to Sappho.

29. B   Difficulty: High

Category: Key Ideas and Details / Detail

Getting to the Answer: All of the details you need to answer this question are in the sixth paragraph (lines 58–66). The first sentence states that the aulos is more like our oboe than our flute, so III is false. This means C and D can be eliminated. The second sentence of the paragraph confirms that the aulos sounded more exciting than the lyre (II). Because (B) is the only remaining answer choice that includes II, you know it has to be the correct answer.

30. F   Difficulty: Medium

Category: Key Ideas and Details / Global

Getting to the Answer: Greek instruments are discussed as a whole at the very beginning of the passage. The author says that our knowledge of Greek instruments comes from "representations on monuments, vases, statues, and friezes and from the testimony of Greek authors" (lines 3–5). These are all secondary sources of information about the instruments, so (F) is the best answer. Choice G is incorrect because quite a bit is known about the tuning of the instruments, as represented in the second paragraph. Choice H is contradicted by the same sentence that supports F. Finally, there is no evidence to suggest that more is known about one type of instrument than the other, so J is incorrect.

Passage IV

Suggested Passage Map notes:

Passage A

¶1: nonspecific defenses = 1st line of defense

¶2: microphages = type of white blood cell (wbc) called APC

¶3: neutrophil = another type of wbc, not APC

¶4: eosinophils, basophils, mast cells = other wbc

Passage B

¶1: 2 types specialized wbc (lymphocytes): B & T cells

¶2: 3 types of T cells: TH, TC, TS

¶3: T cells can't detect free antigens

¶4: B cells CAN detect free antigens

¶5: B and T cells have unique receptors

¶6: B cell clones = plasma B cells

31. C   Difficulty: Low

Category: Craft and Structure / Function

Getting to the Answer: The entire first paragraph lists a variety of nonspecific body defenses against infection. Along with all the others, including skin and mucous, the action of peristalsis is an example of the body's defense against infection, as stated in (C). Choice A is out of scope; though peristalsis takes place in the stomach, the author doesn't describe how the stomach functions. Choice B is a misused detail; it's mentioned along with peristalsis but not the reason why peristalsis itself is in the passage. Choice D is also a misused detail—pH values are associated with secretions.

32. G   Difficulty: High

Category: Key Ideas and Details / Detail

Getting to the Answer: According to the passage, "Macrophages are called antigen-presenting cells" (lines 26–27). This information matches (G).

33. B   Difficulty: Medium

Category: Key Ideas and Details / Global

Getting to the Answer: The second paragraph says that macrophages engulf materials through a process called phagocytosis, and the third paragraph states that neutrophils are phagocytic, like macrophages. This matches (B).

34. J   Difficulty: Medium

Category: Craft and Structure / Vocab-in-Context

Getting to the Answer: A TH cell is a "helper" cell. Additionally, clues in the passage indicate that macrophages/ APCs and B cells cooperate: the third paragraph indicates that T cells interact with APCs, and the fourth paragraph indicates that helper T cells cue B cells to activate. Predict that TH cells "help" or act as intermediaries in the situation, as (J) states.

35. A   Difficulty: High

Category: Key Ideas and Details / Detail

Getting to the Answer: The fifth and sixth paragraphs discuss the activation of B and T cells. The passage states, "When a particular B or T cell gets activated, it begins to divide rapidly to produce identical clones. In the case of B cells, these clones will all produce antibodies of the same structure, capable of responding to the same invading antigens. B cell clones are known as plasma B cells and can produce thousands of antibody molecules per second as long as they live" (lines 89–97). This makes (A) correct.

36. J   Difficulty: Medium

Category: Key Ideas and Details / Detail

Getting to the Answer: The fourth paragraph states that B cells have surface receptors that can "recognize a specific set of foreign antigens (proteins found on the surfaces of foreign cells and viruses)" (lines 78–80). This matches (J).

37. C   Difficulty: High

Category: Integration of Knowledge and Ideas / Synthesis

Getting to the Answer: The introductory information states, "The specific immune system is able to attack very specific disease-causing organisms by means of protein-to-protein interaction and is responsible for our ability to become immune to future infections from pathogens we have fought off already," which matches (C).

38. H   Difficulty: Medium

Category: Integration of Knowledge and Ideas / Synthesis

Getting to the Answer: As the information before Passage A implies, both passages are about the immune system, making (H) correct. Even though the passages focus on different aspects of the system, they are both concerned with the immune system. Passage A provides information about the nonspecific functions of the system, while Passage B provides additional information about the system by addressing the specific functions.

39. A   Difficulty: High

Category: Integration of Knowledge and Ideas / Synthesis

Getting to the Answer: The fourth paragraph in Passage B indicates that B cells can only be activated by TH cells that recognize pathogens the B cell has captured, but the third paragraph indicates that T cells cannot recognize free antigens—they can only detect those displayed on cell surfaces. Additionally, the third paragraph states that there are interactions between T cells and APCs, and the second paragraph specifically states that TH cells will serve as mediators between the macrophages (certain APCs) and B cells. Passage A explains that macrophages are nonspecific functions that can display antigens on their cell walls for the specific system to see. It can thus be logically inferred that a macrophage in the nonspecific division must display information that a TH cell can see and pass to B cells before the B cells can be activated to replicate and produce antibodies, which matches (A).

40. G   Difficulty: Medium

Category: Integration of Knowledge and Ideas / Synthesis

Getting to the Answer: Both authors define their terms, indicating that they do not assume the readers already know them, and they use everyday language to do this. This eliminates F and J. Considering all the different kinds of stories daily newspapers report, H is too broad an answer. There may or may not be science articles in the paper, and even if there are, there is no guarantee that people read them. The only answer left is (G), which

makes sense considering that though the passages are technical, they are in layman's language and all terms are explained, making them accessible to a nonprofessional but interested reader.

SCIENCE TEST

Passage I

1. B   Difficulty: High

Category: Interpretation of Data

Getting to the Answer: When a question asks about a quantity that is not given in the data, think about how that quantity relates to those that *are* given. Blood is a solution in which the solvent (the greatest part of the solution) is water and the solutes (molecules existing in smaller quantities that are dissolved in the solution) are other substances, including sugar. The highest water content per milliliter means the highest water concentration, which means the lowest concentration of other substances. Thus, the blood sample with the highest water content per milliliter is most likely the sample with the lowest sugar concentration, as in (B).

2. H   Difficulty: Medium

Category: Evaluation of Models, Inferences, and Results

Getting to the Answer: Compare blood color to mass in both tables. The higher blood masses generally have higher values for color, which correspond to shades closer to dark red. Therefore, the conclusion in the question stem is not supported by the data. Eliminate F and G because they state that the conclusion is supported. Choice J is incorrect because the tables show that lower masses tend to have lower color values, not higher. Choice (H) correctly states that as blood mass decreases, blood color lightens (color values are lower).

3. C   Difficulty: Low

Category: Interpretation of Data

Getting to the Answer: The data in Tables 1 and 2 show that there is a direct relationship between sugar concentration and mass: mass goes up as sugar concentration goes up. Choice (C) is thus correct.

4. F   Difficulty: Low

Category: Interpretation of Data

Getting to the Answer: Although the passage does not discuss the effects of illness on blood sugar, the question stem states that blood sugar concentration tends to increase during illness. So, the student with the cold is most likely the student with the highest blood sugar concentration. The highest sugar concentration values in both Tables 1 and 2 occur for the samples taken from Student A, so (F) is correct.

5. D   Difficulty: Medium

Category: Interpretation of Data

Getting to the Answer: Since the volumes of the samples in both tables are the same, the heaviest 0.5 mL sample would simply be the one with the largest recorded mass. Although Student A had the sample with the overall highest mass, Student A is not represented in the choices. Student E was a close second and is included among the choices, so (D) is correct.

6. J   Difficulty: Medium

Category: Interpretation of Data

Getting to the Answer: To find the positive difference in mass, locate the mass of the before and after samples for Student C in Tables 1 and 2. The after sample is 1.055 and the before sample is 1.051, so the positive difference is 0.004. Choice G, however, is a trap. The question is asking for the value in *milligrams*, but the data in the tables are in *grams*. There are 1,000 milligrams per gram. To convert the units properly, multiply 0.004 grams by 1,000 to get 4.0 milligrams. This means (J) is correct. Choice F is another trap, set for those who accidentally divide by 1,000 rather than multiply.

Passage II

7. B   Difficulty: Medium

Category: Interpretation of Data

Getting to the Answer: To answer this question, examine the data in Table 2. The pattern established in that table is that for every 0.1 moles of KCl added, the freezing point is lowered by 1.0°C. Because 0.4 moles of KCl yields a

freezing point of −92.0°C, as seen in the last row of the table, A must be incorrect. To reach a freezing point of −93.0°C, 0.1 additional moles will be needed beyond the 0.4 present in Solution 12. Thus, the solution described in the question stem most likely contains 0.5 moles of KCl, as in (B).

8. J   Difficulty: Low

Category: Scientific Investigation

Getting to the Answer: Choices F, G, and H were all factors directly manipulated by the student: the student could have decided to use a substance other than KCl to add to the IPA; the student could have used an amount of IPA other than 200 g; and the student directly varied the amount of KCl added, with values ranging from 0.05 to 0.4 moles. Only (J) describes properties not subject to the direct control of an experimenter.

9. C   Difficulty: Medium

Category: Interpretation of Data

Getting to the Answer: Be careful when data include negatives—it's easy to mistake moving from −80°C to −90°C as an increase, rather than recognize it as the decrease that it actually is. Start by looking at Table 2. As more KCl was added, the freezing point dropped from −88.5°C to −92°C. So, according to Experiment 2, more solute particles mean a lower freezing point, making (C) correct. Choice A is incorrect because the freezing point does indeed change as the number of solute particles changes. Choice B is incorrect because it's the opposite of what you're looking for. Choice D is incorrect because the question stem asks you to draw a conclusion based on the results of Experiment 2 alone, so it doesn't matter that only one solute was tested.

10. F   Difficulty: High

Category: Interpretation of Data

Getting to the Answer: To find the answer to this question, compare the changes reported in the relevant rows of Tables 1 and 2. According to Table 1, when 0.4 moles of KCl are added to 200 g of IPA, the change in boiling point is 119.7°C − 108°C = 11.7°C. This represents an increase. In Table 2, when 0.4 moles of KCl are added to 200 g of IPA, the change in freezing point is −92.0°C − (−88°C) = −4.0°C. This represents a decrease.

Thus, the boiling point is increased more than the freezing point is decreased, and that is a match for (F).

11. A   Difficulty: Low

Category: Interpretation of Data

Getting to the Answer: This question asks about the results of Experiment 1, so look to Table 1. With each increase in the amount of KCl (potassium chloride), the boiling point of the solution increased. Because KCl breaks up into potassium ions and chloride ions, as noted in the description of Experiment 1, more KCl means more of these ions. Choice (A) is thus correct.

12. H   Difficulty: High

Category: Scientific Investigation

Getting to the Answer: The question stem says to assume "that $MgCl_2$ has the same effect on the boiling point of IPA as does KCl per particle produced when dissolved." Thus, to answer this challenging question, you must think in terms of the individual solute particles: 1 K^+ and 1 Cl^- for KCl, and 1 Mg^{2+} and 2 Cl^- for $MgCl_2$. Adding 0.2 moles of $MgCl_2$ results in 3×0.2 moles $= 0.6$ moles of solute particles (0.2 moles of Mg^{2+} and 0.4 moles of Cl^-). According to Table 1, 0.4 moles of *solute particles* (0.2 moles of K^+ plus 0.2 moles of Cl^-) result in a boiling point of 114.4°C, while 0.8 moles of solute particles (0.4 moles of K^+ plus 0.4 moles of Cl^-) result in a boiling point of 119.7°C. Since $0.4 < 0.6 < 0.8$, the boiling point resulting from the addition of 0.2 moles of $MgCl_2$ will most likely be between 114.4°C and 119.7°C, as in (H).

13. D   Difficulty: Medium

Category: Interpretation of Data

Getting to the Answer: Table 1 shows that adding KCl increases the boiling point of both acetone and IPA. Table 2 shows that the freezing point of IPA is depressed by the addition of KCl. Therefore, it is reasonable to conclude that the freezing point of acetone would be depressed as well. The introductory paragraph states that −95°C is the freezing point of acetone, so the correct answer must be lower than this value, which eliminates A, B, and C. Choice (D), −95.5°C, must be correct.

Passage III

14. J   Difficulty: Low

Category: Interpretation of Data

Getting to the Answer: To answer this question, it's necessary to interpret Figure 1 correctly. For δ ^{14}C values, look at the line graph portion of Figure 1. The tombs are numbered 1–10 and each is represented on the x-axis. The correct answer will be the pair of samples for which the C-14 index values are the closest. Go through the answer choices one by one and compare the δ ^{14}C values for the tombs in each choice. The plotted points for the pair in (J) appear to be at roughly the same height, while the pairs in the other choices correspond to C-14 index values that are farther apart. Choice (J) is correct.

15. A   Difficulty: Medium

Category: Interpretation of Data

Getting to the Answer: As with the previous question, answering this question depends on proper interpretation of Figure 1. Both age and δ ^{14}C value are plotted on the y-axis of Figure 1, but the values for age appear along the left side while the values for δ ^{14}C appear along the right. According to the key, the height of the bars represents the age of the samples, and the line with the plotted points represents the C-14 index. If you compare the height of the plotted points to the height of the bars for the same samples, you'll see that they are directly proportional. Since both scales increase as you move from the bottom of the graph to the top, high δ ^{14}C values correspond to greater ages, and lower δ ^{14}C values correspond to lower ages. Choice (A), then, is correct.

16. G   Difficulty: Medium

Category: Evaluation of Models, Inferences, and Results

Getting to the Answer: The question stem doesn't provide much information, so evaluate each answer choice individually. Choice F is directly contradicted by Sample 10 in Study 1, so eliminate it. Choice (G) seems good. The descriptions of Studies 2 and 3 mention that there were 20 m and 40 m, respectively, of soil and rock accumulation over the past 11,000 years, so it's reasonable to assume that this factor was important in the selection of these sites. Choice H doesn't make sense—there was a great deal of soil and rock deposited over both sites.

Choice J is out of scope for this passage—nowhere is land development mentioned. This leaves only (G), which is correct.

17. D   Difficulty: Medium

Category: Interpretation of Data

Getting to the Answer: Follow the trend in Figure 2 to extrapolate data that falls outside the graph's boundaries. The curve in Figure 2 slopes downward, but the $\delta^{14}C$ values along the *y*-axis increase as you move from top to bottom. In other words, the C-14 index *increases* as depth increases. A depth of 25 m is considerably greater than any depth appearing on the graph, so that depth's corresponding C-14 index must be considerably greater than any $\delta^{14}C$ value from the graph. Choice (D) is therefore correct.

18. H   Difficulty: Medium

Category: Evaluation of Models, Inferences, and Results

Getting to the Answer: The passage does not provide a direct answer to this question, but it can be inferred based on the information given. The description of Study 2 mentions that "layers of soil and rock were deposited at a known rate" at the Mexican site, which allowed the researchers to determine age based on depth. As noted in the passage and reiterated in the question stem, 20 m of earth accumulated at the Mexican site but the site in Mali had 40 m of earth accumulate over the same 11,000 year period. Because the average rate of soil and rock accumulation is simply equal to the amount of accumulation per unit time, the rate must have been greater in Mali than in Mexico, as in (H).

19. C   Difficulty: High

Category: Interpretation of Data

Getting to the Answer: To answer this question, begin by going back to the equation that describes how the C-14 index is calculated. The equation appearing after the first paragraph of the passage shows that $\delta^{14}C$ is equal to the $^{14}C/^{12}C$ ratio of the biosphere minus the $^{14}C/^{12}C$ ratio of the sample divided by the $^{14}C/^{12}C$ ratio of the biosphere. $\delta^{14}C$ can only equal 0 if the numerator of the equation equals 0. This is only true when the $^{14}C/^{12}C$ ratio of the biosphere equals the $^{14}C/^{12}C$ ratio of the sample. Choice (C) is correct.

20. G   Difficulty: Medium

Category: Interpretation of Data

Getting to the Answer: This question requires you to make connections between two of the figures to reach an answer: first, move from depth to $\delta^{14}C$ in Figure 2 and, second, move from C-14 index to age in Figure 1. According to Figure 2, a depth of 5 meters corresponds to a C-14 index of approximately 32. In Figure 1, samples 1 and 2 have $\delta^{14}C$ values that are closest to 32, so their ages would be closest to the age of the new sample from the question stem. Because both tombs are slightly less than 3,000 years old, the new sample is most likely about 2,900 years old, as in (G). Be careful about choice H, which might seem right if you moved directly in Figure 1 from the C-14 index points to age in the left axis, instead of looking at the ages that correspond to the heights of the bars under each point.

Passage IV

21. B   Difficulty: Low

Category: Evaluation of Models, Inferences, and Results

Getting to the Answer: The opening paragraph of the passage mentions that each scientist is discussing "events that may have caused" the extinction of the dinosaurs. Thus, it is reasonable to conclude that each of the events discussed by the scientists should have in some way contributed to this extinction. Choice (B), which suggests that the acid rain was mentioned because it is harmful to life, is consistent with this conclusion, making it the correct answer. (This is also supported by Scientist 2's suggestion that acid rain caused food and water to become toxic.) Choice A is incorrect because it suggests the opposite: that acid rain is actually beneficial, which makes little sense in a passage about extinction. Choice C contradicts the information in the passage: CO_2 in the atmosphere helped to cause the acid rain, not vice versa. Choice D also reverses the causality in the passage: fires produced CO_2, which in turn led to the acid rain.

22. G   Difficulty: Medium

Category: Evaluation of Models, Inferences, and Results

Getting to the Answer: The new information about sulfates could only weaken the viewpoint of a scientist who uses sulfates to support his explanation. Only Scientist 2 mentions sulfates, so you can immediately eliminate

F and H, since they include Scientist 1. Scientist 2 states that atmospheric sulfates "led to a breakdown of the ozone layer, allowing high levels of ultraviolet radiation to reach the surface." If, as the new information suggests, sulfates in the atmosphere actually cause radiation to be reflected so that it never reaches the surface, Scientist 2's account would be undermined. Choice (G) is thus correct.

23. D   **Difficulty:** Medium

Category: Evaluation of Models, Inferences, and Results

Getting to the Answer: To answer this question, review what Scientist 2 says about the ozone layer: "SO_4 in the atmosphere led to a breakdown of the ozone layer." If heightened levels of SO_4 break down the ozone layer, then lower levels of SO_4 would help to maintain it. Choice (D) is therefore correct.

24. H   **Difficulty:** Low

Category: Evaluation of Models, Inferences, and Results

Getting to the Answer: Use process of elimination with this question to home in on the correct answer. Choice F is incorrect because only Scientist 1 believes that climate change was caused by the impact of a meteorite; Scientist 2 maintains it was caused by volcanic eruptions. Choice G is incorrect because tidal waves are mentioned only in the account of Scientist 1, and even there they are not explicitly linked to climate change. Choice J can't be correct because only Scientist 2 mentions SO_4. Choice (H), then, is correct. Both scientists connect excess CO_2 to the production of acid rain, while Scientist 1 further suggests that it was responsible for global temperature increases.

25. D   **Difficulty:** Medium

Category: Evaluation of Models, Inferences, and Results

Getting to the Answer: The very first sentence of the passage makes the only reference to the time of the dinosaurs' extinction: "The last of the dinosaurs went extinct approximately 65 million years ago." The meteor described by Scientist 1 would have to have landed at about the same time, so (D) is correct.

26. F   **Difficulty:** High

Category: Evaluation of Models, Inferences, and Results

Getting to the Answer: Scientist 2 makes two claims about sulfates: "the mixing of sulfates with water vapor caused more acid rain" and "SO_4 in the atmosphere led to a breakdown of the ozone layer, allowing high levels of ultraviolet radiation to reach the surface." Thus, a decrease in sulfate levels should lead to less acid rain (which eliminates G and H) and to less radiation reaching the surface (which eliminates J). Choice (F) must therefore be correct. While you can reach this conclusion using process of elimination, it also follows from an understanding of pH: lower pH values indicate greater acidity, while higher pH values indicate lesser acidity. Consequently, an increase in the average pH of rainfall would be expected with fewer sulfates, which is precisely what (F) states.

27. B   **Difficulty:** Medium

Category: Evaluation of Models, Inferences, and Results

Getting to the Answer: Eliminate A and C, because only Scientist 2 mentions sulfates. Scientist 2 states that a large quantity of sulfates was released at the time of the dinosaurs' extinction and that the reduction in the ozone layer that these sulfates caused led to more radiation reaching the surface (which would result in higher temperatures). In such circumstances, it would be reasonable to expect inorganic sulfates to form, so the discovery of such substances dating from 65 million years ago would indeed support Scientist 2. Choice (B) is correct.

Passage V

28. H   **Difficulty:** High

Category: Interpretation of Data

Getting to the Answer: Questions like this one are easier with some chemistry knowledge, so you might want to save it for last if you don't like chemistry. Fortunately, though, there's still a way to the answer without outside knowledge. Two chemical equations appear in the passage. Both have the starting chemicals on the left and the resulting chemicals on the right. The question stem suggests that you start with NaOH and HCl and end with NaCl and H_2O, so you can eliminate F and G, both of which have the order reversed. The only difference between (H) and J is that J has 2 H_2Os on the right side while (H) has just 1. According to the chemical equations in the passage, the total number of each element is the same on each side of the equation: there are 2 Hs and 2 Cls on the left side of the first equation, and 2 of each on the right. The same holds in the second equation:

each side contains 1 Si and 4 each of H and Cl. So, you can determine that J is incorrect because it gives 4 Hs and 2 Os on the right side, but only 2 Hs and 1 O on the left. Choice (H), which properly balances the number of elements on both sides, is correct.

29. B   Difficulty: High

Category: Scientific Investigation

Getting to the Answer: If you glance at the answer choices while thinking through this question, you'll notice that each one consists of two parts, the first concerning the pressure and the second concerning the amount of gas. It's actually easier to start with the second part and consider what happens to the amount of gas. Table 1 shows that the syringe was filled with 40 mL of H_2 and 40 mL of Cl_2 at the beginning of Trial 5, but that no H_2 or Cl_2 was left over after the flash that caused the reaction. That means the total amount of gas has decreased (to nothing), which allows you to eliminate A and C, both of which suggest an increase. To decide between the remaining options, you'll need to determine the effect that the loss of gas has on pressure. Here, it is helpful to have a bit of scientific background knowledge, but it may also be possible to use reasoning to find the correct answer. The flash in Trial 5 leads to the conversion of all the gas to droplets of liquid HCl. This leaves behind an empty space in the syringe, otherwise known as a vacuum. Vacuums are very low pressure—this is why materials are naturally drawn into them, such as is seen in the suctioning power of a vacuum cleaner—so the pressure in the syringe after the reaction had to have decreased. Choice (B) is thus correct.

30. H   Difficulty: Medium

Category: Scientific Investigation

Getting to the Answer: While there is no trial in Experiment 1 that begins with these exact conditions, you can nevertheless reason to the answer by considering the reactions in Table 1 that use more Cl_2 than H_2—Trials 2, 3, and 4. In each of these trials, the amount of Cl_2 left over was equal to the amount of starting Cl_2 minus the amount of starting H_2. So, you can predict that 20 mL of Cl_2 reacting with 10 mL of H_2 will leave behind 10 mL of Cl_2. This matches (H).

31. A   Difficulty: Medium

Category: Scientific Investigation

Getting to the Answer: It can be difficult to predict researchers' assumptions, so work backward from the answer choices on questions like this. Start by eliminating the choices that contain information not included in Experiment 1. Choices C and D refer to solid Si and $SiCl_4$, which appear only in Experiment 2, so you can eliminate both choices. Choice B is incorrect because it contradicts the results of Trials 1, 5, and 6 of Experiment 1—each of these were successful without having Cl_2 left over. Only (A), then, must be true. This makes sense because the results compiled in Table 1 would not be informative if they only reflected what was happening in the middle of the reaction.

32. G   Difficulty: High

Category: Scientific Investigation

Getting to the Answer: This is another question that can be answered either by using background knowledge in chemistry or by making inferences from the patterns established in the passage. The equation following Experiment 1 indicates that 1 H_2 and 1 Cl_2 combine to form 2 HCl; in other words, when there are equal amounts of each, such as in Trials 1 and 5 of Experiment 1, there will be no H_2 or Cl_2 left over after they react. When there is an excess of one of the two, such as the excess Cl_2 in Trial 2 or the excess H_2 in Trial 6, some of that excess substance will remain unreacted. Now, the equation in the question stem states that 2 H_2 and 1 O_2 combine to form 2 H_2O; in other words, you need exactly twice as much H_2 as O_2 to ensure that neither gas is left over at the end. The reaction in the stem involves 10 mL of O_2, so you can expect that to react fully with 20 mL of H_2. However, there are 25 mL of H_2 total, which means that there should be $25 - 20 = 5$ mL of H_2 left over after the reaction. Choice (G) is therefore correct.

33. C   Difficulty: High

Category: Scientific Investigation

Getting to the Answer: According to the description of Experiment 2, $SiCl_4$ and H_2 combined to form liquid HCl. By measuring the changes in mass, students were able to determine the ratio of $SiCl_4$ and H_2 molecules needed to form HCl: "4 molecules of HCl were produced for every 1 molecule of $SiCl_4$ and every 2 molecules of H_2 reacted." Now consider the answer choices one by one to determine whether each could cause an error in these results, most likely by having an impact on the mass changes that the students measured. Choice A could certainly cause an error: if unanticipated reactions produced products other than HCl, then there would be a smaller mass of HCl than there would be if it were the only product, which would impact the ratios that the students calculated. Choice B could also impact these calculations and lead to an error, since only the mass of the HCl that condensed in the condensation chamber was measured. Choice (C) is correct: *nonreactive* impurities would not react with any of the substances that the students weighed, so they should have no impact on the ratios the students calculated. Choice D is incorrect for a similar reason: *reactive* impurities in the H_2 would lead to the formation of products other than HCl, which would affect the mass measurements and the students' calculations.

34. J   Difficulty: Medium

Category: Scientific Investigation

Getting to the Answer: A limiting reagent is a substance that is completely used up in a chemical reaction, thereby limiting how much of the reaction's product can be produced and leaving unreacted any other reagents that are present in excess. According to Table 1, Cl_2 is completely used up in Trials 1, 5, and 6, with excess H_2 left over in Trial 6. Thus, Cl_2 is a limiting reagent for Trial 6, making (J) the correct answer.

Passage VI

35. A   Difficulty: Low

Category: Interpretation of Data

Getting to the Answer: Figure 2 compares slide time to θ. To answer this question, find a value for slide time that contains points for both Earth (represented by the square points) and Mercury (represented by the triangular points). For a slide time of about 0.6 seconds, Earth has a θ of 45° and Mercury has a θ of 85°. Choice (A) is thus correct. Watch out for choices C and D: choice C offers θ values for which Neptune and Earth have approximately equal slide times, while D offers θ values for which Neptune and Mercury are roughly equal.

36. H   Difficulty: Medium

Category: Interpretation of Data

Getting to the Answer: Follow the shape of the given curve to extrapolate beyond the boundaries of the graph. Mercury is represented by the triangular points, so follow the triangles to the far left of the graph in Figure 1 and estimate where the next one would appear for $d_0 = 25$ cm. The slide time is just over 0.7 seconds for $d_0 = 35$ cm and just under 0.7 seconds for $d_0 = 30$ cm. So the slide time for 25 cm should be less than 0.1 seconds lower than the slide time for 30 cm. Choice (H), 0.6 seconds, makes for the best approximation. You could have immediately eliminated J because it is higher than 0.7 seconds, while choices F and G would both be too low.

37. C   Difficulty: Medium

Category: Interpretation of Data

Getting to the Answer: With a question like this that requires interpolating a data point, it can help to draw directly on the figures provided. First draw a curve in Figure 2 that smoothly connects the triangular points representing Mercury's slide times. Then, trace the horizontal line that corresponds to a y-value of 1.2 seconds until it intersects the Mercury curve. Finally, draw a line straight down from that point to the x-axis. The line hits the x-axis somewhere between θ = 35° and θ = 45°. Only (C) falls within this range, making it correct.

38. F   Difficulty: Medium

Category: Interpretation of Data

Getting to the Answer: To answer this question, examine Diagram 1, which shows the box on the track. The distance between the end of the track and the beginning of the box is labeled d_0. If the box slides a distance x down the track, you know that it must be closer to the edge of the track than it started, so eliminate G (which would increase the distance remaining) and H (which would keep the distance remaining constant). As the box slides farther down the track, x increases while the distance remaining must decrease. Thus, J could not be correct, because it suggests that the distance to the end of the track would increase as the box slid farther down the track. Choice (F), then, must be correct, which you can see if you imagine x to be equal to 0, in which case the distance remaining would appropriately be d_0 (because the box hasn't moved yet); and if you imagine x to be equal to d_0, in which case the distance remaining would appropriately be 0 (because the box will have slid all the way down).

39. D   Difficulty: High

Category: Interpretation of Data

Getting to the Answer: This is another question that requires interpolation, so drawing on the figure is again recommended. The question stem mentions a slide time of 0.8 seconds, so trace the line in Figure 2 that corresponds to a y-value of 0.8. This intersects one of Mercury's triangular points at a θ value of 55°, but it does not intersect any of Earth's square points. To find the θ value for Earth, sketch in the curve to connect the squares and then drop down a line to determine the x-value for where the Earth curve intersects 0.8 seconds. You should find that a slide time of 0.8 seconds on Earth corresponds to a θ of approximately 38°. Because 38° is 17° less than 55°, (D) is correct.

40. F   Difficulty: Medium

Category: Interpretation of Data

Getting to the Answer: Apply trends from the figures to make deductions about similar experiments. Based on the acceleration values listed in Table 1 and the results in Figures 1 and 2, slide times are shorter on the surfaces of planets with larger accelerations due to gravity. The acceleration due to gravity on Jupiter is larger than that on any of the given planets, so the slide times on Jupiter should be less than those on any of the three planets, as suggested in (F).

WRITING TEST

MODEL ESSAY

Below is an example of what a high-scoring essay might look like. Notice the author states her position clearly in the introductory paragraph and supports that position with evidence in the following paragraphs. This essay also uses transitions, some advanced vocabulary, and an effective "hook" to draw in the reader.

Teenagers have lots of opinions, many of which we share rather loudly. Taking into consideration the students' feelings about the courses they study in high school has both pros and cons. Some argue that schools should provide students a way to make their preferences known, others feel students are too young to make good decisions about what to study, and others argue that surveying students can help make the curriculum more relevant to them and provide another way to evaluate a teacher's effectiveness. I agree that students' interests should be surveyed as long as they are not, in and of themselves, the basis for creating a curriculum.

From the first perspective, it is argued that high schools should do what colleges do and survey students to see how they feel about their classroom lessons. Studies show that when high school students are engaged because they enjoy their studies and understand the relevance of what they are learning, they are more participatory in class and remember more of what they learn. However, one problem is that schools cannot let students create the lessons, since this would lead to chaos with so many students expressing different opinions. However, if it were made clear that not all suggestions would be used but that there would be some way to pare down the suggestions, implementing only those with most student support, it would be possible for the students' preferences to be included in a lesson. Schools could survey students, compile a list of five top suggestions, then have students vote on them. In this way at least some student suggestions, and hopefully the most popular ones, would be part of the curriculum and promote more interaction and learning in a classroom. Surely this is the goal of education, and therefore it should be encouraged.

On the other hand, there are those who think that only the teachers should be in charge of the curriculum because students are not qualified to make those changes. It's true that students don't have the education, knowledge, and maturity to design lessons, but the argument doesn't say that the curriculum would be totally in the hands of the students, but only that student preferences should be considered. Those who argue that students aren't capable of designing the curriculum have misunderstood the statement. Everybody can benefit from suggestions, including educators, so there is nothing wrong with finding out what students want and trying to incorporate at least some of it into the curriculum. Any good teacher does this already. For example, she tries to make her examples relevant to what the students are interested in, such as teaching math by using basketball or baseball examples. So the argument is already partially in force, and those who misread it by thinking that the entire curriculum would be made up by students are misinterpreting the argument and coming to a wrong conclusion.

Finally, some argue that allowing student surveys could make lessons more interesting and also be a way of evaluating a teacher's effectiveness. I personally think that this would be a better way to evaluate teachers than using test scores, which don't always reflect real learning. But surveys are completely subjective, and it would be very difficult to tell which responses really reflect student satisfaction and which are just written because the student needs to write something. So this option is better than cold test scores, but I also see problems in it and so can't support it fully.

If a school administration makes it really clear that, just because students are being asked to make lesson plan suggestions doesn't mean that all suggestions will be used and that students are not in charge of making the curriculum, then the first perspective—allowing students to give their opinion about what they would like to study—is a good one. This one will make at least some lesson plans more interesting and relevant, and that will lead to better learning.

You can evaluate your essay and the model essay based on the following criteria:

- Is the author's own perspective clearly stated?
- Does the body of the essay assess and analyze an additional perspective?
- Is the relevance of each paragraph clear?
- Does the author start a new paragraph for each new idea?
- Is each sentence in a paragraph relevant to the point made in that paragraph?
- Are transitions clear?
- Is the essay easy to read? Is it engaging?
- Are sentences varied?
- Is vocabulary used effectively? Is college-level vocabulary used?

ACT Practice Test 3
ANSWER SHEET

ENGLISH TEST

1. Ⓐ Ⓑ Ⓒ Ⓓ	11. Ⓐ Ⓑ Ⓒ Ⓓ	21. Ⓐ Ⓑ Ⓒ Ⓓ	31. Ⓐ Ⓑ Ⓒ Ⓓ	41. Ⓐ Ⓑ Ⓒ Ⓓ	51. Ⓐ Ⓑ Ⓒ Ⓓ	61. Ⓐ Ⓑ Ⓒ Ⓓ	71. Ⓐ Ⓑ Ⓒ Ⓓ
2. Ⓕ Ⓖ Ⓗ Ⓙ	12. Ⓕ Ⓖ Ⓗ Ⓙ	22. Ⓕ Ⓖ Ⓗ Ⓙ	32. Ⓕ Ⓖ Ⓗ Ⓙ	42. Ⓕ Ⓖ Ⓗ Ⓙ	52. Ⓕ Ⓖ Ⓗ Ⓙ	62. Ⓕ Ⓖ Ⓗ Ⓙ	72. Ⓕ Ⓖ Ⓗ Ⓙ
3. Ⓐ Ⓑ Ⓒ Ⓓ	13. Ⓐ Ⓑ Ⓒ Ⓓ	23. Ⓐ Ⓑ Ⓒ Ⓓ	33. Ⓐ Ⓑ Ⓒ Ⓓ	43. Ⓐ Ⓑ Ⓒ Ⓓ	53. Ⓐ Ⓑ Ⓒ Ⓓ	63. Ⓐ Ⓑ Ⓒ Ⓓ	73. Ⓐ Ⓑ Ⓒ Ⓓ
4. Ⓕ Ⓖ Ⓗ Ⓙ	14. Ⓕ Ⓖ Ⓗ Ⓙ	24. Ⓕ Ⓖ Ⓗ Ⓙ	34. Ⓕ Ⓖ Ⓗ Ⓙ	44. Ⓕ Ⓖ Ⓗ Ⓙ	54. Ⓕ Ⓖ Ⓗ Ⓙ	64. Ⓕ Ⓖ Ⓗ Ⓙ	74. Ⓕ Ⓖ Ⓗ Ⓙ
5. Ⓐ Ⓑ Ⓒ Ⓓ	15. Ⓐ Ⓑ Ⓒ Ⓓ	25. Ⓐ Ⓑ Ⓒ Ⓓ	35. Ⓐ Ⓑ Ⓒ Ⓓ	45. Ⓐ Ⓑ Ⓒ Ⓓ	55. Ⓐ Ⓑ Ⓒ Ⓓ	65. Ⓐ Ⓑ Ⓒ Ⓓ	75. Ⓐ Ⓑ Ⓒ Ⓓ
6. Ⓕ Ⓖ Ⓗ Ⓙ	16. Ⓕ Ⓖ Ⓗ Ⓙ	26. Ⓕ Ⓖ Ⓗ Ⓙ	36. Ⓕ Ⓖ Ⓗ Ⓙ	46. Ⓕ Ⓖ Ⓗ Ⓙ	56. Ⓕ Ⓖ Ⓗ Ⓙ	66. Ⓕ Ⓖ Ⓗ Ⓙ	
7. Ⓐ Ⓑ Ⓒ Ⓓ	17. Ⓐ Ⓑ Ⓒ Ⓓ	27. Ⓐ Ⓑ Ⓒ Ⓓ	37. Ⓐ Ⓑ Ⓒ Ⓓ	47. Ⓐ Ⓑ Ⓒ Ⓓ	57. Ⓐ Ⓑ Ⓒ Ⓓ	67. Ⓐ Ⓑ Ⓒ Ⓓ	
8. Ⓕ Ⓖ Ⓗ Ⓙ	18. Ⓕ Ⓖ Ⓗ Ⓙ	28. Ⓕ Ⓖ Ⓗ Ⓙ	38. Ⓕ Ⓖ Ⓗ Ⓙ	48. Ⓕ Ⓖ Ⓗ Ⓙ	58. Ⓕ Ⓖ Ⓗ Ⓙ	68. Ⓕ Ⓖ Ⓗ Ⓙ	
9. Ⓐ Ⓑ Ⓒ Ⓓ	19. Ⓐ Ⓑ Ⓒ Ⓓ	29. Ⓐ Ⓑ Ⓒ Ⓓ	39. Ⓐ Ⓑ Ⓒ Ⓓ	49. Ⓐ Ⓑ Ⓒ Ⓓ	59. Ⓐ Ⓑ Ⓒ Ⓓ	69. Ⓐ Ⓑ Ⓒ Ⓓ	
10. Ⓕ Ⓖ Ⓗ Ⓙ	20. Ⓕ Ⓖ Ⓗ Ⓙ	30. Ⓕ Ⓖ Ⓗ Ⓙ	40. Ⓕ Ⓖ Ⓗ Ⓙ	50. Ⓕ Ⓖ Ⓗ Ⓙ	60. Ⓕ Ⓖ Ⓗ Ⓙ	70. Ⓕ Ⓖ Ⓗ Ⓙ	

MATHEMATICS TEST

1. Ⓐ Ⓑ Ⓒ Ⓓ Ⓔ	11. Ⓐ Ⓑ Ⓒ Ⓓ Ⓔ	21. Ⓐ Ⓑ Ⓒ Ⓓ Ⓔ	31. Ⓐ Ⓑ Ⓒ Ⓓ Ⓔ	41. Ⓐ Ⓑ Ⓒ Ⓓ Ⓔ	51. Ⓐ Ⓑ Ⓒ Ⓓ Ⓔ
2. Ⓕ Ⓖ Ⓗ Ⓙ Ⓚ	12. Ⓕ Ⓖ Ⓗ Ⓙ Ⓚ	22. Ⓕ Ⓖ Ⓗ Ⓙ Ⓚ	32. Ⓕ Ⓖ Ⓗ Ⓙ Ⓚ	42. Ⓕ Ⓖ Ⓗ Ⓙ Ⓚ	52. Ⓕ Ⓖ Ⓗ Ⓙ Ⓚ
3. Ⓐ Ⓑ Ⓒ Ⓓ Ⓔ	13. Ⓐ Ⓑ Ⓒ Ⓓ Ⓔ	23. Ⓐ Ⓑ Ⓒ Ⓓ Ⓔ	33. Ⓐ Ⓑ Ⓒ Ⓓ Ⓔ	43. Ⓐ Ⓑ Ⓒ Ⓓ Ⓔ	53. Ⓐ Ⓑ Ⓒ Ⓓ Ⓔ
4. Ⓕ Ⓖ Ⓗ Ⓙ Ⓚ	14. Ⓕ Ⓖ Ⓗ Ⓙ Ⓚ	24. Ⓕ Ⓖ Ⓗ Ⓙ Ⓚ	34. Ⓕ Ⓖ Ⓗ Ⓙ Ⓚ	44. Ⓕ Ⓖ Ⓗ Ⓙ Ⓚ	54. Ⓕ Ⓖ Ⓗ Ⓙ Ⓚ
5. Ⓐ Ⓑ Ⓒ Ⓓ Ⓔ	15. Ⓐ Ⓑ Ⓒ Ⓓ Ⓔ	25. Ⓐ Ⓑ Ⓒ Ⓓ Ⓔ	35. Ⓐ Ⓑ Ⓒ Ⓓ Ⓔ	45. Ⓐ Ⓑ Ⓒ Ⓓ Ⓔ	55. Ⓐ Ⓑ Ⓒ Ⓓ Ⓔ
6. Ⓕ Ⓖ Ⓗ Ⓙ Ⓚ	16. Ⓕ Ⓖ Ⓗ Ⓙ Ⓚ	26. Ⓕ Ⓖ Ⓗ Ⓙ Ⓚ	36. Ⓕ Ⓖ Ⓗ Ⓙ Ⓚ	46. Ⓕ Ⓖ Ⓗ Ⓙ Ⓚ	56. Ⓕ Ⓖ Ⓗ Ⓙ Ⓚ
7. Ⓐ Ⓑ Ⓒ Ⓓ Ⓔ	17. Ⓐ Ⓑ Ⓒ Ⓓ Ⓔ	27. Ⓐ Ⓑ Ⓒ Ⓓ Ⓔ	37. Ⓐ Ⓑ Ⓒ Ⓓ Ⓔ	47. Ⓐ Ⓑ Ⓒ Ⓓ Ⓔ	57. Ⓐ Ⓑ Ⓒ Ⓓ Ⓔ
8. Ⓕ Ⓖ Ⓗ Ⓙ Ⓚ	18. Ⓕ Ⓖ Ⓗ Ⓙ Ⓚ	28. Ⓕ Ⓖ Ⓗ Ⓙ Ⓚ	38. Ⓕ Ⓖ Ⓗ Ⓙ Ⓚ	48. Ⓕ Ⓖ Ⓗ Ⓙ Ⓚ	58. Ⓕ Ⓖ Ⓗ Ⓙ Ⓚ
9. Ⓐ Ⓑ Ⓒ Ⓓ Ⓔ	19. Ⓐ Ⓑ Ⓒ Ⓓ Ⓔ	29. Ⓐ Ⓑ Ⓒ Ⓓ Ⓔ	39. Ⓐ Ⓑ Ⓒ Ⓓ Ⓔ	49. Ⓐ Ⓑ Ⓒ Ⓓ Ⓔ	59. Ⓐ Ⓑ Ⓒ Ⓓ Ⓔ
10. Ⓕ Ⓖ Ⓗ Ⓙ Ⓚ	20. Ⓕ Ⓖ Ⓗ Ⓙ Ⓚ	30. Ⓕ Ⓖ Ⓗ Ⓙ Ⓚ	40. Ⓕ Ⓖ Ⓗ Ⓙ Ⓚ	50. Ⓕ Ⓖ Ⓗ Ⓙ Ⓚ	60. Ⓕ Ⓖ Ⓗ Ⓙ Ⓚ

READING TEST

1. Ⓐ Ⓑ Ⓒ Ⓓ	6. Ⓕ Ⓖ Ⓗ Ⓙ	11. Ⓐ Ⓑ Ⓒ Ⓓ	16. Ⓕ Ⓖ Ⓗ Ⓙ	21. Ⓐ Ⓑ Ⓒ Ⓓ	26. Ⓕ Ⓖ Ⓗ Ⓙ	31. Ⓐ Ⓑ Ⓒ Ⓓ	36. Ⓕ Ⓖ Ⓗ Ⓙ
2. Ⓕ Ⓖ Ⓗ Ⓙ	7. Ⓐ Ⓑ Ⓒ Ⓓ	12. Ⓕ Ⓖ Ⓗ Ⓙ	17. Ⓐ Ⓑ Ⓒ Ⓓ	22. Ⓕ Ⓖ Ⓗ Ⓙ	27. Ⓐ Ⓑ Ⓒ Ⓓ	32. Ⓕ Ⓖ Ⓗ Ⓙ	37. Ⓐ Ⓑ Ⓒ Ⓓ
3. Ⓐ Ⓑ Ⓒ Ⓓ	8. Ⓕ Ⓖ Ⓗ Ⓙ	13. Ⓐ Ⓑ Ⓒ Ⓓ	18. Ⓕ Ⓖ Ⓗ Ⓙ	23. Ⓐ Ⓑ Ⓒ Ⓓ	28. Ⓕ Ⓖ Ⓗ Ⓙ	33. Ⓐ Ⓑ Ⓒ Ⓓ	38. Ⓕ Ⓖ Ⓗ Ⓙ
4. Ⓕ Ⓖ Ⓗ Ⓙ	9. Ⓐ Ⓑ Ⓒ Ⓓ	14. Ⓕ Ⓖ Ⓗ Ⓙ	19. Ⓐ Ⓑ Ⓒ Ⓓ	24. Ⓕ Ⓖ Ⓗ Ⓙ	29. Ⓐ Ⓑ Ⓒ Ⓓ	34. Ⓕ Ⓖ Ⓗ Ⓙ	39. Ⓐ Ⓑ Ⓒ Ⓓ
5. Ⓐ Ⓑ Ⓒ Ⓓ	10. Ⓕ Ⓖ Ⓗ Ⓙ	15. Ⓐ Ⓑ Ⓒ Ⓓ	20. Ⓕ Ⓖ Ⓗ Ⓙ	25. Ⓐ Ⓑ Ⓒ Ⓓ	30. Ⓕ Ⓖ Ⓗ Ⓙ	35. Ⓐ Ⓑ Ⓒ Ⓓ	40. Ⓕ Ⓖ Ⓗ Ⓙ

SCIENCE TEST

1. Ⓐ Ⓑ Ⓒ Ⓓ	6. Ⓕ Ⓖ Ⓗ Ⓙ	11. Ⓐ Ⓑ Ⓒ Ⓓ	16. Ⓕ Ⓖ Ⓗ Ⓙ	21. Ⓐ Ⓑ Ⓒ Ⓓ	26. Ⓕ Ⓖ Ⓗ Ⓙ	31. Ⓐ Ⓑ Ⓒ Ⓓ	36. Ⓕ Ⓖ Ⓗ Ⓙ
2. Ⓕ Ⓖ Ⓗ Ⓙ	7. Ⓐ Ⓑ Ⓒ Ⓓ	12. Ⓕ Ⓖ Ⓗ Ⓙ	17. Ⓐ Ⓑ Ⓒ Ⓓ	22. Ⓕ Ⓖ Ⓗ Ⓙ	27. Ⓐ Ⓑ Ⓒ Ⓓ	32. Ⓕ Ⓖ Ⓗ Ⓙ	37. Ⓐ Ⓑ Ⓒ Ⓓ
3. Ⓐ Ⓑ Ⓒ Ⓓ	8. Ⓕ Ⓖ Ⓗ Ⓙ	13. Ⓐ Ⓑ Ⓒ Ⓓ	18. Ⓕ Ⓖ Ⓗ Ⓙ	23. Ⓐ Ⓑ Ⓒ Ⓓ	28. Ⓕ Ⓖ Ⓗ Ⓙ	33. Ⓐ Ⓑ Ⓒ Ⓓ	38. Ⓕ Ⓖ Ⓗ Ⓙ
4. Ⓕ Ⓖ Ⓗ Ⓙ	9. Ⓐ Ⓑ Ⓒ Ⓓ	14. Ⓕ Ⓖ Ⓗ Ⓙ	19. Ⓐ Ⓑ Ⓒ Ⓓ	24. Ⓕ Ⓖ Ⓗ Ⓙ	29. Ⓐ Ⓑ Ⓒ Ⓓ	34. Ⓕ Ⓖ Ⓗ Ⓙ	39. Ⓐ Ⓑ Ⓒ Ⓓ
5. Ⓐ Ⓑ Ⓒ Ⓓ	10. Ⓕ Ⓖ Ⓗ Ⓙ	15. Ⓐ Ⓑ Ⓒ Ⓓ	20. Ⓕ Ⓖ Ⓗ Ⓙ	25. Ⓐ Ⓑ Ⓒ Ⓓ	30. Ⓕ Ⓖ Ⓗ Ⓙ	35. Ⓐ Ⓑ Ⓒ Ⓓ	40. Ⓕ Ⓖ Ⓗ Ⓙ

ENGLISH TEST

45 Minutes—75 Questions

Directions: Each passage has certain words and phrases that are underlined and numbered. The questions in the right column will provide alternatives for the underlined segments. Most questions require you to choose the answer that makes the sentence grammatically correct, concise, and relevant. If the word or phrase in the passage is already the correct, concise, and relevant choice, select Choice A, NO CHANGE. Some questions will ask a question about the underlined segment. When a question is presented, choose the best answer.

Some questions will ask about part or all of the passage. These questions do not refer to a specific underlined segment. Instead, these questions will accompany a number in a box.

For each question, choose your answer and fill in the corresponding bubble on your answer sheet. Read the passage once before you answer the questions. You will often need to read several sentences beyond the underlined portion to be able to choose the correct answer. Be sure to read enough to answer each question.

Passage I

A Swimming Change

[1]

Until three years ago, I had never considered myself to be athletically talented. I have never been able to hit, catch, throw, or kick a ball with any degree of confidence or accuracy. For years, physical <u>education being</u> often
₁
the worst part of the school day for me. Units on tennis, touch football, volleyball, and basketball were torturous.

1. **A.** NO CHANGE
   B. education, was
   C. education was
   D. education,

I not only dreaded fumbling a pass, <u>so</u> I also feared
₂
being hit in the face by a ball. However, at the beginning of my freshman year of high school, my attitude toward sports changed.

2. **F.** NO CHANGE
   G. and
   H. but
   J. though

GO ON TO THE NEXT PAGE

[2]

Somehow, my good friend Gretchen convinced me

to join <u>our schools</u> swim team.
     3

3. **A.** NO CHANGE

    B. our schools'

    C. our school's

    D. ours school

<u>Knowing that I enjoyed swimming, over the course of</u>
                    4
<u>two summers, it was with Gretchen that I practically</u>
                    4
<u>had lived at the pool.</u>
      4

4. **F.** NO CHANGE

    G. Because we had spent two summers practically living at the pool, it was Gretchen who knew that swimming was enjoyed by me.

    H. Having practically lived at the pool over two summers, the two of us, Gretchen knew it was swimming that I enjoyed.

    J. Gretchen knew I enjoyed swimming, as we had spent two summers practically living at the pool.

My mother had <u>insisted</u> that I take swimming lessons
             5
every summer since I was seven, so I was entirely com-

fortable in the water. I was also eager to start my high

school experience with a new challenge and a new way

to think of myself.

[3]

Of course, I had no idea what I was getting into

when Gretchen and I showed up for the first day of

practice. The team was made up of twenty young

<u>women, most of these swimmers</u> had been participating
           6
in the community swim team for years. I couldn't do

a flip turn at the end of the lane without getting water

up my nose. In contrast, most of the other swimmers,

5. Of the four choices, which is the only one that does NOT indicate that the narrator's mother decided that the narrator must take swimming lessons?

    A. NO CHANGE

    B. suggested

    C. required

    D. demanded

6. **F.** NO CHANGE

    G. women, the majority of them

    H. women most of them

    J. women, most of whom

GO ON TO THE NEXT PAGE

who <u>had been swimming competitively, since</u>
                7

<u>elementary school,</u> were able to gracefully somersault
     7

and begin the next lap. By the end of the first hour of

practice, I was exhausted and waterlogged.

[4]

    However, I had no intention of giving up. <u>I came</u>
                                    8

<u>back the next day and the next for practice.</u> Things
                  8

<u>begun</u> to get serious in the second week, when we started
 9

the regular schedule of four early-morning and five

afternoon practices. Our coach, <u>whom</u> had led the
                        10

team to several state championships, demanded dedi-

cation from everyone on the team. The hard work

<u>eventually paid off. By</u> the end of the first month, I had
         11

discovered that I was good at the butterfly,

7. **A.** NO CHANGE
   B. had been swimming competitively since elementary school,
   C. had been swimming, competitively since elementary school,
   D. had been swimming competitively since elementary school

8. **F.** NO CHANGE
   G. I came back the next day: and the next for practice.
   H. I came back the next day; the next for practice.
   J. I came back the next day; and the next for practice.

9. **A.** NO CHANGE
   B. had been begun
   C. had began
   D. began

10. **F.** NO CHANGE
   G. for whom
   H. who
   J. which

11. **A.** NO CHANGE
   B. eventually paid off, so, as a result
   C. paid off eventually, however, by
   D. paid off, eventually, by

GO ON TO THE NEXT PAGE ⟶

Practice Test 3

a relatively new stroke that was first introduced in the
                                                   12

1930s. I rarely won individual races, but I became a
  12

solid member of our team's medley relay.
                          13

[5]

After that intimidating first season, I continued

swimming. I even will have earned a varsity letter last year.
                       14

Now I'm hoping to earn a spot in the state competition

my senior year. [15]

12. Assuming each of the following creates a true statement, which provides the information most relevant to the narrator's experience on the swim team?

    F. NO CHANGE

    G. a difficult stroke that interested few other members of our team.

    H. which is faster than the backstroke but somewhat slower than the crawl.

    J. which is still sometimes called the dolphin because it incorporates a two-stroke dolphin kick.

13. **A.** NO CHANGE

    B. team's medley relay (it consists of four swimmers).

    C. team's medley relay, which the person swimming backstroke always begins.

    D. team.

14. **F.** NO CHANGE

    G. would have earned

    H. earned

    J. earn

15. If inserted here, which of the following would be the most appropriate sentence to conclude the essay?

    A. My coach continues to schedule demanding practices, but I have come to enjoy the early-morning swims.

    B. For someone who thought she didn't have any athletic talent, I have come a long way.

    C. Gretchen is also still on the team, but she does not swim the medley relay.

    D. I've always enjoyed swimming, so I'm not all that surprised by my success as an athlete.

GO ON TO THE NEXT PAGE

Passage II

Exploring Dubuque's Aquarium

[1]

One lazy day last summer, my parents decided
that my younger sister and I needed a break from our
vacation from academics. They took us to the National
Mississippi River Museum and Aquarium in Dubuque,
Iowa. I was prepared to be bored by this family
educational trip. However, from the moment I walked
through the museum's doors, I was captivated; by all
that there was to learn about life in the Mississippi.

[2]

[1] A large tank stocked with fish and turtles
was there to greet us as we walked into the main hall. [2]
There were also animals I had never before glimpsed,
such as a fish called the long-nosed gar. [3] I was amazed
by this fish in particular. [4] Its long, tubular shape and
distinctive rod-shaped nose that made it appear like
something that lived in the dark depths of the ocean. [5]

This first of five freshwater aquariums offered a close-up
view of familiar animals that I had seen before,

16. F. NO CHANGE
    G. captivated, by
    H. captivated by,
    J. captivated by

17. A. NO CHANGE
    B. is there
    C. are there
    D. were there

18. F. NO CHANGE
    G. nose, which
    H. nose, and this
    J. nose

19. A. NO CHANGE
    B. animals that were familiar sights to me,
    C. familiar animals to which I was no
       stranger,
    D. familiar animals,

GO ON TO THE NEXT PAGE

such as ducks. [20]

[3]

In the next aquarium, I <u>see</u> a catfish bigger than I
                        21
had ever imagined this species could be. According to

the posted information, this specimen weighed more

than 100 pounds. With its long whiskers and slow, lazy

movements, this catfish looked like the grandfather of

all the other fish in the tank.

[4]

<u>I couldn't decide which I liked better, the catfish</u>
                                    22
<u>or the long-nosed gar.</u> The next floor-to-ceiling tank,
           22
which represented the ecosystem of the Mississippi

bayou, held an animal I had never seen: an alligator.

20. To make Paragraph 2 coherent and logical, the best placement of Sentence 5 is:

F. where it is now.

G. before Sentence 1.

H. after Sentence 1.

J. after Sentence 2.

21. A. NO CHANGE

B. had been seeing

C. saw

D. spot

22. Which sentence most effectively connects this paragraph to the preceding paragraph?

F. NO CHANGE

G. Although the catfish was impressive, it was not the biggest animal on display in the museum.

H. After seeing the catfish, I was interested in exhibits that were a bit more hands-on.

J. Until my visit to the museum, I had never really considered what the Mississippi River was like south of my home.

GO ON TO THE NEXT PAGE

At first, I had a hard time spotting the creature—it blended in almost completely with a half-submerged log. [23]

23. At this point, the writer is considering removing the following phrase:

> it blended in almost completely with a half-submerged log.

The primary effect of removing this phrase would be:

A. a smoother transition between sentences.
B. a greater contrast between images.
C. a loss of descriptive information.
D. an increased level of suspense.

Suddenly, though it slid into the water and aimed itself
    24
right at the glass separating me from its ferocious claws

24. F. NO CHANGE
G. Suddenly though it
H. Suddenly, though, it,
J. Suddenly, though, it

and skin-tearing teeth. I had a slightly moment of panic
                                    25
before I remembered that, try as it might, this alligator
would never successfully hunt tourists like me.

25. A. NO CHANGE
B. momentarily slight
C. moment of slight
D. momentarily of slight

As much of the onlookers squealed in delight as the alli-
    26
gator moved through the tank, I noticed his companion.
Far off in a corner slept an enormous snapping turtle.
I could imagine no better roommate for the alligator
than this hook-beaked turtle with rough ridges running
along its shell.

26. F. NO CHANGE
G. a large amount
H. the many
J. many

[5]

Despite my initial expectations, I happily spent the entire day soaking up information about creatures that

GO ON TO THE NEXT PAGE

live in the Mississippi River. In one section of the museum, I held a crayfish. [27] Later, I had the opportunity to touch the cool, sleek skin of a stingray, which can be found where the Mississippi empties into the Gulf of Mexico.

[6]

After seeing all, I could inside the museum, I
                        28
wandered outside, only to find even more exhibits.

Having just enough time, it was that I was able to see
                        29
the otters and watch a riverboat launching, but it was closing time before I was able to see the most impressive thing the museum had to offer. A football-field-sized steamboat from the 1930s is open to tourists. And
                                                    30
operates as a "boat-and-breakfast" that hosts overnight
  30
guests. I'm hoping that my family will plan another educational trip to Dubuque soon so I can experience life on a steamboat.

27. The writer would like to insert a sentence describing the appearance of the crayfish at this point. Which sentence would best accomplish the writer's goal?

   A. Also known as crawdads, crayfish are close relatives of the lobsters that live in freshwater.

   B. At an average length of three inches, the crayfish looks like a miniature lobster, complete with small but effective front pincers.

   C. Although they are found throughout the United States, crayfish populations are densest in Kentucky and Mississippi.

   D. At first, I was a bit nervous to touch the small creature, but then I relaxed and enjoyed the opportunity to look at it so closely.

28.   F. NO CHANGE
     G. all I could inside the museum,
     H. all, I could inside the museum
     J. all I could inside the museum

29.   A. NO CHANGE
     B. It was that I had just enough time, so I was able
     C. Having just enough time, it was possible
     D. I had just enough time

30.   F. NO CHANGE
     G. tourists and that operates
     H. tourists, it operates
     J. tourists and operates

GO ON TO THE NEXT PAGE

Passage III

The Mystery Diner

> The paragraphs in this essay may or may not follow the most logical order. Each paragraph is numbered, and Question 45 will ask you to determine the best placement of Paragraph 6.

[1]

Although secret identities and elaborate disguises are typically associated with the world of spies and villains, <u>it has</u> other uses. For six years,
31

Ruth <u>Reichl the restaurant critic for the *New York Times*,</u>
32
used aliases and costumes as a regular part of her job.

[2]

Dining is big business in New York City, from the neighborhood noodle shops and diners to the upscale

31. A. NO CHANGE
    B. it does have
    C. they do have
    D. and they have

32. F. NO CHANGE
    G. Reichl, the restaurant critic, for the *New York Times*,
    H. Reichl, the restaurant critic for the *New York Times*,
    J. Reichl the restaurant critic for the *New York Times*

GO ON TO THE NEXT PAGE

steak houses and four-star French restaurants. [33] Many of the more than one million people who read the

33. Should the following sentence be inserted into the passage at this point?

> The legendary French restaurant Le Bernardin received a four-star rating from the *Times* shortly after opening in 1986, an honor it has maintained ever since.

A. Yes, because the added sentence emphasizes how important a positive review from the *Times* can be.

B. Yes, because the specific information helps the reader develop a clearer picture of the type of restaurant reviewed by the *Times*.

C. No, because it is unclear whether Reichl was responsible for reviewing this specific restaurant.

D. No, because the specific information about one restaurant leads the reader away from the main topic of the essay.

Times each day <u>look to</u> it for advice on where to eat.
34

34. F. NO CHANGE

G. look with

H. look by

J. looking to

A positive review from the *Times* <u>could have brought</u> a
35
restaurant unimagined success and monthlong waiting lists for reservations. A negative review, on the other hand, can undermine a restaurant's popularity and seriously cut into its profits. Obviously, <u>restaurant owners</u>
36
<u>and workers</u> have a lot at stake when the restaurant
36
critic for the *Times* walks in the door. Waiters and chefs often pull out all the stops to impress the writer

35. A. NO CHANGE

B. can bring

C. will have brought

D. will be bringing

36. F. NO CHANGE

G. restaurant owners and workers;

H. restaurant, owners and workers

J. restaurant owners, and workers

GO ON TO THE NEXT PAGE

that the meal can make or break a restaurant.
37

37. A. NO CHANGE
   B. who's
   C. whose
   D. which

[3]

Reichl acutely aware that she received special treat-
38
ment once restaurant staff recognized her. She would

be graciously greeted and led to the best table in the

restaurant, offered dishes prepared specially by the head

chef, and given multiple courses of amazing desserts.

In other words, the dining experience of the restaurant

critic was nothing like that of the commonly ordinary
39
person walking in from the street.

38. F. NO CHANGE
   G. Reichl, was acutely aware
   H. Reichl very acutely aware
   J. Reichl was acutely aware

39. A. NO CHANGE
   B. common, representative, and average
   C. typical
   D. extravagant

[4]

To remedy this, Reichl decided a solution would be
40
to become, for short periods of time, someone else.
40

Transforming herself into different personas, Reichl
41
used wigs, special makeup, and carefully selected
41
clothing, such as an attractive blonde named
41

40. F. NO CHANGE
   G. she created a solution to the problem by
      becoming,
   H. Reichl decided to become,
   J. Reichl found a way to fix the problem,
      which involved becoming,

41. A. NO CHANGE
   B. With wigs, special makeup, and carefully
      selected clothing, Reichl transformed
      herself into different personas,
   C. Transformed with wigs, special makeup,
      and carefully selected clothing, Reichl's
      different personas,
   D. Reichl used wigs, special makeup, and
      carefully selected clothing, that trans-
      formed herself into different personas,

GO ON TO THE NEXT PAGE →

Chloe, a redhead named Brenda, and an older woman

named Betty. [42]

[5]

Sometimes, Reichl developed a different view about

the quality when she was not treated like a very important

person <u>of a restaurant</u>. Indeed, the difference between the
                  43
treatment she received as herself and as one of her char-

acters was occasionally so great that Reichl would

42. Which of the following true statements would make the most effective and logical conclusion for Paragraph 4?

   F. Reichl found that she could quickly disguise herself as Betty, but it took more time to become Chloe.

   G. Her true identity hidden, Reichl would then dine at a restaurant she was currently evaluating.

   H. After six years at the *Times,* Reichl moved on to become the editor of *Gourmet* magazine.

   J. The former restaurant critic for the *Times* did not always agree with Reichl's methods or her selection of restaurants to review.

43. For the sake of logic and coherence, the under-lined portion should be placed:

   A. where it is now.

   B. after the word *developed*.

   C. after the word *view*.

   D. after the word *quality*.

GO ON TO THE NEXT PAGE ⟶

revise her initial impression of a restaurant and write a worse review. 44

[6]

By becoming an average customer, Reichl encouraged even the most expensive and popular restaurants to improve how they treated all of their customers. After all, waiters could never be certain when they were serving the powerful restaurant critic for the *New York Times*.

44. Would deleting the word *occasionally* from the previous sentence change the meaning of the sentence?

F. Yes, because without this word, the reader would not understand that Reichl had different experiences when she dined in disguise.

G. Yes, because without this word, the reader would think that Reichl always changed her impression of restaurants when she was not recognized and received different treatment as a result.

H. No, because this word repeats an idea that is already presented in the sentence.

J. No, because this word is used only to show emphasis, and it does not contribute to the meaning of the sentence.

Question 45 asks about the preceding passage as a whole.

45. To make the passage flow logically and smoothly, the best place for Paragraph 6 is:

A. where it is now.

B. after Paragraph 1.

C. after Paragraph 3.

D. after Paragraph 4.

GO ON TO THE NEXT PAGE

Passage IV

The Benefits of a Square Foot Garden

[1]

[1] I used to start every spring with great hopes for my backyard vegetable garden. [2] After the last freeze in late March or early April, I devoted an entire weekend to preparing the soil in the garden. [3] I thinned out the rows that had too many plants and spent hours tugging out each weed that threatened to rob my little plants of the nutrients they needed to thrive. [4] Once spring truly arrived, I marked out my rows and scattered the packets of seeds that I <u>hoped, would</u> develop into prizewinning
46
vegetables. [5] In the first few weeks of the season, I was almost always in the garden. 47

[2]

Despite my best intentions, my garden never lived up to the vision I had for it. After I had devoted several weekends to watering and weeding, the garden always started to become more of a <u>burden</u> less of a hobby. By
48
July, the garden was usually in disarray, and I didn't have

46. **F.** NO CHANGE
   G. hoped, would,
   H. hoped would,
   J. hoped would

47. To make Paragraph 1 more logical and coherent, Sentence 3 should be placed:
   A. where it is now.
   B. before Sentence 1.
   C. after Sentence 1.
   D. after Sentence 4.

48. **F.** NO CHANGE
   G. burden:
   H. burden and
   J. burden, but,

GO ON TO THE NEXT PAGE

the energy or time to save it. July and August are always
49
the hottest parts of the year.
49

[3]

This past year, however, my garden was finally the
50
success I had imagined it could be. Instead of planning

the traditional garden of closely planted rows that is
51
modeled after large-scale farming, I tried a new tech-
51
nique. My new approach is called square foot gardening.

[4]

A square foot garden is designed for efficiency.
52

49. **A.** NO CHANGE
    B. The hottest months are July and August.
    C. (July, along with August, provides the hottest temperatures of the year.)
    D. DELETE the underlined portion.

50. Of the following choices, which would be the LEAST acceptable substitution for the underlined word?

    F. on the other hand,
    G. indeed,
    H. though,
    J. in contrast,

51. **A.** NO CHANGE
    B. rows, which is modeled after large-scale farming,
    C. rows, which is based on the techniques for large-scale farming,
    D. rows,

52. Which sentence most effectively links the topic of Paragraph 3 to the topic of Paragraph 4?

    F. NO CHANGE
    G. The technique of square foot gardening was pioneered by Mel Bartholomew.
    H. One of the benefits of a square foot garden is that it is less expensive to maintain than a traditional garden.
    J. My neighbor, who always has a beautiful garden, introduced me to the concept of square foot gardening, and I have been grateful ever since.

GO ON TO THE NEXT PAGE

Practice Test 3

In <u>an ancestral</u> garden, you scatter a packet of seeds
53
down a row. When the plants emerge,

<u>they spend</u> hours thinning each row by pulling out at
54
least half of what was planted. In a square foot garden,

you plant each seed <u>individually, there</u> is never a need for
55
thinning. You create the garden plan one square foot at a

time, until you have a block of 16 squares. Sturdy pieces

of lumber <u>which could make</u> effective borders for each
56
square. Walking paths that are at least two feet wide

separate each 16-square-foot garden. The design is clean

and simple, and it eliminates the problem of getting to the

rows in the middle of a large garden. In fact, <u>you can do</u>
57
all the weeding, watering, and harvesting from the walk-

ing paths.

[5]

In addition to being easier to weed and water, a

square foot garden takes up much less space than a

regular garden. I was able to grow <u>an increased number</u>
58
<u>of more</u> vegetables in two square foot gardens, which
58
took up a total of 32 square feet, than I ever had grown

in my traditional garden, which took up 84 square feet.

Preparing the soil for the smaller space only required

a few hours instead of a whole weekend. There was

so much less weeding to do that the task never felt

53. A. NO CHANGE
    B. a compulsory
    C. a conventional
    D. a devout

54. F. NO CHANGE
    G. he spends
    H. people spend
    J. you spend

55. A. NO CHANGE
    B. individually there
    C. individually so there
    D. individually, so there

56. F. NO CHANGE
    G. that make
    H. make
    J. makes

57. A. NO CHANGE
    B. you could have done
    C. one can do
    D. one is able to do

58. F. NO CHANGE
    G. a larger quantity of more
    H. an increased, bigger quantity
    J. more

GO ON TO THE NEXT PAGE

overwhelming. One season of using the square foot

gardening techniques <u>were all</u> it took for me to convert
                        59
to a completely new outlook on backyard gardening.

59. **A.** NO CHANGE
    B. were just what
    C. was all
    D. could be

Question 60 asks about the preceding passage as a whole.

---

60. If the writer had intended to write an essay detailing how to plan, prepare, and care for a square foot garden, would this essay meet the writer's goal?

    F. No, because the writer relies on generalities rather than specifics when describing her square foot garden.

    G. No, because the writer focuses on comparing two different types of gardens instead of explaining how to begin and care for one type of garden.

    H. Yes, because the writer states specific measurements for her square foot garden.

    J. Yes, because the writer maintains that square foot gardens are superior to traditional gardens.

GO ON TO THE NEXT PAGE

Practice Test 3

Passage V

The Importance of Maintaining Your Car

[1]

Most new car owners glance briefly at the owner's manual before depositing it in the glove compartment of their recently purchased automobile. Owners may dig out their manuals when something goes <u>wrong, such as a flat tire or a flashing engine light</u> but few take the time
61
to learn the basics about maintaining their new purchase. This is truly unfortunate, as a few simple and

routine steps <u>improves the long-term performance of an automobile and decreases</u> the possibility of a traffic
62
accident.

61. A. NO CHANGE
  B. wrong; such as a flat tire or a flashing engine light
  C. wrong, such as a flat tire, or a flashing engine light
  D. wrong, such as a flat tire or a flashing engine light,

62. F. NO CHANGE
  G. improve the long-term performance of an automobile and decreases
  H. improve the long-term performance of an automobile and decrease
  J. improves the long-term performance of an automobile and decrease

[2]

One of the easiest and most overlooked maintenance steps is caring for a car's wiper blades. <u>Most people don't notice a problem to clear the windshield until the blades fail during a rainstorm or heavy snowfall.</u>
63

63. A. NO CHANGE
  B. Most people don't notice a problem until the blades fail to clear the windshield during a rainstorm or heavy snowfall.
  C. To clear the windshield, most people don't notice a problem until the blades fail during a rainstorm or heavy snowfall.
  D. Most people don't notice a problem until the blades fail during a rainstorm to clear the windshield or heavy snowfall.

GO ON TO THE NEXT PAGE ⟹

When a driver's <u>vision being</u> obscured, an accident is
                      64

more likely to happen. Replacing the <u>set</u> blades at a time
                                       65
each year greatly reduces this risk. In addition, frequent-

ly refilling the windshield washer fluid reservoir guaran-

tees that there will always be enough fluid to wash away

grime that accumulates on the windshield.

[3]

Much of car maintenance focuses on preventing

problems before they occur. For example, checking the

levels of coolant, oil, brake fluid, and transmission fluid

can avert serious malfunctions. <u>However,</u> these fluids
                                    66
should be checked monthly and refilled whenever the

need is indicated.

[4]

<u>Cars are becoming more sophisticated every year,</u>
                          67
<u>but car owners without any expertise in mechanics can</u>
                          67
<u>still perform much of the basic upkeep of their vehicle.</u>
                          67
You should change the oil in most cars every 3,000 to

7,000 miles. This task requires a willingness to get a bit

64. F. NO CHANGE
 G. vision, has been
 H. vision is
 J. vision,

65. The underlined word would be most logically placed:

 A. where it is now.
 B. before the word *time*.
 C. before the word *year*.
 D. before the word *risk*.

66. F. NO CHANGE
 G. In general,
 H. Despite this,
 J. After that,

67. Which sentence is the most effective beginning to Paragraph 4?

 A. NO CHANGE
 B. Changing the oil and oil filter regularly is another key to keeping your car's engine performing at its best.
 C. An entire industry now focuses on providing regular car maintenance, such as changing the oil and rotating the tires.
 D. Even if you haven't read your car owner's manual, you probably know that your car needs a tune-up every so often.

GO ON TO THE NEXT PAGE →

Practice Test 3

dirty, <u>so</u> you don't have to be a mechanic to change a
    68
car's oil. Before you get started, read the oil change

<u>section, in your owner's manual</u> and collect all of the
        69

tools you will need. You <u>won't need many tools, but you</u>
                70
<u>will definitely need a car jack.</u> Never get under a car
    70

that is supported only by car <u>jacks—you</u> do not want
               71
to risk being crushed by a car. After you've secured the

car, changing the oil is as straightforward as sliding

under the car with a drain pan to catch the oil and using

a wrench to loosen the oil drain plug. Then follow the

68. F. NO CHANGE
    G. but
    H. for
    J. because

69. A. NO CHANGE
    B. section, in your owner's manual,
    C. section in your owner's manual;
    D. section in your owner's manual,

70. In Paragraph 4, the writer wants to provide an explanation of how to change the oil in an automobile. Which of the following would most logically fit the writer's intention for this paragraph?

    F. NO CHANGE
    G. need to get under the car to open the oil drain, so use car jacks to raise the car and sturdy car jack stands to support it.
    H. may find it helpful to watch someone else change the oil before you try to perform the job on your own.
    J. only need to follow a few basic steps in order to successfully change your car's oil.

71. A. NO CHANGE
    B. jacks, you
    C. jacks you
    D. jacks you,

GO ON TO THE NEXT PAGE ⇨

instructions for changing the oil filter and fill the oil pan to the recommended level with fresh oil. 72

[5]

These simple steps to maintaining the health of a car can be done by just about anyone. However, successfully changing a car's oil does not turn a car owner into a repair expert. More complicated tasks, such as adjusting a carburetor or installing new brake pads, should be performed by a qualified auto mechanic.
73

72. Paragraph 4 of the essay uses the second person (*you*, *your*). Revising this paragraph to remove the second-person pronouns would have the primary effect of:

F. disrupting the logical flow of the essay.

G. making Paragraph 4 more consistent with the essay's overall tone.

H. underscoring the direct advice about regularly changing a car's oil.

J. lightening the essay's formal tone.

73. A. NO CHANGE

B. professionally completed by a qualified

C. performed by a certifiably qualified

D. undertaken by qualifying

Questions 74 and 75 ask about the preceding passage as a whole.

---

74. After rereading the essay, the writer decided that the following sentence contains important information:

> The owner's manual provides instructions on how to test the levels of these different fluids used to lubricate and cool the engine.

Logically, this sentence should be placed:

F. after the last sentence of Paragraph 2.

G. before the first sentence of Paragraph 3.

H. after the last sentence of Paragraph 3.

J. after the last sentence of Paragraph 4.

75. If the writer had intended to write an essay persuading readers to familiarize themselves with the basic safety features and maintenance needs of their cars, would this essay meet the writer's goal?

A. Yes, because the essay repeatedly encourages readers to refer to the owner's manual for their car.

B. Yes, because the essay lists many basic maintenance steps that owners can independently accomplish.

C. No, because the essay encourages readers to go beyond learning about the features of their car and actually perform some of the basic upkeep.

D. No, because the essay does not discuss a car's safety features in any detail.

Practice Test 3

IF YOU FINISH BEFORE TIME IS CALLED, YOU MAY CHECK YOUR WORK ON THIS SECTION ONLY. DO NOT TURN TO ANY OTHER SECTION IN THE TEST. STOP

MATHEMATICS TEST

60 Minutes—60 Questions

Directions: Choose the correct solution to each question and fill in the corresponding bubble on your answer sheet.

Do not continue to spend time on questions if you get stuck. Solve as many questions as you can before returning to any if time permits.

You may use a calculator on this test for any question you choose. However, some questions may be better solved without a calculator.

Note: Unless otherwise stated, you can assume:

1. Figures are NOT necessarily drawn to scale.

2. Geometric figures are two dimensional.

3. The word *line* indicates a straight line.

4. The word *average* indicates arithmetic mean.

1. Tanya used $3\frac{3}{8}$ yards of fabric to make her dress, and she used $1\frac{1}{3}$ yards of fabric to make her jacket. What was the total amount, in yards, that Tanya used for the complete outfit of dress and jacket?

    A. $4\frac{1}{8}$

    B. $4\frac{1}{6}$

    C. $4\frac{4}{11}$

    D. $4\frac{1}{2}$

    E. $4\frac{17}{24}$

2. The product $5x^3y^5 \cdot 6y^2 \cdot 2xy$ is equivalent to which of the following?

    F. $13x^3y^7$

    G. $13x^4y^8$

    H. $60x^3y^7$

    J. $60x^3y^{10}$

    K. $60x^4y^8$

3. Brandon puts 6% of his $36,000 yearly salary into savings, in 12 equal monthly installments. Jacqui deposits $200 every month into savings. At the end of one full year, what is the difference, in dollars, between the amount of money that Jacqui saved and the amount of money that Brandon saved, not including any interest earned?

    A. 216

    B. 240

    C. 480

    D. 1,960

    E. 2,800

GO ON TO THE NEXT PAGE

4. A school is selling T-shirts as a fund-raiser. For the first 100 T-shirts that are sold, the school will earn \$7 per shirt. For each additional shirt that is sold, the school will earn \$10. How much will the school earn if 350 T-shirts are sold?

   F. \$ 245
   G. \$ 250
   H. \$2,450
   J. \$3,200
   K. \$4,200

5. For steel to be considered stainless steel, it must have a minimum of 10.5% chromium in the metal alloy. If a manufacturer has 262.5 pounds of chromium available, what is the maximum amount of stainless steel, in pounds, that the manufacturer can produce?

   A. 27.56
   B. 252
   C. 262.5
   D. 2,500
   E. 25,000

6. A homeowner wants to put a wallpaper border around the top edge of all the walls of his kitchen. The ceiling is rectangular and measures 6.5 meters by 4 meters. What is the required length, in meters, of the border?

   F. 8
   G. 10.5
   H. 13
   J. 21
   K. 26

7. Which of the following expressions is equivalent to $w(x - (y + z))$?

   A. $wx - wy - wz$
   B. $wx - wy + wz$
   C. $wx - y + z$
   D. $wx - y - z$
   E. $wxy + wxz$

8. If $6n - 4 = 3n + 24$, then $n = $?

   F. 28
   G. $\dfrac{28}{3}$
   H. $\dfrac{28}{9}$
   J. $\dfrac{20}{9}$
   K. $\dfrac{3}{28}$

9. To make the color he wants to paint his boat, Marco needs to mix 5 parts white paint with 3 parts blue paint. How many quarts of blue paint will he need to make 24 quarts of this color?

   A. 3
   B. 5
   C. 8
   D. 9
   E. 15

10. What is the real-number value of $m^3 + \sqrt{12m}$ if $5m^2 = 45$?

    F. 27
    G. 33
    H. 38.09
    J. 63
    K. 739.39

GO ON TO THE NEXT PAGE

11. The radius of a sphere is $3\frac{3}{5}$ meters. What is the volume of the sphere, to the nearest cubic meter? Use the formula $V = \frac{4}{3}\pi r^3$.

    A. 42

    B. 45

    C. 96

    D. 157

    E. 195

12. There are 10 peanuts, 6 cashews, and 8 almonds in a bag of mixed nuts. If a nut is chosen at random from the bag, what is the probability that the nut is NOT a peanut?

    F. $\dfrac{5}{12}$

    G. $\dfrac{7}{12}$

    H. $\dfrac{5}{7}$

    J. 10

    K. 14

13. The number of people who shop at an electronics store during a given week is shown in the following matrix:

Adolescents	Adults	Senior Citizens
[75	100	30]

    The ratio of people from each age group who will purchase a product to the number of people in that age group who shop at the store is shown in the following matrix:

Adolescents	0.20
Adults	0.35
Senior Citizens	0.10

    Based on the matrices, how many people will make purchases?

    A. 15

    B. 41

    C. 53

    D. 133

    E. 205

GO ON TO THE NEXT PAGE

Use the following information to answer questions 14–15.

The following table shows the current enrollment in all the English classes offered at King High School.

Course Title	Section	Period	Number of Students
English I	1	5	29
	2	1	27
	3	2	22
English II	1	3	26
	2	6	25
	3	4	24
British Literature	1	6	23
African-American Literature	1	2	26
	2	5	25

14. What is the average number of students per section in English I ?

   F. 22
   G. 25
   H. 26
   J. 27
   K. 29

15. The school has 2 computer labs with 30 computers each. There are 3 broken computers in one lab and 5 broken computers in the other lab. All broken computers are not available to be used by students. For which of the following class periods, if any, are there NOT enough computers available for each English student to use a computer without having to share?

   A. Period 2 only
   B. Period 5 only
   C. Period 6 only
   D. Periods 5 and 6 only
   E. None

16. In the following table, every row, column, and diagonal must have equivalent sums. Which term or value belongs in the lower left cell for this to be true?

m	$-4m$	$3m$
$2m$	0	$-2m$
	$4m$	$-m$

   F. $-4m$
   G. $-3m$
   H. -3
   J. 0
   K. m

GO ON TO THE NEXT PAGE

17. A standard coordinate plane is shown here, with the four quadrants labeled. Suppose point R, denoted by $R(x,y)$, is graphed on this plane, such that $x \neq 0$ and $y \neq 0$.

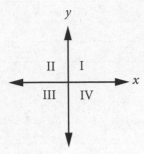

If the product xy is a positive number, then point R is located in:

A. Quadrant I only.

B. Quadrant II only.

C. Quadrant III only.

D. Quadrant I or IV.

E. Quadrant I or III.

18. A party store has 54 packs of plates in stock. The packs are either sets of 8 or sets of 12. If the store has 496 total plates in stock, how many plates would a customer buy if he or she buys all of the packs of 12 that the store has in stock?

F. 144

G. 192

H. 216

J. 312

K. 456

19. At a university, there are 5 females for every 3 males. If there are 6,000 male students, how many students are female?

A. 10,000

B. 12,000

C. 16,000

D. 18,000

E. 30,000

20. In order to determine some information about local gas prices, Sally must find the average cost of gasoline per gallon in her neighborhood. She visits 4 gas stations near her house and finds that the price per gallon at each store is $2.15, $2.05, $2.15, and $1.97, respectively. Among these 4 stations, what is the average price of gasoline per gallon?

F. $2.06

G. $2.07

H. $2.08

J. $2.09

K. $2.10

21. Given $f(x) = -4x + 5$ and $g(x) = \sqrt{x} + 2.5$, what is the value of $f\left(g\left(\frac{1}{4}\right)\right)$?

A. -7

B. -0.5

C. 0

D. 3

E. 6.5

22. Which of the following equations is the slope-intercept form of $3x + 2y = 16$?

F. $y = -\dfrac{3}{2}x + 16$

G. $y = -\dfrac{2}{3}x + 8$

H. $y = \dfrac{3}{2}x + 8$

J. $y = -\dfrac{3}{2}x + 8$

K. $y = -\dfrac{2}{3}x + 16$

GO ON TO THE NEXT PAGE

23. Which value is a solution to the equation $x^2 + 75 = 20x$?

   A.   −15

   B.   −5

   C.   0

   D.   3

   E.   5

24. Given right triangle LMN, what is the value of $\cos N$?

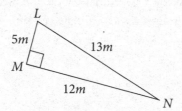

   F. $\dfrac{5}{13}$

   G. $\dfrac{5}{12}$

   H. $\dfrac{12}{13}$

   J. $\dfrac{13}{12}$

   K. $\dfrac{13}{5}$

25. Chord AB passes through the center of circle O, shown here. If radius OC is perpendicular to chord AB and has a length of 7 centimeters, what is the length of chord BC, to the nearest tenth of a centimeter?

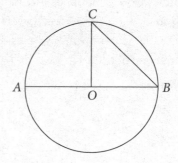

   A.   5.3

   B.   7.0

   C.   9.9

   D.   12.1

   E.   14.0

26. If $(a - b)^2 = 36$ and $ab = 24$, then $a^2 + b^2 = ?$

   F.   −12

   G.   12

   H.   60

   J.   84

   K.   96

27. An Olympic-sized pool is 50 meters long and 25 meters wide. It holds 14,375 cubic meters of water. If the pool is the same depth everywhere, about how many meters deep is the water in the pool?

   A.   Less than 9

   B.   Between 9 and 10

   C.   Between 10 and 11

   D.   Between 11 and 12

   E.   More than 12

GO ON TO THE NEXT PAGE

28. Lucia is beginning a marathon-training program. During her first day of training, she wears a pedometer to get an idea of how far she can currently run. At the end of the run, the pedometer indicates that she took 24,288 steps. Lucia knows from experience that her average running stride (step) is 2.5 feet. Given that 1 mile = 5,280 feet, how many miles did she run on her first day of training?

    F.   1.84

    G.   4.25

    H.   7.6

    J.   11.5

    K.   18.4

29. The following bar graph shows the number of people at the spring prom, according to their grade level at the high school. According to the graph, what fraction of the people at the prom were sophomores?

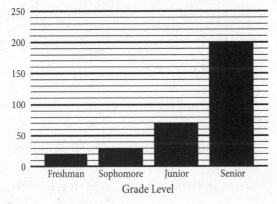

Grade Level

    A. $\dfrac{1}{16}$

    B. $\dfrac{3}{32}$

    C. $\dfrac{3}{29}$

    D. $\dfrac{3}{20}$

    E. $\dfrac{3}{10}$

30. The line that passes through the points (1,1) and (2,16) in the standard (x,y) coordinate plane is parallel to the line that passes through the points $(-10,-5)$ and $(a,25)$. What is the value of a ?

    F. -8

    G.   3

    H.   5

    J.   15

    K.   20

31. What is the x-coordinate of the intersection point, in the (x,y) coordinate system, of the lines $2x + 3y = 8$ and $5x + y = 7$?

    A. -1

    B.   1

    C.   2

    D. $\dfrac{15}{7}$

    E.   3

32. For all pairs of real numbers a and b, where $a = 2b - 8$, $b = ?$

    F. $a + 4$

    G. $2a - 8$

    H. $2a + 8$

    J. $\dfrac{a - 8}{2}$

    K. $\dfrac{a + 8}{2}$

GO ON TO THE NEXT PAGE

33. What is the area, in square millimeters, of parallelogram *RSUT*, shown here? Assume that the dotted line meets side *RT* at a 90° angle.

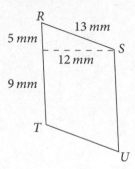

A. 30

B. 39

C. 54

D. 168

E. 182

34. What is the fifth term in the geometric sequence that begins $-108, 36, -12, 4, \ldots$?

F. $-\dfrac{35}{6}$

G. $-\dfrac{8}{3}$

H. $-\dfrac{4}{3}$

J. 0

K. 1

35. The following is a partial map of Centerville, showing 80 square miles: a total of 8 miles of Main Street and a total of 10 miles of Front Street. There is a fire station at the corner of Main and Front Streets, shown as point *F*. The town wants to build a new fire station exactly halfway between the hospital, at *H*, and the school, at *S*. What would be the driving directions to get from the current fire station to the new fire station, by way of Main and Elm streets? All streets and avenues shown intersect at right angles.

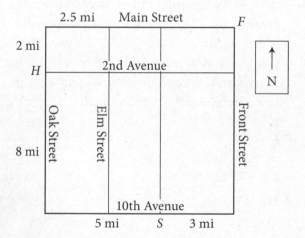

A. 2.5 miles east, 4 miles north

B. 2.5 miles west, 4 miles north

C. 2.5 miles east, 6 miles south

D. 5.5 miles west, 4 miles south

E. 5.5 miles west, 6 miles south

GO ON TO THE NEXT PAGE

36. There are two consecutive even integers. The difference between four times the larger and twice the smaller is 36. If x represents the smaller integer, which of the following equations can be used to determine the smaller integer?

    F. $4x - 2x = 36$

    G. $4(x + 2) - 2x = 36$

    H. $4(x + 1) - 2x = 36$

    J. $(x + 3) - 2x = 36$

    K. $36 - 4x = 2x$

37. A 15-foot supporting wire is attached to a telephone pole 12 feet from the ground. The wire is then anchored to the ground. The telephone pole stands perpendicular to the ground. How far, in feet, is the anchor of the supporting wire from the base of the telephone pole?

    A. 3

    B. 6

    C. 9

    D. 12

    E. 15

38. In the following figure, the sides of the square are tangent to the inner circle. If the area of the circle is 100π square units, what is the perimeter of the square?

    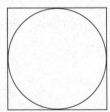

    F. 20

    G. 40

    H. 80

    J. 100

    K. 100π

39. Rectangles $ABCD$ and $EHGF$, shown here, are similar. Using the given information, what is the length of side EH, to the nearest tenth of an inch?

    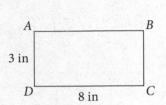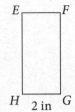

    A. 0.8

    B. 1.3

    C. 5.3

    D. 7.0

    E. 8.0

40. In parallelogram $VWXY$, shown here, points U, V, Y, and Z form a straight line. Given the angle measures as shown in the figure, what is the measure of angle $\angle WYX$?

    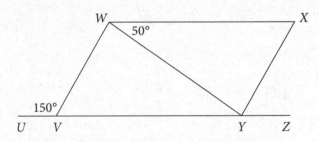

    F. 25°

    G. 30°

    H. 50°

    J. 100°

    K. 150°

GO ON TO THE NEXT PAGE

41. For all nonzero x and y, $\dfrac{\left(16x^2y^2\right)\left(6x^2y^4\right)}{-8x^2y^3} = ?$

    A. $-12y^3$

    B. $-12x^2y^2$

    C. $-12x^2y^3$

    D. $\dfrac{x^2y^2}{12}$

    E. $\dfrac{12}{y}$

42. In the mayoral election, $\dfrac{3}{4}$ of the eligible voters at one site cast a vote. Three-fifths of the votes at this site were for candidate Martinez. If there are 3,500 eligible voters at this site, how many of them voted for Martinez?

    F.   417

    G.   1,575

    H.   2,100

    J.   2,625

    K.   4,725

43. Given that a and b are positive integers and the greatest common factor of a^4b^2 and a^3b is 54, what is a possible value for b?

    A.   2

    B.   3

    C.   6

    D.   9

    E.   27

44. If 40% of x is 70, then what is 180% of x?

    F.   50.4

    G.   126

    H.   154

    J.   175

    K.   315

45. Point M (2,3) and point N (6,5) are points on the coordinate plane. What is the length of segment MN?

    A. $\sqrt{2}$ units

    B. $2\sqrt{3}$ units

    C. $2\sqrt{5}$ units

    D.   6 units

    E.   20 units

46. If $\mathbf{u}$ and $\mathbf{v}$ are vectors such that $\mathbf{u} = \langle -5,1 \rangle$ and $\mathbf{v} = \langle 5,0 \rangle$, which of the following represents $\mathbf{u} + \mathbf{v}$?

    F. $\langle -10,1 \rangle$

    G. $\langle -5,0 \rangle$

    H. $\langle 0,-1 \rangle$

    J. $\langle 0,0 \rangle$

    K. $\langle 0,1 \rangle$

47. What is the equation of a circle in the coordinate plane with center $(-2,3)$ and a radius of 9 units?

    A. $(x-2)^2 + (y+3)^2 = 9$

    B. $(x+2)^2 + (y-3)^2 = 9$

    C. $(x-2)^2 + (y+3)^2 = 81$

    D. $(x+2)^2 + (y-3)^2 = 3$

    E. $(x+2)^2 + (y-3)^2 = 81$

GO ON TO THE NEXT PAGE

48. In the complex number system, $i^2 = -1$. Given that $\dfrac{3}{5-i}$ is a complex number, what is the result of $\dfrac{3}{5-i} \times \dfrac{5+i}{5+i}$?

F. $\dfrac{3}{5+i}$

G. $\dfrac{15+3i}{24}$

H. $\dfrac{15+3i}{26}$

J. $\dfrac{15+i}{26}$

K. $\dfrac{15+i}{24}$

49. Which of the following represents $16^{\frac{3}{2}}$ as an integer?

A. 12

B. 24

C. 64

D. 256

E. 2,048

50. Fifty high school students were polled to see if they owned a cell phone and/or an MP3 player. A total of 35 of the students own a cell phone, and a total of 18 of the students own an MP3 player. How many students own both a cell phone and an MP3 player, assuming all 50 students own at least one of the two items?

F. 0

G. 3

H. 17

J. 32

K. 53

51. Scientists are modeling population trends and have noticed that when a certain population changes, the change is based on a linear function. When $t = 21$, the population is 3. When $t = 35$, the population is 5. Which of the following describes the population as a function of time t ?

A. $p(t) = \dfrac{t}{7}$

B. $p(t) = t - 18$

C. $p(t) = t - 30$

D. $p(t) = 3t - 60$

E. $p(t) = 3t - 100$

52. If 3 people all shake hands with each other, there are a total of 3 handshakes. If 4 people all shake hands with each other, there are a total of 6 handshakes. How many total handshakes will there be if 5 people all shake hands with each other?

F. 7

G. 9

H. 10

J. 11

K. 12

GO ON TO THE NEXT PAGE

53. The following table shows the percentages of a county's budget expenses by category. The remainder of the budget will be placed in the category Miscellaneous. If the same information is to be organized in a circle graph, what will be the degree measure of the central angle for the sector that represents Miscellaneous, rounded to the nearest degree?

Budget Category	Percentage of Budget
Salaries	23
Road Repair	5
Employee Benefits	22
Building Maintenance/ Utilities	18

A. 32

B. 58

C. 68

D. 115

E. 245

54. If $\tan \theta = -\dfrac{4}{3}$ and $\dfrac{\pi}{2} < \theta < \pi$, then $\sin \theta = ?$

F. $-\dfrac{4}{5}$

G. $-\dfrac{3}{4}$

H. $-\dfrac{3}{5}$

J. $\dfrac{3}{5}$

K. $\dfrac{4}{5}$

55. A portion of which of the following systems of inequalities can be approximated by the shaded region shown in the coordinate plane, assuming each grid line on the graph represents 1 unit?

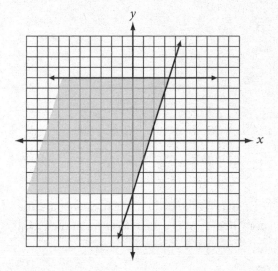

A. $y \le 6$ and $y \ge 3x - 5$

B. $x \le 6$ and $y \ge 3x - 5$

C. $y \le 6$ and $y \le 3x - 5$

D. $x \le 6$ and $y \le -3x - 5$

E. $y \le 6$ and $y \ge \dfrac{1}{3}x - 5$

56. If $f(x) = 3x + 5$ and $g(x) = 4x + 5$, which of the following expressions represents $f(g(x))$?

F. $7x + 5$

G. $7x + 10$

H. $12x + 15$

J. $12x + 20$

K. $12x + 25$

GO ON TO THE NEXT PAGE

57. For what values of x does the graph of the quadratic function $q(x) = 2x^2 + 7x - 4$ cross the x-axis?

    A. $x = -1$, $x = -\dfrac{5}{2}$

    B. $x = -\dfrac{1}{2}$, $x = -4$

    C. $x = -\dfrac{1}{2}$, $x = 4$

    D. $x = \dfrac{1}{2}$, $x = -4$

    E. $x = 1$, $x = \dfrac{5}{2}$

58. In a standard coordinate plane, what are the coordinates of Q', the reflection of the point $Q(r,s)$ over the y-axis?

    F. $(-r,s)$

    G. $(-r,-s)$

    H. $(s,-r)$

    J. $(r,-s)$

    K. $(-s,r)$

59. If $\sin x = \dfrac{1}{2}$ and $\tan x = \dfrac{\sqrt{3}}{3}$, then what is the value of the trigonometric cofunction $\csc x$?

    A. -2

    B. $-\sqrt{3}$

    C. $\dfrac{2}{\sqrt{3}}$

    D. $\sqrt{3}$

    E. 2

60. Find $\cos(75°)$ given that $\cos(75°) = \cos(30° + 45°)$. Use the following table and the formula:

    $$\cos(\alpha + \beta) = \cos(\alpha)\cos(\beta) - \sin(\alpha)\sin(\beta)$$

θ	$\sin\theta$	$\cos\theta$	$\tan\theta$
30°	$\dfrac{1}{2}$	$\dfrac{\sqrt{3}}{2}$	$\dfrac{\sqrt{3}}{3}$
45°	$\dfrac{\sqrt{2}}{2}$	$\dfrac{\sqrt{2}}{2}$	1
60°	$\dfrac{\sqrt{3}}{2}$	$\dfrac{1}{2}$	$\sqrt{3}$

    F. $\dfrac{\sqrt{3} - \sqrt{2}}{4}$

    G. $\dfrac{\sqrt{3} - \sqrt{2}}{2}$

    H. $\dfrac{\sqrt{6} - \sqrt{2}}{4}$

    J. $\dfrac{\sqrt{6} - \sqrt{2}}{2}$

    K. $\dfrac{3 - \sqrt{2}}{4}$

IF YOU FINISH BEFORE TIME IS CALLED, YOU MAY CHECK YOUR WORK ON THIS SECTION ONLY. DO NOT TURN TO ANY OTHER SECTION IN THE TEST. **STOP**

READING TEST

35 Minutes—40 Questions

Directions: The Reading Test includes multiple passages. Each passage includes multiple questions. After reading each passage, choose the best answer and fill in the corresponding bubble on your answer sheet. You may review the passages as often as necessary.

Passage I

PROSE FICTION: This excerpt from a short story describes a conversation between a woman and her husband, who is a twin.

Emily couldn't help but grin broadly after answering the phone. She frequently called us "two peas in a pod," but I'd always felt like anytime we were mentioned outside of my presence, he was
5 "Bruce" and I was "Bruce's twin brother." Because of this, I wasn't surprised to hear my wife giggling uncontrollably as she talked animatedly with to him. Despite the fact she was speaking to someone genetically identical to me, I couldn't help but
10 wonder if she had ever responded so enthusiastically to one of my stories.

"Okay, I'll tell him. Talk to you soon." After Emily hung up, I watched her take a deep, almost wistful breath before walking over to me.
15 "Bruce seems well," I said, trying to sound casual. "He told me about the new job and everything. What did you guys talk about?"

"Not much." Emily replied. She walked behind my chair and patted my shoulder before sitting
20 on the couch and opening her magazine. It didn't appear as if she were really reading. She seemed to stop and start, pausing and reflecting about something unrelated to the smiling celebrities featured in the article.
25 "It's funny to think that he knows some of these people," she said, pointing at her magazine.

I looked at the gleaming teeth and chiseled features of the actors, and then looked over at a picture of Bruce and me resting on the mantel.
30 Looking closely at the photo always made my stomach turn; as with every picture of us, there

was an unmistakable vitality in Bruce's face that wasn't present in mine. It was as if I were wearing a "Bruce" costume; I was trying to mimic one of his
35 trademark smiles, but I always seemed to produce a different failed attempt.

"You all right?" Emily asked, noticing my expression.

I grabbed the picture from the mantel and
40 brought it to her. She looked at it and looked up at me quizzically.

"Can you tell which one is me?" I asked.

She looked back at the picture and pushed her lip out as she looked from one face to the next. Af-
45 ter about five seconds she pointed to my face, then turned and looked at me confidently.

"How could you tell?" I asked.

"Well, it wasn't very hard," she responded. "You are my husband, and I love the way you smile.
50 Bruce looks exactly the same in every picture; it looks practiced. But for you, it always seems like you're thinking about something, even concentrating, to make sure you smile right."

"Really?" I was surprised by how much thought
55 she had put into this.

She took the picture and put it back on the mantel. I could still see the perfection in Bruce's smile and hesitation in mine, but at least Emily found a way to compliment my insecurities.
60 Emily went back to perusing her magazine.

"At least you ended up with a Fairholm," I said, "even if it wasn't the famous one."

"Oh, was I supposed to pursue the famous one?" she shot back.
65 She closed her magazine and put it down on the coffee table. There wasn't an argument coming, but

GO ON TO THE NEXT PAGE

I saw her disappointment. The problem was not that she actually would have married my brother before me; it was the simple fact that I couldn't help but believe that to be the case. I saw myself as second to him and always had. With embarrassing relatives, people will always point out that one can't choose one's family, but when you're a twin, it's not the association that you fear—it's the comparison.

"Do you want to be where he is?" she inquired, with an empty tone.

"This is exactly where I want to be," I replied. "I just never know how to explain to people that I'm an insurance adjuster, not a Hollywood agent. They always want to know how it happened when we had the same upbringing and education. They look at me as if I did something wrong."

"Do you ever call him?" she asked.

"I figure he's busy, and he calls enough," I said.

She cradled her chin in her hand and looked at me in mild disbelief. "You realize that by not calling and turning down his invitations to visit, you make him feel rejected, right?"

"Come on, Emily. He's surrounded by famous people—he doesn't need my approval."

"Maybe not," she sighed, "but his favorite stories to tell me aren't about Hollywood—they're about you two growing up."

"Well, he was popular then, too," I said, shrugging.

"He doesn't look at it that way," she responded. "He would give up a lot to have your approval, Dave. He wants to be your brother, not a competitor."

"It's okay, Emily. I'll call him soon, but I think that he'll be okay either way."

1. From the author's point of view, the narrator can best be described as:
   A. consumed by jealousy.
   B. unsuccessful in his career.
   C. lacking in self-esteem.
   D. proud of his place in the family.

2. Emily is best described as:
   F. aloof and ineffectual.
   G. needling and meddlesome.
   H. caring and diplomatic.
   J. pained and inconsolable.

3. Which of the following statements does NOT describe a feeling Dave has toward his brother?
   A. He is jealous of the reaction his brother gets from Emily during their phone conversation.
   B. He believes he would be better suited for his brother's type of work.
   C. He is resentful of his brother's superior social skills.
   D. He is skeptical of his brother's desire for his approval.

4. The primary focus of the first paragraph is:
   F. Emily's attempt to make her husband jealous.
   G. Emily's desire for the brothers to resolve their differences.
   H. Dave's hope to distance himself from his twin brother.
   J. Dave's feelings of inferiority to his twin brother.

GO ON TO THE NEXT PAGE

5. Lines 83–101 ("Do you ever . . . either way.") suggest that Dave does not contact Bruce because Dave:

   A. believes that Bruce has great need for him but does not want to admit to Emily that she is right.

   B. feels guilty about being distant toward Bruce and worries that he will have to explain himself.

   C. wants to prove to Emily that he is not impressed by Bruce's high-profile job.

   D. still harbors resentment over Bruce getting preferential treatment during their childhood.

6. According to the passage, when Dave looks at the photograph, he sees:

   F. his brother being cruel to him.

   G. two indistinguishable faces.

   H. a comparison unfavorable to him.

   J. his wife paying more attention to Bruce.

7. Which of the following is NOT a basis on which the narrator compares himself with his brother, Bruce?

   A. Fame

   B. Profession

   C. Facial expression

   D. Wealth

8. It can be logically deduced from the passage that Dave and Bruce:

   F. tell Emily different-sounding stories about their shared childhood.

   G. are frequently at odds regarding their different professions.

   H. have often fought over Emily's attention.

   J. were much closer shortly before Bruce moved.

9. Based on the passage, the author would most likely agree that Emily:

   A. should have married Bruce.

   B. is happy in her marriage to Bruce's twin brother.

   C. routinely keeps her phone conversations secret from her husband.

   D. is disappointed that she doesn't know the famous people her brother-in-law knows.

10. According to the passage, the reason Emily tells Dave about the content of Bruce's stories is that Emily:

   F. wants to convince Dave that Bruce does not see himself as better than Dave.

   G. wishes to hear Dave's version of the stories.

   H. sees doing so as a way to make Dave more impressed with his brother.

   J. thinks that doing so will make Dave sympathetic to Bruce's loneliness.

GO ON TO THE NEXT PAGE

Passage II

SOCIAL SCIENCE: This passage discusses the relationship between the media and public opinion.

Large-scale media can likely be traced back to ancient tribes sharing information about the edibility of berries or the aggressiveness of animals. Despite constant evolution, the information
5   most sought after is that regarding personal safety, personal opportunity, and the triumphs and misdeeds of others—the larger the persona and more laudatory or despicable the act, the better. When a story is of continued national interest, however,
10 the focus shifts even further from facts and more to theater. To step back and compose an objective plot of goings-on is a distant possibility, but establishing the hero or villain of the day is paramount. Ultimately, the public's desire to have cold, dry, and
15 correct facts is virtually nonexistent.

Current newscasts exacerbate this by delivering an assault on the senses with meaningless graphics and theatrical music; meanwhile, the monotone newscaster reads verbatim from a teleprompter,
20 often using phrases identical to those on other networks. Additionally, the viewer has probably already read the same story on the Internet earlier. When television was limited to three networks, rather than ubiquitous news-only channels, the
25 newscaster was a national figure and audience members would eagerly await information that was new to them, expecting a relatively thorough explanation of any complicated events. For example, to this day many people, in explaining the Watergate
30 scandal to those too young to know of it, use Walter Cronkite's delineation as the basis for their understanding.

The objective, trustworthy anchorperson has also given way to vociferous demagogues promis-
35 ing truth but delivering oversimplified, bias-driven sound bites. The idea of allowing individuals to draw their own conclusions is notably absent; in fact, many personalities mock those with opinions differing from those presented. The availability of
40 neutral online sources mitigates this slightly, but

not to any large degree. While the actual article may be impartial, electronic periodicals will still sensationalize headlines in order to attract casual readers, and those very headlines sway many read-
45 ers to certain opinions before the article is even read. For example, if a headline mentions an "enraged public," the reader is far more likely to both read and take umbrage at the information than he or she would be if the article mentioned a subject
50 that "irked locals."

In truth, though, the public is as desirous for dry and objective facts as finicky children are for brussels sprouts. The personalities willing to shrug off accountability in favor of wild accusations and
55 bombastic slogans captivate a large demographic, while one would be generous by saying that objective fact-based programs occupy even a niche market. This not only damages the general accuracy of so-called news but also further polarizes the
60 public. People now have the option to receive their news from hosts with a variety of political leanings, and one almost invariably chooses to watch the personality with opinions closest to one's own. This is more harmful than convenient because it
65 allows viewers to simply parrot information they are given, eliminating any thought or scrutiny. It is this intellectual laziness that aids in distancing the general public from factual information: as a growing number become resigned to accepting
70 whatever their favorite host tells them, the more freedom networks have to pass off sensationalist entertainment as news. It boils down to the unfortunate truth that most are far more likely to accept inaccurate information as fact than to question the
75 legitimacy of something that seems to fit with the opinions they already hold.

Those who make the news also obfuscate objective facts. A legion of employees is dedicated solely to the purpose of making the decisions of politi-
80 cal figures sound flawless. Oftentimes, important decisions are made, yet throughout a lengthy press conference, not a single factual implication is discussed. The meeting becomes nothing more than an

GO ON TO THE NEXT PAGE

opportunity for political employees to test their
85 infallible-sounding slogans, while the media dis-
sects the semantics rather than the facts. Semantics, however, are all the media is presented with.

    Despite all these methods of prevarication,
people still are better informed than they were
90 in the past. The public often gains knowledge of
events minutes, rather than days or weeks, after
the fact. The populace has a strong desire for
news in general, and amid all the unscrupulous
presentation methods, facts do exist. However,
95 the profitability of news has put a premium on
presentation, not trustworthiness. Complicating
matters further is the populace's impatience; the
standard consumer would rather be presented
with a minute and potentially inaccurate
100 statement—one that may or may not be retracted
the following day—than suffer through a lengthy
treatise comprised of all the known facts and
nuances of a particular issue. The desire to know
still exists, however; it just happens to be over-
105 shadowed by the public's desire for personal
consensus and the media's desire to reel in the
public.

11. One of the primary points the author
    attempts to make regarding the current
    news media is that:

    A. the media passes off made-up
        stories as facts.

    B. news anchors are not as opinionated
        as they were in decades past.

    C. the media focuses more on presen-
        tation than substance.

    D. the media goes directly against what
        news audiences truly desire to see.

12. In line 3, the author references "the edibility of
    berries" in order to:

    F. emphasize the need for today's farmers to
        plant only edible fruits.

    G. describe a typical wild animal food.

    H. illustrate one kind of information that is
        always important.

    J. comment on the caveman's limited diet.

13. The author brings up Walter Cronkite's coverage
    of Watergate in order to assert that:

    A. Walter Cronkite was a particularly adept
        newsperson.

    B. a previous standard for news rightly
        included clarification of complex issues.

    C. current newscasters are far more forget-
        table than those who came before them.

    D. the expanding number of television
        channels has made individual newscasters
        less famous.

14. By stating that "personal consensus" is of great
    importance to the public (line 105), the author is
    probably suggesting that members of the public:

    F. do not want information that contradicts
        their own beliefs.

    G. work hard to find the source that
        provides information closest to the truth,
        despite the difficulties present.

    H. wish to resolve any moral conflicts
        they may have with practices in news
        reporting.

    J. have difficulty finding news sources reflect-
        ing their personal views.

GO ON TO THE NEXT PAGE

Practice Test 3

15. According to the passage, what type of news stories are sensationalized the most?

    A. Those with a fairly clear chain of events

    B. Those that stay in the public's consciousness for long periods of time

    C. Those that clearly support one political view

    D. Those with the most nationally-relevant information

16. As it is used in line 12, the word *distant* most nearly means:

    F. separated.

    G. different.

    H. reserved.

    J. unlikely.

17. Based on the passage, which of the following headlines would the author be most likely to criticize?

    A. Earthquake Rocks Small Community, Arouses Questions Regarding Preparedness

    B. New Tax Protested by Idaho Farmers

    C. Parents Across Country Outraged at Offensive Song

    D. Governor Says Proposed Legislation Is Too Expensive

18. The author asserts that individuals will often accept potentially inaccurate information because they:

    F. believe that most newscasters are honest.

    G. have no way to research correct facts.

    H. appreciate the opportunity to discuss the information.

    J. have political beliefs similar to those of specific media personalities.

19. In the fourth paragraph, the phrase "even a niche market" (lines 57–58) expresses the author's feeling that:

    A. media companies are greatly influenced by public demand.

    B. cable television networks are willing to present objective facts.

    C. factual news media should look into better marketing practices.

    D. factual news would be profitable with greater exposure.

20. As it is used in line 34, the word *vociferous* most nearly means:

    F. angry.

    G. incompetent.

    H. humorous.

    J. vehement.

GO ON TO THE NEXT PAGE

Passage III

HUMANITIES: James Joyce was among the most influential writers of the early twentieth century and one of the leaders of a literary movement that became known as modernism. The following two passages are excerpted from essays written about Joyce during his lifetime.

Passage A

Although the writer James Joyce has spent the majority of his adult life outside of Ireland, he has always thought of himself as, and will be remembered as, a quintessentially Irish writer. His attach-
5 ment to the nation, and especially his boyhood home of Dublin, is apparent in his works, which are invariably set in Ireland and often focus on the social and political issues of the Irish. One of his earliest works, a collection of short stories, is even
10 entitled *Dubliners*, and his novel *Ulysses*, which is generally considered his greatest work, depicts 1904 Dublin in almost staggering detail. Joyce was often quoted as saying that, were Dublin to be destroyed in some tremendous calamity, it could be re-created
15 brick by brick from the depictions in *Ulysses*; in reading the novel, one finds it difficult to dispute the claim.

In addition to its focus on Dublin, *Ulysses* is somewhat narrowly focused in other ways as well.
20 Its action takes place on a single day, and for the most part it is centered on a single protagonist. Its events are not the grand, sweeping historical landmarks found in other novels, such as Tolstoy's *War and Peace*, but rather the mundane events of
25 everyday life; Joyce considered eating, running errands, and even making trips to the lavatory worthy of inclusion in his masterpiece.

And yet, despite its tight focus, the novel is already considered one of the most globally appealing
30 of all time, a powerful representation of the complete human condition. Almost paradoxically, it is the level of detail in Joyce's microcosm of a single man on a single day in a single city that allows him to make statements and observations that apply to
35 humanity as a whole. Perhaps human existence is

not best contemplated on the great battlefields of history, which are experienced by only a few human beings for small portions of their lives. It might instead be better expressed in the minor struggles and
40 idle musings of an ordinary Irishman who, by the very virtue of his ordinariness, is able to transcend the impediments of time and place in order to appeal to the entirety of the human dilemma.

Passage B

As one contemplates the state of literature in
45 our modern era, it is hard to resist a longing for the great writers of eras gone by. At times, one must take great pains merely to remember that there were once authors such as Dante, Shakespeare, or Dickens: authors who were able to relate stories of
50 great travels and struggles even as they compelled us to mull over the great philosophical questions of all time. They did not waste their time or ours with trivial affairs; their stories were unique and memorable, and they bore repeated readings and reread-
55 ings from generation to generation. These writers never took perverse glee in conveying thoughts and actions that were better off forgotten. They took great care to depict accurately the best and worst aspects of human nature; they were well aware of
60 the impact their works would have on culture and strove to ensure that they would enhance, rather than degrade, the public's intellect; they did not resort to tricks or devices in order to garner readership for their writings; and in all these regards, they
65 are firmly distinguished from writers of the present day, the most notorious of which is the Irish novelist James Joyce.

The goal of art is to enlighten the consciousness of those who partake of it, to lift their minds
70 and souls out of the trenches of ordinary activities and humanity's base instincts. It would seem that modern writers like Joyce have no interest in such enlightenment, instead preferring to revel in every detail of activities that should never have been

GO ON TO THE NEXT PAGE

75 committed to paper in the first place. In basing his
novel *Ulysses* on Homer's *The Odyssey*, Joyce has
sullied the very form of the epic genre. Whereas *The
Odyssey* was a great tale of a noble hero's struggle
against a seemingly insurmountable series of trials
80 in order to restore order and honor to his household, Joyce's book is nearly the direct opposite. The
protagonist is no hero, his actions are listless and
forgettable, and his obsession with obscene and
undignified behavior is virtually nauseating.

85   It is a pity that Homer's epic hero has now been
so distorted by his mere association with Joyce's
antihero. And even more shameful is the waste of
talent, for, subject matter aside, Joyce is no slouch
as a wordsmith. Sadly, it is the literary world's loss
90 that he was not born in a more dignified era where
his talents could have been utilized in a more
appropriate manner.

22. Which of the following best conveys the meaning of "transcend . . . place" (lines 42–43)?

   F. Make a specific statement about a particular group of people.

   G. Write in such a way that precise information is obscured.

   H. Ignore setting in order to focus solely on
character.

   J. Go beyond surface circumstance to reveal
universal truth.

23. Which of the following is NOT a theme in
Joyce's *Ulysses*?

   A. Heroic deeds

   B. Life in Dublin

   C. Everyday common struggles

   D. The human dilemma

Questions 21–23 ask about Passage A.	Questions 24–26 ask about Passage B.

21. Which of the following, if true, would most
significantly weaken the main argument of Passage A?

   A. Historical events are often depicted inaccurately in fictional writing.

   B. Similar philosophical ideas often arise in
cultures that have never had contact with
each other.

   C. People from some cultures find the
thoughts and motivations of people in
other cultures difficult to comprehend.

   D. Thorough knowledge of the place where
one grew up can lead to a stronger understanding of human nature.

24. According to Passage B's first paragraph, the
author is critical of James Joyce's writing on the
grounds that Joyce:

   F. is not as dignified as the great authors of
the past.

   G. lacks proper knowledge of his subject
matter.

   H. copies too closely from the authors who
preceded him.

   J. uses language that is unnecessarily elegant.

GO ON TO THE NEXT PAGE

25. Though he decries Joyce's writing, the author of Passage B admits Joyce's talent by acknowledging that:

    A. Joyce was a product of his time.

    B. writers cannot overcome the constraints of the period in which they live.

    C. Joyce was a skillful writer.

    D. Joyce's writing is comparable to that of Dickens.

26. As used in line 71, the word *base* most nearly means:

    F. unrefined.

    G. foundational.

    H. nauseating.

    J. sophisticated.

Questions 27–30 ask about both passages.

---

27. It can be inferred that the author of Passage A would respond to Passage B's assertion that the goal of art is to enlighten by:

    A. providing evidence that Joyce's writing is more enlightened than older works.

    B. emphasizing the importance of appealing to readers throughout the world.

    C. agreeing that Joyce's attention to detail diminishes the value of his writing.

    D. refusing to acknowledge the significance of great philosophical questions.

28. Which of the following best captures the difference between the two authors' views of Joyce's writing?

    F. The author of Passage A despises its lack of importance, while the author of Passage B disparages its inaccuracy.

    G. The author of Passage A claims that it is insignificant, while the author of Passage B contends that it is obscene.

    H. The author of Passage A admires its universal appeal, while the author of Passage B deplores its lack of decorum.

    J. The author of Passage A laments its irrelevance, while the author of Passage B appreciates its craftsmanship.

29. Which of the following word pairs best reflects the perspective of each author on the word *detail* as used in Passage A (line 12) and Passage B (line 74)?

    A. Passage A: entertainment; Passage B: dismay

    B. Passage A: admiration; Passage B: revulsion

    C. Passage A: enthusiasm; Passage B: shame

    D. Passage A: support; Passage B: glee

30. It can be inferred that the author of Passage B would most likely respond to Passage A's description of Joyce as "a quintessentially Irish writer" (line 4) by:

    F. disagreeing that Joyce was of Irish descent.

    G. disagreeing that Joyce was an exemplary writer.

    H. agreeing that Joyce was a champion linguist.

    J. agreeing that Joyce was an unrelenting mystic.

GO ON TO THE NEXT PAGE

Practice Test 3

Passage IV

NATURAL SCIENCE: This passage discusses the degree to which rattlesnakes pose a threat to humans.

In both recorded and oral history, rattlesnakes are categorized as malevolent beings. Their lance-shaped heads and angular brow-lines make them look the perfect villain, and their venom cements
5 this classification. Publicized reports of bite victims seem to prove the nefarious nature of rattlesnakes.

Unlike mammalian predators such as bears, rattlesnakes do not have the reputation of an animal deserving human respect. One imagines the rattle-
10 snake hiding in our backyards, waiting to strike.

In recent long-term studies, however, the social behavior of rattlesnakes has been found to be quite different than many would expect. Herpetologists, scientists who study snakes, had long suspected
15 a more complex and thoughtful existence for the reptiles and now have hard information to back up their theories. When examined, the sinister opportunist lurking in the shadows better re-sembles a mild-mannered domestic. Unlike the
20 nonvenomous king snake, rattlesnakes are entirely noncannibalistic and tend to spend their entire lives with a single mate. The mating ritual in which two males will extend almost half of their bodies off the ground to wrestle is not lethal, and once bested, a
25 rattlesnake peacefully retreats to find a new den of eligible mates. Female rattlesnakes give birth to live young, and rattlesnakes often share their dens, even hibernating with tortoises without incident.

Sadly, it seems that only those with an existing
30 fascination with snakes are aware of this socially functional rattlesnake. Another discovery that made little stir in the public consciousness is an experiment in which herpetologists tracked snakes with radio transmitters and saw their behavior
35 when humans entered their habitat. While a few snakes did hold their ground and rattle, most saw or sensed a disturbance (snakes cannot hear) and immediately headed in the opposite direction. Many of the snakes that were handled by herpetolo-
40 gists did not coil or strike. This is not to say that a snake will not bite a human if disturbed, but the tendency is to retreat first and give warning second, before striking becomes a possibility.

Describing a more docile nature does not
45 imply that rattlesnakes would make good pets for children, but considering the aggressiveness often displayed by a South American pit viper, the fer-de-lance, one familiar with both would have far less trepidation about passing by a rattlesnake. For one
50 thing, rattlesnakes do coil and rattle, giving humans an opportunity to move away, while fer-de-lance will often strike at passersby without warning. Furthermore, when it comes down to statistics, American hospitals report an average of 7,000
55 snakebite patients a year; generally more than half are actually from nonvenomous snakes thought by victims to be venomous. On average, fewer than six people die of snake envenomation annually, and the vast majority of the serious bites are due to either
60 handling the snake or stepping on it; most people bitten by snakes they were not engaging end up with very mild bites. Compare this with an average of over one million hospital visits for dog bites and twenty annual deaths at the jaws of man's best
65 friend. With such minuscule statistics regarding snakebites, it is curious why they are still viewed as unfathomably dangerous, when bees, lightning—and yes, dogs—are responsible for far more human fatalities. The fer-de-lance, however, is responsible
70 for thousands of deaths annually in Central and South America.

If one is looking for proof that rattlesnakes do not intend to harm humans, one should consider perhaps the most stunning evidence regarding
75 bite behavior. Over half of the bites rattlesnakes administer to humans are "dry," meaning the rattlesnake purposely does not release venom. While I will not posit that this is due to rattlesnakes' possessing an awareness of the well-being of their
80 non-food-source bite victim, there is a great deal of thought present. The snake acknowledges that venom is needed for immobilizing and digesting prey (venom is actually saliva), producing venom

GO ON TO THE NEXT PAGE ⟶

takes time, and the human is not a food source.
85 Therefore, if the snake is not surprised or fearing death, the damage of a rattlesnake bite will likely be far less severe than if the snake used all its venom. This has been known for some time, but in many cases, it is probably better for humans to believe
90 that the snakes are more liberal with venom than they are, simply because a frightened and cornered rattlesnake is very dangerous.

Unfortunately, some people take the traditional view of the rattlesnake and use it as an excuse to
95 harm the animals. People in various areas use the fearsome reputation of rattlesnakes, along with the more docile reality, for profit. Rattlesnake roundups are held, where people collect snakes beforehand and join in a festival celebrating their conquest. The
100 events are billed as both entertainment and as making surrounding residential areas safer for children; however, the vast majority of snakes are collected from uninhabited areas, and people are frequently bitten at the festivals while handling the snakes
105 for the audience. Eventually, the snakes are killed to make clothing or trophies, and these events are estimated to be responsible for 100,000 rattlesnake deaths annually, in comparison to fewer than 6 human deaths from rattlesnakes.
110 Behavior like this provides a better reason for a crotalid mythology. With statistics categorically showing a low level of danger from rattlesnakes to humans and an extremely high level vice versa, it would be a wonder to see what human-related folk-
115 lore rattlesnakes would come up with if they were able to speak or write.

31. In relation to the entire passage, the phrase "the sinister opportunist lurking in the shadows better resembles a mild-mannered domestic" (lines 17–19) most likely implies that:

A. adult rattlesnakes are considerably less aggressive than juveniles.

B. recent studies regarding rattlesnakes found few incidents of aggressive behavior.

C. rattlesnakes are more similar to mammals than once thought.

D. rattlesnakes are entirely predictable in their behavior.

32. The writer's attitude toward rattlesnakes can best be described as:

F. apathetic.

G. solicitous.

H. affrighted.

J. antagonistic.

33. What evidence does the passage give regarding the social ability of rattlesnakes?

A. Rattlesnakes are aware of the uses of their venom.

B. Wrestling between males establishes a social hierarchy.

C. Rattlesnakes can share their habitat with other species.

D. Rattlesnakes rarely eat other snakes.

GO ON TO THE NEXT PAGE

34. The statement "it would be a wonder to see what human-related folklore rattlesnakes would come up with if they were able to speak or write" (lines 113–116) means that:

    F. humans and rattlesnakes present great risks to each other's safety.

    G. humans and rattlesnakes behave in many similar ways.

    H. humans are a much greater threat to rattlesnakes than rattlesnakes are to humans.

    J. humans have traditionally assigned human emotions to rattlesnakes in folklore.

35. According to the passage, what is the correlation between human behavior and serious rattle-snake bites?

    A. There is no statistical relationship.

    B. Humans who move with quick motions provoke strikes.

    C. Humans who actively seek interaction with snakes for entertainment are less likely to receive a "dry" bite.

    D. Rattlesnakes deliver a variable amount of venom based on how threatening humans act.

36. The author refers to "dry" bites (line 76) in order to:

    F. prove that rattlesnakes make conscious decisions about food sources.

    G. do not produce enough venom to inject into a human.

    H. support his contention that rattlesnakes pose no harm to people.

    J. indicate that most rattlesnake bites are not as dangerous to people as supposed.

37. The passage states that the relative likelihood of a human's being killed by a rattlesnake bite is:

    A. greater than that of a dog bite.

    B. less than that of a bee sting.

    C. equal to that of a lightning strike.

    D. comparable to that of the bite of a South American fer-de-lance.

38. Which of the following correctly categorizes a rattlesnake's strategy in venom usage?

    F. The larger the prey or predator, the more venom the rattlesnake uses.

    G. Even when threatened, a rattlesnake reserves venom to use on prey.

    H. Rattlesnakes are aware that they will wound larger animals.

    J. Rattlesnakes normally use venom solely for prey.

39. From the point of view of the author, rattlesnake roundups are:

    A. important ways to control the rattlesnake population.

    B. based on inaccurate ideas about the danger of rattlesnakes.

    C. attempts to rid inhabited areas of unwanted snakes.

    D. appropriate reactions to treacherous reptiles.

40. According to the passage, which of the following is the rattlesnake's most common behavior when confronted with a person?

    F. Immediately bite the intruder

    G. Rattle its tail in warning

    H. Leave the area

    J. Stand its ground

IF YOU FINISH BEFORE TIME IS CALLED, YOU MAY CHECK YOUR WORK ON THIS SECTION ONLY. DO NOT TURN TO ANY OTHER SECTION IN THE TEST.

SCIENCE TEST

35 Minutes—40 Questions

Directions: The Science Test includes multiple passages. Each passage includes multiple questions. After reading each passage, choose the best answer and fill in the corresponding bubble on your answer sheet. You may review the passages as often as necessary.

You may NOT use a calculator on this test.

Passage I

Glaciers are large masses of ice that move slowly over Earth's surface due to the force of gravity and changes in elevation. Glacial *calving* occurs when 1 edge of a glacier borders a body of water. A calving glacier's *terminus* (the lower edge) periodically produces icebergs as they break away from the glacier and fall into the water.

Study 1

A computer was used to create a model of a typical calving glacier. It was hypothesized that a primary factor determining the calving rate is the glacier's velocity at its terminus. Figure 1 shows the calving rate, in meters per year, and length of the computer-generated glacier over a period of 2,000 years.

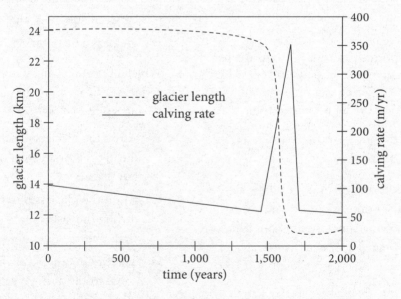

Figure 1

GO ON TO THE NEXT PAGE

Study 2

Four calving glaciers (A–D) were studied over a period of 10 years. The average velocity at the terminus of each glacier was recorded for years 1–5 and again for years 6–10. The calving rate of each glacier was estimated for the same time periods. The results are recorded in Table 1.

	Table 1			
	Years 1–5		Years 6–10	
Glacier	Average velocity (m/yr)	Calving rate (m/yr)	Average velocity (m/yr)	Calving rate (m/yr)
A	72	72	63	64
B	51	52	45	47
C	98	106	256	312
D	160	189	53	54

Study 3

Meteorologists reported unusually high average temperatures in the regions of Glacier C and Glacier D during the same 10-year period examined in Study 2. It was hypothesized that the high temperatures were responsible for the relatively rapid variations in velocity and calving rates evident for Glacier C and Glacier D in Table 1.

1. If the glacier model used in Study 1 is typical of all calving glaciers, the scientists would draw which of the following conclusions about the relationship between glacier length and calving rate?

   A. As calving rate decreases, glacier length always increases.

   B. As calving rate decreases, glacier length always decreases.

   C. A sharp increase in calving rate correlates with a sharp decrease in glacier length.

   D. A sharp increase in calving rate correlates with a sharp increase in glacier length.

2. The meteorologists involved in Study 3 hypothesized that the faster the calving rate, the faster the sea level at a calving glacier's terminus would rise. If this hypothesis is correct, which of the following glaciers from Study 2 experienced the greatest increase in sea level at the terminus during years 6–10 ?

   F. Glacier A

   G. Glacier B

   H. Glacier C

   J. Glacier D

3. Based on the results of Study 2, a calving glacier traveling at a velocity of 80 m/yr would most likely have a calving rate of:

   A. less than 72 m/yr.

   B. between 72 m/yr and 106 m/yr.

   C. between 106 m/yr and 189 m/yr.

   D. greater than 189 m/yr.

4. Which of the following statements best describes the behavior of the glaciers observed during Study 2 ?

   F. All of the glaciers observed traveled faster during the first 5 years than during the last 5 years.

   G. All of the glaciers observed traveled faster during the last 5 years than during the first 5 years.

   H. The calving rate is always less than or equal to the average velocity for all of the glaciers observed.

   J. The calving rate is always greater than or equal to the average velocity for all of the glaciers observed.

GO ON TO THE NEXT PAGE

5. Which of the following graphs best represents the relationship between the calving rate and the average velocity of the glaciers observed in Study 2 for years 6–10 ?

A.

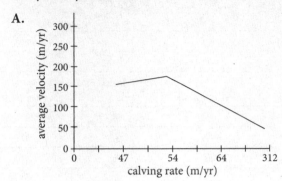

B.

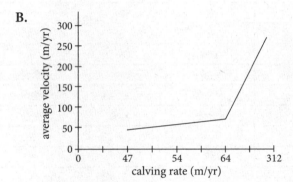

C.

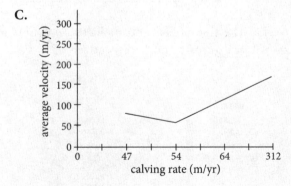

D.

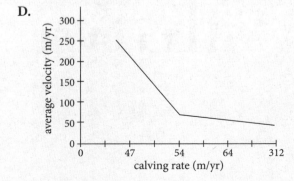

6. If the hypothesis made by the meteorologists in Study 3 is correct, the glacier modeled in Study 1 most likely experienced unusually high temperatures at approximately what time during the simulated 2,000-year study?

F. 500 years

G. 1,000 years

H. 1,500 years

J. 2,000 years

7. Based on Figure 1, what are the approximate values of glacial length and calving rate, respectively, at 1,500 years?

A. 15 km and 125 m/yr

B. 23 km and 125 m/yr

C. 23 km and 350 m/yr

D. 125 km and 350 m/yr

GO ON TO THE NEXT PAGE

Passage II

Allergic rhinitis refers to an inflammatory nasal reaction to small airborne particles called *allergens*. Table 1 shows six specific allergens (three kinds of pollen and three kinds of mold) and the approximate number of reported cases of allergic symptoms each month for a population of 1,000 people living in northern Kentucky during a single year.

	Pollen			Mold		
					Clado-	
Month	Trees	Grass	Weeds	Alternaria	sporium	Aspergillus
January				❀	❀	❀
February				❀	❀	❀
March	❀❀			❀	❀	❀
April	❀❀❀❀			❀	❀	❀
May	❀❀❀	❀❀❀		❀	❀	❀
June		❀❀❀❀		❀	❀	❀
July		❀❀	❀	❀❀	❀	❀
August			❀❀❀	❀❀❀❀	❀❀❀	❀❀❀❀
September			❀❀	❀❀❀	❀❀❀❀	❀❀❀❀
October			❀❀	❀❀❀	❀❀	❀❀
November				❀❀	❀	❀
December					❀	❀

Table 1

Note: Each ❀ equals 100 reported cases of allergic rhinitis.

Weekly tree pollen and total mold spore concentrations were measured in grains per cubic meter (gr/m³) for samples of air taken in southern Iowa for 8 weeks. The tree pollen and mold spore counts are shown in Figures 1 and 2, respectively.

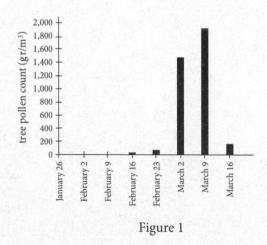

Figure 1

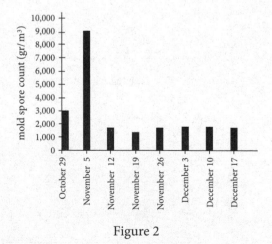

Figure 2

GO ON TO THE NEXT PAGE

8. If the 1,000 patients studied were given special air filters that greatly reduce allergic rhinitis symptoms, which of the following months would have the greatest decrease in the number of allergic rhinitis cases?

F. March

G. June

H. September

J. December

9. Based on Figure 1, the tree pollen count on March 2 was closest to:

A. 75 gr/m^3.

B. 150 gr/m^3.

C. 1,500 gr/m^3.

D. 1,900 gr/m^3.

10. According to Figure 2, the mold spore count in the weeks after November 5:

F. increased.

G. decreased.

H. varied between 1,000 gr/m^3 and 2,000 gr/m^3.

J. remained above 2,000 gr/m^3.

11. Based on the data in Figure 1, the tree pollen count increased the most between which 2 dates?

A. February 16 and February 23

B. February 23 and March 2

C. March 2 and March 9

D. October 29 and November 5

12. According to Figure 1, which of the following conclusions about the tree pollen count is most valid?

F. The tree pollen count was highest on March 9.

G. The tree pollen count was highest on March 16.

H. The tree pollen count was lowest on February 23.

J. The tree pollen count was lowest on March 16.

13. Based on Table 1, most of the cases of allergic rhinitis in May in northern Kentucky were caused by which of the following allergens?

A. Tree and grass pollen

B. Grass and weed pollen

C. Alternaria spores

D. Aspergillus spores

GO ON TO THE NEXT PAGE

Passage III

Simple harmonic motion (SHM) is a type of motion that is *periodic*, or repetitive, and can be described by its frequency of oscillation. Students performed three experiments to study SHM.

Experiment 1

The students assembled the pendulum shown in Diagram 1. The mass at the end of the arm was raised to a small height, *h*, and released. The frequency of oscillation was measured in oscillations per second, or hertz (Hz), and the process was repeated for several different arm lengths. The results are shown in Figure 1.

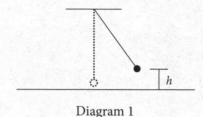

Diagram 1

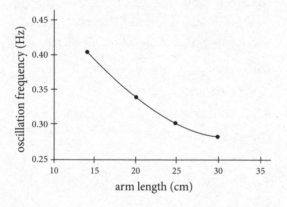

Figure 1

Experiment 2

A spring was suspended vertically from a hook, and a mass was connected to the bottom of the spring, as shown in Diagram 2. The mass was pulled downward a short distance and released, and the frequency of the resulting oscillation was measured. The procedure was repeated with 4 different springs and 4 different masses, and the results are shown in Figure 2.

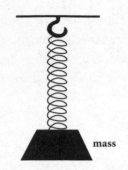

Diagram 2

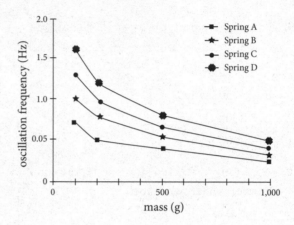

Figure 2

Experiment 3

Using the apparatus from Experiment 2, the mass-spring system was allowed to come to rest, and the *equilibrium length* of the spring was measured. The same 4 masses and 4 springs were used, and the results are shown in Figure 3.

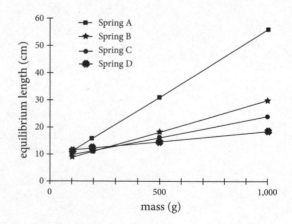

Figure 3

GO ON TO THE NEXT PAGE

14. Based on the results of Experiment 3, for which of the following masses would Spring B, Spring C, and Spring D have approximately equal equilibrium lengths?

    F. 200 g

    G. 275 g

    H. 350 g

    J. 500 g

15. A student has hypothesized that as the length of the arm of a pendulum increases, the oscillation frequency of the pendulum during SHM will decrease. Do the results of Experiment 1 support her hypothesis?

    A. Yes; the oscillation frequency of the pendulum observed in Experiment 1 decreased as the arm length increased.

    B. Yes; although the longest pendulum arm resulted in the highest oscillation frequency, the frequency decreased with increasing arm length for the other 3 lengths tested.

    C. No; the oscillation frequency of the pendulum observed in Experiment 1 increased as the arm length increased.

    D. No; although the longest pendulum arm resulted in the lowest oscillation frequency, the frequency increased with increasing arm length for the other 3 lengths tested.

16. Based on the results of Experiment 2, if an engineer needs the spring that oscillates most slowly after being stretched and released, which of the following springs should be chosen?

    F. Spring A

    G. Spring B

    H. Spring C

    J. Spring D

17. Based on the results of Experiment 3, if a 700 g mass were suspended from Spring A, where would its equilibrium length be found once the system came to rest?

    A. Less than 10 cm

    B. Between 10 cm and 30 cm

    C. Between 30 cm and 50 cm

    D. Greater than 50 cm

18. The students tested a fifth spring, Spring E, in the same manner as in Experiment 2. With a 100 g mass suspended from Spring E, the oscillation frequency was 1.4 Hz. Based on the results of Experiment 2, which of the following correctly lists the 5 springs by their oscillation frequency (with a 100 g mass suspended) from *fastest* to *slowest*?

    F. Spring E, Spring D, Spring C, Spring B, Spring A

    G. Spring D, Spring A, Spring C, Spring B, Spring E

    H. Spring A, Spring B, Spring C, Spring E, Spring D

    J. Spring D, Spring E, Spring C, Spring B, Spring A

Practice Test 3

19. Suppose Experiment 1 were repeated using a larger pendulum mass. Which of the following figures best expresses the comparison between the results that would be found using the larger pendulum mass and the results found using the original mass?

A.

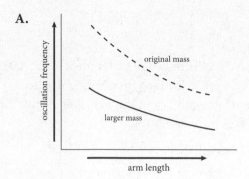

B.

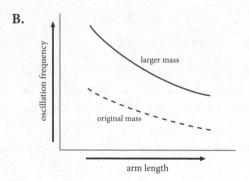

C.

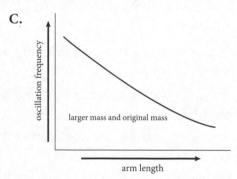

D.

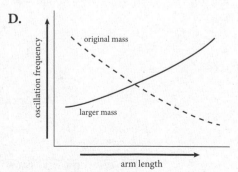

20. According to Figure 1, at which of the following arm lengths will the oscillation frequency come closest to 0.35 Hz ?

F. 13 cm

G. 16 cm

H. 19 cm

J. 21 cm

GO ON TO THE NEXT PAGE

Passage IV

Human beings require a certain percentage of oxygen in the blood for proper respiratory function. The amount of oxygen in the air varies enough with altitude that people normally accustomed to breathing near sea level may experience respiratory problems at significantly higher altitudes. Table 1 shows the average percentage of oxygen saturation in the blood, as well as the average blood concentrations of three enzymes, GST, ECH, and CR, for 3 populations of high-altitude (ha) dwellers and 3 populations of sea-level (sl) dwellers. Enzyme concentrations are given in arbitrary units (a.u.). Figure 1 shows average oxygen partial pressure and average temperature at various altitudes.

Table 1					
Population	Altitude range (m)	Oxygen saturation (%)	Enzyme concentration (a.u.)		
			GST	ECH	CR
ha 1	3,500–4,000	98.1	121.0	89.2	48.8
ha 2	3,300–3,700	99.0	108.3	93.5	45.6
ha 3	3,900–4,200	97.9	111.6	91.9	52.3
sl 1	0–300	98.5	86.7	57.1	44.9
sl 2	0–150	99.2	79.8	65.8	53.1
sl 3	0–200	98.7	82.5	61.4	47.0

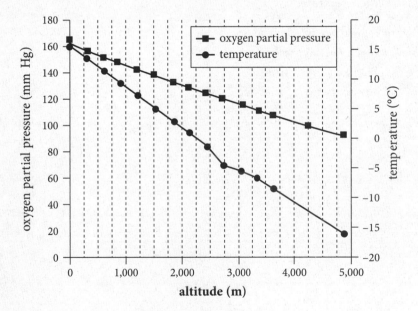

Figure 1

GO ON TO THE NEXT PAGE

21. Based on the data in Table 1, it is reasonable to conclude that the blood of high-altitude dwellers contains a higher concentration of:

    A. CR than ECH.

    B. CR than GST.

    C. ECH than GST.

    D. GST than CR.

22. Based on the information given, one would expect that, compared to the high-altitude dwellers, the sea-level dwellers:

    F. have blood with a lower-percentage oxygen saturation.

    G. have blood with a lower GST concentration.

    H. can tolerate lower oxygen partial pressures.

    J. can tolerate lower temperatures.

23. According to Figure 1, an atmospheric sample found at an oxygen partial pressure of 110 mm Hg was most likely taken from a location with an average temperature of about:

    A.   10°C.

    B.   5°C.

    C.   –7°C.

    D. –13°C.

24. ECH is an enzyme that improves the efficiency of cellular energy production. Assume that people with higher ECH concentrations in the blood can function normally at higher altitudes without any respiratory difficulties. Based on Table 1, people from which population can function normally at the highest altitude?

    F. sl 1

    G. sl 2

    H. ha 2

    J. ha 3

GO ON TO THE NEXT PAGE

25. Assume that a person's blood oxygen saturation percentage is determined only by the oxygen partial pressure at the location at which the person lives and the efficiency of the person's respiratory system at incorporating oxygen into the blood. Which of the following pieces of information supports the hypothesis that people from population ha 2 can incorporate oxygen into their blood more efficiently than can people from population sl 1 ?

   A. Population ha 2 lives in an area where oxygen partial pressure is lower than for population sl 1, yet population ha 2 has the higher blood oxygen saturation percentage.

   B. Population ha 2 lives in an area where oxygen partial pressure is higher than for population sl 1, yet population ha 2 has the lower blood oxygen saturation percentage.

   C. Population ha 2 has a higher CR concentration than does population sl 1.

   D. Population ha 2 has an unusually high GST concentration.

26. If a population living at 1,500–1,800 m were studied, which of the following conclusions about its average enzyme levels would most likely be true?

   F. Its levels of GST, ECH, and CR would be roughly the same as those of the high-altitude populations.

   G. Its levels of GST, ECH, and CR would be roughly the same as those of the sea-level populations.

   H. Its level of GST would be lower than that of the sea-level populations, and its levels of ECH and CR would be lower than those of the high-altitude populations.

   J. Its levels of GST and ECH would be higher than those of the sea-level populations, and its level of CR would be roughly the same as that of both high-altitude and sea-level populations.

GO ON TO THE NEXT PAGE

Passage V

Two students attempt to explain why lakes freeze from the surface downward. They also discuss the phenomenon of the melting of ice under the blades of an ice skater's skates.

Student 1

Water freezes first at the surface of lakes because the freezing point of water decreases with increasing pressure. Under the surface, *hydrostatic pressure* causes the freezing point of water to be slightly lower than it is at the surface. Thus, as the air temperature drops, it reaches the freezing point of water at the surface before reaching that of the water beneath it. Only as the temperature becomes even colder will the layer of ice at the surface become thicker.

Pressure is defined as *force* divided by the *surface area* over which the force is exerted. An ice skater exerts the entire force of his or her body weight over the tiny surface area of two very thin blades. This results in a very high pressure, which quickly melts a small amount of ice directly under the blades.

Student 2

Water freezes first at the surface of lakes because the density of ice is less than that of liquid water. Unlike with most liquids, the volume of a given mass of water expands upon freezing, and the density therefore decreases. As a result, the *buoyant force* of water acting upward is greater than the force of gravity pulling any mass of ice downward, so all ice particles float to the surface upon freezing.

Ice melts under an ice skater's skates because of friction. The energy used to overcome the force of friction is converted to heat, which melts the ice under the skates. The greater the weight of the skater, the greater the force of friction and the faster the ice melts.

27. According to Student 1, which of the following quantities is *greater* for water molecules beneath a lake's surface than for water molecules at the surface?

A. Temperature

B. Density

C. Buoyant force

D. Hydrostatic pressure

28. When 2 ice skaters, wearing identical skates, skated across a frozen lake at the same speed, the ice under the blades of Skater B was found to melt faster than the ice under the blades of Skater A. What conclusion would each student draw about which skater is heavier?

F. Both Student 1 and Student 2 would conclude that Skater A is heavier.

G. Both Student 1 and Student 2 would conclude that Skater B is heavier.

H. Student 1 would conclude that Skater A is heavier; Student 2 would conclude that Skater B is heavier.

J. Student 1 would conclude that Skater B is heavier; Student 2 would conclude that Skater A is heavier.

29. Which student(s), if any, would predict that ice will melt under the blades of an ice skater who is NOT moving?

A. Student 1 only

B. Student 2 only

C. Both Student 1 and Student 2

D. Neither Student 1 nor Student 2

GO ON TO THE NEXT PAGE

30. A beaker of ethanol is found to freeze from the bottom upward, instead of from the surface downward. Student 2 would most likely argue that the density of frozen ethanol is:

    F. greater than the density of water.
    G. less than the density of ice.
    H. greater than the density of liquid ethanol.
    J. less than the density of liquid ethanol.

31. A toy boat was placed on the surface of a small pool of water, and the boat was gradually filled with sand. After a certain amount of sand had been added, the boat began to sink. Based on Student 2's explanation, the boat began to sink because:

    A. hydrostatic pressure became greater than the buoyant force of the water on the boat.
    B. atmospheric pressure became greater than the buoyant force of the water on the boat.
    C. the force of gravity on the boat became greater than the buoyant force of the water on the boat.
    D. the force of gravity on the boat became less than the buoyant force of the water on the boat.

32. According to Student 2, if friction between the ice and the blades of an ice skater's skates were somehow reduced, which of the following quantities must simultaneously decrease at the point where the blades and the ice are in contact?

    F. Pressure exerted by the blades on the ice
    G. Heat produced
    H. Force of gravity on the skater
    J. Freezing point of water

33. Based on Student 2's explanation, the reason a hot air balloon is able to rise above the ground is that the balloon and the air inside it are:

    A. less dense than the air outside the balloon.
    B. more dense than the air outside the balloon.
    C. at a higher pressure than the air outside the balloon.
    D. less buoyant than the air outside the balloon.

GO ON TO THE NEXT PAGE

Passage VI

In many communities, chemicals containing fluoride ions (F^-) are added to the drinking water supply to help prevent tooth decay. Use of F^- is controversial because studies have linked F^- with bone disease. Students performed two experiments to measure F^- levels.

Experiment 1

Five solutions, each containing a different amount of Na_2SiF_6 (sodium silicofluoride) in H_2O, were prepared. Five identical *electrodynamic cells* were filled with equal volumes of each of the 5 solutions, and a sixth identical cell was filled with a *blank* solution (one containing no added Na_2SiF_6). The cells were activated to measure the electrical *conductivity* for each. The conductivities were then corrected by subtracting the conductivity of the blank solution from each value (see Table 1 and Figure 1).

Table 1		
Concentration of F^- (mg/L*)	Measured conductivity (μS/cm**)	Corrected conductivity (μS/cm**)
0.0	15.96	0.00
0.1	16.13	0.17
0.5	16.80	0.84
1.0	17.63	1.67
2.0	19.30	3.34
4.0	22.64	6.68

*mg/L is milligrams per liter.
**μS/cm is microsiemens per centimer.

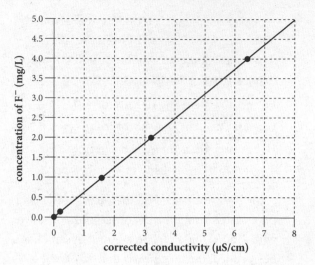

Figure 1

Experiment 2

A water sample was taken directly from the drinking water supply of one community. An electrodynamic cell identical to those used in Experiment 1 was filled with water from this sample, and the cell was activated. The procedure was repeated for water samples from several other communities, and the conductivities were measured. The students then used these measured conductivities and the results from Experiment 1 to calculate fluoride ion concentrations (see Table 2).

Table 2		
Community	Measured conductivity (μS/cm)	Concentration of F^- (mg/L)
Newtown	22.31	3.8
Springfield	16.46	0.3
Lakewood	18.63	1.6
Reading	19.47	2.1

GO ON TO THE NEXT PAGE

34. Students subtracted the measured conductivity of the blank solution from the sample solutions in Experiment 1 in order to:

    F. determine the amount of conductivity solely due to F^-.

    G. calibrate the electrodynamic cells.

    H. correct for non-ionic impurities.

    J. test the solubility of F^-.

35. Based on the results of Experiment 1, if the concentration of F^- in a solution is doubled, then the corrected conductivity of the solution will approximately:

    A. remain the same.

    B. halve.

    C. double.

    D. quadruple.

36. After Experiment 2, a sample was also taken from the drinking water supply of the community of Bluewater and its conductivity was measured to be 20.69 µS/cm. Which of the following correctly lists the drinking water supplies of Newtown, Lakewood, and Bluewater in increasing order of F^- concentration?

    F. Lakewood, Newtown, Bluewater

    G. Bluewater, Newtown, Lakewood

    H. Newtown, Bluewater, Lakewood

    J. Lakewood, Bluewater, Newtown

37. Based on the results of Experiment 1, if a solution with a fluoride ion concentration of 3.0 mg/L had been tested, the corrected conductivity would have been closest to which of the following values?

    A. 2.0 µS/cm

    B. 3.5 µS/cm

    C. 5.0 µS/cm

    D. 6.5 µS/cm

38. If Experiment 1 were repeated to measure the conductivity of chloride ions (Cl^-) in drinking water instead, then which of the following changes in procedure would be necessary?

    F. The solutions should be prepared by adding different concentrations of NaCl (or another chemical containing Cl^-) to H_2O.

    G. The conductivity of the blank solution should be added to the measured conductivities to find the corrected conductivities.

    H. The electrodynamic cells should be set to measure resistivity instead of conductivity.

    J. The solutions should be prepared by adding different concentrations of NaCl (or another chemical containing Cl^-) and Na_2SiF_6 to H_2O.

GO ON TO THE NEXT PAGE

39. Based on the results of Experiments 1 and 2, if the measured conductivities for the samples tested in Experiment 2 were compared with their corrected conductivities, the measured conductivities would be:

    A. lower for all of the samples tested.

    B. higher for all of the samples tested.

    C. lower for some of the samples tested and higher for others.

    D. the same for all of the samples tested.

40. The presence of other negative ions, such as Cl^-, results in an increase in the electrical conductivity of a solution. If all of the samples tested in Experiment 2 contained small concentrations of Cl^-, how would the results have been affected? Compared to the actual F^- concentrations, the calculated F^- concentrations would be:

    F. higher.

    G. lower.

    H. the same.

    J. higher for some of the samples, but lower for others.

IF YOU FINISH BEFORE TIME IS CALLED, YOU MAY CHECK YOUR WORK ON THIS SECTION ONLY. DO NOT TURN TO ANY OTHER SECTION IN THE TEST. STOP

WRITING TEST

40 Minutes—1 Question

Directions: The essay is used to evaluate your writing skills. You will have **40 minutes** to review the prompt and plan and write an essay in English. Before you begin, read everything in this test booklet carefully to make sure you understand the task.

Your essay will be judged based on the evidence it provides of your ability to do the following:

- Assert your own perspective on a complex issue and evaluate the relationship between your perspective and at least one other perspective

- Use reasoning and evidence to refine and justify your ideas

- Present your ideas in an organized way

- Convey your ideas effectively using standard written English

Write your essay on the lined essay pages in the answer booklet. All writing on those lined pages will be scored. Use the unlined pages in this test booklet to plan your essay. Your work on these unlined pages will not be scored.

Put your pencil down as soon as time is called.

DO NOT OPEN THIS BOOKLET UNTIL TOLD TO DO SO.

GO ON TO THE NEXT PAGE

Experiential Education

Experiential education is a philosophy that holds that students learn best through direct experience. Hands-on learning is said to promote deeper understanding because students are able to apply concepts and theories to physical situations. Rather than being required to memorize facts, students are given the opportunity to create physical evidence of logical reasoning and are thus better equipped to apply the same reasoning to new situations. Since all teachers aim to impart critical thinking in their classrooms, should they be expected to provide more hands-on learning opportunities? As educators aim to continuously improve the quality of the education they offer to students, consideration should be given to better incorporating hands-on learning.

Read and carefully consider these perspectives. Each suggests a particular approach regarding experiential education.

Perspective One	Perspective Two	Perspective Three
Some argue that to accept a theory without experiencing it is to learn nothing at all. Teachers need to provide opportunities for experiential involvement if they expect students to truly comprehend each lesson plan objective.	Experiential education is an integral part of readying students to pursue careers in the science, technology, engineering, and math fields, but not all disciplines. If students are expected to perform skill-based tasks in these fields after they graduate, they should be provided a strong foundation on which to build their careers. However, teachers should not be expected to supply experiential learning where it is not appropriate.	Schools cannot be expected to offer hands-on learning for students. Not only is it costly, but also it may not be effective for all learners. Students will be better served if schools invest money in other educational models and opportunities.

Essay Task

Write a clear, well-reasoned essay evaluating multiple perspectives on experimental education. In your essay, be sure to:

- Assert your own perspective on the issue and evaluate the relationship between your perspective and at least one other perspective
- Use reasoning and evidence to refine and justify your ideas
- Present your ideas in an organized way
- Convey your ideas effectively using standard written English

Your perspective may be fully, somewhat, or not at all in agreement with one or more of the three perspectives in the prompt.

GO ON TO THE NEXT PAGE

Planning Your Essay

These pages are not scored.

Use the space below to brainstorm and plan your essay. Consider the following as you think about the prompt:

- Strengths and weaknesses of the three perspectives in the prompt

  ◦ What observations do they offer, and what do they overlook?

  ◦ Why are they persuasive or why are they not persuasive?

- Your own background and identity

  ◦ What is your perspective on this issue, and what are its strengths and weaknesses?

  ◦ What evidence will you use in your essay?

GO ON TO THE NEXT PAGE

GO ON TO THE NEXT PAGE

Practice Test 3

GO ON TO THE NEXT PAGE

Practice Test 3

Practice Test 3

_____

_____

_____

_____

_____

_____

_____

_____

_____

_____

_____

_____

_____

_____

_____

_____

_____

_____

IF YOU FINISH BEFORE TIME IS CALLED, YOU MAY CHECK YOUR WORK ON THIS SECTION ONLY. DO NOT TURN TO ANY OTHER SECTION IN THE TEST.

PRACTICE TEST 3 ANSWER KEY
ENGLISH TEST

1. C	16. J	31. C	46. J	61. D
2. H	17. A	32. H	47. D	62. H
3. C	18. J	33. D	48. H	63. B
4. J	19. D	34. F	49. D	64. H
5. B	20. H	35. B	50. G	65. B
6. J	21. C	36. F	51. D	66. G
7. B	22. G	37. C	52. F	67. B
8. F	23. C	38. J	53. C	68. G
9. D	24. J	39. C	54. J	69. D
10. H	25. C	40. H	55. D	70. G
11. A	26. J	41. B	56. H	71. A
12. G	27. B	42. G	57. A	72. G
13. A	28. G	43. D	58. J	73. A
14. H	29. D	44. G	59. C	74. H
15. B	30. J	45. A	60. G	75. D

MATHEMATICS TEST

1. E	13. C	25. C	37. C	49. C
2. K	14. H	26. J	38. H	50. G
3. B	15. B	27. D	39. C	51. A
4. J	16. G	28. J	40. J	52. H
5. D	17. E	29. B	41. C	53. D
6. J	18. G	30. F	42. G	54. K
7. A	19. A	31. B	43. A	55. A
8. G	20. H	32. K	44. K	56. J
9. D	21. A	33. D	45. C	57. D
10. G	22. J	34. H	46. K	58. F
11. E	23. E	35. E	47. E	59. E
12. G	24. H	36. G	48. H	60. H

READING TEST

1. **C**	9. **B**	17. **C**	25. **C**	33. **C**
2. **H**	10. **F**	18. **J**	26. **F**	34. **H**
3. **B**	11. **C**	19. **A**	27. **B**	35. **C**
4. **J**	12. **H**	20. **J**	28. **H**	36. **J**
5. **D**	13. **B**	21. **C**	29. **B**	37. **B**
6. **H**	14. **F**	22. **J**	30. **G**	38. **J**
7. **D**	15. **B**	23. **A**	31. **B**	39. **B**
8. **F**	16. **J**	24. **F**	32. **G**	40. **H**

SCIENCE TEST

1. **C**	9. **C**	17. **C**	25. **A**	33. **A**
2. **H**	10. **H**	18. **J**	26. **J**	34. **F**
3. **B**	11. **B**	19. **C**	27. **D**	35. **C**
4. **J**	12. **F**	20. **H**	28. **G**	36. **J**
5. **B**	13. **A**	21. **D**	29. **A**	37. **C**
6. **H**	14. **G**	22. **G**	30. **H**	38. **F**
7. **B**	15. **A**	23. **C**	31. **C**	39. **B**
8. **H**	16. **F**	24. **H**	32. **G**	40. **F**

ANSWERS AND EXPLANATIONS

ENGLISH TEST

Passage I

1. C Difficulty: Medium

Category: Usage

Getting to the Answer: Choice (C) forms a complete sentence by using the simple past tense *was*. Choice A creates a sentence fragment; an *-ing* verb needs a helping verb, such as *was* or *is*, to be the main verb in a sentence. Choice B incorrectly uses a comma to separate the subject from the main verb. Choice D omits the verb entirely, creating a sentence fragment.

2. H Difficulty: Medium

Category: Usage

Getting to the Answer: The phrase *not only* in the beginning of the sentence is your clue to the correct answer. Logically, the phrase *not only* is always followed by *but also*. The other choices neither complete the idiom correctly nor convey the necessary contrast between the ideas in the two clauses.

3. C Difficulty: Medium

Category: Punctuation

Getting to the Answer: Add an apostrophe and an *s* to a singular noun to show possession. The narrator and Gretchen attend one school, so (C) is correct. Choice A omits the apostrophe needed to show that the *swim team* belongs to the *school*. Choice B incorrectly treats *school* as a plural, placing the apostrophe after the *s*. Choice D incorrectly uses *ours* and does not make *school* possessive.

4. J Difficulty: Medium

Category: Sentence Structure and Formation

Getting to the Answer: Choice F is incorrect because, as written, the sentence contains a sentence structure error: It is not clear who knows that the writer enjoyed

swimming. Choice (J) corrects the error and uses the active voice. Choices G and H use the passive voice and are wordy.

5. B Difficulty: Low

Category: Knowledge of Language / Precision

Getting to the Answer: Choice (B) indicates that the narrator's mother recommended swimming lessons but did not decide that the narrator *must* take them. Choices A, C, and D all indicate that the mother's mind was made up.

6. J Difficulty: Medium

Category: Sentence Structure and Formation

Getting to the Answer: If a sentence seems to have too many ideas, then it is probably a run-on. By itself, a comma cannot separate two clauses that could be independent sentences, as in F. Choice G replaces *swimmers* with a pronoun but does not correct the run-on. Similarly, H removes the comma but does not address the problem of two complete thoughts that are incorrectly joined. Choice (J) solves the problem by using *whom*, which turns the second half of the sentence into a dependent clause that describes the *women*.

7. B Difficulty: High

Category: Punctuation

Getting to the Answer: This sentence contains a parenthetical phrase. If you omitted "who had been swimming competitively since elementary school," you would still have a complete sentence. Like all parenthetical phrases, this needs to be set off from the rest of the sentence. A comma is used at the beginning of the phrase, so a comma must also be used at the end of the phrase. This makes D incorrect. Choices A and C insert unnecessary commas within the parenthetical phrase.

8. F Difficulty: Medium

Category: Sentence Structure and Formation

Getting to the Answer: Choice (F) is correct because *and* correctly connects the independent clause "I came back the next day" with the phrase "the next for practice" to create a compound sentence. Choices G and J include unnecessary punctuation, and H creates a fragment on the right side of the semicolon.

9. D   Difficulty: Medium

Category: Usage

Getting to the Answer: Trust your ear. *Begin* is an irregular verb; the simple past tense *began* can be used by itself, but the past participle *begun* cannot. Instead, *begun* always appears with *has*, *have*, or *had*, as in "I *have begun* to prepare for the ACT." Choice (D) correctly uses the simple past tense *began*. Choice B creates another verb usage error by inserting *been*. Choice C incorrectly uses *began* with *had*.

10. H   Difficulty: Medium

Category: Usage

Getting to the Answer: Don't panic if you see a question that tests the use of *who* and *whom*. The pronoun *who* serves as a subject, just like the pronouns *he* and *she* replace subjects. The pronoun *whom* serves as an object, just like the pronouns *him* and *her* replace objects. Here, *coach* is the subject of the sentence, so *who*, (H), is correct. Never refer to a person as *which*, as in J.

11. A   Difficulty: Medium

Category: Knowledge of Language / Concision

Getting to the Answer: Don't force a change where one isn't needed. The correct answer for some of the underlined portions will be NO CHANGE. The sentence "The hard work eventually paid off," is correct and concise as it is written. Choice B is verbose, and C and D create run-on sentences.

12. G   Difficulty: Medium

Category: Topic Development / Supporting Material

Getting to the Answer: Start by asking yourself, "Does this information belong here?" The question asks for a sentence that is relevant to the narrator's experience on the swim team. Only (G) is connected to the narrator and the swim team; the sentence explains that the narrator was one of the only swimmers on the team to be interested in the butterfly. The history of the stroke,

F; the relative speed of the stroke, H; and an alternative name for the stroke, J, are not as related to the narrator's personal experience.

13. A   Difficulty: Medium

Category: Knowledge of Language / Concision

Getting to the Answer: The shortest answer is often, but not always, correct. Don't omit portions that add relevant information to the sentence. The sentence is about the narrator's swimming, so her participation in the medley relay is relevant. Choices B and C add descriptions of the medley relay that are not relevant to the topic.

14. H   Difficulty: Medium

Category: Usage

Getting to the Answer: The four choices offer different tenses of the same verb. The clue *last year* indicates that the narrator earned the varsity letter in the past. Choice (H), the simple past tense, is correct. Neither the future perfect tense, F, nor the present tense, J, makes sense with the clue *last year*. Choice G would only make sense if something had prevented the narrator from earning the varsity letter.

15. B   Difficulty: Medium

Category: Topic Development / Supporting Material

Getting to the Answer: Keep the main point of the passage in mind. Before beginning high school, the narrator had never thought of herself as an athlete. Then she joined the swim team and became successful at the sport. Choice (B) is most relevant to the central ideas of the passage. Choices A and C focus too narrowly on details in the passage, while D contradicts the main point of the passage.

Passage II

16. J   Difficulty: Medium

Category: Punctuation

Getting to the Answer: Don't assume that a comma or semicolon is needed just because a sentence is long. Read the sentence aloud to yourself and you should be able to hear that a comma is not needed in the underlined portion. A semicolon, as in F, would only be correct if the second half of the sentence expressed a complete thought. Choices G and H both use an unnecessary comma.

17. A   Difficulty: Low

Category: Usage

Getting to the Answer: When a verb is underlined, check to see whether it agrees with its subject. Watch out for descriptive phrases that separate a verb from its subject. Here, the verb *was* agrees with the singular noun *tank*, so (A) is correct. Choice B uses the present tense, but the surrounding sentences use the past tense. Choices C and D incorrectly use a verb in the plural form.

18. J   Difficulty: Medium

Category: Sentence Structure and Formation

Getting to the Answer: When the word *that* or *which* is underlined, watch out for an incomplete sentence. As it is written, this is a sentence fragment; a complete verb is missing. Removing *that*, as in (J), turns *made* into the main verb of a complete and correct sentence. Choice G does not address the sentence fragment error, and H also fails to provide a clear and appropriate sentence.

19. D   Difficulty: Medium

Category: Knowledge of Language / Concision

Getting to the Answer: If you are *familiar* with a type of animal, then you have almost certainly *seen it before*. Choice (D) creates a concise sentence that does not lose any of the original meaning. The other choices are redundant. Choice B repeats *sights* when *view* has already been used, and C uses the unnecessarily repetitive phrase "to which I was no stranger."

20. H   Difficulty: High

Category: Organization, Unity, and Cohesion / Passage Organization

Getting to the Answer: Scan the paragraph for connecting words and phrases that you can use as clues to determine the most logical order of sentences. In Sentence 5, the word *first* suggests that the sentence should be placed close to the beginning of the paragraph. Sentence 2 says, "There were *also* animals I had never before glimpsed," which indicates that a preceding sentence

discusses animals the writer had glimpsed. Sentence 5, which describes the writer's view of familiar animals, most logically belongs immediately after Sentence 1.

21. C   Difficulty: Low

Category: Sentence Structure and Formation

Getting to the Answer: If an underlined verb agrees with its noun, then determine whether the verb's tense makes sense in the context of the passage. The surrounding verbs are in the past tense, so this sentence should use the simple past tense *saw,* which is (C). Choices A and D use the present tense, and B illogically uses the past progressive "had been seeing."

22. G   Difficulty: High

Category: Organization, Unity, and Cohesion / Transitions

Getting to the Answer: An effective first sentence for a paragraph will introduce the topic of the paragraph and connect that topic to ideas that have come before. Paragraph 3 focuses on the catfish, while Paragraph 4 describes the large alligator and snapping turtle in the bayou tank. Choice (G) would provide an effective connection between these paragraphs, referring to the catfish and introducing the idea that there were even bigger animals on display. Neither F nor H leads into the topic of Paragraph 4. Choice J doesn't provide a transition from the discussion of the catfish in Paragraph 3.

23. C   Difficulty: Medium

Category: Topic Development / Supporting Material

Getting to the Answer: The phrase in question provides a visual image; deleting the phrase would mean losing a description, (C). The removal of the phrase would not affect the transition between sentences, A. Contrary to B, the contrast between images would be decreased. The level of suspense may be somewhat decreased by the loss of the description, but it would not be increased, as stated in D.

24. J   Difficulty: Medium

Category: Punctuation

Getting to the Answer: The word *though* is nonessential and must be set off from the rest of the sentence with proper punctuation. Choice (J) correctly places *though* in between two commas. Choices F and G do not include two commas, and H adds an unnecessary comma after the word *it*.

25. C   Difficulty: Medium

Category: Usage

Getting to the Answer: If something sounds awkward or unusual, there is probably an error. Most words that end in *-ly* are adverbs; they are used to modify verbs, adjectives, or other adverbs. Adverbs cannot be used to describe nouns, such as *moment,* as in A. Choice (C) correctly uses the adjective *slight* to modify *panic.* The sentences formed by B and D don't make sense.

26. J   Difficulty: Low

Category: Usage

Getting to the Answer: The phrase "much of the onlookers" probably sounds strange to you. That's because *much* is used with noncountable things or concepts (as in "there isn't much time") or quantities (as in "there isn't much pizza left"). You could count the number of *onlookers,* so *many,* (J), is correct. Choices G and H also create idiomatic errors.

27. B   Difficulty: Medium

Category: Topic Development / Writer's Purpose

Getting to the Answer: The question tells you that the writer's goal is to describe the appearance of the crayfish, so eliminate the sentence that does not have details about how crayfish look, C. Choice A suggests that crayfish look like lobsters, and D describes the crayfish as small. Neither of these sentences offers the descriptive detail that is given in (B).

28. G   Difficulty: Medium

Category: Punctuation

Getting to the Answer: Trust your ear. You naturally pause when a comma or semicolon is needed in a sentence. A pause between *all* and *I* just doesn't sound right; that's because the full introductory phrase "After seeing all I could inside the museum" should not be interrupted. A comma should not separate a verb (*seeing*) from its object (*museum*). This eliminates F and H. A

comma is needed between an introductory phrase and the complete thought that follows, making (G) correct and J incorrect.

29. D   Difficulty: Medium

Category: Sentence Structure and Formation

Getting to the Answer: Say it simply. The shortest answer here, (D), is correct: it turns the passive construction *it was that* in A and B into the active *I had.* Choice C is unnecessarily wordy.

30. J   Difficulty: High

Category: Sentence Structure and Formation

Getting to the Answer: A sentence must have a subject and verb and must express a complete thought. The sentence that begins *And operates* does not have a subject. Removing the period, (J), creates a grammatically correct sentence. Choice G is awkwardly worded. Choice H creates a run-on sentence; a coordinating conjunction such as *and* needs to be used along with a comma to link two complete thoughts.

Passage III

31. C   Difficulty: Medium

Category: Usage

Getting to the Answer: The pronoun *it* does not agree with its antecedent, "secret identities and elaborate disguises," so A and B are incorrect. Choice (C) corrects the error by using the plural pronoun *they* to refer to the plural antecedent. Choice D fixes the original error but creates a sentence fragment, so it is incorrect.

32. H   Difficulty: Medium

Category: Punctuation

Getting to the Answer: Many English questions will focus on the correct use of commas. Commas should be used to separate an appositive or descriptive phrase from the main part of the sentence. The phrase "the restaurant critic for the *New York Times*" describes the noun *Ruth Reichl,* so the phrase should be set off with commas, as in (H). Choices F and J fail to use both necessary commas. On the other hand, G incorrectly inserts a third comma.

33. D   Difficulty: High

Category: Topic Development / Supporting Material

Getting to the Answer: Only add sentences that are directly connected to the topic of a paragraph. Paragraph 2 discusses the importance of a *Times* review to restaurants in New York City. The suggested sentence provides a specific detail about one restaurant without explaining how the review from the *Times* affected business. Choice (D) best explains why the sentence should not be added.

34. F   Difficulty: Medium

Category: Usage

Getting to the Answer: Trust your ear. You look *to* someone or something for advice. No change is needed. Choice G suggests that the paper is looking along *with* its readers, while H suggests that the readers are looking near the newspaper. Choice J uses an *-ing* verb without a helping verb, creating a sentence fragment.

35. B   Difficulty: Low

Category: Sentence Structure and Formation

Getting to the Answer: Verbs must make sense in the context of the passage. The next sentence says that a negative review *can undermine* a restaurant. Because the two sentences discuss possible results of a review, the underlined verb in this sentence should be in the same tense—*can bring*, (B). Choice A illogically uses the past tense. Choices C and D express certainty in the outcome, which does not match the use of *can* in the following sentence.

36. F   Difficulty: Medium

Category: Punctuation

Getting to the Answer: The subject of the sentence is "restaurant owners and workers," and the verb is *have*. There isn't a descriptive phrase or clause separating the subject and verb, so no comma is needed. A semicolon should be used to connect two complete thoughts, so G is incorrect. Because *restaurant* identifies the type of owners and workers, the comma in H incorrectly separates an adjective from the nouns it describes. A comma should be used with *and* only when separating independent clauses or lists of three or more items, so the comma in J is unnecessary.

37. C   Difficulty: Medium

Category: Usage

Getting to the Answer: To whom does the meal belong? It belongs to the *writer,* so the possessive pronoun *whose* is correct. *Who's*, B, is always a contraction for *who is* or *who has*. Choices A and D introduce sentence structure errors.

38. J   Difficulty: Medium

Category: Sentence Structure and Formation

Getting to the Answer: The sentence is a fragment, so F is incorrect. Choice (J) correctly adds the helping verb *was*, fixes the fragment, and does not introduce new issues. Choice G adds the helping verb but includes an unnecessary comma, and H does not fix the fragment.

39. C   Difficulty: Low

Category: Knowledge of Language / Concision

Getting to the Answer: On the ACT, there's no need to say the same thing twice. *Common, ordinary, representative,* and *average* all have very similar meanings; so A and B use redundant language. Choice (C) makes the sentence concise by using only *typical*. Choice D uses a word that does not make sense in the context of the sentence.

40. H   Difficulty: Medium

Category: Knowledge of Language / Concision

Getting to the Answer: If you have *decided* to do something to solve a problem, you have found a *solution*—there's no need to use both words. Choice (H) eliminates the redundancy and verbosity errors of the other choices.

41. B   Difficulty: High

Category: Sentence Structure and Formation

Getting to the Answer: As a rule, modifying words, phrases, and clauses should be as close as possible to the things or actions they describe. For instance, the list beginning "such as an attractive blonde named Chloe" describes the different personas. Therefore, *different personas* should come right before the list. This eliminates A. Choice (B) correctly uses an introductory phrase and makes *Reichl* the subject of the sentence. Choice C is a sentence fragment; a complete verb is missing. Choice D inserts an unnecessary comma between *clothing* and *that*, and the pronoun *herself* is incorrect in context.

42. G   Difficulty: Medium

Category: Topic Development / Supporting Material

Getting to the Answer: The most logical and effective sentence will be connected to the main topic of the paragraph and make a transition to the following sentence. Paragraph 4 describes how Reichl turned herself into different characters, and Paragraph 5 describes the results of reviewing a restaurant while in disguise. The best link between these ideas is (G). Choice F is a narrow detail that does not connect the two paragraphs, while H and J move completely away from the topic of Reichl's disguises.

43. D   Difficulty: High

Category: Organization, Unity, and Cohesion / Passage Organization

Getting to the Answer: Sometimes it helps to rephrase a question in your own words. For example, this question could be rewritten as "What does the phrase *of a restaurant* describe?" Reichl focuses on the quality of a restaurant, so the best placement is (D). The phrase does not describe *developed*, *view*, or *person*.

44. G   Difficulty: High

Category: Topic Development / Writer's Purpose

Getting to the Answer: The word *occasionally* means *sometimes* so its placement in this sentence indicates that Reichl was sometimes treated very differently when she was in disguise and that sometimes she wasn't. Removing the word *occasionally* would indicate that Reichl always or typically had a different experience as one of her personas, as in (G).

45. A   Difficulty: Medium

Category: Organization, Unity, and Cohesion / Passage Organization

Getting to the Answer: Paragraph 6 describes the effect of Reichl's use of disguises when she reviewed restaurants. Logically, this information should follow the explanation of why and how Ruth dined as different people, the topics of Paragraphs 3 and 4. Paragraph 6 should remain where it is.

Passage IV

46. J   Difficulty: Medium

Category: Punctuation

Getting to the Answer: Trust your ear. A comma indicates a short pause, which you won't hear when you read this part of the sentence aloud. No comma is needed, making (J) the correct answer. A comma can be used to separate a descriptive phrase from the rest of the sentence, as in F and H, but neither "would develop into prizewinning vegetables" nor "develop into prizewinning vegetables" is a descriptive phrase. Choice G incorrectly treats the underlined portion of the sentence as part of a list.

47. D   Difficulty: High

Category: Organization, Unity, and Cohesion / Passage Organization

Getting to the Answer: The paragraph describes events in chronological order, from the last freeze of the year to the time that spring *truly arrived*. Sentence 3 describes thinning out the plants and pulling weeds so the new plants would grow; it would only make sense to do this *after* the seeds have been planted and have started to grow. Sentence 4 is about planting seeds, so Sentence 3 must come after Sentence 4, making (D) the correct answer.

48. H   Difficulty: Medium

Category: Organization, Unity, and Cohesion / Transitions

Getting to the Answer: When you read this sentence aloud, you should be able to hear a short pause between *burden* and *less*. This pause indicates that the conjunction *and* is needed to separate the two descriptions, as in (H). Choice G is incorrect because a colon is used to introduce a brief definition, explanation, or list. Choice J uses the inappropriate conjunction *but*, which doesn't make sense in context.

49. D   Difficulty: Medium

Category: Knowledge of Language / Concision

Getting to the Answer: When "DELETE the underlined portion" is an option, consider whether the underlined portion is relevant to the topic of the sentence or paragraph. Paragraph 2 is about the writer's failure to maintain her garden, not about the weather in July and August. Choice (D) is correct.

50. G **Difficulty:** Low

Category: Organization, Unity, and Cohesion / Transitions

Getting to the Answer: This question asks for the choice that would NOT work in the sentence. In other words, three of the answer choices would make sense in the sentence. The first sentence of Paragraph 3 contrasts with Paragraph 2, so the contrasting transitions in F, H, and J are all possible substitutions for the underlined word. *Indeed,* (G), is a word used to show emphasis, not contrast.

51. D **Difficulty:** Medium

Category: Knowledge of Language / Concision

Getting to the Answer: The shortest answer is often correct. Choices A, B, and C all refer to large-scale farming, which is only loosely related to the topic of gardening. Choice (D) keeps the sentence focused on the topic of Paragraph 3.

52. F **Difficulty:** High

Category: Topic Development / Supporting Material

Getting to the Answer: Before you answer this question, read enough of Paragraph 4 to identify its main idea. Paragraph 3 introduces the topic of square foot gardening, and Paragraph 4 describes several of its advantages. The best link between these ideas is the original sentence, (F). Paragraph 4 doesn't mention the history of square foot gardening or the writer's neighbor, so G and J don't make sense. Choice H is a detail about square foot gardening, but it does not function as a topic sentence for the paragraph.

53. C **Difficulty:** Medium

Category: Knowledge of Language / Precision

Getting to the Answer: This question allows you to choose from among four adjectives, only one of which is correct based on the context. The writer is describing a traditional garden, which means the same thing as a conventional garden. This matches (C). Choices A, B, and D do not reflect the writer's intended meaning: *ancestral* implies that the garden was handed down from generation to generation, *compulsory* means mandatory, and *devout* means religious.

54. J **Difficulty:** Medium

Category: Sentence Structure and Formation

Getting to the Answer: Who spends hours thinning each row? From this sentence, it's unclear: you have no idea who *they* are. Other sentences in Paragraph 4 use the pronoun *you*, so it makes sense to use *you* here.

55. D **Difficulty:** Medium

Category: Sentence Structure and Formation

Getting to the Answer: As written, the sentence is a run-on. Choice (D) inserts a FANBOYS conjunction (in this case, the word *so*) after the comma to correct the error. Choices A, B, and C do not properly combine the two independent clauses in the sentence.

56. H **Difficulty:** Low

Category: Sentence Structure and Formation

Getting to the Answer: As it is written, the sentence does not express a complete thought. To correct the error, remove *which could* so that *make*, (H), becomes the main verb of the sentence. Choice G creates a sentence fragment, and J incorrectly uses the singular rather than the plural form of the verb.

57. A **Difficulty:** Medium

Category: Sentence Structure and Formation

Getting to the Answer: The present tense and the pronoun *you* are used throughout Paragraph 4, so this sentence is correct as it is written.

58. J **Difficulty:** Low

Category: Knowledge of Language / Concision

Getting to the Answer: Remember that the ACT values economy. If you can express an underlined portion in fewer words without changing or losing the original meaning, then the shortest answer is probably correct. The only choice that does not use redundant language is (J).

59. C **Difficulty:** Medium

Category: Usage

Getting to the Answer: The verb in this sentence is separated from its singular subject *one season* by the phrase "of using the square foot garden techniques." Choice (C) corrects the subject-verb agreement error of the original sentence. Incorrect choices A and B use the plural form of the verb, while D uses the future tense, which does not make sense in the context of the sentence.

60. G   Difficulty: High

Category: Topic Development / Writer's Purpose

Getting to the Answer: This question asks about the passage as a whole, so take a moment to think about the main idea of the passage. Paragraphs 1 and 2 describe the writer's failed attempts at a traditional garden, while Paragraphs 3, 4, and 5 focus on the writer's success with a square foot garden. The essay is not instructive; instead, it compares two types of gardens, and that makes (G) correct.

Passage V

61. D   Difficulty: Medium

Category: Punctuation

Getting to the Answer: When a coordinating conjunction such as *but* or *and* combines two independent clauses (meaning two complete thoughts), a comma must come before it. In this sentence, a comma should be inserted after *light,* as in (D). Choice C incorrectly places a comma in a compound phrase and fails to add one before the coordinating conjunction. Choice B incorrectly uses a semicolon between an independent and a dependent clause. You'll likely see at least one semicolon question on the ACT, so remember that a semicolon is used to separate two complete thoughts or to separate items in a series or list when one or more of those items already contains commas.

62. H   Difficulty: Medium

Category: Usage

Getting to the Answer: The answer choices present different forms of the verbs *improve* and *decrease,* so you know the issue is subject-verb agreement. The two underlined verbs need to agree with the plural subject *steps;* only (H) puts both *improve* and *decrease* in the correct form.

63. B   Difficulty: High

Category: Sentence Structure and Formation

Getting to the Answer: As written, the modifying phrase "to clear the windshield" is not logically placed within the sentence, so A is incorrect. Choice (B) correctly places the modifying phrase after the verb *fail.* Choices C and D are incorrect because they misplace the phrase "to clear the windshield."

64. H   Difficulty: Medium

Category: Sentence Structure and Formation

Getting to the Answer: An *-ing* verb needs a helping verb to function as the main verb in a clause or sentence. Changing *being* to *is,* as in (H), corrects the sentence structure error. Choice G inserts an incorrect comma between *vision* and *has been,* while J creates a new sentence structure error by omitting the verb *being.*

65. B   Difficulty: Medium

Category: Sentence Structure and Formation

Getting to the Answer: Something that is *set* is established or predetermined. For the sentence to make sense, *set* should describe *time;* the wiper blades should be replaced at an *established* time each year. Choice (B) is correct. It does not make sense for the *blades,* A, the *year,* C, or the *risk,* D, to be *set,* or established.

66. G   Difficulty: Medium

Category: Organization, Unity, and Cohesion / Transitions

Getting to the Answer: Based on the context, this sentence requires a continuation transition, which matches (G). Eliminate F and H because they are contrast transitions. Choice J is incorrect because *after* is a sequence transition, which doesn't make sense in context.

67. B   Difficulty: Medium

Category: Organization, Unity, and Cohesion / Transitions

Getting to the Answer: To pick the best first sentence for Paragraph 4, you must be able to identify the main idea of the paragraph. If you scan a few sentences of Paragraph 4 before you answer the question, you'll see that the topic of the paragraph is changing a car's oil and oil filter. Only

(B) introduces this topic. Choice A is too general, while C and D refer to car maintenance procedures that are not discussed in Paragraph 4.

68. G   Difficulty: Medium

Category: Organization, Unity, and Cohesion / Transitions

Getting to the Answer: The connecting word *so* is underlined, so consider the relationship between the two parts of the sentence. There is a slight contrast—the first part of the sentence explains what you do need, while the second part identifies what you don't need. The contrasting conjunction *but,* (G), makes the most sense in context. The other choices indicate a cause-and-effect relationship that is not present in the sentence.

69. D   Difficulty: Medium

Category: Punctuation

Getting to the Answer: Information that is key to the main idea of a sentence should not be set off by commas. Here, it's important to know that the section is "in your owner's manual," so commas are incorrect. Choice (D) is correct. Choice C incorrectly uses a semicolon; a complete thought is not expressed by "and collect all of the tools you need."

70. G   Difficulty: High

Category: Topic Development / Supporting Material

Getting to the Answer: Carefully read the question so that you understand the writer's purpose. If the writer wants to explain how to change oil, then the sentence should explain at least one specific step in the process. Choice (G) provides the most detailed information about how to go about changing oil.

71. A   Difficulty: Medium

Category: Punctuation

Getting to the Answer: Use a semicolon to introduce or emphasize what follows. The warning "you do not want to risk being crushed by a car," is certainly worthy of emphasis, so the sentence is correct as it is written. The other choices create run-ons, as the sentence expresses two complete thoughts; additionally, D incorrectly separates a subject noun from its verb with a comma.

72. G   Difficulty: High

Category: Knowledge of Language / Style and Tone

Getting to the Answer: Paragraph 4 uses the informal *you* and *your*, while the rest of the essay uses the more formal third person. Therefore, eliminating the second-person pronouns from Paragraph 4 would make the paragraph match the tone and voice of the rest of the essay, as in (G). Choices H and J are opposite answers: eliminating *you* and *your* would make the advice less direct and would make the essay more formal.

73. A   Difficulty: Low

Category: Knowledge of Language / Concision

Getting to the Answer: A *qualified mechanic* will do a *professional* job, just as a *qualified mechanic* is likely *certified*; B and C use repetitive language. Choice D introduces a sentence structure error. The correct version of the underlined portion is (A).

74. H   Difficulty: Medium

Category: Organization, Unity, and Cohesion / Passage Organization

Getting to the Answer: Knowing the general topic of each paragraph will help you quickly answer a question like this one. The sentence refers to "these different fluids," so look for a part of the passage that discusses fluids. The second and third sentences of Paragraph 3 refer to different fluids (*coolant, oil, brake fluid,* and *transmission fluid*), so the most logical placement for the sentence is at the end of Paragraph 3, as in (H). Paragraph 2 and Paragraph 4 each only refer to one fluid, so F and J are incorrect.

75. D   Difficulty: Medium

Category: Topic Development / Writer's Purpose

Getting to the Answer: Use your Reading Comp skills to answer this question. Does the main idea of the passage fit with this purpose? Not really, as the passage focuses solely on basic maintenance that car owners can do themselves. The passage doesn't discuss the need to learn about a car's safety features. Choice (D) is therefore correct.

MATHEMATICS TEST

1. E   **Difficulty:** Low

Category: Essential Skills / Numbers and Operations

Getting to the Answer: To determine the total amount of fabric used, add the mixed numbers. To add mixed numbers, add the whole-number parts and then add the fractions. The whole-number parts add to 4. To add the fractions, find the least common denominator of 8 and 3, which is 24. Convert each fraction to an equivalent fraction with a denominator of 24: $\frac{3 \times 3}{8 \times 3} = \frac{9}{24}$ and $\frac{1 \times 8}{3 \times 8} = \frac{8}{24}$. Now, add the numerators and keep the denominator the same: $\frac{9}{24} + \frac{8}{24} + \frac{17}{24}$. The total amount of fabric Tanya used was $4\frac{17}{24}$ yards, which is (E).

2. K   **Difficulty:** Low

Category: Essential Skills / Expressions and Equations

Getting to the Answer: To simplify this expression, first multiply the numerical coefficients to get $5 \cdot 6 \cdot 2 = 60$. To multiply the variable terms, keep the base of the variable the same and add the exponents. Remember that x means x^1. Multiply the x terms: $x^3 \cdot x = x^{3+1} = x^4$. Multiply the y terms: $y^5 \cdot y^2 \cdot y = y^{5+2+1} = y^8$. The resulting expression is $60x^4 y^8$, which matches (K).

3. B   **Difficulty:** Low

Category: Essential Skills / Rates, Percents, Proportions, and Unit Conversion

Getting to the Answer: First, find the amount each person saves yearly. Brandon saves 6% of his $36,000 salary, or $0.06 \times 36,000 = \$2,160$ each year. Jacqui saves $200 every month, or $12 \times 200 = \$2,400$ each year. The difference, in dollars, of their savings is $2,400 - 2,160 = \$240$. This makes (B) correct.

4. J   **Difficulty:** Low

Category: Essential Skills / Numbers and Operations

Getting to the Answer: When you are calculating a total price, you usually multiply the number of units sold times the price per unit. The challenge in this word problem is that 100 of the units (T-shirts) were sold at a different price. Calculate the price for the first 100 and add that to the total price of the remaining shirts. The school earned $7 for each of the first 100 shirts and $10 for each of the remaining 250 shirts, for a total of:

$$7(100) + 10(250)$$
$$= 700 + 2,500$$
$$= 3,200$$

Choice (J) is correct.

5. D   **Difficulty:** Medium

Category: Essential Skills / Rates, Percents, Proportions, and Unit Conversion

Getting to the Answer: The amount of chromium is a part of the whole alloy. Use the three-part percent formula, Part = percent × whole. There are 262.5 pounds of chromium available (the part), which must reflect at least 10.5% (the percent) of the whole. Let w represent the whole amount of alloy that can be manufactured and write the algebraic equation $262.5 = 10.5\% \times w$ or, in simpler form, $262.5 = 0.105w$. Divide both sides of the equation by 0.105 to get $w = \frac{262.5}{0.105} = 2,500$ pounds of steel. This matches (D).

6. J   **Difficulty:** Low

Category: Essential Skills / Geometry

Getting to the Answer: A wallpaper border is a strip that surrounds the perimeter of the kitchen. The perimeter of a rectangle = 2(length + width). The kitchen has a length of 6.5 meters and a width of 4 meters, so the amount of border needed is $2(6.5 + 4) = 2(10.5) = 21$ meters, which is (J).

7. A   **Difficulty:** Medium

Category: Essential Skills / Expressions and Equations

Getting to the Answer: To find an equivalent expression for the one given, use the distributive property. First, evaluate the inner parentheses according to the order of operations, or PEMDAS. Distribute the negative sign to $(y + z)$ to get $w(x - y - z)$. Next, distribute the variable w to all terms inside the parentheses to get $wx - wy - wz$. This matches (A).

8. G **Difficulty:** Low

Category: Essential Skills / Expressions and Equations

Getting to the Answer: This is an equation with a variable on both sides. To solve, work to get the n terms isolated on one side of the equation and the numerical terms on the other side. Subtract $3n$ from both sides and then combine like terms to get $3n - 4 = 24$. Now, add 4 to both sides and you'll have $3n = 28$. Finally, divide both sides by 3 to get $n = \dfrac{28}{3}$. Choice (G) is correct.

9. D **Difficulty:** Medium

Category: Essential Skills / Rates, Percents, Proportions, and Unit Conversion

Getting to the Answer: Be careful not to confuse a part:part ratio with a part:whole ratio. The correct ratio between white and blue paint needed to produce the desired color is 5 parts white to 3 parts blue, which gives a total of 8 parts. To find the correct amount of blue paint in 24 quarts of the mixed color, set up a proportion using the ratio of blue paint to the total amount of paint: $\dfrac{3}{8} = \dfrac{b}{24}$. Cross-multiply and solve for b to find that Marco needs $3(24) \div 8 = 9$ quarts of blue paint. This matches (D).

10. G **Difficulty:** Medium

Category: Higher Math / Algebra

Getting to the Answer: First, solve the equation $5m^2 = 45$ for m. Once you obtain a value for m, substitute this into the expression to evaluate and find the answer. To solve the equation, divide both sides of the equation by 5 to get $m^2 = 9$. Take the square root of each side to get $m = 3$ or $m = -3$. Now, evaluate the expression. Because the expression contains the radical $\sqrt{12m}$ and the expression must be a real number, reject the value of $m = -3$. (For a square root, when a radicand, the expression under the radical sign, is negative, the number does not have a value in the set of real numbers.) Substitute 3 for m in the expression:

$$(3)^3 + \sqrt{12(3)} = 27 + \sqrt{36} = 27 + 6 = 33$$

Choice (G) is correct.

11. E **Difficulty:** Medium

Category: Higher Math / Geometry

Getting to the Answer: First, convert the mixed-number radius to a decimal: $3\dfrac{3}{5} = 3.6$. Substitute 3.6 into the formula to get $V = \dfrac{4}{3} \times \pi \times (3.6)^3$. Use the π key on your calculator. If your calculator has fractional capability and follows the correct order of operations, type the entry in as listed above. Otherwise, first find 3.6 to the third power. Multiply the result by 4, then divide by 3. Finally, multiply by π. In either case, the result is approximately 195.43, or 195 to the nearest cubic meter. This makes (E) correct.

12. G **Difficulty:** Medium

Category: Essential Skills / Statistics and Probability

Getting to the Answer: Probability is a ratio that compares the number of favorable, or desired, outcomes to the total number of outcomes. Probability is always a number between 0 and 1. In this question, the number of favorable outcomes is the number of nuts that are NOT peanuts, or $6 + 8 = 14$. The total number of outcomes is $10 + 6 + 8 = 24$. The probability that the nut is NOT a peanut is $\dfrac{14}{24} = \dfrac{7}{12}$, in lowest terms. Choice (G) is correct.

13. C **Difficulty:** Medium

Category: Higher Math / Number and Quantity

Getting to the Answer: The matrices outline how the number of people *in each age group* who shop at the store corresponds to the ratio, written as a decimal, of the number of people *in each age group* who will make purchases. A ratio written as a decimal is essentially a percentage. Interpreting the matrices together, you know that 20% of the 75 adolescents will make a purchase, resulting in $75 \times 0.20 = 15$ adolescent purchases; 35% of the 100 adults will make a purchase, resulting in $100 \times 0.35 = 35$ adult purchases; and 10% of the 30 senior citizens will make a purchase, resulting in $30 \times 0.10 = 3$ senior-citizen purchases. This is a total of $15 + 35 + 3 = 53$ people making purchases, so (C) is correct.

14. H **Difficulty:** Low

Category: Higher Math / Statistics and Probability

Getting to the Answer: This first question simply tests whether you understand how to read the table.

Averages are always calculated by dividing the sum of the terms by the number of terms. Using the three sections of English I (rows 1, 2, and 3) the average number per section is $\frac{29 + 27 + 22}{3} = \frac{78}{3} = 26$, which is (H).

15. B   Difficulty: Medium

Category: Higher Math / Statistics and Probability

Getting to the Answer: Instead of getting overwhelmed by all the data and combinations, try to think of a systematic way to check if each period has enough computers. One good method is to find the total number of students for each period:

Period	1	2	3	4	5	6
Number of Students	27	48	26	24	54	48

The number of computers available is $30 + 30 - 3 - 5$, or 52. This means there aren't enough for Period 5 only, which is (B).

16. G   Difficulty: Medium

Category: Essential Skills / Expressions and Equations

Getting to the Answer: To find the missing value, add the monomials in the first row: $m + (-4m) + 3m = 0$. The first row sums to zero. To be sure, check the rightmost column: $3m + (-2m) + (-m) = 0$. Every row, column, and diagonal must sum to 0. The first column must therefore be $m + 2m + \square = 0$, or $3m + \square = 0$. Isolate the missing term on one side of the equation by subtracting $3m$ from both sides: $\square = -3m$, which is (G).

17. E   Difficulty: Medium

Category: Essential Skills / Geometry

Getting to the Answer: The algebraic expression xy means to multiply the point's x-coordinate by its y-coordinate. If the product is positive, then the x- and y-coordinates are either both positive or both negative, according to the rules for multiplying signed numbers. Quadrant I is the $(+,+)$ quadrant because the x-coordinates are to the right of the origin and the y-coordinates are above the origin. Quadrant III is the $(-,-)$ quadrant because the x-coordinates are to the left of the origin and the y-coordinates are below the origin. The coordinates in either of these two quadrants will give a positive product, making (E) the correct answer.

18. G   Difficulty: High

Category: Higher Math / Algebra

Getting to the Answer: Create a system of linear equations where e represents the number of packs with 8 plates and t represents the number of packs with 12 plates. The first equation should represent the total number of *packs*, each with 8 or 12 plates, or $e + t = 54$. The second equation should represent the total number of *plates*. Because e represents packs with 8 plates and t represents packs with 12 plates, the second equation is $8e + 12t = 496$. Now solve the system using substitution (or elimination if it's faster for you). Solve the first equation for either variable and substitute the result into the second equation:

$$e + t = 54$$
$$e = 54 - t$$

$$8(54 - t) + 12t = 496$$
$$432 - 8t + 12t = 496$$
$$432 + 4t = 496$$
$$4t = 64$$
$$t = 16$$

So, 16 packs have 12 plates. The question asks about packs of 12, so you don't need to find the value of e. But you are not done yet. The question asks how many *plates* a customer would buy if he or she buys all of the packs of 12 the store has, not just the *number of packs*. The customer would buy $16 \times 12 = 192$ plates, which is (G).

19. A   Difficulty: Medium

Category: Essential Skills / Rates, Percents, Proportions, and Unit Conversion

Getting to the Answer: The question describes a comparison of the number of female to male students. This is a ratio, and the ratio of female to male students is 5 to 3, or $\frac{5}{3}$. Let f represent the number of female students. Set up the proportion $\frac{5}{3} = \frac{f}{6,000}$ and cross-multiply to get $3f = 5 \times 6,000$, or $3f = 30,000$. Divide both sides by 3 to get $f = 10,000$ females. This makes (A) correct.

20. H   Difficulty: Low

Category: Essential Skills / Statistics and Probability

Getting to the Answer: The average of a set of terms is equal to the sum of the terms divided by the number of terms. Use the average formula to find the average of all four prices:

$$\frac{\$2.15 + \$2.05 + \$2.15 + \$1.97}{4} = \frac{\$8.32}{4} = \$2.08$$

Choice (H) is correct.

21. A   Difficulty: Medium

Category: Higher Math / Functions

Getting to the Answer: The notation $f(g(x))$ indicates a composition of two functions and is read "f of g of x." It means that the output when x is substituted into $g(x)$ becomes the input for $f(x)$. Substitute $\frac{1}{4}$ for x in $g(x)$, simplify, and then substitute the result into $f(x)$:

$$g\left(\frac{1}{4}\right) = \sqrt{\frac{1}{4}} + 2.5 = \frac{\sqrt{1}}{\sqrt{4}} + 2.5 = \frac{1}{2} + 2.5 = 3$$

$$f(3) = -4(3) + 5 = -12 + 5 = -7$$

Therefore, $f\left(g\left(\frac{1}{4}\right)\right) = -7$, which is (A).

22. J   Difficulty: Medium

Category: Higher Math / Algebra

Getting to the Answer: To find slope-intercept form, $y = mx + b$, solve the given equation for y in terms of x. In other words, you need to isolate y on one side of the equation. First, subtract $3x$ from both sides to get $2y = -3x + 16$. Now, divide all terms on both sides by 2 to get $\frac{2y}{2} = \frac{-3x}{2} + \frac{16}{2}$, which simplifies to $y = -\frac{3}{2}x + 8$. This matches (J).

23. E   Difficulty: Medium

Category: Higher Math / Algebra

Getting to the Answer: To solve a quadratic equation, first write the equation in standard form, $ax^2 + bx + c = 0$, then factor if possible. The rearranged equation is $x^2 - 20x + 75 = 0$. Look for factors of $+75$ ($+$ times $+$, or $-$ times $-$) that when added together will equal -20, the b coefficient. The factors are -5 and -15. The equation,

after factoring, becomes $(x - 5)(x - 15) = 0$. The solutions are the values of x that result in either factor equaling 0, which are $x = 5$ or $x = 15$. Choice (E) matches the first of these values.

24. H   Difficulty: Low

Category: Higher Math / Geometry

Getting to the Answer: Use SOHCAHTOA. Cosine (cos) is "adjacent over hypotenuse," so look at angle N and identify the length of the side adjacent to that angle ($12m$) and the length of the hypotenuse ($13m$). Cos $N = \frac{12m}{13m}$, which reduces to $\frac{12}{13}$. This makes (H) correct.

25. C   Difficulty: Medium

Category: Higher Math / Geometry

Getting to the Answer: The question states that the radius of the circle has a length of 7 cm, and segment OB is a radius, so it also has a length of 7 cm. Because OC is perpendicular to AB, a right angle is formed. To find the length of chord CB, note that it is the hypotenuse of right triangle $\triangle COB$, with legs that each measure 7 cm. Because the legs have the same measure, this is a special right triangle, a 45°-45°-90° triangle, and the sides are in the ratio of $s:s:s\sqrt{2}$. Chord BC is therefore $7\sqrt{2} \approx 9.899$, or 9.9 to the nearest tenth of a centimeter. Alternately, you could use the Pythagorean theorem, $a^2 + b^2 = c^2$, where $a = b = 7$:

$$7^2 + 7^2 = c^2$$
$$49 + 49 = c^2$$
$$c = \sqrt{98} \approx 9.9 \text{ cm}$$

Choice (C) is correct.

26. J   Difficulty: High

Category: Higher Math / Algebra

Getting to the Answer: When you get stuck on a question involving variables, look for ways to rewrite the expressions that will produce like terms to work with. Keep an eye out for the classic quadratic equations.

Start with the first equation: $(a - b)^2 = 36$. This can also be written as $(a - b)(a - b) = 36$. Use FOIL (or recognize the classic quadratic) to expand the left side: $a^2 - 2ab + b^2 = 36$. Now you have something you can work with! Substitute in the value of ab that was given in the question:

$$a^2 - 2(24) + b^2 = 36$$
$$a^2 - 48 + b^2 = 36$$
$$a^2 + b^2 = 84$$

Choice (J) is correct.

27. D   Difficulty: Low

Category: Essential Skills / Geometry

Getting to the Answer: A swimming pool that is the same depth in all parts is a rectangular solid. The amount of water in the pool is the volume of the water. Use the formula $V = lwh$ and substitute the volume, length, and width given in the question: $14{,}375 = 50 \times 25 \times h$, or $14{,}375 = 1{,}250h$. Divide both sides of the equation by 1,250 to get $11.5 = h$. Thus, the depth is between 11 and 12 meters, making (D) the correct choice.

28. J   Difficulty: Medium

Category: Essential Skills / Rates, Percents, Proportions, and Unit Conversion

Getting to the Answer: This question involves a proportion and a unit conversion. You may be tempted to divide the number of steps by the number of feet in Lucia's stride (because the number of steps is already very large), but this isn't correct. To be safe, start by writing a proportion comparing feet and steps.

Let f represent the number of feet Lucia ran. There are 2.5 feet to every 1 of Lucia's steps, and she took 24,288 steps:

$$\frac{2.5 \text{ feet}}{1 \text{ step}} = \frac{f \text{ feet}}{24{,}288 \text{ steps}}$$
$$f = 2.5(24{,}288)$$
$$f = 60{,}720$$

Lucia ran 60,720 feet. Now convert this to miles. There are 5,280 feet in one mile, so divide to get $60{,}720 \div 5{,}280 = 11.5$ miles. This makes (J) correct.

You could also use the factor-label method to answer this question:

$$24{,}288 \text{ steps} \times \frac{2.5 \text{ ft}}{1 \text{ step}} \times \frac{1 \text{ mi}}{5{,}280 \text{ ft}} = 11.5 \text{ miles}$$

29. B   Difficulty: Medium

Category: Essential Skills / Statistics and Probability

Getting to the Answer: The fraction of the people who were sophomores is the ratio of the number of sophomores to the total number of people at the prom. Each horizontal line on the bar graph represents 10 people, so there were 30 sophomores and a total of $20 + 30 + 70 + 200 = 320$ people at the prom. The fraction that were sophomores is $\frac{30}{320} = \frac{3}{32}$, which is (B).

30. F   Difficulty: Medium

Category: Higher Math / Algebra

Getting to the Answer: Parallel lines have the same slope. Use the first pair of points and the slope formula to calculate the slope:

$$\text{Slope} = \frac{y_2 - y_1}{x_2 - x_1} = \frac{16 - 1}{2 - 1} = 15$$

Then use the slope, 15, to figure out the missing coordinate in the second pair of points:

$$\text{Slope} = \frac{y_2 - y_1}{x_2 - x_1}$$
$$15 = \frac{(25 - (-5))}{a - (-10)}$$
$$15 = \frac{30}{a + 10}$$
$$15a + 150 = 30$$
$$15a = -120$$
$$a = -8$$

Choice (F) is correct.

31. B   Difficulty: Medium

Category: Higher Math / Algebra

Getting to the Answer: You can find the point of intersection of two lines by solving the system of equations. Use the elimination method by lining up the equations vertically by like terms:

$$5x + y = 7$$
$$2x + 3y = 8$$

The question asks for the x-coordinate, so multiply one of the equations by a number such that when they are combined, the *y*-values will be eliminated. If you multiply all terms in the top equation by -3, when you combine them, the *y*-values will be eliminated:

$$-3(5x + y = 7) \Rightarrow -15x - 3y = -21$$
$$2x + 3y = 8 \Rightarrow 2x + 3y = 8$$

Add the resulting equations to get $-13x = -13$. Now, divide both sides of this simpler equation by -13 to get $x = 1$, which is (B).

32. K   Difficulty: Medium

Category: Essential Skills / Expressions and Equations

Getting to the Answer: To solve the equation for *b*, isolate *b* on one side of the equation. First, add 8 to both sides of the equation to get $a + 8 = 2b$. Now, divide both sides by 2 to get $\frac{a+8}{2} = \frac{2b}{2}$, which simplifies to $b = \frac{a+8}{2}$. Choice (K) is therefore correct.

33. D   Difficulty: Low

Category: Essential Skills / Geometry

Getting to the Answer: The formula for finding the area of a parallelogram is $A = bh$, where height *h* is the length of the segment that is perpendicular to one of the bases of the parallelogram. In the figure, segment *RT*, of length $9 + 5$, or 14 mm, is the base and the dotted segment, of length 12 mm, is the height. The area of the parallelogram is $14 \times 12 = 168$ mm². Choice (D) is correct.

34. H   Difficulty: Medium

Category: Higher Math / Functions

Getting to the Answer: Only use the geometric sequence formula for questions that ask you about very distant numbers in the sequence. In a geometric sequence, each term is the result of multiplying the previous term by a constant ratio. To find this ratio, divide any term by the term that precedes it: $\frac{-12}{36} = -\frac{1}{3}$. Therefore, the term that follows 4 is $4 \times \left(-\frac{1}{3}\right)$, or $-\frac{4}{3}$. This makes (H) correct.

35. E   Difficulty: High

Category: Higher Math / Geometry

Getting to the Answer: Because all streets and avenues shown intersect at right angles, the map is a rectangle in which opposite sides have the same measures. To find the location halfway between *H* and *S*, first think of the corner of Oak and 10th as the origin, or (0,0). Just as in coordinate geometry, the first coordinate of the ordered pair represents the east-west direction, and the second coordinate represents the north-south direction. The distance from the origin at Oak Street to the school is 5 miles east, which you can call (5,0). The distance from the origin at 10th Avenue to the hospital is 8 miles north, which you can call (0,8). The new station will be halfway between these points, or $\frac{5}{2} = 2.5$ miles east of the origin and $\frac{8}{2} = 4$ miles north of the origin.

Finally, to drive from *F* to the new fire station, you would have to drive $8 - 2.5 = 5.5$ miles west on Main Street, then $10 - 4 = 6$ miles south on Elm Street (the first 2 miles south to get to 2nd Avenue, and then 4 more miles south to be halfway between the hospital and the school). This means (E) is correct.

36. G   Difficulty: High

Category: Essential Skills / Expressions and Equations

Getting to the Answer: Consecutive integers are integers that differ by 1, such as 3, 4, 5. Consecutive even integers are even integers that differ by 2, such as 6, 8, 10, 12. Because the answer choices use the variable *x*, let *x* represent the smaller of the consecutive even integers, so $(x + 2)$ would be the larger of the integers. Four times the larger is represented by $4(x + 2)$ and twice the smaller by $2x$. The key word *difference* means to subtract the smaller from the larger, and the key word *is* means "equal." The equation is $4(x + 2) - 2x = 36$, which matches (G).

37. C   Difficulty: Medium

Category: Higher Math / Geometry

Getting to the Answer: The question states that the telephone pole is perpendicular to the ground and a wire is attached to the pole. This will result in a right triangle.

It helps to draw a quick figure to represent the situation. The thicker side of the triangle represents the telephone pole, and the hypotenuse is the wire:

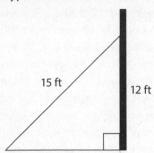

To find out how far the anchor of the supporting wire is from the base of the telephone pole, solve for the length of the missing leg. Use the Pythagorean theorem, which is $a^2 + b^2 = c^2$. Let b represent the missing leg and substitute in the given values to get $12^2 + b^2 = 15^2$, or $144 + b^2 = 225$. Subtract 144 from both sides: $b^2 = 81$. To solve for b, take the square root of both sides: $\sqrt{b^2} = \sqrt{81}$, so $b = 9$ or -9. A length cannot be negative, so the length is 9 feet, making (C) the correct answer.

38. H   Difficulty: Medium

Category: Higher Math / Geometry

Getting to the Answer: The area of a circle is $A = \pi r^2$, where r is the radius of the circle. Use the equation $100\pi = \pi r^2$ and solve for r by dividing both sides by π to arrive at $100 = r^2$. If you take the square root of both sides, then $r = 10$ or -10. Reject the -10 value because a radius length cannot be negative. The radius of the circle is 10, so the diameter of the circle, which is the same as the length of a side of the square, is $2 \times 10 = 20$ units. Be careful here—the question asks for the perimeter of the square, not the side length. The perimeter equals $4(20) = 80$ units, making (H) correct.

39. C   Difficulty: Medium

Category: Essential Skills / Geometry

Getting to the Answer: When figures are similar, the side lengths are in proportion. Let EH represent the missing side length and set up the proportion of shorter side to longer side: $\dfrac{3}{8} = \dfrac{2}{EH}$. Cross-multiply to get $3EH = 16$. Divide both sides by 3 to get $EH = 16 \div 3 \approx 5.3$, to the nearest tenth of an inch. Choice (C) is correct.

40. J   Difficulty: Medium

Category: Essential Skills / Geometry

Getting to the Answer: The figure shown is a parallelogram. Extend the top side out from the parallelogram to make a parallel line to line UZ. Line WY is a transversal to the parallel lines, forming alternate interior angles, $\angle XWY$ and $\angle WYV$, which have the same measures of 50°. Line WV is another transversal line to the parallel lines, forming alternate interior angles $\angle UVW$ and $\angle VWX$. Because they have the same measure, $\angle VWX = 150°$. In addition, $\angle VWX$ and $\angle VYX$ have the same measure—they are opposite angles in a parallelogram. Now $\angle VYX - \angle WYV = \angle WYX$, or $150 - 50 = 100°$. That's (J).

41. C   Difficulty: Medium

Category: Higher Math / Algebra

Getting to the Answer: When multiplying terms with the same base, exponents are *added,* not multiplied. When dividing terms with the same base, exponents are subtracted. You can simplify the numerator, then divide:

$$\frac{\left(16x^2y^2\right)\left(6x^2y^4\right)}{-8x^2y^3} = \frac{96x^4y^6}{-8x^2y^3} = -12x^2y^3$$

Or you can cancel out as much as possible, then simplify. Both methods reveal that (C) is correct:

$$\frac{\left(16x^2y^2\right)\left(6x^2y^4\right)}{-8x^2y^3} = \frac{\left(2y^2\right)\left(6x^2y\right)}{-1} = -12x^2y^3$$

42. G   Difficulty: Medium

Category: Essential Skills / Numbers and Operations

Getting to the Answer: Convert the fractions into decimal equivalents and remember that the key word *of* means to multiply. Because $\dfrac{3}{4}$ of the 3,500 eligible voters cast a vote, this means $0.75 \times 3,500 = 2,625$ votes were cast at the site. Three-fifths of these votes were for Martinez, or $0.6 \times 2,625 = 1,575$ votes for Martinez. Choice (G) is correct.

43. A   Difficulty: Medium

Category: Higher Math / Number and Quantity

Getting to the Answer: To find the greatest common factor, find all factors that the two expressions have in common. In this case, the factors in common are a, a, *a*, and *b*, or a^3b. It is given that the greatest common factor is 54, so think of a cubic number that is a factor of 54. The first cubic numbers are 1^3 (or 1), 2^3 (or 8), and 3^3 (or 27). Twenty-seven is a factor of 54: $27 \times 2 = 54$, so a possible value for *b* is 2. Choice (A) is correct.

44. K   Difficulty: Medium

Category: Essential Skills / Rates, Percents, Proportions, and Unit Conversion

Getting to the Answer: To answer this question, break it up into its parts. First, find the value of *x* given that 40% of *x* is 70. The key word *of* means to multiply. Write this as the equation $0.40x = 70$, then divide both sides by 0.40 to get $x = 175$. Now find 180% of *x*, or 1.80×175, which is 315. This makes (K) the correct answer.

45. C   Difficulty: Medium

Category: Higher Math / Geometry

Getting to the Answer: To find the length of segment *MN*, use the Distance formula: $d = \sqrt{(x_2 - x_1)^2 + (y_2 - y_1)^2}$. Substitute in the coordinates and simplify using the correct order of operations:

$$d = \sqrt{(6 - 2)^2 + (5 - 3)^2}$$
$$d = \sqrt{4^2 + 2^2}$$
$$d = \sqrt{20} = \sqrt{4} \times \sqrt{5} = 2\sqrt{5}$$

Choice (C) is correct.

46. K   Difficulty: Medium

Category: Higher Math / Number and Quantity

Getting to the Answer: To add two vectors, add the first coordinates together and add the second coordinates together:

$$\mathbf{u} + \mathbf{v} = \langle -5 + 5, 1 + 0 \rangle = \langle 0, 1 \rangle$$

Choice (K) is correct.

47. E   Difficulty: Medium

Category: Higher Math / Functions

Getting to the Answer: The equation of a circle, when you know the coordinates of the center (h,k) and the radius *r*, is given by $(x - h)^2 + (y - k)^2 = r^2$. Substitute in the given values to get $(x - (-2))^2 + (y - 3)^2 = 9^2$. This simplifies to $(x + 2)^2 + (y - 3)^2 = 81$, a perfect match for (E).

48. H   Difficulty: High

Category: Higher Math / Number and Quantity

Getting to the Answer: In the complex number system, i^2 is defined to be equal to -1, as you are told in the question stem. Use the distributive property and FOIL to multiply the fractions. Then substitute -1 for i^2 wherever possible and simplify:

$$\frac{3}{5 - i} \times \frac{5 + i}{5 + i} = \frac{3(5) + 3(i)}{5^2 + 5i - 5i - i^2}$$
$$= \frac{15 + 3i}{25 - (-1)}$$
$$= \frac{15 + 3i}{26}$$

Choice (H) is correct.

49. C   Difficulty: Medium

Category: Higher Math / Number and Quantity

Getting to the Answer: To answer this question by hand, rewrite the exponent in a way that makes it easier to evaluate: Use exponent rules to rewrite $\frac{3}{2}$ as a unit fraction raised to a power. Then write the expression in radical form and simplify.

$$16^{\frac{3}{2}} = (16^{\frac{1}{2}})^3$$
$$= (\sqrt{16})^3$$
$$= 4^3$$
$$= 4 \times 4 \times 4$$
$$= 64$$

Choice (C) is correct. Note that you could also use your calculator by entering 16^(3/2) or 16^1.5. Either expression should give 64.

50. G   Difficulty: Medium

Category: Higher Math / Statistics and Probability

Getting to the Answer: The key to answering this question is to first assume that there are no students who have both a cell phone and an MP3 player. If this were the case, then there would be $35 + 18 = 53$ students polled. The question states that 50 students were polled, so therefore 3 students have both electronic devices, making (G) the correct choice.

51. A **Difficulty:** Medium

Category: Higher Math / Functions

Getting to the Answer: You need to determine the relationship between the two variables. You can plug one value of t into each of the answer choices to determine if it results in the correct population. If $t = 21$, then p should equal 3. Check each answer choice and eliminate those that don't yield a p value of 3.

A: $\dfrac{21}{7} = 3$ Keep.

B: $21 - 18 = 3$ Keep.

C: $21 - 30 = -7$ Eliminate.

D: $3 \times 21 - 60 = 63 - 60 = 3$ Keep.

E: $3 \times 21 - 100 = -37$ Eliminate.

Check the second value. If $t = 35$, p should equal 5.

A: $\dfrac{35}{7} = 5$ Keep.

B: $35 - 8 = 27$ Eliminate.

D: $3 \times 35 - 60 = 105 - 60 = 45$ Eliminate.

Choice (A) is the correct answer.

52. H **Difficulty:** High

Category: Higher Math / Statistics and Probability

Getting to the Answer: Make this question easier to visualize by naming the five people A, B, C, D, and E, then systematically writing out the possible combinations (no repeats allowed):

AB, AC, AD, AE

BC, BD, BE

CD, CE

DE

There are 10 distinct combinations, meaning 10 total handshakes, so (H) is correct.

53. D **Difficulty:** Medium

Category: Higher Math / Statistics and Probability

Getting to the Answer: A circle graph uses sectors of a circle to compare the parts of a whole group. The table gives you four of the parts (the four budget categories), but you need to determine the percentage in the category Miscellaneous. The total percentage must sum to 100%, so the percentage for Miscellaneous will be $100 - 23 - 5 - 22 - 18 = 32\%$. To find the number of degrees in a circle graph that corresponds with 32%, set up the ratio, where x represents the number of degrees for the Miscellaneous category. Recall that there are 360° in a whole circle: $\dfrac{32\%}{100\%} = \dfrac{x°}{360°}$. Cross-multiply to arrive at $32 \times 360 = 100x$, or $11{,}520 = 100x$. Divide both sides by 100 to get $x = 115°$, rounded to the nearest degree. Choice (D) is correct.

54. K **Difficulty:** High

Category: Higher Math / Geometry

Getting to the Answer: The information $\dfrac{\pi}{2} < \theta < \pi$ tells you that the angle is in quadrant II of the coordinate plane. In quadrant II, the sine values are positive. So the answer must be positive. Eliminate F, G, and H. You are given the value of tan θ, which is the ratio of the opposite side to the adjacent side of a right triangle (remember SOHCAH-TOA). Sketch this triangle, using leg lengths of 4 and 3:

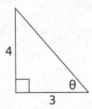

This is a special right triangle, a 3-4-5 Pythagorean triplet, so the hypotenuse is 5 units in length. The sine of an angle is the ratio of the length of the opposite side to the length of the hypotenuse, or $\dfrac{4}{5}$. That's (K).

55. A **Difficulty:** Medium

Category: Higher Math / Algebra

Getting to the Answer: Look at the graphed boundary lines for the inequalities. Find the equation for these boundary lines and then determine whether the shading represents less than (below) or greater than (above) these boundary lines. The horizontal line has a slope of 0 and a y-intercept (where the line crosses the y-axis) of 6, so the equation of this boundary line is $y = 6$. The graph is shaded below this line, so the inequality is $y \leq 6$. Eliminate B and D. The slanted line is increasing from left to right with a change in the y-values of 3 for each change in the x-values of 1, so the slope is $\frac{3}{1} = 3$. The y-intercept is -5. The shading is greater than, or above, this boundary line, so the inequality is $y \geq 3x - 5$. Together, the inequalities match (A).

56. J   Difficulty: High

Category: Higher Math / Functions

Getting to the Answer: Just as you can substitute a number into a function or a composition of functions, you can substitute an expression into a function. The notation $f(g(x))$ means to substitute the expression that defines $g(x)$, the inner function, for x in $f(x)$, the outer function. So, $f(g(x)) = 3(4x + 5) + 5$. Use the distributive property and then combine like terms to get $f(g(x)) = 12x + 15 + 5$, or in simplest form, $12x + 20$. This matches (J).

57. D   Difficulty: Medium

Category: Higher Math / Functions

Getting to the Answer: The graph of the function crosses the x-axis when $q(x) = 0$, so set the equation equal to 0 and solve for x. You can factor (sometimes) or use the quadratic formula to find x:

$$2x^2 + 7x - 4 = 0$$
$$a = 2, b = 7, c = -4$$

$$x = \frac{-b \pm \sqrt{b^2 - 4ac}}{2a}$$
$$= \frac{-7 \pm \sqrt{7^2 - 4(2)(-4)}}{2(2)}$$
$$= \frac{-7 \pm \sqrt{49 + 32}}{4}$$
$$= \frac{-7 \pm \sqrt{81}}{4}$$
$$= \frac{-7 \pm 9}{4}$$

$$x = \frac{-7 + 9}{4} = \frac{1}{2} \text{ or } x = \frac{-7 - 9}{4} = -4$$

Choice (D) is correct.

58. F   Difficulty: Medium

Category: Higher Math / Geometry

Getting to the Answer: This question tests your knowledge of reflections in the coordinate plane. Mentally picture what is happening: When you reflect a point or a figure over the y-axis (the vertical axis), the x-coordinate of each point is the opposite sign of the original and the y-coordinate stays the same. The reflection of the point $Q(r,s)$ after a reflection over the y-axis is therefore $Q'(-r,s)$, which matches (F). Note that you could also pick a nice, easy point, such as (2,5), draw a sketch, and reflect it over the y-axis to see where it lands. You should arrive at $(-2,5)$, which supports the correct answer—change the sign of the x-coordinate and keep the y-coordinate the same.

59. E   Difficulty: Medium

Category: Higher Math / Functions

Getting to the Answer: If you've taken trigonometry in school, be sure to review the relationships between the trigonometric functions. The reciprocal functions, such as $\sec\theta = \frac{1}{\cos\theta}$, $\csc\theta = \frac{1}{\sin\theta}$, and $\cot\theta = \frac{1}{\tan\theta}$, aren't always tested, but they can be quick points if you're already familiar with the concepts. Because $\csc x = \frac{1}{\sin x}$, $\csc x = \frac{1}{\frac{1}{2}} = 2$. The correct answer is (E).

60. H   Difficulty: High

Category: Higher Math / Functions

Getting to the Answer: In this question, you are asked to use the formula $\cos(\alpha + \beta) = \cos(\alpha)\cos(\beta) - \sin(\alpha)\sin(\beta)$ and the table of values to find the value of $\cos(75°)$, which can be written as $\cos(30° + 45°)$. Plug in 30° for α and 45° for β to get $\cos(30°)\cos(45°) - \sin(30°)\sin(45°)$. Now use the table to replace each sine or cosine with the corresponding values from the table: $\frac{\sqrt{3}}{2} \times \frac{\sqrt{2}}{2} - \frac{1}{2} \times \frac{\sqrt{2}}{2}$. Using order of operations, first multiply and then subtract the numerators and keep the denominator: $\frac{\sqrt{6}}{4} - \frac{\sqrt{2}}{4} = \frac{\sqrt{6} - \sqrt{2}}{4}$, which matches (H). Alternately, you could use your calculator to find the value of $\cos(75°)$, which is approximately 0.2588, and then test each answer choice to find the answer closest to this value. Choice (H) will be the only value that is the same.

READING TEST

Passage I

Suggested Passage Map notes:

¶1: Narrator (N) listens to wife Emily (E) talks his twin brother Bruce (B) on phone

¶2–5: E says it's funny to think B knows celebrities

¶6: N thinks B's smile is better than his own

¶7–15: E says she likes N's smile better; B's smile looks practiced

¶16–20: N, an insurance adjuster, feels inferior to B, a Hollywood agent

¶21–28: E says B wants N's approval, N says it'll be fine either way

1. C   Difficulty: Medium

Category: Craft and Structure / Writer's View

Getting to the Answer: The author describes Dave, the narrator ("Bruce's twin brother"), as seeming to regard Bruce as superior to him in many ways. Dave admires Bruce's confident smile; seems to suggest that his wife should have married the more successful, glamorous brother; and says that people look at him "as if I did something wrong" (line 82). The author even mentions Dave's insecurities (line 59). Dave lacks self-esteem, which matches (C). Choices A and B are out of scope because the author does not provide support for either of them. Choice D is opposite, since Dave speaks negatively when comparing himself to his brother.

2. H   Difficulty: Low

Category: Key Ideas and Details / Detail

Getting to the Answer: Emily has a good relationship with both brothers; she has an enjoyable conversation with Bruce and works to make Dave feel better. Also, she wants the brothers to be closer than they are. Because it reflects these details, (H) is the correct answer. Choice F is the opposite; Emily is very attentive. Choices G and J are both extreme and negative distortions of Emily's desire to help relations between the brothers.

3. B   Difficulty: Medium

Category: Key Ideas and Details / Detail

Getting to the Answer: This question is asking you to identify which answer choice is NOT represented in the passage, so the first step is to eliminate choices that ARE contained in the passage. In the first paragraph, Dave is envious of the reaction his wife has when talking to Bruce. This eliminates A. The paragraph about Dave's reaction to the picture captures his negative feelings regarding the difference in their popularity, eliminating C. The final conversation shows Dave as doubtful of Bruce's need for his approval, eliminating D. This leaves (B), which is not found in the passage and is therefore the correct answer.

4. J   Difficulty: Medium

Category: Craft and Structure / Function

Getting to the Answer: The first paragraph starts with a description of Emily on the phone, but the focus quickly shifts to Dave's reaction. It then moves to Dave's making some points about his brother's popularity and questioning whether his own wife has ever reacted so favorably to him. Choice (J) summarizes this well. Choices F and H are not found in the passage, and G occurs much later.

5. D   Difficulty: High

Category: Key Ideas and Details / Inference

Getting to the Answer: Emily attempts to make Dave believe that he is important to Bruce, but Dave still feels he is in Bruce's shadow. It is unclear whether or not Dave entirely believes Emily, but when she brings up Bruce's desire to talk about the brothers' childhood, Dave's response suggests that he does not want to talk about it because it again reminds him of how Bruce has always been the more popular of the two. This makes (D) the correct answer. Choice A is out of scope; the passage does not suggest that Dave does anything to spite Emily. Choice B is incorrect because Dave does not feel guilty; he sees Bruce's success as proof that it doesn't matter whether he calls Bruce or not. Choice C is out of scope; Dave's reasons for not calling Bruce have to do with his feelings toward his brother, not any feelings related to Emily.

6. H   Difficulty: Medium

Category: Key Ideas and Details / Detail

Getting to the Answer: In lines 30–36, Dave explicitly talks about how Bruce's image has positive aspects (*vitality*) that his image lacks. This is a perfect match for (H), which restates this generally. Choices F and J are not found in the passage, and G is contradicted by the fact that both Dave and Emily can tell the difference between the twins.

7. D   Difficulty: Medium

Category: Key Ideas and Details / Detail

Getting to the Answer: This is a NOT question, and because you can't find something that isn't there, you should look for the answer choices that are in the passage and eliminate them. Choice A is in line 62, where the narrator speaks of his brother as the famous one. In line 79, he compares his profession as an insurance adjuster with his brother's career as a Hollywood agent, eliminating B. When he looks at the picture of himself and his brother, the narrator muses about the "unmistakable vitality in Bruce's face that wasn't present in mine" (lines 32–33), making C incorrect. The only choice left is (D), and though it might be assumed that a Hollywood agent earns more than an insurance adjuster, this comparison is never made in the passage.

8. F   Difficulty: Medium

Category: Key Ideas and Details / Inference

Getting to the Answer: With an open-ended question like this, the answer choices must be individually tested. Choice (F) can be logically deduced, especially from the last exchange: Emily mentions that Bruce tells her stories about their childhood, and when Dave makes a comment about Bruce's popularity, Emily responds that "[Bruce] doesn't look at it that way" (line 96). This suggests that there is a difference between the two brothers' childhood stories. Choice G is too extreme and better describes the reaction other people have to the different professions of Bruce and Dave. Choice H is also too extreme: Dave feels competitive with Bruce, but that does not imply that they have fought. Choice J is not supported by the text; their childhood is the only time when it is stated that they spent time together.

9. B   Difficulty: Medium

Category: Craft and Structure / Writer's View

Getting to the Answer: In this passage, the author describes Emily as concerned for her husband when she says, "You are my husband, and I love the way you smile" (lines 48–49). It's Dave, not Emily, who has doubts about whether she married the right brother; Emily seems perfectly happy with the one she has. Match this with answer (B). Choice A is the opposite of Emily's feelings as the author describes them. Choice C is out of scope because it is not supported by the information in the passage, and D is a distortion. Emily comments on the famous people her brother-in-law knows but does not indicate that she wishes she knew them too.

10. F   Difficulty: Medium

Category: Key Ideas and Details / Inference

Getting to the Answer: Emily follows her comment about Bruce's stories by dismissing Dave's comment about Bruce's popularity, saying that Bruce "doesn't look at it that way" (line 96). Her response is in reaction to Dave's frequent comments suggesting that Bruce has been more successful socially and Dave's implication that Bruce feels superior to Dave. This matches (F), which correctly restates this idea. Choice G is not supported by the passage, H is opposite because Emily wants Dave to focus less on his brother's successes, and J is extreme because Bruce wants more attention from his brother but is not necessarily lonely.

Passage II

Suggested Passage Map notes:

¶1: public wants heroes/villains more than facts

¶2: when only 3 channels, newscaster was national figure

¶3: impartial Internet news surrounded by biased headlines

¶4: public polarized by extreme approaches to newscasting

¶5: press conferences present slogans instead of facts

¶6: public better informed but wants immediacy and consensus

11. C **Difficulty:** Medium

Category: Key Ideas and Details / Global

Getting to the Answer: The author is critical of the media throughout the passage and focuses mostly on ways in which the current media is not concerned enough with factual accuracy. Choice (C) matches this nicely. Choice A is too extreme; the author talks about distorting facts, not making them up. Choice B contradicts the third paragraph, which characterizes some news personalities as demagogues with biased views. Choice D contradicts the fourth paragraph; the public's desire for this type of news is one of the reasons for its existence.

12. H **Difficulty:** Medium

Category: Craft and Structure / Function

Getting to the Answer: It might seem odd to open a passage about the news media with a reference to what berries are edible, but the author does this as a general introduction to the kind of information, or news, that has always been important to people. After rereading the applicable part of the passage, predict that edible berries are an example of a food that is safe to eat and that ancient demand for news about the edibility of berries is an example of "the information most sought after [being] that regarding personal safety" (lines 4–5). Choice (H) is a perfect match for that prediction. Choice F is out of scope, and G and J are misused details.

13. B **Difficulty:** Medium

Category: Craft and Structure / Function

Getting to the Answer: The sentence preceding the Walter Cronkite example states that audience members expected to have complicated events explained to them; the Cronkite example follows this logic. Choice (B) matches this perfectly. Choice A may be inferred, but it is not the point the author is making—the author's concern is the treatment of the news, not specific news personalities. This reasoning also eliminates C. Choice D is never mentioned in or suggested by the passage.

14. F **Difficulty:** Medium

Category: Key Ideas and Details / Inference

Getting to the Answer: In order to research this statement, it is a good idea to look back at the fourth paragraph

because it discusses the public. *Personal consensus* applies to the author's point about people looking for news reported by someone with a political opinion similar to their own. Choice (F) matches this. Choices G and J are both contradicted by information given in the fourth paragraph. Choice H is not supported by the passage and contradicts the author's main point.

15. B **Difficulty:** High

Category: Key Ideas and Details / Detail

Getting to the Answer: In the first paragraph, the author states that in stories of "continued national interest" (line 9), the focus shifts from *facts* to *theater* (lines 10–11). Choice (B) is the best match. Choices A, C, and D are not explicitly mentioned as more or less likely to be sensationalized.

16. J **Difficulty:** Medium

Category: Craft and Structure / Vocab-in-Context

Getting to the Answer: The sentence describes objective reporting as a *distant possibility*. Questions like this are easier if you pick a word that means the same thing in context. In this case, you can predict *improbable* or something similar. This matches (J) perfectly. Choices F, G, and H do not address the likelihood of objective reporting.

17. C **Difficulty:** Medium

Category: Craft and Structure / Writer's View

Getting to the Answer: The author is most likely to criticize a headline that sensationalizes or makes a value judgment, and the end of the third paragraph gives an example. Choices A, B, and D are all basically factual and specific. Choice (C) is correct because it refers to a very broad group (like the example in the third paragraph does), makes a value judgment by calling the song offensive, and uses emotional language.

18. J **Difficulty:** Low

Category: Key Ideas and Details / Detail

Getting to the Answer: The fourth paragraph focuses on the flaws of the public and states that individuals who agree with certain politically biased hosts are unlikely to question the validity of the "facts" presented. This matches (J) perfectly. Choices F and G are not explicitly stated by the author. Choice H is the opposite of the author's contention that viewers do not want to draw their own conclusions and prefer to just accept information as fact.

19. A   Difficulty: Medium

Category: Craft and Structure / Writer's View

Getting to the Answer: Overall, the author criticizes news media for emphasizing personalities and opinions rather than facts and clear-eyed consideration of their implications. He mentions niche markets in the context of the "personalities willing to shrug off accountability in favor of wild accusations and bombastic slogans" (lines 53–55) once again accusing the media of ignoring facts in order to "reel in the public" (line 106). The author's overall feeling is that news media cater to what the public wants, which is what (A) states. Choice B is opposite; according to the author, the news media are not willing to present objective facts. Choice C is out of scope because the author is not concerned with marketing practices, and it can be inferred that D is also opposite since the author feels that news media reflect what the audience wants, which may or may not be greater exposure to facts.

20. J   Difficulty: Low

Category: Craft and Structure / Vocab-in-Context

Getting to the Answer: As with all Vocab-in-Context questions, the clues are in the sentences surrounding the word. Here the author is contrasting the "objective, trustworthy anchorperson" (line 33) with *vociferous demagogues* (line 34), the latter of which comes with a negative connotation. Given that H is positive, it can be eliminated. All other answer choices are negative, but think about the author's general point of view. The author doesn't write that reporters are angry but that they are biased, making F incorrect; and there is no suggestion that they are incompetent, eliminating G. The only choice left is the correct one, (J). *Vehement* and *vociferous* are synonyms, both of which mean "loudly insistent."

Passage III

Passage A

¶1: Joyce (J) describes Dublin in *Ulysses* (U)

¶2: *U* focuses on mundane details

¶3: *U* considered globally appealing, represents human cond.

Passage B

¶1: best authors didn't waste time on trivial details

¶2: *U*'s focus on details = undignified

¶3: J isn't bad writer, just in bad era

21. C   Difficulty: Medium

Category: Key Ideas and Details / Global

Getting to the Answer: You should have already noted the main ideas of the passages, so all you need to do here is think about what statements could hinder the main idea of Passage A. The main idea of Passage A is that Joyce, despite or even because of the specific local detail in his work, has managed to create works of universal truth and appeal. Predict that the correct choice will somehow suggest a lack of ability to generate such widespread appeal, leading you to (C) as the correct answer. Choice A is a misused detail; though this author briefly mentions historical events in novels, the idea is not at all central to his point. Choice B is opposite; this might actually help the author's point, as it speaks to universal human ideals. Choice D is opposite; as is the case with B, this statement might actually help the author's point.

22. J   Difficulty: Medium

Category: Key Ideas and Details / Inference

Getting to the Answer: Use a paraphrase as your prediction, but keep in mind that the answer choices may be written in more general language. Here, the quoted phrase talks about escaping the boundaries of time and place to concentrate on greater truths that are independent of these factors. Expect to find a similar paraphrase among the answer choices, leading you to (J) as the correct answer. Choice F is opposite; the author is talking about revealing universal truths, not specific details. Choice G is out of scope; this author never claims that Joyce wrote in such a way as to obscure information. Choice H is a distortion; although ignoring setting gets close to the right idea, focusing on character is not under discussion at this point.

23. A   Difficulty: Medium

Category: Key Ideas and Details / Detail

Getting to the Answer: When answering a NOT question, identify the option that does not appear in the passage.

Passage A praises Joyce's focus on the common man and his daily life, concluding that it "appeal[s] to the entirety of the human dilemma" (lines 43—44). The author gives examples of this focus by citing the fact that Joyce frequently set his stories in Dublin, which eliminates B, that he wrote of "the minor struggles and idle musings of an ordinary Irishman," (lines 39—41), eliminating C, and that, as stated above, it reflects the human dilemma, making D incorrect. The only answer that is not a theme in *Ulysses* is (A), heroic deeds. Indeed, the author of Passage B specifically criticizes Joyce for not writing "of a noble hero's struggle" (line 79).

24. F   Difficulty: Medium

Category: Key Ideas and Details / Detail

Getting to the Answer: One of the main criticisms in the first paragraph of Passage B is that Joyce's subject matter is more base and common than that of earlier authors. Use this idea as the foundation for your prediction, leading you to (F) as the correct answer. Choice G is out of scope; the author of Passage B never questions Joyce's factual knowledge. Choice H is opposite; if anything, Passage B argues that Joyce is too unlike his predecessors. Choice J is out of scope; the author of Passage B never makes claims about the elegance of Joyce's prose.

25. C   Difficulty: Medium

Category: Key Ideas and Details / Detail

Getting to the Answer: The author of Passage B criticizes Joyce for his themes and attention to common activities, but in the last paragraph, the author concedes that "Joyce is no slouch as a wordsmith" (lines 89—90). The author adds that had Joyce been writing in a "more dignified era" (line 91), his talent would have been put to better use. Thus, in the long run, the author admits that Joyce was a talented writer, as (C) states. The author might believe that Joyce was a product of his time, but that doesn't support him as a good writer, making A incorrect. Choice B is out of scope; the author doesn't say this, and D is opposite. The author holds up Dickens as an example of an excellent writer whose themes and goals are quite different from Joyce's.

26. F   Difficulty: Medium

Category: Craft and Structure / Vocab-in-Context

Getting to the Answer: Don't be fooled by familiar words; the challenge of questions like this is in the particular context, not the vocabulary itself. Here, the author uses *base* to describe crude details Joyce often includes, so you should predict something such as *tasteless*, which matches (F), *unrefined*. Choice G is a distortion because it refers to the primary definition of the word. Choice H is a misused detail, referring to the phrase *virtually nauseating* later in the paragraph. Choice J is opposite; the author of Passage B is critical of Joyce's tendency to discuss unrefined activities.

27. B   Difficulty: High

Category: Integration of Knowledge and Ideas / Synthesis

Getting to the Answer: Passage B criticizes Joyce for failing to provide enlightenment for readers, but Passage A has a favorable opinion of Joyce. The author of Passage A discusses how Joyce's works are globally appealing, which matches (B). Choice A is out of scope because Passage A does not discuss the level of enlightenment provided by older works. Choice C is opposite; the author of Passage A believes that Joyce's inclusion of details enhances his writing. Choice D is out of scope because Passage A does not address philosophical questions.

28. H   Difficulty: Medium

Category: Integration of Knowledge and Ideas / Synthesis

Getting to the Answer: Although the question stem asks you to compare the passages, all you really have to do is summarize each author's opinion separately. Passage A is generally favorable towards Joyce, commending him for evoking many universal truths, while Passage B is mostly unfavorable, viewing him as undignified. Use this as the basis for your prediction, which leads you to (H) as the correct answer. Choice F is opposite; the author of Passage A actually considers Joyce a great author, and *inaccuracy* is not really a criticism that Passage B employs. Choice G is opposite; similarly, this is incorrect because the author of Passage A promotes Joyce's significance as a writer. Choice J is a distortion; while Author B does mention Joyce's skill, Author A never laments any aspect of the writing nor deems it irrelevant.

29. B   Difficulty: Low

Category: Integration of Knowledge and Ideas / Synthesis

Getting to the Answer: Keep in mind the authors' general attitudes towards Joyce as you assess their tones at these particular points in the passages. In Passage A, the author is complementing the great degree of detail Joyce uses in describing Dublin, whereas the author of Passage B is expressing disgust at having to read the details of what he considers vulgar or insignificant acts. Use these tones as the basis for your predictions. Choice (B) is correct; this matches the perspectives of the authors. Choice A is a distortion; although both choices here get the general charge right, neither word is quite appropriate to the specific tone of each author. Choice C is a distortion; again, this choice gets the general positive/negative aspects of tone right, but the specifics aren't a good match with each author's attitude. Choice D is opposite; *glee* is contrary to the second author's tone.

30. G   Difficulty: High

Category: Integration of Knowledge and Ideas / Synthesis

Getting to the Answer: The correct choice is likely to involve Passage B's main claim about Joyce's undignified writing. Choice (G) is correct; Passage B argues that Joyce's writing was not exemplary. Choice F is opposite; both authors agree that Joyce was of Irish descent. Choice H is out of scope; the author of Passage B is rarely complementary to Joyce, making this an unlikely choice. Choice J is out of scope; a mystic is someone concerned with religion or the occult, a choice inappropriate for either passage's discussion.

Passage IV

Suggested Passage Map notes:

¶1: rattlesnake (r) thought of as evil

¶2: r has bad reputation

¶3: not cannibals & are monogamous

¶4: 1st instinct = retreat

¶5: low death rate

¶6: majority of bites are "dry" (no venom)

¶7: 100,000 r killed per year

¶8: r should be afraid of humans

31. B   Difficulty: Medium

Category: Key Ideas and Details / Inference

Getting to the Answer: The passage is most concerned with discrediting the myth that rattlesnakes are aggressive and very dangerous, and the selection refers to exactly that: the *sinister opportunist* is the myth, while the *mild-mannered domestic* is closer to fact. Choice (B) can be deduced from this. Choice A is incorrect, as juvenile snakes are not even mentioned. Choice C misuses the detail about rattlesnakes' giving live birth, which is not treated as a recent discovery. Choice D is too extreme; the author describes rattlesnakes as fairly docile but not entirely predictable.

32. G   Difficulty: High

Category: Craft and Structure / Writer's View

Getting to the Answer: The author is sympathetic to rattlesnakes since the author provides several pieces of evidence that disprove the general fear and hatred of them. The real problem is raised in the difficult vocabulary of the answer choices, so use what you know of word prefixes and charge to get a general understanding of the words. First, since the author's view of rattlesnakes is essentially positive, eliminate all negatively-charged words. The *a-* in *apathetic* indicates "away," so *apathetic* means something like "away from sympathy," making F incorrect. Choice H looks very much like the word *frighten*, so assume that it also has a negative charge and eliminate it. In choice J, *anta-* is related to *anti*, meaning "against," and once again indicates a negative word. That leaves choice (G), and even if you did not know that *solicitous* means sympathetic or caring, it is the only answer left and must be correct.

33. C   Difficulty: Medium

Category: Key Ideas and Details / Detail

Getting to the Answer: The passage gives quite a few examples of the social behavior of rattlesnakes, so be prepared to find a restated fact among the answer choices. Choice (C) fits this nicely, because the second paragraph states that rattlesnakes have been known to hibernate with tortoises. Choice A is not a social behavior. Choice B goes beyond the text; the wrestling is used to claim a mate, but the losing snake will leave, rather than take a place within a hierarchy. Choice D also misuses a detail;

rattlesnakes are described as *entirely noncannibalistic* (lines 20—21), meaning they never eat other snakes.

34. H   Difficulty: Medium

Category: Key Ideas and Details / Inference

Getting to the Answer: The mythology referred to is that of the heartless, aggressive rattlesnake. This relates to rattlesnake roundups to which the author clearly objects, so it would follow that the author sees this particular human behavior as heartless and aggressive. Choice (H) matches this perfectly, and the statistical comparison in the seventh paragraph supports this. Choice F contradicts the author's belief that rattlesnakes are not as dangerous as commonly thought. Choices G and J do not relate to the point the author is making.

35. C   Difficulty: Medium

Category: Key Ideas and Details / Detail

Getting to the Answer: The seventh paragraph states that "people are frequently bitten at the festivals while handling snakes for the audience" (lines 103—105), which matches (C). Choice A is incorrect because a relationship is mentioned. Choice B is not mentioned in the text. Choice D is a distortion because rattlesnakes deliver venom based on how threatened they feel, not necessarily based on how threatening humans act.

36. J   Difficulty: High

Category: Craft and Structure / Function

Getting to the Answer: The author defines dry bites as those without venom and says that "Over half of the bites rattlesnakes administer to humans are 'dry'" (lines 75—76). This being the case, they are not as dangerous as bites that inject venom, disproving the popular belief that all rattlesnake bites are potentially fatal. Having predicted this, match it to (J). Choice F is incorrect both because it is an extreme (the word *prove* is extreme) and because it is the opposite of what the author says. Choice G is incorrect because the author does not say that rattlesnakes do not have enough venom to inject into a person, and H is incorrect because the author admits that under the right conditions, rattlesnakes can, indeed, harm humans.

37. B   Difficulty: Medium

Category: Key Ideas and Details / Detail

Getting to the Answer: In the fifth paragraph, the author lists various statistics and states that dogs, bees, and lightning are all responsible for more annual deaths than rattlesnakes and that the fer-de-lance is responsible for substantially more. Choice (B) is the only answer that fits; every other choice is contradicted by the facts given.

38. J   Difficulty: Medium

Category: Key Ideas and Details / Detail

Getting to the Answer: In the sixth paragraph, the author explains that the rattlesnake knows that it needs its venom for food and goes on to state that the only other situation in which a rattlesnake would release all of its venom is when it feels threatened. Choice (J) fits with this; a rattlesnake typically reserves venom for prey. Choice F is incorrect because humans are large in comparison to snakes, but receive mostly "dry" bites. Choice G contradicts the statement about rattlesnakes' potentially using all their venom if threatened. Choice H contradicts the statement that rattlesnakes are not aware of the well-being of nonfood sources.

39. B   Difficulty: Medium

Category: Craft and Structure / Writer's View

Getting to the Answer: The discussion about rattlesnake roundups is in the seventh paragraph, where the author calls them "an excuse to harm the animals" (lines 94—95) based on the popular view of "the fearsome reputation of rattlesnakes" (lines 95—96). Clearly the author disagrees with this reputation, since most of the passage contradicts the view of rattlesnakes as extremely dangerous animals. Thus the author would consider the roundups based on inaccurate information, which matches (B). Choice A is out of scope since population control is not given as a reason for the roundups. Choice C is opposite since the author states that most rattlesnakes caught in a roundup "are collected from uninhabited areas" (lines 102—103). Choice D is also opposite; the author would not consider the reaction appropriate given the view of rattlesnakes presented in the passage.

40. H   Difficulty: Low

Category: Key Ideas and Details / Detail

Getting to the Answer: The rattlesnake's reaction when a person comes into its habitat is detailed in the fourth paragraph. Make a prediction based on the statement that most snakes "immediately headed in the opposite direction" (line 38). This matches (H). Choice F is incorrect because it is not the first reaction of the snake. Though some snakes did rattle a warning before moving away, this was not the most common behavior, making G incorrect. Choice J is the opposite of the given information.

SCIENCE TEST

Passage I

1. C   Difficulty: High

Category: Interpretation of Data

Getting to the Answer: For almost the first 1,000 years plotted in Figure 1, calving rate steadily decreased while glacier length remained roughly constant. This contradicts A and B, so both choices can be eliminated. At the sharp peak around 1,500 years, however, there is a dramatic increase in calving rate and an equally dramatic decrease in glacier length. Choice (C) is thus correct.

2. H   Difficulty: Low

Category: Interpretation of Data

Getting to the Answer: Because the meteorologists proposed a direct relationship between calving rate and change in sea level, this question is really just asking you to find the glacier from Table 1 with the largest calving rate for years 6–10. According to the final column of the table, Glacier C had a calving rate of 312 m/yr during those years, far greater than the rates of the other glaciers, making (H) correct.

3. B   Difficulty: Medium

Category: Interpretation of Data

Getting to the Answer: According to Table 1, all 4 glaciers during both time periods had calving rates that were equal to or slightly greater than their average velocities.

While none of the glaciers from Table 1 had a velocity of 80 m/yr, during years 1–5, glaciers A and C had velocities of 72 m/yr and 98 m/yr, respectively, with calving rates of 72 m/yr and 106 m/yr, respectively. Therefore, a glacier traveling at 80 m/yr could be expected to have a calving rate somewhere between 72 m/yr and 106 m/yr, as in (B).

4. J   Difficulty: Medium

Category: Interpretation of Data

Getting to the Answer: Because there are few clues in the question stem, you'll probably want to use process of elimination to home in on the correct answer. Choice F is contradicted by the behavior of Glacier C in Table 1, while G is contradicted by the behavior of the other glaciers. Even though calving rate is equal to average velocity in the first 5 years for Glacier A, all of the other data in Table 1 feature calving rates that are higher than average velocity. This allows you to eliminate H and to recognize that (J) must be correct.

5. B   Difficulty: Low

Category: Interpretation of Data

Getting to the Answer: Don't be thrown off by the strange scale of the horizontal axis of each choice: the labeled x-values correspond exactly to the calving rates for years 6–10 given in Table 1. Simply find the graph that correctly plots the 4 data points from the last 2 columns of the table. You can do this by selecting test points and eliminating choices that don't include them, or by looking for the 1 graph that consistently shows the direct relationship evident from Table 1, in which every increase in calving rate corresponds to an increase in average velocity. Either way, you'll find that choice (B) is correct.

6. H   Difficulty: Low

Category: Scientific Investigation

Getting to the Answer: The meteorologists in Study 3 hypothesized that high temperatures cause rapid variations in velocity and calving rate. Figure 1 shows a rapid change in calving rate at around 1,500 years. If the hypothesis is true, then the glacier modeled in Study 1 would have been subject to high temperatures at about 1,500 years, meaning (H) is correct.

7. B **Difficulty:** Low

Category: Interpretation of Data

Getting to the Answer: The question is asking you to identify 2 specific values—the glacier length and the calving rate—from Figure 1. To get to the answer, find 1,500 years on the *x*-axis and draw a vertical line extending upward. Find where the vertical line intersects with the glacier length curve and draw a horizontal line back to the *y*-axis on the left side to find that the glacier length is approximately 23 km. This allows you to eliminate A and D. Next, find the point where the calving rate line intersects with the vertical line you drew at 1,500 years, and draw another horizontal line over to the *y*-axis on the right side to find that the calving rate is about 125 m/yr. Choice (B) is thus correct.

Passage II

8. H **Difficulty:** Low

Category: Scientific Investigation

Getting to the Answer: The question stem states that the air filters greatly reduce rhinitis symptoms and asks which month would have the greatest decrease in the number of rhinitis cases. To reach the answer, look at Table 1 and find the month among the 4 listed in the answer choices with the greatest total number of cases. September has far more cases than any of the other 3 months, so it would definitely see the greatest decrease in rhinitis cases if patients used the filters. Choice (H) is correct.

9. C **Difficulty:** Low

Category: Interpretation of Data

Getting to the Answer: To answer this question, just find the relevant value from Figure 1. The bar for March 2 in Figure 1 rises to approximately 1,500 gr/m^3, so (C) is correct.

10. H **Difficulty:** Medium

Category: Interpretation of Data

Getting to the Answer: The question stem asks you to describe the mold spore count in Figure 2 for the weeks after November 5. The spore counts for these weeks fluctuate without a clear trend, but they do stay

within a relatively small range of values, as is correctly described in (H).

11. B **Difficulty:** Low

Category: Interpretation of Data

Getting to the Answer: Be careful to answer the correct question: "increased the most" doesn't necessarily mean the count increased to its largest value, which is the trap set in C. Choice D is also a trap because it relies upon Figure 2 rather than Figure 1. The largest increase in Figure 1 occurs between February 23 and March 2, as in (B).

12. F **Difficulty:** Low

Category: Interpretation of Data

Getting to the Answer: This question asks about the tree pollen count graphed in Figure 1. The largest value for tree pollen count is found on March 9, so (F) is correct. March 16 has neither the highest nor the lowest count, which makes both G and J incorrect. Choice H is incorrect because the first 4 dates in the graph have lower values for tree pollen count than the one from February 23.

13. A **Difficulty:** Low

Category: Interpretation of Data

Getting to the Answer: To answer this question, find the row in Table 1 for the month of May and look for the corresponding column(s) containing the most reported cases of allergic rhinitis (the most ❀ symbols). Tree and grass pollen account for 6 of the 9 total ❀ symbols in May, a majority of the allergic rhinitis cases. Choice (A) is thus correct.

Passage III

14. G **Difficulty:** Medium

Category: Interpretation of Data

Getting to the Answer: Notice that in Figure 3, the lines plotted for Springs B, C, and D intersect at approximately the same mass, which means that their equilibrium lengths are roughly equal there. The exact mass value is not completely clear from the figure, but it appears to be greater than 200 g but less than 300 g, which means that choice (G) must be correct.

15. A   Difficulty: Medium

Category: Evaluation of Models, Inferences, and Results

Getting to the Answer: The curve in Figure 1 is not linear, but it still shows a general trend of the oscillation frequency decreasing as the arm length increases. Thus, the student's hypothesis would be supported, which eliminates C and D. Choice (A) provides an accurate explanation, so (A) is the correct answer.

16. F   Difficulty: Medium

Category: Interpretation of Data

Getting to the Answer: As noted in the passage, oscillation frequency is measured in "oscillations per second"—the faster the spring oscillates, the more oscillations it will complete per second. Thus, the slowest spring will be the one with the lowest value for oscillation frequency. Regardless of the mass attached, Spring A always has the lowest value for oscillation frequency, so (F) is correct.

17. C   Difficulty: Medium

Category: Interpretation of Data

Getting to the Answer: Refer to the line plotted for Spring A in Figure 3. On that line, a mass of 700 g corresponds to an equilibrium length of approximately 40 cm. Choice (C) is therefore correct.

18. J   Difficulty: High

Category: Interpretation of Data

Getting to the Answer: According to Figure 2, an oscillation frequency of 1.4 Hz at a mass of 100 g would be represented by a data point that would fall in between the frequency values for Spring C and Spring D at that mass. Only choices H and (J) place Spring E between Springs C and D, and (J) correctly lists the springs in order of *decreasing* oscillation frequency.

19. C   Difficulty: High

Category: Scientific Investigation

Getting to the Answer: The effects of mass are not mentioned in Experiment 1, so this question requires some background knowledge in physics to answer correctly. While the pendulum arm length will affect the oscillation frequency, the mass attached has no impact on the oscillation frequency of a pendulum, so the plots for the original mass and the larger mass should be identical, as in (C).

20. H   Difficulty: Low

Category: Interpretation of Data

Getting to the Answer: Figure 1 shows the relationship between arm length and oscillation frequency. To find the corresponding arm length, draw a line from 0.35 on the y-axis to the curve. At the point of intersection, draw a line down to the x-axis. The line will be closer to 20 than 15, which is why the correct answer is 19 cm, (H).

Passage IV

21. D   Difficulty: Low

Category: Evaluation of Models, Inferences, and Results

Getting to the Answer: Look at the first 3 rows and last 3 columns of Table 1 to find the enzyme concentration values of populations ha 1, ha 2, and ha 3. The table shows that for all 3 high-altitude populations, GST levels are highest, CR levels are lowest, and ECH levels are in between. Because GST is always higher than CR for these high-altitude populations, (D) is correct.

22. G   Difficulty: Low

Category: Evaluation of Models, Inferences, and Results

Getting to the Answer: This question asks you to compare high-altitude and sea-level dwellers, so use the table and figure provided to evaluate each choice. Choice F is not always true; the oxygen saturation percentages provided in Table 1 are pretty similar for high-altitude and sea-level dwellers. Figure 1 shows that oxygen partial pressure and temperature both decrease at higher altitudes, so it would not be reasonable to conclude that sea-level dwellers can tolerate lower oxygen partial pressures or lower temperatures compared to those who dwell at higher altitudes. Choices H and J can thus be eliminated. Choice (G), however, is directly supported by the data in Figure 1 that shows consistently lower GST values for sea-level dwellers, making (G) the correct answer.

23. C   Difficulty: Medium

Category: Interpretation of Data

Getting to the Answer: The answer to this question comes directly from Figure 1, but you must be careful not to confuse the 2 data sets. Draw a horizontal line from 110 mm Hg on the left vertical axis until it intersects with the oxygen partial pressure data (the line with square points). That intersection happens at about 3,500 m. To find the temperature at this altitude, draw a horizontal line from the temperature plot (the line with circular points) at 3,500 m to the right axis. It intersects somewhere between −5°C and −10°C, meaning the correct answer must be (C). Choice A is a trap that you might select if you accidentally reverse the 2 data sets.

24. H   Difficulty: Medium

Category: Interpretation of Data

Getting to the Answer: Though the question stem provides a lot of new information, it is essentially asking you simply to find the population with the highest ECH concentration. The value of 93.5 a.u. for population ha 2 is higher than any other population's ECH concentration, making (H) correct.

25. A   Difficulty: High

Category: Evaluation of Models, Inferences, and Results

Getting to the Answer: The question stem tells you to assume that only oxygen partial pressure and respiratory efficiency influence oxygen saturation percentage, and it asks you to identify what information would support the idea that population ha 2 has greater respiratory efficiency than population sl 1. The easiest way to make this case would be to show that the other factor, oxygen partial pressure, could not possibly account for the fact that ha 2 has a higher saturation percentage than sl 1. And indeed, according to Figure 1, the oxygen partial pressure at 3,300–3,700 m (where ha 2 lives) is considerably lower than the oxygen partial pressure at 0–300 m (where sl 1 lives). Because this fact supports the hypothesis from the question stem, (A) is correct. Choices B and D are incorrect because they contradict the information from the passage, while C is incorrect because neither the passage nor the question stem suggests a connection between CR concentration and respiratory efficiency.

26. J   Difficulty: High

Category: Scientific Investigation

Getting to the Answer: The question requires you to identify the relationships between altitude and enzyme levels, then predict the levels for a population that lives at an altitude of 1,500–1,800 m, squarely in between the high-altitude and sea-level populations studied in the passage. According to Table 1, GST and ECH levels are consistently higher for the high-altitude populations than for the sea-level populations, while CR levels are roughly constant regardless of altitude. Consequently, it makes sense to predict that the GST and ECH levels of the new population will be higher than those of the sea-level populations but lower than those of the high-altitude populations, while its CR levels would be roughly the same as those of both groups. Choice (J) is thus correct.

Passage V

27. D   Difficulty: Medium

Category: Evaluation of Models, Inferences, and Results

Getting to the Answer: In the passage, Student 1 cites the fact that "the freezing point of water decreases with increasing pressure," and then suggests that, "Under the surface, *hydrostatic pressure* causes the freezing point of water to be slightly lower than it is at the surface." For hydrostatic pressure to cause a decrease in freezing point, it must be higher under the surface, as stated in (D). Choice A is incorrect because it contradicts Student 1's explanation, which suggests that temperature is roughly constant throughout the lake. Choices B and C are incorrect because they are aspects of Student 2's explanation.

28. G   Difficulty: Medium

Category: Evaluation of Models, Inferences, and Results

Getting to the Answer: According to Student 1, pressure causes the ice under ice skates to melt and pressure increases with increasing weight. Student 2 states that friction causes the ice to melt and that the force of friction increases with increasing weight. Therefore, the students would agree that ice would melt faster under the heavier skater, as suggested in (G).

29. A   Difficulty: Medium

Category: Evaluation of Models, Inferences, and Results

Getting to the Answer: Student 1 explains that the ice under ice skates melts due to increased pressure—specifically, having the force of the entire weight of the skater's body distributed over the tiny surface area of the blades of the skates. This heightened pressure would persist regardless of whether the skater is moving, so Student 1 would predict melting from a stationary skater. This allows B and D to be eliminated. Student 2, however, states that "energy used to overcome the force of friction is converted to heat, which melts the ice under the skates." Overcoming the force of friction requires motion, so a stationary skater would generate no heat, suggesting that the ice would not melt on Student 2's account. Because only Student 1 predicts melting under a stationary skater, (A) is correct.

30. H   Difficulty: Medium

Category: Evaluation of Models, Inferences, and Results

Getting to the Answer: Student 2 explains that less dense materials float above more dense materials. On this account, for the frozen ethanol to sink to the bottom, it must be denser than liquid ethanol, making (H) the correct answer. Choice J is the opposite, while F and G are irrelevant because the frozen ethanol described in the question stem does not interact with either liquid or frozen water.

31. C   Difficulty: Medium

Category: Evaluation of Models, Inferences, and Results

Getting to the Answer: You can eliminate A and B due to the mention in both of pressure, which is a concept only Student 1 discusses. Student 2 explains that ice floats on water because "the *buoyant force* of water acting upward is greater than the force of gravity pulling any mass of ice downward." Thus, for an object to sink in water instead, its weight (the force of gravity on that object) must exceed the buoyant force of water on that object, which is precisely what is described in (C).

32. G   Difficulty: Medium

Category: Evaluation of Models, Inferences, and Results

Getting to the Answer: Eliminate F because only Student 1 considers pressure, and eliminate J because Student 1 is the only one who discusses how the freezing point of water could change. Choice H can also be eliminated because the force of gravity will only decrease if the mass of the skater decreases, but this is not required by the question as posed (while decreasing the mass of the skater would be one way to decrease the friction, it is not the only way). Choice (G) must be correct, and this is confirmed by Student 2's statement that "energy used to overcome the force of friction is converted to heat"—less friction means less energy required to overcome friction, which means less heat produced.

33. A   Difficulty: Medium

Category: Evaluation of Models, Inferences, and Results

Getting to the Answer: Recall that Student 2 explains that ice floats on water because it is less dense. Thus, based on the same principle, for a hot air balloon to rise above the surrounding air, it must be less dense than that air, which is precisely what is stated in (A). Choices B and D are both incorrect because they state the opposite (the term *buoyant* is included in D to make it seem more appealing, but "less buoyant" means effectively the same thing as "more dense"). Choice C is incorrect because it involves pressure, which only appeared in Student 1's account.

Passage VI

34. F   Difficulty: Medium

Category: Scientific Investigation

Getting to the Answer: According to the measured conductivity column of Table 1, there is conductivity even in a sample in which F^- is not present. The first paragraph of the passage notes, however, that the students conducting the experiments were interested simply in measuring fluoride levels. Subtracting the conductivity of the sample with no fluoride ions from the other measured values allows the students to determine how much conductivity is due exclusively to F^-. Choice (F) is thus correct. Choice G is incorrect because the correction is applied after the data has already been collected, so it could not be used to calibrate the cells. Choice H is out of scope because the passage does not mention the presence of impurities and non-ionic molecules do not conduct electricity. Choice J is incorrect because solubility is never discussed in the passage and is not a factor in the experiments.

35. C   Difficulty: Low

Category: Interpretation of Data

Getting to the Answer: Either Table 1 or Figure 1 can provide the answer here. Table 1 contains examples of cases in which the F^- concentration is indeed doubled (from 0.5 mg/L to 1 mg/L, for example) and gives the corresponding change in conductivity. Taking care to look in the *corrected* conductivity column, you can see that 2 times the concentration results in 2 times the corrected conductivity. Likewise, Figure 1 makes it clear that relationship between the 2 quantities is linear, which means that any multiplication of the concentration results in the same multiplication of the conductivity. Choice (C) is correct.

36. J   Difficulty: Low

Category: Interpretation of Data

Getting to the Answer: Table 1 and Table 2 both show that there is a direct relationship between measured conductivity and fluoride ion concentration, so ordering the locations by concentration merely requires ordering them by conductivity values. According to Table 2, Newton and Lakewood had conductivity values of 22.31 µS/cm and 18.63 µS/cm, respectively. Thus, in increasing order of F^- concentration, you find Lakewood, Bluewater, and Newton, as in (J).

37. C   Difficulty: Medium

Category: Scientific Investigation

Getting to the Answer: Refer to Table 1 to see where a value of 3.0 mg/L would fit in. This new concentration is between the 2.0 mg/L and 4.0 mg/L values given in the table, so the corrected conductivity should lie midway between 3.34 µS/cm and 6.68 µS/cm. Choices B and D are too close to the extremes of this range, but (C) is almost precisely in the middle, as it should be. Alternatively, you could also find that (C) is correct by looking at Figure 1 and seeing that a fluoride concentration of 3.0 mg/L corresponds to a corrected conductivity of about 5.0 µS/cm.

38. F   Difficulty: Medium

Category: Scientific Investigation

Getting to the Answer: This question requires you to modify Experiment 1 to investigate chloride conductivity rather than fluoride conductivity. According to the

original description of Experiment 1, solutions were prepared by dissolving Na_2SiF_6 in H_2O, which produced F^- ions. To study Cl^- conductivity, the students would need to use a chemical that produced Cl^- ions instead. Choice (F) is thus correct. Choice G is incorrect because it would still be necessary to subtract the blank solution's conductivity to find corrected conductivity values that accounted only for the chloride ions. Choice H is incorrect because resistivity is simply the inverse of conductivity, so this change would just add an extra step in the calculation of conductivity values. Choice J is incorrect because the solutions produced would contain both F^- and Cl^-, which would make it difficult to isolate the conductivity of the chloride ions alone.

39. B   Difficulty: Low

Category: Interpretation of Data

Getting to the Answer: The last sentence of the description of Experiment 1 explains that the corrected conductivity is calculated by *subtracting* the measured conductivity of the blank solution. Because the conductivity of the blank solution is a positive number, this always results in the corrected conductivity's being less than the measured conductivity, as in (B).

40. F   Difficulty: Medium

Category: Scientific Investigation

Getting to the Answer: According to the description of Experiment 2, the students utilized "measured conductivities and the results from Experiment 1 to calculate fluoride ion concentrations." To do this, they would first have to subtract the conductivity of Experiment 1's blank solution from the measured conductivities of the samples to find corrected conductivity values. Then, they could use the graph they plotted in Figure 1 to move from corrected conductivity to F^- concentration. However, as explained in the question stem, the presence of Cl^- in the samples would result in increased values for measured conductivity. This, in turn, would lead to higher values for corrected conductivity and (due to the direct relationship between corrected conductivity and fluoride concentration) to greater values for the calculated F^- concentrations. These calculated values would be higher than the actual values, because a component of the measured conductivity used to calculate them would actually be due to Cl^-, and not just F^-. Choice (F) is thus correct.

WRITING TEST

MODEL ESSAY

Below is an example of what a high-scoring essay might look like. Notice that the author states her position clearly in the introductory paragraph and supports that position with evidence in the following paragraphs. The essay also uses transitions, some advanced vocabulary, and an effective "hook" to draw in the reader.

Teachers often tell us that learning is fun, and the best way to convince us that learning is enjoyable is to give us activities that keep us engaged (and awake). The issue here is whether teachers should provide more hands-on learning experiences because doing so would help all students learn and remember better. On the other hand, others say that it's possible to learn without doing and that schools should use their money for other educational purposes rather than trying to make everything hands-on learning. I believe that the best learning comes from hands-on work.

I know from experience that I learn better when I can actually do something myself. When students do projects such as growing plants, they really learn about the science because they are part of making that science work. This is analogous to learning how to ride a bike. A child can read about it, watch videos on it, and even watch someone actually ride a bike, but he doesn't learn how to do it until he gets on a bike and pedals away. Thus, it is important that the teacher provide opportunities for students to do as much hands-on learning as possible. However, those who think that students don't learn anything unless they actually do it are wrong. There are ideas that can't be experimented with. How can students re-create the Big Bang or evolution? But just because they can't actually do this doesn't mean students don't learn. There is a lot that can be learned from reading and learning from experts. However, if there is a choice between learning by doing and not having that opportunity, learning by doing is the better way to teach and learn.

On the other hand, other people think that experiential education is important only for students who will work in a career that requires that they do things themselves, such as engineering and technology. It is important that students who will enter careers that are skill based have the opportunity to practice this in school. School is supposed to teach what is needed for students later in life, and knowing how to do experiments or re-create what others have done should be part of this. But the people who argue for this say it is important only for students who will need it in their future careers. This means that some students, particularly those who don't know what career they want, will not get the benefit of hands-on experiences. That splits students into two groups: those who learn by doing and those who don't. All students learn well by doing, so it would not be fair to offer it only to some students. How can teachers know what is appropriate for students in their future careers if even the students don't yet know? This solution is not a good one because it assumes things that can't be supported.

Finally, it is shortsighted to argue that rather than create opportunities for hands-on learning, schools should spend their money on other things because learning by doing is expensive and may not be good for all students. There's always the problem that not all students learn in the same way so there's no one kind of learning that is best for everyone. But that doesn't mean teachers shouldn't provide hands-on opportunities. Actually, this is a good way to reach all students because it involves working with your hands, maybe some reading and talking too, and critical thinking, so it uses lots of ways of learning. It is foolish to have the opportunity to do something important and not do it just because some people may not benefit from it or it will cost money. Teachers should give students the opportunity to learn in a hands-on way as much as possible.

In the real world, when we need to learn something new, like how to cook or use a computer program, if it's possible to learn by doing while having someone help and direct us, that is the best way to learn and the way that schools should teach. Studies, and my own experience, show that everyone can benefit from hands-on education; that is the way we learn and remember best.

You can evaluate your essay and the model essay based on the following criteria:

- Is the author's own perspective clearly stated?
- Does the body of the essay assess and analyze an additional perspective?
- Is the relevance of each paragraph clear?
- Does the author start a new paragraph for each new idea?
- Is each sentence in a paragraph relevant to the point made in that paragraph?
- Are transitions clear?
- Is the essay easy to read? Is it engaging?
- Are sentences varied?
- Is vocabulary used effectively? Is college-level vocabulary used?

ACT Practice Test 4
ANSWER SHEET

ENGLISH TEST

1. (A)(B)(C)(D)   11. (A)(B)(C)(D)   21. (A)(B)(C)(D)   31. (A)(B)(C)(D)   41. (A)(B)(C)(D)   51. (A)(B)(C)(D)   61. (A)(B)(C)(D)   71. (A)(B)(C)(D)
2. (F)(G)(H)(J)   12. (F)(G)(H)(J)   22. (F)(G)(H)(J)   32. (F)(G)(H)(J)   42. (F)(G)(H)(J)   52. (F)(G)(H)(J)   62. (F)(G)(H)(J)   72. (F)(G)(H)(J)
3. (A)(B)(C)(D)   13. (A)(B)(C)(D)   23. (A)(B)(C)(D)   33. (A)(B)(C)(D)   43. (A)(B)(C)(D)   53. (A)(B)(C)(D)   63. (A)(B)(C)(D)   73. (A)(B)(C)(D)
4. (F)(G)(H)(J)   14. (F)(G)(H)(J)   24. (F)(G)(H)(J)   34. (F)(G)(H)(J)   44. (F)(G)(H)(J)   54. (F)(G)(H)(J)   64. (F)(G)(H)(J)   74. (F)(G)(H)(J)
5. (A)(B)(C)(D)   15. (A)(B)(C)(D)   25. (A)(B)(C)(D)   35. (A)(B)(C)(D)   45. (A)(B)(C)(D)   55. (A)(B)(C)(D)   65. (A)(B)(C)(D)   75. (A)(B)(C)(D)
6. (F)(G)(H)(J)   16. (F)(G)(H)(J)   26. (F)(G)(H)(J)   36. (F)(G)(H)(J)   46. (F)(G)(H)(J)   56. (F)(G)(H)(J)   66. (F)(G)(H)(J)
7. (A)(B)(C)(D)   17. (A)(B)(C)(D)   27. (A)(B)(C)(D)   37. (A)(B)(C)(D)   47. (A)(B)(C)(D)   57. (A)(B)(C)(D)   67. (A)(B)(C)(D)
8. (F)(G)(H)(J)   18. (F)(G)(H)(J)   28. (F)(G)(H)(J)   38. (F)(G)(H)(J)   48. (F)(G)(H)(J)   58. (F)(G)(H)(J)   68. (F)(G)(H)(J)
9. (A)(B)(C)(D)   19. (A)(B)(C)(D)   29. (A)(B)(C)(D)   39. (A)(B)(C)(D)   49. (A)(B)(C)(D)   59. (A)(B)(C)(D)   69. (A)(B)(C)(D)
10. (F)(G)(H)(J)   20. (F)(G)(H)(J)   30. (F)(G)(H)(J)   40. (F)(G)(H)(J)   50. (F)(G)(H)(J)   60. (F)(G)(H)(J)   70. (F)(G)(H)(J)

MATHEMATICS TEST

1. (A)(B)(C)(D)(E)   11. (A)(B)(C)(D)(E)   21. (A)(B)(C)(D)(E)   31. (A)(B)(C)(D)(E)   41. (A)(B)(C)(D)(E)   51. (A)(B)(C)(D)(E)
2. (F)(G)(H)(J)(K)   12. (F)(G)(H)(J)(K)   22. (F)(G)(H)(J)(K)   32. (F)(G)(H)(J)(K)   42. (F)(G)(H)(J)(K)   52. (F)(G)(H)(J)(K)
3. (A)(B)(C)(D)(E)   13. (A)(B)(C)(D)(E)   23. (A)(B)(C)(D)(E)   33. (A)(B)(C)(D)(E)   43. (A)(B)(C)(D)(E)   53. (A)(B)(C)(D)(E)
4. (F)(G)(H)(J)(K)   14. (F)(G)(H)(J)(K)   24. (F)(G)(H)(J)(K)   34. (F)(G)(H)(J)(K)   44. (F)(G)(H)(J)(K)   54. (F)(G)(H)(J)(K)
5. (A)(B)(C)(D)(E)   15. (A)(B)(C)(D)(E)   25. (A)(B)(C)(D)(E)   35. (A)(B)(C)(D)(E)   45. (A)(B)(C)(D)(E)   55. (A)(B)(C)(D)(E)
6. (F)(G)(H)(J)(K)   16. (F)(G)(H)(J)(K)   26. (F)(G)(H)(J)(K)   36. (F)(G)(H)(J)(K)   46. (F)(G)(H)(J)(K)   56. (F)(G)(H)(J)(K)
7. (A)(B)(C)(D)(E)   17. (A)(B)(C)(D)(E)   27. (A)(B)(C)(D)(E)   37. (A)(B)(C)(D)(E)   47. (A)(B)(C)(D)(E)   57. (A)(B)(C)(D)(E)
8. (F)(G)(H)(J)(K)   18. (F)(G)(H)(J)(K)   28. (F)(G)(H)(J)(K)   38. (F)(G)(H)(J)(K)   48. (F)(G)(H)(J)(K)   58. (F)(G)(H)(J)(K)
9. (A)(B)(C)(D)(E)   19. (A)(B)(C)(D)(E)   29. (A)(B)(C)(D)(E)   39. (A)(B)(C)(D)(E)   49. (A)(B)(C)(D)(E)   59. (A)(B)(C)(D)(E)
10. (F)(G)(H)(J)(K)   20. (F)(G)(H)(J)(K)   30. (F)(G)(H)(J)(K)   40. (F)(G)(H)(J)(K)   50. (F)(G)(H)(J)(K)   60. (F)(G)(H)(J)(K)

READING TEST

1. (A)(B)(C)(D)   6. (F)(G)(H)(J)   11. (A)(B)(C)(D)   16. (F)(G)(H)(J)   21. (A)(B)(C)(D)   26. (F)(G)(H)(J)   31. (A)(B)(C)(D)   36. (F)(G)(H)(J)
2. (F)(G)(H)(J)   7. (A)(B)(C)(D)   12. (F)(G)(H)(J)   17. (A)(B)(C)(D)   22. (F)(G)(H)(J)   27. (A)(B)(C)(D)   32. (F)(G)(H)(J)   37. (A)(B)(C)(D)
3. (A)(B)(C)(D)   8. (F)(G)(H)(J)   13. (A)(B)(C)(D)   18. (F)(G)(H)(J)   23. (A)(B)(C)(D)   28. (F)(G)(H)(J)   33. (A)(B)(C)(D)   38. (F)(G)(H)(J)
4. (F)(G)(H)(J)   9. (A)(B)(C)(D)   14. (F)(G)(H)(J)   19. (A)(B)(C)(D)   24. (F)(G)(H)(J)   29. (A)(B)(C)(D)   34. (F)(G)(H)(J)   39. (A)(B)(C)(D)
5. (A)(B)(C)(D)   10. (F)(G)(H)(J)   15. (A)(B)(C)(D)   20. (F)(G)(H)(J)   25. (A)(B)(C)(D)   30. (F)(G)(H)(J)   35. (A)(B)(C)(D)   40. (F)(G)(H)(J)

SCIENCE TEST

1. (A)(B)(C)(D)   6. (F)(G)(H)(J)   11. (A)(B)(C)(D)   16. (F)(G)(H)(J)   21. (A)(B)(C)(D)   26. (F)(G)(H)(J)   31. (A)(B)(C)(D)   36. (F)(G)(H)(J)
2. (F)(G)(H)(J)   7. (A)(B)(C)(D)   12. (F)(G)(H)(J)   17. (A)(B)(C)(D)   22. (F)(G)(H)(J)   27. (A)(B)(C)(D)   32. (F)(G)(H)(J)   37. (A)(B)(C)(D)
3. (A)(B)(C)(D)   8. (F)(G)(H)(J)   13. (A)(B)(C)(D)   18. (F)(G)(H)(J)   23. (A)(B)(C)(D)   28. (F)(G)(H)(J)   33. (A)(B)(C)(D)   38. (F)(G)(H)(J)
4. (F)(G)(H)(J)   9. (A)(B)(C)(D)   14. (F)(G)(H)(J)   19. (A)(B)(C)(D)   24. (F)(G)(H)(J)   29. (A)(B)(C)(D)   34. (F)(G)(H)(J)   39. (A)(B)(C)(D)
5. (A)(B)(C)(D)   10. (F)(G)(H)(J)   15. (A)(B)(C)(D)   20. (F)(G)(H)(J)   25. (A)(B)(C)(D)   30. (F)(G)(H)(J)   35. (A)(B)(C)(D)   40. (F)(G)(H)(J)

ENGLISH TEST

45 Minutes—75 Questions

Directions: Each passage has certain words and phrases that are underlined and numbered. The questions in the right column will provide alternatives for the underlined segments. Most questions require you to choose the answer that makes the sentence grammatically correct, concise, and relevant. If the word or phrase in the passage is already the correct, concise, and relevant choice, select Choice A, NO CHANGE. Some questions will ask a question about the underlined segment. When a question is presented, choose the best answer.

Some questions will ask about part or all of the passage. These questions do not refer to a specific underlined segment. Instead, these questions will accompany a number in a box.

For each question, choose your answer and fill in the corresponding bubble on your answer sheet. Read the passage once before you answer the questions. You will often need to read several sentences beyond the underlined portion to be able to choose the correct answer. Be sure to read enough to answer each question.

Passage I

The Parthenon

[1]

If you are like most visitors to Athens, you will make your way to the Acropolis, the hill that once served as a fortified, strategic position overlooking the Aegean Sea—to see the Parthenon. This celebrated temple was dedicated in the fifth century BCE to the goddess Athena. There is no more famous building

1. **A.** NO CHANGE
   B. Acropolis. The hill
   C. Acropolis—the hill
   D. Acropolis

GO ON TO THE NEXT PAGE

Practice Test 4

in all of Greece; to climb up its marble steps is <u>to have</u>
                                                     2
<u>beheld</u> a human creation that has attained the stature
 2
of a natural phenomenon like the Grand Canyon.

2. **F.** NO CHANGE
   G. to behold
   H. beholding
   J. to be holding

<u>You should also make an attempt to sample Athenian</u>
                                               3
<u>cuisine while you're there.</u>
        3

3. **A.** NO CHANGE
   B. Also make an attempt to sample Athenian cuisine while you're there.
   C. While you're there, you should also make an attempt to sample Athenian cuisine.
   D. DELETE the underlined sentence.

[2]

Generations of architects <u>have proclaimed</u> the Par-
                                      4
thenon to be the most brilliantly conceived structure in
the Western world. The genius of its construction is

4. **F.** NO CHANGE
   G. has proclaimed
   H. proclaims
   J. are proclaiming

subtle. For example, <u>the temples columns</u> were made to
                              5
bulge outward slightly in order to compensate for the

5. **A.** NO CHANGE
   B. the temples' columns
   C. the temple's column's
   D. the temple's columns

<u>fact, viewed from distance, that straight columns appear</u>
                                6
<u>concave.</u> Using this and other techniques, the architects
    6

6. **F.** NO CHANGE
   G. fact that straight columns, viewed from a distance, appear concave.
   H. view from a distance: straight columns appearing concave.
   J. fact, when viewed from far away, that straight columns appear concave.

strove to create an optical <u>illusion of; uprightness,</u>
                                    7
solidity, and permanence.

7. **A.** NO CHANGE
   B. illusion of: uprightness
   C. illusion of, uprightness
   D. illusion of uprightness,

GO ON TO THE NEXT PAGE →

[3]

Because of this, the overall impression you'll get
8
of the Parthenon will be far different from the one the
ancient Athenians had. Only by standing on the marble
steps of the Parthenon and allowing your imagination to
transport you back to the Golden Age of Athens. You will
9
be able to see the temple's main attraction, the legendary
statue of Athena Parthenos. It was 38 feet high and made

of ivory and over a ton of pure gold. Removed from the
10
temple in the fifth century CE, all that remains is the
10
slight rectangular depression on the floor where it stood.

[4]

Many of the ornate carvings and sculptures that
adorned the walls of the Acropolis is no longer there,
11
either. In the early nineteenth century, the British

diplomat Lord Elgins decision to "protect" the ones that
12
survived by removing them from the Parthenon and carrying
them back to Britain. (He had the permission of the Ottoman
Turks, who controlled Greece at the time, to do so.)

[5]

After they gained independence from the Turks,
they began to demand the sculptures and carvings back
13
from the British, to no avail. Thus, if you want to gain
a complete picture of what the Parthenon once looked
like, you'll have to visit not only the Acropolis of Athens
but the British Museum in London as well.

8. **F.** NO CHANGE
   G. Thus
   H. Rather
   J. Of course

9. **A.** NO CHANGE
   B. Athens; you will
   C. Athens will you
   D. Athens. You may

10. **F.** NO CHANGE
    G. Having been removed from the temple in the fifth century CE,
    H. Given its removal from the temple in the fifth century CE,
    J. The statue was removed from the temple in the fifth century CE;

11. **A.** NO CHANGE
    B. will be
    C. have been
    D. are

12. **F.** NO CHANGE
    G. Elgin's deciding that
    H. Elgin decided to
    J. Elgin's decision to

13. **A.** NO CHANGE
    B. the Turks
    C. the Greeks
    D. who

GO ON TO THE NEXT PAGE

Questions 14 and 15 ask about the preceding passage as a whole.

14. The writer wishes to insert the following material into the essay:

> Some of them were destroyed in 1687 when attacking Venetians bombarded the Acropolis, setting off explosives that had been stored in the Parthenon.

The new material best supports and therefore would most logically be placed in Paragraph:

F. 1.

G. 2.

H. 3.

J. 4.

15. Suppose the editor of an architecture journal had requested that the writer focus primarily on the techniques the ancient Greek architects used in constructing the Parthenon. Does the essay fulfill this request?

A. Yes, because the essay makes it clear that the Parthenon was an amazing architectural achievement.

B. Yes, because the essay explains in the second paragraph the reason the temple's columns bulge outward slightly.

C. No, because the Parthenon's construction is only one of several topics covered in the essay.

D. No, because the author never explains what the architects who designed the Parthenon were trying to accomplish.

GO ON TO THE NEXT PAGE

Passage II

The Legendary Robin Hood

Although there is no conclusive evidence that a man named Robin Hood ever actually existed, the story of Robin Hood and his band of merry men has become one of the most popular traditional tales in English literature. Robin is the hero in a series of ballads dating at least as far back as the fourteenth century. These ballads <u>are telling</u> of discontent among the lower classes

16
in the north of England during a turbulent era that culminated in the Peasants' Revolt of 1381. A good deal of the rebellion against authority stemmed from the restriction of hunting rights. These early ballads reveal the cruelty that was a part of medieval life. Robin Hood was a rebel, and many of the most striking episodes depict him and his companions robbing and killing representatives of authority and <u>they gave</u> the gains to the poor.

17

Their <u>most frequentest</u> enemy was the Sheriff of Not-

18
tingham, a local agent of the central government. Other enemies included wealthy ecclesiastical landowners. While Robin could be ruthless toward those who abused

16. **F.** NO CHANGE
    G. telling
    H. tell
    J. they are telling

17. **A.** NO CHANGE
    B. they were giving
    C. giving
    D. gave

18. **F.** NO CHANGE
    G. even more frequenter
    H. frequent
    J. frequently

GO ON TO THE NEXT PAGE

their power, he was kind to the oppressed. He was a

people's hero as King Arthur was a noble's. ⏹19⏹

    Some scholars have sought to prove that there was

an actual Robin Hood. However, references to the Robin

Hood legends by medieval writers make it clear that the

ballads were the only evidence for Robin's existence

19. The writer is considering adding the following sentence:

> The Broadway musical *Camelot* is based on the legend of King Arthur.

Should the writer make this addition here?

A. Yes, because it bolsters the author's point about King Arthur's wide appeal with a mainstream example.

B. Yes, because it explains King Arthur's significance in popular culture.

C. No, because it provides only one isolated example of a modern adaptation of the legend of King Arthur.

D. No, because it deviates from the paragraph's focus on the legend of Robin Hood.

available to <u>them.</u> A popular modern belief that Robin
        20
was of the time of Richard I most likely stems from the

20. F. NO CHANGE

   G. him.

   H. it.

   J. those writing ballads about him.

antiquary <u>king's fabrication</u>
         21

21. A. NO CHANGE

   B. kings fabrication

   C. kings fabrication,

   D. king's, fabrication

GO ON TO THE NEXT PAGE ⇒

of a "pedigree." 22

22. Suppose that at this point in the passage, the writer wanted to add more information about Richard I. Which of the following additions would be most relevant to the passage as a whole?

    F. A discussion of relevant books on England during the reign of Richard I

    G. A definition of the term *antiquary*

    H. An example of Richard I's interest in King Arthur

    J. A description of the influence Richard I's fabricated pedigree had on later versions of the Robin Hood tale

In the eighteenth century, the nature of the legend was distorted by the suggestion that Robin <u>was as a</u>
23
fallen nobleman. [A] Writers adopted this new element

23. **A.** NO CHANGE

    B. was like as if he was

    C. was a

    D. is as a

<u>as eagerly as puppies.</u> Robin was also given a love
24

24. **F.** NO CHANGE

    G. eagerly

    H. eagerly, like a puppy

    J. like a puppy's eagerness

<u>interest; Maid</u> Marian. [B] Some critics say that these
25
ballads lost much of their vitality and poetic value

by losing the social impulse that prompted their crea-

tion. [C] In the twentieth century, the legend of Robin

Hood inspired several movies and a television series.

Even a Broadway musical <u>basing</u> on the tale. [D] So,
26
whether or not a Robin Hood actually lived in ancient

25. **A.** NO CHANGE

    B. interests—Maid

    C. interest: Maid,

    D. interest—Maid

26. **F.** NO CHANGE

    G. has been based

    H. to base

    J. base

GO ON TO THE NEXT PAGE

Britain, the legendary Robin, has lived in the popular
———————————————————————
                        27

imagination for more than 600 years. [28]

27. **A.** NO CHANGE
    B. Britain, the legendary Robin has
    C. Britain, the legendary, Robin, has
    D. Britain the legendary Robin has

28. The writer wants to divide this paragraph into two paragraphs. The best place to begin a new paragraph would be at Point:

    F. A.
    G. B.
    H. C.
    J. D.

Questions 29 and 30 ask about the preceding passage as a whole.

---

29. Suppose this passage were written for an audience that was unfamiliar with the legend of Robin Hood. The writer could most effectively strengthen the passage by:

    A. citing examples of legendary rebels from Spanish and French literature.

    B. including further evidence of Robin Hood's actual existence.

    C. quoting a few lines from a Broadway musical about ancient Britain.

    D. including a brief summary of the Robin Hood legend.

30. This passage was probably written for readers who:

    F. are experts on how legends are handed down.

    G. are authorities on ancient British civilization and culture.

    H. are convinced that Robin Hood was an actual historical personage.

    J. have some familiarity with the Robin Hood legends.

GO ON TO THE NEXT PAGE ⟩

Passage III

The following paragraphs may or may not be in the most logical order. Each paragraph is numbered in brackets, and Question 45 will ask you to choose the most logical order of the paragraphs.

How Mother Nature Jump-Started My Career

[1]

When Mt. St. Helens erupted, my training as a private pilot paid off. My editor asked me to write a feature story on the volcano. Only scientists and reporters were allowed within a <u>ten-mile radius</u> of the mountain.
31
Eager to see Mt. St. Helens for himself, my brother Jeff volunteered to accompany me as an assistant on the flight.

He had never flown with me before, <u>and I looked</u>
32
<u>forward at the opportunity to show off my skills.</u>
32

[2]

<u>If I could read a newspaper,</u> I entertained thoughts
33
of becoming a photojournalist. I always envisioned

<u>myself</u> in some faraway exotic place, performing
34
dangerous deeds as a foreign correspondent. I was thrilled when I was hired for my first job as a cub reporter for the local newspaper in my rural hometown.

31. **A.** NO CHANGE
    B. radius, consisting of ten miles,
    C. measurement of a ten-mile radius
    D. radius, measuring ten miles,

32. **F.** NO CHANGE
    G. but looked forward to the opportunity of showing off my skills.
    H. and I looked forward to the opportunity to show off my skills.
    J. nevertheless I anticipated being able to show off my skills.

33. **A.** NO CHANGE
    B. Since I found it easy to read a newspaper,
    C. Although I could read a newspaper,
    D. Ever since I could read a newspaper,

34. **F.** NO CHANGE
    G. I
    H. me
    J. it

GO ON TO THE NEXT PAGE

However, some of the glamour began to fade after I covered the umpteenth garden party. Then one day, Mother Nature <u>intervened,</u> giving me the opportunity
35
to cover an international event.

[3]

[A] When we arrived at the airport, <u>filing my flight</u>
36
<u>plan; giving</u> my credentials as a reporter for the Gresh-
36
am *Outlook*. Shortly after leaving Troutdale airport, my Cessna 152 ascended slowly on its way toward Mt. St. Helens. [B] A few other pilots were also circling around the crater. I had to maintain a high enough altitude to avoid both the smoke being emitted <u>from: the crater</u> and
37
the ashen residue already in the atmosphere. [C] Too much exposure to the volcanic particles could put my plane out of service. [D] This element of danger served to increase not only my awareness, but also my excitement. 38

35. **A.** NO CHANGE
   B. intervened:
   C. intervened;
   D. —intervened—

36. **F.** NO CHANGE
   G. I filed my flight plan and gave
   H. filing my flight plan, giving
   J. my flight plan was filed by me, and I gave

37. **A.** NO CHANGE
   B. (from: the crater)
   C. from, the crater,
   D. from the crater

38. The writer is considering adding the following sentence to this paragraph:

   > As we neared the crater, I kept a careful watch for other airplanes in the vicinity.

   If the writer were to add this sentence, it would most logically be placed at Point:

   F. A.
   G. B.
   H. C.
   J. D.

GO ON TO THE NEXT PAGE

[4]

Jeff and I were at first speechless <u>and mute</u> at the
                                      39
awesome sight below us as we circled the crater. It was

as if the spectacular beauty of a Fourth of July celebra-

tion were contained in one natural phenomenon. Jeff

helped me, <u>steadying the plane and took notes,</u> while
                              40

I shot pictures and dictated story ideas to him. ⬚41

[5]

My story appeared as the front-page feature the fol-

lowing day. <u>However,</u> I have realized many of my early
             42
dreams, working as a foreign correspondent in many

different countries. And yet none of my experiences has

surpassed that special pride and excitement I felt cover-

ing my first "international" story.

39. A. NO CHANGE
B. and also mute
C. —and mute—
D. DELETE the underlined portion.

40. F. NO CHANGE
G. steadying the plane and taking notes,
H. steadied the plane and taking notes,
J. steadies the plane and takes notes

41. The writer could most effectively strengthen
the passage at this point by adding which of the
following?

A. A description of Mt. St. Helens

B. The sentence, "Jeff, take this plane lower!"
to add excitement

C. The statement, "A volcano is a vent in
the earth's crust through which lava is
expelled," to inform the reader

D. A discussion of other recent volcanic
eruptions to provide a contrast

42. F. NO CHANGE
G. Since that time,
H. Furthermore,
J. Nevertheless,

GO ON TO THE NEXT PAGE ⇨

Questions 43—45 ask about the preceding passage as a whole.

---

43. Readers are likely to regard the passage as best described by which of the following terms?

   A. Optimistic

   B. Bitter

   C. Nostalgic

   D. Exhausted

44. Is the author's use of the pronoun *I* appropriate in the passage?

   F. No, because, as a rule, one avoids *I* in formal writing.

   G. No, because it weakens the passage's focus on volcanoes.

   H. Yes, because it gives immediacy to the story told in the passage.

   J. Yes, because *I* is, as a rule, appropriate in writing.

45. Choose the sequence of paragraph numbers that will make the passage's structure most logical.

   A. NO CHANGE

   B. 2, 1, 3, 4, 5

   C. 3, 4, 5, 1, 2

   D. 4, 5, 1, 2, 3

Passage IV

Sir Arthur Conan Doyle

[1]

Sherlock Holmes, the <u>ingenious and extremely</u>
                                    46
<u>clever</u> detective, with the deerstalker hat, pipe, and
 46
magnifying glass, is a universally recognizable character.

Everyone knows of Holmes's ability to solve even the

most bizarre mysteries through the application of cold

logic. <u>Therefore, everyone</u> is familiar with the catch-
         47
phrase "Elementary, my dear Watson," Holmes's peren-

nial response to the requests of his baffled sidekick,

Dr. Watson, for an explanation of his amazing <u>tales</u>.
                                                    48

[2]

But how many people know anything about the

creator of Sherlock Holmes, Sir Arthur Conan Doyle?

Fans of Holmes might be surprised to discover that <u>he</u>
                                                    49

did not want <u>to be engraved forever in the memory of</u>
                                50
<u>the people</u> as the author of the Sherlock Holmes stories.
 50

46. F. NO CHANGE
    G. ingenious
    H. ingenious, extremely clever
    J. cleverly ingenious

47. A. NO CHANGE
    B. Although everyone
    C. For this reason, everyone
    D. Everyone

48. F. NO CHANGE
    G. stories
    H. subtractions
    J. deductions

49. A. NO CHANGE
    B. Conan Doyle
    C. they
    D. the detective

50. F. NO CHANGE
    G. to go down in the annals of history
    H. to be permanently thought of forever
    J. to be remembered

GO ON TO THE NEXT PAGE

In fact, Conan Doyle sent Holmes to his death at the
51
end of the second book of short stories and subsequent-

ly felt a great sense of relief. Having had enough of his

famous character by that time, Sherlock Holmes would
52
never divert him again from more serious writing,
52
Conan Doyle promised himself. It took
52

eight years and offering a princely sum of money before
53
Conan Doyle could be persuaded to revive the detective.

[3]

[1] Admirers of Holmes's coldly scientific approach

to his detective work may also be taken aback when they

learn that Conan Doyle has been deeply immersed in
54
spiritualism. [2] Convinced by these experiences of the

validity of paranormal phenomena, that he lectured on
55
spiritualism in towns and villages throughout Britain.

51. **A.** NO CHANGE
    B. Despite this,
    C. Regardless,
    D. Yet

52. **F.** NO CHANGE
    G. the diversion of Sherlock Holmes, Conan Doyle promised himself, would never again keep him from more serious writing.
    H. more serious writing consumed all his time from then on.
    J. Conan Doyle promised himself that Sherlock Holmes would never again divert him from more serious writing.

53. **A.** NO CHANGE
    B. eight years of offer
    C. eight years and
    D. eight years and the offer of

54. **F.** NO CHANGE
    G. is deeply immersed
    H. was deeply immersed
    J. has been immersed deeply

55. **A.** NO CHANGE
    B. phenomena, he lectured
    C. phenomena was he that he lectured
    D. phenomena. He lectured

GO ON TO THE NEXT PAGE

[3] <u>Nevertheless</u>, he and his family attempted to
            56
communicate with the dead by automatic writing

and through a spiritual medium, an individual who

supposedly could contact those in the world beyond.

[4] Conan Doyle claimed to have grasped materialized

hands and watched heavy articles swimming through

the air during sessions led by the medium. [57]

[4]

Doyle seems never to have asked <u>himself: why they</u>
                                        58
would manifest themselves in such curious ways, or to

have reflected on the fact that many of these effects are

the standard trappings of cheating mediums. One has to

wonder, <u>what would Sherlock Holmes have to say?</u>
            59

56. F. NO CHANGE
  G. After
  H. Despite this
  J. For example

57. For the sake of unity and coherence, Sentence 2
should be placed:

  A. where it is now.
  B. before Sentence 1.
  C. after Sentence 3.
  D. after Sentence 4.

58. F. NO CHANGE
  G. himself—why they
  H. himself why those in the other world
  J. himself why they

59. A. NO CHANGE
  B. what would Sherlock Holmes have said?
  C. what is Sherlock Holmes going to say?
  D. what had Sherlock Holmes said?

┌──┐
│ Question 60 asks about the preceding passage │
│ as a whole.   │
└──┘

60. Which of the following would be the most appropriate subtitle for the passage?

  F. The Truth about Spiritualists
  G. Rational or Superstitious?
  H. The Secret Life of Sherlock Holmes
  J. His Religious Beliefs

Practice Test 4

GO ON TO THE NEXT PAGE ⇨

Passage V

Visual Learning

[1]

Traditional educational theories stressed lecture-based methods in which students learned by listening to an instructor, but contemporary studies have noted that students learn best when they see, hear, and experience. Based on these studies, current educational theories emphasize auditory, visual, and experiential learning. Such theories are not <u>fashionable</u>. For example, medical
61
education has stressed this model for decades. Young doctors in their residency training often repeat the mantra, "See it, do it, teach it." Interestingly, much of the development in the visual and experiential learning fields has come from the business world. <u>Many busi-
62
nesses—from corporate management to consulting,
62
utilize presentations.</u> Traditionally, business presenta-
62
tions included slides filled with dense text that merely repeated the presenter's words. Though these slides did

provide a visual aspect, <u>it was</u> difficult to read, which
63
detracted from their effectiveness.

61. **A.** NO CHANGE
     B. popular
     C. groundbreaking
     D. illustrious

62. **F.** NO CHANGE
     G. Many businesses from corporate management to consulting utilize presentations.
     H. Many businesses—from corporate management to consulting utilize presentations.
     J. Many businesses—from corporate management to consulting—utilize presentations.

63. **A.** NO CHANGE
     B. the slide's was
     C. the slides' were
     D. they were

GO ON TO THE NEXT PAGE

[2]

[1] Over the past decade, <u>technological advances</u>
₆₄
<u>have created</u> additional presentation options, business
₆₄
leaders have teamed with public speaking experts to

continue to refine the visual presentation style.

[2] <u>A very important development revealed</u> that less
₆₅
cluttered visual aids work better than denser ones. [3]

This development led to the understanding that text

repeating a presenter's script did not <u>enhance or improve</u>
₆₆
student or audience learning. [4] Studies showed that

visual aids should not simply present a speaker's words,

but instead demonstrate or add to them in some way. [5]

These studies emphasized the efficacy of visual represen-

tations of the presenter's dialogue in the form of <u>graphs,</u>
₆₇
<u>charts, art, or pictures</u>. [68]
₆₇

64. **F.** NO CHANGE
   G. technological advances were creating
   H. as technological advances have created
   J. that technological advances have created

65. **A.** NO CHANGE
   B. On the other hand, a very important development revealed
   C. A very important development similarly revealed
   D. In contrast, a very important development revealed

66. **F.** NO CHANGE
   G. lead to an improvement in
   H. better enhance or improve
   J. improve

67. **A.** NO CHANGE
   B. graphs charts art or pictures
   C. graphs charts, art, or pictures
   D. graphs, charts art, or pictures

68. After reviewing the essay, the writer is considering inserting the following true statement in this paragraph:

   Audio aids, though infrequently used, can also help audiences focus on a presentation.

Should this sentence be added to this paragraph, and if so, what is the most logical placement for it?

   F. Yes, after Sentence 2.
   G. Yes, after Sentence 4.
   H. Yes, after Sentence 5.
   J. No, the sentence should NOT be added.

GO ON TO THE NEXT PAGE

[3]

Several studies <u>have been published in respected</u>
                                    69
<u>journals, that reveal in listeners that aesthetically</u>
                            69
<u>appealing presentations improve comprehension.</u>
                    69

It has been determined by researchers that a learning aid
                                                    70
can be created from any pleasing image, even one that
                            70
is irrelevant. Using this model, many presenters have
    70
begun projecting nature scenes or famous paintings to

accompany <u>presentations. Audience</u> members report
                            71
not being distracted by the irrelevant images. In fact,

most audience members find the pleasing images

helpful in creating a positive environment which, in

turn, helps <u>him or her</u> focus on the presentation.
                72

69. **A.** NO CHANGE

    B. revealing that aesthetically appealing presentations improve comprehension in listeners have been published in respected journals.

    C. in listeners that reveal that aesthetically appealing presentations improve comprehension in respected journals have been published.

    D. have been published in respected journals by revealing in listeners that aesthetically appealing presentations improve comprehension.

70. **F.** NO CHANGE

    G. Researchers have determined that any pleasing image, even an irrelevant one, can serve as a learning aid.

    H. As researchers have determined, that any pleasing image, even an irrelevant one, can serve as a learning aid.

    J. A pleasing image, even an irrelevant one, researchers have determined it can serve as a learning aid.

71. **A.** NO CHANGE

    B. presentations, audience

    C. presentations, and that audience

    D. presentations and that audience

72. **F.** NO CHANGE

    G. one

    H. you

    J. them

GO ON TO THE NEXT PAGE →

[4]

[1] <u>Even more recently, of late,</u> cognitive psycholo-
73
gists have noted that students and audience members

<u>use multiple senses to take in information.</u> [2] In fact,
74
many experts believe that a teacher's or presenter's body

language is the most important factor in student or

audience reaction. [3] Therefore, many education and

public speaking experts <u>are interested in investigat-</u>
75
<u>ing other factors in student and audience reaction.</u> [4]
75
While these developments have not coalesced to form

one paradigm for public speaking and presenting, they

have underscored many of the new theories in the field

of communication. [5] These developments continue to

influence trends in the academic world.

73. **A.** NO CHANGE
   B. Not so long ago, in recent times,
   C. Lately, in addition,
   D. Recently,

74. Given that all of the following are true, which
   choice would provide the most effective and
   logical link between Sentences 1 and 2?

   F. NO CHANGE
   G. learn not only from images, but also from
      body language.
   H. pay more attention to visual images that
      incorporate color or suggest movement.
   J. recall more information when they are
      asked by the presenter or speaker to take
      notes or write questions.

75. At this point, the writer would like to show how
   education and public speaking experts have
   been influenced by the theory about the importance of body language. Given that all of the
   following are true, which choice best achieves
   the writer's purpose?

   A. NO CHANGE
   B. now teach presenters to make purposeful
      movements and focused gestures.
   C. have adjusted the focus of their public
      speaking workshops for teachers and
      business professionals.
   D. question how the size of an audience
      affects the power of a presenter's body
      language.

IF YOU FINISH BEFORE TIME IS CALLED, YOU MAY CHECK YOUR WORK ON THIS SECTION ONLY. DO NOT TURN TO ANY OTHER SECTION IN THE TEST.

Practice Test 4

MATHEMATICS TEST

60 Minutes—60 Questions

Directions: Choose the correct solution to each question and fill in the corresponding bubble on your answer sheet.

Do not continue to spend time on questions if you get stuck. Solve as many questions as you can before returning to any if time permits.

You may use a calculator on this test for any question you choose. However, some questions may be better solved without a calculator.

Note: Unless otherwise stated, you can assume:

1. Figures are NOT necessarily drawn to scale.

2. Geometric figures are two dimensional.

3. The word *line* indicates a straight line.

4. The word *average* indicates arithmetic mean.

1. A *rod* is a unit of length equivalent to 5.5 yards. If a field is 127 yards long, then how many rods long is the field, to the nearest tenth?

   A. 231.9

   B. 69.9

   C. 43.3

   D. 23.1

   E. 4.3

2. Because of increased rents in the area, a pizzeria needs to raise the cost of its $20.00 extra-large pizza by 22%. What will the new cost be?

   F. $20.22

   G. $22.20

   H. $24.00

   J. $24.40

   K. $42.00

3. Increases in membership for five different organizations are given in the following table:

Organization	A	B	C	D	E
Increase in membership	120	210	0	210	180

What is the average increase in membership for the five organizations?

   A. 127.5

   B. 144

   C. 170

   D. 180

   E. 240

GO ON TO THE NEXT PAGE

4. Train A travels 50 miles per hour for 3 hours; Train B travels 70 miles per hour for $2\frac{1}{2}$ hours. What is the difference between the number of miles traveled by Train A and the number of miles traveled by Train B ?

   F. 20

   G. 25

   H. 150

   J. 175

   K. 325

5. Which of the following is a value of b for which $(b - 3)(b + 4)(b + 7) = 0$?

   A. −3

   B. 3

   C. 4

   D. 7

   E. 4 or 7

6. Square $ABCD$ is shown below, with one side measuring 6 centimeters. What is the area of triangle BCD, in square centimeters?

   F. 3

   G. 6

   H. 12

   J. 18

   K. 36

7. If u is an integer, then $(u - 3)^2 + 5$:

   A. must be an even integer.

   B. must be an odd integer.

   C. must be a positive integer.

   D. must be a negative integer.

   E. must be an irrational number.

8. For all nonzero a, b, and c values, $\dfrac{12a^5bc^7}{-3ab^5c^2} = ?$

   F. $\dfrac{-4c^5}{a^4b^4}$

   G. $\dfrac{-4a^4c^5}{b^4}$

   H. $\dfrac{-4ac}{b}$

   J. $-4a^6b^6c^9$

   K. $-4a^4b^4c^5$

9. In the figure below, P and Q lie on the sides of $\triangle WXY$ and $\overline{PQ}$ is parallel to $\overline{WY}$. What is the measure of $\angle QPX$?

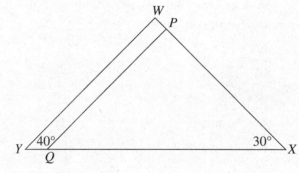

   A. 110°

   B. 120°

   C. 130°

   D. 140°

   E. 150°

GO ON TO THE NEXT PAGE

10. When written in scientific notation,
$740{,}000{,}000 + 800{,}000{,}000 = ?$

    F. 1.54×10^{-9}

    G. 1.54×10^{-8}

    H. 1.54×10^{8}

    J. 1.54×10^{9}

    K. 154×10^{15}

11. A company conducted a taste test of its new soft drink. Of the 1,250 participants, 800 liked the soft drink, 150 didn't like it, and the rest were undecided. What percent of the participants were undecided about the new soft drink?

    A.   24%

    B.   46%

    C.   64%

    D.   76%

    E.   300%

12. Two whole numbers have a greatest common factor of 15 and a least common multiple of 225. Which of the following pairs of numbers will satisfy this condition?

    F.   9 and 25

    G.   15 and 27

    H.   25 and 45

    J.   30 and 45

    K.   45 and 75

13. If $x = 2$ and $y = -3$, then $x^5y + xy^5 = ?$

    A. -60

    B. -192

    C. -390

    D. -582

    E. -972

14. How many units long is one side of a square that has a perimeter of $16 - 24h$ units?

    F. $4 - 6h$

    G. $4 - 24h$

    H. $8h$

    J. $16 - 6h$

    K. $64 - 96h$

15. If $(x - k)^2 = x^2 - 26x + k^2$ for all real numbers x, then $k = ?$

    A.   13

    B.   26

    C.   52

    D.   104

    E.   208

16. Which of the following expressions is a simplified form of $(-2x^5)^3$?

    F. $8x^8$

    G. $-8x^8$

    H. $-2x^{15}$

    J. $-6x^{15}$

    K. $-8x^{15}$

17. Among the points graphed on the number line below, which is closest to e?

    (Note: $e \approx 2.718281828$)

    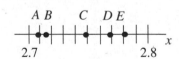

    A. A

    B. B

    C. C

    D. D

    E. E

GO ON TO THE NEXT PAGE

18. In the standard (x,y) coordinate plane, how many times does the graph of the function $f(x) = (x + 1)(x + 2)(x - 3)(x + 4)(x + 5)$ intersect the x-axis?

    F. 15

    G. 9

    H. 5

    J. 4

    K. 1

19. Which of the following is equivalent to the expression $\dfrac{4 + 8x}{12x}$?

    A. $\dfrac{1 + 2x}{3x}$

    B. $\dfrac{1 + 8x}{3x}$

    C. 1

    D. 2

    E. $4\dfrac{2}{3}$

20. Four friends who are about to share an airport shuttle that costs $21.50 per person discover that they can purchase a book of five tickets for $95.00. How much would each of the four save if they can get a fifth person to join them and then divide the cost of the book of five tickets equally among all five people?

    F. $ 2.25

    G. $ 2.50

    H. $ 3.13

    J. $ 9.00

    K. $12.50

21. What is the sum of the polynomials $-2x^2y^2 + x^2y$ and $3x^2y^2 + 2xy^2$?

    A. $-6x^4y^4 + 2x^3y^3$

    B. $-2x^2y^2 + x^2y + 2xy^2$

    C. $x^2y^2 + x^2y + 2xy^2$

    D. $x^2y^2 + x^2y$

    E. $x^2y^2 + 3x^2y$

22. A 12-foot flagpole casts a 7-foot shadow when the angle of elevation of the sun is θ (see figure below). In this scenario, what is $\tan \theta$?

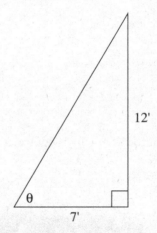

    F. $\dfrac{7}{12}$

    G. 1

    H. $\dfrac{12}{7}$

    J. 19

    K. 84

23. Yuri was x years old 15 years ago. How old will he be 7 years from now?

    A. $x + 7$

    B. $(x - 15) + 7$

    C. $(x + 15) - 7$

    D. $(x - 15) - 7$

    E. $(x + 15) + 7$

GO ON TO THE NEXT PAGE

24. Which of the following is a factor of
$2x^2 - 8x - 24$?

F. $(x - 4)$

G. $(x - 3)$

H. $(x - 2)$

J. $(x + 1)$

K. $(x + 2)$

25. What is the length, in inches, of the hypotenuse of a right triangle with legs measuring 8 inches and 15 inches?

A. $\sqrt{23}$

B. 7

C. $\sqrt{161}$

D. 17

E. 23

26. Which of the following is equivalent to
$\dfrac{4}{\sqrt{5}} + \dfrac{3}{\sqrt{2}}$?

F. $\dfrac{4\sqrt{2} + 3\sqrt{5}}{\sqrt{7}}$

G. $\dfrac{4\sqrt{2} + 3\sqrt{5}}{\sqrt{10}}$

H. $\dfrac{7}{\sqrt{5} + \sqrt{2}}$

J. $\dfrac{7}{\sqrt{7}}$

K. $\dfrac{7}{\sqrt{10}}$

27. The *relative atomic mass* of an element is the ratio of the mass of the element to the mass of an equal amount of carbon. If 1 cubic centimeter of carbon has a mass of 12 grams, what is the relative atomic mass of an element that has a mass of 30 grams per cubic centimeter?

A. 1

B. 1.2

C. 2.5

D. 3

E. 30

28. If $2x + 3 = -5$, what is the value of $x^2 - 7x$?

F. -44

G. -12

H. -4

J. 12

K. 44

29. Which of the following is a graph of the solution set for $8(5 + x) - 1 < 7$?

A.

B.

C.

D.

E.

GO ON TO THE NEXT PAGE

30. A county employee is collecting soil samples from all the houses in a subdivision where trace amounts of an unknown toxin were found in the soil. There are 40 houses in the subdivision. If he starts the first house at 8:00 AM and starts the sixth house at 9:05 AM, how long will it take the employee to collect samples from all the houses in the subdivision, assuming it takes the same amount of time at each house?

    F. 6 hours and 50 minutes

    G. 7 hours and 5 minutes

    H. 7 hours and 14 minutes

    J. 8 hours and 15 minutes

    K. 8 hours and 40 minutes

31. Listed below are five functions, each denoted by $g(x)$ and each involving a real number constant $k > 1$. If $h(x) = 5^x$, which of these 5 functions yields the greatest value for $h(g(x))$, for all $x > 2$?

    A. $g(x) = \dfrac{k}{x}$

    B. $g(x) = \dfrac{x}{k}$

    C. $g(x) = kx$

    D. $g(x) = x^k$

    E. $g(x) = \sqrt[k]{x}$

GO ON TO THE NEXT PAGE

Use the following information to answer questions 32–33.

A hiker planned to hike a small mountain during the course of a day. The hiker began at 7:00 AM at an altitude of 4,000 feet. When the hiker is climbing the mountain, she climbs at a constant speed for an hour. She finished her hike back at 4,000 feet at 1:00 PM. The graph that follows shows the hiker's altitude, in feet, as a function of time.

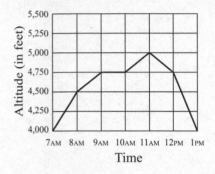

32. What is the closest, in feet, to the total vertical distance (upward and downward) that the hiker traveled between 8:00 AM and 1:00 PM ?

   F.   250

   G. 1,000

   H. 1,500

   J.   1,750

   K. 2,000

33. Which description best describes the hiker's altitude from 9:00 AM to 12:00 PM ?

   A. The hiker stayed at the same altitude, then ascended the mountain.

   B. The hiker ascended the mountain, then descended the mountain at a faster rate.

   C. The hiker descended the mountain at one rate, then descended the mountain at a faster rate.

   D. The hiker ascended the mountain, then stayed at the same altitude, and then descended the mountain.

   E. The hiker stayed at the same altitude, then ascended and descended the mountain at the same rate.

34. A chord 30 centimeters long is 8 centimeters from the center of a circle, as shown in the following figure. What is the radius of the circle, to the nearest tenth of a centimeter?

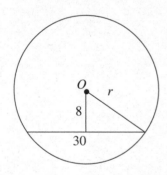

   F. 17.0

   G. 22.8

   H. 31.2

   J.   34.0

   K. 38.0

GO ON TO THE NEXT PAGE

35. If the graphs of $y - 3x = 0$ and $y = ax + 6$ are parallel in the standard (x,y) coordinate plane, then $a = ?$

- **A.** -6
- **B.** -3
- **C.** $\dfrac{1}{3}$
- **D.** 3
- **E.** 6

36. The average of a set of four integers is 14. When a fifth number is included in the set, the average of the set increases to 16. What is the fifth number?

- **F.** 16
- **G.** 18
- **H.** 21
- **J.** 24
- **K.** 26

37. If the system of linear equations that follows has infinitely many solutions, what is the value of k ?

$$12x - 20y = 108$$
$$3x + ky = 27$$

- **A.** -5
- **B.** -3
- **C.** $-\dfrac{1}{4}$
- **D.** $\dfrac{3}{5}$
- **E.** 4

38. A common rule of thumb is that each additional inch of height (H) will add 10 pounds to a person's weight (W). Doctors recommend finding your Body Mass Index (BMI) as a measure of health. BMI is computed as follows (H is in inches, and W is in pounds):

$$BMI = \frac{703W}{H^2}$$

If a 68-inch-tall person typically weighs 150 pounds, which of the following is closest to the expected BMI of a 72-inch-tall person?

- **F.** 1
- **G.** 2
- **H.** 20
- **J.** 26
- **K.** 42

39. At a high school festival, 100 students are signed up to participate in a sporting event: 45 are preparing to compete only in the sack race, 21 will participate only in the balloon toss, and 25 will participate in both the sack race and the balloon toss. How many students are not signed up to participate in either of these events?

- **A.** 9
- **B.** 17
- **C.** 34
- **D.** 66
- **E.** 75

GO ON TO THE NEXT PAGE

40. In the figure below, $\overline{BD}$ is a perpendicular bisector of $\overline{AC}$ in equilateral triangle ABC. If $\overline{BD}$ is $4\sqrt{3}$ units long, how many units long is $\overline{BC}$?

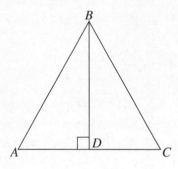

F. $2\sqrt{3}$

G. 4

H. 8

J. $8\sqrt{3}$

K. 16

41. The following figure represents the view of a swimming pool from above. What is the perimeter, in meters, of the pool?

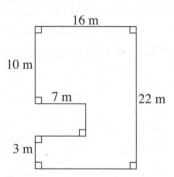

A. 58

B. 83

C. 90

D. 208

E. 352

42. Five books are to be placed on a bookshelf. If all 5 books are placed on the shelf in order, from left to right, in how many different ways can the books be placed?

F. 5

G. 14

H. 60

J. 120

K. 720

43. To make a baby bib, a circle with a radius of 4 inches is cut out of a circle with a radius of 12 inches, as shown in the figure here. Which of the following expressions gives the area of the shaded portion, in square inches?

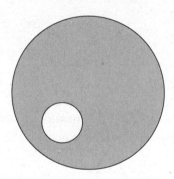

A. $\pi(12 - 2)^2$

B. $\pi12^2 - 2^2$

C. $\pi12^2 - 4^2$

D. $\pi(12 - 4^2)$

E. $\pi(12^2 - 4^2)$

GO ON TO THE NEXT PAGE

44. A scientist has a container of liquid nitrogen that is at a temperature of $-330°F$. If the temperature of the room is $72°F$, how much must the temperature of the liquid nitrogen change to become the room's temperature?

    (Note: "+" indicates a rise in temperature, and "−" indicates a drop in temperature.)

    F. $-330°F$

    G. $-258°F$

    H. $+72°F$

    J. $+402°F$

    K. $+474°F$

45. The area of a rectangular floor is 323 square feet. The width of the floor is 21 feet less than twice the length. How many feet long is the floor?

    A. 8.5

    B. 11

    C. 13.5

    D. 17

    E. 19

46. For the area of a circle to double, the new radius must be the old radius multiplied by which of the following values?

    F. $\dfrac{1}{2}$

    G. $\sqrt{2}$

    H. 2

    J. π

    K. 4

47. If $\log_x 64 = 3$, then $x = ?$

    A. 4

    B. 8

    C. $\dfrac{64}{3}$

    D. $\dfrac{64}{\log 3}$

    E. 64^3

48. If $A = \begin{bmatrix} 3 & -6 \\ 0 & 9 \end{bmatrix}$ and $B = \begin{bmatrix} -3 & 6 \\ 0 & -9 \end{bmatrix}$, then $A - B = ?$

    F. $\begin{bmatrix} 0 & 0 \\ 0 & 0 \end{bmatrix}$

    G. $\begin{bmatrix} 1 & 0 \\ 0 & 1 \end{bmatrix}$

    H. $\begin{bmatrix} -6 & -12 \\ 0 & 18 \end{bmatrix}$

    J. $\begin{bmatrix} 6 & 0 \\ 0 & 0 \end{bmatrix}$

    K. $\begin{bmatrix} 6 & -12 \\ 0 & 18 \end{bmatrix}$

49. If a and b are real numbers, and $a > 0$ and $b < a$, then which of the following inequalities must be true?

    A. $b \leq 0$

    B. $b \geq 0$

    C. $b^2 \geq 0$

    D. $b^2 \geq a^2$

    E. $b^2 \leq a^2$

GO ON TO THE NEXT PAGE

50. The ratio of the lengths of the sides of a right triangle is $2:\sqrt{5}:3$. What is the cosine of the smallest angle in the triangle?

    F. $\dfrac{2}{3}$

    G. $\dfrac{\sqrt{5}}{3}$

    H. $\dfrac{2\sqrt{5}}{5}$

    J. $\dfrac{9}{10}$

    K. 2

51. What is the amplitude of the graph of the trigonometric function with equation
    $y - 2 = 5\cos(4\theta)$?

    (Note: The amplitude is $\dfrac{1}{2}$ the difference between the maximum and the minimum values of y.)

    A. 2

    B. 4

    C. 5

    D. 8

    E. 10

52. A credit score is a number used by financial institutions to determine a person's financial health. One of the factors that affects a person's credit score is the percentage of credit available that he or she is currently utilizing. For example, a person with a credit line of $1,000 who has debt of $900 is utilizing 90% of his or her available credit. Ideally, a person should use no more than 25% of available credit. Angus has been trying to pay down his debt to increase his credit score. Suppose Angus has a credit line of $10,000. The bar graph that follows shows the amount of debt he is currently carrying on that credit line each month. If he continues to pay down this debt at the same rate, how many months from when Angus reached his credit line maximum will it take him to reach 25% utilization?

Reduction of Debt Schedule

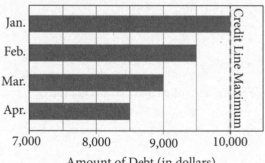

    F. 8

    G. 12

    H. 15

    J. 20

    K. 24

GO ON TO THE NEXT PAGE

53. The measure of the vertex angle of an isosceles triangle is $(x - 10)°$. The base angles each measure $(3x + 18)°$. What is the measure in degrees of one of the base angles?

    A. 12

    B. 22

    C. $37\frac{1}{2}$

    D. $43\frac{1}{2}$

    E. 84

54. To make a set of potholders to give as a gift, Margot needs the following amounts of fabric:

Pieces of Fabric	Length of Each Piece (inches)
6	8
5	12
2	18

    If the fabric costs $1.95 per yard, which of the following would be the approximate cost of fabric for 5 sets of potholders?

    (Note: 1 yard = 36 inches)

    F. $ 8

    G. $ 24

    H. $ 39

    J. $ 58

    K. $117

55. On a used vehicle lot, 50% of the vehicles are cars, $\frac{3}{4}$ of which have automatic transmissions. Of the cars with automatic transmissions, $\frac{1}{3}$ have GPS systems installed. If a vehicle is chosen from the lot at random, what is the probability that it will be a car with an automatic transmission and a GPS system?

    A. $\frac{1}{8}$

    B. $\frac{1}{6}$

    C. $\frac{1}{4}$

    D. $\frac{1}{3}$

    E. $\frac{1}{2}$

56. Given that the list of integers 2, 3, 3, a, b, 8, 9, 12 is written in ascending order, and that the median of the list is 4, which of the following could be a possible value of the product ab ?

    F. 6

    G. 10

    H. 15

    J. 18

    K. 20

57. Which of the following is the equation of the largest circle that can be inscribed in the ellipse with equation $\dfrac{(x - 4)^2}{16} + \dfrac{y^2}{4} = 1$?

    A. $(x - 4)^2 + y^2 = 64$

    B. $(x - 4)^2 + y^2 = 16$

    C. $(x - 4)^2 + y^2 = 4$

    D. $x^2 + y^2 = 16$

    E. $x^2 + y^2 = 4$

GO ON TO THE NEXT PAGE

58. One of the graphs below is that of a cubic function, $g(x) = x^3 + C$, where C is a constant. Which one?

F.

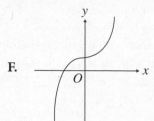

G.

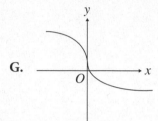

H.

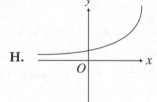

J.

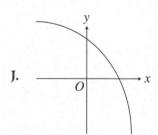

K.

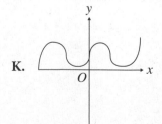

59. Five numbers are given by the expressions x, $2x - 3$, $2x + 1$, $3x - 4$, and $3x + 1$. If the average (arithmetic mean) of these numbers is 10, what is the mode of the numbers?

A. 10

B. 10.5

C. 11

D. 12

E. Cannot be determined from the given information

60. In 4 fair coin tosses, what is the probability of obtaining exactly 3 heads?

(Note: In a fair coin toss, the 2 outcomes, heads and tails, are equally likely.)

F. $\dfrac{1}{16}$

G. $\dfrac{1}{8}$

H. $\dfrac{3}{16}$

J. $\dfrac{1}{4}$

K. $\dfrac{1}{2}$

IF YOU FINISH BEFORE TIME IS CALLED, YOU MAY CHECK YOUR WORK ON THIS SECTION ONLY. DO NOT TURN TO ANY OTHER SECTION IN THE TEST.

Practice Test 4

READING TEST

35 Minutes—40 Questions

Directions: The Reading Test includes multiple passages. Each passage includes multiple questions. After reading each passage, choose the best answer and fill in the corresponding bubble on your answer sheet. You may review the passages as often as necessary.

Passage I

PROSE FICTION: This passage is an excerpt from the short story "Graduation," by John Krupp.

Rosemary sat at her kitchen table, working at a crossword puzzle. Crosswords were nice; they filled the time and kept the mind active. She needed just one word to complete this morning's puzzle; the
5 clue was "a Swiss river," and the first of its three letters was *A*. Unfortunately, Rosemary had no idea what the name of the river was and could not look it up. Her atlas was on the desk, and the desk was in the guest room, currently being occupied by her
10 grandson Victor. Looking up over the tops of her bifocals, Rosemary glanced at the kitchen clock: it was almost 10 a.m. *Land sakes!* Did the boy intend to sleep all day? She noticed that the arthritis in her wrist was throbbing, and she put down her pen. At
15 eighty-seven years of age, she was glad she could still write at all. She had decided long ago that growing old was like slowly turning to stone; you couldn't take anything for granted. She stood up slowly, painfully, and started walking to the guest room.
20 The trip, though only a distance of about twenty-five feet, seemed to take a long while. Late in her ninth decade now, Rosemary often experienced an expanded sense of time, with present and past tense intermingling in her mind. One minute she
25 was padding in her slippers across the living room carpet; the next she was back on the farm where she'd grown up, a sturdy little girl treading the path behind the barn just before dawn. In her mind's eye, she could still pick her way among the stones in the

30 darkness, more than seventy years later. Rosemary arrived at the door to the guest room. It stood slightly ajar, and she peered through the opening. Victor lay sleeping on his side, his arms bent, his expression slightly pained. *Get up, lazy bones*, she
35 wanted to say. Even in childhood, Rosemary had never slept past 4:00 AM.; there were too many chores to do. How different things were for Victor's generation! Her youngest grandson behaved as if he had never done a chore in his life. Twenty-one years
40 old, he had driven down to Florida to visit Rosemary in his shiny new car, a gift from his doting parents. Victor would finish college soon, and his future appeared bright—if he ever got out of bed, that is.
Something Victor had said last night over dinner
45 had disturbed her. Now what was it? Oh yes; he had been talking about one of his college courses—a "gut," he had called it. When she had asked him to explain the term, Victor had said it was a course that you took simply because it was easy to pass.
50 Rosemary, who had not even had a high school education, found the term repellent. If she had been allowed to continue her studies, she would never have taken a "gut." . . . The memory flooded back then, still painful as an open wound all these years
55 later. It was the first day of high school. She had graduated from grammar school the previous year, but her father had forbidden her to go on to high school that fall, saying that she was needed on the farm. After much tearful pleading, she had gotten

GO ON TO THE NEXT PAGE

60 him to promise that next year, she could start high
school. She had endured a whole year of chores instead of books, with animals and rough farmhands
for company instead of people her own age. Now,
at last, the glorious day was at hand. She had put on
65 her best dress (she owned two), her heart racing in
anticipation. But her father was waiting for her as
she came downstairs.

"Where do you think you're going?" he asked.

"To high school, Papa."

70 "No you're not. Take that thing off and
get back to work."

"But Papa, you promised!"

"*Do as I say!*" he thundered.

There was no arguing with Papa when he spoke
75 that way. Tearfully, she had trudged upstairs to
change clothes. Rosemary still wondered what life
would have been like if her father had not been
waiting at the bottom of the stairs that day, or if
somehow she had found the strength to defy him.

1. The author most likely regards Rosemary
   with:

   A. sympathy.

   B. anger.

   C. disappointment.

   D. confusion.

2. It can be inferred from the passage that
   Rosemary is disturbed by Victor's:

   F. intention to drop out of college.

   G. disregard for her harsh upbringing.

   H. willingness to take courses that are
      easy to pass.

   J. inability to get out of bed in the morn-
      ing.

3. The passage suggests that in the year after she
   finished grammar school, Rosemary most
   wanted:

   A. an escape from her father's company.

   B. the opportunity to go to college.

   C. the chance to study challenging subjects.

   D. the company of people her own age.

4. The passage suggests that Rosemary's attitude
   toward the physical afflictions of old age is generally one of:

   F. sadness.

   G. acceptance.

   H. resentment.

   J. optimism.

5. According to the passage, Rosemary does crossword puzzles in order to:

   A. keep her mind active.

   B. practice her handwriting.

   C. learn new geographical facts.

   D. make her more aware of time.

6. As it is used in line 23, the word *expanded* most
   nearly means:

   F. better.

   G. broadened.

   H. unfurled.

   J. abridged.

GO ON TO THE NEXT PAGE

7. In line 41, the author mentions Victor's "shiny new car" in order to illustrate:

   A. the excessive generosity of Rosemary's parents.

   B. the contrast between Rosemary's generation and his.

   C. the strength of Victor's prospects for the future.

   D. the lack of physical hardship in Victor's life.

8. The third paragraph (lines 44–67) primarily portrays Rosemary in her youth as:

   F. resentful of her father's conduct.

   G. eager to continue her education.

   H. undecided about her future career.

   J. proud of her appearance.

9. Rosemary's recollection of growing up on the farm (lines 26–30) is mentioned as an example of her:

   A. nostalgia for her childhood experiences.

   B. determination to overcome her physical disabilities.

   C. ability to recall past and present events at the same time.

   D. disappointment at being denied an education.

10. The author intends the statement that Victor's "future appeared bright" (lines 42–43) to reflect the opinion of:

   F. Rosemary.

   G. Victor.

   H. Victor's parents.

   J. Rosemary's father.

Practice Test 4

GO ON TO THE NEXT PAGE

Passage II

SOCIAL SCIENCE: These two passages reflect two different views concerning the origins of modern liberal economic regulation in the United States. Passage A is from a 1980 newspaper article about the beginning of progressive reforms to the American economy. Passage B was written in the 1990s by a noted economic historian.

Passage A

The Sherman Antitrust Act was introduced into Congress by Senator John Sherman of Ohio, and, after being first rewritten by pro-business Eastern senators, was passed into law in 1890. The Act made
5 illegal "every contract, combination in the form of trust or otherwise, or conspiracy in the restraint of trade." Many have charged, at that time and since, that the decidedly vague wording introduced by the pro-business revisers resulted in the emasculation
10 of the law's antimonopoly message. Nevertheless, the Act was the first law to fight, even symbolically, against economic monopolies in the "open" market economy of the United States.

From the birth of the nation, many politicians
15 and influential business leaders had felt that the most natural and ideal democratic economy was one in which the government played a very limited role in regulating commerce. It was argued that by permitting businesses to pursue their own interests,
20 the government was promoting the interests of the nation as a whole—or as GM chairman Charles E. Wilson reportedly quipped, "What's good for General Motors is good for the nation." Many of the leaders of trusts and monopolies in the 1800s co-
25 opted the then cutting-edge terminology of Charles Darwin's theory of natural selection, arguing that in an unrestrained economy, power and wealth would naturally flow to the most capable according to the principles of "Social Darwinism." Their monopo-
30 lies were thus natural and efficient outcomes of economic development.

Toward the close of the 1800s, however, an increasingly large and vocal number of lower- and middle-class dissenters felt that the laissez-faire[1]
35 policies of the federal government allowed monopolistic trusts like Standard Oil to manipulate consumers by fixing prices, exploit workers by cutting wages, and threaten democracy by corrupting politicians. Most directly, the trusts and
40 monopolies completely destroyed the opportunities for competitors in their industries to do business effectively. The concerns of these working-class dissenters thus created a groundswell of support for the Sherman Antitrust Act, which attempted
45 to outlaw these monopolies and trusts. Even more important than the direct effects of the Act, however, were the signs of a new era of reform against monopolistic economic corruption and the rise of deliberate economic regulation in America. The
50 federal government had finally realized that it had to take a more active role in the economy in order to protect the interests and rights of consumers, workers, and small businesses while tempering the dominating power of big business.

Passage B

55 Some political historians contend that alterations to the powers or role of the federal government are violations of the democratic principles and goals on which the United States was founded. I hold that the evolution of democracy in America
60 has been absolutely necessary and has led to positive reform to correct injustices and suit the needs of changing times. In no arena is this more evident than in the field of economic policy, especially during the presidency of Franklin D. Roosevelt.

65 Roosevelt was a liberal Democrat who looked on his election in 1932 as a mandate from the nation's voters to forge a bold path out of the crippled economy, massive unemployment, and

[1] From the French "to allow to do," an economic policy of non-intervention

Practice Test 4

plummeting farm prices brought on by the Great
70 Depression.[2] Traditionally, it was believed that in
democratic nations, the government should balance
its own budget and not attempt to manipulate the
economy as a whole by spending money. According
to traditional or conservative capitalist economists,
75 busts and booms in an open, unregulated economy
were normal and healthy, part of a natural cycle
that self-regulated excess consumption or overproduction. There was thus no need for government
intervention during recessions. It seemed evident
80 to Roosevelt, however, that the Great Depression
would not "naturally" recede, and that he must, in
his own words, "reform democracy in order to save
it." Roosevelt "pump-primed" the economy using
government funds for the first time in American
85 history by intentional deficit spending. In the Agricultural Adjustment Act, for example, Roosevelt
controlled one of the causes and symptoms of the
economic recession—agricultural overproduction—by using government funds to pay farmers to
90 produce fewer crops. Perhaps more than any other,
this act signaled the end of the laissez-faire economics era and ushered in the modern era of liberal
economic regulation.

Our nation's founders had planned for a mini-
95 malist federal government that would balance its
own books and mind its own business, and for
some 150 years, this attitude seemed intrinsic to the
role of the federal government. The deficit spending and deliberate manipulation of the national
100 economy by the Roosevelt administration marked
a radical revision of the role of the federal government, and it's likely that only the severe crisis of the
Depression could have compelled Americans to
fully embrace the notion that government interven-
105 tion in the economy was both beneficial and necessary. The success of this approach in pulling the
nation out of a crippling depression was undeniable.
Also undeniable was the larger conclusion that the
national government must adapt in both scope and
110 purpose to fit the needs of changing times.

[2] A prolonged and severe economic recession in America during
the 1930s

Questions 11–13 ask about Passage A.

11. The revisions mentioned in line 3 illustrate the:

   A. support for Social Darwinism common in
      the nineteenth century.

   B. resistance from pro-business opponents of
      antitrust reform.

   C. lengthy period of debate that preceded the
      passage of the Sherman Act.

   D. ineffective nature of Congressional
      legislation in the 1890s.

12. The author refers to *Social Darwinism*
    (line 29) in order to:

   F. illustrate the similarities between
      economic evolution and biological
      evolution.

   G. argue that only the strongest corporations
      could survive in a free-market economy.

   H. introduce the terms that monopolists
      utilized to justify their control of
      industries.

   J. provide an example of the influence of
      scientific theories on social and economic
      policy.

GO ON TO THE NEXT PAGE

13. Based on information in the third paragraph of Passage A (lines 32–54), it seems most likely that the author of Passage A would agree with which of the following?

  A. All monopolistic trusts fixed prices and exploited workers.

  B. The overall effects of stifled competition were negative for many Americans.

  C. Outlawing monopolies was a necessary reform to save democracy.

  D. Standard Oil was prevented from freely competing by the Sherman Antitrust Act.

Questions 14–16 ask about Passage B.

---

14. The author cites the Agricultural Adjustment Act (lines 85–86) as:

  F. an important twentieth century antitrust act.

  G. an act that led to a resurgence of laissez-faire economic policy.

  H. a factor leading to the Great Depression.

  J. an example of aggressive government intervention in the economy.

15. According to the passage, Franklin D. Roosevelt was:

  A. a proponent of Social Darwinism.

  B. a leader in introducing government intervention in the economy.

  C. against the Sherman Antitrust Act.

  D. a proponent of a balanced government budget.

16. In the second paragraph of Passage B, the author includes the opinion of "conservative capitalist economists" (line 74) as:

  F. a demonstration of the conservative nature of the economic reforms introduced during the Roosevelt era.

  G. evidence in support of the Agricultural Adjustment Act.

  H. a view about the necessity of government economic regulation that the author will later refute.

  J. an argument that only severe poverty can force radical changes in America.

Questions 17–20 ask about both passages.

---

17. Both passages cite which of the following as a necessary reform to the original design of the American democracy?

  A. Lessening government control of the economy

  B. Abandoning laissez-faire economic policy

  C. Preventing unfair industry domination

  D. Passing laws to limit agricultural overproduction

GO ON TO THE NEXT PAGE

18. The author of Passage B would most likely respond to the description of monopolies as "natural and efficient outcomes of economic development" (lines 30–31) by:

    F. arguing that theories of Social Darwinism were used as justification to promote the interests of the most wealthy.

    G. noting that the most "natural" state of the economy is not necessarily the most preferable.

    H. agreeing that government intervention in the economy is an abandonment of the ideals upon which the country was founded.

    J. noting that the economic policies of Franklin Roosevelt were highly effective in battling such monopolies.

19. What aspect of government economic regulation is emphasized in Passage B but not in Passage A?

    A. Antitrust laws

    B. Deficit spending

    C. Congressional legislation

    D. Laissez-faire policies

20. According to each passage, the term *laissez-faire* describes:

    F. an economic policy that is beneficial to consumers and a period in history that has yet to conclude.

    G. a natural, ideal democratic economy and a government's attempt to balance its own budget without creating interference.

    H. a philosophy that Roosevelt championed and a presidential legacy that is in effect to this day.

    J. an approach that allowed trusts to manipulate consumers and an era that the Agricultural Adjustment Act ended.

Practice Test 4

GO ON TO THE NEXT PAGE

Passage III

HUMANITIES: This passage is an excerpt from *A Short History of Western Civilization, Volume 1*, by John B. Harrison, Richard E. Sullivan, and Dennis Sherman, © 1990 by McGraw-Hill, Inc. Reprinted by permission of McGraw-Hill, Inc.

Enlightenment ideas were put forth by a variety of intellectuals who in France came to be known as the philosophes. *Philosophes* is French for philosophers, and in a sense, these thinkers were rightly
5   considered philosophers, for the questions they dealt with were philosophical: How do we discover truth? How should life be lived? What is the nature of God? But on the whole, the term has a meaning different from the usual meaning of *philosopher*.
10 The philosophes were intellectuals, often not formally trained or associated with a university. They were usually more literary than scientific. They generally extended, applied, popularized, or propagandized ideas of others rather than originating
15 those ideas themselves. The philosophes were more likely to write plays, satires, pamphlets, or simply participate in verbal exchanges at select gatherings than to write formal philosophical books.

It was the philosophes who developed the
20 philosophy of the Enlightenment and spread it to much of the educated elite in Western Europe (and the American colonies). Although the sources for their philosophy can be traced to the Scientific Revolution in general, the philosophes were most
25 influenced by their understanding of Newton, Locke, and English institutions.

The philosophes saw Newton as the great synthesizer of the Scientific Revolution who rightly described the universe as ordered, mechanical,
30 material, and only originally set in motion by God, who since then has remained relatively inactive. Newton's synthesis showed to the philosophes that reason and nature were compatible: Nature functioned logically and discernibly, and what was natu-
35 ral was also reasonable. Newton exemplified the value of reasoning based on concrete experience. The philosophes felt that his empirical methodology was the correct path to discovering truth.

John Locke (1632–1704) agreed with Newton
40 but went further. This English thinker would not exempt even the mind from the mechanical laws of the material universe. In his *Essay Concerning Human Understanding* (1691), Locke pictured the human brain at birth as a blank sheet of paper
45 on which nothing would ever be written except sense perception and reason. What human beings become depends on their experiences—on the information received through the senses. Schools and social institutions could therefore play a great
50 role in molding the individual from childhood to adulthood. Human beings were thus by nature far more malleable than had been assumed. This empirical psychology of Locke rejected the notion that human beings were born with innate ideas or
55 that revelation was a reliable source of truth. Locke also enunciated liberal and reformist political ideas in his *Second Treatise of Civil Government* (1690), which influenced the philosophes. On the whole, Locke's empiricism, psychology, and politics were
60 appealing to the philosophes.

England, not coincidentally the country of Newton and Locke, became the admired model for many of the philosophes. They tended to idealize it, but England did seem to allow greater individual
65 freedom, tolerate religious differences, and evidence greater political reform than other countries, especially France. England seemed to have gone furthest in freeing itself from traditional institutions and accepting the new science of the seventeenth century.
70 Moreover, England's approach seemed to work, for England was experiencing relative political stability and prosperity. The philosophes wanted to see in their own countries much of what England already seemed to have.

GO ON TO THE NEXT PAGE

75   Many philosophes reflected the influence of
Newton, Locke, and English institutions, but
perhaps the most representative in his views was
Voltaire (1694–1778). Of all leading figures of
the Enlightenment, he was the most influential.
80 Voltaire, the son of a Paris lawyer, became the idol
of the French intelligentsia while still in his early
twenties. His versatile mind was sparkling; his wit
was mordant. An outspoken critic, he soon ran
afoul of both church and state authorities. First he
85 was imprisoned in the Bastille; later he was exiled
to England. There he encountered the ideas of
Newton and Locke and came to admire English
parliamentary government and tolerance. In *Letters
on the English* (1732), *Elements of the Philosophy of*
90 *Newton* (1738), and other writings, he popularized
the ideas of Newton and Locke, extolled the virtues
of English society, and indirectly criticized French
society. Slipping back into France, he was hidden
for a time and protected by a wealthy woman who
95 became his mistress. Voltaire's facile mind and pen
were never idle. He wrote poetry, drama, history,
essays, letters, and scientific treatises—ninety
volumes in all. The special targets of his cynical wit
were the Catholic church and Christian institutions.
100 Few people in history have dominated their age
intellectually as did Voltaire.

21. The philosophes can best be described as:

A. writers swept up by their mutual
    admiration of John Locke.

B. professors who lectured in philosophy
    at French universities.

C. intellectuals responsible for popular-
    izing Enlightenment ideas.

D. scientists who furthered the work of
    the Scientific Revolution.

22. From the author's point of view, the philosophes
were:

F. Deservedly influential

G. Seriously misguided

H. Unoriginal in their thinking

J. Excellent writers but poor philosophers

23. According to the passage, Locke felt that schools
and social institutions could "play a great role in
molding the individual" (lines 49–50) primarily
because:

A. human beings were born with certain
    innate ideas.

B. human nature becomes more malleable
    with age.

C. society owes each individual the right to
    an education.

D. the human mind is chiefly influenced by
    experience.

24. Based on the information in the passage, which
of the following best describes Newton's view of
the universe?

   I. The universe was initially set in motion
       by God.

  II. Human reason is insufficient to under-
       stand the laws of nature.

 III. The universe operates in a mechanical
       and orderly fashion.

F. I only

G. I and II only

H. I and III only

J. II and III only

GO ON TO THE NEXT PAGE

25. According to the passage, which of the following works questioned the idea that revelation was a reliable source of truth?

    A. *Letters on the English*

    B. *Second Treatise of Civil Government*

    C. *Elements of the Philosophy of Newton*

    D. *Essay Concerning Human Understanding*

26. The passage supports which of the following statements concerning the relationship between Newton and Locke?

    F. Locke's psychology contradicted Newton's belief in an orderly universe.

    G. Locke maintained that Newton's laws of the material universe also applied to the human mind.

    H. Newton eventually came to accept Locke's revolutionary ideas about the human mind.

    J. Newton's political ideas were the basis of Locke's liberal and reformist politics.

27. According to the passage, the philosophes believed that society should:

    I. allow individuals greater freedom.

    II. free itself from traditional institutions.

    III. tolerate religious differences.

    A. I only

    B. I and II only

    C. II and III only

    D. I, II, and III

28. It can be inferred from the passage that the author regards England's political stability and economic prosperity as:

    F. the reason why the philosophes did not idealize England's achievement.

    G. evidence that political reforms could bring about a better way of life.

    H. the result of Voltaire's activities after he was exiled to England.

    J. an indication that the Scientific Revolution had not yet started there.

29. As it is used in line 83, the word *mordant* most nearly means:

    A. random.

    B. intellectual.

    C. gentle.

    D. biting.

30. What function does the statement that philosophes were "more literary than scientific" (line 12) play in the passage?

    F. It demonstrates how the philosophes' writings contributed to political change.

    G. It compares the number of works that Voltaire authored to Newton's output.

    H. It traces the influences of English literary works on French scientists.

    J. It describes the kinds of literary activities the philosophes commonly engaged in.

GO ON TO THE NEXT PAGE

Passage IV

NATURAL SCIENCE: This passage explores the theory that a large asteroid collided with the Earth 65 million years ago.

Sixty-five million years ago, something triggered mass extinctions so profound that they define the geological boundary between the Cretaceous and Tertiary periods (the K-T Boundary). Approxi-
5 mately 75 percent of all animal species, including every species of dinosaur, were killed off; those that survived lost the vast majority of their numbers. The Earth exists in a region of space teeming with asteroids and comets that on collision have fre-
10 quently caused enormous environmental devasta-tion, including extinctions of animal species. Yet few traditional geologists or biologists considered the effect such impacts may have had on the geologic and biologic history of the Earth. Since
15 gradual geologic processes like erosion or repeated volcanic eruptions can explain the topographical development of the Earth, they felt that there was no need to resort to extraterrestrial explanations.

An important theory proposed in 1980 by
20 physicists Luis and Walter Alvarez challenged this view. The Alvarezes argued that an asteroid roughly six miles in diameter collided with the Earth in the K-T Boundary. Although the damage caused by the meteorite's impact would have been great, the dust
25 cloud that subsequently would have enveloped the planet, completely blotting out the sun for up to a year—the result of soil displacement—would have done most of the harm, according to this theory. The plunge into darkness—and the resulting drasti-
30 cally reduced temperatures—would have inter-rupted plant growth, cutting off the food supply to herbivorous species, the loss of which in turn would have starved carnivores. Additional species would have perished as a result of prolonged atmospheric
35 poisoning, acid rain, forest fires, and tidal waves, all initiated by the asteroid's impact.

Some subsequent research not only tended to support the Alvarez theory but suggested that similar impacts may have caused other sharp breaks
40 in Earth's geologic and biologic history. Research in the composition of the Earth revealed a 160-fold enrichment of iridium all over the world in a thin layer of sediments formed at the K-T Boundary. The presence of this element, which is extremely
45 uncommon in the Earth's crust but very common in asteroids and comets, suggested that a meteorite must have struck Earth at that time. Additional physical evidence of such a strike was found in rock samples, which contained shocked quartz crystals
50 and microtektites (small glass spheres)—both by-products of massive collisions.

Observation of the lunar surface provided fur-ther evidence of the likelihood of a massive strike. Since the moon and the Earth lie within the same
55 swarm of asteroids and comets, their impact histo-ries should be parallel. Although some lunar craters were of volcanic origin, over the last four billion years at least five impact craters ranging from 31 to 58 miles in diameter have marred the lunar surface.
60 Therefore, over the same time span, Earth must have experienced some 400 collisions of similar magnitude. Although such an impact crater had not been found, Alvarez supporters didn't consider finding it necessary or likely. They reasoned that
65 geologic processes over 65 million years, like ero-sion and volcanic eruptions, would have obscured the crater, which in any case probably formed on the ocean floor.

Traditional biologists and geologists resisted
70 the Alvarez theory. They pointed to the absence of any impact crater; to the fact that iridium, while rare at the Earth's surface, was common at its core and could be transported to the surface by volcanic activity; and to the fact that the Alvarezes, though
75 eminent physicists, were not biologists, geologists, or paleontologists.

GO ON TO THE NEXT PAGE

31. According to the Alvarez theory, the mass extinctions of animal species at the end of the Cretaceous period were caused by:

   A. animals being crushed by an enormous asteroid.

   B. processes like erosion and repeated volcanic eruptions.

   C. extreme global warming causing a global firestorm.

   D. environmental conditions following a meteorite impact.

32. Based on the information in the passage, the author probably believes that those who held the traditional views about the topographical development of the Earth were:

   F. proven incorrect by the Alvarezes.

   G. skeptical about the new evidence of iridium.

   H. correct in challenging alternative views.

   J. unreceptive to new evidence.

33. As it is used in line 42, the word *enrichment* most nearly means:

   A. wealth.

   B. improvement.

   C. increase in amount.

   D. reward.

34. The views of scientists who opposed the Alvarez theory would have been strengthened if:

   F. major deposits of iridium were found in the lava flows of active Earth volcanoes.

   G. iridium were absent in sediments corresponding to several episodes of mass extinction.

   H. iridium were absent in fragments of several recently recovered meteorites.

   J. the Alvarezes were biologists as well as physicists.

35. The author's attitude toward the Alvarez theory is best characterized as:

   A. dismissive.

   B. neutral.

   C. skeptical.

   D. supportive.

36. According to the passage, which of the following is the correct order of events in the Alvarez theory explaining the mass extinction of species at the end of the Cretaceous period?

   F. Soil displacement, disappearance of the sun, decline of plant life, fall in temperature

   G. Soil displacement, disappearance of the sun, fall in temperature, decline of plant life

   H. Fall in temperature, decline of plant life, soil displacement, disappearance of the sun

   J. Disappearance of the sun, fall in temperature, decline of plant life, soil displacement

GO ON TO THE NEXT PAGE

37. The author discusses the Alvarezes' description of environmental conditions at the end of the Cretaceous period in order to:

   A. demonstrate that an immense meteorite hit the Earth.

   B. explain why no trace of an impact crater has yet been found.

   C. show that the Earth is vulnerable to meteorite collisions.

   D. clarify how a meteorite may account for mass extinctions.

38. The author's statement (lines 8–9) that "Earth exists in a region of space teeming with asteroids and comets" is important to:

   F. the Alvarezes' claim that an asteroid's impact caused atmospheric poisoning, acid rain, forest fires, and tidal waves.

   G. the Alvarezes' view that the resulting dust cloud, rather than the impact of the meteorite, did most of the harm.

   H. the Alvarezes' argument that frequent damaging collisions must have occurred.

   J. traditionalists' view that topographical development of the Earth can be explained by gradual geologic processes.

39. Supporters of the Alvarezes' theory believe finding the impact crater is not necessary because:

   I. the crater probably is on the ocean floor.

   II. iridium occurs at the Earth's core.

   III. processes like erosion and volcanic eruptions obscured the crater.

   A. I only

   B. I and II only

   C. I and III only

   D. II and III only

40. As it is used in line 2, the word *profound* most nearly means:

   F. at a great depth.

   G. difficult to understand

   H. very important.

   J. sincere

IF YOU FINISH BEFORE TIME IS CALLED, YOU MAY CHECK YOUR WORK ON THIS SECTION ONLY. DO NOT TURN TO ANY OTHER SECTION IN THE TEST. **STOP**

SCIENCE TEST

35 Minutes—40 Questions

Directions: The Science Test includes multiple passages. Each passage includes multiple questions. After reading each passage, choose the best answer and fill in the corresponding bubble on your answer sheet. You may review the passages as often as necessary.

You may NOT use a calculator on this test.

Passage I

The growth of flowering plants and trees can depend on a number of factors, including the type of soil in which the plant is grown and the latitude where it is grown. Table 1, shown here, contains typical soil types, latitudes, and adult heights for several different varieties of a particular flowering plant.

Table 1			
Variety	Soil type	Latitude (degrees)	Height (meters)
Lagerstroemia indica × *fauriei* 'Apalachee'	Soil alone	28	5.2
Lagerstroemia indica 'Catawba'	Soil and organic compost	28	2.7
Lagerstroemia 'Chickasaw'	Soil alone	28	0.9
Lagerstroemia 'Choctaw'	Soil and mulch	28	7.3
Lagerstroemia indica 'Conestoga'	Soil alone	28	2.4
Lagerstroemia fauriei 'Kiowa'	Soil and organic compost	28	8.3
Lagerstroemia 'Miami'	Soil alone	28	6.4
Lagerstroemia 'Natchez'	Soil and mulch	33	5.8
Lagerstroemia 'Natchez'	Soil and natural fertilizer	28	8.6
Lagerstroemia 'Natchez'	Soil and artificial fertilizer	28	7.6
Lagerstroemia indica 'Potomac'	Soil alone	28	4.6
Lagerstroemia 'Tuscarora'	Soil alone	25	4.9

GO ON TO THE NEXT PAGE

The rate of flowering for many trees, such as the pecan tree, depends on the age of the organism. Growth occurs in several distinct phases, which reflect changes in the development of the tree over time. See Figure 1.

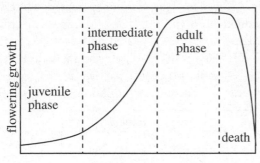

Figure1

1. Based on the information presented in Table 1, if a young *Lagerstroemia* 'Natchez' were planted at a latitude of 28 degrees, its adult height would most likely be:

   A. less than 6.0 meters.

   B. between 6.0 and 6.5 meters.

   C. between 6.5 and 7.5 meters.

   D. greater than 7.5 meters.

2. Flowering growth increases most rapidly during which of the following phases?

   F. Juvenile phase

   G. Intermediate phase

   H. Adult phase

   J. Death

3. Based on the information contained within Table 1, which of the following varieties grown in soil alone reaches the greatest adult height?

   A. *Lagerstroemia indica* 'Conestoga'

   B. *Lagerstroemia* 'Miami'

   C. *Lagerstroemia indica* 'Potomac'

   D. *Lagerstroemia* 'Tuscarora'

4. Seedlings of the plant varieties shown in Table 1 were planted in a patch of soil enriched with organic compost at a latitude of 28 degrees. Which of the following varieties would probably come closest to an adult height of 3 meters?

   F. *Lagerstroemia indica* 'Catawba'

   G. *Lagerstroemia* 'Chickasaw'

   H. *Lagerstroemia fauriei* 'Kiowa'

   J. *Lagerstroemia* 'Natchez'

5. Which of the following hypotheses about flowering trees is supported by the information displayed in Figure 1?

   A. Flowering growth increases at a constant rate throughout the life cycle of the tree.

   B. The flowering growth of juvenile trees begins to increase sharply immediately after they are planted.

   C. The flowering growth of juvenile trees begins to decrease immediately after they are planted.

   D. Young trees experience relatively little flowering growth until they reach a certain point in their development.

6. If a *Lagerstroemia indica* 'Potomac' shrub that is almost 5 meters tall and is located at 28 degrees latitude were observed for one year, what trend of flowering growth would most likely be observed?

   F. The shrub would not produce flowers during that time.

   G. Its flowering growth rate would substantially increase.

   H. Its flowering growth rate would substantially decrease.

   J. Its flowering growth rate would remain about the same.

GO ON TO THE NEXT PAGE

Passage II

The *atomic mass* (A) of an atom is equal to its total number of protons and neutrons, while the *atomic number* (Z) equals its number of protons. *Isotopes* of a given element have the same number of protons but different numbers of neutrons. Isotopes that are *radioactive* have unstable nuclei and decay by emitting alpha (α) particles, beta (β) particles, and/or gamma (γ) rays to become stable.

A series of α and β decay reactions is called a *radioactive decay chain*. This decay process will continue until a relatively stable nucleus is reached—for example, unstable parent nuclei will decay to form daughter nuclei, which if unstable will further decay to form granddaughter nuclei, and so on.

During α decay, an α particle, which consists of 2 protons and 2 neutrons, is emitted from the nucleus, as illustrated in the following reaction equation:

$$^{A}_{Z}X \rightarrow \, ^{A-4}_{Z-2}X' + \, ^{4}_{2}\alpha$$

parent   daughter   alpha particle

During β decay, a neutron is converted to a proton and a high-energy electron, which is emitted as a β particle, as illustrated in the following reaction equation:

$$^{A}_{Z}X \rightarrow \, ^{A}_{Z+1}X' + \, ^{0}_{-1}\beta$$

parent   daughter   beta particle

Scientists performed 2 experiments with 6 different isotopes (A–F) to investigate their decay processes and to measure the radiation they emit during decay.

Experiment 1

Isotope A was placed in a cloud chamber, a device that can detect α and β particles by the paths they produce. Tracks of the particles emitted during decay were observed for 3 generations (parent, daughter, and granddaughter) and the type of decay was recorded. The experiment was repeated with Isotopes B, C, D, E, and F. The results can be found in Table 1, shown here ("+" indicates that a particle of that type was emitted, "−" indicates no emission of that type).

Table 1						
	Parent		Daughter		Granddaughter	
Isotope	α	β	α	β	α	β
A	+	−	+	−	+	−
B	−	+	−	+	+	−
C	+	−	+	−	−	−
D	−	+	+	−	−	+
E	+	−	−	+	−	−
F	−	+	−	−	−	−

Experiment 2

The scientists used a proportional counter, a type of gaseous ionization detector, to measure the radiation energy in megaelectronvolts (MeV) emitted during the decay of Isotopes A–F (see Table 2).

Table 2			
	Radiation energy emitted (MeV)		
Isotope	Parent	Daughter	Granddaughter
A	5.4	5.7	6.3
B	0.1	2.1	5.4
C	6.0	6.8	−
D	0.3	5.0	0.1
E	6.0	1.8	−
F	1.4	−	−

GO ON TO THE NEXT PAGE

7. What is the radiation energy emitted by the daughter nucleus for Isotope B ?

    A. 0.1 MeV

    B. 2.1 MeV

    C. 5.7 MeV

    D. 6.8 MeV

8. According to Table 1, how many total neutrons were emitted from Isotope C ?

    F. 0

    G. 2

    H. 4

    J. 8

9. The scientists examined a seventh isotope, Isotope G, and found the radiation energy emitted by the parent and daughter nuclei to be 6.2 and 0.7 MeV, respectively. Based on the experiments, what particles were most likely emitted during each generation?

	parent	daughter
A.	alpha	alpha
B.	alpha	beta
C.	beta	alpha
D.	beta	beta

10. Based on the data presented in Table 1, which isotope became stable after only one generation?

    F. Isotope A

    G. Isotope C

    H. Isotope E

    J. Isotope F

11. Compared to the atomic mass of the parent nucleus, the atomic mass of the daughter nucleus for Isotope A is:

    A. 4 less.

    B. 4 greater.

    C. 2 less.

    D. 2 greater.

12. Which of the following ranks the total radiation energy emitted over 3 generations for Isotopes A, E, and F from least to greatest?

    F. Isotope A, Isotope E, Isotope F

    G. Isotope E, Isotope F, Isotope A

    H. Isotope F, Isotope A, Isotope E

    J. Isotope F, Isotope E, Isotope A

13. The decay chain $^{212}_{83}X \rightarrow {}^{208}_{81}X' \rightarrow {}^{208}_{82}X''$ could apply to which of the following isotopes?

    A. Isotope A

    B. Isotope B

    C. Isotope E

    D. Isotope F

GO ON TO THE NEXT PAGE

Passage III

Ultraviolet (UV) light, a component of natural sunlight, can be damaging to human skin at high doses. UV light occurs in several ranges, including less damaging UV-A light and more damaging UV-B and UV-C light. Scientists designed 2 experiments to investigate the various factors affecting levels of UV light in a certain region of the United States.

Experiment 1

Scientists studied how levels of UV-A light vary seasonally and with elevation. They measured UV-A energy over a 10-minute span of time for several days to determine an average daily UV-A value for each site. Three sites were studied at 3 different elevations, and measurements from each site were obtained once in the winter and once in the summer. UV-A levels for an average 10-minute period beginning 30 minutes after the sun appeared directly overhead were calculated in millijoules per square centimeter (mJ/cm^2). The results are shown in Table 1.

Table 1		
Season	Elevation (meters above sea level)	Average UV-A level (mJ/cm^2)
Winter	0	1,270
	1,000	1,400
	2,000	1,530
Summer	0	1,580
	1,000	1,740
	2,000	1,900

Experiment 2

Next, the levels of UV-A and UV-B were measured at 0, 1, and 2 hours past the time of day at which the sun was directly overhead during the winter at the site with an elevation of 2,000 meters above sea level. The level of UV-A decreased from 1,620 mJ/cm^2 at 0 hours to 1,430 mJ/cm^2 at 2 hours. The level of UV-B decreased from 48 mJ/cm^2 at 0 hours to 42 mJ/cm^2 at 2 hours.

Experiment 3

UV-B light reaches the Earth's surface at a lower rate than UV-A light, but with higher energy. Levels of UV-B light, in millijoules per square centimeter (mJ/cm^2), were measured at various times of day during the summer at the site with an elevation of 2,000 meters above sea level. The results are shown in Table 2.

Table 2	
Hours after sun is directly overhead	Average UV-B level (mJ/cm^2)
0	68
1	63
2	57
3	49
4	41

14. Which of the following quantities was the independent variable in Experiment 3 ?

    F. Background levels of UV-A light

    G. Background levels of UV-B light

    H. Time of day

    J. Season of the year

15. According to the results of the experiments detailed in the passage, one way to reduce exposure to UV-A light would be to:

    A. spend time in environments with higher levels of UV-B light.

    B. live in an area with shorter summers and longer winters.

    C. live in an area with longer summers and shorter winters.

    D. live in a home with windows designed to filter out UV-B light.

GO ON TO THE NEXT PAGE

16. Based on the results of the experiments from the passage, if a researcher compared UV-B levels when the sun is directly overhead to those when the sun is low on the horizon later in the day, the UV-B levels:

    F. when the sun is overhead would be lower than when the sun is low on the horizon.

    G. when the sun is overhead would be higher than when the sun is low on the horizon.

    H. when the sun is overhead would be the same as when the sun is low on the horizon.

    J. would be measurable only when the sun is overhead.

17. UV-C light is a third type of UV light that was not directly studied in the experiments from the passage. However, if UV-C behaves like the other types of UV light, a new experiment investigating UV-C would most likely reveal that UV-C levels:

    A. decrease from year to year.

    B. increase from year to year.

    C. are higher when the sun is directly overhead.

    D. are lower when the sun is directly overhead.

18. Based on the experimental results from the passage, as the number of hours after the sun is directly overhead increases:

    F. UV-A and UV-B levels both increase.

    G. UV-A levels increase and UV-B levels decrease.

    H. UV-A levels decrease and UV-B levels increase.

    J. UV-A and UV-B levels both decrease.

19. A community near the region studied has an elevation of 3,000 meters above sea level. At a time 30 minutes after the sun is directly over-head, measurement of UV-A levels during the summer would most likely be:

    A. less than 1,580 mJ/cm^2.

    B. between 1,580 and 1,740 mJ/cm^2.

    C. between 1,740 and 1,900 mJ/cm^2.

    D. above 1,900 mJ/cm^2.

20. Based on the passage, which of the following is most likely to be the average UV-B level measured in winter one hour after the sun is directly overhead at the site with the elevation of 2,000 meters?

    F. 45 mJ/cm^2

    G. 48 mJ/cm^2

    H. 57 mJ/cm^2

    J. 63 mJ/cm^2

GO ON TO THE NEXT PAGE

Passage IV

The following experiments were performed to study the motion of gyroscopes, objects that spin quickly around an axis of rotation, which exhibit more complex motion when placed on a surface with their axis tilted. These experiments focus on the gyroscopes' rate of *precession*, or the rate at which they revolve around the point where the axis of rotation touches the surface (see Diagram 1).

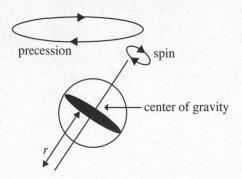

Diagram 1

Experiment 1

A scientist tested several different gyroscopes that differed only in the distance (r) from the gyroscope's center of gravity to the surface (see Diagram 1). A mechanical device was used to spin each gyroscope at the exact same spin rate on the same surface, and the rate of precession was measured for each gyroscope in revolutions per minute (rpm). These precession rates are given in Table 1.

Table 1	
r (centimeters)	Precession rate (rpm)
4	9
6	14
8	19
10	24
12	28

Experiment 2

Next, the scientist used a gyroscope of fixed size and varied the settings on the mechanical device spinning the gyroscope. The precession rate was measured several times for different spin rates, also measured in revolutions per minute (rpm). The results of this experiment are given in Table 2.

Table 2	
Spin rate (rpm)	Precession rate (rpm)
250	41
400	25.5
600	17
750	14
1,200	8.5

Experiment 3

Finally, the scientist placed gyroscopes similar to those used in the first 2 experiments on board a satellite orbiting Earth. It was found that for a gyroscope of fixed size and spin rate, its precession rate on the satellite was about one-eighth of its precession rate on Earth's surface. For example, a precession rate of 24 rpm on Earth would become approximately 3 rpm on the satellite.

21. If, during Experiment 1, the scientists had tested a sixth gyroscope with a center of gravity that was 9 cm from the surface, its precession rate would most likely have been:

    A. 4 rpm.

    B. 9 rpm.

    C. 21.5 rpm.

    D. 23.5 rpm.

GO ON TO THE NEXT PAGE

22. According to the results of Experiment 1, it is reasonable to conclude that the gyroscope's precession rate increases as the gyroscope's center of gravity:

    F. decreases in distance from the surface.

    G. increases in distance from the surface.

    H. moves closer to the axis of rotation.

    J. moves farther away from the axis of rotation.

23. Of the following graphs, which best represents how changes in precession rate are related to changes in spin rate, as demonstrated in Experiment 2 ?

A.

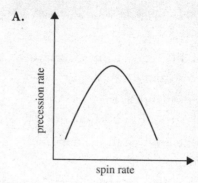

B.

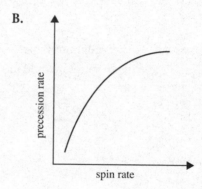

C.

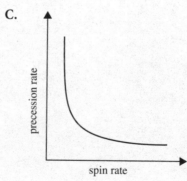

D.

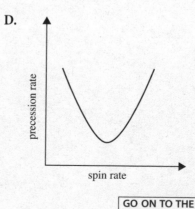

GO ON TO THE NEXT PAGE

24. The hypothesis of the scientist in Experiment 3 was that precession rate is related to the acceleration due to gravity, which decreases as one's distance from Earth increases. To confirm this hypothesis, the scientist should repeat this experiment on:

    F. several different satellites at varying distances from Earth.

    G. another satellite at the exact same distance from Earth as the first satellite.

    H. a satellite orbiting in the opposite direction.

    J. Earth's surface while varying the gyroscope's spin rate.

25. If an r of 6 cm was used throughout Experiment 2, what was the most likely spin rate used in Experiment 1 ?

    A. 400 rpm

    B. 600 rpm

    C. 750 rpm

    D. 1,200 rpm

26. If the information revealed by Experiment 1 had not been considered during the design of Experiment 2, which of the following design shortcomings would most likely have altered Experiment 2's results?

    F. Using gyroscopes with different masses

    G. Using gyroscopes of different sizes

    H. Using gyroscopes with different shapes

    J. Using gyroscopes on surfaces made of different materials

27. Which of the following would constitute the best way to investigate the effect of gyroscope mass on precession rate while keeping the spin rate constant?

    A. Test gyroscopes that are made by different companies.

    B. Test gyroscopes that have a fixed size and shape but are made from different metals with varying densities.

    C. Test gyroscopes that have a fixed size and shape but are measured at different distances from the Earth's surface.

    D. Test gyroscopes that have a fixed mass but vary in size.

GO ON TO THE NEXT PAGE

Passage V

Precipitation is a general term for a form of water, such as rain, snow, sleet, or hail, that falls from the sky to Earth's surface. There are 2 theories that attempt to explain how the tiny water droplets in clouds combine to form precipitation.

Collision-and-Coalescence Theory

As shown in Stage I of Diagram 1, a cloud is initially composed of numerous droplets of liquid water, all of which are of varying sizes but microscopic. As these droplets move about within the cloud, they can collide with one another. These collisions can either result in the droplets' bouncing apart again or sticking together (a process known as *coalescence*) to form a larger droplet (see Stage II). The process continues until the drops formed are so large that they are too heavy to remain suspended in the cloud. Some of these drops will then split apart into smaller droplets that continue the collision and coalescence process, while others will fall to the ground in the form of precipitation (see Stage III).

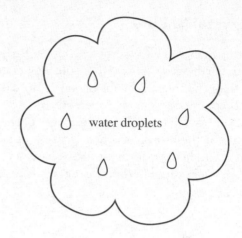

water droplets

Stage I

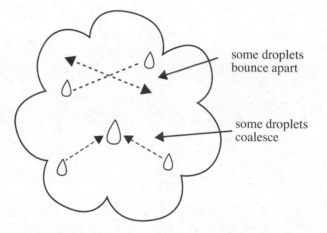

some droplets bounce apart

some droplets coalesce

Stage II

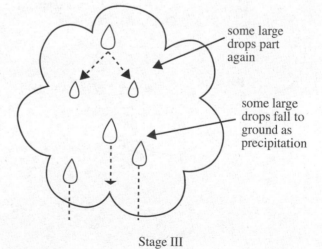

some large drops part again

some large drops fall to ground as precipitation

Stage III

Diagram 1

GO ON TO THE NEXT PAGE

Ice Crystal Theory

In this theory, the tiny droplets in clouds rise to a point in Earth's atmosphere where the temperature is lower than the freezing point of water. Initially, the cloud is composed of many supercooled water droplets that are still in liquid form (see Stage I of Diagram 2). Some of these droplets then freeze around tiny impurities in the air to form miniature ice crystals (see Stage II). Water vapor in the air can then deposit onto the surface of the crystals, while some of the cloud's water droplets evaporate to maintain a constant level of water vapor (see Stage III). The ice crystals quickly become too heavy to remain suspended in the air and fall to the ground, often melting again in the warmer temperatures near the ground to form rain (see Stage IV). The net effect is that the formation of ice crystals takes moisture out of the air, allowing the crystals to grow larger at the expense of the droplets.

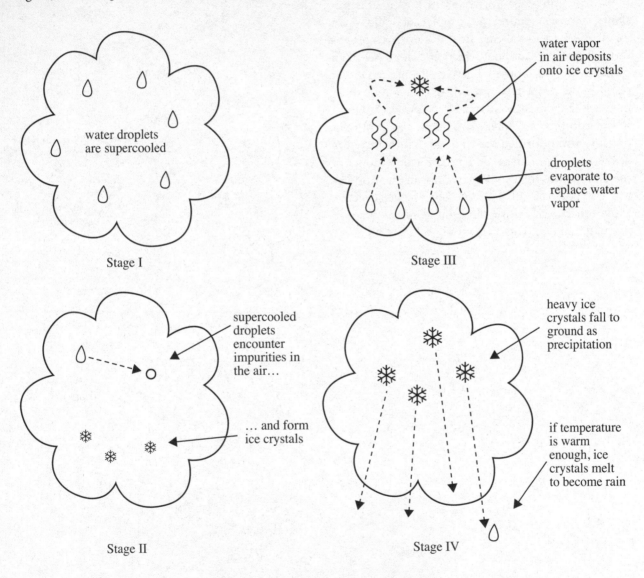

Diagram 2

GO ON TO THE NEXT PAGE

Practice Test 4

28. In which of the following situations would supporters of both theories agree that precipitation would NOT be produced?

    F. A cloud with water droplets colliding and coalescing to produce larger droplets

    G. A cloud with water droplets forming crystals around impurities in the air

    H. A cloud with an insufficient number of water droplets

    J. A cloud containing entities too heavy to remain suspended in the air

29. The Collision-and-Coalescence Theory and the Ice Crystal Theory differ on which of the following points?

    A. Exterior shape of cloud formation

    B. Phase of matter of precipitation before falling from the cloud

    C. Amount of precipitation that reaches the ground

    D. Climate required for precipitation to occur

30. According to the Collision-and-Coalescence Theory, the likelihood of a cloud producing rainfall is greater:

    F. when the droplets collide at a high rate.

    G. when the droplets collide at a variable rate.

    H. when the temperature causes droplets to freeze.

    J. shortly after the last rainfall occurred.

31. A weather balloon travels through a cloud and detects that a high proportion of the cloud's components are too heavy to remain suspended in the air. Both theories would agree that:

    A. there are insufficient impurities in the air to form ice crystals.

    B. the probability of precipitation occurring soon is high.

    C. water droplets in the cloud are colliding at a rapid rate.

    D. the entire cloud is decreasing in altitude.

32. City A has a higher rate of precipitation than City B, despite similar temperatures, humidity levels, and cloud formation rates in both locations. The Ice Crystal Theory would suggest that the higher rate of precipitation in City A most likely results from which of the following?

    F. The greater frequency of thunder-and-lightning storms in City A

    G. Large atmospheric density differences between City A and City B

    H. A greater number of impurities released into the air by factories in City A

    J. The lower rate of air pollution in City A

GO ON TO THE NEXT PAGE

Practice Test 4

33. Which of the following, if true, would best support the Collision-and-Coalescence Theory over the Ice Crystal Theory?

   A. Areas with lower levels of air impurities tend to record less rainfall than those with higher levels.

   B. The amount of water vapor in the atmosphere tends to remain roughly constant over time.

   C. Precipitation can fall from a cloud when its temperature is higher than the freezing point of water.

   D. Water in clouds regularly shifts back and forth between solid, liquid, and gaseous states.

34. Depending on temperature and other conditions, precipitation may change its state before reaching the ground. If precipitation only forms according to the Ice Crystal Theory, which of the following is LEAST likely to occur?

   F. Some ice crystals that fall from a cloud melt to become rain.

   G. Some ice crystals that fall from a cloud partially melt to become sleet.

   H. Some water drops that fall from a cloud freeze to become snow.

   J. Some miniature ice crystals suspended in a cloud melt to become water droplets.

GO ON TO THE NEXT PAGE

Passage VI

Elements from the Periodic Table have a number of different properties that depend on the structure of an element's atoms. For example, some properties depend on the atom's number and arrangement of *electrons* (negatively charged particles), which move in patterns called *shells* (see Diagram 1). The number of electrons in the atom's outermost shell is especially important for determining some elemental properties.

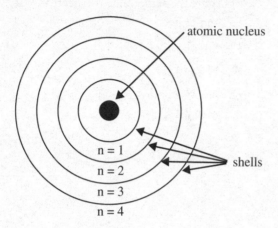

Diagram 1
Note: Drawing is NOT to scale.

Table 1 lists properties for several chemical elements. The table includes each element's atomic symbol; number of shells in the atom (n); number of electrons in the atom's outer shell (e); *atomic radius* (r), distance from the center of the atom's nucleus to the outer shell, in fractions of a meter; *ionization energy* (I), energy in electron volts (eV) required to remove one electron from the atom's outer shell; and *electronegativity* (c), a measure of attraction to electrons in a chemical bond (in Pauling units).

Table 1					
Element	n	e	r ($\times\ 10^{-11}$ m)	I (eV)	c
C	2	4	9.1	11.2	2.5
N	2	5	7.5	14.5	3.0
O	2	6	6.5	13.6	3.5
F	2	7	5.7	17.4	4.0
Si	3	4	14.6	8.2	1.8
P	3	5	12.6	10.5	2.1
S	3	6	10.9	10.4	2.5
Cl	3	7	9.7	13.0	3.0
Ge	4	4	15.2	7.9	1.8
As	4	5	13.3	9.8	2.0
Se	4	6	12.2	9.8	2.4
Br	4	7	11.2	11.8	2.8

35. For any value of n, Table 1 indicates that as e increases, r:

   A. increases only.

   B. sometimes increases and sometimes decreases.

   C. decreases only.

   D. remains unchanged.

GO ON TO THE NEXT PAGE

Practice Test 4

36. Based on Table 1, for an atom with $n = 2$ and $e = 3$, the most likely value of r would be:

   F. 11.7×10^{-11} m.

   G. 8.8×10^{-11} m.

   H. 7.4×10^{-11} m.

   J. 6.2×10^{-11} m.

37. According to information provided in the passage, it is possible to decrease the amount of negative charge in an atom by:

   A.   decreasing the radius of the atom's outer shell.

   B.   forming a chemical bond with the atom.

   C.   applying energy to the atom.

   D.   increasing the number of shells in the atom.

38. The hypothesis that for a given value of n, electronegativity increases as the number of electrons in the atom's outer shell increases, is supported by the data in Table 1 when n is equal to:

   F.   2 only.

   G.   2 or 3 only.

   H.   4 only.

   J.   2, 3, or 4.

39. The most energy will be required to remove an electron from shell:

   A. $n = 3$ in Si.

   B. $n = 3$ in Cl.

   C. $n = 2$ in C.

   D. $n = 2$ in F.

40. Which of the following pairs of elements does not share the same value for electronegativity in Pauling units?

   F.   Se and As

   G.   N and Cl

   H.   Ge and Si

   J.   C and S

WRITING TEST

40 Minutes—1 Question

Directions: The essay is used to evaluate your writing skills. You will have **40 minutes** to review the prompt and plan and write an essay in English. Before you begin, read everything in this test booklet carefully to make sure you understand the task.

Your essay will be judged based on the evidence it provides of your ability to do the following:

- Assert your own perspective on a complex issue and evaluate the relationship between your perspective and at least one other perspective

- Use reasoning and evidence to refine and justify your ideas

- Present your ideas in an organized way

- Convey your ideas effectively using standard written English

Write your essay on the lined essay pages in the answer booklet. All writing on those lined pages will be scored. Use the unlined pages in this test booklet to plan your essay. Your work on these unlined pages will not be scored.

Put your pencil down as soon as time is called.

DO NOT OPEN THIS BOOKLET UNTIL TOLD TO DO SO.

GO ON TO THE NEXT PAGE

Attendance Policies

Students are required to be in attendance during the school day unless they are ill, have a doctor's appointment, or need to attend a funeral. Parents are allowed to take students out of school for other reasons, but prior approval is often required. Truancy, or unexcused absenteeism, is a problem that many schools have yet to solve. Since reducing truancy increases student success, should schools be doing more to prevent unexcused absences? Considering that students rely on educators to offer guidance and support, it is wise for schools to assist students in attending school as regularly as possible.

Read and carefully consider these perspectives. Each suggests a particular approach regarding truancy.

Perspective One	Perspective Two	Perspective Three
Schools should contact law enforcement officers to report students who skip school regularly. In addition to receiving detention for unexcused absences, students who engage in truancy should be given criminal records. This additional consequence will help discourage students from missing school.	Truancy is a symptom rather than a core issue. Students who skip school regularly often do so because of transportation difficulties, social problems, violence concerns, or lack of interest. Addressing the core issues is the key to increasing student attendance, and schools should develop programs to help students overcome obstacles that prevent them from coming to school.	Schools should offer helpful alternative instruction for students who regularly miss school. Whether students are allowed to attend school on the weekends or are required to take classes online, schools should provide students every opportunity to complete their courses and graduate.

Essay Task

Write a clear, well-reasoned essay evaluating multiple perspectives on attendance policies. In your essay, be sure to:

- Assert your own perspective on the issue and evaluate the relationship between your perspective and at least one other perspective

- Use reasoning and evidence to refine and justify your ideas

- Present your ideas in an organized way

- Convey your ideas effectively using standard written English

Your perspective may be fully, somewhat, or not at all in agreement with one or more of the three perspectives in the prompt.

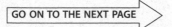
GO ON TO THE NEXT PAGE

Planning Your Essay

These pages are not scored.

Use the space below to brainstorm and plan your essay. Consider the following as you think about the prompt:

- Strengths and weaknesses of the three perspectives in the prompt

  ○ What observations do they offer, and what do they overlook?

  ○ Why are they persuasive or why are they not persuasive?

- Your own background and identity

  ○ What is your perspective on this issue, and what are its strengths and weaknesses?

  ○ What evidence will you use in your essay?

GO ON TO THE NEXT PAGE

Practice Test 4

GO ON TO THE NEXT PAGE

GO ON TO THE NEXT PAGE

Practice Test 4

_____
_____
_____
_____
_____
_____
_____
_____
_____
_____
_____
_____
_____
_____
_____
_____
_____
_____
_____
_____
_____
_____
_____

IF YOU FINISH BEFORE TIME IS CALLED, YOU MAY CHECK YOUR WORK ON THIS SECTION ONLY. DO NOT TURN TO ANY OTHER SECTION IN THE TEST.

PRACTICE TEST 4 ANSWER KEY
ENGLISH TEST

1. **C**	16. **H**	31. **A**	46. **G**	61. **C**
2. **G**	17. **C**	32. **H**	47. **D**	62. **J**
3. **D**	18. **H**	33. **D**	48. **J**	63. **D**
4. **F**	19. **D**	34. **F**	49. **B**	64. **H**
5. **D**	20. **F**	35. **A**	50. **J**	65. **A**
6. **G**	21. **A**	36. **G**	51. **A**	66. **J**
7. **D**	22. **J**	37. **D**	52. **J**	67. **A**
8. **J**	23. **C**	38. **G**	53. **D**	68. **J**
9. **C**	24. **G**	39. **D**	54. **H**	69. **B**
10. **J**	25. **D**	40. **G**	55. **B**	70. **G**
11. **D**	26. **G**	41. **A**	56. **J**	71. **A**
12. **H**	27. **B**	42. **G**	57. **D**	72. **J**
13. **C**	28. **H**	43. **C**	58. **H**	73. **D**
14. **J**	29. **D**	44. **H**	59. **B**	74. **G**
15. **C**	30. **J**	45. **B**	60. **G**	75. **B**

MATHEMATICS TEST

1. **D**	13. **D**	25. **D**	37. **A**	49. **C**
2. **J**	14. **F**	26. **G**	38. **J**	50. **G**
3. **B**	15. **A**	27. **C**	39. **A**	51. **C**
4. **G**	16. **K**	28. **K**	40. **H**	52. **H**
5. **B**	17. **B**	29. **D**	41. **C**	53. **E**
6. **J**	18. **H**	30. **K**	42. **J**	54. **H**
7. **C**	19. **A**	31. **D**	43. **E**	55. **A**
8. **G**	20. **G**	32. **H**	44. **J**	56. **H**
9. **A**	21. **C**	33. **E**	45. **E**	57. **C**
10. **J**	22. **H**	34. **F**	46. **G**	58. **F**
11. **A**	23. **E**	35. **D**	47. **A**	59. **C**
12. **K**	24. **K**	36. **J**	48. **K**	60. **J**

READING TEST

1. **A**	9. **C**	17. **B**	25. **D**	33. **C**
2. **H**	10. **F**	18. **G**	26. **G**	34. **F**
3. **D**	11. **B**	19. **B**	27. **D**	35. **D**
4. **G**	12. **H**	20. **J**	28. **G**	36. **G**
5. **A**	13. **B**	21. **C**	29. **D**	37. **D**
6. **G**	14. **J**	22. **F**	30. **J**	38. **H**
7. **B**	15. **B**	23. **D**	31. **D**	39. **C**
8. **G**	16. **H**	24. **H**	32. **H**	40. **H**

SCIENCE TEST

1. **D**	9. **B**	17. **C**	25. **C**	33. **C**
2. **G**	10. **J**	18. **J**	26. **G**	34. **H**
3. **B**	11. **A**	19. **D**	27. **B**	35. **C**
4. **F**	12. **J**	20. **F**	28. **H**	36. **F**
5. **D**	13. **C**	21. **C**	29. **B**	37. **C**
6. **J**	14. **H**	22. **G**	30. **F**	38. **J**
7. **B**	15. **B**	23. **C**	31. **B**	39. **D**
8. **H**	16. **G**	24. **F**	32. **H**	40. **F**

ANSWERS AND EXPLANATIONS

ENGLISH TEST

Passage I

1. C   Difficulty: High

Category: Punctuation

Getting to the Answer: At first glance, there may not seem to be anything incorrect here. However, the dash after *Aegean Sea* alerts you that the writer has chosen to set off the parenthetical phrase describing *Acropolis* with dashes instead of commas. This means that you have to replace the comma after *Acropolis* with a dash in order to have a matching pair, making (C) correct. If there were a comma after *Aegean Sea*, this underlined part of the sentence would not need to be changed. Knowing that you need to "make it all match" will help you score points on ACT English.

2. G   Difficulty: Medium

Category: Sentence Structure and Formation

Getting to the Answer: "To climb . . . is to have beheld" is unparallel. The two verbs should be in the same form: "to climb . . . is to behold." Choice (G) is correct; it is the only option that offers parallel construction.

3. D   Difficulty: Low

Category: Knowledge of Language / Concision

Getting to the Answer: DELETE the underlined sentence is an option, so check to see if the sentence is either redundant or irrelevant. Athenian cuisine has nothing to do with the subject of the paragraph or the passage, so (D) is correct.

4. F   Difficulty: Medium

Category: Usage

Getting to the Answer: This verb is appropriately plural—the subject, *generations*, is plural—and in the present perfect tense, so (F) is correct. Choices G and H are singular verbs, so they are incorrect. Choice J is incorrect

because generations of architects can't all be proclaiming at the present time.

5. D   Difficulty: Medium

Category: Punctuation

Getting to the Answer: The sentence discusses the columns of the temple, which requires the singular possessive form. Choice (D) correctly indicates that one temple had multiple columns. Choice A is missing a necessary apostrophe. Choice B changes the meaning of the sentence by creating a plural possessive word. Choice C includes the necessary apostrophe but creates a new error by changing the plural *columns* to a singular possessive *column's*.

6. G   Difficulty: Medium

Category: Sentence Structure and Formation

Getting to the Answer: "Viewed from a distance" is a misplaced modifier that has to be moved to a position where it clearly modifies *columns*. Choice (G) accomplishes this. Choices F, H, and J each place the modifying phrase in an incorrect location.

7. D   Difficulty: Medium

Category: Punctuation

Getting to the Answer: The sentence is incorrect as written because the colon is not introducing a short phrase, quotation, explanation, example, or list. There is no need for a semicolon or any other kind of punctuation mark between *of* and *uprightness*, making (D) correct. Don't place a comma before the first element of a series, C, and don't place a colon between a preposition and its objects, B.

8. J   Difficulty: Medium

Category: Organization, Unity, and Cohesion / Transitions

Getting to the Answer: The phrase "Because of this" doesn't make sense here. The optical illusion the architects created is not the reason you'll get a different impression of the Parthenon from the one the ancient

Athenians had; the reason is that the statue of Athena Parthenos isn't there anymore. The introductory phrase that makes sense won't suggest conclusion or contrast; it will emphasize the information in the sentence, making (J) correct.

9. C   Difficulty: Medium

Category: Sentence Structure and Formation

Getting to the Answer: "Only by standing . . . Golden Age of Athens" is a sentence fragment that has to be connected to the sentence after it to fix the error, so you can eliminate A and D. You can't use a semicolon to join the two, B, because then the first clause of the new sentence will still be only a fragment. You have to reverse the subject and verb of the second sentence to attach the fragment to it, as (C) does.

10. J   Difficulty: High

Category: Sentence Structure and Formation

Getting to the Answer: What was removed from the temple? The underlined part of the sentence is an introductory modifying phrase that you know describes the statue, but the word *statue* isn't anywhere in the sentence. As a result, the sentence doesn't make sense at all; it's impossible that "all that remains" in the temple was removed in the fifth century CE. Choice (J) fixes the error and provides the clearest wording.

11. D   Difficulty: Medium

Category: Usage

Getting to the Answer: Quite a few words come between the subject and the verb of this sentence; *many* is the subject of the sentence, not *carvings, walls,* or *Acropolis.* Because *many* is plural, the verb of the sentence has to be plural as well. *Is* has to be changed to *are,* which matches (D).

12. H   Difficulty: High

Category: Sentence Structure and Formation

Getting to the Answer: This sentence is really only a sentence fragment; it has a subject, *decision,* but no verb. Choice (H) rewords the underlined portion to make *Lord Elgin* the subject and *decided* the verb.

13. C   Difficulty: Medium

Category: Knowledge of Language / Ambiguity

Getting to the Answer: *They* is an ambiguous pronoun because it's not immediately clear what group *they* refers to. You can figure out from the context that *they* is *the Greeks;* no other group could have won independence from the Turks and demanded the carvings back from the British. Choice (C) is correct.

14. J   Difficulty: Medium

Category: Organization, Unity, and Cohesion / Passage Organization

Getting to the Answer: What could have been destroyed by explosions in the Parthenon? Carvings. The fact that some of the carvings were destroyed during a war is another good reason that many of them can no longer be found in the Parthenon, as Paragraph 4 states. Therefore, the new material belongs in Paragraph 4, and (J) is correct.

15. C   Difficulty: Medium

Category: Topic Development / Writer's Purpose

Getting to the Answer: The answer to the question is "No." The writer did not fulfill the request, because only the second paragraph discusses techniques of construction at all; even then, only one technique, the bulging of the columns, is described in any detail. The author covers several topics in the essay in addition to construction techniques, including the statue of Athena Parthenos and the fate of the carvings, which matches (C).

Passage II

16. H   Difficulty: Low

Category: Usage

Getting to the Answer: The previous sentence tells you that "Robin is the hero," so look for a verb form that matches the present tense *is* because the sentence continues the discussion of the ballads. In (H), *tell* is in the right tense. Choice F switches to another tense, the present progressive, which makes it sound as if the ballads were literally speaking. Choice G lacks a main verb, creating a sentence fragment. Choice J has the same tense problem as F and compounds it by adding an extra, unnecessary subject, *they.*

17. C **Difficulty:** Medium

Category: Sentence Structure and Formation

Getting to the Answer: You need a verb that is parallel to *robbing* and *killing*, so *giving*, (C), is the correct choice.

18. H **Difficulty:** Medium

Category: Usage

Getting to the Answer: The adjective *frequent* is the correct choice to modify the noun *enemy*, making (H) correct. Choice A uses both the word *most* and the suffix *-est* to indicate the highest degree, or superlative form. Use one or the other, but not both. Likewise, G incorrectly uses *more* and the suffix *-er* together. Both of these express the comparative form—but again, you'd use one or the other, not both at once. In J, *frequently* is an adverb, which can't describe a noun.

19. D **Difficulty:** High

Category: Topic Development / Supporting Material

Getting to the Answer: Eliminate A and B because the proposed sentence discusses a modern adaptation of the King Arthur legend, which does not provide direct support the main focus of the paragraph: the legend of Robin Hood. Choice C is incorrect because even if the sentence included more than one example, it would still be off-topic. Choice (D) is correct; the sentence should not be added because it is irrelevant to the paragraph's main focus.

20. F **Difficulty:** Medium

Category: Usage

Getting to the Answer: This is correct as is, (F). *Them* matches the plural noun it is standing in for: *writers*. Choices G, *him*, and H, *it*, are singular, so they don't. Choice J is too wordy.

21. A **Difficulty:** Medium

Category: Punctuation

Getting to the Answer: Choice (A) is correct because the possessive apostrophe is necessary. Choices B and C are incorrect because they are the plural, not the possessive, form of *king*. Choice D is incorrect because the comma is unnecessary.

22. J **Difficulty:** Medium

Category: Topic Development / Supporting Material

Getting to the Answer: Because this passage is aimed at discussing the historical development of the Robin Hood legend, (J) is most in keeping with the subject matter. Choice F goes way off track; you're asked to add more information on Richard I, not on English history. The main topic of the passage is Robin Hood, not antiquaries, as in G. (Remember, you want the choice that is most relevant to the passage as a whole.) As for H, King Arthur was mentioned earlier in the passage, but only to make a point about Robin Hood. A discussion of Richard I's interest in King Arthur would stray from the topic of the passage.

23. C **Difficulty:** Low

Category: Sentence Structure and Formation

Getting to the Answer: The shortest answer—(C)— is the best choice because it provides a verb, *was*, and an article, *a*. Choices A and D incorrectly imply a comparison between Robin and a nobleman, when the claim was that Robin was a nobleman. Choice B is incoherent.

24. G **Difficulty:** Medium

Category: Knowledge of Language / Style and Tone

Getting to the Answer: The comparison with a puppy doesn't match the matter-of-fact tone of this passage; all choices except (G) can be eliminated.

25. D **Difficulty:** Medium

Category: Punctuation

Getting to the Answer: The only choice that will tie in both parts of the sentence is (D). A dash in this context correctly makes an emphatic pause between *love interest* and its appositive, *Maid Marian*. All the rest of the choices have punctuation errors. Semicolons are used between independent clauses, and the part that would follow the semicolon in A isn't a clause. The plural form of the noun, *interests*, B, doesn't agree with the singular article. Choice C can be ruled out because there is no reason to pause in the middle of a name, and so the comma is incorrectly placed.

26. G   Difficulty: Medium

Category: Usage

Getting to the Answer: The correct verb tense, and the only choice that doesn't create a sentence fragment, is (G). Choices F, H, and J create fragments.

27. B   Difficulty: Medium

Category: Punctuation

Getting to the Answer: The underlined portion includes two commas; check to make sure they are both necessary. Choices A and C are incorrect because the comma after *Robin* is unnecessary. Choice (B) is correct because the comma after *Britain* separates the dependent clause before the comma from the independent clause after the comma. Choice D eliminates the necessary comma after *Britain*, so it is incorrect.

28. H   Difficulty: High

Category: Organization, Unity, and Cohesion / Passage Organization

Getting to the Answer: The passage moves to a discussion of a new time period after Point C, so you should begin a new paragraph there, matching (H). Choices F, G, and J are incorrect because they do not offer logical options.

29. D   Difficulty: Medium

Category: Topic Development / Supporting Material

Getting to the Answer: You're told that the audience is unfamiliar with the story, so it would make sense to include a summary of the Robin Hood legend, (D), something the passage lacks. Choices A and C would do nothing for a reader curious about Robin Hood, because they go off on tangents about other issues. As the passage states that Robin Hood's existence is questionable (*legendary*), B doesn't fit in with the stance of the writer.

30. J   Difficulty: Low

Category: Topic Development / Writer's Purpose

Getting to the Answer: Rarely are ACT English passages written for authorities or experts; they're usually written for the general public, as (J) correctly states in this question. If the passage were directed toward *experts*, F, or *authorities*, G, much of the basic information it presents would be unnecessary and therefore not included. The passage states that the existence of Robin Hood is legendary, so the passage can't be aimed at readers craving confirmation that he "was an actual historical personage." So H is incorrect.

Passage III

31. A   Difficulty: Low

Category: Knowledge of Language / Concision

Getting to the Answer: The shortest answer, (A), is correct. *Ten-mile* is correctly punctuated: the hyphen makes it an adjective modifying *radius*. The other answers—B, C, and D—are wordy and awkward.

32. H   Difficulty: Medium

Category: Usage

Getting to the Answer: You don't look forward *at* something. You look forward *to* something, so F is incorrect. Choice G incorrectly implies that it is the brother who looks forward to the opportunity to show off the narrator's skills. Choice J incorrectly implies a contrast between the two parts of the sentence. Choice (H) is correct.

33. D   Difficulty: Medium

Category: Organization, Unity, and Cohesion / Transitions

Getting to the Answer: *Ever since* means from the time the narrator first could read to the present time of the narrative, which makes sense in context, so (D) is correct. *If* in A signals a hypothetical situation, rather than a period of time. *Since* in B implies a cause-and-effect relationship that doesn't make sense in context. *Although* in C signals a contrast, but there isn't one.

34. F   Difficulty: Low

Category: Usage

Getting to the Answer: It's true that you use *I* and *me*, in G and H, when you're writing about yourself. However, you can't say "I always envisioned I" or "I always envisioned me." Per the rules of grammar, you have to say "I always envisioned myself," as in (F).

35. A   **Difficulty:** Medium

Category: Punctuation

Getting to the Answer: Choice (A) is correct because the comma separates the dependent clause "giving me . . . international event" from the rest of the sentence. You don't need a colon, as in B; colons signal lists or definitions. You don't need a semicolon, as in C, either—a semicolon should be placed between clauses that could stand alone as sentences, but the second part of this sentence can't. Choice D creates a sentence with no verb.

36. G   **Difficulty:** Medium

Category: Sentence Structure and Formation

Getting to the Answer: This is an example of a misplaced modifier. Choices F and H make it sound as if it is the airport, and not the pilot, that is filing the flight plan. Choice J is awkward (it uses a passive construction) and is wordy. Choice (G) is concise, and the verbs *filed* and *gave* are parallel.

37. D   **Difficulty:** Medium

Category: Punctuation

Getting to the Answer: The colon in the original interrupts the flow of the sentence, so A is incorrect. Colons signal lists or definitions, but nothing needs to be equated in this sentence, so B is incorrect as well. Choice C includes unnecessary commas. The correct answer is (D).

38. G   **Difficulty:** Medium

Category: Organization, Unity, and Cohesion / Passage Organization

Getting to the Answer: The sentence should appear after "As we departed Troutdale airport, my Cessna 152 ascended slowly on its way toward Mt. St. Helens," and before "A few other pilots were also circling around the crater." Choice (G) is correct. Choices F, H, and J do not place the sentence in a logical location within the paragraph.

39. D   **Difficulty:** Low

Category: Knowledge of Language / Concision

Getting to the Answer: Because *speechless* and *mute* mean the same thing, it's redundant to use both of them. "DELETE the underlined portion," (D), is correct.

40. G   **Difficulty:** Medium

Category: Usage

Getting to the Answer: *Steadying* and *took* should be in parallel form, so F and H are incorrect. This makes (G)—with *steadying* and *taking*—correct. The verbs in J are parallel, but they're in the present tense, which doesn't fit with the past-tense verbs *shot* and *dictated* in the non-underlined part of the sentence.

41. A   **Difficulty:** Medium

Category: Topic Development / Supporting Material

Getting to the Answer: Jeff and the narrator are circling the mountain, so "a description of Mt. St. Helens," (A), would be appropriate. Choice B contradicts the information in the passage; we're told that the plane must stay high enough to avoid smoke and ash. Choice C sounds as if it belongs in a science textbook rather than in a story. Choice D wanders too far from the direct observation of the Mt. St. Helens volcano, which is the paragraph's focus.

42. G   **Difficulty:** Medium

Category: Organization, Unity, and Cohesion / Transitions

Getting to the Answer: "Since that time," (G), is an appropriate transition. It makes clear the time shift between the day at Mt. St. Helens and the present. The other choices contain inappropriate connecting words. *However* in F and *nevertheless* in J signal contrasts, but there isn't one in the passage. *Furthermore*, H, suggests an elaboration of what came before, but there is no elaboration in the passage.

43. C   **Difficulty:** Medium

Category: Topic Development / Writer's Purpose

Getting to the Answer: Because the author is favorably recalling a memorable past experience, *nostalgic*, (C), is the best choice. The passage is positive in tone. It's definitely not *bitter*, B, or *exhausted*, D. *Optimistic*, A, is close but incorrect. *Optimistic* means "hopeful." The passage focuses on the excitement of the past, not on the good things that might happen.

44. H   **Difficulty:** Medium

Category: Topic Development / Writer's Purpose

Getting to the Answer: The use of *I* is appropriate because this is a firsthand account. First-person narratives are designed to draw the reader in, making the immediacy mentioned in (H) the desired outcome. Choice J is not true, because *I* is not appropriate in all types of writing. The passage is personal and chatty; it's not an example of formal writing. The passage isn't focused on volcanoes in general, as G says, but on the Mt. St. Helens eruption, the narrator's first international story.

45. B   **Difficulty:** High

Category: Organization, Unity, and Cohesion / Passage Organization

Getting to the Answer: The passage reads best if the first and second paragraphs are switched. Choices A, C, and D confuse the time sequence of the narrative, which follows the narrator from early dreams of becoming a photojournalist, to the memorable Mt. St. Helens story, to the present experience as a foreign correspondent.

Passage IV

46. G   **Difficulty:** Low

Category: Knowledge of Language / Concision

Getting to the Answer: The description of Sherlock Holmes as "ingenious and extremely clever" is redundant because *ingenious* and *extremely clever* mean the same thing. You need to use only one of the two to get the point across, so (G) is the only possible option.

47. D   **Difficulty:** High

Category: Organization, Unity, and Cohesion / Transitions

Getting to the Answer: *Therefore* is supposed to be a signal that the sentence that follows is a logical conclusion based on information from the preceding sentence or sentences. The use of *therefore* doesn't make sense here because you can't conclude that everyone knows the phrase "Elementary, my dear Watson," just because everyone knows of Holmes's detective abilities. Choice C is incorrect for the same reason—*for this reason* and

therefore mean the same thing in this context. *Although*, in B, indicates some sort of contrast; this is incorrect because there is no contrast within this sentence or between this sentence and the previous one. Really, there is no need for a structural signal here at all. Choice (D) is correct.

48. J   **Difficulty:** Medium

Category: Knowledge of Language / Precision

Getting to the Answer: You must choose the word that best fits the context of the sentence. The essay discusses Holmes's ability to solve mysteries, which matches (J) since *deductions* are conclusions reached through reasoning. Choices F, G, and H do not make sense in context; the words *tales* and *stories* do not indicate Holmes's logical reasoning skills, and the word *subtractions* is illogical in context.

49. B   **Difficulty:** Medium

Category: Usage

Getting to the Answer: *He* is an ambiguous pronoun because it's unclear whether *he* refers to Conan Doyle or to Sherlock Holmes. You know after reading the entire sentence that *he* is Conan Doyle, so you have to replace *he* with *Conan Doyle* for the sake of clarity. This makes (B) correct.

50. J   **Difficulty:** Medium

Category: Knowledge of Language / Concision

Getting to the Answer: From a grammatical point of view, there is nothing incorrect here; it's just unnecessarily wordy. "To be remembered," (J), is the most concise answer and therefore correct.

51. A   **Difficulty:** Medium

Category: Organization, Unity, and Cohesion / Transitions

Getting to the Answer: *In fact* is the appropriate signal phrase here, so (A) is correct. *Despite this*, *regardless*, and *yet* would all indicate a contrast between this sentence and the previous one. There is no contrast, however; Conan Doyle did not want to be remembered as the author of the Sherlock Holmes stories, so he killed the detective off (at least for a while).

52. J   Difficulty: Medium

Category: Sentence Structure and Formation

Getting to the Answer: A modifying phrase that begins a sentence refers to the noun or pronoun immediately following the phrase. According to that rule, the phrase "having had enough of his famous character by that time" modifies *Sherlock Holmes*, which doesn't make sense. The sentence has to be rearranged so that the introductory phrase describes Conan Doyle. Choice (J) is the choice that accomplishes this.

53. D   Difficulty: Low

Category: Sentence Structure and Formation

Getting to the Answer: The phrase *eight years* and the verb *offering* are connected with the word *and*, so they must have a parallel form. Choice (D) changes the verb to a noun, which matches *years*. Choices A, B, and C are incorrect because they do not offer parallel compounds.

54. H   Difficulty: Medium

Category: Usage

Getting to the Answer: The verb is in the incorrect tense. "Has been deeply immersed" is in the present perfect tense, which is used to describe an action that started in the past and continues to the present or that happened a number of times in the past and may happen again in the future. Because Conan Doyle's immersion in spiritualism is over and done with, you should use the simple past, "was deeply immersed." This makes (H) correct.

55. B   Difficulty: Medium

Category: Sentence Structure and Formation

Getting to the Answer: This is a sentence fragment because there is no subject and verb; all you have is an introductory phrase and a subordinate clause starting with *that*, so A is incorrect. By omitting *that,* you can turn the subordinate clause into a main clause, making *he lectured* the subject and verb, as in (B). Choice C would only work if the sentence began with *so convinced.* Choice D is incorrect because the introductory phrase can't stand alone as a sentence.

56. J   Difficulty: Low

Category: Organization, Unity, and Cohesion / Transitions

Getting to the Answer: Based on the context, the sentence requires a continuation transition, which matches (J). Choices F and H are incorrect because they are contrast transitions. Choice G is incorrect because it is a sequence transition.

57. D   Difficulty: High

Category: Organization, Unity, and Cohesion / Passage Organization

Getting to the Answer: Sentence 2 refers to *these experiences*, so it should come directly after the sentence that describes the paranormal experiences Conan Doyle seemed to have had. Sentence 4 is the one that talks about materialized hands and heavy articles swimming through the air, so Sentence 2 should come after Sentence 4, making (D) correct.

58. H   Difficulty: Medium

Category: Sentence Structure and Formation

Getting to the Answer: There are two problems with the underlined portion of the sentence: the colon does not belong there, and the pronoun *they* is ambiguous because it doesn't refer to anything in particular in the previous sentence. Choice (H) fixes of both of these problems by omitting the colon and by explaining the pronoun.

59. B   Difficulty: Medium

Category: Sentence Structure and Formation

Getting to the Answer: Here, you just have to pick the choice that makes sense. Sherlock Holmes is only a fictional character, so A, C, and D are incorrect; Holmes could not possibly have said anything about Conan Doyle's spiritualism, nor will he ever. You can still wonder, however, what the esteemed detective *would have said*, if he were real. This is the idea behind the last sentence, so since (B) matches that language, it is the correct answer.

60. G   Difficulty: High

Category: Topic Development / Writer's Purpose

Getting to the Answer: The passage contrasts the logical, deductive thinking used by Conan Doyle's fictional character, Sherlock Holmes, with Conan Doyle's own exploration of the paranormal. An appropriate subtitle will reflect this contrast. Choice (G) is the only choice that does.

Passage V

61. C   Difficulty: Medium

Category: Knowledge of Language / Precision

Getting to the Answer: The question provides four words, and you must choose the word that best fits the context of the sentence. The essay indicates that emphasizing auditory, visual, and experiential learning is not a new concept. Choice (C), *groundbreaking*, reflects this idea. Choices A, B, and D do not make sense in context; *fashionable* and *popular* do not refer to how old or new a concept is, and *illustrious* means well-known and respected, which is the opposite of the writer's opinion.

62. J   Difficulty: Medium

Category: Punctuation

Getting to the Answer: The phrase "from corporate management to consulting" is a nonessential phrase that must be properly punctuated. The phrase can be set off from the rest of the sentence with two commas or two dashes, but not a mix of one comma and one dash. Choice (J) fixes the error by changing the comma to a dash. Choices G and H do not fix the issue presented in F.

63. D   Difficulty: Medium

Category: Usage

Getting to the Answer: A pronoun and a verb are underlined, so check to make sure they are both correct. The antecedent is *these slides*, which is plural, so the singular pronoun *it* is incorrect. In addition, the verb must also be plural: *was* should be *were*. Eliminate A and B because they include the singular verb *was*. Choice C is incorrect because the apostrophe makes the word *slides* plural

possessive. Choice (D) is the only option that includes a plural pronoun and verb, so it is correct.

64. H   Difficulty: High

Category: Sentence Structure and Formation

Getting to the Answer: There are several ways to join independent clauses, but only one choice will do so without introducing additional errors. As written, the sentence is a run-on, so F is incorrect. Choice (H) correctly inserts *as* to make the first clause dependent. Choice G does not address the error. Choice J creates a grammatically incorrect sentence.

65. A   Difficulty: Medium

Category: Organization, Unity, and Cohesion / Transitions

Getting to the Answer: When two answer choices have transitions that convey the same meaning and create grammatically correct sentences, you can eliminate both choices because they can't both be right. This sentence is correct as written. Choices B and D use transitions, indicating a contrast, but the idea that people are working on improving visual presentation style does not contrast with the idea that *less cluttered* aids work better than *denser ones*. Choice C uses the transition *similarly*, but the second sentence is an example supporting the first.

66. J   Difficulty: Low

Category: Knowledge of Language / Concision

Getting to the Answer: When the underlined selection consists of two words joined by *and* or *or*, consider whether the two words mean essentially the same thing. If they do, the correct answer choice will eliminate one of them. *Enhance* and *improve*, in this context, mean the same thing, so F is incorrect. Choice (J) omits the redundancy. Choice G is unnecessarily wordy. Choice H does not address the error.

67. A   Difficulty: Low

Category: Punctuation

Getting to the Answer: Items in a list must be separated with commas, so the sentence is correct as written, (A). Choices B, C, and D omit one or more necessary commas.

68. J   Difficulty: Medium

Category: Topic Development / Supporting Material

Getting to the Answer: In questions like this one, first answer the "yes" or "no" part of the question; you'll be able to eliminate at least one answer choice, and usually more. This paragraph focuses solely on how "visual presentation style" is being refined. The topic sentence of the paragraph doesn't discuss audio aids, nor does any other sentence in the paragraph. Therefore, the sentence should NOT be added; (J) is correct.

69. B   Difficulty: High

Category: Sentence Structure and Formation

Getting to the Answer: When you need to determine the correct order of words in a long sentence like this one, start by focusing on the correct placement of descriptive phrases and then eliminate your way to the correct answer. *In respected journals* needs to follow the verb phrase *have been published.* This eliminates C. *In listeners* belongs with *improve comprehension,* which eliminates A and D. Choice (B) is correct.

70. G   Difficulty: Medium

Category: Sentence Structure and Formation

Getting to the Answer: The passive voice will not always be incorrect on the ACT, but passive constructions are generally wordier than active ones, so check for an active version of any underlined passives. "It has been determined by researchers" is a wordy and indirect way of saying "Researchers have determined," so (G) is the best choice here. Choice H is a sentence fragment with no independent clause. Choice J uses incorrect grammatical structure.

71. A   Difficulty: Medium

Category: Punctuation

Getting to the Answer: The end of one sentence and the beginning of the next are underlined, so determine if the sentences should be combined. None of the answer choices offers an option for correctly joining two independent clauses; NO CHANGE is needed, so (A) is correct. Choice B creates a run-on sentence. Choices C and D leave the meaning of the second clause incomplete.

72. J   Difficulty: Medium

Category: Sentence Structure and Formation

Getting to the Answer: When a pronoun is underlined, check that it agrees with its antecedent—the noun it replaces. The underlined pronoun refers back to the audience members, so the third-person plural pronoun *them,* as shown in (J), is correct. Choices F and G use singular pronouns, which don't agree with the plural noun *audience members.* Choice H uses the second-person pronoun *you,* but the writer is not directly addressing the reader.

73. D   Difficulty: Medium

Category: Knowledge of Language / Concision

Getting to the Answer: Check underlined selections for words that are redundant. *Recently* and *of late* mean essentially the same thing, so using them together is redundant. Only (D) eliminates all redundant language.

74. G   Difficulty: High

Category: Organization, Unity, and Cohesion / Transitions

Getting to the Answer: You need to pick the best supporting material to link Sentences 1 and 2, so read Sentence 2 before going to the answer choices. Sentence 2 discusses the importance of body language in presentations; the most effective link to this sentence will introduce this topic. Only (G) mentions body language. Choice F is much more general than (G), repeating ideas that have already been stated in the passage. Choice H focuses on visual images, which were discussed in the previous paragraph, not Sentence 2 of this paragraph. Choice J is unnecessarily wordy, using the passive voice and redundant language.

75. B   Difficulty: Medium

Category: Topic Development / Writer's Purpose

Getting to the Answer: Read the question stems carefully. Frequently, more than one answer choice will be both relevant and consistent, but only one will meet the specific criteria of the question. The writer wants to show how the theory about body language has *influenced* the education and public speaking experts who are the subject of the sentence. Choice (B) explains a specific way these experts have been influenced; they now focus on teaching presenters how to effectively use body language. Choices A and C are both too general; neither shows the specific influence of the body language theory. Choice D is out of scope; audience size isn't discussed in the passage.

MATHEMATICS TEST

1. D   Difficulty: Low

Category: Essential Skills / Rates, Percents, Proportions, and Unit Conversion

Getting to the Answer: When you're converting units, writing out the units will help you determine if you've made a mistake. Arrange the conversion factor in whichever format will allow you to cancel the units you are trying to do away with. Here, "a *rod* is equivalent to 5.5 yards" can be written as $\dfrac{1 \text{ rod}}{5.5 \text{ yd}}$ or $\dfrac{5.5 \text{ yd}}{1 \text{ rod}}$:

$$127 \text{ yd} \cdot \frac{1 \text{ rod}}{5.5 \text{ yd}} \approx 23.1 \text{ rods, (D)}$$

2. J   Difficulty: Low

Category: Essential Skills / Rates, Percents, Proportions, and Unit Conversion

Getting to the Answer: Instead of finding the increase and adding it to the original cost, you can do the computation in one step by adding 100% to the percent increase. When the cost of the pizza is raised by 22%, the new cost will be 122% of the original cost, so multiply the original price by 1.22 to get $20 \cdot 1.22 = \$24.40$, (J).

3. B   Difficulty: Low

Category: Essential Skills / Statistics and Probability

Getting to the Answer: Phrases like "average increase" may sound a little complicated, but there's nothing difficult going on here. The chart shows increases, so you just need to find the average to get the "average increase." Remember, the average of a set of terms is the sum of

the terms divided by the number of terms, so the average here is:

$$\text{Average} = \frac{120 + 210 + 0 + 210 + 180}{5}$$
$$= \frac{720}{5} = 144$$

Choice (B) is correct.

4. G   Difficulty: Low

Category: Essential Skills / Rates, Percents, Proportions, and Unit Conversion

Getting to the Answer: Recall the DIRT formula: **D**istance **is** **r**ate × **t**ime. Use this formula to calculate each train's distance and then subtract the results. Convert the mixed number to a decimal to make it easier to enter into your calculator. Train A travels $50 \times 3 = 150$ miles. Train B travels $70 \times 2.5 = 175$ miles. The difference is $175 - 150$, which is 25 miles, or (G).

5. B   Difficulty: Low

Category: Higher Math / Algebra

Getting to the Answer: When a factored product equals 0, one of the factors must be 0.

$$b - 3 = 0 \rightarrow b = 3$$
$$b + 4 = 0 \rightarrow b = -4$$
$$b + 7 = 0 \rightarrow b = -7$$

Only one of these, 3, appears in the answers, so (B) is correct.

6. J   Difficulty: Low

Category: Essential Skills / Geometry

Getting to the Answer: Because *ABCD* is a square, each side has the same length, which means the base and height of triangle *BCD* both equal 6 centimeters. Substitute these numbers in the formula for the area of a triangle:

$$A = \frac{1}{2}bh$$
$$= \frac{1}{2}(6)(6)$$
$$= 18$$

The area of triangle *BCD* is 18 cm^2, which is (J).

7. C   Difficulty: Medium

Category: Higher Math / Number and Quantity

Getting to the Answer: When a question tests your knowledge of a number property (even/odd, prime/composite, positive/negative, etc.), the easiest way to answer it is to Pick Numbers. Because u is an integer, pick some integers for u. Start with easy numbers (but not 1 because the number 1 has special properties).

If $u = 2$:

$(u - 3)^2 + 5 = (2 - 3)^2 + 5 = (-1)^2 + 5 = 1 + 5 = 6$

This eliminates B, D, and E.

If $u = 3$:

$(u - 3)^2 + 5 = (3 - 3)^2 + 5 = 0 + 5 = 5$

This eliminates A, leaving (C) as the correct answer.

8. G   Difficulty: Low

Category: Higher Math / Algebra

Getting to the Answer: If you forget the rules of exponents, try writing out an example and canceling. For example, $\dfrac{a^2}{a^3} = \dfrac{a \cdot a}{a \cdot a \cdot a} = \dfrac{1}{a}$. When you're dividing, you subtract the exponents when the bases are the same.

$$\frac{12a^5bc^7}{-3ab^5c^2} = \frac{12}{-3} \cdot \frac{a^5}{a} \cdot \frac{b}{b^5} \cdot \frac{c^7}{c^2}$$
$$= -4 \cdot a^4 \cdot \frac{1}{b^4} \cdot c^5$$
$$= \frac{-4a^4c^5}{b^4}$$

This matches (G).

9. A   Difficulty: Medium

Category: Higher Math / Geometry

Getting to the Answer: Whenever you see parallel lines, look for corresponding angles and alternate interior angles. They're most obvious when you're given just two parallel lines and a transversal, so questions that include parallel lines as parts of shapes like triangles or parallelograms can be a little tricky. Because $\overline{PQ}$ is parallel

to $\overline{WY}$, by corresponding angles, $\angle PQX$ has the same measure as $\angle WYX$, so add the measure (40°) to the figure:

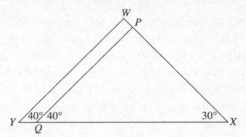

Using the fact that the angles of $\triangle PXQ$ sum to 180 degrees, you find that:

$$40° + 30° + m\angle QPX = 180°$$
$$m\angle QPX = 110°$$

Choice (A) is correct.

10. J   Difficulty: Medium

Category: Essential Skills / Numbers and Operations

Getting to the Answer: Scientific notation is defined as a number between 1 and 10 (not including 10) multiplied by a power of 10, so you can eliminate K right away. Use your calculator (or jot the numbers down quickly) to add the numbers: $740,000,000 + 800,000,000 = 1,540,000,000$. Now move the decimal point (which is to the right of the last 0) until it is between the 1 and the 5. To determine the power of 10, count the number of times you moved the decimal, 9 times. The sum, 1,540,000,000, is a very large number, so the exponent on 10 must be positive, making (J) correct. (Some people forget whether moving the decimal point left or right results in positive powers of 10. It's easier to remember that negative powers of 10 produce tiny decimal numbers, while positive powers produce very large numbers.)

11. A   Difficulty: Low

Category: Essential Skills / Rates, Percents, Proportions, and Unit Conversion

Getting to the Answer: This question is really testing whether you pay attention to detail and work carefully. First, find the *number* of participants who were undecided: $1,250 - 800 - 150 = 300$. Now find the *percent*:

$\dfrac{300}{1,250} = 0.24 = 24\%$, which is (A).

12. K   **Difficulty:** Medium

Category: Essential Skills / Numbers and Operations

Getting to the Answer: The greatest common factor (GCF) is the largest factor that the two numbers share. The least common multiple (LCM) is the smallest number that is a multiple of both numbers. Start with the GCF and choice F: 15 is not a factor of 9 or 25, so these numbers can't have a GCF of 15. On to G: 15 is not a factor of 27, so these numbers can't have a GCF of 15. Choice H: 15 is not a factor of 25, so these numbers can't have a GCF of 15. To choose between the remaining pairs of numbers, try factoring the numbers. Choice J: $30 = 15 \cdot 2$ and $45 = 15 \cdot 3$, so 15 is the GCF here; $30 = 3 \cdot 5 \cdot 2$ and $45 = 3 \cdot 5 \cdot 3$, so the LCM must be $2 \cdot 3 \cdot 3 \cdot 5 = 90$ (not 225). Choice (K) must be correct: $45 = 15 \cdot 3$ and $75 = 15 \cdot 5$, so 15 is the GCF here. Finally, $45 = 3 \cdot 5 \cdot 3$ and $75 = 5 \cdot 5 \cdot 3$, so the LCM is $5 \cdot 5 \cdot 3 \cdot 3 = 225$.

13. D   **Difficulty:** Medium

Category: Essential Skills / Expressions and Equations

Getting to the Answer: This is a straight substitution question. Remember that if you raise a negative number to an odd power, the result is negative. (If the power is even, the result is positive.) Any question that involves negative numbers will require extra attention. It's very easy to lose track of negative signs.

$$\begin{aligned}
x^5 y + xy^5 &= (2)^5(-3) + (2)(-3)^5 \\
&= (32)(-3) + (2)(-243) \\
&= -96 + (-486) \\
&= -582
\end{aligned}$$

Choice (D) is correct.

14. F   **Difficulty:** Medium

Category: Essential Skills / Geometry

Getting to the Answer: The first step is to recall the definition of *perimeter*—the distance around the sides of a figure. For a square, the perimeter is four times the length of a side, which means a side is one-fourth the perimeter. Be careful to divide both terms in the expression by 4 to get $\dfrac{16}{4} - \dfrac{24h}{4} = 4 - 6h$, which is (F).

15. A   **Difficulty:** Medium

Category: Higher Math / Algebra

Getting to the Answer: Memorizing the three classic quadratics will save you valuable time on questions like this. Remember, $(x - y)^2 = x^2 - 2xy + y^2$. You could multiply out the squared binomial (using FOIL), or better yet, write down the formula from memory: $(x - k)^2 = x^2 - 2kx + k^2$, which you're told in the question stem is equal to $x^2 - 26x + k^2$. Because the coefficient of x must be the same in both equations, $-2k = -26$, which yields $k = 13$. Choice (A) is correct.

16. K   **Difficulty:** Medium

Category: Essential Skills / Expressions and Equations

Getting to the Answer: As with every question involving negative numbers, be careful with the negative signs. Also pay attention to the location of the parentheses. Here you need to cube both the -2 and the x^5 because both are inside the parentheses: $(-2x^5)^3 = (-2)^3(x^5)^3 = -8x^{15}$. Choice (K) is therefore correct.

17. B   **Difficulty:** Medium

Category: Higher Math / Number and Quantity

Getting to the Answer: If the labels are missing on a number line, you can find the length of each interval by finding the difference in the endpoints (how much the total interval is) and dividing by the number of subintervals. The unmarked interval goes from 2.7 to 2.8, so it must be 0.1 units long. It's divided into 10 equally spaced subintervals, each of which must be $\dfrac{0.1}{10} = 0.01$ units long.

The number e has an approximate value of 2.718, so you want a point between 2.71 and 2.72. Choice (B) is the closest.

18. H   **Difficulty:** Medium

Category: Higher Math / Functions

Getting to the Answer: You don't have to find the solutions to the equation, just the number of solutions. As long as you know the technique you would use to solve it, you can eyeball the answer in seconds. The graph of a function crosses the x-axis when $y = 0$, so set the equation equal to 0: $(x+1)(x+2)(x-3)(x+4)(x+5) = 0$. There are 5 distinct factors, any of which could equal 0 (for example, if $x = -1$, then $x + 1 = 0$), so there will be 5 x-intercepts, which is (H). Specifically, they are $-1, -2, 3, -4$, and -5, but you don't need to know that to answer the question. If you have a graphing calculator, you could also use it to graph the equation and see how many times the graph intersects the x-axis.

19. A   Difficulty: Medium

Category: Higher Math / Algebra

Getting to the Answer: To reduce a rational expression, you must factor out the same number from the top and the bottom, then cancel. You *cannot* only reduce the 4, neglecting the $8x$ (or vice versa).

$$\frac{4 + 8x}{12x} = \frac{\cancel{4}(1 + 2x)}{\cancel{4}(3x)} = \frac{1 + 2x}{3x}$$

This matches (A).

20. G   Difficulty: Low

Category: Essential Skills / Numbers and Operations

Getting to the Answer: This is a very straightforward question, so don't make careless errors. If 5 people buy 5 tickets for \$95, each pays $\frac{\$95}{5} = \$19$. Because the individual rate is \$21.50, this represents a savings of $\$21.50 - \$19 = \$2.50$ per person, which is (G).

21. C   Difficulty: Low

Category: Essential Skills / Expressions and Equations

Getting to the Answer: Small mistakes will add up quickly—keep yourself focused! The key to this one is that x^2y and $2xy^2$ are NOT like terms. Like terms must have the same exponent on each variable. Combine only the first terms from each expression to get: $(-2x^2y^2 + 3x^2y^2) + x^2y + 2xy^2 = x^2y^2 + x^2y + 2xy^2$, which matches (C).

22. H   Difficulty: Low

Category: Higher Math / Geometry

Getting to the Answer: Use SOHCAHTOA to help you remember which trig function involves which sides of the triangle: $\tan \theta = \frac{\text{opposite}}{\text{adjacent}} = \frac{12}{7}$, which is (H). Note: When answering sine and cosine questions, you can eliminate any answers that are not between -1 and 1, but remember that tangent can get very large or very small.

23. E   Difficulty: Medium

Category: Essential Skills / Expressions and Equations

Getting to the Answer: If you're not sure which operation is appropriate, try Picking Numbers. If Yuri was 10 years old 15 years ago, then he's 25 today. In another 7 years, he will be 32. Plug $x = 10$ into each answer choice to see which one equals 32:

A: $10 + 7 = 17$ Eliminate.

B: $(10 - 15) + 7 = -5 + 7 = 2$ Eliminate.

C: $(10 + 15) - 7 = 25 - 7 = 18$ Eliminate.

D: $(10 - 15) - 7 = -5 - 7 = -12$ Eliminate.

(E): $(10 + 15) + 7 = 25 + 7 = 32$ Correct.

The key to answering this question algebraically is to realize that if Yuri was x years old 15 years ago, he is now $(x + 15)$ years old, not $(x - 15)$ years old. Seven years from now, he'll be another 7 years older, so the expression is $(x + 15) + 7$, which is (E).

24. K   Difficulty: Medium

Category: Higher Math / Algebra

Getting to the Answer: Before factoring a quadratic expression, look for common factors that you can pull out first. Here, you should begin by factoring out a 2 to get $2x^2 - 8x - 24 = 2(x^2 - 4x - 12)$. To factor the simplified quadratic, you need two numbers that multiply to -12 and sum to -4; those numbers are -6 and $+2$, so $2x^2 - 8x - 24 = 2(x - 6)(x + 2)$. The latter factor is (K).

25. D   Difficulty: Medium

Category: Essential Skills / Geometry

Getting to the Answer: When using the Pythagorean theorem, $a^2 + b^2 = c^2$, remember that a and b are the legs and c is the hypotenuse. Wrong answer choices may come from plugging numbers into the wrong part of the formula.

$$8^2 + 15^2 = c^2$$
$$64 + 225 = c^2$$
$$289 = c^2$$
$$c = \sqrt{289} = 17$$

Choice (D) is correct.

26. G   Difficulty: High

Category: Higher Math / Number and Quantity

Getting to the Answer: You add fractions that contain radicals the same way you add regular fractions—find a common denominator and multiply each fraction by whatever it takes to get that denominator. Here, the common denominator is $\sqrt{5} \cdot \sqrt{2} = \sqrt{10}$.

$$\frac{4}{\sqrt{5}} + \frac{3}{\sqrt{2}} = \frac{4}{\sqrt{5}}\left(\frac{\sqrt{2}}{\sqrt{2}}\right) + \frac{3}{\sqrt{2}}\left(\frac{\sqrt{5}}{\sqrt{5}}\right)$$
$$= \frac{4\sqrt{2}}{\sqrt{10}} + \frac{3\sqrt{5}}{\sqrt{10}}$$
$$= \frac{4\sqrt{2} + 3\sqrt{5}}{\sqrt{10}}$$

This matches (G). Note that you could also use your calculator to find the decimal equivalent of the given expression (which is approximately 3.9831) and each of the answer choices until you find a match, but you must enter the expressions very carefully.

27. C   Difficulty: Medium

Category: Essential Skills / Rates, Percents, Proportions, and Unit Converions

Getting to the Answer: Don't worry when you see an unfamiliar term like "relative atomic mass." The test makers don't expect you to be familiar with such terms (including ones they just made up), so they'll tell you everything that you need to know. Use the definition provided to write a ratio in the form of $\frac{\text{mass of unknown element}}{\text{mass of carbon}}$. The result is $\frac{30}{12} = 2.5$, which is (C).

28. K   Difficulty: Medium

Category: Essential Skills / Expressions and Equations

Getting to the Answer: Don't stop until you're sure you've answered the question asked. It's tempting to bubble in the value of x and move on, but that's not what this question is asking for—instead, you need to use the equation to find the value of x and then substitute that value into the other expression:

$$2x + 3 = -5$$
$$2x = -8$$
$$x = -4$$

$$x^2 - 7x = (-4)^2 - 7(-4)$$
$$= 16 + 28 = 44$$

Choice (K) is correct.

29. D   Difficulty: Medium

Category: Higher Math / Algebra

Getting to the Answer: Inequalities work exactly like equalities, except that the direction of the symbol changes if you multiply or divide by a negative number. To save a bit of time here, think about dividing by 8 at the appropriate time rather than distributing it:

$$8(5 + x) - 1 < 7$$
$$8(5 + x) < 8 \quad \text{(Divide by 8.)}$$
$$5 + x < 1$$
$$x < -4$$

The inequality now reads "x is less than -4." The numbers less than -4 on a number line are to the left of -4, which means the correct graph is (D).

30. K   Difficulty: Medium

Category: Essential Skills / Rates, Percent, Proportions, and Unit Conversion

Getting to the Answer: Break the question into steps. First, find how long it took the employee to collect samples from one house, and then use that amount to find how long it should take the employee to collect samples from all of the houses.

The employee *started* the 1st house at 8:00 and *started* the 6th house at 9:05, so it took him 1 hour and 5 minutes, or 65 minutes, to collect samples from 5 houses (not 6 houses because he didn't *finish* the 6th house at 9:05). This gives a unit rate of $65 \div 5 = 13$ minutes per house. Multiply the unit rate by the number of houses in the subdivision (40) to get a total of $13 \times 40 = 520$ minutes to collect samples from all the houses. The answers are given in hours and minutes, so convert 520 minutes to hours and minutes by dividing by 60. The correct answer is $8\frac{2}{3}$ hours, or 8 hours and 40 minutes, making (K) the correct answer.

31. D   Difficulty: High

Category: Higher Math / Functions

Getting to the Answer: You can make abstract questions like this one easier to handle by Picking Numbers. Be sure the numbers you pick obey any restrictions in the question stem. Try $k = 2$ and $x = 4$. (These numbers will make the radical in E easy to calculate.) The question involves a composition of h and g, so start with the inner function, $g(x)$:

A: $g(4) = \dfrac{2}{4} = \dfrac{1}{2}$

B: $g(4) = \dfrac{4}{2} = 2$

C: $g(4) = 2(4) = 8$

(D): $g(4) = 4^2 = 16$

E: $g(4) = \sqrt[2]{4} = 2$

The largest value for $g(x)$ is (D). When this is plugged into $h(g(x)) = 5^{g(x)}$, the largest value of $g(x)$ will produce the largest value of $h(g(x))$. For the values of k and x allowed in this question, (D) is always the largest, so it is correct.

32. H   Difficulty: Medium

Category: Higher Math / Functions

Getting to the Answer: Some questions look tougher than they really are, especially when you are asked to interpret a graph. The question asks for total vertical distance, which is the total change in altitude both while the hiker is ascending the mountain and while she is descending. At 8:00 AM, the hiker is at 4,500 feet of altitude. After 8:00 AM, she ascends 500 feet without descending. After reaching her highest point at 11:00 AM, she descends 1,000 feet by 1:00 PM. Therefore, the total vertical distance traveled is 500 feet + 1,000 feet = 1,500 feet, which is (H).

33. E   Difficulty: Medium

Category: Higher Math / Functions

Getting to the Answer: This question requires no math, but rather an interpretation of the graph. Beginning at 9:00 AM, the hiker had just finished an ascent and did not travel up or down the mountain. Thus, her altitude remained the same. Therefore, either A or (E) is correct. From 10:00 AM to 11:00 AM, she ascended 250 vertical feet. Between 11:00 AM to 12:00 PM, after having reached her highest point, she descended 250 vertical feet at the same rate as during the previous one-hour interval. Choice (E) best describes this progression.

34. F   Difficulty: Medium

Category: Higher Math / Geometry

Getting to the Answer: Even if a question talks about rounding, the correct answer may require no rounding whatsoever. The distance from a point to a line is measured perpendicular to the line, so you can be sure that the triangle shown is a right triangle. Because this distance is perpendicular and measured from the center, it bisects the chord, which means the base of the triangle is 15. Use the Pythagorean theorem to find the length of the hypotenuse, r:

$$a^2 + b^2 = c^2$$
$$8^2 + 15^2 = r^2$$
$$r = \sqrt{8^2 + 15^2} = \sqrt{289} = 17$$

Choice (F) is correct.

35. D   **Difficulty:** Medium

Category: Higher Math / Algebra

Getting to the Answer: Understanding slope-intercept form of a line, $y = mx + b$, is essential on the ACT. When a linear equation is written in the form $y = mx + b$, the slope is the coefficient of x. Rewrite the first equation in this form, $y = 3x$, to find that its slope is 3. In the second equation, the slope is a. To be parallel, the two equations must have the same slope, so $a = 3$, which is (D).

36. J   **Difficulty:** Medium

Category: Essential Skills / Statistics and Probability

Getting to the Answer: The average of a set of terms is the sum of the terms divided by the number of terms. Even if you're not sure what to do on an averages question, plugging the given information into this formula can help you figure out where to go.

For the first four numbers:

$$\frac{\text{sum}}{4} = 14$$
$$\text{sum} = 56$$

When you include the fifth number, x, the new sum will be $56 + x$. The new average is:

$$\frac{56 + x}{5} = 16$$
$$56 + x = 80$$
$$x = 24$$

The fifth number is 24, which is (J). Don't forget to divide by 5 (not 4) in the second equation, because there are now five numbers.

37. A   **Difficulty:** Medium

Category: Higher Math / Algebra

Getting to the Answer: If a system of linear equations has infinitely many solutions, then both equations describe the same line. When two equations represent the same line, one is an exact multiple of the other. Look for a multiple. Because $3 \cdot 4 = 12$ and $27 \cdot 4 = 108$, you can get the first equation by multiplying the second by 4:

$$4(3x + ky) = 4(27)$$
$$12x + 4ky = 108$$

Therefore, $4k = -20$, or $k = -5$. This means (A) is correct.

38. J   **Difficulty:** High

Category: Higher Math / Algebra

Getting to the Answer: Sometimes on the ACT, you will need to put together several pieces of information in the right way to get the answer. Because each extra inch adds approximately 10 pounds, a 72-inch person should weigh about 40 pounds more than a 68-inch person, for a total of 190 pounds. Now use the formula:

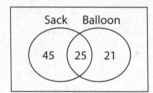

$$BMI = \frac{703W}{H^2} = \frac{703(190)}{72^2} \approx 26$$

Choice (J) is correct.

39. A   **Difficulty:** Low

Category: Essential Skills / Statistics and Probability

Getting to the Answer: It's easy to get confused on "counting" questions. Drawing a Venn Diagram will help you visualize the scenario:

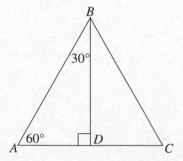

Using the diagram, you can see that $45 + 25 + 21 = 91$ students are signed up for either the sack race, the balloon toss, or both. This means that $100 - 91 = 9$ of the students who signed up to participate in a sporting event at the festival are not signed up for either the sack race or the balloon toss. This makes (A) correct.

40. H   **Difficulty:** Medium

Category: Higher Math / Geometry

Getting to the Answer: Always be on the lookout for special right triangles. What kind of triangles are formed when a perpendicular bisector is added to an equilateral triangle?

Because $\triangle ABC$ is equilateral, each of its angles is 60°. Angle BDA is 90° because $\overline{BD}$ is perpendicular to $\overline{AC}$. Then each half of ABC is a 30°-60°-90° triangle, with side ratios of $x:x\sqrt{3}:2x$. The side opposite the 60° angle is $x\sqrt{3} = 4\sqrt{3}$ units long, so $x = 4$. The hypotenuse, $\overline{BC}$, is $2x = 8$ units long, which is (H).

41. C   Difficulty: Medium

Category: Essential Skills / Geometry

Getting to the Answer: To find the perimeter of a composite figure like this one, it can be easy to leave out some sides. Try marking each side as you add it so that you don't accidentally forget any or add any twice. First find the missing lengths:

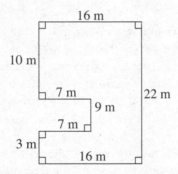

The small horizontal side must be the same length as the small horizontal side above it (7 m), because all the angles are right angles. The interior vertical side must be $22 - (10 + 3) = 9$ meters long, because the total vertical distance on each side of the figure must be the same. Now add the length of each side to find the perimeter: $16 + 22 + 16 + 10 + 7 + 9 + 7 + 3 = 90$, or (C).

42. J   Difficulty: Medium

Category: Higher Math / Statistics and Probability

Getting to the Answer: Permutations are sequences, so order matters. Any of the 5 books could be placed in the first spot on the shelf. Any of the remaining 4 books could be placed in the second spot, any of the remaining 3 books could be placed in the third spot, and so on until there is only 1 remaining book for the fifth spot. You can represent this visually by drawing a line representing each of the shelf's 5 spots, then writing in how many book choices there are for each spot:

$$\underline{5}\ \underline{4}\ \underline{3}\ \underline{2}\ \underline{1}$$

Therefore, the number of possible arrangements is $5 \times 4 \times 3 \times 2 \times 1 = 120$, or (J).

43. E   Difficulty: Medium

Category: Higher Math / Geometry

Getting to the Answer: If your answer doesn't look quite like any of the answer choices, rearrange it so that it does. Don't just pick an answer that looks similar; make sure it actually means the same thing. Parentheses make a big difference, so you should carefully consider where they should be! The outer circle has area $\pi r^2 = \pi(12^2)$. The inner circle has area $\pi r^2 = \pi(4^2)$. The shaded area is $\pi(12^2) - \pi(4^2) = \pi(12^2 - 4^2)$, which is (E).

44. J   Difficulty: Low

Category: Essential Skills / Numbers and Operations

Getting to the Answer: The temperature of the container of liquid nitrogen is lower than the temperature of the room, so it must rise to match the room's temperature. Eliminate F and G, which indicate that a drop in temperature is needed. To find the positive difference, subtract:

$72°F - (-330°F) = 72°F + 330°F = +402°F$, so (J) is correct.

45. E   Difficulty: Medium

Category: Higher Math / Geometry

Getting to the Answer: There are numbers in the answer choices, so Backsolving will work well. Just be sure to plug the answer choices into the right part of the question. Here, they represent possible lengths. Start with C: If the length of the floor is 13.5 feet, then the width will be $2(13.5) - 21 = 27 - 21 = 6$ feet. This would produce an area of $13.5(6) = 81$ square feet, which is not big enough. Try D:

length = 17 feet
width = $2(17) - 21 = 34 - 21 = 13$ feet
area = $17(13) = 221$ square feet

This still isn't big enough, so (E) must be correct:

length = 19 feet
width = $2(19) - 21 = 38 - 21 = 17$ feet
area = $19(17) = 323$ square feet
Perfect!

You could also solve algebraically:

An equation for the width (W) in terms of the length (L) is $W = 2L - 21$.

$$\text{area} = L \cdot W = 323$$
$$L(2L - 21) = 323$$
$$2L^2 - 21L = 323$$
$$2L^2 - 21L - 323 = 0$$
$$(2L + 17)(L - 19) = 0$$
$$2L + 17 = 0 \text{ or } L - 19 = 0$$
$$2L = -17 \text{ or } L = 19$$
$$L = \frac{-17}{2} \text{ or } L = 19$$

Length must be positive, so the length is 19, matching (E).

46. G   Difficulty: Medium

Category: Higher Math / Geometry

Getting to the Answer: Picking Numbers can make a theoretical question much more concrete. Say the original radius was 1. Then the area of the circle would be $\pi r^2 = \pi(1^2) = \pi$. Twice this area would be 2π. Find the radius of a circle with area 2π:

$$\pi r^2 = 2\pi$$
$$r^2 = 2$$
$$r = \sqrt{2}$$

The new radius is $\sqrt{2}$ times the old radius of 1, so (G) is correct.

47. A   Difficulty: Medium

Category: Higher Math / Functions

Getting to the Answer: On some questions, you won't be able to depend on your calculator. You simply have to know the formula or rule. Here, the rule you want is that $\log_b y = x$ translates to $b^x = y$. Use this to rewrite the given logarithmic equation using an exponent: $x^3 = 64$. If you're not sure what number raised to the third power will give you 64, you can always Backsolve. You'll find that $4^3 = 64$, which means (A) is correct.

48. K   Difficulty: Medium

Category: Higher Math / Number and Quantity

Getting to the Answer: Some things in math actually work like you expect them to. To subtract two matrices,

just subtract the elements that are in the same position. After you've subtracted one position, eliminate the answer choices that don't have the correct number in that position. You may be able to get away with only subtracting one or two positions before you eliminate all the wrong answer choices.

$$\begin{bmatrix} 3 & -6 \\ 0 & 9 \end{bmatrix} - \begin{bmatrix} -3 & 6 \\ 0 & -9 \end{bmatrix} = \begin{bmatrix} (3) - (-3) & (-6) - (6) \\ (0) - (0) & (9) - (-9) \end{bmatrix}$$
$$= \begin{bmatrix} 6 & -12 \\ 0 & 18 \end{bmatrix}$$

So (K) is correct.

49. C   Difficulty: Medium

Category: Higher Math / Number and Quantity

Getting to the Answer: When you're Picking Numbers for a question with few limits, don't forget to try both positive and negative integers and fractions. Try $a = 1$ and $b = -2$. This immediately eliminates B. Using these values, $a^2 = 1$ and $b^2 = 4$, which eliminates E. Now try $a = 2$ and $b = 1$. This eliminates A. Using these new values, $a^2 = 4$ and $b^2 = 1$, which eliminates D. Choice (C) must be correct because the square of a number cannot be negative. No matter what b is, b^2 will be greater than or equal to zero.

50. G   Difficulty: Medium

Category: Higher Math / Geometry

Getting to the Answer: On Geometry questions, it usually helps to draw the triangle. Use SOHCAHTOA to remember which trig function involves which sides of the triangle.

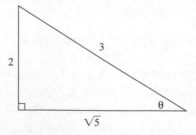

The smallest angle is the one opposite the shortest side. Here, the smallest angle is marked θ. Based on the diagram,

$$\cos \theta = \frac{\text{adjacent}}{\text{hypotenuse}} = \frac{\sqrt{5}}{3} \text{, which is (G).}$$

51. C   Difficulty: High

Category: Higher Math / Functions

Getting to the Answer: A graphing calculator can be a good backup, but understanding the math will always be faster. You could plug this equation into your graphing calculator, find the highest and lowest y-values, find their difference, and divide by 2. Alternatively, you could use algebra and what you know about transformations. Rewrite the equation as $y = 5\cos(4\theta) + 2$. The $+2$ at the end moves the entire graph up 2 units; it doesn't affect the difference between the largest and smallest values. The 4 inside the parentheses affects how often the function repeats itself in the same space on the x-axis. It's the 5 in front that multiplies the y-values and makes the extreme values of the function higher and lower. Cosine usually goes from -1 to 1, so if you multiply all the values by 5, it will go from -5 to 5. The difference is 10, and half of the difference is 5. So the amplitude is 5, or (C).

52. H   Difficulty: Medium

Category: Higher Math / Statistics and Probability

Getting to the Answer: According to the graph, Angus has been paying down his debt at a rate of $500 per month. To reach 25% utilization, he needs to get down to $10,000 \times 0.25 = \$2,500$, which means he needs to pay off $10,000 - \$2,500 = \$7,500$. To do this, it would take $7,500 \div \$500 = 15$ months , making (H) the correct answer.

53. E   Difficulty: Medium

Category: Higher Math / Geometry

Getting to the Answer: The wording of this question is a giveaway. One of the angles is a "vertex angle" and the other two are "base angles." This will allow you to solve the question even if you forgot what an isosceles triangle is! The angles sum to 180 degrees, so:

$$(x - 10) + (3x + 18) + (3x + 18) = 180$$
$$7x + 26 = 180$$
$$7x = 154$$
$$x = 22$$

Base angle $= 3x + 18 = 3(22) + 18 = 84$, making choice (E) correct.

Notice that A and B are the answers to other questions; they are, respectively, the measure of the vertex angle and the value of x. Be sure to solve for the right thing.

54. H   Difficulty: Medium

Category: Essential Skills / Rates, Percents, Proportions, and Unit Conversion

Getting to the Answer: If you don't take the time to read carefully, you'll lose a lot of points on careless mistakes. One set of potholders requires: $(6 \cdot 8) + (5 \cdot 12) + (2 \cdot 18) = 48 + 60 + 36 = 144$ inches of fabric. This is $144 \text{ inches} \times \dfrac{1 \text{ yard}}{36 \text{ inches}} = 4$ yards. Each yard costs $1.95, so one set of potholders costs $4(\$1.95) = \$7.80$. Margot is making 5 sets of potholders, so the total cost is $5(\$7.80) = \$39$, which is (H).

55. A   Difficulty: High

Category: Higher Math / Statistics and Probability

Getting to the Answer: Don't neglect the 50% at the beginning of the question just because it is presented in a different form. Instead, convert 50% to a fraction $\left(\dfrac{1}{2}\right)$ and then think logically—the final probability is $\dfrac{1}{3}$ of $\dfrac{3}{4}$ of $\dfrac{1}{2}$. In math, "of" means multiply, so the probability of randomly choosing a vehicle that is a car with an automatic transmission and a GPS system is $\dfrac{1}{2} \times \dfrac{3}{4} \times \dfrac{1}{3} = \dfrac{1}{8}$. This means (A) is correct.

56. H   Difficulty: High

Category: Essential Skills / Statistics and Probability

Getting to the Answer: The median of a set of numbers is the middle value when the numbers are arranged in ascending or descending order. When there is an even number of terms, the median is the average of the two middle values. Here, there is an even number of terms with a and b in the middle, and you're given that the median is 4, so it must be that $\dfrac{a + b}{2} = 4$. This is equivalent to $a + b = 8$. Thus, the product of a and b must be the product of two numbers that add up to 8. The possible pairs of values for a and b are 1 and 7, 2 and 6, 3 and 5, and 4 and 4, which means the possible products are 7, 12, 15, and 16. Only (H) matches one of these products.

57. C   Difficulty: High

Category: Higher Math / Functions

Getting to the Answer: If you can tell at a glance that a question is going to take several minutes, save it until you've done all the easier questions. In the equation of an ellipse, $\dfrac{(x-h)^2}{a^2} + \dfrac{(y-k)^2}{b^2} = 1$, the center is at (h,k), the length of the horizontal axis is $2a$, and the length of the vertical axis is $2b$. This particular ellipse is shown here:

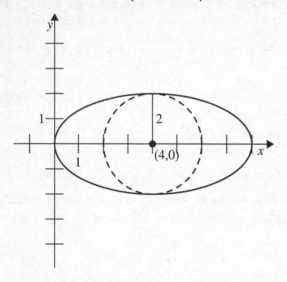

The largest circle possible is dotted on the diagram. Notice that it has the same center as the ellipse and has radius 2 (the shortest dimension of the ellipse). In the equation of a circle, $(x-h)^2 + (y-k)^2 = r^2$, (h,k) is the center and r is the radius. Plug this information into the formula to find this circle's equation: $(x-4)^2 + y^2 = 4$, which is (C).

58. F   Difficulty: Medium

Category: Higher Math / Functions

Getting to the Answer: The highest power in the equation determines the general shape. The graph of $y = x^3$ will always have the general shape of the graph in F. Adding a constant C will move it up by C units (if C is positive—if C is negative the graph will move down). If you're not familiar with the shape of the graph $y = x^3$, you could either plug it into a graphing calculator or plot a few points. Don't worry too much about specific values. As soon as you realize that when x is negative, y will also be negative, you can eliminate all the graphs except (F).

59. C   Difficulty: High

Category: Higher Math / Statistics and Probability

Getting to the Answer: Try not to overthink a question like this—instead, use what you know about finding an average and see where that takes you. The average of a set of terms is the sum of the terms divided by the number of terms. Use this definition along with the average given in the question (10) to solve for x:

$$\text{Average} = \frac{\text{sum of terms}}{\text{number of terms}}$$
$$10 = \frac{x + 2x - 3 + 2x + 1 + 3x - 4 + 3x + 1}{5}$$
$$10 = \frac{11x - 5}{5}$$
$$50 = 11x - 5$$
$$55 = 11x$$
$$5 = x$$

Now, substituting 5 for x in each of the expressions, you get: 5, 2(5) − 3, 2(5) + 1, 3(5) − 4, and 3(5) + 1, which gives the numbers 5, 7, 11, 11, and 16. The *mode* of a data set is the number that occurs most often, which in this case is 11. This means (C) is correct.

60. J   Difficulty: High

Category: Higher Math / Statistics and Probability

Getting to the Answer: ACT probability questions are simple enough that you can write out all the possible outcomes if you need to. Remember that probability is the number of desired outcomes over the number of possible outcomes. The easiest way to think about this question is to look at it backwards. If there are 3 heads, how many tails are there? In 4 coin tosses, if there are 3 heads there must be exactly 1 tail. That tail could be the first, second, third, or fourth toss, so there are 4 ways to get 1 tail and 3 heads. This means the number of desired outcomes is 4. There are 2 possible positions for each coin (heads or tails), so the total number of possible arrangements of heads and tails in 4 tosses is $2 \cdot 2 \cdot 2 \cdot 2 = 16$. Therefore, the probability that in 4 tosses, there will be exactly 3 heads is $\dfrac{4}{16} = \dfrac{1}{4}$. Choice (J) is correct.

If you're in doubt, write it out! All the possible arrangements of 4 coins are as follows:

HHHH	**THHH**	HTTH	THTT
HHHT	HHTT	THTH	TTHT
HHTH	HTHT	TTHH	TTTH
HTHH	THHT	HTTT	TTTT

The ones with 3 heads are in bold type. There are 4 arrangements with exactly 3 heads and 16 total possible arrangements. Again, the probability of getting exactly 3 heads is $\frac{4}{16} = \frac{1}{4}$, so (J) is correct.

READING TEST

Passage I

Suggested Passage Map notes:

¶1: Rosemary (R) - 87 yrs old

¶2: R's youngest grandson V seems lazy

¶3: R appalled by V's explanation of "gut" class

¶4-9: R's father had forbidden her to go to school, wonders what could have been

1. A   Difficulty: Low

Category: Craft and Structure / Writer's View

Getting to the Answer: The author writes that Rosemary "had decided long ago that growing old was like slowly turning to stone; you couldn't take anything for granted" (lines 16–18), that the memory of her childhood was "still painful as an open wound" (line 54), and that she "wondered what life would have been like if her father had not been waiting at the bottom of the stairs that day" (lines 76–78). The writer indicates sympathy for an elderly woman whose life had not gone as she had wished, a match for (A). Choice B is opposite of the information; the author does not use any words that indicate anger at Rosemary. Rosemary may be disappointed by her nephew's "gut" classes, but that's not the same as the author being disappointed in Rosemary, C, and there is no suggestion that the author is confused, as in D, by the narrator.

2. H   Difficulty: Medium

Category: Key Ideas and Details / Inference

Getting to the Answer: Rosemary's unease with Victor's behavior is broadly in response to what she perceives as his laziness, but *laziness* isn't an answer choice. Choice J may be tempting, but Victor isn't unable to get out of bed, he's unwilling to. The third paragraph does specifically talk about something he had said that had *disturbed* her—his willingness to take an easy class, which matches (H). There is no evidence that Victor plans to drop out, so F is not correct, and her upbringing is never discussed with him, so G is incorrect.

3. D   Difficulty: Medium

Category: Key Ideas and Details / Inference

Getting to the Answer: The answer is strongly implied in the passage. The third paragraph notes that Rosemary wanted to go to high school after finishing grammar school. Her father would not permit her to go, so she had to spend time "with animals and rough farmhands for company instead of people her own age," (D). Choice B is flatly contradicted by the third paragraph, which indicates that Rosemary wanted to go to high school, not college. Choices A and C make inferences that are not supported by the passage.

4. G   Difficulty: Medium

Category: Key Ideas and Details / Inference

Getting to the Answer: Lines 16–17 say that Rosemary "had decided long ago that growing old was like slowly turning to stone." This sentiment suggests that she is resigned to the physical problems that accompany old age. *Acceptance*, (G), therefore, is correct. *Sadness*, F, and *resentment*, H, are too negative in tone, while *optimism*, J, is too positive. Rosemary, in short, isn't at all emotional about the aging process.

5. A   Difficulty: Low

Category: Key Ideas and Details / Detail

Getting to the Answer: Rosemary's interest in crossword puzzles is discussed in the opening sentences of the first paragraph. She does them for two reasons: to pass the time and to keep her mind active, (A). The other choices distort details in the first and second paragraphs. Choice B plays on Rosemary's happiness at still being able to write at age 87, C plays on her need to consult an atlas to look up the Swiss river, and D plays on her experience of "an expanded sense of time" as she grows older.

6. G   Difficulty: Medium

Category: Craft and Structure / Vocab-in-Context

Getting to the Answer: The second paragraph describes, among other things, Rosemary's ability to keep "present and past tense intermingling in her mind," which the author infers is a function of her old age. As it is used in the paragraph, *expanded* means *made more extensive*, which matches (G). Since *expanded* doesn't necessarily mean *better*, F is out of scope. An unfurled flag is certainly expanded, but doesn't make sense in the passage, making choice H incorrect. Choice J is opposite; to *abridge* means to *shorten* or *restrict*.

7. B   Difficulty: High

Category: Craft and Structure / Function

Getting to the Answer: In the lines that precede the mention of Victor's "shiny new car," Rosemary considers his easy upbringing and that her "grandson behaved as if he had never done a chore in his life" (lines 38–39). In other words, Victor's car is a symbol of his generation, which has had a much easier time getting through life than did Rosemary's. This contrast is exactly what (B) states. Choice A is incorrect on two counts: Rosemary's parents—her father anyway—can't be described as generous, and her parents have nothing to do with Victor's car, which was a gift from Victor's parents. Similarly, while Rosemary seems to feel that Victor's future prospects are bright, C, and that his life lacks hardship, D, neither has anything to do with his car.

8. G   Difficulty: Medium

Category: Key Ideas and Details / Detail

Getting to the Answer: Paragraph 3 says that Rosemary is disturbed by Victor's dismissive attitude toward his education. She doesn't like the idea that his only reason for taking a course is that he can pass it. In contrast to Victor's attitude, Rosemary, in her youth, was eager to continue her education, (G). Choices F and J refer to details

from the wrong paragraphs, while H introduces an issue that the passage never tackles.

9. C   Difficulty: Medium

Category: Key Ideas and Details / Detail

Getting to the Answer: A few lines before Rosemary recalls what it was like growing up on the farm, the passage says that "Rosemary often experienced an expanded sense of time, with present and past tense intermingling in her mind," (C). Choice D, on the other hand, alludes to recollections from the wrong paragraphs. Choices A and B distort details in Paragraph 2.

10. F   Difficulty: Low

Category: Craft and Structure / Writer's View

Getting to the Answer: The reference to Victor's bright future comes at the end of Paragraph 2, which precedes Rosemary's opinion: "if he [Victor] ever got out of bed." It's clear from the text that it's Rosemary, (F), who thinks that he has a good future. The passage never says what Victor thinks about his own future, G, nor does it say what his parents think about his future, H. And it's extremely unlikely that Victor and Rosemary's father, J, were even alive at the same time.

Passage II

Passage A

¶1: Sherman Antitrust Act (SAA) 1st to fight econ. monopolies

¶2: many politicians felt gov't should stay out of econ.

¶3: by late 1800s, SAA needed to protect consumers

Passage B

¶1: author believes altering gov't = positive reform

¶2: FDR is example of modern liberal econ reg.

¶3: gov't must adapt to changing needs

11. B   Difficulty: High

Category: Key Ideas and Details / Detail

Getting to the Answer: Use evidence in the passage and your own common sense to form a prediction before looking at the answer choices. The passage states that these revisions were written by "pro-business Eastern senators," and that these revisions worked to weaken the effectiveness of the Act. Choice (B) is correct; the pro-business senators resisted the purpose of the bill. Choice A is a misused detail; Social Darwinism is not discussed until the next paragraph, and the author makes no direct connection between it and the revisions. Choice C is a distortion; there is evidence of *debate* because the bill got rewritten, but there is no evidence that the debate took a long time. Choice D is extreme; the author is only discussing this bill, not the nature of all Congressional legislation at that time.

12. H   Difficulty: High

Category: Craft and Structure / Function

Getting to the Answer: Remember to keep straight the opinion of the author and other opinions cited in the passage. The trust leaders used the theory of Social Darwinism to explain why it was natural for them to have monopolies. The author must have included this in order to explain how some people justified the existence of monopolies. Choice (H) is correct; this matches your prediction. Choice F is a distortion; this is what the monopolists thought, not what the author thinks. Choice G is out of scope; the author is not exploring what kind of corporations survived, except to the extent that monopolists artificially stifled competition. Choice J is out of scope; the author is discussing a specific instance, not exploring the general influence of science on policy.

13. B   Difficulty: Medium

Category: Key Ideas and Details / Inference

Getting to the Answer: When a question stem refers you to a section of the passage but does not provide enough information to make a prediction, it is often helpful to take a quick scan through the passage before looking at the answer choices. The third paragraph states that laissez-faire policies created monopolies that had many negative effects. Many people objected to this, which eventually led to the Sherman Antitrust Act and other similar measures. Choice (B) fits with the description of the many negative effects of the trusts. Choice A is extreme; there is not enough evidence in the passage to use the word *all*. Choice C is a misused detail; this idea comes from

Passage B. The author of Passage A never states that it was necessary; maybe there were other ways to handle the situation. Choice D is a distortion; the author would argue that all businesses, even big trusts like Standard Oil, could compete freely after the act.

14. J   Difficulty: Medium

Category: Key Ideas and Details / Detail

Getting to the Answer: Because the answer is in the passage, you should be able to move quickly through Detail questions, saving time for those you find more difficult. Read in the immediate vicinity of the given reference. The prior sentence states that Roosevelt used "government funds for the first time" in "intentional deficit spending." The sentence after the reference points out that this "ushered in the modern era of liberal economic regulation." The Act is an example of active manipulation of the economy by the government, which matches (J). Choice F is a misused detail; Passage A, not Passage B, refers to antitrust acts. Choice G is opposite; the passage states that "this act signaled the end of the laissez-faire economics era." Choice H is opposite; the author says that the Agricultural Adjustment Act helped boost the nation out of the Great Depression.

15. B   Difficulty: Medium

Category: Key Ideas and Details / Detail

Getting to the Answer: The author discusses Franklin D. Roosevelt in the second and third paragraphs. The author quotes Roosevelt as saying that he must "reform democracy in order to save it" (lines 82–83), then describes Roosevelt taking action to end the Depression by instituting deficit spending and "deliberate manipulation of the national economy" (lines 99–100), including paying farmers to produce less. This information matches (B). Choice A is not only opposite but also relevant only to Passage A. Choice C is out of scope, since Passage B has no reference to the Sherman Antitrust Act (and even if it did, it can be assumed that Roosevelt would favor it). Choice D is also opposite; Roosevelt abandoned the traditional idea of a balanced budget to pour government monies into the economy as a way of relieving the Great Depression.

16. H   Difficulty: Medium

Category: Key Ideas and Details / Detail

Getting to the Answer: Opposite choices can be tricky if you do not take the time to read carefully. Many people, including the "conservative capitalist economists," felt that the economy would naturally rise and fall and that the government should not interfere in that process. The author then goes on to state that Roosevelt felt the economy would not naturally recover, and so he instituted policies and spent money to fix it. The author feels that Roosevelt was right to do so. (The author says that Roosevelt's success was *undeniable*.) The author explains the viewpoint of the "conservative capitalist economists" in order to then argue that they were wrong and that Roosevelt was right in working to change the economy. Choice (H) fits nicely with the sentiments of the author. Choice F is opposite; Roosevelt took the opposite view from the "conservative capitalist economists." Choice G is opposite; the viewpoint of the "conservative capitalist economists" was in direct contradiction to policies like the Agricultural Adjustment Act. Choice J is a misused detail; this does not come up until the final paragraph.

17. B   Difficulty: Medium

Category: Integration of Knowledge and Ideas / Synthesis

Getting to the Answer: Watch out for choices that only apply to one of the Paired Passages. Both passages refer to economic reform. Passage A talks about preventing monopolies and trusts, and Passage B speaks in more general terms about spending money to pull the nation out of the Great Depression. Look for something that deals with government intervention in the economy. Choice (B) is mentioned in both passages. Choice A is opposite; both authors seem to agree that some degree of governmental control is necessary. Choice C is a misused detail; this only appears in Passage A. Choice D is a misused detail; this only appears in Passage B.

18. G   Difficulty: Medium

Category: Integration of Knowledge and Ideas / Synthesis

Getting to the Answer: When you are trying to infer how one author would react to an idea in another passage, look for a concept that the author specifically addresses. The author of Passage B argues that it is often a good idea for the government to intervene in the economy.

Therefore, he would probably not accept the argument that something should continue to exist simply because it is the most natural state of affairs. Choice (G) is correct; this fits with Author B's view of laissez-faire economic policy. Choice F is out of scope; we do not know how the author of Passage B feels about the theory of Social Darwinism. Choice C is opposite; this viewpoint is what Author B is arguing against. Choice D is a distortion; Author B never mentions monopolies.

19. B   Difficulty: Low

Category: Integration of Knowledge and Ideas / Synthesis

Getting to the Answer: Use the passages to research your answer. It is tough to make a specific prediction here, so jump into the answer choices and compare each one against the passages. Choice (B) is correct; Passage B mentions Roosevelt's plan to "pump-prime" the depressed American economy through government deficit spending. Choice A is opposite; this appears in Passage A but not Passage B. Choice C is opposite; this is from Passage A, not Passage B. Choice D is opposite; this appears in both passages.

20. J   Difficulty: High

Category: Integration of Knowledge and Ideas / Synthesis

Getting to the Answer: In the third paragraph of Passage A, the author cites many negative consequences of laissez-faire policies and the trusts and monopolies that arose from these policies. In the third paragraph of Passage B, the author states that the Agricultural Adjustment Act "signaled the end of the laissez-faire economics era." These details match (J). Choice F is opposite; Passage A describes how laissez-faire policies negatively affected consumers, and Passage B states that the laissez-faire era ended by the end of the 19th century. Choice G includes misused details that are mentioned in each passage but do not address the question. Choice H is out of scope; Roosevelt's presidential legacy is not discussed.

Passage III

Suggested Passage Map notes:

¶1: philosophes = Enlightenment ideas

¶2: influenced by Newton, Locke, English inst.

¶3: Newton: reason and nature compatible

¶4: Locke: human beings malleable

¶5: English inst.: individual freedom

¶6: philosophe Voltaire = ex. of Enlightenment ideas

21. C   Difficulty: Medium

Category: Key Ideas and Details / Detail

Getting to the Answer: This question asks for a description of the philosophes, so it's back to the first two paragraphs. Lines 12–15 say that they took the ideas of others and popularized them. The first sentence of the second paragraph (lines 19–22) goes on to state that they "developed the philosophy of the Enlightenment and spread it to much of the educated elite in Western Europe (and the American colonies)." Thus, (C) is correct. Choices B and D are contradicted by information in the first paragraph, which states that the philosophes were generally neither professors nor scientists. Choice A, on the other hand, is too narrow in scope: true, the philosophes were influenced by Locke, but they were also influenced by Newton and English institutions.

22. F   Difficulty: Medium

Category: Craft and Structure / Writer's View

Getting to the Answer: This author says the philosophes "were rightly considered philosophers," (lines 4–5), that they were intellectuals, and that they "developed the philosophy of the Enlightenment and spread it to much of the educated elite in Western Europe (and the American colonies)" (lines 19–22). The author seems to admire these people and acknowledge their influence on the educated world, matching (F). Choice G is the opposite of the author's opinion, and H seems to criticize the philosophes for basing their thinking on the previous ideas of "Newton, Locke, and English institutions" (lines 25–26). Choice J is contradicted by the statement that the philosophes "were rightly considered philosophers" (lines 4–5).

23. D   Difficulty: Medium

Category: Key Ideas and Details / Detail

Getting to the Answer: The answer to a question that contains a line reference is found in the lines around that reference. Locke's idea that "schools and social institutions could . . . play a great role in molding the individual" (lines 49–51) comes up right after his belief that humans

are shaped by their experiences, (D). Choice A is contradicted by lines 43–46, while B and C distort details in the fourth paragraph.

24. H   Difficulty: High

Category: Key Ideas and Details / Inference

Getting to the Answer: Your passage map should have pointed you to the third paragraph, where Newton is discussed. This paragraph says that Newton believed that "the universe [was]...originally set in motion by God," Option I, and that "the universe operates in a mechanical and orderly fashion," Option III. However, this paragraph doesn't say that Newton believed that "human reason is insufficient to understand the laws of nature," Option II; if anything, it implies just the opposite. Choice (H), Options I and III only, is correct.

25. D   Difficulty: Medium

Category: Key Ideas and Details / Detail

Getting to the Answer: Lines 54–55 reveal that it was Locke who questioned the notion that "revelation was a reliable source of truth." Thus, you're looking for a work written by him, so you can immediately eliminate A, *Letters on the English*, and C, *Elements of the Philosophy of Newton*, both of which were authored by Voltaire. The remaining two works, *Second Treatise of Civil Government*, B, and *Essay Concerning Human Understanding*, (D), were both written by Locke; but *Second Treatise of Civil Government*, B, is a political, not a philosophical, work, so it can be eliminated as well. That leaves (D) as the correct answer.

26. G   Difficulty: Medium

Category: Key Ideas and Details / Inference

Getting to the Answer: The first sentence of Paragraph 4 states that Locke "agreed with Newton but went further." Specifically, Locke also thought that the human mind was subject to "the mechanical laws of the material universe" (lines 41–42), (G). The other choices distort details in the third and fourth paragraphs.

27. D   Difficulty: Medium

Category: Key Ideas and Details / Global

Getting to the Answer: The philosophes—as the fifth paragraph shows—were greatly influenced by an England that allowed more individual freedom, was more tolerant of religious differences, and was freer of traditional political institutions than other countries, particularly France. Indeed, the philosophes wanted other countries to adopt the English model. Thus (D), Options I, II, and III, is correct.

28. G   Difficulty: High

Category: Craft and Structure / Writer's View

Getting to the Answer: This question also asks about England, so refer back to the fifth paragraph. In the second-to-last sentence of the paragraph, the philosophes cite England's political stability and prosperity as evidence that England's system worked. The last sentence of the paragraph goes on to say that the philosophes "wanted to see in their own countries much of what England already seemed to have" (lines 72–75). Choice (G), therefore, is correct. Choice F, on the other hand, flatly contradicts the gist of the fifth paragraph. Finally, H and J distort details from the wrong part of the passage.

29. D   Difficulty: Medium

Category: Craft and Structure / Vocab-in-Context

Getting to the Answer: *Mordant* is a word the author uses to describe Voltaire's humor in the sixth paragraph. Think about the other words the author uses to describe Voltaire: *versatile, sparkling, outspoken.* Consider also that Voltaire was imprisoned, then exiled because of his criticism of church and state. Now go back to the phrase *mordant wit.* Given the context, this must mean something about a sarcastic, critical humor. *Biting*, choice (D), is another word with the same meaning, and it is correct. Choice A is opposite. The author states that Voltaire offended both church and state, so there were specific, not random targets. Choice B confuses the word *intelligentsia* (highly educated people) with Voltaire's intelligence, and C is opposite of the correct meaning.

30. J   Difficulty: Medium

Category: Craft and Structure / Function

Getting to the Answer: The notion that the philosophes were "more literary than scientific" appears in the middle of the first paragraph. A few lines further down, the paragraph furnishes a list of the types of literary works produced by the philosophes, so (J) is correct. The passage never mentions any *political change*, F, nor does it

compare the literary outputs of Newton and Voltaire, G. Finally, H is out because the philosophes were not scientists.

Passage IV

Suggested Passage Map notes:

¶1: 65 mil yrs ago — mass extinction

¶2: 1980 — Alvarezes' asteroid theory

¶3: research supports theory + additional meteor strikes

¶4: moon surface info also supports theory

¶5: trad. bio/geo resisted theory

31. D   Difficulty: Low

Category: Key Ideas and Details / Detail

Getting to the Answer: This question emphasizes the importance of reading all the choices before selecting one. The second paragraph tells us that the Alvarezes believed conditions created by the impact of a meteorite led to mass extinctions, making (D) correct. The impact of the asteroid, A, caused great damage, but it didn't do "most of the harm"—see the third sentence. Processes like B and C are the explanations of the traditional scientists.

32. H   Difficulty: High

Category: Craft and Structure / Writer's View

Getting to the Answer: To fully accept the validity of a theory, scientists require verifiable and repeatable evidence. Until that is available, scientists are correct in continuing to challenge the theory and pursuing their own research into it., This makes choice (H) correct. Keep in mind that the question is about traditionalists, meaning that the alternative view must be that of the Alvarezes. The traditionalists' arguments are given only briefly, and the author clearly believes the Alvarezes have added something valuable to the study of mass extinctions, but the traditional view has not been proven wrong conclusively, as in F. And as the last paragraph indicates, traditionalists have produced their own theories to account for new evidence, such as iridium's reaching the Earth's surface via volcanic activity, as in J. Choice G is a distortion; the traditionalists were not skeptical about iridium itself, but of the Alvarezes' explanation of its origin.

33. C   Difficulty: Medium

Category: Craft and Structure / Vocab-in-Context

Getting to the Answer: As it is used in the sentence, *enrichment* means "increase in amount," (C). It wouldn't make sense for the Earth to have *wealth*, A, *improvement*, B, or *reward*, D, of iridium.

34. F   Difficulty: Low

Category: Key Ideas and Details / Global

Getting to the Answer: The arguments of Alvarez-theory opponents are given in the last paragraph: no crater, iridium comes from the Earth's core, and the Alvarezes are only physicists. If sufficient iridium deposits come from the Earth's core in lava flows, (F), Alvarez supporters can't rely on them as evidence of meteorite impact. The Alvarezes didn't say extinctions never occurred without asteroid impacts, G, or that all meteorites contain iridium, H. Choice J contradicts one of the arguments against the Alvarezes, not their opponents.

35. D   Difficulty: Medium

Category: Craft and Structure / Writer's View

Getting to the Answer: In the first sentence of the second paragraph, the author calls the Alvarez theory important. The bulk of the passage explains and supports this theory, so (D) is correct. The implication is that the author believes the Alvarezes were on the right track, so we want a positive answer. Choices A and C are negative, and B is neutral.

36. G   Difficulty: High

Category: Key Ideas and Details / Detail

Getting to the Answer: According to the information in the second paragraph, soil displacement was the immediate result of a meteorite's impact; it "blotted out" the sun, which reduced temperatures and caused plants to die, which matches (G). None of the other answer choices are in the correct order.

37. D   Difficulty: Medium

Category: Craft and Structure / Function

Getting to the Answer: Look back at the second paragraph; details there clarify how the impact led to extinctions—the meteorite didn't simply smash all species into

extinction. Choice A is incorrect not only because it uses the extreme word *demonstrate*, meaning *prove*, but also because the Alvarezes' intent was to link a meteorite strike with extinction, not just prove that one had occurred. The lack of a known crater site, B, is mentioned at the end of the fourth paragraph, but that's not relevant to the discussion in the second paragraph. The conditions that result from meteorite collisions aren't evidence that the Earth is vulnerable to such collisions, as in C. Choice (D) is correct.

38. H   Difficulty: Medium

Category: Key Ideas and Details / Global

Getting to the Answer: The large number of asteroids implied by *teeming* in the first paragraph explains why Alvarez supporters believe frequent collisions capable of producing enormous damage must have occurred. This makes it very likely that a meteorite strike caused the massive environmental changes that resulted in dinosaur extinction. This matches (H). The fact that an impact would result in certain effects, F, or the idea that the dust cloud would do more harm than the impact itself, G, and the traditional view about gradual processes, J, are not related to the number of impacts that are likely.

39. C   Difficulty: Medium

Category: Key Ideas and Details / Detail

Getting to the Answer: The two sentences at the end of the fourth paragraph offer the answer; only I and III explain this position, and (C) is correct. Iridium relates to a different argument entirely.

40. H   Difficulty: Low

Category: Craft and Structure / Vocab-in-Context

Getting to the Answer: All three answer choices are possible meanings for the word *profound*, but only one makes sense in the passage. The author doesn't mention the depth of the crater, or of anything else for that matter, making F out of scope. Something very hard to understand might be profound, but the passage is very clear, so G would be the wrong definition. *Sincere*, J, is another definition of profound, but it doesn't make sense in the context of the passage. This leaves (H), which is correct. The entire passage is about dinosaur extinction, indicating its high level of importance.

SCIENCE TEST

Passage I

1. D   Difficulty: Low

Category: Interpretation of Data

Getting to the Answer: Finding the answer to this question depends on locating the appropriate part of Table 1. There are 2 rows in the table that refer to *Lagerstroemia* 'Natchez' grown at a latitude of 28 degrees. (Ignore the row containing *Lagerstroemia* 'Natchez' grown at a latitude of 33 degrees.) Reading across the 2 rows, you can see that the plants have heights of 8.6 and 7.6 meters. Both of these values are greater than 7.5 meters tall, so (D) presents the most reasonable expectation for the height of an adult plant of the same variety.

2. G   Difficulty: Low

Category: Interpretation of Data

Getting to the Answer: Flowering growth is represented by the *y*-axis of Figure 1. The slope of the line indicates the rate of increase for flowering growth, so you should look for the segment that has the steepest positive slope. According to the figure, flowering growth increases only slightly in the Juvenile and Adult phases, and it decreases during the Death phase. The only phase containing a large increase in flowering growth, indicated by a steep upward slope, is the Intermediate phase, (G).

3. B   Difficulty: Low

Category: Interpretation of Data

Getting to the Answer: This question merely requires you to read the table accurately. The 4 varieties mentioned in the answer choices typically grow to heights of 2.4, 6.4, 4.6, and 4.9 meters, respectively. Choice (B) has the greatest adult height, making it correct.

4. F   Difficulty: Medium

Category: Interpretation of Data

Getting to the Answer: Take a look at Table 1 and examine the information given about each plant variety. Of the 2 varieties with data about growth in soil and organic compost, *Lagerstroemia indica* 'Catawba' reaches a typical height of 2.7 meters while *Lagerstroemia fauriei* 'Kiowa' grows to 8.3 meters tall, which means H can safely be eliminated. *Lagerstroemia* 'Chickasaw' only includes data for when it is grown in soil alone (with a typical height of 0.9 meters), but the passage offers no reason to suspect that adding organic compost would triple its growth, so G can be eliminated too. *Lagerstroemia* 'Natchez' also has no data about growth with organic compost, but it consistently reaches heights of more than double the desired value when grown at 28 degrees of latitude, allowing J to be eliminated as well. *Lagerstroemia indica* 'Catawba' is the only variety that comes close to a height of 3 meters, so (F) is correct.

5. D   Difficulty: Medium

Category: Evaluation of Models, Inferences, and Results

Getting to the Answer: To answer this question, simply compare the statement in each choice to the information in Figure 1—only 1 choice should agree closely with the data. Choice A cannot be correct since the rate of increase for flowering growth (the slope of the curve) changes in each phase. Choices B and C don't match the data either—the curve tapers upward slightly during the Juvenile phase, indicating neither a sharp increase nor a decrease but rather a gradual increase in flowering growth. Choice (D) is correct: Figure 1 shows that flowering growth remains relatively low until the onset of the Intermediate phase.

6. J   Difficulty: Medium

Category: Evaluation of Models, Inferences, and Results

Getting to the Answer: The introductory paragraph states that Table 1 includes a plant's typical adult height—for *Lagerstroemia indica* 'Potomac,' that height is 4.6 meters. The question asks about a "*Lagerstroemia indica* 'Potomac' shrub that is almost 5 meters tall," which would almost certainly be an adult since it is close to the typical height from the table. To find the trend for its flowering growth, look at the adult phase in Figure 1. The flowering growth rate increases only slightly during the beginning of the adult phase and then plateaus, meaning that the general trend is for flowering growth to stay about the same during this phase. Choice (J) is thus correct.

Passage II

7. B **Difficulty:** Low

Category: Interpretation of Data

Getting to the Answer: Radiation energy emitted can be found in Table 2. Simply look up the value for the Isotope B row and the Daughter column. The radiation emitted by the daughter nucleus for Isotope B is 2.1 MeV, as in (B).

8. H **Difficulty:** Medium

Category: Interpretation of Data

Getting to the Answer: Look at Table 1 to determine the decay reaction Isotope C underwent during each generation. The parent and daughter nuclei both underwent alpha decay, but the granddaughter nucleus did not decay further. According to the passage, alpha decay involves the emission of 2 neutrons and 2 protons. Since Isotope C underwent alpha decay twice, $2 \times 2 = 4$ neutrons were emitted. The correct answer is (H).

9. B **Difficulty:** Medium

Category: Scientific Investigation

Getting to the Answer: Compare the values for Isotope G to the values of Isotopes A–F in Table 2. Isotope G (6.2 MeV and 0.7 MeV) is most similar to Isotope E (6.0 MeV and 1.8 MeV), which underwent alpha and then beta decay. Alternatively, compare Table 1 to Table 2 to determine the range of radiation energy emitted for alpha and beta decay. Radiation energy emitted from alpha decay ranges from 5.0 to 6.8 MeV, and from beta decay, it ranges from 0.1 to 2.1 MeV. For Isotope G, 6.2 MeV (parent) falls between 5.0 and 6.8 MeV and 0.7 MeV (daughter) falls between 0.1 and 2.1 MeV. Hence, the particles emitted during decay of the parent and of the daughter are most likely alpha and beta, respectively. The correct answer is (B).

10. J **Difficulty:** Medium

Category: Interpretation of Data

Getting to the Answer: The second paragraph of the passage states that when an isotope is stable, it no longer emits radiation. According to Table 1, the daughter and granddaughter of Isotope F did not emit alpha or beta

particles. Thus, Isotope F was stable after 1 generation. The correct answer is (J). Isotopes C and E became stable after 2 generations, and Isotope A did not become stable and continued to decay after 3 generations.

11. A **Difficulty:** Medium

Category: Interpretation of Data

Getting to the Answer: Look at Table 1 to determine which particle was emitted from the parent nucleus for Isotope A. According to the table, the parent underwent alpha decay. Alpha decay as defined in the third paragraph of the passage results in the emission of an alpha particle, which consists of 2 protons and 2 neutrons. Atomic mass is the sum of protons and neutrons, as noted in the first paragraph. If 2 protons and 2 neutrons were emitted, the atomic mass of the daughter nucleus would be 4 less than that of the parent, as in (A).

12. J **Difficulty:** Medium

Category: Interpretation of Data

Getting to the Answer: Refer to Table 2 to determine the total radiation energy emitted over 3 generations for Isotopes A, E, and F. For Isotope A, the total energy of the 3 generations is $5.4 + 5.7 + 6.3 = 17.4$ MeV. The total radiation energy emitted for Isotope E is $6.0 + 1.8 = 7.8$ MeV. The total radiation energy for Isotope F is 1.4 MeV. Thus, the appropriate ranking for energy emitted from least to greatest is Isotope F, Isotope E, and Isotope A. The correct answer is (J). Watch out for trap answer F, which ranks the isotopes from greatest to least energy emitted.

13. C **Difficulty:** High

Category: Evaluation of Models, Inferences, and Results

Getting to the Answer: During the first decay in the question stem, the atomic mass decreases by 4 (from 212 to 208) and the atomic number decreases by 2 (from 83 to 81), which indicates alpha decay. During the second decay, the atomic mass does not change but the atomic number increases by 1 (from 81 to 82), which indicates beta decay. Look at Table 1 to see which isotope underwent first alpha decay and then beta decay. Only Isotope E matches that series. Choice (C) is thus correct.

Passage III

14. H   Difficulty: Medium

Category: Scientific Investigation

Getting to the Answer: The independent variable is the quantity that is manipulated by researchers and that impacts the dependent variable (or variables) that the researchers measure. Table 2 and the description for Experiment 3 both indicate that the experiment studied how levels of UV-B light varied based on the time of day during which they were measured. The time of day is thus the independent variable, and (H) is correct. Choice F is incorrect because Experiment 3 only considered UV-B levels. Choice G is incorrect because UV-B level was the dependent variable in Experiment 3, the one that the researchers measured. Choice J is incorrect because Experiment 3 was limited to a single season, the summer.

15. B   Difficulty: Medium

Category: Interpretation of Data

Getting to the Answer: To answer this question, begin by considering the trends that are revealed by the experimental results. The results of Experiment 1 indicate that UV-A levels are greater during the summer and at higher elevations, while the results of Experiment 2 show that UV-A levels are lower the more time has passed after the sun has been directly overhead. Choice (B) is correct because living in an area with shorter summers and longer winters would mean fewer days with higher UV-A levels and more days with lower UV-A levels. Choice A is incorrect because there is no suggestion in the passage of an inverse relationship between UV-A levels and UV-B levels—if anything, the results of Experiment 2 suggest a direct relationship since levels of both decrease 2 hours after the sun is directly overhead. Choice C is the opposite of (B) and would likely result in greater UV-A levels. Choice D is incorrect because windows that filter out UV-B light would not necessarily filter out UV-A light as well.

16. G   Difficulty: Low

Category: Interpretation of Data

Getting to the Answer: Essentially, this question is asking how UV-B levels change from when the sun is overhead, in the middle of the day, to when it is low on the horizon, near the end of the day. Experiments 2 and 3 both investigate the relationship between time of day and UV-B levels, though it is probably easier to see this relationship in Experiment 3. According to Table 2, UV-B levels decrease every hour after the sun is directly overhead, so you should predict that UV-B levels will be lower when the sun is low on the horizon. This corresponds to (G).

17. C   Difficulty: Medium

Category: Scientific Investigation

Getting to the Answer: The question stem asks you to predict how UV-C light would behave if it acted like UV-A and UV-B light did in the experiments from the passage. Here, it's a good idea to examine the answer choices to narrow down what data from the passage will be relevant. Choices A and B concern the change in UV levels from year to year, but this was not investigated in any of the experiments, so both choices can be eliminated. The remaining choices concern the relative UV levels when the sun is directly overhead, so consider the findings from Experiments 2 and 3, which investigated this directly. In Experiment 2, both UV-A and UV-B levels were higher when the sun was directly overhead, while in Experiment 3, the highest UV-B levels were recorded at that time as well. Thus, if UV-C light behaved in the same way, its levels would be higher when the sun is directly overhead, as stated in (C).

18. J   Difficulty: Low

Category: Interpretation of Data

Getting to the Answer: While working on previous questions, you should have found that both UV-A and UV-B are higher when the sun is overhead and lower at later times of day, as reflected in the results from Experiments 2 and 3. That means that both levels *decrease* as the number of hours after the sun is overhead *increases*. Choice (J) is the only choice that captures these relationships accurately.

19. D   Difficulty: Medium

Category: Scientific Investigation

Getting to the Answer: This question may look complex, but the mention of UV-A levels, the summer, and measuring 30 minutes after the sun is overhead all point to the design of Experiment 1, particularly the information in the second half of Table 1. Since the elevation mentioned in the question stem is higher than all of those in the table, and because UV-A levels increase with greater elevation, predict that the levels of UV-A in this community will be higher than all of the values in the "Summer" portion of Table 1. Only (D) matches this prediction.

20. F   Difficulty: Low

Category: Scientific Investigation

Getting to the Answer: Experiment 2 investigated the change in UV-B levels over time at an elevation of 2,000 meters during winter. According to the description of that experiment, the UV-B measurement when the sun is directly overhead is 48 mJ/cm^2, and after 2 hours, it is 42 mJ/cm^2. The only answer choice that has a value between 42 mJ/cm^2 and 48 mJ/cm^2 is (F). Choice J is a trap because it reflects the value of UV-B after 1 hour in the summer, as listed in Table 2.

Passage IV

21. C   Difficulty: Medium

Category: Scientific Investigation

Getting to the Answer: The question is asking you to predict a result for circumstances that were not tested in the original experiment, so look for the trend in Experiment 1's results. According to Table 1, every 2 cm added to r results in an additional 4 or 5 rpm for the precession rate, so the relationship between r and precession rate is direct and roughly linear. Thus, a gyroscope with an r of 9 cm should have a precession rate that is halfway between the precession rates for gyroscopes with r values of 8 cm and 10 cm, which are 19 rpm and 24 rpm, respectively. Halfway between those values is 21.5 rpm, which corresponds to (C).

22. G   Difficulty: Low

Category: Interpretation of Data

Getting to the Answer: The results of Experiment 1 are presented in Table 1, so look for the general trend there. As the r value increases, so does the precession rate. Since r is a measure of how far the center of gravity is from the surface, (G) accurately reflects the direct relationship between these 2 quantities. Choices H and J are incorrect because Experiment 1 did not vary the distance of the center of gravity from the axis of rotation.

23. C   Difficulty: Medium

Category: Interpretation of Data

Getting to the Answer: To answer this question, you don't have to figure out the exact shape of the graph—just enough to distinguish it from the incorrect answer choices. The results of Experiment 2 consistently show a decrease in precession rate as spin rate increases, with no sign in Table 2 of this trend reversing. This best fits with (C), which also shows the precession rate (y-axis) decreasing as the spin rate (x-axis) increases. Choice A shows an initial increase in precession rate before it decreases, which is not supported by the data in the table. Choice B shows the opposite trend—precession rate increasing as spin rate increases. Choice D shows an initial decrease in precession rate, but the subsequent increase is not supported by the data in Table 2.

24. F   Difficulty: Medium

Category: Scientific Investigation

Getting to the Answer: To test a hypothesis about precession rate and the acceleration due to gravity, the scientist would have to measure the precession rate at multiple locations that varied with respect to this quantity. The question tells you that gravitational acceleration decreases as distance from the Earth increases. Thus, one way to test this hypothesis would be to measure gyroscopes at different distances from Earth, which matches (F). Choice G would not provide any new data because a satellite at the exact same distance would experience the same gravitational acceleration as was encountered in Experiment 3. Choice H is incorrect because nothing in the passage or question stem indicates that orbital direction has an impact on acceleration due to gravity. Choice J would more or less replicate Experiment 2, which revealed nothing about the effect of gravitational acceleration on precession.

25. C   Difficulty: High

Category: Interpretation of Data

Getting to the Answer: In order to answer this question, you'll need to relate 3 quantities together: r, spin rate, and precession rate. So start working on this question by considering the information revealed in Tables 1 and 2. Table 1 relates r and precession rate for a fixed spin rate, while Table 2 relates spin rate and precession rate for a fixed r, which you're told in the question stem is equal to 6 cm. Call the fixed spin rate used in Experiment 1 s. Based on Table 1, when the spin rate is s and r is 6 cm, the precession rate is 14 rpm. Now, to find the value of s, just look for a matching precession rate in Table 2. When r is 6 cm (as it is for all of the entries in Table 2, according to the question stem) and the precession rate is 14 rpm, the spin rate is 750 rpm. So, you can conclude that s, the spin rate from Experiment 1, is 750 rpm, which matches (C).

26. G   Difficulty: High

Category: Scientific Investigation

Getting to the Answer: This question is effectively asking you to identify a variable that the researcher needed to control (that is, to keep constant) to ensure useful results in Experiment 2. The question stem says to assume that the results of Experiment 1 were not taken into account during Experiment 2's design, which suggests that the relevant variable is precisely the one that was manipulated during Experiment 1. According to the description of Experiment 1, the gyroscopes "differed only in the distance (r) from the gyroscope's center of gravity to the surface." As Table 1 reveals, different r values produced different precession rates. This helps to explain why the scientist "used a gyroscope of fixed size" in Experiment 2: if the scientist had used gyroscopes with varying r values while also altering their spin rates, some of the precession rates measured would have differed from those found in Table 2—and this would have made it impossible to isolate the effect of changing spin rate on precession rate. Because using gyroscopes of various sizes would have altered the results of Experiment 2, (G) is correct. Choices F, H, and J all concern quantities that are not investigated in any of the experiments discussed in the passage.

27. B   Difficulty: High

Category: Scientific Investigation

Getting to the Answer: Always keep in mind that a well-designed experiment should involve manipulating only the variable being tested while keeping other quantities constant. To investigate the effects of gyroscope mass, you need to find a way to vary mass without changing other properties of the gyroscope, such as its size and shape. A fixed size and shape means a fixed volume, and the only way to alter the mass of an object without

altering its volume is to alter its density, meaning its ratio of mass to volume. This can be done by using different materials that differ in density—for example, a gyroscope made of a denser metal like lead would have a greater mass than a gyroscope (of the same size and shape) made of a less dense metal like aluminum. Choice (B) is thus correct. Choice A is not specific enough to be correct: although gyroscopes from different companies could potentially have different masses, they might also differ in size and shape. Choice C would involve altering the acceleration due to gravity—and thus the weight—of the gyroscopes, but weight is different from mass (weight is equal to mass times the acceleration due to gravity). Choice D would test the effect of r on precession rate (as was investigated in Experiment 1), not the effect of mass.

Passage V

28. H   Difficulty: Low

Category: Evaluation of Models, Inferences, and Results

Getting to the Answer: The two theories differ on the details, but both describe how water droplets in clouds come together in some way until they become too heavy and fall to the ground. If there were an insufficient number of water droplets in a cloud, they would not be able to coalesce enough to form large water droplets (as in the first theory) or to evaporate to replace the water vapor that deposits onto miniature ice crystals (as in the second theory). According to either theory, no precipitation would form without enough water droplets, so (H) is correct. Choices F and G are incorrect because F would lead to precipitation in the first theory and G would lead to precipitation in the second. Choice J would lead to precipitation according to either, because the first theory involves large water drops that are too heavy while the second theory involves heavy ice crystals.

29. B   Difficulty: Medium

Category: Evaluation of Models, Inferences, and Results

Getting to the Answer: The major point of difference between the 2 theories concerns what actually forms in the clouds to become precipitation. According to the Collision-and-Coalescence Theory, large water drops become precipitation, while the Ice Crystal Theory maintains that precipitation results from the formation of ice crystals. Water drops are liquid but ice crystals are solid, meaning precipitation forms as 2 different phases of matter under the 2 theories, as in (B). Choices A, C, and D are incorrect because they concern aspects of precipitation that are not addressed in either theory as described in the passage.

30. F   Difficulty: Medium

Category: Evaluation of Models, Inferences, and Results

Getting to the Answer: The first theory described in the passage maintains that rainfall occurs after large water drops are formed from the repeated collision and coalescence of smaller droplets. According to this theory, rainfall is more likely to occur if more droplets coalesce, and more droplets are likely to coalesce if more of them collide. Consequently, a greater rate of collision translates to a higher probability of rainfall, making (F) correct. Choice G is incorrect because a variable rate could mean fewer collisions and therefore less coalescence and fewer raindrops, reducing the likelihood of rain. Choice H is incorrect because cold temperatures are necessary for the Ice Crystal Theory but not for the Collision-and-Coalescence Theory. Choice J is incorrect because the description of the theory in the passage does not address the time between rainfalls.

31. B   Difficulty: Medium

Category: Evaluation of Models, Inferences, and Results

Getting to the Answer: The Collision-and-Coalescence Theory maintains that water drops fall to the ground once they become "too heavy to remain suspended in the cloud." Similarly, the Ice Crystal Theory holds that "ice crystals quickly become too heavy to remain suspended in the air and fall to the ground." Thus, both theories agree that precipitation is the result of entities that are too heavy to stay suspended, so if a weather balloon discovers that there are many of these large entities within a cloud, it is highly likely that precipitation will soon follow. Choice (B) is correct. Choice A is incorrect because only the second theory concerns impurities in the air, while C is incorrect because only the first theory discusses colliding water droplets. Choice D is incorrect because the downward motion of entire clouds is not addressed in either theory as described in the passage.

32. H   Difficulty: Medium

Category: Evaluation of Models, Inferences, and Results

Getting to the Answer: According to the Ice Crystal Theory as described in the passage, precipitation is the result of the formation of ice crystals that become so heavy they can no longer be suspended in the air. For this process to begin, water droplets in the cloud must "freeze around tiny impurities in the air to form miniature ice crystals." Thus, air impurities play a crucial role in the production of precipitation. A city that produces more of these impurities could be expected to have higher rates of precipitation according to the Ice Crystal Theory, precisely as is suggested in (H). Choices F and G cannot be correct because the description of the Ice Crystal Theory mentions neither thunder-and-lightning storms nor atmospheric density. Choice J is incorrect because it suggests an opposite result: less air pollution would lead to fewer impurities in the air, which would mean fewer ice crystals forming and less precipitation.

33. C   Difficulty: High

Category: Evaluation of Models, Inferences, and Results

Getting to the Answer: The question asks you to find a statement that makes the Collision-and-Coalescence Theory more likely to be true than the Ice Crystal Theory. Assess each answer choice individually and eliminate any that fail to provide the appropriate support. The Ice Crystal Theory requires that water droplets "freeze around tiny impurities in the air to form miniature ice crystals." In this theory, fewer impurities means fewer crystals, which means less rainfall and other precipitation—so eliminate A for supporting the Ice Crystal Theory. The Ice Crystal Theory also maintains that "water droplets evaporate to maintain a constant level of water vapor," so B is more consistent with it than with the Collision-and-Coalescence Theory, meaning B can be eliminated too. According to the Ice Crystal Theory, ice crystals that eventually become precipitation form after "tiny droplets in clouds rise to a point in Earth's atmosphere where the temperature is lower than the freezing point of water." However, if precipitation could form in clouds at higher temperatures, then precipitation could occur without the formation of ice crystals, which directly contradicts the Ice Crystal Theory. Moreover, this would be consistent with the Collision-and-Coalescence Theory, which only requires the presence of liquid water droplets for precipitation. Choice (C) supports the Collision-and-Coalescence Theory while weakening the Ice Crystal Theory, so it must be correct. This is confirmed by evaluating D, which is incorrect because only the Ice Crystal Theory depends on water's changing between phases of matter.

34. H   Difficulty: High

Category: Evaluation of Models, Inferences, and Results

Getting to the Answer: Because the question asks for the *least* likely outcome, use process of elimination to remove any answer choices that seem likely to happen in the Ice Crystal Theory. According to the passage, in the final stage of the theory, "ice crystals quickly become too heavy to remain suspended in the air and fall to the ground, often melting again in the warmer temperatures near the ground to form rain." Choice F closely reflects this account, so eliminate it. Similarly, it makes sense that in slightly colder temperatures, the ice crystals might melt only partially; therefore, G can be eliminated too. Choice (H) seems unlikely to occur in the Ice Crystal Theory because water drops do not fall from the cloud (as they do in the Collision-and-Coalescence Theory); only ice crystals fall from the cloud, so don't eliminate this choice just yet. Choice J is not mentioned directly in the passage, but the Ice Crystal Theory maintains that some water droplets become water vapor (moving from liquid to gas) even though the temperature is so cold; so it is plausible that small ice crystals sometimes turn back into water droplets (moving from solid to liquid). Thus, J should be eliminated and (H) should be recognized as the correct answer.

Passage VI

35. C   Difficulty: Medium

Category: Interpretation of Data

Getting to the Answer: The question asks you to identify the trend between e and r for any value of n. If you look at Table 1, you'll see that n can be either 2, 3, or 4. Start by looking at the $n = 2$ data. As the values of e increase from 4 to 7, the values of r decrease steadily from 9.1 to 5.7. In other words, the 2 variables are inversely related. Next, look at the $n = 3$ data—the same inverse relationship

holds, as it does for the $n = 4$ data. Choice (C), then, is the correct answer.

36. F   Difficulty: Medium

Category: Interpretation of Data

Getting to the Answer: This question requires you to extrapolate for a value that doesn't appear in Table 1, so use the trends in the data to make a prediction. You saw in the previous question that for a given value of n, higher values of e yield lower values of r, and vice versa. For $n = 2$, the lowest value of e given is 4, with a corresponding r of 9.1×10^{-11} m. If the trend continues as expected, you can predict that a lower e of 3 would have a higher value for r. Choice (F) is correct because it's the only value of r greater than 9.1×10^{-11} m.

37. C   Difficulty: High

Category: Interpretation of Data

Getting to the Answer: While having background knowledge in chemistry could potentially help here, there is enough information directly in the passage to answer this question. The opening paragraph of the passage describes electrons as "negatively charged particles," so anything that removes electrons would decrease an atom's negative charge. According to the second paragraph, the ionization energy is the "energy in electron volts (eV) required to remove one electron from the atom's outer shell." Thus, applying energy to an atom could allow for the removal of an electron, which would decrease the atom's negative charge. Choice (C) is therefore correct. Choice A is incorrect because, for a given n, smaller r values are associated with larger e values, meaning greater numbers of negatively-charged electrons in the outer shell. Choice B is incorrect because the passage offers no information about the impact of forming chemical bonds on the negative charge in an atom. Choice D is incorrect because shells contain electrons and adding more shells would only add more negative charge.

38. J   Difficulty: Medium

Category: Evaluation of Models, Inferences, and Results

Getting to the Answer: This question asks you to examine the trend between the number of electrons in an atom's outer shell (e) and electronegativity (c) when the value of n is fixed. Look for the trend between e and c

for each value of n separately. For $n = 2$, c increases as e increases. Eliminate H because it doesn't contain $n = 2$. For $n = 3$, c again increases as e increases. Eliminate F because it doesn't contain $n = 3$. For $n = 4$, once again, c increases as e increases. Because the trend holds for all the values of n in the table, the correct answer must be (J).

39. D   Difficulty: Medium

Category: Interpretation of Data

Getting to the Answer: According to the passage, the "energy in electron volts (eV) required to remove one electron from the atom's outer shell" is the ionization energy, symbolized in Table 1 by I. As can be seen by examining the table, the n values listed in the answer choices correspond to the outer shell for each element, so answering this question merely requires finding the highest value of I in Table 1. The I values for Si, Cl, C, and F are 8.2, 13.0, 11.2, and 17.4, respectively. Of these, 17.4, the value for F, is greatest, so the correct answer is (D).

40. F   Difficulty: Medium

Category: Interpretation of Data

Getting to the Answer: According to the passage, Pauling units are the units of measurement for electronegativity, which is represented by the variable c in Table 1. N and Cl share a c value of 3.0, Si and Ge share a c value of 1.8, and C and S share a c value of 2.5. The elements As and Se have the same value for I, but c is 2.0 for As and 2.4 for Se. So (F) is correct.

WRITING TEST

MODEL ESSAY

Below is an example of what a high-scoring essay might look like. Notice the author states her position clearly in the introductory paragraph and supports that position with evidence in the following paragraphs. This essay also uses transitions, some advanced vocabulary, and an effective "hook" to draw in the reader.

"Be cool; stay in school," is the type of saying that may sound silly to high school students. Even though that phrase isn't really sophisticated, it does provide very wise advice. Attending school is incredibly important, and some people argue that unexcused absences should be reported to the police. Other people want to focus on treating the underlying causes of truancy rather than doling out harsh punishments. Still others think that schools should provide alternative instruction options for students who have trouble getting to school on a regular basis. All three options have the same goal, which is to help students most at risk for missing school, and I think that schools should incorporate the best parts of all three approaches into their truancy-reduction policies.

The idea of having a police record because I skipped school is extremely scary and would certainly prevent me from missing school. If students know that their school will report them to the police after a specific number of unexcused absences, they will be more likely to find a way to get to school. Teenagers don't always do the right thing because it's a good idea but rather because not doing the right thing will get them in a lot of trouble. For example, many high school students turn in their assignments on time because they don't want teachers to deduct points for late submissions. The fear of consequence can promote good behavior in both homework habits and school attendance.

While avoiding a harsh consequence is a good reason to get to school, it's sometimes not compelling enough for students who are struggling with issues that make attending school very difficult. The best way to increase attendance for these students is to address the underlying problems. If students have transportation trouble, schools should help coordinate carpools and bus schedules. School counselors should be available to help students who have social issues or violence concerns. As for lack of interest, schools can offer before- and after-school activities such as intramural sports and social clubs to give students a reason to stay throughout the day.

Even with the best efforts, some students will invariably struggle with attendance. For those students, schools should offer as many opportunities for them to complete their coursework as possible. It is in society's best interest to facilitate education, especially for at-risk youth. Now that technology allows students to learn from nearly anywhere, schools should offer students the option to study remotely. Students will benefit from a high school diploma, of course, and they will be able to say that their teachers did everything they could to give them the best chance at a good life.

Attending school isn't just about learning facts. The school environment provides students with the opportunity to learn how to employ necessary social skills, collaborate with peers, and communicate effectively. The only way for students to develop these skills is to actually attend school. Every measure should be taken to reduce truancy, including the threat of a criminal record, the mitigation of underlying causes, and the option to pursue alternative instruction. That way, students don't have to just take our "be cool; stay in school" word for it — they'll show up because, really, with all those measures in place, how could they not?

You can evaluate your essay and the model essay based on the following criteria:

- Is the author's own perspective clearly stated?
- Does the body of the essay assess and analyze an additional perspective?
- Is the relevance of each paragraph clear?
- Does the author start a new paragraph for each new idea?
- Is each sentence in a paragraph relevant to the point made in that paragraph?
- Are transitions clear?
- Is the essay easy to read? Is it engaging?
- Are sentences varied?
- Is vocabulary used effectively? Is college-level vocabulary used?

ACT Practice Test 5
ANSWER SHEET

ENGLISH TEST

1. (A)(B)(C)(D)   11. (A)(B)(C)(D)   21. (A)(B)(C)(D)   31. (A)(B)(C)(D)   41. (A)(B)(C)(D)   51. (A)(B)(C)(D)   61. (A)(B)(C)(D)   71. (A)(B)(C)(D)
2. (F)(G)(H)(J)   12. (F)(G)(H)(J)   22. (F)(G)(H)(J)   32. (F)(G)(H)(J)   42. (F)(G)(H)(J)   52. (F)(G)(H)(J)   62. (F)(G)(H)(J)   72. (F)(G)(H)(J)
3. (A)(B)(C)(D)   13. (A)(B)(C)(D)   23. (A)(B)(C)(D)   33. (A)(B)(C)(D)   43. (A)(B)(C)(D)   53. (A)(B)(C)(D)   63. (A)(B)(C)(D)   73. (A)(B)(C)(D)
4. (F)(G)(H)(J)   14. (F)(G)(H)(J)   24. (F)(G)(H)(J)   34. (F)(G)(H)(J)   44. (F)(G)(H)(J)   54. (F)(G)(H)(J)   64. (F)(G)(H)(J)   74. (F)(G)(H)(J)
5. (A)(B)(C)(D)   15. (A)(B)(C)(D)   25. (A)(B)(C)(D)   35. (A)(B)(C)(D)   45. (A)(B)(C)(D)   55. (A)(B)(C)(D)   65. (A)(B)(C)(D)   75. (A)(B)(C)(D)
6. (F)(G)(H)(J)   16. (F)(G)(H)(J)   26. (F)(G)(H)(J)   36. (F)(G)(H)(J)   46. (F)(G)(H)(J)   56. (F)(G)(H)(J)   66. (F)(G)(H)(J)
7. (A)(B)(C)(D)   17. (A)(B)(C)(D)   27. (A)(B)(C)(D)   37. (A)(B)(C)(D)   47. (A)(B)(C)(D)   57. (A)(B)(C)(D)   67. (A)(B)(C)(D)
8. (F)(G)(H)(J)   18. (F)(G)(H)(J)   28. (F)(G)(H)(J)   38. (F)(G)(H)(J)   48. (F)(G)(H)(J)   58. (F)(G)(H)(J)   68. (F)(G)(H)(J)
9. (A)(B)(C)(D)   19. (A)(B)(C)(D)   29. (A)(B)(C)(D)   39. (A)(B)(C)(D)   49. (A)(B)(C)(D)   59. (A)(B)(C)(D)   69. (A)(B)(C)(D)
10. (F)(G)(H)(J)   20. (F)(G)(H)(J)   30. (F)(G)(H)(J)   40. (F)(G)(H)(J)   50. (F)(G)(H)(J)   60. (F)(G)(H)(J)   70. (F)(G)(H)(J)

MATHEMATICS TEST

1. (A)(B)(C)(D)(E)   11. (A)(B)(C)(D)(E)   21. (A)(B)(C)(D)(E)   31. (A)(B)(C)(D)(E)   41. (A)(B)(C)(D)(E)   51. (A)(B)(C)(D)(E)
2. (F)(G)(H)(J)(K)   12. (F)(G)(H)(J)(K)   22. (F)(G)(H)(J)(K)   32. (F)(G)(H)(J)(K)   42. (F)(G)(H)(J)(K)   52. (F)(G)(H)(J)(K)
3. (A)(B)(C)(D)(E)   13. (A)(B)(C)(D)(E)   23. (A)(B)(C)(D)(E)   33. (A)(B)(C)(D)(E)   43. (A)(B)(C)(D)(E)   53. (A)(B)(C)(D)(E)
4. (F)(G)(H)(J)(K)   14. (F)(G)(H)(J)(K)   24. (F)(G)(H)(J)(K)   34. (F)(G)(H)(J)(K)   44. (F)(G)(H)(J)(K)   54. (F)(G)(H)(J)(K)
5. (A)(B)(C)(D)(E)   15. (A)(B)(C)(D)(E)   25. (A)(B)(C)(D)(E)   35. (A)(B)(C)(D)(E)   45. (A)(B)(C)(D)(E)   55. (A)(B)(C)(D)(E)
6. (F)(G)(H)(J)(K)   16. (F)(G)(H)(J)(K)   26. (F)(G)(H)(J)(K)   36. (F)(G)(H)(J)(K)   46. (F)(G)(H)(J)(K)   56. (F)(G)(H)(J)(K)
7. (A)(B)(C)(D)(E)   17. (A)(B)(C)(D)(E)   27. (A)(B)(C)(D)(E)   37. (A)(B)(C)(D)(E)   47. (A)(B)(C)(D)(E)   57. (A)(B)(C)(D)(E)
8. (F)(G)(H)(J)(K)   18. (F)(G)(H)(J)(K)   28. (F)(G)(H)(J)(K)   38. (F)(G)(H)(J)(K)   48. (F)(G)(H)(J)(K)   58. (F)(G)(H)(J)(K)
9. (A)(B)(C)(D)(E)   19. (A)(B)(C)(D)(E)   29. (A)(B)(C)(D)(E)   39. (A)(B)(C)(D)(E)   49. (A)(B)(C)(D)(E)   59. (A)(B)(C)(D)(E)
10. (F)(G)(H)(J)(K)   20. (F)(G)(H)(J)(K)   30. (F)(G)(H)(J)(K)   40. (F)(G)(H)(J)(K)   50. (F)(G)(H)(J)(K)   60. (F)(G)(H)(J)(K)

READING TEST

1. (A)(B)(C)(D)   6. (F)(G)(H)(J)   11. (A)(B)(C)(D)   16. (F)(G)(H)(J)   21. (A)(B)(C)(D)   26. (F)(G)(H)(J)   31. (A)(B)(C)(D)   36. (F)(G)(H)(J)
2. (F)(G)(H)(J)   7. (A)(B)(C)(D)   12. (F)(G)(H)(J)   17. (A)(B)(C)(D)   22. (F)(G)(H)(J)   27. (A)(B)(C)(D)   32. (F)(G)(H)(J)   37. (A)(B)(C)(D)
3. (A)(B)(C)(D)   8. (F)(G)(H)(J)   13. (A)(B)(C)(D)   18. (F)(G)(H)(J)   23. (A)(B)(C)(D)   28. (F)(G)(H)(J)   33. (A)(B)(C)(D)   38. (F)(G)(H)(J)
4. (F)(G)(H)(J)   9. (A)(B)(C)(D)   14. (F)(G)(H)(J)   19. (A)(B)(C)(D)   24. (F)(G)(H)(J)   29. (A)(B)(C)(D)   34. (F)(G)(H)(J)   39. (A)(B)(C)(D)
5. (A)(B)(C)(D)   10. (F)(G)(H)(J)   15. (A)(B)(C)(D)   20. (F)(G)(H)(J)   25. (A)(B)(C)(D)   30. (F)(G)(H)(J)   35. (A)(B)(C)(D)   40. (F)(G)(H)(J)

SCIENCE TEST

1. (A)(B)(C)(D)   6. (F)(G)(H)(J)   11. (A)(B)(C)(D)   16. (F)(G)(H)(J)   21. (A)(B)(C)(D)   26. (F)(G)(H)(J)   31. (A)(B)(C)(D)   36. (F)(G)(H)(J)
2. (F)(G)(H)(J)   7. (A)(B)(C)(D)   12. (F)(G)(H)(J)   17. (A)(B)(C)(D)   22. (F)(G)(H)(J)   27. (A)(B)(C)(D)   32. (F)(G)(H)(J)   37. (A)(B)(C)(D)
3. (A)(B)(C)(D)   8. (F)(G)(H)(J)   13. (A)(B)(C)(D)   18. (F)(G)(H)(J)   23. (A)(B)(C)(D)   28. (F)(G)(H)(J)   33. (A)(B)(C)(D)   38. (F)(G)(H)(J)
4. (F)(G)(H)(J)   9. (A)(B)(C)(D)   14. (F)(G)(H)(J)   19. (A)(B)(C)(D)   24. (F)(G)(H)(J)   29. (A)(B)(C)(D)   34. (F)(G)(H)(J)   39. (A)(B)(C)(D)
5. (A)(B)(C)(D)   10. (F)(G)(H)(J)   15. (A)(B)(C)(D)   20. (F)(G)(H)(J)   25. (A)(B)(C)(D)   30. (F)(G)(H)(J)   35. (A)(B)(C)(D)   40. (F)(G)(H)(J)

ENGLISH TEST

45 Minutes—75 Questions

Directions: Each passage has certain words and phrases that are underlined and numbered. The questions in the right column will provide alternatives for the underlined segments. Most questions require you to choose the answer that makes the sentence grammatically correct, concise, and relevant. If the word or phrase in the passage is already the correct, concise, and relevant choice, select Choice A, NO CHANGE. Some questions will ask a question about the underlined segment. When a question is presented, choose the best answer.

Some questions will ask about part or all of the passage. These questions do not refer to a specific underlined segment. Instead, these questions will accompany a number in a box.

For each question, choose your answer and fill in the corresponding bubble on your answer sheet. Read the passage once before you answer the questions. You will often need to read several sentences beyond the underlined portion to be able to choose the correct answer. Be sure to read enough to answer each question.

Passage I

American Jazz

One of the earliest music forms to originate in the
1
United States was jazz. Known as truly Mid-American

1. **A.** NO CHANGE
   B. One of the most earliest
   C. The most early
   D. The earliest

because of it's origins in several locations in middle
2
America, this music developed almost simultaneously in

New Orleans, Saint Louis, Kansas City, and Chicago.

2. **F.** NO CHANGE
   G. its
   H. its's
   J. its,

GO ON TO THE NEXT PAGE

At the start of the twentieth century, musicians all along the Mississippi River familiar with West African folk music ☐3 blended it with European classical music from the early nineteenth century.

3. At this point, the writer is considering adding the following phrase:

   —rich with syncopation—

   Given that it is true, would this be a relevant addition to make here?

   A. Yes, because it can help the reader have a better understanding of the music being discussed.

   B. Yes, because it helps explain to the reader why this music became popular.

   C. No, because it fails to explain the connection between this music and the button accordion.

   D. No, because it is inconsistent with the style of this essay to mention specific musical forms.

This combination <u>adopted</u> by artists in the region
4
who began to use minor chords and syncopation in their own music, ragtime and blues. At the same time, brass bands and gospel choirs adopted jazz music, and it became a true blend of cultures. Eventually, a unique music <u>style developed; based on</u> a blend of the
5
many different cultures in America at the time.

4. F. NO CHANGE

   G. was adopted

   H. having been adopted

   J. being adopted

5. A. NO CHANGE

   B. style developed based on

   C. style developed based on,

   D. style, developed based on

<u>It was American jazz and</u> became the first indigenous
6
American style to affect music in the rest of the world.

6. F. NO CHANGE

   G. This style, known as American jazz,

   H. Being known as American jazz, it

   J. It being American jazz first

GO ON TO THE NEXT PAGE

[1] One of the true greats of American jazz was Cabell "Cab" Calloway III. [2] He was born in New York in 1907, but his family moved to Chicago during his teen years. [3] Growing up, Cab made his living working
7

as a shoe shiner and he was a waiter. [4] During
8
these years, he also spent time at the racetrack,

where he walked horses to keep them in good shape.

9 [5] After graduating from high school in Chicago,

where Cab got his first performance job in a revue
10
called "Plantation Days." [6] His strong and impressive

7. Which of the following alternatives to the underlined portion would NOT be acceptable?
   A. earned his living by
   B. made his living from
   C. made his living on
   D. earned his living

8. F. NO CHANGE
   G. as well
   H. being
   J. DELETE the underlined portion

9. The writer is considering deleting the following clause from the preceding sentence (placing a period after the word *racetrack*):

   > where he walked horses to keep them in good shape.

   Should the writer make this deletion?
   A. Yes, because the information is unrelated to the topic addressed in this paragraph.
   B. Yes, because the information diminishes the musical accomplishments and successes of Cab Calloway.
   C. No, because the information explains the reference to the racetrack, which might otherwise puzzle readers.
   D. No, because the information shows how far Cab Calloway came in his life.

10. F. NO CHANGE
    G. it was there that
    H. was where
    J. DELETE the underlined portion

GO ON TO THE NEXT PAGE

voice soon gained him <u>popularity in the top jazz circles</u>
11

of the United States. 12

Many others have followed Cab's lead and have

added to the <u>richly</u> tradition of American jazz. Like
13
other folk music forms, American jazz has a rich history

and unique sound that <u>means it'll stick around for a</u>
14
<u>while.</u>
14

11. **A.** NO CHANGE

   B. popularity: in the top jazz circles

   C. popularity, in the top jazz circles,

   D. popularity in the top jazz circles,

12. Upon reviewing this paragraph and finding that some information has been left out, the writer composes the following sentence incorporating that information:

   > He became widely known as "the man in the zoot suit with the reet pleats."

   This sentence would most logically be placed after sentence:

   F. 3.

   G. 4.

   H. 5.

   J. 6.

13. **A.** NO CHANGE

   B. rich

   C. mostly rich

   D. richest of

14. **F.** NO CHANGE

   G. causes it to be an enduring institution with a timeless appeal.

   H. makes many people enjoy it.

   J. ensures its continued vitality.

Question 15 asks about the preceding passage as a whole.

15. Suppose the writer's goal was to write a brief essay focusing on the history and development of American jazz music. Would this essay successfully fulfill this goal?

A. Yes, because the essay describes the origins of American jazz music and one of its important figures.

B. Yes, because the essay mentions the contributions American jazz music has made to other folk music traditions.

C. No, because the essay refers to other musical forms besides American jazz music.

D. No, because the essay focuses entirely on one American jazz musician, Cab Calloway.

GO ON TO THE NEXT PAGE

Passage II

My Grandfather's Internet

[1]

My grandfather is possibly the least technologically capable writer in the <u>world. He refused</u> to use anything
16
but his pen and paper to write until last year.

(He <u>said,</u> he didn't need any keys or mouse pads
17
between his words and himself.)

Consequently, when he <u>has went</u> to buy a
18

computer—<u>because of the knowledge that</u> his editor
19
refused to read another hand-written novel—he

resisted connecting it to the Internet for several

months. He said he had no need to find information

<u>when he had a set of encyclopedias right there in his</u>
20
<u>office on a World Wide Web.</u>
20

[2]

Grandpa is fascinated by all the things he can do on

the World Wide Web. He has found that chat rooms are

16. F. NO CHANGE

G. world he refused

H. world refusing,

J. world, and has been refusing

17. A. NO CHANGE

B. said

C. said, that

D. said, that,

18. F. NO CHANGE

G. had went

H. went

J. goes

19. A. NO CHANGE

B. due to the fact that

C. because

D. so

20. F. NO CHANGE

G. on a World Wide Web when he had a set
of encyclopedias right there in his office.

H. when he had a set of encyclopedias right
there on a World Wide Web in his office.

J. when he had a set of encyclopedias on a
World Wide Web right there in his office.

GO ON TO THE NEXT PAGE

wonderful places to have long conversations with people

interesting enough to be characters in his books.

For example, he says, by clicking the "close" button
21

he can just ignore them who aren't interesting.
22
Grandpa's favorite website is Google.com. Google.com

is a search engine that searches millions of sites for

whatever word he types in, which is very

convenient when he needs to know how the native
23
people of Africa developed the game mancala.

For him, Grandpa says that, in merely a few seconds, to
24
be able to find anything he wants is a source of pure joy.
24

[3]

Grandpa's editor, however, was clever and, knowing

exactly how my grandfather could use it, described how

the Internet would improve his life. However, Grandpa
25
could get instant feedback and praise from the

publishing company, read online reviews, and do

research for his characters much faster. Finally, Grandpa

connected to the Internet, and he hasn't logged off yet.

[4]

[1] As for his writings, Grandpa uses the Internet

not only for research but also for making them more

21. A. NO CHANGE
    B. To illustrate,
    C. On the one hand,
    D. On the other hand,

22. F. NO CHANGE
    G. the people
    H. it
    J. their talking

23. A. NO CHANGE
    B. convenient, when
    C. convenient. When
    D. convenient; when

24. F. NO CHANGE
    G. For him, Grandpa says that to be able
        to find anything he wants, is a source of
        pure joy for him, in merely a few seconds.
    H. Grandpa says a source of pure joy for
        him is that he is able to find anything he
        wants, in merely a few seconds.
    J. Grandpa says that being able to find
        anything he wants in merely a few seconds
        is a source of pure joy for him.

25. A. NO CHANGE
    B. Additionally, Grandpa
    C. Conversely, Grandpa
    D. Grandpa

 GO ON TO THE NEXT PAGE

creative and checking his word choice. [2] Explaining

his new vocabulary to his editor, <u>Grandpa points</u> to his
                                        26
new computer and admits that an Internet connection

was a good idea after all. [3] I am sure Grandpa hasn't

explored the entire Internet yet, <u>but I am sure he</u>
                                        27
<u>will continue to find new and better ways of using it.</u> [28]
        27

26. **F.** NO CHANGE
    G. pointing
    H. having pointed
    J. Grandpa has pointed

27. **A.** NO CHANGE
    B. and he probably won't explore the rest of it either.
    C. and so his editor will have to teach him to find things faster.
    D. and his editor knows just that.

28. Upon reviewing Paragraph 4 and realizing that some information has been left out, the writer composes the following sentence:

    > He uses the dictionary and thesaurus websites religiously.

    The most logical placement for this sentence would be:

    F. before Sentence 1.
    G. after Sentence 1.
    H. after Sentence 2.
    J. after Sentence 3.

Questions 29 and 30 ask about the essay as a whole.

---

29. The writer is considering deleting the first sentence of Paragraph 1. If the writer removed this sentence, the essay would primarily lose:

    A. information about aspects of technology that his grandfather does not use.
    B. humor that sets the mood for the piece.
    C. important details about the Internet that his grandfather might enjoy.
    D. a justification for his grandfather's reluctance to use the Internet.

30. For the sake of logic and coherence, Paragraph 3 should be placed:

    F. where it is now.
    G. before Paragraph 1.
    H. after Paragraph 1.
    J. after Paragraph 4.

GO ON TO THE NEXT PAGE

Passage III

Chickasaw Wandering

<u>In</u> the twilight of a cool autumn evening, I
31
walked with a gathering of people to the center of

a field in Oklahoma. Although I didn't know

<u>more of the people who</u> walked with me,
32

<u>a few of them I did know quite well.</u> We were Chickasaw
33

Indians, and some of us <u>had waited</u> for years to make
34
this journey across the Chickasaw territory to the

ornately decorated capital of Tishomingo.

For my whole life I had been shown <u>other</u>
35
<u>Chickasaw's pictures</u>—many of them the ancestors of the
35

31. **A.** NO CHANGE
    B. On
    C. With
    D. From

32. **F.** NO CHANGE
    G. more of the people whom
    H. most of the people who
    J. most of the people whom

33. The writer wants to balance the statement made
in the earlier part of this sentence with a related
detail that suggests the unity of the people.
Given that all of the following choices are true,
which one best accomplishes this goal?

    A. NO CHANGE
    B. we each had our own reasons for being
there.
    C. I hoped I would get to know some of
them.
    D. I felt a kinship with them.

34. **F.** NO CHANGE
    G. were waiting
    H. had been in waiting
    J. waited

35. **A.** NO CHANGE
    B. pictures in which other Chickasaw were
present
    C. pictures of other Chickasaw
    D. other Chickasaw whose pictures had been
taken

GO ON TO THE NEXT PAGE

people, who walked along with me, to the Festival that
36

evening. My father and grandmother helped preserve
37
tribal history by collecting books and newspaper
37
clippings. Books about the history and traditions of
37
our tribe were stacked on the bookshelves, and framed

portraits of members of our tribe decorated the

walls of these rooms. When I was growing up,

I would often find my father or grandmother in

one of the rooms, my father reading a book and my
38
grandmother listening to ancient tribal music.
38

That room held everything I knew about being a
39

Chickasaw, and unlike many Chickasaw, my family
40
had moved away from Oklahoma all the way to Seattle.

Once a year, the tribe held a Festival and Annual

Meeting that was always well attended. Before they
41
moved to Seattle, my grandmother and father had

always attended this event. However, the tribe owned no

land in Seattle on which a ceremonial house could be

---

36. F. NO CHANGE

    G. people who, walked along with me

    H. people, who walked along, with me

    J. people who walked along with me

37. A. NO CHANGE

    B. Some of those pictures had been reprinted in books my father and grandmother collected.

    C. My grandmother and father proudly displayed these pictures in their homes.

    D. Like other Chickasaw, my father and grandmother had each set aside a room in their own home to the tribe.

38. F. NO CHANGE

    G. my father read a book and my grandmother listened

    H. my father having read a book and my grandmother listening

    J. my father who had read a book and my grandmother who would listen

39. A. NO CHANGE

    B. Her rooms

    C. Those rooms

    D. This room

40. F. NO CHANGE

    G. Chickasaw unlike

    H. Chickasaw, unlike

    J. Chickasaw. Unlike

41. Given that all of the choices are true, which one provides information most relevant to the main focus of this paragraph?

    A. NO CHANGE

    B. notable for its exquisite dancing.

    C. in south central Oklahoma.

    D. that lasted several days.

GO ON TO THE NEXT PAGE ⇒

built and <u>Chickasaw ceremonies conducted.</u> Since I had
                        42
never been to Oklahoma, I had never been to a Chicka-

saw event or walked in our territory.

<u>Still</u>, I had never even known any other Chickasaw
  43
children. Finally, my father, grandmother, and I all took a

trip to participate in the Festival. As we walked together

through the open plain, hundreds of <u>crickets chirping</u>
                                              44
softly from the grass. The insects accompanied our march

like the spirits of our ancestors singing to us on our way

home.

42. F. NO CHANGE
    G. Chickasaw ceremonies were conducted there.
    H. there were Chickasaw ceremonies conducted there.
    J. the conducting of Chickasaw ceremonies.

43. A. NO CHANGE
    B. Meanwhile
    C. In fact
    D. On the other hand

44. F. NO CHANGE
    G. crickets, which chirped
    H. crickets that chirped
    J. crickets chirped

Question 45 asks about the essay as a whole.

---

45. Suppose the writer's goal had been to write an essay describing the history of the Chickasaw people. Would this essay successfully accomplish this goal?

    A. Yes, because it describes events that take place in the past.
    B. Yes, because it contains detailed information about the Chickasaw.
    C. No, because it focuses on an individual's limited experiences.
    D. No, because it is narrated from one person's point of view.

GO ON TO THE NEXT PAGE

Passage IV

Topping the Washington Monument

During the midday hours of December 6, 1884, engineers and workers braced themselves for the days 46 dangerous mission. [A] Winds that rushed past the workers

at speeds of nearly sixty miles per hour threatened to 47

postpone and delay the capstone ceremony marking 48

the placement of the capstone atop the Washington Monument. 49

Eighty-five years of fundraising and planning had brought about this moment. In 1799, attorney and 50 Congressman John Marshall proposed a monument 50

46. F. NO CHANGE
   G. days'
   H. day's
   J. days's

47. A. NO CHANGE
   B. had been threatened
   C. will have threatened
   D. threatens

48. F. NO CHANGE
   G. to a later time
   H. by delaying
   J. DELETE the underlined portion

49. The writer is considering deleting the following from the preceding sentence:

   marking the placement of the capstone atop the Washington Monument.

   If the writer were to delete this phrase, the essay would primarily lose:

   A. a minor detail in the essay's opening paragraph.
   B. an explanation of the term *capstone ceremony*.
   C. the writer's opinion about the significance of the capstone ceremony
   D. an indication of the capstone ceremony's significance to the American people.

50. F. NO CHANGE
   G. attorney, and Congressman
   H. attorney and Congressman,
   J. attorney, and Congressman,

GO ON TO THE NEXT PAGE

to honor the young nation's Revolutionary War hero and
51

first president. Architect Robert Mills, who planned
52
the monument that would memorialize Washington.

[B] The monument would be in the form of a 500-foot

obelisk made of marble and topped with a 100-pound

capstone of aluminum.

In 1861, construction on the monument was halted
53
for because supplies and men were needed to fight the
53
Civil War. [C] Fifteen years passed before work

resumed on the monument. The workers had the
54

entire monument's history in their minds during

they're attempt to place its capstone.
55

The crowd cheered as, attached to the top of the
56
monument, the capstone was hoisted up. [D] More than
56

51. Which of the following alternatives to the underlined portion would NOT be acceptable?

　A. in honor of

　B. honoring

　C. for honor of

　D. that would honor

52. F. NO CHANGE

　G. Mills, planner of

　H. Mills planned

　J. Mills creating

53. A. NO CHANGE

　B. was halted and then because

　C. was halted; because

　D. was halted because

54. F. NO CHANGE

　G. started

　H. began

　J. restarted again

55. A. NO CHANGE

　B. they're attempt to place it's

　C. their attempt to place its

　D. their attempt to place it's

56. F. NO CHANGE

　G. As the crowd cheered, the capstone was hoisted up and attached to the top of the monument.

　H. As the crowd cheered, attached to the top of the monument, the capstone was hoisted up.

　J. The capstone was hoisted up as the crowd cheered and attached to the top of the monument.

GO ON TO THE NEXT PAGE ⇨

eight <u>decades and more than eighty years</u> of planning and
57

57. A. NO CHANGE
     B. decades amounting to more than eighty years
     C. decades—over eighty years—
     D. decades

building had come to a <u>conclusion, the</u> Washington
58
Monument was finally complete.

58. F. NO CHANGE
     G. conclusion, and the
     H. conclusion, though the
     J. conclusion the

Questions 59 and 60 ask about the essay as a whole.

---

59. The writer wants to add the following sentence to the essay:

> During the Civil War, the monument stood only 176 feet tall, and the ground around it served as grazing land for livestock used to feed the Union army.

The sentence would most logically be placed at Point:

A. A in Paragraph 1.
B. B in Paragraph 2.
C. C in Paragraph 3.
D. D in Paragraph 3.

60. Suppose the writer had intended to write a brief essay that describes the entire process of designing and building the Washington Monument. Would this essay successfully fulfill the writer's goal?

F. Yes, because it offers such details as the materials used to make the capstone and shaft of the monument.
G. Yes, because it explains in detail each step in the design and construction of the monument.
H. No, because it focuses primarily on one point in the development of the monument rather than on the entire process.
J. No, because it is primarily a historical essay about the early stages in the development of the monument.

GO ON TO THE NEXT PAGE

Passage V

Why Lions Roar

Research by biologists and environmental scientists has found several reasons that lions roar. Lions, which live in groups called prides, are very social creatures that communicate with one another in many ways. Roaring, the sound most often associated with lions, <u>perform</u> several key functions within the pride.
61

One of these <u>defense</u> involves protecting the pride's
62
land. When prides take large pieces of land and claim them as their own, they will roar to keep away intruders,

<u>those are usually</u> other lions. This "No Trespassing"
63

warning serves to keep the peace <u>because</u> it helps prevent
64
competing prides from fighting over food or for mates.

<u>Lions also roar</u> to stay in contact with one another
65
when members of a pride are separated by long distances.

61. **A.** NO CHANGE
    B. perform,
    C. performs,
    D. performs

62. **F.** NO CHANGE
    G. One of these, defense,
    H. One of these being defense,
    J. One of these is defense and it

63. **A.** NO CHANGE
    B. most often these are
    C. and are typically
    D. usually

64. Which of the following alternatives to the underlined portion would be the LEAST acceptable?

    F. although
    G. in that
    H. since
    J. as

65. **A.** NO CHANGE
    B. It's also the case that roaring is employed
    C. In addition, roaring is a way
    D. Roaring is also used

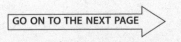
GO ON TO THE NEXT PAGE

Practice Test 5

Like all large cats, lions have acute <u>hearing, which</u>
                                              66
<u>makes it possible for</u> them to hear other members of
        66

66. Which of the following alternatives to the
       underlined portion would NOT be acceptable?

   F. hearing, thereby allowing

   G. hearing, making it possible for

   H. hearing, makes it possible for

   J. hearing, thereby making it possible for

their pride from great distances. <u>Frequently, everyday</u>
                                           67

67. **A.** NO CHANGE

   B. Quite regularly, everyday

   C. Many times, everyday

   D. Everyday

activities like hunting <u>call upon animals' sharp instincts</u>;
                                    68
in order to reunite, the pride members roar to find one

another.

68. Given that all of the choices are true, which
       is the best replacement for the underlined
       selection to provide a logical reason for the
       action described in the second clause of the
       sentence?

   F. NO CHANGE

   G. disperse a pride over large areas of land

   H. require the pride to travel some distance

   J. involve the entire pride

    <u>Finally</u>, lions use roars to attract potential mates.
                69
During mating season, males will try to attract females

from the pride by roaring, displaying their manes,

69. **A.** NO CHANGE

   B. Nevertheless

   C. Second

   D. Thus

<u>they rub</u> against females, and fighting one another.
     70
Often a male that does not belong to a pride will try to

enter the pride and mate with females inside the pride.

70. **F.** NO CHANGE

   G. rubbing

   H. rubbed

   J. rub

When this occurs, the <u>alpha or, dominant, male</u>
                              71
instructs all the other males in the pride to roar

71. **A.** NO CHANGE

   B. alpha, or dominant, male

   C. alpha or dominant male,

   D. alpha or, dominant male

GO ON TO THE NEXT PAGE ⟶

toward the outsider. <u>The outsider is scared during his</u>
72
<u>preparation for the fight partly by the roaring.</u>
72

The combined roaring of the males <u>make</u> the pride
73
sound much larger than it actually is.

    Future research on lions will help us understand

more about the reasons they roar. What is already

<u>clear, is that</u> often the lion's roar is meant to be heard.
74
Whether communicating with one another or threaten-

ing intruders, lions roar to get attention.

72. **F.** NO CHANGE

    G. The purpose of the roaring is to help scare the outsider during his preparation for the fight.

    H. Fear in the outsider is raised, during preparation for the fight, by the roaring.

    J. The roaring helps scare the outsider during his preparation for the fight.

73. **A.** NO CHANGE

    B. have the effect of making

    C. are intended to make

    D. makes

74. **F.** NO CHANGE

    G. clear is that,

    H. clear is, that

    J. clear is that

Question 75 asks about the essay as a whole.

---

75. Suppose the writer's goal had been to explain some natural phenomenon. Would this essay have accomplished this goal?

    A. Yes, because it presents some of the reasons lions roar.

    B. Yes, because it deals with a scientific topic.

    C. No, because it does not attempt to explain why lions roar.

    D. No, because it focuses only on lions and not other animals.

IF YOU FINISH BEFORE TIME IS CALLED, YOU MAY CHECK YOUR WORK ON THIS SECTION ONLY. DO NOT TURN TO ANY OTHER SECTION IN THE TEST. **STOP**

MATHEMATICS TEST

60 Minutes—60 Questions

Directions: Choose the correct solution to each question and fill in the corresponding bubble on your answer sheet.

Do not continue to spend time on questions if you get stuck. Solve as many questions as you can before returning to any if time permits.

You may use a calculator on this test for any question you choose. However, some questions may be better solved without a calculator.

Note: Unless otherwise stated, you can assume:

1. Figures are NOT necessarily drawn to scale.

2. Geometric figures are two dimensional.

3. The word *line* indicates a straight line.

4. The word *average* indicates arithmetic mean.

1. In a class, 10 students are receiving honors credit. This number is exactly 20% of the total number of students in the class. How many students are in the class?

   A. 12

   B. 15

   C. 18

   D. 20

   E. 50

2. What value of k satisfies the following proportion?

$$\frac{14}{21} = \frac{k}{27}$$

   F. 4

   G. 16

   H. 18

   J. 22

   K. 25

3. What is the fifth term of the arithmetic sequence 7, 4, 1, … ?

   A. −5

   B. −2

   C. 1

   D. 4

   E. 14

4. At a certain time of day, Carrie casts a 380-centimeter-long shadow, and Wade casts a 400-centimeter-long shadow (assume that Carrie and Wade are standing vertically on level ground). If Wade is 180 centimeters tall, how many centimeters tall is Carrie?

   F. 160

   G. 171

   H. 180

   J. 189

   K. 200

GO ON TO THE NEXT PAGE

5. If *G*, *H*, and *K* are distinct points on the same line, and $\overline{GK} \cong \overline{HK}$, then which of the following must be true?

   A. *G* is the midpoint of $\overline{HK}$

   B. *H* is the midpoint of $\overline{GK}$

   C. *K* is the midpoint of $\overline{GH}$

   D. *G* is the midpoint of $\overline{KH}$

   E. *K* is the midpoint of $\overline{KG}$

6. Four pieces of high-tension wire, each 1.2 meters long, are cut from the end of a spool of wire that is 50 meters long. How many meters of wire are left?

   F. 45.2

   G. 45.8

   H. 46.8

   J. 47.2

   K. 47.8

7. The combined length of 3 pieces of rope is 80 feet. The lengths of the pieces are in the ratio 2:3:5. If the longest of the three existing pieces is cut in half, how many feet long will each half be?

   A. 12

   B. 16

   C. 20

   D. 24

   E. 40

8. Which of the following represents the solution to the inequality $3x + 12 \geq 4(x + 2)$?

   F. ⊶ (line with open circle at 4, shaded left, marks at 0, 4)

   G. (line with open circle at 4, shaded left, marks at 0, 4)

   H. (line with closed circle at 4, shaded right, marks at 0, 4)

   J. (line with closed circle at 4, shaded left, marks at 0, 4)

   K. (line with closed circles at −4 and 4, shaded between, marks at −4, 0, 4)

9. A walkway, 31 by $32\frac{1}{2}$ feet, surrounds a pool that is $27\frac{1}{2}$ by 29 feet, as shown here.

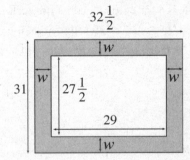

   What is the width, *w*, of the walkway in feet?

   A. $1\frac{1}{4}$

   B. 1

   C. $1\frac{1}{2}$

   D. $1\frac{3}{4}$

   E. $3\frac{1}{2}$

GO ON TO THE NEXT PAGE

10. If $x^5 = 500$ (and x is a real number), then x lies between which two consecutive integers?

   F. 2 and 3

   G. 3 and 4

   H. 4 and 5

   J. 5 and 6

   K. 6 and 7

11. If $47 - x = 188$, then $x = ?$

   A. -235

   B. -141

   C. 4

   D. 141

   E. 235

12. The toll for driving a segment of a certain freeway is $1.50 plus 25 cents for each mile traveled. Joy paid a $25 toll for driving a segment of the freeway. How many miles did she travel?

   F. 10

   G. 75

   H. 94

   J. 96

   K. 100

13. A local skating rink is hosting a skate-a-thon for charity. Each person who enters must skate a minimum of 3 hours before earning any money for the charity. After the first 3 hours, participants earn $20 per half hour of continuous skating. Which expression represents the total amount earned by a person who skates h hours, assuming he or she skates at least 3 hours?

   A. $10h$

   B. $20h - 3$

   C. $20(h - 3)$

   D. $40h - 120$

   E. $40h$

14. Which of the following is a simplified form of $5a - 5b + 3a$?

   F. $5(a - b + 3)$

   G. $(a - b)(5 + 3a)$

   H. $a(8 - 5b)$

   J. $8a - 5b$

   K. $2a - 5b$

15. In the parallelogram below, what is the measure of angle FEG ?

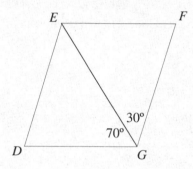

   A. $30°$

   B. $40°$

   C. $50°$

   D. $60°$

   E. $70°$

16. What is the slope of any line that is parallel to the line $4x + 3y = 9$?

   F. -4

   G. $-\dfrac{4}{3}$

   H. $\dfrac{4}{9}$

   J. 4

   K. 9

GO ON TO THE NEXT PAGE

17. If $x > 0$ and $3x^2 - 7x - 20 = 0$, then $x = ?$

    A. $\dfrac{5}{3}$

    B. 3

    C. 4

    D. 7

    E. 20

18. The lengths of the sides of a triangle are 2, 5, and 6 centimeters. How many centimeters long is the shortest side of a similar triangle that has a perimeter of 26 centimeters?

    F. 4

    G. 7

    H. 10

    J. 12

    K. 13

19. A shirt that normally sells for $24.60 is on sale for 15% off. How much does it cost during the sale, to the nearest dollar?

    A. $ 4

    B. $10

    C. $20

    D. $21

    E. $29

20. If $f(x) = x^3 - x^2 - x$, what is the value of $f(-3)$?

    F. -39

    G. -33

    H. -21

    J. -15

    K. 0

21. If a function is defined by the rule $r \clubsuit s = r(r - s)$ for all integers r and s, then $4 \clubsuit (3 \clubsuit 5)$ equals which of the following?

    A. -8

    B. -2

    C. 2

    D. 20

    E. 40

22. There are three feet in a yard. If 2.5 yards of fabric cost $4.50, what is the cost per foot?

    F. $ 0.60

    G. $ 0.90

    H. $ 1.50

    J. $ 1.80

    K. $11.25

23. Melba is making a circular spinner for a board game. She divides a circle into 8 congruent sectors. What is the arc measure, in degrees, of each sector?

    A. 30

    B. 40

    C. 45

    D. 60

    E. 75

24. A salesperson earns $7h + 0.04s$ dollars, where h is the number of hours worked, and s is the total amount of her sales. What does she earn for working 15 hours with $120.50 in sales?

    F. $109.82

    G. $153.20

    H. $226.10

    J. $231.50

    K. $848.32

GO ON TO THE NEXT PAGE

25. The following figures show regular polygons and the sum of the degrees of the angles in each polygon. Based on these figures, which equation represents the number of degrees in a regular polygon as a function of the number of sides, n, the polygon has?

 180°   360°   540°   720°

A. $f(n) = 60n$

B. $f(n) = 180n$

C. $f(n) = 180(n - 2)$

D. $f(n) = 20n^2$

E. Cannot be determined from the given information

26. $|6(-12) + 8(4)| = ?$

F. -104

G. -40

H. -6

J. 40

K. 104

27. When $-1 \leq a \leq 1$ and $-4 \leq b \leq 3$, what is the greatest possible value of the expression $a \times b$?

A. 4

B. 3

C. 2

D. -3

E. -12

28. A baker makes 186 cupcakes. Some have chocolate icing and some have vanilla icing, and both kinds are made with and without sprinkles, as shown in the table that follows. Because they are more popular, the baker used chocolate icing on $\frac{2}{3}$ of the cupcakes. If a cupcake with chocolate icing is chosen at random, what is the probability that it will have sprinkles?

	Chocolate Icing	Vanilla Icing	Total
With Sprinkles		40	
Without Sprinkles			104
Total			186

F. $\frac{21}{93}$

G. $\frac{21}{62}$

H. $\frac{41}{93}$

J. $\frac{21}{41}$

K. Cannot be determined from the given information

29. What is the value of $-1\begin{bmatrix} 4 & 3 \\ 2 & 1 \end{bmatrix} + 2\begin{bmatrix} 1 & 2 \\ 3 & 4 \end{bmatrix}$?

A. $\begin{bmatrix} -2 & -1 \\ -4 & -7 \end{bmatrix}$

B. $\begin{bmatrix} -1 & -2 \\ -3 & -4 \end{bmatrix}$

C. $\begin{bmatrix} -2 & 1 \\ 3 & 4 \end{bmatrix}$

D. $\begin{bmatrix} -2 & 1 \\ 4 & 7 \end{bmatrix}$

E. $\begin{bmatrix} 1 & 2 \\ 3 & 4 \end{bmatrix}$

GO ON TO THE NEXT PAGE

30. A triangle has sides of length 3.5 inches and 6 inches. Which of the following CANNOT be the length of the third side, in inches?

    F. 2

    G. 3

    H. 4

    J. 5

    K. 6

31. The entire graph of a function, *F*, is shown in the standard (x, y) coordinate plane below. One of the following sets is the range of the function. Which set is it?

    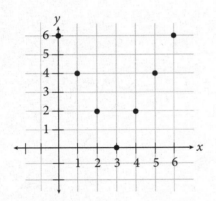

    A. $\{y: y \geq 0\}$

    B. $\{y: 0 \leq y \leq 6\}$

    C. $\{x: 0 \leq x \leq 6\}$

    D. $\{0, 2, 4, 6\}$

    E. $\{0, 1, 2, 3, 4, 5, 6\}$

32. The probability of rain today is 60 percent, and the independent probability of rain tomorrow is 75 percent. What is the probability that it will rain neither today nor tomorrow?

    F. 10%

    G. 15%

    H. 45%

    J. 55%

    K. 65%

33. If the length of a square is increased by 2 inches and the width is increased by 3 inches, a rectangle is formed. If each side of the original square is *b* inches long, what is the area of the new rectangle, in square inches?

    A. $2b + 5$

    B. $4b + 10$

    C. $b^2 + 6$

    D. $b^2 + 5b + 5$

    E. $b^2 + 5b + 6$

34. What is the circumference of a circle in the standard (x, y) coordinate plane, given by the equation $(x + 3)^2 + (y - 2)^2 = 100$?

    F. 10π

    G. 20π

    H. 25π

    J. 100π

    K. 200π

GO ON TO THE NEXT PAGE

35. The school band has a collection of 300 pieces of music. Of these, 10% are movie theme songs. Out of the rest of the pieces of music, 80 are marches. How many of the band's pieces of music are neither marches nor movie theme songs?

    A. 190

    B. 198

    C. 210

    D. 220

    E. 270

36. A basketball team made 1-point (free throws), 2-point, and 3-point baskets. Twenty percent of the baskets they made were worth 1 point, 70% of their baskets were worth 2 points, and 10% of their baskets were worth 3 points. To the nearest tenth, what was the average point value of their baskets?

    F. 1.4

    G. 1.7

    H. 1.8

    J. 1.9

    K. 2.0

37. If $g = 4q + 3$ and $h = 2q - 8$, what is g in terms of h ?

    A. $g = \dfrac{h + 8}{2}$

    B. $g = \dfrac{4h + 11}{2}$

    C. $h = \dfrac{g - 3}{4}$

    D. $2h + 11$

    E. $2h + 19$

38. What is the largest possible product for two odd integers whose sum is 42 ?

    F. 117

    G. 185

    H. 259

    J. 377

    K. 441

39. In the figure that follows, lines l and m are parallel, lines n and p are parallel, and the measures of two angles are as shown. What is the value of x ?

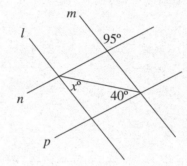

    A. 40

    B. 45

    C. 50

    D. 70

    E. 85

40. In the (x,y) coordinate plane, what is the y-intercept of the line $12x - 3y = 12$?

    F. −4

    G. −3

    H. 0

    J. 4

    K. 12

GO ON TO THE NEXT PAGE

41. In the final round of a trivia competition, contestants were asked to name as many states that begin with the letter M as they could in 30 seconds. The bar graph below shows the number of states the contestants were able to name. Based on the graph, what was the median number of states that contestants were able to name?

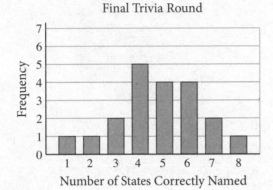

Final Trivia Round

A. 4

B. 5

C. 6

D. 7

E. Cannot be determined from the given information

42. For what value of a would the following system of equations have no solution?

$$-x + 6y = 7$$
$$-5x + 10ay = 32$$

F. $\dfrac{5}{3}$

G. 3

H. 6

J. 30

K. 60

43. The figure below shows a square overlapping with a rectangle. One vertex of the rectangle is at the center of the square. What is the area of the shaded region, in square inches?

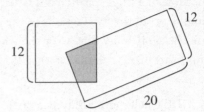

A. 9

B. 18

C. 36

D. 72

E. 144

44. If $p - q = -4$ and $p + q = -3$, then $p^2 - q^2 = ?$

F. 25

G. 12

H. 7

J. -7

K. -12

GO ON TO THE NEXT PAGE

45. The table below shows a summary of a high-density lipoprotein, or HDL, cholesterol study. An HDL level less than 40 mg/dL is considered to be a major risk factor for heart disease. Based on the table, if a single participant is selected at random from all the participants in the study, what is the probability that he or she will be at risk for heart disease and be at least 36 years old?

HDL Cholesterol Study Results

Age Group	< 40 mg/dL	40-60 mg/dL	> 60 mg/dL	Total
18-25	9	22	17	48
26-35	16	48	34	98
36-45	19	35	40	94
Older than 45	12	27	21	60
Total	56	132	112	300

A. $\dfrac{19}{300}$

B. $\dfrac{1}{12}$

C. $\dfrac{31}{300}$

D. $\dfrac{14}{75}$

E. $\dfrac{31}{56}$

46. Based on the circle graph shown below, if there are 1,000 residents in Englebrook who are age 17 or younger, how many residents are 36 through 55 years old?

Age Distribution of Englebrook Residents

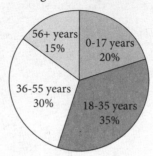

F. 300

G. 700

H. 1,300

J. 1,500

K. 3,000

47. If x^n is the simplified form of the expression below, what is the value of n?

$$\frac{\sqrt[3]{x} \cdot x^{\frac{5}{2}} \cdot x}{\sqrt{x}}$$

A. $\dfrac{3}{10}$

B. $\dfrac{5}{6}$

C. $\dfrac{7}{6}$

D. $\dfrac{7}{3}$

E. $\dfrac{10}{3}$

GO ON TO THE NEXT PAGE

48. What is the value of the expression $\cos\left(\dfrac{5\pi}{12}\right)$

given that $\dfrac{5\pi}{12} = \dfrac{2\pi}{3} - \dfrac{\pi}{4}$ and that

$\cos(x - y) = (\cos x)(\cos y) + (\sin x)(\sin y)$?

(Note: Use the following table of values.)

θ	$\sin\theta$	$\cos\theta$
$\dfrac{\pi}{4}$	$\dfrac{\sqrt{2}}{2}$	$\dfrac{\sqrt{2}}{2}$
$\dfrac{2\pi}{3}$	$\dfrac{\sqrt{3}}{2}$	$-\dfrac{1}{2}$
$\dfrac{5\pi}{6}$	$\dfrac{1}{2}$	$-\dfrac{\sqrt{3}}{2}$

F. $-\dfrac{\sqrt{3}}{4}$

G. $-\dfrac{\sqrt{3}}{2}$

H. $\dfrac{2 - \sqrt{3}}{4}$

J. $\dfrac{-1 - \sqrt{2}}{2}$

K. $\dfrac{\sqrt{6} - \sqrt{2}}{4}$

49. If $x > 0$ and $y > 0$, $\dfrac{\sqrt{x}}{x} + \dfrac{\sqrt{y}}{y}$ is equivalent to

which of the following?

A. $\dfrac{2}{\sqrt{xy}}$

B. $\dfrac{\sqrt{x} + \sqrt{y}}{\sqrt{xy}}$

C. $\dfrac{x + y}{xy}$

D. $\dfrac{\sqrt{x} + \sqrt{y}}{\sqrt{x + y}}$

E. $\dfrac{x + y}{\sqrt{xy}}$

50. Line segments $\overline{WX}$, $\overline{XY}$, and $\overline{YZ}$, which represent the 3 dimensions of the rectangular box shown below, have lengths of 12 centimeters, 5 centimeters, and 13 centimeters, respectively. What is the cosine of $\angle ZWY$?

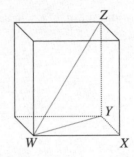

F. $\dfrac{13\sqrt{2}}{12}$

G. 1

H. $\dfrac{12}{13}$

J. $\dfrac{\sqrt{2}}{2}$

K. $\dfrac{5}{13}$

GO ON TO THE NEXT PAGE

Use the following information to answer questions 51–52.

In the standard (x,y) coordinate plane, points P and Q have coordinates $(2,3)$ and $(12,-15)$, respectively.

51. If M is the midpoint of $\overline{PQ}$, what are the coordinates of M?

A. $(6,-12)$

B. $(6,-9)$

C. $(6,-6)$

D. $(7,-9)$

E. $(7,-6)$

52. If line L is perpendicular to $\overline{PQ}$, which of the following could be the equation of line L?

F. $y = -\dfrac{9}{5}x + \dfrac{33}{5}$

G. $y = -\dfrac{5}{9}x + \dfrac{5}{33}$

H. $y = \dfrac{5}{9}x + 3$

J. $y = \dfrac{9}{5}x + 3$

K. $y = \dfrac{9}{5}x + \dfrac{33}{5}$

---

53. The equation $x^2 - 8x + k = 0$ has exactly one solution for x. What is the value of k?

A. 0

B. 4

C. 8

D. 16

E. 32

54. Suppose a quadratic function is given by the equation $Q(x) = (x + 4)(x - 1)$. If $R(x)$ is a reflection of $Q(x)$ over the y-axis, through which two points must the graph of $R(x)$ pass?

F. $(-4,0)$ and $(1,0)$

G. $(-1,0)$ and $(4,0)$

H. $(0,-4)$ and $(0,1)$

J. $(0,-1)$ and $(0,4)$

K. $(-4,1)$ and $(4,-1)$

55. Given that $i = \sqrt{-1}$, which of the following shows the product $\left(2 + \sqrt{-9}\right)\left(-1 + \sqrt{-4}\right)$ written in the form $a + bi$?

A. $-8 + i$

B. $-8 - i$

C. $4 + i$

D. $4 - i$

E. $8 + i$

56. Suppose that m will be randomly selected from the set $\{-2, -1, 0, 1, 2\}$ and that n will be randomly selected from the set $\{-3, -2, -1, 0\}$. What is the probability that $mn < 0$?

F. $\dfrac{3}{20}$

G. $\dfrac{1}{5}$

H. $\dfrac{3}{10}$

J. $\dfrac{5}{9}$

K. $\dfrac{3}{5}$

GO ON TO THE NEXT PAGE

57. What is the smallest positive value for θ where the graph of $f(x) = \sin 2\theta$ reaches its minimum value?

   A. $\dfrac{\pi}{4}$

   B. $\dfrac{\pi}{2}$

   C. $\dfrac{3\pi}{4}$

   D. π

   E. $\dfrac{3\pi}{2}$

58. In the standard (x,y) coordinate plane, if the distance between the points $(10,r)$ and $(r,6)$ is 4 coordinate units, which of the following could be the value of r ?

   F. 3

   G. 4

   H. 7

   J. 8

   K. 10

59. A state-wide hospital system in a certain state uses patient identifiers that consist of 6 alphanumeric characters (letters A-Z and numbers 0-9) with the constraints that the letters I and O cannot be used and the first character cannot be a zero. Which of the following expressions gives the number of distinct patient identifiers that are possible assuming that repetition of both letters and numbers is allowed?

   A. $24^3 + 9 + 10^2$

   B. $24^3 \cdot 9 \cdot 10^2$

   C. $1^{33} \cdot 5^{34}$

   D. $33 \cdot 34^5$

   E. $33 \cdot 5 \cdot 34!$

60. How many different integer values of x satisfy the inequality $\dfrac{1}{5} < \dfrac{3}{x} < \dfrac{1}{3}$?

   F. 1

   G. 2

   H. 3

   J. 4

   K. 5

IF YOU FINISH BEFORE TIME IS CALLED, YOU MAY CHECK YOUR WORK ON THIS SECTION ONLY. DO NOT TURN TO ANY OTHER SECTION IN THE TEST. **STOP**

Practice Test 5

READING TEST

35 Minutes—40 Questions

Directions: The Reading Test includes multiple passages. Each passage includes multiple questions. After reading each passage, choose the best answer and fill in the corresponding bubble on your answer sheet. You may review the passages as often as necessary.

Passage I

PROSE FICTION: This passage is adapted from Nathaniel Hawthorne's short story "Rappaccini's Daughter."

Giovanni still found no better occupation than to look down into the garden beneath his window. From its appearance, he judged it one of those botanic gardens that were of earlier date in Padua
5 than elsewhere in Italy or in the world. Or, not improbably, it might once have been the pleasure-place of an opulent family; for there was the ruin of a marble fountain in the center, sculptured with rare art, but so woefully shattered that it was
10 impossible to trace the original design from the chaos of remaining fragments. The water, however, continued to gush and sparkle into the sunbeams as cheerfully as ever. A little gurgling sound ascended to the young man's window, and made
15 him feel as if the fountain were an immortal spirit that sung its song unceasingly and without heeding the vicissitudes around it, while one century embodied it in marble and another scattered the perishable embellishments on the soil. All about
20 the pool into which the water subsided grew various plants that seemed to require a plentiful supply of moisture for the nourishment of gigantic leaves, and, in some instances, flowers gorgeously magnificent. There was one shrub in particular,
25 set in a marble vase in the midst of the pool, that bore a profusion of purple blossoms, each of which had the luster and richness of a gem; and the whole together made a show so resplendent that it seemed enough to illuminate the garden, even had

30 there been no sunshine. Every portion of the soil was peopled with plants and herbs, which, if less beautiful, still bore tokens of assiduous care, as if all had their individual virtues, known to the scientific mind that fostered them. Some were placed in
35 urns, rich with old carving, and others in common garden pots; some crept serpent-like along the ground or climbed on high, using whatever means of ascent was offered them. One plant had wreathed itself round a statue of Vertumnus, which was thus
40 quite veiled and shrouded in a drapery of hanging foliage, so happily arranged that it might have served a sculptor for a study.

While Giovanni stood at the window he heard a rustling behind a screen of leaves, and became
45 aware that a person was at work in the garden. His figure soon emerged into view, and showed itself to be that of no common laborer, but a tall, emaciated, sallow, and sickly-looking man, dressed in a scholar's garb of black. He was beyond the
50 middle term of life, with gray hair, a thin, gray beard, and a face singularly marked with intellect and cultivation, but which could never, even in his more youthful days, have expressed much warmth of heart.

55 Nothing could exceed the intentness with which this scientific gardener examined every shrub that grew in his path: it seemed as if he were looking into their inmost nature, making observations in regard to their creative essence, and discovering
60 why one leaf grew in this shape and another in that, and why such and such flowers differed

GO ON TO THE NEXT PAGE ⟹

among themselves in hue and perfume. Nevertheless, in spite of this deep intelligence on his part, there was no approach to intimacy between himself and these
65 vegetable existences. On the contrary, he avoided their actual touch or the direct inhaling of their odors with a caution that impressed Giovanni most disagreeably; for the man's demeanor was that of one walking among malignant influences, such as savage beasts, or
70 deadly snakes, or evil spirits, which, should he allow them one moment of license, would wreak upon him some terrible fatality. It was strangely frightful to the young man's imagination to see this air of insecurity in a person cultivating a garden, that most simple and
75 innocent of human toils, and which had been alike the joy and labor of the unfallen parents of the race. Was this garden, then, the Eden of the present world? And this man, with such a perception of harm in what his own hands caused to grow—was he the Adam?
80   The distrustful gardener, while plucking away the dead leaves or pruning the too luxuriant growth of the shrubs, defended his hands with a pair of thick gloves. Nor were these his only armor. When, in his walk through the garden, he came to the magnificent plant
85 that hung its purple gems beside the marble fountain, he placed a kind of mask over his mouth and nostrils, as if all this beauty did but conceal a deadlier malice; but, finding his task still too dangerous, he drew back, removed the mask, and called loudly, but in the infirm
90 voice of a person affected with inward disease.

1. Of the plants mentioned in the passage, which of the following did Giovanni find to be the most exceptional?

    A. The plant wreathed around the statue

    B. The plant that crept along the ground

    C. The plant with the gigantic leaves

    D. The plant with the purple blossoms

2. In order to ensure that he is safe from the plants, the gardener:

         I. handles them only indirectly.

        II. avoids looking directly at them.

       III. avoids breathing their odors.

    F. I and II only

    G. I and III only

    H. II and III only

    J. I, II, and III

3. Given the descriptions in the passage, the author would agree that compared to Giovanni, the gardener is a:

    A. more religious man.

    B. less cautious man.

    C. more cautious man.

    D. less religious man.

4. Which of the following actions performed by the gardener disturbs Giovanni?

         I. Indicating disregard or disapproval of the plants

        II. Avoiding directly inhaling the odors of the plants

       III. Looking at the inmost nature of the plants

    F. I only

    G. II only

    H. III only

    J. I and II only

5. As described in the third paragraph (lines 55–79), the gardener's actions suggest that he is a man who:

    A. is very alert.

    B. knows all there is to know about plants.

    C. loves nature.

    D. resembles Adam.

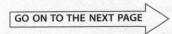

Practice Test 5

6. The narrator suggests that the plant with "a profusion of purple blossoms" (line 26) could:

    F. sprout precious gems.

    G. seemingly produce light.

    H. overrun the garden.

    J. grow very quickly.

7. The narrator takes the point of view of:

    A. a gardener.

    B. Giovanni.

    C. a scientist.

    D. an unknown third party.

8. When Giovanni questions whether the garden is "the Eden of the present world" and whether the gardener is Adam (lines 76–79), he is expressing his belief that the gardener:

    F. goes about his work with great care.

    G. has every reason to be distressed by the plants.

    H. should treat the plants with reverence.

    J. should not appear so afraid of the plants.

9. According to the passage, Giovanni characterizes the area beneath his window as a:

    A. botanic garden.

    B. center for rare art.

    C. place for people with plants.

    D. pleasure-place for the community.

10. In the third paragraph (lines 55–79), the author suggests that the gardener's relationship with the plants was partly characterized by:

    F. the gardener's impatience with the plants.

    G. the gardener's interest in understanding the plants.

    H. the gardener's desire to harm the plants.

    J. the gardener's anger toward the plants.

GO ON TO THE NEXT PAGE

Passage II

SOCIAL SCIENCE: This passage is adapted from "Look First to Failure" by Henry Petroski, which appeared in the October 2004 issue of *Harvard Business Review*. It discusses a paradox in the field of engineering.

Engineering is all about improvement, and so it is a science of comparatives. "New, improved" products are ubiquitous, advertised as making teeth whiter, wash fluffier, and meals faster. Larger
5 engineered systems are also promoted for their comparative edge: the taller building with more affordable office space, the longer bridge with a lighter-weight roadway, the slimmer laptop with greater battery life. If everything is a new, improved
10 version of older technology, why do so many products fail, proposals languish, and systems crash?

To reengineer anything—be it a straight pin, a procurement system, or a Las Vegas resort—we first
15 must understand failure. Successes give us confidence that we are doing something right, but they do not necessarily tell us what or why. Failures, on the other hand, provide incontrovertible proof that we have done something wrong. That is invaluable
20 information.

Reengineering anything is fraught with risk. Take paper clips. Hundreds of styles were introduced in the past century, each claiming to be an improvement over the classic Gem design. Yet
25 none displaced it. The Gem maintains its privileged position because, though far from perfect, it strikes an agreeable balance between form and function. Each challenger may improve on one aspect of the Gem but at the expense of another. Thus, a
30 clip that is easier to attach to a pile of papers is also more likely to fall off. Designers often focus so thoroughly on the advantages that they fail to appreciate (or else ignore) the disadvantages of their new design.

35 Imagine how much more complex is the challenge of reengineering a jumbo jet. The overall external form is more or less dictated by aerodynamics. That form, in turn, constrains the configuration of the interior space, which must
40 accommodate articulated human passengers as well as boxy luggage and freight. As much as shipping clerks might like fuselages with square corners, they must live with whale bellies. It is no wonder that Boeing invited stakeholders, including
45 willing frequent flyers, to participate in designing its Dreamliner—so the users would buy into the inevitable compromises. The resulting jetliner will succeed or fail depending on how convincingly those compromises are rationalized.

50 Logically speaking, basing a reengineering project—whether of a product or a business process—on successful models should give designers an advantage: They can pick and choose the best features of effective existing designs.
55 Unfortunately, what makes things work is often hard to express and harder to extract from the design as a whole. Things work because they work in a particular configuration, at a particular scale, and in a particular culture. Trying to reverse-
60 engineer and cannibalize a successful system sacrifices the synergy of success. Thus John Roebling, master of the suspension bridge form, looked for inspiration not to successful examples of the state of the art but to historical failures.
65 From those he distilled the features and forces that are the enemies of bridges and designed his own to avoid those features and resist those forces. Such failure-based thinking gave us the Brooklyn Bridge, with its signature diagonal cables, which
70 Roebling included to steady the structure in winds he knew from past example could be its undoing.

But when some bridge builders in the 1930s followed effective models, including Roebling's,
75 they ended up with the Tacoma Narrows Bridge, the third-longest suspension bridge in the world and the largest ever to collapse in the wind. In the process of "improving" on Roebling's design, the

GO ON TO THE NEXT PAGE

very cables that he included to obviate failure were
80 left out in the interests of economy and aesthetics.

　　When a complex system succeeds, that success masks its proximity to failure. Imagine that the *Titanic* had not struck the iceberg on her maiden voyage. The example of that "unsinkable" ship
85 would have emboldened success-based shipbuilders to model larger and larger ocean liners after her. Eventually the *Titanic* or one of those derivative vessels would probably have encountered an iceberg with obvious consequences. Thus, the failure of the
90 *Titanic* contributed much more to the design of safe ocean liners than would have her success. That is the paradox of engineering—and of reengineering.

11. All of the following are mentioned as constraints on the design of a jumbo jet EXCEPT:

　A. the shape of the human body.

　B. fuel consumption.

　C. aerodynamics.

　D. freight handling.

12. When the author states Boeing wants stakeholders to "buy into" the Dreamliner's inevitable compromises (line 46), he means the company hopes that:

　F. passengers will be willing to invest in the company to support Dreamliner development.

　G. engineers will be able to satisfy all the needs of passengers, freight handlers, and pilots.

　H. users will be willing to pay extra to have their specific needs met.

　J. users will understand and accept that the jet will not meet all their needs perfectly.

13. The author believes the sinking of the *Titanic* contributed more to the safety of ocean travel than its success would have because:

　A. engineers realized they could not be so careless.

　B. later ships carried more lifeboats.

　C. shipbuilders were able to learn from mistakes in the *Titanic*'s design before they built more ships with the same weaknesses.

　D. passengers were more likely to take out insurance before a voyage.

14. With which of the following quotes would the author most strongly agree?

　F. "Giving up is the only sure way to fail." (Gena Showalter)

　G. "The definition of insanity is doing something over and over again and expecting a different result." (Albert Einstein)

　H. "Mistakes are the portal to discovery." (James Joyce)

　J. "If everyone is moving forward together, then success takes care of itself." (Henry Ford)

15. According to the passage, which of the following contributed to the failure of the Tacoma Narrows Bridge?

　A. The engineers copied the design for the Brooklyn Bridge too closely.

　B. The wind at Tacoma Narrows was stronger than in Brooklyn.

　C. The engineers ignored the aesthetic aspect of the design.

　D. The final design omitted diagonal cables.

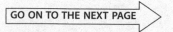
GO ON TO THE NEXT PAGE

16. The author inserts the final paragraph (lines 81–92) in order to:

    F. emphasize that the designers of the *Titanic* should have studied earlier ships more thoroughly.

    G. make the point that all ocean liners will eventually encounter icebergs and sink.

    H. illustrate how the failure of a complex design may contribute more to long-term technical development than its success would have.

    J. point out that the designs of ocean liners and bridges both involve significant risks.

17. The main purpose of the Gem paper clip example is to show that:

    A. paper clips are indispensable to modern business.

    B. attempting to redesign a paper clip is a waste of time.

    C. engineers should study the effectiveness of the paper clip before beginning a design project.

    D. redesigning a successful product risks damaging its effectiveness.

18. According to the passage, the Gem paper clip continues to be the most popular because:

    F. it features an excellent compromise between ease of attachment and security.

    G. it was invented long before alternative designs.

    H. people are familiar with the name and don't want to risk trying new products.

    J. it is unlikely to fall off in use.

19. In the context of this passage, "failure-based thinking" (line 68) refers to:

    A. a counterproductive habit engineers adopt that inhibits their creativity.

    B. the process of taking inspiration from analyzing the causes of past failures.

    C. an example of how cannibalizing a successful system can create synergy.

    D. an approach to design that was discredited with the collapse of the Tacoma Narrows Bridge.

20. When the author claims engineering is a "science of comparatives" (line 2), he means that:

    F. engineers are always compared to other scientists.

    G. engineered products are only better if they are bigger or faster than other products.

    H. engineers' designs are generally evaluated based on whether they offer improvements over previous designs of the same product.

    J. engineering tools are used to compare the discoveries of scientists.

GO ON TO THE NEXT PAGE

Passage III

HUMANITIES: The following passages are excerpted from two books that discuss fairy tales. Passage A was written by a specialist in psychology and children's literature and was published in 1965. Passage B was written by a folklore methodologist and was published in 1986.

Passage A

Most of the stories that our society tells have only enjoyed a comparatively short period of popularity in comparison with the sweep of human history, flaming into popular consciousness in books,
5   television, or film for a period reaching anywhere from a few months to a few centuries. Fads come and go as fickle as the weather, and today's hit may be tomorrow's forgotten relic. But one particular kind of story that our society tells, the fairy tale,
10 has a kind of popularity that is uniquely persistent. Literally since time immemorial, fairy tales have been told and retold, refined and adapted across generations of human history. Folk tales that spoke to people in some deeper way, and thus proved
15 popular, endured and were passed down through the ages. Tales that had only temporal and fleeting appeal are long since lost. Since, as we know, it is a truism that time sifts out the literary wheat and discards the chaff, fairy tales can be said to have
20 undergone the longest process of selection and editing of any stories in human history.

Consider, for example, the story of Snow White. Here is reflected the tale of the eternal struggle for supremacy between the generations. The evil
25 mother queen grows jealous of the competition of the young Snow White for supremacy in the realm of youth and beauty, so she contrives to do away with her rival. The innocent Snow White survives by a twist of whim and circumstance, and then
30 retreats into the forest—the traditional symbol of the site of psychological change—where she hides among the Seven Dwarves. Small supernatural spirits or homunculi, often depicted in folk tales as tiny elves, spirit men, trolls, or fairies, represent
35 unconscious forces, and thus Snow White must care for and nurture the Seven Dwarves while she undergoes her psychological transformation. The dwarves' mining activities can be said to symbolize this process of mental delving into the depths in
40 hopes of uncovering the precious materials of the developing psyche.

Yet Snow White's road to her new identity is not without incident. The breaching of the secure space by the disguised queen mother and Snow
45 White's giving in to the temptation of the apple—representative of the same youth and beauty that the queen seeks to deprive her of—causes her to fall into the slumberous mock death. Only the prince can deliver Snow White and metaphorically
50 resurrect her with a kiss, itself a motif that suggests her entry into the identity of a mature person ready to leave the dwarves and forest of the unconscious behind and take on adult responsibilities.

The popularity of this tale, and others like
55 it, across time and in widely scattered societies confirms its power in tapping into unconscious forces and common motifs that all humans share. All humans in all ages experience generational rivalry and the impact that it has on patterns of
60 growth and maturity. The specific symbols used to represent these dynamics are less important than their universality; indeed the very adaptability of the symbolism is what allows tales to remain popular over time. By dramatizing these
65 psychological progressions, the fairy tale helps its audience to process the ill-understood unconscious psychological forces that are a part of human life. Can it be any wonder that such powerful avenues to the cosmic unconscious can be shown to have
70 remained popular across the eons?

GO ON TO THE NEXT PAGE

Passage B

The contention that folklore represents a cosmic tale that encapsulates cross-cultural human universalities in narrative form is naïve in the extreme. The notion that folk tales somehow

75 embody a symbolically encoded map of human consciousness suffers from a fundamental flaw: It assumes that each tale has a more-or-less consistent form. In fact, the forms of most folk tales that we have today recorded in collections

80 and in the popular media represent nothing more than isolated snapshots of narratives that have countless forms, many of which are so different as to drastically change the interpretations that some critics want to say are universal.

85 Consider, for example, the story of Little Red Riding Hood. Some psychological interpretations might conjecture, for example, that this is a tale about obedience and parental authority. Straying from the path in the forest, in this context, might

90 represent rebelling against that authority, and the wolf then symbolizes the dangerous unconscious forces from which parents seek to protect Little Red. The red color of the riding hood might be seen as representing the subdued emotions of

95 anger and hostility. Being consumed by the wolf signifies a period of isolation and transformation. Finally, the rescuing huntsman at the end of the story then symbolizes the return of parental authority to deliver the innocent child from being

100 metaphorically consumed by ill-understood emotional states.

It is an apparently consistent analogy, and one that is difficult to dispute, until one investigates the circumstances of the composition and recording

105 of the version of Little Red Riding Hood that we have today. Earlier editions of the story simply don't have many of the components that critics would like to present as so-called "universal symbols." For example, in the vast majority of the older and

110 simpler versions of this tale, the story ends after the wolf eats the girl. So there can be no theme of parental rescue because, in all but a few of the examples of this tale, there is no rescue and no kind huntsman. In some versions the girl even saves

115 herself, completely contradicting the assumption that it is a story about rescue. Story elements such as the path, the hunter, and the happy ending, which are seen as essential symbolic components of our interpretation above, were introduced to this

120 ancient tale by the Brothers Grimm in the 19th century. Even the introduction of the "symbolic" red garment dates only from the seventeenth century, when it was put into the story by Charles Perrault.

125 In fact, every fairy tale known to the study of folklore has so many different versions that there are encyclopedic reference books to catalog the variations and the differences between them. A creature that is an elf in one country and era

130 might be a troll in another. A magic object represented as a hat in one version of a tale might be a cloak in ten other tellings. If folk tales actually represent universal human truths in symbolic form, the symbols in them would have to reflect universal

135 consistency across time. Any attempt to pinpoint a consistent symbolic meaning or underlying scheme in such a field of moving, blending, and ever-changing targets is doomed to fail before it even begins. Instead, we should embrace all

140 such variations on a theme, searching for insights into the cultural conditions that prompt such divergence.

GO ON TO THE NEXT PAGE

Questions 21–23 ask about Passage A.

Questions 24–26 ask about Passage B.

---

21. As it is used in line 4, the word *flaming* most nearly means:

   A. on fire.

   B. dangerous.

   C. important.

   D. prominent.

22. The word *avenues* in line 68 conveys the author's belief that fairy tales offer:

   F. boulevards for navigating historic cities.

   G. beginnings of life-changing adventures.

   H. approaches for understanding common experiences.

   J. homecomings for people's true feelings toward others.

23. In discussing fairy tales in lines 8–21, the author of Passage A suggests that:

   A. which stories endure and which are forgotten has nothing to do with the characters featured in the story.

   B. stories written by a single author and not endlessly retold and edited will not become popular.

   C. many folk tales that spoke deeply to their audiences have been lost and forgotten over the ages.

   D. folk tales undergo selection and editing, as do other types of literature.

24. The final sentence of Passage B provides information about:

   F. the author's opinion that only fairy tales written in modern times can be accurately interpreted.

   G. folklore methodologists who seek out oral versions of folk tales themselves instead of getting them from books.

   H. the earliest recorded versions of folk tales, which are more accurate and authoritative than later versions.

   J. the variations among versions of fairy tales, which can tell us something about the cultures in which these versions developed.

25. The author of Passage B specifically disagrees with critics who extract simple symbolic interpretations from fairy tales because of their:

   A. disregard for the rigorous principles of modern psychology.

   B. willingness to assume that minor details of a specific version of a folk tale are universal.

   C. failure to make proper use of reference materials pertaining to folklore methodology.

   D. naïve view of the complexity of human nature.

GO ON TO THE NEXT PAGE ⟶

26. The statement that "there can be no theme of parental rescue . . . huntsman" in Passage B (lines 111–114) suggests that fairy tales:

    F. cannot be said to have a single authoritative form.

    G. are generally not interested in historical accuracy.

    H. should make a greater effort to capture universal human themes.

    J. are usually not concerned with themes of rescue.

Questions 27–30 ask about both passages.

---

27. The authors of both passages state that fairy tales are:

    A. intuitively meaningful.

    B. critically misunderstood.

    C. historically changeable.

    D. symbolically rich.

28. Which of the following best describes the primary disagreement that the author of Passage B would most likely raise against the statement in Passage A (lines 32–37) that "Small supernatural spirits . . . transformation"?

    F. The specific details in different versions of this folk tale show too much variation to make any consistent interpretations based on this particular version.

    G. The popularity of this tale is no indication of its value in expressing a psychological truth.

    H. This version of the tale is not necessarily the most accurate, because it is recent and may have deviated too much from the true version over time.

    J. Small supernatural spirits could represent many things other than unconscious forces.

29. The author of Passage A would probably respond to the statement in lines 78–84 of Passage B with the argument that:

    A. many modern folk tales originated relatively recently and haven't been subjected to centuries of editing.

    B. the changes in the symbolism of more-recent revisions of folk tales are less important psychologically than the broad themes.

    C. there is no evidence that the symbolism of folk tales is related to psychological forces.

    D. Snow White is a poor example to use as evidence because it has changed so much over time.

30. With which of the following statements about fairy tales would the authors of both passages most likely agree?

    F. The popularity of fairy tales is due to their deeper meanings.

    G. Fairy tales speak to all humans in the language of universal psychological symbols.

    H. Fairy tales have resulted from a compositional process very different from that of modern literature written by a single author.

    J. The study of folklore is undergoing extensive changes because of new information about different versions of particular tales.

Practice Test 5

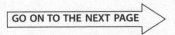

Passage IV

NATURAL SCIENCE: This passage is adapted from an article about particle accelerators. It describes two different devices used to accelerate subatomic particles.

In linear accelerators, particles are accelerated in a straight line, with the target at the end of the line. Low energy accelerators such as cathode ray tubes and X-ray generators use a single pair of electrodes
5 with a DC voltage of a few thousand volts between them. In an X-ray generator, the target is one of the electrodes.

Higher energy accelerators use a linear array of plates to which an alternating high energy field is
10 applied. As the particles approach a plate, they are accelerated toward it by an opposite polarity charge applied to the plate. As they pass through a hole in the plate, the polarity is switched so that the plate now repels the particles, which are now acceler-
15 ated by it toward the next plate. Normally, a stream bunches particles that are accelerated, so a carefully controlled AC voltage is applied to each plate to repeat this for each bunch continuously.

As the particles approach the speed of light,
20 the switching rate of the electric fields becomes so high as to operate at microwave frequencies, and so microwave cavities are used in higher energy machines instead of simple plates. High energy linear accelerators are often called linacs.

25 Linear accelerators are very widely used. Every cathode ray tube contains one, and they are also used to provide an initial low-energy kick to particles before they are injected into circular accelerators. They can also produce proton beams,
30 which can produce "proton-heavy" medical or research isotopes, as opposed to the "neutron-heavy" ones made in reactors.

In circular accelerators, the accelerated particles move in a circle until they reach sufficient levels of
35 energy. The particle track is bent into a circle using dipole magnets. The advantage of circular accelerators over linacs is that components can be reused to accelerate the particles further, as the particle passes a given point many times. However, they suffer a

40 disadvantage in that the particles emit synchrotron radiation.

When any charged particle is accelerated, it emits electromagnetic radiation. As a particle travelling in a circle is always accelerating
45 towards the center of the circle, it continuously radiates. This has to be compensated for by some of the energy used to power the accelerating electric fields, which makes circular accelerators less efficient than linear ones. Some circular accelera-
50 tors have been deliberately built to generate this radiation (called synchrotron light) as X-rays—for example, the Diamond Light Source being built at the Rutherford Appleton Laboratory in England. High energy X-rays are useful for X-ray
55 spectroscopy of proteins, for example.

Synchrotron radiation is more powerfully emitted by lighter particles, so these accelerators are invariably electron accelerators. Consequently, particle physicists are increasingly using heavier
60 particles, such as protons, in their accelerators to achieve higher levels of energy. The downside is that these particles are composites of quarks and gluons, which makes analyzing the results of their interactions much more complicated.

65 The earliest circular accelerators were cyclotrons, invented in 1929 by Ernest O. Lawrence. Cyclotrons have a single pair of hollow "D"-shaped plates to accelerate the particles and a single dipole magnet to curve the track of the particles. The particles are
70 injected in the center of the circular machine and spiral outwards toward the circumference.

Cyclotrons reach an energy limit because of relativistic effects at high energies, whereby particles gain mass rather than speed. As the
75 Special Theory of Relativity means that nothing can travel faster than the speed of light in a vacuum, the particles in an accelerator normally travel very close to the speed of light. In high energy accelerators, there is a diminishing return in speed as the
80 particle approaches the speed of light. The effect of

GO ON TO THE NEXT PAGE

the energy injected using the electric fields is therefore to increase their mass markedly, rather than their speed. Doubling the energy might increase the speed a fraction of a percent closer to that of light, but the main effect is
85 to increase the relativistic mass of the particle.

Cyclotrons no longer accelerate electrons when they have reached an energy for about 10 million electron volts. There are ways of compensating for this to some extent—namely, the synchrocyclotron and the isochro-
90 nous cyclotron. They are nevertheless useful for lower energy applications.

To push the energies even higher—into billions of electron volts—it is necessary to use a synchrotron. This is an accelerator in which the particles are contained
95 in a doughnut-shaped tube, called a storage ring. The tube has many magnets distributed around it to focus the particles and curve their track around the tube, and microwave cavities similarly distributed to accelerate them. The size of Lawrence's first cyclotron was a mere
100 four inches in diameter. Fermilab now has a ring with a beam path of four miles.

31. The main idea of the passage is that:

   A. linear accelerators are more efficient than circular accelerators.

   B. particles in accelerators cannot travel at the speed of light.

   C. linear and circular accelerators have important, but different, uses.

   D. the cyclotron is a useful type of circular accelerator.

32. The passage states that magnets affect particles by:

   F. influencing the direction particles travel.

   G. creating curved particles.

   H. increasing the acceleration of particles.

   J. causing an increase in the particles' energy levels.

33. The passage states that which of the following causes an increase in particle mass in high-energy accelerators?

   A. A particle reaching the speed of light

   B. Acceleration of a particle in a vacuum

   C. Using a mixture of different particles

   D. Injecting energy using electric fields

34. As it is used in line 62, the word *quarks* most nearly refers to:

   F. objects made up of electrons.

   G. objects made up of radiation.

   H. components of protons.

   J. components of gluons.

35. According to the passage, which of the following CANNOT be a result of using a circular accelerator?

   A. Particles that emit electromagnetic radiation

   B. Reuse of components to accelerate particles

   C. Particles that emit synchrotron radiation

   D. An initial low kick of energy in particles

36. With which of the following statements would the author most likely agree?

   F. Linear accelerators are of limited use.

   G. Using particles such as protons in particle acceleration experiments is not possible, since they are composites of quarks and gluons.

   H. Circular accelerators have improved little since Lawrence's first cyclotron.

   J. Depending on the desired result, both linear and circular accelerators are valuable tools.

GO ON TO THE NEXT PAGE

37. According to the passage, what is one effect of particles passing through the hole in the plates and the polarity switching in higher energy accelerators?

    A. The mass of the particles increases.

    B. The charge of the particles changes.

    C. The particles lose energy.

    D. The particles are repelled and accelerated toward the next plate.

38. The passage suggests that the greatest difference between a cyclotron and a synchrotron is that:

    F. cyclotrons are not useful.

    G. synchrotrons accelerate particles in a circle.

    H. synchrotrons can overcome limitations that cyclotrons cannot.

    J. synchrotrons are capable of causing particles to curve more closely to the edge of the tube.

39. How does the information about the size of Lawrence's first cyclotron and the size of Fermilab's ring function in the passage?

    A. It suggests that, over time, there has been progress in improving the size and capabilities of particle accelerators.

    B. It proves that cyclotrons are important for particle acceleration because they were invented by Lawrence.

    C. It indicates that the inventors at Fermilab were more capable than Lawrence was.

    D. It emphasizes the difference between cyclotrons and synchrotrons.

40. The author's approach to the passage is most similar to that of:

    F. an interested amateur reporting on an online encyclopedia entry to a group of similarly interested people.

    G. a noted scientist working with accelerators and explaining them to other scientists.

    H. a professor explaining types and uses of accelerators to a class of aspiring science researchers.

    J. a high school student writing a paper for a science class.

SCIENCE TEST

35 Minutes—40 Questions

Directions: The Science Test includes multiple passages. Each passage includes multiple questions. After reading each passage, choose the best answer and fill in the corresponding bubble on your answer sheet. You may review the passages as often as necessary.

You may NOT use a calculator on this test.

Passage I

Metabolism is the process by which organisms convert food into energy. Metabolism occurs through a number of *metabolic pathways*, each of which is critical to the organism's survival. Even while at rest, an organism will undergo metabolism, although at a lower rate than while active. When an organism is at rest, the measurement of its ability to metabolize is called the *Basal Metabolic Rate* (BMR). Numerous factors affect an organism's BMR. Researchers decided to conduct a series of studies to investigate some of these factors.

Study 1

The researchers investigated humans and bears (including hibernating bears) at various ages. Their BMRs were evaluated relative to the average peak metabolic rate of each species (the values for both bears not in hibernation and bears in hibernation are compared to the average for bears not in hibernation). The results are shown in Table 1.

	Table 1		
	BMR (% of average peak)		
Age (years)	Human	Bear (not in hibernation)	Bear (in hibernation)
1	42	50	30
7	75	80	30
14	85	100	30
21	100	80	30
28	86	40	30
35	72	0	0

Study 2

The average weight of a human male who is 1.8 m tall is approximately 73 kg. The researchers measured the relative BMR of several male individuals, aged 25, who were approximately 1.8 m tall and who had varying weights. The results are shown in Table 2.

Table 2	
Weight (kg)	BMR (% of average peak)
62	90
63	92
65	93
67	94
69	96
71	98
73	100

Study 3

The researchers investigated the BMR of several 25-year-old males weighing 73 kg at different internal body temperatures. The results are shown in Table 3.

Table 3	
Internal body temperature (°C)	BMR (% of average peak)
35.0	72
35.5	78
36.0	85
36.5	93
37.0	100
37.5	108
38.0	115
38.5	122
39.0	129

GO ON TO THE NEXT PAGE

1. Based on the results of Study 2, if the researchers had collected data for a 68-kg male who was 1.8 m tall, his measured relative BMR would most likely have been:

   A. 91%.

   B. 93%.

   C. 95%.

   D. 97%.

2. A researcher hypothesized that a 25-year-old male who was 1.8 m tall with an above-average weight would have a relative BMR that is greater than 100%. Do the results of Study 2 support this hypothesis?

   F. Yes, because as weight increases, BMR increases.

   G. Yes, because as weight increases, BMR decreases.

   H. No, because as weight increases, BMR increases.

   J. No, because as weight increases, BMR decreases.

3. Which of the following accurately characterizes a difference between Study 1 and Study 2 ?

   A. In Study 1, relative BMR was recorded; in Study 2, absolute BMR was recorded.

   B. In Study 1, absolute BMR was recorded; in Study 2, relative BMR was recorded.

   C. In Study 1, only 1 species was investigated; in Study 2, 2 different species were investigated.

   D. In Study 1, 2 different species were investigated; in Study 2, only 1 species was investigated.

4. Which of the following statements about bears is supported by Study 1 ? As a bear's age increases from 1 to 35 years, the bear's BMR:

   F. increases only.

   G. decreases only.

   H. increases, then decreases.

   J. decreases, then increases.

5. Suppose that a 25-year-old man loses a significant amount of weight in a relatively short period of time. If researchers were to measure his relative BMR before and after his weight loss, they would most likely find that his BMR afterwards:

   A. decreased, because lower weights correspond to lower BMRs.

   B. decreased, because lower weights correspond to higher BMRs.

   C. increased, because lower weights correspond to lower BMRs.

   D. increased, because lower weights correspond to higher BMRs.

6. Which of the following hypotheses best explains why a hibernating bear's BMR is lower than a non-hibernating bear's?

   F. A bear's energy needs are considerably higher while hibernating.

   G. A bear's energy needs are considerably lower while hibernating.

   H. A bear has a higher internal body temperature during hibernation.

   J. A bear tends to weigh significantly more during hibernation.

7. Based on the passage, which of the following internal body temperatures would most likely lead to weight gain in a human male?

   A. 35.0°C

   B. 36.5°C

   C. 37.0°C

   D. 39.0°C

GO ON TO THE NEXT PAGE

Passage II

For centuries, physicians attempted to treat patients by transfusion, the transfer of blood from a healthy person to a patient. This was not reliably successful until the discovery of blood groups and blood types in the mid-20th century. A person is said to have a certain blood type if his or her red blood cells have a particular set of molecules, called antigens, on the cells' surfaces. The primary antigens are A and B; if a person's blood cells have neither A nor B antigens, he or she is designated type "O." Also significant is the Rh antigen, which is inherited separately from the A and B antigens; the presence of the Rh antigen is designated by a "+."

A significant complication that can occur from giving blood to someone of a different type is that the recipient's blood contains antibodies (proteins that react with antigens), which recognize and attack any blood group antigen not normally present in the person's blood. A recipient cannot safely receive blood donated by someone with an incompatible blood type. Table 1 presents a sample of transfusion compatibility for some blood types.

Table 1						
Recipient's blood type		Compatible with transfusion from:				
ABO type	Rh type	A−	A+	B−	B+
AB	+	Yes	Yes	Yes	Yes
AB	−	Yes	No	Yes	No
B	+	No	No	Yes	Yes
B	−	No	No	Yes	No

The set of antigens present on an individual's red blood cells is an aspect of his or her phenotype, the physical and biochemical properties of that person. The phenotype is determined by the genotype, which is the set of genes that code for those properties. Humans have two copies, or alleles, of each gene; these alleles may be the same or different. For example, the A, B, and o alleles are different versions of the gene for ABO type, while the Rh+ and Rh− alleles are different versions of the gene for Rh type. Each parent passes one allele of each gene on to offspring, so a child's genotype consists of two alleles per gene, one from each parent. Table 2 presents the ABO phenotypes that result from each possible genotype.

Table 2	
Genotype	Phenotype (ABO type)
AA	A
Ao	A
BB	B
Bo	B
AB	AB
oo	O

8. Based on the passage, an individual with A+ blood could safely receive a transfusion from which of the following blood types?

   F. All blood types
   G. All Rh+ blood types
   H. A+ and A−
   J. A+ and B+

9. A child with a blood group phenotype AB+ could have parents with which of the following phenotypes?

   A. O+ and AB+
   B. A− and B−
   C. A+ and B−
   D. A+ and O−

10. Suppose that a patient with blood type B+ is in need of a transfusion, but the blood bank has only A+, A−, B+, and B− available. Based on Table 1, which of those blood types would be suitable for the patient to receive?

    F. A+ only
    G. A+ and A−
    H. B+ only
    J. B+ and B−

GO ON TO THE NEXT PAGE

11. Based on the information provided in the passage, which of the following blood types would be safe for any transfusion recipient to receive, regardless of the recipient's blood type?

    A. AB−

    B. AB+

    C. O−

    D. O+

12. Which of the following ABO blood types would NOT be possible for the offspring of a woman with type A blood and a man with type AB blood?

    F. O

    G. A

    H. B

    J. AB

13. A physician orders a blood transfusion for a patient with A+ blood and later discovers that her patient was given O+ blood. Should the physician be confident that this is a safe transfusion?

    A. No, because anti-O antibodies in the patient's blood will attack the O antigen in the donor blood, causing an adverse reaction.

    B. No, because anti-Rh antibodies in the patient's blood will attack the Rh antigen in the donor blood, causing an adverse reaction.

    C. Yes, because the O antigen in the donor blood will not react with the anti-A antibodies in the patient's blood.

    D. Yes, because the patient's blood does not contain any antibodies that will attack antigens in the donor blood.

Passage III

Earth's magnetic field has two distinct poles, labeled North and South. Certain materials, such as iron and steel, are sensitive to Earth's magnetic field. The origin and behavior of the magnetic field is modeled by *dynamo theory*, which links the magnetic field with the geological activity of Earth's molten core. Diagram 1 depicts Earth's geological layers from crust to core.

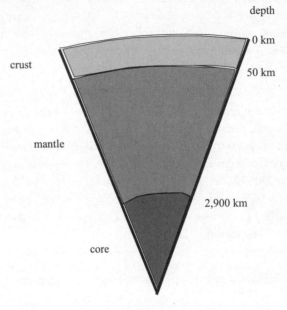

Diagram 1

Note: Diagram is not drawn to scale.

Evidence has been found of complete reversals in the polarity of the magnetic field, called *geomagnetic reversals*. Concentrated deposits of rock with reversed magnetic properties have been found on the ocean floor. The magnetic anomalies observed suggest that Earth undergoes a geomagnetic reversal sporadically over time spans of thousands of years (the last geomagnetic reversal occurred approximately 780,000 years ago). Two scientists discuss the possible causes of geomagnetic reversal.

GO ON TO THE NEXT PAGE

Scientist 1

Dynamo theory suggests that a constantly moving fluid can help maintain a magnetic field. Earth's core is made of molten nickel and iron. The constant motion of this portion of the core creates eddy currents, which in turn help to create Earth's magnetic field. The motions of the molten core can often be chaotic, and in turn disturb the magnetic field. It is this necessary by-product of the dynamo effect that causes spontaneous geomagnetic reversal.

Scientist 2

Earth's molten core is responsible for the creation, maintenance, and shifts of the magnetic field. The motions of the core, in accordance with dynamo theory, create a magnetic field from eddy currents. The motions of tectonic plates and other seismic events can have a powerful effect on Earth's core. Such events can disrupt the motion of the core to such an extent that the magnetic field effectively turns off. When the regular motions of the core resume, the resulting magnetic field will either remain as it was, or emerge as a reversal of its previous state.

14. Dynamo theory can be applied to other planets that have molten cores, and hotter planets are more likely to have molten cores. Based on this information, which of the following planets would the theory most likely NOT apply to?

    F. Neptune

    G. Mars

    H. Venus

    J. Mercury

15. Which of the following pairs of statements best accounts for Earth's geomagnetic reversal according to the viewpoints of the 2 scientists?

	Scientist 1	Scientist 2
A.	Magnetic field resets after seismic disturbance	Natural consequence of the dynamo effect
B.	Seismic disturbance caused by magnetic field	Natural consequence of the dynamo effect
C.	Natural consequence of the dynamo effect	Magnetic field resets after seismic disturbance
D.	Natural consequence of the dynamo effect	Seismic disturbance caused by magnetic field

    A. A

    B. B

    C. C

    D. D

16. Based on Scientist 2's account, seismic activity that affects Earth's molten core must be able to resonate to depths of at least:

    F.   50 km.

    G.   700 km.

    H.   1,500 km.

    J.   2,900 km.

17. Which of the following statements is most consistent with the ideas expressed by Scientist 1 ?

    A. The motion of molten nickel and iron creates a magnetic field.

    B. The motion of molten nickel and iron counteracts magnetic fields already in existence.

    C. The melting of nickel and iron creates a magnetic field.

    D. Nickel and iron are found only in Earth's core.

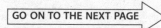
GO ON TO THE NEXT PAGE

Practice Test 5

18. Which of the following hypotheses would both scientists agree upon?

    F. The dynamo theory accounts for shifts in Earth's magnetic field.

    G. Eddy currents create seismic disturbances.

    H. Seismic disturbances cause geomagnetic reversal.

    J. The dynamo theory is relevant only every few thousand years.

19. According to the passage, which of the following is a reliable indicator of the polarity of Earth's magnetic field at a particular point in time?

    A. Molten nickel and iron

    B. Deposits of magnetized rock

    C. Seismic activity

    D. Shifts in solar magnetism

20. If it were discovered that the polarity of the Earth's magnetic field can be directly altered only by the activity of the Sun's magnetic field, how would this affect the viewpoints of each scientist?

    F. It would strengthen the viewpoint of Scientist 1 only.

    G. It would weaken the viewpoint of Scientist 2 only.

    H. It would strengthen the viewpoints of both scientists.

    J. It would weaken the viewpoints of both scientists.

21. In a computer simulation, the effect of seismic activity on the motion of Earth's molten core was studied. Which of the following findings would be consistent with Scientist 2's viewpoint? The seismic activity would:

    A. be caused by the motion of the molten core.

    B. cause significant disturbances in the molten core.

    C. have no effect on the motion of the molten core.

    D. cause eddy currents in the molten core.

GO ON TO THE NEXT PAGE

Passage IV

Faraday's Law relates changes in magnetic fields to the production of electric voltage. *Magnetic flux* is a measure of the magnetic field in a region of space. It can be thought of as the mathematical product of the magnetic field and an area defined by a loop of wire in that field. The unit of magnetic flux is the weber, abbreviated Wb. Any instance of change in magnetic flux produces a voltage, also known as an *electromotive force* (emf). This relationship is commonly called *electromagnetic induction*.

Students conducted 3 experiments to study electromagnetic induction.

Experiment 1

A magnet was passed at varying speeds through a coiled wire with a diameter of 2 cm, as shown in Diagram 1. The various speeds created corresponding changes to the magnetic flux within the coil. A voltmeter was used to measure the maximum induced emf in units of volts (V). The results are shown in Table 1.

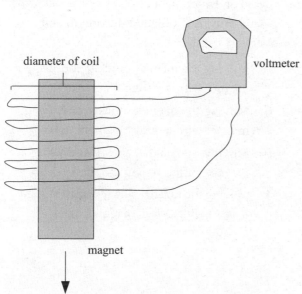

Diagram 1

Table 1		
Trial	Change in magnetic flux (Wb)	Maximum emf (V)
1	0.3	0.22
2	0.5	0.41
3	0.7	0.63
4	0.9	0.85

Experiment 2

A coiled wire was rotated at various speeds within a constant magnetic field, creating corresponding changes to the magnetic flux within the coil. Special connectors called "slip rings" allow the coil of wire to rotate without tangling the wires. The slip rings also connect the coil electrically to a voltmeter, which was used to measure the maximum resulting emf. This setup is illustrated in Diagram 2, and the results are recorded in Table 2.

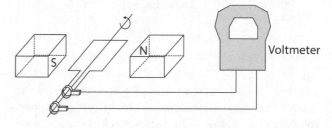

Diagram 2

Table 2		
Trial	Change in magnetic flux (Wb)	Maximum emf (V)
5	0.2	0.2
6	0.4	0.4
7	0.6	0.6

GO ON TO THE NEXT PAGE

Experiment 3

A coiled wire was mounted on a pole and a metal ring was placed on the pole, as shown in Diagram 3. (Note that the battery powering the current is not depicted.)

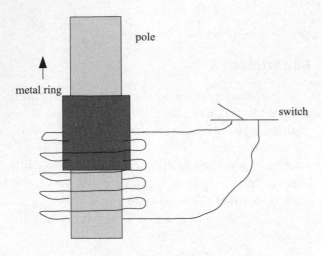

Diagram 3

A current was sent through the wire, producing a magnetic field that caused the metal ring to float up the pole. The students used the same amount of current in each trial and kept the diameter of the coils fixed, but used wires with differing numbers of coils. The height that the metal ring reached on the pole was recorded for each trial. The results are shown in Table 3.

Table 3		
Trial	Number of coils	Height (cm)
8	50	1.1
9	100	1.5
10	150	2.1

22. Based on Table 3, it can be concluded that the magnetic field generated by the wires in Experiment 3:

F. did not change as the number of coils in the wire increased.

G. increased as the number of coils in the wire increased.

H. decreased as the number of coils in the wire increased.

J. decreased as the amount of current passing through the wire increased.

23. In Experiment 2, if the coil were slowed down to a rotational velocity of 0 m/s, the resulting emf would correspond to the emf recorded in:

A. Trial 5.

B. Trial 6.

C. Trial 7.

D. none of the trials.

24. Based on Experiment 1, which of the following would provide the highest maximum emf reading?

F. Moving the magnet quickly and using a magnet with a strong magnetic field

G. Moving the magnet quickly and using a magnet with a weak magnetic field

H. Moving the magnet slowly and using a magnet with a strong magnetic field

J. Moving the magnet slowly and using a magnet with a weak magnetic field

GO ON TO THE NEXT PAGE

25. Based on the results of Experiment 1, the relationship between change in magnetic flux and maximum induced emf is best represented by which of the following graphs?

A.
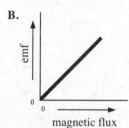

B.
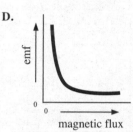

C.
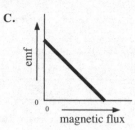

D.
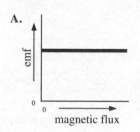

26. In which of the following trials from Experiment 1 was the magnet moved at the slowest speed?

F. Trial 1

G. Trial 2

H. Trial 3

J. Trial 4

27. If a new trial were conducted that repeated the conditions of Trial 9, except with double the current passing through the wire, which of the following would most likely be the recorded height of the metal ring?

A. 0.7 cm

B. 1.1 cm

C. 1.5 cm

D. 2.9 cm

28. Suppose that the students repeated the conditions of Trials 1–4 of Experiment 1, except that they used a coil with a diameter of 4 cm instead of 2 cm. Based on the passage, how would the results of this new experiment most likely compare to the original results of Experiment 1 ?

F. Maximum emf and change in magnetic flux would both decrease in the new experiment.

G. Maximum emf would decrease but change in magnetic flux would increase in the new experiment.

H. Maximum emf and change in magnetic flux would both increase in the new experiment.

J. Maximum emf would increase but change in magnetic flux would decrease in the new experiment.

GO ON TO THE NEXT PAGE

Passage V

An acid is defined as any substance that can donate a hydrogen ion in a solution, while a base is defined as any substance that can accept a hydrogen ion. Acids and bases are measured by the pH scale, as indicated in Table 1.

Table 1 shows how pH level corresponds to hydrogen ion concentration in moles per liter, indicated by $[H^+]$.

Table 1	
$[H^+]$ (mol/L)	pH level
1×10^0	0
1×10^{-1}	1
1×10^{-2}	2
1×10^{-3}	3
1×10^{-4}	4
1×10^{-5}	5
1×10^{-6}	6
1×10^{-7}	7
1×10^{-8}	8
1×10^{-9}	9
1×10^{-10}	10
1×10^{-11}	11
1×10^{-12}	12
1×10^{-13}	13
1×10^{-14}	14

Table 2 shows categorizations of acidic and basic solutions according to pH level. (Note that fractional pHs should be rounded to the nearest whole number before referencing the table.)

Table 2	
Category	pH level
highly acidic	0–3
slightly acidic	4–6
neutral	7
slightly basic	8–10
highly basic	11–14

Table 3 lists several strong acids and bases. A 1 mol/L solution of a strong acid should have a pH lower than 2, while a 1 mol/L solution of a strong base should have a pH higher than 12.

Table 3	
Strong bases	Strong acids
sodium hydroxide	nitric acid
calcium hydroxide	sulfuric acid
barium hydroxide	hydrobromic acid

Table 4 presents the approximate hydrogen ion concentration in several common substances.

Table 4	
Substance	$[H^+]$ (mol/L)
ammonia	1×10^{-11}
baking soda	1×10^{-9}
lemon juice	1×10^{-2}
milk	1×10^{-6}
vinegar	1×10^{-3}
water	1×10^{-7}

29. An unknown solution is tested in order to determine if it is an acid or a base. Its hydrogen ion concentration is found to be 1×10^{-11} mol/L. Based on the passage, this solution would be considered:

   A. highly acidic.

   B. slightly acidic.

   C. highly basic.

   D. slightly basic.

GO ON TO THE NEXT PAGE

30. Based on Table 4, which of the following substances has the greatest hydrogen ion concentration?

    F. Ammonia

    G. Lemon juice

    H. Milk

    J. Vinegar

31. According to the passage, which of the following substances would be classified as highly acidic?

    A. Milk

    B. Vinegar

    C. Baking soda

    D. Ammonia

32. Based on information in the passage, which of the following is the most accurate statement?

    F. As hydrogen ion concentration increases, a solution becomes more dangerous.

    G. A solution with a pH close to 0 is considered neutral.

    H. The difference in hydrogen ion concentration is greater between highly acidic and highly basic solutions than between slightly acidic and slightly basic solutions.

    J. The difference in hydrogen ion concentration is greater between slightly basic and highly basic solutions than between slightly acidic and highly acidic solutions.

33. Assuming a concentration of 1 mol/L, which of the following substances has the highest pH level?

    A. Baking soda

    B. Nitric acid

    C. Barium hydroxide

    D. Vinegar

34. The hydrogen ion concentration, or $[H^+]$, of a solution is inversely proportional to the solution's hydroxide ion concentration, or $[OH^-]$. For example, a solution with a pH of 2 has a pOH of 12, and a solution with a pH of 11 has a pOH of 3. Based on this information, assuming a 1 mol/L solution, which of the following has the highest pOH ?

    F. Sulfuric acid

    G. Calcium hydroxide

    H. Water

    J. Ammonia

GO ON TO THE NEXT PAGE

Passage VI

Carbonated beverages are liquids that have undergone carbonation, a process in which carbon dioxide gas becomes dissolved in them. A group of students proposed a hypothesis that the presence of carbonation in various bottled liquids would affect *balance time* (the time it takes a liquid to reach equilibrium after being initially off-balance). Diagram 1 shows the bottle held by 2 fixed points on a hinged incline. After the hinge is closed and the angle of inclination becomes zero, the liquid in the bottle completes its balance time when it no longer moves within the bottle.

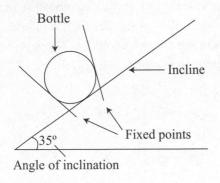

Diagram 1

Each student tested the hypothesis in different trials and recorded average balance times. The initial angle of inclination is 35° for all 3 experiments. Identical 2-L glass bottles were used in all 3 experiments.

Experiment 1

The students added 1 L of clear fruit juice, which is uncarbonated, to an empty bottle. After sealing it, they placed it between the fixed points and closed the hinge. The balance time was then recorded. Next, they added 1 L of the same juice to a second empty bottle, sealed and shook it, and found its balance time. They repeated these 2 procedures with 2 additional liquids: carbonated seltzer that contained a lot of froth, and root beer that was originally carbonated, but was then allowed to become flat (that is, to lose its dissolved carbon dioxide). The results of these trials are shown in Table 1.

		Balance time (seconds)	
Trial	Liquid	Without shaking	With shaking
1	Clear fruit juice	20.01	19.89
2	Carbonated seltzer	21.35	22.97
3	Root beer	20.15	22.48

Table 1

Experiment 2

The students added 1 L of the flat root beer to an empty bottle. After sealing and shaking the bottle, they set it aside for 10 minutes. After the 10 minutes elapsed, they found the bottle's balance time before and immediately after shaking it again (Trial 4). After conducting these measurements, they set the bottle aside for an additional 90 minutes and found the balance time before and immediately after shaking it a third time (Trial 5). The results can be seen in Table 2.

	Balance time (seconds)	
Trial	Before shaking	After shaking
4	20.83	22.67
5	20.04	22.45

Table 2

Experiment 3

The students added 1 L of the flat root beer to an empty bottle and 1 L of carbonated seltzer to a second empty bottle. They then sealed both bottles. After shaking both bottles and seeing froth form, the students set them aside for observation. At 10 minutes into the experiment, fewer bubbles were visible in the bottle that contained the root beer. At 90 minutes into the experiment, there were no bubbles remaining in the root beer.

GO ON TO THE NEXT PAGE

35. Which of the following conclusions is most strongly supported by the results of Experiment 3 ? Ten minutes after being shaken, root beer:

    A. had a lower level of carbonation than seltzer.

    B. had a higher level of carbonation than seltzer.

    C. had a greater quantity of liquid than seltzer.

    D. achieved balance time twice as fast as seltzer.

36. When comparing Trials 1 through 5 in Experiments 1 and 2, in which two trials, after shaking, are the balance times the most similar?

    F. Trials 1 and 5

    G. Trials 1 and 3

    H. Trials 2 and 4

    J. Trials 3 and 5

37. In Experiment 2, shaking the bottle of root beer resulted in:

    A. decreasing the number of bubbles in the beverage.

    B. increasing the balance time of the bottle of root beer.

    C. decreasing the balance time of the bottle of root beer.

    D. increasing the mass of the bottle of root beer.

38. Based on the results of the experiments, is it likely that bubbles were present immediately before the bottle was shaken in Trial 4 ?

    F. Based on Experiment 1, it is likely the bubbles were present before shaking.

    G. Based on Experiment 1, it is unlikely the bubbles were present before shaking.

    H. Based on Experiment 3, it is likely the bubbles were present before shaking.

    J. Based on Experiment 3, it is unlikely the bubbles were present before shaking.

39. Suppose a sixth trial existed in which the same bottle of root beer was set aside for an additional 90 minutes after the fifth trial was completed. Based on the results of Experiment 2, what would the balance time most likely be if the students do not shake the bottle?

    A. Less than 20.83 seconds

    B. Between 20.83 seconds and 22.45 seconds

    C. Between 22.45 seconds and 22.67 seconds

    D. Greater than 22.67 seconds

40. Based on the results of Trials 3–5 and Experiment 3, if the students had added 1 L of the flat root beer to an empty bottle, then sealed the bottle and shook it, how long would it most likely take for the bubbles to become too few to affect the bottle's balance time?

    F. 0 minutes

    G. Between 0 minutes and 10 minutes

    H. Between 10 minutes and 90 minutes

    J. More than 90 minutes

Practice Test 5

IF YOU FINISH BEFORE TIME IS CALLED, YOU MAY CHECK YOUR WORK ON THIS SECTION ONLY. DO NOT TURN TO ANY OTHER SECTION IN THE TEST.

Practice Test 5 467

WRITING TEST

40 Minutes—1 Question

Directions: The essay is used to evaluate your writing skills. You will have **40 minutes** to review the prompt and plan and write an essay in English. Before you begin, read everything in this test booklet carefully to make sure you understand the task.

Your essay will be judged based on the evidence it provides of your ability to do the following:

- Assert your own perspective on a complex issue and evaluate the relationship between your perspective and at least one other perspective

- Use reasoning and evidence to refine and justify your ideas

- Present your ideas in an organized way

- Convey your ideas effectively using standard written English

Write your essay on the lined essay pages in the answer booklet. All writing on those lined pages will be scored. Use the unlined pages in this test booklet to plan your essay. Your work on these unlined pages will not be scored.

Put your pencil down as soon as time is called.

DO NOT OPEN THIS BOOKLET UNTIL TOLD TO DO SO.

GO ON TO THE NEXT PAGE

Collegiate Fields of Study

Students pursuing higher education with the intent to commit to a particular field of study often determine that a different concentration is a better fit and subsequently make a change. Many students base their initial field of study on their interests, strengths, and experiences in high school. Some students complete the program they originally selected, but many others find that college unearths new passions and prospects. Additionally, collegiate study often exposes students to job markets that help students evaluate the availability of jobs in their desired field; this is often a driving factor in changing their concentration since students seek financial security upon graduation. Should high schools incorporate career-oriented programs to help students make better decisions regarding their majors? Making better-informed choices before entering college will help students wisely allocate their time and money during their college careers and prevent graduates from entering a career field without background knowledge regarding job availability.

Read and carefully consider these perspectives. Each discusses the importance of providing high school students with the necessary knowledge to choose appropriate fields of study in college.

Perspective One	Perspective Two	Perspective Three
High schools should hold career-oriented seminars at least once a semester during the regular school day to help students make informed decisions when choosing collegiate fields of study. These seminars will help students explore career options, post-graduate position availability, and job requirements. Armed with this knowledge, students can make better-informed choices that will help them to avoid spending unnecessary time and money in both college and job markets.	High schools should retain their current primary focus but offer optional after-school career-focused seminars conducted by professionals so students can learn about options before attending college. Students who take advantage of this resource will be able to make better decisions, and these seminars will allow teachers to continue to focus on the core curriculum and assist students academically.	High schools should partner with colleges and professionals to embed career-oriented options into current courses. The job market information will be relevant to the class in which it is presented. Although students will only receive career-based information centered on the courses in which they are enrolled, this approach guarantees that each student is offered course-specific advice.

GO ON TO THE NEXT PAGE

Essay Task

Write a clear, well-reasoned essay evaluating multiple perspectives on academic programs that assist students in choosing appropriate fields of study. In your essay, be sure to:

- Assert your own perspective on the issue and evaluate the relationship between your perspective and at least one other perspective

- Use reasoning and evidence to refine and justify your ideas

- Present your ideas in an organized way

- Convey your ideas effectively using standard written English

Your perspective may be fully, somewhat, or not at all in agreement with one or more of the three perspectives in the prompt.

Planning Your Essay

These pages are not scored.

Use the space below to brainstorm and plan your essay. Consider the following as you think about the prompt:

- Strengths and weaknesses of the three perspectives in the prompt

  ○ What observations do they offer, and what do they overlook?

  ○ Why are they persuasive or why are they not persuasive?

- Your own background and identity

  ○ What is your perspective on this issue, and what are its strengths and weaknesses?

  ○ What evidence will you use in your essay?

GO ON TO THE NEXT PAGE

GO ON TO THE NEXT PAGE

_____

_____

_____

_____

_____

_____

_____

_____

_____

_____

_____

_____

_____

_____

_____

_____

_____

_____

_____

IF YOU FINISH BEFORE TIME IS CALLED, YOU MAY CHECK YOUR WORK ON THIS SECTION ONLY. DO NOT TURN TO ANY OTHER SECTION IN THE TEST.

PRACTICE TEST 5 ANSWER KEY
ENGLISH TEST

1. **A**	16. **F**	31. **A**	46. **H**	61. **D**
2. **G**	17. **B**	32. **H**	47. **A**	62. **G**
3. **A**	18. **H**	33. **D**	48. **J**	63. **D**
4. **G**	19. **C**	34. **F**	49. **B**	64. **F**
5. **B**	20. **G**	35. **C**	50. **F**	65. **A**
6. **G**	21. **D**	36. **J**	51. **C**	66. **H**
7. **C**	22. **G**	37. **D**	52. **H**	67. **D**
8. **J**	23. **A**	38. **F**	53. **D**	68. **G**
9. **C**	24. **J**	39. **C**	54. **F**	69. **A**
10. **J**	25. **D**	40. **J**	55. **C**	70. **G**
11. **A**	26. **F**	41. **C**	56. **G**	71. **B**
12. **J**	27. **A**	42. **F**	57. **D**	72. **J**
13. **B**	28. **G**	43. **C**	58. **G**	73. **D**
14. **J**	29. **D**	44. **J**	59. **C**	74. **J**
15. **A**	30. **H**	45. **C**	60. **H**	75. **A**

MATHEMATICS TEST

1. **E**	13. **D**	25. **C**	37. **E**	49. **B**
2. **H**	14. **J**	26. **J**	38. **K**	50. **J**
3. **A**	15. **E**	27. **A**	39. **B**	51. **E**
4. **G**	16. **G**	28. **G**	40. **F**	52. **H**
5. **C**	17. **C**	29. **D**	41. **B**	53. **D**
6. **F**	18. **F**	30. **F**	42. **G**	54. **G**
7. **C**	19. **D**	31. **D**	43. **C**	55. **A**
8. **J**	20. **G**	32. **F**	44. **G**	56. **H**
9. **D**	21. **E**	33. **E**	45. **C**	57. **C**
10. **G**	22. **F**	34. **G**	46. **J**	58. **K**
11. **B**	23. **C**	35. **A**	47. **E**	59. **D**
12. **H**	24. **F**	36. **J**	48. **K**	60. **K**

READING TEST

1. **D**	9. **A**	17. **D**	25. **B**	33. **D**
2. **G**	10. **G**	18. **F**	26. **F**	34. **H**
3. **C**	11. **B**	19. **B**	27. **C**	35. **D**
4. **J**	12. **J**	20. **H**	28. **F**	36. **J**
5. **A**	13. **C**	21. **D**	29. **B**	37. **D**
6. **G**	14. **H**	22. **H**	30. **H**	38. **H**
7. **D**	15. **D**	23. **D**	31. **C**	39. **A**
8. **J**	16. **H**	24. **J**	32. **F**	40. **H**

SCIENCE TEST

1. **C**	9. **C**	17. **A**	25. **B**	33. **C**
2. **F**	10. **J**	18. **F**	26. **F**	34. **F**
3. **D**	11. **C**	19. **B**	27. **D**	35. **A**
4. **H**	12. **F**	20. **J**	28. **H**	36. **J**
5. **A**	13. **D**	21. **B**	29. **C**	37. **B**
6. **G**	14. **F**	22. **G**	30. **G**	38. **H**
7. **A**	15. **C**	23. **D**	31. **B**	39. **A**
8. **H**	16. **J**	24. **F**	32. **H**	40. **H**

ANSWERS AND EXPLANATIONS

ENGLISH TEST

Passage I

1. A   **Difficulty:** Low

Category: Usage

Getting to the Answer: The superlative adjective form will use *-est* or *most*—not both. This sentence needs (A), NO CHANGE. *Earliest* is the correct superlative adjective to refer to all *music forms*. Choice B uses *most* with *earliest*, which is grammatically incorrect. Choice C uses *most early*, which is also incorrect; *most* is only used with words that do not have an *-est* superlative form. Choice D uses the right adjective, but creates a subject-verb agreement error; "The earliest . . . forms" does not agree with the singular verb form *was*.

2. G   **Difficulty:** High

Category: Punctuation

Getting to the Answer: *It's* is a contraction of *it is* or *it has*. If neither of these makes sense when substituted for the contraction, the contraction is incorrect. It doesn't make sense to say "because of it is (or has) having," so we know F is incorrect. Choice (G) substitutes the correct singular possessive adjective, *its*, meaning that the *origins* belong to American jazz. Choice H uses a spelling that is never correct, and J adds an incorrect comma.

3. A   **Difficulty:** High

Category: Topic Development / Supporting Material

Getting to the Answer: Just determining whether or not the suggested information is relevant gives you a 50/50 chance of getting the question right. First, determine if the new information is relevant or not. Here, it is, since the paragraph discusses the way that different musical forms came together to form American jazz; eliminate C and D. Choice B is out of scope for the paragraph, which concerns the development, not the popularity, of American jazz. Choice (A) is correct, because a syncopated style helpfully connects the West African folk music with the syncopation of ragtime and blues.

4. G   **Difficulty:** Medium

Category: Sentence Structure and Formation

Getting to the Answer: The answer choices include difference verb forms. Choose the form that creates a complete sentence. Choices F, H, and J all create fragments. Therefore, (G) is correct.

5. B   **Difficulty:** Medium

Category: Punctuation

Getting to the Answer: If a semicolon is used to combine clauses, the clauses must be independent. This sentence incorrectly places a semicolon between an independent and a dependent clause. Choice (B) eliminates the incorrect semicolon. Choice C incorrectly inserts a comma between a preposition and its object. Choice D separates a subject from its verb with a comma, which is also incorrect.

6. G   **Difficulty:** Medium

Category: Knowledge of Language / Ambiguity

Getting to the Answer: When an underlined selection includes a pronoun, make sure its antecedent is clear and unambiguous. There are several singular nouns in the sentence previous to this one (*style, blend, America, the time*) that could be antecedents for the pronoun *It*. Choice (G) replaces the pronoun with the appropriate noun. Choices H and J do not address the ambiguity issue.

7. C   **Difficulty:** Medium

Category: Usage

Getting to the Answer: When an English Test question has a stem, read it carefully. This one asks you to determine the unacceptable choice, which means three of the choices will be correct in context. Although "made his living on" is a properly constructed idiom, it is inappropriate in this context, since it refers to the location where the living was made, such as on a boat, rather than the occupation itself. Choice (C) is the correct choice here. Choices A, B, and D are all acceptable in the sentence.

8. J   Difficulty: Medium

Category: Knowledge of Language / Concision

Getting to the Answer: When DELETE is an option, check to see if the underlined selection is necessary to the meaning of the sentence. *He was* isn't necessary here; "working as a shoe shiner and a waiter" properly provides a compound object for the preposition, so (J) is correct. Choice G uses incorrect grammatical structure, and H leaves the meaning of the second clause incomplete.

9. C   Difficulty: High

Category: Topic Development / Supporting Material

Getting to the Answer: When asked about deleting information, read the sentence without the selection in question. The information that Cab Calloway "spent time at the racetrack" doesn't make sense coming directly after a sentence that discusses the jobs he held, unless we also know that Calloway worked at the track. Choice (C) is correct; without this explanation, readers might be confused. Choice A is incorrect; the information does relate to the topic at hand. Choice B is also wrong; the information has nothing to do with Calloway's accomplishments or successes. Other information in the sentence tells us how far Cab Calloway came in his life; it's not necessary to keep this clause for the reason that D suggests.

10. J   Difficulty: Medium

Category: Sentence Structure and Formation

Getting to the Answer: Although DELETE will not always be the correct answer when it's offered, always consider the possibility that the selection is either redundant or used incorrectly. As written, this sentence is a fragment, with no independent clause. Eliminating *where*, as (J) suggests, corrects this error. Choice G is unnecessarily wordy. Choice H does not address the fragment error.

11. A   Difficulty: Medium

Category: Punctuation

Getting to the Answer: The ACT tests only a few very specific punctuation rules; make sure your answer choice follows these rules. Choice (A) is correct; no punctuation is needed here. Choice B inserts a colon which, on the ACT, will only be correct when used to introduce a brief explanation, definition, or list. Choice C treats the phrase

"in the top jazz circles" as nonessential information set off by commas, but the sentence does not make sense when read without it. Choice D inserts an unneeded comma before a prepositional phrase.

12. J   Difficulty: Medium

Category: Organization, Unity, and Cohesion / Passage Organization

Getting to the Answer: Because NO CHANGE is not an answer choice, the sentence must be relevant; you'll need to determine its most logical placement. *Widely known* is a good context clue. It doesn't make sense that he was well-known when he was a shoe-shiner and waiter, when he was walking racehorses, and when he first began performing, so you can eliminate F, G, and H. Choice (J) places the sentence logically.

13. B   Difficulty: Medium

Category: Usage

Getting to the Answer: The word that follows is a noun, so you need an adjective rather than an adverb. Eliminate A. Choices C and D are awkwardly worded, so (B) is correct.

14. J   Difficulty: Medium

Category: Knowledge of Language / Style and Tone

Getting to the Answer: In addition to following the rules of grammar, style, and usage, the correct answer choice must also be consistent with the tone of the passage. The phrase "it'll stick around for a while" is too informal and slangy for the rest of this passage. Choice (J) matches the professional tone of the essay and provides a logical conclusion. Choice G is unnecessarily wordy. Choice H doesn't provide a logical conclusion to the passage; it concerns jazz's popularity rather than its endurance.

15. A   Difficulty: Medium

Category: Topic Development / Writer's Purpose

Getting to the Answer: Once you determine whether or not the passage satisfies the conditions in the question stem, you can immediately eliminate two of the four choices. First, you'll need to determine whether or not this essay focuses on "the history and development of American jazz music." Since it does, you can eliminate both *no* choices, C and D. Now focus on the reasoning.

Choice B misstates the information in the passage, which tells us that jazz developed from folk music, not the other way around. Choice (A) is the correct choice here.

Passage II

16. F   Difficulty: Medium

Category: Sentence Structure and Formation

Getting to the Answer: Approximately 25% of ACT English Test questions will require NO CHANGE. This sentence contains no error, so (F) is correct. Choice G creates a run-on sentence. Choice H would be acceptable if the comma were placed after *world*, but is incorrect punctuated this way. Choice J introduces a verb tense that is inappropriate in context.

17. B   Difficulty: Medium

Category: Punctuation

Getting to the Answer: When commas are the issue, remember your tested rules. This sentence does not meet any of the tested conditions for proper comma usage; (B) is correct. Choice A separates the verb from its object. Choices C and D do not address the error; *said that* would be acceptable without the commas but, as written, these choices are incorrect.

18. H   Difficulty: Medium

Category: Usage

Getting to the Answer: When a verb is underlined, check that it is in the correct tense and is properly formed. Choices F and G incorrectly use *went* with *has* and *had*, respectively; the correct past participle for the verb *to go* is *gone*. Choice J uses the present tense, which is incorrect in context. This sentence discusses something that happened in the past, so (H) is correct.

19. C   Difficulty: Low

Category: Knowledge of Language / Concision

Getting to the Answer: Many ACT Knowledge of Language questions will have four answer choices that are grammatically correct; your goal is to find the best one, which is often the most concise option. *Because* is all that is needed here; (C) is the best choice. Choices A and

B are unnecessarily wordy. Choice D creates an illogical relationship between the clauses; the editor's refusal to read hand-written manuscripts was the cause, not the result, of Grandpa's decision to buy a computer.

20. G   Difficulty: Medium

Category: Sentence Structure and Formation

Getting to the Answer: When the underlined portion contains modifying phrases, check for proper placement. A modifying phrase should be close to the noun it modifies. The only logical entity that is "on a World Wide Web" is *information*, so that phrase must occur at the beginning of the selection. Choice (G) is correct.

21. D   Difficulty: Medium

Category: Organization, Unity, and Cohesion / Transitions

Getting to the Answer: Make sure Connections words properly relate the words or clauses they connect. The second sentence here provides a different point than the first; Grandpa is saying that he can talk to interesting people for a long time or he can ignore uninteresting people. Choice (D) uses the appropriate connection. Choices A and B indicate that the second sentence will provide a specific example of the first, but this is not the case. Choice C suggests that the writer will introduce a contrasting perspective after discussing Grandpa's use of the "close" button, but the writer does not do so.

22. G   Difficulty: Low

Category: Usage

Getting to the Answer: When the underlined word is a pronoun, make sure its antecedent is clear and that it is in the proper case. Since you wouldn't say *them people*, F is incorrect; *those* would be the proper pronoun here. However, since *those* is not among the answer choices, you'll need to find a logical replacement for the pronoun. Choice (G) correctly indicates who isn't interesting. Choice H incorrectly uses *it* to refer to people. Choice J creates a sentence that is grammatically incorrect.

23. A   Difficulty: Medium

Category: Punctuation

Getting to the Answer: If you read the sentence and don't find a problem with it, don't be afraid to choose

NO CHANGE. It will be the correct choice about 25% of the time. This sentence contains no error; (A) is correct here. Choice B treats the phrase "which is very convenient" as nonessential information, but the sentence does not make sense without it. The second sentence created by C is a fragment. Choice D misuses the semicolon, which is only correct when combining two independent clauses.

24. J   Difficulty: High

Category: Sentence Structure and Formation

Getting to the Answer: When an entire sentence is underlined, choose the clearest revision. As written, this sentence is wordy and convoluted. While not much briefer, (J) is easier to understand; "in merely a few seconds" is placed directly after the phrase it modifies, "being able to find anything he wants," and "for him" follows the phrase it modifies, "a source of pure joy." Choices F, G, and H are all less concise and more awkward than (J); additionally, G incorrectly places a comma between the sentence's subject and predicate verb.

25. D   Difficulty: Medium

Category: Organization, Unity, and Cohesion / Transitions

Getting to the Answer: Make sure transition words are both logical and necessary. This sentence needs nothing to link it to the sentence that precedes it. Choice (D) eliminates the unnecessary word. Choices A and C incorrectly use contrast words to link the two sentences. Choice B uses *additionally*, which means the second sentence is building upon the first sentence. This is not the case either.

26. F   Difficulty: Medium

Category: Sentence Structure and Formation

Getting to the Answer: Unless context makes it clear that more than one time frame is being referenced, verb tenses should remain consistent. This sentence needs (F), NO CHANGE; the present tense is correct in context. Choices G and H create sentence fragments. Choice J introduces a verb tense that is inappropriate in context.

27. A   Difficulty: Low

Category: Topic Development / Supporting Material

Getting to the Answer: Don't just read for errors in grammar and usage; read for logic as well. Here, (A) is the only choice that is both consistent with the passage and uses the proper contrast transition *but*. Nothing in the passage indicates that Grandpa won't continue to explore the Internet, as B suggests, or that his editor believes this to be the case, as in D. Choice C doesn't follow logically from the first clause of the sentence.

28. G   Difficulty: Medium

Category: Organization, Unity, and Cohesion / Passage Organization

Getting to the Answer: When asked to add information, read the new sentence into the passage at the suggested points to determine its best placement. This sentence adds information about how Grandpa uses the websites he accesses, so placing it before Sentence 1, as F suggests, is illogical. Choices H and J both place the new information too far from the discussion of Grandpa's use of the Internet. Choice (G) is the most logical place for this new sentence.

29. D   Difficulty: Medium

Category: Topic Development / Supporting Material

Getting to the Answer: Whenever you are asked to consider deleting something, think about why the author included that information. What purpose does it serve? The first sentence of this passage tells us that Grandpa does not know how to use technology. This explains why Grandpa did not want to use the Internet; (D) is correct. Choice A misstates a detail from the passage; the sentence in question tells us only that Grandpa does not like to use technology, not the specific technologies he avoids. The first sentence is not particularly humorous, which eliminates B. Choice C can be eliminated as well, since no details about the Internet are provided.

30. H   Difficulty: Medium

Category: Organization, Unity, and Cohesion / Passage Organization

Getting to the Answer: When asked about the logical placement for a paragraph, pay attention to any unexplained shifts in the text. If there's a place that needs a transition, that is likely where the paragraph should go. Because Paragraph 1 ends by saying the Grandpa doesn't see the need for the Internet, and Paragraph 2 describes Grandpa's reaction to the Internet, this is a logical place for a paragraph describing how Grandpa was convinced to try the Internet. Choice (H) is correct.

Passage III

31. A   Difficulty: Low

Category: Usage

Getting to the Answer: Most idiom questions will hinge on preposition usage. This sentence needs (A), NO CHANGE; "In the twilight" is the appropriate idiom in this context. Choice B is idiomatically incorrect usage. Choices C and D would require more information to be correct; neither "With the twilight" nor "From the twilight" is an acceptable idiom by itself.

32. H   Difficulty: High

Category: Usage

Getting to the Answer: Some constructions might be grammatically correct but inappropriate in context. Although "more of the people who" is a grammatically correct construction, it is used incorrectly here, so F is incorrect. It was "most of the people" the writer did not know; (H) makes the correction without introducing a new error. Choice G does not address the error; additionally, it uses the objective pronoun form *whom* where *who* is correct. Choice J corrects the incorrect use of *more*, but adds a new error by changing *who* to *whom*.

33. D   Difficulty: Medium

Category: Topic Development / Writer's Purpose

Getting to the Answer: Read question stems carefully and use Keywords to determine the correct answer choice. The Keyword in this question stem is *unity*. Choice (D) mentions *kinship*, which suggests a family-like relationship between the writer and the other walkers. Choice A indicates that the writer knew some of the people, but you can know people without feeling unity with them.

Choice B's mention of each walker having his or her own reasons for being there suggests the opposite of unity. Being interested in knowing people, as C suggests, does not convey unity.

34. F   Difficulty: High

Category: Sentence Structure and Formation

Getting to the Answer: The answer choices are all in the past tense. Determine which fits best with the overall past-tense narration of the story. The people had been waiting to make their journey, but by the time of the narration they are no longer waiting; they are making the journey. Thus, the answer should express that the people waited prior to the past-tense event of making the journey together. Choices G and J reference an event that was either ongoing in the past or else happened at one time in the past; eliminate them. Choice H is unnecessarily wordy. Only (F) places the waiting prior to the journey, without being too wordy; (F) is therefore correct.

35. C   Difficulty: High

Category: Knowledge of Language / Ambiguity

Getting to the Answer: As written, the sentence does not make clear whether the writer is talking about pictures of other Chickasaw or pictures belonging to other Chickasaw, so A is incorrect. Choice (C) makes this clear. Choice B is unnecessarily wordy. Choice D changes the meaning of the phrase, indicating that it was *Chickasaw*, and not *pictures*, that the writer had been shown.

36. J   Difficulty: Medium

Category: Punctuation

Getting to the Answer: Only very specific comma uses are tested on the ACT. If commas are used in any other way, they will be incorrect. The underlined selection does not meet any of the tested requirements for comma usage; (J) is correct. Choice F treats the phrase "who walked along with me" as nonessential information, but the sentence does not make sense without it. Choice G inserts a comma within a phrase modifying "people." Choice H treats another necessary phrase, "who walked along," as nonessential.

37. D   Difficulty: High

Category: Organization, Unity, and Cohesion / Transitions

Getting to the Answer: Each sentence in the passage must lead logically into the next. Look at the sentence preceding the selection and the one that follows. You need to find a choice that transitions from the idea of the pictures the writer had been shown and somewhere that "Books . . . were stacked on the bookshelves." Choice (D) does this best. Choices A, B, and C all explain where the pictures came from but do not lead logically into the sentence that follows.

38. F   Difficulty: High

Category: Sentence Structure and Formation

Getting to the Answer: The verbs here must be in the proper format not to create a run-on sentence or change the intended meaning. Choice G creates a run-on, whereas H and J both unnecessarily reference another time frame when the father read the book. Choice (F) is correct.

39. C   Difficulty: Low

Category: Knowledge of Language / Precision

Getting to the Answer: Remember to read for logic as well as grammar and usage. We know there are two rooms: the father's and the grandmother's; (C) correctly conveys this. Choices A and D refer to a single room, but the writer has been talking about two rooms. Choice B seems to indicate that both rooms belong to the writer's grandmother, but this contradicts the passage.

40. J   Difficulty: Medium

Category: Organization, Unity, and Cohesion / Transitions

Getting to the Answer: Connection words, such as conjunctions, must logically join the ideas they are used to combine. The two clauses here do not relate to one another in a way that makes it logical for them to be joined into a single sentence; one clause concerns the rooms displaying pictures of Chickasaw and the other, the writer's family's move to Seattle, so a change is needed and F is incorrect. Choice (J) correctly makes each clause a separate sentence. Choices G and H create run-on sentences.

41. C   Difficulty: High

Category: Topic Development / Supporting Material

Getting to the Answer: When NO CHANGE is offered as an option, you'll need to determine the logic and relevance of any potential new material. The information in the underlined sentence, while related to the topic being discussed, does not logically lead from the idea that the writer and his family had moved to Seattle to the reason they were then unable to attend the Annual Meetings. This means you can eliminate A. By pointing out the location of these meetings, (C) connects the two ideas: the meetings were too far away from the family's new home. Choice B is out of scope—dancing at the Festivals is never mentioned in the passage—and still fails to logically connect the ideas. Choice D also fails to provide a logical reason for the writer's family not attending the meetings.

42. F   Difficulty: Medium

Category: Knowledge of Language / Concision

Getting to the Answer: Be wary of answer choices that are significantly longer than the original selection. Barring errors of grammar or logic, these will be incorrect. There is no need to make this sentence any longer; (F) is correct. Choices G, H, and J are all wordier than the original and violate the parallel structure required for the compound "built and . . . conducted."

43. C   Difficulty: Low

Category: Organization, Unity, and Cohesion / Transitions

Getting to the Answer: Connections words and phrases must logically combine the ideas they connect. This sentence builds on the preceding one by giving more evidence to make the point of the first sentence. Choice (C) correctly reflects this relationship. Choices A and D use inappropriate contrast connections. Choice B indicates two events occurring simultaneously, which is illogical in context.

44. J   Difficulty: Medium

Category: Sentence Structure and Formation

Getting to the Answer: A sentence can have multiple verbs and still be a fragment. Remember, the *-ing* verb form by itself can never be the predicate (main) verb in a sentence. As written, this sentence is a fragment; neither clause is independent. Choice (J) gives the sentence a correct predicate verb, *chirped*. Choices G and H do not address the error.

45. C   Difficulty: High

Category: Topic Development / Writer's Purpose

Getting to the Answer: When asked whether an essay accomplishes a certain purpose, first decide whether or not it accomplishes that purpose, and then choose the answer that reflects your reasoning. The question stem asks if this essay fulfills the goal of describing the history of the Chickasaw people. Since the passage focuses primarily on the narrator's own story, you can eliminate the *yes* choices, A and B. Choice D's reasoning is that the essay is narrated from one person's point of view, but history can be narrated in that way. It is not the style of the narration but rather the fact that the essay focuses on the narrator's personal experiences that makes the essay ill-suited for the stated purpose. Choice (C) is correct here.

Passage IV

46. H   Difficulty: Medium

Category: Punctuation

Getting to the Answer: When apostrophe use is the issue, use context to determine whether a plural or a possessive is required; eliminate answer choices that use the apostrophe in ways that are never correct. As written, this sentence uses the plural *days*, which doesn't make sense in context, so you can eliminate F. Although there are circumstances in which a noun ending in *s* will be made possessive by adding *'s*, the rules for this usage are quite complicated and are not tested on the ACT; eliminate J. Since the sentence is discussing one specific day (December 6, 1884), the plural possessive in G can also be eliminated. *Day's*, the singular possessive, is what is called for here; (H) is correct.

47. A   Difficulty: Low

Category: Usage

Getting to the Answer: Use context to determine the appropriate tense of underlined verbs. There is no

contextual reason to change verb tenses in this sentence; since *rushed* is in the past tense, (A) *threatened* is correct. Choice B changes the meaning of the sentence, making the wind the object of the threat, rather than its cause. Choice C uses a tense that indicates actions that will happen in the future, but these actions have already occurred. Choice D uses the singular verb form *threatens* with the plural noun *winds*.

48. J   Difficulty: Low

Category: Knowledge of Language / Concision

Getting to the Answer: Whenever DELETE is presented as an option, check the underlined selection for relevance and redundancy. Here, *postpone* and *delay* mean essentially the same thing, so eliminate F; (J), DELETE, is the correct choice here. Choice G still contains redundant wording; "to a later time" is included in the meaning of *postpone*. Choice H is also redundant; there is no other way to *postpone* something than *by delaying* it.

49. B   Difficulty: Medium

Category: Topic Development / Supporting Material

Getting to the Answer: Remember your "purpose of a detail" skills from ACT Reading; that's what question stems like this one are asking for. Here, the phrase marked for deletion is the definition of *capstone ceremony*; (B) correctly explains what the essay would lose if the clause were deleted. Since the term *capstone ceremony* is not something most people are familiar with, this *detail* is not *minor*, as A suggests. Nothing in the phrase reflects the writer's opinion or the ceremony's significance to the American people, which eliminates C and D.

50. F   Difficulty: Medium

Category: Punctuation

Getting to the Answer: Remember your tested comma rules; if a comma is used in any other way in the underlined selection, it will be incorrect. A comma is not required, so (F) is correct. Choices G and J insert commas between the two parts of a compound; this is never correct comma usage. Choice H treats "attorney and Congressman" as nonessential information, but leaving it out makes it unclear who John Marshall was.

51. C   Difficulty: Medium

Category: Usage

Getting to the Answer: The question asks which answer choice is not acceptable, so eliminate any choice that fits well in the sentence. Choices A, B, and D are all idiomatically correct and should therefore be eliminated. Choice (C) is awkwardly worded and is therefore correct.

52. H   Difficulty: Medium

Category: Sentence Structure and Formation

Getting to the Answer: A sentence may be a fragment even if it contains multiple nouns and verb forms. As written, this sentence consists of a single dependent clause, so eliminate F. Only (H) creates a complete sentence by adding an appropriate predicate verb, *planned*. Choices G and J do not address the fragment error.

53. D   Difficulty: Medium

Category: Sentence Structure and Formation

Getting to the Answer: The word *because* signals a dependent clause. When joining an independent and dependent clause, it is not appropriate to use the same conjunctions and punctuation you use to join two independent clauses; eliminate C. No additional conjunctions are needed so, A and B are incorrect. Choice (D) correctly omits any unnecessary punctuation or conjunctions.

54. F   Difficulty: Medium

Category: Knowledge of Language / Precision

Getting to the Answer: If two answer choices mean the same thing and work in grammatically similar ways, you can eliminate them both, since only one answer choice can be correct. Since work was done on the monument, stopped, and then started again, *resumed*, (F), is the most appropriate. Choices G and H do not convey the idea that this work was a continuation of work that was done in the past. Choice J is redundant; *again* is indicated by the prefix *re-* in *restarted*.

55. C   Difficulty: Medium

Category: Usage

Getting to the Answer: Replacing contractions with the full phrase can help you determine correct usage.

They're is a contraction of *they are*, so first determine if the contraction is appropriate here. Since "during they are attempt" doesn't make sense, you can quickly eliminate A and B. Now turn to the difference between the remaining choices: the possessive *its* versus the contraction *it's*. Try replacing the contraction with *it is* or *it has*; neither makes sense, so you can eliminate D as well. Choice (C) is correct here.

56. G   Difficulty: Medium

Category: Sentence Structure and Formation

Getting to the Answer: In most cases, a descriptive phrase will modify the first noun that follows it. As written, this sentence refers to the capstone as "attached to the top of the monument." However, this doesn't make sense, since the sentence concerns placing the capstone there, so eliminate F. Choice (G) creates the most logical sentence: the crowd cheers while the capstone is hoisted up, then the capstone is attached. Choices H and J make it sound as if the crowd, not the capstone, was "attached to the top of the monument."

57. D   Difficulty: Low

Category: Knowledge of Language / Concision

Getting to the Answer: Look for words and phrases that mean the same thing; using them together will not be correct on the ACT. *Eight decades* and *eighty years* are the same amount of time. Choice (D) eliminates the redundancy. Choices A, B, and C all include redundant information.

58. G   Difficulty: Medium

Category: Sentence Structure and Formation

Getting to the Answer: When a comma appears in the middle of an underlined portion, check for a run-on sentence. Both halves of the sentence are independent clauses, so they must be connected properly. Eliminate F and J. Choice H is grammatically correct, but it creates an inappropriate contrast between the two clauses. Therefore, (G) is correct.

59. C   Difficulty: Medium

Category: Organization, Unity, and Cohesion / Passage Organization

Getting to the Answer: The sentence refers to *Civil War*, so it must occur soon after the Civil War is mentioned. Paragraph 1 does not mention a war, so eliminate A. Choice B is incorrect because while paragraph 2 mentions a war, it mentions the Revolutionary War, not the Civil War. Only (C) occurs directly after the mention of the Civil War, so (C) is correct.

60. H   Difficulty: Medium

Category: Topic Development / Writer's Purpose

Getting to the Answer: Question stems like this one appear frequently on the ACT. Answer the *yes* or *no* part of the question first, then tackle the reasoning behind your choice. The question stem asks if this essay would satisfy an assignment to write about "the entire process of designing and building the Washington Monument." Since the passage focuses primarily on the capstone ceremony, you can immediately eliminate the *yes* choices, F and G. Choice J's reasoning is that the essay focuses on "the early stages" of the monument's construction, but the opposite is true. Choice (H) is correct here.

Passage V

61. D   Difficulty: Medium

Category: Usage

Getting to the Answer: The test maker frequently places a plural object near a verb with a singular subject. Always determine the proper subject of an underlined noun; it will generally not be the noun closest to it in the sentence. The singular *Roaring*, not the plural *lions*, is the subject of the verb *perform*, so eliminate A. Choice (D) puts the verb in the proper singular form without introducing any additional errors. Choice B does not address the error and also incorrectly places a comma between the verb and its object. Choice C corrects the agreement error, but also inserts the incorrect comma.

62. G   Difficulty: High

Category: Punctuation

Getting to the Answer: Always read for logic as well as usage and style. As written, this sentence uses the plural *these* to modify the singular *defense*. This is incorrect, so eliminate F. By putting commas around *defense*, (G) makes

"One of these" refer to *functions* and identifies *defense* as a function of roaring. Choice H creates a sentence that is grammatically incorrect. Choice J is unnecessarily wordy.

63. D   Difficulty: Medium

Category: Sentence Structure and Formation

Getting to the Answer: There are several ways to correct a run-on sentence, but only one answer choice will do so without introducing any new errors. This sentence is a run-on; the underlined selection begins a new independent clause, which means A is incorrect. Choice (D) corrects the error by making the final clause dependent. Choice B does not address the error. Choice C eliminates the run-on error, but it is unnecessarily wordy.

64. F   Difficulty: Low

Category: Organization, Unity, and Cohesion / Transitions

Getting to the Answer: Read question stems carefully. You can determine the least acceptable transition word simply by finding the one that is inconsistent with the other three. Because NO CHANGE is not given as an option, you're looking for the connection that cannot be substituted for *because*. *In that*, *since*, and *as* can all mean *because*; therefore, G, H, and J are all considered acceptable. *Although* indicates contrast, not cause-and-effect, and is therefore unacceptable, so (F) is correct.

65. A   Difficulty: Low

Category: Knowledge of Language / Concision

Getting to the Answer: Be suspicious of answer choices that are significantly longer than the original selection. They won't always be incorrect, but make sure the longer phrase is necessary for logic or grammatical correctness. There is no reason for a longer sentence; (A) is correct. Choices B and C are unnecessarily wordy, and D is in passive voice.

66. H   Difficulty: Medium

Category: Sentence Structure and Formation

Getting to the Answer: When asked which alternative is not acceptable, look for the answer choice that contains a grammatical error, is too wordy, or is irrelevant. Choice (H) does not properly join the two clauses, creating an improperly formed second clause. Choices F, G, and J correctly make the second clause dependent on the first, so (H) is correct.

67. D   **Difficulty:** Medium

Category: Knowledge of Language / Concision

Getting to the Answer: Use context clues to determine when words are used redundantly. Something that is described as *everyday* can be assumed to be done *frequently*; (D) eliminates the redundancy. Choices A, B, and C all use words or phrases that are redundant with *everyday*.

68. G   **Difficulty:** High

Category: Topic Development / Writer's Purpose

Getting to the Answer: Remember the first rule in the Kaplan Method: Read until you have enough information to answer the question. The second clause here tells us the pride members have to *reunite*, so the logical answer choice will concern their being separated. Choice (G) is the choice most consistent with the question stem. Neither F nor J involves the pride becoming separated. Although H mentions the pride traveling, it does not indicate that the lions become separated when they do so.

69. A   **Difficulty:** Medium

Category: Organization, Unity, and Cohesion / Transitions

Getting to the Answer: Transition words and phrases must logically connect the ideas they combine. Each paragraph in this essay describes a way in which roaring helps lions survive. This paragraph discusses the final use lions have for their roars; *Finally* is the best transition here, so (A) is correct. Choice B uses *Nevertheless*, which indicates a contrast that is not present here. Choice C uses *Second*, but this is the essay's third point. Choice D signifies a conclusion, which is inappropriate in this context.

70. G   **Difficulty:** Low

Category: Sentence Structure and Formation

Getting to the Answer: Run-on sentences can be corrected in a number of ways, but only one answer choice will do so without introducing additional errors. As written, this sentence is a run-on, so you can eliminate F right away. Choices (G), H, and J all make the second clause dependent, but only (G) follows the rules of parallel

structure required in the series "roaring . . . displaying . . . and fighting."

71. B   **Difficulty:** High

Category: Punctuation

Getting to the Answer: Commas are never correct when used to separate a subject and verb. As written, the sentence treats the word *dominant* as nonessential information, so A is incorrect; the sentence does not make sense without *dominant*. Choice (B) correctly sets off the phrase *or dominant* from the rest of the sentence; the sentence is still both logical and grammatically correct with this information removed. Choice C incorrectly places a comma between a subject and its predicate verb. Choice D places a comma after a coordinating conjunction, which is also incorrect.

72. J   **Difficulty:** Medium

Category: Sentence Structure and Formation

Getting to the Answer: In most cases, the passive voice will make a sentence unnecessarily wordy and may cause modifier errors as well. This sentence is written in the passive voice, making it unclear what the phrase "by the roaring" is intended to modify, so F is incorrect. Choice (J) creates the clearest sentence. The passive voice in G and H makes them unnecessarily wordy.

73. D   **Difficulty:** Medium

Category: Usage

Getting to the Answer: Don't mistake the object of a preposition for the subject of a verb. Here, the plural *makes* is the object of the preposition *of*; the subject of the verb here is the singular *roaring*. Choice A is incorrect; B, C, and (D) all correct the agreement error, but B and C are unnecessarily wordy. Thus, (D) is correct.

74. J   **Difficulty:** Medium

Category: Punctuation

Getting to the Answer: Remember your tested comma rules. If a sentence doesn't satisfy one or more of those requirements, commas will be incorrect. This sentence does not meet any of the tested requirements for comma usage; (J) is correct. Choice F puts a comma between the sentence's subject and its predicate verb. Choice G incorrectly places a comma between *that* and the clause it introduces. The comma in H separates the verb *is* from its object.

75. A   Difficulty: Low

Category: Organization, Unity, and Cohesion / Passage Organization

Getting to the Answer: Because lions' roaring is a natural phenomenon, and the entire passage is about why lions roar, the answer here is *yes*. Eliminate C and D. Dealing with a scientific topic is not sufficient for accomplishing the stated goal, so B is incorrect. Only (A) remains, and it is correct.

MATHEMATICS TEST

1. E   Difficulty: Low

Category: Essential Skills / Rates, Percents, Proportions, and Unit Conversion

Getting to the Answer: This is a great question for Back-solving because you know 20% of the answer should turn out to be 10. Alternatively, you could use your knowledge that Percent $= \dfrac{\text{part}}{\text{whole}}$. 100% to set up an equation. Let x be the number of students in the class. Then 20% of x is 10:

$$0.2x = 10$$
$$x = 50$$

That's (E).

2. H   Difficulty: Low

Category: Essential Skills / Rates, Percents, Proportions, and Unit Conversion

Getting to the Answer: Whenever you see a proportion (two fractions set equal to each other), you can cross-multiply to solve.

$$\frac{14}{21} = \frac{k}{27}$$
$$14(27) = 21k$$
$$k = \frac{378}{21} = 18$$

Choice (H) is correct.

3. A   Difficulty: Low

Category: Higher Math / Functions

Getting to the Answer: Even if you forget what "arithmetic" means, you should still be able to recognize the pattern. Each term is 3 less than the previous term.

Fourth term $= 1 - 3 = -2$

Fifth term $= (-2) - 3 = -5$

Choice (A) is correct. Be sure not to stop too soon—the fourth term is a tempting, but wrong, answer choice.

4. G   Difficulty: Medium

Category: Essential Skills / Rates, Percents, Proportions, and Unit Conversion

Getting to the Answer: Solve word problems one step at a time. Pay attention to the units and what you are comparing. Set up and solve a proportion to find Carrie's height:

$$\frac{\text{Carrie's height}}{\text{Carrie's shadow}} = \frac{\text{Wade's height}}{\text{Wade's shadow}}$$
$$\frac{x}{380} = \frac{180}{400}$$
$$400x = 180(380)$$
$$x = \frac{180(380)}{400} = 171$$

Carrie is 171 centimeters tall, which is (G).

5. C   Difficulty: Low

Category: Essential Skills / Geometry

Getting to the Answer: On questions like this that don't include a diagram, drawing one is an excellent idea. $\overline{GK} \cong \overline{HK}$ means that the line segments $\overline{GK}$ and $\overline{HK}$ are congruent, or equal in length. For these two segments to have equal lengths, the points must be arranged like this:

K is the midpoint of $\overline{GH}$, so (C) is correct.

6. F Difficulty: Low

Category: Essential Skills / Numbers and Operations

Getting to the Answer: On early questions, you can sometimes let your calculator do most of the work for you: wire cut off = 4(1.2) = 4.8 yards; wire remaining = 50 − 4.8 = 45.2 yards, which is (F).

7. C Difficulty: Medium

Category: Essential Skills / Rates, Percents, Proportions, and Unit Conversion

Getting to the Answer: Use the ratio to set up an equation. Let x represent an unknown part of the combined length of the rope. If the lengths of the pieces are in the ratio 2:3:5, then $2x + 3x + 5x = 80$ feet. This simplifies to $10x = 80$, or $x = 8$. Because the longest piece is given by $5x$, its length is 5(8), or 40 feet. Cutting this in half gives a final length of 20 feet, which is (C).

8. J Difficulty: Medium

Category: Higher Math / Algebra

Getting to the Answer: You solve an inequality just like an equation. The only difference is that if you multiply or divide both sides by a negative number (usually in the last step of the solution), you must reverse (flip) the inequality symbol. Start by distributing the 4:

$$3x + 12 \geq 4(x + 2)$$
$$3x + 12 \geq 4x + 8$$
$$-x \geq -4$$
$$x \leq 4$$

Now find the number line that matches. Pay attention to the dot at 4 and the shading. Because x is less than or equal to 4, the dot should be solid (closed) and the graph should be shaded to the left of 4, which matches the number line in (J).

9. D Difficulty: Medium

Category: Essential Skills / Numbers and Operations

Getting to the Answer: This may look like a geometry question, but it's really just testing your ability to work with mixed numbers. Examine the diagram carefully. You can use either dimension to find w, so focus on only one dimension. Using the length, the walkway is $32\frac{1}{2}$ feet

long, of which 29 feet is the pool, so the walkway is only $32\frac{1}{2} - 29 = 3\frac{1}{2}$ feet. This is split, half on each side of the pool, so the width, w, of the walkway in feet is:

$$3\frac{1}{2} \div 2 = \frac{7}{2} \times \frac{1}{2} = \frac{7}{4} = 1\frac{3}{4}$$

Choice (D) is correct.

10. G Difficulty: Low

Category: Higher Math / Number and Quantity

Getting to the Answer: You can use your calculator to quickly find the fifth root of 500 (by entering 500 raised to the one-fifth power, which is approximately 3.47), or you can compare the fifth power of the integers in the answer choices.

$2^5 = 32$

$3^5 = 243$

$4^5 = 1,024$ Stop.

If $x^5 = 500$, then x must be between 3 and 4, because 500 is between 3^5 and 4^5, so (G) is correct.

11. B Difficulty: Low

Category: Essential Skills / Expressions and Equations

Getting to the Answer: You can use your calculator for the arithmetic here. It will take only a few seconds and will help you avoid mistakes.

$$47 - x = 188$$
$$47 = 188 + x$$
$$-141 = x$$

That's (B).

12. H Difficulty: Low

Category: Essential Skills / Numbers and Operations

Getting to the Answer: There is no need to set up an equation to answer this question. Just think logically and carry out a few simple arithmetic steps. Everyone pays $1.50, and the rest of the toll is based on the number of miles traveled. Subtract $1.50 from Joy's toll to see how much is based on distance traveled: $25.00 − $1.50 = $23.50. Then divide that amount by 25 cents per mile:

$$\frac{\$23.50}{\$0.25\,\text{per mile}} = 94\,\text{miles}$$

Choice (H) is correct.

13. D   Difficulty: Medium

Category: Essential Skills / Expressions and Equations

Getting to the Answer: Use the information in the question to write your own expression, then look for the answer choice that matches. Simplify your expression only if you don't find a match. If participants earn $20 *per half hour* that they skate, then they earn 20 × 2 = $40 *per hour*. Multiply this amount by the number of hours (not including the first 3 hours). This can be expressed as 40(h − 3). This is not one of the answer choices, so simplify by distributing the 40 to get 40h − 120, which is (D).

If you're struggling with the algebra, try Picking Numbers. Pick a number of hours a participant might skate, like 5. They don't earn anything for the first 3 hours, but they earn $20 per half hour for the last 2 hours, which is 20 times 4 half hours, or $80. Now, find the expression that gives you an answer of $80 when h = 5 hours. The expression in (D) gives 40(5) − 120 = 200 − 120 = 80.

14. J   Difficulty: Low

Category: Essential Skills / Expressions and Equations

Getting to the Answer: Before you try anything too fancy, check for like terms. Combine the like terms 5a and 3a to find that 5a − 5b + 3a = 8a − 5b, which is (J).

15. E   Difficulty: Medium

Category: Essential Skills / Geometry

Getting to the Answer: Even if you forget all the properties of a parallelogram, you can figure out questions like this by using the fact that opposite sides are parallel. Redraw the diagram, and it's clear that ∠FEG and ∠EGD are alternate interior angles. Therefore, the measure of ∠FEG is also 70°, so (E) is correct.

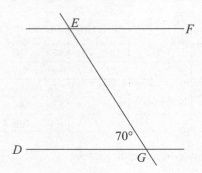

16. G   Difficulty: Medium

Category: Higher Math / Algebra

Getting to the Answer: The easiest way to find the slope of a line is to write the equation in slope-intercept form, $y = mx + b$.

$$4x + 3y = 9$$
$$3y = -4x + 9$$
$$y = -\frac{4}{3}x + 3$$

The slope, m, is the coefficient of x, or $-\frac{4}{3}$, which matches (G).

17. C   Difficulty: Medium

Category: Higher Math / Algebra

Getting to the Answer: When you factor a quadratic equation, make sure one side is equal to zero before you begin. Then you know that one factor or the other must be equal to zero. Because 3 is a prime number, the two binomial factors must look like (3x ± ___)(x ± ___). One of the last two numbers must be positive and the other negative, because they multiply to a negative number (−20). At this point you can use trial and error with the factors of −20 to find (3x + 5)(x − 4) = 0. If the product is equal to zero, then one of the factors must be equal to zero, so 3x + 5 = 0 or x − 4 = 0. The first equation gives you a negative value for x, which contradicts the question stem (x > 0), while the second equation gives you x = 4, which matches (C).

If factoring is not your strong suit, there are lots of other options. You could Backsolve, use the quadratic formula, or graph the equation in your graphing calculator to see where it crosses the x-axis.

18. F   Difficulty: Medium

Category: Higher Math / Geometry

Getting to the Answer: In similar shapes, each side is scaled up or down by the same factor, and the perimeter is also scaled up or down by that same factor. The perimeter of the original triangle is 2 + 5 + 6 = 13. Because the similar triangle has a perimeter twice as long, each side must also be twice as long. The smallest side is 2(2) = 4, making (F) the correct answer.

19. D   Difficulty: Low

Category: Essential Skills / Rates, Percents, Proportions, and Unit Conversion

Getting to the Answer: You can often save a step in percentage questions if you figure out what percentage is left. If the shirt is 15% off, then the sale price is 100% − 15% = 85% of the original price. Thus, during the sale, it costs $24.60(0.85) = $20.91 ≈ $21, which is (D).

20. G   Difficulty: Medium

Category: Higher Math / Functions

Getting to the Answer: To find the value of a function for a specified input, simply plug in the number for each x and see what you get. Be sure to follow the correct order of operations when simplifying.

$$f(x) = x^3 - x^2 - x$$
$$f(-3) = (-3)^3 - (-3)^2 - (-3)$$
$$= -27 - 9 + 3$$
$$= -33$$

Choice (G) is correct.

21. E   Difficulty: Medium

Category: Higher Math / Functions

Getting to the Answer: Don't panic. This is nothing more than a plug-and-chug question, along with using the correct order of operations. Start in the parentheses (as always), apply the rule, and work your way out: (3 ❖ 5) = 3(3 − 5) = 3(−2) = −6; then, 4 ❖ (−6) = 4 [4 − (−6)] = 4(10) = 40. Choice (E) is correct.

22. F   Difficulty: Medium

Category: Essential Skills / Rates, Percents, Proportions, and Unit Conversion

Getting to the Answer: Writing out the units on conversion questions will help you avoid mistakes. First find the cost per yard: $\frac{4.50 \text{ dollars}}{2.5 \text{ yards}} = 1.80 \frac{\text{dollars}}{\text{yard}}$.

Then find the cost per foot (notice that yards cancel):

$1.80 \frac{\text{dollars}}{\text{yard}} \cdot \frac{1 \text{ yard}}{3 \text{ feet}} = 0.60 \frac{\text{dollars}}{\text{foot}}$

Choice (F) is correct.

23. C   Difficulty: Medium

Category: Higher Math / Geometry

Getting to the Answer: In a circle, arc measure is the same as the measure of the central angle of the sector. Thus, the arc measures of a circle must sum to 360 degrees. Because all 8 sectors of Melba's spinner are congruent, divide 360 by 8 to get an arc measure of 45 degrees, which is (C).

24. F   Difficulty: Low

Category: Essential Skills / Expressions and Equations

Getting to the Answer: Questions like this may seem complicated at first, but all you need to do is plug the given numbers into the formula. Here, $h = 15$ and $s = 120.50$.

$$7h + 0.04s$$
$$= 7(15) + 0.04(120.50)$$
$$= 105 + 4.82$$
$$= 109.82$$

Choice (F) is correct.

25. C   Difficulty: Medium

Category: Higher Math / Functions

Getting to the Answer: Don't let the function notation throw you. You are looking for an equation that gives the number of degrees in an n-sided regular polygon. One way to answer the question is to make a table and look for a pattern, or a rule, which is exactly what a function is. Notice in the figure, that each time the number of sides goes up by 1, the sum of the angle measures goes up by 180°. Make a third column in the table to discover a relationship and a fourth column to express the relationship using function notation.

Number of Sides, n	Sum of the Angles	Pattern	Function Notation
3	180°	180° × 1	$f(3) = 180 \times (3 - 2)$
4	360°	180° × 2	$f(4) = 180 \times (4 - 2)$
5	540°	180° × 3	$f(5) = 180 \times (5 - 2)$
6	720°	180° × 4	$f(6) = 180 \times (6 - 2)$
n			$f(n) = 180 \times (n - 2)$

The final function notation matches (C).

26. J   Difficulty: Low

Category: Essential Skills / Numbers and Operations

Getting to the Answer: Absolute value is a special type of parentheses, so follow the same order of operations as usual. Here, you need to multiply the two pairs of numbers, then add the results, and finally, take the absolute value of the sum:

$$|6(-12) + 8(4)| = |-72 + 32|$$
$$= |-40|$$
$$= 40$$

Choice (J) is correct.

27. A   Difficulty: Medium

Category: Higher Math / Number and Quantity

Getting to the Answer: Pick Numbers for questions like this. Because the operation involved is multiplication, you can focus on the endpoints of the ranges given. Multiply all combinations of the endpoints and choose the greatest possible product. Because a falls between -1 and 1, use those endpoints for a, and because b falls between -4 and 3, use those endpoints for b:

$a \times b = -1 \times (-4) = 4$

$a \times b = -1 \times 3 = -3$

$a \times b = 1 \times (-4) = -4$

$a \times b = 1 \times 3 = 3$

The greatest possible product of a and b is 4, which is (A).

28. G   Difficulty: High

Category: Essential Skills / Statistics and Probability

Getting to the Answer: The table is not complete, so your first step is to fill in the missing values. Start with what you know and work from there. It may not be necessary to complete the entire table, but rather only what you need to answer the question.

You know there are 186 cupcakes total and that 104 are without sprinkles, which means $186 - 104 = 82$ have sprinkles. Because you already know that 40 of those cupcakes have vanilla icing, this means $82 - 40 = 42$ of the cupcakes with sprinkles have chocolate icing. You also know that $\frac{2}{3}$ of the total number of cupcakes have

chocolate icing, which means there are $\frac{2}{3} \times 186 = 124$ cupcakes with chocolate icing, total, so you can fill this number in the "Total" row of that column. You do not need to fill in any more of the table because the question only asks about cupcakes with chocolate icing that have sprinkles. There are 124 cupcakes with chocolate icing total and 42 of them have sprinkles, so the probability of randomly choosing one with sprinkles is $\frac{42}{124}$, or $\frac{21}{62}$, which is (G).

29. D   Difficulty: Medium

Category: Higher Math / Number and Quantity

Getting to the Answer: Matrices behave exactly as you would expect (except when multiplying one matrix by another), so don't let this question intimidate you. The numbers in front of the matrices (-1 and 2) are called scalars, and you simply multiply each entry in the matrix by the scalar (just like distributing inside a set of parentheses):

$$-1\begin{bmatrix} 4 & 3 \\ 2 & 1 \end{bmatrix} + 2\begin{bmatrix} 1 & 2 \\ 3 & 4 \end{bmatrix} = \begin{bmatrix} -4 & -3 \\ -2 & -1 \end{bmatrix} + \begin{bmatrix} 2 & 4 \\ 6 & 8 \end{bmatrix}$$

To add the two resulting matrices, simply add the corresponding entries (the numbers that sit in the same spots):

$$\begin{bmatrix} -4 & -3 \\ -2 & -1 \end{bmatrix} + \begin{bmatrix} 2 & 4 \\ 6 & 8 \end{bmatrix} = \begin{bmatrix} -4+2 & -3+4 \\ -2+6 & -1+8 \end{bmatrix}$$
$$= \begin{bmatrix} -2 & 1 \\ 4 & 7 \end{bmatrix}$$

Choice (D) is correct.

30. F   Difficulty: Medium

Category: Higher Math / Geometry

Getting to the Answer: There will usually be one question that tests your knowledge of the Triangle Inequality Theorem. If you're not sure how to proceed, try drawing a sketch. The Triangle Inequality Theorem states that any side of a triangle is less than the sum of and more than the difference between the other two sides, so the third side must be at least $6 - 3.5 = 2.5$ inches. Choice (F) is too small.

31. D   **Difficulty:** Medium

Category: Higher Math / Functions

Getting to the Answer: The range of a function is the set of all possible y-values. (Remember, alphabetical order: domain = x and range = y.) Eliminate C. The graph consists of discrete points, not continuous segments, so the range will be a set of discrete values, not an interval. Eliminate A and B. To choose between (D) and E, look at the coordinates of the points: The y-coordinates of the points, from left to right, are 6, 4, 2, 0, 2, 4, and 6. Thus, the range is the set {0, 2, 4, 6}. This matches (D). (Note that the set in E is the domain of the function.)

32. F   **Difficulty:** Medium

Category: Essential Skills / Statistics and Probability

Getting to the Answer: To find the probability that an event will *not* occur, subtract the probability that it *will* occur from 1. The probability that it will rain today is 60%, so the probability that it will not rain today is 100% − 60% = 40%. The probability that it will rain tomorrow is 75%, so the probability that it will not rain tomorrow is 100% − 75% = 25%.

To find the probability that two independent events will both occur, multiply the individual probabilities. Thus, to get the probability that it will not rain today or tomorrow, multiply 40% and 25%:

(40%)(25%) = (0.40)(0.25) = 0.10 = 10%

The answer is (F).

33. E   **Difficulty:** Medium

Category: Higher Math / Geometry

Getting to the Answer: The area of a rectangle is $A = lw$. In this question, the dimensions of the rectangle are algebraic expressions. When you multiply binomials, don't forget to use FOIL.

The new length is $b + 2$, and the new width is $b + 3$, so the area is:

$$\text{Area} = l \cdot w$$
$$= (b + 2)(b + 3)$$
$$= b^2 + 3b + 2b + 6$$
$$= b^2 + 5b + 6$$

That's (E).

34. G   **Difficulty:** Medium

Category: Higher Math / Geometry

Getting to the Answer: To find the circumference of a circle, you need to know the length of the radius so you can use the formula $C = 2\pi r$. In the standard (x,y) coordinate plane, the equation of a circle is given by the equation $(x + h)^2 + (y - k)^2 = r^2$, where (h,k) is the center of the circle and r is the length of the radius. Here, r^2 is 100, so $r = 10$. Thus, the circumference of the circle is $2\pi(10) = 20\pi$, which is (G).

35. A   **Difficulty:** Medium

Category: Essential Skills / Rates, Percents, Proportions, and Unit Conversion

Getting to the Answer: Answer this question one step at a time. First, find the number of movie theme songs:

10% of 300 = 0.10 × 300 = 30

Then subtract the number of movie theme songs and marches from the total number of pieces of music:

300 − (30 + 80) = 300 − 110 = 190

So (A) is the correct answer.

36. J   **Difficulty:** Medium

Category: Essential Skills / Statistics and Probability

Getting to the Answer: To make the question a little easier to follow, Pick Numbers for the total number of baskets. Imagine that they made a total of 100 baskets. If the team made 100 baskets, then they made 20 1-point baskets, 70 2-point baskets, and 10 3-point baskets. The average point value of all the baskets is the total number of points divided by the total number of baskets:

$$\frac{20(1) + 70(2) + 10(3)}{100} = \frac{20 + 140 + 30}{100}$$
$$= \frac{190}{100}$$
$$= 1.9$$

Choice (J) is correct.

37. E   **Difficulty:** High

Category: Higher Math / Algebra

Getting to the Answer: The question is asking for the value of g in terms of h. The two given equations do not show a direct relationship between g and h, so you must solve for q in the second equation to get q in terms of h, and then substitute this value for q in the first equation. To solve for q in the second equation, isolate q by first adding 8 to both sides of the equation, which gives $h + 8 = 2q$. Divide both sides by 2 to get $\frac{h + 8}{2} = q$. Use this value of q in the first equation: $g = 4q + 3$ becomes

$$g = 4\left(\frac{h + 8}{2}\right) + 3.$$

Factor out a 2 from the numerator and the denominator of the first term to get $g = 2(h + 8) + 3$. Distributing the 2 gives $g = 2h + 16 + 3$, or $g = 2h + 19$, which is (E).

38. K   Difficulty: Medium

Category: Essential Skills / Numbers and Operations

Getting to the Answer: On this type of question, you want the numbers to be either as close together or as far apart as possible (because you are asked for an extreme value). Try a few possibilities; you should see a pattern.

$3 \times 39 = 117$

$5 \times 37 = 185$

$7 \times 35 = 245$

The products are increasing, so it looks like you want the two numbers to be as close together as possible. Because half of 42 is 21, try 21×21, which is 441. Because (K) is the largest possible answer choice, you can be sure it's correct.

39. B   Difficulty: Medium

Category: Essential Skills / Geometry

Getting to the Answer: Parallel lines provide lots of information—look for congruent and supplementary angles.

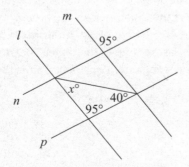

Because both sets of lines are parallel, the missing angle in the triangle corresponds to the angle marked 95°. The three interior angles of the triangle sum to 180°.

$$40° + 95° + x° = 180°$$
$$x° = 45°$$

Choice (B) is correct.

40. F   Difficulty: Medium

Category: Higher Math / Algebra

Getting to the Answer: Don't jump right in to using your graphing calculator; often some simple algebra is the best route to the correct answer. The easiest way to find the y-intercept (the value of y when the graph crosses the y-axis) is to plug in $x = 0$:

$$12(0) - 3y = 12$$
$$-3y = 12$$
$$y = -4$$

This means (F) is correct.

41. B   Difficulty: Medium

Category: Higher Math / Statistics and Probability

Getting to the Answer: The median of a data set is the middle number when the data values are arranged in ascending (or descending) order. If there is an even number of terms, the median is the average of the two middle terms. Use the frequency (along the vertical axis) and the bar heights to list out the values: There is one 1, one 2, two 3s, five 4s, four 5s, four 6s, two 7s, and one 8. The list of data values is:

1, 2, 3, 3, 4, 4, 4, 4, 4, **5, 5,** 5, 5, 6, 6, 6, 6, 7, 7, 8

There are 20 terms in all, so the median is the average of the 10th and 11th terms, which are both 5s. Thus, the median is 5, making (B) the correct answer.

42. G   Difficulty: High

Category: Higher Math / Algebra

Getting to the Answer: If a system of equations has no solution, there are no values of x and y that make both equations true. Graphically, that means the two linear equations never intersect and are therefore parallel (have the same slope but different *y*-intercepts). Write both equations in slope-intercept form, then set the slopes equal and solve for *a*:

$$-x + 6y = 7$$
$$6y = x + 7$$
$$y = \boxed{\frac{1}{6}}x + \frac{7}{6}$$
$$-5x + 10ay = 32$$
$$10ay = 5x + 32$$
$$y = \boxed{\frac{5}{10a}}x + \frac{32}{10a}$$

$$\frac{1}{6} = \frac{5}{10a}$$
$$10a = 30$$
$$a = 3$$

The correct answer is (G).

43. C   Difficulty: High

Category: Higher Math / Geometry

Getting to the Answer: Sometimes the answer choices give you a hint about how to answer the question. Here, they are simple enough that you know you don't have to do any fancy calculations. In fact, they're different enough that you might even be able to eyeball the answer. Draw in lines that go from the center of the square to the edge at right angles.

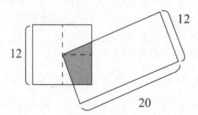

The gray triangle is the same size as the white triangle. (The portion of the upper 90° angle formed by the gray triangle is the same as the portion of the rectangle's 90° angle formed by the gray triangle. Therefore, the portion of the lower 90° angle formed by the white triangle is also the same.) If you move the gray triangle to where the white triangle is, the shaded area is exactly $\frac{1}{4}$ of the square.

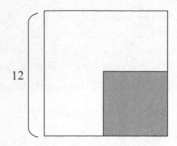

Because the area of the square is $12 \times 12 = 144$, the area of the shaded region is $\frac{1}{4}(144) = 36$. Choice (C) is correct.

44. G   Difficulty: Medium

Category: Higher Math / Algebra

Getting to the Answer: Always be on the lookout for the three classic quadratics—they'll save you a lot of time. Here, $p^2 - q^2$ is a difference of squares, which can be factored relatively easily. Once you have the factors in place, check the question stem again to see what you can plug in.

$$p^2 - q^2 = (p + q)(p - q)$$
$$= (-3)(-4)$$
$$= 12$$

Choice (G) is correct.

45. C   Difficulty: Medium

Category: Higher Math / Statistics and Probability

Getting to the Answer: This question requires careful reading of the table. The first criterion is fairly straightforward—you're looking for a participant with an HDL level in the < 40 range, so focus on that column in the table. The second criterion is a bit trickier—*at least 36 years old* means 36 years old or older, so you'll need to use the values in the rows for 36-45 and Older than 45. There were 19 in the 36-45 age group who were considered at risk, and 12 in the Older than 45 age group, resulting in a total of $19 + 12 = 31$ out of 300 participants (the total in the last row, last column of the table). The probability of randomly selecting one participant from either of these two groups is $\frac{31}{300}$, which is (C).

46. J   Difficulty: Medium

Category: Higher Math / Statistics and Probability

Getting to the Answer: Note that you are given the number of residents in a specific age group here, not the total number of residents, so in this case you will have to work backward to get the total. According to the circle graph, 20% of residents are age 17 or younger, and this corresponds to 1,000 residents. So if x is the total number of residents, you know that 1,000 is 20% of x. Therefore, $1{,}000 = 0.2x$. Divide both sides of this equation by 0.2 to find that $x = 5{,}000$. So there are 5,000 residents total and 30% of them are 36 through 55 years old. Multiply 5,000 by 30% (or 0.3) to determine that 1,500 residents are 36 through 55 years old. That's (J).

47. E   Difficulty: High

Category: Higher Math / Number and Quantity

Getting to the Answer: Write each factor in the expression in exponential form (using fractional exponents for the radicals). Then use exponent rules to simplify the expression. Add the exponents of the factors that are being multiplied and subtract the exponent of the factor that is being divided:

$$\frac{\sqrt[3]{x} \cdot x^{\frac{5}{2}} \cdot x}{\sqrt{x}} = \frac{x^{\frac{1}{3}} \cdot x^{\frac{5}{2}} \cdot x^{1}}{x^{\frac{1}{2}}}$$

$$= x^{\frac{1}{3} + \frac{5}{2} + \frac{1}{1} - \frac{1}{2}} = x^{\frac{2}{6} + \frac{15}{6} + \frac{6}{6} - \frac{3}{6}}$$

$$= x^{\frac{20}{6}} = x^{\frac{10}{3}}$$

The question states that n is the power of x, so the value of n is $\dfrac{10}{3}$. That's (E).

48. K   Difficulty: High

Category: Higher Math / Functions

Getting to the Answer: Because your calculator can evaluate both $\cos \dfrac{5\pi}{12}$ and each of the answer choices, this is an excellent opportunity to check your work using your calculator. Just make sure you set it to radians instead of degrees. Using the given equation and the table of values, you get:

$$\cos\left(\frac{2\pi}{3} - \frac{\pi}{4}\right) = \left(\cos\frac{2\pi}{3}\right)\left(\cos\frac{\pi}{4}\right) + \left(\sin\frac{2\pi}{3}\right)\left(\sin\frac{\pi}{4}\right)$$

$$= \left(-\frac{1}{2}\right)\left(\frac{\sqrt{2}}{2}\right) + \left(\frac{\sqrt{3}}{2}\right)\left(\frac{\sqrt{2}}{2}\right)$$

$$= -\frac{\sqrt{2}}{4} + \frac{\sqrt{6}}{4} = \frac{\sqrt{6} - \sqrt{2}}{4}$$

This matches (K).

49. B   Difficulty: High

Category: Higher Math / Algebra

Getting to the Answer: You could using Picking Numbers to answer this question, but there are a lot of terms to evaluate, so algebra is actually a more efficient route. Notice that most of the answer choices contain radicals in the denominator, so reduce each term before you find a common denominator and add:

$$\frac{\sqrt{x}}{x} + \frac{\sqrt{y}}{y} = \frac{1}{\sqrt{x}} + \frac{1}{\sqrt{y}}$$

$$= \frac{1}{\sqrt{x}}\left(\frac{\sqrt{y}}{\sqrt{y}}\right) + \frac{1}{\sqrt{y}}\left(\frac{\sqrt{x}}{\sqrt{x}}\right)$$

$$= \frac{\sqrt{y} + \sqrt{x}}{\sqrt{xy}}$$

Reverse the order of the terms in the numerator and you have a match for (B).

Note: If you're not sure about the first step (reducing the original terms), think of the radicals in terms of fractional exponents:

$$\frac{\sqrt{x}}{x} = \frac{x^{\frac{1}{2}}}{x^{1}} = \frac{1}{x^{1-\frac{1}{2}}} = \frac{1}{x^{\frac{1}{2}}} = \frac{1}{\sqrt{x}}$$

50. J   Difficulty: High

Category: Higher Math / Geometry

Getting to the Answer: If you're not sure where to get started, try working backwards. What are you looking for? The cosine of $\angle ZWY$. What do you need to find that? The lengths of the hypotenuse and the adjacent leg, WZ and WY. How can you find those lengths? By using the given side lengths and your knowledge of right triangles. Now that you've figured out how to get from what you have to what you need, you can go ahead and get there. $\triangle WXY$ is a right triangle. You know that WX is 12 and XY is 5, so WY must be 13. (If you didn't spot the 5:12:13 triplet, you could have used the Pythagorean theorem.) $\triangle WYZ$ is also a right triangle. You know that WY and YZ are both 13, so WZ must be $13\sqrt{2}$. (Again, you could have used the Pythagorean theorem if you didn't spot the 45°-45°-90° triangle.) The cosine of an angle is the adjacent leg over the hypotenuse, so the cosine of $\angle ZWY$ is WY over WZ, or $\dfrac{13}{13\sqrt{2}} = \dfrac{1}{\sqrt{2}} = \dfrac{\sqrt{2}}{2}$. Choice (J) is correct.

51. E   Difficulty: Low

Category: Essential Skills / Geometry

Getting to the Answer: The coordinates of the midpoint are the averages of the coordinates of the endpoints. The average of the x-values is $\dfrac{2+12}{2} = 7$, and the average of the y-values is $\dfrac{3+(-15)}{2} = -6$, so the coordinates of the midpoint, M, are $(7, -6)$, which is (E).

52. H   Difficulty: Medium

Category: Higher Math / Geometry

Getting to the Answer: Finding the equation of a line that is perpendicular to another line (or line segment) involves slope. Perpendicular lines have negative-reciprocal slopes, so find the slope of $\overline{PQ}$ and then choose the line that has the negative-reciprocal slope. (The y-intercept doesn't matter in this question, and there is no requirement that line L passes through the midpoint found in the previous question.) The slope of $\overline{PQ}$ is:

$$m = \frac{y_2 - y_1}{x_2 - x_1}$$
$$= \frac{-15 - 3}{12 - 2}$$
$$= \frac{-18}{10}$$
$$= -\frac{9}{5}$$

Be careful—don't pick choice A. You want a line that has a slope that is the negative reciprocal of $-\dfrac{9}{5}$, which is $\dfrac{5}{9}$, so (H) is correct.

53. D   Difficulty: Medium

Category: Higher Math / Algebra

Getting to the Answer: When you solve a quadratic equation by factoring, each factor will give you a solution. If the equation has only one solution, that means the factors are the same. To get a middle term of $-8x$, you must have factors of $(x - 4)$ and $(x - 4)$. Multiply it out to get $(x - 4)(x - 4) = x^2 - 4x - 4x + 16$, which simplifies to $x^2 - 8x + 16$. This means that $k = 16$, which is (D).

54. G   Difficulty: Medium

Category: Higher Math / Functions

Getting to the Answer: Think this question through logically, one step at a time. The equation for $Q(x)$ is given in factored form, so you know its roots (x-intercepts); they are the values of x that make the equation equal 0, which are -4 and 1. Thus, the graph of $Q(x)$ passes through the points $(-4, 0)$ and $(1, 0)$. If $R(x)$ is a reflection of $Q(x)$ over the y-axis, which is a horizontal reflection, the x-coordinates of these points will take on the opposite signs. This means the graph of $R(x)$ must pass through $(4, 0)$ and $(-1, 0)$, which is (G).

55. A   Difficulty: High

Category: Higher Math / Number and Quantity

Getting to the Answer: Each of the factors in this product has two terms, so they behave like binomials. This means you can use FOIL to find the product. To avoid messy numbers, simplify the two radicals first using the definition of i. Write each of the numbers under the radicals as a product of -1 and the number, take the square roots, and then FOIL the resulting expressions. You'll also need to use the property that $i^2 = -1$:

$$\left(2 + \sqrt{-9}\right)\left(-1 + \sqrt{-4}\right) = \left(2 + \sqrt{-1 \times 9}\right)\left(-1 + \sqrt{-1 \times 4}\right)$$
$$= (2 + 3i)(-1 + 2i)$$
$$= -2 + 4i - 3i + 6i^2$$
$$= -2 + i + 6(-1)$$
$$= -8 + i$$

Choice (A) is correct.

56. H   Difficulty: High

Category: Higher Math / Statistics and Probability

Getting to the Answer: This question takes a bit of thought: For *mn* to be less than 0 (a negative number), either the first number selected is negative and the second is positive, or the reverse. These are two independent events, so once you find the probability of each event, you'll need to add them. Also keep in mind that if either number is 0, then the product will not be less than 0 (it will be equal to 0), so selecting a 0 from either set of numbers is not a desired outcome.

$$P(\text{negative then positive}) = \frac{2}{5} \times \frac{0}{4} = 0$$

$$P(\text{positive then negative}) = \frac{2}{5} \times \frac{3}{4} = \frac{6}{20} = \frac{3}{10}$$

The probability that either of these two events will occur is $\frac{3}{10}$, which is (H).

57. C   Difficulty: High

Category: Higher Math / Functions

Getting to the Answer: Answering this question requires some knowledge of the unit circle and/or the graph of a sine curve. First figure out where the graph of sine reaches a minimum, then worry about where the 2θ comes in. The sine function first reaches its minimum (of -1) at $\frac{3\pi}{2}$, so:

$$2\theta = \frac{3\pi}{2}$$

$$\theta = \frac{3\pi}{2} \times \frac{1}{2} = \frac{3\pi}{4}$$

Choice (C) is correct.

58. K   Difficulty: High

Category: Higher Math / Geometry

Getting to the Answer: Backsolving is a great option here if you're not sure how to set this question up algebraically or if you're not confident about your variable manipulation skills. Plug the given coordinates into the Distance formula, $\left(\sqrt{(x_2 - x_1)^2 + (y_2 - y_1)^2}\right)$, set the distance equal to 4, and solve for *r*:

$$\sqrt{(r - 10)^2 + (6 - r)^2} = 4$$

$$(r - 10)^2 + (6 - r)^2 = 16$$

$$\left(r^2 - 20r + 100\right) + \left(36 - 12r + r^2\right) = 16$$

$$2r^2 - 32r + 136 = 16$$

$$2r^2 - 32r + 120 = 0$$

$$r^2 - 16r + 60 = 0$$

$$(r - 10)(r - 6) = 0$$

$$r = 10 \text{ or } r = 6$$

Only 10 is an answer choice, so (K) is correct. To Backsolve, you still need to know the Distance formula to figure out whether F, G, H, and J are correct, but notice that (K) gives the points (10,6) and (10,10). Because the *x*-coordinate is the same, you can see that the distance between the points is $10 - 6 = 4$ without using the formula.

59. D   Difficulty: High

Category: Higher Math / Statistics and Probability

Getting to the Answer: Think of each character in the patient identifier as a slot to be filled and use the Fundamental Counting Principle. The first character can be 1 of 24 letters (not 26 because I and O cannot be used) or 1 of 9 numbers (not 10 because the first character cannot be 0), for a total of 33 possibilities for the first character. Each of the remaining characters can be 1 of 24 letters or 1 of 10 numbers, for a total of 34 possibilities for each character. Thus, the total number of possibilities is $33 \cdot 34 \cdot 34 \cdot 34 \cdot 34 \cdot 34$, which can be written as $33 \cdot 34^5$. Choice (D) is correct.

60. K   Difficulty: Medium

Category: Essential Skills / Numbers and Operations

Getting to the Answer: Each question is worth the same amount, so don't spend too much time on any one. Questions that ask how many different values of something there are tend to be particularly lengthy, so it's a good idea to save them for the end of the test. One way to solve this is to make all of the numerators 3: The result is $\frac{3}{15} < \frac{3}{x} < \frac{3}{9}$.

This inequality is true for all values of *x* between 9 and 15. That's 10, 11, 12, 13, and 14: five integer values of *x*, making (K) correct.

READING TEST

Passage I

Suggested Passage Map notes:

¶1: Giovanni (G) admires garden below

¶2: G sees old, sickly gardener

¶3: Gardener avoids touching plants

¶4: Gardener wears mask to shield himself

1. D   Difficulty: Medium

Category: Key Ideas and Details / Detail

Getting to the Answer: Good notes will help lead you quickly to the section of the passage you need to research. In lines 24–29, Giovanni notices "one shrub in particular" that seems to "illuminate the garden." The plant he is speaking about is the one with "a profusion of purple blossoms." In the next sentence, he considers other plants that are *less beautiful* than the one with purple blossoms. This should lead you to (D). Choice A is a misused detail; the plant that is wreathed around the statue (lines 38–42) is shown in a positive light, but these lines do not indicate that Giovanni finds the plant to be exceptional. Choice B is a misused detail; in lines 36–38, there is information about plants that "crept serpent-like along the ground," yet no specific plant on the ground is mentioned, nor are any viewed as being special. Choice C is a misused detail; in lines 22–23, "gigantic leaves" are mentioned, but not a specific plant's leaves.

2. G   Difficulty: Medium

Category: Key Ideas and Details / Detail

Getting to the Answer: If you are able to determine that a certain numbered statement is correct (or incorrect), you can include (or eliminate) all answer choices that include that statement. Normally, you would start with the statement that appears most frequently, but all statements here appear an equal number of times. Your notes should indicate that the narrator discusses the gardener's interaction with the plants principally in paragraphs 3 and 4. Skim those paragraphs for the information in the three statements. In line 66, you see that the gardener avoids the "actual touch or the direct inhaling of [the plants']

odors." Paragraph 4 offers alternate confirmation of these two statements. Based on this, you know that Statements I and III are valid; eliminate all choices that don't include both of them (F and H). A quick skim of the paragraphs offers no support for Statement II; eliminate J. Choice (G) is correct; the passage supports both statements.

3. C   Difficulty: Medium

Category: Craft and Structure / Writer's View

Getting to the Answer: Consider what the author writes about the gardener. In line 82, he states that the gardener wears gloves to protect himself. He also wears other "armor," the mask that he puts over his mouth and nostrils, in line 86. In lines 65–74, Giovanni is disturbed by the fact that the gardener takes so much caution with the plants, indicating that Giovanni himself would not take these types of precautions. A good prediction is that the gardener is a cautious man. Choice (C) matches this. Choices A and D are distortions; Giovanni alludes to Adam and the Garden of Eden, but this does not indicate that the gardener is more or less religious. Choice B is opposite; the narrator depicts the gardener as being very cautious, behavior that disturbs Giovanni.

4. J   Difficulty: Medium

Category: Key Ideas and Details / Detail

Getting to the Answer: In Roman numeral questions, start with the statements that appears most frequently. Statements I and II appear more frequently than the third one does, so start there. In line 67, the gardener "impressed Giovanni most disagreeably" by avoiding the inhalation of the plants' odors; Statement II is valid then. Eliminate F and H. (Note that this means you don't have to investigate Statement III.) In the following lines, Giovanni becomes upset that "the man's demeanor was that of one walking among malignant influences," which supports Statement I. Choice (J) is the correct choice.

5. A   Difficulty: Medium

Category: Key Ideas and Details / Inference

Getting to the Answer: Some questions will ask you to read between the lines. Although this can sometimes be difficult, remember that the answer will always be supported by information in the passage. The gardener, in lines 65–66, avoids directly touching the plants or "inhaling . . . their odors." Yet he is also described as a *scientific gardener*, who seems to be *looking into* the nature of the plants. You can infer that he is observant and seems to understand the essence of the plants. Predict that he is "focused" or "attentive." Choice (A) matches this prediction. Choice B is extreme; lines 55–62 indicate that the gardener knows a lot about plants. The narrator suggests, however, that he discovers this information as he works, not that he already knows all there is to know about plants. Choice C is opposite; the fact that he refuses to touch or smell the plants goes against the idea that he loves nature. Choice D is a misused detail; Giovanni mentions Adam in line 79, but there is no indication that the gardener actually resembles him.

6. G   Difficulty: Medium

Category: Key Ideas and Details / Inference

Getting to the Answer: Don't over-infer. The correct choice will be closely related to something stated in the passage. In lines 29–30, the plant is described as seemingly able to "illuminate the garden, even had there been no sunshine." From this, you can infer that the plant seemed capable of producing light, which matches (G). Choice F is a distortion; in line 27 the narrator states that each blossom "had the luster and richness of a gem." To say that the plant could sprout gems stretches the metaphor too far. Choice H is a distortion; the narrator suggests that the plant could shed light on the garden, not overrun it like a weed. Choice J is out of scope; nowhere in the passage is there any indication that the plant grows very quickly.

7. D   Difficulty: Low

Category: Craft and Structure / Writer's View

Getting to the Answer: Take the time to predict an answer before looking at the answer choices; this will help you avoid being tempted by incorrect answer choices. The passage is not told directly from Giovanni's point of view; the reader understands what Giovanni is thinking, yet this information comes from an unidentified narrator. Look for this among the choices; (D) matches. Choice A is a misused detail; the narrator refers to the gardener in the third person. Choice B is a misused detail; the narrator refers to Giovanni in the third person. Choice C is a misused detail; the gardener is described as being scientific, yet that does not indicate that the narrator is a scientist.

8. J   Difficulty: Medium

Category: Craft and Structure / Function

Getting to the Answer: Read the referenced lines carefully to determine the author's intent. These statements are made after the narrator describes Giovanni as being disturbed by the insecurities the gardener shows while cultivating the garden. The narrator mentions Eden to show how far the gardener's behavior is from the "joy and labor" of Adam in the ideal garden—he should display more positive feelings for the plants he tends. Choice (J) matches this prediction. Choice F is a misused detail; Giovanni seems to recognize this in the gardener earlier in the paragraph, but this has no relation to the references to Adam and Eden. Choice G is opposite; Giovanni finds the gardener's behavior inexplicable. Choice H is a distortion; while these are Biblical references, Giovanni never implies that the gardener should show the plants respect, religious or otherwise.

9. A   Difficulty: Low

Category: Key Ideas and Details / Detail

Getting to the Answer: When you don't receive line references, good notes will help you know where to research. Your notes should indicate that every paragraph but the first focuses on Giovanni's observation of the gardener, so look to the first paragraph. Choice (A) is correct; in lines 3–4, Giovanni refers to the garden as "one of those botanic gardens," different from most in the world. Choice B is a distortion; rare art is mentioned in line 9, but this refers specifically to the marble fountain, not to the garden as a whole. Choice C is a distortion; this answer is a misreading of lines 30–31, where the narrator states that "the soil was peopled with plants and herbs." He is not referring to actual people, but the plants that populate the garden. Choice D is a distortion; in lines 6–7, the narrator states that the garden "might once have been the pleasure-place of an opulent family." He never states that it was such a locale for "the community."

10. G   Difficulty: High

Category: Key Ideas and Details / Global

Getting to the Answer: When given line references in the question stem, go back to those lines in the text and, if necessary, read the sentences before and after those lines. The paragraph begins by describing the gardener as examining the plants intently and "looking into [the plants'] inmost nature," "discovering why one leaf grew in this shape and another in that" (lines 59–61). He seems interested in understanding what the plants are made up of. The remainder of the paragraph discusses his apparent fear of the plants. Look for one of these ideas in the correct choice. Choice (G) matches the first part of the paragraph. Choice F is opposite; the paragraph indicates that he is quite patient, intently seeking to understand the plants' inmost qualities. Choice H is a distortion; the gardener seems to fear the plants may harm him, but he does not seem to want to harm the plants. Choice J is out of scope; there is no indication that the gardener is angry with the plants.

Passage II

Suggested Passage Map notes:

¶1: Eng. focuses on improvement

¶2: Re-eng. starts w/ understanding failure

¶3: Ex. of failed re-eng.: paperclip

¶4: Ex. of eng. compromises: jumbo jet

¶5: Ex. of re-eng. based on failure: Roebling bridge

¶6: Re-eng. of Roebling created failure (TNB)

¶7: Failures contribute more than successes (Titanic)

11. B   Difficulty: Low

Category: Key Ideas and Details / Detail

Getting to the Answer: You are looking for three things that ARE mentioned and one that IS NOT. Don't get the two confused. First, check your notes to see that the author mentions jumbo jet design in paragraph 4. Research the passage, and cross off each choice that is referenced in the paragraph. Choice (B) is not referenced in this paragraph. Choice A is opposite; the author mentions this in line 40. Choice C is opposite; the author mentions this in line 38. Choice D is opposite; the author mentions this in line 41.

12. J   Difficulty: Medium

Category: Craft and Structure / Vocab-in-Context

Getting to the Answer: The test makers frequently give you uncommon usages of common words. You need to read carefully to understand the intended meaning of the phrase. The Boeing example starts by pointing out that the plane's design will be limited in ways that will make it impossible to satisfy everyone. You can assume that the company wants to come close enough to satisfying all the plane's users, not that those users will be happy with the final design. Choice (J) matches the thrust of the text. Choice F is out of scope; the author doesn't discuss such investments. Choice G is extreme; the passage tells you that there will be compromises. Choice H is out of scope; the cost to users is not mentioned.

13. C   Difficulty: Medium

Category: Key Ideas and Details / Detail

Getting to the Answer: You need to find the details used as evidence for this belief. Therefore, your answer will come straight from the passage. Your passage notes should send you to the last paragraph. The author asks you to "imagine" that the *Titanic* hadn't sunk on her first trip. In the author's opinion, there would have been many ships designed even larger than the *Titanic*, eventually resulting in a catastrophic sinking. Look for an answer choice that reflects this idea. Choice (C) is correct. Choice A is out of scope; there is no evidence that ship designers were careless before the *Titanic* sank. Choice B is out of scope; the number of lifeboats is not mentioned. Choice D is out of scope; the passage never discusses insurance.

14. H   Difficulty: Medium

Category: Craft and Structure / Writer's View

Getting to the Answer: Your map should tell you that the entire passage is focused on learning from mistakes. As the author writes, "Failures . . . provide incontrovertible proof that we have done something wrong. That is invaluable information" (lines 17–20). To support this, he gives examples of reengineering the paper clip and jet plane and the tragedy of the *Titanic*, which, he writes, "contributed much more to the design of safe ocean liners than would have her success" (lines 90–91). Thus, the author would agree with James Joyce, (H), emphasizing the importance of mistakes in discovering ways to succeed. It cannot be assumed that he would agree with F, since giving up is not discussed in the passage. Similarly, repeating the same approach and expecting success, G, is irrelevant, and Ford's quote, J, is also out of scope; the author does not equate teamwork with success.

15. D   Difficulty: Medium

Category: Key Ideas and Details / Detail

Getting to the Answer: Use your notes to find the correct paragraph, and predict the answer before looking at the choices; you will reach your answer more quickly and be less likely to fall into traps set by the test maker. Based on your notes, you should go directly to paragraph 6. It tells you that the engineers for the Tacoma Narrows Bridge tried to improve on Roebling's design for the Brooklyn Bridge and left out "the very cables that he included to obviate failure." The prior paragraph identifies those cables. Choice (D) is correct. Choice A is opposite; deviations from the design of the Brooklyn Bridge were the cause of the failure of the Tacoma Narrows Bridge. Choice B is out of scope; the author doesn't discuss any difference in the wind strength between the two bridges. Choice C is opposite; the engineers' concern for "economy and aesthetics" were what caused them to leave out the critical cables.

16. H   Difficulty: High

Category: Craft and Structure / Function

Getting to the Answer: Use your notes to help you understand the writer's purpose in selecting this specific example. Because this is the final paragraph, it is likely that its meaning will be closely related to the overall purpose of the passage. Lines 81–86 state that the *Titanic*'s failure contributed more to ocean liner safety than its success would have. Note that the correct choice may not be stated so specifically; (H) is correct. Choice F is a distortion; the author's point is about design in general, not just the *Titanic*. Choice G is a distortion; the article is not about the fate of ocean liners. Choice J is out of scope; this is true, but it's not the function of the paragraph.

17. D   Difficulty: Medium

Category: Craft and Structure / Function

Getting to the Answer: Focus on how an example fits into the overall point the author is making. Use your notes to locate the paper clip example—paragraph 3. The author points out that challengers to the Gem may be able to improve on one aspect of its design but not another. This reiterates the topic sentence, "Reengineering anything is fraught with risk." The example is probably meant to emphasize this point. Choice (D) is correct.

Choice A is out of scope; the paragraph is not about the importance of paper clips. Choice B is extreme; the example points out the risks of reengineering in general. Choice C is a distortion; the author does not recommend that all engineers should study the paper clip's specific design.

18. F   Difficulty: Low

Category: Key Ideas and Details / Detail

Getting to the Answer: Use your notes to research paragraph 3. To avoid traps, predict your answer before reading the choices. The paragraph tells you that the Gem clip is easy to use and doesn't fall off. Challengers have improved on one aspect of the Gem clip but have sacrificed the other. Choice (F) addresses the compromise predicted. Choice G is out of scope; function, not timing, determines success. Choice H is out of scope; brand awareness and familiarity are not mentioned. Choice J is a distortion; this mentions only one of the benefits the author lists rather than the Gem's successful balance of features.

19. B   Difficulty: Medium

Category: Key Ideas and Details / Detail

Getting to the Answer: When dealing with unfamiliar or passage-specific terms, read around the reference carefully. "Failure-based thinking" in this reference is related to Roebling's successful design of the Brooklyn Bridge. A careful reading shows you that Roebling was able to succeed because he understood where others had failed. You need to look for a positive use of "failure" in your answer choice. Choice (B) matches this prediction. Choice A is out of scope; the author doesn't discuss such a habit. Choice C is a distortion; this choice can be tempting because it uses several keywords from the paragraph, but the passage says cannibalizing can sacrifice synergy, not create it. Choice D is opposite; the Tacoma Bridge collapse supports the author's theory because the designers of that bridge failed to use "failure-based thinking."

20. H   Difficulty: Medium

Category: Craft and Structure / Vocab-in-Context

Getting to the Answer: To answer this question, you need to understand the author's use of the term in context. First, read the entire sentence and, if necessary, the sentences before and after. *So* in the middle of the sentence tells you that the first and second halves of the sentence are closely linked. From this, you conclude that *comparatives* relates to improvements. You need to look for an answer choice that tells you that engineering is measured by its ability to make improvements. Choice (H) is correct. Choice F is out of scope; the comparison is between products, not individuals. Choice G is a distortion; "bigger" and "faster" are only two possible measures of improvement. Choice J is out of scope; the author doesn't deal with such comparisons.

Passage III

Suggested Passage Map notes:

Passage A

¶1: Fairy tales (ft) passed down for centuries

¶2: Ft ex. Snow White includes symbolism

¶3: Snow White's new identity = mature adult

¶4: Ft popular b/c shared human experiences

Passage B

¶1: Fairy tales (ft) do NOT represent shared human experiences

¶2: Ft ex. LRRH seems to be about obedience, parental auth.

¶3: Older versions of LRRH didn't include obedience, parental auth.

¶4: All ft have variations, symbols not universal

21. D   Difficulty: Medium

Category: Craft and Structure / Vocab-in-Context

Getting to the Answer: The word in question appears in the context of the author comparing stories of short-lived interest to those of fairy tales, which have been told "since time immemorial" (line 11). Of the short-lived stories, some come "flaming into popular consciousness . . . for a period reaching anywhere from a few months to a few centuries." For that period of time, they become prominent and grab the listener's interest. Match this with (D). All other answers have the wrong definition in the context of the passage. Though C is tempting, there is no indication that these stories are important; just that they

are of relatively fleeting interest. Completely unimportant stories, such as Facebook anecdotes, can be interesting but not particularly important.

22. H   Difficulty: Low

Category: Craft and Structure / Writer's View

Getting to the Answer: Read the sentence referenced in the question stem to make a prediction. The passage states that these avenues are used to get at "the cosmic unconscious," so predict that the author believes fairy tales are one method to help people process common human experiences. Choice (H) matches this prediction. Choice F reflects the standard meaning of the word *avenues*, which doesn't fit here. Choices G and J don't make sense in context.

23. D   Difficulty: Medium

Category: Key Ideas and Details / Inference

Getting to the Answer: Correct answers to Inference questions will only be a step removed from what is stated in the passage. The lines indicated in the passage, along with those preceding them, discuss how popular fairy tales survive, while unpopular ones die out ("time . . . discards the chaff"). Look for an answer close to that. Choice (D) matches the passage's emphasis on *editing* and *appeal*. Choice A is out of scope; characters are not discussed at this point. Choice B is a distortion; a story written by one author could enjoy popularity, at least temporarily. Choice C is opposite; such tales would have *endured*.

24. J   Difficulty: Medium

Category: Key Ideas and Details / Detail

Getting to the Answer: Don't range too far from the text given and the ideas in that text when drawing your conclusion. The final sentence of Passage B states that we should acknowledge the many variations among versions of fairy tales and search "for insights into the cultural conditions that prompt such divergence." In other words, we should reflect on what these variations tell us about the specific cultures in which they appear. This matches (J) nicely. Choice F is a distortion; the author of Passage B indicates that there is no accurate interpretation of fairy tales, regardless of when they were written. Choice G is out of scope; the passage doesn't explore the difference between written and "oral versions" of the stories. Choice

H is a distortion; the author of Passage B does not suggest that any version of a tale is more valid or authoritative than any other.

25. B   Difficulty: Medium

Category: Key Ideas and Details / Detail

Getting to the Answer: Remember not to confuse something said by one author with something said by the other author. You know that the author of Passage B disagrees with the kinds of symbolic interpretations made in Passage A, and this question asks specifically why. Predict something about the way that such interpretations fail to take multiple versions of tales into account. Choice (B) matches this prediction. Choice A is opposite; if anything, Author B thinks that Author A pays too much attention to psychology. Choice C is out of scope; the problem that Author B sees goes beyond simple failure to use reference materials. Choice D is a misused detail; Author B criticizes not the "naïve view of . . . human nature," but rather the naïve view of folklore methodology.

26. F   Difficulty: High

Category: Key Ideas and Details / Inference

Getting to the Answer: Beware of answer choices that pull from details in the passage but have nothing to do with the inference at hand. The indicated section of the passage makes the argument that an interpretation based on details about the huntsman can't be valid when most versions of the folk tale don't have a huntsman in them. Predict something along the lines of fairy tales having too many variations to interpret. Choice (F) is the best match for this prediction. Choice H is a distortion; this original idea comes from Passage A. Choice G is out of scope; the passage doesn't raise the question of historical accuracy. Choice J is a distortion; the author is not arguing about how often certain themes appear in fairy tales, but rather against the universality of themes at all.

27. C   Difficulty: Medium

Category: Integration of Knowledge and Ideas / Synthesis

Getting to the Answer: Some questions don't lend themselves easily to prediction; work your way through the answer choices if you need to. This question calls for a detail that the passages have in common, but it doesn't

give you any real hints as to where to look. Eliminate wrong answers, paying special attention to those that come from one passage only. Choice (C) is the correct choice. Both authors admit that fairy tales have changed over time. Author A uses the idea of fairy tales changing to introduce the idea of their lasting significance in the first paragraph, and Author B uses the fact that they change as the basis of the argument against universal interpretation. Choice A is a distortion; only Passage A states this. Choice B is a distortion; this idea appears only in Passage B. Choice D is a distortion; this appears only in Passage A. The author of Passage B would not agree that symbolic interpretation of folk tales is valid.

28. F   Difficulty: Medium

Category: Integration of Knowledge and Ideas / Synthesis

Getting to the Answer: Return to the main point made by Author B. The correct answer should be consistent with this overall idea. The main argument made by Author B is that it isn't possible to interpret the symbolism of specific tales as reflecting general psychological truth, so eliminate any answer choice that contradicts that idea. Only (F) captures the central argument of Author B against this type of interpretation. Choice G is out of scope; Author B does not address the "popularity" of such tales. Choice H is a distortion; Author B does not believe that there is such a thing as a definitive version of a tale. Choice J is a distortion; this choice doesn't reflect the overall opinion of Author B that interpretations can't be made at all.

29. B   Difficulty: High

Category: Integration of Knowledge and Ideas / Synthesis

Getting to the Answer: In questions asking what one author might say to the other, be careful not to confuse the respective viewpoints of the authors. Author A mentions that these motifs are common to all humans in "widely scattered" (line 55) societies across time, so Author A would probably argue that the specifics of a given version are less important than these universal psychological trends. This prediction matches (B). Choice A is out of scope; Author A makes no mention of recent versions of folk tales or advances in methodology. Choice C is opposite; Author A believes in the relevance of "psychological forces." Choice D is opposite; Author A chooses Snow White as the principal example of his argument.

30. H   Difficulty: Low

Category: Integration of Knowledge and Ideas / Synthesis

Getting to the Answer: For broadly stated questions, work through the choices, eliminating clearly incorrect answers, and then return to the passages to support your choice. Because a prediction for this question might be difficult, check and eliminate answer choices that don't match both passages. Because both authors would concur that folk tales are developed and passed down through generations (certainly a unique "compositional process"), they would agree with (H). Choice F is a distortion; only Author A emphasizes this. Choice G is a distortion; the contention that folk tales have "universal" truth comes from Passage A only. Choice J is out of scope; neither passage says anything about "new information about...particular tales."

Passage IV

Suggested Passage Map notes:

¶1: Low energy linear acc. use 1 pair of electrodes

¶2: High energy linear acc. use multiple plates

¶3: Microwave cavities used in high energy machines (linacs)

¶4: Linear acc. widely used

¶5: Circular acc. can accelerate particles further but emit radiation

¶6: Circular acc. less efficient than linear acc.

¶7: Physicists use heavier particles to ↑ energy

¶8: 1st circular acc. were cyclotrons (1929, Lawrence)

¶9: Cyclotrons reach an energy limit

¶10: Cyclotrons used for lower energy app.

¶11: Synchrotrons used for high energy app.

31. C   Difficulty: Low

Category: Key Ideas and Details / Global

Getting to the Answer: Be sure to predict an answer before looking at the answer choices; predicting will help you avoid trap answers. Throughout this passage, the author discusses how linear and circular accelerators work

and how they differ in their uses. Choice (C) matches this prediction well. Choice A is a misused detail; although this does appear, it is not the main idea of the entire passage. Choice B is a misused detail; this appears in the passage, but it is not the main idea. Choice D is a misused detail; based on the passage, cyclotrons do seem to be a useful type of circular accelerator, but as this answer does not mention linear accelerators, it cannot be the main idea of the entire passage.

32. F   Difficulty: Medium

Category: Key Ideas and Details / Detail

Getting to the Answer: Think of Detail questions as matching questions. The answer choice will always match a detail stated directly in the passage. In lines 95–97, the author writes, "The tube has many magnets distributed around it to focus the particles and curve their track around the tube." The author similarly describes the function of magnets in lines 35–36. The magnets, by focusing the particles and their curve, influence the direction in which the particles travel; use this as your prediction. Choice (F) matches this prediction well. Choice G is a distortion; this misconstrues the statement that the magnets curve the particles' track "around the tube" (line 97). The particles' track is curving, not the particles themselves. Choice H is a distortion; the microwave cavities accelerate the particles (lines 98–99), not the magnets. Choice J is out of scope; there is no indication that the magnets impact the energy levels of the particles.

33. D   Difficulty: Medium

Category: Key Ideas and Details / Detail

Getting to the Answer: On Detail questions, avoid incorrect choices that contain details from the passage not relevant to the question being asked. According to lines 80–82, "The effect of the energy injected using the electric fields is therefore to increase their mass." Choice (D) is correct. Choice A is a distortion; the passage states that particles do not reach the speed of light. Choice B is a distortion; accelerating particles does not always result in increasing their mass. Choice C is out of scope; there is no indication in the passage that using a mixture of different particles will cause particle mass to increase.

34. H   Difficulty: Medium

Category: Craft and Structure / Vocab-in-Context

Getting to the Answer: Read the entire sentence that contains the vocabulary word to decipher its meaning; then look at the choices. In lines 58–61, the author states that heavier particles, such as protons, are being used in accelerators. In the following sentence, you see that "these particles are composites of quarks and gluons." It follows that quarks help make up protons. Choice (H) matches this prediction. Choice F is a misused detail; electron accelerators are mentioned in lines 56–58, but there is no indication that electrons are what make up a quark. Choice G is out of scope; there is no indication that a quark is made up of radiation. Choice J is a distortion; gluons and quarks seem to be roughly equivalent. Neither is a component of the other.

35. D   Difficulty: Medium

Category: Key Ideas and Details / Detail

Getting to the Answer: Some questions will ask you what CANNOT be possible. Make sure you take the time to read the question carefully, so that you don't select what is possible. In lines 26–29, the passage states that linear accelerators "are also used to provide an initial low-energy kick to particles before they are injected into circular accelerators." These lines show that linear accelerators provide this kick, not the circular accelerator, as (D) suggests. Choice A is opposite; in lines 43–44, the author states that "When any charged particle is accelerated, it emits electromagnetic radiation," which means that the circular accelerator can cause this. Choice B is opposite; in lines 37–38, the author states that the parts of circular accelerators "can be reused to accelerate the particles further." Choice C is opposite; in lines 39–41, the author states that circular accelerators "suffer a disadvantage in that the particles emit synchrotron radiation."

36. J   Difficulty: Medium

Category: Craft and Structure / Writer's View

Getting to the Answer: It can be assumed that an author will agree with anything in the passage and anything that is in line with the passage. The author describes both linear and circular accelerators, stating that linear accelerators are in wide use, and they can produce "'proton-heavy' medical or research isotopes" (lines 30–31). Though

the author doesn't explain how research isotopes are used, it can be assumed that they have some benefits. Circular accelerators "are useful for X-ray spectroscopy of proteins" (line 54–55), so they also have benefits. Since they are both useful, the correct answer is (J). Choice F is opposite, as is G, since the author states in lines 58–61 that physicists are using protons in accelerators. Choice H is a distortion; the passage mentions other types of circular accelerators developed since Lawrence's first cyclotron, such as the synchrotron.

37. D   Difficulty: Medium

Category: Key Ideas and Details / Detail

Getting to the Answer: To get more points on Test Day, predict answers; this will keep you from being tempted to pick incorrect choices that distort or misuse information from the passage. Your notes can help direct you to the second paragraph. Lines 12–15 include the information needed to answer this question. Once the particles have passed through the hole in the plate, the plate repels the particles, which are accelerated toward the next plate. Choice (D) matches this. Choices A, B, and C are out of scope; the author does not provide support for any of those answer choices.

38. H   Difficulty: High

Category: Key Ideas and Details / Inference

Getting to the Answer: Remember that even though the answers for Inference questions will not be directly stated in the passage, they will be supported by information in the passage. Use your notes to find where the author discusses these items. The author writes that synchrotrons can push energy levels higher than cyclotrons can. Look for this distinction among the choices. Choice (H) is correct. Choice F is extreme; as stated in lines 90–91, cyclotrons are still useful for lower energy applications. Choice G is a distortion; circular accelerators accelerate particles in a circle, and cyclotrons and synchrotrons are both types of circular accelerators. Choice J is out of scope; the author never indicates that synchrotrons cause particles to move closer to the edge of the tube.

39. A   Difficulty: Medium

Category: Craft and Structure / Function

Getting to the Answer: When you come across Function questions, remember that context is crucial to understanding the purpose of a particular passage element. After discussing the "storage ring," the author recalls the earliest cyclotron, from 1929, and shows the size difference between it and a modern counterpart. You can predict that the author means to show the progress made in the technology. Choice (A) matches this prediction. Choice B is a misused detail; the passage indicates that cyclotrons are important, but not because Lawrence invented them. Choice C is a distortion; the author is not criticizing Lawrence's abilities, but demonstrating the scope of improvements made since his invention. This is not, however, the author's purpose in making this statement. Choice D is a distortion; this is not the purpose of this reference.

40. H   Difficulty: High

Category: Craft and Structure / Writer's View

Getting to the Answer: Note not only the difficult language and concepts in this passage, but also how the author explains a lot of the jargon and otherwise uses common terms. The approach is most likely that of someone who is knowledgeable about accelerators, such as a professor, and is explaining them to a group of somewhat less knowledgeable but highly interested students, a match for (H). The level of jargon and information is mostly beyond that of amateurs and high school students, making F and J incorrect. A noted scientist speaking to a group of other scientists would not need to explain basic information about accelerators, eliminating G.

SCIENCE TEST

Passage I

1. C   Difficulty: Low

Category: Interpretation of Data

Getting to the Answer: According to Table 2, which presents the results of Study 2, a 67-kg male of the specified height has a relative BMR of 94% of average peak, while a 69-kg male has a relative BMR of 96%. It is reasonable to conclude that a 68-kg male would have a relative BMR that falls between those values, which makes (C) the correct answer.

2. F   Difficulty: Medium

Category: Evaluation of Models, Inferences, and Results

Getting to the Answer: Table 2 shows that as body weight increases, so does the relative BMR. Extrapolating from this trend, a male who weighed more than 73 kg would have a BMR higher than 100% of the average peak. The researcher's hypothesis is supported by the results of Study 2, so (F) is correct.

3. D   Difficulty: Low

Category: Scientific Investigation

Getting to the Answer: According to the descriptions of the studies in the passage, Study 1 investigated both humans and bears (including bears in hibernation), while Study 2 investigated only human subjects. Choice (D) is thus correct. Choices A and B are incorrect because relative BMR was recorded in both studies. Choice C is incorrect because it reverses the number of species investigated by each study.

4. H   Difficulty: Low

Category: Interpretation of Data

Getting to the Answer: According to Table 1, the BMR of a bear rises as the bear begins to age but drops after the age of 14. Choice (H) reflects this trend in its entirety.

5. A   Difficulty: Medium

Category: Scientific Investigation

Getting to the Answer: The question stem describes an individual who loses weight, so turn to the results of Study 2, which investigated the effect of weight on BMR. According to Table 2, individuals who weigh less have lower relative BMRs. Consequently, an individual who lost weight could be expected to see a decrease in BMR. Choice (A) is thus correct.

6. G   Difficulty: Medium

Category: Evaluation of Models, Inferences, and Results

Getting to the Answer: According to the introduction to the passage, metabolism is how organisms convert food into energy, and BMR is simply the rate at which metabolism occurs while an organism is at rest. During hibernation, a bear is essentially in a kind of prolonged sleep, allowing it to survive through winter months when food may be scarce. It stands to reason, then, that a bear has a lower BMR because it has less need for energy while hibernating. Choice (G) is thus correct. Choice F is incorrect because it suggests the opposite—but a higher need for energy would actually correspond to a higher BMR. Choice H is incorrect because the results of Study 3 showed that higher internal body temperatures were correlated with higher BMRs. Choice J is incorrect because the results of Study 2 showed that heavier weights were associated with higher BMRs.

7.   A   Difficulty: Medium

Category: Interpretation of Data

Getting to the Answer: The effect of internal temperature on relative BMR was investigated in Study 3, so look to Table 3 for guidance on this question. According to the table, BMR increases as body temperature increases. Thus, the lowest temperature will result in the lowest BMR, while the highest temperature will result in the highest BMR. In order to gain weight, an organism would need to convert less of the food it consumes into energy, which means it would need to have a lower BMR. Consequently, you're looking for the choice with the lowest temperature, so (A) is correct. All of the other choices are associated with higher relative BMRs, which would be less likely to result in weight gain.

Passage II

8.   H   Difficulty: Medium

Category: Interpretation of Data

Getting to the Answer: A+ is not one of the recipients listed in Table 1, but its transfusion compatibility can be inferred from the pattern established in the table or from the description in the second paragraph, which states that a recipient's antibodies "recognize and attack any blood group antigen not normally present in the person's blood." An A+ individual's blood cells contain the A and Rh antigens, but not the B antigen. Thus, an A+ individual can safely receive blood of any non-B type. Choices F, G, and J can be eliminated, because they each include at least one blood type containing the B antigen. Choice (H) is correct because it is the only option that exclusively contains blood types without the B antigen.

9.   C   Difficulty: High

Category: Interpretation of Data

Getting to the Answer: According to the passage, children receive one allele for ABO type and one allele for Rh type from each parent. In order to have AB blood, a child will need to have one parent passing on the A allele and the other parent passing on the B allele, which means that A and D can be eliminated. To have Rh+ blood, the child will need to have at least one parent who has the Rh antigen, so B can also be eliminated. Choice (C) is correct because the child could receive the A allele and the Rh+ allele from the first parent and the B allele from the second parent.

10.   J   Difficulty: Low

Category: Interpretation of Data

Getting to the Answer: Based on Table 1, a recipient with B+ blood can safely receive transfusions from both B+ and B− blood. Choice (J) is thus correct.

11.   C   Difficulty: High

Category: Interpretation of Data

Getting to the Answer: According to the second paragraph of the passage, a blood transfusion recipient's antibodies will "recognize and attack any blood group antigen not normally present in the person's blood." Thus, in order for a blood type to be safe for any transfusion recipient, it should completely lack the blood group antigens discussed in the passage. The first paragraph of the passage notes that type O blood cells lack both the A and B antigens and implies that a "−" indicates the lack of the Rh antigen. Thus, type O−blood will completely be lacking in antigens, making it safe for any transfusion recipient. Choice (C) is correct.

12.   F   Difficulty: Medium

Category: Interpretation of Data

Getting to the Answer: Based on Table 2, a man with type AB blood would have to have a genotype of AB, while a woman with type A blood could have a geno-type of AA or Ao. In order to produce a child with type O blood, both parents would have to be able to pass on an o allele to their offspring, but the father can only pass on an A or a B. Thus, type O blood is not possible for this couple's offspring, making (F) correct. Choice G is incorrect because type A blood would be the result if the father passed on an A allele (the child's genotype would then be AA or Ao). Choice H is incorrect because type B blood would be the result if the father passed on a B allele and the mother passed on an o allele. Choice J is incorrect because type AB blood would be the result if the father passed on a B allele and the mother passed on an A allele.

13. D   Difficulty: Medium

Category: Interpretation of Data

Getting to the Answer: The second paragraph indicates that a transfusion is unsafe when the recipient's antibodies "recognize and attack any blood group antigen not normally present in the person's blood." O+ blood cells include only the Rh antigen because, as noted in the first paragraph, type O simply refers to the absence of A and B antigens. Because the patient has A+ blood, which includes an Rh antigen, he has no anti-Rh antibodies, so it will be safe for him to receive O+ blood. Choice (D) is thus correct. Choices A and B are incorrect because they suggest that the transfusion is unsafe, while C is incorrect because there is no such thing as an O antigen and because A+ blood would not contain anti-A antibodies.

Passage III

14. F   Difficulty: Low

Category: Evaluation of Models, Inferences, and Results

Getting to the Answer: According to the question stem, hotter planets are more likely to have molten cores, meaning that dynamo theory can be applied to them. Because planets are generally hotter the closer they are to the Sun, the planet that is farthest from the Sun would be the least likely to have a molten core. Neptune is much farther from the Sun than Mercury, Venus, and Mars, so (F) is correct.

15. C   Difficulty: Medium

Category: Evaluation of Models, Inferences, and Results

Getting to the Answer: According to the passage, Scientist 1 believes that geomagnetic reversal is a natural consequence of dynamo theory, whereas Scientist 2 believes it to be caused by seismic events. Choice (C) accurately summarizes the views of both scientists.

16. J   Difficulty: Medium

Category: Interpretation of Data

Getting to the Answer: Scientist 2 suggests that seismic activity can affect the molten core of the Earth. Diagram 1 shows that the core is found at a depth of 2,900 km. Choice (J) is thus correct.

17. A   Difficulty: Medium

Category: Evaluation of Models, Inferences, and Results

Getting to the Answer: Scientist 1 states that the constant motion of molten nickel and iron in the core "creates eddy currents, which in turn help to create Earth's magnetic field." Choice (A) is thus correct.

18. F   Difficulty: Medium

Category: Evaluation of Models, Inferences, and Results

Getting to the Answer: Scientist 1 believes that the dynamo theory, which contends that the Earth's magnetic field is the result of motion in the liquid core, fully accounts for geomagnetic reversal. Scientist 2, while attributing geomagnetic reversal to the effects of seismic activity, does not dispute the dynamo theory itself. Choice (F) is thus correct. Choice G is incorrect because neither scientist attributes seismic disturbances to eddy currents. Choice H is incorrect because only Scientist 2 believes it. Choice J is incorrect because both scientists agree that dynamo theory generally explains the existence of the Earth's magnetic field, not just during times of geomagnetic reversal.

19. B   Difficulty: Medium

Category: Evaluation of Models, Inferences, and Results

Getting to the Answer: The introductory text states that scientists found evidence of geomagnetic reversal in magnetized rock deposits on the ocean floor. Thus, the best evidence of the polarity of the magnetic field at a particular point in time can be found in these deposits, (B).

20. J   Difficulty: Medium

Category: Evaluation of Models, Inferences, and Results

Getting to the Answer: Both scientists argue that geomagnetic reversal is a result of activity within the Earth's molten core. Scientist 1 thinks that these reversals spontaneously arise from the motions of molten nickel and iron, while Scientist 2 believes that seismic disturbances disrupt these motions, sometimes resulting in a geomagnetic reversal. Neither scientist suggests that geomagnetic reversals can be caused by an external source like the Sun's magnetic field, so the information in the question stem would weaken both scientists' accounts. Choice (J) is thus correct.

21. B   Difficulty: Medium

Category: Evaluation of Models, Inferences, and Results

Getting to the Answer: Scientist 2 believes that seismic activity "can disrupt the motion of the core to such an extent that the magnetic field effectively turns off." These disruptions will sometimes result in geomagnetic reversals. Because Scientist 2 contends that seismic activity can significantly disturb the motions of the core, (B) is correct. Choice A is incorrect because it reverses the direction of causality suggested by Scientist 2; seismic activity affects the core, but not vice-versa. Choice C is incorrect because it directly contradicts Scientist 2's account. Choice D is incorrect because Scientist 2 suggests that eddy currents spontaneously arise from the core's motion, but never suggests that these currents are caused by seismic activity.

Passage IV

22. G   Difficulty: Medium

Category: Interpretation of Data

Getting to the Answer: The description of Experiment 3 states that the current generates a magnetic field, which causes the ring to move up the pole. According to Table 3, as the number of coils in the wire increased, so did the height reached by the metal ring. It follows, then, that

a greater number of coils produces a stronger magnetic field, capable of moving the ring up a greater distance. The relationship between magnetic field and number of coils is direct, so (G) is correct. Choices F and H are incorrect because they do not accurately describe the relationship between number of coils and magnetic field. Choice J is incorrect because the amount of current passing through the wire was held constant.

23. D   Difficulty: Medium

Category: Scientific Investigation

Getting to the Answer: In Experiment 2, the rotation of the wire caused a change in magnetic flux, which produced a voltage. If the wire is not rotating, there will be no change in magnetic flux and no voltage produced. Therefore, none of the existing data points account for this case. Choice (D) is thus correct.

24. F   Difficulty: High

Category: Scientific Investigation

Getting to the Answer: The introduction to the passage states that magnetic flux depends on the strength of the magnetic field, while the description of Experiment 1 suggests that the speed of the magnet corresponds to changes in magnetic flux. Moreover, Table 1 shows that higher magnetic flux changes correlate with higher emf readings. Thus, in order to produce the highest emf, you need to create the largest change in magnetic flux, which requires moving the magnet more quickly and having a magnet with a stronger magnetic field. Choice (F) is correct.

25. B   Difficulty: Medium

Category: Interpretation of Data

Getting to the Answer: According to Table 1, which provides the results of Experiment 1, maximum induced emf increases as the change in magnetic flux increases. Thus, you are looking for a graph with a positive slope. The only choice that satisfies this requirement is (B).

26. F   Difficulty: Low

Category: Interpretation of Data

Getting to the Answer: According to the description of Experiment 1, the magnet's "various speeds created corresponding changes to the magnetic flux within the coil." In other words, the greater the speed, the greater the change in magnetic flux. To find the trial with the lowest speed, then, you merely need to identify which of the trials had the lowest change in magnetic flux. Trial 1 was lower than any of the other trials in Experiment 1, so (F) is correct.

27. D   Difficulty: Medium

Category: Scientific Investigation

Getting to the Answer: The description of Experiment 3 states that the current sent through the wire produced "a magnetic field that caused the metal ring to float up the pole." From this, it is reasonable to conclude that a larger current would produce a larger magnetic field, which would cause the ring to move farther up the pole. In Trial 9, the ring reached a height of 1.5 cm, so in this new trial the height should be even greater. The only value above 1.5 cm is found in (D), making it the correct answer.

28. H   Difficulty: Medium

Category: Scientific Investigation

Getting to the Answer: According to the introduction of the passage, magnetic flux is "the mathematical product of the magnetic field and an area defined by a loop of wire in that field." Consequently, a larger area (created by a loop with a larger diameter) would create a larger magnetic flux, which means that the changes in magnetic flux caused by passing a magnet through the coil would be greater in the new experiment. Choices F and J can be eliminated because they suggest that the change in magnetic flux would decrease. Because there is a direct relationship between change in magnetic flux and maximum induced emf, as indicated by the results in Table 1, the value for emf could also be expected to increase in the new experiment, which eliminates G. Choice (H) is thus correct.

Passage V

29. C   Difficulty: Low

Category: Interpretation of Data

Getting to the Answer: Table 1 shows the link between pH and hydrogen ion concentration. According to Table 1, a concentration of 1×10^{-11} mol/L corresponds to a pH

of 11. According to Table 2, a solution with a pH of 11 is categorized as highly basic. Choice (C) is thus correct.

30. G   Difficulty: Medium

Category: Interpretation of Data

Getting to the Answer: Read the question carefully to make sure you understand what is being asked. The hydrogen ion concentrations in Table 4 are given in terms of 10 to a negative power, where $1 \times 10^{-2} = 0.01$, $1 \times 10^{-3} = 0.001$, and so on. From this, it can be seen that the smaller the number in the exponent (the closer the exponent is to 0), the larger the concentration. With an exponent of -2, which is closer to 0 than any of the others provided in the table, lemon juice has the greatest concentration of hydrogen ions. Choice (G) is thus correct.

31. B   Difficulty: Medium

Category: Interpretation of Data

Getting to the Answer: To answer this question, you must synthesize the information from multiple tables. Table 2 provides the pH level of highly acidic solutions, Table 1 shows how pH level corresponds to hydrogen ion concentration, and Table 4 lists the hydrogen ion concentrations for the substances in the answer choices. From Tables 1 and 2, you can deduce that a highly acidic solution has a hydrogen ion concentration of 1×10^{-3} mol/L or higher. In Table 4, only vinegar falls within this range. Thus, (B) is correct.

32. H   Difficulty: Medium

Category: Interpretation of Data

Getting to the Answer: According to Table 2, highly acidic solutions have a pH between 0 and 3, slightly acidic solutions have a pH between 4 and 6, slightly basic solutions have a pH between 8 and 10, and highly basic solutions have a pH between 11 and 14. Because each 1-point increase in pH corresponds to a 10-fold increase in hydrogen ion concentration (as is clear from Table 1), the difference in [H+] is much greater between highly acidic and highly basic solutions than it is between slightly acidic and slightly basic solutions. Choice (H) is thus correct. Choice F is incorrect because the passage never discusses what makes a solution "dangerous." Choice G is incorrect because a solution with a pH close to 0 is highly acidic, not neutral. Choice J is incorrect because the difference between highly and slightly acidic solutions is the same as the difference between highly and slightly basic solutions, according to Table 2.

33. C   Difficulty: Medium

Category: Interpretation of Data

Getting to the Answer: The passage explains that 1 mol/L solutions of strong acids have pH values less than 2, while 1 mol/L solutions of strong bases have pH values greater than 12. According to Table 3, barium hydroxide is a strong base, so it must have a pH of greater than 12, which is higher than the pH of any of the other solutions given. Choice (C) is thus correct. Choice A is incorrect because baking soda has a pH of 9, as indicated by cross-referencing Table 4 with Table 1. Choices B and D are incorrect because nitric acid and vinegar are both acids with pH values below 7.

34. F   Difficulty: Medium

Category: Interpretation of Data

Getting to the Answer: The question stem explains that pH and pOH are inversely proportional: as pH goes down, pOH goes up. Therefore, the solution with the lowest pH will have the highest pOH. Sulfuric acid (listed in Table 3) is the only strong acid listed among the answer choices, so it will have the lowest pH (below 2 at a concentration of 1 mol/L). Choice (F) is thus correct.

Passage VI

35. A   Difficulty: Low

Category: Evaluation of Models, Inferences, and Results

Getting to the Answer: Experiment 3 does not include a table of results, but does describe the relevant results in the text: "At 10 minutes into the experiment, fewer bubbles were visible in the bottle that contained the root beer." This suggests that, ten minutes after being shaken, the root beer had fewer bubbles and thus a lower level of carbonation than the seltzer. Choice (A) is correct. Choice B is incorrect because it states the opposite. Choice C is incorrect because there was 1 L of liquid in each bottle. Choice D is incorrect because balance time

wasn't measured in Experiment 3.

36. J   Difficulty: Low

Category: Interpretation of Data

Getting to the Answer: This question can be answered simply by comparing data in Tables 1 and 2. The question is asking for the most similar balance times after the liquids have been shaken, which is reported in the right-most column of each table. According to the tables, the balance time after shaking for Trial 3 was 22.48 seconds and for Trial 5 was 22.45 seconds. These are by far the closest in value, so (J) is correct.

37. B   Difficulty: Medium

Category: Interpretation of Data

Getting to the Answer: The results for Experiment 2 are found in Table 2. For both of the trials, the balance time after shaking was longer than the balance time before shaking. Thus, it can be concluded that shaking the bottle of root beer increased its balance time, (B). Choice A is incorrect because the number of bubbles weren't measured in Experiment 2, though it is more likely that they would have increased, not decreased. Choice C is incorrect because it states the opposite of what the results show. Choice D is incorrect because the bottle was sealed, so its mass should have remained constant.

38. H   Difficulty: Medium

Category: Scientific Investigation

Getting to the Answer: According to the description of Experiment 2, the first measurement of balance time in Trial 4 occurred after setting aside the bottle for 10 minutes, so this question is really asking if bubbles would still be present 10 minutes after the root beer was shaken. This is directly investigated in Experiment 3, when bubbles in the root beer were compared to bubbles in the seltzer: "At 10 minutes into the experiment, fewer bubbles were visible in the bottle that contained the root beer." This suggests that there were still bubbles present before the bottle was shaken in Trial 4, so (H) is correct. Choice F is incorrect because it cites the wrong experiment, while G and J are incorrect because they reach the opposite conclusion.

39. A **Difficulty:** Medium

Category: Scientific Investigation

Getting to the Answer: According to the description of Trial 5 in Experiment 2, the bottle of root beer was set aside for 90 minutes after being shaken before having its balance time recorded. The scenario in the question stem merely involves a repetition of the conditions in Trial 5, so similar results should be expected. The original balance time before shaking for Trial 5 was 20.04 seconds, so the balance time in this new trial would likely be slightly above 20 seconds as well. Choice (A) is thus correct.

40. H **Difficulty:** Medium

Category: Scientific Investigation

Getting to the Answer: According to the description of Experiment 3, there were no bubbles remaining in the bottle after setting it aside for 90 minutes, although there were bubbles present after setting it aside for only 10 minutes. Moreover, balance time in Trial 4 (after a 10-minute wait) was longer than the original balance time without shaking in Trial 3, while balance time in Trial 5 (after a 90-minute wait) was back to around 20 seconds. It can therefore be inferred that it takes somewhere between 10 and 90 minutes for the bubbles to become too few to affect the balance time. Choice (H) is thus correct.

WRITING TEST

MODEL ESSAY

Below is an example of what a high-scoring essay might look like. Notice the author states her position clearly in the introductory paragraph and supports that position with evidence in the following paragraphs. This essay also uses transitions, some advanced vocabulary, and an effective "hook" to draw in the reader.

High school is a time to master a solid educational base and explore future opportunities, therefore high schools need to expose students to career opportunities. The best way to accomplish this goal is to require students to attend in-school seminars that are held on a regular basis. Having information about a variety of careers provides an excellent basis to keep exploring, and that basis should be introduced in high school to give students a jump start on their thinking about careers.

Because exploring options is so important to deciding on a career, students should be required to attend career seminars in assemblies held during the regular school day. While attending such events once a semester is a good start, it would make sense for the number of seminars to increase as graduation approaches. Freshmen should be expected to attend just two seminars a year, as they are likely least sure of their future careers, while juniors and seniors should attend a few each semester. The seminars for freshmen and sophomores should focus on the myriad of options available to entice students to study hard and earn the grades required to be admitted to competitive college programs. For juniors and seniors, the information should be more focused and provide real-life examples of what someone can actually do with a Gen Ed degree versus a bachelors in STEM. Students need to learn whether it's worth it to spend tens of thousands of dollars on a degree that will require additional training after graduation, such as a Bachelor of Philosophy. If students know that the job market is looking for people with Bachelors degrees in the sciences, technology, engineering, and math fields, hopefully they'll pursue degrees that will provide options for paying back mountains of student debt.

At my high school in Miami, only about half of the graduating class each year goes directly on to college, leaving hundreds of students who are entering into the job market without much guidance. The students who need these seminars the most are the least likely to spend their free time after school attending a lecture about jobs, so it is imperative that schools make students attend job information sessions during the day. Many of those students do not have a family background that encourages college or professional careers, and those students would likely not attend seminars that they feel is of no interest to them. By bringing professions right into the school day , students will learn their options after graduation. Someone who is considering continuing to work part-time at a restaurant could learn from a career lecture how much career advancement is possible in companies many students don't think of often, such as rental car companies like Hertz and retail clothing stores like Banana Republic.

The idea to embed career-oriented options into current courses misses the fact that not all students take the same courses, so those who do not take courses with career options embedded in them will not be exposed to these opportunities. Also, if the options are taught in a class relevant to it, who would choose which classes and options to incorporate? Furthermore, this option would take up class time and teachers may not be able to teach everything they need to. The argument states that all students would be given course-specific advice, but to guarantee that every student gets that advice means that there will have to be a lot of options offered in every class, from art to history, and a lot of classes interrupted. This approach takes up school time. The same professionals and college representatives can give seminars and not have to develop whole programs that would go into high school classes. This may be overkill. We don't need to have entire embedded programs to be exposed to career possibilities.

When all students have the opportunity to learn about careers and future financial security, they can make better decisions about what to study in college, and presumably graduate into a society which values and recompenses their expertise.

You can evaluate your essay and the model essay based on the following criteria:

- Is the author's own perspective clearly stated?
- Does the body of the essay assess and analyze an additional perspective?
- Is the relevance of each paragraph clear?
- Does the author start a new paragraph for each new idea?
- Is each sentence in a paragraph relevant to the point made in that paragraph?
- Are transitions clear?
- Is the essay easy to read?
- Is it engaging?
- Are sentences varied?
- Is vocabulary used effectively?
- Is college-level vocabulary used?

ACT Practice Test 6
ANSWER SHEET

ENGLISH TEST

1. Ⓐ Ⓑ Ⓒ Ⓓ   11. Ⓐ Ⓑ Ⓒ Ⓓ   21. Ⓐ Ⓑ Ⓒ Ⓓ   31. Ⓐ Ⓑ Ⓒ Ⓓ   41. Ⓐ Ⓑ Ⓒ Ⓓ   51. Ⓐ Ⓑ Ⓒ Ⓓ   61. Ⓐ Ⓑ Ⓒ Ⓓ   71. Ⓐ Ⓑ Ⓒ Ⓓ
2. Ⓕ Ⓖ Ⓗ Ⓙ   12. Ⓕ Ⓖ Ⓗ Ⓙ   22. Ⓕ Ⓖ Ⓗ Ⓙ   32. Ⓕ Ⓖ Ⓗ Ⓙ   42. Ⓕ Ⓖ Ⓗ Ⓙ   52. Ⓕ Ⓖ Ⓗ Ⓙ   62. Ⓕ Ⓖ Ⓗ Ⓙ   72. Ⓕ Ⓖ Ⓗ Ⓙ
3. Ⓐ Ⓑ Ⓒ Ⓓ   13. Ⓐ Ⓑ Ⓒ Ⓓ   23. Ⓐ Ⓑ Ⓒ Ⓓ   33. Ⓐ Ⓑ Ⓒ Ⓓ   43. Ⓐ Ⓑ Ⓒ Ⓓ   53. Ⓐ Ⓑ Ⓒ Ⓓ   63. Ⓐ Ⓑ Ⓒ Ⓓ   73. Ⓐ Ⓑ Ⓒ Ⓓ
4. Ⓕ Ⓖ Ⓗ Ⓙ   14. Ⓕ Ⓖ Ⓗ Ⓙ   24. Ⓕ Ⓖ Ⓗ Ⓙ   34. Ⓕ Ⓖ Ⓗ Ⓙ   44. Ⓕ Ⓖ Ⓗ Ⓙ   54. Ⓕ Ⓖ Ⓗ Ⓙ   64. Ⓕ Ⓖ Ⓗ Ⓙ   74. Ⓕ Ⓖ Ⓗ Ⓙ
5. Ⓐ Ⓑ Ⓒ Ⓓ   15. Ⓐ Ⓑ Ⓒ Ⓓ   25. Ⓐ Ⓑ Ⓒ Ⓓ   35. Ⓐ Ⓑ Ⓒ Ⓓ   45. Ⓐ Ⓑ Ⓒ Ⓓ   55. Ⓐ Ⓑ Ⓒ Ⓓ   65. Ⓐ Ⓑ Ⓒ Ⓓ   75. Ⓐ Ⓑ Ⓒ Ⓓ
6. Ⓕ Ⓖ Ⓗ Ⓙ   16. Ⓕ Ⓖ Ⓗ Ⓙ   26. Ⓕ Ⓖ Ⓗ Ⓙ   36. Ⓕ Ⓖ Ⓗ Ⓙ   46. Ⓕ Ⓖ Ⓗ Ⓙ   56. Ⓕ Ⓖ Ⓗ Ⓙ   66. Ⓕ Ⓖ Ⓗ Ⓙ
7. Ⓐ Ⓑ Ⓒ Ⓓ   17. Ⓐ Ⓑ Ⓒ Ⓓ   27. Ⓐ Ⓑ Ⓒ Ⓓ   37. Ⓐ Ⓑ Ⓒ Ⓓ   47. Ⓐ Ⓑ Ⓒ Ⓓ   57. Ⓐ Ⓑ Ⓒ Ⓓ   67. Ⓐ Ⓑ Ⓒ Ⓓ
8. Ⓕ Ⓖ Ⓗ Ⓙ   18. Ⓕ Ⓖ Ⓗ Ⓙ   28. Ⓕ Ⓖ Ⓗ Ⓙ   38. Ⓕ Ⓖ Ⓗ Ⓙ   48. Ⓕ Ⓖ Ⓗ Ⓙ   58. Ⓕ Ⓖ Ⓗ Ⓙ   68. Ⓕ Ⓖ Ⓗ Ⓙ
9. Ⓐ Ⓑ Ⓒ Ⓓ   19. Ⓐ Ⓑ Ⓒ Ⓓ   29. Ⓐ Ⓑ Ⓒ Ⓓ   39. Ⓐ Ⓑ Ⓒ Ⓓ   49. Ⓐ Ⓑ Ⓒ Ⓓ   59. Ⓐ Ⓑ Ⓒ Ⓓ   69. Ⓐ Ⓑ Ⓒ Ⓓ
10. Ⓕ Ⓖ Ⓗ Ⓙ   20. Ⓕ Ⓖ Ⓗ Ⓙ   30. Ⓕ Ⓖ Ⓗ Ⓙ   40. Ⓕ Ⓖ Ⓗ Ⓙ   50. Ⓕ Ⓖ Ⓗ Ⓙ   60. Ⓕ Ⓖ Ⓗ Ⓙ   70. Ⓕ Ⓖ Ⓗ Ⓙ

MATHEMATICS TEST

1. Ⓐ Ⓑ Ⓒ Ⓓ Ⓔ   11. Ⓐ Ⓑ Ⓒ Ⓓ Ⓔ   21. Ⓐ Ⓑ Ⓒ Ⓓ Ⓔ   31. Ⓐ Ⓑ Ⓒ Ⓓ Ⓔ   41. Ⓐ Ⓑ Ⓒ Ⓓ Ⓔ   51. Ⓐ Ⓑ Ⓒ Ⓓ Ⓔ
2. Ⓕ Ⓖ Ⓗ Ⓙ Ⓚ   12. Ⓕ Ⓖ Ⓗ Ⓙ Ⓚ   22. Ⓕ Ⓖ Ⓗ Ⓙ Ⓚ   32. Ⓕ Ⓖ Ⓗ Ⓙ Ⓚ   42. Ⓕ Ⓖ Ⓗ Ⓙ Ⓚ   52. Ⓕ Ⓖ Ⓗ Ⓙ Ⓚ
3. Ⓐ Ⓑ Ⓒ Ⓓ Ⓔ   13. Ⓐ Ⓑ Ⓒ Ⓓ Ⓔ   23. Ⓐ Ⓑ Ⓒ Ⓓ Ⓔ   33. Ⓐ Ⓑ Ⓒ Ⓓ Ⓔ   43. Ⓐ Ⓑ Ⓒ Ⓓ Ⓔ   53. Ⓐ Ⓑ Ⓒ Ⓓ Ⓔ
4. Ⓕ Ⓖ Ⓗ Ⓙ Ⓚ   14. Ⓕ Ⓖ Ⓗ Ⓙ Ⓚ   24. Ⓕ Ⓖ Ⓗ Ⓙ Ⓚ   34. Ⓕ Ⓖ Ⓗ Ⓙ Ⓚ   44. Ⓕ Ⓖ Ⓗ Ⓙ Ⓚ   54. Ⓕ Ⓖ Ⓗ Ⓙ Ⓚ
5. Ⓐ Ⓑ Ⓒ Ⓓ Ⓔ   15. Ⓐ Ⓑ Ⓒ Ⓓ Ⓔ   25. Ⓐ Ⓑ Ⓒ Ⓓ Ⓔ   35. Ⓐ Ⓑ Ⓒ Ⓓ Ⓔ   45. Ⓐ Ⓑ Ⓒ Ⓓ Ⓔ   55. Ⓐ Ⓑ Ⓒ Ⓓ Ⓔ
6. Ⓕ Ⓖ Ⓗ Ⓙ Ⓚ   16. Ⓕ Ⓖ Ⓗ Ⓙ Ⓚ   26. Ⓕ Ⓖ Ⓗ Ⓙ Ⓚ   36. Ⓕ Ⓖ Ⓗ Ⓙ Ⓚ   46. Ⓕ Ⓖ Ⓗ Ⓙ Ⓚ   56. Ⓕ Ⓖ Ⓗ Ⓙ Ⓚ
7. Ⓐ Ⓑ Ⓒ Ⓓ Ⓔ   17. Ⓐ Ⓑ Ⓒ Ⓓ Ⓔ   27. Ⓐ Ⓑ Ⓒ Ⓓ Ⓔ   37. Ⓐ Ⓑ Ⓒ Ⓓ Ⓔ   47. Ⓐ Ⓑ Ⓒ Ⓓ Ⓔ   57. Ⓐ Ⓑ Ⓒ Ⓓ Ⓔ
8. Ⓕ Ⓖ Ⓗ Ⓙ Ⓚ   18. Ⓕ Ⓖ Ⓗ Ⓙ Ⓚ   28. Ⓕ Ⓖ Ⓗ Ⓙ Ⓚ   38. Ⓕ Ⓖ Ⓗ Ⓙ Ⓚ   48. Ⓕ Ⓖ Ⓗ Ⓙ Ⓚ   58. Ⓕ Ⓖ Ⓗ Ⓙ Ⓚ
9. Ⓐ Ⓑ Ⓒ Ⓓ Ⓔ   19. Ⓐ Ⓑ Ⓒ Ⓓ Ⓔ   29. Ⓐ Ⓑ Ⓒ Ⓓ Ⓔ   39. Ⓐ Ⓑ Ⓒ Ⓓ Ⓔ   49. Ⓐ Ⓑ Ⓒ Ⓓ Ⓔ   59. Ⓐ Ⓑ Ⓒ Ⓓ Ⓔ
10. Ⓕ Ⓖ Ⓗ Ⓙ Ⓚ   20. Ⓕ Ⓖ Ⓗ Ⓙ Ⓚ   30. Ⓕ Ⓖ Ⓗ Ⓙ Ⓚ   40. Ⓕ Ⓖ Ⓗ Ⓙ Ⓚ   50. Ⓕ Ⓖ Ⓗ Ⓙ Ⓚ   60. Ⓕ Ⓖ Ⓗ Ⓙ Ⓚ

READING TEST

1. Ⓐ Ⓑ Ⓒ Ⓓ   6. Ⓕ Ⓖ Ⓗ Ⓙ   11. Ⓐ Ⓑ Ⓒ Ⓓ   16. Ⓕ Ⓖ Ⓗ Ⓙ   21. Ⓐ Ⓑ Ⓒ Ⓓ   26. Ⓕ Ⓖ Ⓗ Ⓙ   31. Ⓐ Ⓑ Ⓒ Ⓓ   36. Ⓕ Ⓖ Ⓗ Ⓙ
2. Ⓕ Ⓖ Ⓗ Ⓙ   7. Ⓐ Ⓑ Ⓒ Ⓓ   12. Ⓕ Ⓖ Ⓗ Ⓙ   17. Ⓐ Ⓑ Ⓒ Ⓓ   22. Ⓕ Ⓖ Ⓗ Ⓙ   27. Ⓐ Ⓑ Ⓒ Ⓓ   32. Ⓕ Ⓖ Ⓗ Ⓙ   37. Ⓐ Ⓑ Ⓒ Ⓓ
3. Ⓐ Ⓑ Ⓒ Ⓓ   8. Ⓕ Ⓖ Ⓗ Ⓙ   13. Ⓐ Ⓑ Ⓒ Ⓓ   18. Ⓕ Ⓖ Ⓗ Ⓙ   23. Ⓐ Ⓑ Ⓒ Ⓓ   28. Ⓕ Ⓖ Ⓗ Ⓙ   33. Ⓐ Ⓑ Ⓒ Ⓓ   38. Ⓕ Ⓖ Ⓗ Ⓙ
4. Ⓕ Ⓖ Ⓗ Ⓙ   9. Ⓐ Ⓑ Ⓒ Ⓓ   14. Ⓕ Ⓖ Ⓗ Ⓙ   19. Ⓐ Ⓑ Ⓒ Ⓓ   24. Ⓕ Ⓖ Ⓗ Ⓙ   29. Ⓐ Ⓑ Ⓒ Ⓓ   34. Ⓕ Ⓖ Ⓗ Ⓙ   39. Ⓐ Ⓑ Ⓒ Ⓓ
5. Ⓐ Ⓑ Ⓒ Ⓓ   10. Ⓕ Ⓖ Ⓗ Ⓙ   15. Ⓐ Ⓑ Ⓒ Ⓓ   20. Ⓕ Ⓖ Ⓗ Ⓙ   25. Ⓐ Ⓑ Ⓒ Ⓓ   30. Ⓕ Ⓖ Ⓗ Ⓙ   35. Ⓐ Ⓑ Ⓒ Ⓓ   40. Ⓕ Ⓖ Ⓗ Ⓙ

SCIENCE TEST

1. Ⓐ Ⓑ Ⓒ Ⓓ   6. Ⓕ Ⓖ Ⓗ Ⓙ   11. Ⓐ Ⓑ Ⓒ Ⓓ   16. Ⓕ Ⓖ Ⓗ Ⓙ   21. Ⓐ Ⓑ Ⓒ Ⓓ   26. Ⓕ Ⓖ Ⓗ Ⓙ   31. Ⓐ Ⓑ Ⓒ Ⓓ   36. Ⓕ Ⓖ Ⓗ Ⓙ
2. Ⓕ Ⓖ Ⓗ Ⓙ   7. Ⓐ Ⓑ Ⓒ Ⓓ   12. Ⓕ Ⓖ Ⓗ Ⓙ   17. Ⓐ Ⓑ Ⓒ Ⓓ   22. Ⓕ Ⓖ Ⓗ Ⓙ   27. Ⓐ Ⓑ Ⓒ Ⓓ   32. Ⓕ Ⓖ Ⓗ Ⓙ   37. Ⓐ Ⓑ Ⓒ Ⓓ
3. Ⓐ Ⓑ Ⓒ Ⓓ   8. Ⓕ Ⓖ Ⓗ Ⓙ   13. Ⓐ Ⓑ Ⓒ Ⓓ   18. Ⓕ Ⓖ Ⓗ Ⓙ   23. Ⓐ Ⓑ Ⓒ Ⓓ   28. Ⓕ Ⓖ Ⓗ Ⓙ   33. Ⓐ Ⓑ Ⓒ Ⓓ   38. Ⓕ Ⓖ Ⓗ Ⓙ
4. Ⓕ Ⓖ Ⓗ Ⓙ   9. Ⓐ Ⓑ Ⓒ Ⓓ   14. Ⓕ Ⓖ Ⓗ Ⓙ   19. Ⓐ Ⓑ Ⓒ Ⓓ   24. Ⓕ Ⓖ Ⓗ Ⓙ   29. Ⓐ Ⓑ Ⓒ Ⓓ   34. Ⓕ Ⓖ Ⓗ Ⓙ   39. Ⓐ Ⓑ Ⓒ Ⓓ
5. Ⓐ Ⓑ Ⓒ Ⓓ   10. Ⓕ Ⓖ Ⓗ Ⓙ   15. Ⓐ Ⓑ Ⓒ Ⓓ   20. Ⓕ Ⓖ Ⓗ Ⓙ   25. Ⓐ Ⓑ Ⓒ Ⓓ   30. Ⓕ Ⓖ Ⓗ Ⓙ   35. Ⓐ Ⓑ Ⓒ Ⓓ   40. Ⓕ Ⓖ Ⓗ Ⓙ

ENGLISH TEST

45 Minutes—75 Questions

Directions: Each passage has certain words and phrases that are underlined and numbered. The questions in the right column will provide alternatives for the underlined segments. Most questions require you to choose the answer that makes the sentence grammatically correct, concise, and relevant. If the word or phrase in the passage is already the correct, concise, and relevant choice, select Choice A, NO CHANGE. Some questions will ask a question about the underlined segment. When a question is presented, choose the best answer.

Some questions will ask about part or all of the passage. These questions do not refer to a specific underlined segment. Instead, these questions will accompany a number in a box.

For each question, choose your answer and fill in the corresponding bubble on your answer sheet. Read the passage once before you answer the questions. You will often need to read several sentences beyond the underlined portion to be able to choose the correct answer. Be sure to read enough to answer each question.

Passage I

My Old-Fashioned Father

My father, though he is only in his early 50s, is stuck in his old-fashioned <u>ways. He has a</u> general
¹
mistrust of any innovation or technology that he

can't immediately grasp, and he always <u>tells us, that</u> if
²
something isn't broken, then you shouldn't fix it.

He <u>has run</u> a small grocery store in town, and if you
³
were to look at a snapshot of his back office taken

1. **A.** NO CHANGE
   B. ways he has a
   C. ways having a
   D. ways, and still has a

2. **F.** NO CHANGE
   G. tells us, that,
   H. tells us that,
   J. tells us that

3. **A.** NO CHANGE
   B. was running
   C. runs
   D. ran

GO ON TO THE NEXT PAGE

when he opened the store in 1975, you would <u>see that</u>
<u>not much has changed since</u>. He is the most disorgan-
ized person I know and still uses a pencil and paper to

keep track of his <u>inventory.</u> His small office is about to

burst with all the various documents, notes, and receipts

he has accumulated over the <u>years, his filing cabinets</u>

have long since been filled up. The centerpiece of all the

clutter is his ancient typewriter, which isn't even electric.

In the past few years, Father's search for replacement

typewriter ribbons has become an increasingly difficult

task, because they are no longer being produced. He is

perpetually tracking down the few remaining places that

still have these antiquated ribbons in their dusty inven-

tories. When people ask him why he doesn't upgrade

his equipment, he tells them, "Electric typewriters won't

work in a blackout. All I need is a candle and some

paper, and I'm fine." Little does Father <u>know, however,</u>

<u>is that</u> the "upgrade" people are speaking of is not to an

electric typewriter but to a computer.

4. **F.** NO CHANGE
   G. not be likely to see very much that has changed since
   H. be able to see right away that not very much has changed since
   J. not change very much

5. Assuming that all are true, which of the following additions to the word "inventory" is most relevant in context?

   A. inventory of canned and dry goods.
   B. inventory, refusing to consider a more current method.
   C. inventory, which he writes down by hand.
   D. inventory of goods on the shelves and in the storeroom.

6. **F.** NO CHANGE
   G. years; his filing cabinets
   H. years, and besides that, his filing cabinets
   J. years and since his filing cabinets

7. **A.** NO CHANGE
   B. know, besides, that
   C. know, however, that
   D. know, beyond that,

GO ON TO THE NEXT PAGE

Practice Test 6

[1] Hoping to bring Father out of the dark ages, my sister, and I bought him a brand new computer for his fiftieth birthday. [2] We offered to help him to transfer all of his records onto it and to teach him how to use it. [3] Eagerly, we told him about all the new spreadsheet programs that would help simplify his recordkeeping

and organize his accounts; and emphasized the advantage of not having to completely retype any document when he found a typo. [4] Rather than offering us a look of joy for the life-changing gift we had presented him, however, he again brought up the blackout scenario. [5] To Father, this is a concrete argument, although our town hasn't had a blackout in five years, and that one only lasted an hour or two. 11 12

My father's state-of-the-art computer now serves as a very expensive bulletin board for the hundreds of adhesive notes he uses to keep himself organized.

8. **F.** NO CHANGE
   G. me and my sister
   H. my sister and I
   J. my sister and I,

9. **A.** NO CHANGE
   B. On the other hand,
   C. In addition
   D. Rather,

10. **F.** NO CHANGE
    G. accounts and
    H. accounts and,
    J. accounts, we

11. The purpose of including this fact about the town's blackout history is to:
    A. make the father appear delusional.
    B. suggest that the father's reasons not to update his technology are ill-founded.
    C. add an interesting detail to set the scene.
    D. foreshadow an event that occurs later in the story.

12. The author wants to include the following statement in this paragraph:

    We expected it to save him a lot of time and effort.

    The most logical placement for this sentence would be:

    F. before Sentence 1.
    G. after Sentence 1.
    H. after Sentence 4.
    J. after Sentence 5.

GO ON TO THE NEXT PAGE

Sooner than later, we fully expect it will completely dis-
                    13
appear under the mounting files and papers in the

back office. In the depths of that disorganized office, the
                              14
computer will join the cell phone my mom gave him
                    14
a few years ago. Interestingly enough, every once in a
        14
while, that completely forgotten cell phone will ring

from under the heavy clutter of the past. ⬜15

13. **A.** NO CHANGE

    B. Sooner rather than later

    C. Sooner or later

    D. As soon as later

14. **F.** NO CHANGE

    G. Deep in the disorganization of that office's, the computer will join the cell phone my mom gave him a few years back.

    H. In the disorganized depths of the office, the computer will soon be joined by the cell phone my mom gave him a few years ago.

    J. The computer will join the cell phone my mom gave him a few years back in the disorganized depths of that office.

15. Which of the following would provide the most appropriate conclusion for the passage?

    A. It's hard to say what else might be lost in there.

    B. We tell my father it's a reminder that he can't hide from the future forever.

    C. We have no idea who might be calling.

    D. Maybe one day I will try to find it and answer it.

GO ON TO THE NEXT PAGE ⇨

Passage II

Breaking Baseball's Color Barrier

A quick perusal of any modern major league baseball team will reveal a roster of players of multiple ethnicities <u>from the farthest</u> reaches of the globe.
16
Second only to soccer, baseball has evolved into a global

sport and <u>a symbol among races for equality.</u>
17
Its diversity today presents a stark contrast to the state of the sport just sixty years ago. As late as the 1940s, there existed an unwritten rule in baseball that prevented all but white players <u>to participate</u> in
18
the major leagues. This rule was known as the "color barrier" or "color line." The color line in baseball actually predated the birth of the major leagues. Prior to the official formation of any league of professional baseball teams, there existed an organization of amateur baseball clubs known as the National Association of Baseball Players, <u>which was the precursor to today's</u>
19
<u>National League.</u> On December 11, 1868, the governing
19
body of this association had unanimously adopted a rule

16. **F.** NO CHANGE
G. from the most far
H. from the most farthest
J. from farther

17. **A.** NO CHANGE
B. among races for equality a symbol
C. a symbol for equality among races
D. for equality among races a symbol

18. **F.** NO CHANGE
G. to be able to participate
H. from participating
J. to participation

19. Is the underlined portion relevant here?

A. Yes, because it helps familiarize the reader with the range of baseball associations that once existed.

B. Yes, because it helps clarify the development the author traces.

C. No, because the names of the organizations are not important.

D. No, because it is inconsistent with the style of the essay to provide specific historical data.

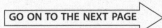

that effectively barred any team that <u>had, any "colored</u>
                                                              20
<u>persons"</u> on its roster. However, when baseball started to
20

organize into leagues <u>by</u> professional teams in the early
                       21
1880s, the National Association of Baseball Players'

decree no longer had any weight, especially in the newly

formed American Association. <u>For a brief period in</u>
                                                      22
<u>those early years, a few African Americans played side</u>
                             22
<u>by side with white players on major league diamonds.</u>
                             22

[1] Most baseball historians believe that the first

African American to play in the major leagues was

Moses "Fleet" Walker. [2] <u>Walker was a catcher</u> for the
                                                   23
Toledo Blue Stockings of the American Association

between 1884 and 1889. [3] During that time, a few

other African Americans, <u>including</u> Walker's brother
                                    24

Weldy, <u>would be joining him</u> on the Blue Stockings.
                          25
[4] Unfortunately, this respite from segregation did not

last for very long; as Jim Crow laws took their hold on

the nation, many of the most popular white ballplayers

20. **F.** NO CHANGE
    G. had any, "colored persons"
    H. had any "colored persons"
    J. had any "colored persons,"

21. **A.** NO CHANGE
    B. of
    C. from
    D. about

22. The writer is considering deleting the under-
    lined portion. Should the writer make this
    deletion?

    F. Yes, because the information is not
        relevant to the topic of the paragraph.

    G. Yes, because the information contradicts
        the first sentence of the paragraph.

    H. No, because the information shows
        that white players did not object to
        integration.

    J. No, because the statement provides
        a smooth transition to the specific
        information about early African American
        players in the next paragraph.

23. **A.** NO CHANGE
    B. Walker, being a catcher
    C. Walker, a catcher
    D. Walker who was a catcher

24. **F.** NO CHANGE
    G. that included
    H. who would include
    J. including among them

25. **A.** NO CHANGE
    B. joined him
    C. were to join him
    D. will join him

GO ON TO THE NEXT PAGE

started to refuse to take the field with their African American teammates. [5] By the 1890s, the color barrier had fully returned to baseball, where it would endure for more than half a century. [26]

Jackie Robinson would become the first African American to cross the color line at the time when 27 he debuted for the Brooklyn Dodgers in 1947. For Robinson's landmark achievements on and off the

diamond, he will forever be recognized as a hero of the 28

civil rights movement and a sports icon. His response to 29 the prejudices of American society during the 1940s and 1950s opened the door for the multi-racial and multi-national face of modern baseball, and fans of the sport worldwide will be forever in his debt.

26. Upon reviewing this paragraph, the author discovers that he has neglected to include the following information:

A handful of African Americans played for other teams as well.

This sentence would be most logically placed after:

F. Sentence 1.
G. Sentence 2.
H. Sentence 3.
J. Sentence 4.

27. A. NO CHANGE
B. when
C. while
D. when the time came that

28. F. NO CHANGE
G. one day be recognized
H. forever recognize
J. be admired by a lot of people for being

29. Which choice best maintains the essay's positive tone while emphasizing the unique role that Robinson played?

A. NO CHANGE
B. The path that he blazed through
C. The stance he took against
D. His collaboration in the face of

GO ON TO THE NEXT PAGE

Question 30 asks about the essay as a whole.

30. Suppose the writer had been assigned to develop a brief essay on the history of baseball. Would this essay successfully fulfill that goal?

   F. Yes, because it covers events in baseball over a period of more than a century.

   G. Yes, because it mentions key figures in baseball history.

   H. No, because people played baseball before 1868.

   J. No, because the focus of this essay is on one particular aspect of baseball history.

GO ON TO THE NEXT PAGE

Practice Test 6

Passage III

The Bear Mountain Bridge

When the gleaming Bear Mountain Bridge officially opened to traffic on Thanksgiving Day in <u>1924, it</u>
                                                                                     31
was known as the Harriman Bridge, after Edward H. Harriman, wealthy philanthropist and patriarch of the family most influential in the bridge's construction. Before <u>they were</u> constructed, there were no bridges
                    32
spanning the Hudson River south of Albany. By the early 1920s, the ferry services used to transport people back and forth across the river had become woefully inadequate. In February of 1922, in an effort to alleviate some of the burden on the ferries and create a permanent link across the Hudson, the New York State Legislature <u>had authorized</u> a group of private investors,
               33
led by Mary Harriman, to build a bridge. The group,

known as the Bear Mountain Hudson Bridge Company (BMHBC), was allotted thirty years to <u>build, construct,</u>
                                                       34
<u>and maintain</u> the structure, at which time the span
   34
would be handed over to New York State.

The BMHBC invested almost $4,500,000 into the suspension bridge and hired the world-renowned design team <u>of Howard Baird and George Hodge</u> as
            35

31. A. NO CHANGE
    B. 1924; it
    C. 1924. It
    D. 1924 and it

32. F. NO CHANGE
    G. the bridges were
    H. it was
    J. it were

33. A. NO CHANGE
    B. authorized
    C. was authorized
    D. would authorize

34. F. NO CHANGE
    G. build and construct and maintain
    H. construct and maintain
    J. construct, and maintain

35. A. NO CHANGE
    B. of Howard Baird, and George Hodge
    C. of Howard Baird and, George Hodge
    D. of, Howard Baird and George Hodge

GO ON TO THE NEXT PAGE

Practice Test 6

architects. [36] Baird and Hodge enlisted the help of John

36. The purpose of including the cost of the bridge is to:

    F. provide a piece of information critical to the point of the essay.

    G. insert a necessary transition between the second and third paragraphs.

    H. add a detail contributing to the reader's understanding of the magnitude of the project.

    J. provide an explanation of how the group raised money to invest in the bridge.

A. Roebling and Sons, <u>who were</u> instrumental in the
                      37
steel work of the Brooklyn Bridge and would later work on the Golden Gate and George Washington Bridges.

    Amazingly, the bridge took only twenty months and eleven days to complete, and not one life was lost. [38] It was a technological marvel and would stand as a model for the suspension bridges of the future. At the time of the Harriman Bridge's completion, it was, at 2,257 feet,

37. A. NO CHANGE

    B. who was

    C. a company

    D. a company that had been

38. If the writer were to delete the preceding sentence, the essay would lose primarily:

    F. information about how long the project had been expected to take.

    G. a warning about the dangers of large-scale construction projects.

    H. crucial information about the duration of the project.

    J. a necessary transition between Paragraphs 3 and 4.

the longest single-span steel suspension bridge in the world. <u>Therefore, the</u> two main cables used in the
              39
suspension were 18 inches in diameter, and each contained 7,752 individual steel wires wrapped in 37 thick strands. If completely unraveled, the single wires in both

39. A. NO CHANGE

    B. Nonetheless, the

    C. At the same time, the

    D. The

GO ON TO THE NEXT PAGE ⟹

cables would be 7,377 miles <u>longer</u>. The bridge links
40
Bear Mountain on the western bank of the Hudson

to Anthony's Nose on the eastern <u>side, it lies</u> so precisely
41
on an east-west plane that one can check a compass by

it. It carries Routes 6 and 202 across the Hudson and is

the point of river crossing for the Appalachian Trail.

In an attempt to recoup some of its investment after

the bridge <u>opened, the BMHBC charged</u> an exorbitant
42
toll of eighty cents per crossing. Even with the high

toll, however, it operated at a loss for thirteen of its first

sixteen years. Finally it was acquired, more than ten

years earlier than planned, by the New York State Bridge

Authority. The bridge was renamed the Bear Mountain

Bridge. <u>Moreover,</u> the Bear Mountain Bridge sees
43

<u>more than</u> six million vehicles cross its concrete decks
44
each year.

40. F. NO CHANGE
    G. long
    H. in total length
    J. lengthy

41. A. NO CHANGE
    B. side, lies
    C. side, lying
    D. side; and it lies

42. F. NO CHANGE
    G. opened the BMHBC charged
    H. opened: the BMHBC charged
    J. opened; the BMHBC charged

43. A. NO CHANGE
    B. In contrast
    C. Besides that fact
    D. Today

44. F. NO CHANGE
    G. over
    H. even more than
    J. a higher amount than

GO ON TO THE NEXT PAGE

Question 45 asks about the essay as a whole.

45. Suppose the author had been assigned to write a brief history of bridge building in the United States. Would this essay successfully fulfill that requirement?

   A. Yes, because it provides information on the entire process from the initial funding through the opening of the bridge.

   B. Yes, because Bear Mountain Bridge is historically significant.

   C. No, because it focuses on only one bridge.

   D. No, because the essay is primarily concerned with the financial aspects of building and maintaining the bridge.

GO ON TO THE NEXT PAGE ▷

Passage IV

The Dream of the American West

As the sun <u>was slowly rising</u> over the Atlantic Ocean
                    46
and painted New York harbor a spectacular fiery orange,

I started my old Toyota's engine. At this early hour, there

was still some semblance of the night's tranquility left

on the city sidewalks, but I knew that, as the minutes

ticked by, <u>the streets would flood with humanity.</u>
                    47

I smiled <u>with</u> the thought that soon all the wonderful
                  48
chaos of New York City would be disappearing behind

me as I <u>embarked on my trip to the other side of</u> the
                      49
country.

<u>As the morning sun climbed into the sky,</u>
                      50

46. F. NO CHANGE
   G. rising slowly
   H. rose slowly
   J. continued to rise

47. The author wants to contrast the statement about the quiet of the night streets with a related detail about the daytime activity. Assuming that all of the choices are true, which of the following best accomplishes that goal?

   A. NO CHANGE
   B. some people might appear.
   C. everything would be different.
   D. the tranquility would be unbroken.

48. F. NO CHANGE
   G. along with
   H. at
   J. all because of

49. A. NO CHANGE
   B. embarked on this journey across
   C. traveled to the other side of
   D. traveled across

50. Which of the following alternatives to the underlined portion would NOT be acceptable?

   F. At sunrise,
   G. Watching the morning sun climb into the sky,
   H. The morning sun climbed into the sky,
   J. As the sun rose,

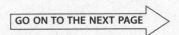

GO ON TO THE NEXT PAGE

I shuddered with excitement to think that my final stop
would be in California, where the sun itself ends its
journey across America. Like the sun, however, I still
had quite a journey before me.

I had been planning this road trip across the United States for as long as I could remember. In my life, I had been fortunate enough to see some of the most beautiful countries in the world. However, it had always bothered me that although I'd stood in the shadow of the Eiffel Tower, marveled in the desert heat at the Pyramids of Giza, I'd never seen any of the wonders of my own country, except those found in my hometown of New York City. All of that was about to change.

As I left the city, the tall buildings began to give way to smaller ones, then to transform into the quaint rows of houses that clustered in the crowded suburbs. Trees and grass, then the yellow-green of cornfields and the golden

wash of wheat were slowly replacing the familiar mazes of cement and steel. My world no longer stretched

51. The writer is considering revising this sentence by deleting the underlined portion. If she did so, the paragraph would primarily lose:

   A. information about the reasons for the writer's trip.
   B. information about the writer's destination.
   C. a description of the writer's planned route.
   D. a comparison between the sunrise in New York and the sunset in California.

52. F. NO CHANGE
   G. Eiffel Tower and had marveled in the desert heat at the Pyramids of Giza,
   H. Eiffel Tower and marveled in the desert heat at the Pyramids of Giza
   J. Eiffel Tower, and had marveled, in the desert heat, at the Pyramids of Giza

53. Given that all are true, which of the following provides the most effective transition between the third paragraph and the description of the Midwest in the fourth paragraph?

   A. NO CHANGE
   B. In fact, there were changes on the horizon almost immediately.
   C. My excitement hadn't diminished.
   D. I realized that people who lived in other areas might feel the same way about visiting New York.

54. Assuming that all are true, which of the following provides information most relevant to the main focus of the paragraph?

   F. NO CHANGE
   G. appearing before me
   H. racing past my window
   J. becoming monotonous

GO ON TO THE NEXT PAGE →

vertically toward the sky, it now spread horizontally
                     55
toward eternity. For two days, I pushed through the

wind-whipped farmlands of Mid-America, hypnotized

by the beauty of the undulating yet unbroken lines. At

night, the breeze from my car would stir the wheat fields

to dance beneath the moon, and the silos hid in the

shadows, quietly imposing their simply serenity upon
                                        56
everything.

55. A. NO CHANGE
    B. the sky but it now spread
    C. the sky; it now spread
    D. the sky spreading

56. F. NO CHANGE
    G. simple
    H. simplest
    J. simpler

Then, as the night's shadows gave way to light, there
                    57

57. A. NO CHANGE
    B. nights shadows
    C. shadows from the night
    D. night shadow

seemed to be a great force rising to meet the sun as it
                                                58
made its reappearance.
        58

58. F. NO CHANGE
    G. sun as it reappeared
    H. reappearing sun
    J. sun as it was also rising

Still, I had no idea what I was looking at. Then, there
59

59. A. NO CHANGE
    B. Even so,
    C. At first,
    D. Eventually,

was no mistaking it. The unbroken lines of Mid-America
          60
had given way to the jagged and majestic heights of the

Rockies and the gateway to the American West.

60. F. NO CHANGE
    G. mistake to be made
    H. chance to mistake it
    J. having made a mistake

GO ON TO THE NEXT PAGE

Passage V

Traveling at the Speed of Sound

The term "supersonic" refers to anything that travels faster than the speed of sound. When the last of the supersonic Concorde passenger planes made its final trip across the Atlantic in <u>November of 2003, an interesting</u> chapter in history was finally closed. The

61
fleet of supersonic Concorde SSTs, or

"Supersonic Transports," <u>they were</u> jointly operated

62
by Air France and British Airways, had been making the intercontinental trip across the Atlantic for almost thirty years. These amazing machines cruised at Mach 2, more than twice the speed of sound. They flew <u>to a height</u> almost twice that of standard passenger

63
airplanes. The Concorde routinely made the trip from New York to London in less than three hours and was much more expensive than normal transatlantic flights. <u>Furthermore,</u> the majority of the passengers

64
who traveled on the Concorde were celebrities or the extremely wealthy, it also attracted ordinary people who simply wanted to know how it felt to travel faster than the speed of sound. Some would save money for years just to gain that knowledge.

What is the speed of sound? Many people are surprised to learn that there is no fixed answer to this question. The speed <u>that</u> sound travels through a given

65
medium depends on a number of factors. To understand

61. A. NO CHANGE
B. November, of 2003 an interesting
C. November of 2003 an interesting
D. November of 2003; an interesting

62. F. NO CHANGE
G. those were
H. which were
J. which being

63. A. NO CHANGE
B. at an altitude
C. toward an altitude
D. very high

64. F. NO CHANGE
G. Despite
H. Though
J. Along with

65. A. NO CHANGE
B. to which
C. at which
D. where

GO ON TO THE NEXT PAGE

the speed of sound, we must first understand what a "sound" really is. [66]

The standard dictionary definition of sound is "a vibration or disturbance transmitted, like waves through water, through a material medium such as a gas." Our

ears are able to pick up those sound waves and <u>convert</u>
₆₇
them into what we hear. This means that the speed at

which sound travels through gas <u>directly depends on</u>
₆₈
<u>what gas it is traveling through, and the temperature</u>
₆₈
<u>and pressure of the gas.</u> When discussing aircraft
₆₈
breaking the speed of sound, that gas medium, of course, is air. As air temperature and pressure decrease

<u>with altitude,</u> so does the speed of sound. An airplane
₆₉
flying at the speed of sound at sea level is traveling

66. The purpose of this paragraph, as it relates to the surrounding paragraphs, is primarily to:

F. provide an example of the main idea before continuing discussion of that idea.

G. transition from a discussion of certain aircraft to the science behind them.

H. present a counterargument to the main thesis before refuting that counterargument.

J. transition from the general topic of aircraft to a story about specific airplanes.

67. Which of the following alternatives to the underlined portion would be the LEAST acceptable?

A. change

B. translate

C. alter

D. transform

68. F. NO CHANGE

G. depends directly on the type, temperature, and pressure of the gas it is traveling through

H. directly depends on what gas it is and also on the temperature and pressure of that gas

J. depends directly on the type, temperature, and pressure of the gas

69. A. NO CHANGE

B. with height

C. with a drop in altitude

D. at higher altitudes

GO ON TO THE NEXT PAGE

roughly at 761 mph; <u>however</u> when that same plane
70
climbs to 20,000 feet, the speed of sound is only about

707 mph. This is why the Concorde's cruising altitude

was so much higher than that of a regular passenger

aircraft; <u>planes can reach supersonic speeds more easily</u>
71
<u>at higher altitudes.</u>
71

In the years since the Concorde <u>has been</u>
72
decommissioned, only fighter pilots and astronauts

have been able to experience the sensation of

breaking "the sound barrier." <u>But that is all about</u>
73
<u>to change very soon.</u> Newer and faster supersonic
73
passenger planes are being developed that will

be technologically superior to the Concorde

and much cheaper to operate. <u>Now,</u> supersonic
74
passenger travel will be available not only to the rich

and famous, <u>but also be for</u> the masses so they, too, can
75
experience life at supersonic speeds.

70. F. NO CHANGE
    G. however,
    H. and so,
    J. even so

71. Given that all are true, which of the following provides the most logical conclusion for this sentence?

    A. NO CHANGE
    B. they're much faster
    C. they use much more fuel than regular aircraft
    D. they're rarely visible because they fly above the cloud cover

72. F. NO CHANGE
    G. came to be
    H. was
    J. had been

73. A. NO CHANGE
    B. Soon, however, that is about to change.
    C. Soon, however, that will change.
    D. That is about to change soon.

74. F. NO CHANGE
    G. Nearby,
    H. Soon,
    J. Upcoming,

75. A. NO CHANGE
    B. but also be available to
    C. but also to
    D. but for

IF YOU FINISH BEFORE TIME IS CALLED, YOU MAY CHECK YOUR WORK ON THIS SECTION ONLY. DO NOT TURN TO ANY OTHER SECTION IN THE TEST.

MATHEMATICS TEST

60 Minutes—60 Questions

Directions: Choose the correct solution to each question and fill in the corresponding bubble on your answer sheet.

Do not continue to spend time on questions if you get stuck. Solve as many questions as you can before returning to any if time permits.

You may use a calculator on this test for any question you choose. However, some questions may be better solved without a calculator.

Note: Unless otherwise stated, you can assume:

1. Figures are NOT necessarily drawn to scale.

2. Geometric figures are two dimensional.

3. The word *line* indicates a straight line.

4. The word *average* indicates arithmetic mean.

1. The eighth grade girls' basketball team played a total of 13 games this season. If they scored a total of 364 points, what was the mean (average) score per game?

    A. 13
    B. 16
    C. 20
    D. 28
    E. 32

2. When $4\frac{3}{7}$ is written as an improper fraction in simplest form, what is the numerator of the fraction?

    F. 12
    G. 21
    H. 27
    J. 28
    K. 31

3. If $4x + 18 = 38$, then $x = ?$

    A. 3
    B. 4.5
    C. 5
    D. 14
    E. 20

4. John weighs 1.5 times as much as Ellen. If John weighs 144 pounds, how many pounds does Ellen weigh?

    F. 84
    G. 96
    H. 104
    J. 164
    K. 216

GO ON TO THE NEXT PAGE

5. What positive number when divided by its reciprocal gives a result of $\frac{9}{16}$?

   A. $\frac{3}{16}$

   B. $\frac{3}{4}$

   C. $\frac{4}{3}$

   D. $\frac{16}{9}$

   E. $\frac{16}{3}$

6. If $\sqrt[3]{x} = \frac{1}{4}$, then $x = $?

   F. $\frac{1}{256}$

   G. $\frac{1}{64}$

   H. $\frac{1}{12}$

   J. $\frac{1}{\sqrt[3]{4}}$

   K. 64

7. If $x^2 + 14 = 63$, then x could be which of the following?

   A. 4.5

   B. 7

   C. 14

   D. 24.5

   E. 49

8. Two vectors are given by $\mathbf{v}_1 = \langle 7, -3 \rangle$ and $\mathbf{v}_2 = \langle a, b \rangle$. If $\mathbf{v}_1 + \mathbf{v}_2 = \langle 5, 5 \rangle$, then what is the value of a ?

   F. -2

   G. 2

   H. 5

   J. 8

   K. 12

9. Based on past graduations, a university estimates that 6% of the graduating class will not attend the graduation ceremony. Based on this estimate, if there are 1,250 graduates, how many will not attend the ceremony?

   A. 75

   B. 140

   C. 220

   D. 350

   E. 425

10. $5.2^3 + 6.8^2 = $?

   F. 46.24

   G. 94.872

   H. 120.534

   J. 140.608

   K. 186.848

GO ON TO THE NEXT PAGE

11. Lexi uses her debit card to make a purchase totaling $40. When she records the debit in her checkbook register, she accidentally adds $40 to her balance rather than subtracting it, which results in an inaccurate total. Because of her error, Lexi's checkbook register shows:

    A. $80 less than it should.

    B. $40 less than it should.

    C. $20 more than it should.

    D. $40 more than it should.

    E. $80 more than it should.

12. $3^3 \div 9 + (6^2 - 12) \div 4 = ?$

    F. 3

    G. 6.75

    H. 9

    J. 12

    K. 15

13. If bananas cost $0.24 and oranges cost $0.38, what is the total cost of x bananas and y oranges?

    A. $(x + y)(\$0.24 + \$0.38)$

    B. $\$0.24x + \$0.38y$

    C. $\$0.62(x + y)$

    D. $\dfrac{\$0.24}{x} + \dfrac{\$0.38}{y}$

    E. $\$0.38x + \$0.24y$

14. In the following figure, all of the small triangles are the same size. What percent of the entire figure is shaded?

    F. 8

    G. 24

    H. $33\dfrac{1}{3}$

    J. 50

    K. $66\dfrac{2}{3}$

15. In a high school senior class, the ratio of girls to boys is 5:3. If there are a total of 168 students in the senior class, how many girls are there?

    A. 63

    B. 100

    C. 105

    D. 147

    E. 152

16. On her first three geometry tests, Sarah scored an 89, a 93, and an 84. If there are four tests total and Sarah needs at least a 90 average for the four, what is the lowest score she can receive on the final test?

    F. 86

    G. 90

    H. 92

    J. 94

    K. 96

GO ON TO THE NEXT PAGE

Practice Test 6   535

17. What is the solution set of $3x - 11 \geq 22$?

    A. $x \geq -11$

    B. $x < -3$

    C. $x \geq 0$

    D. $x > 3$

    E. $x \geq 11$

18. Dillon is going to randomly pick a domino from a pile of dominos that are all facing downward. Of the dominos in the pile, 48 have an even number of dots on them. He randomly picks a single domino. If the probability that he picks a domino with an even number of dots is $\frac{3}{4}$, how many dominos are in the pile?

    F. 36

    G. 48

    H. 56

    J. 64

    K. 72

19. What is the value of $3x - 8y$ when $x = 4$ and $y = -\frac{1}{2}$?

    A. -4

    B. 8

    C. 12

    D. 16

    E. 28

20. Court reporters type every word spoken during trials and hearings so that there is a written record of what transpired. Suppose a certain court reporter can type 3.75 words per second, and a trial transcript contains 25 pages with an average of 675 words per page. If this court reporter typed the transcript at his typical rate, how long was he actively typing?

    F. 1 hour, 15 minutes

    G. 1 hour, 40 minutes

    H. 2 hours, 10 minutes

    J. 2 hours, 30 minutes

    K. 3 hours

21. In the following figure, lines m and l are parallel and the measure of $\angle a$ is 68°. What is the measure of $\angle f$?

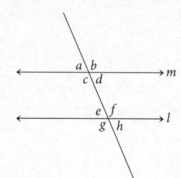

    A. 22°

    B. 68°

    C. 80°

    D. 112°

    E. 292°

GO ON TO THE NEXT PAGE

22. On a map, the scale is the ratio of the distance shown on the map to the actual distance. A geography teacher has a map on her wall with a scale of 1 inch:100 miles. She uses the school's copier to shrink the large wall map down to the size of a piece of paper to hand out to each of her students. To do this, she makes the map $\frac{1}{4}$ of its original size. Suppose on the students' maps, the distance between two cities is 2.5 inches. How many actual miles apart are those cities?

F. 25

G. 250

H. 800

J. 1,000

K. 1,200

23. A piece of letter-sized paper is $8\frac{1}{2}$ inches wide and 11 inches long. Suppose you want to cut strips of paper that are $\frac{5}{8}$ of an inch wide and 11 inches long. What is the maximum number of strips of paper you could make from 1 piece of letter-sized paper?

A. 5

B. 6

C. 12

D. 13

E. 14

24. In the following figure, $\overline{MN}$ and $\overline{PQ}$ are parallel. Point A lies on $\overline{MN}$, and points B and C lie on $\overline{PQ}$. If $AB = AC$ and $\angle MAB$ has a measure of 55°, what is the measure of $\angle ACB$?

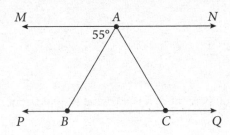

F. 35°

G. 55°

H. 65°

J. 80°

K. 125°

25. What is the slope of the line that passes through the points $(-10,0)$ and $(0,-6)$?

A. $-\frac{5}{3}$

B. $-\frac{3}{5}$

C. $\frac{3}{5}$

D. $\frac{5}{3}$

E. 0

26. For all x, $(x+4)(x-4)+(2x+2)(x-2) = ?$

F. $x^2 - 2x - 20$

G. $3x^2 - 12$

H. $3x^2 - 2x - 20$

J. $3x^2 + 2x - 20$

K. $3x^2 + 2x + 20$

GO ON TO THE NEXT PAGE

27. What is the length of a line segment with endpoints $(3, -6)$ and $(-2, 6)$?

   A.   1

   B.   5

   C.   10

   D.   13

   E.   15

28. If 60 percent of h is 80, what is 30 percent of h ?

   F.   30

   G.   40

   H.   50

   J.   60

   K.   70

29. Set A contains 7 consecutive even integers. If the average of Set A's integers is 46, which of the following is the smallest integer of Set A ?

   A.   36

   B.   38

   C.   40

   D.   42

   E.   44

30. Which of the following statements describes the total of the first n terms of the arithmetic sequence below?

$$1, 3, 5, 7, 9, \ldots$$

   F.   The total is always equal to 25 regardless of n.

   G.   The total is always equal to $2n$.

   H.   The total is always equal to $3n$.

   J.   The total is always equal to n^2.

   K.   There is no consistent pattern for the total.

31. Which of the following matrices is equal to the matrix product $\begin{bmatrix} -2 & 0 \\ 1 & -3 \end{bmatrix} \cdot \begin{bmatrix} 2 \\ 2 \end{bmatrix}$?

   A. $\begin{bmatrix} -4 & 0 \\ 2 & -6 \end{bmatrix}$

   B. $\begin{bmatrix} -4 & 2 \\ 2 & -6 \end{bmatrix}$

   C. $\begin{bmatrix} 0 & 0 \\ 0 & 0 \end{bmatrix}$

   D. $\begin{bmatrix} -4 \\ -4 \end{bmatrix}$

   E. $\begin{bmatrix} -4 \\ -6 \end{bmatrix}$

32. A playground is $(x + 7)$ units long and $(x + 3)$ units wide. If a square of side length x is sectioned off from the playground to make a sandpit, which of the following could be the remaining area of the playground?

   F. $x^2 + 10x + 21$

   G. $10x + 21$

   H. $2x + 10$

   J. $21x$

   K.   21

33. Assume m and n are nonzero integers such that $m > 0$ and $n < 0$. Which of the following *must* be negative?

   A. $-n^m$

   B. $-mn$

   C. m^n

   D. $-n - m$

   E. $n - m$

GO ON TO THE NEXT PAGE

34. The point $(-3,-2)$ is the midpoint of the line segment in the standard (x,y) coordinate plane with endpoints $(1,9)$ and (m,n). Which of the following is (m,n) ?

   F. $(-7,-13)$

   G. $(-2,7)$

   H. $(-1,3.5)$

   J. $(2,5.5)$

   K. $(5,20)$

35. If $f(x) = 16x^2 - 20x$, what is the value of $f(3)$?

   A. -12

   B. 36

   C. 84

   D. 144

   E. 372

36. What is the length of side AC in triangle ABC graphed on the following coordinate plane?

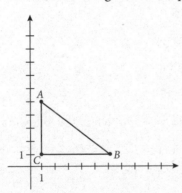

   F. 3

   G. 4

   H. 5

   J. 6

   K. 7

37. If $f(x) = \dfrac{1}{3}x + 13$ and $g(x) = 3x^2 + 6x + 12$, which expression represents $f(g(x))$?

   A. $x^2 + 12x + 4$

   B. $\dfrac{x^2}{3} + 2x + 194$

   C. $x^2 + 2x + 17$

   D. $x^2 + 2x + 25$

   E. $x^2 + 2x + 54$

38. What is the equation of a line that is perpendicular to the line $y = \dfrac{2}{3}x + 5$ and contains the point $(4,-3)$?

   F. $y = \dfrac{2}{3}x + 4$

   G. $y = -\dfrac{2}{3}x + 3$

   H. $y = -\dfrac{3}{2}x + 3$

   J. $y = -\dfrac{3}{2}x - 9$

   K. $y = -\dfrac{3}{2}x + 9$

39. The formula for converting a Fahrenheit temperature reading to Celsius is $C = \dfrac{5}{9}(F - 32)$, where C is the reading in degrees Celsius and F is the reading in degrees Fahrenheit. Which of the following is the Fahrenheit equivalent to a reading of $95°$ Celsius?

   A. $35°F$

   B. $53°F$

   C. $63°F$

   D. $203°F$

   E. $207°F$

GO ON TO THE NEXT PAGE

40. When 3 times x is increased by 5, the result is less than 11. Which of the following is a graph of the real numbers x for which the previous statement is true?

F.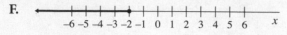

G.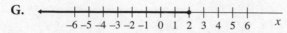

H.

J.

K.

41. In the following triangle, what is the value of $\cos R$?

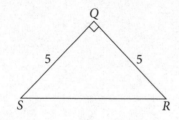

A. $\dfrac{\sqrt{2}}{6}$

B. $\dfrac{\sqrt{2}}{5}$

C. $\dfrac{\sqrt{2}}{2}$

D. $2\sqrt{2}$

E. $5\sqrt{2}$

42. Marvin has two saltwater fish tanks in his home. One has tangs and angelfish in a ratio of 5 to 2. The second tank has tangs and puffers in a ratio of 2 to 3. Marvin wants to put a tank in his office with angelfish and puffers using the same ratio he has at home to make it easier to buy food for them in bulk. What ratio of angelfish to puffers should he use?

F. 2:3

G. 2:5

H. 5:2

J. 5:7

K. 4:15

43. The volume of a sphere is given by the formula $V = \dfrac{4}{3}\pi r^3$, where r is the radius of the sphere. What is the volume, in cubic inches, of a sphere that has a diameter of 6 inches?

A. 3π

B. 9π

C. 27π

D. 36π

E. 288π

44. For all $x \neq -1$, which of the following is equivalent to $\dfrac{x^2 - 5x - 6}{x + 1} + x + 1$?

F. $x - 5$

G. $2x - 5$

H. $x^2 - 5x - 6$

J. $\dfrac{2x - 5}{x + 1}$

K. $\dfrac{x^2 - 4x - 5}{x + 1}$

GO ON TO THE NEXT PAGE

45. Which of the following expressions is the greatest monomial factor of $60a^3b + 45a^2b^2$?

    A. $15a^2b$

    B. $15a^3b^2$

    C. $15a^5b^3$

    D. $180a^3b^2$

    E. $180a^5b^3$

Use the following information to answer questions 46–47.

The population of fish in a certain pond from 1985 to 1995 is shown in the graph below.

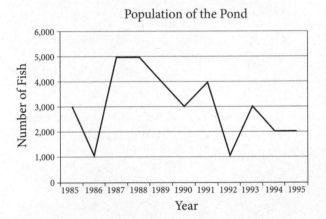

Population of the Pond

46. Which of the following best describes the percent change in the population from 1985 to 1995 ?

    F. 33.33% increase

    G. 33.33% decrease

    H. 50% decrease

    J. 333.33% increase

    K. 333.33% decrease

47. Which of the following years contains the median population for the data?

    A. 1986

    B. 1989

    C. 1990

    D. 1991

    E. 1995

---

48. The table below shows the results of a study identifying the number of males and females with and without college degrees who were unemployed or employed at the time of the study. If one person from the study is chosen at random, what is the probability that that person is an employed person with a college degree?

	Unemployed	Employed	Totals
Female Degree	12	188	200
Female No Degree	44	156	200
Male Degree	23	177	200
Male No Degree	41	159	200
Totals	120	680	800

    F. $\dfrac{73}{160}$

    G. $\dfrac{10}{17}$

    H. $\dfrac{73}{136}$

    J. $\dfrac{17}{20}$

    K. $\dfrac{73}{80}$

GO ON TO THE NEXT PAGE

49. Which of the following expressions gives the number of distinct permutations of the letters in GEOMETRY ?

   A. $8!(2!)$

   B. $8!$

   C. $\dfrac{8!}{2!}$

   D. $\dfrac{8!}{6!}$

   E. $\dfrac{8!}{(6!)(2!)}$

50. The graph below represents the solution set to which inequality, assuming each grid line represents 1 unit?

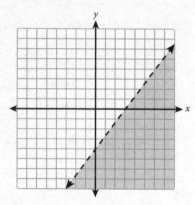

   F. $y < -\dfrac{4}{3}x - 4$

   G. $y > -\dfrac{3}{4}x - 4$

   H. $y < \dfrac{3}{4}x - 4$

   J. $y < \dfrac{4}{3}x - 4$

   K. $y > \dfrac{4}{3}x - 4$

51. A function h is defined by $h(x,y,z) = 4xy^2 - yz^3$. What is the value of $h(2,-1,3)$?

   A. -35

   B. -19

   C. -1

   D. 19

   E. 35

52. The radius of a circle is increased so that the radius of the new circle is triple that of the original circle. How many times larger is the area of the new circle than that of the original circle?

   F. $\dfrac{1}{3}$

   G. 3

   H. 6

   J. 6π

   K. 9

53. The function $f(x) = 0.5\sin(2x)$ is graphed below over the domain $[0,2\pi]$. What is the period of the function?

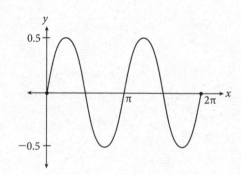

   A. $\dfrac{\pi}{4}$

   B. $\dfrac{\pi}{2}$

   C. π

   D. 2π

   E. 4π

GO ON TO THE NEXT PAGE

54. For what value of x is the equation $\sqrt[3]{4x - 12} + 25 = 27$ true?

   F. -5

   G. -1

   H. -2.5

   J. 5

   K. 6.5

55. The chord shown in the figure is 8 units long. If the chord is 3 units from the center of the circle, what is the area of the circle?

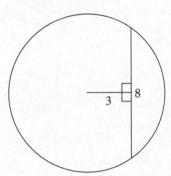

   A. 9π

   B. 16π

   C. 18π

   D. 25π

   E. 28π

56. If $f(x) = 3^{3x + 3}$ and $g(x) = 27^{\left(\frac{2}{3}x - \frac{1}{3}\right)}$, for what value of x, if any, does the graph of $f(x)$ intersect the graph of $g(x)$?

   F. -4

   G. $-\dfrac{7}{4}$

   H. $-\dfrac{10}{7}$

   J. 2

   K.   The graphs do not intersect.

57. What value of x satisfies the equation $\log_3 (5x - 40) - \log_3 5 = 2$?

   A. 17

   B. 9

   C. 1

   D. -9

   E. -17

58. A finite arithmetic sequence has five terms. The first term is 4. What is the difference between the mean and the median of the five terms?

   F. 0

   G. 1

   H. 2

   J. 4

   K. 5

GO ON TO THE NEXT PAGE

59. In the following triangle, if $\cos \angle BAC = 0.6$ and the hypotenuse of the triangle is 15, what is the length of side BC?

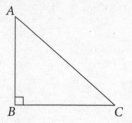

- **A.** 3
- **B.** 5
- **C.** 10
- **D.** 12
- **E.** 15

60. The table below shows several points that lie on the graph of a parabola. Based on the data in the table, what is the value of y when $x = -4$?

x	y
-2	3
0	-3
2	-5
4	-3
6	3
8	13

- **F.** -13
- **G.** -5
- **H.** 5
- **J.** 13
- **K.** Cannot be determined from the given information

IF YOU FINISH BEFORE TIME IS CALLED, YOU MAY CHECK YOUR WORK ON THIS SECTION ONLY. DO NOT TURN TO ANY OTHER SECTION IN THE TEST. STOP

READING TEST

35 Minutes—40 Questions

Directions: The Reading Test includes multiple passages. Each passage includes multiple questions. After reading each passage, choose the best answer and fill in the corresponding bubble on your answer sheet. You may review the passages as often as necessary.

Passage I

PROSE FICTION: This passage is adapted from *The Age of Innocence*, by Edith Wharton (1920).

It was generally agreed in New York that the Countess Olenska had "lost her looks."

She had appeared there first, in Newland Archer's boyhood, as a brilliantly pretty little girl
5 of nine or ten, of whom people said that she "ought to be painted." Her parents had been continental wanderers, and after a roaming babyhood she had lost them both, and been taken in charge by her aunt, Medora Manson, also a wanderer, who was
10 herself returning to New York to "settle down."

Poor Medora, repeatedly widowed, was always coming home to settle down (each time in a less expensive house), and bringing with her a new husband or an adopted child, but after a few
15 months she invariably parted from her husband or quarrelled with her ward, and, having got rid of her house at a loss, set out again on her wanderings. As her mother had been a Rushworth, and her last unhappy marriage had linked her to one of
20 the crazy Chiverses, New York looked indulgently on her eccentricities, but when she returned with her little orphaned niece, whose parents had been popular in spite of their regrettable taste for travel, people thought it a pity that the pretty child should
25 be in such hands.

Everyone was disposed to be kind to little Ellen Mingott, though her dusky red cheeks and tight curls gave her an air of gaiety that seemed unsuitable in a child who should still have been in
30 black for her parents. It was one of the misguided Medora's many peculiarities to flout the unalterable

rules that regulated American mourning, and when she stepped from the steamer her family was scandalized to see that the crepe veil she wore for
35 her own brother was seven inches shorter than those of her sisters-in-law, while little Ellen wore a crimson dress and amber beads.

But New York had so long resigned itself to Medora that only a few old ladies shook their
40 heads over Ellen's gaudy clothes, while her other relations fell under the charm of her high spirits. She was a fearless and familiar little thing, who asked disconcerting questions, made precocious comments, and possessed outlandish arts, such
45 as dancing a Spanish shawl dance and singing Neapolitan lovesongs to a guitar. Under the direction of her aunt, the little girl received an expensive but incoherent education, which included "drawing from the model," a thing never
50 dreamed of before, and playing the piano in quintets with professional musicians.

Of course no good could come of this, and when, a few years later, poor Chivers finally died, his widow again pulled up stakes and departed
55 with Ellen, who had grown into a tall bony girl with conspicuous eyes. For some time no more was heard of them; then news came of Ellen's marriage to an immensely rich Polish nobleman of legendary fame. She disappeared, and when a few years later
60 Medora again came back to New York, subdued, impoverished, mourning a third husband, and in quest of a still smaller house, people wondered that her rich niece had not been able to do something for her. Then came the news that Ellen's own

GO ON TO THE NEXT PAGE

65 marriage had ended in disaster, and that she was
herself returning home to seek rest and oblivion
among her kinsfolk.

These things passed through Newland Archer's
mind a week later as he watched the Countess
70 Olenska enter the van der Luyden drawing room
on the evening of the momentous dinner. In the
middle of the room she paused, looking about
her with a grave mouth and smiling eyes, and in
that instant, Newland Archer rejected the general
75 verdict on her looks. It was true that her early
radiance was gone. The red cheeks had paled;
she was thin, worn, a little older-looking than
her age, which must have been nearly thirty. But
there was about her the mysterious authority of
80 beauty, a sureness in the carriage of the head, the
movement of the eyes, which, without being in the
least theatrical, struck him as highly trained and
full of a conscious power. At the same time she was
simpler in manner than most of the ladies present,
85 and many people (as he heard afterward) were
disappointed that her appearance was not more
"stylish"—for stylishness was what New York most
valued. It was, perhaps, Archer reflected, because
her early vivacity had disappeared; because she
90 was so quiet—quiet in her movements, her voice,
and the tones of her voice. New York had expected
something a good deal more resonant in a young
woman with such a history.

1. The author describes which of the following
practices as undesirable to New York society?
   A. Playing the piano
   B. Performing Spanish shawl dances
   C. Traveling
   D. Adopting children

2. With which of the following would the author
most likely agree regarding New York society as
it pertains to Medora?
   F. It is rigid and unaccepting of different
behavior.
   G. It is usually whimsical, with few solid
rules.
   H. It is often based on unrealistic
expectations.
   J. It is snobbish but occasionally accepting of
less common behavior.

3. It is most reasonable to infer that, after the death
of Medora's third husband, Ellen did not help
her aunt primarily because:
   A. Ellen was no longer wealthy, since her
own marriage had failed.
   B. Medora had become embittered because
she hadn't heard from Ellen for so long.
   C. Ellen resented the incoherent education
she received from her aunt.
   D. receiving help from her niece would
interfere with Medora's desire to be
eccentric.

GO ON TO THE NEXT PAGE

4. Based on the characterization of Newland Archer in the last paragraph, he can best be described as:

   F. reflective and nonjudgmental.

   G. likable but withdrawn.

   H. disinterested but fair.

   J. stylish and gregarious.

5. In her descriptions of Medora, the author intends to give the impression that Medora is:

   A. eccentric and peripatetic.

   B. impoverished and resentful.

   C. kind and loyal.

   D. precocious and pretty.

6. As it is used in line 31, the word *flout* most nearly means:

   F. eliminate.

   G. exemplify.

   H. disregard.

   J. float.

7. What does the narrator suggest is a central characteristic of Medora Manson?

   A. Arrogance

   B. Immodesty

   C. Nonconformity

   D. Orthodoxy

8. Which of the following characters learns to do something otherwise unheard of by New York society?

   F. Ellen Mingott

   G. Newland Archer

   H. Medora Manson

   J. Count Olenska

9. The author includes reference to Medora's mother and Medora's marriage to "one of the crazy Chiverses" (lines 19–20) in order to indicate that:

   A. she had an unhappy childhood.

   B. her eccentricities were not surprising.

   C. she was the perfect person to raise Ellen.

   D. she was a wanderer.

10. One can reasonably infer from the passage that on the occasion of the dinner, Newland and Ellen:

   F. had not seen each other for some time.

   G. were interested in becoming romantically involved.

   H. were both disappointed with New York society.

   J. had just met, but were immediately attracted to each other.

GO ON TO THE NEXT PAGE

Passage II

SOCIAL SCIENCE: The following passage is excerpted from a magazine article discussing scientific research on traditional methods of predicting the timing and character of the Indian monsoon.

Can traditional rules of thumb provide accurate weather forecasts? Researchers in Junagadh, India, are trying to find out. Most farmers in the region grow one crop of peanuts or castor per year. In a
5 wet year, peanuts give the best returns, but if the rains are poor, the more drought-tolerant castor is a better bet. In April and May, before the monsoon comes, farmers decide what to plant, buy the seed, prepare the soil and hope for the best. An accurate
10 forecast would be extremely helpful.

Little wonder, then, that observant farmers have devised traditional ways to predict the monsoon's timing and character. One such rule of thumb involves the blooming of the *Cassia fistula*
15 tree, which is common on roadsides in southern Gujarat. According to an old saying which has been documented as far back as the 8th century, the monsoon begins 45 days after *C. fistula's* flowering peak. Since 1996, Purshottambhai Kanani, an
20 agronomist at Gujarat Agricultural University, has been collecting data to test this rule. He records the flowering dates of trees all over the university's campus and plots a distribution to work out when the flowering peak occurs. While not perfect,
25 *C. fistula* has so far done an admirable job of predicting whether the monsoon will come early or late.

Similarly, with help from local farmers, Dr. Kanani has been investigating a local belief
30 regarding the direction of the wind on the day of Holi, a Hindu festival in spring. The wind direction at certain times on Holi is supposed to indicate the strength of the monsoon that year. Wind from the north or west suggests a good monsoon, whereas
35 wind from the east indicates drought. Each year before Holi, Dr. Kanani sends out postcards to more than 400 farmers in Junagadh and neighbouring districts. The farmers note the wind direction at the specified times, and then send the postcards back.

40 In years of average and above-average monsoons (1994, 1997, 1998, and 2001), the wind on Holi tended to come from the north and west. In the drier years of 1995 and 1996 the majority of farmers reported wind from the east (Dr. Kanani did not
45 conduct the study in 1999 and 2000). As with the *C. fistula* results, the predictions are not especially precise, but the trend is right.

Dr. Kanani first became interested in traditional methods in 1990, when an old saying attributed to
50 a tenth-century sage named Bhadli—that a storm on a particular day meant the monsoon would come 72 days later—proved strikingly correct. This prompted Dr. Kanani to collect other rules from old texts in Gujarati and Sanskrit.

55 Not all of his colleagues approve. Damaru Sahu, a meteorologist at Gujarat Agricultural University and a researcher for India's director-general of meteorology, says that traditional methods are "OK as a hobby." But, he goes on, they cannot be relied
60 upon, and "may not be applicable to this modern age." Yet Dr. Sahu concedes that meteorological science has failed to provide a useful alternative to traditional methods. For the past 13 years, he notes, the director-general for meteorology has
65 predicted "normal monsoon" for the country. Every year, the average rainfall over the whole country is calculated, and this prediction is proved correct. But it is no use at all to farmers who want to know what will happen in their region.

70 Dr. Kanani hopes that his research will put traditional methods on a proper scientific footing. He and his colleagues have even set up a sort of peer-review forum for traditional meteorology. Each spring, he hosts a conference for 100 local
75 traditional forecasters, each of whom presents a monsoon prediction with supporting evidence—the behaviour of a species of bird, strong flowering in a certain plant, or the prevailing wind direction that season. Dr. Kanani records these predictions and
80 publishes them in the local press.

GO ON TO THE NEXT PAGE →

548   Practice Test 6

He has also started a non-governmental organisation, the Varsha Vigyan Mandal, or Rain Science Association, which has more than 400 members. Its vice-president, Dhansukh
85 Shah, is a scientist at the National Directorate of Meteorology in Pune. By involving such mainstream meteorologists as Dr. Shah in his work, Dr. Kanani hopes to bring his unusual research to the attention of national institutions. They could
90 provide the funding for larger studies that could generate results sufficiently robust to be published in peer-reviewed science journals.

11. According to the passage, all of the following traditional methods of weather prediction have been scientifically tested EXCEPT:

   A. wind direction during the Hindi festival of Holi.

   B. the behavior of certain bird species.

   C. the flowering *Cassia fistula* trees.

   D. a tenth-century prediction connecting storm activity to later monsoons.

12. The author uses the phrase "useful alternative" (line 62) in order to show that:

   F. modern meteorology rarely provides an accurate forecast.

   G. equipment needed for accurate forecasting is too expensive for many in India.

   H. modern meteorology doesn't give as reliable predictions as traditional methods do.

   J. today's science is not yet able to provide specific meteorological forecasts needed by farmers.

13. According to the passage, a good monsoon is associated with winds from the:

   A. north.

   B. south.

   C. east.

   D. southwest.

14. The author's attitude toward traditional methods of weather forecasting may reasonably be described as:

   F. curious as to their development.

   G. cautious hopefulness that they are useful.

   H. skeptical regarding their real scientific value.

   J. regretful of the fad of interest in these methods.

15. According to the passage, which of the discussed methods gives the most advanced prediction of monsoon arrival?

   A. The behavior of the birds

   B. The flowering of the *C. fistula* tree

   C. The wind direction on Holi

   D. Bhadli's prediction based on storms

16. The function of the second paragraph in relation to the passage as a whole is most likely to provide:

   F. a reason that farmers need techniques to predict monsoons earlier.

   G. examples of the inexact nature of predictions made from traditional methods.

   H. an explanation of the ancient saying that the rest of the passage will examine.

   J. an introduction to the modern research of traditional methods.

GO ON TO THE NEXT PAGE

Practice Test 6

17. According to the passage, the purpose of Dr. Kanani's springtime conferences is to:

    A. record the traditional methods of weather prediction before they disappear.

    B. help gain acceptance for traditional methods in the academic community.

    C. publish the methods in the local press.

    D. facilitate the exchange of ideas between farmers from far-flung regions of India.

18. According to the passage, the reason farmers use traditional methods to predict the weather is that:

    F. traditional methods are more accessible to rural populations.

    G. "normal" monsoons can still be very different from each other.

    H. they need to anticipate the local conditions for the coming growing season.

    J. traditional methods get the basic trends right.

19. The author uses the term "admirable job" (line 25) to indicate that:

    A. the flowering of the *C. fistula* tree provides remarkably predictive data on the coming monsoon.

    B. precision isn't everything.

    C. predictions based on the peak of *C. fistula*'s flowering do provide some reliable answers.

    D. sometimes rules of thumb are better than complex formulas.

20. According to Damaru Sahu, traditional weather prediction:

    F. can be curiously accurate.

    G. has a defined place in meteorology.

    H. is useful in some ways despite its lack of scientific foundation.

    J. appeals to an instinct different than the rational brain.

GO ON TO THE NEXT PAGE

Passage III

HUMANITIES: One of the most enjoyable ways to analyze culture is through music. By analyzing musical styles and lyrics, one can explore quintessential characteristics of particular cultures.

Passage A

Country music has its roots in the southern portions of the United States, specifically in the remote and undeveloped backcountry of the central and southern areas of the Appalachian

5 mountain range. Recognized as a distinct cultural region since the late nineteenth century, the area became home to European settlements in the eighteenth century, primarily led by Ulster Scots from Ireland. Early inhabitants have been

10 characterized as fiercely independent, to the point of rudeness and inhospitality. It was in this area that the region's truly indigenous music, now known as country music, was born.

Rooted in spirituals as well as folk music,

15 cowboy songs, and traditional Celtic melodies, country music originated in the 1920s. The motifs are generally ballads and dance tunes, simple in form and accompanied mostly by guitar, banjo, and violin. Though today there are many genres of

20 country music, all have their roots in this mélange of sources.

The term "country" has replaced the original pejorative term, "hillbilly." Hillbillies referred to Appalachian inhabitants who were considered poor,

25 uneducated, isolated, and wary; the name change reflects a more accepting characterization of these mountain dwellers.

Hank Williams put country music on the map nationally, and is credited with the movement of

30 country music from the South to more national prominence. Other early innovators include the Carter family, Ernest Tubb, Woody Guthrie, Loretta Lynn, and Bill Monroe, father of bluegrass music. More recently, Faith Hill, Reba

35 McEntire, and Shania Twain have carried on the tradition.

What might be considered the "home base" of country music is in Nashville, Tennessee, and the legendary music hall, the Grand Ole Opry. Founded

40 in 1925 by George D. Hay, it had its genesis in the pioneer radio station WSM's program *Barn Dance*. Country singers are considered to have reached the pinnacle of the profession if they are asked to become members of the Opry. While noted

45 country music performers and acts take the stage at the Opry numerous times, Elvis Presley performed there only once, in 1954. His act was so poorly received that it was suggested he return to his job as a truck driver.

50 The offshoots and relatives of country music highlight the complexity of this genre. In a move away from its mountain origins, and turning a focus to the West, honky-tonk music became popular in the early twentieth century. Its name is

55 a reference to its roots in honky-tonk bars, where the music was played. Additionally, Western Swing emerged as one of the first genres to blend country and jazz musical styles, which required a great deal of skill and creativity. Some of the most talented

60 and sophisticated musicians performing in any genre were musicians who played in bluegrass string bands, another relative of country music.

Country music has always been an expression of American identity. Its sound, lyrics, and performers

65 are purely American, and though the music now has an international audience, it remains American in its heart and soul.

Passage B

A style of music closely related to country is the similarly indigenous music known as

70 bluegrass, which originated in the Appalachian highland regions extending westwards to the Ozark Mountains in southern Missouri and northern Arkansas. Derived from the music brought over by European settlers of the region,

75 bluegrass is a mixture of Scottish, Welsh, Irish,

> GO ON TO THE NEXT PAGE

and English melodic forms, infused, over time, with African-American influences. Indeed, many bluegrass songs, such as "Barbara Allen" and "House Carpenter" preserve their European roots,
80 maintaining the traditional musical style and narratives almost intact. Story-telling ballads, often laments, are common themes. Given the predominance of coal mining in the Appalachian region, it is not surprising that ballads relating to
85 mining tragedies are also common.

   Unlike country music, in which musicians commonly play the same melodies together, bluegrass highlights one player at a time, with the others providing accompaniment. This tradition of
90 each musician taking turns with solos, and often improvising, can also be seen in jazz ensembles. Traditional bluegrass music is typically played on instruments such as banjo, guitar, mandolin, bass, harmonica, and Dobro (resonator guitar).
95 Even household objects, including washboards and spoons, have, from time to time, been drafted for use as instruments. Vocals also differ from country music in that, rather than featuring a single voice, bluegrass incorporates baritone and tenor
100 harmonies.

   Initially included under the catch-all phrase "folk music," and later referred to as "hillbilly," bluegrass did not come into his own category until the late 1950s, and appeared first in the
105 comprehensive guide, *Music Index*, in 1965. Presumably it was named after Bill Monroe's Blue Grass band, the seminal bluegrass band. A rapid, almost frenetic pace, characterizes bluegrass tempos. Even today, decades after their most
110 active performing era, The Foggy Mountain Boys members Lester Flatt, a bluegrass guitarist and mandolinist, and Earl Scruggs, known for his three-finger banjo picking style, are widely considered the foremost artists on their instruments.
115   Partially because of its pace and complexity, bluegrass has often been recorded for movie soundtracks. "Dueling Banjos," played in the movie *Deliverance*, exemplifies the skill required by the feverish tempo of the genre. The soundtrack for

120 *O Brother, Where Art Thou?* incorporates bluegrass and its musical cousins folk, country, gospel, and blues. Bluegrass festivals are held throughout the country and as far away as the Czech Republic. Interactive, often inviting audience participation, they feature performers
125 such as Dolly Parton and Alison Krauss.

   Central to bluegrass music are the themes of the working class—miners, railroad workers, farmers. The phrase "high, lonesome sound" was coined to represent the bluegrass undertones of intensity and cheerlessness,
130 symbolizing the hard-scrabble life of the American worker. As with so much of a nation's traditional music, and for better or worse, bluegrass music reflects America.

> ## Questions 21–23 ask about Passage A.

21. According to the passage, country music originated from all of the following EXCEPT:

   A. Celtic melodies.

   B. spirituals.

   C. jazz.

   D. cowboy songs.

22. Which of the following would be the most logical place to hear the best of country music?

   F. Honky-tonk bars

   G. Ireland

   H. The Appalachian backcountry

   J. The Grand Ole Opry

23. As it is used in line 23, the word *pejorative* most nearly means:

   A. traditional.

   B. accurate.

   C. disparaging.

   D. mountain dwelling.

GO ON TO THE NEXT PAGE

Questions 24–26 ask about Passage B.

24. If a song were a lament with Welsh and African-American derivation, the author of Passage B would classify it as:

F. bluegrass.

G. country.

H. jazz.

J. hillbilly.

25. According to the passage, the instruments played in bluegrass music are:

A. both typical and unusual.

B. derived from African-American influences.

C. made famous by the piece "Dueling Banjos."

D. restricted to those used in the Ozarks.

26. In addition to highlighting one player at a time, bluegrass music differs from country music because it often:

F. features harmonies sung by bass and tenor voices.

G. features a single voice.

H. is characterized by musicians commonly playing the same melodies together.

J. is played on instruments such as the banjo and guitar.

Questions 27–30 ask about both passages.

27. It can be inferred that laments and high, lonesome sounds both reflect:

A. the influence of Irish music.

B. the challenges of American life.

C. songs sung by Shania Twain.

D. hillbilly music.

28. As it is used in the introductory information, *quintessential* most nearly means:

F. old-fashioned.

G. representative.

H. charming.

J. unconventional.

29. Passage A states that there were "talented and sophisticated" (lines 59–60) musicians playing bluegrass music. Which sentence in Passage B suggests this claim?

A. "Central to bluegrass music are the themes of the working class—miners, railroad workers, farmers."

B. "Partially because of its pace and complexity, bluegrass has often been recorded for movie soundtracks."

C. "Lester Flatt, a bluegrass guitarist and mandolinist, and Earl Scruggs, known for his three-finger banjo picking style, are widely considered the foremost artists on their instruments."

D. "A style of music closely related to country is the similarly indigenous music known as bluegrass . . ."

30. It can be inferred that both authors would agree that:

F. country and bluegrass music are popular genres.

G. both genres—country and bluegrass—are showcased at the Grand Ole Opry.

H. music genres can evolve.

J. country and bluegrass music are gaining in acceptance.

GO ON TO THE NEXT PAGE

Passage IV

NATURAL SCIENCE: The following passage appeared in *Science* magazine as "Pluto: The Planet That Never Was" by Govert Schilling. (© *Science*, Inc., 1999)

Nearly 70 years ago, Pluto became the ninth member of the sun's family of planets, but now it's on the verge of being cast out of that exclusive clan. The International Astronomical Union (IAU)
5 is collecting votes on how to reclassify the icy body: as the first (and largest) of the so-called trans-Neptunian objects, or as the 10,000th entry in the growing list of minor bodies orbiting the sun. In either case, Pluto may officially lose its planetary
10 status, leaving the solar system with only eight planets.

Children's books and planetariums may not acknowledge the loss. And Brian Marsden of the Harvard-Smithsonian Center for Astrophysics
15 in Cambridge, Massachusetts, who launched the discussion six years ago, says no one is trying to demote Pluto. "If anything, we're going to add to Pluto's status," he says, "by giving it the honor of a very special designation."

20 Cold comfort for Pluto, maybe, but its reclassification will at least end a long identity crisis, which began soon after its 1930 discovery at Lowell Observatory in Flagstaff, Arizona, by Clyde Tombaugh, who died in 1997. Pluto turned
25 out to be much smaller than all the other planets (according to recent estimates, its diameter is only 2200 kilometers), and its orbit is strangely elongated. It didn't belong with either the Earth-like rocky planets or the gas giants.

30 A clue to its true nature came in 1992, when David Jewitt of the University of Hawaii, Honolulu, and Jane Luu, then at the University of California, Berkeley, discovered a small, icy object beyond the orbit of Neptune. Provisionally cataloged as
35 1992 QB1, this ice dwarf measures a mere 200 kilometers in diameter. Since then many more trans-Neptunian objects (TNOs) have been detected, some of which move in very Pluto-like orbits around the sun.

40 These "supercomets" populate the Kuiper Belt, named after Dutch-American astronomer Gerard Kuiper, who predicted its existence in the early 1950s. "Pluto fits the picture [of the solar system] much better if it's viewed as a TNO," says Luu, who
45 is now at Leiden University in the Netherlands.

At present, more than 70 TNOs are known, and apparently, Pluto is just the largest member of this new family, which explains why it was found more than 60 years before number two. If astronomers
50 had known about the other TNOs back in the 1930s, Pluto would never have attained the status of a planet, Luu says: "Pluto was lucky."

A couple of months ago, the kinship between Pluto and the TNOs led Richard Binzel of the
55 Massachusetts Institute of Technology to propose that Pluto be made the first entry in a new catalog of TNOs for which precise orbits have been determined. It would then enter the textbooks as something like TN-1 (or TN-0, as some
60 astronomers have suggested).

Marsden agrees that Pluto is a TNO, but he doesn't like the idea of establishing a new catalog of solar system objects, arguing that astronomers already have a perfectly serviceable
65 list of numbered minor bodies (mostly asteroids). "The question is: Do we want to recognize [trans-Neptunian objects] with a different designation?" he asks. He points out that the Centaurs—TNOs that have been nudged well inside Neptune's
70 orbit—have been classified as asteroids and says he sees "no reason for introducing a new designation system for objects of which we have representations in the current [catalog of minor bodies]."

Instead of making Pluto the founding member
75 of a new catalog, Marsden wants to add it to the existing list. "The current number is 9826," he says. "With the current detection rate, we should arrive at number 10,000 somewhere in January or February." He notes that asteroids 1000, 2000,
80 3000, and so on have all been honored by the IAU

GO ON TO THE NEXT PAGE

with special names, including Leonardo and Isaac Newton. "What better way to honor Pluto than to give it this very special number?"

But the prospect of lumping Pluto with the solar
85 system's riffraff outrages supporters of a new TNO category. "It's the most idiotic thing" she's ever heard, says Luu. "Pluto is certainly not an asteroid," she says.

To try to settle the issue, Mike A'Hearn of the
90 University of Maryland, College Park, is collecting e-mail votes from 500 or so members of IAU divisions on the solar system, comets and asteroids, and other relevant topics. "I wanted to arrive at a consensus before Christmas [1998]," he says,
95 "but it may take a while, since the community as a whole doesn't seem to have a consensus." Neither proposal has attracted a majority. Although many people opposed Marsden's proposal, a comparable number were unhappy with Binzel's idea, A'Hearn
100 says, because Pluto would still be an anomaly, being much larger than the other trans-Neptunian objects. A'Hearn says that if no consensus can be reached, Pluto will probably not end up in any catalog at all, making it the ultimate outcast of the
105 solar system.

However the debate settles out, Pluto's career as a planet seems to be ending, and even astronomers are wistful at the prospect. "No one likes to lose a planet," says Luu. A'Hearn agrees. "It will probably
110 always be called the ninth planet" by the general public, he says.

31. According to the passage, regarding the view that Pluto should be categorized as an asteroid, Jane Luu expressed which of the following?

A. Shock

B. Excitement

C. Confusion

D. Forceful opposition

32. It can be inferred that Pluto's original designation as a planet would have never happened if scientists had:

F. understood its size from the beginning.

G. seen the icy core of Pluto sooner.

H. been able to detect the many smaller TNOs when Pluto was discovered.

J. understood the popular misconceptions about Pluto's planethood that would follow.

33. With which of the following statements would the author agree in regard to reclassifying Pluto?

A. It should be classified as a TNO.

B. It should be classified as an IAU.

C. It should remain a planet.

D. Its future classification is unclear.

34. According to the passage, large objects similar to the makeup and orbit of Pluto found nearer to the sun than Neptune are called:

F. Centaurs.

G. IAUs.

H. TNOs.

J. ice dwarves.

GO ON TO THE NEXT PAGE

35. According to lines 66–73, the central issue in the debate over Pluto is:

    A. whether Pluto is more similar to the rocky planets or the gas giants.

    B. the distance of Pluto from the sun.

    C. whether or not the unique qualities of Pluto warrant the creation of a new classification category for all TNOs.

    D. scientists' conception of Pluto versus the view of the general public.

36. As used in line 64, the term *serviceable* most nearly means:

    F. able to be fixed.

    G. adequate.

    H. beneficial.

    J. durable.

37. One slightly less scientific concern expressed by most of the scientists in the passage is:

    A. the role of the IAU in making classification decisions.

    B. respect for the views of the public.

    C. who gets the credit for Pluto's reclassification.

    D. the preservation of Pluto's fame and importance.

38. According to the passage, what is the major reason for lack of consensus regarding the status of Pluto?

    F. The general population resists the scientific community's belief that Pluto is not a planet.

    G. Pluto seems very different than the other members of any classification.

    H. Pluto's strange orbit makes it asteroid-like, but its surface more closely resembles a planet.

    J. There have been numerous discoveries of other Pluto-like objects nearer to the sun than to Neptune.

39. Details in the passage suggest that Pluto is much different from other planets in:

    A. its distance from the sun and the shape of its orbit.

    B. its size and the shape of its orbit.

    C. the year of its discovery and its size.

    D. its shape and surface composition.

40. Pluto's size accounts for:

    F. its classification as a TNO.

    G. its dissimilarity to asteroids.

    H. its early discovery relative to other TNOs.

    J. its bizarre orbit.

Practice Test 6

SCIENCE TEST

35 Minutes—40 Questions

Directions: The Science Test includes multiple passages. Each passage includes multiple questions. After reading each passage, choose the best answer and fill in the corresponding bubble on your answer sheet. You may review the passages as often as necessary.

You may NOT use a calculator on this test.

Passage I

Soil, by volume, consists on average of 45% minerals, 25% water, 25% air, and 5% organic matter (including both living and nonliving organisms). Time and topography shape the composition of soil and cause it to develop into layers known as *horizons*. The soil horizons in a particular area are collectively known as the *soil profile*. The composition of soil varies in each horizon, as do the most common minerals, as can be seen in the soil profile depicted in Diagram 1. Diagram 1 also shows the depth of each horizon and the overall density of the soil.

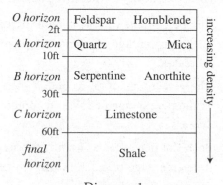

Diagram 1

Table 1 lists the zinc and calcium contents (as percentages) in the minerals that compose soil.

Table 1		
Mineral	Zinc content (%)	Calcium content (%)
Feldspar	35–40	0–10
Hornblende	30–35	10–20
Quartz	25–30	20–30
Mica	20–25	30–40
Serpentine	15–20	40–50
Anorthite	10–15	50–60
Limestone	5–10	60–70
Shale	0–5	70–80

Table 2 shows the average percentage of minerals that compose granite and sandstone, two rock types that are commonly found in soil.

Table 2		
Mineral	Percentage of mineral in:	
	Sandstone	Granite
Feldspar	30	54
Hornblende	2	0
Quartz	50	33
Mica	10	10
Serpentine	0	0
Anorthite	0	0
Limestone	5	0
Shale	0	0
Augite	3	3

GO ON TO THE NEXT PAGE

1. An analysis of an unknown mineral found in soil revealed its zinc content to be 32% and its calcium content to be 12%. Based on the data in Table 1, geologists would most likely classify this mineral as:

   A. hornblende.

   B. anorthite.

   C. serpentine.

   D. mica.

2. Geologists digging down into the A horizon would most likely find which of the following minerals?

   F. Limestone

   G. Shale

   H. Serpentine

   J. Mica

3. Based on the data presented in Diagram 1 and Table 1, which of the following statements best describes the relationship between the zinc content of a mineral and the depth below surface level at which it is dominant? As zinc content increases:

   A. depth increases.

   B. depth decreases.

   C. depth first increases, then decreases.

   D. depth first decreases, then increases.

4. If geologists were to drill 30 feet into the Earth, which of the following minerals would they most likely encounter?

   F. Quartz, mica, and limestone

   G. Feldspar, shale, and serpentine

   H. Feldspar, quartz, and anorthite

   J. Hornblende, limestone, and serpentine

5. If augite is most commonly found in soil in close proximity to the other minerals that make up granite, then augite would most likely be found at a depth of:

   A. less than 10 feet.

   B. between 10 feet and 30 feet.

   C. between 30 feet and 60 feet.

   D. greater than 60 feet.

6. Based on the passage, how is the percentage of zinc content related to the percentage of calcium content in the minerals that make up soil?

   F. The percentage of zinc content increases as the percentage of calcium content increases.

   G. The percentage of zinc content increases as the percentage of calcium content decreases.

   H. Both the percentage of zinc content and the percentage of calcium content remain constant.

   J. There is no discernible relationship between the percentage of zinc content and the percentage of calcium content.

GO ON TO THE NEXT PAGE

Passage II

Students conducted the following studies to determine the melting points of several materials. They attempted to melt the materials by submerging them in a variety of aqueous solutions that were heated to their boiling points. They used the following equation to calculate the boiling points of these solutions:

$$\Delta T_b = K_b \times m \times i,$$

where

ΔT_b = increase in boiling point above pure solvent

K_b = $0.512 \dfrac{°C \times kg}{mol}$

m = molality = $\dfrac{mol \; solute}{kg \; solvent}$

i = number of ions present per molecule of solute

Study 1

In order to prepare various solutions of sodium chloride (NaCl), 100.00 g of H_2O were added to a beaker. A known quantity of NaCl was dissolved into the water and the resulting boiling point of the solution was recorded. This procedure was repeated with different amounts of NaCl as shown in Table 1.

	Table 1		
Solution	Mass of H_2O (g)	Amount of NaCl (mol)	Boiling point (°C)
1	100.00	0	100.00
2	100.00	0.085	100.88
3	100.00	0.171	101.75
4	100.00	0.257	102.63
5	100.00	0.342	103.50

Study 2

In order to prepare various solutions of calcium chloride ($CaCl_2$), 100.00 g of H_2O were added to a beaker. A known quantity of $CaCl_2$ was dissolved into the water and the resulting boiling point of the solution was recorded. This procedure was repeated with different amounts of $CaCl_2$ as shown in Table 2.

	Table 2		
Solution	Mass of H_2O (g)	Amount of $CaCl_2$ (mol)	Boiling point (°C)
6	100.00	0.270	104.15
7	100.00	0.360	105.53
8	100.00	0.450	106.91
9	100.00	0.541	108.29
10	100.00	0.631	109.67

Study 3

Each solution from Studies 1 and 2 was brought to a boil. A small sample of a material was placed in each solution. If the material melted, a "Y" was marked in Table 3. If the material did not melt, an "N" was marked in Table 3. This procedure was repeated for all eight materials.

	Table 3									
	Solution									
Material	1	2	3	4	5	6	7	8	9	10
1	Y	Y	Y	Y	Y	Y	Y	Y	Y	Y
2	N	Y	Y	Y	Y	Y	Y	Y	Y	Y
3	N	N	Y	Y	Y	Y	Y	Y	Y	Y
4	N	N	N	N	Y	Y	Y	Y	Y	Y
5	N	N	N	N	N	Y	Y	Y	Y	Y
6	N	N	N	N	N	N	N	Y	Y	Y
7	N	N	N	N	N	N	N	N	N	Y
8	N	N	N	N	N	N	N	N	N	N

GO ON TO THE NEXT PAGE

Practice Test 6

7. Which of the following modifications to Solution 5 of Study 1 would result in an increase in its boiling point?

   I. Increasing the K_b of the solution

   II. Increasing the amount of NaCl

   III. Replacing the NaCl with an equal amount of $CaCl_2$

   A. I only

   B. I and II only

   C. II and III only

   D. I, II, and III

8. In Study 1, what was the boiling point of the solution with 0.171 mol of NaCl ?

   F. 100.00°C

   G. 100.88°C

   H. 101.75°C

   J. 109.67°C

9. Based on the results of the studies from the passage, the boiling point of Material 5 is most likely:

   A. less than 102.63°C.

   B. between 102.63°C and 103.50°C.

   C. between 103.50°C and 104.15°C.

   D. greater than 104.15°C.

10. If a sixth solution had been prepared during Study 2 using 0.721 mol $CaCl_2$, its boiling point would most likely be closest to which of the following?

    F. 108.75°C

    G. 111.07°C

    H. 113.72°C

    J. 115.02°C

11. A ninth material was submerged in Solutions 1–6 as in Experiment 3. Which of the following is LEAST likely to be a plausible set of results for this material?

	Solution					
	1	2	3	4	5	6
A.	Y	Y	Y	Y	N	N
B.	Y	Y	Y	Y	Y	Y
C.	N	N	N	N	Y	Y
D.	N	N	N	N	N	N

    A. A

    B. B

    C. C

    D. D

12. Which of the following best explains why the students recorded data for their solutes in mol rather than g or kg ?

    F. The H_2O was already measured in kg.

    G. The units for mass are less accurate.

    H. The change in boiling point depends on molality.

    J. The melting points of the various materials do not depend on the masses of the materials.

13. Would the results of Studies 1–3 support the claim that Material 7 has a lower melting point than Material 8 ?

    A. Yes, because in Solution 10, Material 7 melted and Material 8 did not.

    B. Yes, because in Solution 10, Material 8 melted and Material 7 did not.

    C. No, because the melting point of Material 8 cannot be determined from the data.

    D. No, because the melting point of Material 7 cannot be determined from the data.

GO ON TO THE NEXT PAGE

Passage III

Engineers designing a roadway needed to test the composition of the soil that would form the roadbed. In order to determine whether their two sampling systems (System A and System B) give sufficiently accurate soil composition measurements, they first conducted a study to compare the two systems.

Soil samples were taken with varying levels of *humidity* (concentration of water). The concentrations of the compounds that form the majority of soil were measured. The results for the sampling systems were compared with data on file with the US Geological Survey (USGS), which compiles extremely accurate data. The engineers' and USGS' results are presented in Table 1 below.

Table 1					
Concentration (mg/L) of:	Level of Humidity				
	10%	25%	45%	65%	80%
Nitrogen (N)					
USGS	105	236	598	781	904
System A	112	342	716	953	1,283
System B	196	408	857	1,296	1,682
Potassium Oxide (K_2O)					
USGS	9.4	9.1	8.9	8.7	8.2
System A	9.4	9.0	8.7	8.5	8.0
System B	9.5	9.2	9.0	8.8	8.3
Calcium (Ca)					
USGS	39.8	24.7	11.4	5.0	44.8
System A	42.5	31.4	10.4	8.0	42.9
System B	37.1	23.2	11.6	11.1	45.1
Phosphorus Oxide (P_2O_5)					
USGS	69.0	71.2	74.8	78.9	122.3
System A	67.9	69.9	72.2	76.7	123.1
System B	74.0	75.6	78.7	82.1	126.3
Zinc (Zn)					
USGS	0.41	0.52	0.64	0.74	0.70
System A	0.67	0.80	0.88	0.97	0.93
System B	0.38	0.48	0.62	0.77	0.73

Note: Each system concentration measurement is the average of 5 measurements.

GO ON TO THE NEXT PAGE

14. The hypothesis that increasing humidity increases the concentration of a compound is supported by the results for each of the following EXCEPT:

    F. nitrogen.

    G. potassium oxide.

    H. phosphorus oxide.

    J. zinc.

15. At a humidity level of 25%, it could be concluded that System B LEAST accurately measures the concentration of which of the following compounds, relative to the data on file with the USGS?

    A. N

    B. Ca

    C. K_2O

    D. P_2O_5

16. The engineers hypothesized that the concentration of potassium oxide (K_2O) decreases as the level of humidity increases. This hypothesis is supported by:

    F. the data from the USGS only.

    G. the System A measurements only.

    H. the data from the USGS and the System B measurements only.

    J. the data from the USGS, the System A measurements, and the System B measurements.

17. Do the results in Table 1 support the conclusion that System B is more accurate than System A for measuring the concentration of zinc?

    A. No, because the zinc measurements from System A are consistently higher than the zinc measurements from System B.

    B. No, because the zinc measurements from System A are closer to the data provided by the USGS than the zinc measurements from System B.

    C. Yes, because the zinc measurements from System B are consistently lower than the zinc measurements from System A.

    D. Yes, because the zinc measurements from System B are closer to the data provided by the USGS than the zinc measurements from System A.

GO ON TO THE NEXT PAGE

18. The relationship between humidity level and calcium concentration, as measured by System B, is best represented by which of the following graphs?

    F.

    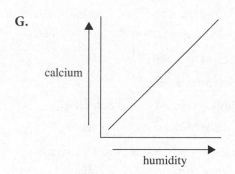

    G.

    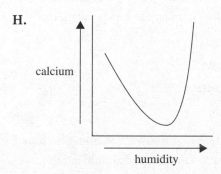

    H.

    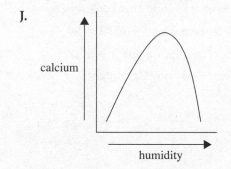

    J.

19. After conducting their comparisons, the engineers used System B to test a soil sample at the future road site. They measured the concentrations, in mg/L, of selected compounds in the sample and found that they were: potassium oxide = 9.1, calcium = 17.3, and zinc = 0.57. Based on the data in Table 1, the engineers should predict that the level of humidity is approximately:

    A. 16%.

    B. 37%.

    C. 49%.

    D. 57%.

GO ON TO THE NEXT PAGE

Practice Test 6   **563**

Passage IV

Diabetes is a metabolic disorder that causes hyperglycemia (higher-than-normal blood glucose levels). The most common form is type 2 diabetes, which occurs when the body does not produce enough insulin or has a lowered level of response to insulin (insulin resistance). Insulin is a hormone produced in the pancreas that helps regulate blood glucose levels by stimulating cells to absorb and metabolize glucose. Typically occurring in adults, type 2 diabetes has developed in an increasing number of individuals over 45 years old. Three scientists offered hypotheses to explain the cause of type 2 diabetes.

Scientist 1

Studies have shown that the consumption of sugar-sweetened drinks in excess is associated with an increased risk of type 2 diabetes. Thus, the cause of type 2 diabetes is an overconsumption of sugar. When sugar intake is high, the insulin in the body is unable to normalize the increased blood glucose levels. In a study of individuals 18–25 years old who consumed more than the daily recommended amount of sugar, although their insulin levels were normal, their blood glucose levels were significantly elevated. When these individuals received small injections of supplemental insulin once a day, their blood sugar did not return to normal levels.

Scientist 2

Type 2 diabetes primarily occurs as a result of obesity and lack of exercise. Experimental data have shown that diets high in fat but not high in sugar are associated with an increased risk of type 2 diabetes. In a study of healthy young men, those put on a high-fat diet had twice the blood glucose levels compared to those put on a high-carbohydrate diet. Excess fat in the bloodstream breaks down into free radicals that impair insulin action, causing cells to become insulin resistant and blood glucose levels to rise. Studies have also shown that the lack of exercise causes 7% of type 2 diabetes cases. Regular exercise can boost the body's efficiency to regulate blood glucose levels.

Scientist 3

Type 2 diabetes is not caused by lifestyle or diet but inherited. Studies have shown an increased risk of type 2 diabetes in people with a parent or sibling who has type 2 diabetes. More than 36 genes that contribute to the risk of type 2 diabetes have been found. Individuals have about a 15–20% chance of developing type 2 diabetes if one of their parents has it and a roughly 50% chance if both parents have it. The chance of siblings having type 2 diabetes is 25–50%.

20. The liver helps to regulate the amounts of glucose, protein, and fat in the blood. About eighty percent of people with diabetes have buildup of fat in the liver. This information, if true, would strengthen the viewpoint of:

    F. Scientist 1 only.
    G. Scientist 2 only.
    H. both Scientist 1 and Scientist 2.
    J. neither Scientist 1 nor Scientist 2.

21. Scientists 1 and 2 would most likely agree that the occurrence of type 2 diabetes in an individual is associated with the patient's:

    A. lifestyle.
    B. diet.
    C. genetics.
    D. age.

22. According to the passage, adults who have had their pancreas removed should exhibit:

    F. increased blood insulin levels.
    G. decreased blood sugar levels.
    H. increased blood sugar levels.
    J. decreased body fat content.

GO ON TO THE NEXT PAGE

23. Suppose that an individual had an 18% chance of developing type 2 diabetes. Based on the passage, Scientist 3 would most likely predict that this individual has:

    A. a high-sugar diet.

    B. a high-fat diet.

    C. one parent with type 2 diabetes.

    D. two parents with type 2 diabetes.

24. Suppose a 50-year-old patient developed type 2 diabetes. Which of the following statements is most consistent with the information in the passage?

    F. Scientist 1 would conclude that the patient consumes excess fat daily.

    G. Scientist 2 would conclude that the patient has a high-sugar diet.

    H. Scientist 3 would conclude that the patient fails to exercise.

    J. Scientist 3 would conclude that the patient had at least one parent with type 2 diabetes.

25. Which of the following discoveries, if accurate, would support the viewpoint of Scientist 1 ?

    A. High intake of sugar causes insulin resistance.

    B. High intake of fat causes impaired insulin action.

    C. Low intake of sugar causes increased insulin production.

    D. Low intake of sugar causes increased free radical production.

26. Which of the following arguments could Scientist 3 use as an effective counter to Scientist 2's claim that lack of exercise causes 7% of type 2 diabetes cases?

    F. The 7% that lacked exercise also have family histories of type 2 diabetes.

    G. More than 36 genes that contribute to the risk of type 2 diabetes have been found.

    H. The 7% that lacked exercise did not receive insulin injections.

    J. Scientist 2's hypothesis would suggest that more than 7% of type 2 diabetes cases should be due to lack of exercise.

GO ON TO THE NEXT PAGE

Practice Test 6

Passage V

Human blood is composed of approximately 45% *formed elements*, including blood cells, and 50% plasma. The formed elements of blood are further broken down into red blood cells, white blood cells, and platelets. The mass of a particular blood sample is determined by the ratio of formed elements to plasma; the formed elements weigh approximately 1.10 grams per milliliter (g/mL) and plasma approximately 1.02 g/mL. This ratio varies according to an individual's diet, health, and genetic makeup.

The following studies were performed by a phlebotomist to determine the composition and mass of blood samples from three different individuals, each of whom was required to fast overnight before the samples were taken.

Study 1

A 10-mL blood sample was taken from each of the three patients. The densities of the blood samples were measured using the *oscillator technique*, which determines fluid densities by measuring sound velocity transmission.

Study 2

Each 10-mL blood sample was spun for 20 minutes in a centrifuge to force the heavier formed elements to separate from the plasma. The plasma was then siphoned off and its mass recorded.

Study 3

The formed elements left over from Study 2 were analyzed using the same centrifuge, except this time they were spun at a slower speed for 45 minutes so that the red blood cells, white blood cells, and platelets could separate out. The mass of each element was then recorded. The results of the three studies are shown in Table 1.

Table 1					
Patient	Plasma (g)	Red blood cells (g)	White blood cells (g)	Platelets (g)	Total density (g/mL)
A	4.54	2.75	1.09	1.32	1.056
B	4.54	2.70	1.08	1.35	1.054
C	4.64	2.65	1.08	1.34	1.050

27. The results of the studies indicate that the blood sample with the lowest density is the sample with the most:

   A. plasma.

   B. red blood cells.

   C. white blood cells.

   D. platelets.

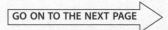
GO ON TO THE NEXT PAGE

28. Which of the following offers the most reasonable explanation for why the phlebotomist required each patient to fast overnight before taking blood samples?

F. It is more difficult to withdraw blood from patients who have not fasted.

G. Fasting causes large, temporary changes in the composition of blood.

H. Fasting ensures that blood samples are not affected by temporary changes caused by consuming different foods.

J. Blood from patients who have not fasted will not separate when spun in a centrifuge.

29. Which of the following best explains why the amount of plasma, red blood cells, white blood cells, and platelets do not add up to 10.50 g in Patient C ?

A. Some of the red blood cells might have remained in the plasma, yielding low red blood cell measurements.

B. Some of the platelets might not have separated from the white blood cells, yielding high white blood cell counts.

C. The centrifuge might have failed to fully separate the plasma from the formed elements.

D. There are likely components other than plasma, red and white blood cells, and platelets in blood.

30. Based on the data collected from the studies, it is reasonable to conclude that, as total blood density increases, the mass of red blood cells:

F. increases only.

G. increases, then decreases.

H. decreases only.

J. decreases, then increases.

31. Suppose that a 10-mL blood sample from a fourth individual contains approximately 5 mL of plasma and approximately 5 mL of formed elements. The mass of this blood sample would most likely be:

A. less than 10.0 g.

B. between 10.0 and 12.0 g.

C. between 12.0 and 14.0 g.

D. greater than 14.0 g.

32. The phlebotomist varied which of the following techniques between Study 2 and Study 3 ?

F. The volume of blood taken from each patient

G. The mass of blood taken from each patient

H. The instrument used to separate the elements of the blood samples

J. The amount of time the samples were left in the centrifuge

33. The patient with the greatest mass of red blood cells is:

A. Patient A.

B. Patient B.

C. Patient C.

D. not possible to determine from the information given.

GO ON TO THE NEXT PAGE

Passage VI

A student performed experiments to determine the relationship between the amount of electrical current carried by a material and the physical dimensions and temperature of a sample of that material. Current is measured in amperes (A) and the resistance to the flow of current is measured in ohms (Ω). Current and resistance are related to voltage, measured in volts (V), by Ohm's law: $V = A \times \Omega$. (Note that Ohm's law can also be written as $V = I \times R$, where V is voltage, I is current, and R is resistance.)

Experiment 1

The student used several lengths of an iron rod with a 1-cm diameter. The rods were heated or cooled to the specified temperatures and used to complete the circuit shown in Diagram 1. The circuit contains a battery and an ammeter, which measures current in milliamperes (mA). The results are presented in Table 1.

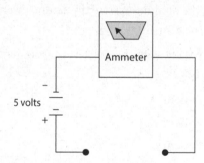

Diagram 1

Table 1			
Trial	Length (cm)	Temperature (°C)	Current (mA)
1	16	80	20
2	16	20	40
3	12	80	27
4	12	20	53
5	10	80	32
6	10	20	64
7	8	80	40
8	8	20	80

Experiment 2

The student then repeated the experiment, this time using 1-cm diameter rods made from either iron or copper. The results are presented in Table 2.

Table 2				
Trial	Material	Length (cm)	Temperature (°C)	Current (mA)
9	Iron	16	80	20
10	Copper	16	80	100
11	Iron	16	20	40
12	Copper	16	20	200
13	Iron	12	80	27
14	Copper	12	80	135
15	Iron	12	20	53
16	Copper	12	20	265

34. Based on the experimental results, which of the following most accurately describes the relationships between current and rod length and between current and temperature?

   F. Current is directly related to length and inversely related to temperature.

   G. Current is inversely related to both length and temperature.

   H. Current is inversely related to length and directly related to temperature.

   J. Current is directly related to both length and temperature.

35. Based on the information from the passage, which of the following rods would have the highest value for resistance?

   A. A 12-cm iron rod at 20°C

   B. A 16-cm copper rod at 20°C

   C. A 16-cm iron rod at 80°C

   D. A 12-cm copper rod at 80°C

GO ON TO THE NEXT PAGE

36. The *conductivity* of a material is a measure of how readily a length of the material allows the passage of an electric current. Conductivity is represented by σ, the Greek letter sigma, with standard units of siemens per meter (S/m). Siemens are equivalent to inverse ohms (that is, $1/\Omega$). Based on this information, which of the following equations accurately describes the relationship between conductivity and resistance?

    F. $\Omega = \dfrac{1}{\sigma}$

    G. $\sigma = \Omega \times m$

    H. $\sigma = \dfrac{1}{\Omega \times m}$

    J. $\Omega = \sigma \times m$

37. If the rod used in Trial 4 of Experiment 1 were heated to a temperature of 50°C, the current it then conducts would most likely be:

    A. less than 27 mA.

    B. between 27 and 53 mA.

    C. between 53 and 80 mA.

    D. greater than 80 mA.

38. What would happen to the results of Experiment 2 if the student replaced the 5-V battery with a 10-V battery instead?

    F. The recorded current values would increase for both the copper and the iron rods.

    G. The recorded current values would increase for the copper rods but decrease for the iron rods.

    H. The recorded current values would decrease for the copper rods but increase for the iron rods.

    J. The recorded current values would decrease for both the copper and the iron rods.

39. Suppose the student took an iron rod of 8 cm and a copper rod of 8 cm, both with a 1-cm diameter, and attached them end to end, creating a composite rod with a length of 16 cm. Based on the results of Experiment 2, at a temperature of 20°C, this composite rod would most likely conduct a current of:

    A. less than 20 mA.

    B. between 20 and 40 mA.

    C. between 40 and 200 mA.

    D. greater than 200 mA.

40. Which of the following variables was NOT directly manipulated by the student in Experiment 2 ?

    F. Material

    G. Length

    H. Temperature

    J. Current

IF YOU FINISH BEFORE TIME IS CALLED, YOU MAY CHECK YOUR WORK ON THIS SECTION ONLY. DO NOT TURN TO ANY OTHER SECTION IN THE TEST. **STOP**

GO ON TO THE NEXT PAGE

WRITING TEST

40 Minutes—1 Question

Directions: The essay is used to evaluate your writing skills. You will have **40 minutes** to review the prompt and plan and write an essay in English. Before you begin, read everything in this test booklet carefully to make sure you understand the task.

Your essay will be judged based on the evidence it provides of your ability to do the following:

- Assert your own perspective on a complex issue and evaluate the relationship between your perspective and at least one other perspective

- Use reasoning and evidence to refine and justify your ideas

- Present your ideas in an organized way

- Convey your ideas effectively using standard written English

Write your essay on the lined essay pages in the answer booklet. All writing on those lined pages will be scored. Use the unlined pages in this test booklet to plan your essay. Your work on these unlined pages will not be scored.

Put your pencil down as soon as time is called.

DO NOT OPEN THIS BOOKLET UNTIL TOLD TO DO SO.

GO ON TO THE NEXT PAGE

Scientific Research

A great deal of pure research, undertaken without specific goals but generally to further humankind's understanding of itself and its world, is subsidized at least partly, if not fully, by the nation's government to help drive progress and promote outcomes that improve overall quality of life for citizens. Though pure research often involves considerable time, energy, and money without any assurances of positive outcomes, it can result in economic, medical, and technological benefits. However, it can also result in negative, harmful, and perhaps irreversible outcomes, in which case taxpayer dollars can be wasted and society put at risk. Should governments fund research when the outcome is unclear? Given that taxpayers prefer that their dollars be spent efficiently and effectively, it may be unwise to allocate significant funding to endeavors that may not benefit society as a whole.

Read and carefully consider these perspectives. Each discusses government funding of scientific research.

Perspective One	Perspective Two	Perspective Three
Governments should fund as much pure research as they can afford when the intent is to benefit the mass population. Without the government's money, many research projects would have to cease unless alternative funding is secured. Even research without clear, positive consequences should be pursued because the outcome may prove beneficial, and the research can always be paused or stopped entirely if negative repercussions begin to emerge.	Governments should be very cautious and limit efforts to fund research programs with unclear consequences. Rather, these programs should demonstrate their worth and intended results when seeking government money. Governments should evaluate the merit and benefit of each program on a case-by-case basis and fund only those projects that are designed to create—and will likely achieve—clear and acceptable outcomes.	Governments should partner with private contributors to fund research. Private contributors include companies doing research and development as well as nonprofit foundations. These partnerships will distance the government from taking responsibility for any unintended or undesired consequences and relieve the burden on the taxpayer for efforts that do not prove beneficial. Additionally, this approach incentivizes research teams to provide results-based research that can generate private funding, thus increasing the chance that the research will prove useful to multiple entities, including the government.

GO ON TO THE NEXT PAGE

Essay Task

Write a clear, well-reasoned essay evaluating multiple perspectives on government funding of scientific research. In your essay, be sure to:

- Assert your own perspective on the issue and evaluate the relationship between your perspective and at least one other perspective

- Use reasoning and evidence to refine and justify your ideas

- Present your ideas in an organized way

- Convey your ideas effectively using standard written English

Your perspective may be fully, somewhat, or not at all in agreement with one or more of the three perspectives in the prompt.

Planning Your Essay

These pages are not scored.

Use the space below to brainstorm and plan your essay. Consider the following as you think about the prompt:

- Strengths and weaknesses of the three perspectives in the prompt

  ○ What observations do they offer, and what do they overlook?

  ○ Why are they persuasive or why are they not persuasive?

- Your own background and identity

  ○ What is your perspective on this issue, and what are its strengths and weaknesses?

  ○ What evidence will you use in your essay?

GO ON TO THE NEXT PAGE

GO ON TO THE NEXT PAGE

_____

_____

_____

_____

_____

_____

_____

_____

_____

_____

_____

_____

_____

_____

_____

_____

_____

_____

_____

_____

_____

_____

_____

IF YOU FINISH BEFORE TIME IS CALLED, YOU MAY CHECK YOUR WORK ON THIS SECTION ONLY. DO NOT TURN TO ANY OTHER SECTION IN THE TEST.

PRACTICE TEST 6 ANSWER KEY

ENGLISH TEST

1. **A**	16. **F**	31. **A**	46. **H**	61. **A**
2. **J**	17. **C**	32. **H**	47. **A**	62. **H**
3. **C**	18. **H**	33. **B**	48. **H**	63. **B**
4. **F**	19. **B**	34. **H**	49. **D**	64. **H**
5. **B**	20. **H**	35. **A**	50. **H**	65. **C**
6. **G**	21. **B**	36. **H**	51. **B**	66. **G**
7. **C**	22. **J**	37. **D**	52. **G**	67. **C**
8. **H**	23. **A**	38. **J**	53. **A**	68. **J**
9. **A**	24. **F**	39. **D**	54. **F**	69. **D**
10. **G**	25. **B**	40. **G**	55. **C**	70. **G**
11. **B**	26. **H**	41. **C**	56. **G**	71. **A**
12. **G**	27. **B**	42. **F**	57. **A**	72. **H**
13. **C**	28. **F**	43. **D**	58. **H**	73. **C**
14. **F**	29. **B**	44. **F**	59. **C**	74. **H**
15. **B**	30. **J**	45. **C**	60. **F**	75. **C**

MATHEMATICS TEST

1. **D**	13. **B**	25. **B**	37. **C**	49. **C**
2. **K**	14. **H**	26. **H**	38. **H**	50. **J**
3. **C**	15. **C**	27. **D**	39. **D**	51. **E**
4. **G**	16. **J**	28. **G**	40. **J**	52. **K**
5. **B**	17. **E**	29. **C**	41. **C**	53. **C**
6. **G**	18. **J**	30. **J**	42. **K**	54. **J**
7. **B**	19. **D**	31. **D**	43. **D**	55. **D**
8. **F**	20. **F**	32. **G**	44. **G**	56. **F**
9. **A**	21. **D**	33. **E**	45. **A**	57. **A**
10. **K**	22. **J**	34. **F**	46. **G**	58. **F**
11. **E**	23. **D**	35. **C**	47. **C**	59. **D**
12. **H**	24. **G**	36. **G**	48. **F**	60. **J**

READING TEST

1. **C**	9. **B**	17. **B**	25. **A**	33. **D**
2. **J**	10. **F**	18. **H**	26. **F**	34. **F**
3. **A**	11. **B**	19. **C**	27. **B**	35. **C**
4. **F**	12. **J**	20. **H**	28. **G**	36. **G**
5. **A**	13. **A**	21. **C**	29. **C**	37. **D**
6. **H**	14. **G**	22. **J**	30. **H**	38. **G**
7. **C**	15. **D**	23. **C**	31. **D**	39. **B**
8. **F**	16. **J**	24. **F**	32. **H**	40. **H**

SCIENCE TEST

1. **A**	9. **C**	17. **D**	25. **A**	33. **A**
2. **J**	10. **G**	18. **H**	26. **F**	34. **G**
3. **B**	11. **A**	19. **B**	27. **A**	35. **C**
4. **H**	12. **H**	20. **G**	28. **H**	36. **H**
5. **A**	13. **A**	21. **B**	29. **D**	37. **B**
6. **G**	14. **G**	22. **H**	30. **F**	38. **F**
7. **D**	15. **A**	23. **C**	31. **B**	39. **C**
8. **H**	16. **J**	24. **J**	32. **J**	40. **J**

ANSWERS AND EXPLANATIONS

ENGLISH TEST

Passage I

1. A   Difficulty: Low

Category: Sentence Structure and Formation

Getting to the Answer: When a period appears in the underlined portion, check to see if each sentence is complete. Here, each sentence is complete and correct; therefore, (A), NO CHANGE, is correct. Choice B creates a run-on sentence. Choices C and D create sentences that are awkward and overly wordy.

2. J   Difficulty: Medium

Category: Punctuation

Getting to the Answer: The ACT tests very specific punctuation rules. If punctuation is used in a way not covered by these rules, it will be incorrect. No commas are required in the underlined selection; (J) is correct. Choices F, G, and H all contain unnecessary commas.

3. C   Difficulty: Medium

Category: Sentence Structure and Formation

Getting to the Answer: When a verb is underlined, make sure it places the action properly in relation to the other events in the passage. This passage is written primarily in the present tense; *runs*, (C), is the best answer here. Choices A and B use verb tenses that do not make sense in context. The past tense verb in D is inconsistent with the rest of the passage.

4. F   Difficulty: Medium

Category: Knowledge of Language / Concision

Getting to the Answer: Very rarely will a correct answer choice be significantly longer than the original selection. The underlined selection is grammatically and logically correct, so check the answer choices for a more concise version. You can eliminate G and H, both of which are wordier than the original. Choice J may be tempting because it's shorter than the underlined selection, but it changes the meaning of the sentence; the back office, not the reader, is what hasn't changed. Choice (F) is correct.

5. B   Difficulty: Medium

Category: Topic Development / Supporting Material

Getting to the Answer: When an English Test question contains a question stem, read it carefully. More than one choice is likely to be both relevant and correct, but only one will satisfy the conditions of the stem. This paragraph deals with the author's father's refusal to give up his old-fashioned ways. Choice (B) is the most consistent choice. Choices A and D describe the items being inventoried, which is irrelevant to the point of the paragraph. Choice C is redundant; since we already know he uses paper and pencil to keep his inventory, it's understood that he's writing it by hand.

6. G   Difficulty: Medium

Category: Sentence Structure and Formation

Getting to the Answer: Commas cannot be used to combine independent clauses. Here, the comma connects two independent clauses. Choice (G) correctly replaces the comma with a semicolon. Choice H corrects the run-on error but is unnecessarily wordy. Choice J leaves the meaning of the second clause incomplete.

7. C   Difficulty: High

Category: Sentence Structure and Formation

Getting to the Answer: Beware of answer choices that make changes to parts of the selection that contain no error; these choices will rarely be correct. As written, this sentence uses incorrect grammatical structure; the verb *is* is incorrect here, so you should eliminate A. Choice (C) eliminates it without introducing additional errors. Choices B and D correct the sentence's grammatical error, but neither uses the necessary contrast transition to relate this sentence to the one before it.

8. H   Difficulty: Low

Category: Punctuation

Getting to the Answer: Commas are used in a series of three or more; they are incorrect in compounds. "My sister and I" is a compound; no comma is needed, so F is incorrect. Choice (H) corrects the error without adding any new ones. Choice G uses the incorrect pronoun case; because you wouldn't say "me bought him a brand new computer," *me* is incorrect in the compound as well. Choice J incorrectly separates the sentence's subject and its predicate verb with a comma.

9. A   Difficulty: High

Category: Organization, Unity, and Cohesion / Transitions

Getting to the Answer: When a transition word or phrase is underlined, make sure it properly relates the ideas it connects. The underlined word is the transition between the offer to help transfer records and the information about other ways the computer could be helpful. The second sentence is a continuation of the first, so you can eliminate B and D, both of which suggest a contrast. Choosing between (A) and C is a little more difficult, but remember that new errors may be introduced in answer choices. *In addition* in C would be acceptable if it were followed by a comma, but as written, it's incorrect. Choice (A) is correct.

10. G   Difficulty: Medium

Category: Punctuation

Getting to the Answer: Semicolons can only combine independent clauses. Here, the second clause is not independent, so the semicolon is incorrect; eliminate F. Choice (G) correctly eliminates the semicolon. Choice H incorrectly places a comma after the conjunction. Choice J creates a run-on sentence.

11. B   Difficulty: High

Category: Topic Development / Writer's Purpose

Getting to the Answer: When asked about the purpose of particular information, consider the purpose of the larger section. This paragraph describes the father's resistance to technology, which stems in part from his desire to be able to work even in blackout conditions. The information about the town's history shows that blackout

conditions seldom occur, making the father's reason a bad one. Choice (B) reflects this reasoning, and it is correct. Choice A is too extreme; the father's reason may be poor, but that does not make him delusional. Choices C and D do not relate to the purpose of the paragraph.

12. G   Difficulty: Medium

Category: Organization, Unity, and Cohesion / Passage Organization

Getting to the Answer: When asked to add new information, read it into the passage at the points suggested to choose its most logical placement. There are three pronouns in this new sentence; clarity requires that it be placed somewhere that these pronouns have logical antecedents. Placing it after Sentence 1, as (G) suggests, gives each pronoun a clear antecedent: *we* is the author and his sister, *him* is their father, and *it* is the computer. Choice F puts the siblings' hopes about how a computer could help their father before the information that they bought him one. Choice H's placement makes the antecedent for *it* Father's *blackout scenario*, which doesn't make sense in context. Placing the new sentence where Choice J suggests gives the pronoun the antecedent *blackout*, which is also illogical.

13. C   Difficulty: Medium

Category: Usage

Getting to the Answer: Idiom questions often offer more than one idiomatically correct answer choice; use context to determine which is appropriate. "Sooner than later" is idiomatically incorrect, so you should eliminate A; these are comparison words, but nothing is compared here. Both B and (C) offer proper idioms, but (C) is the one that's appropriate here. Choice D is also incorrect idiomatic usage.

14. F   Difficulty: Medium

Category: Sentence Structure and Formation

Getting to the Answer: Remember to read for logic as well as for grammar and usage. The best version of this sentence is the way it is written; (F) is correct. Choice G redundantly uses the possessive *office's* where possession has already been indicated by *of*. Choice H misstates the information in the passage; the writer's father received the cell phone before the computer. Choice J incorrectly indicates that "the disorganized depths of that office" is where the writer's father received his cell phone, not where the cell phone ended up.

15. B   Difficulty: Low

Category: Organization, Unity, and Cohesion / Passage Organization

Getting to the Answer: When asked to add information, consider both subject matter and tone. This essay is about the author's father's resistance to technology. Choice (B) concludes the essay by referencing something stated at the beginning: that the writer's father tries to *hide* from the future. Choices A, C, and D, while relevant to the paragraph, do not provide strong conclusions to a passage about the father's aversion to technology.

Passage II

16. F   Difficulty: Medium

Category: Usage

Getting to the Answer: *More* or *-er* adjectives are used to compare two items; for more than two, use *most* or *-est*. This sentence is correct as written, (F); *farthest* is appropriate when comparing all areas of the globe. Choice G uses *most far*, which is incorrect in context. Choice H combines *most* with the *-est* suffix, which is never correct. Choice J uses *farther*, which indicates a comparison that is not present here.

17. C   Difficulty: Medium

Category: Sentence Structure and Formation

Getting to the Answer: The fact that the underlined portion contains multiple prepositions (*among* and *for*) is a clue to look for a misplaced modifier. It makes the most sense to describe equality as being *among races*, eliminating A and B. Choice D awkwardly places the noun after its modifying phrases, so (C) is correct.

18. H   Difficulty: Medium

Category: Usage

Getting to the Answer: Most ACT idiom questions will hinge on preposition usage. "Prevented . . . to participate" is idiomatically incorrect, so you can eliminate F. The proper idiom in this context is "prevented . . . from

participating," (H). Choices G and J are both idiomatically incorrect.

19. B   Difficulty: Medium

Category: Topic Development / Supporting Material

Getting to the Answer: When you're asked whether a piece of text is relevant, first determine the topic of the paragraph. This paragraph is about the evolution of the *color line* in baseball. Therefore, information that talks about the development of the industry and the shift in authority is relevant to the paragraph; (B) is correct. Choice A is incorrect because, although the text does talk about previous associations, knowing that range doesn't further the purpose of the paragraph. Choices C and D can be eliminated, since they indicate that the information is irrelevant.

20. H   Difficulty: Medium

Category: Punctuation

Getting to the Answer: A verb should not be separated from its object by a comma. As written, this sentence places an incorrect comma between the verb *had* and its object; eliminate F. Choice (H) eliminates the comma without introducing any additional errors. Choices G and J both add incorrect commas.

21. B   Difficulty: Medium

Category: Usage

Getting to the Answer: When a preposition is underlined, you're most likely being tested on idioms. Select the choice that sounds the most correct when read with the following noun phrase—in this case, *professional teams*. Because the leagues are made up *of* professional teams, (B) is correct here. Choices A, C, and D all suggest an incorrect relationship between the leagues and the teams.

22. J   Difficulty: Medium

Category: Topic Development / Supporting Material

Getting to the Answer: Determining whether or not the underlined text should be deleted will help you quickly eliminate two answer choices. If you eliminate the underlined selection, the passage skips abruptly from the decree losing its force to a discussion of specific African American players. The underlined text introduces those players generally, as a result of the decree losing its impact, and therefore provides a necessary transition, as indicated in (J). Choices F and G can be eliminated, since they advocate deleting the selection. The reasoning in H is not supported by the passage.

23. A   **Difficulty:** Medium

Category: Sentence Structure and Formation

Getting to the Answer: Expect about 25% of your English Test questions to have no error. This sentence is correct as written, (A). Choices B, C, and D all create sentence fragments.

24. F   **Difficulty:** Medium

Category: Usage

Getting to the Answer: The phrase "including Walker's brother Weldy" is properly used here to modify "a few other African Americans"; no change is needed, so (F) is correct. Choice G is incorrect because no comma is used to introduce a clause beginning with *that*. Choices H and J make the sentence wordier unnecessarily.

25. B   **Difficulty:** Medium

Category: Sentence Structure and Formation

Getting to the Answer: Use context to determine appropriate verb tense usage. The previous sentence says that Walker *was* a catcher; the introductory phrase in this sentence refers us to the same time period. Only (B) uses a consistent tense. Choices A, C, and D all refer to future actions.

26. H   **Difficulty:** Medium

Category: Organization, Unity, and Cohesion / Passage Organization

Getting to the Answer: Since NO CHANGE is not presented as an option, you'll need to find the most logical placement for the new sentence. *Other teams* must contrast with teams already mentioned, and the only place that happens is in Sentences 2 and 3. Sentence 2 talks about one player for the Blue Stockings, and Sentence 3 mentions some additional players for the same team. Sentence 4 turns to the time when segregation returned, so the information about African Americans playing for other teams must come before that, between Sentences 3 and 4, (H).

27. B   **Difficulty:** Low

Category: Knowledge of Language / Concision

Getting to the Answer: When you don't spot an error in grammar or usage, check for errors of style. "At the time when" is a longer way of saying *when*; (B) is correct here. Choice C uses *while*, which indicates a continuing period of time, but this sentence refers to a specific moment when Jackie Robinson crossed the color line. Choice D is even wordier than the original.

28. F   **Difficulty:** Medium

Category: Knowledge of Language / Precision

Getting to the Answer: Make sure your selection reflects the meaning of the sentence. The best version of this sentence is the way it is written, (F). Choice G changes the meaning of the sentence, implying that Robinson has yet to be recognized as a hero. Choice H also changes the sentence's meaning, indicating that Robinson is doing the recognizing rather than being recognized. Choice J is unnecessarily wordy.

29. B   **Difficulty:** High

Category: Knowledge of Language / Style and Tone

Getting to the Answer: A question that asks about the essay's tone will likely include only answer choices that are grammatically correct. Be as picky as possible when determining which choice best fits the stated tone and emphasis. Choice A is too neutral, so it should be eliminated. Choice C does not emphasize the uniqueness of Robinson's role; eliminate it. Choice D mentions collaboration, which emphasizes teamwork rather than uniqueness, so it is also incorrect. Someone who blazes a path goes where no one has gone before. Thus, only (B) maintains a positive tone while showing that Robinson played a unique role.

30. J   **Difficulty:** Medium

Category: Topic Development / Writer's Purpose

Getting to the Answer: This question format appears frequently on the ACT; it's asking for the passage's main idea. This essay is about the color barrier in baseball; it would not fulfill an assignment to write about the history of baseball, so you can eliminate F and G. The fact that baseball was played before 1868, H, is not the reason this essay does not fulfill an assignment on baseball's history. Choice (J) correctly states the reasoning: the essay focuses only on one aspect of the game.

Passage III

31. A   Difficulty: Medium

Category: Punctuation

Getting to the Answer: An introductory phrase should be separated from the rest of the sentence by a comma. This introductory phrase is set off by a comma; the sentence is correct as written, (A). Choices B and C incorrectly treat the introductory phrase as an independent clause. Choice D incorrectly connects a dependent and an independent clause with the conjunction *and*.

32. H   Difficulty: Medium

Category: Usage

Getting to the Answer: When a pronoun is underlined, check whether it matches its antecedent. The underlined portion refers to the bridge, so the correct answer will be singular; eliminate F and G. Choice J contains a subject-verb agreement error; the singular *it* requires the singular *was*. Choice (H) is correct.

33. B   Difficulty: Medium

Category: Sentence Structure and Formation

Getting to the Answer: Make sure verb tenses make sense within the chronology of the passage. The past perfect is used in this sentence, but this tense is only correct when used to describe one past action completed before another. That is not the case here, so A is incorrect; (B) correctly replaces the verb with its past tense form. Choice C changes the meaning of the sentence (the legislature did the authorizing; it wasn't authorized by someone else) and creates a sentence that is grammatically incorrect. Choice D uses a conditional verb phrase, which is inappropriate in context.

34. H   Difficulty: Low

Category: Knowledge of Language / Concision

Getting to the Answer: When the underlined selection contains a compound, check to see if the words mean the

same thing. If so, the correct answer choice will eliminate one of them. *Build* and *construct* mean the same thing, so you can eliminate F and G right away. The only difference between (H) and J is a comma, which is incorrect in a compound; eliminate J.

35. A   Difficulty: Medium

Category: Punctuation

Getting to the Answer: Where the only difference among the answer choices is comma placement, remember your tested rules. This sentence needs NO CHANGE, (A). Choice B incorrectly places a comma between items in a compound. Choice C places a comma after the conjunction in a compound, which is also incorrect. Choice D incorrectly inserts a comma between a preposition and its object.

36. H   Difficulty: Medium

Category: Topic Development / Writer's Purpose

Getting to the Answer: Read the sentence without the material in question to determine what it adds to the paragraph and therefore why it was included. Looking at the paragraph as a whole, you can see that the author mentions the amount of money invested, the prominence of the architects, and the accomplishments of the firm the architects brought in to help. Removing one of these details detracts from that description; (H) is the best choice here. Choice F can be eliminated because this is not the only detail that supports the larger point; in and of itself, it's not critical. Removing this one phrase wouldn't impact the transition, as G suggests. Choice J is a trap. The segment in question does concern finances, but the text only mentions the amount of money invested, not how it was raised.

37. D   Difficulty: High

Category: Usage

Getting to the Answer: On the ACT, *who* will only be correct when used to refer to people. Despite the fact that it's named after a person, "John A. Roebling and Sons" is the name of a company, so *who* isn't appropriate. That eliminates A and B. Choice C might be tempting because it's shorter than (D), but when C is read into the sentence, it creates a grammatical problem: "a company . . . and would later" requires another verb. Choice (D) is correct.

38. J   Difficulty: Medium

Category: Topic Development / Supporting Material

Getting to the Answer: Consider context when you're asked about the role a piece of text plays. A question that asks what would be lost if text were deleted is really just asking for the function of that text. If you read the paragraphs before and after the sentence in question, you'll see that what is missing is a clear transition; (J) is correct. Choice F distorts the meaning of the sentence, which discusses how long the project actually took, not how long it was expected to take. Choice G is out of scope; danger is only mentioned in this one sentence and then only in terms of how few lives were lost constructing the bridge. Choice H overstates the significance of the detail regarding construction time.

39. D   Difficulty: Medium

Category: Organization, Unity, and Cohesion / Transitions

Getting to the Answer: When transition words are underlined, focus on the relationship between the sentences or clauses they combine. The preceding sentence talks about the length of the bridge, and the sentence in which the underlined segment appears goes on to describe the cables in more detail. Since the second isn't a result of the first, you can eliminate A. Choice B inaccurately suggests an inconsistent or contradictory relationship between the sentences. Choice C is illogical; these are facts about the bridge, not events occurring simultaneously. The best choice here is no transition at all, as in (D).

40. G   Difficulty: Low

Category: Usage

Getting to the Answer: When you're tested on Usage, wrong answer choices may have the wrong word in context. They may also be wordy or passive. *Longer* means a comparison: one thing is longer *than* something else. Since this sentence doesn't offer a comparison, *longer* can't be correct. Eliminate F. Choices (G) and H are both grammatically correct in context, but H is unnecessarily wordy. *Lengthy*, in J, is not correct when used to describe a specific length.

41. C   Difficulty: Medium

Category: Sentence Structure and Formation

Getting to the Answer: When the underlined portion contains a comma, check for a run-on. Because the comma separates two independent clauses, A is incorrect. Choice B eliminates the subject of the second clause, so it is incorrect. Choice D incorrectly combines a semicolon and a FANBOYS conjunction. Choice (C) makes the second clause dependent and correctly separates the clauses with a comma. Choice (C) is correct.

42. F   Difficulty: Medium

Category: Punctuation

Getting to the Answer: Introductory phrases and clauses should be set off from the rest of the sentence by a comma. The comma here is used correctly, so no change is needed; (F) is correct. Choice G eliminates the comma, making the sentence difficult to understand. Both the colon in H and the semicolon in J would work only if the first clause were independent, which it is not.

43. D   Difficulty: Medium

Category: Organization, Unity, and Cohesion / Transitions

Getting to the Answer: When a transition word is underlined, check to see what ideas are being connected by the transition. The previous sentence mentions that the bridge was renamed, and the sentence beginning with the underlined portion switches to the present tense to describe the number of vehicles that cross the bridge daily. There is no logical contrast between these ideas, so B and C can be eliminated. Choice A indicates a continuation of the previous thought, but that does not fit the context; eliminate it. Choice (D) is correct, because it transitions from the past-tense description in the previous sentence to the present-tense description of the bridge's daily activity.

44. F   Difficulty: Medium

Category: Usage

Getting to the Answer: This sentence is correct as written, (F). Choice G replaces *more than* with *over*, which, despite its common usage, is actually a preposition that indicates location, not amount. Choice H is unnecessarily wordy. Choice J is also wordy and uses *amount*, which is incorrect for a countable noun like *vehicles*.

45. C   Difficulty: Medium

Category: Topic Development / Writer's Purpose

Getting to the Answer: As you read ACT English passages, develop a sense of the topic or *big idea*, just like you do in Reading; this question format is very common on the ACT. This passage is about one specific bridge, so it would not satisfy the requirement set out in the question stem. You can therefore eliminate A and B right away. Now turn to the reasoning. Choice D misstates the topic of the passage; (C) is correct.

Passage IV

46. H   Difficulty: Medium

Category: Sentence Structure and Formation

Getting to the Answer: Verbs in a compound should be in the same tense. The compound verb in this clause is "was . . . rising . . . and painted." Since the second verb is in the past tense, the first should be as well, so F is incorrect; (H) is correct. Choice G uses the gerund verb form without the necessary helping verb. Choice J is unnecessarily wordy.

47. A   Difficulty: Medium

Category: Topic Development / Writer's Purpose

Getting to the Answer: Read English Test question stems carefully. Often, all of the choices will be relevant and grammatically correct, but only one will fulfill the requirements of the stem. This question stem asks for a detail that shows a contrast between the quiet night streets and the daytime activity. The original text does this best. The verb in B does not convey the difference in the streets at these two times as well as *flood* in (A). Choice C is too general. Choice D does not provide the necessary contrast.

48. H   Difficulty: Medium

Category: Usage

Getting to the Answer: Use your Kaplan resources to familiarize yourself with commonly tested idioms. Although all four answer choices form idioms that would be correct in some contexts, one smiles *at* someone or something; (H) is correct.

49. D   Difficulty: Medium

Category: Knowledge of Language / Concision

Getting to the Answer: When you don't spot an error in grammar or usage, look for errors in style. Choice A is a wordy way of saying *traveled across*, (D). Choices B and C are unnecessarily wordy as well.

50. H   Difficulty: Low

Category: Sentence Structure and Formation

Getting to the Answer: Read question stems carefully. This one asks which answer choice would NOT be acceptable, which means that three of the choices will be correct in context. Choices F, G, and J are appropriate introductory clauses, but (H) is an independent clause, which makes the sentence a run-on.

51. B   Difficulty: Medium

Category: Topic Development / Supporting Material

Getting to the Answer: Use your Reading skills for questions like this one that ask for the function of a detail. The underlined portion tells us that the writer's journey will end in California. Choice (B) is correct. The underlined selection does not mention the reasons for the writer's trip, describe her route, or make any comparisons, so A, C, and D are incorrect.

52. G   Difficulty: Medium

Category: Punctuation

Getting to the Answer: Use commas in a list or series only if there are three or more items. Since the writer only mentions two places she has been, the first comma here is incorrect; eliminate F. Choice (G) corrects this without introducing any additional errors. Choice H eliminates the incorrect comma but removes the one at the end of the selection, which is needed to separate the introductory clause from the rest of the sentence. Choice J does not address the error.

53. A   Difficulty: Medium

Category: Organization, Unity, and Cohesion / Transitions

Getting to the Answer: To identify the most effective transition, you'll need to read both paragraphs. Paragraph 3

is about how the author has traveled to foreign countries but, within the United States, she only knows New York City. Paragraph 4 describes her drive through the Midwest. The text as written takes the reader from New York City (tall buildings) to the less populated areas, leading to the description of the cornfields. Choice (A), NO CHANGE, is the best choice here. Choice B misstates the passage; the cornfields didn't appear *almost immediately*, but gradually. Choice C and D do not provide appropriate transitions between the paragraphs.

54. F   Difficulty: Medium

Category: Topic Development / Supporting Material

Getting to the Answer: When you're asked to identify the *most relevant* choice, use context clues. The paragraph is about the change the author experiences as she drives from New York across the country. That contrast is clear in the passage as written; (F) is the best choice here. Choices G and H do not relate to the paragraph's topic. Choice J is opposite; the writer describes many different settings, which is the opposite of *monotonous*.

55. C   Difficulty: Medium

Category: Sentence Structure and Formation

Getting to the Answer: There are a number of ways to correct a run-on sentence, but only one answer choice will do so without introducing any additional errors. Each of the clauses in this sentence is independent; (C) corrects the run-on by replacing the comma with a semicolon. Choice B omits the comma necessary with the coordinating conjunction *but*. Choice D loses the contrast between the clauses that is present in the original.

56. G   Difficulty: Medium

Category: Usage

Getting to the Answer: When a single adverb is underlined, you are most likely being tested on idioms. Determine what is being modified. The underlined portion modifies the noun *serenity*, so it should be an adjective. Eliminate F. Choices H and J compare this serenity to other states of being, but there is no such comparison in the passage. Choice (G) is correct.

57. A   Difficulty: Medium

Category: Punctuation

Getting to the Answer: Only two apostrophe uses are tested on the ACT: possessive nouns and contractions. The noun here is possessive; the apostrophe is used correctly in (A). Choice B uses the plural *nights* instead of the possessive. Choice C is unnecessarily wordy and uses the idiomatically incorrect "shadows from the night." Choice D changes the meaning of the sentence.

58. H   Difficulty: Medium

Category: Knowledge of Language / Concision

Getting to the Answer: If you don't spot a grammar or usage error, check for errors in style. As written, this sentence is unnecessarily wordy, so F is incorrect; (H) provides the best revision. Choices G and J are still unnecessarily wordy.

59. C   Difficulty: Medium

Category: Organization, Unity, and Cohesion / Transitions

Getting to the Answer: When a transition word or clause is underlined, determine the relationship between the ideas being connected. Look at the relationship between the sentences in this paragraph. The ideas are presented chronologically—that is, in the order in which they happened. Choice (C), *At first*, is the best transition into this series of events. Choices A and B imply contradiction or qualification, which is incorrect in context. Choice D implies that a lot went on prior to the writer's not having any idea what she was looking at, but this is presented as the first in a series of events.

60. F   Difficulty: High

Category: Sentence Structure and Formation

Getting to the Answer: The correct answer will rarely be longer than the original selection. This question requires no change, so (F) is correct. The pronoun's antecedent appears in the previous sentence ("what I was looking at"), and the *-ing* verb form is used correctly. Choices G, H, and J are wordy; additionally, G introduces the passive voice unnecessarily.

Passage V

61. A   Difficulty: Low

Category: Punctuation

Getting to the Answer: Commas are used to combine an independent and a dependent clause. This sentence is correct as written, (A), with the comma properly placed after the introductory clause. Choice B places the comma incorrectly; *of 2003* is part of the introductory clause. Choice C omits the necessary comma. Choice D incorrectly uses a semicolon between a dependent and an independent clause.

62. H   Difficulty: Medium

Category: Sentence Structure and Formation

Getting to the Answer: The underlined portion introduces nonessential information, so it should not form an independent clause. Choices F and G both make the clause an independent one; they should be eliminated. The passage is in the past tense, making the present tense verb in J incorrect. Choice (H) is correct.

63. B   Difficulty: Medium

Category: Knowledge of Language / Precision

Getting to the Answer: Precision questions require you to look at context; frequently, words will have similar meanings but be used differently. *Height* means "the distance from the top to the bottom of something"; *altitude* means "height above sea level." Since *altitude* is correct in this context, you can eliminate A. Choices (B) and C both use *altitude,* but "at an altitude" is the correct idiom here; (B) is correct. Choice D creates a grammatically incorrect sentence.

64. H   Difficulty: High

Category: Organization, Unity, and Cohesion / Transitions

Getting to the Answer: When a transition word is underlined, check the logic of the transition as well as the grammar and punctuation. The sentence contrasts the famous and wealthy passengers with passengers who were ordinary people. Eliminate F and J because they do not express contrast. While G presents a contrast, it is grammatically incorrect. *Despite* creates a dependent clause requiring an *-ing* or *-ed* verb form, which is not

present in the sentence. Choice (H) is correct, both logically and grammatically.

65. C   Difficulty: High

Category: Usage

Getting to the Answer: Words like *that,* which are commonly misused in everyday speech, can make a question more challenging. Sound doesn't travel a speed, it travels *at* a speed; eliminate A. Only (C) makes the correction. Sound doesn't travel *to* a speed, as in B; *where,* D, will only be correct on the ACT when used to indicate location or direction.

66. G   Difficulty: Medium

Category: Topic Development / Writer's Purpose

Getting to the Answer: When asked about the purpose of a paragraph in relation to others, take a few seconds to summarize the paragraph in question, the one before it, and the one after it. The previous paragraph introduced the topic of supersonic aircraft. The paragraph in question transitions to questions of science, which are then discussed in the following paragraph. Choice (G) is correct. The paragraph does not provide an example or a counterargument, making F and H incorrect. The passage does not move from the general topic to a specific story, making J incorrect.

67. C   Difficulty: Medium

Category: Knowledge of Language / Precision

Getting to the Answer: Read English Test question stems carefully. This one asks for the LEAST acceptable alternative, which means that three of the choices will be correct in the sentence. All of the answer choices mean "change," so read each of them into the sentence. "Change them into," "translate them into," and "transform them into" are all appropriate usage, but "alter them into" is not because it changes the meaning. Choice (C) is correct here.

68. J   Difficulty: High

Category: Knowledge of Language / Concision

Getting to the Answer: Look for constructions that repeat words unnecessarily; these will be incorrect on the ACT. The sentence tells us that the speed at which sound travels through gas depends on three things: what kind of gas it is, the temperature, and the pressure; "it is traveling through" is redundant, so F is incorrect. Choice (J) is the most concise answer, and it does not lose any of the meaning of the underlined selection. Choices G and H do not address the error.

69. D   Difficulty: High

Category: Knowledge of Language / Ambiguity

Getting to the Answer: Don't choose the shortest answer if it fails to make the writer's meaning clear. "Air temperature and pressure decrease with altitude" isn't clear; "air temperature" and "pressure" themselves do not have altitude, and we're not told to what the altitude is referring, so A is incorrect. Choice (D) makes the writer's meaning clear; when altitudes are higher, the decrease in temperature and pressure occur. Choice B does not address the error and even compounds it by replacing *altitude* with *height*. Choice C contradicts the facts in the passage; higher, not lower, altitudes have this effect.

70. G   Difficulty: Medium

Category: Punctuation

Getting to the Answer: Beware of answer choices that make unnecessary changes to the sentence. The information provided in the two clauses contrasts, so *however* is correct, but it requires a comma to separate it from the rest of the clause. Eliminate F. Choice (G) is correct. Choice H creates an inappropriate cause-and-effect relationship between the clauses. Choice J does not address the punctuation error.

71. A   Difficulty: Medium

Category: Organization, Unity, and Cohesion / Passage Organization

Getting to the Answer: When you're asked to choose the most logical conclusion, first determine the sentence's function within the paragraph. The first half of this sentence previews a reason that the Concorde cruises at a higher altitude than regular planes, and it ties that reason back to the contrast between the speed of sound at two different altitudes. You need, then, a conclusion to the sentence that both explains why the planes would fly higher and does so in light of the information about altitude in the preceding sentence. The best choice here is (A); the original version of the sentence is the most logical.

Choice B doesn't provide a reason; it simply repeats information that has already been stated. Choice C is out of scope; fuel consumption isn't mentioned in the passage. Choice D is a result of the plane's higher altitude, not its cause.

72. H   Difficulty: High

Category: Sentence Structure and Formation

Getting to the Answer: The use of *since* creates a specific marking point in the past and requires a verb that does the same. You need a simple past verb with *since*; (H) is correct. Choice F uses a tense that indicates an action that is ongoing, but the decommissioning of the Concorde has been completed. Choice G is unnecessarily wordy. The past perfect in J is only correct when used to indicate one past action completed prior to another stated past action, which is not the case here.

73. C   Difficulty: Medium

Category: Knowledge of Language / Concision

Getting to the Answer: The phrases *about to* and *very soon* are redundant, making A, B, and D all incorrect. Furthermore, sentences beginning with coordinating (FANBOYS) conjunctions will not be correct on the ACT, which is an additional error in A. Only (C) correctly removes the redundancy.

74. H   Difficulty: Medium

Category: Organization, Unity, and Cohesion / Transition

Getting to the Answer: When a transition word is underlined, check to see if it makes sense in the context. The sentence discusses upcoming advances to supersonic travel. Choice F places the advances in the present, which does not match the future-tense *will* later in the sentence. Choice G is about location rather than time, which does not fit the context. Choices (H) and J both refer to a future time, but only (H) makes sense in context. The answer must be an adverb in order to describe when the advances will take place, but *Upcoming*, choice J, is an adjective. Choice (H) is therefore correct.

75. C   Difficulty: Medium

Category: Sentence Structure and Formation

Getting to the Answer: Here, the items combined by "not only . . . but also" are "to the rich and famous" and "be for the masses." These items are correlated in the sentence, but they are not parallel in structure; eliminate A. Choices B and D do not address the error in parallel structure. Choice (C) corrects the error.

MATHEMATICS TEST

1. D   Difficulty: Low

Category: Essential Skills / Statistics and Probability

Getting to the Answer: The basketball team scored 364 points in 13 games, so they scored an average of $\frac{364}{13} = 28$ points per game. Choice (D) is correct.

2. K   Difficulty: Low

Category: Essential Skills / Numbers and Operations

Getting to the Answer: To convert a mixed number to an improper fraction, you have two options:

Option 1: Rewrite the whole number part using the denominator of the fraction part, then add. Here, the result is $\frac{28}{7} + \frac{3}{7} = \frac{31}{7}$.

Option 2: Use the shortcut rule, which is: Multiply the whole number by the denominator of the fraction and add the numerator, then write the result over the original denominator. Here, you get $4 \times 7 + 3 = 28 + 3 = 31$ over 7, or $\frac{31}{7}$.

Using either method, you arrive at a numerator of 31, which is (K).

3. C   Difficulty: Low

Category: Essential Skills / Expressions and Equations

Getting to the Answer: To solve for x, you need to isolate it on one side of the equation. To do this, subtract 18 from both sides, then divide by 4. The result is:

$$4x + 18 = 38$$
$$4x = 20$$
$$x = 5$$

Choice (C) is correct. Note that you could also Backsolve to answer this question, but the algebra is quicker.

4. G   Difficulty: Low

Category: Essential Skills / Numbers and Operations

Getting to the Answer: Because John weighs *more* than Ellen, begin by eliminating J and K, as doing so will reduce the chance of a miscalculation error. According to the question, John's 144 pounds represents 1.5 times Ellen's weight. Therefore, Ellen's weight must be $\frac{144}{1.5} = 96$ pounds. Choice (G) is correct.

If you're not sure whether to multiply or divide by 1.5, you could also set up an equation and solve it. Let $J =$ John's weight and $E =$ Ellen's weight. Translating from English to math gives:

$$J = 1.5E$$
$$144 = 1.5E$$
$$\frac{144}{1.5} = E$$
$$E = 96$$

5. B   Difficulty: Medium

Category: Essential Skills / Numbers and Operations

Getting to the Answer: To find the reciprocal of a number, swap the numerator and the denominator. You could use algebra to answer the question, but Backsolving is likely to be quicker. As usual, start with C:

The reciprocal of $\frac{4}{3}$ is $\frac{3}{4}$ and $\frac{4}{3} \div \frac{3}{4} = \frac{4}{3} \times \frac{4}{3} = \frac{16}{9}$. This is too big (and it's the flip of what you're looking for), so try (B) next:

The reciprocal of $\frac{3}{4}$ is $\frac{4}{3}$ and $\frac{3}{4} \div \frac{4}{3} = \frac{3}{4} \times \frac{3}{4} = \frac{9}{16}$. Choice (B) is correct.

6. G   Difficulty: Medium

Category: Higher Math / Number and Quantity

Getting to the Answer: The inverse operation of cube rooting is cubing, so cube both sides of the equation to solve for x:

$$\sqrt[3]{x} = \frac{1}{4}$$
$$x = \left(\frac{1}{4}\right)^3 = \frac{1}{4} \times \frac{1}{4} \times \frac{1}{4} = \frac{1}{64}$$

That's (G).

7. B   Difficulty: Low

Category: Higher Math / Algebra

Getting to the Answer: Isolate the variable, then solve for x. To do this, subtract 14 from both sides, then take the square root:

$$x^2 + 14 = 63$$
$$x^2 = 49$$
$$x = \pm 7$$

Choice (B) matches the positive value of x.

8. F   Difficulty: Medium

Category: Higher Math / Number and Quantity

Getting to the Answer: Don't let the vector notation scare you. Adding vectors works exactly as you would expect it to: To add two vectors, add the corresponding components. The question only asks about the value of a, so focus on the first entries only: $7 + a = 5$, which gives $a = 5 - 7$, or -2. Choice (F) is correct.

9. A   Difficulty: Low

Category: Essential Skills / Rates, Percents, Proportions, and Unit Conversion

Getting to the Answer: The quickest way to answer this question is to estimate. While you may or may not know 6% of 1,250 off the top of your head, 10% of 1,250 is 125. Because 6% < 10%, the correct answer must be less than 125. Only (A) works.

To solve this the more traditional way, multiply 1,250 by the decimal form of 6%: $1,250 \times 0.06 = 75$.

10. K   Difficulty: Low

Category: Essential Skills / Numbers and Operations

Getting to the Answer: When the choices are spaced far apart, estimation is generally the quickest way to the correct answer. To estimate, round 5.2 to 5 and 6.8 to 7. Because $5^3 + 7^2 = 125 + 49 = 174$, the correct answer will be close to 174. That would be (K).

11. E   Difficulty: Low

Category: Higher Math / Number and Quantity

Getting to the Answer: You certainly could reason this question out logically, but it's much easier to just pick a

starting balance, make the error described in the question, and see which answer choice matches. Suppose Lexi starts with a balance of $100. If she accidentally adds $40 to this amount, the incorrect new balance is $140. If she had subtracted instead, the correct balance would have been $60. Thus the incorrect balance is $140 - $60 = $80 more than is should be. Choice (E) is correct.

12. H   Difficulty: Medium

Category: Essential Skills / Numbers and Operations

Getting to the Answer: To answer this question, you'll need to follow the order of operations (PEMDAS).

First, evaluate the parentheses:

$$3^3 \div 9 + (6^2 - 12) \div 4$$
$$= 3^3 \div 9 + (36 - 12) \div 4$$
$$= 3^3 \div 9 + 24 \div 4$$

Next, simplify the exponent:

$$3^3 \div 9 + 24 \div 4 = 27 \div 9 + 24 \div 4.$$

Then, take care of any multiplication and/or division, from left to right: $27 \div 9 + 24 \div 4 = 3 + 6$.

Finally, take care of any addition and/or subtraction, from left to right: $3 + 6 = 9$.

So (H) is correct.

13. B   Difficulty: Low

Category: Essential Skills / Expressions and Equations

Getting to the Answer: Each banana costs $0.24, so the price of x bananas is $0.24x$. Similarly, each orange costs $0.38, so the price of y oranges is $0.38y$. Therefore, the total price of x bananas and y oranges is $0.24x + 0.38y$. That's (B).

14. H   Difficulty: Low

Category: Essential Skills / Rates, Percents, Proportions, and Unit Conversion

Getting to the Answer: To find the percent shaded, divide the number of shaded triangles by the total number of triangles. There are 24 small triangles in all, and 8 of them are shaded: $\frac{8}{24} = \frac{1}{3} = 33\frac{1}{3}\%$. Choice (H) is correct.

15. C   Difficulty: Medium

Category: Essential Skills / Rates, Percents, Proportions, and Unit Conversion

Getting to the Answer: The ratio of girls to boys is 5:3, so the ratio of girls to the total number of seniors is 5:(3 + 5), or 5:8. Call g the number of girls in the senior class. Set up a proportion and cross-multiply to solve for g:

$$\frac{5}{8} = \frac{g}{168}$$
$$8g = 840$$
$$g = 105$$

There are 105 girls in the senior class, which is (C).

16. J   Difficulty: Medium

Category: Essential Skills / Statistics and Probability

Getting to the Answer: When a question about averages involves a missing value (here, the final test score), it often helps to think in terms of the sum instead. For Sarah's exam scores to average at least a 90, they must sum to at least $90 \times 4 = 360$. She already has an 89, a 93, and an 84, so she needs at least $360 - (89 + 93 + 84)$, which gives $360 - 266 = 94$ points on her final test. Choice (J) is correct.

17. E   Difficulty: Low

Category: Essential Skills / Expressions and Equations

Getting to the Answer: Treat inequalities just as you would equations. The only exception is that if you multiply or divide by a negative number, you must flip the inequality symbol.

$$3x - 11 \geq 22$$
$$3x \geq 33$$
$$x \geq 11$$

This matches (E).

18. J   Difficulty: Medium

Category: Essential Skills / Statistics and Probability

Getting to the Answer: Probability is the number of desired outcomes divided by the total number of possible outcomes. Here, you're given the probability $\left(\frac{3}{4}\right)$ and the number of desired outcomes (48). You're looking

for the total number of possible outcomes (the number of dominos in the pile). Let d represent the number of dominos in the pile. Set up an equation using the definition of probability and the given information:

$$P(\text{even \# dots}) = \frac{\text{\# with even \# dots}}{\text{total \# dominos in pile}} = \frac{3}{4}$$
$$\frac{3}{4} = \frac{48}{d}$$
$$3d = 192$$
$$d = 64$$

Choice (J) is correct.

19. D   Difficulty: Low

Category: Essential Skills / Expressions and Equations

Getting to the Answer: This is a straightforward substitution question, so just be careful of the negative signs. Plug in 4 for x and $-\frac{1}{2}$ for y and simplify:

$$3x - 8y$$
$$= 3(4) - 8\left(-\frac{1}{2}\right)$$
$$= 12 - (-4)$$
$$= 12 + 4$$
$$= 16$$

That's (D).

20. F   Difficulty: Medium

Category: Essential Skills / Rates, Percents, Proportions, and Unit Conversion

Getting to the Answer: Whenever multiple rates are given, pay very careful attention to the units. As you read the question, decide how and when you will need to convert units. Use the factor-label method as needed. The answer choices are given in hours and minutes, so start by converting the given typing rate from words per second to words per minute:

$$\frac{3.75 \text{ words}}{1 \text{ second}} \times \frac{60 \text{ seconds}}{1 \text{ minute}} = \frac{225 \text{ words}}{1 \text{ minute}}$$

Next, find the number of words in the 25-page transcript:

$$\frac{675 \text{ words}}{1 \text{ page}} \times 25 \text{ pages} = 16{,}875 \text{ words}$$

Finally, let m be the number of minutes it takes the court reporter to type the whole transcript. Set up a proportion and solve for m:

$$\frac{225 \text{ words}}{1 \text{ minute}} = \frac{16{,}875 \text{ words}}{m \text{ minutes}}$$

$$225m = 16{,}875$$

$$m = 75$$

Because 75 minutes is not an answer choice, convert it to hours and minutes: 75 minutes = 1 hour, 15 minutes, making (F) the correct answer.

21. D   Difficulty: Low

Category: Essential Skills / Geometry

Getting to the Answer: When two parallel lines are cut by a transversal, half of the angles will be acute and half will be obtuse. Each acute angle will have the same measure as every other acute angle. The same is true of every obtuse angle. Furthermore, the acute angles will be supplementary to the obtuse angles. Based on the information provided, $\angle a$ is an acute angle measuring 68°. Based on the figure, $\angle f$ is an obtuse angle, so $\angle a$ must be supplementary to $\angle f$. Therefore, the measure of $\angle f$ is $180° - 68° = 112°$. Choice (D) is correct.

22. J   Difficulty: Medium

Category: Essential Skills / Rates, Percents, Proportions, and Unit Conversion

Getting to the Answer: If the student copy is $\frac{1}{4}$ the size of the wall map, then 2.5 inches on the student map would be $2.5 \times 4 = 10$ inches on the wall map. Now set up a proportion to find the actual distance between the cities using the scale of the wall map:

$$\frac{1}{100} = \frac{10}{x}$$

$$x = 1{,}000$$

The correct answer is (J).

23. D   Difficulty: Medium

Category: Essential Skills / Numbers and Operations

Getting to the Answer: The piece of paper is $8\frac{1}{2}$ inches wide. To find the number of $\frac{5}{8}$-inch wide strips of paper you can cut, divide:

$$8\frac{1}{2} \div \frac{5}{8} = \frac{17}{2} \div \frac{5}{8}$$

$$= \frac{17}{2} \times \frac{8}{5}$$

$$= \frac{136}{10} = \frac{68}{5} = 13.6$$

Thus, you can make 13 strips of paper that are $\frac{5}{8}$ of an inch wide and 11 inches long, and you will have a small, thin strip of paper left over. Choice (D) is correct.

24. G   Difficulty: Medium

Category: Essential Skills / Geometry

Getting to the Answer: This is a pair of parallel lines cut by a transversal, but this time, there's also a triangle thrown into the mix. Begin with segment AB. This is a transversal, so $\angle MAB$ and $\angle ABC$ are alternate interior angles and $m\angle MAB = m\angle ABC = 55°$. Because triangle ABC is isosceles with $AB = AC$, $m\angle ACB$ is also 55° (base angles of an isosceles triangle have equal measures). Choice (G) is correct.

25. B   Difficulty: Low

Category: Higher Math / Algebra

Getting to the Answer: Use the slope formula to find the slope of the line:

$$m = \frac{y_2 - y_1}{x_2 - x_1}$$

$$= \frac{-6 - 0}{0 - (-10)}$$

$$= -\frac{6}{10}$$

$$= -\frac{3}{5}$$

That's (B).

26. H   Difficulty: Medium

Category: Higher Math / Algebra

Getting to the Answer: This question seems long, but it actually isn't that complicated. FOIL the first pair of binomials, FOIL the second pair, then add the results by combining like terms:

$$(x + 4)(x - 4) = x(x) + x(-4) + 4(x) + 4(-4)$$

$$= x^2 - 4x + 4x - 16$$

$$= x^2 - 16$$

(If you noticed the difference of squares above, that will save you some time.)

$$(2x + 2)(x - 2) = 2x(x) + 2x(-2) + 2(x) + 2(-2)$$
$$= 2x^2 - 4x + 2x - 4$$
$$= 2x^2 - 2x - 4$$

Finally, add the two polynomials by combining like terms:

$$\boxed{x^2} \boxed{-16} + \boxed{2x^2} - 2x \boxed{-4} = 3x^2 - 2x - 20$$

Choice (H) is correct.

27. D   Difficulty: Medium

Category: Higher Math / Geometry

Getting to the Answer: To find the distance between two points that don't have either the same x-coordinates or the same y-coordinates, plug the points into the Distance formula and evaluate:

$$\begin{aligned}
\text{Distance} &= \sqrt{(x_2 - x_1)^2 + (y_2 - y_1)^2} \\
&= \sqrt{(-2 - 3)^2 + (6 - (-6))^2} \\
&= \sqrt{(-5)^2 + 12^2} \\
&= \sqrt{25 + 144} \\
&= \sqrt{169} \\
&= 13
\end{aligned}$$

Choice (D) is correct.

28. G   Difficulty: Medium

Category: Essential Skills / Rates, Percents, Proportions, and Unit Conversion

Getting to the Answer: Look for shortcuts; you could write an equation and solve for h, but is there a faster way? Examine the two percents: 30 percent is half of 60 percent, so 30 percent of h will be half of 60 percent of h, or half of 80, which is 40. That's (G).

29. C   Difficulty: Medium

Category: Higher Math / Statistics and Probability

Getting to the Answer: Because the integers in Set A are consecutive, their average must equal their middle term. In a set of 7 integers, the middle one is the fourth term.

To find the smallest term, count backward from 46: 46, 44, 42, 40. That's (C). You can also answer this question by using Backsolving. Start with (C). If 40 is the smallest integer of Set A, then the next six consecutive integers must be 42, 44, 46, 48, 50, and 52. Take the average of these 7 integers:

$$\frac{40 + 42 + 44 + 46 + 48 + 50 + 52}{7} = \frac{322}{7} = 46$$

This matches the condition in the question stem: The average of these consecutive integers equals 46, so (C) must be the correct answer.

30. J   Difficulty: Medium

Category: Higher Math / Functions

Getting to the Answer: Test the sum for 2, then 3, then 4, then 5 terms of the sequence to see if a relationship can be determined. If $n = 2$, the sum is $1 + 3 = 4$. If $n = 3$, the sum is $1 + 3 + 5 = 9$. If $n = 4$, the sum is $1 + 3 + 5 + 7 = 16$. If $n = 5$, the sum is $1 + 3 + 5 + 7 + 9 = 25$. The sum is always equal to the square of n. Therefore, the correct answer is (J).

31. D   Difficulty: Medium

Category: Higher Math / Number and Quantity

Getting to the Answer: To multiply two matrices, the sizes (# of rows by # of columns) must match in a certain way. Here, the size of the first matrix is 2×2 and the size of the second is 2×1. If you multiply a 2×2 matrix by a 2×1 matrix (which is possible because the middle dimensions match), the result will be a 2×1 matrix (the outer dimensions when the sizes are written as a product). This means you can eliminate A, B, and C, which are all 2×2 matrices. To multiply the matrices, multiply each element in the first row of the first matrix by the corresponding element in the second matrix and add the products. Then repeat the process using the second row of the first matrix:

$$\begin{bmatrix} -2 & 0 \\ 1 & -3 \end{bmatrix} \cdot \begin{bmatrix} 2 \\ 2 \end{bmatrix} = \begin{bmatrix} -2(2) + 0(2) \\ 1(2) + (-3)(2) \end{bmatrix} = \begin{bmatrix} -4 \\ -4 \end{bmatrix}$$

Choice (D) is correct.

32. G **Difficulty:** Medium

Category: Higher Math / Geometry

Getting to the Answer: This is an area question with a twist—you're cutting a piece out of the rectangle. To find the area of the remaining space, you will need to subtract the area of the sandpit from the area of the original playground. Recall that the area of a rectangle is length $\times$ width. The dimensions of the original playground are $x + 7$ and $x + 3$, so its area is $(x + 7)(x + 3)$ which FOILS to $x^2 + 10x + 21$. The sandpit is a square with side x, so its area is x^2. Remove the pit from the playground, and the remaining area is $x^2 + 10x + 21 - x^2 = 10x + 21$. Choice (G) is correct.

33. E **Difficulty:** High

Category: Higher Math / Number and Quantity

Getting to the Answer: Because $m > 0$, m is a positive number; likewise, because $n < 0$, n is a negative number. Consider each answer choice and decide whether the expression must be positive, negative, or could be either depending on the values of m and n. Keep in mind that m and n can be even or odd integers.

A: $-n^m \rightarrow$ If m is even, n^m is positive so $-n^m$ is negative. However, when m is odd, n^m is negative, so $-n^m$ is positive. Eliminate this choice.

B: $-mn \rightarrow$ Because one number is positive and the other is negative, the product mn must be negative, so $-mn$ must be positive. Eliminate this choice.

C: $m^n \rightarrow m$ is positive, so m raised to any exponent will also be positive. A negative exponent simply means to take the reciprocal of the number, not to give the number a negative sign. Eliminate this choice.

D: $-n - m \rightarrow -n$ equals $-(-\text{number})$, which is positive, and m is positive, so $-n - m$ is a positive minus a positive. If $m > -n$, then $-n - m$ will be negative. However, if $-n > m$, then $-n - m$ will be positive. Eliminate this choice.

(E): $n - m \rightarrow n$ is negative and m is positive, so $n - m$ is a negative minus a positive. This must be negative, so (E) is the correct answer.

34. F **Difficulty:** Medium

Category: Essential Skills / Geometry

Getting to the Answer: Use the midpoint formula and the given midpoint to solve for m and n:

$$M = \left(\frac{x_1 + x_2}{2}, \frac{y_1 + y_2}{2} \right)$$

$$(-3, -2) = \left(\frac{1 + m}{2}, \frac{9 + n}{2} \right)$$

Once you have the formula set up and all the given information plugged in, separate the coordinates into two equations and solve for the variables:

$$-3 = \frac{1 + m}{2} \quad \text{and} \quad -2 = \frac{9 + n}{2}$$
$$-6 = 1 + m \qquad\qquad -4 = 9 + n$$
$$-7 = m \qquad\qquad\quad -13 = n$$

Thus $(m, n) = (-7, -13)$, which is (F).

35. C **Difficulty:** Low

Category: Higher Math / Functions

Getting to the Answer: When given a function and a value of x, plug in the number value for each x in the equation and simplify. Make sure you follow the order of operations:

$$f(x) = 16x^2 - 20x$$
$$f(3) = 16(3)^2 - 20(3)$$
$$= 16(9) - 60$$
$$= 144 - 60 = 84$$

Choice (C) is the answer.

36. G **Difficulty:** Low

Category: Essential Skills / Geometry

Getting to the Answer: To find the length of a line segment on the coordinate plane, you would normally need to use the Distance formula. This requires the coordinates of the segment's two endpoints. Because A (1,5) and C (1,1) have the same x-coordinate, a much faster way is to simply subtract the y-coordinate of C from the y-coordinate of A. The length of segment AC is $5 - 1$, or 4. Choice (G) is correct.

37. C   Difficulty: Medium

Category: Higher Math / Functions

Getting to the Answer: With nested functions, work from the inside out. To answer this question, substitute the entire rule for $g(x)$ for x in the function $f(x)$, then simplify:

$$f\big(g(x)\big) = \frac{1}{3}\big(3x^2 + 6x + 12\big) + 13$$
$$= x^2 + 2x + 4 + 13$$
$$= x^2 + 2x + 17$$

Choice (C) is correct.

38. H   Difficulty: Medium

Category: Higher Math / Algebra

Getting to the Answer: Perpendicular lines have negative-reciprocal slopes. Because the line in the question has a slope of $\frac{2}{3}$ (the coefficient of x), the line you are looking for must have a slope of $-\frac{3}{2}$. Eliminate F and G. The question also says that this line contains the point $(4, -3)$. Plugging all of this information into the equation of a line, $y = mx + b$, will allow you to find the final missing piece of the equation—the y-intercept:

$$y = mx + b$$
$$-3 = -\frac{3}{2}(4) + b$$
$$-3 = -6 + b$$
$$3 = b$$

With a slope of $-\frac{3}{2}$ and a y-intercept of 3, the line is $y = -\frac{3}{2}x + 3$, which matches (H).

39. D   Difficulty: Medium

Category: Higher Math / Algebra

Getting to the Answer: This looks like a chemistry or physics question, but in fact it's just a "plug in the number and solve for the missing quantity" question. Be sure to plug 95 in for C (not F). To clear the fraction (rather than distributing it), multiply both sides of the equation by the reciprocal of $\frac{5}{9}$:

$$C = \frac{5}{9}(F - 32)$$
$$95 = \frac{5}{9}(F - 32)$$
$$\frac{9}{5} \times 95 = F - 32$$
$$F - 32 = 171$$
$$F = 171 + 32 = 203$$

Choice (D) is correct.

40. J   Difficulty: Medium

Category: Higher Math / Algebra

Getting to the Answer: First, translate from English to math: "3 times x is increased by 5" translates to $3x + 5$, and "the result is less than 11" translates to < 11. Put these together to write an inequality and then solve for x:

$$3x + 5 < 11$$
$$3x < 6$$
$$x < 2$$

This inequality is graphed with an open circle at 2 (because x cannot equal 2) and shaded to the left, where the numbers are less than 2. Your graph should look like (J).

41. C   Difficulty: Medium

Category: Higher Math / Geometry

Getting to the Answer: Because $QS = QR$, triangle QRS must be a 45°-45°-90° triangle and the hypotenuse is $5\sqrt{2}$.

Remember that $\cos = \dfrac{\text{adjacent}}{\text{hypotenuse}}$. Therefore:

$$\cos R = \frac{5}{5\sqrt{2}}$$
$$= \frac{1}{\sqrt{2}}$$
$$= \frac{1}{\sqrt{2}} \times \frac{\sqrt{2}}{\sqrt{2}} = \frac{\sqrt{2}}{2}$$

Choice (C) is correct.

Answers & Explanations

42. K   Difficulty: High

Category: Essential Skills / Rates, Percents, Proportions, and Unit Conversion

Getting to the Answer: You need to find the ratio of angelfish to puffers. You're given two ratios: tangs to angelfish and tangs to puffers.

Both of the given ratios contain tangs, but the tang amounts (5 and 2) are not the same. To directly compare them, find a common multiple (10). Multiply each ratio by the factor that will make the number of tangs equal to 10:

tangs to angelfish: (5:2) × (2:2) = 10:4

tangs to puffers: (2:3) × (5:5) = 10:15

Now that the number of tangs are the same in both ratios, you can merge the two ratios to compare angelfish to puffers directly: **4:10:15**. So the proper ratio of angelfish to puffers is 4:15, which is (K).

43. D   Difficulty: Low

Category: Higher Math / Geometry

Getting to the Answer: This question is testing whether you can substitute into a formula correctly. Because you are told the diameter is 6, you know the radius, r, of the sphere is 3. Plug this value into the formula and simplify:

$$V = \frac{4}{3}\pi(3)^3 = \frac{4}{3}\pi(27) = 36\pi$$

Choice (D) is correct.

44. G   Difficulty: Medium

Category: Higher Math / Algebra

Getting to the Answer: To simplify the given expression, look for factors in the fraction term that will cancel. Use the denominator as a hint as to how to factor the numerator. Be careful—you cannot simply cancel the $x + 1$ in the denominator with the $x + 1$ at the end of the expression.

$$\frac{x^2 - 5x - 6}{x + 1} + x + 1 = \frac{(x+1)(x-6)}{x+1} + x + 1$$
$$= x - 6 + x + 1$$
$$= 2x - 5$$

Choice (G) is correct.

45. A   Difficulty: Medium

Category: Higher Math / Algebra

Getting to the Answer: Don't let the language throw you—*greatest monomial factor* just means the greatest common factor. Look for the largest number that divides evenly into 60 and 45. (Use the answer choices as a hint). The number is 15, so eliminate D and E. Next, look for the highest power of each variable that appears in *both* terms: a^2 and plain b. Thus, the greatest monomial factor is $15a^2b$, which is (A).

46. G   Difficulty: Low

Category: Higher Math / Statistics and Probability

Getting to the Answer: Percent change is calculated by dividing the amount of change by the original amount. In 1985, the population was 3,000; in 1995, the population was 2,000. Thus the amount of change was 1,000. Divide this by the original amount (the 1985 population) to find that the percent change was $1,000 \div 3,000 = 0.3333$, or 33.33%. The population went *down* from 1985 to 1995, so this is a decrease of 33.33%, which is (G).

47. C   Difficulty: Medium

Category: Higher Math / Statistics and Probability

Getting to the Answer: This question requires brute force. You need to list the data value corresponding to each year, order the values from least to greatest, find the median (the middle value), match it to a year in the graph, and then select the correct answer.

85	86	87	88	89	90
3,000	1,000	5,000	5,000	4,000	3,000
91	92	93	94	95	
4,000	1,000	3,000	2,000	2,000	

Order the data, keeping the year labels:

86	92	94	95	85	90
1,000	1,000	2,000	2,000	3,000	3,000
93	89	91	87	88	
3,000	4,000	4,000	5,000	5,000	

The median of this group is the sixth value, or 3,000. The years 1985, 1990, and 1993 all had populations of 3,000. The only one of these years among the answer choices is 1990, which is (C).

48. F   Difficulty: Medium

Category: Higher Math / Statistics and Probability

Getting to the Answer: Identify which pieces of information from the table you need. The question asks for the probability that a randomly chosen person from the study is employed and has a college degree, so you need the total of both females and males with college degrees who are employed compared to all the participants in the study. There are 188 employed females with a college degree and 177 employed males with a college degree for a total of 365 employed people with a college degree out of 800 participants, so the probability is $\frac{365}{800}$, which reduces to $\frac{73}{160}$, (F).

49. C   Difficulty: High

Category: Higher Math / Statistics and Probability

Getting to the Answer: Distinct permutations are permutations without repetition. You need to find the number of unique orderings of the letters GEOMETRY. If all eight letters were different, the number of unique orderings would be 8!. Because the E is repeated, you must divide by 2! to account for the repeated E. The result is $\frac{8!}{2!}$, which is (C).

Note that this process is the same as using the formula for "indistinguishable" outcomes: $\frac{n!}{a! \times b! \times \ldots}$. The number of letters is 8 (so $n = 8$), and there are 2 indistinguishable E's, so $a = 2$ and there is no b.

50. J   Difficulty: Low

Category: Higher Math / Geometry

Getting to the Answer: To match an inequality to its graph, you need to consider three things: the equation of the line, whether the line should be solid or dashed, and the direction of the shading. You can use any, or all, of these things to eliminate choices. Here, the shading is below (or less than) the line, so the inequality symbol should be <. Eliminate G and K. The line is dashed, but all the symbols are strict inequalities, so this doesn't help. The y-intercept of the line is -4 and the line rises 4 units for each 3 units that it runs, so the slope is $\frac{4}{3}$. This means the correct inequality is $y < \frac{4}{3}x - 4$, which is (J).

51. E   Difficulty: Medium

Category: Higher Math / Functions

Getting to the Answer: Occasionally, you may encounter a function that is defined in terms of two or three independent variables. These functions behave just as you would expect them to. As with any function, substitute the given values for the corresponding variables and simplify. Here, $x = 2$, $y = -1$, and $z = 3$.

$$h(x,y,z) = 4xy^2 - yz^3$$
$$h(2,-1,3) = 4(2)(-1)^2 - (-1)(3)^3$$
$$= 4(2)(1) - (-1)(27)$$
$$= 8 + 27$$
$$= 35$$

Choice (E) is correct.

52. K   Difficulty: Medium

Category: Higher Math / Geometry

Getting to the Answer: Write the formula for the area of a circle, using r to represent the radius of the original circle in the question: $A = \pi r^2$. This is the area of the original circle. Then write the formula for the area of the new larger circle, using $3r$ as the radius: $A = \pi(3r)^2 = \pi(9r^2) = 9\pi r^2$.

Now, divide the two areas (area of the new circle by the area of the original circle) to find out how many times larger the area of the new circle is compared to the area of the original circle.

$$\frac{\text{area of new circle}}{\text{area of original circle}} = \frac{9\pi r^2}{\pi r^2} = 9$$

Choice (K) is correct.

53. C   Difficulty: High

Category: Higher Math / Functions

Getting to the Answer: You don't really have to know anything about trig functions to answer this question. You just need to know the definition of *period*: The period of a repeating function is the distance along the x-axis required for the function to complete one full cycle. For a sine curve, this means one full wave (one up "bump" and one down "bump"). Here, that happens between 0 and π, which means the period is π. Choice (C) is correct.

If you happen to know the normal period of sine, which is 2π, you could also set the x term $(2x)$ equal to that period and solve for x. You'll get $2x = 2\pi$, which simplifies to $x = \pi$.

54. J   Difficulty: High

Category: Higher Math / Algebra

Getting to the Answer: Solving equations that involve radicals may seem daunting, but they work just like other equations. In fact, they're usually easier to solve than quadratic equations because you don't have to worry about factoring. As a general rule, you need to: 1) isolate the radical part; 2) eliminate the radical by squaring both sides of the equation if the radical is a square root, cubing both sides if it's a cube root, and so on; and 3) isolate the variable. To solve the equation here, the steps are:

$$\sqrt[3]{4x - 12} + 25 = 27$$
$$\sqrt[3]{4x - 12} = 2$$
$$\left(\sqrt[3]{4x - 12}\right)^3 = 2^3$$
$$4x - 12 = 8$$
$$4x = 20$$
$$x = 5$$

Choice (J) is correct. Note that you could also use Backsolving to answer this question.

55. D   Difficulty: Medium

Category: Higher Math / Geometry

Getting to the Answer: The chord is perpendicular to the line segment from the center of the circle, so that line segment must be its perpendicular bisector. This allows you to add the following measures to the figure:

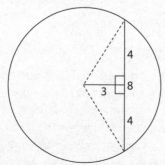

The two right triangles have legs 3 and 4, so they are both 3-4-5 right triangles with hypotenuse 5. This hypotenuse

is also the radius of the circle, so plug that into the area formula to solve:

$$A = \pi r^2$$
$$= \pi(5)^2$$
$$= 25\pi$$

The correct answer is (D).

56. F   Difficulty: High

Category: Higher Math / Functions

Getting to the Answer: Don't let the function notation intimidate you. The graphs of two functions intersect when the function equations are equal. Therefore, you need to set the equations equal to each other and solve for x.

$$f(x) = g(x)$$
$$3^{3x + 3} = 27^{\left(\frac{2}{3}x - \frac{1}{3}\right)}$$

When the equations have variables in the exponents, you must rewrite one or both of them so that either the bases are the same or the exponents themselves are the same. In this question, the two bases seem different at first glance but, because 27 is actually 3^3, you can rewrite the equation as:

$$3^{3x + 3} = \left(3^3\right)^{\left(\frac{2}{3}x - \frac{1}{3}\right)}$$

This simplifies to $3^{3x+3} = 3^{2x-1}$. Now that the bases are equal, set the exponents equal to each other and solve for x:

$$3x + 3 = 2x - 1$$
$$x + 3 = -1$$
$$x = -4$$

Choice (F) is correct.

57. A   Difficulty: High

Category: Higher Math / Functions

Getting to the Answer: To solve a logarithmic equation, rewrite the equation in exponential form and solve for the variable. To rewrite the equation, use the translation $\log_b y = x$ means $b^x = y$. The left side of the given equation has two logs, so you'll need to combine them first using properties of logs before you can translate. Don't worry about the right-hand side of the equation just yet.

$$\log_b x - \log_b y = \log_b \left(\frac{x}{y}\right)$$

$$\log_3(5x - 40) - \log_3 5 = \log_3 \left(\frac{5x - 40}{5}\right)$$

$$= \log_3 (x - 8)$$

Now the equation looks like $\log_3 (x - 8) = 2$, which can be rewritten as $3^2 = x - 8$. Simplifying yields $9 = x - 8$, or $17 = x$. Choice (A) is correct.

58. F   Difficulty: High

Category: Higher Math / Functions

Getting to the Answer: Fortunately, "cannot be determined" is not one of the answer choices here, because that would be very tempting. There is in fact enough information to answer this question. You just have to use what you know about arithmetic sequences—specifically, that to get from one term to the next, you add the same number each time. Here, you don't know what that number is, so call it n. The five terms in the sequence are:

4

$4 + n$

$4 + n + n$

$4 + n + n + n$

$4 + n + n + n + n$

These terms are already listed in order, so the median is the middle term, which is $4 + n + n$, or $4 + 2n$. The mean is the sum of all the terms divided by the number of terms: $\frac{20 + 10n}{5} = 4 + 2n$. Thus, the mean and the median have the same value, making the difference between them equal to 0, which is (F).

59. D   Difficulty: High

Category: Higher Math / Geometry

Getting to the Answer: You are given the cosine of $\angle BAC$ and the length of the hypotenuse of the triangle, so begin

by using these and SOHCAHTOA to find the length of the side adjacent to $\angle BAC$ (which is AB):

$$\cos A = \frac{\text{adjacent}}{\text{hypotenuse}}$$

$$0.6 = \frac{AB}{15}$$

$$AB = 0.6(15) = 9$$

So the adjacent side, $\overline{AB}$, is 9, and triangle ABC is a right triangle with a leg length of 9 and a hypotenuse of length 15. Triangle ABC must therefore be a 3-4-5 right triangle (scaled up by a factor of 3), and $\overline{BC}$ must have a length of 12. Choice (D) is correct.

60. J   Difficulty: High

Category: Higher Math / Geometry

Getting to the Answer: The question states that the points lie on the graph of a parabola (which is a nice, symmetric U shape), so use what you know about parabolas to answer the question. Notice that the x-values in the table increase by 2 each time. To find the y-value when $x = -4$, you just need to imagine adding one extra row to the top of the table. Now, think about symmetry—you can see from the points in the table that $(2,-5)$ is the vertex of the parabola. The points $(0,-3)$ and $(4,-3)$ are equidistant from the vertex, as are the points $(-2,3)$ and $(6,3)$. This means the point whose x-value is -4 should have the same y-value as the last point in the table $(8,13)$. So, when $x = -4$, $y = 13$. Choice (J) is correct.

READING TEST

Passage I

Suggested Passage Map notes:

¶1: Countess Olenska (CO) no longer pretty

¶2: CO 1st in NY as little girl adopted by aunt Medora (M)

¶3: M repeatedly widowed, NY accepting of M's eccentricities

¶4: All kind to Ellen (E) [aka CO], M not follow mourning rules

¶5: E was well-liked, fearless child; E's odd edu.

¶6: E married Polish nobleman, ended in disaster

¶7: NY expected CO to be more stylish and vibrant

1. C   Difficulty: Low

Category: Key Ideas and Details / Detail

Getting to the Answer: Remember that the correct answer to Detail questions will be directly stated in the passage. Your notes should guide you as you locate specific references to the details in question. Line 23 mentions Ellen's parents' "regrettable taste for travel" in the context of describing what the people of New York thought. Predict something like "travel." Choice (C) matches this prediction. Choice A is a misused detail; Medora does teach her niece to play the piano, but nothing in the passage suggests that this was undesirable. Choice B is a misused detail; Spanish shawl dances are described as "outlandish," but this is within the context of Medora and Ellen's eccentric, but accepted, behaviors. Choice D is a misused detail; while Medora often adopted children, this is never described as undesirable.

2. J   Difficulty: High

Category: Craft and Structure / Writer's View

Getting to the Answer: Consider how the author writes about New York society. In lines 24–25, she writes that "people thought it a pity that the pretty child [Ellen] should be in such hands," meaning that they did not feel the eccentric Medora was a good influence on Ellen. People call Medora "misguided" (line 30), and the author notes that she scandalized her family by not adhering to the "unalterable rules" of mourning (lines 31–32). All in all, New York society seems to have some rigid and snobbish rules. On the other hand, New Yorkers "looked indulgently on [Medora's] eccentricities" (lines 20–21), and New York "resigned itself to Medora" (lines 38–39). The author's view of New York society as it pertains to Medora seems to be mixed, which matches (J). Choice F doesn't take into account New York society's acceptance of Medora's odd behavior, G is opposite, and H is not mentioned in the passage.

3. A   Difficulty: Medium

Category: Key Ideas and Details / Inference

Getting to the Answer: To answer Inference questions, you will have to go beyond what is directly stated in the passage. However, the correct answer choice will be supported by evidence from the passage, so make sure you make a prediction that has solid textual support. You can predict, based on lines 56–67, that Ellen was unable to help her aunt because her own marriage to the immensely rich Polish nobleman "had ended in disaster." Choice (A) matches this prediction. Choice B is a distortion; since both Medora and Ellen left New York the amount of their communication over the years is unknown. Choice C is a distortion; while the author tells you that Ellen had an incoherent education, nothing in the passage suggests that she resented this. Choice D is a distortion; though the passage makes it clear that Medora was eccentric, this is in no way related to receiving help from her niece.

4. F   Difficulty: Medium

Category: Key Ideas and Details / Global

Getting to the Answer: Generalization questions require you to synthesize information, sometimes from the entire passage. Predicting an answer is particularly important for questions like this. Make sure you can support your prediction with information in the passage. Lines 68–70 suggest that Newland has spent time thinking about Ellen, and lines 74–93 describe Newland's observations of Ellen. Newland is not disappointed that Ellen is not as "stylish" as others expected (lines 84–87). You can predict that Newland is thoughtful and, unlike many of the other characters in the passage, nonjudgmental. Choice (F) matches this prediction. Choice G is out of scope; it might seem reasonable to conclude that Newland is likable, but the passage does not provide any evidence to directly support this. Also, there is nothing to suggest that he is withdrawn. Choice H is opposite; Newland's observations about Ellen in the last paragraph clearly indicate that he is interested in her. Choice J is a distortion; Newland's observation that Ellen is not as stylish as New York society might expect says nothing about his own stylishness, nor does the author ever describe his level of sociability.

5. A   Difficulty: Medium

Category: Craft and Structure / Writer's View

Getting to the Answer: Wharton writes that Medora has "many peculiarities" (line 31) and that "New York looked indulgently on her eccentricities" (lines 20–21). This matches the first part of answer choice (A). Since you may not know what *peripatetic* means, hold on to (A) while you research the other answers. Though Wharton states that each time Medora returns to New York she looks for a less expensive house, indicating reduced circumstances, this doesn't necessarily mean that Medora is impoverished, and there is no suggestion that she is resentful. Eliminate B. Medora may be kind (she does, after all, take in orphaned Ellen), but *loyal* doesn't describe someone who "invariably parted from her husband or quarrelled with her ward" (lines 15–16), eliminating C. Choice D mixes up Medora with Ellen; these words describe Ellen as a child, so D is incorrect. Choice (A) must be correct, even if you don't know that *peripatetic* means "traveling from place to place."

6. H   Difficulty: Medium

Category: Craft and Structure / Vocab-in-Context

Getting to the Answer: The word *flout* is used in the author's description of Medora wearing a veil considered too short for acceptable mourning and dressing Ellen in a crimson dress and amber beads" (line 37). Both of these are examples of Medora's "misguided . . . many peculiarities" (lines 30–31), which go against accepted New York behavior. Thus (H), *disregard*, is a good match. Choice F is too strong to describe Medora's behavior, as she does partially follow, rather than totally eliminate, the rules of mourning. Choice G is opposite, and while J looks similar to the word *flout*, it doesn't make sense in the passage.

7. C   Difficulty: Medium

Category: Key Ideas and Details / Global

Getting to the Answer: Make sure you have good evidence for your prediction, and the right answer choice will be easy to find. Line 21 mentions Medora's *eccentricities*, line 31 mentions her *peculiarities*, and line 44 mentions the *outlandish arts* that Medora teaches Ellen. From these descriptions, you can predict that Medora is unconventional or eccentric. Choice (C) matches this prediction. Choice A is out of scope; although Medora does not adhere to conventions, as indicated by lines 31–32, there is nothing to suggest that this is attributable to arrogance.

Choice B is a distortion; the description of the short veil that Medora wore to her brother's funeral in lines 34–36 might suggest immodesty, but the author makes clear that this is evidence of Medora's willingness to flout social conventions and never mentions any immodest dress or behavior. Choice D, which means following established practice, is opposite; you are told in lines 31–32 that one of her peculiarities is to "flout the unalterable rules that regulated American mourning."

8. F   Difficulty: Low

Category: Key Ideas and Details / Detail

Getting to the Answer: Detail questions like this one are straightforward, but it can sometimes be difficult to find exactly where in the passage the relevant information comes from. Make sure that you are answering the specific question being asked so that other details don't distract you. Medora teaches Ellen "drawing from the model" (line 49), which is described as "a thing never dreamed of before," so predict Ellen or Countess Olenska. Choice (F) matches your prediction. Choice G is out of scope; Newland is not described as having learned anything at all, let alone something controversial. Choice H is a distortion; Medora teaches Ellen, but the passage does not mention Medora learning anything herself. Choice J is a distortion; Count Olenska is only mentioned indirectly as the rich nobleman whom Medora marries. The passage makes it clear that Ellen is Countess Olenska; don't be fooled by this initially tempting, but incorrect, choice.

9. B   Difficulty: Medium

Category: Craft and Structure / Function

Getting to the Answer: Locate where the author mentions Medora's mother and read the next few lines. The author writes that "her mother had been a Rushworth" (line 18), that Medora married "one of the crazy Chiverses" (lines 19–20), and that because of these two conditions, "New York looked indulgently on her eccentricities" (lines 20–21). In other words, given her mother and her marriage, people were not surprised by Medora's unconventional life, which matches (B). There is no support for A, so it is out of scope. Choice C is opposite; New Yorkers "thought it a pity that the pretty child should be in such hands" (lines 24–25), and D is true but not relevant to Medora's eccentricities.

10. F   Difficulty: High

Category: Key Ideas and Details / Inference

Getting to the Answer: Remember that Inference questions will have details in the wrong answer choices that are meant to throw you off. Making a good prediction before reviewing the choices will guard against this. The beginning of the passage (line 4) implies that Newland knew Ellen when he was young. Lines 55–59 state that no one had heard from Ellen for some time, and after a few years, she came back to New York, as Medora had done before her. Predict that at the dinner, Newland and Ellen had not seen one another for an extended period of time. Choice (F) matches your prediction. Choice G is extreme; although Newland is clearly paying attention to Ellen in the last paragraph, there is nothing to suggest that either of them is interested in a romantic relationship. Choice H is extreme; while Ellen's lack of *stylishness* (lines 86–87) might suggest that she is not interested in New York society's conventions, it goes too far to say that she is disappointed. Choice J is opposite; the passage clearly portrays Ellen and Newland's encounter as a re-acquaintance.

Passage II

Suggested Passage Map notes:

¶1: Researchers in Junagadh, India, attempt accurate forecast

¶2: 1st trad. rule: monsoon begins 45 days after *Cassia fistula* tree blooms

¶3: 2nd trad. rule: north or west wind = good monsoon, east = drought

¶4: Trad. rules not exact, but general trend is correct

¶5: Dr. K started in 1990 when old saying was exactly correct

¶6: Meteorologist Sahu disagrees w/ Dr. K

¶7: Dr. K hopes research will show trad. methods are valid; holds conference

¶8: Dr. K started NGO to support further research

11. B   Difficulty: Medium

Category: Key Ideas and Details / Detail

Getting to the Answer: More difficult Detail questions can be approached using elimination and careful reading. Remember the EXCEPT. For EXCEPT questions, review the answer choices methodically, eliminating those which fail to meet the conditions of the question stem. The passage deals in some depth with both the flowering of the *C. fistula* tree, C, and the wind during Holi, A, so you can eliminate those first. Paragraph 5 states that Dr. Kanani became interested in traditional methods when a tenth-century rule of thumb "proved strikingly correct," which suggests that D has been tested. In contrast, the bird behavior is merely listed as an example of a rule of thumb uncovered in one of Kanani's conferences, making (B) the correct answer.

12. J   Difficulty: Medium

Category: Craft and Structure / Function

Getting to the Answer: Identify the paragraph in which these words appear; it ends with the statement that farmers need more precise forecasts than traditional methods provide. However, science has not developed good alternatives for farmers in different regions. Match this with (J). Choice F is opposite; the author writes that "Every year, the average rainfall over the whole country is calculated, and this prediction is proved correct" (lines 65–67). Choice G isn't mentioned in the passage, and H is a distortion.

13. A   Difficulty: Low

Category: Key Ideas and Details / Detail

Getting to the Answer: Your map should tell you that information about the winds observed during the Holi festival is in the third paragraph. In that paragraph, the author states that "the north or west suggests a good monsoon, whereas wind from the east indicates drought" (lines 33–35), which matches (A). Choices B and C are the wrong direction, and D, southwest, is not mentioned.

14. G   Difficulty: Medium

Category: Craft and Structure / Writer's View

Getting to the Answer: Inference questions encompassing the whole text will draw on evidence from the entire passage. A good prediction depends on your ability to synthesize the major ideas from throughout the passage. The passage mentions several traditional methods and their general accuracy. Even the scientific skepticism described in the passage admits a place for traditional methodology. The passage validates traditional methods, so predict that the author finds these methods to be valuable. Choice (G) matches this prediction. Choice F is out of scope; while the author briefly discusses the origins of some methods, she never expresses more interest in the development of the methods. Choice H is a distortion; the skepticism gets relatively little treatment and is followed by a detailed discussion of the progress toward making a real science of traditional methods. Choice J is opposite; the author never casts interest in traditional methods as a fad, and, as noted before, mentions the success of traditional methods more than once.

15. D   Difficulty: Low

Category: Key Ideas and Details / Detail

Getting to the Answer: Look to your notes to find specific locations for tested details. According to paragraph 5, Bhadli's storm method offers a 72-day warning. None of the other cited methods provide the same sort of accuracy over such a specific and extended time period, so look for Bhadli's method among the choices. Choice (D) matches this prediction. Choice A is a distortion; while the author mentions bird behavior as a possible predictor discussed at a conference, no information is given about the nature of this prediction. Choice B is a distortion; the flowering of the *Cassia fistula* tree does provide a specific and accurate prediction, but it gives only 45 days' advance warning. Choice C is a distortion; while the passage describes a loose correlation between the character of the monsoon and the wind direction on Holi, this method doesn't predict when the monsoon will arrive.

16. J   Difficulty: Low

Category: Craft and Structure / Function

Getting to the Answer: Beware of answer choices that present details that are narrower than the main point of the paragraph or sum up surrounding paragraphs instead of the target of the question. Focus on the overall topic of the paragraph and how it helps build the story or argument in the passage. The passage in general

describes the accuracy of traditional methods of weather prediction. The paragraph provides an example of a traditional method and introduces you to Dr. Kanani and his interest in applying scientific rigor to these methods; this can serve as your prediction. Choice (J) matches this prediction. Choice F is a misused detail; this sums up the first paragraph. Choice G is a misused detail; this accounts only for the last sentence of the cited paragraph. Choice H is a distortion; while the ancient saying is examined in the passage, this choice casts this examination as the central issue.

17. B   Difficulty: Low

Category: Key Ideas and Details / Detail

Getting to the Answer: For Detail questions, rely on your notes to direct your research to the relevant part of the passage. The topic sentences of the paragraph, lines 70–73, read: "Dr. Kanani hopes that his research will put traditional methods on a proper scientific footing. He and his colleagues have even set up a sort of peer-review forum." Predict that the conference's goal is this establishment of traditional methods as worthy subjects of scientific inquiry. Choice (B) matches this prediction. Choice A is out of scope; the passage never discusses the disappearance of traditional methods. Choice C is a misused detail; while Dr. Kanani does, in fact, publish the methods in the local press, this is not the objective of the conference. Choice D is out of scope; the passage never mentions the exchange of ideas between geographically distant farmers.

18. H   Difficulty: Medium

Category: Key Ideas and Details / Inference

Getting to the Answer: Beware of general answer choices. Attack the question stem, get a good understanding of what it's really asking, and make a solid prediction. The question asks you for the reason farmers predict the weather using traditional methods. What do they hope to accomplish? When the question is rephrased, the answer seems more obvious; predict that the correct choice, according to the first paragraph, will show that they want to know what to plant, so they need to know what's coming. Choice (H) matches this prediction. Choice F is out of scope; the passage never mentions the accessibility of the methods. Choice G is a distortion; while "'normal' monsoons" are discussed in paragraph 6, this is in reference to modern meteorology, not traditional methods of forecasting. Choice J is a distortion; while traditional methods do get the basics right, the question asks why the farmers are trying to get the basics right in the first place.

19. C   Difficulty: Medium

Category: Craft and Structure / Function

Getting to the Answer: Eliminate answers that are inconsistent with the central concerns of the passage. Reread the specific reference and the surrounding text, which identifies the flowering of *C. fistula* as a monsoon predictor that isn't "perfect," but still of value and interest. Predict that the correct choice will account for both an appreciation of this traditional method and an awareness of its limitations. Choice (C) matches this prediction. Choice A is extreme; while the author feels that the predictive data are useful and noteworthy, calling them "remarkably predictive" goes too far. Choice B is out of scope; the author never attempts to generalize on the relative value of precision. Choice D is out of scope; again, the author neither casts traditional methods as rules of thumb and scientific methods as complex formulas nor attempts to elevate one over the other.

20. H   Difficulty: Low

Category: Key Ideas and Details / Detail

Getting to the Answer: Consult your notes to direct your research to the relevant text. Sahu says in lines 58–61 that traditional prediction may be "OK as a hobby," but "may not be applicable to this modern age." Then he concedes that modern era forecasts are not always helpful to farmers in the way traditional methods claim to be. That some utility exists despite scientific skepticism serves as a good prediction and an accurate paraphrase of his attitude. Choice (H) summarizes Sahu's attitude and matches this prediction. Choice F is opposite; the author identifies Sahu as claiming the methods "cannot be relied upon" (lines 59–60). Choice G is opposite; Sahu rejects traditional methods from the scientific view. Choice J is out of scope; Sahu never mentions the appeal of the methods, only their trustworthiness as predictors.

Passage III

Suggested Passage Map notes:

Passage A

¶1: Country music (C) born in central & southern Appalachians

¶2: Originated in 1920s from multiple sources

¶3: The term "country" replaced "hillbilly"

¶4: Hank Williams 1st to take country national; artists

¶5: Nashville, TN = country home w/ Grand Ole Opry (1925)

¶6: C relatives = honky tonk, Western Swing

¶7: C expresses Am. identity

Passage B

¶1: Bluegrass (B) origin and description

¶2: B diff. from C: highlight 1 musician at a time, diff. instruments, vocal harmonies

¶3: Own category in late 1950s, named after Bill Monroe's band

¶4: Today: movies, festivals

¶5: B themes = working class; reflects Am.

21. C   Difficulty: Medium

Category: Key Ideas and Details / Detail

Getting to the Answer: Use your Passage Map to locate this detail; the second paragraph should include the necessary information. Use the list of the sources of country music ("spirituals as well as folk music, cowboy songs, and traditional Celtic melodies") to make your prediction. Choice (C) is correct because country music is not rooted in jazz. Rather, jazz was combined with country music to create Western Swing. Paragraph 6 states, "Additionally, Western Swing emerged as one of the first genres to blend country and jazz musical styles, which required a great deal of skill and creativity." Choice A is opposite; paragraph 2 describes the many sources of country music with the sentence, "Rooted in spirituals as well as folk music, cowboy songs, and traditional Celtic melodies, country music originated in the 1920s." Choice

B is opposite; spirituals influenced the development of country music. Choice D is opposite; country music is rooted in cowboy songs.

22. J   Difficulty: Medium

Category: Key Ideas and Details / Detail

Getting to the Answer: The answer to a Detail question is stated in the passage. However, because all answer choices are in the passage, be careful to assess each one in terms of the actual question asked. A look at your notes or a quick scan of the passage should provide enough information to make a prediction about where to find the best country music. Match that prediction to the correct answer. Choice (J) is correct; in paragraph 5, the author writes "Country singers are considered to have reached the pinnacle of the profession if they are asked to become members of the Opry." To hear the best music, it makes sense to go to the place where those at the pinnacle, or top of their field, perform. Choice F is a misused detail; one would hear honky-tonk music, a derivative of country, but not country music itself, in these bars. Choice G is a misused detail; Ireland is the original home of the Ulster Scots, many of whom settled in Appalachia. Choice H is a misused detail; though country music had its origins in the mixture of music created in Appalachia, the author does not state that it is the place to hear the best music.

23. C   Difficulty: High

Category: Craft and Structure / Vocab-in-Context

Getting to the Answer: As with all Vocab-in-Context questions, use the surrounding clues to define the word in question. The word appears in paragraph 3, where the original term *hillbillies* is used to describe "Appalachian inhabitants who were considered poor, uneducated, isolated, and wary." The more accepting word *country* has replaced *hillbillies*, indicating that *pejorative* is an adjective used to highlight the negative characteristics described in the paragraph. This matches (C), since *disparaging* means "belittling, or bad." Choice A is a synonym for *original* rather than a word that means *negative*. Choice B is out of scope, as the author never expresses that the negative view is accurate, and D refers to where the people live rather than describing the term (i.e., it is not a mountain-dwelling term).

24. F   Difficulty: Low

Category: Craft and Structure / Writer's View

Getting to the Answer: Both passages introduce several genres of American music, but this question refers to Passage B, so research the passage carefully. In the first paragraph, the author introduces bluegrass music and writes that it is "a mixture of Scottish, Welsh, Irish, and English melodic forms, infused, over time, with African-American influences" (lines 75–77) and that laments "are common themes" (line 82). These are exactly the components of the song in the question, making (F) correct. The other answers refer to Passage A and are described as having different derivations.

25. A   Difficulty: Medium

Category: Key Ideas and Details / Detail

Getting to the Answer: Locate the paragraph in which bluegrass instruments are described, and match those descriptions with the correct answer choice. Your notes point to only one paragraph in which musical instruments are mentioned. Scan the answer choices, then reread the information in that paragraph to determine which answer choice characterizes the information given. Choice (A) is correct; musical instruments are described in the second paragraph and include typical ones such as "banjo, guitar, mandolin, bass, harmonica, and Dobro (resonator guitar)." But the paragraph goes on to include far less typical ones, such as "household objects, including washboards and spoons," which are not usually considered musical instruments, but are sometimes included in a bluegrass band. Choice B is a misused detail; African-American influences are provided as one more source of the bluegrass genre, but instrumentation is not referenced. Choice C is a misused detail; this is an example of a bluegrass piece used in a movie soundtrack. Choice D is out of scope; the reference to the Ozark mountains concerns the origin of bluegrass and has nothing to do with a description of musical instruments.

26. F   Difficulty: High

Category: Key Ideas and Details / Detail

Getting to the Answer: The answer to a Detail question is stated in the passage. Locate the paragraph in which the differences between country and bluegrass music are discussed. Paragraph 2 includes the information you need to answer the question. Be sure to keep straight which details describe each genre of music. Choice (F) is correct. Paragraph 2 details two characteristics of bluegrass music: first, that "bluegrass highlights one player at a time, with the others providing accompaniment," and second, that "bluegrass incorporates baritone and tenor harmonies." Choice G is opposite; country music features a single voice. Choice H is opposite; country musicians commonly play the same melodies together. Choice J is a distortion; which instruments are used is not cited as a difference between the music styles.

27. B   Difficulty: Medium

Category: Key Ideas and Details / Inference

Getting to the Answer: Locate the paragraphs that mention laments and high, lonesome sound, and consider what the author means by including these two details. The reference to *laments* in the first paragraph and the reference to "high, lonesome sound" in the last paragraph are examples of "the hard-scrabble life of the American worker," which matches (B). Choice A is out of scope; the elements mentioned in the question stem do not necessarily reflect Irish music; bluegrass has multiple sources. Choice C is a misused detail; Shania Twain is an example of a country singer and is mentioned in Passage A only. Choice D is a misused detail; though bluegrass was originally called *hillbilly*, this is the name for the genre, not the theme.

28. G   Difficulty: Medium

Category: Craft and Structure / Vocab-in-Context

Getting to the Answer: Vocab-in-Context questions require that you understand the context of a cited word or phrase. Locate the reference, and focus your research on the text immediately preceding and immediately following the word or phrase in question. The introductory paragraph states, "One of the most enjoyable ways to analyze culture is through music." Look for an answer choice that indicates that music can provide specific insight about a culture as a whole. Choice (G) matches this prediction. Choices F, H, and J are distortions; *quintessential* does not mean old-fashioned, charming, or conventional (typical).

29. C   Difficulty: Medium

Category: Integration of Knowledge and Ideas / Synthesis

Getting to the Answer: When asked to use a quote to find support in one paragraph for information in another, be sure to read the quote in the context of the paragraph. First, find the paragraph in which the quote from Passage A appears, then match the quote to one in Passage B. Choice (C) is correct; Flatt and Scruggs are mentioned in Passage B, paragraph 3, in which they are characterized as "the foremost artists on their instruments." The best artists are certainly "talented and sophisticated." Choice A is a misused detail; this quote refers to bluegrass themes, whereas the question asks for one that supports talented and sophisticated musicians. Choice B is out of scope; the "pace and complexity" of the music does not necessarily relate to the skill of the musicians themselves. Choice D is out of scope; the relation between bluegrass and country music refers to the kinship of the genres, not the musicians.

30. H   Difficulty: Medium

Category: Integration of Knowledge and Ideas / Synthesis

Getting to the Answer: When looking for something on which both authors would agree, first determine what each one actually states in the passage, then consider what must be true based on those statements. The evolution, or gradual change, in music, as with anything else, must start from somewhere, so look to the parts of each passage that detail the genesis of the music genres, then consider the progression from there. Choice (H) is correct; both authors detail the various music sources that became either country or bluegrass. In the first passage, the author mentions "folk music, cowboy songs, and traditional Celtic melodies," and in the second passage, the author refers to "Scottish, Welsh, Irish, and English melodic forms, infused, over time, with African-American influences." Both authors affirm that the two music genres are *indigenous*. Thus, it must be true that both country and bluegrass music have evolved from their various roots to become American music, supporting agreement on the fact that music can evolve. Choice F is out of scope; each passage mentions how its particular music genre is popular (as explained in the next sentence in the explanation—the Czech festivals and international growth), but both authors don't describe why *both* genres are popular, only their own. Choice G is a misused detail; the Grand Ole Opry showcases country music only, not bluegrass. Choice J is out of scope; the passages don't each discuss both genres, only their own.

Passage IV

Suggested Passage Map notes:

¶1: 1999, Pluto about to lose planet status

¶2: Marsden says Pluto given special status, not demoted

¶3: Discussion started in 1930, Pluto small & elongated orbit

¶4: 1992 Jewitt and Luu discovered QB1, Luu says Pluto is a TNO

¶5: 70 TNOs are known, Pluto is biggest

¶6: Binzel suggests Pluto be made 1st entry in TNO catalog

¶7: Marsden agrees Pluto is TNO, but doesn't want new way of classifying TNOs

¶8: Marsden wants to give Pluto its own special number in an existing asteroid catalog

¶9: Luu disagrees w/ Marsden

¶10: A'Hearn trying to settle dispute

¶11: General public will still think of Pluto as 9th planet

31. D   Difficulty: Low

Category: Key Ideas and Details / Detail

Getting to the Answer: Luu strongly disagrees with the view that Pluto should be labeled an asteroid (lines 84–88). She goes so far as to use the term *idiotic* in reference to others in her profession, so predict something like *indignation*. Choice (D) matches this prediction. Choice A is a distortion; while *shock* may be an initially tempting choice, it's clear that Luu's surprise stems from her disagreement with the opinion, not her lack of preparation to hear it. Choice B is opposite; *excitement* suggests some degree of positive response, which Luu clearly does not display. Choice C is opposite; Luu quite clearly expresses her feelings on the classification controversy.

32. H   Difficulty: Medium

Category: Key Ideas and Details / Inference

Getting to the Answer: If you get stuck, eliminating answers that have no support in the passage will greatly reduce the number of choices. The passage states that, if astronomers had known about the other TNOs, Pluto would not have been named a planet (lines 49–52). The size of Pluto is indicated as the reason it was discovered before the others. You can infer that a better system of detection would have discovered other TNOs, eliminating Pluto's status as a planet. Account for this in your prediction. Choice (H) matches your prediction. Choice F is a distortion; Pluto's size does indeed make it different from the other planets, but the lack of this knowledge is not cited as the sole reason for its initial classification. Choice G is a distortion; although the icy Pluto is said to belong with neither the *rocky planets* nor the *gas giants* (lines 28–29), this information is included as a way to differentiate Pluto from the planets, and the lack of this knowledge initially is not identified as the reason for Pluto's original classification. Choice J is a distortion; the controversy that would later surround Pluto's initial classification as a planet was never drawn into the discussion of the original classification.

33. D

Category: Craft and Structure / Writer's View

Difficulty: Medium

Getting to the Answer: As interested as the author is in how to describe Pluto, at no point does the author offer a personal opinion. Because of this, you cannot assume that the author would agree with anything other than a neutral statement, as (D) is. The author does not side with those who would call Pluto a TNO, making A incorrect, nor those who argue that it should remain a planet, C. Choice B is a distortion; IAU stands for International Astronomical Union, not a classification.

34. F

Category: Key Ideas and Details / Detail

Difficulty: Low

Getting to the Answer: Your notes on the passage should show the location of key details and terminology so you can quickly find them as you research the question stem.

Neptune is mentioned only a few times; the fourth paragraph mentions Neptune in relation to trans-Neptunian objects, and the seventh paragraph mentions Neptune and Centaurs, one of the answer choices. Sure enough, an examination of the description reveals that Centaurs, a great prediction, are asteroids similar to Pluto "nudged" inside Neptune's orbit. Choice (F) matches this prediction. Choice G is a misused detail; the passage states that IAU stands for International Astronomical Union. Choice H is a misused detail; TNO stands for trans-Neptunian objects, things beyond Neptune. Choice J is a misused detail; the term "ice dwarf" is used in connection with the discovery of a TNO.

35. C

Category: Key Ideas and Details / Inference

Difficulty: Low

Getting to the Answer: Inference questions such as this ask that you interpret the referenced lines, drawing on your reading of the passage as a whole. The quote making up the majority of the referenced lines comes from a scientist who, in the passage, takes a position against creating a new classification. Your prediction should reflect the issue of whether the existing categories are suitable. Choice (C) matches this prediction. Choice A is a misused detail; this is certainly discussed in the passage, but this doesn't pertain to the cited lines or the speaker in question. Choice B is a misused detail; distance from the sun and from Neptune is significant to certain classification schemes, but this is not the central issue in Pluto's specific case. Choice D is a misused detail; that the scientific community and general public have differing opinions is irrelevant to the cited lines.

36. G   Difficulty: High

Category: Craft and Structure / Vocab-in-Context

Getting to the Answer: Vocab-in-Context questions require that you understand the context of a cited word or phrase. Locate the reference and focus your research on the text immediately preceding and immediately following the word or phrase in question. Investigating the word in question contextualizes it within the argument of a scientist who "doesn't like the idea of establishing a new catalog of solar system objects" (lines 62–63) and argues

that "astronomers already have a perfectly serviceable list of numbered minor bodies" (lines 64–65). Predict something like *sufficient* to replace the word in question. Choice (G) matches this prediction. Choice F invokes the most common meaning of the word, which doesn't make sense in context and is usually a trap answer; the scientist does *not* want to change the system. Choices H and J don't work in context, since describing a particular classification system as *beneficial* or *durable* is awkward.

37. D   Difficulty: Low

Category: Key Ideas and Details / Global

Getting to the Answer: Remember that Global questions will attempt to make tempting answer choices out of issues discussed in the passage only briefly. A recurring theme throughout the passage is giving Pluto a "very special designation" (line 19) or honor (line 80), which differs from the predominantly scientific concerns over Pluto's classification discussed elsewhere. Predict an answer that touches on this idea of honoring or distinguishing Pluto in some way. Choice (D) matches this prediction. Choice A is out of scope; the role of the IAU is never discussed by the cited experts. Choice B is a misused detail; the author does relay some information about the ways in which public opinion is unlikely to change, but this is not a significant concern for scientists dealing with deeper issues. Choice C is out of scope; none of the cited scientists seem particularly concerned with being credited for solving the problem.

38. G   Difficulty: Medium

Category: Key Ideas and Details / Detail

Getting to the Answer: The passage ends with a discussion of one scientist's attempt to find consensus about Pluto's status. In this part of the passage, the major ideas are listed. Binzel's idea is rejected because Pluto "would still be an anomaly." Luu forcefully asserts that "Pluto is certainly not an asteroid." Both criticisms are based on the idea that neither category adequately describes Pluto, so predict that the correct answer will focus on the inadequacy of any categorization scheme. Choice (G) matches this prediction. Choice F is a misused detail; the public's recognition of Pluto's controversial status or a potential change in category are not significant issues to scientists. Choice H is a distortion; Pluto's orbit plays little role in the discussion of its classification, and its surface is never mentioned. Choice J is a misused detail; the existence of Pluto-like objects nearer to the sun than Neptune functions as a criticism of only one theory.

39. B   Difficulty: Medium

Category: Key Ideas and Details / Detail

Getting to the Answer: Detail questions will sometimes require a broad approach to information from a variety of locations in the text. Your notes will help you to sort out the specifics. Lines 24–27 discuss Pluto's size in relation to other planets, and lines 27–28 describe its orbit as anomalous. A good prediction will account for both. Choice (B) matches this prediction. Choice A is a misused detail; distance from the sun versus distance from Neptune is significant only in certain classification systems for non-planets. Choice C is out of scope; the year of Pluto's discovery in relation to those of other planets is never discussed. Choice D is out of scope; Pluto's shape is not compared to other planets.

40. H   Difficulty: High

Category: Key Ideas and Details / Detail

Getting to the Answer: Tougher Detail questions will require an investigation of several sections of text. Count on your notes to direct you, even when the search is fairly extensive. Lines 24–27 tell you that Pluto is smaller than other planets, which is why scientists need to reclassify it, yet its large size compared to asteroids and TNOs (lines 101–102) is what keeps many scientists confused about its proper category. Lines 46–49 cite Pluto's size as the exact reason that it was found 60 years before the next body like it. Your prediction should account for this classification difficulty as well as Pluto's early discovery. Choice (H) matches this prediction. Choice F is a distortion; categorizing of Pluto as a TNO is only a proposed solution to the classification problem and takes into consideration issues other than size, most importantly, its relation to Neptune. Choice G is opposite; it is Pluto's relatively small size that potentially allows it the same classification as an asteroid. Choice J is a misused detail; the passage never relates Pluto's size to the nature of the planet's orbit.

SCIENCE TEST

Passage I

1. A   Difficulty: Low

Category: Interpretation of Data

Getting to the Answer: The question stem tells you that you're looking for a mineral composed of 32% zinc and 12% calcium. Table 1 lists the percentages of calcium and zinc in a variety of minerals, so look there for an answer. According to Table 1, hornblende is composed of 30 to 35% zinc and 10 to 20% calcium. Choice (A) is thus correct.

2. J   Difficulty: Low

Category: Interpretation of Data

Getting to the Answer: Diagram 1 presents the most common minerals in each soil horizon. A geologist digging down into the A horizon would encounter mostly quartz and mica. Quartz isn't included as a possible answer, but mica is. Choice (J) is thus correct. Choice F is incorrect because limestone isn't commonly found until the C horizon. Choice G is incorrect because shale isn't common until the final horizon. Choice H is incorrect because serpentine is commonly found in the B horizon.

3. B   Difficulty: Medium

Category: Interpretation of Data

Getting to the Answer: Based on Diagram 1, you can see that the minerals are arranged in Table 1 so that the shallowest are at the top of the table and the deepest are at the bottom. However, as you move down the table, you'll notice that zinc content decreases, which indicates an inverse relationship between depth and zinc content. In other words, as zinc content *increases*, depth *decreases*. Choice (B) is thus correct.

4. H   Difficulty: Low

Category: Interpretation of Data

Getting to the Answer: Based on Diagram 1, the only minerals geologists wouldn't commonly find at a depth of 30 feet or lower (to the bottom of the B Horizon) are limestone and shale. You can eliminate F, G, and J because each contains one of these minerals. Choice (H), then, is correct.

5. A   Difficulty: Medium

Category: Interpretation of Data

Getting to the Answer: The mineral content of granite is located in Table 2, so start there. Table 2 shows that granite is composed of feldspar, quartz, mica, and augite. If augite is found close to the other minerals in granite, then it should be located at roughly the same depth as feldspar, quartz, and mica. Now use Diagram 1 to find the depths at which those three minerals are most commonly found. Feldspar is found in the O horizon, at a depth of 2 feet or less, while quartz and mica are found in the A horizon, at a depth of 2 to 10 feet. So you should definitely expect to find augite at depths of less than 10 feet, as in (A).

6. G   Difficulty: Low

Category: Interpretation of Data

Getting to the Answer: Zinc content percentage and calcium content percentage are found in Table 1, so examine it for an answer. Moving down the table, zinc content steadily decreases as calcium content steadily increases. The two quantities are inversely related, making (G) correct.

Passage II

7. D   Difficulty: Medium

Category: Scientific Investigation

Getting to the Answer: To answer this question, examine the formula that is provided at the beginning of the passage: $\Delta T_b = K_b \times m \times i$. This equation indicates that the boiling point will increase more if K_b, m, or i is increased. Item I would increase K_b, item II would increase m, and item III would increase i (because $CaCl_2$ splits into 3 ions, while NaCl only splits into 2 ions). Because all three items would increase the boiling point of Solution 5, (D) is correct.

8. H   Difficulty: Low

Category: Interpretation of Data

Getting to the Answer: The results for Study 1 are presented in Table 1. Table 1 shows that for 0.171 mol of NaCl, the boiling point is increased to 101.75°C. Choice (H) is thus correct.

9. C   Difficulty: Medium

Category: Interpretation of Data

Getting to the Answer: This question asks about the melting point of Material 5. Table 3 provides data about when Material 5 melted, indicating that it did not melt in Solution 5, but that it did melt in Solution 6. Therefore, its melting point will be somewhere between the boiling points of those solutions. Table 1 shows that Solution 5 has a boiling point of 103.50°C and Table 2 shows that Solution 6 has a boiling point of 104.15°C, so Material 5's melting point must fall somewhere in between those values. Choice (C) is thus correct.

10. G   Difficulty: Medium

Category: Interpretation of Data

Getting to the Answer: Table 2 provides the boiling points for solutions consisting of various amounts of $CaCl_2$ added to water. The trend seems linear: for each increase of roughly 0.9 mol $CaCl_2$, the boiling point increases by roughly 1.4°C. The highest amount of $CaCl_2$ on the table is 0.631 mol, roughly 0.9 less than the amount in the question stem. Therefore, the increase will be roughly 1.4° higher than 109.67°C, or 111.07°C. Choice (G) is thus correct. Choice F is between the boiling points for Solutions 9 and 10, which is too low. Choices H and J are too high.

11. A   Difficulty: Medium

Category: Scientific Investigation

Getting to the Answer: Table 3 gives an indication of the points at which each material begins to melt. Based on the information from Tables 1 and 2, a higher-numbered solution corresponds to a higher boiling point. It would be highly implausible for a material to melt at a low temperature but not at a higher temperature, which is the trend depicted in (A). The other choices are incorrect because they are all possibilities already revealed in

Study 3's results: B corresponds to the results for Material 1, C to the results for Material 4, and D to the results for Materials 6, 7, and 8.

12. H   Difficulty: High

Category: Scientific Investigation

Getting to the Answer: The equation for boiling point elevation given in the passage indicates that the increase in temperature depends upon the molality of the solution. As noted in the explanation of the equation, molality is defined as moles (mol) of solute over kilograms (kg) of solvent. Thus, the students recorded the moles of a solute, rather than its mass, in order to make the calculation of molality—and the subsequent calculation of change in boiling point—easier. Choice (H) is correct. Choice F makes little sense; measuring the solvent's mass does nothing to prevent measuring the solute's mass. Choice G is a false statement; moles are usually calculated on the basis of mass, so if anything mass measurements are more accurate. Choice J is true but irrelevant to the question.

13. A   Difficulty: Medium

Category: Evaluation of Models, Inferences, and Results

Getting to the Answer: Table 3 shows that Material 7 melted in Solution 10, whereas Material 8 did not. That means that Material 7 must have a melting point of no more than 109.67°C (the boiling point of Solution 10), while Material 8 must have a melting point higher than that temperature. Thus, the results do support the claim that Material 7 has the lower melting point, making (A) correct. Choice B is incorrect because it reverses the results for the materials. Choice C is incorrect because the exact melting point of Material 8 does not need to be determined to support the claim—it only has to be shown to have a higher melting point than Material 7. Choice D is incorrect because the approximate melting point of Material 7 can be determined: it must be between the boiling point temperatures of Solutions 9 and 10.

Passage III

14. G   Difficulty: Medium

Category: Evaluation of Models, Inferences, and Results

Getting to the Answer: According to Table 1, the concentrations of nitrogen, phosphorus oxide, and zinc all tend to increase as humidity level increases, regardless of which of the three data sources is considered. For potassium oxide, however, the trend is reversed: the concentration decreases as humidity increases. Choice (G) is thus correct.

15. A   Difficulty: Low

Category: Interpretation of Data

Getting to the Answer: To answer this question, compare the System B data to the USGS data at 25% humidity for the 4 compounds given as answer choices. For nitrogen (N), the USGS concentration is 236 mg/L, while System B measures it as 408 mg/L, which is close to double. For calcium (Ca), USGS has 24.7 mg/L and System B has 23.2 mg/L, a much smaller difference, meaning B can be eliminated. For potassium oxide (K_2O), USGS has 9.2 mg/L and System B has 9.1 mg/L, a very small difference, allowing you to eliminate C too. Finally, for phosphorus oxide (P_2O_5), USGS has 71.2 mg/L and System B has 75.6 mg/L, still smaller than the difference seen in nitrogen, meaning D can also be eliminated. Nitrogen shows by far the biggest difference, whether this is calculated in absolute or relative terms, so (A) is correct.

16. J   Difficulty: Low

Category: Evaluation of Models, Inferences, and Results

Getting to the Answer: From Table 1, you can see that the potassium oxide concentration continually decreases from 9.4 mg/L to 8.2 mg/L as humidity increases from 10% to 80% in the USGS data, continually decreases from 9.4 to 8.0 in System A, and continually decreases from 9.5 to 8.3 in System B. Because the data from all 3 sources support the hypothesis that potassium oxide levels decrease with increasing humidity, (J) is correct.

17. D   Difficulty: Medium

Category: Evaluation of Models, Inferences, and Results

Getting to the Answer: The question asks you to determine which system is more accurate, so ultimately you're trying to find the one that is closer to the USGS data, which is described in the passage as "extremely accurate." Looking at the data for zinc, you can see that the measurements from System B are always closer to the data from the USGS than are the measurements from System A. Therefore, you know the answer to the question is yes, allowing you to eliminate A and B. Choice C, though, is incorrect because it gives the wrong reasoning: System B does give lower measurements than System A, but that alone doesn't make it more accurate. The measurements from System B are more accurate because they are closer to the data from the USGS than are the measurements from System A. Choice (D) is thus correct.

18. H   Difficulty: Medium

Category: Interpretation of Data

Getting to the Answer: To answer this question, look at the row in the table that represents calcium concentrations for System B. You can see that the numbers gradually decrease from 10% humidity to 65% humidity, then increase quickly from 65% to 85% humidity. The only graph that shows values decreasing and then rapidly increasing is (H).

19. B   Difficulty: High

Category: Scientific Investigation

Getting to the Answer: Examine the System B data in Table 1 to answer this question. According to the table, a potassium oxide level of 9.1 mg/L falls between the values for 25% humidity (9.2) and 45% humidity (9.0), a calcium level of 17.3 mg/L also falls between the values for 25% (23.2) and 45% (11.6), and a zinc level of 0.57 mg/L likewise falls between the values for 25% (0.48) and 45% (0.62). Therefore, the level of humidity for this sample should almost certainly be some value between 25% and 45%. Only (B) falls within this range.

Passage IV

20. G   Difficulty: Low

Category: Evaluation of Models, Inferences, and Results

Getting to the Answer: What are Scientist 1's and Scientist 2's viewpoints? Scientist 1 believes that type 2 diabetes is caused by excess sugar consumption, and Scientist 2 says that type 2 diabetes is caused by obesity as a result of a high-fat diet and lack of exercise. If new research suggested that 80% of people with diabetes have buildup of fat in the liver, this information would support the view of Scientist 2 only. The correct answer is (G).

21. B   Difficulty: Low

Category: Evaluation of Models, Inferences, and Results

Getting to the Answer: Scientist 1 states that "the cause of type 2 diabetes is an overconsumption of sugar," while Scientist 2 states that "diets high in fat but not high in sugar are associated with an increased risk of type 2 diabetes." Thus, both scientists would mostly likely agree that the occurrence of type 2 diabetes in an individual is associated with the patient's diet. The correct answer is (B). Choice A is only mentioned by Scientist 2, and C is only mentioned by Scientist 3. Age is mentioned in the introductory text, but even though type 2 diabetes is more prevalent in adults, the passage does not suggest that age causes type 2 diabetes, so D is also incorrect.

22. H   Difficulty: Medium

Category: Evaluation of Models, Inferences, and Results

Getting to the Answer: The passage states that type 2 diabetes occurs "when the body does not produce enough insulin," and explains that "Insulin is a hormone produced in the pancreas that helps regulate blood glucose levels." If the pancreas is removed, the body would not produce insulin, and would thus be unable to regulate blood glucose levels, thereby causing type 2 diabetes to develop. None of the answer choices state this explicitly, but (H) gives the major symptom of diabetes that was stated in the introductory paragraph: elevated blood glucose levels (hyperglycemia). Choices F and G are incorrect because they state the opposite of what you should expect. You can also eliminate J because you're given no reason to suspect a link between the pancreas and body fat content.

23. C   Difficulty: Medium

Category: Evaluation of Models, Inferences, and Results

Getting to the Answer: According to Scientist 3, type 2 diabetes is inherited. Eliminate A and B, which correspond to the hypotheses of Scientists 1 and 2, respectively. Scientist 3 states "individuals have about a 15–20% chance of developing type 2 diabetes if one of their parents has it and a roughly 50% chance if both parents have it." 18% falls within the 15–20% range. Therefore, Scientist 3 would probably predict that an individual with an 18% chance of developing type 2 diabetes has one parent with type 2 diabetes. The correct answer is (C).

24. J   Difficulty: Medium

Category: Evaluation of Models, Inferences, and Results

Getting to the Answer: Remember to keep straight who said what. If a 50-year-old developed type 2 diabetes, Scientist 1 would likely conclude the patient has a high-sugar diet, Scientist 2 would likely conclude the patient has a high-fat diet and/or lacks exercise, and Scientist 3 would likely conclude the patient inherited it from one or both parents. The only answer choice that correctly matches one of these predictions is (J).

25. A   Difficulty: High

Category: Evaluation of Models, Inferences, and Results

Getting to the Answer: According to Scientist 1, the elevated blood glucose levels in individuals with normal insulin levels did not return to normal when they received small injections of supplemental insulin. It can thus be inferred that although insulin levels were normal, the body had a lowered response to insulin, indicating insulin resistance. Look for a choice that supports the idea that a high-sugar diet causes or is otherwise related to lowered response to insulin. Choice (A) does just that. Choices B and D are incorrect because they mention fat intake and free radical production, respectively, which were only discussed by Scientist 2. Choice C is incorrect because Scientist 1 discussed the effects of a high-sugar diet, not a low-sugar one.

26. F   Difficulty: High

Category: Evaluation of Models, Inferences, and Results

Getting to the Answer: Scientist 3 believes that "type 2 diabetes is not caused by lifestyle or diet but inherited." To challenge Scientist 2's claim that the lack of exercise causes 7% of type 2 diabetes cases, Scientist 3 would have to explain how the actual cause of the occurrence of type 2 diabetes in these individuals is due to inheritance, rather than lifestyle. Choice (F) does precisely that: if the individuals who didn't exercise also had family histories of diabetes, then Scientist 3 could claim that the patients actually developed diabetes because of their genetics, not their lifestyles. Even though Scientist 3 actually states the information in G, it does not directly address Scientist 2's claim from the question stem. Choice H is incorrect because insulin injections are only discussed by

Scientist 1. Choice J is incorrect because Scientist 2 does not suggest that type 2 diabetes solely results from lack of exercise, but also blames diets high in fat.

Passage V

27. A   Difficulty: Low

Category: Interpretation of Data

Getting to the Answer: To answer this question, turn to the results of the studies in Table 1. According to the table, the lowest-density blood sample is 1.050 g/mL, that of Patient C. Looking at each column, you can see that Patient C has more platelets than Patient A but fewer than Patient B, fewer white blood cells than Patient A, the fewest red blood cells, but the most plasma. Choice (A), then, is correct.

28. H   Difficulty: Medium

Category: Scientific Investigation

Getting to the Answer: According to the passage, the purpose of the studies was "to determine the composition and mass of blood samples." Thus, the phlebotomist has an interest in avoiding anything that could alter the composition or mass of the blood on a temporary basis because it would skew the results of the studies. The passage also states that diet can affect the composition of blood, so it would make sense that the phlebotomist would try to control this factor by requiring the patients to fast. Choice (H) is thus correct. Choice F is incorrect because you're given no reason to suspect that taking blood is easier if a patient has fasted. Choice G is incorrect because if fasting could greatly change the composition of blood, then the phlebotomist would likely have made sure the patients avoided it by eating something beforehand. Choice J is incorrect because you're given no indication in the passage that anything the patient does can affect the ability of blood to separate in a centrifuge.

29. D   Difficulty: High

Category: Scientific Investigation

Getting to the Answer: According to Table 1, Patient C had a density of 1.050 g/mL, which amounts to a 10.50 g mass for a 10-mL sample. However, if you add up the masses of the components listed in Table 1, you get a total of less than 10.50 g (9.71 g, to be specific). The question is asking you to explain this discrepancy. To find the best explanation, consider each of the possibilities offered in the answer choices. Choice A does not offer an adequate explanation, because if some red blood cells remained in the plasma, then they would have been weighed along with the plasma, which means their mass would have been included. Choice B also falls short; the mass of the platelets would have been included when the white blood cells were weighed. Choice C suffers from a similar problem: if some of the formed elements remained in the plasma, their masses would simply be included when the plasma was weighed. By process of elimination, (D) must be correct. And this makes sense because the only components that were weighed were plasma, red blood cells, white blood cells, and platelets. If there were additional components, their masses would not be included in Table 1. This is also consistent with the opening of the passage, which claims that blood is 45% formed elements and 50% plasma, leaving 5% of the blood unaccounted for.

30. F   Difficulty: Low

Category: Interpretation of Data

Getting to the Answer: Go back to Table 1 and look at the columns for total density and red blood cell mass. (Circle each column if you tend to get distracted by the other information.) Reading the table from the bottom up, you can see that, as total density increases, the mass of the red blood cells also increases, (F).

31. B   Difficulty: Medium

Category: Interpretation of Data

Getting to the Answer: The introduction to the passage states that "formed elements weigh approximately 1.10 grams per milliliter (g/mL) and plasma approximately 1.02 g/mL." Here, you have about 5 mL of plasma, so the total mass of plasma is roughly 5 mL $\times$ 1.02 g/mL = 5.1 g. You also have about 5 mL of formed elements, so the total mass of formed elements is about 5 mL $\times$ 1.10 g/mL = 5.5 g. The total mass of the sample would then be around 5.1 g + 5.5 g = 10.6 g. It may be a bit higher due to elements other than the plasma and formed elements, but the total mass is still likely to be between 10.0 and 12.0 g, as in (B).

32. J   Difficulty: Low

Category: Scientific Investigation

Getting to the Answer: The passage explains that the phlebotomist placed the blood samples in a centrifuge for 20 minutes in Study 2 and at a slower speed for 45 minutes in Study 3. Only (J) captures any element of this difference. Choice F is incorrect because you're told at the beginning of the passage that 10 mL of blood were taken from each patient. Choice G is incorrect because, while the mass of the blood samples did vary from patient to patient, the masses weren't intentionally varied by the phlebotomist from Study 2 to Study 3. Choice H is incorrect because a centrifuge was used in both Studies 2 and 3.

33. A   Difficulty: Low

Category: Interpretation of Data

Getting to the Answer: To answer this question, simply compare the masses in the red blood cell column of Table 1. According to the table, Patient A has a red blood cell mass of 2.75 g, Patient B a mass of 2.70 g, and Patient C a mass of 2.65 g. Because Patient A has the greatest mass of red blood cells, (A) is correct.

Passage VI

34. G   Difficulty: Medium

Category: Interpretation of Data

Getting to the Answer: Since the question asks about length and temperature, the simplest data set to consider is Table 1, because Table 2 includes another variable, type of material. Comparing the odd-numbered trials (all conducted at 80°C) or the even-numbered trials (all conducted at 20°C) shows that the shorter the rod, the higher the current, which is an inverse relationship. Choices F and J can be eliminated. Comparing any trials which hold length of the rod constant while changing the temperature, such as Trials 1 and 2, show that as temperature goes down, current through the rod goes up, which is another inverse relationship. Because both length and temperature are inversely related to current, (G) is correct.

35. C   Difficulty: Medium

Category: Interpretation of Data

Getting to the Answer: The passage states that voltage, current, and resistance are related through Ohm's law, $V = A \times \Omega$, where Ω stands for resistance in ohms and A stands for current in amperes. In the circuit used for these experiments, the voltage is held constant at 5 V, as indicated by the battery in Diagram 1. This means that if current goes up, resistance must have gone down. Conversely, the lowest current will result from the highest resistance. Because each of the rods featured in the answer choices was tested in Experiment 2, to find the rod with the highest resistance, you merely need to find the one with the lowest recorded current in Table 2. The rod in Trial 9 conducted a current of only 20 mA, less than any of the others, so it must have the highest resistance. Choice (C) is thus correct.

36. H   Difficulty: High

Category: Interpretation of Data

Getting to the Answer: According to the question stem, conductivity uses the units of siemens per meter ($\sigma = S/m$) and siemens are equal to inverse ohms ($S = 1/\Omega$). Putting these two equations together, you can see that the units of conductivity are equivalent to inverse ohms divided by meters ($\sigma = [1/\Omega]/m$), which simplifies to $\sigma = 1/(\Omega \times m)$. Choice (H) is thus correct.

37. B   Difficulty: Low

Category: Interpretation of Data

Getting to the Answer: According to Table 1, the rod in Trial 4 conducted 53 mA of electricity at 20°C. A rod of the same length was used in Trial 3, but it was heated to 80°C and conducted only 27 mA. Because 50°C is in between these two values, it is reasonable to assume that the current conducted will fall somewhere between 27 and 53 mA. Choice (B) is therefore correct.

38. F   Difficulty: Medium

Category: Scientific Investigation

Getting to the Answer: The introduction to the passage mentions Ohm's law, $V = I \times R$, which shows that voltage and current are directly related. Because the resistance

values wouldn't change (the same rods would be used), the increase in voltage with the 10-V battery would lead to higher recorded values for current, regardless of the material of the rods. Thus, since both the copper and iron rods would conduct larger currents with a 10-V battery, (F) is correct.

39. C   Difficulty: Medium

Category: Interpretation of Data

Getting to the Answer: According to the results of Experiment 2, copper conducts electricity more effectively than iron. Thus, a 16-cm composite rod that was half-copper and half-iron would be expected to conduct electricity better than a 16-cm iron rod but worse than a 16-cm copper rod. According to Table 2, a 16-cm iron rod at 20°C conducts 40 mA, while a 16-cm copper rod at that temperature conducts 200 mA. Thus, the composite rod should conduct a current of somewhere between 40 and 200 mA, as in (C).

40. J   Difficulty: Low

Category: Scientific Investigation

Getting to the Answer: The variables that are directly manipulated in an experiment are the independent variables, so this question is asking for the one variable that is not an independent variable. In both experiments, the dependent variable—in other words, the variable that was observed and measured—was the current recorded by the ammeter. Thus, current was not directly manipulated by the student, so (J) is correct.

WRITING TEST

MODEL ESSAY

Below is an example of what a high-scoring essay might look like. Notice the author states her position clearly in the introductory paragraph and supports that position with evidence in the following paragraphs. This essay also uses transitions, some advanced vocabulary, and an effective "hook" to draw in the reader.

I fully agree that pure scientific research is vital to increase our understanding of ourselves and our world, and that this research, even without specific goals, can result in important benefits to society. To fund this research, a consortium of government, pharmaceutical companies, and nonprofit agencies should be formed, pooling money but giving no one group entire oversight or responsibility.

Many life-changing discoveries have been found without purposely looking for them. Alexander Fleming did not set out to discover penicilin, but in doing so accidentally saved millions of people from death. Putting a man on the moon did not help people on Earth, but it certainly taught us a lot about our universe. This kind of pure research must continue, and the cost should be shared by the government, drug companies, and nonprofit groups. This type of research can be prohibitively expensive; thus, monies must be drawn from various sources, each contributing as much as possible. No single organization can completely fund ongoing research, especially if there is no stated goal other than to hopefully discover something beneficial. Tax payers, pharmaceutical company investors, and nonprofit group members expect results, which may be long in coming, or, indeed, continually elusive. However, efforts must continue. As Thomas Edison said, "Just because something doesn't do what you planned it to do doesn't mean it's useless."

Consider also that pharmaceutical companies are always searching for new therapeutic drugs. They send scientists out into the field to come back with anything interesting, which is then researched and, if promising, developed into a new drug. Such is the relation between blood sugar and diabetes, leading to the insulin that my diabetic cousin takes; without insulin, he would not survive. If a drug company develops an important drug, it can make millions of dollars from the sale of it, leading to funding more research. Nonprofit organizations also have a stake in pure research, since another accidental discovery could prove to be financially beneficial. Finally, if the government shares the burden of underwriting research, it is not at risk for being fully blamed if the research does not produce positive results. Taxpayers would be more liable to accept a minimal loss in a good cause rather than a major loss in an unsure endeavor. A partnership would ensure continued funding and the funders, as well as all citizens, would benefit from discoveries.

On the other hand, people who say the government should fund only research which has demonstrated its worth do not understand the function of pure research. It is not possible for researchers to say with certainty that they are going to find a cure for cancer. Researchers have to be able to say they are searching for something as yet unknown with the hope that it will be beneficial. And what is a clear and acceptable outcome? If cancer researchers find a cure for diabetes, but not cancer, is that acceptable if it is not the stated intention? A great deal of science is luck and perserverance. According to this perspective, if a researcher wanted government funding to work in the Amazonian rain forest with the general intent of exploring indigenous plants, the government would be unable to fund the project because there is no clearly beneficial objective. But that is exactly how quinine, a now widely used treatment for malaria, was found, and the general exploration was certainly worth funding. Finally, it is unlikely that pure research, no matter who funds it, will result in disaster. Researchers are very careful to prevent this, and even if a disaster did happen, it would not be the fault of whom is funding the research.

It is quite clear that pure research is invaluable, as the examples of penicilin, quinine, and insulin support. It cannot be dependent on the whims, finances, and oversight of any one group but must be a concerted effort among all and for all who may benefit.

You can evaluate your essay and the model essay based on the following criteria:

- Is the author's own perspective clearly stated?
- Does the body of the essay assess and analyze an additional perspective?
- Is the relevance of each paragraph clear?
- Does the author start a new paragraph for each new idea?
- Is each sentence in a paragraph relevant to the point made in that paragraph?
- Are transitions clear?
- Is the essay easy to read?
- Is it engaging?
- Are sentences varied?
- Is vocabulary used effectively?
- Is college-level vocabulary used?

ACT Practice Test 7
ANSWER SHEET

ENGLISH TEST

1. A B C D	11. A B C D	21. A B C D	31. A B C D	41. A B C D	51. A B C D	61. A B C D	71. A B C D
2. F G H J	12. F G H J	22. F G H J	32. F G H J	42. F G H J	52. F G H J	62. F G H J	72. F G H J
3. A B C D	13. A B C D	23. A B C D	33. A B C D	43. A B C D	53. A B C D	63. A B C D	73. A B C D
4. F G H J	14. F G H J	24. F G H J	34. F G H J	44. F G H J	54. F G H J	64. F G H J	74. F G H J
5. A B C D	15. A B C D	25. A B C D	35. A B C D	45. A B C D	55. A B C D	65. A B C D	75. A B C D
6. F G H J	16. F G H J	26. F G H J	36. F G H J	46. F G H J	56. F G H J	66. F G H J	
7. A B C D	17. A B C D	27. A B C D	37. A B C D	47. A B C D	57. A B C D	67. A B C D	
8. F G H J	18. F G H J	28. F G H J	38. F G H J	48. F G H J	58. F G H J	68. F G H J	
9. A B C D	19. A B C D	29. A B C D	39. A B C D	49. A B C D	59. A B C D	69. A B C D	
10. F G H J	20. F G H J	30. F G H J	40. F G H J	50. F G H J	60. F G H J	70. F G H J	

MATHEMATICS TEST

1. A B C D E	11. A B C D E	21. A B C D E	31. A B C D E	41. A B C D E	51. A B C D E
2. F G H J K	12. F G H J K	22. F G H J K	32. F G H J K	42. F G H J K	52. F G H J K
3. A B C D E	13. A B C D E	23. A B C D E	33. A B C D E	43. A B C D E	53. A B C D E
4. F G H J K	14. F G H J K	24. F G H J K	34. F G H J K	44. F G H J K	54. F G H J K
5. A B C D E	15. A B C D E	25. A B C D E	35. A B C D E	45. A B C D E	55. A B C D E
6. F G H J K	16. F G H J K	26. F G H J K	36. F G H J K	46. F G H J K	56. F G H J K
7. A B C D E	17. A B C D E	27. A B C D E	37. A B C D E	47. A B C D E	57. A B C D E
8. F G H J K	18. F G H J K	28. F G H J K	38. F G H J K	48. F G H J K	58. F G H J K
9. A B C D E	19. A B C D E	29. A B C D E	39. A B C D E	49. A B C D E	59. A B C D E
10. F G H J K	20. F G H J K	30. F G H J K	40. F G H J K	50. F G H J K	60. F G H J K

READING TEST

1. A B C D	6. F G H J	11. A B C D	16. F G H J	21. A B C D	26. F G H J	31. A B C D	36. F G H J
2. F G H J	7. A B C D	12. F G H J	17. A B C D	22. F G H J	27. A B C D	32. F G H J	37. A B C D
3. A B C D	8. F G H J	13. A B C D	18. F G H J	23. A B C D	28. F G H J	33. A B C D	38. F G H J
4. F G H J	9. A B C D	14. F G H J	19. A B C D	24. F G H J	29. A B C D	34. F G H J	39. A B C D
5. A B C D	10. F G H J	15. A B C D	20. F G H J	25. A B C D	30. F G H J	35. A B C D	40. F G H J

SCIENCE TEST

1. A B C D	6. F G H J	11. A B C D	16. F G H J	21. A B C D	26. F G H J	31. A B C D	36. F G H J
2. F G H J	7. A B C D	12. F G H J	17. A B C D	22. F G H J	27. A B C D	32. F G H J	37. A B C D
3. A B C D	8. F G H J	13. A B C D	18. F G H J	23. A B C D	28. F G H J	33. A B C D	38. F G H J
4. F G H J	9. A B C D	14. F G H J	19. A B C D	24. F G H J	29. A B C D	34. F G H J	39. A B C D
5. A B C D	10. F G H J	15. A B C D	20. F G H J	25. A B C D	30. F G H J	35. A B C D	40. F G H J

ENGLISH TEST

45 Minutes—75 Questions

Directions: Each passage has certain words and phrases that are underlined and numbered. The questions in the right column will provide alternatives for the underlined segments. Most questions require you to choose the answer that makes the sentence grammatically correct, concise, and relevant. If the word or phrase in the passage is already the correct, concise, and relevant choice, select Choice A, NO CHANGE. Some questions will ask a question about the underlined segment. When a question is presented, choose the best answer.

Some questions will ask about part or all of the passage. These questions do not refer to a specific underlined segment. Instead, these questions will accompany a number in a box.

For each question, choose your answer and fill in the corresponding bubble on your answer sheet. Read the passage once before you answer the questions. You will often need to read several sentences beyond the underlined portion to be able to choose the correct answer. Be sure to read enough to answer each question.

Passage I

My Cousin Nicola

My father and his two younger brothers emigrated from Italy to New York in the early 1970s. Only their older sister Lucia, <u>which</u> was already married, remained
1

1. A. NO CHANGE
    B. whom
    C. who
    D. she who

behind in their small home <u>town, this village</u> lies in the
2
shadow of Mount Vesuvius. Growing up in America, my cousins and I were as close as brothers and sisters, but

2. F. NO CHANGE
    G. town, it can be seen where it
    H. town it
    J. town that

we hardly <u>known</u> our family across the Atlantic. When
3
I was a young child, my parents and I went to Italy to visit Aunt Lucia and her family for a week. I first met my

3. A. NO CHANGE
    B. knew
    C. had knew
    D. been known

GO ON TO THE NEXT PAGE ⇨

cousin <u>Nicola however,</u> I remember that we were not
      4

only about the same age, <u>and</u> we also got along well. But
        5

because <u>I being</u> so young, I remember little else. I hadn't
      6
seen him again up until this last summer.

    Nicola decided that he wanted to join the Italian
Air Force after finishing high school. Before beginning
his service, though, he wanted to travel for a bit. <u>He
                  7
had never been to America, even though so many of his
          7
relatives live here, but he had been to England already.</u>
           7
When the rest of the cousins heard the news, they were

<u>ecstatic</u>. Most of them had never met Nicola or, like me,
 8

4. **F.** NO CHANGE

   G. Nicola, so then

   H. Nicola because

   J. Nicola then.

5. **A.** NO CHANGE

   B. so

   C. but

   D. then

6. **F.** NO CHANGE

   G. I, who was

   H. I was

   J. I,

7. Assuming that each choice is true, which one
provides the most relevant information about
Nicola's travel plans?

   A. NO CHANGE

   B. He had never been to America, so he
called my father and asked if he could
come spend the summer with us in
New York.

   C. He had never been to America, which is
most easily reached from Italy by plane.

   D. Because it was expensive for his whole
family to travel overseas, Nicola had
never been to America before.

8. Three of these choices indicate that the cousins
looked forward to meeting Nicola. Which choice
does NOT do so?

   F. NO CHANGE

   G. excited

   H. apprehensive

   J. thrilled

GO ON TO THE NEXT PAGE

hadn't seen him, since we were kids; they were eager to
                                     9
get to know him.

Two weeks later, we picked Nicola up at JFK
Airport. Right away, I was surprised by his height. I am
the tallest of all the cousins in America, and Nicola was
easily a couple of inches taller than me. In addition to
our height, he and I had another similarity: we were both
musicians. The moment I saw the acoustic guitar slung
over his shoulder, I knew he and I would get along just
fine. None of them plays an instrument, and I always
          10

thought that I was the only musician in the family (even
                                          11
though some relatives have lovely singing voices). I was
                    11
happy to find out I was wrong.

Throughout that summer, Nicola and I shared
the gift of music. We would sing and play our guitars
long into the night, only stopping when my mother
came downstairs and forced us to quit. We liked many
of the same bands, and we taught each other to play
our favorite songs. Taught to him as a child before she
                                  12
passed away in Italy, I was taught by him the Italian folk
                12
songs of our grandmother more importantly. It was
                12
through those songs that I truly connected to the beauty
of our ancestry. On the night before Nicola returned to

9. **A.** NO CHANGE
   B. hadn't seen him since we were kids
   C. hadn't seen him since we were kids;
   D. hadn't seen, him since we were kids,

10. **F.** NO CHANGE
    G. us
    H. the Americans
    J. my American cousins

11. **A.** NO CHANGE
    B. in the family, which has at least 20
        members that I know of
    C. in the family
    D. DELETE the underlined portion

12. **F.** NO CHANGE
    G. Teaching him as a child before she passed
        away, our grandmother in Italy more
        importantly taught to me many of the
        Italian folk songs.
    H. Teaching him as a child, more importantly,
        by our grandmother in Italy, I was taught
        by him many Italian folk songs.
    J. More importantly, however, he taught
        me many of the Italian folk songs our
        grandmother in Italy had taught him as a
        child before she passed away.

GO ON TO THE NEXT PAGE

Italy, my father <u>would have thrown</u> a big party for all of
13
the relatives.

Nicola and I played the folk songs of <u>our</u>
14
<u>grandmothers</u> country for the American side of our
14
family. When we were done, my Uncle Vittorio had a

tear in his eye. Since coming to America so long ago, he

had never been able to return to Italy. In the music and

our singing, Nicola and I brought the beautiful country

back to Uncle Vittorio.

13. **A.** NO CHANGE
    B. will have thrown
    C. threw
    D. throws

14. **F.** NO CHANGE
    G. our grandmother's
    H. our grandmothers'
    J. are grandmother's

Question 15 asks about the preceding passage
as a whole.

---

15. Suppose the writer's goal had been to write a
    personal narrative that emphasizes the value
    of family. Would this passage accomplish this
    purpose?

    A. Yes, because it shows how connecting
    with distant family can be meaningful.

    B. Yes, because it shows how much closer
    the narrator is to Nicola than to his
    American cousins.

    C. No, because the narrator and Nicola are
    not closely related.

    D. No, because the passage does not mention
    any family members besides Nicola.

GO ON TO THE NEXT PAGE

Passage II

The Handsome Bean

On the ground floor of the apartment <u>building</u>
16
<u>where, I live,</u> the Handsome Bean coffee shop is
16
almost always bustling with customers. During the
warm months, the shop sets up outdoor tables on the
sidewalk, and the chatter of conversation mixed with
the aroma of coffee often floats in through my window
to wake me in the mornings. Next to the Handsome
Bean is a used bookstore, and the two shops share many
of the same customers. People come to find a book and
stay to enjoy a cup of coffee. Across the street from the
building is the neighborhood Little League field. ⯐17⯐

The Handsome Bean often <u>sponsors</u> a local team.
18
During the games, the coffee shop offers a discount to

16. **F.** NO CHANGE
    G. building where I live,
    H. building, where I live
    J. building where I live

17. The purpose of including the location of the Little League field is to:
    A. introduce the kind of team the Handsome Bean sponsors.
    B. transition from a discussion of the Handsome Bean to a discussion of baseball.
    C. add a detail that helps the reader picture the scene.
    D. downplay the importance of the Handsome Bean.

18. **F.** NO CHANGE
    G. had sponsored
    H. was a sponsor of
    J. supported

GO ON TO THE NEXT PAGE

parents whose children are competing across the street.

[19] It is a pleasure to have as a neighbor a business that

19. At this point, the writer wants to add a sentence that provides additional detail about the customers who come to the Handsome Bean. Which of the following sentences would best achieve the writer's purpose?

   A. In addition to this discount, the shop offers all patrons a punch card to receive a tenth coffee for free.

   B. The shop also sells ice cream, so it often gets very crowded with children and parents after the Little League games are over.

   C. The Handsome Bean also provides uniforms for an elementary school soccer team.

   D. The Little League field doesn't have a concession stand, so the coffee shop doesn't have much competition for the parents' business.

children. And adults enjoy so much.
      20

20. F. NO CHANGE

   G. children and adults

   H. children and that adults

   J. children. Adults

Over the past few years, I have become friends with
                            21
Mary, the owner of the shop. The store's main counter is
      21

21. Which choice most effectively leads the reader into the topic of this paragraph?

   A. NO CHANGE

   B. Mary, the shop's owner, has a great appreciation for history.

   C. The Handsome Bean has only been open for a couple of years, but the owner, Mary, has taken great care to make it look like it has been there for decades.

   D. Before Mary, the shop's owner, opened the Handsome Bean, the space had been unoccupied for six months.

GO ON TO THE NEXT PAGE

a century-old antique that Mary bought and restored to its <u>originally conditional</u>, and the photos that adorn the
22

22. F. NO CHANGE
     G. original conditional
     H. original condition
     J. conditionally original

back wall <u>depicts</u> our town during the 1920s and 1930s.
23
My favorite detail of the shop, however, is the original tin ceiling. One afternoon, while staring at the intricate patterns etched into the tin tiles, I noticed a name camouflaged within the ornate design: Harvey. I pointed it out to Mary, and she said the original owner of the building was named Harvey Wallaby. Her guess was that he had probably written it there more than 70 years ago. 24 That night after the coffee shop had closed, Mary and I etched our names into the ceiling right next to Harvey's, hoping that our names would similarly be discovered in the far-off future.

23. A. NO CHANGE
     B. depict
     C. has depicted
     D. shows

24. The writer is considering deleting the sentence below from the passage:

     > Her guess was that he had probably written it there more than 70 years ago.

     If the writer were to delete this sentence, the essay would primarily lose:

     F. an additional detail about the building that houses the coffee shop.
     G. a depiction of the action taken by Mary and the writer.
     H. an emphasis on the original owner's influence.
     J. a description of the shop's interior.

On Friday nights, the Handsome Bean has live entertainment, usually in the <u>form of, a</u> band or a poetry
25
reading. For a small-town coffee shop, the Handsome

25. A. NO CHANGE
     B. form; of a
     C. form, of a
     D. form of a

GO ON TO THE NEXT PAGE ⟹

Bean attracts a good amount of talented musicians and
26

poets. It being that I am amazed by the performances,
27
they transpire within its cozy walls.
27

[1] The clientele of the coffee shop is as varied as the selection of flavored brews. [2] In the mornings, the Handsome Bean is abuzz with the 9-to-5 crowd stopping in for some java before heading off to work. [3] During the day, the tables are home to local artists lost in their thoughts and cappuccinos. [4] The evening finds the Handsome Bean filled with bleary-eyed college students loading up on caffeine so they can cram all night for their upcoming exams or finishing
28
their research papers with looming due dates. [5] Then there's me, sitting in the corner, maybe talking to Mary or reading the paper, smiling at the thought that the best cup of coffee in town is found right beneath my bedroom window. [6] In the afternoons, a group of high school students who stops by to have an ice cream cone
29

or an egg cream. 30

26. **F.** NO CHANGE
    G. better amount
    H. better number
    J. good number

27. **A.** NO CHANGE
    B. Amazing the performances, it is that I know they
    C. I am amazed by the performances that
    D. Amazing the performances, they

28. **F.** NO CHANGE
    G. finish
    H. finishes
    J. finalizing

29. **A.** NO CHANGE
    B. students that
    C. students, and they
    D. students

30. For the sake of logic and coherence, Sentence 6 should be placed:
    F. where it is now.
    G. before Sentence 2.
    H. before Sentence 4.
    J. before Sentence 5.

GO ON TO THE NEXT PAGE

Passage III

Mr. Midshipman Marryat

> The paragraphs below may or may not be in the most logical order. A number in brackets appears above each paragraph. At the end of the passage, Question 45 will ask you to determine the most logical place for Paragraph 1.

[1]

Born to an upper-class English family in 1792, Marryat had a thirst for <u>naval adventure</u> and exploration
31
very early in his childhood. As a young boy at private school, he tried to run away to sea a number of times.

<u>Finally, his exasperated parents</u> at last granted him his
32

wish in 1806; <u>they were</u> enlisted in the British Royal
33
Navy as a midshipman. Marryat had the luck to be assigned to sail upon the frigate *HMS Imperieuse* under

the command of Lord Cochrane. Cochrane, <u>that's</u>
34
naval exploits are legendary, would later serve as the

31. A. NO CHANGE
  B. naval, adventure,
  C. naval, adventure
  D. naval adventure;

32. F. NO CHANGE
  G. His exasperated parents
  H. In the end, his exasperated parents
  J. Ultimately, the result was that his exasperated parents

33. A. NO CHANGE
  B. they
  C. he
  D. and he

34. F. NO CHANGE
  G. who's
  H. whose
  J. who the

inspiration for <u>a number of</u> Marryat's fictional
35

35. The writer is considering deleting the phrase "a number of." If the writer decided to delete the phrase, would the meaning of the sentence change?

   A. Yes, because without this phrase, the reader would think that all of Marryat's fictional characters were based on Cochrane.

   B. Yes, because without this phrase, the reader would not understand that Marryat used Cochrane as a model for more than one fictional character.

   C. No, because this phrase is an example of wordiness that should be eliminated from the sentence.

   D. No; although the phrase adds a detail about Marryat's character, this detail is not essential to the meaning of the sentence.

characters. 36

36. At this point, the writer is considering adding the sentence below:

> The well-known writer Patrick O'Brian also modeled his Captain Jack Aubrey after Cochrane.

Should the writer make this addition?

   F. Yes, because if readers know that other writers were inspired by Cochrane, they will better understand that Cochrane was an impressive person.

   G. Yes, because the added detail provides information about a writer who used a style similar to Marryat's.

   H. No, because the essay doesn't reveal the relationship between O'Brian and Marryat.

   J. No, because the detail distracts from the main focus of the essay.

GO ON TO THE NEXT PAGE

[2]

Unlike most of the other <u>famous</u> authors who have
₃₇
spun tales of brave British naval officers fighting for
king and country on the high seas, Frederick Marryat
actually served as a captain in the British navy. While
others could only use their imagination and accounts
to describe what life must have been like for a young
man rising through the ranks from lowly midshipman
to all-powerful captain <u>from historical records</u>, Marryat
₃₈
needed only to dip into the vast library of adventure
stored in his memory.

[3]

Marryat's three years aboard the *Imperieuse* were
filled with experiences that would later serve him well
in his writing career. The *Imperieuse* saw much action
off the coast of Spain, where Marryat took part in
capturing a Spanish castle and numerous vessels in the
Mediterranean. Marryat willingly accepted any chance
to distinguish himself in the eyes of his revered <u>captain</u>
₃₉
<u>and literary inspiration, Cochrane</u>. In fact, Marryat once
₃₉
jumped into the turbulent sea to save the life of another

midshipman who <u>had fallen</u> overboard. Not only did
₄₀
Marryat have the privilege of knowing first-hand a
character as illustrious as Cochrane, but his own bold
experiences as a midshipman would also be the basis for
his most famous novel, *Mr. Midshipman Easy*.

37. Which of the following would NOT be an equivalent replacement for the underlined portion?
   A. prominent
   B. beloved
   C. well-known
   D. noteworthy

38. The best placement for the underlined portion is:
   F. where it is now.
   G. after the word *accounts*.
   H. after the word *others*.
   J. after the word *adventure*.

39. A. NO CHANGE
   B. captain, and literary inspiration Cochrane.
   C. captain and literary inspiration Cochrane.
   D. captain and, literary inspiration, Cochrane.

40. F. NO CHANGE
   G. would have fallen
   H. had been falling
   J. falls

GO ON TO THE NEXT PAGE

[4]

As Marryat quickly climbed through the ranks of the British navy, <u>many feats were accomplished by him.</u>
                                        41
These included single-handedly saving his ship during a horrific storm and fighting in a number of sea battles against the United States navy during the War of 1812.

He <u>therefore</u> earned a medal from the Royal Humane
        42
Society for inventing a special lifeboat.

[5]

<u>Marryat earned his greatest acclaim for his novels</u>
                                        43
<u>and short stories during this time</u>, which were published
                    43
in England while he was at sea. He retired from the navy shortly after being awarded the rank of post captain in

1825 to concentrate <u>for writing</u> full-time. Marryat's
                        44
thrilling stories of sea adventure still live on today because, as the old cliché goes, the best stories are the ones that are true.

41. A. NO CHANGE
  B. his accomplishment of many feats occurred
  C. his many feats were accomplished
  D. he accomplished many feats

42. F. NO CHANGE
  G. also
  H. again
  J. thirdly

43. A. NO CHANGE
  B. During this time, Marryat earned his greatest acclaim for his novels and short stories
  C. His greatest acclaim was earned by him, for his novels and short stories during this time
  D. During this time for his novels and short stories, earned him his greatest acclaim

44. F. NO CHANGE
  G. at writing
  H. on writing
  J. with writing of

Question 45 asks about the preceding passage as a whole.

45. The most logical placement of Paragraph 1 is:
  A. where it is now.
  B. after Paragraph 2.
  C. after Paragraph 3.
  D. after Paragraph 4.

GO ON TO THE NEXT PAGE

Passage IV

The Toughest Task in Sports

[1]

I've often heard others make the comment that the hardest single act in all of sports is to hit a major league fastball. I'm not going to deny that hitting a ball traveling at upwards of 95 miles per hour is a daunting task, but I can think of something even tougher than taking a major league at-bat: stopping a crank shot in lacrosse. <u>Football quarterbacks facing oncoming</u>
              46
<u>defensive linemen are also in a difficult position.</u>
              46

[2]

Lacrosse <u>that is</u> often referred to as "the fastest sport
        47
on two feet," and with good reason. The game is often

<u>brutally</u>, and the best players normally possess a bit of
  48

<u>toughness and</u> a bit of finesse. Using sticks known as
  49
"crosses" to pass a hard rubber ball back and forth through the air, players on two teams sprint around

46. **F.** NO CHANGE
    G. Also in a challenging position are football quarterbacks facing oncoming defensive linemen.
    H. (Football quarterbacks also face a daunting task when they are rushed by defensive linemen.)
    J. DELETE the underlined portion.

47. **A.** NO CHANGE
    B. which has been
    C. is
    D. DELETE the underlined portion.

48. **F.** NO CHANGE
    G. brutal
    H. brute
    J. brutality

49. **A.** NO CHANGE
    B. toughness; and
    C. toughness
    D. toughness, and,

GO ON TO THE NEXT PAGE

a field; <u>they then attempted</u> to set up a shot on the
                          50
opposing team's goal. As in hockey or soccer, the only

thing that stands between the ball and the goal is the

goalkeeper. Using just his body and his crosse, the goalie

must protect the six-foot by six-foot goal from being

penetrated by a ball that is less than eight inches in

circumference.

[3]

This brings me to the heart of my argument. A

regulation lacrosse ball is almost an inch narrower than

a regulation baseball, with an unstitched, smooth rubber

surface. The fastest baseball pitch on record was clocked

at 100.9 mph, <u>because</u> only a handful of major league
                  51
pitchers can approach even the upper nineties in speed.

In men's lacrosse, because the crosse acts as a lever, the

fastest crank shots on <u>goal, can</u> reach 110 mph. Even at
                          52
the high school level, crank shots of more than 90 mph

<u>made by high school players</u> are not uncommon. Unlike
                53
a baseball pitcher throwing his fastball from a fixed

position on the mound, a lacrosse player may shoot

50. **F.** NO CHANGE
      G. they must attempt
      H. one then attempts
      J. one must attempt

51. **A.** NO CHANGE
      B. before
      C. though
      D. moreover,

52. **F.** NO CHANGE
      G. goal, can,
      H. goal can
      J. goal can,

53. **A.** NO CHANGE
      B. made by these high school players
      C. shot by high school players
      D. DELETE the underlined portion.

GO ON TO THE NEXT PAGE ⟶

from anywhere on the field. 54 This means that a lacrosse goalie may be asked to stop a crank shot from only six feet away! To make the goalie's job even more

absurd, a lacrosse player may shoot from over his
55
shoulder, from his side, or drop his stick down and wind up from the ground. On top of that, the best players
56
often employ a variety of fakes, and most have the ability to shoot left-handed or right-handed, depending upon their angle to the goal.

[4]

Like hitting a major league fastball, stopping a
57
crank shot in lacrosse is tough. Both of these endeavors,
57

54. The writer is considering adding a comma and the following information to the end of the preceding sentence:

which is usually grass.

Should the writer make this addition?

F. Yes, because it allows the reader to picture the field.

G. Yes, because it adds a detail that supports the rest of the sentence.

H. No, because it distracts from the focus on the game.

J. No, because it weakens the claim in the following sentence.

55. A. NO CHANGE

B. insurmountable

C. harrowing

D. difficult

56. Of the following possible replacements for the underlined portion, which would be LEAST acceptable?

F. In addition

G. On the other hand

H. Furthermore

J. What's more

57. Which choice is the most effective and logical transition from the topic of Paragraph 3 to the topic of Paragraph 4?

A. NO CHANGE

B. The combination of these unknown variables makes stopping a crank shot in lacrosse tougher than hitting a major league fastball.

C. Though baseball is less challenging than lacrosse, both sports require tremendous skill and dedication from athletes.

D. There is little question that stopping a crank shot in lacrosse is among the toughest tasks an athlete can face.

GO ON TO THE NEXT PAGE

however, require the same set of skills. One must
       58
possess superlative athleticism, great hand-eye

coordination, and catlike quickness. Above all, you must
                                                  59
be fearless.
59

58. **F.** NO CHANGE

     G. requires

     H. required

     J. would have required

59. **A.** NO CHANGE

     B. one must be

     C. they must be

     D. he must have been

> Question 60 asks about the preceding passage as a whole.

60. Suppose that the writer had wanted to write an essay comparing the strategies used by baseball pitchers and lacrosse goalies. Would this essay fulfill the writer's goal?

     F. Yes, because the writer compares both sports throughout the essay.

     G. Yes, because the writer details the challenges that lacrosse goalies face.

     H. No, because the writer does not provide any specific details about baseball pitchers.

     J. No, because the writer focuses on comparing the difficulty of hitting a ball pitched by a major league pitcher to the difficulty of blocking a crank shot in men's lacrosse.

GO ON TO THE NEXT PAGE

Passage V

Thomas Edison, Tinfoil Cylinders, and MP3 Players

[1]

Thomas Edison first recorded sounds on tinfoil cylinders in the 1870s, and since then, <u>formats for recording music have come and gone</u> at a breakneck pace. Innovation in recording music has been constant, and the popularity and lifespan of the newest format have always been transitory at best. Those first tinfoil cylinders, which were hailed as a miracle in their day, quickly progressed to wax cylinders, then hard plastic cylinders and, within a decade, were completely replaced by the next "miracle," the gramophone disc record.

[2]

The vinyl phonograph record, which sounded, soon <u>better</u> supplanted the gramophone in the 1940s. This newfangled format dominated the music landscape for the next 30 years, but like its predecessors, it would eventually fall into obsolescence. The vinyl <u>record being</u> no longer mass-marketed to the public. For that matter, neither is its successor, the 8-track cartridge of the 1970s.

[3]

It may seem curious to a 40-year-old man today that the average high-school student is well acquainted

61. A. NO CHANGE
   B. formats for recording music have come and gone,
   C. formats for recording music, have come and gone
   D. formats, for recording music have come and gone

62. The most logical placement for the underlined word would be:
   F. where it is now.
   G. before the word *vinyl*.
   H. after the word *sounded*.
   J. before the word *gramophone*.

63. A. NO CHANGE
   B. record, having been
   C. record is
   D. record,

GO ON TO THE NEXT PAGE

with the older vinyl record format <u>so</u> has never even
64
heard of an 8-track cartridge. DJs and those who mix

popular music still <u>uses and appreciates</u> the vinyl
65

<u>record format cherished by them</u>. They have kept
66

records from disappearing into oblivion. 67

[4]

That same 40-year-old man witnessed the rise and
fall of the cassette tape, so he may not be surprised that
many in today's recording industry view the compact
disc as similarly spiraling toward its own doom. For

the first <u>time, though</u> it is not the sound quality of
68
the recording that is ushering in the change. Now the

64. F. NO CHANGE
　　G. yet
　　H. thus
　　J. or

65. A. NO CHANGE
　　B. use and appreciates
　　C. uses and appreciate
　　D. use and appreciate

66. F. NO CHANGE
　　G. record format that they cherish.
　　H. format for records they play on turntables.
　　J. record format.

67. The writer is considering adding a comma and the following information to the end of the preceding sentence:

> along with the 8-track and the more recent recording format, the cassette tape.

Should the writer make this addition?

　　A. Yes, because it adds details relevant to the focus of the passage.
　　B. Yes, because it reinforces the passage's main argument.
　　C. No, because it distracts from the passage's main topic of vinyl records.
　　D. No, because it weakens the passage's main argument.

68. F. NO CHANGE
　　G. time; though
　　H. time, though,
　　J. time though,

GO ON TO THE NEXT PAGE ⟹

driving force is something <u>different</u> the quality of the
                                    69
player itself.

[5]

A standard audio compact disc can store only about
700 megabytes worth of digital data, which equates to
only a few hours' worth of songs. <u>Moreover,</u> recently
                                        70
introduced small personal music players, such as the
iPod, can have up to an impressive 60 gigabytes' worth
of storage space. For those who are music lovers, this
has completely changed the experience of listening to
their favorite songs. <u>Contrasting by</u> the few hours' worth
                          71
of songs stored on a single CD, a 60-gigabyte MP3
player can store a month's worth of uninterrupted music
on a machine about the size of an old cassette tape.

<u>It's no wonder that MP3 players are among the most</u>
                                    72
<u>popular technology purchases for people of all ages.</u>
                                    72

[6]

Has the apex in the climb toward better and better
ways to play recorded music been reached? For those
who believe it has, history teaches that they are wrong;
such a proclamation will surely prove to be shortsighted
when the next "miracle" in music arrives.

69. **A.** NO CHANGE
    B. different;
    C. different:
    D. different,

70. **F.** NO CHANGE
    G. In contrast
    H. Despite
    J. Subsequently

71. **A.** NO CHANGE
    B. Compared to
    C. While
    D. In contrast of

72. In this paragraph, the writer wants to help
    readers understand the storage capacity and size
    of the new personal music players. Which true
    statement would best help the writer accomplish
    this goal?

    F. NO CHANGE
    G. It is not unreasonable to expect that
    technological improvements will soon
    allow personal music players to have an
    even more compact size and store twice
    as many songs.
    H. Experts in the music industry predict
    that personal music players will quickly
    replace compact disc players, just as
    compact disc players so recently replaced
    vinyl record players.
    J. Entire music libraries that were once
    confined to the living room wall can now fit
    into a music lover's pocket and be taken and
    listened to anywhere.

GO ON TO THE NEXT PAGE

Questions 73–75 ask about the preceding passage as a whole.

73. Paragraphs 5 and 6 of this essay are written in the third person, using the pronouns *those*, *their*, and *they*. If the writer revised these paragraphs using the second-person pronouns *you* and *your*, the essay would primarily:

A. gain a sense of urgency by suggesting actions to be taken by the reader.

B. gain a more personal tone by speaking directly to the reader.

C. lose the formal and removed tone that matches the content and purpose of the essay.

D. lose a sense of the author's knowledge on the subject by personalizing the essay.

74. After reading the essay, the writer realized that some information had been left out. The writer then composed the sentence below to convey that information:

> Though the gramophone record's disc shape proved to have longevity, the gramophone record itself did not.

The most effective and logical placement of this sentence would be before the first sentence of Paragraph:

F. 2.

G. 3.

H. 4.

J. 5.

75. Suppose the writer had set out to write an essay explaining the process of recording sounds in a variety of formats. Does this essay meet that purpose?

A. Yes, because the essay describes the different recording formats used since the 1870s.

B. Yes, because the writer provides specifics about how each new recording format has improved upon earlier formats.

C. No, because the essay discusses a limited number of recording formats.

D. No, because the essay does not discuss the mechanics of how sounds are recorded and played back in different formats.

IF YOU FINISH BEFORE TIME IS CALLED, YOU MAY CHECK YOUR WORK ON THIS SECTION ONLY. DO NOT TURN TO ANY OTHER SECTION IN THE TEST. **STOP**

MATHEMATICS TEST

60 Minutes—60 Questions

Directions: Choose the correct solution to each question and fill in the corresponding bubble on your answer sheet.

Do not continue to spend time on questions if you get stuck. Solve as many questions as you can before returning to any if time permits.

You may use a calculator on this test for any question you choose. However, some questions may be better solved without a calculator.

Note: Unless otherwise stated, you can assume:

1. Figures are NOT necessarily drawn to scale.

2. Geometric figures are two dimensional.

3. The word *line* indicates a straight line.

4. The word *average* indicates arithmetic mean.

1. Khristina walked $1\frac{2}{3}$ miles on Sunday and $2\frac{3}{4}$ on Monday. What was the total distance, in miles, that she walked over those two days?

    A. $3\frac{1}{2}$

    B. $3\frac{5}{7}$

    C. $3\frac{11}{12}$

    D. $4\frac{1}{4}$

    E. $4\frac{5}{12}$

2. The expression $2y^3 \cdot 3xy^2 \cdot 6xy^2$ is equivalent to which of the following?

    F. $11x^2y^7$

    G. $11x^2y^{12}$

    H. $36x^2y^7$

    J. $36xy^{12}$

    K. $36x^2y^{12}$

3. Ms. Ruppin is a machinist who works 245 days a year and earns a salary of $51,940. She recently took an unpaid day off from work to attend a bridge tournament. The company pays temporary replacements $140 a day. How much less did the company have to pay in salary by paying the replacement instead of Ms. Ruppin that day?

    A. $ 72

    B. $113

    C. $140

    D. $196

    E. $212

GO ON TO THE NEXT PAGE

4. On his first four 100-point tests this quarter, a student has earned the following scores: 52, 70, 76, 79. What score must the student earn on the fifth 100-point test in order to earn an average Ftest grade of 75 for all five tests?

    F. 69

    G. 70

    H. 71

    J. 98

    K. The student cannot earn an average of 75.

5. Relative humidity is found by dividing the grams of water vapor per cubic meter of air by the maximum possible grams of water vapor per cubic meter of air, then converting to a percentage. If on a given day the air has 6.7 grams of water vapor per cubic meter, and the maximum possible at that temperature is 19.2 grams of water vapor per cubic meter, what is the relative humidity, to the nearest percent?

    A. 19%

    B. 30%

    C. 35%

    D. 67%

    E. 87%

6. A fence completely surrounds a pool that is 30 feet by 10 feet. What is the approximate length, in feet, of the fence?

    F. 20 feet

    G. 40 feet

    H. 60 feet

    J. 80 feet

    K. 160 feet

7. A film that is 3 hours 40 minutes long must be cut into two equal parts. What will be the duration of each part?

    A. 1 hour 10 minutes

    B. 1 hour 30 minutes

    C. 1 hour 50 minutes

    D. 1 hour 55 minutes

    E. 2 hours 20 minutes

8. If $2x - 5 = 7x + 3$, then $x = ?$

    F. $-\dfrac{8}{5}$

    G. $-\dfrac{5}{8}$

    H. $-\dfrac{2}{5}$

    J. $\dfrac{2}{5}$

    K. $\dfrac{8}{9}$

9. What two numbers should be placed in the blanks below so that each pair of consecutive numbers has the same difference?

$$13, \underline{\quad}, \underline{\quad}, 49$$

    A. 22, 31

    B. 23, 39

    C. 24, 38

    D. 25, 37

    E. 26, 39

GO ON TO THE NEXT PAGE

10. If x is a real number such that $x^3 = 729$, then $\sqrt{x} + x^2 = ?$

    F. 9

    G. 21

    H. 53

    J. 84

    K. 90

11. Which of the following is the decimal equivalent of $\dfrac{3}{7}$?

    (Note that a bar indicates a numerical pattern that is repeated.)

    A. $0.\overline{428571}$

    B. 0.42857142

    C. $0.428571\overline{42}$

    D. 0.4285714286

    E. $0.4285714\overline{286}$

12. If a ball is randomly chosen from a bag with exactly 10 purple balls, 10 yellow balls, and 8 green balls, what is the probability that the ball chosen will NOT be green?

    F. $\dfrac{2}{7}$

    G. $\dfrac{2}{5}$

    H. $\dfrac{1}{2}$

    J. $\dfrac{9}{14}$

    K. $\dfrac{5}{7}$

13. In the figure below, lines l and m are parallel and $a = 110$. Which of the following is equal to the sum of b, c, and d ?

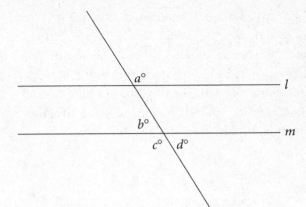

    A. 250

    B. 260

    C. 270

    D. 280

    E. 290

GO ON TO THE NEXT PAGE

Use the following information to answer questions 14–15.

Erin hiked a small mountain over the course of a day. She began at 7 AM at an altitude of 4,000 feet. As she climbed the mountain, Erin climbed at a constant speed during each one-hour interval. She finished her hike back at 4,000 feet at 1 PM. Erin's altitude, as a function of time, is shown in the graph below.

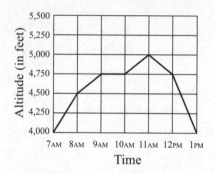

14. For how long, in hours and minutes, was Erin at or above 4,500 feet?

   F. 1 hour 20 minutes

   G. 3 hours

   H. 4 hours

   J. 4 hours 20 minutes

   K. 5 hours

15. Which graph best represents the absolute value of the velocity that Erin traveled, in vertical feet per hour?

(Note: Ignore acceleration and deceleration at the beginning and end of each one-hour interval.)

A.
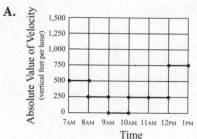

B.
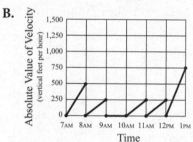

C.
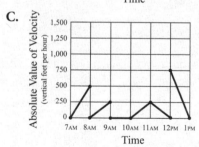

D.
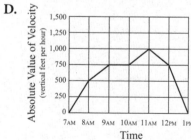

E.
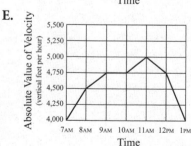

GO ON TO THE NEXT PAGE

16. What expression must be in the center cell of the table below so that the sums of each row, each column, and each diagonal are equivalent?

$-3x$	$4x$	$-7x$
$-6x$	?	$2x$
$3x$	$-8x$	$-x$

   F. $-6x$

   G. $-4x$

   H. $-2x$

   J. $2x$

   K. $4x$

17. If an object travels at a speed of 3 feet per second, how many feet does it travel in half an hour?

   A. 1,800

   B. 2,400

   C. 3,600

   D. 4,200

   E. 5,400

18. Leila has 5 necklaces, 8 pairs of earrings, and 3 hair clips. How many distinct sets of accessories, each consisting of a necklace, a pair of earrings, and a hair clip, can Leila choose?

   F.   16

   G.   55

   H.   64

   J.   120

   K.   360

19. At a factory, 90,000 tons of grain are required to make 150,000 tons of bread. How many tons of grain are required to produce 6,000 tons of bread?

   A.   3,600

   B. 10,000

   C. 25,000

   D. 36,000

   E. 60,000

20. In a certain set of integers, the ratio of even numbers to odd numbers is 2:3. What percent of the numbers in the set are even?

   F.   20

   G. $33\dfrac{1}{3}$

   H.   40

   J.   60

   K. $66\dfrac{2}{3}$

21. For all positive integers a, b, and c, which of the following is FALSE?

   A. $\dfrac{a \cdot b}{c \cdot b} = \dfrac{a}{c}$

   B. $\dfrac{a \cdot a}{b \cdot b} = \dfrac{a^2}{b^2}$

   C. $\dfrac{a \cdot b}{b \cdot a} = 1$

   D. $\dfrac{a + b}{b} = \dfrac{a}{b} + 1$

   E. $\dfrac{a + b}{c + b} = \dfrac{a}{c} + 1$

22. What is the slope-intercept form of $-3x - y + 7 = 0$?

   F. $y = 3x - 7$

   G. $y = 3x + 7$

   H. $y = -7x + 3$

   J. $y = -3x - 7$

   K. $y = -3x + 7$

GO ON TO THE NEXT PAGE

Practice Test 7

23. Which of the following is a solution to the equation $x^2 - 8x = 8x$?

   A. 32

   B. 16

   C. 8

   D. 4

   E. −4

24. Which of the following expressions describes the indicated values on the number line shown here?

   F. $x \leq 1$

   G. $x \geq 1$

   H. $|x| \leq 1$

   J. $|x| \geq 1$

   K. $x \geq |1|$

25. A chord 30 centimeters long is 8 centimeters from the center of a circle, as shown below. What is the radius of the circle, to the nearest tenth of a centimeter?

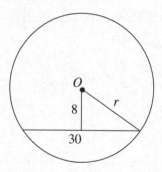

   A. 38.0

   B. 34.0

   C. 31.2

   D. 22.8

   E. 17.0

26. The velocity, in meters per second, of an object is given by the equation $V = \frac{5}{3}t + 0.05$, where t is the amount of time that has passed, in seconds. After how many seconds will the object be traveling at 0.575 meters per second?

   F. 0.28

   G. 0.315

   H. 0.365

   J. 0.525

   K. 0.57

27. A city has decided to store an estimated 15,000 cubic yards of sand for later distribution to the city's beaches. If this sand were spread evenly over the entire soccer field shown below, about how many yards deep would the sand be?

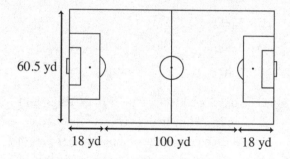

   A. Less than 1

   B. Between 1 and 2

   C. Between 2 and 3

   D. Between 3 and 4

   E. More than 4

GO ON TO THE NEXT PAGE

28. The hypotenuse of right $\triangle ABC$ shown below is 18 feet long. The cosine of $\angle A$ is $\frac{4}{5}$. About how many feet long is $\overline{AC}$?

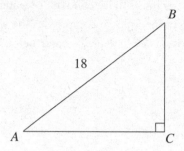

F. 15.2

G. 14.4

H. 13.9

J. 12.6

K. 10.8

29. The pictograph that follows shows the number of beds in each of several hotels, rounded to the nearest 50 beds. According to the graph, what fraction of the beds in these four hotels are at the Bedtime Hotel?

	Key = 100 beds

Hotel	Number of Beds
Comf-E	🛏🛏
Just Like Home	🛏🛏
Budget	🛏🛏🛏🛏
Bedtime	🛏🛏🛏

A. $\frac{1}{4}$

B. $\frac{1}{3}$

C. $\frac{2}{5}$

D. $\frac{5}{11}$

E. $\frac{1}{2}$

30. Points B and C lie on $\overline{AD}$ as shown. The length of $\overline{AD}$ is 38 units, $\overline{AC}$ is 26 units long, and $\overline{BD}$ is 20 units long. If it can be determined, how many units long is $\overline{BC}$?

A   B   C   D

F. 6

G. 8

H. 12

J. 18

K. Cannot be determined from the given information

31. What is the x-coordinate of the point in the standard (x,y) coordinate plane at which the two lines $y = 4x + 10$ and $y = 5x + 7$ intersect?

A. 3

B. 4

C. 7

D. 10

E. 22

32. Meri read 96 pages in 2 hours and 40 minutes. What was Meri's average rate in pages per hour?

F. 24

G. 30

H. 36

J. 42

K. 48

GO ON TO THE NEXT PAGE

33. If an integer is randomly chosen from the first 50 positive integers, what is the probability that an integer with a digit of 3 is selected?

    A. $\dfrac{1}{10}$

    B. $\dfrac{7}{25}$

    C. $\dfrac{3}{10}$

    D. $\dfrac{2}{5}$

    E. $\dfrac{3}{5}$

34. If $s = 4 + t$, then $(t - s)^3 = ?$

    F. -64

    G. -12

    H. -1

    J. 12

    K. 64

35. A zoo has the shape and dimensions, in yards, given in the figure below. The viewing point for the giraffes is halfway between points B and F. Which of the following is the location of the viewing point from the entrance at point A ?

    (Note: The zoo's borders run east/west or north/south.)

    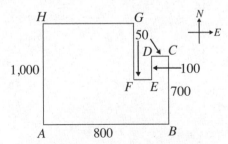

    A. 400 yards east and 350 yards north

    B. 400 yards east and 500 yards north

    C. 600 yards east and 350 yards north

    D. 750 yards east and 300 yards north

    E. 750 yards east and 350 yards north

36. In a contest, the weight of a first-place watermelon is 15 pounds less than 3 times the weight of the second-place watermelon. If w is the weight of the second-place watermelon, which of the following expresses the weight, in pounds, of the first-place watermelon?

    F. $w - 5$

    G. $w + 15$

    H. $w - 15$

    J. $3w + 15$

    K. $3w - 15$

37. If xy is negative, which of the following CANNOT be negative?

    A. $y - x$

    B. $x - y$

    C. $x^2 y$

    D. xy^2

    E. $x^2 y^2$

38. Which of the following sets of numbers has the property that the sum of any two numbers in the set is also a number in the set?

        I. The set of even integers

        II. The set of odd integers

        III. The set of prime numbers

    F. I only

    G. III only

    H. I and II only

    J. I and III only

    K. I, II, and III

GO ON TO THE NEXT PAGE

39. The sides of a triangle are in the ratio of exactly 15:17:20. A second triangle, similar to the first, has a longest side of length 12. To the nearest tenth of a unit, what is the length of the shortest side of the second triangle?

    A. 15.9

    B. 10.2

    C. 9.0

    D. 7.0

    E. Cannot be determined from the given information

40. In the figure shown, WXZY is a trapezoid, point X lies on $\overline{WT}$, and the angle measures are as marked. What is the measure of $\angle ZXT$?

    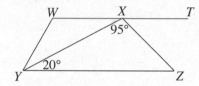

    F. 20°

    G. 30°

    H. 40°

    J. 55°

    K. 65°

41. What are the values of θ, between 0° and 360°, when $\sin \theta = \dfrac{\sqrt{3}}{2}$?

    A. 30° and 150° only

    B. 60° and 120° only

    C. 45° and 135° only

    D. 60° and 150° only

    E. 60° only

42. Of 896 seniors at a certain university, approximately $\dfrac{1}{3}$ are continuing their studies after graduation, and approximately $\dfrac{2}{5}$ of those continuing their studies are going to law school. Which of the following is the best estimate of how many seniors are going to law school?

    F. 120

    G. 180

    H. 240

    J. 300

    K. 360

43. If $a = -2$, $b = 4$, and $c = 7$, then $(a + b)(c - a) = ?$

    A. −30

    B. −10

    C. 10

    D. 18

    E. 30

44. If $\log_7 7^{\sqrt{7}} = x$, then x is between which of the following pairs of consecutive integers?

    F. 0 and 1

    G. 2 and 3

    H. 4 and 5

    J. 6 and 7

    K. 7 and 8

GO ON TO THE NEXT PAGE

45. The chart below shows the distribution of employees at a company into different teams in different departments. According to the chart, how many total employees are there?

Department	Number of Teams	Employees per Team
Development	1	4
Marketing	2	3
Accounting	3	2
Public Relations	5	5

- A. 14
- B. 25
- C. 41
- D. 84
- E. 154

46. The percent increase from 6 to 16 is equal to the percent increase from 12 to what number?

- F. 16
- G. 22
- H. 23
- J. 32
- K. 36

47. A circle in the standard (x,y) coordinate plane is tangent to the x-axis at 4 and tangent to the y-axis at 4. Which of the following is an equation of the circle?

- A. $x^2 + y^2 = 4$
- B. $x^2 + y^2 = 16$
- C. $(x - 4)^2 + (y - 4)^2 = 4$
- D. $(x - 4)^2 + (y - 4)^2 = 16$
- E. $(x + 4)^2 + (y + 4)^2 = 16$

48. Liza drove at an average speed of 40 miles per hour for 2 hours and then increased her average speed by 25% for the next 3 hours. Her average speed for the 5 hours was r miles per hour. What is the value of r?

- F. 44
- G. 45
- H. 46
- J. 47
- K. 48

49. The number of executives at a large company, by division, can be modeled using the following matrix.

Marketing	Human Resources	Operations	Legal
[20	12	40	10]

The company is downsizing and the head of Human Resources estimates the proportion of current executives who will be laid off within the next year. The estimates are shown in the following matrix.

$$
\begin{matrix}
\text{Marketing} \\
\text{Human Resources} \\
\text{Operations} \\
\text{Legal}
\end{matrix}
\begin{bmatrix}
0.3 \\
0.5 \\
0.2 \\
0.4
\end{bmatrix}
$$

Given these matrices, what is the head of Human Resources' estimate of the number of current executives in these departments who will be laid off within the next year?

- A. 24
- B. 27
- C. 30
- D. 32
- E. 36

GO ON TO THE NEXT PAGE

50. The probability distribution of the discrete random variable X is shown in the table below. Based on the probability distribution, what is the expected value of X ?

X	Probability $P(X = x)$
10	$\frac{1}{5}$
11	$\frac{1}{10}$
12	$\frac{3}{10}$
13	$\frac{3}{20}$
14	$\frac{1}{4}$

F. $10\frac{4}{5}$

G. 11

H. 12

J. $12\frac{3}{20}$

K. $13\frac{1}{20}$

51. Which of the following is the solution set for all real numbers x such that $x - 2 < x - 5$?

A. The empty set

B. The set containing all real numbers

C. The set containing all negative real numbers

D. The set containing all nonnegative real numbers

E. The set containing only zero

52. The figure shown here represents the function $g(x) = \sqrt{x}$.

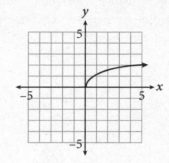

Suppose $h(x)$ is a transformation of $g(x)$ and is given by the equation $h(x) = \sqrt{x + 1} + 3$. Which of the following correctly states the domain and range of $h(x)$?

F. Domain: $x \geq -1$; Range: $y \geq 0$

G. Domain: $x \geq -1$; Range: $y \geq 3$

H. Domain: $x \geq 0$; Range: $y \geq 0$

J. Domain: $x \geq 1$; Range: $y \geq -3$

K. Domain: $x \geq 1$; Range: $y \geq 3$

53. Diane wants to draw a circle graph showing the favorite teachers at her school. When she polled her classmates, 25% said Mr. Green, 15% said Ms. Brown, 35% said Mrs. White, 5% said Mr. Blue, and the remaining classmates said teachers other than Mr. Green, Ms. Brown, Mrs. White, or Mr. Blue. The teachers other than Mr. Green, Ms. Brown, Mrs. White, or Mr. Blue will be grouped together in an Other sector. What will be the degree measure of the sector that represents Other?

A. 144°

B. 72°

C. 36°

D. 20°

E. 15°

GO ON TO THE NEXT PAGE

Practice Test 7

54. The first and seventh terms in a sequence are 1 and 365, respectively. If each term after the first in the sequence is formed by multiplying the preceding term by 3 and subtracting 1, what is the sixth term?

F.   40

G.   41

H.   121

J.   122

K.   123

55. A portion of which of the following systems of inequalities is represented by the shaded region of the graph below?

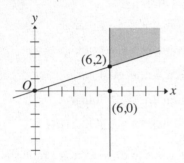

A. $y \geq \dfrac{1}{3}x$ and $x \geq 6$

B. $y \geq 3x$ and $x \geq 6$

C. $y \leq \dfrac{1}{3}x$ and $x \geq 6$

D. $y \leq 3x$ and $x \geq 6$

E. $y \leq \dfrac{1}{3}x$ and $x \leq 6$

56. If $f(x) = 2(x + 7)$, then $f(x + c) = ?$

F. $2(x + 7) + c$

G. $2x + c + 7$

H. $2x + c + 14$

J. $2x + 2c + 7$

K. $2x + 2c + 14$

57. A formula for the volume, V, of a right circular cylinder is $V = \pi r^2 h$, where r is the radius and h is the height. The cylindrical swimming pool shown here is filled completely with water and has a radius of 6 feet and a depth of 4 feet.

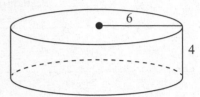

If 1 cubic foot of water weighs approximately 62.4 pounds, then the weight, in pounds, of the water in the swimming pool is:

A.   less than 20,000.

B.   between 20,000 and 25,000.

C.   between 25,000 and 30,000.

D.   between 30,000 and 35,000.

E.   more than 35,000.

58. A triangle, $\triangle ABC$, is reflected across the y-axis to create the image $\triangle A'B'C'$ in the standard (x,y) coordinate plane (for example, A reflects to A'). If the coordinates of point A are (v,w), what are the coordinates of point A'?

F. $(v,-w)$

G. $(-v,w)$

H. $(-v,-w)$

J. (w,v)

K.   Cannot be determined from the given information

GO ON TO THE NEXT PAGE

59. If $a = 6c + 7$ and $b = 3 - 2c$, which of the following expresses a in terms of b?

A. $a = \dfrac{16 - b}{3}$

B. $a = \dfrac{17 - b}{2}$

C. $a = 16 - 3b$

D. $a = 25 - 12b$

E. $a = 6b + 7$

60. In complex numbers, where $i^2 = -1$, what is the simplified form of the expression $\dfrac{(2i + 2)^2}{(2i - 2)^2}$?

F. $\dfrac{i + 1}{i - 1}$

G. $\dfrac{i}{4}$

H. $\dfrac{4}{i}$

J. 1

K. -1

IF YOU FINISH BEFORE TIME IS CALLED, YOU MAY CHECK YOUR WORK ON THIS SECTION ONLY. DO NOT TURN TO ANY OTHER SECTION IN THE TEST. STOP

READING TEST

35 Minutes—40 Questions

Directions: The Reading Test includes multiple passages. Each passage includes multiple questions. After reading each passage, choose the best answer and fill in the corresponding bubble on your answer sheet. You may review the passages as often as necessary.

Passage I

LITERARY NARRATIVE: This passage is adapted from the novel *My Doggie and I* by R.M. Ballantyne.

I possess a doggie—not a dog, observe, but a doggie. If he had been a dog I would not have presumed to intrude him on your notice. A dog is all very well in his way—one of the noblest of
5 animals, I admit, and preeminently fitted to be the companion of man, for he has an affectionate nature, which man demands, and a forgiving disposition, which man needs—but a dog, with all his noble qualities, is not to be compared to a
10 doggie.

Freely admit that you don't at once perceive the finer qualities, either mental or physical, of my doggie, partly owing to the circumstance that he is shapeless and hairy. The former quality is
15 not attractive, while the latter tends to veil the amiable expression of his countenance and the luster of his speaking eyes. But as you come to know him he grows upon you; your feelings are touched, your affections stirred, and your love
20 is finally evoked. As he resembles a doormat, or rather a scrap of a very ragged doormat, and has an amiable spirit, I have called him "Dumps." I should not be surprised if you did not perceive any connection here. You are not the first who
25 has failed to see it; I never saw it myself.

When I first met Dumps, he was scurrying towards me along a sequestered country lane. It was in the Dog Days. Dust lay thick on the road; the creature's legs were remarkably short though
30 active, and his hair being long he swept up the dust in clouds as he ran. He was yelping, and I

observed that one or two stones appeared to be racing with, or after, him. The voice of an angry man also seemed to chase him, but the owner of
35 the voice was at the moment concealed by a turn in the lane, which was bordered by high stone walls.

Rabies, of course, flashed into my mind. I grasped my stick and drew close to the wall. The
40 hairy whirlwind, if I may so call it, came wildly on, but instead of passing me, or snapping at my legs as I had expected, it stopped and crawled towards me in a piteous, supplicating manner that at once disarmed me. If the creature had lain
45 still, I should have been unable to distinguish its head from its tail; but as one end of him whined, and the other wagged, I had no difficulty.

Stooping down with caution, I patted the end that whined, whereupon the end that wagged
50 became violently demonstrative. Just then the owner of the voice came round the corner. He was a big, rough fellow, in ragged garments, and armed with a thick stick, which he seemed about to fling at the little dog, when I checked him with
55 a shout—

"You'd better not, my man, unless you want your own head broken!"

You see, I am a pretty well-sized man myself, and, as I felt confidence in my strength, my stick,
60 and the goodness of my cause, I was bold.

"What d'you mean by ill-treating the little dog?" I demanded sternly, as I stepped up to the man.

GO ON TO THE NEXT PAGE

"A man may do as he likes with his own,
65 mayn't he?" answered the man, with a sulky
scowl.

"A 'man' may do nothing of the sort," said I
indignantly, for cruelty to dumb animals always
has the effect of inclining me to fight, though I
70 am naturally of a peaceable disposition. "There
is an Act of Parliament," I continued, "which
goes by the honored name of Martin, and if you
venture to infringe that Act I'll have you taken up
and prosecuted."

75 While I was speaking I observed a peculiar
leer on the man's face, which I could not account
for. He appeared, however, to have been affected
by my threats, for he ceased to scowl, and assumed a deferential air as he replied, "Well, sir, it
80 do seem rather hard that a man's head should be
broken for kindness."

"Kindness!" I exclaimed, in surprise.

"Ay, kindness, sir. That there animal loves me,
it do, like a brother, and the love is mutual. We've
85 lived together now—off an' on—for the matter of
six months. Well, I get employment in a factory
about fifteen miles from here, in which no dogs
is allowed. Of course, I can't give up that employment, sir, can I? Neither can my doggie give up
90 his master that he's so fond of, so I'm obliged to
leave him in the charge of a friend, with strict
orders to keep him locked up till I'm fairly gone.
Well, off I goes, but he manages to escape and
runs after me. Now, what can a feller do but drive
95 him home with sticks an' stones, though it do get
to my heart to do it? But if he goes to the factory,
he's sure to be shot, or dragged, or drowned, or
something; so you see, sir, it's out of pure kindness I'm chasing him."

100 I confess that I felt somewhat doubtful of the
truth of this story; but, in order to prevent any
expression of my face betraying me, I stooped
and patted the dog while the man spoke. It
received my attentions with evident delight. A
105 thought suddenly flashed on me:

"Will you sell your little dog?" I asked.

1. The narrator implies that his "doggie" differs
from a "dog" in that his "doggie":

   A. may be less impressive at first sight.

   B. is older than a puppy but not a dog.

   C. is forgiving of humans, no matter what.

   D. is a majestic creature, both handsome and
   good-natured.

2. According to paragraph 2, which of the following accurately describes Dumps?

   F. His eyes are dull, and his body is shapeless.

   G. Observers are quickly struck by his wise
   demeanor.

   H. He has kind-looking eyes that are often hidden behind his hair.

   J. His abundant hair gives him the appearance
   of a well-groomed carpet.

3. The description in paragraphs 3–4 suggests that
Dumps was running:

   A. at a leisurely pace, stopping to sniff the
   grass.

   B. in a desperate manner, looking for help.

   C. as though compelled by immobilizing ter-
   ror.

   D. to fetch a stick as part of his favorite game.

4. As it is used in line 54, *checked* most nearly
means:

   F. prevented.

   G. square patterned.

   H. verified.

   J. assaulted.

GO ON TO THE NEXT PAGE

Practice Test 7

5. The author places the word *man* in quotes (line 67) in order to:

   A. compare the narrator's recognition of the dog owner's large size to his own stature.

   B. indicate that the narrator is ironically agreeing with the dog owner's assertion.

   C. signal that the narrator is attempting to start a violent fight with the dog owner despite his typical peaceful nature.

   D. imply that the narrator considers the dog owner inhumane regarding his treatment of animals.

6. According to lines 75–81, the dog's owner stops scowling at the narrator because:

   F. after listening to the narrator, he decides that the dog is unlikely to bite the narrator.

   G. he shifts his concern away from his dog's behavior to anxiety about being late for his job at the factory.

   H. he is concerned about the narrator's mention of breaking the law and wants to make a better impression.

   J. the narrator has stopped threatening to hit the dog with a stick and is offering to help.

7. Throughout the passage, the narrator's attitude toward the reader is best described as:

   A. considerate and wanting the reader to think well of him.

   B. argumentative about how pets are commonly perceived.

   C. fearful that the reader will disagree with his unorthodox views.

   D. deceptive in order to gain a favorable opinion from the reader.

8. Which choice best reflects the dog owner's explanation as to why chasing the dog with a stick is actually a demonstration of kindness?

   F. The dog belongs to the owner, so the owner is entitled to treat the dog as he chooses.

   G. The owner cannot take the dog to his factory job, but the dog escapes and runs after him so he must drive the dog back.

   H. Dogs love running after thrown sticks, and this activity will provide the dog with exercise before the owner goes to work at the factory.

   J. The men who work at the factory have a record of mistreating animals, especially dogs.

9. The narrator most likely doubts the dog owner's story (lines 100–105) because:

   A. the owner is so eager to sell the dog that the narrator doubts he really cares for it.

   B. the narrator cannot believe that a man with his temperament could hold down a job.

   C. it seems unlikely that the dog would actually be harmed as the owner claims.

   D. the owner seems to claim he loves the dog only after being threatened with legal prosecution.

10. The passage implies that the narrator wants to buy the dog primarily because:

    F. he believes the dog will make the great companion he's been looking for.

    G. he cares for animals and suspects that the dog's owner is treating it badly.

    H. he fears the dog's owner and hopes to appease him by offering him money.

    J. the dog's owner wishes that the dog didn't have to be alone while he's at work.

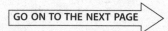

GO ON TO THE NEXT PAGE

Passage II

SOCIAL STUDIES: The following two passages were written in the early 1990s and present two viewpoints about the ways that the public responds to the results of scientific research.

Passage A

The way that people in present-day industrial societies think about science in the modern world actually tends to cultivate the very unscientific perception that science supplies us with

5 unquestionable facts. If there is one unquestionable fact about science, it is that science is inherently uncertain. Research consists not so much of a search for truth as a search for some degree of certainty in an uncertain world. Every research study, every

10 experiment, and every survey incorporates an extensive statistical analysis that is meant to be taken as qualifying the probability that the results are consistent and reproducible. Yet policy makers, public relations interests, and so-called experts in

15 the popular media continue to treat the results of every latest study as if they were surefire truths.

History is filled with examples of the fallibility of scientific certainties. From the medieval monks who believed the sun orbited around Earth and

20 the world was only 4,000 years old, to the early twentieth-century scientists who thought that X-rays were a hoax and that exploding a nuclear bomb would set off a chain reaction that would destroy all matter in the universe, it has been

25 demonstrated repeatedly that science deals primarily with possibilities and is subject to the same prejudices as other kinds of opinions and beliefs. Yet statistics are complicated, and in our need to feel that we live in a universe of predictable

30 certainties, it is tempting to place our faith in the oversimplified generalities of headlines and sound bites rather than the rigorous application of probabilities. Ironically, even though the intent of science is to expand the realm of human

35 knowledge, an unfounded prejudice stemming from a desire for scientific constancy can actually discourage inquiry.

Science serves an important practical function; predictability and reproducibility are vital to

40 making sure that our bridges remain standing, our nuclear power plants run smoothly, and our cars start in the morning so we can drive to work. When these practicalities become everyday occurrences, they tend to encourage a complacent faith in the

45 reliability and consistency of science. Yet faced with so many simple conveniences, it is important to remember that we depend on the advance of science for our very survival. With progress expanding into those gray areas at the boundaries

50 of scientific exploration, caution and prudence are just as important as open-mindedness and imagination. As technological advances engage increasingly complex moral questions within fields such as pharmaceutical developments,

55 indefinite extension of life, and the potential for inconceivably potent weapons, an understanding of the limitations of science becomes just as important as an understanding of its strengths.

Passage B

While it is important that scientific knowledge

60 be taken into consideration in significant matters of public interest, such consideration must be tempered with critical rigor. In the early days during the ascendance of science as a practical discipline, the public was inclined to view every

65 new advance and discovery with a healthy skepticism. In the late 19th century, when Italian astronomer Giovanni Schiaparelli first detected seas and continents on the planet Mars, many people balked at the idea of Earth-like topography on the

70 Red Planet. Just a few decades later, when fellow Italian astronomer Vincenzo Cerulli provided evidence that the seas and continents Schiaparelli

GO ON TO THE NEXT PAGE

observed were merely optical illusions, public disbelief proved to be entirely appropriate.

75 Since then, the historic tendency of the public to question scientific findings has unfortunately been lost. Yet in present-day industrial societies, and especially where public policy is at issue, response to scientific research needs more than ever to pursue an informed,

80 critical viewpoint. Who performs a research study, what kind of study it is, what kinds of review and scrutiny it comes under, and what interests support it are every bit as important as a study's conclusions.

Studies of mass media and public policy reveal that,

85 all too often, scientific findings presented to the public as objective and conclusive are actually funded at two or three degrees of removal by corporate or political interests with a specific agenda related to the outcome of those findings. For example, some critics question

90 the issue of whether a study of the effectiveness of a new drug is more likely to produce favorable results when the study is funded by the pharmaceutical company that owns the drug patent. In cases where such findings conflict with the interests of the funding

95 parties, analysts sometimes wonder if information was repressed, altered, or given a favorable public relations slant in order to de-emphasize dangerous side effects. Some critics of company-funded studies argue that the level of misrepresentation included in such studies

100 borders on immoral.

Part of the problem grows from the public's willingness to place blind faith in the authority of science without an awareness of the interests that lie behind the research. Public officials then, in turn, may

105 sometimes be too willing to bend in the face of public or private political pressure rather than pursuing the best interests of the constituency. Issues such as genetics, reproductive health, and preventative care are particularly fraught with political angst. Where the

110 safety of individuals is at stake, a precautionary principle of allowing for unpredictable, unforeseen negative effects of technological advances should be pursued.

It is the duty of active citizens in a free society to educate themselves about the real-world application

115 of risk-assessment and statistical analysis, and to resist passive acceptance of the reassurances of self-styled scientific authorities. The most favorable approach to policy decisions based on realistic assessments finds a middle ground between the

120 alarmism of political "Chicken Littles" and the recklessness of profit-seeking risk takers.

Questions 11–13 ask about Passage A.

---

11. According to the passage, policy makers consider the results of studies:

   A. with concern.

   B. as unquestioned truth.

   C. as debatable.

   D. as false.

12. The word *probabilities* in line 33 is used to express the author's belief that:

   F. scientific theories will eventually be proven true.

   G. current scientific findings will be regarded as outdated by future scientists.

   H. viewing scientific results as possibly wrong is a wise approach.

   J. refusing to question science is unavoidable because people prefer certainty.

13. As it is used in line 44, the word *complacent* most nearly means:

   A. conceited.

   B. dangerous.

   C. unquestioned.

   D. dissatisfied.

GO ON TO THE NEXT PAGE

Questions 14–16 ask about Passage B.

14. Which of the following is an example of a scientific discovery greeted with skepticism by the public?

 F. A pharmaceutical study funded by a drug patent holder

 G. Schiaparelli's detection of continents on Mars

 H. The statement that X-rays are a hoax

 J. Darwin's theory of evolution

15. The author of Passage B uses the first paragraph to explain:

 A. a new scientific hypothesis.

 B. a historical contrast.

 C. a public policy generality.

 D. the underlying cause of an issue.

16. With which of the following statements would the author of Passage B most likely agree?

 F. People should not unquestioningly accept the results of scientific studies.

 G. More government control and regulation are needed to ensure that science serves the best interests of the public.

 H. Society should place less emphasis on modern conveniences and more on understanding the limitations of science.

 J. The results that scientists derive from research are less reliable now than they were in former times.

Questions 17–20 ask about both passages.

17. What does the author of Passage A believe is the biggest obstacle to reaching the solution described by the author of Passage B in lines 113–117 ("It is the duty . . . authorities")?

 A. Policymakers are too willing to bend to public pressure when it comes to regulating scientific research.

 B. The interests that fund research are the same interests that stand to profit by favorable results, making impartiality impossible.

 C. Statistics are too abstract when compared with the concrete evidence of technological conveniences.

 D. Unanswered ethical questions are increasingly coming under scrutiny at the forefront of our most advanced scientific research.

18. Both passages refer to which of the following?

 F. Present-day industrial societies

 G. Early twentieth-century scientists

 H. Critics of company-funded studies

 J. Significant matters of public interest

GO ON TO THE NEXT PAGE

19. According to Passage B, which of the following is an example of the "fallibility of scientific certainties" (lines 17–18) mentioned in Passage A?

    A. Medieval monks who believed the sun orbited around Earth

    B. People who balked at the idea of Earth-like topography on Mars

    C. Issues such as genetics, reproductive health, and preventative care

    D. Early twentieth-century scientists who thought that X-rays were a hoax

20. The authors of both passages mention the term *pharmaceutical* in order to:

    F. highlight a particular scientific field in which moral questions may arise.

    G. point out an example of the recklessness of profit-seeking risk takers.

    H. identify unfounded prejudice stemming from a desire for scientific constancy.

    J. cite the usefulness of the current approach regarding drug testing and analysis.

GO ON TO THE NEXT PAGE

Passage III

HUMANITIES: This passage is adapted from a Wiki-pedia article titled "Walter Scott."

Born in Edinburgh in 1771, the young Walter
Scott survived a childhood bout of polio that would
leave him lame in his right leg for the rest of his
life. After studying law at Edinburgh University,
5 he followed in his father's footsteps and became
a lawyer in his native Scotland. Beginning at age
25, he started dabbling in writing, first translating
works from German, then moving on to poetry. In
between these two phases of his literary career, he
10 published a three-volume set of collected Scottish
ballads, *The Minstrelsy of the Scottish Border*. This
was the first sign of his interest in Scotland and
history in his writings.

After Scott had founded a printing press, his
15 poetry, beginning with *The Lay of the Last Minstrel*
in 1805, brought him great fame. He published a
number of other poems over the next ten years,
including in 1810 the popular *Lady of the Lake*,
portions of which (translated into German) were
20 set to music by Franz Schubert. Another work from
this time period, *Marmion*, produced some of his
most quoted (and most often misattributed) lines,
such as

Oh! what a tangled web we weave
25 *When first we practise to deceive!*

When Scott's press became embroiled in
financial difficulties, Scott set out, in 1814, to write
a successful (and profitable) work. The result was
Waverley, a novel that did not name its author. It
30 was a tale of the last Jacobite rebellion in the United
Kingdom, the "Forty-Five," and the novel met
with considerable success. There followed a large
number of novels in the next five years, each in the
same general vein. Mindful of his reputation as a
35 poet, he maintained the anonymity he had begun
with *Waverley*, always publishing the novels under a
name such as "Author of Waverley" or attributed as
"Tales of . . ." with no author. Even when it was clear
that there would be no harm in coming out into

40 the open, he maintained the façade, apparently out
of a sense of fun. During this time, the nickname
"The Wizard of the North" was popularly applied
to the mysterious best-selling writer. His identity as
the author of the novels was widely rumored, and
45 in 1815 Scott was given the honour of dining with
George, Prince Regent, who wanted to meet "the
author of Waverley."

In 1820, Scott broke away from writing about
Scotland with *Ivanhoe*, a historical romance set
50 in twelfth-century England. It too was a runaway
success and, as he did with his first novel, he
unleashed a slew of books along the same lines.
As his fame grew during this phase of his career,
he was granted the title of Baronet, becoming Sir
55 Walter Scott. At this time he organized the visit
of King George IV to Scotland, and when the
King visited Edinburgh in 1822, the spectacular
pageantry Scott had concocted to portray the King
as a rather tubby reincarnation of Bonnie Prince
60 Charlie made tartans and kilts fashionable and
turned them into symbols of national identity.

Beginning in 1825, Scott fell into dire financial
straits again, and his company nearly collapsed.
That he was the author of his novels became general
65 knowledge at this time as well. Rather than declare
bankruptcy he placed his home, Abbotsford House,
and income into a trust belonging to his creditors,
and proceeded to write his way out of debt. He
kept up his prodigious output of fiction (as well as
70 producing a biography of Napoleon Bonaparte)
through 1831. By then his health was failing, and
he died at Abbotsford in 1832. Though not in the
clear by then, his novels continued to sell, and he
made good his debts from beyond the grave. He
75 was buried in Dryburgh Abbey; nearby, fittingly, a
large statue can be found of William Wallace—one
of Scotland's great historical figures.

Scott was responsible for two major trends
that carry on to this day. First, he popularized the
80 historical novel; an enormous number of imitators
(and imitators of imitators) would appear in
the nineteenth century. It is a measure of Scott's

GO ON TO THE NEXT PAGE ⟹

influence that Edinburgh's central railway station, opened in 1854, is called Waverley Station. Second, his Scottish novels rehabilitated Highland culture after years in the shadows following the Jacobite rebellions.

Scott was also responsible, through a series of pseudonymous letters published in the *Edinburgh Weekly News* in 1826, for retaining the right of Scottish banks to issue their own banknotes, which is reflected to this day by his continued appearance on the front of all notes issued by the Bank of Scotland.

21. The main idea of the passage is that:

    A. historical novels can be very successful in rehabilitating a country's culture.

    B. Sir Walter Scott's writings achieved both financial success and cultural impact.

    C. Scott became known more for his financial failures than for his literary talents.

    D. the success of Scott's novels was largely due to the anonymity of the author.

22. According to the passage, Walter Scott turned to writing novels because:

    F. his childhood bout with polio made it difficult for him to continue working as a lawyer.

    G. his printing press business was being sued over copyright violations.

    H. his three-volume set of Scottish ballads did not sell well.

    J. his printing press business was losing money.

23. According to the author, Scott published *Waverly* anonymously because:

    A. he didn't want to damage his reputation as a lawyer.

    B. he had fun watching people try to determine who the author was.

    C. his novels sold faster without an author's name on them.

    D. he was afraid writing fiction would take away from his reputation as a poet.

24. The author would most likely describe Scott's effect on how Scotland was viewed as:

    F. damaging, since Scott degraded Scottish culture by popularizing tartans and kilts.

    G. unimportant, since Scott's novels were no more than popular fiction.

    H. ground-breaking, since Scott was the first to write serious analyses of Scottish history.

    J. positive, since Scott made Scottish culture acceptable again after years of neglect.

25. Based on the passage, it is reasonable to assume that Scott's reputation after his death:

    A. remained favorable.

    B. waned because there were no more of his novels being published.

    C. declined because he died without paying all of his debts.

    D. was debased because of all his imitators.

GO ON TO THE NEXT PAGE

26. As it is used in line 40, the word *façade* most nearly means:

    F. pretense.

    G. building front.

    H. bluff.

    J. character.

27. The author most likely uses *fittingly* (line 75) when describing the presence of a statue of William Wallace near Scott's grave in Dryburgh Abbey because:

    A. Scott's first major novel was about the achievements of William Wallace.

    B. Scott wrote novels about Scottish history, and Wallace is a famous historical figure from Scotland.

    C. Scott was a very religious man and deserved to be buried in an abbey.

    D. Wallace was an avid fan of Scott's poetry.

28. The passage suggests that the author's attitude toward Sir Walter Scott is:

    F. restrained and skeptical.

    G. derisive and contemptuous.

    H. interested and appreciative.

    J. passionate and envious.

29. Based on the fifth paragraph (lines 62–77), it is reasonable to infer that Sir Walter Scott's attitude toward his debts was:

    A. irresponsible, since he left them to be taken care of after his death.

    B. resentful, for he believed that they were caused by his partners.

    C. impatient, because he became annoyed that his creditors hounded him so.

    D. accepting, since he acknowledged his responsibility and tried to pay them back.

30. The author's use of *dabbling* in line 7 suggests that:

    F. Scott sought to establish himself in a field in which he had little experience.

    G. the financial losses eventually suffered by Scott's printing press began with this activity.

    H. Scott's inexperience led to the poor quality of his literary work.

    J. Scott's initial work led to his interest in Scottish history.

GO ON TO THE NEXT PAGE

Passage IV

NATURAL SCIENCE: The following is adapted from Wikipedia articles titled "Lemur" and "Ring-tailed Lemur."

Lemurs are part of a suborder of primates known as prosimians, and make up the infraorder Lemuriformes. This type of primate was the evolutionary predecessor of monkeys and apes
5   (simians). The term "lemur" is derived from the Latin word *lemures*, which means "spirits of the night." This likely refers to many lemurs' nocturnal behavior and their large, reflective eyes. It is generically used for the members of the four
10 lemuriform families, but it is also the genus of one of the lemuriform species. The two flying lemur species are not lemurs, nor are they even primates.

Lemurs are found naturally only on the island of Madagascar and some smaller surrounding islands,
15 including the Comoros (where it is likely they were introduced by humans). While they were displaced in the rest of the world by monkeys, apes, and other primates, the lemurs were safe from competition on Madagascar and differentiated into a number of
20 species. These range in size from the tiny 30-gram pygmy mouse lemur to the 10-kilogram indri. The larger species have all become extinct since humans settled on Madagascar, and since the early twentieth century the largest lemurs reach about seven
25 kilograms. Typically, the smaller lemurs are active at night (nocturnal), while the larger ones are active during the day (diurnal).

All lemurs are endangered species, due mainly to habitat destruction (deforestation) and hunting.
30 Although conservation efforts are underway, options are limited because of the lemurs' limited range and because Madagascar is desperately poor. Currently, there are approximately 32 living lemur species.

35 The ring-tailed lemur is a relatively large prosimian, belonging to the family Lemuridae. Ring-tailed lemurs are the only species within the genus *Lemur* and are found only on the island of Madagascar. Although threatened by habitat
40 destruction and therefore listed as vulnerable by the IUCN Red List, ring-tailed lemurs are the most populous lemurs in zoos worldwide; they reproduce readily in captivity.

Mostly grey with white underparts, ring-tailed
45 lemurs have slender frames; their narrow faces are white with black lozenge-shaped patches around the eyes and black vulpine muzzles. The lemurs' trademark, their long, bushy tails, are ringed in black and white. Like all lemurs, ring-tailed lemurs
50 have hind limbs longer than their forelimbs; their palms and soles are padded with soft, leathery skin and their fingers are slender and dexterous. On the second toe of their hind limbs, ring-tailed lemurs have claws specialized for grooming purposes.

55 The very young animals have blue eyes while the eyes of all adults are a striking yellow. Adults may reach a body length of 46 centimeters (18 inches) and a weight of 5.5 kilograms (12 pounds). Their tails are longer than their bodies, at up to
60 56 centimeters (22 inches) in length.

Found in the southwest of Madagascar and ranging farther into highland areas than any other lemur, ring-tailed lemurs inhabit deciduous forests with grass floors or forests along riverbanks
65 (gallery forests); some may also inhabit dry, open brush where few trees grow. Ring-tailed lemurs are thought to require primary forest (that is, forests that have remained undisturbed by human activity) in order to survive; such forests are now being
70 cleared at a troubling rate.

While primarily frugivores (fruit-eating), ring-tailed lemurs will also eat leaves, seeds, and the odd insect. Ring-tailed lemurs are diurnal and primarily arboreal animals, forming troops of up
75 to 25 individuals. Social hierarchies are determined by sex, with a distinct hierarchy for each gender; females tend to dominate the troop, while males will alternate between troops. Lemurs claim a sizable territory, which does not overlap with those

GO ON TO THE NEXT PAGE

80 of other troops; up to 5.6 kilometers (3.5 miles)
of this territory may be covered in a single day's
foraging.

   Both vocal and olfactory signals are important
to ring-tailed lemurs' communication: 15 distinct
85 vocalizations are used. A fatty substance is exuded
from the lemurs' glands, which the lemurs run
their tails through; this scent is used by both sexes
to mark territory and to challenge would-be rivals
amongst males. The males vigorously wave their
90 tails high in the air in an attempt to overpower the
scent of others.

   The breeding season runs from April to June,
with the female fertile period lasting for only a day.
Gestation lasts for about 146 days, resulting in a
95 litter of either one or two. The young lemurs begin
to eat solid food after two months and are fully
weaned after five months.

31. According to the passage, lemurs survived on
the island of Madagascar because:

   A. their large, reflective eyes allowed them to
   move around at night when predators were
   asleep.

   B. their ability to mark their territory by scent
   gave them adequate territory for foraging.

   C. monkeys, apes, and other primates were not
   a threat to them on Madagascar.

   D. their strong social hierarchy allowed them
   to band together for safety.

32. According to the passage, the social organization
of the ring-tailed lemur:

   F. places females at the top of the hierarchy.

   G. functions to ensure adequate food supplies.

   H. has followed the same structure since
   antiquity.

   J. is notable for its equality of the sexes.

33. As it is used in line 73, the word *odd* most nearly
means:

   A. strange.

   B. unusual.

   C. eerie.

   D. occasional.

34. According to the passage, why are ring-tails the
most populous species of lemurs in zoos?

   F. They inhabit deciduous forests, which make
   the lemurs' capture relatively easy.

   G. They have no difficulty giving birth in a zoo
   environment.

   H. Their attractive appearance makes them
   popular with patrons.

   J. Their eating preferences are easily
   accommodated.

35. The passage suggests that the rate at which
primary forests are being cleared is *troubling*
(line 70) because:

   A. it is causing significant soil erosion in the
   lemurs' primary habitat.

   B. valuable hardwoods are being destroyed.

   C. lemurs' predators inhabit the cleared area.

   D. lemurs need to live in primary forests to
   survive.

36. All of the following are given as ways in
which ring-tailed lemurs use olfactory signals
EXCEPT:

   F. to put male challengers on notice.

   G. to mask the scent of other lemurs.

   H. to signify group identification.

   J. to mark their territory.

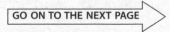

GO ON TO THE NEXT PAGE

Practice Test 7

37. According to the passage, which of the following describes a characteristic of the infraorder Lemuriformes?

    A. They are nocturnal.

    B. They evolved before monkeys and apes did.

    C. They include two species of flying lemurs.

    D. They are found only on Madagascar.

38. Which of the following can reasonably be inferred from information in the second paragraph (lines 13–27)?

    F. The pygmy mouse lemur is diurnal.

    G. The larger species of lemur were hunted for their fur.

    H. The indri lemur is extinct.

    J. Lemurs are descended from monkeys.

39. When ring-tailed lemurs grow from young animals to adults:

    A. they become less aggressive.

    B. they no longer need primary forests.

    C. their eye color changes.

    D. they become known as flying lemurs.

40. Which of the following questions is NOT answered by the passage?

    F. Will conservationists be able to prevent the extinction of lemurs?

    G. Why did lemurs survive on Madagascar?

    H. How many offspring can a female lemur produce per year?

    J. What makes up the lemur's diet?

IF YOU FINISH BEFORE TIME IS CALLED, YOU MAY CHECK YOUR WORK ON THIS SECTION ONLY. DO NOT TURN TO ANY OTHER SECTION IN THE TEST. STOP

664 Practice Test 7

SCIENCE TEST

35 Minutes—40 Questions

Directions: The Science Test includes multiple passages. Each passage includes multiple questions. After reading each passage, choose the best answer and fill in the corresponding bubble on your answer sheet. You may review the passages as often as necessary.

You may NOT use a calculator on this test.

Passage I

In the 1920s, scientists developed numerous models of the atom, most of which posited a central nucleus surrounded by electrons. See Diagram 1.

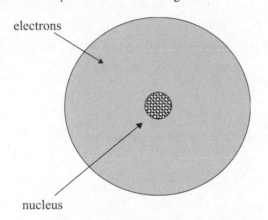

Diagram 1

The protons and neutrons in the atom's nucleus have positive and neutral charges, respectively, whereas electrons have a negative charge. In the process of becoming ionized, an atom gains or loses electrons, thereby obtaining an overall positive or negative charge. Additionally, after atoms have become energized, they release such energy in the form of light. Electrons are thought to be responsible for this process.

In the 1920s, two scientists debated the way in which electrons surround an atom's nucleus.

Scientist 1: Bohr model

Electrons move around an atom's nucleus in precise, co-planar, concentric circular orbits. Any given orbit can only hold a certain number of electrons. Once the orbit is filled with electrons, the next level orbit must be used. For this reason, some atoms will be larger (have a larger radius) than others.

Additionally, if electrons become energized, they will "jump" from one orbit to the next. When they return to their normal energy level, they emit energy in the form of light. This accounts for the fact that excited atoms emit very specific and well-defined colors of light. If the position of electrons is not specified, the precise wavelengths of light that are emitted cannot be explained.

Scientist 2: Electron cloud model

The precise location of electrons cannot be detected. Electrons move around a nucleus in a cloud. In this cloud, certain regions have a higher probability of containing electrons than others. The cloud extends all around the nucleus in 3 dimensions. The uncertainty of any one electron's position and the nature of its existence as a charged particle contribute to an understanding of the wave-particle nature of matter and energy.

GO ON TO THE NEXT PAGE
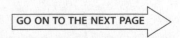

Practice Test 7

Though this model is seemingly at odds with a number of assumptions about the stability of matter in larger-scale reality, it is anchored to a concept called the *wave function*. The wave function helps to specify the distinct shape of the probability clouds surrounding a nucleus. This explains how the position of the electrons can be random and yet localized.

1. Which of the following statements is most consistent with the electron cloud model?

    A. Electrons orbit the nucleus of an atom in fixed paths.

    B. Electrons are found in the nucleus of an atom.

    C. Electrons exhibit almost random patterns of movement around a nucleus.

    D. Electrons have a fixed position outside the nucleus.

2. By suggesting that the position of an electron follows the wave function, Scientist 2 supports which of the following claims?

    F. The probability of an electron's position depends on its orbit.

    G. The color of emitted light depends on the charge of an atom.

    H. Protons and neutrons are also subject to the wave-particle duality.

    J. Electron configuration affects an atom's shape and corresponding properties.

3. According to the passage, a similarity between the Bohr model and the electron cloud model is that:

    A. electrons do not have a fixed position.

    B. the charge of electrons is based on probability.

    C. protons and neutrons are composed of many smaller particles.

    D. the atom is indivisible.

4. According to Scientist 1, which of the following observations provides the strongest evidence that electrons do NOT lie in a probability cloud surrounding the nucleus?

    F. Electrons have a fixed position around the nucleus.

    G. The light emitted by energized electrons is specific and predictable.

    H. Electrons behave according to the wave function.

    J. The charge of electrons is constant.

GO ON TO THE NEXT PAGE

Practice Test 7

5. After the 1920s, it was observed that a single electron will exhibit patterns of motion that imply both that it is a distinct particle and also that the path it takes correlates to a probability. Which model does this observation strengthen?

   A. The electron cloud model, because the observation supports wave-particle duality

   B. The electron cloud model, because the observation shows that an electron travels in a distinct path

   C. The Bohr model, because the observation indicates that electrons travel in orbits

   D. The Bohr model, because the observation confirms that electrons behave according to probability

6. Scientist 2 implies that the Bohr model is *weakened* by observing that:

   F. electrons have a greater chance of lying in specific areas around the nucleus than others.

   G. electrons behave like photons.

   H. the precise position of electrons cannot be known.

   J. the orbits of electrons are not circular.

7. Which of the following diagrams is most consistent with the Bohr model of the atom?

   A.

   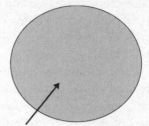

   protons, neutrons, electrons

   B.

   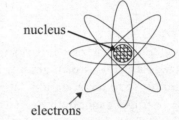

   nucleus

   electrons

   C.

   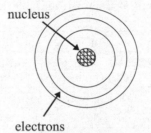

   nucleus

   electrons

   D.

   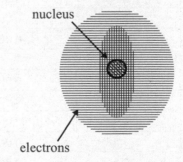

   nucleus

   electrons

GO ON TO THE NEXT PAGE

Practice Test 7

Passage II

Scientists noted an increase in acid rainfall and reports of respiratory ailments in a certain community. They suspected that both of these outcomes were due to increased levels of airborne pollutants, such as carbon monoxide and sulfur dioxide, entering the atmosphere in that community. Common sources of gaseous pollutants are factories, motor vehicles, or industrial processes that burn fossil fuels and release byproducts of their reactions into the air. To determine the sources of these pollutants, scientists conducted the following studies.

Study 1

The scientists found that one likely source of pollutant gases was a network of highways located near the community. Sampling stations at ground level were set up near two major highways so that air samples could be measured and analyzed daily. The results of these analyses, with pollutant levels in parts per million (ppm), are shown in Table 1.

Table 1		
Date	Carbon monoxide level (ppm)	Sulfur dioxide level (ppm)
Highway 1		
January 6	2.3	0.002
January 7	3.2	0.002
January 8	2.9	0.003
January 9	2.6	0.002
January 10	2.1	0.004
Highway 2		
January 6	3.4	0.004
January 7	3.8	0.006
January 8	4.9	0.004
January 9	3.4	0.003
January 10	3.2	0.002

Study 2

Scientists also suspected that another source of pollutants was from the community's power plant, an older coal-burning plant. Air samples were recorded from the tops of two different monitoring towers near the power plant's two main smokestacks, which emit most of the byproducts created in the electricity-generating process. The results are shown in Table 2.

Table 2			
Date	Ozone level (ppm)	Carbon monoxide level (ppm)	Sulfur dioxide level (ppm)
Tower 1			
January 6	0.05	3.3	0.005
January 7	0.06	3.2	0.006
January 8	0.11	3.3	0.009
January 9	0.15	4.3	0.013
January 10	0.10	4.2	0.009
Tower 2			
January 6	0.04	2.0	0.004
January 7	0.05	2.9	0.005
January 8	0.06	3.0	0.008
January 9	0.05	2.8	0.006
January 10	0.04	2.1	0.004

8. How is the design of Study 1 different from the design of Study 2, in terms of sampling methods?

F. In Study 1, sampling was done weekly, while in Study 2, sampling was done every day.

G. In Study 1, air was sampled at ground level, while in Study 2, air was sampled at the tops of two towers.

H. In Study 1, ozone levels were sampled, while in Study 2, ozone levels were not sampled.

J. In Study 1, only carbon monoxide was sampled, while in Study 2, only sulfur dioxide was sampled.

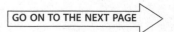 GO ON TO THE NEXT PAGE

Practice Test 7

9. In order to obtain more information about the relationship between carbon monoxide, sulfur dioxide, and respiratory ailments, which of the following studies should be carried out next?

   A. Studying how asthma is affected by changes in temperature throughout the year

   B. Assessing the rates of respiratory illness in communities with different average levels of carbon monoxide and sulfur dioxide

   C. Adding large amounts of carbon monoxide and sulfur dioxide to the air surrounding Highway 1

   D. Encouraging carpools to decrease traffic levels in the highways around this community

10. Scientists suspected that sulfur dioxide emissions from the power plant were contributing to acid rain, which in turn was affecting the acidity of lakes in the surrounding countryside. In order to test this hypothesis, which of the following should the scientists do next?

    F. Sample sulfur dioxide levels near the power plant's smaller smokestacks.

    G. Measure the number of respiratory ailments suffered by people living near the lakes.

    H. Increase the amount of coal burned by the power plant.

    J. Measure the acidity of the water at a number of lakes with varying levels of atmospheric sulfur dioxide.

11. What hypothesis concerning respiratory ailments were the scientists hoping to test in Study 1 ?

    A. Pollutants from vehicular highway traffic cause an increase in respiratory ailments.

    B. Emissions from coal-burning power plants cause a decrease in respiratory ailments.

    C. Rainfall in the communities located near the highways causes a decrease in respiratory ailments.

    D. Acid rain tends to deposit pollutants into areas where highway traffic is least frequent.

12. Given the results of Studies 1 and 2, all of the following actions would help to reduce levels of airborne pollutants EXCEPT:

    F. building more highways in the areas surrounding the community.

    G. placing limits on the amount of highway traffic near the community.

    H. reducing the amount of coal burned at the power plant.

    J. installing filters in the power plant's smokestacks that remove sulfur dioxide from the plant's emissions.

13. As carbon monoxide emissions are carried away from their sources, they tend to diffuse (become less concentrated). Which of the following would be the most likely approximate carbon monoxide level near Highway 1 on January 7 if the sampling station were set up closer to the roadway?

    A. 1.0 ppm
    B. 2.0 ppm
    C. 3.0 ppm
    D. 4.0 ppm

14. Which of the following accurately describe(s) the results of Study 2 ?

    I. Ozone levels and sulfur dioxide levels increased, then decreased in both towers.

    II. Carbon monoxide levels in Tower 2 were always greater than those in Tower 1.

    III. January 9 showed the highest emissions for all pollutants at both towers.

    F. I only
    G. II only
    H. I and II only
    J. I, II, and III

GO ON TO THE NEXT PAGE

Passage III

Conductivity is the ability of a sample of a material to transmit electricity. All materials have electrical properties that divide them into three broad categories: *conductors*, *insulators*, and *semiconductors*. A conductor is a substance that allows an electric charge to travel from one object to another. An insulator is a substance that prevents an electric charge from traveling between objects. Substances with a level of conductivity between that of a conductor and that of an insulator are called semi-conductors. The unit of current is the ampere (A), and an *ammeter* is an instrument used to measure the current flowing in a circuit, as can be seen in Diagram 1.

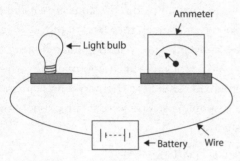

Diagram 1

A scientist carried out three studies to determine the validity of the hypothesis that a wire conducts more current when the diameter of the wire increases or when the temperature of the wire decreases.

Study 1

Wires were made from five different materials. Each strand of wire had a diameter of exactly 4 millimeters (mm). The strands of wire connecting the battery, light bulb, and ammeter were a total of 0.5 meters (m) long and were kept at a temperature of 50°C. Table 1 displays the current, in milliamps (mA), recorded by the ammeter.

Table 1	
Material	Current (mA)
Silicon carbide (SiC)	4.6
Copper (Cu)	9.4
Rubber	0.0
Zinc telluride (ZnTe)	5.2
Steel	3.5

Study 2

The conditions in Study 1 were repeated, except the diameter of the wires was increased to 6 mm. The length between the battery, the light bulb, and the ammeter was held constant at 0.5 m and the wires were kept at 50°C. Table 2 displays the findings.

Table 2	
Material	Current (mA)
Silicon carbide (SiC)	6.5
Copper (Cu)	11.3
Rubber	0.0
Zinc telluride (ZnTe)	7.1
Steel	5.4

Study 3

Study 2 was repeated at 30°C. Table 3 displays the findings.

Table 3	
Material	Current (mA)
Silicon carbide (SiC)	7.3
Copper (Cu)	12.1
Rubber	0.0
Zinc telluride (ZnTe)	8.9
Steel	6.6

GO ON TO THE NEXT PAGE

15. Which of the following ranges represents the amperage of all five wires with diameters of 6 mm at 30°C ?

    A. 5.4 mA to 11.3 mA

    B. 0.0 mA to 9.4 mA

    C. 0.0 mA to 11.3 mA

    D. 0.0 mA to 12.1 mA

16. The scientist hypothesized that increasing the diameter of a wire increases the amount of current it conducts. The results from the studies for each of the following materials support the scientist's hypothesis EXCEPT the results for:

    F. silicon carbide.

    G. rubber.

    H. copper.

    J. steel.

17. According to the results of the studies, a wire made from ZnTe would conduct the most current under which of the following conditions?

    A. 1-mm diameter, 0.5-m length at 40°C

    B. 4-mm diameter, 0.5-m length at 40°C

    C. 4-mm diameter, 0.5-m length at 20°C

    D. 8-mm diameter, 0.5-m length at 20°C

18. What would the ammeter read if the scientist used wires of 4-mm diameter at 30°C and a total length of 0.5 m, but if the material for the wire from the battery to the ammeter was copper, the wire from the ammeter to the light bulb was rubber, and the wire from the light bulb back to the battery was steel?

    F. 0.0 mA

    G. 3.5 mA

    H. 9.4 mA

    J. 12.9 mA

19. How would the current conducted by the materials most likely be affected if Study 3 was repeated and the temperature of the wires was increased to 100°C ?

    A. The current would decrease, with the exception of rubber.

    B. The current would remain unchanged.

    C. The current would either increase or decrease, depending on the type of material.

    D. The current would increase, with the exception of rubber.

20. Based on the results of the studies, which of the following best describes the properties of rubber?

    F. Rubber's capacity as a conductor increases with temperature.

    G. Rubber's capacity as an insulator increases with temperature.

    H. Rubber's capacity as an insulator increases with diameter.

    J. Rubber's capacity as an insulator is unaffected by temperature or diameter.

21. Which of the following effects would be the most appropriate for the scientist to investigate next in order to learn more about the ability of wires to conduct current?

    A. The effect of temperature on conductivity

    B. The effect of diameter on current conducted

    C. The effect of choice of material on conductivity

    D. The effect of wire length on current conducted

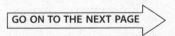

Passage IV

The climate (long-term meteorological conditions) of a region consists of the average weather (short-term meteorological conditions) in that region over a period of years. Climate is measured by monitoring the variation in temperature, humidity, atmospheric pressure, wind, and precipitation. A microclimate is a smaller area within a climate region that has its own unique climate. Scientists performed the following studies to investigate the microclimates of neighboring rural and urban (population greater than 50,000 people) areas.

Study 1

Monthly average air temperatures and relative humidity for neighboring rural and urban areas were collected over a period of 11 years. Results indicated that, compared to the relative humidity of the rural area, the relative humidity of the urban area was 2% lower in the winter and 6% lower in the summer. Figure 1 shows the average temperature for August (summer) and February (winter) for the rural and urban areas.

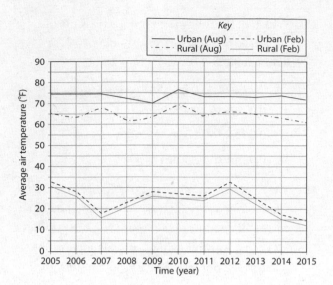

Figure 1

Study 2

Annual precipitation and cloud cover were recorded for the same neighboring rural and urban areas over the same period of 11 years. Results showed that the rural area had on average 5% fewer cloudy or hazy days than the urban area for each year. Figure 2 shows the total accumulated precipitation for each year.

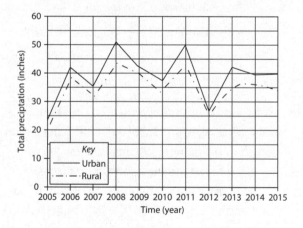

Figure 2

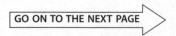

Practice Test 7

Study 3

An anemometer was used to measure the wind velocity at a standard height of 33 feet for the same neighboring rural and urban areas. Figure 3 shows the monthly average wind velocity over a year. The scientists also measured air quality and found that urban air had about 10 times more dust particles than rural air.

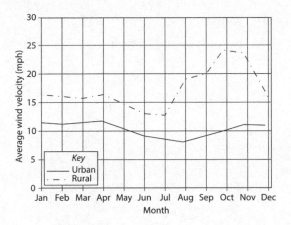

Figure 3

22. According to Study 1, the greatest difference in average air temperature during the summer between the urban and rural areas occurred in which of the following years?

F. 2007

G. 2010

H. 2012

J. 2014

23. According to Study 3, average wind velocities in the rural area were closest for which of the following pairs of months?

A. January and April

B. April and July

C. July and September

D. September and November

24. Suppose new evidence showed that buildings increase frictional drag on air flowing over built-up terrain. Based on Study 3, would it be justified to conclude that the rural area has more buildings than the urban area?

F. Yes, because the average wind velocity is lower for the rural area than for the urban area.

G. Yes, because the average air temperature is lower for the rural area than for the urban area.

H. No, because the average wind velocity is higher for the rural area than for the urban area.

J. No, because the average air temperature is higher for the rural area than for the urban area.

25. Based on Study 1, what conclusion can be drawn from the fact that the difference in relative humidity between the urban and rural areas is less in the winter than in the summer?

A. The relative humidity is higher for the urban area than for the rural area.

B. The average winter air temperature is higher for the urban area than for the rural area.

C. Relative humidity differences correlate with average air temperature differences.

D. Relative humidity differences correlate with average wind velocity differences.

GO ON TO THE NEXT PAGE

26. Scientists hypothesized that building materials and road surfaces in urban areas absorb heat during the day and release it at night, increasing the air temperature. Do the results of Study 1 support this hypothesis?

    F. Yes; the recorded summer temperatures in the urban area were lower than those in the rural area.

    G. Yes; the recorded summer temperatures in the urban area were higher than those in the rural area.

    H. No; the recorded humidity in the urban area was lower than that in the rural area.

    J. No; the recorded humidity in the urban area was higher than that in the rural area.

27. Given that dust particles act as hygroscopic nuclei, encouraging rain production, which of the following best explains why the rural area received less rain than the urban area in Study 2 ?

    A. The wind velocity was higher at the urban area than the rural area.

    B. There were more dust particles in the air at the urban area to become nuclei.

    C. There were fewer cloudy days in the urban area.

    D. Higher relative humidity in the urban area allowed the air to hold more moisture.

28. At a third area located near the other two, the scientists determined the average summer air temperature to be 75°F and the average annual precipitation to be 40 inches. Based on the data from the studies, the scientists should predict that the average wind velocity is most likely:

    F. between 8 and 12 mph.

    G. between 12 and 15 mph.

    H. between 15 and 20 mph.

    J. between 20 and 25 mph.

GO ON TO THE NEXT PAGE

Passage V

The movement of planets and other celestial bodies in the solar system is governed by the force of gravity. Gravitational effects are determined by considering many factors, such as a body's mass and the distance between bodies. Table 1 lists the masses and radii for several planets.

Table 1		
Planet	Mass (kg)	Radius (km)
Saturn	5.68×10^{26}	58,232
Jupiter	1.90×10^{27}	69,911
Earth	5.97×10^{24}	6,371
Venus	4.87×10^{24}	6,052
Mercury	3.29×10^{23}	2,440

Figure 1 shows the acceleration due to gravity of an object at various distances from the center of 3 planets.

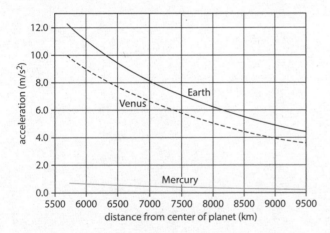

Figure 1

Perihelion is the point in a planet's orbit at which it is closest to the sun. Figure 2 shows how the orbital velocity of the same 3 planets varies as each planet approaches and recedes from perihelion (a negative distance means the planet is approaching perihelion, positive means the planet is receding).

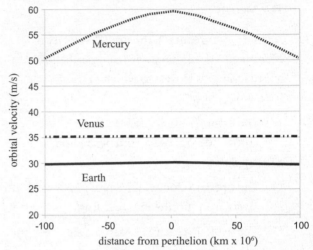

Figure 2

29. According to Figure 2, as Mercury approaches perihelion and then recedes from it, its orbital velocity:

   A. increases, then decreases.

   B. decreases, then increases.

   C. decreases only.

   D. increases only.

30. Suppose that a planet was found to have a mass between that of Saturn and Jupiter. Based on Table 1 and assuming a similar density, which of the following would be the most likely radius for the planet?

   F. 2,240 km

   G. 6,197 km

   H. 63,452 km

   J. 87,128 km

GO ON TO THE NEXT PAGE

31. Which of the planets listed on Table 1 has the greatest mass?

    A. Saturn

    B. Jupiter

    C. Earth

    D. Mercury

32. According to Figure 2, the orbital velocity of Mercury 75×10^6 km away from perihelion, approaching, is closest to which of the following?

    F. The orbital velocity of Mercury 100×10^6 km away from perihelion, approaching

    G. The orbital velocity of Mercury 75×10^6 km away from perihelion, receding

    H. The orbital velocity of Mercury 50×10^6 km away from perihelion, receding

    J. The orbital velocity of Mercury 50×10^6 km away from perihelion, approaching

33. According to Figure 1, does an object fall faster towards Earth or towards Venus from a distance of 8,000 km ?

    A. Venus, because the acceleration due to gravity from Venus is higher

    B. Venus, because the acceleration due to gravity from Venus is lower

    C. Earth, because the acceleration due to gravity from Earth is higher

    D. Earth, because the acceleration due to gravity from Earth is lower

34. If a new planet were found in the solar system with a mass of 8.5×10^{23} kg and a radius of 5,423 km, which of the following would be most reasonable, based on the information provided in the passage, to predict as its velocity at perihelion?

    F. 60 m/s

    G. 45 m/s

    H. 30 m/s

    J. 15 m/s

GO ON TO THE NEXT PAGE

Passage VI

The following chemical equation represents a typical acid-base neutralization reaction:

$$HCl + NaOH \rightarrow H_2O + NaCl$$

Table 1 lists common pH indicators and the pH ranges over which a distinct color change occurs.

Table 1	
Indicator	pH range
Methyl yellow	2.9 − 4.0
Bromocresol green	3.8 − 5.4
Methyl red	4.4 − 6.2
Phenol red	6.8 − 8.4
Phenolphthalein	8.3 − 10.0
Alizarine	10.1 − 12.0

In the process of acid-base titration, the *equivalence point* is the point at which equal concentrations of an acid and base are present. When an acid or base is added to a solution at its equivalence point, changes in pH are typically much more drastic than they are at other points in the titration process. Figure 1 shows the pH of Solution A and Solution B versus the amount of an NaOH solution added.

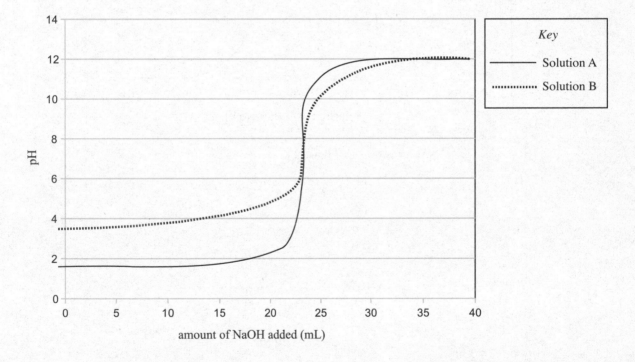

Figure 1

GO ON TO THE NEXT PAGE

Figure 2 shows the reaction rate for Solutions A and B (as a percentage of the reaction rate at their equivalence point) versus the amount of NaOH solution added.

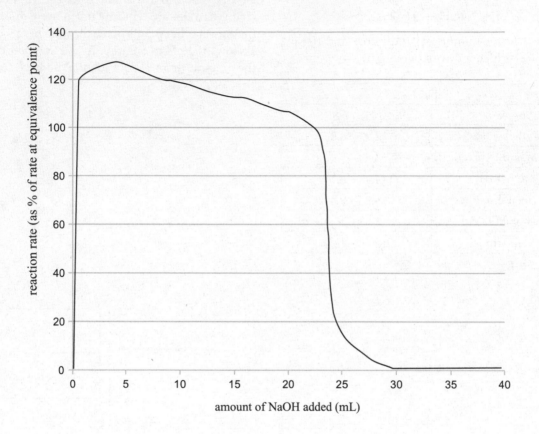

Figure 2

Practice Test 7

35. If the experimental setup were reversed and Solution A were titrated into a beaker of NaOH, which of the following graphs would best represent the corresponding titration curve?

A. pH

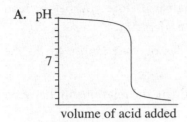

volume of acid added

B. pH

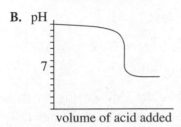

volume of acid added

C. pH

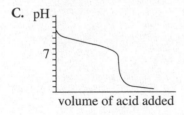

volume of acid added

D. pH

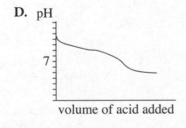

volume of acid added

36. Based on Table 1 and Figure 1, which indicator changes color in a pH range that includes the equivalence point of Solution A ?

F. Bromocresol green

G. Methyl red

H. Phenol red

J. Alizarine

37. If the chemical reaction associated with the chemical equation shown in the passage takes place completely (with negligible unused reactants), the pH of the resulting solution should be approximately:

A. 0.

B. 2.

C. 7.

D. 14.

38. According to Figure 2, for which of the following volumes of NaOH does the reaction rate exceed the reaction rate at the equivalence point?

F. 0 mL

G. 5 mL

H. 25 mL

J. 30 mL

39. In the chemical equation shown in the passage, the sodium in NaOH becomes part of which of the following compounds?

A. Water

B. Table salt

C. Hydrochloric acid

D. Sodium hydroxide

40. Based on Figures 1 and 2, the amount of NaOH for which the reaction rate is highest also corresponds to:

F. the equivalence point of Solution A.

G. the equivalence point of Solution B.

H. a high pH in Solution A.

J. a low pH in Solution B.

IF YOU FINISH BEFORE TIME IS CALLED, YOU MAY CHECK YOUR WORK ON THIS SECTION ONLY. DO NOT TURN TO ANY OTHER SECTION IN THE TEST. **STOP**

WRITING TEST

40 Minutes—1 Question

Directions: The essay is used to evaluate your writing skills. You will have **40 minutes** to review the prompt and plan and write an essay in English. Before you begin, read everything in this test booklet carefully to make sure you understand the task.

Your essay will be judged based on the evidence it provides of your ability to do the following:

- Assert your own perspective on a complex issue and evaluate the relationship between your perspective and at least one other perspective

- Use reasoning and evidence to refine and justify your ideas

- Present your ideas in an organized way

- Convey your ideas effectively using standard written English

Write your essay on the lined essay pages in the answer booklet. All writing on those lined pages will be scored. Use the unlined pages in this test booklet to plan your essay. Your work on these unlined pages will not be scored.

Put your pencil down as soon as time is called.

DO NOT OPEN THIS BOOKLET UNTIL TOLD TO DO SO.

GO ON TO THE NEXT PAGE

Student Loans

Despite the rising cost of higher education, financial experts agree that a college diploma is worth the investment. As students enroll in college to increase their lifetime earning potential, broaden their opportunities, and pursue careers, many worry about the challenge of paying off student loans once they graduate. Student loan repayment includes both the original amount borrowed as well as interest accrued over time, which often takes students years to repay. Should colleges and financial institutions be expected to develop programs and policies to address student concern regarding loans? Given the fact that affording college is a primary factor in deciding whether or not to pursue higher education, it is prudent for institutions to develop practices to better assist students in financing their degrees.

Read and carefully consider these perspectives. Each suggests a particular way of thinking about student loans.

Perspective One	Perspective Two	Perspective Three
Student loans should not be subject to interest rates if a student is able to pay off the loan within a reasonable amount of time. Financial lenders, including the United States government, should not be making a profit on loans that students need to complete their degrees. Should a student request additional time to repay the loan beyond the agreed-upon repayment schedule, interest or a penalty fee can then be applied to the remaining balance.	Higher education is a commodity and is subject to supply and demand principles inherent in a capitalist market. Colleges, financial institutions, and the United States government should not make special accommodations for college students. All loans should be held to the same standard and should not differ according to a borrower's intended use.	The amount of money students can borrow should be proportional to the annual salary they are projected to earn once they graduate. Students should not be allowed to borrow more money than they can pay back in a reasonable amount of time. Reducing or eliminating interest rates does not address the more concerning issue of disproportionate debt and future earning potential.

Essay Task

Write a clear, well-reasoned essay evaluating multiple perspectives on student loans. In your essay, be sure to:

- Assert your own perspective on the issue and evaluate the relationship between your perspective and at least one other perspective
- Use reasoning and evidence to refine and justify your ideas
- Present your ideas in an organized way
- Convey your ideas effectively using standard written English

Your perspective may be fully, somewhat, or not at all in agreement with one or more of the three perspectives in the prompt.

GO ON TO THE NEXT PAGE

GO ON TO THE NEXT PAGE

Planning Your Essay

These pages are not scored.

Use the space below to brainstorm and plan your essay. Consider the following as you think about the prompt:

- Strengths and weaknesses of the three perspectives in the prompt

  - What observations do they offer, and what do they overlook?

  - Why are they persuasive or why are they not persuasive?

- Your own background and identity

  - What is your perspective on this issue, and what are its strengths and weaknesses?

  - What evidence will you use in your essay?

GO ON TO THE NEXT PAGE

GO ON TO THE NEXT PAGE

Practice Test 7

IF YOU FINISH BEFORE TIME IS CALLED, YOU MAY CHECK YOUR WORK ON THIS SECTION ONLY. DO NOT TURN TO ANY OTHER SECTION IN THE TEST.

STOP

PRACTICE TEST 7 ANSWER KEY

ENGLISH TEST

1. **C**	16. **G**	31. **A**	46. **J**	61. **A**
2. **J**	17. **A**	32. **G**	47. **C**	62. **H**
3. **B**	18. **F**	33. **C**	48. **G**	63. **C**
4. **J**	19. **B**	34. **H**	49. **A**	64. **G**
5. **C**	20. **G**	35. **A**	50. **G**	65. **D**
6. **H**	21. **C**	36. **J**	51. **C**	66. **J**
7. **B**	22. **H**	37. **B**	52. **H**	67. **A**
8. **H**	23. **B**	38. **G**	53. **D**	68. **H**
9. **C**	24. **F**	39. **A**	54. **H**	69. **C**
10. **J**	25. **D**	40. **F**	55. **D**	70. **G**
11. **C**	26. **J**	41. **D**	56. **G**	71. **B**
12. **J**	27. **C**	42. **G**	57. **B**	72. **J**
13. **C**	28. **G**	43. **B**	58. **F**	73. **B**
14. **G**	29. **D**	44. **H**	59. **B**	74. **F**
15. **A**	30. **H**	45. **B**	60. **J**	75. **D**

MATHEMATICS TEST

1. **E**	13. **A**	25. **E**	37. **E**	49. **A**
2. **H**	14. **J**	26. **G**	38. **F**	50. **J**
3. **A**	15. **A**	27. **B**	39. **C**	51. **A**
4. **J**	16. **H**	28. **G**	40. **K**	52. **G**
5. **C**	17. **E**	29. **A**	41. **B**	53. **B**
6. **J**	18. **J**	30. **G**	42. **F**	54. **J**
7. **C**	19. **A**	31. **A**	43. **D**	55. **A**
8. **F**	20. **H**	32. **H**	44. **G**	56. **K**
9. **D**	21. **E**	33. **B**	45. **C**	57. **C**
10. **J**	22. **K**	34. **F**	46. **J**	58. **G**
11. **A**	23. **B**	35. **D**	47. **D**	59. **C**
12. **K**	24. **J**	36. **K**	48. **H**	60. **K**

READING TEST

1. **A**	9. **D**	17. **C**	25. **A**	33. **D**
2. **H**	10. **G**	18. **F**	26. **F**	34. **G**
3. **B**	11. **B**	19. **B**	27. **B**	35. **D**
4. **F**	12. **H**	20. **F**	28. **H**	36. **H**
5. **D**	13. **C**	21. **B**	29. **D**	37. **B**
6. **H**	14. **G**	22. **J**	30. **F**	38. **H**
7. **A**	15. **B**	23. **D**	31. **C**	39. **C**
8. **G**	16. **F**	24. **J**	32. **F**	40. **F**

SCIENCE TEST

1. **C**	9. **B**	17. **D**	25. **C**	33. **C**
2. **J**	10. **J**	18. **F**	26. **G**	34. **G**
3. **A**	11. **A**	19. **A**	27. **B**	35. **A**
4. **G**	12. **F**	20. **J**	28. **F**	36. **H**
5. **A**	13. **D**	21. **D**	29. **A**	37. **C**
6. **H**	14. **F**	22. **J**	30. **H**	38. **G**
7. **C**	15. **D**	23. **A**	31. **B**	39. **B**
8. **G**	16. **G**	24. **H**	32. **G**	40. **J**

ANSWERS AND EXPLANATIONS

ENGLISH TEST

Passage I

1. C   Difficulty: Medium

Category: Usage

Getting to the Answer: Use *who* or *whom* to refer to a person. The underlined word begins a description of Lucia; the correct pronoun is *who*, because Lucia is a person. Choice (C) is correct. *Which*, in A, is incorrect when used to refer to a person. Choice B uses the objective case *whom*; you wouldn't say "*her* was already married," so "*whom* was already married" is incorrect. *She who*, in D, makes the sentence unnecessarily wordy and awkward.

2. J   Difficulty: Medium

Category: Sentence Structure and Formation

Getting to the Answer: Independent clauses should either be joined by a semicolon or connected with a coordinating conjunction; otherwise, one of the clauses must be made subordinate. As written, the sentence is a run-on. None of the answer choices offers a semicolon or a comma and a coordinating conjunction, but (J) makes the second clause dependent by using *that*. Choices G and H do not address the run-on error.

3. B   Difficulty: Medium

Category: Sentence Structure and Formation

Getting to the Answer: Use context to determine appropriate verb tenses. This sentence uses the simple past tense *were* and doesn't indicate any time shift, so the simple past tense *knew* makes the most sense. Choice (B) is correct. Choice A uses the past participle *known* without the necessary helping verb *had*. Choice C incorrectly uses *had knew*; the past participle of *know* is *known*. Choice D uses *been known* without the necessary helping verb *had*; it also creates a sentence that is grammatically incorrect.

4. J   Difficulty: Medium

Category: Organization, Unity, and Cohesion / Transitions

Getting to the Answer: Remember to read for logic, as well as grammar and usage. This sentence inappropriately uses the contrast word *however*. Choice J correctly uses *then*, a transition word indicating time. Choices G and H use cause-and-effect transitions, which are inappropriate in context.

5. C   Difficulty: Medium

Category: Usage

Getting to the Answer: When an idiomatic construction begins with *not only*, it must conclude with *but also*. Only (C) correctly completes the idiom. *And*, A, *so*, B, and *then*, D, all fail to correctly complete the idiom.

6. H   Difficulty: Medium

Category: Sentence Structure and Formation

Getting to the Answer: The *-ing* form can serve several functions; when used as a verb, it requires a helping verb to be correct. *I being* here is grammatically incorrect; (H) substitutes the correct verb form *was*. Choice G creates a grammatically incorrect sentence, and J omits the verb.

7. B   Category: Topic Development / Writer's Purpose

Difficulty: Medium

Getting to the Answer: With Writer's Purpose questions like this one, you need to identify the choice that matches the purpose stated in the question stem. The question asks you to select the sentence that gives the most relevant information about Nicola's travel plans. Only (B) tells you about Nicola's plans; he intends to spend the summer with his family in New York. Choice A mentions Nicola's trip to England, which is out of scope for the passage. Choice C provides general information about the easiest way to travel from Italy to America, but it doesn't tell you anything about Nicola's specific plans to visit America. Choice D also focuses on the past, explaining why Nicola had not previously come to America; this doesn't match the question stem's call for information about Nicola's travel plans.

8. H   Difficulty: Medium

Category: Knowledge of Language / Precision

Getting to the Answer: Always read question stems carefully; it's easy to miss an important word like NOT or EXCEPT. The question asks for the word that does NOT show that the cousins looked forward to meeting Nicola. The only negatively charged word here is *apprehensive*, which suggests that the cousins feared Nicola's arrival. Choice (H) is correct. Choices F, G, and J all use positively charged words that indicate the cousins were looking forward to Nicola's visit.

9. C   Difficulty: Medium

Category: Punctuation

Getting to the Answer: A phrase set off between commas must be nonessential: that is, the sentence must still make sense without it. As written, this sentence treats the phrase "hadn't seen him" as nonessential, but "like me, since they were kids" does not make sense—this phrase must remain in the sentence. Choice (C) eliminates the incorrect comma without introducing any additional errors. Choices B and D create run-on sentences; additionally, D incorrectly inserts a comma between a verb and its object.

10. J   Difficulty: High

Category: Knowledge of Language / Ambiguity

Getting to the Answer: When a pronoun is underlined, first determine to what or whom it refers. In this case, the reference is unclear. The last plural noun is *musicians*, but that refers to the narrator and Nicola, who do play instruments. Eliminate F. Choice G clearly refers to the narrator and Nicola, so it should also be eliminated. Choice H is ambiguous: to which Americans does the sentence refer? Choice (J) correctly identifies the group mentioned earlier in the paragraph: the narrator's American cousins.

11. C   Difficulty: Medium

Category: Knowledge of Language / Concision

Getting to the Answer: The shortest answer isn't always correct—D omits a phrase necessary for the sentence to make sense. Choices A and B include information irrelevant to the topic of the writer meeting Nicola. That leaves (C), which eliminates the irrelevant information without losing the logic of the sentence.

12. J   Difficulty: Medium

Category: Sentence Structure and Formation

Getting to the Answer: As a general rule, descriptive phrases modify the nouns that immediately follow them. As written, this sentence tells us that *I* was "Taught to him before she passed away in Italy." Choice (J) is the most concise and logical version of this sentence. Choice G incorrectly indicates that the grandmother, not Nicola, taught the songs to the writer. Choice H gives the introductory phrase no logical noun to modify, making its grammatical structure incorrect.

13. C   Difficulty: Low

Category: Sentence Structure and Formation

Getting to the Answer: A verb is underlined, so start by checking to see if the tense is correct. The simple past tense is used in this paragraph: *shared* and *connected*. The correct tense here is the simple past *threw*, as in (C). Choice A uses the conditional tense "would have thrown," but the sentence describes something the writer's father actually did, not something hypothetical. Choice B uses the future perfect tense, but the sentence describes something that happened in the past, not an upcoming event. Choice D uses the present tense, but the action happened in the past.

14. G   Difficulty: Low

Category: Punctuation

Getting to the Answer: "Possessive versus plural" questions can often be answered quickly: does the sentence refer to more than one grandmother or something belonging to a grandmother? This sentence is discussing the country that *belongs* to the grandmother, so an apostrophe is needed to make *grandmother* possessive. Only (G) does this without introducing an additional error. Choice F is missing the necessary apostrophe; *grandmothers* is plural, not possessive. Choice H uses the plural possessive *grandmothers'*, but only one grandmother is discussed in the paragraph. Choice J corrects the punctuation error but substitutes the homophone *are* for the plural possessive pronoun *our*.

15. A   Category: Topic Development / Writer's Purpose

Difficulty: Medium

Getting to the Answer: When asked about the purpose of the passage as a whole, consider its topic and tone. The narrator describes a personal experience getting to know his cousin from Italy. The tone is positive, emphasizing their similarities and ending with a scene in which family members are touched emotionally by the singing of family folk songs. Thus, the passage accomplishes the stated purpose; eliminate C and D. Choice B is a distortion; the differences between Nicola and the narrator's American cousins are not the reason the essay accomplishes the stated purpose. Thus, (A) is correct.

Passage II

16. G   Difficulty: Medium

Category: Punctuation

Getting to the Answer: When the only difference in the answer choices is the use of commas, focus on sentence structure. Are there items in a list that need to be separated by commas? A nonessential phrase that needs to be set off from the rest of the sentence with a pair of commas? An introductory phrase or clause that needs to be separated from the rest of the sentence? This sentence treats the phrase *I live* as nonessential, but removing it creates a sentence fragment. Choice (G) properly places a comma between the introductory phrase describing the location of the Handsome Bean coffee shop and the sentence's independent clause. Choice H creates an introductory clause with no noun to modify, which is grammatically incorrect. Choice J fails to set off the introductory phrase from the body of the sentence, making the sentence difficult to understand.

17. A   Difficulty: Medium

Category: Topic Development / Writer's Purpose

Getting to the Answer: When you're asked the purpose of including a detail, read around that detail for context. By describing the proximity of the Little League field, the writer provides a context for the teams the Handsome Bean often sponsors. Without this information, the following sentence would not fit well in the context. Thus, (A) is correct. There is no change of topic, so B is incorrect. While the information helps the reader picture the scene, C misses the function of introducing the sponsored team in the following sentence. Choice D does not match the tone of the passage, which portrays the Handsome Bean positively.

18. F   Difficulty: Low

Category: Sentence Structure and Formation

Getting to the Answer: Use context to determine the answers to questions with underlined verbs. The verbs in this paragraph are in the present tense: *come, stay, is,* and *offers.* The present tense *sponsors* is correct, so no change is needed, (F). Choice G uses the past perfect *had sponsored*, incorrectly suggesting that the coffee shop sponsored the Little League team before another past event. Choices H and J use the past tense, which is inconsistent with the rest of the paragraph.

19. B   Difficulty: Medium

Category: Topic Development / Supporting Material

Getting to the Answer: Read question stems carefully. Often, all four answer choices to Supporting Material questions will be relevant to the passage, but only one will fulfill the specific requirements of the question. The question asks for additional detail about the customers who come to the coffee shop. Only (B) focuses on customers—the parents and children who come for ice cream after the Little League games. Choice A focuses on an additional discount provided by the coffee shop, not on the customers of the shop. Choice C provides a detail about another sport supported by the coffee shop; this doesn't match the purpose stated in the question stem. Choice D provides more information about the Little League field, not about the coffee shop's customers.

20. G Difficulty: Medium

Category: Sentence Structure and Formation

Getting to the Answer: When the end of one sentence and the beginning of the next are underlined, consider whether one or both are sentence fragments. As written, both of these sentences are fragments, since neither expresses a complete thought. Choice (G) correctly combines the two fragments into a single sentence. Choice H is unnecessarily wordy. Choice J does not address the error.

21. C Difficulty: Medium

Category: Organization, Unity, and Cohesion / Passage Organization

Getting to the Answer: Remember the first step in the Kaplan Method: read the passage and identify the issue. Here, you need to select the sentence that best introduces the topic of the paragraph, so you'll need to read the paragraph. The paragraph describes the antique décor of the coffee shop—its "century-old" counter, the photos from the 1920s and 1930s, and the "original tin ceiling." Choice (C) effectively leads into this description by explaining that the owner wants the shop to "look like it has been there for decades." Choice A focuses on the friendship between the writer and Mary; this doesn't connect with the details of the antique counter, old photos, and original tin ceiling. Choice B is too general; (C) provides a more specific reason for the decorating decisions Mary has made. Choice D explains that the space was vacant before the Handsome Bean opened, but this doesn't introduce the description of the décor.

22. H Difficulty: Low

Category: Usage

Getting to the Answer: The object of a preposition must be a noun, pronoun, or gerund (-*ing* verb form functioning as a noun). For this sentence to make sense, the noun *condition* is required as the object of *to*. Since nouns can only be modified by adjectives, (H) is correct. Choices F and G use the adjective *conditional* as the object of the preposition, which is grammatically incorrect. Although *original* can function as a noun, it could not then be modified by an adverb, so J is incorrect.

23. B Difficulty: Medium

Category: Usage

Getting to the Answer: The ACT will often separate a tested verb from its subject with an intervening phrase or clause. Make sure that you've correctly identified the subject with which an underlined verb must agree. As in many sentences on the ACT, a description separates the subject and verb here; the subject of the verb *depicts* is the plural *photos*. The plural form *depict* is needed; (B) is correct. Choices C and D do not address the error; additionally, C introduces an unwarranted verb tense change.

24. F Difficulty: High

Category: Topic Development / Supporting Material

Getting to the Answer: To answer this type of question, focus on the function of the sentence. What purpose does it serve in the paragraph? The sentence provides the reader with the information that the building is at least 70 years old. Therefore, if the sentence were deleted, you would lose information about the age of the building. Choice (F) is correct. Choice G refers to Mary and the writer etching their names in the ceiling, but the sentence does not describe this action. Choice H relates the sentence to the influence of the original owner; however, the time at which Harvey etched his name has little to do with his influence on Mary, the writer, or anyone else. Choice J treats the sentence as a description of the interior of the coffee shop, but no description of the ceiling is given in this sentence.

25. D Difficulty: Medium

Category: Punctuation

Getting to the Answer: A comma should not be inserted between a preposition and its object. This sentence requires no comma; (D) is correct. Choice B uses a semicolon, which is only correct when used to connect two independent clauses. Choice C treats "usually in the form" as a nonessential phrase. However, deleting this phrase does not leave a logical sentence, so C is incorrect.

26. J Difficulty: Medium

Category: Usage

Getting to the Answer: Use *number* for items that are countable and *amount* for quantities that are not. The talented musicians and poets are countable, so *number* should be used instead of *amount*. Since the number of talented performers isn't compared to anything, *good* is the correct adjective. The answer is (J). Choices F and G use *amount* where *number* would be correct; additionally, Choice G uses the comparative adjective *better*, but nothing is compared here. Choice H also uses *better*, which is correct only in a comparison.

27. C   Difficulty: Medium

Category: Knowledge of Language / Concision

Getting to the Answer: Be aware of phrases like "It being that"; they add no real meaning to the sentence and provide no clear antecedent for the pronoun. "It being that" is unnecessary here, but eliminating it creates a run-on sentence. Choice (C) eliminates the unnecessary language and makes the second clause subordinate. Choices B and D both use incorrect grammatical structure.

28. G   Difficulty: Medium

Category: Sentence Structure and Formation

Getting to the Answer: Elements in a compound must be parallel in structure. The conjunction "or" creates a compound: students load up on caffeine "so they can cram all night . . . or finishing their research papers." Choice (G) makes the two verbs, *cram* and *finish*, parallel. Choices H and J do not address the parallelism error.

29. D   Difficulty: Medium

Category: Sentence Structure and Formation

Getting to the Answer: A sentence may have multiple nouns and verbs and still be a fragment. A complete sentence requires a subject and a verb in an independent clause that expresses a complete thought. The subject here is "a group of high school students," but the clause "who stops by to have an ice cream cone or an egg cream" describes the students without providing a predicate verb. Choice (D) eliminates the pronoun, making *stops* the predicate verb. Choice B does not address the error and incorrectly uses *that* to refer to people. Choice C creates an error in subject-verb agreement.

30. H   Difficulty: Medium

Category: Organization, Unity, and Cohesion / Passage Organization

Getting to the Answer: When you need to add or move information, read the new information into the passage at the suggested points to determine its logical placement. The paragraph describes different customers at the coffee shop throughout a typical day, starting in the morning and ending in the evening. This sentence talks about customers who come to the coffee shop in the afternoon, so it should be placed between Sentence 3, which talks about daytime customers, and Sentence 4, which describes customers in the evening. Choice (H) is correct. Choices F and J both place the information about customers in the afternoon after information about customers in the evening. Choice G places the information about afternoon customers before the information about morning customers.

Passage III

31. A   Difficulty: Low

Category: Punctuation

Getting to the Answer: Remember your tested comma rules. If a sentence doesn't satisfy a tested condition, the comma will be incorrect. No change is needed here. Choice B treats *naval*, *adventure*, and *exploration* as three items in a list, but *naval* is an adjective, not a noun. Choice C places a comma between the adjective *naval* and *adventure*, the noun it describes. Choice D adds a semicolon, but the second clause is not independent.

32. G   Difficulty: Low

Category: Knowledge of Language / Concision

Getting to the Answer: Always read until you have enough information to identify the issue. A problem that isn't apparent in the underlined portion may be clear when you consider the whole sentence. The sentence is grammatically correct, but it uses redundant language: *Finally* and *at last* mean the same thing. Choice (G) is the most concise and is therefore correct. Choice H changes *Finally* to *In the end*, but this doesn't correct the redundancy problem. Choice J makes the redundancy problem worse by using both *Ultimately* and *the result*.

33. C   Difficulty: Medium

Category: Usage

Getting to the Answer: Every pronoun must have a clear and logical antecedent. Marryat, not his parents, enlisted in the British navy, so the pronoun here should be *he*, not *they*. Both (C) and D correct the pronoun, but D introduces a new error; a comma, not a semicolon, is used with a coordinating conjunction (*and*). Choice B does not address the error.

34. H   Difficulty: Low

Category: Usage

Getting to the Answer: Remember the difference between *who's* and *whose*. *Who's* always stands for *who is* or *who has*, while *whose* shows possession. The *naval exploits* were Cochrane's, so the pronoun *whose* is correct here, as in (H). Choice F uses *that's*, which is a contraction for *that is*; "that is naval exploits are legendary" doesn't make sense in context. Choice G uses *who's*, a contraction for *who is* or *who has*; "who is (or has) naval exploits are legendary" doesn't make sense. Choice J creates a grammatically incorrect sentence.

35. A   Difficulty: Medium

Category: Topic Development / Supporting Material

Getting to the Answer: Use your elimination skills here. Once you've answered the question *yes* or *no*, you can immediately eliminate two choices and focus your attention on the remaining two. The question asks you if the phrase "a number of" adds meaning to the sentence, so take a look at the sentence without the phrase. Omitting the phrase leaves you with Cochrane "as the inspiration for Marryat's fictional characters." A reader could easily assume that this means that Cochrane was the inspiration for all of Marryat's characters, which definitely changes the meaning of the sentence. Choice (A) provides the correct answer. Choice B is incorrect because *characters* is plural, which indicates that Cochrane was a model for more than one character. Choices C and D incorrectly state that omitting the phrase would not change the meaning of the sentence.

36. J   Difficulty: Medium

Category: Topic Development / Supporting Material

Getting to the Answer: When you're asked about adding a new phrase or sentence, consider both relevance and tone. The focus of this essay is Marryat and how his adventures at sea influenced his writing. The description of Cochrane as an inspiration for Marryat is directly related to the essay's focus, but the information that Cochrane inspired another writer is irrelevant. The sentence should not be added because it is not connected to the main idea of the essay, so (J) is correct. Choices F and G would both incorrectly add the sentence to the essay. Choice H is incorrect because even adding an explanation of the relationship between O'Brian and Marryat would not make this detail relevant to the topic of the essay.

37. B   Difficulty: Medium

Category: Knowledge of Language / Precision

Getting to the Answer: The question asks which choice would NOT be equivalent, so determine which answer choice stands out from the rest. Choices A, C, and D all convey that the authors are widely known. Choice (B) has a different sense. *Beloved* means well loved, which is not the same as being widely known. Thus, (B) is correct.

38. G   Difficulty: Medium

Category: Sentence Structure and Formation

Getting to the Answer: The question asks you to correctly place the prepositional phrase in the sentence, so start by determining what came "from historical records." The sentence explains that Marryat had vast experiences at sea, while other writers had only "their imaginations and accounts." It makes sense that these accounts came "from historical records," so the placement in (G) is correct. Choice F indicates that the captain himself, not stories about him, came "from historical records." Choice H indicates that the other writers came "from historical records," which doesn't make sense. Choice J indicates that Marryat's memories of adventures came "from historical records"; this contradicts the information in the passage.

39. A **Difficulty:** Medium

Category: Punctuation

Getting to the Answer: Not every underlined portion will contain an error; about 25% of English Test questions will require no change. In this sentence, "captain and literary inspiration" describes Cochrane; (A) correctly sets "Cochrane" off from the rest of the sentence. Choices B and D incorrectly place commas within a compound; commas are used to set off items in a series of three or more. Choice C omits the comma necessary to set off "Cochrane" from the rest of the sentence.

40. F **Difficulty:** Medium

Category: Sentence Structure and Formation

Getting to the Answer: Verb tenses must make sense in the context of the sentence, so consider whether one action logically occurs before another. This sentence tells you about two past events—a midshipman falling overboard and Marryat jumping into the sea to save him. The first event was the midshipman falling, so the past perfect "had fallen" in (F) is correct. Choice G uses the conditional "would have fallen," but Marryat didn't prevent the midshipman from falling into the sea; he jumped in after the midshipman. Choice H illogically suggests that the midshipman was still in the process of falling overboard when Marryat jumped in to save him. Choice J incorrectly uses the present tense; all of the actions in this sentence took place in the past.

41. D **Difficulty:** Low

Category: Knowledge of Language / Concision

Getting to the Answer: The passive voice is not always incorrect, but it is generally wordier than the active. If a passive construction can be easily made active, the correct answer choice will do so. Marryat is the one who accomplished the feats, so an active sentence will focus on him, rather than his actions. Choice (D) makes *he* the subject and uses the active verb *accomplished*. Choices A and C make *feats*, not Marryat, the subject, requiring passive and unnecessarily wordy constructions. Choice B is also unnecessarily wordy.

42. G **Difficulty:** Medium

Category: Organization, Unity, and Cohesion / Transitions

Getting to the Answer: When a transition word is underlined, check both the grammar and the logic of the transition. The underlined word connects Marryat's successes at sea with his earning a medal for inventing a special lifeboat. The second idea does not follow from the first, making F incorrect. Choice H suggests that Marryat won medals for his earlier feats, which is not supported by the paragraph. Choice J inappropriately begins a list with its third item. Choice (G) is correct; the best transition is simply to add the final item to Marryat's list of successes.

43. B **Difficulty:** Medium

Category: Sentence Structure and Formation

Getting to the Answer: Modifying words and phrases should be as close as possible to the person, thing, or action they describe. Marryat's "novels and short stories" were published in England while he was at sea; (B) makes this clear. In A, "during this time" seems to be what was published in England, which is illogical. Choice C is awkwardly worded, and "by him" is redundant with "His greatest acclaim." The sentence created by D is grammatically incorrect.

44. H **Difficulty:** Medium

Category: Usage

Getting to the Answer: Many ACT Usage questions hinge on preposition choice. The correct idiom here is "concentrate on writing," as in (H). Choice F uses "concentrate for"; you might concentrate for a period of time, but you don't concentrate *for* writing. Choice G uses "concentrate at"; you might concentrate at a place, such as school, but you don't concentrate *at* writing. Choice J uses two prepositions that are inappropriate in context. You don't concentrate *with* writing; additionally, "writing of full-time" suggests that Marryat was writing about the topic of full-time.

45. B **Difficulty:** Medium

Category: Organization, Unity, and Cohesion / Passage Organization

Getting to the Answer: The first paragraph in a passage typically introduces the passage's topic. Only Paragraph 2

uses Marryat's full name: *Frederick Marryat*. This paragraph also introduces the topic: Marryat wrote about the adventures he had at sea. This makes Paragraph 2 a better opening paragraph than Paragraph 1; (B) is correct. Choice C interrupts the chronology by placing information about Marryat's enlistment in the navy after details about his first few years in the navy. Choice D similarly disrupts the chronological order by placing information about Marryat's enlistment in the navy after all of the details about his experiences in the navy.

Passage IV

46. J   Difficulty: Low

Category: Knowledge of Language / Concision

Getting to the Answer: When DELETE is an option, read the underlined selection for relevance. The first paragraph compares the challenge of hitting a major league fastball to that of stopping a crank shot in lacrosse. The rest of the passage focuses on lacrosse, returning to the comparison to baseball in the third and fourth paragraphs. The description of quarterbacks is out of scope, so it should be deleted, (J). Choices G and H also concern the challenge faced by quarterbacks.

47. C   Difficulty: Medium

Category: Sentence Structure and Formation

Getting to the Answer: The words *that* and *which* often begin dependent clauses; when one of these words is included in an underlined portion, make sure it doesn't create a sentence fragment. As written, this sentence has no predicate verb. *Lacrosse* is the subject, but "is often referred to" is the verb for the clause that begins with *that* and describes *Lacrosse*. Removing *that* makes "is often referred to" the main verb; (C) is correct. Choices B and D do not correct the fragment error.

48. G   Difficulty: Medium

Category: Usage

Getting to the Answer: An adverb can modify a verb, adjective, or another adverb; it cannot be used to modify a noun. Here, the adverb *brutally* is used to modify the noun *game*. The adjective form *brutal* in (G) is correct. Although *brute*, H, can be used as an adjective, it is

incorrect in this context. Choice J uses *brutality*, which is a noun, where the adjective form is needed.

49. A   Difficulty: Medium

Category: Punctuation

Getting to the Answer: When the main difference in the answer choices is punctuation, remember your tested rules. A comma is not needed to separate two items connected with *and*. No change is needed, making (A) correct. Choice B uses a semicolon, which would only be correct if an independent clause followed it. Choice C omits the conjunction, making the meaning of the sentence unclear. Choice D inserts a comma after *and*; commas are incorrect after the conjunctions in compounds.

50. G   Difficulty: High

Category: Sentence Structure and Formation

Getting to the Answer: A pronoun and a verb are underlined, so you have several things to check. Make sure that the pronoun has a clear antecedent and is used consistently. Then make sure that the verb agrees with its subject and is in the correct tense. The pronoun *they* correctly refers to the *players*, but this paragraph is written in the present tense (*is, possess, stands, sprint*). The present tense *attempt* in (G) is correct. Choice F incorrectly uses the past tense. Choices H and J both incorrectly use the pronoun *one*, which does not agree with its plural antecedent *players*.

51. C   Difficulty: Medium

Category: Organization, Unity, and Cohesion / Transitions

Getting to the Answer: The underlined portion is a transition word, so check whether the sentence is logically and grammatically correct. The transition connects the fastest recorded pitch speed with the fact that few pitchers can pitch at speeds in the upper nineties. The first idea is not the result of the second, so A is incorrect. The passage is citing statistics where no temporal relationship is implied; eliminate B. Choice D turns the sentence into a run-on. Choice (C) correctly contrasts the fastest recorded pitch with the idea that few pitchers come close to that record.

52. H   Difficulty: High

Category: Punctuation

Getting to the Answer: If you're not sure how to approach a tough Punctuation question, try boiling the sentence down to its basics. Identify the subject and verb in each clause. Remember that a single comma should not separate a subject from its verb. Eliminate the introductory phrase and dependent clause from this sentence, and you're left with "the fastest crank shots on goal, can reach 110 mph." The subject is "crank shots," and the verb is "can reach." There should be no comma separating them, so (H) is correct. Choice F treats "the fastest crank shots on goal" as a nonessential phrase, but the sentence does not make sense without it. Choice G inserts two commas, treating *can* as nonessential. However, *can* is a necessary part of the verb phrase "can reach." Choice J places the comma between the two verbs in the verb phrase, which will never be correct.

53. D   Difficulty: Medium

Category: Knowledge of Language / Concision

Getting to the Answer: Always consider redundancy when DELETE is an answer choice. "By high school players" is redundant in a sentence that begins "Even at the high school level." Choice (D) removes the redundant language. Choices B and C both contain redundancies.

54. H   Difficulty: Low

Category: Topic Development / Supporting Material

Getting to the Answer: When asked whether to add new information, first consider whether it is relevant. The information about the composition of the field is not relevant to the point about the difficulty of stopping a lacrosse shot. Eliminate F and G. Choice (H) accurately describes the irrelevance of the new information, so it is correct.

55. D   Difficulty: High

Category: Knowledge of Language / Precision

Getting to the Answer: When the answer choices are all single words with similar meanings, you are likely being tested on Precision. Choose the word that best describes the challenging job of the goalie. Choice A does not fit; to be absurd is to be ridiculous or meaningless,

which does not apply to the goalie's job. Choice B is incorrect because a task cannot be *more* insurmountable; if it is insurmountable, the task cannot be done, and there is no way to have a higher degree of that failure. A *harrowing* event is deeply disturbing. While the goalie's job is challenging, we do not get a sense that the narrator is disturbed by the job. Rather, the narrator seems in awe of lacrosse goalies. Thus, C is incorrect. Choice (D), *difficult*, accurately describes the goalie's job.

56. G   Difficulty: Low

Category: Organization, Unity, and Cohesion / Transitions

Getting to the Answer: Think about what relationships these transitions depict. The preceding sentence gives an explanation of why a lacrosse goalie has a difficult task. This sentence adds to that explanation, telling you that players can make fake moves to trick the goalie. Choices F, H, and J all use transitions that indicate one idea is being added to another. Only (G) indicates a different relationship; "On the other hand" suggests a contrast between the ideas in the two sentences.

57. B   Difficulty: Medium

Category: Organization, Unity, and Cohesion / Passage Organization

Getting to the Answer: When asked to connect paragraphs, be sure you read through them, considering both subject matter and tone. The keyword *however* in the second sentence of Paragraph 4 tells you that there must be some sort of contrast between the first and second sentences. The second sentence also refers to "Both of these endeavors," so the sentence in question should discuss both hitting a major league pitch and blocking a crank shot. Only (B) meets both of these requirements. Choices A and C do not provide the contrast indicated by *however*; additionally, the slang phrase "is tough" in A is inconsistent with the tone of the rest of the passage. Choice D does not mention hitting a major league pitch, making "Both of these endeavors" in the second sentence illogical.

58. F   Difficulty: Medium

Category: Usage

Getting to the Answer: Get in the habit of *matching* verbs with their subject nouns. Since the subject of the underlined verb is the plural *Both*, this sentence needs no change, (F). Choice G is singular and does not agree with the plural subject *both*. Choice H changes the verb to the past tense, but the passage is in the present tense. Choice J uses the conditional *would have*, but there is nothing conditional or hypothetical about the writer's opinion.

59. B   Difficulty: Medium

Category: Sentence Structure and Formation

Getting to the Answer: A pronoun is underlined, so the issue may be pronoun-antecedent agreement, ambiguity, or a pronoun shift. Check context clues. The preceding sentence uses the third-person pronoun *One*. Because the underlined sentence adds a thought to the preceding sentence, the pronouns should be consistent. This makes (B) correct. Choice A uses the second-person pronoun *you*. Choice C shifts to the third-person plural *they*. Choice D shifts from *One* to *he*; it also illogically changes the verb tense.

60. J   Difficulty: Medium

Category: Topic Development / Writer's Purpose

Getting to the Answer: This type of question requires you to determine the main idea of the passage. Your Reading skills will come in handy here. In the first paragraph, the writer argues that "stopping a crank shot in men's lacrosse" is "even tougher than taking a major league at-bat." All of the following details support this position. Choice (J) correctly identifies the main idea of the passage. Choices F and G are both automatically out, because the passage does not go into any depth about the strategies employed by baseball pitchers. Choice H is incorrect because the passage provides details in Paragraph 3 about the speeds achieved by baseball pitchers.

Passage V

61. A   Difficulty: Medium

Category: Punctuation

Getting to the Answer: If you're not sure whether a phrase or clause should be set off from the sentence by commas, try reading the sentence without it. If the sentence no longer makes sense, then the commas are incorrect. The sentence is correct as written, (A). Choice B incorrectly separates the prepositional phrase "at a

breakneck pace" from the verb it describes. Choices C and D both incorrectly insert a comma between the subject *formats* and the verb phrase "have come and gone."

62. H   Difficulty: High

Category: Sentence Structure and Formation

Getting to the Answer: More than one placement may create a grammatically correct sentence, so make sure that the sentence is also logical. What word in this sentence does *better* most logically describe? The main idea of the sentence is that the vinyl record replaced the gramophone, so something about the vinyl record must have been better than the gramophone. It makes the most sense to describe the vinyl record as sounding better, as in (H). Choice F places *better* before *supplanted*, which means *replaced*, but the sentence isn't comparing the way the vinyl record replaced the gramophone to the way another technology replaced the gramophone. Choice G puts *better* before *vinyl*, but *vinyl* isn't being compared to anything in the sentence that results. Choice J creates an illogical sentence, indicating that the gramophone was the better recording format even though it was replaced by the vinyl record.

63. C   Difficulty: Medium

Category: Sentence Structure and Formation

Getting to the Answer: The *-ing* verb form cannot be the predicate (main) verb in a sentence. As written, this sentence is a fragment. Choice (C) corrects this by providing a predicate verb without introducing any additional errors. Choices B and D do not address the error.

64. G   Difficulty: High

Category: Organization, Unity, and Cohesion / Transitions

Getting to the Answer: With Transitions questions, focus on the relationship between ideas. The two ideas here are contrasted—the average high school student knows about one type of recording but not the other. Choice (G) has the only contrasting transition word. Choices F and H incorrectly indicate a cause-and-effect relationship; it doesn't make sense that familiarity with the vinyl record would lead to unfamiliarity with the 8-track. Choice J uses *or*, which doesn't make sense in context. It wouldn't seem *curious* that younger people had either heard of one of these recording techniques or not heard of the other; what's *curious* is that they are familiar with the older one, but not the more recent.

65. D   Difficulty: Medium

Category: Usage

Getting to the Answer: A compound subject joined with *and* requires a plural verb form. The subject here is *DJs and those*, so the two verbs need to be in the plural form. Choice (D) is correct. Choices B and C change one verb but not the other.

66. J   Difficulty: Medium

Category: Knowledge of Language / Concision

Getting to the Answer: Redundant information may be contained within the underlined selection, or the underlined information may be redundant because of information elsewhere in the sentence or paragraph. Since we already know that DJs and music-mixers *appreciate* vinyl recordings, it is redundant to also say that they *cherish* them; (J) is correct. Choice G does not address the error. Choice H is unnecessarily wordy.

67. A   Difficulty: Medium

Category: Topic Development / Supporting Material

Getting to the Answer: When asked whether to add new information, note the context surrounding the proposed addition. The passage focuses on changes in music-playing technology, so the new information is relevant, adding an interesting detail. Eliminate C and D. The passage does not make an argument, so B is incorrect. Choice (A) correctly states the reason for making the addition.

68. H   Difficulty: Medium

Category: Punctuation

Getting to the Answer: Aside words like *though*, *for example*, and *however* should be set off with commas, since the sentence would still make sense without them. Choice (H) places the commas correctly. Choices F and J only use one of the necessary commas to separate *though* from the rest of the sentence. Choice G uses a semicolon, which is correct only when used to combine independent clauses.

69. C   Difficulty: High

Category: Punctuation

Getting to the Answer: Colons are used to introduce or emphasize a brief definition, explanation, or list. The information after the underlined selection serves as an explanation of the *something different* to which the writer refers. Choice (C) correctly places a colon before this information. Choice A uses no punctuation, which makes the sentence hard to understand. Choice B incorrectly uses a semicolon between an independent clause and an explanatory phrase. Choice D uses a comma, which doesn't set off the explanation as well as the colon does.

70. G   Difficulty: Medium

Category: Organization, Unity, and Cohesion / Transitions

Getting to the Answer: When a transition word is underlined, check whether it makes sense logically and grammatically. The transition connects the fact that older technologies could not hold much music to the fact that newer technologies can hold more. These ideas stand in contrast to each other. Eliminate F and J because they lack contrast. Choice H is a contrast transition, but it makes the sentence ungrammatical. *Despite* cannot be a modifying phrase on its own, so eliminate H. Choice (G) is correct.

71. B   Difficulty: Medium

Category: Usage

Getting to the Answer: Read idioms for both proper construction and logic in context. *Contrasting by* is idiomatically incorrect; the best choice here is (B), *Compared to*. Choice C uses incorrect grammatical structure. Choice D is idiomatically incorrect.

72. J   Difficulty: Medium

Category: Topic Development / Writer's Purpose

Getting to the Answer: Read all question stems carefully. The correct answer choice will maintain the passage's tone and satisfy the stated purpose. The question stem asks for a choice that will "help readers understand the [MP3 player's] storage capacity and size," so you can immediately eliminate Choices F and H, which address the player's popularity, not its storage capacity. Both G and (J) discuss the MP3 player's storage capacity, but

(J)'s information is more specific and better satisfies the requirement of the question stem by focusing on the current technology rather than future improvements.

73. B   Difficulty: High

Category: Knowledge of Language / Style and Tone

Getting to the Answer: Read the paragraphs in question with the suggested changes. How do they affect the essay? If the writer uses the pronouns *you* and *your*, he is directly addressing the reader. The effect is a more personal tone, (B). Choice A mentions suggested actions, which are not present in Paragraphs 5 and 6. The tone of the essay is not "formal and removed," as C indicates. Choice D focuses on the writer's knowledge, but changing the pronouns would not affect the facts presented by the writer.

74. F   Difficulty: Medium

Category: Organization, Unity, and Cohesion / Passage Organization

Getting to the Answer: The first sentence of a paragraph typically introduces the topic of the paragraph, so look for the paragraph that contains details related to this sentence. Paragraph 2 explains how the gramophone record was replaced by the vinyl phonograph record. The new sentence introduces the idea that the gramophone record's popularity did not last, so the beginning of Paragraph 2 is the most logical placement. Choice (F) is correct. The gramophone is not mentioned in Paragraphs 3, 4, or 5.

75. D   Difficulty: Medium

Category: Topic Development / Writer's Purpose

Getting to the Answer: This is a question about the main idea of the essay. By determining the main idea, you can quickly eliminate two answer choices. The main idea of the essay is that recording formats have changed and improved rapidly over the past 135 years and are likely to continue changing rapidly. This main idea does not include any technical explanation of how sounds are recorded, so you can immediately eliminate A and B. Choice C can also be ruled out since, far from discussing "a limited number of recording formats," this essay mentions nearly all of them; (D) is correct.

MATHEMATICS TEST

1. E   Difficulty: Low

Category: Essential Skills / Numbers and Operations

Getting to the Answer: To add or subtract fractions, you must first write them over the same denominator.

$$1\frac{2}{3} + 2\frac{3}{4} = \frac{5}{3} + \frac{11}{4} = \frac{20}{12} + \frac{33}{12} = \frac{53}{12} = 4\frac{5}{12}$$

Or, alternatively, plug the numbers into your calculator: $1.6667 + 2.75 = 4.4167$. When you enter (E) into your calculator, you get the same result.

2. H   Difficulty: Low

Category: Essential Skills / Expressions and Equations

Getting to the Answer: The signs (multiplication dots) between these terms say to *multiply*—keep that in mind as you apply the rules for exponents. Be careful not to leave any parts out or multiply by any part more than once. First, multiply the number parts together: $2 \cdot 3 \cdot 6 = 36$, which immediately eliminates F and G. Then, x times x is x^2, which eliminates J. Now multiply the ys to get $y^3 \cdot y^2 \cdot y^2 = y^{3+2+2} = y^7$, so (H) is correct. Remember that you're counting the number of ys that are being multiplied, so add the exponents.

3. A   Difficulty: Low

Category: Essential Skills / Numbers and Operations

Getting to the Answer: Make sure you solve for what the question is asking. Incorrect answer choices will often be other parts of the question or steps along the way. Ms. Ruppin earns $\frac{\$51,940}{245} = \$212$ per day. The company will save $\$212 - \$140 = \$72$ by paying the replacement instead, which is (A). Note that E is Ms. Ruppin's pay and C is the replacement's pay. Don't fall for the traditional traps.

4. J   Difficulty: Medium

Category: Essential Skills / Statistics and Probability

Getting to the Answer: Answering questions about averages always starts the same way: Set up the formula using the given information. The average is equal to the sum of the terms divided by the number of terms. Let x be the fifth test score. Then the equation for this question is:

$$\frac{52 + 70 + 76 + 79 + x}{5} = 75$$

$$\frac{277 + x}{5} = 75$$

$$277 + x = 375$$

$$x = 98$$

Choice (J) is correct.

5. C   Difficulty: Low

Category: Essential Skills / Rates, Percents, Proportions, and Unit Conversion

Getting to the Answer: This may seem like a complicated question, but the first sentence tells you everything you need to answer the question. Divide the amount of water vapor per cubic meter, 6.7 grams, by the maximum, 19.2 grams:

$$\frac{6.7}{19.2} \approx 0.34896 = 34.896\% \approx 35\%$$

Choice (C) is correct.

6. J   Difficulty: Low

Category: Essential Skills / Geometry

Getting to the Answer: Try to translate what you're asked for into concepts that you know. This question asks for the distance around the pool, also known as the perimeter. To find the perimeter of a rectangle, add up all the sides, keeping in mind that opposite sides have the same lengths: $2(30) + 2(10) = 80$ feet, which is (J).

7. C   Difficulty: Low

Category: Essential Skills / Numbers and Operations

Getting to the Answer: Keep careful track of units. A film that is 3 hours 40 minutes long will be a total of $(3 \times 60) + 40 = 220$ minutes long. Half that is $\frac{220}{2} = 110$ minutes, or 1 hour 50 minutes, making (C) the correct answer.

8. F   Difficulty: Low

Category: Essential Skills / Expressions and Equations

Getting to the Answer: Watching your positives and negatives is key! Subtracting when you mean to add (or vice versa) will lead you straight to an incorrect answer choice.

$$2x - 5 = 7x + 3$$

$$-5 = 5x + 3$$

$$-8 = 5x$$

$$-\frac{8}{5} = x$$

Choice (F) is correct.

9. D   Difficulty: Low

Category: Higher Math / Functions

Getting to the Answer: Sometimes Backsolving will be much easier than trying to work out the algebra. You're not going to be able to tell whether you need a larger or smaller number here, so start with A and work your way down until you have the answer.

A: $22 - 13 = 9$ and $49 - 31 = 18$. The difference between the first pair and the last pair is not the same. Eliminate.

B: $23 - 13 = 10$ and $49 - 39 = 10$. So far so good, but what about going from the second to the third number? $39 - 23 = 16$, which is not the same as the difference between the other pairs. Eliminate.

C: $24 - 13 = 11$ and $49 - 38 = 11$. However, $38 - 24$ is 14, not 11. Eliminate.

(D): $25 - 13 = 12$, $49 - 37 = 12$, and $37 - 25 = 12$. With a difference of 12, the sequence 13, 25, 37, 49 works. Choice (D) is correct.

If you would rather approach the question algebraically, imagine that you're adding the same thing three times in order to get from 13 to 49 (since you always add the same amount to get the next number). This means that:

$$13 + 3x = 49$$

$$3x = 36$$

$$x = 12$$

The difference is 12, which means the next two numbers are $13 + 12 = 25$ and $25 + 12 = 37$. You can check that $37 + 12 = 49$. Choice (D) is correct.

10. J   Difficulty: Medium

Category: Higher Math / Algebra

Getting to the Answer: Keeping the values for $\sqrt{x}$, x, and x^2 straight is important. It's easy to quit a step too soon and confuse x with $\sqrt{x}$.

$$x = \sqrt[3]{729} = 729^{\frac{1}{3}} = 9$$
$$\sqrt{x} + x^2 = \sqrt{9} + 9^2 = 3 + 81 = 84$$

Choice (J) is correct.

11. A   Difficulty: Low

Category: Essential Skills / Numbers and Operations

Getting to the Answer: If you divide 3 by 7 on your calculator, it will most likely stop after 8 or 10 digits. This should be enough, however, for you to see which numbers repeat. Here, the 428571 all repeat, so write the bar over all 6 digits. Choice (A) is correct.

12. K   Difficulty: Medium

Category: Essential Skills / Statistics and Probability

Getting to the Answer: Pay close attention to words like "not" and "except"—these will make all the difference in a question. Probability is defined as the ratio of the number of desired outcomes to the total number of possible outcomes. The total number of balls in the bag is $10 + 10 + 8 = 28$. The number of non-green balls is $10 + 10 = 20$. The probability of choosing a ball that isn't green is $\frac{20}{28} = \frac{5}{7}$, which is (K).

13. A   Difficulty: Low

Category: Essential Skills / Geometry

Getting to the Answer: Remember the rules for parallel lines and transversals. All acute angles are equal, and all obtuse angles are equal. If a is 110, then the corresponding angle below it has the same measure. If you also remember that the angle measure of a straight line is 180°, you're in good shape.

$$110 + d = 180 \rightarrow d = 70$$

$b + c = 180$ (because the two angles form a straight line)

$$b + c + d = 180 + 70 = 250$$

Choice (A) is correct.

14. J   Difficulty: Medium

Category: Higher Math / Functions

Getting to the Answer: When a question includes a graph, be sure to fully understand it before trying to answer the question. Erin reached an altitude of 4,500 feet at 8 AM. She stayed at or above 4,500 feet until the final hour of her hike. This suggests that she was at or above 4,500 feet for at least 4 full hours. She descended the final 750 feet at a constant speed in one hour. More specifically, she descended the 250 feet from 4,750 feet to 4,500 feet in 20 minutes. Therefore, she was at or above 4,500 feet for 4 hours 20 minutes, which is (J).

15. A   Difficulty: High

Category: Higher Math / Functions

Getting to the Answer: The question states that during each one-hour interval, Erin traveled at a constant speed. Therefore, a graph showing her speed should remain constant (horizontal on the graph) within each one-hour interval. The only graph that does this is graph (A). All other graphs show a change in speed during each interval, which suggests an acceleration or deceleration and, ultimately, movement at speeds that are not constant.

16. H   Difficulty: Low

Category: Essential Skills / Expressions and Equations

Getting to the Answer: You don't need to calculate every row, column, and diagonal—because they should all be equal, you just need to look at one row or column that doesn't contain the middle square and one row, column, or diagonal that does contain the middle square. The first column sums to $-3x - 6x + 3x = -6x$. The second column should have the same sum. Call the missing square m:

$$4x + m - 8x = -6x$$
$$m - 4x = -6x$$
$$m = -2x$$

Choice (H) is correct.

17. E   Difficulty: Medium

Category: Essential Skills / Rates, Percents, Proportions, and Unit Conversion

Getting to the Answer: Sometimes, part of the challenge of questions involving units of measurement is making such units—here, seconds and hours—consistent. To keep the units organized, consider using the factor-label method:

$$\frac{3 \text{ ft}}{1 \text{ sec}} \times \frac{60 \text{ sec}}{1 \text{ min}} \times 30 \text{ min} = 5,400 \text{ ft}$$

Choice (E) is correct.

18. J   Difficulty: Low

Category: Higher Math / Statistics and Probability

Getting to the Answer: Once you know the rule, all questions like this are straightforward. Simply multiply the number of possibilities for each type to arrive at $5 \times 8 \times 3 = 120$, or (J).

19. A   Difficulty: Medium

Category: Essential Skills / Rates, Percents, Proportions, and Unit Conversion

Getting to the Answer: Blindly doing calculations is not a good way to approach a question like this—many wrong answers involve doing the wrong calculations with the given numbers. Make a plan before you start manipulating numbers. Set up a proportion using the ratio of grain to bread. Be sure to keep track of the zeroes.

$$\frac{90,000}{150,000} = \frac{x}{6,000}$$

$$\frac{9}{15} = \frac{x}{6,000}$$

$$54,000 = 15x$$

$$3,600 = x$$

Choice (A) is the answer.

20. H   Difficulty: Medium

Category: Essential Skills / Rates, Percents, Proportions, and Unit Conversion

Getting to the Answer: When you know that the given parts add up to the whole, then you can turn a part-to-part ratio into two part-to-whole ratios—put each term of the ratio over the sum of the terms. Here, because all the numbers in the set must be either even or odd, the parts do add up to the whole. The sum of the terms in the ratio 2:3 is 5, so the part-to-whole ratio for even numbers in the set to all the numbers in the set is 2:5. Use this to find the percent:

$$\frac{\text{Even numbers}}{\text{All the numbers}} = \frac{2}{5} \times 100\% = \frac{200\%}{5} = 40\%$$

That's (H).

21. E   Difficulty: Medium

Category: Higher Math / Algebra

Getting to the Answer: If you're not comfortable simplifying the expressions on the left to see if they match the expressions on the right, you can Pick Numbers for a, b, and c, although this is likely to take more time. Algebraically, choice A is true because you can cancel the factor b in the numerator and denominator of the expression on the left. Choice B is true based on rules of exponents: $a^1 \cdot a^1 = a^{1+1} = a^2$, and the same for b. Choice C is true because both the numerator and the denominator equal ab, and anything divided by itself equals 1 (except for zero, but that's not relevant here). Choice D is true: $\frac{a+b}{b} = \frac{a}{b} + \frac{b}{b} = \frac{a}{b} + 1$. Choice (E) is false because you cannot divide the first terms and the second terms separately. When you divide, you can only divide out factors (things that are multiplied in both the numerator and denominator), not terms (things that are added or subtracted in the numerator and denominator).

22. K   Difficulty: Medium

Category: Higher Math / Algebra

Getting to the Answer: Even if you forgot what slope-intercept form looks like, the answer choices tell you to solve for y. Before you start moving the x term and the constant, notice that if you add y to both sides of the equation, your work is done. The result is $-3x + 7 = y$, which matches (K).

23. B   **Difficulty:** Medium

Category: Higher Math / Algebra

Getting to the Answer: Before you factor a quadratic equation, make sure one side is equal to zero. Here, $x^2 - 8x = 8x$ becomes $x^2 - 16x = 0$.

$$x^2 - 16x = 0$$
$$x(x - 16) = 0$$
$$x = 0 \text{ or } x - 16 = 0$$
$$x = 0 \text{ or } x = 16$$

The latter answer is (B).

24. J   **Difficulty:** Medium

Category: Higher Math / Number and Quantity

Getting to the Answer: Be sure not to be tempted by answers that are partly right. The inequality $x \geq 1$ describes the right half of the values on the number line but leaves out the left half. The selected values on the number line consist of 1, everything greater than 1, -1, and everything less than -1. The easiest way to describe this set is that the absolute value of x, or its distance from zero on the number line, is greater than or equal to 1. This can be written in mathematical notation as $|x| \geq 1$. Thus, (J) is correct.

25. E   **Difficulty:** Medium

Category: Higher Math / Geometry

Getting to the Answer: Even if a question talks about rounding, the correct answer may require no rounding whatsoever. The distance from a point to a line is measured perpendicularly, so you can be sure that the triangle is a right triangle. Because this distance is perpendicular and measured from the radius, it bisects the chord, which means the base of the triangle is 15. Use the Pythagorean theorem (or your knowledge of common Pythagorean triplets) to find the length of the hypotenuse, r:

$$8^2 + 15^2 = r^2$$
$$r = \sqrt{8^2 + 15^2}$$
$$= \sqrt{64 + 225}$$
$$= \sqrt{289} = 17$$

That's (E).

26. G   **Difficulty:** Medium

Category: Higher Math / Algebra

Getting to the Answer: Don't confuse your variables—here you're given V and you need to solve for t:

$$V = \frac{5}{3}t + 0.05$$
$$0.575 = \frac{5}{3}t + 0.05$$
$$0.525 = \frac{5}{3}t$$
$$t = \left(\frac{3}{5}\right)0.525 = 0.315$$

Choice (G) is correct.

27. B   **Difficulty:** Medium

Category: Higher Math / Geometry

Getting to the Answer: If a question seems confusing, try rewording it in simpler terms. The sand over the soccer field will make a rectangular prism, and you're looking for the height if the volume is 15,000 cubic yards. The volume of a rectangular prism is length times width times height. The length of this soccer field is $100 + 18 + 18 = 136$ yards, the width is 60.5 yards, and the height is unknown. Put this information into an equation with the volume of sand:

$$l \cdot w \cdot h = V$$
$$136 \cdot 60.5 \cdot h = 15,000$$
$$8,228h = 15,000$$
$$h \approx 1.82$$

The value of h is between 1 and 2, making (B) the correct answer.

28. G   **Difficulty:** Medium

Category: Higher Math / Geometry

Getting to the Answer: Most of the trigonometry on the ACT simply tests whether you know the definitions of sine, cosine, and tangent. Remember the method for finding the three basic trigonometric functions: SOHCAHTOA tells you that cosine is calculated by dividing the adjacent side by the hypotenuse. Let x be the length of $\overline{AC}$.

$$\cos A = \frac{\text{adjacent}}{\text{hypotenuse}}$$

$$\frac{4}{5} = \frac{x}{18}$$

$$5x = 4(18)$$

$$5x = 72$$

$$x = 14.4$$

Choice (G) is correct.

29. A   Difficulty: Medium

Category: Higher Math / Statistics and Probability

Getting to the Answer: Don't automatically start calculating the actual numbers of beds—the graph is already sufficient to answer this question. Bedtime has 2.5 pictures of beds (each representing 100 actual beds). There's a total of $1.5 + 2 + 4 + 2.5 = 10$ pictures of beds. So the fraction of the total beds that are at Bedtime is $\frac{2.5}{10} = \frac{25}{100} = \frac{1}{4}$, which is (A).

30. G   Difficulty: Medium

Category: Essential Skills / Geometry

Getting to the Answer: Sometimes drawing a good diagram (or strategically using the one given) will be key to answering a question. Here, you should add the given measures to the figure to get started:

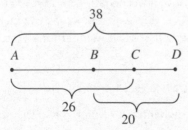

Because $26 + 20 = 46$, the overlapping part, *BC*, must be $46 - 38 = 8$, which is (G). If you didn't see that right away, you can always calculate from one piece to another. If $AC = 26$ and $AD = 38$, *CD* must be 12. If $CD = 12$ and $BD = 20$, *BC* must be 8, which again is (G).

31. A   Difficulty: Medium

Category: Higher Math / Algebra

Getting to the Answer: The intersection of two lines is simply the one (*x,y*) point that makes both equations true.

You can solve this like any system of equations.

$$4x + 10 = 5x + 7$$

$$10 = x + 7$$

$$3 = x$$

Choice (A) is correct. If you had accidentally solved for the *y*-coordinate, you would have gotten E. Look out for traps like this in coordinate geometry questions.

32. H   Difficulty: Medium

Category: Essential Skills / Rates, Percents, Proportions, and Unit Conversion

Getting to the Answer: To get Meri's rate in pages per hour, take the 96 pages and divide by the time in hours. The time is given as "2 hours and 40 minutes." Forty minutes is $\frac{2}{3}$ of an hour, so you can express Meri's time as $2\frac{2}{3}$ hours, or $\frac{8}{3}$ hours:

$$\text{Pages per hour} = \frac{96 \text{ pages}}{\frac{8}{3} \text{ hours}}$$

$$= 96 \times \frac{3}{8} = 36 \text{ pg/hr}$$

This matches (H).

33. B   Difficulty: High

Category: Higher Math / Statistics and Probability

Getting to the Answer: If an integer is chosen randomly from the first 50 integers, the probability of choosing any particular number is $\frac{1}{50}$, and the probability of choosing an integer with a digit of 3 is the number of integers with a digit of 3 divided by 50. The integers 3, 13, 23, 30, 31, 32, 33, 34, 35, 36, 37, 38, 39, and 43 are the only integers with 3s in them, for a total of 14 different integers, so the probability is $\frac{14}{50}$ or $\frac{7}{25}$, which is (B).

34. F   Difficulty: Medium

Category: Higher Math / Algebra

Getting to the Answer: This question is much easier than it looks. Plug the expression given for *s* into the cubed expression and see what happens:

$$\left(t - \boxed{s}\right)^3 = \left(t - \left(\boxed{4 + t}\right)\right)^3$$
$$= (t - 4 - t)^3$$
$$= (-4)^3 = (-4)(-4)(-4) = -64$$

That's (F).

35. D   Difficulty: High

Category: Higher Math / Geometry

Getting to the Answer: Feel free to draw all over your test booklet—that's what it's there for. This question tests your ability to read coordinates and to find a midpoint (although you may not realize this at first glance). Set up a coordinate system to compare points B and F. Because you're trying to find the distance relative to A, make A (0,0). Then B is at (800,0). Use the labeled distances to find the x-value of F, which is 700 (AB − DC − FE), and the y-value, which is 600 (CB − DE). This means F is at (700,600). The lookout point is at the midpoint of B and F, so you can use the midpoint formula:

$$\left(\frac{800 + 700}{2}, \frac{0 + 600}{2}\right) = (750,300)$$

Using these coordinates, the lookout is 750 yards to the right (east) of point A and 300 yards up (north), which is (D).

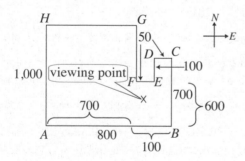

36. K   Difficulty: Low

Category: Essential Skills / Expressions and Equations

Getting to the Answer: Carefully translate potentially intimidating word problems. "Fifteen pounds less than" tells you to subtract 15 from some quantity. That quantity is three times the weight of the second-place watermelon, or 3w, so 3w − 15 is the correct expression. Choice (K)

is correct. Picking Numbers can also help if you have difficulty translating. Pick w = 10. Three times this quantity is 30 and 15 less than 30 is 15. Substitute 10 for w in each of the answer choices, eliminating any choice that does not equal 15:

F: 10 − 5 = 5   Eliminate.
G: 10 + 15 = 25   Eliminate.
H: 10 − 15 = −5   Eliminate
J: 3(10) − 15 = 15   Eliminate.
(K): 3(10) − 15 = 15   Keep.

The only expression that works is (K).

37. E   Difficulty: Medium

Category: Higher Math / Number and Quantity

Getting to the Answer: If you remembered that any number squared is positive, a quick look at the answer choices would tell you that (E), x^2y^2, will be positive for any nonzero values of x and y, and is therefore the correct answer. If you didn't remember that, you should make a note of it, because it's a very important concept. You can also solve this one by Picking Numbers. If xy is negative, then either x or y is negative and the other is positive because a negative times a positive equals a negative. Picking a couple of pairs of numbers for x and y will tell you that both x − y and y − x can be either positive or negative depending on the exact values of x and y; x^2y will be negative if y is negative, and xy^2 will be negative if x is negative. However, any values you pick for x and y will give you a positive number for x^2y^2, so again, (E) is correct.

38. F   Difficulty: High

Category: Higher Math / Number and Quantity

Getting to the Answer: Picking numbers is the easiest, fastest way to answer this question. Choose a pair of numbers from each set and add them together. If you are unable to prove immediately that a set does not have the property described in the question stem, you may want to choose another pair. In set I, if you add 2 and 4, you get 6. Adding 12 and 8 gives you 20. Adding −2 and 8 gives you 6. Because each sum is a member of the set of even integers, set I seems to be true. For set II, adding 3 and 5 yields 8, which is not an odd integer. Therefore, II is not true. Finally, if you add two primes, say 2 and 3, you get 5. That example is true. If you add 3 and 5, however, you get 8, and 8 is not a prime number. Therefore, only set I has the property, and the answer is (F).

39. C   Difficulty: Medium

Category: Higher Math / Geometry

Getting to the Answer: Similar triangles have equal angles and proportional sides. Be sure to keep track of which side is proportional to which—the longest side of one triangle goes with the longest side of the other triangle and so on. Use the given ratio and the fact that the longest side of the second triangle has length 12 to set up a proportion comparing the longest sides of both triangles and the shortest sides of both triangles:

$$\frac{12}{20} = \frac{x}{15}$$
$$20x = 12(15)$$
$$20x = 180$$
$$x = 9$$

Choice (C) is correct.

40. K   Difficulty: Medium

Category: Essential Skills / Geometry

Getting to the Answer: The angles of triangle YXZ sum to 180 degrees, so:

$$m\angle YZX + 20° + 95° = 180°$$
$$m\angle YZX = 65°$$

The bases of the trapezoid, $\overline{WX}$ and $\overline{YZ}$, are parallel, making $\angle YZX$ and $\angle TXZ$ alternate interior angles relative to transversal XZ. This means $m\angle TXZ = 65°$, which is (K).

41. B   Difficulty: High

Category: Higher Math / Functions

Getting to the Answer: Knowing the basic trig values for benchmark angles (multiples of 30° and 45°) would certainly help here. However, Backsolving also works because there are numbers in the answer choices. Use your calculator to find the sine of each angle (make sure your calculator is in "degree" mode first). Note that $\frac{\sqrt{3}}{2}$ is approximately equal to 0.866.

$\sin 30° = 0.5$
$\sin 45° \approx 0.7071$
$\sin 60° \approx 0.866$
$\sin 120° \approx 0.866$
$\sin 135° \approx 0.7071$
$\sin 150° = 0.5$

Choice (B) is correct.

42. F   Difficulty: Medium

Category: Essential Skills / Numbers and Operations

Getting to the Answer: When given two ratios, make sure you check whether the second one is a fraction of the first group or a fraction of the total. The number of students continuing their studies $= \frac{1}{3}(896) \approx 299$.

Of that 299, the number of students going to law school is $\frac{2}{5}(299) \approx 120$, which is (F).

43. D   Difficulty: Medium

Category: Essential Skills / Numbers and Operations

Getting to the Answer: Knowing what each letter in the mnemonic "PEMDAS" represents will make simple number operations questions a breeze on Test Day. Substitute the values for a, b, and c, and evaluate the expression following the order of operations: $(a + b)(c - a) = (-2 + 4)[7 - (-2)] = (2)(9) = 18$. Choice (D) is the correct answer.

44. G   Difficulty: High

Category: Higher Math / Functions

Getting to the Answer: If you remember your properties of logs, this question is very straightforward. Because $\log_b b^x = x$, the value of x is $\sqrt{7} \approx 2.65$, which lies between 2 and 3. Choice (G) is correct.

If you don't remember this property, you'll have to rewrite the logarithmic equation as an exponential equation and solve: $\log_7 7^{\sqrt{7}} = x$ is equivalent to the exponential form $7^x = 7^{\sqrt{7}}$. The bases are the same (7), so the exponents must be equal. This means $x = \sqrt{7} \approx 2.65$, which lies between 2 and 3.

45. C   Difficulty: Low

Category: Essential Skills / Statistics and Probability

Getting to the Answer: If a question that involves reading a table or chart seems easy, it probably is. All you have to do is be careful that you don't make an arithmetic error. Carefully calculate the number of employees by division, then add to find the total:

$$\text{Development} = 1 \times 4 = 4$$
$$\text{Marketing} = 2 \times 3 = 6$$
$$\text{Accounting} = 3 \times 2 = 6$$
$$\text{Public Relations} = 5 \times 5 = 25$$
$$\text{Total: } 4 + 6 + 6 + 25 = 41$$

That's (C).

46. J   Difficulty: Medium

Category: Essential Skills / Rates, Percents, Proportions, and Unit Conversion

Getting to the Answer: Even though this question uses the word *percent*, you are never asked to find the actual percent itself. Set this question up as a proportion to get the answer more quickly. Use the definition: percent change equals amount of change divided by original amount.

$$\frac{16 - 6}{6} = \frac{x - 12}{12}$$
$$\frac{10}{6} = \frac{x - 12}{12}$$
$$120 = 6(x - 12)$$
$$120 = 6x - 72$$
$$192 = 6x$$
$$32 = x$$

Choice (J) is correct.

47. D   Difficulty: High

Category: Higher Math / Geometry

Getting to the Answer: Concepts such as "tangent to" are less scary if you work on becoming more comfortable

with math vocabulary. It also helps to draw a sketch like the one below:

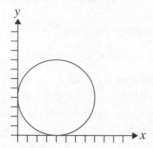

As you can see in the sketch, the center of the circle is at (4,4), and the radius is 4. In the equation of a circle, $(x - h)^2 + (y - k)^2 = r^2$, the center is at (h,k), and the radius is r. Plug in the information you know to get $(x - 4)^2 + (y - 4)^2 = 4^2$, which is (D). If you're stuck, try plugging in a few points. For example, using either (4,0) or (0,4) eliminates all answers except B and (D), and (4,8) eliminates B.

48. H   Difficulty: High

Category: Essential Skills / Rates, Percents, Proportions, and Unit Conversion

Getting to the Answer: The average speed is the total distance traveled divided by the total hours traveled. Liza drove at 40 miles per hour for 2 hours, for a total of 40×2, or 80 miles. If she increased her speed by 25%, then she increased her speed by $0.25(40) = 10$, so her new speed was $40 + 10 = 50$ miles per hour. So she drove at 50 miles per hour for the next 3 hours, for a total of $50 \times 3 = 150$ miles. She went 80 miles and then 150 miles, for a total of 230 miles, and she drove for 2 hours and then for 3 hours, for a total of 5 hours. Liza's average rate for the trip was 230 miles divided by 5 hours, or 46 miles per hour, making (H) the correct answer.

49. A   Difficulty: Medium

Category: Higher Math / Number and Quantity

Getting to the Answer: Even if you're not sure how to perform operations on matrices, you can probably reason out the answer. The number of people who will leave Marketing is $0.3(20) = 6$. You can compute the number for each department, then add them all together. This will give you the same result as multiplying the matrices.

$$\begin{bmatrix} 20 & 12 & 40 & 10 \end{bmatrix} \begin{bmatrix} 0.3 \\ 0.5 \\ 0.2 \\ 0.4 \end{bmatrix}$$

$$= 20(0.3) + 12(0.5) + 40(0.2) + 10(0.4)$$
$$= 6 + 6 + 8 + 4 = 24$$

Choice (A) is correct.

50. J   Difficulty: Medium

Category: Higher Math / Statistics and Probability

Getting to the Answer: The expected value of a random discrete variable is the weighted average of all possible values that the variable can take on. The weights are determined by the probability distribution. To find the expected value, multiply each possible value by its given probability and then add the products:

$$E(X) = \frac{1}{5}(10) + \frac{1}{10}(11) + \frac{3}{10}(12) + \frac{3}{20}(13) + \frac{1}{4}(14)$$

$$= 2 + \frac{11}{10} + \frac{36}{10} + \frac{39}{20} + \frac{14}{4}$$

$$= \frac{40}{20} + \frac{22}{20} + \frac{72}{20} + \frac{39}{20} + \frac{70}{20}$$

$$= \frac{243}{20} = 12\frac{3}{20}$$

Choice (J) is correct.

51. A   Difficulty: Medium

Category: Higher Math / Algebra

Getting to the Answer: Don't get too caught up in the language—figure out what the solution is, then think about which answer choice means that. Subtract x from both sides: $-2 < -5$. When is -2 less than -5? Never. What set has nothing in it? The empty set, which is (A).

52. G   Difficulty: High

Category: Higher Math / Functions

Getting to the Answer: The fastest route to the correct answer here (because you're given a graph of the parent square root function) is to write the domain and range of $g(x)$ and then adjust the values based on the transformation. The x-values of the curve shown in the

graph begin at 0 and extend to the right indefinitely, so the domain is $x \geq 0$. The transformation $(x + 1)$ shifts the graph to the left 1 unit, so the domain of $h(x)$ is $x \geq -1$. Eliminate H, J, and K. Likewise, the y-values of the curve shown in the graph begin at 0 and extend upward indefinitely, so the range is $y \geq 0$. The transformation $(+ 3)$ shifts the graph up 3 units, so the range of $h(x)$ is $y \geq 3$. This means (G) is correct.

Note that you could also quickly sketch the graph of $h(x)$ to find its domain and range. The graph would look like the dashed curve below:

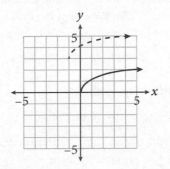

53. B   Difficulty: High

Category: Higher Math / Statistics and Probability

Getting to the Answer: Once you're strong on the basics, combining two concepts on seemingly complex questions like this one will be a breeze! The percent who chose one of the four named teachers is 25% + 15% + 35% + 5% = 80%. This means that 20% of the answers were grouped under "Other." A circle has 360 degrees, so the measure of the Other sector will be 20% of 360, or 0.2(360) = 72 degrees, which is (B).

54. J   Difficulty: Medium

Category: Higher Math / Functions

Getting to the Answer: Because you're looking for the sixth term of the sequence, call the sixth term x. Every term in this sequence is formed by multiplying the previous term by 3 and then subtracting 1, so the seventh term must be formed by multiplying the sixth term, x, by 3, and then subtracting 1; in other words, the seventh term is equal to $3x - 1$. Because the seventh term is 365, you have $365 = 3x - 1$. You can solve for x by adding 1 to both sides of the equation and then dividing by 3. The result is $x = 122$, which is (J).

55. A   Difficulty: Medium

Category: Higher Math / Geometry

Getting to the Answer: A great way to test inequalities is to plug in a point or two. All the points in the shaded region of the graph should work in *both* inequalities. However, a more algebraic approach may save some time. Because only values of x greater than 6 are shaded, $x \geq 6$ should be one of the inequalities, eliminating E. Because the area *above* the slanted line is shaded, the other inequality should have a $\geq$ symbol, eliminating C and D. To choose between (A) and B, examine the slanted line more closely. From the dot at the origin to the dot at (6,2), the line rises 2 units and runs 6 units, so the slope of the line is $\frac{1}{3}$, making (A) the correct answer.

56. K   Difficulty: High

Category: Higher Math / Functions

Getting to the Answer: The question asks you to evaluate the function $f(x)$, replacing x with $(x + c)$. Replace any instance of x in the function definition with $x + c$. This means that $2(x + 7)$ will be $2(x + c + 7)$. Use the distributive property and multiply each term in parentheses by 2 to get $2x + 2c + 2(7)$, or $2x + 2c + 14$, which is (K).

57. C   Difficulty: Medium

Category: Higher Math / Geometry

Getting to the Answer: If the answer choices are ranges of numbers, you might be able to save time by rounding numbers and estimating values. Start by finding the volume of the swimming pool: $V = \pi r^2 h = \pi(6)^2(4) = \pi(36)(4) = 144\pi$ cubic feet. To find the weight of the water in the pool, multiply the pool's volume in cubic meters by the weight of 1 cubic foot: 144π cubic feet × 62 pounds per cubic feet = $8,928\pi$ pounds. Because the answer choices consist of large ranges of numbers, you can estimate the volume by rounding π to the nearest whole number, which is 3. Using 3 as an estimate for π, $8,928\pi$ pounds is approximately 26,784 pounds, making (C) correct.

58. G   Difficulty: Medium

Category: Higher Math / Geometry

Getting to the Answer: Drawing a triangle and flipping it over the y-axis will help you visualize this situation and

others like it. Choose nice coordinates to represent A and see what happens to those coordinates:

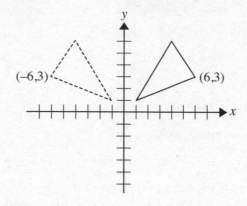

Based on the diagram, the y-coordinate stays the same, and the x-coordinate goes from positive to negative. This means that (v,w) will become $(-v,w)$, which is (G).

59. C   Difficulty: High

Category: Higher Math / Algebra

Getting to the Answer: To get a in terms of b, you'll first need to get c in terms of b, because c is the variable the two equations have in common.

$$b = 3 - 2c$$
$$b + 2c = 3$$
$$2c = 3 - b$$
$$c = \boxed{\frac{3 - b}{2}}$$

$$a = 6\boxed{c} + 7$$
$$a = 6\left(\frac{3 - b}{2}\right) + 7$$
$$a = 3(3 - b) + 7$$
$$a = 9 - 3b + 7$$
$$a = 16 - 3b$$

A perfect match for (C)!

60. K   Difficulty: High

Category: Higher Math / Number and Quantity

Getting to the Answer: You don't have to know anything about complex numbers ahead of time. All the information you need is in the question stem. Treat i as a variable, write the squared binomials as repeated multiplication, FOIL, and replace i^2 with -1 whenever it appears:

$$\frac{(2i + 2)^2}{(2i - 2)^2} = \frac{(2i + 2)(2i + 2)}{(2i - 2)(2i - 2)}$$

$$= \frac{4i^2 + 4i + 4i + 4}{4i^2 - 4i - 4i + 4}$$

$$= \frac{4(-1) + 8i + 4}{4(-1) - 8i + 4}$$

$$= \frac{8i}{-8i} = -1$$

Choice (K) is correct.

READING TEST

Passage I

Suggested Passage Map notes:

¶1: dog vs. doggie

¶2: describes doggie look; doggie grows on you; called "Dumps"

¶3: meeting Dumps: dog running; angry man

¶4: afraid of dog, but dog whines

¶5: owner wants to hurt dog

¶6–9: argue about dog

¶10: narrator threatens owner

¶11–12: owner changes and claims kindness to dog

¶13: owner story: loves dog, got new job, dog escapes, must drive dog back

¶14–15: narrator doubts story, offers to buy dog

1. A **Difficulty:** High

Category: Key Ideas and Details / Inference

Getting to the Answer: Review the narrator's discussion of dogs in paragraph 1. In paragraph 2, the narrator notes that people may not initially notice his doggie's "finer qualities," but they will see his "amiable spirit" after getting to know him. Predict that while *both* dogs and the narrator's doggie are companionable, the main distinction is that his doggie must be less initially appealing; this matches (A).

Choice B is incorrect because the narrator never discusses the relative ages of any dog or doggie. Choice C cannot be correct because a "forgiving disposition" (lines 7–8) is attributed to *dogs*, while the correct answer must reflect a trait of his *doggie*. Likewise, D reflects the narrator's description of dogs in paragraph 1.

2. H **Difficulty:** Medium

Category: Key Ideas and Details / Detail

Getting to the Answer: List the characteristics of Dumps before looking at the answer choices. The narrator states that his "finer qualities" are not obvious but goes on to describe his other features in lines 11–25. Predict: Dumps is mangy-looking, but friendly. This matches (H). Choice F is incorrect because his eyes are described as having a "luster" rather than being "dull." Choice G is the opposite; the narrator claims "you don't at once perceive" his mental qualities. Choice J is a distortion because while the dog is certainly hairy, he resembles a "ragged doormat" rather than something "well-groomed."

3. B **Difficulty:** Medium

Category: Key Ideas and Details / Inference

Getting to the Answer: Consider the scene in paragraphs 3–4. Dumps is described as "active," "yelping," and running so quickly that he was kicking up stones. The narrator also notes hearing "the voice of an angry man." Though the narrator expects the dog to "snap" at him, the dog instead approaches him in a "piteous" manner. This matches (B). Choice A does not match the description of a dog running "wildly." Choice C is too extreme; the dog is trying to escape the "angry man," but he is running away, so he is clearly not so upset that he is "immobilized." Choice D is a distortion: the narrator states in the next paragraph that the owner "seemed about to fling" a "thick stick" at the dog (lines 53–54), not toss a stick in a playful manner.

4. F **Difficulty:** Low

Category: Vocabulary-in-Context

Getting to the Answer: The dog's owner is ready to throw a stick at the dog, so the narrator "checks" him by shouting a threat. The narrator is trying to *stop* the owner from hurting the dog, so predict "checked" means *stopped*. This matches (F), "prevented." The scene has nothing to do with a square design, G, and the narrator is not merely "verifying" something, H, but shouting to prevent an act of violence. "Assaulted," J, is too extreme for a verbal response and lacks the necessary connotation of preventing the throw.

5. D   Difficulty: High

Category: Craft and Structure / Function

Getting to the Answer: When stopped, the owner scowls and claims that "A man may do as he likes with his own." The narrator responds with indignation, showing the owner and the reader that animal welfare is important to him. The word "man" is emphasized to indicate that the narrator is using it sarcastically; he does not think the owner is acting like a "man" at all, which matches (D). Choice A is a misused detail; the narrator does refer to the other man as "big" in paragraph 5, but he is not using the word "man" to describe the other man's size. Instead, he is using it to question his humanity. Choice B is opposite, as the narrator does not agree with the owner, answering him "indignantly." Choice C is a distortion. Although the narrator states that "cruelty" to animals "has the effect of inclining me to fight," his actions are not physical.

6. H   Difficulty: Low

Category: Key Ideas and Details / Detail

Getting to the Answer: In lines 65–66, the owner initially responded to the narrator's words with a "sulky scowl." In response, the narrator mentions an Act of Parliament and makes a threat. At this, the owner stops scowling, seeming "to have been affected by my threats." The owner was worried about the narrator's threats of prosecution, (H). Choice F is out of scope; the owner never seems worried that the dog will bite, and the dog has been behaving kindly towards the narrator since running up to him. Choice G is incorrect because the owner does not discuss his factory job until a later paragraph and never mentions being late to work. Choice J distorts the passage: the owner, not the narrator, was about to throw a stick at the dog.

7. A   Difficulty: High

Category: Craft and Structure / Writer's View

Getting to the Answer: Consider the narrator's tone and comments directed toward the reader. Although

the introduction might appear to be argumentative, the narrator includes comments to the reader in lines 2–3 and lines 22–25 that display a thoughtful attitude. He will later explain his behavior in lines 69–70: "I am naturally of a peaceable disposition." Clearly, the narrator doesn't want the reader to think him a brute. This tone matches (A). Choice B is opposite; the narrator is mindful of the reader, though he argues with the dog owner in the passage. Choice C is extreme; the narrator never expresses fear that anyone will disagree with his views about dogs, doggies, or animal welfare. Choice D is also extreme. The narrator seems to desire the reader to have a favorable opinion of him, but nothing suggests that he is so concerned that he's misrepresenting the events.

8. G   Difficulty: Medium

Category: Key Ideas and Details / Detail

Getting to the Answer: Locate the paragraph that contains the owner's explanation about "kindness" (lines 83–99) and review his story. To prevent the dog from following him to the factory, the owner chases him home "out of pure kindness." This matches (G). Choice F is a misused detail; the owner does make this claim in lines 64–66, but this is before he's trying to explain his behavior towards the dog as kindness. Choice H is out scope, as no mention is made of playing fetch, and the owner even admits that the throwing of "sticks an' stones" is meant to drive the dog home. Choice J is a distortion. While the owner does claim that the dog might be harmed at the factory, he does not claim that the men at the factory "have a record" of these types of actions in the past.

9. D   Difficulty: High

Category: Key Ideas and Details / Inference

Getting to the Answer: In lines 83–99, the owner explains his motivation for his treatment of the dog. After hearing this, the narrator is "somewhat doubtful of the truth of this story." The narrator had just seen the owner mistreating his dog, despite his claims, and his initial "scowl" morphs to a "deferential air" (line 79) as soon as the narrator threatens to have him arrested for his behavior. It seems that the owner is putting on an act to avoid prosecution, (D). Choice A is out of scope; the passage concludes before the purchase of the dog is discussed, so we don't know anything about the owner's eagerness. The narrator calls the owner "big" and "rough" (line 52) but never questions his employability, B, only his treatment of animals. Choice C is a distortion; the narrator's suspicion of the story stems from the owner's contradictory actions and behaviors, not his assumptions about conditions at the owner's workplace.

10. G   Difficulty: Medium

Category: Key Ideas and Details / Inference

Getting to the Answer: Keep in mind both the characters' actions and motivations as well as the timing. Immediately after the owner's story about why chasing the dog with sticks is "kindness," the narrator doubts this explanation and has the sudden thought of buying the dog (lines 100–105). The narrator has considered everything that's happened thus far and realizes that the win-win-win scenario for himself, the owner, and the dog is for him to buy the dog, (G). Choice F is a distortion. The first paragraphs do establish that the dog is "amiable," but the narrator is immediately motivated by his concern for the dog's welfare. Choice H is opposite; rather, he acts assertively towards the owner, as in lines 59–60: "as I felt confidence in my strength, my stick, and the goodness of my cause, I was bold." Choice J is also a distortion, as the narrator believes the owner is just pretending to have concern for the dog's welfare.

Passage II

Suggested Passage Map notes:

Passage A

¶1: Present-day people think science is unquestionable

¶2: History shows that science is not always correct

¶3: People think science remains constant, but questioning leads to progress

Passage B

¶1: Historically people were skeptical about science

¶2: Scientific research should be questioned

¶3: Pharma. company studies should be scrutinized

¶4: Policy decisions should be based on balance of faith and doubt

11. B   Difficulty: Low

Category: Key Ideas and Details / Detail

Getting to the Answer: The first mention of policy makers is in paragraph 1, lines 13–16, where the author writes that they "treat the results of every latest study as if they were surefire truths." In other words, they accept the results without question, which matches (B). Choices A, C, and D are opposites.

12. H   Difficulty: Low

Category: Craft and Structure / Writer's View

Getting to the Answer: Because the question cites a specific part of the passage, reread the relevant text to make a prediction. In line 33, the author uses the word *probabilities* to refer to the scientific discipline that studies the comparative chances of events taking place, which matches (H). Choice F is opposite; the author believes that science is uncertain, so theories will not necessarily be proven true. Choice G is out of scope; the author does not include information about how future scientists will impact current data. Choice J is a distortion; the author does state that "an unfounded prejudice stemming from a desire for scientific constancy can actually discourage inquiry," but that is not related to the idea that science is an implementation of probabilities.

13. C Difficulty: Medium

Category: Craft and Structure / Function

Getting to the Answer: The word *complacent* follows examples of predictable events, including a car starting and a power plant running without problems. Since we assume these events will always be the same, we become used to them and don't question them at all. In the same way, we have a "a complacent faith in the reliability and consistency of science" and assume that study results are always correct. Choice (C), *unquestioned*, is a synonym for *complacent*. All other choices are incorrect definitions based on the context provided.

14. G   Difficulty: Medium

Category: Key Ideas and Details / Detail

Getting to the Answer: If you have not made notes about various scientific studies in your map, scan through the passage looking for each of the answer choices, and

Answers & Explanations

eliminate those that were not accepted by the public. Choice F is questioned by "some critics," who we cannot assume are the general public. Choice H is in Passage A, not Passage B, and J isn't in the passages at all. That leaves (G) as the correct answer.

15. B   Difficulty: Medium

Category: Craft and Structure / Function

Getting to the Answer: Use your passage notes to help predict an answer for a Function question that refers to an entire paragraph. The first paragraph of Passage B outlines the way that skepticism toward science has changed over time. Choice (B) matches the function of paragraph 1. Choice A is out of scope; no new hypothesis is introduced in this paragraph. Choice C is a misused detail; paragraph 2 introduces the issue of public policy, but this question asks specifically about paragraph 1. Choice D is a misused detail; underlying causes are discussed in the third paragraph, not the first.

16. F   Difficulty: High

Category: Key Ideas and Details / Inference

Getting to the Answer: Remember not to make too big a logical leap; the correct inference will not stray far from the text. The author believes that people are too ready to believe the results of scientific studies. Choice (F) fits well with the text and represents a logical, supportable inference. Choice G is out of scope; neither author supports the idea of government control and regulation. Choice H is a misused detail; this idea applies to Passage A. Choice J is out of scope; the belief that the reliability of science has decreased isn't discussed in the passage.

17. C   Difficulty: High

Category: Integration of Knowledge and Ideas / Synthesis

Getting to the Answer: Keeping track of each author's primary viewpoints or beliefs can help you to more quickly evaluate and eliminate answer choices. Passage B describes a solution in which people understand enough about science to assess its reliability for themselves, but Passage A claims that people don't do this because they desire a world of certainties. The contrast between striving for more knowledge and clinging to easy beliefs is captured in (C). Choice A is a distortion; the actions and attitudes of policymakers don't prevent people from

becoming better educated. Choice B is a misused detail; Passage B discusses the difficulties of obtaining impartial results, but this is not relevant to the question. Choice D is out of scope; the author of Passage A discusses ethical questions, but this is not related to the solution specified in Passage B.

18. F   Difficulty: Low

Category: Key Ideas and Details / Detail

Getting to the Answer: Remember that the answers to Detail questions are always stated directly. By turning first to the passages, you can accurately predict the correct answer and not be misled by misused details. Passage A includes the phrase "present-day industrial societies" in the first sentence, and Passage B mentions "present-day industrial societies" in the second paragraph. Choice (F) matches your research. Choice G is a misused detail; this phrase is from paragraph 2 in Passage A. Choice H is a misused detail; this is included in paragraph 3 in Passage B. Choice J is a misused detail; this is mentioned in the first paragraph of Passage B only.

19. B   Category: Key Ideas and Details / Detail

Difficulty: Medium

Getting to the Answer: Prediction is key in Detail questions. Wrong answer choices will often reference other details erroneously. In paragraph 2, the passage directly states, "In the late 19th century, when Italian astronomer Giovanni Schiaparelli first detected seas and continents on the planet Mars, many people balked at the idea of Earth-like topography on the Red Planet," which shows the fallibility, or inaccuracy, of a scientific certainty. Use this as a prediction. Choice (B) matches the prediction. Choice A is a misused detail; this example is mentioned in Passage A, not Passage B. Choice C is a distortion; the author of Passage B discusses this in paragraph 4, but these are not examples of the fallibility of scientific certainties. Choice D is a misused detail; this example is mentioned in Passage A, not Passage B.

20. F   Difficulty: Medium

Category: Integration of Knowledge and Ideas / Synthesis

Getting to the Answer: When a question stem includes a specific line reference, you usually need to read a little before and a little after those particular lines in order to understand the full context of the quoted portion. The word cited in the question stem comes from the third paragraphs of Passage A and Passage B. Passage A says, "technological advances engage increasingly complex moral questions within fields such as pharmaceutical developments," and Passage B states, "Some critics of company-funded studies argue that the level of misrepresentation included in such studies borders on immoral." Choice (F) matches with the references to moral questions in both passages. Choice G is a misused detail; this is mentioned in Passage B only, in the last paragraph. Choice H is a misused detail; this is mentioned in Passage A only, in the third paragraph. Choice J is a misused detail; drug testing and analysis is discussed in paragraph 3 of Passage A but not in paragraph 3 of Passage B.

Passage III

Suggested Passage Map notes:

¶1: Walter Scott (S) born in Scotland in 1771, wrote Scottish ballads

¶2: S poetry brought fame

¶3: 1814, S started writing novels anonymously for $

¶4: 1820 S wrote *Ivanhoe* set in England, became Baronet

¶5: wrote for $ until his death in 1832

¶6: S (1) popularized historical novel, (2) rehabilitated Highland culture

¶7: S responsible for Scottish banks retaining right to issue own banknotes

21. B   Difficulty: Medium

Category: Key Ideas and Details / Global

Getting to the Answer: This question focuses on the big picture. You should be predicting the purpose and main idea of every passage so you can deal with questions like this quickly. Your notes should tell you that the author is writing more about Scott's achievements than about his weaknesses. You can predict that the answer will be favorable overall. Choice A is out of scope; this choice lacks a sufficient focus on Scott. Choice (B) matches your prediction. Scott's success is stressed throughout, and the last two paragraphs point out Scott's impact in several areas. Choice C is a distortion; although you read that

Scott had financial difficulties, the financial aspect is much less important than is the success of his writing. Choice D is a distortion; the passage offers no support for this claim.

22. J   Difficulty: Medium

Category: Key Ideas and Details / Detail

Getting to the Answer: On Detail questions, first find the appropriate section in the passage. Read the question carefully; sometimes a single word can make a major difference in selecting the correct answer. Note that the question asks about why Scott started writing novels, not poetry, so look to paragraph 3, where the author first talks about Scott's novels. The first line tells you that financial difficulties led Scott to write a novel, which met with great success. Look for a choice that matches this idea. Choice F is out of scope; the author doesn't list this outcome as a result of Scott's polio. Choice G is out of scope; nothing in the passage mentions "copyright violations." Choice H is out of scope; the author doesn't reference whether the ballads sold well or not. Choice (J) fits the prediction.

23. D   Difficulty: Low

Category: Key Ideas and Details / Detail

Getting to the Answer: If your notes don't help, titles, whether italicized or capitalized, are easier to spot when skimming. In the third paragraph, you see that the author references *Waverly* to mention that Scott left his name off it because he was "mindful of his reputation as a poet." Use this as your prediction. Choice A is a distortion; your research tells you that it was his reputation as a poet, not as a lawyer, that concerned Scott. Choice B is a misused detail; the author tells you that Scott found writing anonymously *fun* only after he believed that it would not damage his reputation as a poet. Choice C is out of scope; although the fact that Scott was "widely rumored" to be the author indicates that there was public interest in the novels' author, there is nothing to suggest that interest spurred sales. Choice (D) matches the prediction.

24. J   Difficulty: Medium

Category: Craft and Structure / Writer's View

Getting to the Answer: Use the passage to help you understand the author's view of this concept. First find where he refers to Scott and Scottish history, and

Answers & Explanations

then focus on the tone of that discussion. Consider the author's overall attitude toward Scott, which is positive. In paragraph 4, the author mentions Scott's popularization of the tartan and kilt and writes that he turned them into symbols of national identity. Also, in paragraph 6, you see in lines 85–86 that Scott's novels "rehabilitated Highland culture after years in the shadows." Choice F is opposite; the author's tone is more admiring than this. Choice G is opposite; to say that Scott "rehabilitated Highland culture" sounds important. Choice H is a distortion; Scott wrote novels, not "serious analyses of Scottish history." Choice (J) matches the research above.

25. A   Difficulty: Medium

Category: Key Ideas and Details / Global

Getting to the Answer: When in doubt, keep in mind the overall tone that the author takes in the passage. This question asks about Scott's reputation after his death. Since the overall structure of the passage is chronological, it is likely that the answer will come toward the end. The last three paragraphs give evidence of Scott's continued popularity: you read that his novels continued to sell after his death, eventually covering his debts; that Edinburgh's central railroad station was named after his first successful novel; and that his picture is on Scottish currency today. You can predict that his reputation has only grown or is still positive. Choice (A) matches the prediction, and a quick check of the other choices shows that this is the only one with a positive description. Choice B is opposite; the passage clearly states that Scott's novels continued to sell well after his death. Choice C is a distortion; his debts were unpaid, but this did not affect Scott's reputation. Choice D is a distortion; the passage does mention such imitators (lines 80–81), but the author doesn't suggest that they damaged Scott's reputation.

26. F   Difficulty: High

Category: Vocab-in-Context

Getting to the Answer: Sir Walter Scott never put his own name to his novels, but instead attributed them to "the author of *Waverly*," or to no author at all. He continued to do this even when his novels became so popular that it would not have hurt his reputation to reveal his name. Nevertheless, he "maintained the façade," meaning that he continued to hide his own authorship under the pretense that he was not the author of the

novels, a match for (F). Choice G is another definition of *façade*, but it doesn't make sense in the context of the passage. Choice H has a negative connotation, while the author says Scott maintained the pretense "out of a sense of fun." Choice J also doesn't make sense in the sentence.

27. B   Difficulty: Low

Category: Craft and Structure / Function

Getting to the Answer: To understand the function of a word in context, reading the entire sentence it appears in should be enough. Ask yourself why the placement of this statue would be fitting—the author has not referred to Wallace before this point. The author has, however, previously stressed Scott's affinity for his native land, Scotland, for which Wallace is a great historical figure. Look for a connection with Scotland among the choices. Choice A is out of scope; nothing in the passage suggests that Scott ever wrote a novel about Wallace. Choice (B) fits your prediction. Choice C is out of scope; this fails to address the issue of Wallace. Choice D is out of scope; the passage doesn't support this.

28. H   Difficulty: Medium

Category: Craft and Structure / Writer's View

Getting to the Answer: You will need to answer this question from your overall impression of the passage rather than any specific paragraph. First, you need to decide whether the author's attitude is positive or negative. Look to the close of the passage; you know that the author believes Scott was responsible for two major trends. The focus on Scott's achievements indicates that the author admires Scott's work. Choice F is a distortion; nothing indicates that the author is skeptical toward Scott's achievements. Choice G is opposite; both of these adjectives are too negative. Choice (H) matches your prediction. Choice J is out of scope; the passage gives no such indication of jealousy.

29. D   Difficulty: Low

Category: Key Ideas and Details / Global

Getting to the Answer: Paragraph references focus your research. Use your notes and reference the passage as needed. The author writes that Sir Walter refused to declare bankruptcy, insisting on putting his home and income into a trust that would eventually pay back his creditors completely. Predict that he was committed to paying his debts back. Choice A is opposite; the passage clearly contradicts this. Choice B is out of scope; the author never discusses the cause of Scott's debts. Choice C is out of scope; the author doesn't mention such annoyance on Scott's part. Choice (D) matches the prediction.

30. F   Difficulty: Low

Category: Craft and Structure / Writer's View

Getting to the Answer: Read the complete sentence for context. You may need to read the ones before and after as well. The prior sentence states that Scott was working as a lawyer, after which you read the first mention of Scott's writings. The subsequent sentences make clear that the emphasis has shifted to Scott's literary career. So the sentence including *dabbling* deals with Scott's first forays into writing. Look for a choice that captures that idea. Choice (F) matches the thrust of the prediction. Choice G is a misused detail; Scott's printing press is not mentioned until paragraph 3, and the author draws no connection between his *dabbling* and his financial troubles. Choice H is a distortion; he was certainly inexperienced, but there is no evidence that his work was inferior. Choice J is a distortion; *dabbling* refers to Scott's writing, not to his interest in history.

Passage IV

Suggested Passage Map notes:

¶1: Lemur (L) part of suborder of primates, nocturnal; flying lemurs not primates

¶2: L found on Madagascar, larger are nocturnal, smaller are diurnal

¶3: All L species are endangered b/c deforestation and hunting

¶4: Ring-tailed lemur (RTL) most populous L in zoos

¶5: RTL physical characteristics

¶6: RTL baby v. adult characteristics

¶7: RTL live in forests or open brush, require primary forests

¶8: RTL behavior, territory

¶9: RTL communication

¶10: RTL breeding

31. C   Category: Key Ideas and Details / Detail

Difficulty: Low

Getting to the Answer: Wrong answers on Detail questions often include material relevant to other sections of the passage. Be sure you research the passage carefully to interpret the context correctly. You are looking for a factor that is responsible for the lemurs' survival. Your notes should help you find your way to paragraph 2, where the author first discusses Madagascar. The author says the lemurs "were safe from competition" on the island. That should factor into the correct choice. Choice A is a misused detail; the author does mention that lemurs have large reflective eyes, but doesn't relate this to survival. Choice B is a misused detail; scent marking is related to their social organization, not their survival. Choice (C) paraphrases the relevant sentence in paragraph 2. Choice D is a misused detail; the author mentions *hierarchy* later, but not as an explanation for the lemurs' survival.

32. F   Difficulty: Medium

Category: Key Ideas and Details / Detail

Getting to the Answer: Taking good notes and marking the passage will help you on Detail questions that lack line references. From your notes, you should see that social organization is discussed in paragraph 8. The writer states that there are separate hierarchies for each gender and that "females tend to dominate the troop." Look for this among the choices. Choice (F) matches your prediction. Choice G is a distortion; the author does reference *foraging*, but not in the context of social organization. Choice H is out of scope; the author doesn't offer support for such a sweeping statement. Choice J is opposite; the author writes that females tend to dominate the troop.

33. D   Difficulty: Medium

Category: Vocab-in-Context

Getting to the Answer: Since *odd* is a common word, it's important to think about it the specific context of what the author has written. He uses the word when describing what ring-tailed lemurs usually eat—fruit, leaves, and seeds, plus an insect every now and then. Thus *odd* refers to occasionally, as (D) says. All other answer choices are possible definitions of *odd*, but none make sense in the sentence.

34. G   Difficulty: Medium

Category: Key Ideas and Details / Detail

Getting to the Answer: The answers to Detail questions are stated directly in the passage—you can find the answer with research. This point is fairly obscure and may not be reflected in your notes. If you have to, skim for *zoo*, which appears in paragraph 4. The author states that ring-tailed lemurs are the most populous lemurs in zoos and follows that by writing "they reproduce readily in captivity." Use that as your prediction. Choice F is out of scope; the author doesn't make such a contention. Choice (G) is a good paraphrase of the text referenced above. Choice H is out of scope; the author does not make this point. Choice J is a distortion; the author addresses *foraging*, but not in connection with zoos.

35. D   Difficulty: Medium

Category: Key Ideas and Details / Inference

Getting to the Answer: When given a line reference, move quickly and read at least that entire sentence to discern context. The author indicates that lemurs need to live in primary forest to survive. The clearing will likely endanger the lemurs' continued survival. Look for a match to this idea. Choice A is out of scope; the author does not refer to this. Choice B is out of scope; the author does not refer to this. Choice C is out of scope; the author doesn't reference such predators here. Choice (D) matches the research above.

36. H   Difficulty: Low

Category: Key Ideas and Details / Detail

Getting to the Answer: This is an EXCEPT question. That means you need to find three choices that are mentioned in the text and one that is not mentioned. Don't confuse the two. Your notes can help you to locate "olfactory signals"; they appear in paragraph 9. Work through the paragraph, crossing off the three choices that do appear. Choice F is opposite; this appears in line 88–89. Choice G is opposite; this appears in line 90–91. The author does not reference (H), which makes it the correct answer. Choice J is opposite; this appears in line 88.

37. B   Difficulty: Medium

Category: Key Ideas and Details / Detail

Getting to the Answer: Detail questions are answered directly in the passage. Referencing it before making a prediction will help you avoid misused details. Note that the question concerns all Lemuriformes, not only ring-tailed lemurs. This leads you to the first paragraph, which discusses lemurs in general. You may be unsure exactly which characteristic to predict, so compare this paragraph to the choices. Choice A is a distortion; many lemurs are nocturnal, but not all lemurs are. Choice (B) makes sense. Paragraph 1 states that lemurs represent the "evolutionary predecessor" of monkeys and apes, a paraphrase of what you see here. Choice C is opposite; at the end of paragraph 1, the author clearly states that these species are not actually lemurs (*Lemuriformes*). Choice D is opposite; the first sentence in paragraph 2 states that lemurs are found on Madagascar "and some smaller surrounding islands."

38. H   Difficulty: Medium

Category: Key Ideas and Details / Inference

Getting to the Answer: You need to "read between the lines" to find the correct answer. But don't make too great a logical leap. Check your notes for the second paragraph, and read it again if necessary. The question is very open-ended, so work through the choices and compare them to the information in the paragraph. Choice F is opposite; the author states that the pygmy mouse lemur is the smallest species and that smaller species are typically nocturnal, not diurnal. Choice G is out of scope; the author does not discuss why certain species of lemur have become extinct. Choice (H) works. The author writes that the indri was the largest lemur. The next sentence states that "the larger species" are all extinct. Therefore, you can infer that the indri is extinct. Choice J is opposite; in paragraph 1, you learn that lemurs are described as evolutionary *predecessors* of monkeys, meaning monkeys are descended from them.

39. C   Difficulty: Medium

Category: Key Ideas and Details / Detail

Getting to the Answer: Your map should note that paragraphs 5 and 6 describe the physical attributes of ring-tailed lemurs, and paragraph 6 states that "the very young animals have blue eyes while the eyes of all adults are a striking yellow." Since there's no other reference to anything else that changes when ring-tailed lemurs become adults, (C) has to be the correct answer. Choice A is out of scope; there's nothing in the passage that supports this. Choice B is contradicted by the sentence "Ring-tailed lemurs are thought to require primary forest" (lines 66–67). D is opposite; flying lemurs are not lemurs at all, as lines 11–12 state.

40. F   Difficulty: Medium

Category: Key Ideas and Details / Detail

Getting to the Answer: Because this question asks which question is not answered, it functions as an EXCEPT question. Find the issue that is not addressed in the passage. The answers to these questions could fall anywhere in the passage. Your notes, though, should help you find the information you need. The author touches on (F) in paragraph 3, saying that "options are limited." This implies that the question of survival has not been fully answered. If you're unsure at this point, work through the others to see that they are answered. Choice G is opposite; this is answered in the second sentence of paragraph 2. Lemurs survived because they did not have to compete with monkeys and apes. Choice H is opposite; looking at the last paragraph, you see that the female is fertile for only one day a year, and that gestation lasts 146 days. So the female can have only one litter, and the author states that a litter consists of one or two babies. Choice J is opposite; this is answered in paragraph 8. The author states lemurs eat fruit, "leaves, seeds, and the odd insect."

SCIENCE TEST

Passage I

1. C   Difficulty: Medium

Category: Evaluation of Models, Inferences, and Results

Getting to the Answer: According to Scientist 2, the positions of electrons are "random and yet localized" as they move around the nucleus. They don't follow fixed orbits, but they are more likely to be in some places than others. Thus, one way to describe the movement of electrons would be to say that it's "almost random," as in (C). Choice A is incorrect because it better describes the Bohr model. Choices B and D are incorrect because they contradict both models; both suggest that electrons move around the nucleus in some way.

2. J   Difficulty: High

Category: Evaluation of Models, Inferences, and Results

Getting to the Answer: Scientist 2 mentions the wave function in order to explain the way in which an electron's possible position is given boundaries. These boundaries determine the shape of an atom, which in turn helps to define many of its properties. Choice (J) is thus correct. Choice F conflates the two models, but only the Bohr model describes orbits and only the electron cloud model deals with probabilities. Choice G is incorrect because neither scientist suggests a dependence between charge and the color of light emitted by an atom. Choice H is incorrect because Scientist 2 only discusses the wave-particle duality with respect to electrons.

3. A   Difficulty: Low

Category: Evaluation of Models, Inferences, and Results

Getting to the Answer: Although the two models offer differing accounts of how electrons move around the nucleus, both agree that electrons move rather than remaining in a fixed position. Choice (A) is thus correct. Choice B is incorrect because neither view suggests that charge is based on probability; only the electron cloud model discusses probability, but there it is applied only to position, not charge. Choice C is incorrect because neither scientist discusses the composition of protons and neutrons. Choice D is incorrect because both views discuss the components of atoms, suggesting that atoms can in fact be divided into smaller parts.

4. G   Difficulty: Medium

Category: Evaluation of Models, Inferences, and Results

Getting to the Answer: Scientist 1 cites the fact that excited electrons emit very specific wavelengths of light when reverting to lower energy orbits, and makes the following argument in favor of the Bohr model: "If the position of electrons is not specified, the precise wave-lengths of light that are emitted cannot be explained." This poses a direct challenge to the view of Scientist 2, so (G) is correct. Choice F is incorrect because it contradicts the views of both scientists. Choice H is incorrect because it's cited by Scientist 2 as support for the probability cloud idea. Choice J is incorrect because it's a fact agreed to by both scientists.

5. A **Difficulty:** High

Category: Evaluation of Models, Inferences, and Results

Getting to the Answer: According to Scientist 2, "[t]he uncertainty of any one electron's position and the nature of its existence as a charged particle contribute to an understanding of the wave-particle nature of matter and energy." The findings mentioned in the question stem further support this wave-particle duality. Therefore, (A) is correct. Choice B is incorrect because traveling in distinct paths is part of the Bohr model. Choices C and D are incorrect because they suggest the observation supports the Bohr model. Choice D also wrongly supplies reasoning in favor of the electron cloud model rather than the Bohr model.

6. H **Difficulty:** Medium

Category: Evaluation of Models, Inferences, and Results

Getting to the Answer: Scientist 2 begins by stating that "[t]he precise location of electrons cannot be detected." This challenges the idea from the Bohr model that electrons travel in fixed paths, which would allow their locations to be identified precisely. Choice (H) is therefore correct. Choice F is incorrect because it is not inconsistent with the Bohr model (Scientist 1 would say that electrons have a 100% chance of occupying one of the fixed orbit paths, and a 0% chance of being elsewhere). Choices G and J and incorrect because they are not discussed by Scientist 2.

7. C **Difficulty:** Medium

Category: Evaluation of Models, Inferences, and Results

Getting to the Answer: According to Scientist 1's account of the Bohr model, "[e]lectrons move around an atom's nucleus in precise, co-planar, concentric circular

orbits." Choice (C) is the only option that reflects this. Choice A in incorrect because it shows an atom without a nucleus. Choice B shows an atom with orbiting electrons, but the electrons do not orbit in co-planar, concentric circles. Choice D would be a better representation of the electron cloud model.

Passage II

8. G **Difficulty:** Low

Category: Scientific Investigation

Getting to the Answer: This question simply requires you to find the answer choice that reflects differences in sampling between the two studies. The passage notes that sampling was conducted "at ground level" for Study 1 but "from the tops of two different monitoring towers" for Study 2. Choice (G) is thus correct. Choice F contradicts the passage—in both experiments, sampling was done on a daily basis. Choice H is tempting, but it switches the studies, making the statement untrue. Choice J does not work either—both pollutants mentioned were sampled in each experiment.

9. B **Difficulty:** Medium

Category: Scientific Investigation

Getting to the Answer: Although several of these procedures might be worthwhile, only (B) correctly proposes studying all three variables mentioned in the question stem (carbon monoxide, sulfur dioxide, and respiratory ailments). Choice A includes a respiratory ailment (asthma), but it is incorrect because temperature was not one of the variables mentioned. Choices C and D are incorrect because they describe procedures that would not provide any information about respiratory ailments.

10. J **Difficulty:** Medium

Category: Scientific Investigation

Getting to the Answer: To test the hypothesis from the question stem, you'd need an experiment that relates sulfur dioxide and the acidity of lakes. Only (J) connects sulfur dioxide to the acidity of lake water, so it is correct. Choice F is incorrect because it doesn't provide a link between sulfur dioxide and lake acidity.

Choice G might be tempting because the passage does mention respiratory ailments, but G also fails to provide a direct link between sulfur emissions and lake acidity. Choice H is also incorrect: while the amount of coal burned might increase the amount of sulfur dioxide emitted by the plant, doing this alone won't tell you anything about the link between sulfur dioxide and the acidity of the lake.

11. A   Difficulty: Medium

Category: Scientific Investigation

Getting to the Answer: The first paragraph describes the motivation behind the studies: "Scientists noted an increase in acid rainfall and reports of respiratory ailments in a certain community. They suspected that both of these outcomes were due to increased levels of airborne pollutants, such as carbon monoxide and sulfur dioxide, entering the atmosphere in that community." Because Study 1 involved measuring the levels of these pollutants near two highways, it is reasonable to conclude that the scientists were trying to determine if pollution from traffic was the source of these respiratory problems. This fits well with the hypothesis expressed in (A). Choice B is incorrect because the power plant is only a factor in Study 2, not Study 1. Choice C incorrectly states that Study 1 was concerned with measuring rainfall. Choice D is incorrect because it fails to involve respiratory ailments.

12. F   Difficulty: Medium

Category: Interpretation of Data

Getting to the Answer: The studies in this passage indicate that emissions from highway traffic and from power plants contribute to increases in airborne pollutants. Building more highways, as in (F), would consequently increase, rather than reduce, highway traffic and subsequent pollution, making (F) the best answer. Choice G is incorrect because it would help: highway traffic is indicated as a source of pollutants, so traffic limits would help reduce pollution due to highway vehicles. Choice H would also help: burning coal is the source of the power plant's pollutant emissions, so reducing coal burning would reduce emission levels. Choice J is incorrect for a similar reason: filters would decrease the amount of sulfur dioxide reaching the outside air, thereby reducing nearby levels of this airborne pollutant.

13. D   Difficulty: Medium

Category: Interpretation of Data

Getting to the Answer: If emissions become less concentrated farther away from their sources, what would you expect to happen if you moved closer to the source? You could expect emissions measured closer to a source (the roadway, in this case) to be more concentrated. Thus, the correct answer will be larger than the data point for Highway 1 on January 7 in Table 1, which is 3.2 ppm. Choice (D) is the only option larger than 3.2 ppm, so it is correct. Choices A, B, and C are all smaller than 3.2 ppm.

14. F   Difficulty: Medium

Category: Interpretation of Data

Getting to the Answer: Look carefully at Table 2, which compiles the results of Study 2. According to the table, ozone and sulfur dioxide levels both show an increase followed by a decrease in both towers, supporting statement I. Because I is true, G can be eliminated. Carbon monoxide levels were always greater in Tower 1, not Tower 2, so statement II is false, meaning that H and J can also be eliminated. Choice (F) must therefore be correct. This can be confirmed by determining that statement III is false: Tower 2 had the highest level of emissions on January 8, not January 9.

Passage III

15. D   Difficulty: Medium

Category: Interpretation of Data

Getting to the Answer: Each of the tables includes rubber, which always produces an amperage of 0.0 mA. This means A can be eliminated. Study 2 and Study 3 both use 6 mm wire, but only Study 3 was conducted at 30°C, so use Table 3 to find the range. The highest value is 12.1 mA, so the range is 0.0 mA to 12.1 mA. Choice (D) matches this range. Choices B and C give the ranges for Study 1 and Study 2, respectively.

16. G   Difficulty: Low

Category: Evaluation of Models, Inferences, and Results

Getting to the Answer: Comparing the data in Tables 1 and 2 shows that for most of the materials tested in these experiments, the current carried by the wire increases as the diameter of the wire increases. The exception is rubber, which does not carry current in any of these trials, so it is the only material that does not support the hypothesis that a larger diameter results in more current carried. Choice (G) is thus correct.

17. D   Difficulty: Medium

Category: Interpretation of Data

Getting to the Answer: Start by looking at what happens to current when the diameter of a zinc telluride (ZnTe) wire increases. Tables 1 and 2 show that when the diameter increases, the amount of current conducted increases. For temperature, comparing Tables 2 and 3 shows that when temperature decreases, current increases. Thus, to find the wire that would carry the largest current, you want the wire with the largest diameter and the lowest temperature. Choice (D) is thus correct.

18. F   Difficulty: Medium

Category: Scientific Investigation

Getting to the Answer: The conditions described in the question stem differ from the setup of any of the studies conducted in the passage, but the key is to focus on the most important information. The materials of the wires are copper, rubber, and steel. According to the results of the 3 studies, rubber always yields an ammeter reading of 0.0 mA. This makes it an insulator, according to the definition provided in the introductory paragraph, that is, "a substance that prevents an electric charge from traveling between objects." Because the rubber wire interrupts the flow of charge in the circuit, no current will be conducted, so the ammeter will read 0.0 mA. Choice (F) is thus correct.

19. A   Difficulty: Medium

Category: Scientific Investigation

Getting to the Answer: The scientist hypothesized that decreasing the temperature increases the amount of current a wire will carry, and this hypothesis was generally supported by a comparison of the results in Tables 2 and 3, with the exception of rubber, which never conducted a current. Consequently, if the temperature of a wire were instead *increased*, the amount of current carried would *decrease*, except for rubber, which would remain

unchanged at 0.0 mA. Choice (A) is thus correct. Choice B is incorrect because only the current for rubber would remain unchanged. Choice C is incorrect because the current would never increase at a higher temperature; it would only decrease or remain unchanged. Choice D is incorrect because the current would decrease for most of the materials.

20. J   Difficulty: Medium

Category: Evaluation of Models, Inferences, and Results

Getting to the Answer: You can see by looking at the tables that rubber conducts 0.0 mA of electricity throughout all three studies. Because it prevents the flow of current, this makes it an insulator, based on the definition provided in the passage. However, because the results of all three studies are the same for rubber, it does not appear that its capacity as an insulator is affected by changes to its diameter or temperature. Choice (J) is thus correct.

21. D   Difficulty: Low

Category: Scientific Investigation

Getting to the Answer: The question asks you to identify which effect the scientist should investigate next to learn more. Choice A, however, was revealed by comparing the results of Studies 2 and 3, while B was revealed by comparing Studies 1 and 2. Choice C was investigated in all of the studies. That leaves (D), which is correct because wire length was held constant throughout all of the studies, so it would be an appropriate choice to manipulate in a future study to determine its effect on current conducted.

Passage IV

22. J   Difficulty: Low

Category: Interpretation of Data

Getting to the Answer: The question stem points you to the top two curves in Figure 1. To find the greatest difference, determine the average air temperature in August for the urban area (the solid line) and rural area (the dash-dot line) for each of the years listed in the answer choices. The respective August urban and rural temperatures were approximately 75°F and 68°F in 2007; 77°F and 70°F in 2010; 73°F and 66°F in 2012; and 74°F and 63°F in 2014. The differences in temperature between urban and rural are 7°F in 2007, 2010, and 2012, and 11°F in 2014. Therefore, the correct answer is (J). Alternatively, rather than calculate the exact differences, you could eyeball the graph and estimate; it shouldn't be too hard to see that the gap between the top two curves is wider for 2014 than for the other years.

23. A   Difficulty: Low

Category: Interpretation of Data

Getting to the Answer: Look at Figure 3 to find out which pair of months had the closest average wind velocities. According to Figure 3, the average wind velocity for the rural area was approximately 16 mph for January, 16 mph for April, 13 mph for July, 20 mph for September, and 23 mph for November. Since the average wind velocities for January and April are about the same, the correct answer is (A).

24. H   Difficulty: Medium

Category: Evaluation of Models, Inferences, and Results

Getting to the Answer: The question stem mentions Study 3, in which the scientists studied wind velocity and air quality. Eliminate G and J, which mention average air temperature (the focus of Study 1). The new evidence states that buildings increase frictional drag on air flowing over built-up terrain. An increase in frictional drag would lead to lower wind velocity, which means that having more buildings lowers wind velocity. According to Figure 3, the average wind velocity is lower for the urban area than for the rural area, which suggests that there are more buildings in the urban area. Thus, the conclusion in the question stem that the rural area has more buildings than the urban area would NOT be justified based on the results. The correct answer is (H). Even if you were unaware of what effect frictional drag would have on wind velocity, you could still eliminate F because it provides the reasoning that wind velocity is lower for the rural area, which is directly contradicted by Figure 3.

25. C   Difficulty: Medium

Category: Evaluation of Models, Inferences, and Results

Getting to the Answer: According to Study 1, "compared to the relative humidity of the rural area, the relative humidity of the urban area was 2% lower in the winter and 6% lower in the summer." Figure 1 shows a similar relationship for average air temperature differences. The difference in the average summer air temperatures between the urban and rural areas is greater than the difference in the average winter air temperatures. Thus, because they follow similar trends, you can conclude that relative humidity differences and average air temperature differences are correlated. The correct answer is (C). Choice A is not true according to the passage: the relative humidity is lower for the urban area. Choice B is true but does not answer the question, which concerns both winter and summer temperature differences. Choice D is incorrect because it mentions wind velocity, which was measured in Study 3 and not Study 1.

26. G   Difficulty: Medium

Category: Evaluation of Models, Inferences, and Results

Getting to the Answer: The hypothesis from the question stem suggests that since building materials and road surfaces increase the air temperature of urban areas, urban areas would have higher air temperature than rural areas. According to Figure 1, the summer temperatures of the urban area during August are higher than those of the rural area during August. Therefore, yes, the results do support the hypothesis. Eliminate H and J. Choice (G) correctly states summer temperatures in the urban area were higher than those in the rural area, making (G) the correct answer.

27. B   Difficulty: Medium

Category: Scientific Investigation

Getting to the Answer: Make sure your response draws from the information given in the passage and question stem. According to Study 3, there are about 10 times more dust particles in the air of the urban area than of the rural area. Given that dust particles act as hygroscopic nuclei, it is likely that the urban areas will have more rain because of the higher level of dust in the air at those areas. And, indeed, Figure 2 shows that the urban area received more precipitation than the rural area. Thus, the correct answer is (B). Choices A, C, and D are not true statements. According to the passage, compared to the urban area, the rural area had higher wind velocity, fewer clouds, and higher relative humidity.

28. F   Difficulty: Medium

Category: Interpretation of Data

Getting to the Answer: Based on Figure 1, 75°F is approximately the average air temperature for the urban area in the summer, while Figure 2 suggests that the average annual precipitation for the urban area is about 40 inches. Therefore, this third area is likely also an urban area, which could be expected to have a similar wind velocity to the urban area that was studied. According to Figure 3, the wind velocity for the urban area varied between about 8 and 12 mph. Thus, it is reasonable to expect that this third area will have an average wind velocity of somewhere between 8 and 12 mph, as in (F).

Passage V

29. A   Difficulty: Medium

Category: Interpretation of Data

Getting to the Answer: Based on Figure 2, Mercury speeds up as it approaches perihelion and slows down as it moves away. Choice (A) is thus correct. Choice B suggests the opposite trend. Choice C suggests that orbital velocity decreases, but that happens only as the planet moves away from perihelion. Choice D suggests that orbital velocity increases, but that happens only as the planet moves toward perihelion.

30. H   Difficulty: Low

Category: Interpretation of Data

Getting to the Answer: A planet with a mass in between that of Jupiter and Saturn, assuming a similar density, would have a radius that lies between the radii of Jupiter and Saturn, that is, between 58,232 and 69,911 km. Only (H) falls into this range. Choice F suggests a radius less than that of Mercury. Choice G suggests a radius between that of Earth and Venus. Choice J suggests a radius larger than that of Jupiter.

31. B   Difficulty: Low

Category: Interpretation of Data

Getting to the Answer: According to Table 1, Saturn has a mass of 5.68×10^{26} kg, Jupiter a mass of 1.90×10^{27} kg,

Earth a mass of 5.97×10^{24} kg, and Mercury a mass of 3.29×10^{23} kg. Of these, Jupiter has the greatest mass, so (B) is correct.

32. G   Difficulty: Medium

Category: Interpretation of Data

Getting to the Answer: Based on Figure 2, Mercury's orbital velocity at 75×10^6 km away from perihelion is roughly 53 m/s. The next point at which it has this orbital velocity is 75×10^6 km as it recedes from perihelion. Choice (G) is thus correct. This can also be seen from the symmetry of Mercury's curve in Figure 2: the velocity at a particular distance while approaching is always equal to the velocity at that same distance while receding. Choice F is incorrect because it corresponds to a velocity of about 50 m/s. Choices H and J are incorrect because both correspond to a velocity of about 56 m/s.

33. C   Difficulty: Medium

Category: Interpretation of Data

Getting to the Answer: Acceleration is simply the change in velocity per unit of time, so a larger acceleration due to gravity will cause a falling object to reach a given velocity more quickly—in other words, it will cause the object to fall faster. Because Earth has a higher acceleration due to gravity than does Venus, objects on Earth fall faster than objects on Venus. Choice (C) is thus correct.

34. G   Difficulty: Medium

Category: Interpretation of Data

Getting to the Answer: According to Table 1, Mercury has a mass of 3.29×10^{23} kg and a radius of 2,440 km, while Venus has a mass of 4.87×10^{24} kg and a radius of 6,052 km. The mass and radius of the new planet in the question stem fall in between the values for Mercury and Venus, so it is reasonable to predict that it would have a velocity at perihelion that falls in between Mercury's velocity of about 59 m/s and Venus's velocity of about 35 m/s. Choice (G) is correct because it is the only value that falls within this range.

Passage VI

35. A   Difficulty: Medium

Category: Interpretation of Data

Getting to the Answer: As can be seen in Figure 1, titration of a strong base into a strong acid generates a curve that starts with an acidic pH (a value considerably less than 7), followed by a sharp increase to a basic pH (a value considerably greater than 7). Titration of a strong acid into a strong base would show the reverse behavior, starting well above pH 7 and finishing well below pH 7. Choice (A) is thus correct. Choice B has an appropriate appearance, but it is incorrect because it bottoms out near a neutral pH (near 7) instead of an acidic pH. Choices C and D are incorrect because their curves do not match the general shape seen in Figure 1.

36. H   Difficulty: Medium

Category: Interpretation of Data

Getting to the Answer: This question asks about the equivalence point, which is defined in the passage as "the point at which equal concentrations of an acid and base are present." The passage also notes that the change in pH immediately after and immediately before the equivalence point will be drastic, so you should look for the point in the middle of the sharp increase for Solution A in Figure 1. Based on the figure, the equivalence point for Solution A is found at a pH of about 7 (after approximately 24 mL of NaOH have been added). According to Table 1, phenol red has a pH range of 6.8 – 8.4, making it the only indicator that includes pH 7 in its range. Choice (H) is thus correct. Choices F and G are incorrect because they change colors at too low of a pH, while J is incorrect because it changes colors at too high of a pH.

37. C   Difficulty: Low

Category: Interpretation of Data

Getting to the Answer: This question is easier to answer if you remember from high school chemistry that 7 is a neutral pH. The passage describes the chemical equation as "a typical acid-base neutralization reaction." Thus, if it goes to completion without excess reactants, the resulting solution should have a neutral pH of 7. Choice (C) is correct. Choices A and B present acidic pH values, while D presents a basic pH.

38. G   Difficulty: Medium

Category: Interpretation of Data

Getting to the Answer: Figure 2 presents the reaction rate as a percentage of the rate at the equivalence point. Thus, any percentage value greater than 100% corresponds to a reaction rate that is faster than the rate at the equivalence point. The curve in Figure 2 is above 100% between approximately 1 mL and 24 mL. Choice (G) is correct because it is the only option with a volume in this range.

39. B   Difficulty: Medium

Category: Interpretation of Data

Getting to the Answer: Familiarity with the names of elements and simple compounds will help to answer this question. According to the reaction presented in the passage, sodium (Na) moves from NaOH to NaCl as the reaction proceeds forward. NaCl is sodium chloride, commonly known as table salt. Choice (B) is correct. Choices A and C are incorrect because water (H_2O) and hydrochloric acid (HCl) do not contain sodium. Choice D is incorrect because sodium hydroxide (NaOH) is where the sodium is found before the reaction, not after it.

40. J   Difficulty: Medium

Category: Interpretation of Data

Getting to the Answer: Because the question asks about a reaction rate, look at Figure 2 first. The highest reaction rate (with a value of over 125%) is found after about 5 mL of NaOH have been added. Figure 1 shows low pH values for both solutions at 5 mL of NaOH. Choice (J) is correct because it is the only option that features a low pH. Choices F and G are incorrect because both points are found after about 24 mL of NaOH have been added, when the reaction rate is only 100%. Choice H is incorrect because a high pH in Solution A is only found after about 25 mL or more of NaOH have been added, when the reaction rate drops below 100%.

WRITING TEST

MODEL ESSAY

Below is an example of what a high-scoring essay might look like. Notice the author states her position clearly in the introductory paragraph and supports that position with evidence in the following paragraphs. This essay also uses transitions, some advanced vocabulary, and an effective "hook" to draw in the reader.

In today's world the truth of the matter is that a high school diploma no longer makes a job applicant competitive; a college degree is now required for most high-paying jobs which also offer advancement opportunities. Given the high cost of a college education—and even community college fees may be beyond the reach of some students—taking out a student loan is almost a given for the college student. The question is, however, how these loans should be structured. Several options are offered, but the fairest and most workable is that of no-interest government and bank loans.

Firstly, as the issue states, student loans can take years to repay, even when the former students earn good salaries and repay the loan month by month. This is simply because the cost of a college education is so high. The average cost of a four-year college ranges from almost $10,000 per year to over $35,000. For all but the wealthiest of students, paying for college without a loan is prohibitive. My cousin spent years trying to pay off her student loans and, in the long run, defaulted and had to declare bankruptcy. Surely this is not the intention of either the government, other lending institutions, or colleges.

Loans are not special entitlements; they are fundamental to allow students of all economic backgrounds to attend college. As such, the government should not be making money from student loans. Interest is essentially a fee charged for borrowing money, with some sort of collateral insuring repayment. In the case of a college loan, that collateral is the student's future earning capacity. Granted, the principal must be repaid, but beyond that, taking money out of earnings cuts into the former student's ability to use that money for other purchases, including housing, which are so vital in driving the country's economy. Charging only the principal needed to pay for college insures that students can not only pay the yearly tuition, but are also more likely to be able to settle the entire loan and after graduation, contribute to the economy as a whole. In the special circumstance that some students need more time, it is then fair to add some further amount of payment as recognition that the original agreement was not fulfilled. This is the fairest solution and one that provides the greatest opportunity for students to go to college and pay off their loans.

The second option defines a college education as a commodity, which is something that can be bought and sold and also implies choice. Although it can be argued that a college education can be bought, it is not the same as oil or wheat. It is not used for the moment but for the future and it cannot be compared to loans for items that people choose to buy, such as cars or refrigerators. Loans to support an educated populace as the backbone of our society are not the same as car loans and should not be treated as such. If we truly believe in education, we must make allowances for the loans required to fund it. As we have all learned, college is an investment in the future. It has become less and less a personal choice and more of a requirement for job consideration. When considered on a supply and demand basis, it is even more important, since studies show that jobs requiring a college degree are in more and more demand. A capitalist market requires the ability to be competitive and creative; this is exactly what a college education provides. Educated students are far more important than almost anything else a loan can support, and any accommodations, including making college loans less expensive than other loans, is for the benefit of society and the future, and should be promoted, not prohibited.

Finally, the third point of view is simply ridiculous. There is absolutely no way to determine how much money a person will earn in the future. We can make considered guesses—lawyers will earn more than waiters—but there is no guarantee that the lawyer will not be fired and the waiter will not become a restaurant owner. Basing the loan amount on future earnings can also mean that the graduate has no opportunity to change his career from a high-earning one, such as a lawyer, to one that may truly be his heart's desire, such as being an artist. Furthermore, even if one were to train to be a lawyer, it is possible that he will not find a job that pays him the same amount of money the loan projected him to earn. At one time, investment counselors were earning a lot of money, and therefore would have been low-risk borrowers, but after the investment scandal several years ago, many investment counselors are doing other jobs, have no job, or may even be in jail. College graduates are just starting their careers; how well they do, what they earn, and whether they stay in their original jobs are unknown and cannot be used to determine a loan amount.

College loans should be as accessible and easy to repay as possible. There is nothing more important than an educated and far-sighted generation of college graduates. They are the ones who will run the government, captain business, and teach children. To deprive them of their college opportunity by making it too hard for them to either get or repay adequate loans is to deprive this country of those who will steer its future.

You can evaluate your essay and the model essay based on the following criteria:

- Is the author's own perspective clearly stated?
- Does the body of the essay assess and analyze an additional perspective?
- Is the relevance of each paragraph clear?
- Does the author start a new paragraph for each new idea?
- Is each sentence in a paragraph relevant to the point made in that paragraph?
- Are transitions clear?
- Is the essay easy to read?
- Is it engaging?
- Are sentences varied?
- Is vocabulary used effectively?
- Is college-level vocabulary used?

ACT Practice Test 8
ANSWER SHEET

ENGLISH TEST

1. (A)(B)(C)(D)	11. (A)(B)(C)(D)	21. (A)(B)(C)(D)	31. (A)(B)(C)(D)	41. (A)(B)(C)(D)	51. (A)(B)(C)(D)	61. (A)(B)(C)(D)	71. (A)(B)(C)(D)
2. (F)(G)(H)(J)	12. (F)(G)(H)(J)	22. (F)(G)(H)(J)	32. (F)(G)(H)(J)	42. (F)(G)(H)(J)	52. (F)(G)(H)(J)	62. (F)(G)(H)(J)	72. (F)(G)(H)(J)
3. (A)(B)(C)(D)	13. (A)(B)(C)(D)	23. (A)(B)(C)(D)	33. (A)(B)(C)(D)	43. (A)(B)(C)(D)	53. (A)(B)(C)(D)	63. (A)(B)(C)(D)	73. (A)(B)(C)(D)
4. (F)(G)(H)(J)	14. (F)(G)(H)(J)	24. (F)(G)(H)(J)	34. (F)(G)(H)(J)	44. (F)(G)(H)(J)	54. (F)(G)(H)(J)	64. (F)(G)(H)(J)	74. (F)(G)(H)(J)
5. (A)(B)(C)(D)	15. (A)(B)(C)(D)	25. (A)(B)(C)(D)	35. (A)(B)(C)(D)	45. (A)(B)(C)(D)	55. (A)(B)(C)(D)	65. (A)(B)(C)(D)	75. (A)(B)(C)(D)
6. (F)(G)(H)(J)	16. (F)(G)(H)(J)	26. (F)(G)(H)(J)	36. (F)(G)(H)(J)	46. (F)(G)(H)(J)	56. (F)(G)(H)(J)	66. (F)(G)(H)(J)	
7. (A)(B)(C)(D)	17. (A)(B)(C)(D)	27. (A)(B)(C)(D)	37. (A)(B)(C)(D)	47. (A)(B)(C)(D)	57. (A)(B)(C)(D)	67. (A)(B)(C)(D)	
8. (F)(G)(H)(J)	18. (F)(G)(H)(J)	28. (F)(G)(H)(J)	38. (F)(G)(H)(J)	48. (F)(G)(H)(J)	58. (F)(G)(H)(J)	68. (F)(G)(H)(J)	
9. (A)(B)(C)(D)	19. (A)(B)(C)(D)	29. (A)(B)(C)(D)	39. (A)(B)(C)(D)	49. (A)(B)(C)(D)	59. (A)(B)(C)(D)	69. (A)(B)(C)(D)	
10. (F)(G)(H)(J)	20. (F)(G)(H)(J)	30. (F)(G)(H)(J)	40. (F)(G)(H)(J)	50. (F)(G)(H)(J)	60. (F)(G)(H)(J)	70. (F)(G)(H)(J)	

MATHEMATICS TEST

1. (A)(B)(C)(D)(E)	11. (A)(B)(C)(D)(E)	21. (A)(B)(C)(D)(E)	31. (A)(B)(C)(D)(E)	41. (A)(B)(C)(D)(E)	51. (A)(B)(C)(D)(E)
2. (F)(G)(H)(J)(K)	12. (F)(G)(H)(J)(K)	22. (F)(G)(H)(J)(K)	32. (F)(G)(H)(J)(K)	42. (F)(G)(H)(J)(K)	52. (F)(G)(H)(J)(K)
3. (A)(B)(C)(D)(E)	13. (A)(B)(C)(D)(E)	23. (A)(B)(C)(D)(E)	33. (A)(B)(C)(D)(E)	43. (A)(B)(C)(D)(E)	53. (A)(B)(C)(D)(E)
4. (F)(G)(H)(J)(K)	14. (F)(G)(H)(J)(K)	24. (F)(G)(H)(J)(K)	34. (F)(G)(H)(J)(K)	44. (F)(G)(H)(J)(K)	54. (F)(G)(H)(J)(K)
5. (A)(B)(C)(D)(E)	15. (A)(B)(C)(D)(E)	25. (A)(B)(C)(D)(E)	35. (A)(B)(C)(D)(E)	45. (A)(B)(C)(D)(E)	55. (A)(B)(C)(D)(E)
6. (F)(G)(H)(J)(K)	16. (F)(G)(H)(J)(K)	26. (F)(G)(H)(J)(K)	36. (F)(G)(H)(J)(K)	46. (F)(G)(H)(J)(K)	56. (F)(G)(H)(J)(K)
7. (A)(B)(C)(D)(E)	17. (A)(B)(C)(D)(E)	27. (A)(B)(C)(D)(E)	37. (A)(B)(C)(D)(E)	47. (A)(B)(C)(D)(E)	57. (A)(B)(C)(D)(E)
8. (F)(G)(H)(J)(K)	18. (F)(G)(H)(J)(K)	28. (F)(G)(H)(J)(K)	38. (F)(G)(H)(J)(K)	48. (F)(G)(H)(J)(K)	58. (F)(G)(H)(J)(K)
9. (A)(B)(C)(D)(E)	19. (A)(B)(C)(D)(E)	29. (A)(B)(C)(D)(E)	39. (A)(B)(C)(D)(E)	49. (A)(B)(C)(D)(E)	59. (A)(B)(C)(D)(E)
10. (F)(G)(H)(J)(K)	20. (F)(G)(H)(J)(K)	30. (F)(G)(H)(J)(K)	40. (F)(G)(H)(J)(K)	50. (F)(G)(H)(J)(K)	60. (F)(G)(H)(J)(K)

READING TEST

1. (A)(B)(C)(D)	6. (F)(G)(H)(J)	11. (A)(B)(C)(D)	16. (F)(G)(H)(J)	21. (A)(B)(C)(D)	26. (F)(G)(H)(J)	31. (A)(B)(C)(D)	36. (F)(G)(H)(J)
2. (F)(G)(H)(J)	7. (A)(B)(C)(D)	12. (F)(G)(H)(J)	17. (A)(B)(C)(D)	22. (F)(G)(H)(J)	27. (A)(B)(C)(D)	32. (F)(G)(H)(J)	37. (A)(B)(C)(D)
3. (A)(B)(C)(D)	8. (F)(G)(H)(J)	13. (A)(B)(C)(D)	18. (F)(G)(H)(J)	23. (A)(B)(C)(D)	28. (F)(G)(H)(J)	33. (A)(B)(C)(D)	38. (F)(G)(H)(J)
4. (F)(G)(H)(J)	9. (A)(B)(C)(D)	14. (F)(G)(H)(J)	19. (A)(B)(C)(D)	24. (F)(G)(H)(J)	29. (A)(B)(C)(D)	34. (F)(G)(H)(J)	39. (A)(B)(C)(D)
5. (A)(B)(C)(D)	10. (F)(G)(H)(J)	15. (A)(B)(C)(D)	20. (F)(G)(H)(J)	25. (A)(B)(C)(D)	30. (F)(G)(H)(J)	35. (A)(B)(C)(D)	40. (F)(G)(H)(J)

SCIENCE TEST

1. (A)(B)(C)(D)	6. (F)(G)(H)(J)	11. (A)(B)(C)(D)	16. (F)(G)(H)(J)	21. (A)(B)(C)(D)	26. (F)(G)(H)(J)	31. (A)(B)(C)(D)	36. (F)(G)(H)(J)
2. (F)(G)(H)(J)	7. (A)(B)(C)(D)	12. (F)(G)(H)(J)	17. (A)(B)(C)(D)	22. (F)(G)(H)(J)	27. (A)(B)(C)(D)	32. (F)(G)(H)(J)	37. (A)(B)(C)(D)
3. (A)(B)(C)(D)	8. (F)(G)(H)(J)	13. (A)(B)(C)(D)	18. (F)(G)(H)(J)	23. (A)(B)(C)(D)	28. (F)(G)(H)(J)	33. (A)(B)(C)(D)	38. (F)(G)(H)(J)
4. (F)(G)(H)(J)	9. (A)(B)(C)(D)	14. (F)(G)(H)(J)	19. (A)(B)(C)(D)	24. (F)(G)(H)(J)	29. (A)(B)(C)(D)	34. (F)(G)(H)(J)	39. (A)(B)(C)(D)
5. (A)(B)(C)(D)	10. (F)(G)(H)(J)	15. (A)(B)(C)(D)	20. (F)(G)(H)(J)	25. (A)(B)(C)(D)	30. (F)(G)(H)(J)	35. (A)(B)(C)(D)	40. (F)(G)(H)(J)

ENGLISH TEST

45 Minutes—75 Questions

Directions: Each passage has certain words and phrases that are underlined and numbered. The questions in the right column will provide alternatives for the underlined segments. Most questions require you to choose the answer that makes the sentence grammatically correct, concise, and relevant. If the word or phrase in the passage is already the correct, concise, and relevant choice, select Choice A, NO CHANGE. Some questions will ask a question about the underlined segment. When a question is presented, choose the best answer.

Some questions will ask about part or all of the passage. These questions do not refer to a specific underlined segment. Instead, these questions will accompany a number in a box.

For each question, choose your answer and fill in the corresponding bubble on your answer sheet. Read the passage once before you answer the questions. You will often need to read several sentences beyond the underlined portion to be able to choose the correct answer. Be sure to read enough to answer each question.

Passage I

A Screenwriting Career

[1]

Wanting to have success as a Hollywood screenwriter, if you do, you should be aware of the difficulties that come along with this career and its development. Very few budding screenwriters attain success by selling, let alone producing, their screenplays.

On the other hand, even successful screenwriters report living stressful and dissatisfied, though wealthy, lives.

[2]

The first difficulty encountered by budding screenwriters is the lack of a formal career path. A recent college graduate cannot approach the

1. A. NO CHANGE
   B. If you want to succeed as a Hollywood screenwriter,
   C. Whether or not wanting to succeed as a Hollywood screenwriter,
   D. Having decided if you want to or not succeed as a Hollywood screenwriter,

2. F. NO CHANGE
   G. For this reason
   H. Nowadays
   J. Furthermore

career center at his or her school or <u>find time for</u>
                                              3
<u>extracurricular activities.</u> While several successful
       3
screenwriters have written guides that outline

possibilities for success, their proposed suggestions

only highlight the <u>fruitlessness</u> of their experiences.
                         4

[3]

Unlike its value in other professional pursuits,

<u>a college education was</u> not necessarily a career boost
             5
for a budding screenwriter. In fact, a college educa-

tion can have the reverse effect on a screenwriter. The

academic study of literature or film may help a budding

screenwriter to produce higher quality work, but such

an education delays its recipient from competing in the

film industry. <u>This also tends to hold true for actors.</u>
                                    6

While a college graduate spends his or her late teens

and early twenties studying, the budding screenwriters

who do not attend college <u>begins honing</u> their craft
                                    7
and competing for work several years earlier.

3. Assuming that all are true, which choice is the most logical and appropriate in context?

   A. NO CHANGE

   B. read the classified ads in order to find screenwriting opportunities.

   C. understand the difficulties of his or her chosen career.

   D. stumble into an opportunity to work in the field.

4. Which choice best conveys that there is no one path to becoming a screenwriter?

   F. NO CHANGE

   G. difficulty

   H. rewards

   J. disparity

5. A. NO CHANGE

   B. a college education has been

   C. a college education is

   D. it is, a college education

6. F. NO CHANGE

   G. Actors also find this to be true for themselves.

   H. This has similar repercussions for actors.

   J. DELETE the underlined portion.

7. A. NO CHANGE

   B. begins to hone

   C. begin honing

   D. has begun honing

GO ON TO THE NEXT PAGE

In a career path that usually requires years to develop, late entry can create a substantial disadvantage. ⬚8

8. Suppose the writer had intended to write a paragraph discouraging those interested in writing screenplays from pursuing a college education. Does the paragraph fulfill this purpose?

   F. Yes, because it mentions the value of education.

   G. Yes, because it provides reasons why pursuing an education can be harmful.

   H. No, because the author does not express an opinion about the value of education.

   J. No, because the focus is on screenwriting rather than education.

[4]

Moreover, the debt of a college education
acquired at a prestigious school may lead many young
       9
screenwriters to surrender early to the allure of steady, if not glamorous, work and pay. Those without college

9. **A.** NO CHANGE

   B. though universities offer work-study programs to help students pay for school, many graduate with debt; this burden

   C. the burden of student loans

   D. student loans which

educations often cannot escape to "fallback" careers;
                                     10
this lack of options bolsters their drive to succeed.
 10
Furthermore, those without college educations are less

10. **F.** NO CHANGE

   G. careers; this,

   H. careers so, this

   J. careers this

averse to the low-wage jobs, aspiring screenwriters are
                          11
forced to take in order to pay living expenses while saving blocks of time to hone their craft.

11. **A.** NO CHANGE

   B. jobs, these aspiring screenwriters

   C. jobs aspiring, screenwriters,

   D. jobs that aspiring screenwriters

GO ON TO THE NEXT PAGE ⟹

[5]

The very few screenwriters who succeed often find
that's the realities of their day-to-day lives are far different
12
from their glamorous preconceptions and the media's
idealistic portrayals. While they can earn very high
salaries, successful Hollywood screenwriters often feel
more stressed and powerless than they did when they
struggled. A Hollywood screenwriter's reputation always
hinges on the success of his or her last screenplay. It
13
produces a high level of stress and pressure to

continually produce more and better work.
14
Furthermore, the Hollywood hierarchy places studio
executives, producers, directors, and star actors above
screenwriters in both pay and importance. Thus,
even the most successful screenwriters must yield
creative power to individuals who often have very little
knowledge of the craft of screenwriting.

[6]

Regardless of the hardships of initially succeeding
and then thriving in the screenwriting profession, young
people move to Los Angeles every year to pursue this
career. If one is among these people, please research and
15
learn as much as possible about the vicissitudes as well
as the potential triumphs of this profession.

12. **F.** NO CHANGE
    G. that the realities of there
    H. there the realities of their
    J. that the realities of their

13. **A.** NO CHANGE
    B. This volatile situation
    C. The screenplay
    D. They

14. **F.** NO CHANGE
    G. churn out improving and increasing
    H. be more productive and improved
    J. raising the stakes of

15. **A.** NO CHANGE
    B. one is among them
    C. finding yourself among these people
    D. you are among these people

GO ON TO THE NEXT PAGE

Passage II

The Swallows of San Juan Capistrano

[1]

The oldest building still in use in California is the Mission at San Juan Capistrano, the seventh in the chain of California missions built by Spanish priests in the late eighteenth and early nineteenth centuries. The mission has gained fame as the <u>well-known summer residence</u>
16

of the swallows of San Juan Capistrano. ⬜17

[2]

[1] For centuries, these cliff swallows have migrated to and from California every year in a cloud-like formation. [2] The swallows leave the town of San Juan Capistrano, halfway between San Diego and Los Angeles, around October 23. [3] They then journey 7,000 miles to spend the winter in Argentina. [4] Every spring, the birds faithfully return from Argentina to nest and <u>for bearing</u> their young in the valley near the mission.
18
[5] On March 19, mission bells ring, a fiesta is held,

and a parade <u>snaking</u> through the streets as throngs of
19
locals and tourists celebrate the birds' return.

16. **F.** NO CHANGE
    G. seasonal residence for the summer
    H. summer residence
    J. residential summer home

17. The primary purpose of this paragraph is to:
    A. introduce the story of the founding of the mission.
    B. transition into a discussion of the architecture of the mission.
    C. set the scene for a discussion of the swallows.
    D. persuade the reader that the mission is important.

18. **F.** NO CHANGE
    G. with bearing
    H. bearing
    J. bear

19. **A.** NO CHANGE
    B. snaked
    C. snakes
    D. is snaking

GO ON TO THE NEXT PAGE

[3]

According to legend, the swallows were seeking refuge from an innkeeper who had destroyed their muddy <u>nests when they discovered</u> the mission.
20

20. **F.** NO CHANGE
    G. nests when discovering
    H. nests, when
    J. nests, when finding

Biologists have a different explanation for how the birds <u>might of</u> developed their fondness for the mission.
21

21. **A.** NO CHANGE
    B. might have
    C. may of
    D. may

<u>Although</u> observing the swallows' behavior and
22
noting that the birds build their nests out of mud, biologists have postulated that the swallows really chose the mission due to its proximity to two rivers. These rivers provide the swallows with ample mud for building their funnel-like nests <u>of which</u> they
23

22. **F.** NO CHANGE
    G. Indeed
    H. After
    J. Before

23. **A.** NO CHANGE
    B. to which
    C. by which
    D. which

GO ON TO THE NEXT PAGE

return year after year. [24]

[4]

[1] One aspect of the legend, however, rings true. [2] The swallows, sensing that they will be protected within the mission walls, return to the compound every spring. [3] Despite this, beyond the church walls, the
<u>   25   </u>
entire city has sought to protect the swallows. San Juan Capistrano municipal ordinances declare the city a bird sanctuary and outlaw the destruction or damaging of swallow nests.

[5]

[1] Although the <u>community clearly</u> sees the
                    26
importance of providing a home for the swallows, some problems have arisen in recent years. [2] Due to the city's growth and development, the number of insects has declined, causing many of the swallows to locate farther from the mission in the town center and closer to the open areas where their food source thrives. [3] Large groups of swallows have found other nesting sites in the <u>area, usually in the hills</u> due to disruptions from
        27

24. Of the following true statements, which is the best choice to insert here in order to further support the biologists' explanation that the swallows chose the mission because of its proximity to two rivers?

   F. The swallows will repair a damaged nest instead of building an entirely new nest.
   G. The rivers also supply insects upon which the swallows feed.
   H. Both rivers are also home to a wide variety of fish.
   J. The location of the mission near the rivers also provides other advantages for the swallows.

25. A. NO CHANGE
    B. Finally
    C. In fact
    D. Next

26. F. NO CHANGE
    G. community, clearly
    H. community clearly,
    J. community clear

27. A. NO CHANGE
    B. area; usually in the hills,
    C. area—usually in the hills—
    D. area, having been usual in the hills,

GO ON TO THE NEXT PAGE

recent restorations of the <u>old, historic</u> buildings at the
                                    28
mission. [4] Fortunately, city and mission officials have

started to respond to these problems. [5] For example,

<u>to attempt at enticing</u> the birds back home, mission
                    29
workers have strewn insects about the mission's

grounds.

28. **F.** NO CHANGE

    G. old and historic

    H. historic

    J. olden times

29. **A.** NO CHANGE

    B. in an attempt to entice

    C. in an attempt's enticement

    D. in an attempt of enticing

Question 30 asks about the preceding passage
as a whole.

30. The writer is considering adding the following
    sentence to further explain how residents of
    San Juan Capistrano feel about the swallows:

> Many residents and visitors miss the huge
> clouds of swallows descending upon the
> mission as in the past decades.

The most logical place to insert this sentence
would be directly after:

    F. Sentence 5 in Paragraph 2.

    G. Sentence 3 in Paragraph 4.

    H. Sentence 1 in Paragraph 5.

    J. Sentence 3 in Paragraph 5.

Passage III

Root for the Home Team?

If you are young and love football, it is advantageous to live near a large sporting-goods store that carries a wide variety of paraphernalia from different teams. My daughter and I visit our local store at least once a year to buy another new football jersey for yet another team. Although my daughter is a fan of our <u>city</u>
31
professional team, she frequently changes her jersey to match that of her favorite player.

A free agent is a professional football player who is no longer under contract with a team, which means he can choose the team <u>which</u> he wants to play.
32

In the NFL today, players can become free agents easily. ☐33☐ Things were much different when I was growing up.

31. A. NO CHANGE
    B. city's
    C. cities
    D. cities'

32. F. NO CHANGE
    G. at which
    H. for which
    J. DELETE the underlined portion.

33. The writer is considering adding a comma and the following to the end of the preceding sentence:

    > so they often switch teams many times in their careers.

    Should the writer make this addition?

    A. Yes, because it adds an interesting detail about why players become free agents.
    B. Yes, because it provides a necessary link between being a free agent and switching teams.
    C. No, because it distracts from the focus on the parent-daughter relationship.
    D. No, because it is irrelevant to the point being made about free agents.

GO ON TO THE NEXT PAGE

My favorite player was on the same team for his entire

career I had one jersey. My daughter has bought over
    34

eight team jerseys in the past six years! At seventy-five

dollars a shirt, this is not a sustainable trend.

There are many disadvantages to free agency.
                               35

When my daughter and I went to pre-season training
   35

practice to get a preview of this year's home team, we

constantly consulted the team roster to figure out the

new line-up, because there were so many new players.

At one point, a number of fans even started to cheer for

a player who, was no longer with the team, because they
                  36

did not realize someone new was wearing his number.

A second disadvantage of free agency is

having some camaraderie and cohesion.
   37

Football is the ultimate team sport, in which players

must depend upon each other to win. A team
          38

trains strategizes and plays together for months. The
   39

players learn each other's strengths and weaknesses.

34. **F.** NO CHANGE
    G. career, so I had
    H. career, because I had
    J. career, and then I had

35. **A.** NO CHANGE
    B. free agency: for when my
    C. free agency, when my
    D. free agency when my

36. **F.** NO CHANGE
    G. player who was no longer with the team
    H. player, who was no longer, with the team
    J. player who was no longer, with the team

37. **A.** NO CHANGE
    B. lack of
    C. total
    D. wholehearted

38. **F.** NO CHANGE
    G. to win on each other
    H. upon winning with each other
    J. DELETE the underlined portion.

39. **A.** NO CHANGE
    B. trains, strategizes, and plays,
    C. trains strategizes, and plays
    D. trains, strategizes, and plays

GO ON TO THE NEXT PAGE ⇒

Eleven players are on the field at one time, <u>and their goal</u>
40
is to stop the other team from progressing down the

field. If any one of those eleven players leaves the team,

it <u>disrupt</u> the dynamics and cohesion that the entire team
41
has worked together to build.

<u>A third disadvantage is the loss</u> of team dynasties.
42
When I was a teenager, my home team made the play-

offs for three years in a row. Since free agency was in-

troduced, our team has not made it back to the playoffs

for ten years. When the team did return <u>10 years later,</u>
43
my daughter fell in love with both the team and our star

quarterback. That player moved to another team;

<u>because</u> our home team has not had a winning season
44

since he left, his new team has won the Superbowl for

the last two years. ⬜45

40. F. NO CHANGE
    G. because their goal
    H. yet their goal
    J. or their goal

41. A. NO CHANGE
    B. disrupted
    C. disrupts
    D. disrupting

42. F. NO CHANGE
    G. A loss is the third disadvantage
    H. A disadvantage is the third loss
    J. The third loss is a disadvantage

43. A. NO CHANGE
    B. to the Super Bowl
    C. 10 years' later
    D. DELETE the underlined portion.

44. F. NO CHANGE
    G. however
    H. therefore
    J. while

45. Which of the following sentences, if added, would best conclude the essay?
    A. Football is a great sport that will never decrease in popularity.
    B. Free agency has a variety of benefits, but the negatives outweigh the positives.
    C. Free agency allows players to change teams frequently, which has made it increasingly difficult to root for a home team that never stays the same.
    D. One thing will never change, and that is the home team.

GO ON TO THE NEXT PAGE

Practice Test 8   **739**

Passage IV

> The paragraphs below may or may not be in the most logical order. A number in brackets appears above each paragraph. Question 49 will ask you to determine the most logical place for Paragraph 3.

The Right to Write

[1]

Going to see a play is a cultural tradition that has been passed on for thousands of years. Although theater is a form of art and entertainment, it is also a highly competitive business, especially for playwrights. Many plays are written, but <u>it is only</u> a select few are produced
                                46
and seen by the public, and often with strings attached.

Playwright José Rivera is an example of a contemporary playwright <u>that</u> has fought for the right to have his work
           47
produced and seen in the way he intended it.

[2]

Rivera was born in San Juan, Puerto Rico, in 1955, but his family moved to New York when he was four years old. <u>Yet</u> many of Rivera's relatives had already
        48
moved to the Bronx, a bustling neighborhood in New York, Rivera's father wanted to live in a place that felt more like a small town. So they moved to a quarter acre of land in Long Island, New York, which at the time had dirt roads and woods.

46. **F.** NO CHANGE
    G. there are only
    H. only
    J. there only is

47. **A.** NO CHANGE
    B. who
    C. which
    D. whom

48. **F.** NO CHANGE
    G. Meanwhile,
    H. However,
    J. Although

[3]

49 From an early age, Rivera knew that he wanted to be a writer. As a kid, he wrote comic strips, a novel

about baseball, and essays in response to photographs, from *Life* magazine. When he was in middle school,

he saw a play that inspired him when he saw the play that he wanted to become a playwright.

He writes several plays during high school and in college.

[4]

Rivera, after graduating, returned to New York, from college determined to continue writing.

49. The most logical placement of Paragraph 3 is
   A. where it is now.
   B. after Paragraph 1.
   C. after Paragraph 4.
   D. after Paragraph 5.

50. F. NO CHANGE
   G. photographs from
   H. photographs from:
   J. photographs; from

51. A. NO CHANGE
   B. that when he saw the play he wanted
   C. that he wanted when he saw that play
   D. DELETE the underlined portion.

52. F. NO CHANGE
   G. is writing
   H. has written
   J. wrote

53. A. NO CHANGE
   B. Rivera returned from college after graduating, to New York,
   C. After graduating from college, Rivera returned to New York,
   D. Rivera, from graduating, returned to New York,

GO ON TO THE NEXT PAGE

He worked at a bookstore and became <u>then</u> a copy
₅₄
editor at a publishing company. Eventually, Rivera
found an artistic home in a playwriting group called
the Theater Matrix; the group met on Monday nights to
share their work. One of <u>them</u> he wrote and produced,
₅₅
The House of Roman Iglesia, received a good review by
The New York Times. This was an important step in

Rivera's <u>career receiving</u> a good review from a major
₅₆
publication led to more work. The famous television
producer Norman Lear read the review and immediately
offered Rivera a job writing for Embassy Television in
California.

[5]

In order to make a living, Rivera accepted the job.
He learned a lot from the process of writing for televi-
sion shows, but there were sacrifices he had to make.
He missed writing plays and living in New York. [57]
Rivera also discovered that in the entertainment busi-
ness, he was often labeled and identified by his ethnicity.
Rivera was proud of his cultural heritage but wanted to
be acknowledged for his talent.

54. **F.** NO CHANGE
G. (Place before *became*)
H. (Place before *publishing*)
J. (Place after *company*)

55. **A.** NO CHANGE
B. those
C. the work
D. the plays

56. **F.** NO CHANGE
G. career, receiving
H. career; receiving
J. career receiving.

57. If the writer wanted to reinforce the main point made in Paragraph 5, which sentence would she add here?

A. He also missed the reward of owning his work, because his writing became the property of the television shows.

B. California is a beautiful state with a variety of places to visit, from beaches to major cities.

C. He had the opportunity to write for television shows such as *Family Matters* and *Eerie, Indiana*.

D. While in California, he became a founding member of a theater company in the city of Los Angeles.

GO ON TO THE NEXT PAGE

[6]

After many years of hard work and perseverance, Rivera has received the recognition he deserves through countless productions of his plays and the numerous awards he has won for playwriting. Despite the challenges of show business, José Rivera <u>has became</u> an
58
important playwright whose work has an impact on audiences worldwide.

58. **F.** NO CHANGE
    G. is became
    H. has become
    J. have become

Questions 59 and 60 ask about the preceding passage as a whole.

59. Does this essay successfully describe the challenges faced by playwrights in the entertainment business?

    A. The essay is not successful; it is a neutral biography of the playwright José Rivera.

    B. The essay is not successful; it portrays playwriting as a fun and rewarding career.

    C. The essay is successful; it describes playwriting as an impossible dream for only the very lucky.

    D. The essay is successful; it demonstrates the challenges through the life and work of José Rivera.

60. The writer is considering adding the following sentence:

    The contrast between small-town and city life became an influence on Rivera's work.

    The best placement for this detail is in:

    F. Paragraph 1.
    G. Paragraph 2.
    H. Paragraph 5.
    J. Paragraph 6.

GO ON TO THE NEXT PAGE

Passage V

Signature of the Time

[1] The home of Tyler Gregory looks like an abandoned bureaucratic archive. [2] Almost all of the available space <u>being crammed with old books or</u> covered with folios and documents. [3] Dr. Gregory, a psychologist, first began collecting old documents
₆₁

as a hobby. [4] What was initially a <u>hobby quickly became a life's</u> passion and devotion. [5] Predictably,
₆₂
₆₂
several papers in Dr. Gregory's collection, which includes a faded but detailed inn receipt,

<u>is</u> signed by John Hancock. [6] Proudly displayed,
₆₃

the John Hancock documents <u>had represented</u>
₆₄
Dr. Gregory's work: graphology. [7] Unlike other rare

and vintage document enthusiasts, Dr. Gregory collects only documents that bear famous signatures. [65]

61. **A.** NO CHANGE
    B. was crammed with old books or is
    C. is crammed with old books or
    D. crammed with old books or

62. **F.** NO CHANGE
    G. hobby, quickly became a life's
    H. hobby quickly became a life's,
    J. hobby: quickly became a life's

63. **A.** NO CHANGE
    B. are
    C. was
    D. DELETE the underlined portion.

64. **F.** NO CHANGE
    G. represent
    H. represented
    J. would have represented

65. To maintain the logic and coherence of this paragraph, Sentence 7 should be placed:
    A. where it is now.
    B. after Sentence 1.
    C. after Sentence 3.
    D. after Sentence 4.

GO ON TO THE NEXT PAGE

Graphology, <u>a growing field,</u> is used to authenticate
₆₆
documents in court trials and other legal proceedings,

but it has other, less familiar uses as well. Psychologists

can use graphology to analyze a patient's psyche.

Many patients cannot explain their problems,

<u>but psychologists have techniques to help patients learn</u>
₆₇
<u>to express themselves.</u> Psychologists and graphologists
₆₇
have noted that handwriting is a subconscious

expression of inner thoughts. Many of the issues

involuntarily revealed by a subject's handwriting remain

unknown to the subject herself. Unlike the patients of

most psychologists <u>use</u> graphology, however,
₆₈
Dr. Gregory's subjects are dead. Dr. Gregory once

practiced clinical <u>psychology in the past,</u> but his
₆₉
interest in graphology is a more historical one. He

studies the handwriting of historical figures, hoping

to better understand their personalities. Dr. Gregory's

interest in historical personalities stems from an

interdisciplinary desire to apply psychological theories

to the explanation of historical events. Historians

66. Which of the following true choices provides
information that is most relevant and
meaningful to the essay in its entirety?

F. NO CHANGE

G. or handwriting analysis,

H. which has been practiced for decades,

J. as a professional endeavor,

67. After reviewing the essay, the writer wants to
insert a statement at this point that would lead
into the next sentence. Given that all of the
choices are true, which one best accomplishes
the writer's purpose?

A. NO CHANGE

B. and this is one reason they seek help from
professionals.

C. but their handwriting often can.

D. so analyzing the psyche can be
challenging.

68. F. NO CHANGE

G. used to

H. who use

J. being used

69. A. NO CHANGE

B. psychology for a time,

C. psychology at an earlier period in his life,

D. psychology,

GO ON TO THE NEXT PAGE

and political scientists have long sought to apply psychology and its theories to their work, but they have not always met with success. While such theories as organizational psychology and cognitive dissonance have illuminated some historical decisions, they have done so neither definitively nor broadly. The scarcity of information regarding the personalities of historical figures has been the biggest obstacle. [70]

Unlike current in-depth information from multiple media sources, scarcely any record exists of the private personalities and lives of history's greatest figures. [71]

70. The primary purpose of mentioning psychology in this paragraph is to:

    F. provide introductory information about Dr. Gregory.

    G. explain its relation to graphology.

    H. discuss the psychology of preserving historical documents.

    J. downplay its importance in understanding personalities.

71. If the writer were to delete the previous sentence, the paragraph would primarily lose:

    A. a motivation for Dr. Gregory's interest in graphology.

    B. an important detail about the difficulty in applying psychological theories to historical figures.

    C. a reason for the broad agreement about the analyses of historical figures.

    D. a cause for the friends of well-known figures to write accounts of them.

GO ON TO THE NEXT PAGE ⇨

Practice Test 8

The records that do exist paint skewed pictures, for
                                                    72
they come almost entirely from friends, enemies, or
 72
the historical figures themselves. Thus, Dr. Gregory

uses graphology to study and understand the

personalities and inner lives of important men and

women who lived so long ago.

Dr. Gregory, along with most graphologists,

believes that a person's signature reveals more about

that person's personality than normal handwriting. The

signature legally and traditionally conveys the mark of

an individual. This supports Dr. Gregory's belief that the
                                                      73
shape of a signature also serves as a psychological stamp.

According to Dr. Gregory, a person has been both
                                           74
consciously and unconsciously imprinting key aspects

of his personality while he forms a signature. Those

aspects have led Dr. Gregory to infer many personal

details about historical figures. Such details are now

being used by historians in their analysis of historical

decisions.

72. Of the following alternatives to the underlined
    portion, which choice would NOT be
    acceptable?

    F. pictures; they
    G. pictures. They
    H. pictures, as they
    J. pictures they

73. A. NO CHANGE
    B. belief, that
    C. belief that,
    D. belief: that

74. F. NO CHANGE
    G. had been
    H. will be
    J. is

GO ON TO THE NEXT PAGE

Practice Test 8

Question 75 asks about the preceding passage as a whole.

75. Suppose the writer had intended to write a short essay about an example of one area of study influencing another area of study. Would this essay achieve the writer's goal?

A. Yes, because the essay explains how personality traits determined through analyzing a historical individual's handwriting can be used to form a psychological study of such figures and their roles in historical events.

B. Yes, because the essay compares the research process of graphologists to the research process of historians.

C. No, because the essay focuses on Dr. Gregory's personal life rather than his area of study.

D. No, because the essay does not discuss the findings of historians who have applied psychological theories to historical figures and events.

IF YOU FINISH BEFORE TIME IS CALLED, YOU MAY CHECK YOUR WORK ON THIS SECTION ONLY. DO NOT TURN TO ANY OTHER SECTION IN THE TEST. STOP

MATHEMATICS TEST

60 Minutes—60 Questions

Directions: Choose the correct solution to each question and fill in the corresponding bubble on your answer sheet.

Do not continue to spend time on questions if you get stuck. Solve as many questions as you can before returning to any if time permits.

You may use a calculator on this test for any question you choose. However, some questions may be better solved without a calculator.

Note: Unless otherwise stated, you can assume:

1. Figures are NOT necessarily drawn to scale.

2. Geometric figures are two dimensional.

3. The word *line* indicates a straight line.

4. The word *average* indicates arithmetic mean.

---

1. Three points, A, B, and C, lie on the same line. The length of $\overline{AB}$ is 8 units, and the length of $\overline{BC}$ is 2 units. Which of the following gives all of the possible lengths for $\overline{AC}$?

   A. 6 only

   B. 10 only

   C. 6 and 10 only

   D. Any number less than 6 or greater than 10

   E. Any number greater than 6 and less than 10

2. If a "sump" number is defined as one in which the sum of the digits of the number is greater than the product of the digits of the same number, which of the following is a "sump" number?

   F. 123

   G. 234

   H. 332

   J. 411

   K. 521

3. In a raffle, Mark must draw a ticket at random from a bag. The probability that he will draw a winning ticket is 0.3. What is the probability that he will draw a losing ticket?

   A. 0.0

   B. 0.1

   C. 0.7

   D. 1.0

   E. 1.3

4. Mandy buys a winter coat that is on sale for 20% off, and then she uses a coupon worth an additional 15% off of the sale price. What percentage of the original price has she saved?

   F. 32%

   G. 34%

   H. 35%

   J. 38%

   K. 40%

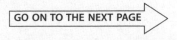
GO ON TO THE NEXT PAGE

5. On Monday, Tom received a bag of candy for his birthday and ate half of it. On Tuesday he ate half of the remaining candy, and on Wednesday he ate half of what remained from Tuesday. If 6 pieces of candy then remained, how many pieces of candy did he receive originally?

   A. 18
   B. 24
   C. 36
   D. 48
   E. 96

6. If $R = 4x$ and $S = 3y - x$, then what is the value of $R + S$?

   F. $3x + 3y$
   G. $3x - 3y$
   H. $4x + 3y$
   J. $4x - 3y$
   K. $5x + 3y$

7. In the figure below, l_1 is parallel to l_2, l_3 is parallel to l_4, and the lines intersect as shown. What is the measure of angle y ?

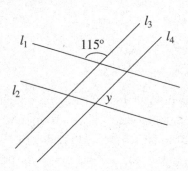

   A. 60°
   B. 65°
   C. 70°
   D. 75°
   E. Cannot be determined from the given information

8. If $f(x) = -x^2 - 7x + 5$, then $f(-3) = $?

   F. -25
   G. -7
   H. 14
   J. 17
   K. 35

9. The average of five numbers is 85. If each of the numbers is increased by 4, what is the average of the five new numbers?

   A. 80
   B. 81
   C. 85
   D. 87
   E. 89

10. The expression $3x + 9y$ is equivalent to which of the following?

   F. $3(x + y)$
   G. $12(x + y)$
   H. $3(x + 3y)$
   J. $3xy$
   K. $12xy$

11. For each month on his phone bill, Mark pays $20 plus a fixed amount for every minute of long distance calls. In May he used 80 long distance minutes and his bill was $28. In June he used 20 more long distance minutes than in May. What was the charge on his phone bill in June?

   A. $20.00
   B. $28.20
   C. $29.00
   D. $30.00
   E. $32.50

GO ON TO THE NEXT PAGE

12. When the positive integer p is divided by 7, the remainder is 5. What is the remainder when $5p$ is divided by 7?

    F. 0

    G. 1

    H. 2

    J. 3

    K. 4

13. The hands of a clock are both pointing to 12 at noon. By 8 PM, what is the number of degrees the *hour* hand has moved?

    A. 80°

    B. 96°

    C. 120°

    D. 160°

    E. 240°

14. Six model cars are to be placed on a bookshelf. If all 6 cars are placed on the shelf in order, from left to right, in how many different ways can the cars be placed?

    F. 5

    G. 14

    H. 60

    J. 120

    K. 720

15. Which of the following equations has both $x = 5$ and $x = -7$ as solutions?

    A. $(x - 5)(x + 7) = 0$

    B. $(x - 5)(-x + 7) = 0$

    C. $(x + 5)(x + 7) = 0$

    D. $(x + 5)(x - 7) = 0$

    E. $x - 5 = x + 7$

16. There are 5,280 feet in a mile. Gary walked 220 feet to the bus stop, and the bus took him three-fourths of a mile to school. What is the ratio of his distance walking to the distance he rode the bus?

    F. 1:6

    G. 1:8

    H. 1:9

    J. 1:12

    K. 1:18

17. If 30% of x equals 60, then $x = $?

    A. 2

    B. 18

    C. 200

    D. 1,800

    E. 2,000

18. Maria keeps a record of the amount of money in her piggy bank. She takes $1.25 out of the piggy bank to buy a candy bar. When figuring the new amount of money in the piggy bank, she accidentally adds $1.25 to the total rather than subtracting it. Assuming she had recorded the correct amount of money prior to this error, the total amount of money she now has recorded is:

    F. $2.50 less than it should be.

    G. $1.25 less than it should be.

    H. the correct amount.

    J. $1.25 more than it should be.

    K. $2.50 more than it should be.

GO ON TO THE NEXT PAGE

Practice Test 8

19. Suppose you want to buy a salad for lunch. The price on the menu is $3.99, and the cashier is going to add a sales tax of 7% of the $3.99 (rounded to the nearest cent) to the price of the salad. You are going to pay with a five-dollar bill. How much change should the cashier return to you?

    A.   7¢

    B.   27¢

    C.   28¢

    D.   73¢

    E.   93¢

20. For which nonnegative value of x is the expression $\dfrac{1}{x^2 - 4}$ undefined?

    F.   0

    G.   2

    H.   4

    J.   8

    K.   16

21. What is the correct ordering of π, $3\frac{1}{4}$, and 3.5, from greatest to least?

    A. $\pi > 3\frac{1}{4} > 3.5$

    B. $\pi > 3.5 > 3\frac{1}{4}$

    C. $3.5 > 3\frac{1}{4} > \pi$

    D. $3.5 > \pi > 3\frac{1}{4}$

    E. $3\frac{1}{4} > 3.5 > \pi$

22. Bo and Duke are driving from Town X to Town Y. Their total trip time is 5 hours, including 48 minutes they spent on the side of the road fixing the car. If they were driving at 70 miles per hour the whole way, how far away, in miles, is Town Y from Town X ?

    F.   123

    G.   280

    H.   294

    J.   336

    K.   350

23. There are 3 routes from Bay City to Riverville. There are 4 routes from Riverville to Straitstown. There are 3 routes from Straitstown to Frog Pond. If a driver must pass through Riverville and Straitstown exactly once, how many possible ways are there to go from Bay City to Frog Pond?

    A.   6

    B.   10

    C.   12

    D.   24

    E.   36

24. Which of the following gives all of the solutions of $x^2 + x = 30$?

    F.   −6 and 5

    G.   −5 and 6

    H.   −2 and 15

    J.   2 and 15

    K.   15 only

GO ON TO THE NEXT PAGE

Practice Test 8

25. If $(a - b)^2 = 81$ and $ab = \dfrac{3}{2}$, then $a^2 + b^2 = ?$

    A. -18

    B. 18

    C. 27

    D. 84

    E. 90

26. The probability distribution of the discrete random variable Y is shown in the table below. If a random number generator uses this distribution to generate a value for Y, what is the probability that the value will be an even number?

Y	Probability $P(Y = y)$
0	$\dfrac{1}{5}$
1	$\dfrac{1}{10}$
2	$\dfrac{3}{10}$
3	$\dfrac{3}{20}$
4	$\dfrac{1}{4}$

    F. $\dfrac{3}{200}$

    G. $\dfrac{1}{4}$

    H. $\dfrac{11}{20}$

    J. $\dfrac{13}{20}$

    K. $\dfrac{3}{4}$

27. Given the complex number i such that $i^2 = -1$, what is the value of $i^2 - i^4$?

    A. -2

    B. -1

    C. 0

    D. 1

    E. 2

28. $\overline{AB}$ is a line segment in the standard (x,y) coordinate plane with endpoints A and B. If point A has the coordinates $(5,-4)$ and the midpoint of $\overline{AB}$ has coordinates $(-2,4)$, what are the coordinates of point B ?

    F. $(-9,12)$

    G. $(-3,-16)$

    H. $(3,-16)$

    J. $(3,-1)$

    K. $(9,12)$

GO ON TO THE NEXT PAGE

Practice Test 8

Use the following information to answer questions 29–31.

The following table shows the amount of trash collected by 30 participants in a litter cleanup drive.

Pounds of trash	10	15	20	25	30
Number of participants	12	9	4	4	1

29. What is the mode of the number of pieces of trash collected by the participants in the litter cleanup drive?

    A. 10

    B. 15

    C. 20

    D. 25

    E. 30

30. The goal of the litter cleanup drive was to collect 500 pounds of trash. What percent of this goal did the 30 participants achieve?

    F.   8

    G. 20

    H. 56

    J.   93

    K. 100

31. What was the average amount of trash collected by each of the 30 participants in the litter cleanup drive?

    A. Between 10 and 11 pounds

    B. Between 11 and 12 pounds

    C. Between 15 and 16 pounds

    D. Between 19 and 20 pounds

    E. Between 20 and 21 pounds

32. Three parallel lines are intersected by transversals, as shown below. The points of intersection are labeled. $\overline{QR}$ measures 3 inches, $\overline{RS}$ measures 5 inches, and $\overline{UV}$ measures 7 inches. What is the length of $\overline{TU}$, in inches?

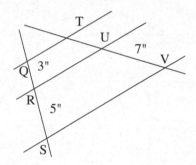

    F. $\dfrac{15}{7}$

    G. 3

    H. 4

    J. $\dfrac{21}{5}$

    K. $\dfrac{35}{3}$

GO ON TO THE NEXT PAGE

33. In the figure below, the circle centered at O has radii $\overline{OA}$ and $\overline{OB}$. $\triangle AOB$ is a right isosceles triangle. If the area of $\triangle AOB$ is 18 square units, what is the area of the circle, in units?

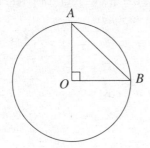

   A. 12π

   B. 18π

   C. 36π

   D. 72π

   E. 81π

34. Which of the following represents the same set as the figure shown below?

   F. $x \leq -5$ or $x > 4$

   G. $x > -5$ or $x \leq 4$

   H. $x \geq -5$ or $x < 4$

   J. $x > -5$ and $x \leq 4$

   K. $x \geq -5$ and $x < 4$

35. A circle in the standard (x,y) coordinate plane has the equation $(x + 3)^2 + (y - 4)^2 = 25$. What is the diameter of the circle?

   A. $\sqrt{5}$

   B. $2\sqrt{5}$

   C. 5

   D. 10

   E. 50

36. During fairly heavy traffic, the number of cars that can safely pass through a stoplight during a left turn signal is directly proportional to the length of time in seconds that the signal is green. If 9 cars can safely pass through a light that lasts 36 seconds, how many fewer cars can safely pass through a light that lasts 24 seconds?

   F. 3

   G. 4

   H. 5

   J. 6

   K. 7

37. The numbers 84 and 96 are both divisible by n, a real positive integer. Neither 18 nor 16 is divisible by n. What is the sum of the digits of n?

   A. 1

   B. 3

   C. 4

   D. 5

   E. 6

38. In the standard (x,y) coordinate plane, line R is parallel to the x-axis. What is the slope of R?

   F. -1

   G. 0

   H. 1

   J. Undefined

   K. Cannot be determined from the given information

39. Which of the following lines has the same slope as $y = 2x - 1$?

   A. $-y = 2x - 1$

   B. $y = 3x - 1$

   C. $y = 4x + 2$

   D. $4y = 2x + 6$

   E. $5y = 10x + 2$

GO ON TO THE NEXT PAGE

40. The two triangles in the figure below share a common side. What is $\sin(x + y)$?

(Note: For all x and y, $\sin(x + y) = \sin x \cos y + \sin y \cos x$.)

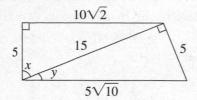

F. $\dfrac{1}{5\sqrt{10}}$

G. $\dfrac{12\sqrt{5} + \sqrt{10}}{30}$

H. $\dfrac{6\sqrt{5} + 3\sqrt{10}}{20}$

J. $\dfrac{2\sqrt{2} + \sqrt{10}}{3}$

K. $5\sqrt{10}$

41. Set C includes all numbers between 0 and 5, inclusive. Set D includes all numbers between 3 and 7, inclusive. Which of the following inequalities correctly describes x, where x is the union of set C and set D?

A. $0 \le x \le 3$

B. $0 \le x \le 5$

C. $0 \le x \le 7$

D. $3 \le x \le 5$

E. $3 \le x \le 7$

42. The graph of the function $f(x) = \cos x$ in the standard (x,y) coordinate plane is reflected over the x-axis, shifted right π units, and then shifted down a units. Which of the following functions represents the graph after the 3 transformations have been applied?

F. $f'(x) = -\cos(x - \pi) - a$

G. $f'(x) = -\cos(x + \pi) - a$

H. $f'(x) = -\cos(x + \pi) + a$

J. $f'(x) = \cos(-x - \pi) - a$

K. $f'(x) = \cos(-x + \pi) - a$

43. In $\triangle RST$, $\angle R$ is a right angle and $\angle S$ measures $60°$. If $\overline{ST}$ is 8 inches long, what is the area of $\triangle RST$ in square inches?

A. 8

B. $8\sqrt{3}$

C. 16

D. 32

E. $32\sqrt{3}$

44. If $(x^{3b-1})^2 = x^{16}$ for all x, then $b = ?$

F. 1

G. $\dfrac{5}{3}$

H. $\dfrac{5}{4}$

J. 3

K. $\dfrac{16}{3}$

GO ON TO THE NEXT PAGE

45. The figure below is composed of a square and a semicircle. The radius of the semicircle is r and the side of the square is $2r$. Suppose r is doubled. How many times the area of the original figure is the area of the new figure?

A. 2

B. 3

C. 4

D. 8

E. 10

46. For what value of x would the following system of equations have an infinite number of solutions?

$$\begin{cases} 4a - b = 4 \\ 16a - 4b = 8x \end{cases}$$

F. 2

G. 4

H. 6

J. 16

K. 24

47. Sally and Samir left their camp at the same time. Sally walked at a constant rate of 3 miles per hour. She walked 20 minutes north, then 40 minutes east. Samir walked at a constant rate of 2 miles per hour. He walked 20 minutes south, then 40 minutes east. Which of the following is an expression for the number of miles apart Samir and Sally were one hour after they left camp?

A. $1(3 - 2)$

B. $\sqrt{\left(1 - \dfrac{2}{3}\right)^2 + \left(2 - \dfrac{4}{3}\right)^2}$

C. $\sqrt{\left(1 + \dfrac{2}{3}\right)^2 + \left(2 - \dfrac{4}{3}\right)^2}$

D. $\sqrt{\left(1 + \dfrac{2}{3}\right)^2 + \left(2 + \dfrac{4}{3}\right)^2}$

E. $\sqrt{\left(1 - \dfrac{2}{3}\right)^2 + \left(2 + \dfrac{4}{3}\right)^2}$

48. Which of the following functions best describes the curve in the figure below?

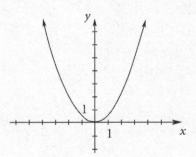

F. $f(x) = -2x^2$

G. $f(x) = -x^2$

H. $f(x) = |x|$

J. $f(x) = \dfrac{1}{2}x^2$

K. $f(x) = 2x^2$

GO ON TO THE NEXT PAGE

49. In the figure below, for which point (x,y) is the product xy the greatest?

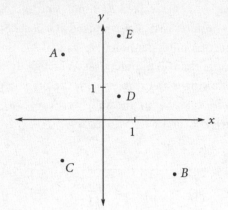

A. A

B. B

C. C

D. D

E. E

50. If $g(x) = x^2 - 3x$ and $h(x) = 2x + 5$, which of the follow expressions represent $g(h(x))$?

F. $2x^2 - 6x + 5$

G. $4x^2 - 6x + 10$

H. $4x^2 + 4x + 10$

J. $4x^2 + 14x + 10$

K. $4x^2 + 17x + 25$

51. Given the vertices of $\triangle ABC$ in the standard (x,y) coordinate plane below, what is the area of $\triangle ABC$ in square units?

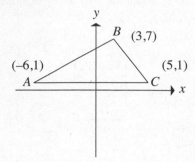

A. 22

B. 32

C. 33

D. 40

E. 66

52. If $-3x^2y^3 > 0$, which of the following CANNOT be true?

F. $x = y$

G. $x < 0$

H. $x > 0$

J. $y < 0$

K. $y > 0$

53. If the first and second terms of a geometric sequence are 6 and 18, what is the expression for the value of the 25th term of the sequence?

A. $a_{25} = 6^{25} \times 3$

B. $a_{25} = 6^{24} \times 3$

C. $a_{25} = 3^{24} \times 6$

D. $a_{25} = 3^{25} \times 6$

E. $a_{25} = 3^{25} \times 18$

GO ON TO THE NEXT PAGE

54. Which function could have been used to generate the data given in the table below?

x	-3	-2	-1	0	1	2	3
$g(x)$	12	8	6	5	4.5	4.25	4.125

F. $g(x) = -4x$

G. $g(x) = -3x - 3$

H. $g(x) = x^2 + 3$

J. $g(x) = \left(\dfrac{1}{2}\right)^x + 4$

K. $g(x) = -2^x + 4$

55. If $0° \leq n \leq 90°$ and $\cos n = \dfrac{15}{17}$, then $\tan n = ?$

A. $\dfrac{8}{17}$

B. $\dfrac{8}{15}$

C. $\dfrac{17}{15}$

D. $\dfrac{15}{8}$

E. $\dfrac{17}{8}$

56. For every cent decrease in the price of milk, a grocery store sells 10 more gallons of milk per day. Right now, the store is selling 65 gallons of milk per day at \$2.25 per gallon. Which of the following expressions represents the number of gallons that will be sold per day if the cost is reduced by c cents?

F. $65(2.25 - c)$

G. $2.25(10c + 65)$

H. $(2.25 - c)(10c + 65)$

J. $2.25 - c$

K. $65 + 10c$

57. A group of 100 students are being divided into 10 teams for a relay race. Each student will draw and keep a token from a bag of tokens numbered 00 through 99. Students who draw tokens numbered with the same tens digit will be on the same team. (Students with numbers between 00 and 09, for example, will be on the same team.) Ann is the first student to draw, and she draws 56. If Elizabeth is the second student to draw, what is the probability that she will be on Ann's team?

A. $\dfrac{1}{8}$

B. $\dfrac{1}{9}$

C. $\dfrac{1}{10}$

D. $\dfrac{1}{11}$

E. $\dfrac{1}{99}$

58. Suppose the graph of $g(x)$ passes through the point $(5, -1)$. If $g(x)$ is reflected over the line $y = 3$, through which point must the reflected graph pass?

F. $(3, -1)$

G. $(1, -1)$

H. $(5, 1)$

J. $(5, 3)$

K. $(5, 7)$

GO ON TO THE NEXT PAGE

59. In the figure below, line *l* has the equation $y = x$. Line *m* is perpendicular to *l* and intercepts the *x*-axis at (3,0). Which of the following is an equation for *m* ?

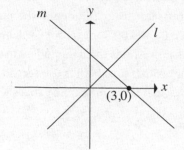

A. $y = x + 3\sqrt{2}$

B. $y = x + 3$

C. $y = -x + 3$

D. $y = -x + 3\sqrt{2}$

E. $y = -3x + 3$

60. What is the smallest possible value for the product of two real numbers that differ by 8 ?

F. -64

G. -16

H. -8

J. 0

K. 16

IF YOU FINISH BEFORE TIME IS CALLED, YOU MAY CHECK YOUR WORK ON THIS SECTION ONLY. DO NOT TURN TO ANY OTHER SECTION IN THE TEST. **STOP**

Practice Test 8

READING TEST

35 Minutes—40 Questions

Directions: The Reading Test includes multiple passages. Each passage includes multiple questions. After reading each passage, choose the best answer and fill in the corresponding bubble on your answer sheet. You may review the passages as often as necessary.

Passage I

PROSE FICTION: *This passage is adapted from* Howard's End, *by E. M. Forster (1910). Two sisters, Helen and Margaret, are attending an orchestra performance with friends and family.*

It will be generally admitted that Beethoven's *Fifth Symphony* is the most sublime noise that has ever penetrated into the ear of man. All sorts and conditions are satisfied by it. Whether you are like
5 Mrs. Munt, and tap surreptitiously when the tunes come—of course, not so as to disturb the others— or like Helen, who can see heroes and shipwrecks in the music's flood; or like Margaret, who can only see the music; or like Tibby, who is profoundly
10 versed in counterpoint, and holds the full score of the symphony open on his knee; or like Fraulein Mosebach's young man, who can remember nothing but Fraulein Mosebach: in any case, the passion of your life becomes more vivid, and you are bound
15 to admit that such a noise is cheap at two shillings. It is cheap, even if you hear it in the Queen's Hall, dreariest music-room in London, though not as dreary as the Free Trade Hall, Manchester; and even if you sit on the extreme left of that hall, so that the
20 brass bumps at you before the rest of the orchestra arrives, it is still cheap.

"Whom is Margaret talking to?" said Mrs. Munt, at the conclusion of the first movement. She was again in London on a visit to Wickham Place.
25 Helen looked down the long line of their party, and said that she did not know.

"Would it be some young man or other whom she takes an interest in?"

"I expect so," Helen replied. Music enwrapped
30 her, and she could not be bothered by the distinction that divides young men whom one takes an interest in from young men whom one knows.

"You girls are so wonderful in always having— Oh dear! One mustn't talk."
35 For the Andante had begun—very beautiful, but bearing a family likeness to all the other beautiful andantes that Beethoven had written, and, to Helen's mind, rather disconnecting the heroes and shipwrecks of the first movement from the
40 heroes and goblins of the third. She heard the tune through once, and then her attention wandered, and she gazed at the audience, or the organ, or the architecture. Then Beethoven started decorating his tune, so she heard him through once more, and
45 then she smiled at her Cousin Frieda. But Frieda, listening to classical music, could not respond. Herr Liesecke, too, looked as if wild horses could not make him inattentive; there were lines across his forehead, his lips were parted, his glasses at right
50 angles to his nose, and he had laid a thick, white hand on either knee. And next to her was Aunt Juley, so British, and wanting to tap. How interesting that row of people was! What diverse influences had gone into the making of them! Here Beethoven,
55 after humming and hawing with great sweetness, said "Heigho," and the Andante came to an end. Applause ensued, and a round of praise volleying from the audience. Margaret started talking to her new young man; Helen said to her aunt: "Now
60 comes the wonderful movement: first of all the goblins, and then a trio of elephants dancing"; and Tibby implored the company generally to look out for the transitional passage on the drum.

GO ON TO THE NEXT PAGE

"On the what, dear?"

65 "On the drum, Aunt Juley."

"No—look out for the part where you think you are done with the goblins and they come back," breathed Helen, as the music started with a goblin walking quietly over the universe, from end to end.

70 Others followed him. They were not aggressive creatures; that was what made them so terrible to Helen. They merely observed in passing that there was no such thing as splendor or heroism in the world. Helen could not contradict them, for once,

75 she had felt the same, and had seen the reliable walls of youth collapse. Panic and emptiness! Panic and emptiness! The goblins were right. Her brother raised his finger; it was the transitional passage on the drum.

80 Helen pushed her way out during the applause. She desired to be alone. The music had summed up to her all that had happened or could happen in her life.

She read it as a tangible statement, which could

85 never be superseded. The notes meant this and that to her, and they could have no other meaning, and life could have no other meaning. She pushed right out of the building and walked slowly down the outside staircase, breathing the autumnal air, and

90 then she strolled home.

1. Helen would most likely agree with which of the following statements about her relationship with Margaret?

A. Helen disapproves of Margaret's actions.

B. Helen's feelings toward Margaret are affected by Helen's jealousy of the attention Margaret receives from suitors.

C. Helen is not interested in Margaret's actions, at least as long as the music is playing.

D. They are drawn together principally by their mutual love of music.

2. Helen can most accurately be characterized as:

F. creative and effervescent.

G. analytical yet optimistic.

H. imaginative and introspective.

J. curt and insensitive.

3. Which of the following statements does NOT describe one of Helen's reactions to the goblins?

A. She feels that their presence is a denial of the good in the world.

B. She is frightened by the goblins' aggressive nature.

C. She cannot deny the viewpoint that the goblins seem to represent.

D. She believes that the goblins will return after they appear to have left.

4. As it is used in line 43, the word *decorating* most nearly means:

F. dressing up.

G. glamorizing.

H. awarding.

J. embellishing.

GO ON TO THE NEXT PAGE

5. Which of the following does the author mention as images the music brings to the listeners' minds?

   A. Wild horses
   B. Shipwrecks
   C. Queen's Hall
   D. Drums

6. According to the passage, when Tibby listens to the symphony he is:

   F. most interested in the technical aspects of the music.
   G. caught up in imagery that the music conveys to him.
   H. distracted from the performance as a whole because of his focus on the drum.
   J. depressed by his dreary surroundings.

7. Which of the following statements most accurately expresses Helen's feelings as she leaves after the symphony?

   A. Helen feels alienated by the indifference of her companions.
   B. Helen is meditative, pondering the music's immutable meaning.
   C. Helen is upset with Tibby's constant focus on the technical aspects of the music.
   D. Helen is relieved to have escaped the crowding and discomfort of the performance hall.

8. It can most reasonably be inferred from the passage that the reason Aunt Juley refrains from tapping along with the music is because:

   F. Aunt Juley is concentrating instead on the drum.
   G. Aunt Juley does not want to distract Helen.
   H. British custom only permits snapping one's fingers along with the music.
   J. Aunt Juley feels it would not be appropriate.

9. All of the following characters are deeply interested in the music EXCEPT:

   A. Herr Liesecke.
   B. Margaret.
   C. Fraulein Mosebach's young man.
   D. Tibby.

10. According to the passage, the reason why Helen's attention returns to the Andante after it had wandered is because she:

   F. hears changes in the tune.
   G. is directed to do so by Tibby.
   H. no longer wishes to speak with Mrs. Munt.
   J. believes the Andante is nearing its end.

GO ON TO THE NEXT PAGE

Passage II

SOCIAL SCIENCE: *The following passage is adapted from the article "What Causes Overweight and Obesity" released by the National Heart, Lung and Blood Institute.*

The past 10 years have seen a dramatic rise in "diseases of affluence" in the United States. Americans suffer from type II diabetes, obesity, and cardiovascular disease in epidemic proportions.
5 Indeed, American culture is often perceived to be entrenched in fast-food, excessive consumption, and minimal physical exertion. Supermarkets and restaurants in the United States serve a panoply of processed foods loaded with sugar, preservatives,
10 trans-fats and cholesterol. Children develop poor eating habits—from sugar-laden cereals to school lunches drenched in saturated fat—that, unfortunately, last into adulthood. While changes in diet are partly responsible for American obesity, the
15 primary cause of obesity is the sedentary lifestyle that 40 percent of Americans currently lead.

For most of human history, people worked as farmers, hunters, laborers, and tradesmen—all physically demanding occupations. Blacksmiths
20 hammered metal, servants washed dirty linen, and farmers lifted hay bales by hand. At the time, the only sources of work energy were animals or man power. However, these lifestyles afforded people vast stretches of idle time—winter months, reli-
25 gious holidays, and festivals—to rest and recover. Furthermore, routine and leisure activities also required more physical exertion. For all but the wealthy, everyday life was similar to a balanced gym routine. Despite high mortality from infectious
30 diseases and malnutrition (and debilitating physical injuries suffered in far more hazardous working environments than today's workplace), physical fitness was standard.

Urbanization and industrialization during
35 the 19th and 20th centuries drastically changed people's life-styles. Agricultural advances have led to increasingly larger farms manned by fewer workers. Machines are used for most aspects of farming, from sowing seeds to harvesting. Manu-
40 facturing, meanwhile, transformed into a system of mass production facilitated by machines—a process that does not require the range or degree of physical exertion from workers as was necessitated by preindustrial fabrication. People began to move
45 less and sit more. During the 20th century, increasingly elaborate systems of government and finance brought about the most sedentary workplace of all: the office building. Suddenly massive complexes peopled by legions of clerks, salespeople, analysts,
50 and secretaries manning telephones, computers, and typewriters began to fill the American city. Urbanization condensed all aspects of living into a few square blocks. The conveniences of the modern urban environment are also conducive to inactivity.

55 Transportation has also exacerbated the problem by offering city dwellers numerous options for travel, none of which require any real physical exertion. Therefore, the average 9-to-5 worker can go to work, run errands, and seek entertainment with
60 little more effort than what is required to walk to and from a car or a mass transit station.

Leisure has likewise contributed to the obesity epidemic. Watching television and playing video games have supplanted sports, leisurely strolls,
65 and horse-riding as popular pastimes. Pre-studies have revealed a positive correlation between hours of television viewing and levels of obesity. In fact, video games are found to play an especially significant role in childhood obesity.

70 Despite the proliferation of gimmick diets and fancy gadgets, losing weight is actually a simple matter of burning more calories than one consumes. Active living initiatives are working hard to bring more movement into the average
75 American's life. Urban planners are designing cities that include more sidewalks, crosswalks, parks, and

GO ON TO THE NEXT PAGE →

bicycle trails. Education programs and advertising campaigns seek to reform the deleterious habits of adults and create more active lifestyles in children.
80 Parents and nutritionists are working together to banish some of the more egregious offenders—fries, pizza, and soda—from public school cafeterias.

In the 21st century, the stakes for combating obesity in the United States are increasingly high.
85 As an overweight baby boom generation enters its twilight, insurance providers and health care professionals are encountering alarming rates of diabetes and heart disease. American life expectancy has begun to drop from all-time highs during
90 the late 1990s. Even more concerning is the earlier onset of obesity in younger generations. Given that the World Health Organization has estimated 60 percent of the global population get insufficient exercise, finding a way to get people back in shape is
95 perhaps the greatest health care issue that the world currently faces.

11. According to the author, pre-industrial revolution farmers faced challenges of:

A. winter weather.

B. obesity.

C. disease.

D. poor eating habits.

12. According to the passage, all of the following are aspects of pre-industrial culture responsible for promoting physical fitness EXCEPT:

F. the hazardous conditions of the 19th century workplace.

G. the variation of physical activity required by most occupations.

H. the absence of alternative energy source for performing tasks.

J. the vigor of pastime activities.

13. The function of lines 17–33 is to:

A. provide examples of typical pre-industrial occupations that have been rendered obsolete.

B. cite occupations that necessitated human energy for successful completion.

C. recommend jobs that modern Americans should pursue to counter obesity.

D. explain why consuming foods rich in calories was more acceptable in past eras.

14. The third paragraph details the effects of industrialization on the workplace by:

F. citing the hazards of the modern workplace.

G. lamenting the working conditions in office buildings.

H. praising the efficiency of modern farming and manufacturing.

J. indicating specific ways in which modern workers do less physical work.

15. The author mentions 9–5 workers (lines 58–61) in order to:

A. give an example of people who do not get a lot of exercise.

B. prove that pre-industrial revolution farm workers are superior to modern office workers.

C. criticize urbanization.

D. support nutritional initiatives to combat obesity.

16. All of the following are cited as those working to make people more active and improve diets EXCEPT:

F. urban planners.

G. advertisers.

H. nutritionists.

J. physicians.

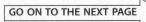
GO ON TO THE NEXT PAGE

Practice Test 8

Reading Test

GO ON TO THE NEXT PAGE

17. According to the passage, losing weight:

   A. is essential to avoiding health problems in later life.

   B. can be achieved only through excessive levels of physical exertion.

   C. is possible when caloric intake exceeds energy burned through activity.

   D. requires a deficit between consumption and metabolism.

18. The author most likely mentions diets and exercise machines to:

   F. contrast public opinion with the simplicity of losing weight.

   G. give examples of effective weight loss techniques.

   H. critique nontraditional methods of combating obesity.

   J. emphasize the ease of using modern exercise machines.

19. Based on the passage, health-conscious families and experts' attitudes toward public school lunches can best be described as:

   A. ambivalent.

   B. inimical.

   C. apathetic.

   D. enthralled.

20. The author most likely mentions *life expectancy* in lines 88–89 in order to:

   F. emphasize the longevity of Americans during the 1990s.

   G. indicate that obesity has innocuous effects on older Americans.

   H. illustrate long-term effects of obesity in the U.S. population.

   J. contrast American health with the health of people in other countries.

GO ON TO THE NEXT PAGE

Passage III

HUMANITIES: *This passage is excerpted from "Mr. Bennett and Mrs. Woolf," by Irving Howe. Reprinted by permission of* The New Republic, *© 1990, The New Republic, LLC.*

Literary polemics come and go, sparking a season of anger and gossip, and then turning to dust. A handful survive their moment: Dr. Johnson's demolition of Soames Jenyn, Hazlitt's attack on
5 Coleridge. But few literary polemics can have been so damaging, or so lasting in consequences, as Virginia Woolf's 1924 essay "Mr. Bennett and Mrs. Brown," about the once widely read English novelists Arnold Bennett, H. G. Wells, and John
10 Galsworthy. For several literary generations now, Woolf's essay has been taken as the definitive word finishing off an old-fashioned school of fiction and thereby clearing the way for literary modernism. Writing with her glistening charm, and casting
15 herself as the voice of the new (always a shrewd strategy in literary debate), Woolf quickly seized the high ground in her battle with Bennett. Against her needling thrusts, the old fellow never had a chance.

The debate has been nicely laid out by Samuel
20 Hynes in *Edwardian Occasions*, and I owe to him some of the following details. It all began in 1917, with Woolf's review of a collection of Bennett's literary pieces, a rather favorable review marred by the stylish snobbism that was becoming a trade-
25 mark of the Bloomsbury circle. Bennett, wrote Woolf, had a materialistic view of the world—"he had been worrying himself to achieve infantile realisms." A catchy phrase, though exactly what "in- fantile realisms" meant Woolf did not trouble to say.
30 During the next few years she kept returning to the attack, as if to prepare for "Mr. Bennett and Mrs. Brown." More than personal sensibilities or rivalries of status was involved here, though both were quite visible; Woolf was intent upon discrediting, if not
35 simply dismissing, a group of literary predecessors who enjoyed a large readership.

In 1923 Bennett reviewed Woolf's novel *Jacob's Room*, praising its "originality" and "exquisite" prose but concluding that "the characters do not
40 vitally survive in the mind." For Bennett, this was a fatal flaw. And for his readers, too—though not for the advanced literary public that by now was learn- ing to suspect this kind of talk about "characters surviving" as a lazy apology for the shapeless and
45 perhaps even mindless Victorian novel.

A year later Woolf published her famous essay, brilliantly sketching an imaginary old lady named Mrs. Brown whom she supplied with anecdotes and reflections as tokens of inner being. These
50 released the sort of insights, suggested Woolf, that would not occur to someone like Bennett, a writer obsessed with dull particulars of setting (weather, town, clothing, furniture, and so on). Were Bennett to write about a Mrs. Brown, he would describe
55 her house in conscientious detail but never pen- etrate her essential life, for—what a keen polemi- cist!— "he is trying to hypnotize us into the belief that, because he has made a house, there must be a person living there." (Herself sensitive to the need
60 for a room with a view, Woolf seemed indifferent to what a house might mean for people who had risen somewhat in the world. For a writer like Bennett, however, imagining a house was part of the way to locate "a person living there.") And in a quiet
65 putdown of Bennett's novel *Hilda Lessways* (not one of his best), Woolf gave a turn of the knife: "One line of insight would have done more than all those lines of description."

From the suave but deadly attack of "Mr. Bennett
70 and Mrs. Brown" Bennett's literary reputation never quite recovered. He remained popular with the general public, but among literary readers, the sort that became the public for the emerging modern- ists, the standard view has long been that he was a
75 middling, plodding sort of Edwardian writer whose work has been pushed aside by the revolutionary achievements of Lawrence, Joyce, and to a smaller extent Woolf herself.

GO ON TO THE NEXT PAGE

When Bennett died in 1930, Woolf noted in
80 her diary that "he had some real understanding power, as well as a gigantic absorbing power
[and] direct contact with life"—all attributes, you
might suppose, handy for a novelist but for her
evidently not sufficient. In saying this, remarks
85 Hynes, "Woolf gave Bennett, perhaps, the 'reality
gift' that [she] doubted in herself, the gift that she
despised and envied." Yes; in much of her fiction
Woolf resembles Stevens's man with the blue guitar
who "cannot bring a world quite round/Although I
90 patch it as I can." Still, none of this kept Woolf from
steadily sniping at Bennett's "shopkeeping view
of literature." Bennett was a provincial from the
Five Towns; Bennett was commercially successful;
Bennett was an elder to be pulled down, as elders
95 must always be pulled down even if they are also
admired a little.

21. Which of the following statements best
characterizes the author's view of Virginia
Woolf?

    A. Woolf criticized others only in areas
where she felt strong, leaving her own
weaknesses out of the discussion.

    B. Woolf only disparaged Bennett and
his school of authors because she
envied the strides they had made.

    C. Woolf almost single-handedly
changed the prevailing opinion about
a particular writer and laid the path
for a new school of literature.

    D. Woolf's views toward the venerated
authors of the day were abusive, and
her reputation has rightly suffered as
a result of those attacks.

22. As it is used in line 1, the word *polemics* most
nearly means:

    F. attacks.

    G. reviews.

    H. controversies.

    J. friendships.

23. In the first paragraph, the author compares
Woolf's polemic against Bennett to other literary
attacks. This comparison supports the author's
view that:

    A. Bennett's dull style of writing would soon
have fallen out of fashion anyway.

    B. many such attacks are remembered as
turning points for the arts.

    C. Woolf fought with other authors often.

    D. Woolf's criticisms of Bennett were
especially important and memorable.

24. According to the passage, Bennett's literary output was marked by:

    F. description of the scene rather than
insight into the characters.

    G. the use of colorful characters who
frequently reveal their deepest emotions.

    H. fewer essays than Woolf wrote.

    J. exhaustive description of minute details.

25. It can be reasonably inferred from the passage
that the author means to:

    A. demonstrate an effective strategy for
writing a literary polemic.

    B. suggest a new interpretation of a well-
known literary polemic.

    C. analyze one literary polemic and its effect
on the literature of its era.

    D. assess the significance of a literary
polemic in the context of similar works.

GO ON TO THE NEXT PAGE

26. Based on the passage, it is most reasonable to infer that Woolf's phrase *infantile realisms* (lines 27–28) means:

    F. a focus on things rather than on people.

    G. the values of the Bloomsbury Circle.

    H. the type of writing that doesn't survive in the reader's mind.

    J. the superficial details of Mrs. Brown's house.

27. In the final sentence of the passage, the author suggests that Woolf believed that "elders must always be pulled down." This same sentiment is most closely exemplified by which of the following examples from the passage?

    A. The author's view of Woolf's novel *Jacob's Room*

    B. The author's view of *Edwardian Occasions* by Samuel Hynes

    C. The author's comparison of Woolf to "Stevens's man with the blue guitar"

    D. The author's reference to Bennett's *Hilda Lessways* as "not one of his best"

28. Bennett's general opinion of Woolf's novel *Jacob's Room* was that it was:

    F. inferior to other novels published at that time.

    G. a keen example of a new style of literature.

    H. a success, despite one or two minor failings.

    J. generally original and inspired, but with significant problems.

29. It is Woolf's opinion that the thoughts and feelings of characters are more important than the details of a scene because:

    A. scenic descriptions were part of a literary style that she disliked.

    B. scenic details cannot convey a sense of the character within.

    C. good authors know to include at least one line of insight into a character.

    D. scenic details create characters that are easily forgettable.

30. In the last paragraph, the function of the phrase "he had some real understanding power, as well as a gigantic absorbing power [and] direct contact with life" (lines 80–82) is to present:

    F. Woolf retracting her criticism of Bennett.

    G. Woolf excoriating Bennett.

    H. Bennett praising Woolf.

    J. Woolf praising Bennett.

GO ON TO THE NEXT PAGE

Passage IV

NATURAL SCIENCE: *Fossil fuels are energy-rich substances formed from the remains of organisms. Both coal and petroleum help power commercial energy throughout the world.*

Passage A

Coal is a solid fossil fuel formed from the remains of land plants that flourished 300 to 400 million years ago. It is composed primarily of carbon but also contains small amounts of sulfur. When the
5   sulfur is released into the atmosphere as a result of burning, it can form SO_2, a corrosive gas that can damage plants and animals. When it combines with H_2O in the atmosphere, it can form sulfuric acid, one of the main components of acid rain, which has
10 been demonstrated to be an environmental hazard. Burning coal has also been shown to contain trace amounts of mercury and radioactive materials, similarly dangerous substances. The type of coal that is burned directly affects the amount of sulfur that is
15 released into the atmosphere.

The formation of coal goes through discrete stages as, over millions of years, heat and pressure act on decomposing plants. Coal begins as peat, partially decayed plant matter, which is still found
20 today in swamps and bogs, and can be burned, but produces little heat. As the decayed plant material is compressed over time, lignite is formed. Lignite is a sedimentary rock with low sulfur content and, like peat, also produces a small amount of heat
25 when burned. With further compaction, lignite loses moisture, methane, and carbon dioxide, and becomes bituminous coal, the form of coal most widely used. Bituminous coal is also a sedimentary rock, but it has a high sulfur content.

30 Anthracite, or hard coal, is a metamorphic rock formed when heat and pressure are added to bituminous coal. Anthracite coal is most desirable because it burns very hot and also contains a much smaller amount of sulfur, meaning that it burns cleaner.

35 However, the supplies of anthracite on Earth are limited. In the United States, most anthracite is extracted from the valleys of northeastern Pennsylvania, which is known as the Coal Region. The major American reserve of bituminous coal is
40 in West Virginia, while the largest coal producer in the world is The People's Republic of China. The United States and China are also foremost among the world's coal consumers. There are many other coal-producing areas throughout the world, though
45 in some cases, the coal is essentially tapped out, or other, cleaner sources of coal are preferred.

Coal is extracted from mines. For subsurface mines, machines dig shafts and tunnels underground to allow the miners to remove the mate-
50 rial. Buildup of poisonous gases, explosions, and collapses are all dangers that underground miners must face. The Sago Mine disaster of January 2006 in West Virginia—where only 1 of 13 trapped miners survived an explosion—shows how extracting
55 these underground deposits of solid material is still a very dangerous process. Strip mining, or surface mining, is cheaper and less hazardous than underground mining. However, it often leaves the land scarred and unsuitable for other uses.

Passage B

60 Petroleum, or crude oil, is a thick liquid that contains organic compounds of hydrogen and carbon, called hydrocarbons. The term "crude oil" refers to both the unprocessed petroleum and the products refined from it, such as gasoline, heating
65 oil, and asphalt. Petroleum contains many types of hydrocarbons in liquid, solid and gaseous forms, as well as sulfur, oxygen, and nitrogen.

When organic material such as zooplankton and algae settled on the bottom of oceans millions of
70 years ago, the material mixed with mud and was covered in sediment more quickly than it could decay. Thousands of years later, the sediments that contained the organic material were subjected to

GO ON TO THE NEXT PAGE ⟹

intense amounts of heat and pressure, changing
75 it into a waxy material called kerogen. From this
substance, liquid hydrocarbons can be produced to
create oil shale. When more heat was added to the
kerogen, it liquefied into the substance we know
as oil. Since hydrocarbons are usually lighter than
80 rock or water, they migrate upward through the
permeable rock layers until they reach impermeable
rocks. The areas where oil remains in the porous
rocks are called reservoirs.

Oil is traditionally pumped out of the layer of
85 reserves found under the surface of Earth. In order
to penetrate the earth, an oil well is created using
an oil rig, which turns a drill bit. After the hole
is drilled, a casing—a metal pipe with a slightly
smaller diameter than the hole—is inserted and
90 bonded to its surroundings, usually with cement.
This strengthens the sides of the hole, or wellbore,
and keeps dangerous pressure zones isolated. This
process is repeated with smaller bits and thinner
casings, going deeper into the surface to reach
95 the reservoir. Drilling fluid is pushed through the
casings to break up the rock in front of the bit and
to clean away debris and lower the temperature of
the bit, which grows very hot. Once the reservoir is
reached, the top of the wellbore is usually equipped
100 with a set of valves encased in a pyramidal iron cage
called a Christmas Tree.

The natural pressure within the reservoir is
usually high enough to push the oil or gas up to the
surface. But sometimes, additional measures, called
105 secondary recovery, are required. This is especially
true in depleted fields. Installing thinner tubing
is one solution, as are surface pump jacks—the
structures that look like horses repeatedly dipping
their heads.
110 It is impossible to remove all of the oil in a single
reservoir. In fact, a 30 percent to 40 percent yield
is typical. However, technology has provided a few
ways to increase drilling yield, including forcing
water or steam into the rock to "push" out more
115 of the oil. Even with this technique, only about 50
percent of the deposit will be extracted.

There are also more unconventional sources
of oil, including oil shale and tar sands. The
hydrocarbons obtained from these sources require
120 extensive processing to be useable, reducing their
value. The extraction process also has a particularly
large environmental footprint.

Questions 31–33 ask about Passage A.

31. According to the first paragraph, all of the
following are released or formed when coal
is burned EXCEPT:

A. SO_2.

B. sulfuric acid.

C. hydrocarbons.

D. mercury.

32. The passage suggests that which of the
following has the smallest amount of
moisture, methane, and carbon dioxide?

F. Lignite

G. Peat

H. Bituminous coal

J. Kerogen

33. The author contrasts bituminous coal with
anthracite in order to:

A. indicate that bituminous coals burns
cleaner.

B. compare the amount of mercury in
each one.

C. suggest that burning anthracite is
better for the environment.

D. recommend replacing all coals with
oil.

GO ON TO THE NEXT PAGE

Practice Test 8

Questions 34–36 ask about Passage B.

34. As it is used in line 122, the phrase *environmental footprint* most likely means:

  F. indentations in the surface of the earth.

  G. the positive environmental results of extracting oil.

  H. the effect that a person or activity has on the environment.

  J. irreversible damage to the earth.

35. According to the passage, the second step in extracting the oil is:

  A. drilling a hole.

  B. pushing in draining fluid.

  C. topping with valves.

  D. inserting a pipe.

36. What is most likely true about an oil field in which a pump jack is installed?

  F. Oil is being extracted in the safest way.

  G. The oil reserves in the field are greatly diminished.

  H. About 60 percent of the available oil is recovered.

  J. The wellbore is strengthened.

Questions 37–40 ask about both passages.

37. Both passages include details regarding all of the following EXCEPT:

  A. the transformation of organic material into usable energy sources.

  B. the lengthy nature of converting organic material into fossil fuel.

  C. the limited supply of fossil fuels.

  D. evidence to support the claim that solar power is a safer energy source than oil or coal.

38. The formation of both coal and oil requires all of the following EXCEPT:

  F. proper extraction techniques

  G. pressure.

  H. heat.

  J. organic material.

39. Fossil fuel is formed in a multi-step process, as stated in Passage A, where the author writes that "The formation of coal goes through discrete stages . . ." Which sentence in Passage B confirms a similar multistep process for the formation of oil?

  A. The areas where oil remains in the porous rocks are called reservoirs.

  B. The natural pressure within the reservoir is usually high enough to push the oil or gas up to the surface.

  C. When more heat was added to the kerogen, it liquefied into the subtance we know as oil.

  D. Petroleum contains many different types of hydrocarbons in liquid, solid, and gaseous forms, as well as sulfur, oxygen, and nitrogen.

40. The final sentence in each passage conveys which of the following?

  F. The land cannot recover after fossil fuels have been extracted.

  G. The process of extracting coal and oil present environmental repercussions.

  H. New technology can reduce the amount of sulfur released into the air.

  J. Lead is as hazardous to both people and the environment as coal and oil.

IF YOU FINISH BEFORE TIME IS CALLED, YOU MAY CHECK YOUR WORK ON THIS SECTION ONLY. DO NOT TURN TO ANY OTHER SECTION IN THE TEST.

SCIENCE TEST

35 Minutes—40 Questions

Directions: The Science Test includes multiple passages. Each passage includes multiple questions. After reading each passage, choose the best answer and fill in the corresponding bubble on your answer sheet. You may review the passages as often as necessary.

You may NOT use a calculator on this test.

Passage I

A panel of engineers designed and built a pressurized structure to be used for shelter by geologists during extended research missions near the South Pole. The design consisted of 4 rooms, each with its own separate heating and air pressure control systems. During testing, the engineers found the daily average air temperature, in degrees Celsius (°C), and daily average air pressure, in millimeters of mercury (mm Hg), in each room. The data for the first 5 days of their study are given in Table 1 and Table 2.

Table 1				
	Daily average air temperature (°C)			
Day	Room 1	Room 2	Room 3	Room 4
1	19.64	19.08	18.67	18.03
2	20.15	19.20	18.46	18.11
3	20.81	19.19	18.62	18.32
4	21.06	19.51	19.08	18.91
5	21.14	19.48	18.60	18.58

Table 2				
	Daily average air pressure (mm Hg)			
Day	Room 1	Room 2	Room 3	Room 4
1	748.2	759.6	760.0	745.2
2	752.6	762.0	758.7	750.3
3	753.3	760.2	756.5	760.4
4	760.1	750.8	755.4	756.8
5	758.7	757.9	754.0	759.5

GO ON TO THE NEXT PAGE

1. The lowest daily average air pressure recorded during the first 5 days of the study was:

   A. 762.0 mm Hg.

   B. 745.2 mm Hg.

   C. 21.14 mm Hg.

   D. 18.03 mm Hg.

2. According to Table 2, daily average air pressures were recorded to the nearest:

   F. 0.01 mm Hg.

   G. 0.1 mm Hg.

   H. 1   mm Hg.

   J. 10   mm Hg.

3. Which of the following graphs best represents a plot of the daily average air temperature versus the daily average air pressure for Room 4 ?

   A.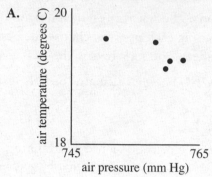

   B.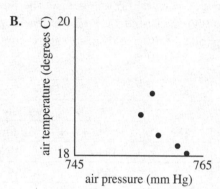

   C.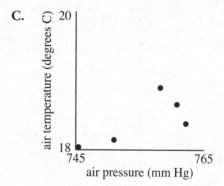

   D.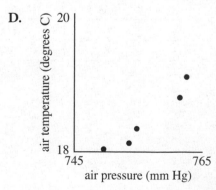

GO ON TO THE NEXT PAGE

4. Which of the following most accurately describes the changes in the daily average air pressure in Room 3 during days 1–5 ?

   F. The daily average air pressure increased from day 1 to day 4 and decreased from day 4 to day 5.

   G. The daily average air pressure decreased from day 1 to day 2, increased from day 2 to day 4, and decreased again from day 4 to day 5.

   H. The daily average air pressure increased only.

   J. The daily average air pressure decreased only.

5. Suppose the *heat absorption modulus* of a room is defined as the quantity of heat absorbed by the contents of the room divided by the quantity of heat provided to the entire room. Based on the data, would you be justified in concluding that the heat absorption modulus of Room 1 was higher than the heat absorption modulus of any of the other rooms?

   A. Yes, because the quantity of heat provided to Room 1 was greater than the quantity of heat provided to any of the other rooms.

   B. Yes, because the quantity of heat not absorbed by the contents of Room 1 was greater than the quantity of heat not absorbed by the contents of any of the other rooms.

   C. No, because the quantity of heat absorbed by the contents of Room 1 was less than the quantity of heat absorbed by the contents of any of the other rooms.

   D. No, because the information provided is insufficient to determine heat absorption modulus.

6. If the geologists were to use equipment that malfunctions in warm environments, which room would be most likely to cause the equipment to malfunction?

   F. Room 1

   G. Room 2

   H. Room 3

   J. Room 4

GO ON TO THE NEXT PAGE

Passage II

Microbiologists have observed that certain species of bacteria are *magnetotactic*, that is, sensitive to magnetic fields. Several species found in the bottom of swamps in the Northern Hemisphere tend to orient themselves toward magnetic north (the northern pole of the earth's magnetic field). Researchers conducted the following series of experiments on magnetotactic bacteria.

Study 1

A drop of water filled with magnetotactic bacteria was observed under high magnification. The direction of the first 500 bacterial migrations across the field of view was observed for each of five trials and the tally for each trial recorded in Table 1. Trial 1 was conducted under standard laboratory conditions. In Trial 2, the microscope was shielded from all external light and electric fields. In Trials 3 and 4, the microscope was rotated clockwise 90° and 180°, respectively. For Trial 5, the microscope was moved to another laboratory at the same latitude.

Table 1				
	Direction			
Trial	North	East	South	West
1	474	7	13	6
2	481	3	11	5
3	479	4	12	5
4	465	9	19	7
5	480	3	11	6

Study 2

The north pole of a permanent magnet was positioned near the microscope slide. The magnet was at the 12:00 position for Trial 6 and was moved 90° clockwise for each of three successive trials. All other conditions were as in Trial 1 of Study 1. The results were tallied and recorded in Table 2.

Table 2				
	Direction			
Trial	12:00	3:00	6:00	9:00
6	470	6	15	9
7	8	483	3	6
8	17	4	474	5
9	5	19	9	467

7. What serves as the control in Study 1 ?

   A. Trial 1

   B. Trial 2

   C. Trial 3

   D. Trial 5

8. The hypothesis that light was NOT the primary stimulus affecting the direction of bacterial migration is:

   F. supported by a comparison of the results of Studies 1 and 2.

   G. supported by a comparison of the results of Trials 1 and 2 of Study 1.

   H. supported by a comparison of the results of Trials 3 and 4 of Study 1.

   J. not supported by any of the results noted in the passage.

GO ON TO THE NEXT PAGE

9. If the south pole of the permanent magnet used in Study 2 had been placed near the microscope slide, what would the most likely result have been?

   A. The figures for each trial would have remained approximately the same, since the strength of the magnetic field would be unchanged.

   B. The bacteria would have become disoriented, with approximately equal numbers moving in each direction.

   C. The major direction of travel would have shifted by 180° because of the reversed direction of the magnetic field.

   D. The bacteria would still have tended to migrate toward Earth's magnetic north, but would have taken longer to orient themselves.

10. It has been suggested that magnetic sensitivity helps magnetotactic bacteria orient themselves downward. Such an orientation would be most advantageous from an evolutionary standpoint if:

    F. organisms that consume magnetotactic bacteria were mostly bottom-dwellers.

    G. the bacteria could only reproduce by migrating upwards to the water's surface.

    H. bacteria that stayed in the top layers of water tended to be dispersed by currents.

    J. the nutrients necessary for the bacteria's survival were more abundant in bottom sediments.

11. Researchers could gain the most useful new information about the relationship between magnetic field strength and bacterial migration by repeating Study 2 with:

    A. incremental position changes of less than 90°.

    B. a magnet that rotated slowly around the slide in a counterclockwise direction.

    C. more and less powerful magnets.

    D. larger and smaller samples of bacteria.

12. Which of the following statements is supported by the results of Study 1 ?

    F. The majority of magnetotactic bacteria migrate toward the Earth's magnetic north pole.

    G. The majority of magnetotactic bacteria migrate toward the north pole of the nearest magnet.

    H. The majority of magnetotactic bacteria migrate toward the 12:00 position.

    J. The effect of the Earth's magnetic field on magnetotactic bacteria is counteracted by electric fields.

GO ON TO THE NEXT PAGE

Practice Test 8   777

Science Test

13. If each diagram below represents a microscopic field, which diagram best reflects the results of Trial 7 from Study 2 ?

A.

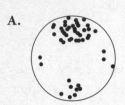

B.

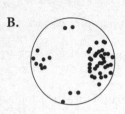

C.

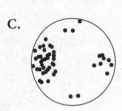

D.

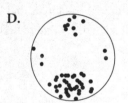

Passage III

A student performed three studies with a battery and four different light bulbs.

Study 1

The student connected the battery to a fixed outlet designed to accept any of the four bulbs. She then placed four identical light sensors at different distances from the outlet. Each sensor was designed so that a green indicator lit up upon the sensor's detection of incident light, while a red indicator remained illuminated when no light was detected. The student darkened the room and recorded the state of each sensor while each bulb was lit. The results are shown in Table 1.

Table 1				
Sensor distance (cm)	Sensor indicator color			
	Bulb 1	Bulb 2	Bulb 3	Bulb 4
50	green	green	green	green
100	red	green	green	green
150	red	red	green	green
200	red	red	red	green

Study 2

The battery produced an *electromotive force*, or voltage, of 12 volts (V). The student was given a device called an *ammeter*, which is used to measure the current passing through an electric circuit. She completed the circuit by connecting the battery, the ammeter, and each of the four light bulbs, one at a time. She measured the associated current in amperes (A) for each bulb and calculated the *impedance* (Z), or effective resistance to the flow of current, in ohms (Ω) for each bulb, using the following formula:

$$Z = \text{voltage} \div \text{current}$$

GO ON TO THE NEXT PAGE

778 Practice Test 8

Practice Test 8

The results are shown in Table 2.

Table 2		
Bulb	Current (A)	Z (Ω)
1	0.2	60
2	0.3	40
3	0.4	30
4	0.6	20

Study 3

The *power rating* (P) of each light bulb was printed near its base. P is a measure of the energy consumption of the bulb per unit time and is related to the *brightness* (B) of the light at a given distance from the bulb. B is calculated in watts per square meter (W/m^2), using the following formula:

$$B = \frac{P}{4\pi r^2}$$

where r is the distance in meters (m) from the bulb, and P is measured in watts (W).

The student calculated B for each bulb at a distance of 1 m. The results are shown in Table 3.

Table 3		
Bulb	P (W)	B (W/m^2)
1	2.4	0.19
2	3.6	0.29
3	4.8	0.38
4	7.2	0.57

14. If the student had tested a fifth light bulb during Study 2 and measured the current passing through it to be 1.2 A, the Z associated with this bulb would have been:

    F.   1 Ω.
    G. 10 Ω.
    H. 14.4 Ω.
    J. 100 Ω.

15. Based on the results of Study 2, a circuit including the combination of which of the following batteries and light bulbs would result in the highest current in the circuit? (Assume Z remains constant for a given light bulb.)

    A. A 10 V battery and Bulb 1
    B. An 8 V battery and Bulb 2
    C. A 6 V battery and Bulb 3
    D. A 5 V battery and Bulb 4

16. With Bulb 3 in place in the circuit in Study 1, how many of the sensors were unable to detect any incident light?

    F. 1
    G. 2
    H. 3
    J. 4

17. Which of the following equations correctly calculates B (in W/m^2) at a distance of 2 m from Bulb 2 ?

    A. $B = \dfrac{2}{4\pi(3.6)^2}$

    B. $B = \dfrac{2}{4\pi(2.4)^2}$

    C. $B = \dfrac{3.6}{4\pi(2)^2}$

    D. $B = \dfrac{2.4}{4\pi(2)^2}$

GO ON TO THE NEXT PAGE

18. Another student used the approach given in Study 3 to calculate B at a distance of 1 m from a fifth light bulb. He determined that, for this fifth bulb, $B = 0.95$ W/m². Accordingly, P for this bulb was most likely closest to which of the following values?

    F. 0.1 W

    G. 6 W

    H. 12 W

    J. 18 W

19. One difference between Study 1 and Study 2 is that, in Study 1:

    A. 4 light sensors were used.

    B. 4 different light bulbs were used.

    C. the voltage of the battery was varied.

    D. the current was highest for Bulb 1.

20. According to Table 3, which light bulb with a brightness greater than 0.30 W/m² has the lowest power consumption?

    F. Bulb 1

    G. Bulb 2

    H. Bulb 3

    J. Bulb 4

Passage IV

The electrons in a solid occupy *energy states* determined by the type and spatial distribution of the atoms in the solid. The probability that a given energy state will be occupied by an electron is given by the *Fermi-Dirac distribution function*, which depends on the material and the temperature of the solid. Fermi-Dirac distribution functions for the same solid at 3 different temperatures are shown in Figure 1.

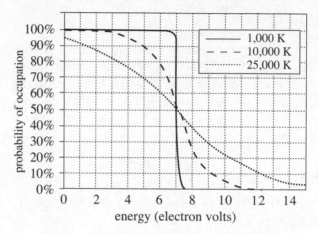

Figure 1

(Note: 1 electron volt (eV) $= 1.66 \times 10^{-19}$ joules (J); eV and J are both units of energy. At energies above 15 eV, the probability of occupation at each temperature continues to decrease.)

21. The information in Figure 1 supports which of the following statements about energy states?

    A. Cooler materials have a larger range of energy states than hotter materials.

    B. Materials have the same range of energy states regardless of temperature.

    C. Cooler materials are more capable of occupying higher energy states than hotter materials.

    D. Hotter materials are more capable of occupying higher energy states than cooler materials.

GO ON TO THE NEXT PAGE

22. The steepness of the slope of each distribution function at the point where its value equals 50% is inversely proportional to the average *kinetic energy* of the atoms in the solid. Which of the following correctly ranks the 3 functions, from *least* to *greatest*, according to the average kinetic energy of the atoms in the solid?

    F. 25,000 K; 10,000 K; 1,000 K
    G. 25,000 K; 1,000 K; 10,000 K
    H. 10,000 K; 1,000 K; 25,000 K
    J. 1,000 K; 10,000 K; 25,000 K

23. Based on Figure 1, the probability of an electron occupying an energy state of 20 eV at a temperature of 1,000 K is:

    A. less than 5%.
    B. between 5% and 50%.
    C. between 50% and 90%.
    D. greater than 90%.

24. Based on Figure 1, which of the following sets of Fermi-Dirac distribution functions best represents an unknown solid at temperatures of 2,000 K, 20,000 K, and 50,000 K ?

F.

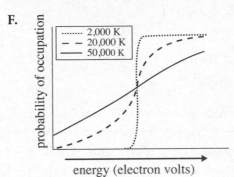

G.

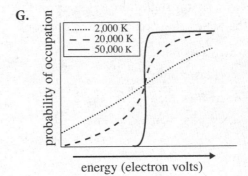

H.

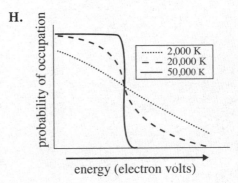

J.

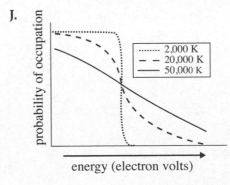

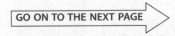

GO ON TO THE NEXT PAGE

Practice Test 8

25. Based on Figure 1, the probability of a 5 eV energy state being occupied by an electron will equal 80% when the temperature of the solid is closest to:

    A.   500 K.

    B.   5,000 K.

    C. 20,000 K.

    D. 30,000 K.

26. The *de Broglie wavelength* of an electron energy state decreases as the energy of the state increases. Based on this information, over all energies in Figure 1, as the de Broglie wavelength of an electron energy state decreases, the probability of that state being occupied by an electron:

    F. increases only.

    G. decreases only.

    H. increases, then decreases.

    J. decreases, then increases.

Passage V

Soft drinks consist of carbonated water (carbon dioxide gas dissolved in water), sweeteners, colors, and flavors. Students hypothesized that the amount of CO_2 dissolved in water depends upon the pressure and temperature. The following experiments were performed to study the solubility of CO_2 in 5 different soft drinks (A, B, C, D, and E).

Experiment 1

To simulate a 12-fluid-ounce can of soft drink at various temperatures, students filled a 355-milliliter (mL) cylinder with 330 mL of Soft Drink A. The cylinder was then sealed and placed in a water bath at room temperature (25°C), as depicted in Diagram 1. After 10 minutes, a pressure gauge was attached and used to measure the air pressure of the headspace (the unfilled space of the cylinder). Additional trials were performed at 35°C and at a refrigerated temperature of 4°C. The experiment was repeated for Soft Drinks B, C, D, and E. The results are shown in Table 1.

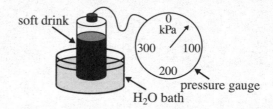

Diagram 1

Table 1			
Soft Drink	Pressure (kPa) at:		
	4°C	25°C	35°C
A	130	237	366
B	114	234	353
C	149	284	394
D	123	243	382
E	109	228	347

GO ON TO THE NEXT PAGE

Experiment 2

The cylinder used in Experiment 1 was completely filled (no headspace) with uncarbonated Soft Drink A. At a pressure of 1 atmosphere (atm) and room temperature, the students then dissolved CO_2 into the soft drink until the solution reached its maximum CO_2 concentration. From the maximum concentration, the solubility of CO_2 was calculated and recorded in millimoles per liter-atmosphere (mmol/L-atm). Additional trials were performed at 4°C and 35°C. The experiment was repeated for Soft Drinks B, C, D, and E. The results are shown in Table 2.

Table 2			
Soft Drink	CO_2 solubility (mmol/L-atm) at:		
	4°C	25°C	35°C
A	65.92	34.09	25.00
B	65.91	34.08	24.92
C	66.00	34.15	25.03
D	65.95	34.11	24.96
E	65.87	34.04	24.84

27. Which of the following bar graphs best represents the pressures of the container contents from Experiment 1 at 25°C ?

A.

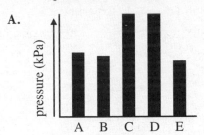

B.

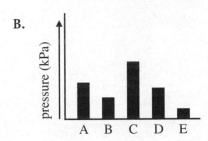

C.

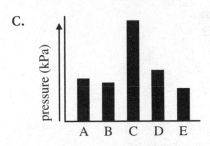

D.

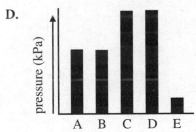

GO ON TO THE NEXT PAGE

28. Which of the following pairs of figures best depicts the change in position of the needle on the pressure gauge while attached to the container holding Soft Drink C in Experiment 1 ?

<u>needle position at 4°C</u>   <u>needle position at 35°C</u>

F.
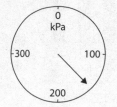

G.
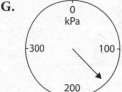

H.
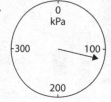

J.
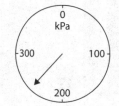

29. A student hypothesized that, at a given pressure and temperature, the higher the sugar content of a soft drink, the higher the solubility of CO_2 in that soft drink. Do the results of Experiment 2 and all of the information in the table below support this hypothesis?

Soft Drink	Sugar content (grams per 12 ounces)
A	23
B	32
C	38
D	40
E	34

A. Yes; Soft Drink A has the lowest sugar content and the lowest CO_2 solubility.

B. Yes; Soft Drink D has a higher sugar content and CO_2 solubility than Soft Drink C.

C. No; the higher a soft drink's sugar content, the lower the soft drink's CO_2 solubility.

D. No; there is no clear relationship in these data between sugar content and CO_2 solubility.

30. According to the results of Experiment 1, as the temperature of the soft drink increases, the pressure:

F. decreases only.

G. increases only.

H. decreases, then increases.

J. increases, then decreases.

GO ON TO THE NEXT PAGE

31. Which of the following figures best illustrates the apparatus used in Experiment 2 ?

A.

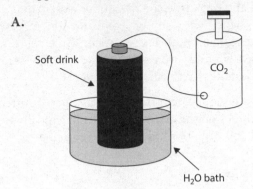

B.

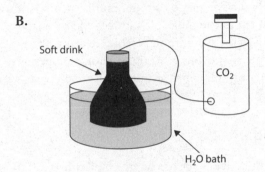

C.

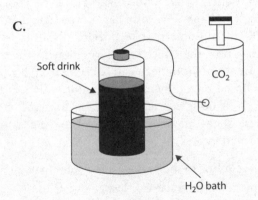

D.

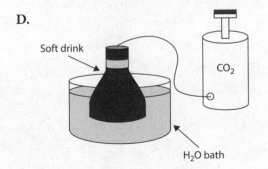

32. Which of the following statements best explains why, in Experiment 1, the students waited 10 minutes before recording the pressure of the air above the soft drink? The students waited to allow:

F. all of the CO_2 to be removed from the container.

G. time for the soft drink in the container to evaporate.

H. the contents of the container to adjust to the temperature of the H_2O bath.

J. time for the pressure gauge to stabilize.

33. Table 2 shows that the soft drink's CO_2 solubility:

A. increases as temperature increases.

B. decreases as temperature increases.

C. sometimes increases and sometimes decreases as temperature increases.

D. is not affected by changes in temperature.

GO ON TO THE NEXT PAGE

Practice Test 8

Passage VI

Straight-chain conformational isomers are simple carbon compounds that differ only by rotation about one or more single carbon bonds. Essentially, these isomers represent the same compound in slightly different positions (or conformations). One example of such isomers can be found with butane (C_4H_{10}), in which the first and last carbon atoms of the chain can be thought of as methyl (CH_3) groups. As bonds in the carbon chain rotate, these 2 methyl groups can occupy different positions in space relative to one another. The conformational isomers of butane are classified into 4 categories, based on the angle between the 2 bonds to the methyl groups. These isomers are depicted as *Newman projections* (a perspective which highlights the angle between the methyl group bonds) in Diagram 1.

1. In the *anti* conformation, the bonds connecting the methyl groups are rotated 180° with respect to each other.

2. In the *gauche* conformation, the bonds connecting the methyl groups are rotated 60° with respect to each other.

3. In the *eclipsed* conformation, the bonds connecting the methyl groups are rotated 120° with respect to each other.

4. In the *totally eclipsed* conformation, the bonds connecting the methyl groups are rotated 0° with respect to each other.

Diagram 1

The anti conformation is the lowest energy and most stable state of the butane molecule since it allows for the methyl groups to maintain maximum separation from each other. The methyl groups are much closer to each other in the gauche conformation, but this still represents a relative minimum or *meta-stable* state, due to the relative orientations of the other hydrogen atoms in the molecule. Molecules in the anti or gauche conformations tend to maintain their shape. The eclipsed conformation represents a relative maximum energy state, while the totally eclipsed conformation is the highest energy state of all of butane's conformational isomers.

Two organic chemistry students offered different hypotheses on the *active shape* (the chemically functional conformation) of a butane molecule.

Student 1

The active shape of a butane molecule is always identical to the molecule's lowest-energy shape. Any other shape would be unstable. Because the lowest-energy shape for a straight-chain conformational isomer of butane is the anti conformation, its active shape is always the anti conformation.

Student 2

The active shape of a butane molecule is dependent upon the energy state of the shape. However, a butane molecule's shape may also depend on temperature and its initial isomeric state. Specifically, in order to convert from the gauche conformation to the anti conformation, the molecule must pass through either the eclipsed or totally eclipsed conformation. If the molecule is not given enough energy to reach either of these states, its active shape will be the gauche conformation.

34. According to the passage, molecules in conformations with relatively low energy tend to:

   F. convert to the totally eclipsed conformation.

   G. convert to the eclipsed conformation.

   H. maintain their shape.

   J. be unstable.

GO ON TO THE NEXT PAGE

35. The information in the passage indicates that when a compound changes from one straight-chain conformational isomer to another, it still retains its original:

   A. energy state.

   B. shape.

   C. number of single carbon bonds.

   D. temperature.

36. Student 2's views differ from Student 1's views in that only Student 2 believes that a butane molecule's active shape is partially determined by its:

   F. initial isomeric state.

   G. energy state.

   H. stability.

   J. proximity of methyl groups.

37. A student rolls a ball along the curved path shown below. Given that points closer to the ground represent states of lower energy, the ball coming to rest at the position shown corresponds to a butane molecule settling into which conformational isomer?

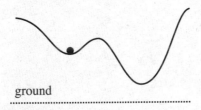

   A. Anti

   B. Gauche

   C. Eclipsed

   D. Totally eclipsed

38. Suppose butane molecules are cooled so that each molecule is allowed to reach its active shape. Which of the following statements is most consistent with the information presented in the passage?

   F. If Student 1 is correct, all of the molecules will be in the anti conformation.

   G. If Student 1 is correct, all of the molecules will have shapes different from their lowest-energy shapes.

   H. If Student 2 is correct, all of the molecules will be in the anti conformation.

   J. If Student 2 is correct, all of the molecules will have shapes different than their lowest-energy shapes.

GO ON TO THE NEXT PAGE

39. Which of the following diagrams showing the relationship between a given butane molecule's shape and its relative energy is consistent with Student 2's assertions about the energy of butane molecules, but is NOT consistent with Student 1's assertions about the energy of butane molecules?

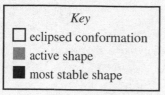

Key

☐ eclipsed conformation
▩ active shape
■ most stable shape

A.

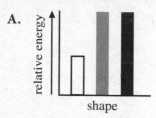

B.

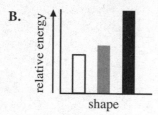

C.

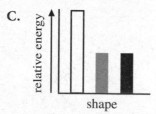

D.

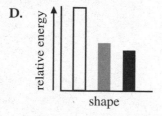

40. Student 2 argues that a butane molecule can sometimes settle into a gauche conformation, even though this is not its lowest energy state. Which of the following findings, if true, would most effectively *counter* the argument he presents for this claim?

F. Once a molecule has settled into a given conformation, all of its single carbon bonds are stable.

G. Enough energy is always available in the environment to overcome local energy barriers.

H. During molecule formation, the hydrogen bonds are formed before the carbon bonds.

J. Molecules that change their isomeric conformation tend to lose their chemical functions.

IF YOU FINISH BEFORE TIME IS CALLED, YOU MAY CHECK YOUR WORK ON THIS SECTION ONLY. DO NOT TURN TO ANY OTHER SECTION IN THE TEST. STOP

Practice Test 8

WRITING TEST

40 Minutes—1 Question

Directions: The essay is used to evaluate your writing skills. You will have **40 minutes** to review the prompt and plan and write an essay in English. Before you begin, read everything in this test booklet carefully to make sure you understand the task.

Your essay will be judged based on the evidence it provides of your ability to do the following:

- Assert your own perspective on a complex issue and evaluate the relationship between your perspective and at least one other perspective

- Use reasoning and evidence to refine and justify your ideas

- Present your ideas in an organized way

- Convey your ideas effectively using standard written English

Write your essay on the lined essay pages in the answer booklet. All writing on those lined pages will be scored. Use the unlined pages in this test booklet to plan your essay. Your work on these unlined pages will not be scored.

Put your pencil down as soon as time is called.

DO NOT OPEN THIS BOOKLET UNTIL TOLD TO DO SO.

GO ON TO THE NEXT PAGE

Access to Technology

To help ready students to become productive members of the workforce, schools concentrate on providing a strong foundation on which students can build their careers. Since job applicants who are proficient in word processing applications, email programs, and storage tools are more likely to be hired than applicants who do not have technology experience, it is to the benefit of students that schools offer technology instruction in high school. Given the importance of technology in today's society, should schools be responsible for providing ongoing access to computers for every student? Since many students will need to use computers in various capacities throughout their lifetimes, how well a school provides access to technology directly affects its student body.

Read and carefully consider these perspectives. Each discusses the importance of student access to technology.

Perspective One	Perspective Two	Perspective Three
Schools should be encouraged to incorporate technology objectives into homework assignments and class projects, but schools do not have an obligation to provide unlimited access to computers. Teachers can provide time during the school day for students to use on-site computer labs, which will allow students the tools they need to complete assignments that require computer technology.	Schools should be required to provide personal computers for students to use at least throughout their high school careers, if not during middle and elementary school as well. Unlimited access to a personal computer for every student will foster continual development of technological abilities, which is a highly valued skill set.	Schools and computer companies should work together to provide significant student discounts so that the majority of parents who have school-age children can afford to purchase at least one personal computer. Students who do not have their own computers can use their schools' computer labs or go to their local libraries to complete homework assignments that require computer technology.

Essay Task

Write a clear, well-reasoned essay evaluating multiple perspectives on student access to technology. In your essay, be sure to:

- Assert your own perspective on the issue and evaluate the relationship between your perspective and at least one other perspective

- Use reasoning and evidence to refine and justify your ideas

- Present your ideas in an organized way

- Convey your ideas effectively using standard written English

Your perspective may be fully, somewhat, or not at all in agreement with one or more of the three perspectives in the prompt.

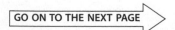
GO ON TO THE NEXT PAGE

Practice Test 8

Planning Your Essay

These pages are not scored.

Use the space below to brainstorm and plan your essay. Consider the following as you think about the prompt:

- Strengths and weaknesses of the three perspectives in the prompt

  ◦ What observations do they offer, and what do they overlook?

  ◦ Why are they persuasive or why are they not persuasive?

- Your own background and identity

  ◦ What is your perspective on this issue, and what are its strengths and weaknesses?

  ◦ What evidence will you use in your essay?

GO ON TO THE NEXT PAGE

_____

_____

_____

_____

_____

_____

_____

_____

_____

_____

_____

_____

_____

_____

_____

_____

_____

_____

_____

_____

GO ON TO THE NEXT PAGE

Practice Test 8

IF YOU FINISH BEFORE TIME IS CALLED, YOU MAY CHECK YOUR WORK ON THIS SECTION ONLY. DO NOT TURN TO ANY OTHER SECTION IN THE TEST.

STOP

PRACTICE TEST 8 ANSWER KEY

ENGLISH TEST

1. **B**	16. **H**	31. **B**	46. **H**	61. **C**
2. **J**	17. **C**	32. **H**	47. **B**	62. **F**
3. **B**	18. **J**	33. **B**	48. **J**	63. **B**
4. **J**	19. **C**	34. **G**	49. **A**	64. **G**
5. **C**	20. **F**	35. **A**	50. **G**	65. **D**
6. **J**	21. **B**	36. **G**	51. **D**	66. **G**
7. **C**	22. **H**	37. **B**	52. **J**	67. **C**
8. **G**	23. **B**	38. **F**	53. **C**	68. **H**
9. **C**	24. **G**	39. **D**	54. **G**	69. **D**
10. **F**	25. **C**	40. **F**	55. **D**	70. **G**
11. **D**	26. **F**	41. **C**	56. **H**	71. **B**
12. **J**	27. **C**	42. **F**	57. **A**	72. **J**
13. **B**	28. **H**	43. **D**	58. **H**	73. **A**
14. **F**	29. **B**	44. **J**	59. **D**	74. **J**
15. **D**	30. **J**	45. **C**	60. **G**	75. **A**

MATHEMATICS TEST

1. **C**	13. **E**	25. **D**	37. **B**	49. **C**
2. **J**	14. **K**	26. **K**	38. **G**	50. **J**
3. **C**	15. **A**	27. **A**	39. **E**	51. **C**
4. **F**	16. **K**	28. **F**	40. **G**	52. **K**
5. **D**	17. **C**	29. **A**	41. **C**	53. **C**
6. **F**	18. **K**	30. **J**	42. **F**	54. **J**
7. **B**	19. **D**	31. **C**	43. **B**	55. **B**
8. **J**	20. **G**	32. **J**	44. **J**	56. **K**
9. **E**	21. **C**	33. **C**	45. **C**	57. **D**
10. **H**	22. **H**	34. **J**	46. **F**	58. **K**
11. **D**	23. **E**	35. **D**	47. **C**	59. **C**
12. **K**	24. **F**	36. **F**	48. **J**	60. **G**

READING TEST

1. **C**	9. **C**	17. **D**	25. **C**	33. **C**
2. **H**	10. **F**	18. **F**	26. **F**	34. **H**
3. **B**	11. **C**	19. **B**	27. **C**	35. **D**
4. **J**	12. **F**	20. **H**	28. **J**	36. **G**
5. **B**	13. **B**	21. **C**	29. **B**	37. **D**
6. **F**	14. **J**	22. **F**	30. **J**	38. **F**
7. **B**	15. **A**	23. **D**	31. **C**	39. **C**
8. **J**	16. **J**	24. **F**	32. **H**	40. **G**

SCIENCE TEST

1. **B**	9. **C**	17. **C**	25. **C**	33. **B**
2. **G**	10. **J**	18. **H**	26. **G**	34. **H**
3. **C**	11. **C**	19. **A**	27. **C**	35. **C**
4. **J**	12. **F**	20. **H**	28. **G**	36. **F**
5. **D**	13. **B**	21. **D**	29. **D**	37. **B**
6. **F**	14. **G**	22. **J**	30. **G**	38. **F**
7. **A**	15. **D**	23. **A**	31. **A**	39. **D**
8. **G**	16. **F**	24. **J**	32. **H**	40. **G**

ANSWERS AND EXPLANATIONS

ENGLISH TEST

Passage I

1. B   **Difficulty:** Medium

Category: Knowledge of Language / Concision

Getting to the Answer: Look for the answer choice that expresses the sentence's idea in the clearest, most concise way. The clearest version here is (B): "If you want to succeed as a Hollywood screenwriter." This is grammatically correct and sets up the if–then relationship between the clauses. Choice A is awkward and unnecessarily wordy. Choices C and D create sentences that are grammatically incorrect.

2. J   **Difficulty:** Medium

Category: Organization, Unity, and Cohesion / Transitions

Getting to the Answer: When a transition word or phrase is underlined, check for the logic of the transition and then for correct grammar and punctuation. The paragraph discusses the difficulties of pursuing a career in screenwriting, and the previous sentence mentions one difficulty. The sentence containing the underlined portion discusses another difficulty: that those who obtain these careers are stressed and dissatisfied. Although the sentence mentions these people being wealthy, it does so in contrast to the main part of the sentence, which is a disadvantage of pursuing this career. Thus, the sentence is a continuation of the idea that this career is challenging, making (J) correct. Choice F incorrectly contrasts the ideas. The first difficulty does not provide a reason for the second, making G incorrect. Choice H is irrelevant, because time is not being discussed.

3. B   **Difficulty:** Medium

Category: Topic Development / Supporting Material

Getting to the Answer: Don't forget to read for logic as well as for grammar and usage. The preceding sentence explains that screenwriters don't have "a formal career path." The first part of the sentence in question gives an example of what a formal career path might involve—going to a school career center for help. The correct answer will provide another example along these lines. Someone with a formal career path could find job opportunities in the classified ads, but a screenwriter cannot. Choice (B) is correct. Choice A refers to "extracurricular activities," which is out of scope for a sentence concerning a career path. There's no reason to believe that a college graduate can't understand how difficult it is to become a screenwriter, as C suggests. Choice D is an example of something involved in an *informal* career path, not a formal one.

4. J   **Difficulty:** Medium

Category: Knowledge of Language / Precision

Getting to the Answer: When asked which choice best conveys a certain meaning, choose the answer that conveys that meaning most precisely. The only choice that conveys the difference in how successful screenwriters have achieved their success is (J). The other choices convey either the challenges, as in F and G, or the benefits, as in H.

5. C   **Difficulty:** Medium

Category: Sentence Structure and Formation

Getting to the Answer: A passage should not change tense for no reason. The passage is in the present tense, making the past tense verb in A incorrect. There is no reason to discuss the ongoing nature of a college education in the past, so the verb tense in B is incorrect. Choice D creates a grammatically incorrect sentence. Choice (C), with the present tense, is correct.

6. J   **Difficulty:** Low

Category: Knowledge of Language / Concision

Getting to the Answer: When "DELETE the underlined portion" is an option, read the underlined selection for relevance. The topic of this paragraph, and the entire essay, is the career of screenwriting. No matter how it is worded, a sentence about an acting career is out of scope. This sentence should be deleted, (J).

7. C   Difficulty: Medium

Category: Usage

Getting to the Answer: The ACT often separates a subject from its verb with an intervening phrase or clause containing another noun. Although the singular noun *college* is closer to the verb *begins* in this sentence, its subject is the plural *screenwriters*. The verb needs to be in the plural form, which eliminates all answer choices but (C). Choice B does not address the error. *Has begun* in D is also singular.

8. G   Difficulty: Medium

Category: Topic Development / Writer's Purpose

Getting to the Answer: When asked if a paragraph fulfills a certain purpose, consider its topic and scope. The topic of this paragraph is pursuing a college education on the path to becoming a screenwriter, and the author expresses the judgment that a college education can delay entry into the screenwriting profession. Thus, the paragraph does fulfill the goal of discouraging aspiring screenplay writers from pursuing a college education. Eliminate H and J. Choice F is opposite; mentioning the value of education does not discourage people from pursuing an education. Choice (G) is correct.

9. C   Difficulty: Medium

Category: Knowledge of Language / Concision

Getting to the Answer: Be wary of answer choices that are significantly longer than the underlined selection; they will rarely be correct. As written, the underlined portion is unnecessarily wordy and the phrase "at a prestigious school" is misleading, since it is not just some colleges that the writer deems irrelevant for screenwriters. Choice (C) corrects this error by focusing only on the student loans. Choice B is much wordier than the original and includes irrelevant information about "work-study programs." Choice D creates a sentence fragment.

10. F   Difficulty: Medium

Category: Punctuation

Getting to the Answer: To check if a semicolon is correctly used, try replacing it with a period and making the second clause a separate sentence. If two complete sentences are formed, then the semicolon is correct. A

semicolon is correctly used here to join two independent clauses. No change is needed, (F). Choice G incorrectly inserts a comma between *this* and the noun it modifies. Choice H incorrectly places a comma after *so*; a comma should be placed before a coordinating conjunction. Choice J creates a run-on sentence.

11. D   Category: Punctuation

Difficulty: Medium

Getting to the Answer: If you're unsure about punctuation, read the sentence without the descriptive words and phrases to focus on its structure. Stripped of some of the descriptive phrases, this sentence becomes easier to deal with: "Those without college educations are less averse to the jobs, aspiring screenwriters are forced to take." There is no reason for a comma here. Choice (D) correctly uses *that* to indicate that the phrase "aspiring screenwriters are forced to take" is meant to modify *jobs*. Choice B creates a run-on sentence. Choice C incorrectly treats *screenwriters* as inessential information.

12. J   Difficulty: Low

Category: Usage

Getting to the Answer: Many words can function as more than one part of speech; use context to help you eliminate choices that use these words incorrectly. The word *that's* in the underlined selection is a contraction of the pronoun *that* and the verb *is*, but context tells us that this sentence requires *that* to be used as a conjunction. Choice (J) uses *that* correctly and does not introduce any new errors. Choice G replaces the correct possessive pronoun *their* with its homophone *there*; familiarize yourself with the correct uses of *their*, *there*, and *they're* before Test Day. Choice H creates a grammatically incorrect sentence.

13. B   Difficulty: Medium

Category: Knowledge of Language / Ambiguity

Getting to the Answer: When a pronoun is underlined, always determine to what it refers. We know that something about the described scenario produces stress, but the exact referent is unclear, making A incorrect. Choice D is similarly unclear. It does not make sense for the screenplay to be the source of the stress, but rather the position the writer is in; eliminate C. Choice (B) correctly identifies the situation as the source of the stress, removing the ambiguity.

14. F   Difficulty: Medium

Category: Usage

Getting to the Answer: About one in four English Test questions will require no change. This sentence is correct as written, (F). Choice G illogically states the screenwriter's work must be *increasing*. Choice H suggests that screenwriters face pressure to "be . . . work," which does not make sense. Choice J is idiomatically incorrect; *to raise*, not *to raising*, is the correct infinitive.

15. D   Difficulty: Medium

Category: Knowledge of Language / Style and Tone

Getting to the Answer: When some answer choices contain *you* and others contain *one*, determine which pronoun matches the style of the passage. This passage never uses *one*, but it does use *you* in the first sentence. Furthermore, the remainder of the sentence directly addresses the reader with *please*. Eliminate A and B. Choice (D) is more straightforwardly worded than C, so (D) is correct.

Passage II

16. H   Difficulty: Medium

Category: Knowledge of Language / Concision

Getting to the Answer: The underlined selection may repeat something said elsewhere in the sentence, so take the whole sentence into consideration before choosing an answer. This sentence already indicates that the mission *gained fame*, so it is unnecessary to repeat that it is *well-known*. Eliminate F. Choice G unnecessarily uses the adjective *seasonal* along with *summer*; summer is a season, so you can eliminate G. Choice J describes the *home* as *residential*, but a home is, by definition, residential. Choice (H) is the only choice that eliminates all redundant language.

17. C   Difficulty: Low

Category: Topic Development / Writer's Purpose

Getting to the Answer: When asked about the purpose of a paragraph, consider both its topic and the surrounding context. Read further in the passage if necessary. The topic of the paragraph is the Mission at San Juan Capistrano, which is famous as a summer home for swallows. The following paragraph discusses the migration of these swallows, and they are the focus of the rest of the passage. Choice (C) describes the purpose of introducing these swallows. Choices A, B, and D are irrelevant to the purpose of the passage.

18. J   Difficulty: Medium

Category: Sentence Structure and Formation

Getting to the Answer: Items in a compound must be parallel in form. The two verbs joined by *and* in the original sentence are *nest* and *bearing*. Only (J) provides the needed parallel verb. Choices F, G, and H all use the *-ing* form, violating the rules of parallel structure.

19. C   Difficulty: Medium

Category: Sentence Structure and Formation

Getting to the Answer: Items in a series or list require parallel structure. There are three verbs in this series. The first two verbs, *ring* and *is*, are in the simple present tense, so the underlined verb should be also. Choice (C) is correct. Choices A, B, and D all violate the rules of parallel structure.

20. F   Difficulty: Medium

Category: Sentence Structure and Formation

Getting to the Answer: NO CHANGE will be the answer to about 25% of English Test questions. This sentence is correct as written, so (F) is the answer. The past tense verb *discovered* used after the past progressive *were seeking* indicates that the birds found the mission while in the process of looking for *refuge*. Choices G and J omit the pronoun *they*, suggesting that it was the innkeeper, not the birds, who found the mission. Choice H creates a grammatically incorrect sentence.

21. B   Difficulty: Low

Category: Usage

Getting to the Answer: The preposition *of* cannot be part of a verb phrase. The preposition *of* in the original version should actually be the verb *have*. Choice (B) corrects this error. Choices A and C both use the preposition *of* instead of the verb *have*. Choice D omits the verb *have*, leaving the grammatically incorrect *may developed*.

22. H **Difficulty:** Medium

Category: Organization, Unity, and Cohesion / Transitions

Getting to the Answer: When a transition word is underlined, determine what two ideas are being connected. Here, the transition word connects the discovery that the birds create their nests out of mud and the idea that the swallows chose the mission because it was near rivers. The following sentence explains that the rivers are a source of mud, so these ideas are not in contrast; eliminate F. *Indeed* cannot be used to create a subordinate clause, making G ungrammatical. It would make more sense for the biologists to postulate about the reason the swallows wanted to live near rivers after discovering that they needed mud for their nests, so (H) is correct.

23. B **Difficulty:** Low

Category: Usage

Getting to the Answer: Many word choice questions will present you with four grammatically correct idioms; use context to determine which is correct. *Of which*, A, *to which*, B, and *by which*, C, are all proper idioms, but the only one that makes sense in context is (B): the swallows *return to* their nests. Choice D omits the preposition, incorrectly suggesting that the birds return the nests to some person or place.

24. G **Difficulty:** Medium

Category: Topic Development / Supporting Material

Getting to the Answer: When an English Test question has a question stem, read it carefully. Frequently, all of the answer choices will be both consistent and relevant, but only one will fulfill the requirements of the stem. Only one sentence gives a specific reason for the swallows choosing the mission based on its location near two rivers. Choice (G) explains that the rivers provide a food supply for the swallows, which is a logical reason for the swallows to live nearby. Choice F provides information about swallow nest-building, not about swallows choosing the mission based on its location near the rivers. Choice H provides a detail about the rivers, but it is unclear how this detail relates to the swallows. Choice J is a generalization; it doesn't tell you anything specific about the *other advantages* provided by the rivers.

25. C **Difficulty:** Medium

Category: Organization, Unity, and Cohesion / Transitions

Getting to the Answer: The underlined portion is a transitional phrase, so check for errors in both logic and grammar. The previous sentence describes the swallows' returning to the mission for protection, and the sentence with the underlined portion explains that the whole city protects the swallows. Choice A includes a contrast transition, which is illogical here; both ideas involve protecting the swallows. Choices B and D are sequential transitions, which do not make sense in the context. The idea that the whole city protects the swallows serves to reinforce that they can return to the mission for protection, making the emphasis transition in (C) correct.

26. F **Difficulty:** Medium

Category: Punctuation

Getting to the Answer: Remember your tested comma rules; no other uses will be correct on the ACT. The sentence is correct as written; no change is needed, (F). Choices G and H both incorrectly insert a comma between the noun *community* and its verb *sees*. Choice J uses an adjective (*clear*), instead of an adverb, to modify the verb *sees*.

27. C **Difficulty:** Medium

Category: Punctuation

Getting to the Answer: Dashes may be used to offset supplementary material within a sentence. Here, "usually in the hills" is descriptive information about *the area*. Such descriptive phrases can be offset from the main sentence with commas or dashes; (C) correctly uses dashes to offset and emphasize the phrase. Choice A omits one of the commas necessary to correctly offset the phrase. Choice B uses a semicolon, but the second clause is not independent. Choice D is awkward and unnecessarily wordy.

28. H **Difficulty:** Medium

Category: Knowledge of Language / Concision

Getting to the Answer: Two words that convey the same information are redundant and incorrect on the ACT. All historic buildings are old, so F and G are both incorrect. Choice J is unnecessarily wordy. Choice (H) is the most concise answer and is therefore correct.

29. B   **Difficulty:** Medium

Category: Usage

Getting to the Answer: Some idioms will be properly constructed but incorrect in context. The phrase *in an attempt* requires the infinitive verb form; (B) is correct. Choice A uses *to attempt at*, which is idiomatically incorrect. Choices C and D change the infinitive *to attempt* to the noun *an attempt*; this creates an illogical sentence in C and an idiomatically incorrect one in D.

30. J   **Difficulty:** Medium

Category: Organization, Unity, and Cohesion / Passage Organization

Getting to the Answer: Since NO CHANGE is not offered as an option, you'll need to find the most logical place to insert the new sentence. Paragraph 5 discusses the problems that "have arisen in recent years," so this sentence about a problem with the swallows belongs in paragraph 5; eliminate F and G. Sentences 2 and 3 in Paragraph 5 explain the specific problems that are leading to a decline in the swallow migration. It is reasonable that one result of the changes discussed in Sentences 2 and 3 would be the lack of "huge clouds of swallows descending upon the mission as in the past decades." The best placement for the new sentence is after Sentence 3 in Paragraph 5; (J) is correct.

Passage III

31. B   **Difficulty:** Low

Category: Punctuation

Getting to the Answer: The possessive form of most singular nouns is formed by adding *'s*. Context tells us that the singular possessive, not the plural, form is needed here. Choice (B) retains the singular form and places the apostrophe correctly. Choice C creates the plural of the noun and does not show possession. Choice D creates the plural possessive of the noun, but the context is referring to one city.

32. H   **Difficulty:** Medium

Category: Usage

Getting to the Answer: Be sure to read ACT passages for logic as well as grammatical correctness. The word *which* modifies *team*, and a preposition is necessary. Choice (H) is the correct answer, because it adds the preposition *for*. Choice G introduces an incorrect preposition. Omitting the selection, as J suggests, changes the meaning of the sentence. The player is not choosing which team to play against, but rather which team to join.

33. B   **Difficulty:** High

Category: Topic Development / Supporting Material

Getting to the Answer: When asked whether information should be added, consider whether the new information is relevant. If it is relevant, consider what it adds. The narrator brings up the topic of free agents in order to explain why the daughter continues to need new jerseys, so the fact that being a free agent leads players to switch teams is relevant; the team-switching is the reason the daughter's favorite players keep changing jerseys. Thus, C and D are incorrect. Choice A is also incorrect; the new information tells us a result, not a cause, of becoming a free agent. Choice (B) accurately describes the reason the information should be added—namely, that it provides the missing link.

34. G   **Difficulty:** Medium

Category: Sentence Structure and Formation

Getting to the Answer: A complete sentence must have a subject and predicate verb that express a complete thought. In this case, there are two subjects and predicates that create a run-on sentence and an incomplete thought. Choice (G) properly uses the conjunction *so* to join two independent clauses expressing connected thoughts. Choice H creates a grammatically correct sentence, but it suggests an illogical cause-and-effect relationship. Choice J creates an illogical sentence; presumably, the narrator had one jersey while his or her favorite player was on the team, not after.

35. A   Difficulty: Low

Category: Sentence Structure and Formation

Getting to the Answer: Make sure independent clauses are properly separated. The sentences in question are correctly separated by a period because they express two separate, complete thoughts. This matches (A). Choice B is incorrect because, while the colon draws the reader's attention to a specific point directly related to what precedes it, the words *for when* makes the sentence structure awkward. The first sentence says there are *many* disadvantages to free agency, but the information in the second sentence expresses only one disadvantage. Choice C is incorrect because the comma separates two independent clauses. Choice D is incorrect because it also creates a run-on.

36. G   Difficulty: Medium

Category: Punctuation

Getting to the Answer: When a word or phrase is set off from the rest of the sentence with commas, the sentence must make sense without that phrase. The sentence is grammatically incorrect as written. A comma incorrectly separates *who* from the remainder of the phrase. Choice (G) corrects this by removing the comma. Choices H and J maintain an incorrect use of a comma, which breaks up the thought.

37. B   Difficulty: Medium

Category: Knowledge of Language / Precision

Getting to the Answer: The answer choices have different meanings, which indicates that you are being tested on precision. Choose the answer that makes the most sense in the context. The sentence introduces a disadvantage related to camaraderie and cohesion. Because those are both good things, it would be a disadvantage to be without them. Choice (B) conveys this meaning. Choice A is too neutral to make sense, whereas C and D are too positive.

38. F   Difficulty: Low

Category: Usage

Getting to the Answer: When DELETE is an option, first determine if the underlined information is necessary to the meaning of the sentence. The underlined information

is necessary to the sentence, which means J can be eliminated. In the correct answer, (F), *upon* correctly precedes the direct object *each other*. Choice G uses incorrect prepositions, *to* and *on*, and separates the direct object from *depend*. Choice H is illogical; the players depend on each other, not on winning.

39. D   Difficulty: Low

Category: Punctuation

Getting to the Answer: A list must be set off with serial commas. Choice (D) is the correct answer because it correctly places the commas between each item. Choice A is incorrect because it omits the commas. Choice B is incorrect because it uses a comma to separate the adverb *together* from the verb it modifies, *plays*. Choice C is incorrect because the comma that separates the first item from the second is missing.

40. F   Difficulty: Low

Category: Organization, Unity, and Cohesion / Transitions

Getting to the Answer: When determining whether two thoughts are correctly combined, check for the logic of the transition as well as proper grammar and punctuation. Because the players' attempt to block the other team is not a result of the number of players, the cause-and-effect transition *because* is inappropriate; eliminate G. No contrast is needed, making H incorrect. *Or* does not make sense in context; it would be illogical for the team either to have eleven players on the field or to try to stop the other team from progressing. Thus, J is incorrect. The sentence is correct as written, so (F) is the correct answer.

41. C   Difficulty: Low

Category: Usage

Getting to the Answer: When a verb is underlined, check to see if it matches the subject. The subject, *it*, is singular, requiring the plural verb *disrupts*, (C). Choice A requires a plural subject, B makes an unwarranted shift to past tense, and D creates a fragment.

42. F   Difficulty: Medium

Category: Sentence Structure and Formation

Getting to the Answer: Make sure modifying phrases are placed so as to modify logical things. Choice (F) is the correct answer because it concludes the sequence of three major disadvantages to free agency and correctly modifies "the loss of team dynasties." Choice G is incorrect because *loss* should modify *team dynasties*. Choices H and J are incorrect because the adverb *third* should modify *disadvantage*, not *loss*.

43. D   Difficulty: Medium

Category: Knowledge of Language / Concision

Getting to the Answer: Read the sentence without the underlined information to see if it still makes sense, and eliminate answer choices that contain redundant language. In the context of the paragraph, the sentence still makes sense without the underlined information. Choice (D) is the correct answer. Choice B contains redundant language. Adding an apostrophe to *years* in C is grammatically incorrect, and the phrase is redundant.

44. J   Difficulty: High

Category: Organization, Unity, and Cohesion / Transitions

Getting to the Answer: Remember to read for logic, as well as grammar and usage. Choice (J) is the only choice that logically connects ideas in this sentence by setting up the contrast between the simultaneous failure of the home team and the success of the player's new team. Choice F is incorrect because it creates a causal relationship between the home team failing and the player's new team winning (as a result of the home team's failure). Choices G and H cannot introduce dependent clauses, making the sentence ungrammatical.

45. C   Difficulty: Medium

Category: Organization, Unity, and Cohesion / Passage Organization

Getting to the Answer: Read question stems carefully. Often, the wrong answer choices will be consistent with the passage but fail to answer the question posed. The question stem is looking for the choice that best reflects the main idea of the essay. This paragraph concerns the author's dislike of what free agency has done to his experience of football; choice (C) makes this point best. Choice A is a general opinion that does not relate to the specific argument in the essay. Choice B is incorrect because the author does not describe any benefits of

free agency. Choice D is incorrect because it takes the opposite point of view from the main point of persuasion in the essay.

Passage IV

46. H   Difficulty: Medium

Category: Sentence Structure and Formation

Getting to the Answer: Be aware of phrases like *it is only*, because they add no real meaning to the sentence and provide no clear antecedent for the pronoun. *It is only* is unnecessary here. Choice (H) eliminates the unnecessary language and makes the second clause subordinate. Choices G and J both use incorrect grammatical structure.

47. B   Difficulty: Medium

Category: Usage

Getting to the Answer: Use *who* or *whom* to refer to a person. The underlined word refers to José Rivera; the correct pronoun is *who*, because José Rivera is a person. Choice (B) is correct. *Which*, in C, is incorrect when used to refer to a person. Choice D uses the objective case *whom*; you wouldn't say "him has fought for the right," so "whom has fought for the right" is incorrect.

48. J   Difficulty: Medium

Category: Organization, Unity, and Cohesion / Transitions

Getting to the Answer: Remember to read for logic, as well as grammar and usage. This sentence inappropriately uses the coordinating conjunction *Yet*. *Although*, a subordinating conjunction that introduces subordinate clauses, is the best choice here. Choice (J) is correct. Choice G is inappropriate for the context. Choice H cannot be used as a conjunction.

49. A   Difficulty: Medium

Category: Organization, Unity, and Cohesion / Passage Organization

Getting to the Answer: When you need to consider moving information, first read it to determine the main idea. Then consider the context of this information in the essay as a whole to determine its logical placement. The paragraph describes the early years in Rivera's schooling when he discovered he wanted to be a writer. In the essay as a whole, this information is in the right sequence; the paragraph before describes his childhood and the paragraph after describes his employment as an adult. Choice (A) is the correct answer. Choices B, C, and D would place the information out of sequence.

50. G   Difficulty: Low

Category: Punctuation

Getting to the Answer: A comma should not be inserted between a preposition and its object. The concluding conjunction *and* completed the list of the different things Rivera wrote. The direct object, *photographs*, and the indirect object, Life *magazine*, are part of one thought. Choice (G) is the correct answer. Choice H uses a colon, which is only correct when it follows an independent clause in order to introduce some information. Choice J uses a semicolon, which is only correct when used to connect two independent clauses.

51. D   Difficulty: Low

Category: Knowledge of Language / Concision

Getting to the Answer: When DELETE is an option, read the underlined selection for relevance. Eliminate answer choices that contain redundant language. It is redundant to use "he saw a play" and "when he saw the play" together; (D) eliminates the redundancy. Choices A, B, and C all contain redundant language.

52. J   Difficulty: Low

Category: Sentence Structure and Formation

Getting to the Answer: When a verb is underlined, check to see if the tense is correct. The simple present tense, *writes*, is used in this sentence to describe an event that happened in the past. The correct tense here is the simple past tense, *wrote*, as in (J). Choice G uses the present continuous tense, and H uses the present perfect tense, but the sentence describes something that happened in the past.

53. C   Difficulty: High

Category: Sentence Structure and Formation

Getting to the Answer: Remember to read for logic, as well as grammar and usage. In the underlined portion, the

subject and predicate are split by misplaced prepositional phrases. The subject is *Rivera*, and the predicate is "returned to New York determined to continue writing." The prepositional phrase, "After graduating from college," modifies the action. Choice (C) is the correct answer. Choices B and D both contain misplaced modifiers.

54. G   Difficulty: Low

Category: Sentence Structure and Formation

Getting to the Answer: When you need to consider moving information, read it into the passage at the suggested points to determine its logical placement. *Then* modifies *became*, so (G) is the correct answer. Choice F is awkward, and H and J are illogical.

55. D   Difficulty: Medium

Category: Knowledge of Language / Ambiguity

Getting to the Answer: A pronoun must clearly refer to its antecedent. In A, it is unclear to whom or what *them* refers. The last plural entity was the group of people, but that does not make sense in the context. Choice B is unclear for the same reasons. While C and (D) both clearly refer to Rivera's writing, it makes more sense to refer to "one of the plays" than "one of the work," because *work* is singular. Choice (D) is correct.

56. H   Difficulty: Medium

Category: Punctuation

Getting to the Answer: When the only difference in the answer choices is punctuation, remember your tested rules. A semicolon is used to join independent clauses closely related in meaning. Choice (H) is the correct answer. Choice G is incorrect because a comma cannot join two independent clauses without a conjunction. Choice J is incorrect because the period is placed in the middle of the predicate.

57. A   Difficulty: Medium

Category: Topic Development / Supporting Material

Getting to the Answer: Read question stems and the paragraph that is being added to carefully. Often, all four answer choices to Supporting Material questions will be somewhat relevant to the passage, but only one will fulfill the specific requirements of the question. The question asks for a detail that supports Paragraph 5, which is about the sacrifices Rivera had to make to be a writer. Choice (A) is the only answer choice that supports this idea. Choices B and C are incorrect because they are off topic and do not support the main idea. Choice D is incorrect because it describes the writing he did for television as an opportunity, which is a positive change.

58. H **Difficulty:** Medium

Category: Sentence Structure and Formation

Getting to the Answer: When a verb is underlined, check to see if the tense is correct. The correct tense here is the past continuous tense, *has become*, as in (H). *Has became* is an incorrect construction, making (F) incorrect. Choice G uses *is*, which cannot be used with *became*. Choice J uses the past continuous tense, but José Rivera is singular, not plural as *have* would imply.

59. D **Difficulty:** Medium

Category: Topic Development / Writer's Purpose

Getting to the Answer: By determining the main idea of the passage, you can quickly eliminate two answer choices. The main idea of the essay is that being a playwright is challenging, but there are people like José Rivera who have succeeded despite the odds. Choice (D) is the correct answer. Choice A is incorrect because the essay is persuasive, not merely biographical. Choice B is incorrect because it conveys the opposite of what the passage is arguing. Choice C is too extreme; the passage portrays playwriting as challenging, but not impossible.

60. G **Difficulty:** Medium

Category: Organization, Unity, and Cohesion / Passage Organization

Getting to the Answer: The first sentence of a paragraph typically introduces the topic of the paragraph, so look for the paragraph that contains details related to the sentence in question. Paragraph 2 describes Rivera's upbringing and contrasts the "bustling neighborhood of the Bronx" with the "dirt roads and woods" of Long Island. Choice (G) is the correct answer. Choices F, H, and J can be eliminated because the detail does not support the main idea of any of these paragraphs.

Passage V

61. C **Difficulty:** Medium

Category: Sentence Structure and Formation

Getting to the Answer: Remember that an *-ing* verb form by itself cannot serve as the predicate (main) verb in a sentence. As written, this sentence is a fragment. Choice (C) corrects this error by replacing *being* with *is* and does not introduce any additional errors. Choice B uses verb tenses inconsistently. Choice D does not address the error.

62. F **Difficulty:** Medium

Category: Punctuation

Getting to the Answer: Remember the tested punctuation rules. If punctuation isn't needed for one of those reasons, it will be incorrect on the ACT. This sentence is correct as written, (F); no additional punctuation is needed in the underlined portion. Choice G incorrectly places a comma between the subject "What was initially a hobby" and the verb phrase "quickly became." Choice H incorrectly places a comma between a possessive noun (which functions grammatically as an adjective) and the noun it modifies. Choice J uses a colon, but what follows is not a brief definition, explanation, or list of what comes before.

63. B **Difficulty:** Medium

Category: Usage

Getting to the Answer: Don't fall for the common test makers' trick of putting a singular noun near a verb with a plural subject. Always determine the correct subject of an underlined verb. The subject of the verb *is* is not the singular *receipt* that immediately precedes it, but the plural *papers* ("several papers . . . is signed by John Hancock"). The underlined verb must be in the plural form; (B) is correct. Choices A and C both use singular verb forms, which do not agree with the plural subject. Choice D eliminates the verb, creating a sentence fragment.

64. G **Difficulty:** Medium

Category: Sentence Structure and Formation

Getting to the Answer: The past perfect verb tense is only correct when describing an action that was completed prior to another stated past action. Checking context, you can see that the verbs used to describe Dr. Gregory's collection of signatures are all in the present tense: *includes* and *are* (the correction to the underlined *is* in question 63). The verb here should also be in the present tense; (G) is correct. Choice F uses the past perfect, but there is no stated past action here to justify this tense. Choice H uses the past tense, which is inconsistent with the rest of the description of the collection. Choice J uses the conditional, but there is nothing hypothetical about the meaning of the Hancock documents.

65. D   Difficulty: Medium

Category: Organization, Unity, and Cohesion / Passage Organization

Getting to the Answer: When you need to determine the best placement for a sentence, look for Keywords that show how the sentence relates to other ideas in the paragraph. Sentence 7 identifies the type of documents that Dr. Gregory collects, and Sentences 5 and 6 specifically describe some of those documents. The keyword *Predictably* in Sentence 5 tells you that Sentence 7 should come right before sentence 5; it is only predictable for Dr. Gregory to have documents signed by Hancock if it has already been stated that Dr. Gregory collects famous signatures. Choice (D) is correct. Choice A disrupts the logical general-to-specific order set up in the paragraph; it also interrupts the transition between Sentence 6, which gives the name of Dr. Gregory's field, and the beginning of Paragraph 2, which provides an explanation of that field. Choice B interrupts the description of Dr. Gregory's home. Choice C interrupts the explanation of how Dr. Gregory's interest in collecting documents developed.

66. G   Difficulty: Medium

Category: Topic Development / Supporting Material

Getting to the Answer: Since NO CHANGE is offered as an answer choice, you must first decide whether a change is warranted. If so, you must then decide what the change should be. Graphology is discussed throughout the essay, so a definition of the term would be relevant and helpful to readers. Choice (G) provides this definition. The other choices do not provide information related to the topic discussed in the rest of the essay—the analysis of the handwriting of historical figures.

67. C   Difficulty: Medium

Category: Topic Development / Writer's Purpose

Getting to the Answer: Remember the first step of the Kaplan Method: read until you have enough information to identify the issue. To determine the best transition to the following sentence, you must first read that sentence. The sentence following the underlined portion explains how psychologists and graphologists use handwriting. Only (C) mentions handwriting, identifying it as a tool to diagnose patients' problems. This is the most logical lead-in to the next sentence. Choice A changes the focus from handwriting to the general topic of how patients learn to express themselves. Choice B similarly moves the topic to an explanation of why patients seek help; this doesn't lead in to the next sentence's explanation of how psychologists use handwriting. Choice D is too general; it doesn't lead in to the specific information of why handwriting analysis can be helpful.

68. H   Difficulty: Medium

Category: Sentence Structure and Formation

Getting to the Answer: As written, the sentence contains an incomplete first clause. The idea of using graphology needs to be properly connected to the psychologists who use it for the sentence to be complete. Choice (H) properly connects these ideas; it is the psychologists who use graphology. Choice G changes the meaning of the sentence; the sentence is about those who use graphology, not those who are accustomed to it. Choice J creates a grammatically incorrect sentence by forming the phrase "psychologists being used graphology."

69. D   Difficulty: Medium

Category: Knowledge of Language / Concision

Getting to the Answer: If a sentence is grammatically correct, check for errors in style. The sentence already tells you that "Dr. Gregory *once* practiced clinical psychology," so there is no need to repeat the information that this occurred "in the past." Choice (D) eliminates this redundant language. Choices B and C both contain unnecessary language.

70. G   Difficulty: Medium

Category: Topic Development / Writer's Purpose

Getting to the Answer: The purpose of a part of the passage will always fit with the overall purpose. The passage discusses Dr. Gregory's interest in graphology, focusing on his use of graphology on historical documents. Thus, we can expect the information about psychology to relate to graphology, and it does; the paragraph explains that graphology can be used to determine a person's psychology. Choice (G) is correct. Choice F is incorrect because Dr. Gregory has already been introduced at this point in the passage. Choice H distorts the text; the focus is on learning about historical figures, not the people who preserve historical documents. Choice J is incorrect as well; the author mentions challenges in understanding historical figures' personalities, but that does not mean psychology is generally unimportant in understanding personalities.

71. B   Difficulty: High

Category: Topic Development / Supporting Material

Getting to the Answer: When considering the effect of deleting material, think about what information it adds to the surrounding text. The sentence says that few records exist of the lives and personalities of historical figures, thus reinforcing the idea in the previous paragraph that it is difficult to apply psychological theories to historical figures. Choice (B) accurately reflects this idea. Choice A is out of scope; the passage does not suggest that Dr. Gregory turns to graphology because he cannot use other means to analyze historical figures. Choice C is the opposite of true; the lack of records is a reason there is not broad agreement. Choice D is a distortion; the passage does not suggest that the lack of historical records led friends of historical figures to write about them.

72. J   Difficulty: Medium

Category: Sentence Structure and Formation

Getting to the Answer: You need to find the choice that is NOT acceptable; in other words, the correct answer will create an error in the sentence. It is not acceptable to connect two independent clauses, such as the ones in this sentence, without the proper punctuation and/or conjunction. Choice (J) creates a run-on sentence. Choice F correctly uses a semicolon to connect two independent

clauses. Choice G forms two complete sentences. Choice H keeps the second clause dependent, replacing *for* with *as*.

73. A   Difficulty: Medium

Category: Punctuation

Getting to the Answer: Don't expect to find a grammatical or stylistic error in every underlined selection. About 25% of your English Test questions will require no change. No punctuation is needed here; the sentence is correct as written, (A). Choice B incorrectly inserts a comma before that, which is used here as a conjunction. Choice C incorrectly uses a comma after that; commas are not correct after conjunctions. Choice D uses a colon, which would be appropriate only if it also eliminated that, but it does not.

74. J   Difficulty: High

Category: Sentence Structure and Formation

Getting to the Answer: Use context to make sure verb tenses properly sequence the actions discussed in a sentence. As indicated by the word *while*, the two actions in this sentence take place at the same time. The second verb, *forms*, is in the present tense, so the underlined verb should also be in the present tense. Choice (J) is correct. Choices F and G both put the action of "imprinting key aspects of his personality" in the past; this would only make sense if the rest of the sentence were also in the past tense. Choice H indicates that the action of "imprinting key aspects of his personality" takes place in the future, not *while* he "forms a signature."

75. A   Difficulty: High

Category: Topic Development / Writer's Purpose

Getting to the Answer: To make sure you understand the question, take a moment to put it in your own words. Here, you might rephrase the questions as "Does the essay talk about how one area of study can influence another?" The essay explains how Dr. Gregory, a psychologist, has used graphology to identify personality traits in historical figures; the essay concludes by explaining that these "details are now being used by historians in their analysis of historical decisions." This satisfies the condition of the question stem, so you can eliminate both "no" answers, C and D. Now move on to the reasoning. Choice (A) is an accurate paraphrase of the main idea of the essay. Choice B is incorrect because the essay does not compare different research processes.

MATHEMATICS TEST

1. C   Difficulty: Low

Category: Essential Skills / Geometry

Getting to the Answer: It may be helpful to draw a number line and plot the possible positions for point C. B is 8 units away from A, and C is 2 units away from B, so there are only 2 possible positions for C—2 units before B or 2 units after B. Therefore, C must be either 6 units or 10 units away from A, which matches (C).

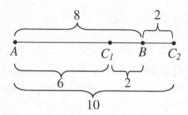

2. J   Difficulty: Low

Category: Essential Skills / Numbers and Operations

Getting to the Answer: Here you have a strange word, "sump," which describes a number that has a certain relationship between the sum and the product of its digits. To answer this question, find the sum and the product of the digits for each answer choice. You're told that for a "sump" number, the sum should be greater than the product. Choice (J), 411, has a sum of 6 and a product of 4, so that's the one you're looking for.

3. C   Difficulty: Low

Category: Essential Skills / Statistics and Probability

Getting to the Answer: Don't get thrown off when you see probability expressed as a decimal rather than as a ratio or as a fraction. You could think of 0.3 as a 30% chance of something happening, or a probability of $\frac{3}{10}$. Because you know that every ticket either will win or will not win, the probability that Mark will draw a winning ticket and the probability that he will draw a losing ticket

will add up to 1. The probability that he will draw a losing ticket is $1.0 - 0.3 = 0.7$, which is (C). If it is easier for you to think in terms of percents, look at the question this way: If Mark has a 30% chance of drawing a winning ticket, the other 70% of the time he will draw a losing ticket. That's $\frac{70}{100}$, or 0.7, which is (C).

4. F   Difficulty: Medium

Category: Essential Skills / Rates, Percents, Proportions, and Unit Conversion

Getting to the Answer: Be careful on questions that involve multiple percent discounts. You can't simply add the percents. Instead, choose a nice starting price, such as $100, and apply each discount, one at a time. If the coat is on sale for 20% off, then Mandy pays 80% of the original price, which is $0.8(\$100) = \$80$. If she then uses a 15% off coupon, she pays 85% of the sale price, or $0.85(80) = \$68$. Thus, she saved $\$100 - \$68 = \$32$ out of $100, or 32%. Choice (F) is correct.

5. D   Difficulty: Low

Category: Essential Skills / Numbers and Operations

Getting to the Answer: Try translating the question into algebra. You are looking for the amount of candy that Tom started with, which you can call x. Tom reduced that number by half 3 times, and ended up with 6 pieces.

$$\left(\frac{1}{2}\right)\left(\frac{1}{2}\right)\left(\frac{1}{2}\right)x = 6$$
$$\frac{1}{8}x = 6$$
$$x = 6 \cdot 8 = 48$$

Choice (D) is correct. If you get confused trying to answer this question using algebra, you can always Backsolve. The correct answer choice, divided in half three times, will equal 6.

6. F   Difficulty: Low

Category: Essential Skills / Expressions and Equations

Getting to the Answer: This question asks you to combine two algebraic expressions. Pay attention to the signs as you combine like terms and you won't have any trouble. $R + S$ is equivalent to $4x + 3y - x$. Combining the x terms will give you the answer, $3x + 3y$, which matches (F).

7. B   Difficulty: Medium

Category: Essential Skills / Geometry

Getting to the Answer: If you are familiar with the properties of parallel lines that are intersected by transversals, this question will be quick and easy for you. In a figure like this one, formed by intersecting parallel lines, you only need the measure of one angle to quickly find the measure of every other angle. Start with the angle you know and work your way around the figure until you reach *y*.

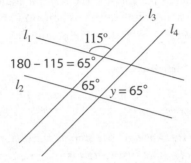

The angle adjacent to the angle that measures 115° must be supplementary to 115°, so its measure is $180° - 115° = 65°$. That angle and the angle to the right of l_3 are alternate interior angles, so they have the same measure, and that angle corresponds to angle *y*, so angle *y* must also measure 65°. Choice (B) is correct.

8. J   Difficulty: Medium

Category: Higher Math / Functions

Getting to the Answer: Once you get the hang of function notation, questions like this one are very straightforward. All you need to do is to substitute the given value for the variable. Be careful to get the signs right when substituting a negative value! Replace each *x* with −3 and apply the rules of PEMDAS:

$$f(x) = -\boxed{x}^2 - 7\boxed{x} + 5$$
$$f(-3) = -\left(\boxed{-3}\right)^2 - 7\left(\boxed{-3}\right) + 5$$
$$= -(9) + 21 + 5$$
$$= 17$$

Choice (J) is correct.

9. E   Difficulty: Medium

Category: Essential Skills / Statistics and Probability

Getting to the Answer: If you increase or decrease each of a set of numbers by the same amount, the average of those numbers will also increase or decrease by the same amount. This question is not so difficult if you imagine using specific numbers. If the average of 5 numbers is 85, each of the five numbers could be 85. Now, if you increase each of those numbers by 4, the average will be $\frac{5(89)}{5}$, or 89. Choice (E) is correct.

10. H   Difficulty: Low

Category: Essential Skills / Expressions and Equations

Getting to the Answer: This question involves factoring. If you are not comfortable with factoring, be sure to practice questions like this before Test Day. To simplify this expression, you can factor out a 3. This will give you the new, equivalent expression, $3(x + 3y)$, which matches (H). When in doubt, you can Pick Numbers for the variables and find the equivalent expression.

11. D   Difficulty: Medium

Category: Essential Skills / Numbers and Operations

Getting to the Answer: Word problems like this one give you all the information you need, but in a roundabout way. Stay on your toes and remember to ask yourself what you are really looking for. For instance, don't forget that the June bill will be $20 plus the cost of *100* long distance minutes, not 20. First, determine the price per minute based on what Mark was charged in May. Subtract the $20 fee from his total of $28, and you will find that he paid $8 for 80 minutes of long distance. That means that 1 minute costs 10 cents. In June he talked 100 minutes, and 100 minutes times 10 cents per minute is $10. Add this to his monthly $20, and the total bill is $30, which is (D).

12. K   Difficulty: Medium

Category: Essential Skills / Numbers and Operations

Getting to the Answer: If *p* divided by 7 leaves a remainder of 5, you can say that $p = 7n + 5$, where *n* represents some integer. Multiply both sides by 5 to get $5p = 35n + 25$. The remainder when you divide 7 into $35n$ is 0. The remainder when you divide 7 into 25 is 4, so the remainder when you divide $5p$ by 7 is $0 + 4 = 4$, which is (K).

For most people, this one's a lot easier to do by Picking Numbers. Think of an example for p and try it out. Let p equal 12, for example, because when you divide 12 by 7, the remainder is 5. (p could also be 19, 26, 33, or any of infinitely many more possibilities.) Now multiply your chosen p by 5 to get $12 \times 5 = 60$. Divide 60 by 7 and see what the remainder is: 60 divided by 7 is 8, remainder 4. Thus, (K) is correct.

13. E   Difficulty: Medium

Category: Higher Math / Geometry

Getting to the Answer: Always be on the lookout for basic geometric figures. If you remember that a clock is just a circle, and you are familiar with the properties of circles, you will have all of the tools you need to answer this question. You already know that a whole circle is 360°. You also know that a clock is divided into 12 hours. Use this information to calculate how many degrees the hour hand will move in 1 hour; the result is $\frac{360°}{12} = 30°$, so the hour hand will move 30° in one hour. In the 8 hours between noon and 8 PM, the hour hand will move a total of $8 \times 30° = 240°$, which is (E).

14. K   Difficulty: Medium

Category: Higher Math / Statistics and Probability

Getting to the Answer: Permutations are sequences, so order matters. Any of the 6 cars could be placed in the first spot on the shelf. Any of the remaining 5 cars could be placed in the second spot, any of the remaining 4 cars could be placed in the third spot, and so on until there is only 1 remaining car for the sixth spot. You can represent this visually by drawing a line representing each of the shelf's 6 spots, and then writing in how many car choices there are for each spot:

$$\underline{6} \; \underline{5} \; \underline{4} \; \underline{3} \; \underline{2} \; \underline{1}$$

Then use the Fundamental Counting Principle to find that the number of possible arrangements is $6 \times 5 \times 4 \times 3 \times 2 \times 1 = 720$, which is (K).

15. A   Difficulty: Low

Category: Higher Math / Algebra

Getting to the Answer: Be sure to be familiar with the properties of zero before Test Day! Remember that when the product of two factors is zero, at least one of those factors must equal zero. You could substitute the two values for x into each answer choice to find which equation has both 5 and -7 as solutions, but all that work is not necessary. When you have an equation in which the product of two binomials is zero, one of the binomials will have to equal zero. So, if $(x - 5)(x + 7) = 0$, then $x - 5 = 0$ or $x + 7 = 0$. The solutions to this equation, then, would be $x = 5$ and $x = -7$. Choice (A) is correct.

16. K   Difficulty: Low

Category: Essential Skills / Rates, Percents, Proportions, and Unit Conversion

Getting to the Answer: To compare the distances using a ratio, you need to first write them in the same unit of measure. One fourth of a mile is $5,280 \div 4 = 1,320$ feet, so three-fourths of a mile is $3(1,320) = 3,960$ feet. Thus, the ratio of walking distance to riding distance is 220:3,960, which reduces to 1:18. That's (K).

17. C   Difficulty: Low

Category: Essential Skills / Rates, Percents, Proportions, and Unit Conversion

Getting to the Answer: Focus on what you are looking for in percent questions like this. Don't make the mistake of calculating 30 percent of 60. Percentages can be much more workable if you convert them to decimals. If 30% of x is 60, solve for x using the equation $0.3x = 60$. The result is $x = \frac{60}{0.3} = 200$, which is (C).

18. K   Difficulty: Low

Category: Higher Math / Number and Quantity

Getting to the Answer: Make this abstract question more concrete by Picking Numbers. Suppose the starting balance is $10. Maria accidentally adds $1.25 to the total, so her record now shows $10 + $1.25 = $11.25. She should have subtracted $1.25 from the total, so her record should show $10 - $1.25 = $8.75. The difference between what the record now shows and what it should show is

$11.25 − $8.75 = $2.50. Because she added incorrectly, the amount recorded is more than it should be, so (K) is the correct answer.

19. D   Difficulty: Medium

Category: Essential Skills / Rates, Percents, Proportions, and Unit Conversion

Getting to the Answer: Getting comfortable converting percentages to decimals will save you some time. To increase a number by 7%, you don't need to calculate 7% and add it to the original number. Instead, multiply the original number by 1.07. To calculate the total charge for the salad with sales tax, multiply to get a total of (1.07)($3.99) = $4.2693.

The price, rounded to the nearest cent, is $4.27. Subtract the price from $5.00 to find that the amount of change should be 73¢, which is (D).

20. G   Difficulty: Medium

Category: Higher Math / Algebra

Getting to the Answer: If you remember what causes a rational expression to be "undefined," you can answer this question quickly using algebra. The denominator can't be zero, so you're looking for the value of x that will give the denominator $(x^2 − 4)$ a value of 0. Find it by setting up an equation:

$$x^2 − 4 = 0$$
$$(x − 2)(x + 2) = 0$$
$$x = 2 \text{ or } x = −2$$

Because the question asks for a nonnegative value of x, the answer is 2, which is (G). You can also Backsolve by plugging in each answer choice for x, and see which one results in a denominator of zero.

21. C   Difficulty: Low

Category: Essential Skills / Numbers and Operations

Getting to the Answer: Comparing values is always easier when all the values are expressed in the same form. The numbers in this question would be much easier to compare if they were all decimals, so convert them. You might remember that π has a value of approximately 3.14. The mixed number $3\frac{1}{4}$ is equivalent to 3.25. These

numbers are much easier to compare, but don't forget to order them from *greatest* to *least*:

$$3.5 > 3.25 > 3.14, \text{ so } 3.5 > 3\frac{1}{4} > π$$

Choice (C) is correct.

22. H   Difficulty: Medium

Category: Essential Skills / Rates, Percents, Proportions, and Unit Conversion

Getting to the Answer: Other than having to convert minutes to hours, this is a very straightforward question. Use the DIRT equation: Distance is rate times time. The total travel time was 5 hours minus 48 minutes, or 4 hours and 12 minutes. Because 12 minutes is 12 ÷ 60 = 0.2 hours, the total travel time was 4.2 hours. Bo and Duke drove at a rate of 70 miles per hour, so the total distance is 4.2(70) = 294 miles. Choice (H) is correct.

23. E   Difficulty: Medium

Category: Higher Math / Statistics and Probability

Getting to the Answer: In order to find the number of possibilities, multiply the number of possibilities in each step. There are 3 routes from Bay City to Riverville and 4 routes from Riverville to Straitstown—that's 3 × 4 = 12 routes so far. There are 3 more routes from Straitstown to Frog Pond, so there are 12 × 3 = 36 total routes from Bay City to Frog Pond, which is (E).

24. F   Difficulty: Medium

Category: Higher Math / Algebra

Getting to the Answer: The answer choices in this question give you a clue that the question involves a quadratic that can be factored. You could also substitute the values given in each of the answer choices for x to see which ones work. Backsolving or algebra may be faster for you—use whichever will get you to the answer more quickly.

$$x^2 + x = 30$$
$$x^2 + x − 30 = 0$$
$$(x + 6)(x − 5) = 0$$
$$x + 6 = 0 \text{ or } x − 5 = 0$$
$$x = −6 \text{ or } x = 5$$

Choice (F) is correct.

Answers & Explanations

25. D   Difficulty: High

Category: Higher Math / Algebra

Getting to the Answer: When you get stuck on a question involving variables, look for ways to rewrite the expressions that will produce like terms to work with. Keep an eye out for the classic quadratic equations.

Start with the first equation, $(a - b)^2 = 81$. This can also be written as $(a - b)(a - b) = 81$. Use FOIL (or recognize the classic quadratic) to multiply the binomials on the left side. The result is $a^2 - 2ab + b^2 = 81$. Now you have something you can work with! Substitute in the value of ab that was given in the question:

$$a^2 - 2\left(\frac{3}{2}\right) + b^2 = 81$$
$$a^2 - 3 + b^2 = 81$$
$$a^2 + b^2 = 84$$

Thus, (D) is correct.

26. K   Difficulty: Medium

Category: Higher Math / Statistics and Probability

Getting to the Answer: This question tests your ability to read a probability distribution table. You also need to recall that 0 is an even number (because it sits between two odd numbers, −1 and 1). The probability that the randomly generated number will be even is $P(Y = 0)$ + $P(Y = 2) + P(Y = 4)$, which is $\frac{1}{5} + \frac{3}{10} + \frac{1}{4}$. Write each fraction over a denominator of 20 and add: $\frac{4}{20} + \frac{6}{20} + \frac{5}{20} = \frac{15}{20}$, which simplifies to $\frac{3}{4}$, making (K) the correct answer.

27. A   Difficulty: Medium

Category: Higher Math / Number and Quantity

Getting to the Answer: You don't have to know about imaginary numbers to answer a question like this. Because you are given that $i^2 = -1$, plug in −1 for i^2. Remember that $i^4 = (i^2)^2$.

$i^2 - i^4 = i^2 - (i^2)^2 = (-1) - (-1)^2 = -1 - 1 = -2$, which is (A).

28. F   Difficulty: Medium

Category: Essential Skills / Geometry

Getting to the Answer: Don't forget what you are really looking for in this question. You will use the Midpoint formula, but be sure to solve for an endpoint (*B*) rather than the midpoint. Remember that the *x*-coordinate of the midpoint of a line segment is the average of the *x*-coordinates of the endpoints. The *y*-coordinate of the midpoint is the average of the *y*-coordinates of the endpoints. Use the Midpoint formula:

$$\text{Midpoint} = \left(\frac{x_1 + x_2}{2}, \frac{y_1 + y_2}{2}\right)$$

First, calculate the *x*-coordinate of *B* by solving for x_2:

$$\frac{5 + x_2}{2} = -2$$
$$5 + x_2 = -4$$
$$x_2 = -9$$

The *x*-coordinate of *B* is −9. You could continue by finding the *y*-coordinate in the same way, but that is not necessary because only (F) has the correct *x*-coordinate.

29. A   Difficulty: Low

Category: Essential Skills / Statistics and Probability

Getting to the Answer: The mode is the number that appears most often in a set of data. The largest number of people who collected the same amount of trash was the 12 people who collected 10 pounds of trash, so 10 is the mode of this set of data. That's (A).

30. J   Difficulty: Medium

Category: Essential Skills / Rates, Percents, Proportions, and Unit Conversion

Getting to the Answer: The total amount of trash collected by the 30 participants was $12(10) + 9(15) + 4(20) + 4(25) + 1(30) = 120 + 135 + 80 + 100 + 30 = 465$ pounds of trash. The goal of the drive was to collect 500 pounds of trash, so you need to figure out what percent 465 is of 500. Divide to find that the participants reached $\frac{465}{500} = 93\%$ of the goal, which is (J).

31. C **Difficulty:** Medium

Category: Higher Math / Statistics and Probability

Getting to the Answer: The total amount of trash collected by the 30 participants was 12(10) + 9(15) + 4(20) + 4(25) + 1(30) = 120 + 135 + 80 + 100 + 30 = 465 pounds of trash. Because there were 30 participants, the average amount of trash collected by each one was $\frac{465}{30} = 15.5$ pounds, making (C) the correct answer.

32. J **Difficulty:** Medium

Category: Higher Math / Geometry

Getting to the Answer: Whenever 3 or more parallel lines are intersected by 2 transversals, the transversals are divided proportionally by the parallel lines. The ratio of the length of $\overline{TU}$ to the length of $\overline{UV}$ will be equal to the ratio of the length of $\overline{QR}$ to the length of $\overline{RS}$. Therefore, you can set up the following proportion:

$$\frac{x}{7} = \frac{3}{5}$$
$$5x = 21$$
$$x = \frac{21}{5}$$

That's (J).

33. C **Difficulty:** High

Category: Higher Math / Geometry

Getting to the Answer: To answer this question, you will have to remember the area formulas for both triangles and circles. To find the area of a circle, use the equation $A = \pi r^2$. You don't know the value of r yet, but you might have noticed that the sides of $\triangle AOB$ are also radii of the circle. Use the area formula for triangles $\left(A = \frac{1}{2}bh\right)$ and the given area, 18, to find the base and height of the triangle. In this case, the base and height are both equal and are both radii of the circle.

$$\frac{1}{2}(r)(r) = 18$$
$$r^2 = 36$$

The area of a circle is πr^2, and you now know that r^2 is 36, so the area of this circle is 36π, which is (C). Even if you were completely stuck, you could narrow down your options and make a strategic guess. The area of the circle must be more than 4 times the area of the triangle, so you can eliminate A and B, which are less than 4 times the area of the triangle.

34. J **Difficulty:** Medium

Category: Essential Skills / Expressions and Equations

Getting to the Answer: The symbol ≤ means less than or equal to, and ≥ means greater than or equal to. You will use one of these symbols when you want to include a number in a set. The bold part of the number line represents the numbers that should be included in the set, including 4 and excluding −5. The shading includes numbers that are to the right of (greater than) −5 and to the left of (less than) and including (equal to) 4. Therefore, $x > -5$ and $x \le 4$, which matches (J).

35. D **Difficulty:** Medium

Category: Higher Math / Geometry

Getting to the Answer: This question is much simpler than it first appears. You just need to know the formula for the equation of a circle. The formula for the equation of a circle is $(x - h)^2 + (y - k)^2 = r^2$, where the center of the circle is (h,k) and r is the radius of the circle. Therefore, in this question, $r^2 = 25$ which makes $r = 5$. Be careful—C is a trap! The question asks for the diameter of the circle, which is twice the radius, so the correct answer is 10, or (D).

36. F **Difficulty:** Medium

Category: Essential Skills / Rates, Percents, Proportions, and Unit Conversion

Getting to the Answer: To answer a question that says "directly proportional," set two ratios equal to each other and solve for the missing amount. Don't forget to match the units in the numerators and in the denominators on both sides.

Let *c* equal the number of cars that can safely pass through a light that lasts 24 seconds. Set up the proportion and solve for *c*:

$$\frac{9 \text{ cars}}{36 \text{ seconds}} = \frac{c \text{ cars}}{24 \text{ seconds}}$$
$$9(24) = 36(c)$$
$$216 = 36c$$
$$6 = c$$

Choice J is a trap! The question asks how many *fewer* cars can pass through the 24-second light, so the correct answer is $9 - 6 = 3$, which is (F).

37. B   Difficulty: High

Category: Essential Skills / Numbers and Operations

Getting to the Answer: "Divisible by" means the same as "is a factor of," so think of all of the integers that are factors of both 84 and 96; they are 1, 2, 3, 4, 6, and 12. Now, 1, 2, 3, 4, and 6 are all factors of either 18 or 16, so they can be eliminated. The only integer left is 12. The digits of 12 (1 and 2) add up to 3, making (B) the correct answer.

38. G   Difficulty: Low

Category: Higher Math / Algebra

Getting to the Answer: If you are tempted to say you don't have enough information to answer this question, look again. Knowing that line *R* is parallel to the *x*-axis is an important clue. The *x*-axis is the horizontal axis. Any line that is parallel to the *x*-axis is also horizontal, and the slope of a horizontal line is always 0. Remember, slope is change in *y* over change in *x*. If the line is horizontal, there is no change in *y*. This means (G) is correct.

39. E   Difficulty: Medium

Category: Higher Math / Algebra

Getting to the Answer: The quickest way to compare the slopes among equations is to use algebra to put the equations in slope-intercept form: $y = mx + b$. In slope-intercept form, the slope is represented by *m*. Therefore, the slope of the line in the question, $y = 2x - 1$, is 2. Which of the answer choices has a slope of 2? A and D may appear to at first, but be careful—they are not in slope-intercept form. In slope-intercept form, A is $y = -2x + 1$

and D is $y = \frac{1}{2}x + \frac{3}{2}$. Neither has a slope of 2. Choices B and C are already in slope-intercept form, with slopes that do not equal 2. Take a look at (E):

$$5y = 10x + 2$$
$$y = 2x + \frac{2}{5}$$

The slope of this line is 2, so (E) is correct.

40. G   Difficulty: High

Category: Higher Math / Functions

Getting to the Answer: Use SOHCAHTOA to find the sine and cosine of each angle. The presence of the complicated formula in the note warns you that this question will take a while, so it's a good one to leave for the end of the test. The question stem tells you how to calculate $\sin(x + y)$, so your job is to find $\sin x$, $\cos x$, $\sin y$, and $\cos y$ and plug those values into the given equation.

Because $\sin = \dfrac{\text{opposite}}{\text{hypotenuse}}$, $\sin x = \dfrac{10\sqrt{2}}{15}$ and $\sin y = \dfrac{5}{5\sqrt{10}}$.

Because $\cos = \dfrac{\text{adjacent}}{\text{hypotenuse}}$, $\cos x = \dfrac{5}{15}$ and $\cos y = \dfrac{15}{5\sqrt{10}}$.

Plug those values into the formula:
$\sin(x + y) = \sin x \cos y + \sin y \cos x$

$$\frac{10\sqrt{2}}{15} \cdot \frac{15}{5\sqrt{10}} + \frac{5}{5\sqrt{10}} \cdot \frac{5}{15} = \frac{150\sqrt{2}}{75\sqrt{10}} + \frac{25}{75\sqrt{10}}$$

$$= \frac{150\sqrt{2} + 25}{75\sqrt{10}} = \frac{6\sqrt{2} + 1}{3\sqrt{10}} = \frac{\sqrt{10}(6\sqrt{2} + 1)}{\sqrt{10}(3\sqrt{10})}$$

$$= \frac{6\sqrt{20} + \sqrt{10}}{3 \cdot 10} = \frac{12\sqrt{5} + \sqrt{10}}{30}$$

This matches (G).

41. C   Difficulty: Low

Category: Higher Math / Number and Quantity

Getting to the Answer: The union of two sets includes all the elements that appear in either set. In this case, that means all the numbers between 0 and 5 and all the numbers between 3 and 7. You can combine these ranges and say that the union includes all the numbers between 0 and 7. Because $0 \leq x \leq 7$ includes all the numbers between 0 and 7, including both 0 and 7, (C) is correct.

42. F   Difficulty: High

Category: Higher Math / Functions

Getting to the Answer: Don't spend a lot of time comparing the answer choices. They are very similar and are likely to confuse you. Instead, apply the rules of transformations to the original function, one at a time, and then look for a match. First, a reflection over the x-axis is a vertical reflection, so apply a negative sign to the entire function (not just the x); the result is $-\cos x$. Shifting the graph right π units can be achieved by subtracting π from the x-value only (remember, horizontal translations are the opposite of what you expect); now you have $-\cos(x - \pi)$. Finally, shifting the graph down a units can be achieved by subtracting a from the whole equation to get $-\cos(x - \pi) - a$. Thus, the final function is $f'(x) = -\cos(x - \pi) - a$, which matches (F).

43. B   Difficulty: Medium

Category: Higher Math / Geometry

Getting to the Answer: Did you recognize that $\triangle RST$ is a 30°-60°-90° triangle? You should always be on the lookout for special triangles. Drawing a quick sketch of $\triangle RST$ may help you to organize the information in this question. Because $\angle R$ is a right angle, you know that the side opposite $\angle R$, $\overline{ST}$, will be the hypotenuse.

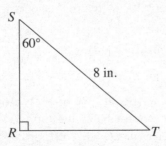

Remember that a 30°-60°-90° triangle has sides in the ratio $x : x\sqrt{3} : 2x$. This allows you to calculate the other two sides of $\triangle RST$. Because $2x = 8$, $x = 4$. $\overline{RT}$ is 4 inches

long and $\overline{SR}$ is $4\sqrt{3}$ inches long. These two sides are the base and height of $\triangle RST$, so you can plug their lengths into the area formula for triangles:

$$\begin{aligned} A &= \frac{1}{2}bh \\ &= \frac{1}{2}(4)\left(4\sqrt{3}\right) \\ &= 8\sqrt{3} \end{aligned}$$

Choice (B) is correct.

44. J   Difficulty: High

Category: Higher Math / Algebra

Getting to the Answer: This question is not as difficult as it may appear. It's primarily testing your knowledge of rules of exponents. When an exponent is raised to another exponent, multiply the exponents. Because the variable you want to solve for is part of an exponent, try to make the bases the same so that you can compare the exponents.

$$(x^{3b-1})^2 = x^{16} \rightarrow x^{6b-2} = x^{16}$$

Now that the bases are the same, set up an equation comparing the exponents:

$$\begin{aligned} 6b - 2 &= 16 \\ 6b &= 18 \\ b &= 3 \end{aligned}$$

That's (J).

45. C   Difficulty: High

Category: Higher Math / Geometry

Getting to the Answer: The area of the original figure is the area of the square plus the area of the semicircle. The square has sides of length $2r$, so its area is $(2r)^2 = 4r^2$. The area of the semicircle is $\frac{1}{2}\pi r^2$, so the area of the original figure is $4r^2 + \frac{1}{2}\pi r^2$. If r is doubled, the new figure will be composed of a square with sides of length $4r$ and a semicircle with radius $2r$. The new figure's area will be:

$$(4r)^2 + \frac{1}{2}\pi(2r)^2 = 16r^2 + \frac{1}{2}\pi 4r^2 = 16r^2 + 2\pi r^2$$

The new area compared to the original area is:

$$\frac{16r^2 + 2\pi r^2}{4r^2 + \frac{1}{2}\pi r^2} = \frac{2r^2(8+\pi)}{\frac{1}{2}r^2(8+\pi)} = \frac{2}{\frac{1}{2}} = 4$$

So, the new figure has 4 times the area of the original figure. Choice (C) is correct.

To make the question more concrete, you could Pick Numbers. If $r = 1$, then the area of the original figure is $2^2 + \frac{1}{2}\pi(1^2) = 4 + \frac{1}{2}\pi$. When r is doubled, it becomes 2, and the area of the new figure is $4^2 + \frac{1}{2}\pi(2^2) = 16 + 2\pi$. This is $\frac{16 + 2\pi}{4 + \frac{1}{2}\pi} = 4$ times the area of the original figure.

46. F **Difficulty:** Medium

Category: Higher Math / Algebra

Getting to the Answer: A system of equations has an infinite number of solutions when both equations represent the same line. So, you just have to find the value of x that will make the second equation equivalent to the first one. Compare the two equations. The left side of the second equation is 4 times the left side of the first equation. If the term on the right side of the second equation is also 4 times the term on the right side of the first equation, the two equations will be equivalent.

$$4(4a - b) = 4(4)$$
$$16a - 4b = 16$$
$$\text{So:}$$
$$16 = 8x$$
$$2 = x$$

Choice (F) is correct. Note that you could also write each equation in slope-intercept form and find the value of x that makes the y-intercepts the same.

47. C **Difficulty:** High

Category: Higher Math / Geometry

Getting to the Answer: This question combines rates with plane geometry. The first step is to figure out where Samir and Sally have gone. Only then can you come up with an expression that describes the distance between

them. Sally walked north for 20 minutes, or $\frac{1}{3}$ of an hour. Since she was walking at a rate of 3 miles per hour, she went $\frac{1}{3}(3) = 1$ mile north. She walked east for 40 minutes, or $\frac{2}{3}$ of an hour, so she went $\frac{2}{3}(3) = 2$ miles east. Samir walked south at a rate of 2 miles per hour for $\frac{1}{3}$ of an hour, so he went $\frac{1}{3}(2) = \frac{2}{3}$ miles south. Then he went $\frac{2}{3}(2) = \frac{4}{3}$ miles east. A sketch will help you see where they are:

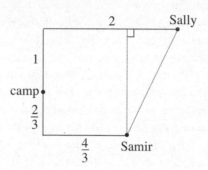

The distance between them is the hypotenuse of a right triangle. The height of the triangle is the north-south distance between them, and the base of the triangle is the east-west distance. The north-south distance is $1 + \frac{2}{3}$, and the east-west distance is $2 - \frac{4}{3}$. Don't bother to simplify these, because the answer choices don't either. Instead, plug them into the Pythagorean theorem, which can be written as $c = \sqrt{a^2 + b^2}$, to find that the hypotenuse of this triangle must be $\sqrt{\left(1 + \frac{2}{3}\right)^2 + \left(2 - \frac{4}{3}\right)^2}$, which is (C).

48. J **Difficulty:** Medium

Category: Higher Math / Functions

Getting to the Answer: The graph is a parabola that opens up, so it must be of the form $f(x) = ax^2$. This means you can eliminate F, G, and H. To choose between (J) and K, pick a point on the graph and try it in each answer choice.

The point $\left(1, \frac{1}{2}\right)$ is a great point to test—it only works for (J). (Even if you're not sure what the y-value of that point on the graph is, you can see that it is between 0 and 1. Choice (J) is the only equation that produces a y-value between 0 and 1 when $x = 1$.)

49. C   Difficulty: Medium

Category: Essential Skills / Geometry

Getting to the Answer: Think logically: A positive product will be greater than a negative product. You should be able to determine where x and y are each positive and negative based on the quadrant in which each point lies. Remember that a negative number times a negative number is positive. The product will only be positive when either both coordinates are positive or both are negative, so it must be (C), D, or E. Choice D clearly has a small product (because both coordinates are less than 1), so the answer is either (C) or E. Notice that E's x-coordinate is less than 1, which means its product, xy, is less than y. Choice (C)'s x- and y-coordinates both have large values, more than making up for its y being slightly smaller than E's y (thinking in terms of absolute value, because the product gets rid of the negatives). Thus, (C) will have the largest product.

50. J   Difficulty: Medium

Category: Higher Math / Functions

Getting to the Answer: As with any composition, work from the inside out. Substitute the value (the expression) for $h(x)$ into $g(x)$ for each x and simplify:

$$g\big(h(x)\big) = g(2x + 5)$$

$$g(x) = x^2 - 3x$$
$$g(2x + 5) = (2x + 5)^2 - 3(2x + 5)$$
$$= (2x + 5)(2x + 5) - 3(2x) - 3(5)$$
$$= 4x^2 + 10x + 10x + 25 - 6x - 15$$
$$= 4x^2 + 14x + 10$$

This matches (J).

51. C   Difficulty: Medium

Category: Higher Math / Geometry

Getting to the Answer: You don't need to use the distance formula to answer this question. Look for a quick way to find the base and height of the triangle. The area of a triangle is $A = \frac{1}{2}bh$. Because the base of this triangle, $\overline{AC}$, is a horizontal line segment (both vertices have the same y-coordinate), you can determine its length by finding the difference between the x-coordinates of A and C. The length of the base is $5 - (-6) = 11$.

The height will be the shortest distance from the base to B, so you can calculate the height by finding the difference between the y-coordinates of B and any point on the base: $7 - 1 = 6$.

Now use the area formula:

$$A = \frac{1}{2}bh$$
$$= \frac{1}{2}(11)(6)$$
$$= 33$$

Choice (C) is correct.

52. K   Difficulty: Medium

Category: Higher Math / Number and Quantity

Getting to the Answer: Stop and think about what it means to say that a number is greater than 0. That's just another way of saying that the number is positive. Your task is to find which of the answer choices will always yield a positive result for $-3x^2y^3$. Since one of the factors (-3) is negative, exactly one of the other 2 factors must also be negative. You know x^2 will never be negative, because any real number squared will always be positive or zero. That means that y^3 must be negative, and when y^3 is negative, y must also be negative. Therefore, y cannot be greater than 0. Choice (K) is correct.

53. C   Difficulty: High

Category: Higher Math / Functions

Getting to the Answer: In a geometric sequence, when you are looking for a term that is fairly far out in the sequence, use the formula $a_n = a_1(r^{n-1})$, where a_n is the nth

term in the sequence, a_1 is the first term in the sequence, and r is the amount by which each preceding term is multiplied to get the next term (called the common ratio).

The first two terms in this sequence are 6 and 18, so r is $\frac{18}{6} = 3$. You're given that a_1 is 6 and you're looking for the 25th term, so n is 25. Plug each of these values into the formula and simplify to get $a_{25} = 6(3^{25-1}) = 6 \times 3^{24}$. That's equivalent to (C).

54. J   Difficulty: High

Category: Higher Math / Functions

Getting to the Answer: You could try plugging each pair of values into each answer choice until you find one that works for all the pairs of values in the table, but this is likely to use up valuable time. Instead, examine the patterns in the table and try to eliminate at least 2 or 3 answer choices. The x-values increase by 1 each time, while the y-values decrease by varying amounts (not a constant change). This means the function cannot be linear, so eliminate F and G. Choice H is a parabola that has been shifted up 3 units, so it should pass through the point (0,3). According to the table, the graph passes through (0,5), so eliminate G as well. To choose between (J) and K, choose an easy pair of values from the table, such as (0,5), and check each function. Choice (J) gives

$$g(0) = \left(\frac{1}{2}\right)^0 + 4 = 1 + 4 = 5;$$ choice K gives $g(0) = -2^0 + 4 = -1 + 4 = 3$. This means (J) is correct. (Note that -2^0, which equals -1, is not the same as $(-2)^0$, which equals 1.)

55. B   Difficulty: High

Category: Higher Math / Geometry

Getting to the Answer: Don't worry when a trig question doesn't include a diagram. You have all of the information you need, and you can always draw your own triangle if you are confused. Imagine a triangle with angle n. If $\cos n = \frac{15}{17}$, then you can assume that the adjacent side is 15 and the hypotenuse is 17, because $\cos = \frac{\text{adjacent}}{\text{hypotenuse}}$.

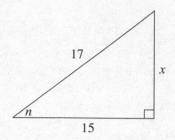

Tangent equals $\frac{\text{opposite}}{\text{adjacent}}$, so all you need now is the length of the side opposite angle n. Use the Pythagorean theorem:

$$15^2 + x^2 = 17^2$$
$$225 + x^2 = 289$$
$$x^2 = 64$$
$$x = 8$$

So, $\tan n = \frac{8}{15}$, making (B) the correct answer.

56. K   Difficulty: Medium

Category: Essential Skills / Expressions and Equations

Getting to the Answer: Some word problems include unnecessary information. Do you really need to know the current price of milk? Imagine the price of milk drops by 3 cents. How many gallons of milk would you expect the grocery store to sell? You know there will be 10 extra gallons sold for every cent decrease, so 3(10) more than the current 65 gallons will be sold. This is represented by the expression $65 + 10c$, which is (K).

57. D   Difficulty: Medium

Category: Higher Math / Statistics and Probability

Getting to the Answer: Probability is the ratio between the number of *favorable* outcomes and the number of total *possible* outcomes. For Elizabeth to be on Ann's team, she has to draw one of the remaining tokens that has the number 5 in the tens digit. 56 is no longer available, so that leaves 50 through 55, plus 57, 58, and 59. That makes 9 tokens that would put Elizabeth on Ann's team, or 9 possibilities for a favorable outcome. Now how many tokens are there for Elizabeth to draw from? There were 100 to start with, but Ann took one, so there are 99. That leaves a probability of $\frac{9}{99}$, which reduces to $\frac{1}{11}$, (D).

58. K   **Difficulty:** High

Category: Higher Math / Functions

Getting to the Answer: A quick sketch is needed to answer this question. You don't need anything fancy, just a graph that includes the given point, (5,−1), and the line $y = 3$ (which is a horizontal line that crosses through the y-axis at 3).

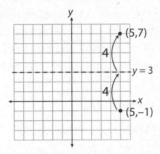

The only real rule to remember here is that if you reflect a point over a line, the distance from the line should remain the same. The point (5,−1) is 4 units below the horizontal line $y = 3$, so the reflected point will be 4 units above the line, or (5,3+4) = (5,7). Choice (K) is correct.

59. C   **Difficulty:** High

Category: Higher Math / Algebra

Getting to the Answer: When lines in the coordinate plane are perpendicular, the slopes of the two lines are negative reciprocals. Because *m* is perpendicular to *l*, and *l* has a slope of 1, the slope of *m* must be −1. That eliminates A, B, and E. To distinguish between (C) and D, you'll need to find the y-intercept of line *m*. Because the slope is −1, the line goes down 1 unit for every unit it goes to the right. You can also think of it as going up 1 unit for every unit it goes to the left. Start at (3,0) and count units until you reach the y-axis: (3,0), (2,1), (1,2), (0,3). The y-intercept of line *m* is 3, so (C) is correct.

60. G   **Difficulty:** High

Category: Higher Math / Number and Quantity

Getting to the Answer: Sometimes trial-and-error is the best way to approach a question. Try a few different values for the two numbers. Let the answer choices be clues as to which numbers you experiment with. To

get the smallest possible product, you want to have a negative product. That means that one of the factors will have to be negative, and the other will have to be positive. Don't forget that the factors differ by 8. So, use numbers that are close to zero. You'll find that 4 and −4 give you the smallest possible product, −16. Choice (G) is correct.

READING TEST

Passage I

Suggested Passage Map notes:

¶1: Audience listens to Beethoven's *5th Symph.* in Queen's Hall

¶2-6: Mrs. Munt (MM) asks Helen (H) who Margaret (M) is talking to, but H doesn't know and doesn't care

¶7-9: H listens to music and observes people around her

¶10: H imagines goblins that represent fleeting youth

¶11: H leaves, wanting to be alone

¶12: H feels music perfectly represented meaning of life

1. C   **Difficulty:** Medium

Category: Key Ideas and Details / Inference

Getting to the Answer: When the passage offers you little information about the subject of the question, make a conservative inference based only on what the text supports. Helen and Margaret interact very little in the passage, though you do see in lines 29–32 that Helen appears uninterested in Margaret's conversation with the young man. Helen is too engrossed in the symphony being played. Don't make too big a leap here; they don't seem that close, but this is just a single incident in the course of a novel. Choice (C) is correct as it captures the sense of this section nicely. Choice A is extreme; Helen "could not be bothered" by Margaret's conversation. She does not express disapproval. Choice B is out of scope; the passage does not suggest that Helen is jealous of Margaret. Choice D is out of scope; the passage doesn't allow you to draw much of a conclusion about what draws them together.

2. H   Difficulty: High

Category: Key Ideas and Details / Global

Getting to the Answer: When answer choices consist of pairs of words, both words in a choice have to be correct for that choice to be correct. Consult your notes to come up with a prediction for Helen's personality. She certainly gives the music great consideration, to the exclusion of communing with those in her party. Predict something like "given to deep thought" or "tending to keep to herself." Both of the adjectives in (H) match the prediction and the gist of the text. Choice F is a distortion; her analysis of the music definitely shows creativity, but she does not display an animated personality. Choice G is a distortion; Helen does analyze the music, but the results of her analysis are more pessimistic: "there was no such thing as splendor or heroism in the world . . . Panic and emptiness!" (lines 72–77). Choice J is extreme; Helen doesn't speak much to those around her, but these adjectives are too strong to be supported by the text.

3. B   Difficulty: Low

Category: Key Ideas and Details / Detail

Getting to the Answer: With "NOT" questions, find the section that the question draws from, then cross off the three answer choices mentioned there. Your notes should help you see that Helen considers the goblins in depth in lines 66–79. Compare the choices to the description here and work your way to the one NOT mentioned. In lines 65–66, Helen says, "They were not aggressive creatures; that was what made them so terrible to Helen." This line directly contradicts (B), which is the correct choice. Choice A is opposite; in lines 72–74, Helen feels that the goblins communicate the sense that "there was no such thing as splendor or heroism in the world." Choice C is opposite; in lines 74–77, Helen admits she "could not contradict them . . . The goblins were right" in their pessimistic worldview. Choice D is opposite; in lines 66–67, Helen warns her aunt to "look out for the part where you think you are done with the goblins and they come back."

4. J   Difficulty: Medium

Category: Craft and Structure / Vocab-in-Context

Getting to the Answer: There are several meanings for the word *decorating*, but you're looking for the one which fits into the sentence. In the surrounding lines, the author writes that the Andante portion of the music had "a family likeness to all the other beautiful andantes that Beethoven had written." Because the tune sounded like other music she had heard, Helen's *attention wandered*. She paid attention again, when "Beethoven started decorating his tune." In context, this must mean that the music changed, was no longer so familiar, and had new elements. Predict this answer and match it with (J)—embellishing means to make more interesting or entertaining. Even if you don't know that definition, you can eliminate all other answer choices because none of them makes sense in a passage about listening to music.

5. B   Difficulty: Medium

Category: Key Ideas and Details / Detail

Getting to the Answer: All answer choices are mentioned in the passage, but only one is what listeners imagine when hearing the music, so you'll have to research each answer. In lines 7–8 the author writes that "Helen, . . . can see . . . shipwrecks in the music's flood," making shipwrecks, (B), is the correct answer. Choice A, wild horses, are referred to in line 47 to describe how attentive Herr Liesecke is. Queen's Hall, C, is mentioned in line 17 as the "dreariest music-room in London," and drums, D, (line 63) are not in any listener's imagination but a part of the music to which Tibby wants his fellow listeners to pay particular attention.

6. F   Difficulty: Low

Category: Key Ideas and Details / Detail

Getting to the Answer: Remember that "according to the passage" indicates a Detail question; the answer will be a paraphrase of something directly stated in the passage. Your notes can remind you where the author discusses Tibby (paragraphs 1, 7, and 10). He listens to the symphony with "the full score . . . open on his knee" and draws the company's attention to "the transitional passage on the drum." Predict that he is fascinated by details within the performance. Choice (F) correctly matches the thrust of this prediction and of the text. Choice G is a misused detail; this more correctly defines Helen. Choice H is a distortion; Tibby's attention to the drum exemplifies his focus on the more technical aspects of the music. Choice J is a distortion; the author refers to the hall as dreary, but nothing indicates that this affects Tibby in this way.

7. B   **Difficulty:** Medium

Category: Key Ideas and Details / Inference

Getting to the Answer: Good notes and a good sense of the passage help when you don't receive a line or paragraph reference. The symphony performance takes up most of the passage, so research the last few paragraphs. The symphony leaves Helen with a hopeless feeling, but also feelings of certainty and acceptance of that outcome—a sense of resolution. Look for a match to this idea among the choices. Choice (B) correctly captures Helen's sentiments as she leaves. Choice A is out of scope; the passage paints Helen as unconcerned with her companions, who also seem anything but indifferent. Choice C is a out of scope; the passage does not describe Helen's reaction to Tibby. Choice D is a distortion; though Helen "pushed her way out" of the hall, nothing indicates that conditions in the hall affected her decision to leave.

8. J   **Difficulty:** Medium

Category: Key Ideas and Details / Inference

Getting to the Answer: With Prose Fiction passages, be careful to keep straight which character does or thinks what. This passage contains a number of different characters. Use your notes to find where the author mentions Aunt Juley—principally in lines 51–52. He describes her as "so British, and wanting to tap." You also might have found the reference to Mrs. Munt in line 5: she would tap along with the music, but surreptitiously. You can infer that tapping must be frowned upon, and Aunt Juley is aware of that. Choice (J) is the most reasonable inference based on the text. Choice F is a misused detail; Tibby draws Aunt Juley's attention to the drum, but this comes after her decision not to tap. Choice G is a distortion; the passage does not suggest that Aunt Juley was considering how her tapping might affect Helen. Choice H is out of scope; "snapping one's fingers" is not mentioned in the passage.

9. C   **Difficulty:** Medium

Category: Key Ideas and Details / Detail

Getting to the Answer: Use your notes to whittle down the choices, then research further as needed. In lines 12–13, you read that, though the music enthralls nearly everyone else, he "can remember nothing but Fraulein Mosebach." He must be infatuated with her, and not the music. Choice

(C) logically follows from this portion of the passage. Choice A is opposite; the author writes, "wild horses could not make him inattentive" (lines 47–48). Choice B is opposite; though Margaret seems interested in the young man she is speaking with, when the performance is going on, she "can only see the music" (lines 8–9). Choice D is opposite; the author describes Tibby's interest in the music in multiple spots in the passage.

10. F   **Difficulty:** Low

Category: Key Ideas and Details / Detail

Getting to the Answer: If your notes don't help, skim the passage, especially when looking for italicized or capitalized text. The author deals with the Andante in paragraph 7. Helen listened to the Andante *once more* after "Beethoven started decorating his tune." Predict that she was drawn by a change in the music. Choice (F) matches the prediction nicely. Choice G is a misused detail; Tibby does gesture her way, but this occurs later in the passage. Choice H is a distortion; the two women had already stopped speaking once the Andante began. Choice J is out of scope; the author doesn't indicate that Helen believed this.

Passage II

Suggested Passage Map notes:

¶1: recent ↑ type II diabetes, obesity, heart disease

¶2: historically people were more active

¶3: urban. & industr. changed lifestyles, more sedentary

¶4: Leisure is less active

¶5: Burning more calories than consuming = lose weight

¶6: Preventing these diseases is extremely important

11. C   **Difficulty:** Low

Category: Key Ideas and Details / Detail

Getting to the Answer: As your map tells you, farmers in this era are discussed in the first paragraph, but the only one of the answers mentioned there is disease, which matches (C). Winter is mentioned as an idle time (line 24), but not having to work so hard is not necessarily a challenge. Obesity and poor eating habits are afflictions of the modern world, not the pre-industrial one.

12. F   Difficulty: Low

Category: Key Ideas and Details / Detail

Getting to the Answer: Whenever a question uses the phrase "EXCEPT," eliminating obviously wrong answer choices first can make finding the correct choice easier. The author lists several aspects of pre-industrial life that contributed to overall physical fitness. The author never suggests that (F), hazardous conditions of the 19th-century workplace, were conducive to being fit. Choice G is incorrect because author mentions variation in activity in paragraph 2. Choice H is incorrect because the second paragraph cites animal and manpower as the primary sources of pre-industrial work energy. Choice J is incorrect because paragraph 4 discusses the physicality of pre-industrial pastimes.

13. B   Difficulty: Medium

Category: Craft and Structure / Writer's View

Getting to the Answer: When answer choices begin with verbs, eliminate choices that don't match the author's purpose. Put yourself in the author's shoes and ask yourself, "Why would I include that information?" The author mentions these occupations to support the main idea of the second paragraph—jobs in pre-industrial society required more physical activity. Choice (B) matches the prediction well. Choice A is out of scope; the passage does not mention jobs that are obsolete. Choice C is extreme; while the passage focuses on obesity, the author does not recommend specific occupations for people. Choice D is a misused detail; caloric intake and nutrition are mentioned in the first paragraph, not the second.

14. J   Difficulty: Medium

Category: Key Ideas and Details / Inference

Getting to the Answer: It is sometimes helpful to consider information from the author's viewpoint to determine what it implies. The author describes how the modern workplace promotes obesity by showing ways in which modern work requires less energy from people. Choice (J) is correct. Choice F is opposite; the passage describes pre-industrial work as hazardous. Choice G is extreme; the word "lament" is too strong for the context of the passage, which does not refer to grieving. Choice H is extreme; the passage does not praise modern working conditions.

15. A   Difficulty: Medium

Category: Craft and Structure / Function

Getting to the Answer: Nine-to-five workers are examples of people who have "numerous options for travel, none of which require any real physical exertion" (lines 56–57), which matches (A). Choice B is a distortion; the word "prove" is too extreme, and the author doesn't write that farmers are superior to office workers. Choice C is also a distortion; though the author seems to blame urbanization for some aspects of obesity, the author doesn't go so far as to criticize it. Choice D is out of scope—initiatives are in paragraph 4 and nutritional initiatives have nothing to do with making people more active.

16. J   Difficulty: Medium

Category: Key Ideas and Details / Detail

Getting to the Answer: By reviewing lines 70–82, you'll see that all answers except (J) are in the paragraph. Although it can be assumed that physicians are also working toward better health, they are not specifically mentioned.

17. D   Difficulty: High

Category: Key Ideas and Details / Detail

Getting to the Answer: Wrong answers on Detail questions often employ language from the passage. Look for the idea that matches your prediction, not the exact wording. Lines 71–73 state that losing weight requires burning more calories than one consumes. Choice (D) expresses the same basic concept. Choice A is out of scope; while the passage suggests that weight loss is beneficial, the author never directly states this information. Choice B is extreme; the passage does not state that excessive levels of exercise are required for weight loss. Choice C is opposite; the passage states that one must burn more calories than are consumed, not consume more calories than are burned.

18. F   Difficulty: High

Category: Craft and Structure / Writer's View

Getting to the Answer: Writer's View questions require you to figure out why the author does what he does. Consider how the information relates to the paragraph topic and passage as a whole. The paragraph topic relates measures that people could take to combat obesity. The author mentions gimmick diets and exercise machines as a means of explaining how losing weight is simpler than people realize. Choice (F) matches your prediction. Choice G is opposite; the passage does not suggest that these methods are effective. Choice H is a distortion; the author's purpose is not to criticize these methods, but rather to focus on the simplicity of losing weight. Choice J is a distortion; the passage focuses more on the ease, or rather simplicity, of losing weight, not of using exercise machines.

19. B   Difficulty: High

Category: Key Ideas and Details / Inference

Getting to the Answer: Questions that ask about tone often require you to choose between subtle shades of emotion. A little vocabulary study can help make such differences clear. The author states that parents and nutritionists have banished certain foods from public schools, indicating hostility to such foods. Choice (B) fits this prediction. Choice A is incorrect because the passage doesn't mention any uncertainty in feelings. Choice C is incorrect because the passage clearly indicates that parents and nutritionists care and thus are not apathetic. Choice D is incorrect because "enthralled," or "fascinated," is not at all mentioned in the passage.

20. H   Difficulty: Medium

Category: Craft and Structure / Writer's View

Getting to the Answer: Remember that a Writer's View answer will always be consistent with the main idea of the passage. The last paragraph discusses the increasing need to deal with the obesity problem. Choice (H) supports this. Choice F is a misused detail; while Americans during the 1990s lived longer, this choice has nothing to do with the paragraph topic. Choice G is opposite; the passage does not characterize the effects of obesity as innocuous, or harmless. Choice J is out of scope; American health is not directly compared to the health of people in other countries.

Passage III

Suggested Passage Map notes:

¶1: Woolf (W) essay "Mr. Bennett and Mrs. Brown" = enduring literary criticism

¶2: Hynes described debate, W said Bennett (B) was materialistic, wanted to discredit B

¶3: 1923 B said W characters don't "survive in the mind"

¶4: W said B obsessed with dull details

¶5: B's literary reputation didn't recover

¶6: W noted after B died that he had some skill, but she felt he had to be pulled down

21. C   Difficulty: High

Category: Craft and Structure / Writer's View

Getting to the Answer: Questions that encompass the whole passage will often offer choices that distort or misuse details from the passage. Your notes should give you a good read on "big-picture" questions like this. The author seems to feel that Woolf treated Bennett harshly, detracting from her own reputation, at least in his eyes. The passage makes clear that Bennett's career was never the same and that Woolf's essay paved the way for literary modernism. Choice (C) matches that idea. Choice A is a distortion; the author of the passage compares the authors' strengths and weaknesses, but you receive no indication as to what Woolf considered her own advantages or disadvantages compared to Bennett et al. Choice B is a distortion; the passage lists only the slightest of praise on Woolf's part for Bennett and his peers. Choice D is out of scope; the author references no such repercussions for Woolf.

22. F   Difficulty: Medium

Category: Craft and Structure / Vocab-in-Context

Getting to the Answer: The word *polemic* is used throughout the passage, which focuses on Woolf's criticism of Arnold Bennett. Criticism best matches (F), attack. Choice G is too neutral, H implies an opposite side, which isn't in the passage, and J is opposite.

23. D   Difficulty: Medium

Category: Craft and Structure / Writer's View

Getting to the Answer: Ask yourself what the writer is attempting to accomplish—why he says what he does. In the paragraph, the author claims that only a *handful* of such disputes "survive their moment," after which he lists two presumably famous ones. But he follows that by saying that few others "can have been so damaging, or so lasting in consequences." Predict that the author feels that this polemic may have been the most important one yet. Choice (D) matches this prediction. Choice A is a distortion; the author doesn't indicate this. Choice B is extreme; even among the others in the *handful*, none is characterized by the author as being so pivotal. Choice C is a distortion; the author doesn't use the comparison to make this point.

24. F   Difficulty: Medium

Category: Key Ideas and Details / Detail

Getting to the Answer: Use your notes to help find the paragraph where the author discusses this. Discussion of Bennett's work appears in several paragraphs, but the most in-depth treatment comes in paragraph 4: for example, "a writer obsessed with dull particulars of setting" (lines 52–53), and "he would describe her house in conscientious detail but never penetrate her essential life." Choice (F) correctly matches these ideas. Choice G is opposite; this contradicts the information found in paragraph 4. Choice H is out of scope; you know of the one essay Woolf wrote attacking Bennett, but not any more than that on this subject. Choice J is extreme; the passage indicates that Bennett did focus on certain details, but it doesn't indicate that he did so to the degree suggested here.

25. C   Difficulty: Medium

Category: Key Ideas and Details / Global

Getting to the Answer: Some questions will be so generally worded that making a prediction won't be feasible. Start working through the choices, and you should see which part of the passage to research. All of the choices reference the term "polemic." The author deals with this term most directly in the first paragraph. Compare the choices against that paragraph, only researching further as required. The passage deals primarily with Woolf's polemic and its effect on twentieth century literature, which matches (C). Choice A is out of scope; the author would likely agree that Woolf provides a great example of a successful polemic, but he never offers advice about formulating such a work. Choice B is a distortion; the author doesn't offer a "new interpretation." He discusses and expands on the generally understood view of the dispute. Choice D is out of scope; the author mentions other polemics only as an introduction to discussing Woolf's essay. He doesn't rank or compare multiple polemics.

26. F   Difficulty: Medium

Category: Craft and Structure / Vocab-in-Context

Getting to the Answer: Always try to make a prediction based on context before moving to the choices. When you go to the reference, you'll remember that even the author seems unsure of what Woolf means in using this phrase. Directly before this, however, you read that Woolf wrote that Bennett "had a materialistic view of the world." Look for a choice that incorporates this idea. Choice (F) is correct. Choice G is a distortion; this group is mentioned before the comment on Bennett, but there is no indication that he and the group are related in any way. Choice H is a distortion; this quotes a criticism that Bennett made about Woolf. Choice J is a misused detail; this may be an example of the concept, but it is too specific to represent the entire meaning of the phrase.

27. C   Difficulty: High

Category: Craft and Structure / Writer's View

Getting to the Answer: Take the citation given and put it in your own words. Then review each specific example to see if it matches the general idea of your paraphrase. The quotation refers to Woolf's criticism of a writer whom most observers of that era considered well established and successful. Work through the choices, looking for a match to this general idea. The analogy suggests that Woolf tried to achieve something but couldn't. The *Yes* that begins that sentence (lines 87–90) indicates a continuation of the idea in the previous sentence—a criticism of Woolf, who supposedly envied the *reality gift* displayed by Bennett. Choice (C) matches well. Choice A is a distortion; the author doesn't express an opinion of *Jacob's Room*. He only cites Bennett's opinion of it. Choice B is out of scope; the author refers to this book as an authority for his own essay, but expresses no "view" on it. Choice D is a distortion; this parenthetical comment by the author is not strong enough to "pull down" Bennett's reputation.

28. J   Difficulty: Medium

Category: Key Ideas and Details / Detail

Getting to the Answer: A good set of notes will help you to move quickly, even when you don't receive a line reference. Your notes should show you that the author addresses *Jacob's Room* in paragraph 3. Bennett praised the novel's *originality* and writing style but concluded that "the characters do not vitally survive in the mind." Bennett found this to be a serious deficiency. Only (J) matches the thrust of the citation. Choice F is out of scope; Bennett never compares the work to other novels. Choice G is out of scope; the author does not cite Bennett referring to this. Choice H is opposite; Bennett feels the novel does well in small ways but fails where it counts.

29. B   Difficulty: Medium

Category: Key Ideas and Details / Inference

Getting to the Answer: Find the relevant spot in the text, and predict an inference that is close to something said in the text. You find Woolf's opinion on "details of scene" in paragraph 4. As the author paraphrases, Woolf charged that Bennett would describe Mrs. Brown's "house in conscientious detail but never penetrate her essential life." Predict that such details can't capture a character's inner feelings. Choice (B) accurately matches this prediction. Choice A is a distortion; Woolf criticizes much of the work of these writers, but such feelings are not her reason for devaluing details of scene. Choice C is a distortion; this draws from Woolf's quote on one of Bennett's works. Choice D is a distortion; she might feel this way, but this pulls more from a comment made by Bennett.

30. J   Difficulty: Medium

Category: Craft and Structure / Function

Getting to the Answer: This is the only paragraph in which Woolf gives credit to Bennett, beginning with the quote in the question. Here Woolf is praising Bennett, making (J) correct. Choice F is opposite; Woolf doesn't say she retracts her criticism, but only gives faint praise

upon Bennett's death. Choice G is opposite because to excoriate is to severely criticize. Choice H is also opposite; Woolf is praising Bennett, not the other way around.

Passage IV

Suggested Passage Map notes:

Passage A

¶1: Type of coal burned affects amt of sulfur released

¶2: Stages of bituminous coal formation

¶3: Anthracite coal is formed from bit. coal, burns cleaner than bit. coal

¶4: Anth. coal limited, US & China biggest consumers

¶5: Subsurface mining is dangerous, strip mining less dangerous but worse for land

Passage B

¶1: Crude oil refers to petroleum and processed products

¶2: Formed from organic material, heat, pressure to create reservoirs

¶3: Oil wells extract oil from reservoirs

¶4: Secondary recovery required if pressure is low

¶5: At most 50% can be extracted

¶6: Unconventional sources less valuable and higher environ. footprint

31. C   Difficulty: Medium

Category: Key Ideas and Details / Detail

Getting to the Answer: The best way to approach this kind of question is to eliminate all answers which are in the passage; the one that's left is the correct answer. The question points you to paragraph 1, where you read that SO_2 and sulfuric acid are formed in the atmosphere, while mercury is released when coal is burned. The only answer left is (C), which, in Passage B, refers to petroleum compounds of hydrogen and carbon.

32. H   Difficulty: High

Category: Key Ideas and Details / Inference

Getting to the Answer: The best way to answer a question like this is to research each answer separately, using your notes or scanning the passage for the words. Look for an answer that the author specifically indicates has low levels of moisture, methane, and carbon dioxide. Since the author states, "With further compaction, lignite loses moisture, methane, and carbon dioxide, and becomes bituminous coal," it must be true that the bituminous coal has less moisture, methane, and carbon dioxide than lignite. Since peat is found in swamps and bogs, it would have more moisture than both lignite and bituminous coal. Choice (H) is the best choice. Choice F is a misused detail; lignite is a sedimentary rock that has *more* moisture, methane, and carbon dioxide than bituminous coal. Choice G is a misused detail; peat is found in swamps and bogs, so it would have more moisture than both lignite and bituminous coal. Choice J is out of scope; kerogen is waxy material found in shale that can be heated to produce oil (Passage B), not coal.

33. C   Difficulty: Medium

Category: Craft and Structure / Function

Getting to the Answer: As your map tells you, the second paragraph describes how bituminous coal is formed, and the third paragraph provides details about anthracite. The author clearly states that anthracite burns cleaner, making A the opposite of the information. Having detailed all the environmental dangers involved in burning bituminous coal (paragraph 1), a cleaner burning fuel is obviously better for the environment, as (C) states. Choice B is out of scope, since there's no reference to mercury in anthracite, and D is also out of scope; the author never mentions oil (that's in Passage B) and doesn't recommend one fuel over another.

34. H   Difficulty: Medium

Category: Craft and Structure / Vocab-in-Context

Getting to the Answer: Questions like this require you to consider the meaning of the phrase in the context not only of the sentence in which it appears, but also in terms of the surrounding sentences. The phrase relates to the *extraction process* of oil shale and tar sands. In the last paragraph, the author writes, "The hydrocarbons obtained from these sources require extensive processing to be usable, reducing their value. The extraction process also has a particularly large environmental footprint," which sounds negative. An environmental footprint refers to how much a person or action affects the health of the environment. In this case, it's a big, and seemingly negative, effect, which matches (H). Choice F is a distortion; in this case, "footprint" does not refer to the imprint of a foot, but to the effect on the environment of the extraction of oil. Choice G is opposite; the phrase "extensive processing" seems like a negative one, as it is associated with a reduction in value. Choice J is out of scope; the author does not state that all effects on the environment, even negative ones, are irreversible.

35. D   Difficulty: Medium

Category: Key Ideas and Details / Detail

Getting to the Answer: Use your notes to research where to find the details about how oil is pumped from under the Earth's surface. All the information about the process of extracting oil is in paragraph 3. Look for keywords that signal the steps in the process, such as *after* and "the process is repeated." Paragraph 3 outlines the steps in erecting a well: "An oil well is created using an oil rig, which turns a drill bit. After the hole is drilled, a casing—a metal pipe with a slightly smaller diameter than the hole—is inserted and bonded to its surroundings, usually with cement." In these three steps, drilling the hole is the second one; thus, (D) is the correct answer. Choice A is a misused detail; drilling a hole is the first step in the process. Choice B is a misused detail; draining fluid is pushed in after casings are in place, one of the last steps in extraction. Choice C is a misused detail; topping the wellbore is the very last part of the procedure.

36. G   Difficulty: High

Category: Key Ideas and Details / Inference

Getting to the Answer: It's hard to predict the answer to a question like this, since many things could be inferred. Rather than make a prediction, use the answers to research the passage. Pump jacks are mentioned in paragraph 4, where it states that they are used in one particular circumstance. Determine what that circumstance is, then match it with the correct answer. When writing about pump jacks in paragraph 4, the author states, "But sometimes, additional measures, called secondary recovery, are required. This is especially true in depleted fields . . . " Depleted fields are those in which the oil reserves are greatly diminished, meaning very low. Choice

(G) correctly matches the circumstances described in paragraph four. Choice F is out of scope; the passage does not provide any information about the safety of using pump jacks. Choice H is opposite; paragraph five states that even with new technology, only about 50% of the oil can be recovered. Choice J is a misused detail; the wellbore (paragraph 3) is the drilling hole, strengthened by metal pipes, not pump jacks.

37. D   Difficulty: Low

Category: Integration of Knowledge and Ideas / Synthesis

Getting to the Answer: Read the question carefully. Though not worded in the most straightforward way, it's really just saying that, given the information in the passage, it can be inferred that both authors would agree on three of the four answers; the one on which the authors would not agree is the correct one. The key here is that the passages must include information relevant to the question. If there is no information given, there is no basis from which to draw an inference. Look for an answer that is not referred to in any part of either passage. Neither author says anything about solar power, so we don't have evidence regarding the safety of solar power; therefore, (D) is correct. Choice A is opposite; here's a point of agreement. Both authors write about organic material being used as an energy source. Choice B is opposite; in passage A, the author writes: "Coal is a solid fossil fuel formed from the remains of land plants that flourished 300 to 400 million years ago," and in passage B the author notes that "organic material such as zooplankton and algae settled on the bottom of ocean[s] millions of years ago." Both statements clearly mean that both oil and coal are created from organic material, and the process takes a very long time. Choice C is opposite; in passage A, the author refers to limited supplies of anthracite (paragraph 3), while the reference to "depleted fields" in passage B (paragraph 4) indicates that, at least in some oil fields, the supply has dwindled.

38. F   Difficulty: Low

Category: Integration of Knowledge and Ideas / Synthesis

Getting to the Answer: Use your notes to research where to find the details about how coal and oil are formed. The information you need regarding the formation of coal and oil is located in the second paragraph of each passage. According to the passages, extraction does not affect the formation of coal and oil since extraction occurs millions of years after the formation of fossil fuels; therefore, (F) is correct. Choice G is opposite; passage A states, "The formation of coal goes through discrete stages as, over millions of years, heat and pressure act on decomposing plants." Passage B states, "Thousands of years later, the sediments that contained the organic material were subjected to intense amounts of heat and pressure, changing it into a waxy material called kerogen." Choice H is opposite; heat is mentioned in the second paragraphs of both Passages A and B. Choice J is opposite; organic material is mentioned in the second paragraphs of both Passages A and B.

39. C   Difficulty: Medium

Category: Integration of Knowledge and Ideas / Synthesis

Getting to the Answer: The formation of oil is described in the third paragraph, a likely place to research when looking for support for a multi-step process. Though the information in paragraph 3 is not given in a step-by-step process with key words such as "first" and "then," look for a phrase that indicates a process which evolves over time, with different steps at different points. The phrase "when more heat is added" means that the addition of heat is a step taken after a previous one. Even though the passage says that this takes a long time, it's still a step-by-step procedure, which results in oil as we know it. Choice (C) matches this description. Choice A is out of scope; this answer is about the terminology for an oil field, not the process of oil formation. Choice B is out of scope; how oil is pushed to the surface is irrelevant to how it is formed. Choice D is out of scope; the components of oil are also irrelevant.

40. G   Difficulty: Medium

Category: Integration of Knowledge and Ideas / Synthesis

Getting to the Answer: When answering Function questions, consider the author's purpose in doing something. Read both final sentences, focusing on each author's tone. Both authors include negative descriptions of the consequences of extracting fossil fuels. In passage A, the author states, "However, it often leaves the land scarred and unsuitable for other uses." Passage B states "The extraction process also has a particularly large environmental footprint." Given the information that sulfur is dangerous, it is likely that the authors would agree that extracting coal and oil results in negative consequences. Choice (G) matches these descriptions. Choice F is a distortion; both passages mention negative impacts of extracting fossil fuels, but only Passage A conveys the idea that the land may not recover. The "environmental footprint" mentioned in Passage B does not guarantee irreparable harm to the land. Choice H is out of scope; new technology is mentioned only in passage B, where it is referenced as a way to increase oil recovery. Since it is not discussed at the end of both Passages A and B it cannot be the correct answer. Choice J is out of scope; since neither author writes about lead, you can eliminate this answer choice.

SCIENCE TEST

Passage I

1. B   Difficulty: Low

Category: Interpretation of Data

Getting to the Answer: Searching for the lowest value of the 20 listed in Table 2 would be time consuming, so start instead with the lowest value among the answer choices. Choice D, like C, is far lower than the values in Table 2—in fact, both are values from Table 1. Eliminate both. Choice (B) is correct because it is the lowest value in Table 2, recorded in Room 4 on Day 1. Choice A is the highest value in Table 2.

2. G   Difficulty: Low

Category: Interpretation of Data

Getting to the Answer: All of the values in Table 2 include one digit after the decimal point, so they are recorded to the nearest 0.1 mm Hg. Choice (G) is correct. Choice F is a trap for those who mistakenly refer to Table 1, in which values are recorded to the nearest 0.01°C.

3. C   Difficulty: Medium

Category: Interpretation of Data

Getting to the Answer: Pick one data point at a time and check it against the answer choices, eliminating any that don't contain that data point. Start by checking for the point from Day 1 (745.2 mm Hg, 18.03°C). Eliminate A, B, and D, because they don't contain this point. Only (C) correctly represents this data point, so it must be the correct answer. And, indeed, it does contain all of the data points for Room 4.

4. J   Difficulty: Low

Category: Interpretation of Data

Getting to the Answer: Circle the Room 3 column in Table 2 if possible, to ensure that you look at the right data. Reading down the column, you can see that the average daily air pressure decreases every day. Choice (J) matches this perfectly. Choice F describes the pressure changes for Room 1. Choice G describes the temperature changes (in Table 1) for Room 3. Choice H is the opposite of the correct answer.

5. D   Difficulty: Medium

Category: Evaluation of Models, Inferences, and Results

Getting to the Answer: The only data provided in the passage are average daily air temperatures and pressures; there is nothing to indicate the quantity of heat provided to a room nor the quantity of heat absorbed by the contents of a room. Because the information necessary to calculate heat absorption modulus is absent, you would not be justified in concluding that Room 1 has a higher heat absorption modulus. Choice (D) is thus correct.

6. F   Difficulty: Low

Category: Interpretation of Data

Getting to the Answer: According to Table 1, the highest average air temperature on each day can be found in Room 1. Therefore, that room would be the most likely to cause the equipment to malfunction. Choice (F) is correct.

Passage II

7. A   Difficulty: Low

Category: Scientific Investigation

Getting to the Answer: In any experiment, the control condition is the one used as a baseline, providing a standard of comparison to judge the experimental effects of the other conditions. In Study 1, there would be no way to know what the effect of, say, rotating the microscope was on bacterial migration if you didn't know how the bacteria migrated before you rotated the microscope. In short, the control condition is the trial that is run without any experimental manipulations. For Study 1, that would be Trial 1, (A).

8. G   Difficulty: Medium

Category: Evaluation of Models, Inferences, and Results

Getting to the Answer: In order to be able to tell whether light was the stimulus affecting the direction of bacterial migration, you have to compare two trials, one with light present and the other with light absent. If there is no difference in the direction of bacterial migration between the two trials, then light does not have an effect and is not the primary stimulus. The two trials you need to compare are Trial 1 and Trial 2 of Study 1, because "Trial 1 was conducted under standard laboratory conditions" (with the light on) but "[i]n Trial 2, the microscope was shielded from all external light." Because the results of the trials differed only minimally, they support the theory that light was not the primary stimulus. Choice (G) is thus correct.

9. C   Difficulty: Medium

Category: Scientific Investigation

Getting to the Answer: The data show that the bacteria are sensitive to magnetic fields and tend to migrate in the direction of magnetic north. In Study 2, this meant that the bacteria moved toward the permanent magnet because the magnet's north pole was facing the slide. If the magnet's south pole faced the slide instead, the magnetic field would be reversed and the bacteria would migrate in exactly the opposite direction, away from the magnet. That makes (C) the correct answer. Choice A is incorrect because the direction, not the strength, of the magnetic field is what determined how the bacteria

migrated. Choice B is incorrect because there is no reason to believe that the bacteria could become "disoriented." Choice D is incorrect because the proximity of the permanent magnet overpowered the effects of the Earth's magnetic field, as can be seen in the results of Study 2.

10. J   Difficulty: Medium

Category: Evaluation of Models, Inferences, and Results

Getting to the Answer: The question stem asks for the reasoning that would be "most advantageous from an evolutionary standpoint," which means that you need to identify the condition that would most aid the survival or reproductive capacity of bacteria that oriented themselves downward. Choice F is incorrect because it concerns the survival of organisms that consume the bacteria, not the bacteria themselves. Choice G is incorrect because it would grant evolutionary advantage to bacteria that oriented themselves upward, not downward. Choice H is incorrect because there is no clear indication of what effect dispersal would have on the bacteria—it could be good or bad, depending on circumstances. Choice (J) is the only remaining option, so it must be correct. And, indeed, if necessary nutrients were more abundant in bottom sediments, bacteria that oriented themselves downward would have an obvious evolutionary advantage in terms of survival.

11. C   Difficulty: Medium

Category: Scientific Investigation

Getting to the Answer: To gain new information about the relationship between magnetic field strength and bacterial migrations, the researchers should vary the magnetic field strength and observe the effect on bacterial migrations. Choice (C) is correct because it suggests using more and less powerful magnets, which would produce a variety of magnetic field strengths, exactly as required. None of the other choices would create variation in magnetic field strength.

12. F   Difficulty: Medium

Category: Evaluation of Models, Inferences, and Results

Getting to the Answer: In each of the trials of Study 1, bacterial migrations were largely found to be in the direction of magnetic north. Shielding from light and electric fields, rotation of the microscope, and movement of the microscope to another lab all had no distinct effect on the direction of migration. Thus, it is reasonable to conclude from Study 1 that most magnetotactic bacteria migrate towards Earth's magnetic north pole. Choice (F) is correct. Choice G presents a conclusion supported by the results of Study 2. Choice H is only supported by Trial 6 of Study 2, when the permanent magnet was placed at the 12:00 position. Choice J is incorrect because the first two trials of Study 1 showed that electric fields have no real impact on bacterial migration.

13. B   Difficulty: Medium

Category: Interpretation of Data

Getting to the Answer: To answer this question, refer to Table 2. Based on the data for Trial 7 in the table, 483 bacteria moved in the 3:00 direction on the microscope slide, whereas only a few moved in other directions. Only (B) has a high density of dots at the 3:00 location (that is, to the right) and a low density of dots at other places on the field.

Passage III

14. G   Difficulty: Medium

Category: Scientific Investigation

Getting to the Answer: The equation in Study 2 tells you how to calculate the answer: Z = voltage $\div$ current = 12 V $\div$ 1.2 A = 10 Ω. Thus, (G) is correct. You could also answer this question by noticing the inverse relationship between current and impedance in Table 2: when current doubles, Z is halved. Thus, since 1.2 A is twice the current seen in Bulb 4, you should expect the impedance to be half of 20 Ω.

15. D   Difficulty: High

Category: Scientific Investigation

Getting to the Answer: The equation in the passage tells you that Z = voltage $\div$ current, which means that current = voltage $\div$ Z. Plugging in the Z values from Table 2 yields the following results: For A, current = 10 V $\div$ 60 Ω = $\frac{1}{6}$ A. For B, current = 8 V $\div$ 40 Ω = $\frac{1}{5}$ A. For C,

current = 6 V $\div$ 30 Ω = $\frac{1}{5}$ A. Finally, for (D), current = 5 V $\div$ 20 Ω = $\frac{1}{4}$ A. Choice (D), then, results in the largest current, making it correct.

16. F   Difficulty: Low

Category: Interpretation of Data

Getting to the Answer: According to Table 1, Bulb 3 produced one red indicator light and three green indicator lights. The text above Table 1 explains that green indicators illuminate when light is detected and red indicators illuminate when no light is detected. For Bulb 3, then, only one sensor did not detect any light. Choice (F) is thus correct.

17. C   Difficulty: Medium

Category: Interpretation of Data

Getting to the Answer: First, find the equation for B in the passage. It's listed in Study 3 as $B = \frac{P}{4\pi r^2}$. The text explains that P is the power rating in watts and r is the distance in meters from the bulb. You're given r in the question stem (2 meters), but you'll need to find P. P is listed in Table 3 as 3.6 watts for Bulb 2. Plugging in P = 3.6 and r = 2 gives you (C). Choice A is the result if you accidentally swap the values of P and r. Choices B and D are the results if you mistakenly use the P for Bulb 1.

18. H   Difficulty: High

Category: Interpretation of Data

Getting to the Answer: Because you are not permitted to use your calculator during the Science Test, there must be a way to estimate when a question looks like it requires a complex calculation. Because $B = \frac{P}{4\pi r^2}$, that means $P = 4\pi r^2 B$. You're given in the question stem that the bulb is 1 m away, so you can plug r = 1 into the equation. You're also given that B = 0.95 W/m². Plugging in these values yields: $P = 4\pi(1\text{ m})^2(0.95\text{ W/m}^2)$. Because π is slightly larger than 3 and 0.95 is slightly smaller than 1, you can round to get: $P \approx 4(3)(1\text{ m}^2)(1\text{ W/m}^2)$ = 12 W. Choice (H) is thus correct. Alternatively, you could notice that 0.95 is just less than double the B value for Bulb 4, so you could infer that the power of the new bulb should be a bit less than double Bulb 4's power of 7.2 W.

19. A   Difficulty: Low

Category: Scientific Investigation

Getting to the Answer: To answer this question, look at the descriptions of the two studies and the accompanying tables of results. According to the passage, there were 4 light sensors used in Study 1, but no light sensors in Study 2, so (A) is correct. Choice B is incorrect because 4 different light bulbs were used in both studies. Choice C is incorrect because a 12 V battery was used for both studies. Choice D is incorrect because Table 2 shows that the current was actually lowest for Bulb 1.

20. H   Difficulty: Medium

Category: Interpretation of Data

Getting to the Answer: According to Table 3, Bulb 1 and Bulb 2 have brightness values below 0.30 W/m², so F and G can be eliminated. Bulb 3's brightness is greater than 0.30 W/m² and its power rating is less than that of Bulb 4. Choice (H) is thus correct.

Passage IV

21. D   Difficulty: High

Category: Evaluation of Models, Inferences, and Results

Getting to the Answer: Figure 1 shows how energy relates to the probability of occupation. According to the passage, the figure shows the same solid at 3 different temperatures. The hottest solid (25,000 K) is able to reach energy states beyond 14 electron volts, which is a higher value than the two cooler solids. Choice (D) is thus correct. Choices A and B are incorrect because hotter materials have a larger range of energy states than cooler ones. Choice C is incorrect because it is the opposite of what Figure 1 shows.

22. J   Difficulty: High

Category: Interpretation of Data

Getting to the Answer: All three curves happen to intersect at 50% probability with 7 eV of energy, so look at their slopes at this point. "Inversely proportional" means that the average kinetic energy is lower for steeper slopes. The 1,000 K curve has the steepest slope and therefore the lowest average kinetic energy. The 10,000 K curve has the

next steepest slope and therefore the next lowest kinetic energy, while the 25,000 K curve has the least steep slope and the highest kinetic energy. Choice (J) is correct.

23. A   Difficulty: Low

Category: Interpretation of Data

Getting to the Answer: The 1,000 K curve in Figure 1 appears to reach 0% at energies above approximately 8 eV. The note under the graph says that the curves all continue to decrease beyond 15 eV, so the value of the 1,000 K curve should still be approximately 0% at an energy of 20 eV. Clearly, the probability will be less than 5%, so (A) is correct.

24. J   Difficulty: Medium

Category: Interpretation of Data

Getting to the Answer: The temperatures given in the question stem are simply double the values presented in Figure 1, so you can expect the curves to follow the same trends that were seen there. One of the trends in Figure 1 that applies to all three curves is that probability decreases as energy increases. This means that F and G can be eliminated, because both show the opposite. The other trend from Figure 1 is that the curves become shallower as temperature increases. This same trend is evident in (J), so it is the correct answer. Watch out for the trap in H: the solid line is used to represent the hottest material in the answer choices here but the coolest material in Figure 1, so H looks deceptively similar to Figure 1.

25. C   Difficulty: High

Category: Interpretation of Data

Getting to the Answer: Locate the point in Figure 1 corresponding to an 80% probability of occupation for a 5 eV energy state. It lies between the 10,000 K and 25,000 K curves. The temperature of the solid, then, must be between 10,000 K and 25,000 K. Choice (C) must be correct because it is the only option in this range.

26. G   Difficulty: Medium

Category: Interpretation of Data

Getting to the Answer: It doesn't matter whether you've ever heard of the de Broglie wavelength before—or whether you can even pronounce it! Everything you need to know is in the question stem. As the de Broglie wavelength decreases, the energy increases. What happens to probability as energy increases? Figure 1 clearly shows that the values on all three curves decrease with increasing energy. Choice (G), then, is correct.

Passage V

27. C   Difficulty: Medium

Category: Interpretation of Data

Getting to the Answer: The bars on the graph need to represent the values in the 25°C column of Table 1. Soft Drink C has by far the largest value of 284 kPa, while Soft Drink D has the second largest value of 243 kPa. Choices A and D can be eliminated because they show those two soft drinks as tied. Choice B can also be eliminated because it suggests that Soft Drink A has a higher pressure than Soft Drink D. Only (C) accurately reflects the decreasing order of C, D, A, B, and E.

28. G   Difficulty: Low

Category: Interpretation of Data

Getting to the Answer: The question asks you to identify how the pressure gauge would look for Soft Drink C at temperatures of 4°C and 35°C. According to Table 1, Soft Drink C has a pressure of 149 kPa at 4°C and 394 kPa at 35°C. Thus, the first gauge should have the needle half way between 100 and 200, while the second gauge should point way past 300, almost reaching back to 0 at the top. Choice (G) includes gauges that follow precisely this pattern, so it is correct.

29. D   Difficulty: Medium

Category: Evaluation of Models, Inferences, and Results

Getting to the Answer: To answer this question, look for correlations between the two sets of data. According to the new table, Soft Drink D has the highest sugar content (40 grams per 12 ounces) but, according to Table 2, it always has lower CO_2 solubility than Soft Drink C. This means higher sugar content doesn't always correlate with higher solubility. Therefore, the hypothesis is not supported, allowing A and B to be eliminated. Choice C is also incorrect because Soft Drink D has the highest

sugar content but not the lowest solubility (Soft Drink E is lowest in solubility). Choice (D), then, is correct.

30. G   Difficulty: Low

Category: Interpretation of Data

Getting to the Answer: According to Table 1, for all soft drinks the pressure values for 4°C are lower than the pressure values for 25°C, which are lower than the pressure values for 35°C. Thus, pressure always increases with increasing temperature and (G) is correct.

31. A   Difficulty: Medium

Category: Scientific Investigation

Getting to the Answer: Refer to the description of Experiment 2 in the passage to answer this question. According to the description of that experiment, "[t]he cylinder used in Experiment 1 was completely filled (no headspace)." Choices B and D can be eliminated because they show the soft drink in a flask, not in the original cylinder from Experiment 1. Choice C can be eliminated because the cylinder it depicts includes headspace. Choice (A) is correct because it accurately shows the cylinder completely filled with soft drink.

32. H   Difficulty: Medium

Category: Scientific Investigation

Getting to the Answer: Even though the passage does not state explicitly why the students waited 10 minutes before measuring the pressure, the reasoning can be inferred from what the passage does state. The description of Experiment 1 notes that the water bath was initially 25°C, but does not mention the temperature of the soft drink. However, for the pressure measurement to be accurate for the indicated temperature, the contents of the cylinder must be at that temperature, not just the water bath. Thus, waiting 10 minutes allows the soft drink and its headspace to reach the same temperature as the water bath. Choice (H) is therefore correct. Choice F is incorrect because the CO_2 was only removed in Experiment 2, not Experiment 1. Choice G is incorrect because the evaporation of the soft drink is never considered in the passage. Choice J is incorrect because the pressure gauge isn't even attached to the cylinder until after 10 minutes, so that time can't be used for stabilizing the pressure gauge.

33. B   Difficulty: Low

Category: Interpretation of Data

Getting to the Answer: According to Table 2, every soft drink's CO_2 solubility decreases as temperature increases from 4°C to 35°C. Choice (B) is thus correct.

Passage VI

34. H   Difficulty: Medium

Category: Evaluation of Models, Inferences, and Results

Getting to the Answer: According to the passage, "[t]he anti conformation is the lowest energy and most stable state of the butane molecule," and "[m]olecules in the anti or gauche conformations tend to maintain their shape." Choice (H), then, is a perfect match. Choices F and G are incorrect because they wrongly suggest that molecules in low energy conformations do change their shapes. Choice J is incorrect because it contradicts the passage's claim that the lowest energy conformation is the most stable.

35. C   Difficulty: Medium

Category: Evaluation of Models, Inferences, and Results

Getting to the Answer: The first paragraph of the passage states that straight-chain conformational isomers "differ only by rotation about one or more single carbon bonds." The implication here is that, if the only difference is rotation, then the number of single carbon bonds must remain constant. Choice (C) is thus correct. Choice A is incorrect because, as explained in the passage, the different conformational isomers vary with respect to energy, with anti being the lowest energy and totally eclipsed being the highest. Choice B is incorrect because *shape* is just another word for *conformational isomer*. Choice D is incorrect because, according to Student 2, temperature can have an impact on which conformational isomer is favored.

36. F   Difficulty: Medium

Category: Evaluation of Models, Inferences, and Results

Getting to the Answer: According to the passage, Student 1 believes that a molecule's active shape is *always* identical to its lowest-energy shape. Student 2, however, believes that "a butane molecule's shape may also depend on temperature and its initial isomeric state." Temperature does not appear among the options, but initial isomeric state does, so (F) is correct. The other choices are incorrect because both Student 1 and Student 2 would agree that energy state, stability, and the proximity of methyl groups have an influence on butane's active shape.

37. B   Difficulty: High

Category: Interpretation of Data

Getting to the Answer: Try to find structural similarities between the passage and the new situation. The larger valley represents the lowest energy state because it is closest the ground, while the smaller valley is lower in energy than its immediate surroundings, but relatively higher in energy compared to the larger valley. Thus, the larger valley corresponds to the anti conformation, the lowest energy state of butane, while the smaller valley corresponds to the second-lowest energy state, the gauche conformation. Indeed, the passage describes the gauche conformation as "a relative minimum or *meta-stable* state." Choice (B) is thus correct. Choice A is incorrect because anti corresponds to the larger valley. Choice C is incorrect because eclipsed corresponds to the smaller hill. Choice D is incorrect because totally eclipsed corresponds to the larger hills at the far left and far right of the figure.

38. F   Difficulty: Medium

Category: Evaluation of Models, Inferences, and Results

Getting to the Answer: According to the passage, Student 1 believes that a molecule's active shape and its lowest-energy shape are the same thing. Therefore, Student 1 believes that all butane molecules in their active shape will be in the anti conformation. Choice (F) is thus correct. Choice G is incorrect because it directly contradicts Student 1's view. Choice H is incorrect because Student 2 believes that the active shape of butane will sometimes be the gauche conformation. Choice J is incorrect because Student 2 believes that the active shape of butane will sometimes be the anti conformation, which is the lowest in energy.

39. D   Difficulty: High

Category: Evaluation of Models, Inferences, and Results

Getting to the Answer: According to the passage, Student 2 believes that the energy of a molecule's active shape may be slightly higher than that of its most stable shape, while Student 1 believes that a molecule's most stable shape and its active shape are always the same. Choice (D) depicts a situation in which the active shape has a higher energy than the most stable shape, so it is correct. Choices A and B are incorrect because both students would agree that the energy of the eclipsed conformation is higher than that of either the active or most stable shape. Choice C is incorrect because Student 1 believes that the active shape and most stable shape are always the same, but you're looking for a choice Student 1 would disagree with.

40. G   Difficulty: High

Category: Evaluation of Models, Inferences, and Results

Getting to the Answer: Student 2 uses the following argument to contend that the gauche conformation can serve as the active shape of butane: "in order to convert from the gauche conformation to the anti conformation, the molecule must pass through either the eclipsed or totally eclipsed conformation. If the molecule is not given enough energy to reach either of these states, its active shape will be the gauche conformation." Choice (G), however, suggests that the energy to overcome these local barriers is always present in the environment, which would mean that a butane molecule would never settle into a gauche conformation, since it would always have enough energy to convert to anti. Choice (G) is therefore correct. None of the other choices are directly relevant to Student 2's argument.

WRITING TEST

MODEL ESSAY

Below is an example of what a high-scoring essay might look like. Notice the author states her position clearly in the introductory paragraph and supports that position with evidence in the following paragraphs. This essay also uses transitions, some advanced vocabulary, and an effective "hook" to draw in the reader.

The question posed is if schools should provide computers to all students so that they can become proficient in using computers, since in today's world, computers are important for jobs and general communication. Since there is no going back to a pre-computer time, and the odds are that computer use will continue to grow, it will be necessary for everyone to know how to use a computer. The question is how schools will contribute to this and the fairest and most workable solution is for schools and business to work together to lower the cost of computers to a point at which most parents can afford to buy them.

When schools and business, presumably those which manufacture and sell computers, such as Apple, work together to lower the cost of computers, most parents who need computers for their children can buy them at a large discount. This will allow most students to have continuous access to computers, and reduce the number of students who still need to use the school computer center. In this way students with their own computers can not only do their schoolwork, but also have the opportunity to explore computer use for a myriad of programs, increasing their computer literacy and thus their competitiveness in the future job market. Indeed, some studies have shown that playing computer games can increase critical thinking, eye-hand coordination, and quick decision-making—all skills which are useful not only in school but in so many other activities. It has been demonstrated, for example, that the best airline pilots play computer games, which promote high-level coordination and decision-making skills.

Furthermore, computers are essentially online libraries—a fount of knowledge in almost every subject, and a boon to students writing research papers or even just looking for an academic site where they can supplement their school program. Computers also offer Power Point, illustration programs, and a host of other programs to enhance a presentation. In terms of future employment, a brief scan of newspaper and online job searches shows that many companies require employees to be computer literate. A few hours on a school computer, limited to only the required work, does not provide this comfortable, creative, and, in today's world, necessary tool. Given the volume of computer sales, companies can well afford to reduce their prices in special circumstances. As a marketing tool, this may also ensure a customer for life; one who will purchase the same brand as his purchasing power and need for upgrades allow.

On the other hand, those who posit that students should have access to school computers in a computer lab overlook several problems. School computer labs are open during school hours and an hour or two before and after school, which may not be enough time for all students who need to use computers to take their turns in a lab. Consider also that many students have after-school jobs, sports team practice, or family obligations, and may not be able to take advantage of time in the computer lab. If teachers give students class projects, that work may require that several students work on computers at the same time and in the same place, possibly for hours at a time. This becomes unworkable. In general, this option is not necessarily a poor one, but one which cannot be well-implemented for all students.

Finally, others argue that schools should give computers to all high school students throughout their years in school, and perhaps all middle school and elementary students as well. If all students have computers, there is no doubt that they will be very proficient at using them, and that will be beneficial for their careers in a world of technology. However, I live in Los Angeles and I know from experience that there are problems with giving students their own computers. The school board did just that in Los Angeles and has run into trouble with students using the computers for inappropriate reasons. Also, given the size of the Los Angeles school district and other very large school districts, giving every student a computer, even if it's only for high school students, will cost a great deal of money, and some school districts may not be able to support it. If that is the case, we create two groups: the haves and have-nots. This is inequitable and not something the schools should support.

To reiterate, a partnership between schools and computer companies is the best one because it provides either personal or school computers for all students, and is not a financial burden for parents. It is vital today that all students be computer literate, and this will become even more vital in the future. School is the proper place to prepare students for their working or college careers, and it is incumbent on them to provide all the tools needed for this. Thus, when businesses and schools work together to make computers affordable and available, all students will have the tools they need for school and career success.

You can evaluate your essay and the model essay based on the following criteria:

- Is the author's own perspective clearly stated?
- Does the body of the essay assess and analyze an additional perspective?
- Is the relevance of each paragraph clear?
- Does the author start a new paragraph for each new idea?
- Is each sentence in a paragraph relevant to the point made in that paragraph?
- Are transitions clear?
- Is the essay easy to read? Is it engaging?
- Are sentences varied?
- Is vocabulary used effectively? Is college-level vocabulary used?